EXAMINATI
REGULATIO
2015

UNIVERSITY OF OXFORD

EXAMINATION REGULATIONS 2015

[FOR THE ACADEMIC YEAR 2015–16]

OXFORD UNIVERSITY PRESS

OXFORD
UNIVERSITY PRESS

Great Clarendon Street, Oxford, OX2 6DP,
United Kingdom

Oxford University Press is a department of the University of Oxford.
It furthers the University's objective of excellence in research, scholarship,
and education by publishing worldwide. Oxford is a registered trade mark of
Oxford University Press in the UK and in certain other countries

© Oxford University Press 2015

The moral rights of the author have been asserted

First Edition published in 2015
Impression: 1

Published in the United States of America by Oxford University Press
198 Madison Avenue, New York, NY 10016, United States of America

British Library Cataloguing in Publication Data
Data available

Library of Congress Control Number: 2015943761

ISBN 978-0-19-873935-7

Printed in Great Britain by
Ashford Colour Press Ltd, Gosport, Hampshire

PREFACE

This book contains the regulations of the University relating to the various degrees, diplomas and certificates conferred by the University together with regulations made by boards, and certain other relevant information.

There is a range of other documents of importance to those involved in examinations:

Student Handbook (Proctors' and Assessor's Memorandum) available online at: http://www.admin.ox.ac.uk/proctors/info/pam

Policy and Guidance for Examiners and others involved in University Examinations available online at: http://www.admin.ox.ac.uk/edc/policiesandguidance/ pgexaminers/

The Examination Regulations are now available online at: http://www.admin.ox.ac. uk/examregs/. The online version, along with the print version, is maintained by the Education Policy Support Section, who may be contacted via examinationregulationsenquiries@admin.ox.ac.uk.

DATES OF TERMS 2015–16

2015
Michaelmas: Thursday 1 October to Thursday 17 December

2016
Hilary: Thursday 7 January to Saturday 19 March
Trinity: Wednesday 20 April to Wednesday 6 July
Michaelmas: Saturday 1 October to Saturday 17 December

[1]DATES OF FULL TERM 2015–2016

2015
Michaelmas: Sunday 11 October to Saturday 5 December

2016
Hilary: Sunday 17 January to Saturday 12 March
Trinity: Sunday 24 April to Saturday 18 June
Michaelmas: Sunday 9 October to Saturday 3 December

DATES OF EXTENDED TERMS 2015–16

For Part I candidates in Materials, Economics, and Management
2016
Trinity: Sunday 24 April to Saturday 25 June

2017
Trinity: Monday 24 April to Saturday 24 June

For Part II candidates in Molecular and Cellular Biochemistry
2015
Michaelmas: Friday 18 September to Saturday 12 December

2016
Michaelmas: Friday 16 September to Saturday 10 December

For Part II candidates in Chemistry
2015
Michaelmas: Thursday 24 September to Tuesday 22 December

2016
Hilary: Tuesday 5 January to Wednesday 23 March
Trinity: Monday 4 April to Saturday 9 July
Michaelmas: Thursday 22 September to Tuesday 20 December

---

[1] Undergraduates will be required by their colleges to come into residence in the week preceding the beginning of Full Term.

For Part II candidates in Materials Science

2015
Michaelmas: Friday 11 September to Saturday 12 December

2016
Hilary: Friday 8 January to Saturday 19 March
Trinity: Friday 1 April to Saturday 2 July
Michaelmas: Friday 9 September to Saturday 10 December

For Master of Business Administration

2015
Michaelmas: Monday 21 September to Friday 18 December

2016[1]
Hilary: Monday 11 January to Friday 8 April
Trinity: Monday 25 April to Friday 1 July
Long vacation term: Monday 4 July to Friday 2 September
Long vacation term: Monday 5 September to Saturday 10 September

For further information please see the notice published by Council in the University Gazette of 22 January 2015 at http://www.ox.ac.uk/gazette/2014–2015

---

[1] The above dates are provisional and subject to minor changes. Please contact the departmental administrator for further information.

CONTENTS

PROVISIONAL DATES OF EXAMINATIONS

The provisional start dates of examinations and examination entry deadlines which were previously published in this volume are now produced as a separate document. This document is published in mid-September in the *University Gazette* and on the University website (www.ox.ac.uk), and is circulated directly to colleges and depart-   5
ments. The reason for this change is that the publication lead-time for this volume requires the inclusion of dates likely to change before the start of the academic year. The revised publication arrangements have led to greater reliability of published information on examination dates and entry deadlines, to the benefit of those who make use of it.   10

NOTE ON CONVENTIONS GOVERNING THE
REVISED USE OF HEADINGS IN THIS EDITION

As a result of changes in the structure of University legislation, with effect from 1 October 2002, all former decrees concerning examinations were formally converted into regulations. In order to maintain continuity with earlier editions of this volume   15
the following conventions have been observed as far as is practicable:

1. All former decrees governing the award of a degree, diploma, or certificate in general terms (as opposed to those decrees dealing with examinations in particular subjects leading to the award of such a qualification) are headed GENERAL REGULATIONS.   20

2. All former decrees relating to a particular subject course are headed SPECIAL REGULATIONS.

3. All elements of examination legislation which were regulations under the previous dispensation, and remain so under the new structure, are also to be found under the heading SPECIAL REGULATIONS.   25

4. In order to distinguish between the two types of Special Regulation described above, those which were formerly decrees are to be found under a sub-heading 'A', while those which were formerly regulations under a sub-heading 'B'.

REGULATIONS ON THE NUMBER AND LENGTH OF TERMS

Made by Council on 8 May 2002

1. The academic year shall be divided into three terms and three vacations.

2. (1) The first, or Michaelmas, Term shall begin on and include 1 October and end on and include 17 December.

   (2) The second, or Hilary, Term shall begin on and include 7 January and end on and include 25 March or the Saturday before Palm Sunday, whichever is the earlier.

   (3) The third, or Trinity, Term shall begin on and include 20 April or the Wednesday after Easter, whichever is the later, and end on and include 6 July.

3. (1) In each term there shall be prescribed by Council a period of eight weeks to be known as Full Term, beginning on a Sunday, within which lectures and other instruction prescribed by statute or regulation shall be given.

   (2) The dates on which each Full Term will begin and end in the next academic year but one shall be published by the Registrar in the *University Gazette* during Hilary Term.

REGULATIONS FOR MATRICULATION OF STUDENT MEMBERS

Made by Council on 8 May 2002

1. In these regulations, unless the context requires otherwise, 'college' means any college, society, or Permanent Private Hall or any other institution designated by Council by regulation as being permitted to present candidates for matriculation.

Academic qualifications

2. (1) In order to be matriculated as student members candidates must show evidence of an appropriate educational background and good standards of literacy and numeracy.[1]

   (2) The University sets no formal 'Course Requirements' other than for the First Examination for the Degree of Bachelor of Medicine; candidates must, however, show that they are qualified to study the particular course they wish to take at Oxford.

   (3) Acceptance by a college for presentation for matriculation will be deemed to be adequate evidence of an appropriate educational background, of good standards of literacy and numeracy, and of qualifications to study the course.

3. All candidates for matriculation shall supply to the Registrar such particulars as Council may from time to time determine, and may be required to produce to the Registrar (through the authorities of their colleges) evidence of their qualification to be matriculated.

4. Certificates in a language other than English must be accompanied by an English translation certified as correct by a duly authorised official of the country to which the candidate belongs.

Presentation for matriculation

5. Unless regulation 6 below applies, every head of a college or in their absence their deputies shall present to the Vice-Chancellor for matriculation all members of their college who are prospective student members of the University within a fortnight from the date of their admission to the college.

6. A person who wishes to become a Senior Student under the provisions of the Regulations for Senior Student Status, or a graduate of another university who is applying for admission as a Probationer Research Student or as a student for any of the Degrees of Master of Fine Art, Master of Letters, Master of Philosophy, Master of Science, Master of Studies, Magister Juris, Master of Business Administration, Master

---

[1] GCSE passes at grade C and above in English Language, in a Mathematics or Science Subject, and in a language other than English and at least two A-level passes (or the equivalent in AS levels or a mixture of A and AS levels) would normally satisfy these requirements, as would an appropriate level of attainment in other qualifications such as Scottish Highers, the Irish Leaving Certificate, BTEC National Certificate, an Open University Foundation Course Credit, the European and International Baccalaureates, and degrees of other universities.

of Public Policy, Bachelor of Philosophy, Bachelor of Civil Law, or Bachelor of Divinity must be presented to the Vice-Chancellor for matriculation by the head of his or her college or deputy within one month from the date of his or her admission to membership of his or her college.

7. A candidate who is matriculated during vacation shall be deemed to have been matriculated on the first day of the term following the vacation.

8. A person who becomes a student member by incorporation under regulations 1.7–1.18 of the Regulations for Degrees, Diplomas, and Certificates shall be deemed to have been matriculated on the first day of the term in which he or she was incorporated (or, in the case of a person incorporated during vacation, on the first day of the term following the vacation).

9. The procedure at the matriculation ceremony shall be in accordance with the arrangements laid down in the Regulations of Congregation for the Conduct of Ceremonies in Congregation.

Provisional matriculation

10. (1) Any person who is eligible to be matriculated may, if in the opinion of the head of his or her college there is good reason for that person not to be presented for matriculation under regulation 5 above, and on payment of the matriculation fee (if payable), be 'provisionally matriculated' (in absence) in accordance with arrangements made by Council and shall then be treated for all purposes as a member of the University until the end of the term in which he or she is provisionally matriculated.

(2) The duty under regulation 5 above of a head of a college to present any person for matriculation within a specified period from the date of his or her admission to the college shall be deemed to have been satisfied by that provisional matriculation, subject to the following conditions:

(*a*) any person who is matriculated not later than the term following the date of his or her provisional matriculation shall be deemed for all purposes to have been matriculated on the date of his or her provisional matriculation;

(*b*) if any person has not been matriculated in or before the term following his or her provisional matriculation, his or her provisional matriculation shall, unless Council determines otherwise, be cancelled but the fee shall not be returned.

11. Notwithstanding the provisions of regulation 10 above, any person who has been provisionally matriculated and who is a student for the degree of M.St in International Human Rights Law, or who, in accordance with arrangements approved by Council, spends the first two terms of his or her studies at any of the universities approved by Council under the ERASMUS postgraduate exchange scheme for Law and Economics may be matriculated up to the end of the third term after the term in which he or she was provisionally matriculated, and the duty under regulation 5 above of a head of a college to present any person for matriculation within a specified period from the date of his or her admission to the college shall be deemed to have been satisfied by that provisional matriculation, subject to the following conditions:

(1) any person who is matriculated not later than the third term after the term in which he or she was provisionally matriculated shall be deemed for all purposes to have been matriculated on the date of his or her provisional matriculation;

(2) if any person has not been matriculated in or before the third term after the term in which he or she was provisionally matriculated, his or her provisional matriculation shall, unless Council determines otherwise, be cancelled but the fee shall not be returned.

12. The matriculation fee (if payable), the particulars which the candidate is required to supply under the provisions of regulation 3 above, and (if requested) evidence of his or her qualification to be matriculated shall be sent by the authorities of the candidate's college to the Registrar with a request that the candidate be provisionally matriculated.

St Catherine's Society

13. All persons who were matriculated through St Catherine's Society shall be deemed to have been matriculated through St Catherine's College, except that those who were matriculated in Michaelmas Term 1961 or later and who were not reading for the Degree of Bachelor of Arts shall be deemed to have been matriculated through Linacre College.

Matriculation for Theological Courses of members of certain institutions in Oxford

14. In each academic year, subject to the approval of Council, Ripon College, Cuddesdon, shall be permitted, subject to the conditions laid down in regulations 15–17 below, to present for matriculation by the University:

(1) not more than twenty-two full-time-equivalent qualified candidates offering themselves for the qualifications listed in regulation 17 below other than the M.Th. in Applied Theology or the Diploma in Applied Theology; and

(2) not more than fourteen qualified candidates offering themselves for the M.Th. in Applied Theology or the Diploma in Applied Theology.

15. No person may be matriculated under the authority of these regulations unless the institution presenting that person for matriculation can certify that he or she is a minister of religion or a genuine candidate for the ministry.

16. Before presenting any candidate for matriculation under the authority of these regulations, the institution presenting him or her shall consult the Board of the Faculty of Theology and Religion or such nominee or nominees as the board may appoint to act for it.

17. Persons matriculated under the authority of regulations 14–16 above shall have in relation to the University the same privileges and obligations as if they had been matriculated through a college, except that they may not (unless they migrate to a college listed in Statute V) offer themselves for any degree, diploma, or certificate examinations of the University other than those for:

(1) the Honour School of Theology and Religion or any joint Honour School which includes Theology;

(2) the Diploma in Theology or a Certificate in Theology or the Degree of Bachelor of Theology;

(3) the Degree of Master of Studies or Master of Philosophy in Theology, or Master of Studies or Master of Philosophy in Philosophical Theology, or Master of Theology in Applied Theology, or the Diploma in Applied Theology;

(4) the Degree of Bachelor of Divinity or Doctor of Divinity.

REGULATIONS FOR RESIDENCE IN THE UNIVERSITY

Made by Council on 8 May 2002

1. Where under any statute or regulation a student member is required, in order to be admitted to any examination or degree or obtain any other qualification of the University, to keep a number of terms or any other period of residence in the University these regulations shall apply for the purpose of:

    (1) defining the place or places of residence; and

    (2) calculating any period of residence necessary to satisfy that requirement.

2. Residence as defined by those regulations is called 'statutory residence'.

3. In these regulations, unless the context otherwise requires, 'college' means any college, society, or Permanent Private Hall or any other institution designated by Council by regulation as being permitted to present candidates for matriculation as student members of the University.

Place of residence

4. (1) Unless regulations 4(2), 6, or 7 below apply, student members who are reading for a degree awarded on passing the Second Public Examination must reside, for the period prescribed for that degree, within six miles from Carfax.

    (2) A student member to whom paragraph (1) above applies may reside within twenty-five miles from Carfax if he or she:

        (*a*) holds the status of Senior Student or has already satisfied the examiners in a Second Public Examination; or

        (*b*) resides in the home of his or her parent or guardian.

5. Unless regulations 6 or 7 below apply, student members who are reading for any other degree of the University shall reside, for the period prescribed for that degree, within twenty-five miles from Carfax.

6. The Proctors may, upon the application in writing of the head or another officer of the applicant's college, authorise a student member to reside and keep terms in a house or flat situated more than the number of miles from Carfax prescribed in his or her case if there are special circumstances which appear to the Proctors to justify such authorisation.

7. All student members who are engaged on part-time courses, or who are exceptionally permitted to undertake their research in a well-found laboratory outside Oxford under the provisions of the Regulations for the Degree of Doctor of Philosophy, shall be exempt from the residence limit.

8. If any student member (other than one engaged on a part-time course, or one exceptionally permitted to undertake his or her research in a well-found laboratory outside Oxford under the provisions of the Regulations for the Degree of Doctor of Philosophy) shall reside more than the number of miles from Carfax prescribed in his or her case without the permission of the Proctors, he or she shall not be permitted to count such residence towards any period or periods during which he or she is required to reside to obtain a degree or other qualification from the University.

9. (1) If any student member is dissatisfied with a decision by the Proctors under regulation 6 above or regulation 14 below, he or she, or his or her college, may within fourteen days of the date of the decision appeal in writing to the Chair of the Education Committee of Council.

(2) The appeal shall be adjudged expeditiously by the Chair or another member of that committee, other than one of the Proctors, nominated by the Chair.

Calculating periods of residence

10. Whenever the required time for any degree or other qualification is reckoned in terms, 'term' shall mean a term as prescribed in regulation 2 of the Regulations on the Number and Length of Terms.

11. A person on whom any degree has not yet been conferred shall not be reckoned as having completed a term of residence for his or her degree unless he or she has resided within the University for six weeks of each such term.

12. Whenever the required time for any degree or other qualification is reckoned in years, a year shall be deemed to be the equivalent of three terms. (For example, if three years are required, nine terms shall be understood, if four years, twelve terms, and so on.)

13. If a student member is presented for matriculation during the course of a term he or she shall be entitled to count the whole of that term as one term's residence if he or she has been residing at a place of residence authorised under these regulations for the whole of that term.

14. A person who wishes to become a Senior Student under the provisions of the Regulations for Senior Student Status, or a graduate of another university who is applying for admission as a Probationer Research Student or as a student for any of the Degrees of Master of Fine Art, Master of Letters, Master of Philosophy, Master of Science, Master of Studies, Magister Juris, Master of Business Administration, Master of Public Policy, Bachelor of Philosophy, or Bachelor of Civil Law, may be given permission by the Proctors to count towards his or her statutory residence any period not exceeding one calendar month during which he or she has resided, before his or her matriculation, under conditions approved by his or her college, within the relevant distance from Carfax as specified in these regulations.

15. Any person who has been given dispensation from the requirements of regulation 11 (1) of the Regulations for Matriculation of Student Members only after he or she has come into residence shall be permitted to reckon as part of his or her statutory residence under these regulations any period, not exceeding one term, during which he or she has resided before his or her matriculation, under conditions approved by his or her college, within the appropriate distance from Carfax as specified in these regulations.

16. If a student member is suspended from access to the premises and facilities of the University, the period of suspension shall not count towards the fulfilment of that student's statutory residence requirements.

Dispensations

17. Council may by regulation provide for student members to be excused from any required period of statutory residence up to a specified limit.

REGULATIONS FOR SENIOR STUDENT STATUS

Made by Council on 8 May 2002

1. The following may be admitted to the status and privileges of a Senior Student, subject to the decision of the Education Committee of Council in any case of doubt or difficulty:

(1) persons who have obtained a degree at another university after having pursued a course of study extending over three years of full-time study, or its equivalent on a part-time basis;

(2) persons who, having been a student at a university in a European country, have successfully completed a course of study on a full-time, or equivalent part-time, basis deemed to be equivalent to that of an undergraduate degree qualification;

(3) persons who have obtained a degree at another university and have also been selected to come to Oxford by some body recognized for the purposes of this regulation by the University;

(4) persons who, though not eligible under paragraphs (1) or (2) or (3) above, have satisfied the Education Committee of Council that they are well-qualified to be admitted as Senior Students.

2. The status and privileges of Senior Students shall be as follows:

(1) The term in which they are matriculated shall be reckoned, for the purposes of any provisions respecting the standing of members of the University, as the fourth term from their matriculation.

(2) They shall not be required to pass the First Public Examination as a condition for the Degree of Bachelor of Arts or of Master of Biochemistry or Chemistry or Computer Science or Earth Sciences or Engineering or Mathematics or Mathematics and Computer Science or Computer Science and Philosophy or Mathematics and Philosophy or Mathematics and Physics (after transfer to that Honour School for their Part C examination from the Master of Mathematics in Mathematics, the Master of Physics in Physics, or the Master of Physics and Philosophy in Physics and Philosophy following their Part B examinations) or Physics or Physics and Philosophy, or the Preliminary Examination in Fine Art as a condition for the Degree of Bachelor of Fine Art, as the case may be.

(3) They shall be entitled to supplicate for the Degree of Bachelor of Arts, or of Bachelor of Fine Art, or of Master of Biochemistry or Chemistry or Computer Science or Computer Science and Philosophy or Earth Sciences or Engineering or Mathematics or Mathematics and Computer Science or Mathematics and Philosophy or Mathematics and Physics (after transfer to that Honour School for their Part C examination from the Master of Mathematics in Mathematics, the Master of Physics in Physics, or the Master of Physics and Philosophy in Physics and Philosophy following their Part B examinations) or Physics or Physics and Philosophy, as the case may be, if they have kept statutory residence, as defined in the relevant regulations, for six terms in the case of courses of study lasting three years, or

nine terms in the case of courses of study lasting four years, and have obtained a place, or have been declared to have deserved Honours under the Regulations for the Conduct of Examinations, in the Results List of an Honour School of the Second Public Examination or the Final Examination in Fine Art, or they are entitled under the relevant regulations to supplicate for one of those degrees as if they had obtained Honours in such an examination.

3. Any persons who desire to become Senior Students under the provisions of these regulations shall send their applications, through an officer of a college, society, or Permanent Private Hall or another institution designated by Council by regulation as being permitted to present candidates for matriculation, to the Registrar and shall at the same time produce all necessary certificates and information in support of their applications.

REGULATIONS FOR READMISSION AND MIGRATION

Made by Council on 8 May 2002

1. In these regulations, unless the context requires otherwise, 'college' means any college, society, or Permanent Private Hall or any other institution designated by Council by regulation as being permitted to present candidates for matriculation.

2. If any person has been expelled by any college, that person shall not be readmitted to the college without the written permission of the Proctors if:

(1) his or her expulsion has taken place while he or she was still subject to any penalty imposed by the Proctors or the Disciplinary Court or the Appeal Court; or

(2) the Proctors have given specific notice in writing to the college that the consent of the Proctors will be required.

3. A student member of the University may migrate from any college to any other, and a graduate of the University who is a minister of religion or a candidate for the ministry may migrate to Ripon College, Cuddesdon, in order to read for the Honour School of Theology and Religion, for any joint Honour School which includes Theology, for the Diploma in Theology, for the Certificate in Theology, or for the Degree of Bachelor of Theology, if in each case he or she has first obtained:

(1) written permission for his or her migration from the college to which he or she belongs; and

(2) a certificate signed by the two Proctors that they have seen that permission and do not oppose his or her migration.

4. If the Proctors decline to give their consent under regulation 2 above, or to sign the certificate specified in regulation 3 (2) above, the person concerned may dispute the Proctors' decision in accordance with Statute XVII.

5. No person who has previously been admitted as a member by any college within the University shall be admitted as a member by any other without the production of the proper certificates.

6. In granting a certificate of migration, the Proctors, with the consent of the Vice-Chancellor, may append such conditions as to residence during the next three terms as may appear to them desirable.

7. If any permission or testimonial required under the provisions of regulations 2 and 3 above is refused, the Vice-Chancellor may nevertheless, if he or she thinks fit, grant consent in writing for the migration.

8. If any student member of the University has been expelled by the authorities of any college, that person shall not be readmitted to membership of the University unless the Vice-Chancellor has heard the case and has given consent in writing for the readmission of that person; and it shall be the duty of the authorities of colleges to satisfy themselves that any person applying to them for admission has not previously been so expelled.

9. Any student member of the University migrating or having been readmitted to membership of the University except under the conditions laid down above shall forfeit all the privileges of the University from the date of his or her migration or

readmission; except that the two Proctors, if they are satisfied that there was no reason why that person should not have been allowed to migrate or to be readmitted, may exempt him or her from the penalties imposed by this regulation, and any person so exempted shall pay to the University through the Registrar a further sum equivalent to one-half of the matriculation fee payable at the date of the exemption. 5

10. (1) Nothing in regulations 2–9 above shall be taken to apply to any person:

    (*a*) who becomes a member of another college by virtue of his or her election to any office or emolument;

    (*b*) who, being a graduate of the University, becomes a member of another college in order to pursue a further course of study (other than one 10 which continues the academic programme for which he or she has already been admitted as a Probationer Research Student).

(2) It shall be the responsibility of the head or bursar of the college of which a person becomes a member under paragraph (1) (*a*) or (*b*) above to include the name of that person in the termly schedule of the names of the members 15 of the college who are liable to pay composition fees to the University, unless that person's name is included in the schedule prepared by the head or bursar of any other college of which the person is already a member.

NOTES

1

REGULATIONS FOR THE CONDUCT OF UNIVERSITY EXAMINATIONS

It is suggested that these regulations are read in conjunction with the Education Committee Policy and Guidance for examiners and others involved in University examinations.[1]

Part 1 Introduction

1.1. (1) These regulations shall, unless otherwise stated in any statute or in these or any other regulations, apply to University Examinations (including the First as well as the Second Public Examination) for all degrees except those referred to in paragraph (3) below.

(2) They also apply to University Examinations for all certificates and diplomas awarded by the University, and to any Examination described as a qualifying examination.

(3) They do not apply to University Examinations for the degree of Doctor of Divinity, Medicine, Civil Law, Letters, Science, Music and Philosophy or Master of Letters, Master of Science by Research, and Master of Studies in Legal Research, or Bachelor of Divinity.

1.2. In these regulations unless the context otherwise requires:

(1) 'college' means any college, society, or Permanent Private Hall or any other institution designated by Council by regulation as being permitted to present candidates for matriculation;

(2) 'examiners' includes all persons approved to examine candidates for University Examinations to which these regulations apply;

(3) 'examination' includes the submission and assessment of a thesis, dissertation, essay, practical work, or other coursework and any other exercise which is not undertaken in formal examination conditions but counts towards or constitutes the work for a degree or other academic award;

(4) 'University Examination' means a group or number of examinations which a candidate must pass to obtain a degree or other award or to qualify as a candidate for a degree or other award of the University;

(5) 'supervisory body' means a Board of the Division or Faculty or other university body which has supervision over a University Examination;

(6) 'Board of Examiners' means the body of examiners, including external examiners, who are appointed to conduct a University Examination but does not include assessors.

(7) 'Senior Tutor' means the Senior Tutor or other proper officer of a candidate's college.

---

[1] Available at: http://www.admin.ox.ac.uk/edc/policiesandguidance/.

(8) words and expressions in the singular include the plural and those in the plural include the singular.

1.3. For the purpose of these regulations unless regulation 1.4 below applies a person is a member of the college through which he or she pays fees or has compounded for the payment of fees to the University, and of no other college.   5

1.4. A person who is a tutor or fellow of a college shall for the purpose of these regulations be deemed to be a member of that college.

1.5. Where in these regulations examiners are distinguished as junior and senior, seniority shall, unless the context reguires otherwise, be determined in accordance with regulations made by Council.   10

1.6. References in these regulations to Full Term and any other University Term shall bear the meaning attributed to them by Council Regulations on the Number and Length of Terms.

1.7. Council may authorise a supervisory body to make special regulations for a University Examination modifying the effect of these regulations on that Examination   15
to the extent permitted by Council.

Part 2 Number of Examiners

2.1. It is the duty of every supervisory body:

    (1) to ensure that there is a sufficient number of suitably qualified examiners to prepare and examine every part of the University Examination for which it   20
is responsible;

    (2) to arrange for their nomination in accordance with Part 4 below.

2.2. Except in the cases mentioned in regulation 2.3 below, every candidate in an examination shall be examined by at least two examiners or by one examiner and one assessor.   25

2.3. Regulations 2.2 above shall not apply to:

    (1) an examination which is part of a Preliminary Examination or Moderations (but not Honour Moderations) in the First Public Examination; or

    (2) an examination which is exempted from the requirement set out in regula-   30
tion 2.2 with the written permission of the Chair of the Education Committee.

Doctor of Clinical Psychology and Postgraduate Certificate in Supervision of Applied Psychological Practice

2.4. (1) The membership and terms of reference of the Board of Examiners for the   35
Degree of Doctor of Clinical Psychology and the Postgraduate Certificate in Supervision of Applied Psychological Practice shall be determined by the Oxford Institute of Clinical Psychology Training.

    (2) The Course Directors shall deposit annually with the Proctors the procedures for nomination of examiners, and the terms of reference and con-   40
ventions of the Board of Examiners for each of these awards.

    (3) Nominations of examiners shall be subject to regulation 4.8 and 4.13 in Part 4 of these regulations.

Part 3 Qualifications of Examiners

3.1. Examiners, other than examiners appointed under regulation 2.4 above or   45
external examiners appointed under Part 4 of these regulations, must be members of a Faculty or department of the University.

3.2. The Pro-Vice-Chancellor (Education) and Proctors may for good cause dispense with the requirements of regulation 3.1 above.

3.3. Except in the cases referred to in regulation 3.4 below, no more than two persons who are, or have been during the two preceding years, on the teaching staff of the same college shall be nominated to serve at the same time:

    (1) as moderators in the same part of a First Public Examination; or

    (2) as public examiners in the same Final Honour School.

3.4. Regulation 3.3 above does not apply to persons who are appointed to examine in separate subjects or in the separate parts of a University Examination which is divided into separate formal parts.

3.5. The Pro-Vice-Chancellor (Education) and Proctors may for good cause dispense with the requirements of regulation 3.3 above.

Part 4 Examiners: Nominations and Vacancies

4.1. It is the duty of every supervisory body to establish and maintain standing orders for:

    (1) the number of examiners for any University Examination for which that supervisory body is responsible;

    (2) the examiners' period of office;

    (3) the appointment of a chair of examiners;

    (4) the composition and constitution (including the arrangements for appointment of the chair and rules as to quorum) of any nominating committee to whom responsibilities are delegated under regulations 4.4 or 4.5 below; and

    (5) the period of service of the members of that committee and the filling of vacancies.

4.2. The standing orders made under regulation 4.1 above shall be submitted:

    (1) to the Proctors and the Registrar[1] before the beginning of each academic year; and

    (2) the Education Committee with the examiners' report at the conclusion of the Examination.

4.3. Examiners must be nominated to the Pro-Vice-Chancellor (Education) and Proctors by the supervisory body in accordance with those standing orders.

4.4. Unless there is provision to the contrary in any regulation, the responsibility for making nominations in respect of any University Examination which is under the joint supervision of more than one supervisory body shall be delegated to a nominating committee appointed jointly for this purpose by the supervisory bodies concerned.

4.5. A single supervisory body responsible for making nominations in respect of any other University Examination may delegate its responsibility to a nominating committee consisting of not fewer than three persons appointed by it for this purpose.

---

[1] References to the Registrar in this section should normally be taken to refer to the Head of Examinations and Assessments at the Examination Schools, who acts on behalf of the Registrar.

4.6. The Proctors and the Registrar shall be informed annually of the membership of each nominating committee.

4.7. (1) Every nomination shall be made by a majority of votes.

(2) When the votes are equal the chair of the relevant board or other body or nominating committee acting on its behalf shall have an additional, casting vote.

(3) Where the nomination is made by a casting vote and is forwarded to the Pro-Vice-Chancellor (Education) and Proctors for their approval, they shall be informed that it has been made by a casting vote.

Doctor of Clinical Psychology and Postgraduate Certificate in Supervision of Applied Psychological Practice

4.8. (1) Nominations of examiners for the Degree of Doctor of Clinical Psychology and the Postgraduate Certificate in Supervision of Applied Psychological Practice shall be made by a committee comprising two persons elected by the Oxford Institute of Clinical Psychology Training and two persons elected by the Medical Sciences Board.

(2) Nominations made under this regulation must be made in writing by at least three of the members of the nominating committee and shall be subject to the approval of the Pro-Vice-Chancellor (Education) and Proctors.

Notice of vacancies

4.9. By the Friday of the last week of each Full Term the Registrar shall send to each supervisory body, or its nominating committee acting on its behalf (as the case may be), the vacancies in examinerships to be filled in the following term.

Notice of nominations

4.10. Each supervisory body, or its nominating committee acting on its behalf (as the case may be), shall, unless regulation 4.11 below applies, submit to the Registrar, by 5 p.m. on the first Tuesday of the Full Term in which any vacancy has to be filled in accordance with Part 5 of these regulations, nominations of new examiners, signed by not fewer than two of the members of the board or other body or committee in question.

4.11. Nominations of new examiners for the Degree of Bachelor of Philosophy and Master of Philosophy in subjects other than Classical Archaeology shall be submitted by 5 p.m. on Friday in the sixth week of the Full Term in which a vacancy has to be filled in accordance with Part 5 of these regulations.

4.12. If notice of a vacancy in an examinership is not received by the Monday before the Full Term in which it is to be filled in accordance with regulation 4.9 above, the Pro-Vice-Chancellor (Education) shall fix the date by which nominations in writing must be received in accordance with those regulations, and the date for any meeting of the board or other body or nominating committee which may be necessary to make a nomination.

Submission of nominations

4.13. The chair of the board or other body or of the nominating committee acting on its behalf shall be responsible for the submission of nominations under regulations 4.10–4.12 above when duly signed by the persons specified.

External examiners

4.14. Regulations 4.15–4.19 below apply to the appointment of external examiners.

4.15. Each supervisory body or nominating committee acting on its behalf *must* nominate as an external examiner for each University Examination for the Second

Public Examination for which it is responsible a person to act as an external arbiter of standards and *may* nominate a person as an external examiner to provide academic expertise not otherwise obtainable from within the University.

4.16. A person nominated under regulation 4.15 above may be approved and designated by the Pro-Vice-Chancellor (Education) and Proctors as an external examiner. An external examiner who fails to submit the annual report required by the University may continue in office only with the permission of the Pro-Vice-Chancellor (Education) and the Proctors.

4.17. A person holding a post in the University or any college or other Oxford institution associated with the University in the examination of candidates may not be approved or designated as an external examiner.

4.18. Unless they are appointed to examine separate subjects or in separate parts of a University Examination divided into formal parts, no two persons who are, or have been during the preceding two years, on the teaching staff of the same university or other institution shall normally be nominated to serve at the same time as external examiners in the same University Examination.

4.19. External examiners shall be entitled to a retaining fee up to but not exceeding an amount determined from time to time by the Planning and Resource Allocation Committee of Council.

Additional examiners

4.20. A supervisory body may at any time, if it is necessary or desirable to do so, nominate additional examiners to serve on a Board of Examiners for one University Examination only, and the provisions of any standing orders shall not apply to the time of their nomination.

Final Honour Schools divided into Parts

4.21. If any Final Honour School is divided into Parts there shall be a separate Board of Examiners for each Part.

Part 5 Examiners: Period of Office, Casual Vacancies, Resignation, and Removal

5.1. (1) Examiners (except additional examiners) shall take up their office on the first day of the Full Term following the approval of their nomination by the Pro-Vice-Chancellor (Education) and Proctors.

(2) Additional examiners shall take up their office immediately after that date.

5.2. (1) Subject to the provisions of this Part examiners shall serve for the period designated in its standing orders by the supervisory body responsible for the University Examination for which they are appointed.

(2) Each supervisory body shall notify the Proctors and the Registrar before the beginning of each academic year of the number of examiners and the period of their office.

5.3. Examiners who have not held office for the full period may be renominated either for a full period or for such period as together with the period of office they have in fact completed will constitute a full period.

5.4. If it is necessary for the due regulation of the succession among examiners in any University Examination that an examiner or examiners shall retire before the end of the normal period of service, then the junior shall retire.

5.5. The Pro-Vice-Chancellor (Education) and Proctors may dispense from any of the requirements of regulations 5.1–5.4 above if they consider it reasonable to do so.

5.6. (1) An examiner may, on account of sickness or other urgent cause, obtain from the Pro-Vice-Chancellor (Education) and Proctors leave of absence for a period extending over not more than one University Examination, and a suitably qualified person shall be appointed to act as his or her substitute during that period.

(2) If leave of absence is granted before the first day of the Full Term in which or following which the University Examination in question is to begin, the substitute shall be nominated by the supervisory body or (as the case may be) the nominating committee concerned.

(3) If leave of absence is granted on or after that day the substitute shall be appointed by the Pro-Vice-Chancellor (Education) and Proctors.

5.7. If an examiner appears to the Pro-Vice-Chancellor (Education) or the Proctors to be acting in the conduct of his or her office in a manner which is inconsistent with proper standards of academic rigour, integrity, impartiality, or fairness, or may otherwise bring discredit upon the examination process or the University, he or she shall (without prejudice to any other action which may be taken) be removed from office by the Pro-Vice-Chancellor (Education) or Proctors as the case may be.

5.8. (1) If an examiner dies or resigns or is removed from office under this Part a suitably qualified person shall be appointed to act as his or her substitute.

(2) Where death, resignation, or removal occurs before the first day of Full Term in which or following which the University Examination in question is to begin, the substitute shall be nominated in accordance with regulation 5.6 (2) above and shall serve for the residue of the period of office of the person whom he or she succeeds.

(3) Where death, resignation, or removal occurs after that date the substitute shall be appointed by the Pro-Vice-Chancellor (Education) and Proctors and shall serve for the next University Examination only.

5.9. Examiners appointed under regulations 5.6 and 5.7 above shall:

(1) take up their office forthwith; and

(2) receive such remuneration (if any) as is determined from time to time by the Pro-Vice-Chancellor (Education) and Proctors.

5.10. If a person who is appointed an examiner by virtue of his or her office is for any reason unable to act he or she shall nominate a deputy who shall be a member of a faculty to act in his or her place with the approval of the Pro-Vice-Chancellor (Education) and the Proctors.

Part 6 Chairs of Examiners

6.1. The supervisory body responsible for a University Examination shall appoint a chair of examiners as soon as practicable and in accordance with its standing orders for approval by the Pro-Vice-Chancellor (Education) and Proctors.

6.2. Except with the permission of the Pro-Vice-Chancellor (Education), an external examiner shall not be eligible to serve as chair.

6.3. Until a chair has been appointed the senior examiner who is a member of a Faculty shall fulfil the duties of the chair. Seniority shall be determined by reference to the rules for academic precedence and standing as made from time to time by Council.

6.4. As well as performing the specific duties laid down in these or any other regulations the chair shall be responsible generally for ensuring that the business of his or her Board of Examiners is properly conducted and that the requirements of these regulations are fulfilled by that Board. 5

6.5. It shall be the duty of each chair of examiners to ensure that account is taken of the *Policy and Guidance for Examiners and others involved in University Examinations* published periodically by the Proctors and by the Education Committee so far as it is applicable to the University Examination for which his or her Board of Examiners is responsible. 10

6.6. (1) The chair shall convene at least one meeting of the examiners before each University Examination for which they are responsible and by this and other means ensure that all arrangements for its proper conduct have been made and understood. 15

(2) An external examiner shall not be required to attend such a meeting but shall be informed by the chair of its proceedings and decisions.

6.7. The chair of the Board of Examiners for each single Final Honour School shall designate the examiners required for any joint Final Honour School in which any of the examinations correspond with an examination in the single School. 20

Part 7 Assessors

7.1. A Board of Examiners may in accordance with the provisions of this Part appoint as assessors other persons who are not examiners in the same University Examination to act with them in setting and/or marking any particular part of a University Examination. 25

7.2. (1) Unless paragraph (3) below applies an assessor must hold the same qualifications as an examiner as provided in regulation 3.1 above.

(2) The Pro-Vice-Chancellor (Education) and Proctors may for good cause dispense with the requirements of regulation 7.2 (1) above. 30

(3) A person who holds a post of lector in either the University or one of the colleges in the language concerned may be appointed to act as an assessor in an oral examination in any of the following Final Honour Schools:

Modern Languages

History and Modern Languages 35

Philosophy and Modern Languages

Classics and Modern Languages

English and Modern Languages

European and Middle Eastern Languages.

7.3. Where an examination forms part of more than one University Examination a person may be appointed to act as an assessor of that examination for all University Examinations of which it forms a part. 40

7.4. The chair of the Board of Examiners concerned must apply to the Pro-Vice-Chancellor (Education) and Proctors for their approval of the appointment of any assessor, and an appointment shall not be effective until that approval is given.

7.5. The Proctors shall inform the Registrar of the names of all persons appointed as assessors.   5

7.6. Persons acting as assessors shall make a report to the Board of Examiners on the parts of the University Examinations submitted to them, but shall have no right of voting on the place of any candidate in a Results List nor on the question of his or her having satisfied the examiners or having been adjudged worthy of distinction.

7.7. An assessor shall if invited by the Board of Examiners take part in any *viva*   10
voce examination.

7.8. The remuneration of assessors shall be according to a scale drawn up by the Planning and Resource Allocation Committee of Council.

7.9. The provisions of regulations 5.6, 5.7, and 5.8 above which concern leave of absence, death, resignation, and removal in the case of examiners shall apply, with any   15
necessary modifications, to assessors.

7.10. The Pro-Vice-Chancellor (Education) and Proctors shall have power to give and vary directions necessary for the carrying out of the provisions of this Part.

Part 8 Approval of Conventions and Submission of Papers to Examiners   20

Approval of conventions

8.1. The conventions to be used in the assessment of candidates in any University Examination shall be approved by the supervisory body responsible for the course and the Examination and be published to prospective candidates not less than one whole term before the Examination takes place or, where assessment takes place in the first   25
term of a course, at the beginning of that term.

Submission of papers to examiners

8.2. The papers proposed for any written examination shall be submitted to all the examiners in the University Examination concerned according to a timetable determined by the chair of the examiners under this Part.   30

8.3. Each chair of examiners shall determine a timetable for the submission of papers under regulation 8.2 above which shall allow sufficient time for

    (1) the due consideration and approval of the proposed papers by all the examiners;

    (2) the production and proof-reading of the papers and their presentation in   35
camera-ready copy; and

    (3) the delivery of two camera-ready copies of each paper to the Examination Schools not later than five weeks before the first day of the University Examination in question.

8.4. In the Final Honour School of Oriental Studies it shall be sufficient if the paper   40
in each main subject and, where appropriate, additional language, is submitted to the chair of the examiners and the examiners acting together in the conduct of the examination in that main subject and additional language.

Part 9 Times for Holding Examinations and Entry of Names of Candidates

Times for holding Examinations

9.1. The Registrar and the Education Committee shall, after consultation with the Pro-Vice-Chancellor (Education) and Proctors, fix the days on which each University Examination shall begin and shall give public notice of such days.

9.2. The chair of examiners in each University Examination shall, on the advice of the Registrar, state and give public notice of the date time and place of the beginning of each examination, and shall afterwards give such notice as he or she shall deem necessary of the further attendance required of candidates.

Entry of names of candidates

9.3. (1) The Registrar shall be given the names of all candidates for all University Examinations except those referred to in paragraph (2) of this regulation.

(2) For the Examination for the Postgraduate Certificate in Education names shall be given in the manner prescribed by the regulations governing that Examination.

9.4. Using the designated forms, candidates shall be required to

(1) state the University Examination for which they intend to enter;

(2) state the options they intend to offer, if the regulations of the University Examination for which they are entering permit the offering of options;

(3) declare their intention of abiding by all University Regulations governing the conduct of examinations; and

(4) provide such other declaration as may be required by the special regulations for the University Examination in question.

9.5. The Registrar shall fix the days for entering names after consultation with the Education Committee, and he or she shall give public notice of the place and hour at which he or she will receive names.

Late entries

9.6. Where a candidate whose name has not been entered for an examination by the date fixed by the Registrar under the provisions of regulation 9.5 above wishes his or her name to be entered after that date, the procedure shall be as follows:

(1) the candidate shall apply in writing through the Senior Tutor to the Registrar for his or her name to be so entered;

(2) the Registrar shall determine whether the candidate proposes to offer part of the examination which has not already been offered by some other candidate whose name has been entered under the provisions of regulations 9.3–9.5 above and whether any other change in the conduct of the examination, as already arranged, would be involved;

(3) if no change in the conduct of the examination as referred to in paragraph (2) would be involved, the Registrar shall, subject to the payment by the candidate of a late-entry fee, grant permission for the candidate to be admitted to the examination;

(4) if some such change would be involved, the Registrar shall ask the chair of examiners whether he or she is, nevertheless, willing to consent to the candidate being admitted to the examination, and if the chair consents

the Registrar shall, subject to the payment by the candidate of a late-entry fee, grant permission for the candidate to be admitted to the examination;

(5) if the chair of examiners refuses to give the consent referred to in paragraph (4), the Registrar shall refer the matter to the Proctors for decision, and, if they give permission, this shall be subject to the payment by the candidate of a late-entry fee;

(6) the late-entry fee payable under paragraphs (3), (4), and (5) shall be such sum as the Education Committee shall from time to time determine, and different sums may be specified in respect of permission given under different paragraphs.

9.7. (1) Notwithstanding the provisions of regulation 9.6 above, the Divisional Board of Social Sciences may make provision for late entry, as appropriate, in the regulations for the Postgraduate Certificate in Education.

(2) Candidates permitted to enter late for these examinations shall pay such sum as the Education Committee shall from time to time determine.

Late alteration of options

9.8. Where the regulations for a University Examination permit the offering of options and a candidate wishes to alter his or her choice of options, the procedure shall be as follows:

(1) The candidate shall apply in writing through the Senior Tutor to the Registrar for the alteration to be made.

(2) The Registrar shall determine whether the candidate proposes to offer a part of the examination which has not already been offered by some other candidate whose name has been entered under the provisions of regulations 9.3–9.5 above and whether any other change in the conduct of the examination, as already arranged, would be involved.

(3) If no change in the conduct of the examination as referred to in paragraph (2) would be involved, the Registrar shall, subject to the payment by the candidate of a late-alteration fee, grant permission for the alteration to be made.

(4) If some such change would be involved, the Registrar shall ask the chair of examiners whether he or she is, nevertheless, willing to consent to the alteration, and, if the chair consents, the Registrar shall, subject to the payment by the candidate of a late alteration fee, grant permission for the alteration to be made.

(5) If the chair of examiners refuses to give the consent referred to in paragraph (4), the Registrar shall refer the matter to the Proctors for decision, and, if they give permission, this shall be subject to the payment by the candidate of a late-alteration fee.

(6) A candidate or his or her college may within fourteen days of the date of the Proctors' decision appeal in writing to the Chair of the Education Committee (who may nominate another member of the committee, other than one of the Proctors, to adjudicate the appeal).

(7) The late-alteration fee payable under paragraphs (3), (4), and (5) above shall be such sum as the Education Committee shall from time to time determine, and different sums may be specified in respect of permission given under different paragraphs.

Waiver of fees

9.9. The Proctors may waive the payment of any fee payable under regulations 9.6 and 9.8 above if it appears to them to be reasonable to do so.

Processing of entries

9.10. The Registrar shall acknowledge to the candidates the receipt of all completed forms and shall return to the candidate for completion or correction any form which is incomplete or is not in accordance with any relevant regulation.

9.11. Candidates must notify the Registrar of any subsequent changes in the   5
information given on their form.

9.12. If, through change of name, migration or otherwise the Registrar entertains any reasonable doubt about the identity of a candidate offering himself or herself for any University Examination, he or she may require such further evidence of identity as he or she may deem necessary.   10

Transmission of names of candidates and their options to the examiners

9.13. The Registrar shall assign a candidate number to each candidate and shall send the lists of numbers to the chair of the examiners in the University Examination for which the candidates have been entered.

Examination for the Degree of Doctor of Clinical Psychology validated by the   15
University

9.14. Notwithstanding any provision of regulations in this Part to the contrary, the entry of names, late entries, late alterations of names and candidates, and transmission of names of candidates and lists of subjects to the examiners for the examination for the Degree of Doctor of Clinical Psychology shall be governed by regulations laid   20
down from time to time by the Directorate of the Oxford Doctoral Course in Clinical Psychology and lodged annually with the Proctors.

Part 10 Dictation of Papers, Use of Word-Processors, Calculators, Computers & other Materials

Dictation and the use of word-processors   25

10.1. Unless permitted by the Proctors under Parts 12 or 13 of these regulations or under any other regulation, the use of word-processing and the dictation of papers in any University Examination is prohibited.

10.2. (1) If the Proctors permit the use of a word-processor, whether for the candidate's own use or for use by an amanuensis during the dictation of   30
papers, the Proctors shall specify in each case such detailed arrangements as they deem appropriate for the preparation and use of any equipment and computer software during the examination and for the conduct of the examination.

   (2) The Proctors shall also specify the detailed arrangements to be made for   35
the printing, handing in and recording of the candidate's script, and the number of copies to be made.

   (3) The Proctors shall send the details of these arrangements promptly to the chair of the examiners of the relevant examination, with copies to the Senior Tutor, and to the Registrar.   40

   (4) The arrangements for the collection of the examination paper by the invigilator and for the invigilation of the candidate shall take place in accordance with regulation 15.5 and 15.6 below.

10.3. The costs of arrangements made under regulation 10.2 above shall not fall on the candidate.   45

Use of calculators

10.4. Unless any regulation provides otherwise the following conditions shall apply in any University Examination in which candidates are permitted to use hand-held pocket calculators.

(1) The candidate shall ensure that the power supply of the calculator is adequately charged. 5

(2) No calculator for which a mains supply is essential will be allowed.

(3) Any calculator deemed by the Proctors or examiners to cause a disturbance will be prohibited.

(4) Output by the calculator shall be by visible display only. 10

(5) Candidates shall clear any user-entered data or programmes from the memories of their calculators immediately before starting each examination.

(6) No storage media external to the calculator are permitted.

(7) Input to the calculator during the examination shall be by its own keys or switches only. 15

(8) The examiners, invigilators, Proctors and the Registrar may inspect any calculator during the course of the examination.

Use of computers

10.5. Unless any regulation provides otherwise, in any University Examination 20 which requires use of computers the following conditions apply:

(1) No material such as cassettes, discs, or any other device on which machine readable files can be stored may be taken into the examination room.

(2) No password or username other than any specified on the examination paper shall be used. 25

(3) The examination paper shall contain a list of files, if any, which it is permitted to access. None of these files shall be deleted, written to, or tampered with in any way. No other file shall be accessed (except any files created by candidates during the course of the examination).

(4) Any files which candidates are permitted to access during the examination 30 shall be previously submitted for approval to all examiners conducting that examination.

(5) If it is permitted to access remotely held files which are held in a file store containing other files, the permitted files shall be accessed by user names and passwords which are used solely for the purposes of the examination, 35 and they shall not be revealed to the candidates until the start of the examination and shall be specified on the examination paper.

(6) In the event of any computer failure not involving the loss of any files in use in the examination and lasting less than one half hour, or not more than two separate failures, together lasting less than one half hour, the 40 examination shall be extended by the amount of time lost.

(7) In the event of any computer failure not covered by (6), the examination in question shall cease forthwith. An entirely new paper shall be set at a time and place which shall have been previously announced in the timetable for the examination: but it shall be open to any candidate who shall have 45 submitted work during or at the end of the sitting of the original paper to elect to be assessed upon that work and not to sit the new paper.

(8) If any examination is aborted on a second occasion the examiners shall determine the outcome of that examination by an alternative method after consultation with the Proctors.

Use of pencils

10.6. Except for the drawing of diagrams, no candidate may use pencil for the writing of an examination unless prior permission has been obtained from the Proctors.

Use of dictionaries

10.7. (1) Unless any regulation provides otherwise, the use of dictionaries of any kind shall not be permitted in any University Examination.

(2) This regulation shall not apply to candidates whose course of study commenced prior to Michaelmas Term 2009. Such a candidate whose native language is not English and who wishes to take into any examination a bilingual dictionary (covering English and the candidate's native language) must at the time of entering for the examination obtain permission from the Proctors through the Senior Tutor. Permission shall not be given where regulations or examiners' instructions have previously forbidden the use of dictionaries.

Part 11 Religious Festivals and Holidays Coinciding with Examinations

11.1. A candidate in any University Examination who is forbidden, for reasons of faith, from taking papers on religious festivals or other special days which may coincide with days on which examinations are set, may, through his or her Senior Tutor, apply to the Proctors for approval of alternative examination arrangements.

11.2. A candidate in any University Examination who is fasting, for reasons of faith, during religious festivals or other special days which may coincide with days on which examinations are set, may, through his or her Senior Tutor, apply to the Proctors for approval of alternative examination arrangements.

11.3. An application under 11.1 or 11.2 above shall be made as soon as possible after matriculation and in any event not later than the date of entry of the candidate's name for the first examination for which alternative arrangements are sought and shall specify the faith of the candidate concerned and the details of any days specially affected.

11.4. (1) If the Proctors approve the application they shall notify the Registrar who shall make reasonable efforts to ensure that an examination timetable is set such that alternative arrangements are not required.

(2) If the Proctors do not approve the application they shall give reasons for their decision.

(3) Where a request is made after the date specified in 11.3 the Proctors may still approve the application and shall follow the procedure set out in 11.4(1) above.

11.5. If it is not practicable to adjust the timetable in the manner described in regulation 11.4(1) above, the Registrar shall notify the Proctors and the candidate's Senior Tutor and identify another date or time when the candidate must take that part, which will, whenever possible, be no earlier than the date prescribed for the part in question.

11.6. Following such notification, the Senior Tutor shall make arrangements for the candidate to be examined at that alternative time and shall submit these arrangements to the Proctors for approval.

11.7. The Proctors shall notify the Chair of Examiners and the Registrar of alternative arrangements approved under this regulation.   5

11.8. When a candidate is to be examined on a date or at a time fixed by the Registrar under regulation 11.5 above, the invigilation of the candidate shall be carried out in accordance with regulation 15.5 below.

Costs
11.9. The costs of arrangements made under this Part shall not fall on the candidate.   10

Appeals under this Part
11.10. A candidate who is dissatisfied with a decision made by the Proctors under regulation 11.4 above, or his or her college, may appeal against that decision in accordance with the provisions of regulation 18.1 below.

Part 12 Candidates with Special Examination Needs   15

Application of Part 12
12.1. (1) This Part is concerned with candidates for University Examinations who have a physical or mental impairment which has a substantial and long-term adverse effect on their ability to carry out normal day-to-day activities.

(2) This Part shall apply to them if the impairment which they have significantly affects their ability to undertake any examination at or within the time allotted to it, or at the place where it is to be held, or in the manner in which it is normally undertaken by candidates.   20

(3) This Part in any case applies to every candidate who has a specific learning difficulty such as dyslexia, dyspraxia, dysgraphia, dyscalculia, or attention deficit disorder.   25

(4) Candidates to whom this Part applies are called 'candidates with special examination needs' and those falling within paragraph (3) of this regulation are called 'candidates with specific learning difficulties'.

General Rules   30
12.2. A candidate in any University Examination with special examination needs may apply to the Proctors through the Senior Tutor of his or her college for alternative examination arrangements relating to his or her condition. They may also apply to the Registrar through the Senior Tutor of his or her college for the condition to be taken into account by the examiners as a special factor that may affect his or her performance in examinations.   35

12.3. (1) An application under regulation 12.2 above shall be made as soon as possible after matriculation and in any event not later than the date of entry of the candidate's name for the first examination for which alternative arrangements are sought.   40

(2) The application must be supported by a statement from an educational psychologist or other suitably qualified medical practitioner (called in these regulations 'the consultant') approved by the Proctors.

(3) The consultant's statement must be based on an assessment of the candidate carried out by that person and on such further assessment of the candidate as the consultant considers necessary in order to form a judgement.   45

(4) The Proctors shall issue guidance periodically on the qualifications of consultants and the nature of the assessments that will be considered appropriate.

12.4. (1) Where an application is made in respect of a candidate who is confirmed under regulation 12.3 above to have special examination needs, the Proctors shall ensure that arrangements are made for the examination of that candidate which are appropriate for him or her and fair in all the circumstances.

(2) These arrangements may include but are not limited to the provision of a room for the examination of the candidate, permission under Part 10 of these regulations for the dictation of papers and the use of a word-processor or other materials and equipment, the provision of an ama-nuensis, and the granting of extra time for the examination.

(3) The Proctors shall have regard to any recommendation made by the consultant in deciding what arrangements they should make.

12.5. Candidates who are confirmed under regulation 12.3 above to have a specific learning difficulty shall, where appropriate, be given extra time by the Proctors. Additional examination adjustments may be permitted on the recommendation of the consultant.

12.6. In the case of a candidate with a specific learning difficulty the Proctors shall also ensure that the appropriate statements explaining the effects of a specific learning difficulty are supplied to the chair of the examiners of the relevant University Examination and the Registrar shall ensure that they are placed on the candidate's examination scripts and any other work submitted for assessment, in order to assist the examiners in adjudicating the merits of the candidate's work.

Visually-impaired candidates

12.7. (1) This additional regulation applies to candidates who are visually-impaired.

(2) Where any college has a visually-impaired candidate for any University Examination, the Senior Tutor shall, not less than three months before the date of the Examination, inform the Proctors who will make the necessary arrangements (including provision for papers in Braille if appropriate) in consultation with the Chair of Examiners and the Registrar.

(3) When papers in Braille or another format are required, the chair concerned shall submit a copy of the necessary manuscripts to the Registrar at least eight weeks before the date of the beginning of the University Examination.

Codes of practice

12.8. In exercising their powers under this Part the Proctors and chairs of examiners shall take full account of any relevant code of practice or other guidance adopted by the University in relation to persons who have a disability.

Invigilation

12.9. The invigilation of candidates with special examination needs for whom an examination room is provided shall be carried out in accordance with regulation 15.5 below.

Continuity of arrangements

12.10. Alternative arrangements approved by the Proctors under this Part shall normally apply to all University Examinations taken by the candidate during his or her course of study.

12.11. (1) It shall be the responsibility of the candidate to apply for any subsequent change to these arrangements which he or she may wish, and to inform the Proctors of any material change in his or her circumstances which might affect the suitability of those arrangements.

(2) In considering any request made under paragraph (1) the Proctors shall obtain and take into account the views of the consultant.

Appeals under this Part
12.12. A candidate who is dissatisfied with any decision made by the Proctors under this Part, or his or her college, may appeal against that decision in accordance with the provisions of regulation 18.1 below.

Costs
12.13. The costs of arrangements made under this Part shall not fall on the candidate.

Part 13 Factors Affecting Performance in an Examination

Application of Part 13
13.1. This Part is concerned with candidates whose performance in a University Examination may be significantly affected by acute illness or some other urgent cause, not falling within regulation 12.1 above, which the candidate wishes to be brought to the attention of the examiners before, during or after an examination.

Factors affecting performance
13.2. If a candidate considers that his or her performance in any part of a University Examination is likely to be or has been affected by factors of which the examiners have no knowledge, the candidate shall through the Senior Tutor of his or her college inform the Registrar of this factor.

13.3. The Registrar shall pass this information on to the chair of the examiners except in cases where it is received after marks have been finalised by examiners. In such cases, the information will be passed to the Proctors who will determine whether the application meets one of the criteria given in 13.4 below.

13.4. (1) Applications under this part received after the final meeting of examiners will normally only be passed to examiners by the Proctors if they are received within three months of the publication of results and if one of the following applies:

(*a*) The candidate's condition is such as to have prevented him or her from making an earlier submission;

(*b*) The candidate's condition is not known or diagnosed until after the final meeting of the examiners;

(*c*) There has been a procedural error that has prevented the candidate's information from being submitted.

(2) If the Proctors decide not to pass the information on they shall give reasons for their decision.

13.5. (1) If the University Examination is one in which Honours may be awarded the examiners may adopt one of the following courses, taking account of the information passed to them:

(*a*) if they consider the candidate has submitted enough work to allow them to determine his or her proper class, they shall award the candidate the class his or her performance merits;

(*b*) if they are unable to adopt course (a) but consider, on the evidence of the work submitted, that but for the illness or other urgent cause affecting the candidate's performance, he or she would have obtained Honours, they may deem the candidate to have obtained Honours and publish his or her name accordingly at the foot of the Results List under the words 'declared to have deserved Honours';

(*c*) if they are unable to adopt course (a) or course (b) but are nevertheless satisfied with the work submitted, they may include the candidate's name on the Results List to show that the candidate has satisfied the examiners;

(*d*) if they are unable to adopt course (a), (b), or (c) they shall fail the candidate.

(2) Where the examiners have adopted course (b), (c), or (d) above it shall be open to the candidate to apply to Education Committee for consideration of his or her standing for Honours at a future examination.

(3) If the University Examination is one in which Honours are not awarded the examiners may adopt one of the following courses, taking account of the information passed to them:

(*a*) if they consider that the candidate has submitted enough work to allow them to determine that it is of sufficient standard to enable the candidate to pass the Examination, they shall include his or her name in the Results List;

(*b*) if they are unable to adopt course (a) they shall fail the candidate.

Appeals under this Part

13.6. A candidate or his or her college who is dissatisfied with any decision made by the Proctors or by the examiners under this Part, may appeal against that decision in accordance with the provisions of regulations 18.1. or 18.2. below.

Part 14 Late Submission, Non-submission, Non-appearance and Withdrawal from Examinations

14.1. This Part provides for candidates who wish to withdraw from any University Examination after their names have been entered under Part 9 of these regulations or who do not appear at the time and place appointed for taking any examination for which they have been entered or who do not submit a thesis or other exercise at the time and place appointed.

14.2. (1) A candidate who fails to appear for any part of a University Examination (including a viva voce examination other than as specified in (2) below) or who fails to submit a thesis (or other exercise) will be deemed to have failed the entire Examination or, in the case of a Second Public Examination taken over more than one year, the entire Part of the Examination unless a successful submission under Part 14 has been made.

(2) This regulation shall not apply where candidates (a) fail to appear for, or to submit work in respect of, optional papers supplementary to the compulsory elements of the examination; (b) fail to appear for a viva voce examination which has the sole purpose of confirming their final position in a Results List.

Late submission and non-submission of a thesis or other written exercise

14.3. A candidate in any University Examination may, through his or her college, request the Proctors to accept an application that the candidate will be or has been prevented by illness or other urgent cause from submitting a thesis (or other exercise) at the appointed time and place for any part of a University Examination.   5

14.4. (1) A request under 14.3. above must be submitted in writing by the Senior Tutor or other proper officer of the candidate's college, with sufficient evidence to support it.

(2) Where non-submission is caused by illness a medical certificate from a qualified medical practitioner must be sent, and this certificate must   10 specify, with dates, the reason why the illness will prevent or has prevented the candidate from submitting the thesis (or other exercise).

14.5. Where the candidate wishes to be permitted to present such thesis (or other exercise) later than the date prescribed by any statute, or regulation, the procedure shall be as follows: 15

(1) the candidate shall include this request in the submission made to the Proctors under 14.3 above;

(2) in cases where a significant extension of time is requested, or where the proposed new submission date is beyond the date by which the thesis (or other exercise) may reasonably be assessed for consideration at the rele-   20 vant meeting of the examiners, or where the request is made after the original date for submission, the Proctors shall consult the chair of examiners about any such application and shall then decide whether or not to grant permission.

14.6. (1) If the Proctors accept a submission under 14.3. above they shall send a   25 copy of their decision promptly to the chair of examiners of the University Examination concerned and inform the candidate's college and the Registrar.

(2) If the Proctors decide not to accept the submission they shall give reasons for their decision.   30

14.7. If the Proctors accept a submission under 14.3., they may authorise the examiners either:

(1) to accept a submission at a later date as provided for under 14.5. above. The examiners shall accept and mark such a thesis (or other exercise) as if it had been submitted by the prescribed date; or   35

(2) if other work that the candidate has already submitted in the Examination is of sufficient merit, to act as if he or she had completed the part of the University Examination which he or she was unable to attend.

14.8. (1) Where it is decided under 14.7.(2) above or 14.16.(2) below that the examiners are to act as if the candidate had completed the part of the   40 University Examination concerned, and the University Examination is one in which Honours may be awarded, the examiners may adopt one of the following courses:

(*a*) if they consider the candidate has submitted enough work to allow them to determine his or her proper class, they may award the   45 candidate the class his or her performance merits;

(*b*) if they are unable to adopt course (a) but consider, on the basis of the work submitted, that but for the candidate's absence he or she would have obtained classified Honours, they may deem the candidate to have obtained Honours and publish his or her name accordingly at   50 the foot of the Results List under the words 'declared to have deserved Honours';

(*c*) if they are unable to adopt course (a) or course (b) but are nevertheless satisfied with the work submitted, they may include the candidate's name on the Results List to show that the candidate has satisfied the examiners;

(*d*) if they are unable to adopt course (a), (b), or (c) they shall fail the candidate.

(2) Where the examiners have adopted course (b), (c), or (d) above it shall be open to the candidate to apply to Education Committee for consideration of his or her standing for Honours at a future examination.

(3) Where it is decided under 14.7.(2) above or 14.16.(2) below that the examiners are to act as if the candidate had completed the parts of the University Examination concerned, and the University Examination is one in which Honours are not awarded, the examiners may adopt one of the following courses:

(*a*) if they consider the candidate has submitted enough work to allow them to determine whether it is of a sufficient standard to enable the candidate to pass the Examination they may include his or her name in the Results List;

(*b*) if they are unable to adopt course (a), they shall fail the candidate.

14.9. If a candidate fails to submit a thesis (or other exercise) by the required time for submission without prior permission, but submits it on the prescribed date of submission, the examiners shall mark the submitted work and impose an academic penalty according to the established conventions agreed by the relevant supervisory body and the candidate shall pay a late presentation fee. A candidate may apply to the Proctors in writing through the Senior Tutor of his or her college to request that the examiners take into account the circumstances of the late submission. Such an application should be made within five working days of the notification of late submission. If the Proctors accept the application, they shall forward it to the chair of examiners. If the Proctors decide not to accept the application, they shall inform the Senior Tutor in writing of the reasons why.

14.10. If a candidate fails to submit a thesis (or other exercise) on time without prior permission, but submits after the prescribed date of submission, the Proctors shall enquire into the circumstances. If they permit the candidate to remain in the Examination, then they shall instruct the examiners to accept and mark the work, and forward to the chair of examiners an account of the circumstances of the late submission. They may give leave to the examiners to impose an academic penalty according to the established conventions agreed by the relevant supervisory body. It shall be a condition of any permission granted under this regulation that the candidate shall pay a late presentation fee.

14.11. Where provided for by regulation, submissions must be accompanied by a declaration of authorship and originality. The examiners are under no obligation to mark any submission not so accompanied. This declaration should be in a sealed envelope (which may be included inside the envelope used to hand in the written work). In the event that the Declaration of Authorship is submitted late, the Proctors may recommend that the examiners apply an academic penalty.

14.12. The Proctors may waive the payment of any fee payable under 14.9. or 14.10. if it appears to them to be reasonable to do so.

Non-appearance at an examination

14.13. (1) A candidate in any University Examination may, through his or her college, request the Proctors to accept a submission that the candidate will be or has been prevented by illness or other urgent cause from presenting himself or herself at the appointed time or place for any part of a University Examination.   5

(2) For the purposes of this regulation a candidate will be deemed to have presented himself or herself for a written paper if he or she was present in the place designated for that examination and had the opportunity to see the question paper there.   10

14.14. (1) A request under regulation 14.13 above must be submitted in writing by the Senior Tutor or other proper officer of the candidate's college, with sufficient evidence to support it.

(2) Where non-appearance is caused by illness a medical certificate from a qualified medical practitioner must be sent, and this certificate must   15
specify, with dates, the reason why the illness will prevent or has prevented the candidate from attending the examination.

14.15. (1) If the Proctors accept a submission under regulation 14.13 above they shall send a copy of their decision promptly to the chair of examiners of the University Examination concerned and inform the candidate's col-   20
lege and the Registrar.

(2) If the Proctors decide not to accept the submission they shall give reasons for their decision.

14.16. If the Proctors accept a submission under 14.13 above they may authorise the examiners either: 25

(1) to examine the candidate at another place or time under such arrangements as they deem appropriate with invigilation carried out in accordance with regulation 15.5 below; or

(2) if other work that the candidate has already submitted in the Examination is of sufficient merit, to act as if he or she had completed   30
the part of the University Examination which he or she was unable to attend, in accordance with 14.8 above.

Withdrawal before the Examination begins

14.17. A candidate whose name has been entered for a University Examination may withdraw from that Examination at any time before the start or (as the case may   35
be) date for submission of the first paper or other assessed exercise in the Examination.

Withdrawal after the Examination has started

14.18. A candidate who wishes to withdraw from a University Examination at any time after the start of the first paper or date for submission of the first paper or other exercise must inform his or her college as soon as possible.   40

14.19. (1) A candidate may not withdraw from a University Examination at any time after the start or date for submission of the first paper or other exercise in the Examination unless it is a result of acute illness or other urgent cause. If the candidate's college is satisfied with the reason given the Senior Tutor must as soon as possible notify the Registrar.   45

(2) On receipt of the notice given under paragraph (1) above the Registrar shall inform the chair of the relevant examiners.

Appeals under this Part

14.20. A candidate or his or her college who is dissatisfied with any decision made by the Proctors or by the examiners under this Part, may appeal against that decision in accordance with the provisions of regulations 18.1 or 18.2 below.

Part 15 Supervision and Invigilation of Examinations

Attendance at examinations by examiners

15.1. (1) Before the start of any examination at least one examiner shall be present to check the question paper and shall remain for the first 30 minutes of the examination (or for the duration of the paper if so required by the chair of the examiners) in case of query.

(2) An external examiner shall not be required to attend.

(3) The chair of the examiners may appoint an assessor to attend in the place of an examiner.

Invigilators

15.2. (1) The Registrar shall draw up for the approval of the Proctors a list of persons whom he or she deems suitable to invigilate examinations.

(2) No student member of the University shall be eligible to act as an invigilator unless he or she is a graduate student in at least the third year of his or her registration for graduate study.

(3) Approved invigilators shall comply with any requirements made by Proctors, in consultation with the Registrar, with regard to their training, conduct, attendance or the discharge of their duties.

(4) The Proctors may remove from the list the name of any person who in their opinion should no longer act as an invigilator.

(5) The Registrar shall, in consultation with the chair of the examiners, arrange for individuals from the approved list to invigilate each examination.

(6) No person who is appointed to act as an amanuensis in any examination may also invigilate that examination.

Invigilation

15.3. Unless the Proctors otherwise determine, one invigilator shall be required for the first fifty candidates and one for each additional fifty candidates or fraction of that number.

Remuneration of invigilators

15.4. Persons other than examiners appointed to supervise or to invigilate under this Part shall be paid in accordance with the scale drawn up by the Education Committee.

Invigilation in cases to which regulation 10.2 or Parts 11, 12, or 13 apply

15.5. (1) When a candidate is to be examined on a date or at a time or place fixed by the Proctors, or as the case may be by a chair of examiners, under regulation 10.2 or Parts 11, 12, or 13 above, paragraphs (2)–(6) of this regulation and regulation 15.6 below shall apply.

(2) Whenever possible the examination shall take place in a room managed by the Registrar who shall be responsible for the appointment of an invigilator and other necessary arrangements.

(3) If the examination takes place in a room provided by the candidate's college, the Senior Tutor shall appoint as invigilator for that part of the examination a person whose name is on the list of invigilators or some other suitable person whose name shall be approved by the Proctors.

(4) If the examination is to take place at a time different from the time fixed for other candidates the Senior Tutor shall make arrangements to be approved by the Proctors for the isolation and supervision of the candidate during the period which begins at the time when the part of the examination is due to be taken by him or her and ends at the time at which it is taken by other candidates (or the other way round) which will ensure that the candidate is unable directly or indirectly to communicate in person, by telephone or by electronic or any other means with any other candidate, unless the Proctors otherwise permit.

(5) When these arrangements are approved by the Proctors they shall communicate them to the chair of the examiners and the Registrar.

(6) The provisions of this regulation shall apply with any necessary modification to practical examinations.

15.6. (1) Where the Proctors have given permission for an examination to be held in a place or at a time other than that appointed for the examination, the invigilator or another person approved by the Proctors shall attend the Examination Schools at least 15 minutes before the examination begins, to receive the examination paper and any necessary writing materials from the Examination Schools, and should bring their University Card or other reliable evidence of their identity.

(2) The invigilator should sign the list kept by the Registrar of examination papers which are issued in this way.

(3) The candidate's work must be handed as soon as possible after the time appointed for the collection of papers to the Registrar, who shall make the appropriate entry in his or her register.

Part 16 Marking and Assessment

Adjudication on the merits of candidates

16.1. (1) Every examiner who takes part in adjudicating on the merits of a candidate shall give careful attention to the examination of such candidates.

(2) No examiner adjudicating on the merits of any candidate shall take account of any circumstances, not forming part of, or directly resulting from, the examination itself, except as provided in Parts 12 or 13 of these regulations.

(3) The work of any candidate to whom Parts 12 or 13 of these regulations applies shall be assessed with due and careful regard to the circumstances of that candidate and any relevant code of practice or guidelines adopted by the University in relation to such candidates.

(4) In the case of a candidate against whom an order has been made by a University Court under section 11 (3) or section 21 (1)(*e*) of Statute XI or by the Appeal Court in similar terms (intentional or reckless breach of examination regulations), the examiners shall give effect to that order.

(5) Where the Proctors have a recommendation to the examiners in respect of a candidate under section 32 (3) of Statute XI (breach of examination regulations which is neither intentional nor reckless) the examiners shall give due weight to the recommendation in assessing the candidate's work.

Examination conventions

16.2. (1) In adjudicating on the merits of candidates the examiners shall follow and apply the conventions approved under regulation 8.1 above subject to the right of the Board of Examiners in exceptional circumstances to make minor adjustments to the conventions during any particular Examination.

(2) In cases of doubt or difficulty arising under (1), the examiners shall consult the Proctors.

(3) Nothing in this regulation shall affect the authority of the examiners in the making of academic judgements on the performance of each candidate.

Viva voce Examination

16.3. In any University Examination in which candidates are examined viva voce the examiners shall determine the order in which they are to be examined.

16.4. Only one candidate at a time shall be examined viva voce in any one University Examination, but in cases approved by the Pro-Vice-Chancellor (Education) and Proctors the examiners in any University Examination may be permitted to divide themselves into groups which may examine candidates simultaneously.

16.5. (1) Except in the circumstances referred to in paragraph (2) below no examiner, other than an examiner in the Preliminary Examination in Medicine or in the Second Examination for the Degree of Bachelor of Medicine, or in the Honour School of Oriental Studies shall examine viva voce any candidate who belongs to any college in which he or she is tutor or in which he or she has been tutor during the previous two years or who has been instructed by him or her (otherwise than at a lecture or class open to all members of the University) within the previous two years.

(2) The Pro-Vice-Chancellor (Education) and Proctors may relieve any Board of Examiners of the restriction imposed by this regulation if it would cause difficulty in the conduct of the Examination in question.

Submission of theses or other exercises: exceeding word limits and departure from title or subject-matter

16.6. (1) Where a candidate for any University Examination in which a thesis (or other exercise) may be, or is required to be, submitted as part of that Examination presents a thesis (or other exercise) which exceeds the word limit prescribed by the relevant statute, or regulation, the examiners, if they agree to proceed with the examination of the work, may reduce the mark by up to one class (or its equivalent).[1]

(2) Where a candidate submits such a thesis (or other exercise), the title or subject matter of which differs from that which was approved by the supervisory body concerned, the examiners (if they agree to proceed with

---

[1] 'Reduction by one class' means a reduction from a II(i) to a II(ii) in the case of a mark which would otherwise have led to classification as a II(i).

the examination of the work) may similarly reduce the mark by up to one class (or its equivalent).[1]

Illegible scripts

16.7. (1) If a chair of examiners considers that a script of a candidate in an examination is illegible (whether the whole script or any part thereof as identified by the chair), he or she shall inform the Senior Tutor of that candidate's college.

(2) Should the Senior Tutor dispute the illegibility of any such script (or part thereof as identified by the chair of examiners), the question shall be referred to the Proctors, whose ruling on the question shall be conclusive.

(3) Where it is accepted that a script (or part thereof) is illegible, the Senior Tutor shall either:

(*a*) arrange with the Registrar for the script to be transcribed in accordance with the procedure agreed between the Proctors and the Registrar; or

(*b*) arrange for the candidate to dictate his or her script (or each required part thereof) to a typist under the invigilation of a Master of Arts of the University or any other person who is deemed by the Proctors to be suitable, having first submitted in advance to the Proctors proposals for (i) the appointment of a typist and an invigilator for the transcription of the script and (ii) the timing and venue for the exercise.

(4) It shall be the responsibility of the Registrar or the Senior Tutor, as the case may be, to ensure that the transcription exercise is conducted in accordance with the arrangements approved by the Proctors.

(5) During the transcription exercise the candidate shall dictate his or her script (or each required part thereof) to the typist in the presence of the invigilator, with the exception (unless otherwise identified by the chair of examiners) of work which constitutes rough notes. The candidate shall ensure that the typescript is in every respect identical in form and content to the original script. The use of any recording device is not permitted. Only one fair copy shall be made of each dictated script (or required part thereof), for submission to the examiners.

(6) Academic dress and sub-fusc clothing need not be worn by any of the participants during the transcription exercise.

(7) The cost of the typing and invigilation shall not be a charge on the University.

(8) Following completion of the transcription exercise, it shall be the responsibility of the Registrar (for transcriptions under (3)(*a*) above) or the Senior Tutor (for transcriptions under (3)(*b*) above) to make available to the chair of examiners both the original script and the typescript.

(9) The examiners shall read the typescript page by page with the original script beside it and shall immediately report any discrepancy to the Proctors.

---

[1] 'Reduction by one class' means a reduction from a II(i) to a II(ii) in the case of a mark which would otherwise have led to classification as a II(i).

16.8. (1) If in voting upon the place to be assigned to a candidate in any Results List the examiners shall be equally divided, the chair of the examiners in that Examination shall (unless paragraph (2) below applies) have a second or casting vote.

(2) If the candidate in question shall be of the same college as the chair of the examiners or of any college in which he or she is tutor or in which he or she has been tutor during the previous two years, or shall have been privately taught by him or her during the past two years, then the casting vote shall be with the senior of the examiners who is not disqualified on that ground.

16.9. Candidates whose performance is not sufficient for the award of Honours but have satisfied the examiners at 'pass' standard shall be awarded a pass.

Part 17 Publication of Results

Honours Examinations

17.1. As soon as the examiners in an Honours Examination have examined and fully considered the work of all the candidates they shall:

(1) distribute candidates (identified only by their examination numbers) judged to have shown merit into three classes according to merit;

(2) except in the case of Honour Moderations (other than Classics) distribute the candidates in the second class into two divisions;

(3) forthwith provide the information determined under (1) and (2) above to the Registrar using the Registrar's Results Lists.

17.2. Where a University Examination in which Honours are awarded is divided into several Parts then (unless the regulations for the specific Examination otherwise provide) in respect of all Parts save the last:

(1) the examiners shall determine the candidates (identified only by their examination numbers) who have shown sufficient merit to obtain Honours in each Part; and

(2) forthwith provide the information determined under paragraph (1) above to the Registrar; and

(3) the respective chairs of the examiners shall deposit the candidates' exercises with the Registrar for the use of the examiners in any succeeding Examination.

17.3. If a candidate in any Honour Moderations has not been judged by the moderators to be worthy of Honours but has satisfied the moderators at 'pass' standard they shall give notice of that fact at the close of the Examination to the Registrar.

17.4. If a candidate in any Final Honour School or in the Final Examination for the Degree of Bachelor of Fine Art has not been judged by the examiners to be worthy of Honours but has satisfied them at 'pass' standard the examiners shall give notice of that fact at the close of the Examination to the Registrar.

17.5. (1) If a candidate in any Honour School of the First or Second Public Examination or in the Final Examination for the Degree of Bachelor of Fine Art is disqualified by standing from obtaining Honours in that

Examination, but has in the judgement of the examiners shown sufficient merit to entitle him or her to obtain Honours, but for such disqualification, the examiners shall give notice of that fact on the Results List submitted to the Registrar at the close of the Examination.

(2) A candidate to whom this regulation applies shall be entitled to supplicate for the Degree of Bachelor of Arts or of Fine Art (as the case may) in the same manner as if he or she had obtained Honours in the Examination.

17.6. If the regulations for any University Examination in which Honours are awarded also permit the award of a merit or a distinction in any part of that Examination the examiners shall give notice to the Registrar at the close of the examination of the names of all the candidates whose work in that part has been adjudged worthy of either accolade.

Other Examinations

17.7. The examiners in any Preliminary or Qualifying Examination or in any examination for a graduate taught programme or for a diploma or certificate except the Diploma in Law or the Certificate in Management Studies shall:

(1) determine the candidates (identified only by their examination number) who have satisfied them;

(2) if the regulations governing the particular Examination permit, determine the candidates who have shown sufficient merit to obtain a distinction; and

(3) forthwith provide the information determined under paragraphs (1) and (2) above to the Registrar using the Registrar's Results Lists.

17.8. In an Examination where a candidate is not required to pass in all subjects at one and the same Examination the examiners shall provide a Results List with the agreed results to date.

Approved musical exercises for the Degree of Bachelor of Music

17.9. At the close of the Examination of the Musical Exercises for the Degree of Bachelor of Music submitted to them in any term, the examiners shall notify the Registrar of the candidates whose exercises have been approved by them.

Candidates who have failed

17.10. If a candidate in any University Examination has been judged by the examiners to have failed the examination the examiners shall give notice of that fact, at the close of the examination to the Registrar by inclusion on the Registrar's Results List.

Notification of results

17.11. All notifications submitted to the Registrar under this Part shall be made in a form of Results List as provided by the Registrar, unless he or she otherwise agrees.

17.12. All information submitted to the Registrar under this Part shall (unless any examiner shall have been excused by the Proctors) be certified by the signature of all the examiners who have acted together in the assessment of the candidates in the Examination.

17.13. On receipt of the information provided under regulations 17.11 to 17.12 above, the Registrar shall arrange the publication of results to each candidate.

17.14. (1) After results have been released to candidates, examiners shall have no power to alter such Results Lists except under paragraph (2)–(4) below.

(2) Examiners may submit to the Deputy Registrar a change in an individual assessment mark or grade without further consent in instances where an examination overall outcome is not changed.

(3) Examiners may, with the written consent of the Pro-Vice-Chancellor (Education) and Proctors, amend an individual assessment mark or grade where such change will result in a change in the overall examination outcome.

(4) Examiners may, with the written consent of the Pro-Vice-Chancellor (Education) and Proctors, issue a further Results List or Lists to provide results of candidates omitted from the original list.

Custody of records

17.15. The Results Lists drawn up and duly signed shall be circulated and published by the Registrar according to the requirements of the Education Committee and subject to the provisions of the Data Protection Act and the signed copy shall remain in the custody of the Registrar, and any question thereafter arising, with respect to the result of any Examination, shall be determined by reference to such lists.

Forms of Certificates

17.16. (1) Degree certificates and other certificates for diplomas and other certificate courses shall be issued to successful candidates in forms prescribed by the Registrar.

(2) When a candidate has obtained a distinction in his or her Examination, or in any part of it for which a distinction may be awarded, the certificate or diploma, as the case may be, which is issued shall record that fact.

Part 18 Appeals from Decisions of the Proctors and Examiners

Appeals from decisions under Parts 11, 12, 13, and 14

18.1. (1) A candidate who is dissatisfied with a decision made by the Proctors under Parts 11, 12, 13, or 14 above, may, or his or her college may, appeal against it in accordance with the procedures set out in this regulation.

(2) An appeal must be made within 14 days of the date of the Proctors' decision.

(3) Any such appeal must be made in writing to the Chair of the Education Committee.

(4) The appeal shall be determined expeditiously by the Chair or another member of the Committee, other than one of the Proctors, nominated by the Chair.

Appeals from decisions of examiners

18.2. Appeals from decisions of examiners shall be made in accordance with the Procedures for Handling Complaints (including Academic Appeals) laid down and published by the Proctors under section 20 of Statute IX and any Council Regulations made under that section and not otherwise.

Part 19 Proctors' Disciplinary Regulations for Candidates in Examination

Made by the Proctors on 1 October 2003
Approved by Council on 30 October 2003

1. These regulations are made by the Proctors in the exercise of their powers under   5
section 22 of Statute IX and are designated by Council as disciplinary regulations
under section 2 (2) of Statute XI. In accordance with that Statute, candidates who
deliberately or recklessly breach any of the following regulations may be subject to
disciplinary procedures.

2. In these regulations: (1) 'examination' includes where the context so permits the   10
submission and assessment of a thesis, dissertation, essay, Transfer of Status materials,
Confirmation of Status materials, or other coursework which is not undertaken in
formal examination conditions but is a requirement for, counts towards or constitutes
the work for a degree or other academic award; and (2) 'examination room' means
any room designated by the Registrar or his or her deputy or approved by the Proctors   15
as a place for one or more candidates to take an examination.

3. No candidate shall cheat or act dishonestly, or attempt to do so, in any way,
whether before, during or after an examination, so as to obtain or seek to obtain an
unfair advantage in an examination.

4. No candidate shall plagiarise by presenting someone else's work as their own,   20
or by incorporating other people's work or ideas into their own work without full
acknowledgement. This includes: verbatim quotation, cutting and pasting from the
internet, and paraphrasing without clear acknowledgement; collusion; inaccurate
citation; failure to acknowledge assistance; use of material written by professional
agencies or other persons; and autoplagiarism.   25

5. Unless specifically permitted by the Special Subject Regulations for the examination concerned, no candidate shall submit to the examiners any work which he or
she has previously submitted partially or in full for examination at this University or
elsewhere. Where earlier work by the candidate is citable, he or she shall reference it
clearly.   30

6. No person shall dishonestly give help to a candidate before, during or after an
examination so as to give, or attempt to give, that candidate an unfair advantage in an
examination.

7. No candidate shall take, or attempt to take, into an examination any un-
authorised material (including revision notes), item or device (including a mobile   35
telephone or any device capable of receiving or communicating information) nor use
or attempt to use such material, item or device.

8. No candidate shall copy from the script of another candidate or in any other
way dishonestly receive help from another person in an examination.

9. Candidates may not communicate with any person other than an invigilator   40
during an examination.

10. No candidate may leave or re-enter an examination room unless permitted by
an invigilator.

11. No candidate shall enter an examination room more than thirty minutes after an
examination has started except with the permission of the Proctors or an invigilator.   45

12. No candidate shall unless permitted by the Proctors or an invigilator leave an
examination room:

(1) within thirty minutes of the beginning of an examination; or

(2) within thirty minutes of the time at which it is due to end.

13. No candidate may smoke in an examination room or in any building in which an examination is being held, or behave in any other way which distracts or is likely to distract other candidates.

14. Candidates may not use paper in an examination except that which is provided for them.

15. At the end of each examination candidates must hand back to an invigilator all the paper provided for writing their answers, including paper used for rough drafts and paper which has not been used. No paper may be removed from the examination room other than the question-paper for the examination that has just been completed.

16. Unless regulation 17 below applies, all articles or equipment to be used in an examination must be carried into the examination room in a transparent bag.

17. Candidates must offer non-transparent bags for inspection and, unless special permission is given by an invigilator, must deposit them at the place designated for the deposit of bags and other personal belongings.

18. Candidates must present themselves for examinations in full academic dress.

19. Candidates must follow the directions of the invigilators and the Proctors during an examination, including a direction to leave the examination room and the building in which the examination is being held.

Part 20 Proctors' Administrative Regulations for Candidates in Examinations

Made by the Proctors on 1 October 2005

1. These regulations shall apply to all university examinations, including any examination described in any regulation as a qualifying examination.

2. In these regulations 'college' means any college, society, or Permanent Private Hall or any other institution designated by Council by regulation as being permitted to present candidates for matriculation.

3. It is the responsibility of each candidate to ensure that he or she hands in all the material he or she wishes to be considered by the examiners and to comply with regulations relating to the submission of written work such as dissertations, essays, and project reports. Once a candidate has submitted a piece of work, he or she may not withdraw that piece of work and substitute a revised version in the same examination without the Proctors' consent.

4. During every written paper, each candidate shall display his or her University Card face up on the desk at which he or she is writing.

5. A candidate who is taken ill while sitting a written paper may (with an invigilator's permission) leave the room and return while the examination is in progress, to resume the paper on one occasion only (and no extra time shall be allowed). If the candidate is unable to complete the paper concerned because he or she has been taken ill a second time, he or she should inform an invigilator so that the incomplete script can be handed in. It is the candidate's responsibility to obtain a medical certificate, in accordance with the relevant provisions of the General Regulations for the Conduct of University Examinations, explaining how his or her performance in the paper concerned may have been affected by illness.

6. A candidate may not withdraw from an examination after the written part of the examination is complete. The point of completion shall be deemed to be the conclusion of the last paper for which the candidate has entered, or the time by which a dissertation or other written material is due to be submitted, whichever is the later.

7. Concerns about the conduct of an examination must not be raised directly with Examiners. A candidate on a taught course may communicate with Examiners about such matters only through the Senior Tutor or equivalent officer of his or her college. If such a candidate wishes to raise a query or make a complaint about the conduct of his or her examination, such query or complaint must be notified to the Senior Tutor or equivalent officer of his or her college not later than three months after the notification of the results of the examination concerned (when the matter will be dealt with in accordance with the Council Regulations governing the handling of complaints submitted to the Proctors). A candidate for a research degree or higher doctorate may communicate a query or complaint about the conduct of his or her examination direct to the Proctors: this must be done not later than three months after the notification of the results of the examination concerned (in accordance with the procedures set out in the Council Regulations governing the handling of complaints submitted to the Proctors).

NOTES

2

GENERAL REGULATIONS FOR THE FIRST AND SECOND PUBLIC EXAMINATION

Part 1 General

5

1.1. These regulations apply to the following degrees of the University:

Bachelor of Arts	Master of Engineering
Bachelor of Fine Art	Master of Mathematics
Master of Biochemistry	Master of Mathematics and Computer Science
Master of Chemistry	Master of Mathematics and Philosophy
Master of Computer Science	Master of Mathematics and Physics
Master of Computer Science and Philosophy	Master of Physics
Master of Earth Sciences	Master of Physics and Philosophy

1.2. In these regulations where the context admits:

(1) the expression 'statutory residence' means residence at any place authorised by the Regulations for Residence in the University ('the Residence Regulations');

(2) references to divisions and faculty boards shall include a reference to the Committee for the Ruskin School of Art; and

(3) 'college' means any college, society, or Permanent Private Hall or any other institution designated by Council by regulation as being permitted to present candidates for matriculation.

1.3. Any member of the University may be admitted to a degree to which these regulations apply if he or she:

(1) has kept statutory residence for the period prescribed in these regulations for the degree in question; and

(2) has employed himself or herself in study and hearing lectures and has (unless exempt) passed the First and Second Public Examinations in accordance with the requirements laid down by regulation.

Part 2 Residence

2.1. A member reading for the Degree of Bachelor of Arts or of Fine Art must unless regulation 2.2 below applies keep nine terms of statutory residence.

2.2. A member who has taken Honour Moderations in Classics as the First Public Examination or who intends to apply for Honours in the Second Public Examination in Mathematics and Philosophy (Part II) or Physics and Philosophy (Part C) must keep twelve terms of statutory residence.

2.3. A member reading for any of the Master's degrees referred to in regulation 1.1 above must keep twelve terms of statutory residence.

2.4. The Proctors may, for any reason judged by them to be sufficient and on such conditions as they think fit, excuse a member reading for a degree to which these regulations apply from up to three terms of statutory residence.

2.5. (1) If any member is dissatisfied with a decision by the Proctors under regula-   5
tion 2.4 above, he or she, or his or her college, may within fourteen days of the date of the decision appeal in writing to the Chair of the Education Committee of Council.

(2) The appeal shall be adjudged expeditiously by the Chair or another member of that committee, other than one of the Proctors, nominated by the Chair.   10

2.6. Applications for dispensation under regulation 2.4 above must be made through the applicant's college.

2.7. A member who is granted dispensation from statutory residence under regulation 2.4 above must nevertheless, unless expressly exempted, pay in respect of any term for which he or she is excused residence any university fee which would have been   15
payable if he or she had actually resided.

2.8. Council may permit time spent outside Oxford, as part of an academic programme approved by it, to be counted towards residence for the purposes of these regulations.

Part 3 First Public Examination   20

3.1. The First Public Examination shall include Honour Moderations, Moderations, and Preliminary Examinations in the subjects respectively listed in Table 1, Table 2, and Table 3

3.2. The examinations shall be conducted by Moderators under the supervision of the divisional and faculty boards assigned to each subject respectively in Table 1,   25
Table 2, and Table 3

TABLE 1: HONOUR MODERATIONS

Subject	Board(s)
Archaeology and Anthropology	Social Sciences Division
Classics	Faculty of Classics

TABLE 2: MODERATIONS

Subject	Board(s)
Law	Faculty of Law

TABLE 3: PRELIMINARY EXAMINATIONS *(For the explanation of the asterisks see regulation 3.10)*   35

Subject	Board(s)
Ancient and Modern History	Faculties of Classics and History
*Archaeology and Anthropology	Social Sciences Division
Biological Sciences	Mathematical, Physical and Life Sciences Division
Biomedical Sciences	Medical Sciences Division
Chemistry	Mathematical, Physical and Life Sciences Division
Classical Archaeology and Ancient History	Social Sciences Division and Faculty of Classics
*Classics	Faculty of Classics
Classics and English	Faculties of Classics and English Language and Literature

Computer Science	Mathematical, Physical and Life Sciences Division	
Computer Science and Philosophy	Mathematical, Physical and Life Sciences Division and Faculty of Philosophy	
Earth Sciences	Mathematical, Physical and Life Sciences Division	
Economics and Management	Social Sciences Division	5
Engineering Science	Mathematical, Physical and Life Sciences Division	
English and Modern Languages	Faculties of English Language and Literature and Medieval and Modern Languages	
English Language and Literature	Faculty of English Language and Literature	10
European and Middle Eastern Languages	Faculties of Medieval and Modern Languages and Oriental Studies	
Fine Art	Committee for Ruskin School of Art	
Geography	Social Sciences Division	15
History	Faculty of History	
History and Economics	Faculty of History and Social Sciences Division	
History and English	Faculties of History and English Language and Literature	
History and Modern Languages	Faculties of History and Medieval and Modern Languages	20
History and Politics	Faculty of History and Social Sciences Division	
History of Art	Faculty of History	
Human Sciences	Social Sciences Division	
Materials Science	Mathematical, Physical and Life Sciences Division	25
Mathematics	Mathematical, Physical and Life Sciences Division	
Mathematics and Computer Science	Mathematical, Physical and Life Sciences Division	
Mathematics and Philosophy	Mathematical, Physical and Life Sciences Division and Faculty of Philosophy	30
Modern Languages	Faculty of Medieval and Modern Languages	
Molecular and Cellular Biochemistry	Medical Sciences Division	
Music	Faculty of Music	
Oriental Studies	Faculty of Oriental Studies	35
Philosophy and Modern Languages	Faculties of Philosophy and Medieval and Modern Languages	
Philosophy, Politics, and Economics	Faculty of Philosophy and Social Sciences Division	
Physics	Mathematical, Physical and Life Sciences Division	40
Physics and Philosophy	Mathematical, Physical and Life Sciences Division and Faculty of Philosophy	
Psychology, Philosophy, and Linguistics	Medical Sciences Division and Faculties of Philosophy and Linguistics, Philology and Phonetics	45
Theology	Faculty of Theology	

3.3. The boards shall from time to time make and publish Special Regulations respecting the examinations under their supervision and shall publish lists of subjects and (where appropriate) of books which may be offered for examination, maintaining as far as possible a distinction between the subjects and any books prescribed in the First and Second Public Examinations respectively.

3.4. Special Regulations made and lists drawn up by boards under regulation 3.3 above shall not have effect until:

    (1) they have been approved by or on behalf of the Education Committee of Council;

(2) in the case of regulations made and lists drawn up by faculty boards or other bodies within the Humanities and Social Sciences Divisions, they have also first been approved by the Humanities Board or the Social Sciences Board as appropriate;

(3) they have then been duly published, and if necessary approved by Congregation, in accordance with the procedure laid down in sections 13–18 of Statute VI.

Method of examining

3.5. Subject to regulation 3.6 below the examinations shall be conducted in writing.

3.6. A board may specify by Special Regulation that an examination shall be partly aural, oral, practical, or visual.

Admission to the First Public Examination

3.7. No person who is not a student member of the University may be admitted to the First Public Examination.

3.8. Candidates may be admitted to Honour Moderations at any time not earlier than the third term from matriculation, but no candidate who has exceeded the sixth term from matriculation inclusively, or the eighth term in the case of candidates for Honour Moderations in Classics, shall be capable of obtaining Honours.

3.9. Candidates may be admitted to each of the Moderations listed in Table 4, not earlier than the term from matriculation specified in each case.

TABLE 4: ADMISSION TO MODERATIONS

Moderations	*Earliest term from matriculation*
Law	2nd

3.10. (1) Candidates shall not be admitted to any of the Preliminary Examinations which has the same title as any Honour Moderations or Moderations, and which is one of those marked with an asterisk in Table 3, unless they have either failed the examination for the Honour Moderations or Moderations with the same title or, subject to the consent of the Proctors, have been prevented by illness or other urgent and reasonable cause from taking that examination.

(2) If any member of the University is dissatisfied with a decision by the Proctors under paragraph (1) above, he or she, or his or her college, may within fourteen days of the date of the decision appeal in writing to the Chair of the Education Committee of Council.

(3) The appeal shall be adjudged expeditiously by the Chair or another member of the committee, other than one of the Proctors, nominated by the Chair.

3.11. Candidates may be admitted to each of the Preliminary Examinations listed in Table 5, not earlier than the term from matriculation specified in each case.

TABLE 5: ADMISSION TO PRELIMINARY EXAMINATIONS

Preliminary Examination	*Earliest term from matriculation*
Ancient and Modern History	3rd
Biological Sciences	3rd
Biomedical Sciences	3rd

Chemistry	2nd
Classical Archaeology and Ancient History	3rd
Classics	2nd
Computer Science	3rd
Computer Science and Philosophy	3rd
Earth Sciences	2nd
English and Modern Languages:	
English	3rd
Modern Language	2nd
Fine Art	3rd
History	3rd
History and Economics	3rd
History and English	3rd
History and Modern Languages	3rd
History and Politics	3rd
Mathematics	3rd
Mathematics and Computer Science	3rd
Mathematics and Philosophy	3rd
Modern Languages	2nd
Molecular and Cellular Biochemistry	2nd
Music	3rd
Oriental Studies:	
Arabic, Chinese, Egyptology and Ancient Near	3rd
Eastern Studies, Japanese, Turkish	
Other languages	2nd
Philosophy and Modern Languages	2nd
Philosophy, Politics, and Economics	2nd
Physics	3rd
Physics and Philosophy	3rd
Psychology, Philosophy, and Linguistics	2nd
Theology and Religion	2nd

3.12. No person whose name has been placed in any Results List issued by Moderators shall be admitted again as a candidate in the same Honours Examination.

Passing the First Public Examination

3.13. A candidate shall be deemed to have passed the First Public Examination if he or she has satisfied the Moderators in any one of the parts of the examination as set out in Table 1, Table 2, and Table 3

3.14. Any person who has satisfied the Moderators in Part I of the First Examination for the Degree of Bachelor of Medicine shall be deemed to have passed the First Public Examination.

3.15. (1) A candidate who fails to satisfy the examiners in his or her initial examination for the First Public Examination shall be permitted to re-enter for the examination on one further occasion in accordance with the special regulations governing re-sits in the programme concerned.

(2) A further exceptional opportunity to re-sit the examination at the next opportunity shall require application to and approval on behalf of the Education Committee.

(3) A candidate who passes the First Public Examination whether at the first attempt or after re-sitting the examination shall be deemed to have

reached the University's threshold standard for embarking on the Final Honour School.

Part 4 Second Public Examination

4.1. The Second Public Examination shall, except in the case of the Degree of Bachelor of Fine Art, consist of a Final Examination in the Honour Schools in each of the subjects listed in Table 6.

TABLE 6: HONOUR SCHOOLS

Subject	*Board(s)*
Ancient and Modern History	Faculties of Classics and History
Archaeology and Anthropology	Social Sciences Division
Biological Sciences	Mathematical, Physical and Life Sciences Division
Cell and Systems Biology	Medical Sciences Division
Chemistry	Mathematical, Physical and Life Sciences Division
Classical Archaeology and Ancient History	Social Sciences Division and Faculty of Classics
Classics and English	Faculties of Classics and English Language and Literature
Classics and Modern Languages	Faculties of Classics and Medieval and Modern Languages
Classics and Oriental Studies	Faculties of Classics and Oriental Studies
Computer Science (three-year and four-year)	Mathematical, Physical and Life Sciences Division
Computer Science and Philosophy (three-year and four-year)	Mathematical, Physical and Life Sciences Division and Faculty of Philosophy
Earth Sciences (four-year)	Mathematical, Physical and Life Sciences Division
Economics and Management	Social Sciences Division
[**Until MT 2017:** Engineering, Economics, and Management	Mathematical, Physical and Life Sciences and Social Sciences Divisions]
Engineering Science	Mathematical, Physical and Life Sciences Division
English Language and Literature	Faculty of English Language and Literature
English and Modern Languages	Faculties of English Language and Literature and Medieval and Modern Languages
European and Middle Eastern Languages	Faculties of Medieval and Modern Languages and Oriental Studies
Experimental Psychology	Medical Sciences Division
Geography	Social Sciences Division
Geology (three-year)	Mathematical, Physical and Life Sciences Division
History	Faculty of History
History and Economics	Faculty of History and Social Sciences Division
History and English	Faculties of History and English Language and Literature
History and Modern Languages	Faculties of History and Medieval and Modern Languages

History and Politics	Faculty of History and Social Sciences Division
History of Art	Faculty of Modern History
Human Sciences	Social Sciences Division
Jurisprudence	Faculty of Law
Literae Humaniores	Faculties of Classics and Philosophy
[**Until MT 2018**: Materials, Economics, and Management	Mathematical, Physical and Life Sciences and Social Sciences Divisions]
Materials Science	Mathematical, Physical and Life Sciences Division
Mathematics (three-year and four-year)	Mathematical, Physical and Life Sciences Division
Mathematics and Computer Science (three-year and four-year)	Mathematical, Physical and Life Sciences Division
Mathematics and Philosophy	Mathematical, Physical and Life Sciences Division and Faculty of Philosophy
Mathematical and Theoretical Physics (after transfer to that Honour School for the Part C examination from the Honour Schools of Mathematics, Physics, or Physics and Philosophy)	Mathematical, Physical and Life Sciences Division
Mathematics and Statistics (three-year and four-year)	Mathematical, Physical and Life Sciences Division
Medical Sciences	Medical Sciences Division
Modern Languages	Faculty of Medieval and Modern Languages
Molecular and Cellular Biochemistry	Medical Sciences Division
Music	Faculty of Music
Neuroscience	Medical Sciences Division
Oriental Studies	Faculty of Oriental Studies
Philosophy and Modern Languages	Faculties of Philosophy and Medieval and Modern Languages
Philosophy, Politics, and Economics	Faculty of Philosophy and Social Sciences Division
Philosophy and Theology	Faculties of Philosophy and Theology and Religion
Physics (three-year and four-year)	Mathematical, Physical and Life Sciences Division
Physics and Philosophy	Mathematical, Physical and Life Sciences Division and Faculty of Philosophy
Psychology, Philosophy, and Linguistics	Medical Sciences Division and Faculties of Philosophy and Linguistics, Philology and Phonetics
Theology and Religion	Faculty of Theology and Religion
Theology and Oriental Studies	Faculties of Theology and Religion and Oriental Studies

4.2. The examinations shall be conducted by the Public Examiners under the supervision of the divisional or faculty boards assigned to each school in Table 6.

4.3. The Second Public Examination for the Degree of Bachelor of Fine Art shall consist of a Final Honour School under the supervision of the Committee for the Ruskin School of Art.

4.4. The boards shall from time to time make and publish Special Regulations respecting the examinations under their supervision and shall publish lists of subjects and (where appropriate) of books which may be offered for examination.

4.5. Special Regulations made and lists drawn up by boards under regulation 4.5 above shall not have effect until:

(1) they have been approved by or on behalf of the Education Committee of Council;

(2) in the case of regulations made and lists drawn up by faculty boards or other bodies within the Humanities and Social Sciences Divisions, they have also first been approved by the Humanities Board or the Social Sciences Board as appropriate;

(3) they have then been duly published, and if necessary approved by Congregation, in accordance with the procedure laid down in sections 13–18 of Statute VI.

Method of examining

4.6. Every candidate in a Second Public Examination shall be examined in writing; and any candidate who seeks Honours may be examined viva voce where Special Regulations made by the divisional board, board of a faculty, or other body responsible for an examination (or jointly by the relevant bodies where an examination is a joint responsibility) expressly provide.

4.7. A board may specify by Special Regulation that an examination shall be partly aural, oral, practical, or visual.

Admission to the Second Public Examination

4.8. No person who is not a student member of the University may be admitted to the Second Public Examination.

4.9. No person may be admitted to the Second Public Examination unless he or she has passed or been exempted from the First Public Examination.

4.10. No person may be admitted as a candidate in any Final Honour School unless he or she:

(1) has satisfied the conditions, if any, which are required by regulations (including Special Regulations) relating to the School in which he or she is a candidate; and

(2) will by the end of the term in which the examination is taken have kept statutory residence for the number of terms which, under Part 2 or 5 of these regulations or the Regulations for Senior Student Status, is appropriate to his or her status and to the School in which he or she is a candidate.

Maximum time allowed for Honours

4.11. No person may be admitted as a candidate in any Final Honour School after the lapse of twelve terms from the term of matriculation inclusively, except in the following cases:

(1) A candidate who has obtained Honours in some other Final Honour School may be admitted not more than six terms after the date on which he or she first obtained Honours in a Final Honour School.

(2) A candidate who has obtained Honours (or has satisfied the Moderators under the Regulations for the Conduct of Examinations) in Honour Moderations may be admitted as a candidate in Part II of the examination in Chemistry or in Molecular and Cellular Biochemistry or in Materials Science up to the end of the eighteenth term.

(3) A candidate in any of the following Final Honour School examinations may be admitted up to the end of the fifteenth term:

(*a*) any Final Honour School, if the candidate has obtained Honours (or has satisfied the Moderators under the Regulations for the Conduct of Examinations) in Honour Moderations in either the fifth or sixth term, or the eighth term in the case of Honour Moderations in Classics, from matriculation;

(*b*) the second part of any Final Honour School which is divided into two parts, except the Honour School of Biological Sciences, the Honour School of Geology, and the Honour School of Physics (three-year course);

(*c*) the third part of any Final Honour School which is divided into three parts;

(*d*) the Honour School of Classics and Modern Languages, English and Modern Languages, European and Middle Eastern Languages, Jurisprudence, Modern Languages, Modern History and Modern Languages, or Philosophy and Modern Languages, if the candidate is certified by his or her college to have spent an academic year of approved residence in an appropriate country or appropriate countries;

(*e*) the examination in Chinese or Japanese, or, if the candidate is certified to have spent an academic year abroad on a course approved by the Board of the Faculty of Oriental Studies, the examination in Arabic, or Hebrew, or Persian, or Turkish, in the Honour School of Oriental Studies.

(4) A person whose position is not covered in any of paragraphs 4.11 (1)–(3) may be admitted as a candidate in a Final Honour School for which there is at least one other candidate, subject to the approval of the Education Committee.

(5) A person who is admitted under (4) above within six terms of the term in which they were originally due to be examined for a part of a Final Honour School or the relevant Part, shall normally be examined in accordance with the regulations pertaining to the orginal examination.

(6) A person who is admitted under (4) above seven or more terms after the term in which they were originally due to be examined for a part of a Final Honour School or the relevant Part, shall normally be examined in accordance with the current regulations.

4.12. The candidate's college shall be required to notify the University of any change in the candidate's status between entry and the date of the examination.

4.13. No person whose name has been placed in any Results Listand recorded as achieving a classified result by the Public Examiners (other than a candidate who has been declared to have deserved Honours under the Regulations for the Conduct of Examinations) shall be admitted again as a candidate in the same Final Honour School, but this regulation shall not affect the regulations concerning the Final Honour Schools of Modern Languages and Oriental Studies which enable candidates under certain conditions to offer themselves again in the same School.

4.14. (1) No person whose name has been placed in any Results List by the Public Examiners (with the exceptions in regulations 4.12 and 4.13 above) shall be admitted as a candidate in a second Final Honour School having papers in common with the first, except with the permission of the Proctors.

(2) If any member of the University is dissatisfied with a decision by the Proctors under paragraph (1) above, he or she, or his or her college, may within fourteen days of the date of the decision appeal in writing to the Chair of the Education Committee of Council.

(3) The appeal shall be adjudged expeditiously by the Chair or another member of the committee, other than one of the Proctors, nominated by the Chair.

Passing the Second Public Examination

4.15. Candidates shall be deemed to have passed the Second Public Examination if they either have obtained Honours, or satisfied the examiners, in any one of the Honour Schools listed in Table 5, and Table 6, or in the Final Examination in Fine Art.

Part 5 Foundation Course at the Department for Continuing Education

5.1. Any member of the University who has successfully completed the course for a Foundation Certificate at the Department for Continuing Education (whether or not he or she was a member when he or she did so) may apply for admission to the Degree of Bachelor of Arts if he or she has:

(1) kept statutory residence in accordance with regulations 5.2 and 5.3 below; and

(2) passed the Second Public Examination.

5.2. A person who has successfully completed the course for the Foundation Certificate in English Literature may be admitted as a candidate in the Final Honour School of English Language and Literature if by the end of the term in which the examination is held he or she has kept statutory residence for six terms.

5.3. A person who has successfully completed the course for any Foundation Certificate may not be admitted as a candidate in any Final Honour School more than nine terms inclusively from the term of matriculation.

Part 6 Degrees awarded on passing the Second Public Examination

6.1. The Degree of Bachelor of Arts shall be awarded to members of the University who have obtained Honours, or have satisfied the examiners but have not obtained Honours, in any Final Honour School other than the School of Fine Art or the Schools listed in Table 7 below, subject to these regulations and to the Special Regulations for the Second Public Examination concerned.

6.2. The Degree of Bachelor of Fine Art shall be awarded to members of the University who have obtained Honours, or who have satisfied the examiners, in the Final Honour School for that degree, subject to these regulations and to the Special Regulations for that School.

6.3. The Master's Degrees to which these regulations apply shall be awarded to members of the University who have obtained Honours in the Second Public Examination in the relevant Final Honour Schools, as set out in Table 7 below, subject also to the conditions laid down in the Special Regulations for each School.

TABLE 7: MASTER'S DEGREES

Degree	Final Honour School
Master of Biochemistry	Molecular and Cellular Biochemistry
Master of Chemistry	Chemistry
Master of Computer Science	Computer Science (four-year course)
Master of Computer Science and Philosophy	Computer Science and Philosophy (four-year course)
Master of Earth Sciences	Earth Sciences
Master of Engineering	Engineering Science

	[Until MT 2017: Engineering, Economics, and Management]
	[Until MT 2018: Materials, Economics, and Management]
	Materials Science
Master of Mathematics	Mathematics (four-year course)
	Mathematics and Statistics (four-year course)
Master of Mathematics and Computer Science	Mathematics and Computer Science (four-year course)
Master of Mathematics and Philosophy	Mathematics and Philosophy (four-year course)
Master of Physics	Physics (four-year course)
Master of Mathematics and Physics	Mathematical and Theoretical Physics (after transfer to that Honour School for the Part C examination from the Honour Schools of Mathematics,Physics, or Physics and Philosophy)
Master of Physics and Philosophy	Physics and Philosophy (four-year course)

5

10

15

SPECIAL REGULATIONS FOR SPECIFIC FIRST PUBLIC EXAMINATIONS

Special Regulations for the Honour Moderations in Archaeology and Anthropology

A

Honour Moderations in Archaeology and Anthropology shall be under the supervision of the Social Sciences Board and shall consist of such subjects as it shall by regulation prescribe.

B

1. Every Candidate shall offer four papers of three hours each, as follows:

Paper (1) Introduction to world archaeology.

Paper (2) Introduction to anthropological theory.

Paper (3) Perspectives on human evolution.

Paper (4) The nature of archaeological enquiry.

2. All candidates will be required to undertake a course of practical work, including laboratory work.

All candidates will be assessed on their practical ability.

Class co-ordinators shall make available to the chair of the examiners records showing the extent to which each candidate has pursued an adequate course of practical work.

Honour Moderations in Classics

A

The subjects of the examination shall be as prescribed by regulation from time to time by the Board of the Faculty of Classics and the Board of the Faculty of Philosophy.

B

[For students starting before MT 2015: Candidates shall take one of the following courses: IA, IB, IC, IIA, IIB.

Any candidate whose native language is not English may bring a bilingual (native language to English) dictionary for use in any examination paper where candidates are required to translate Ancient Greek and/or Latin texts into English.

Course IA

The examination will consist of the following papers.

I. HOMER, *ILIAD*

One paper (3 hours) of translation and questions. Compulsory passages for translation and commentary will be set from *Iliad* I–IX and XVI–XXIV. Candidates will be expected to have knowledge of the whole poem. They will also be required to scan a short passage.

II. VIRGIL, *AENEID*

One paper (3 hours) of translation and questions. Compulsory passages for translation and commentary will be set from *Aeneid* I–VI and XII. Candidates will be expected to have knowledge of the whole poem. They will also be required to scan a short passage.

III, IV. TEXTS AND CONTEXTS

An essay paper and a translation paper (each 3 hours). Candidates are expected to have considered the general topics as well as the particular texts and archaeological material specified. In the essay paper they will be required to answer a compulsory picture question, and three essay questions. A syllabus of images from which items will be selected for the picture question will be posted on WebLearn under "Texts and Contexts". In the translation paper candidates will be required to translate six passages, three Greek and three Latin, set from the texts listed under α for each topic.   5

1. *The Persian Wars and Cultural Identities*
    α Herodotus 7.1–53, 8.56–110
    β Aeschylus, *Persians*
      Herodotus 1.1–32, 131–40; 3.61–88, 150–160; 7.54–239; 8.1–55
      Bisitun Inscription of Darius 1–15, 51–76   10
    Archaeological material: Identities in Greek and Persian art
2. *Dionysus, Drama, and Athens*
    α Euripides, *Bacchae* 1–1167
      Aristophanes, *Frogs* 1–459, 830–1533
    β Remainder of *Bacchae*   15
      Remainder of *Frogs*
      Archaeological material: Theatres, theatre images, and Dionysian iconography
3. *Love and Luxury*
    α Cicero, *pro Caelio* 17–53 (*... dedisti.*)
      Catullus 1–16, 31–7, 42–5, 48–51, 53, 69–70, 75–6, 79, 83–6, 95, 99–101, 116   20
      Propertius 1.1–3, 6, 11, 14
    β Remainder of *pro Caelio*
      Catullus 64.31–266
      Remainder of Propertius 1
    Archaeological material: Love pictures and Vesuvian villas   25
4. *Class*
    α Petronius, *Cena Trimalchionis* 26.7–36, 47–78
      Juvenal 3, 5
    β Remainder of *Cena Trimalchionis*
      Juvenal 1, 4, 6, 7, 9   30
      Pliny, *Epistulae* 7.29, 8.6
      Tacitus, *Annals* 14.42–5
    Archaeological material: Houses, tombs, and the archaeology of public entertainment.

V. PHILOSOPHY SPECIAL SUBJECT

All candidates must offer one Philosophy Special Subject, chosen from either   35
Group A or Group B. Candidates may not combine a subject from Group B with a
Classical Special Subject (VI) from Group E. One three-hour paper will be set in each
subject.

A.
1. *Early Greek Philosophy*   40

   Candidates will be expected to have studied:
   (*a*) Heraclitus, Parmenides, Empedocles, and Anaxagoras; and **any one** of the
        following:
   (*b*) Early Ionian Philosophy;
   (*c*) Zeno;   45
   (*d*) Early Atomism.

A general knowledge of pre-Socratic philosophy will also be expected. The subject shall be studied in Diels, *Die Fragmente der Vorsokratiker*, sixth or any later edition, edited by Kranz (Berlin, 1951 and later).

The texts prescribed are:

(a) Heraclitus (Diels-Kranz 22), B 1, 2, 10, 12, 17, 18, 21, 26, 28–32, 40, 41, 45, 50–62, 64, 67, 78–80, 88, 90, 93, 94, 101, 101a, 102, 103, 107, 108, 111, 113–15, 117–19, 123–6, and the first part of A 22 (Aristotle *Eudemian Ethics* 1235^{a}25–7); Parmenides (Diels-Kranz 28), B 1–9, 19; Empedocles (Diels-Kranz 31), B 6, 8, 11–13, 17, 28–30, 35, 112, 115, 117, 134, 146; Anaxagoras (Diels-Kranz 59), B 1–17, 21, 21a;

(b) (i) early Ionian philosophy: Anaximander (Diels-Kranz 12) A 9 and B 1; Anaximenes (Diels-Kranz 13) B 2; Aristotle *Metaphysics* A 3.983^{a}24–984^{a}18, *Physics* III 4.203^{a}16–18 and 203^{b}3–15; Xenophanes (Diels-Kranz 21), B 1, 7, 10–12, 14–16, 18, 23–9, 32, 34–6, 38; Aristotle *Metaphysics* A 5.986^{b}10–27;

(ii) Zeno: Zeno (Diels–Kranz 29) B 1–4; Plato *Parmenides* 127a7–128e4; Aristotle *Physics* VI 2.233^{a}21–31 and 9.239^{b}5–240^{a}18;

(iii) early atomists: Leucippus (Diels-Kranz 67) B 2; Democritus (Diels-Kranz 68) B 4, 6–8, 9, 10, 11, 117, 118, 125, 156, 164, 167; Aristotle *De Generatione et Corruptione* I 8.324^{b}35–325^{a}36, *Metaphysics* A4.985^{b}3–22.

Where Diels-Kranz B-texts are prescribed, the prescription includes only what Diels-Kranz print in spaced type.

A compulsory question will contain passages for translation and comment from (a). A second compulsory question will contain passages for comment (not for translation). At least one passage will be taken from (a), and at least one from each of (b)–(d). Essay questions will also be set which will include questions on (a) and on each of (b)–(d).

2. Plato, *Meno* and *Euthyphro*

The paper will include questions on the philosophical topics discussed in the dialogues. Candidates will be expected to have read *Meno* in Greek and *Euthyphro* in English. There will be a compulsory question containing passages for translation and comment from *Meno*; any passages for comment from *Euthyphro* will be accompanied by a translation (to be taken from *The Last Days of Socrates*, tr. Tredennick & Tarrant (Penguin, revised 1993)).

B.

1. *General Philosophy*

As specified for section I of Introduction to Philosophy in the Preliminary Examination for Philosophy, Politics, and Economics.

2. *Moral Philosophy*

As specified for section II of Introduction to Philosophy in the Preliminary Examination for Philosophy, Politics, and Economics.

3. *Introduction to Logic*

As specified for section III of Introduction to Philosophy for the Preliminary Examination for Philosophy, Politics, and Economics.

VI. CLASSICAL SPECIAL SUBJECT

All candidates must offer one Classical Special Subject, chosen from one of the groups C–F. Candidates must not combine a subject from Group E with a Philosophy Special Subject (V) from Group B. One three-hour paper will be set in each subject.

C.

1. *Thucydides and the West*

The prescribed text is Thucydides VI. Compulsory passages for translation and comment will be set from this book. Candidates will also be expected to be familiar with Thucydides VII and Plutarch, *Nicias*.

2. *Aristophanes' Political Comedy*

The prescribed plays are *Knights, Wasps*, and *Lysistrata*. Compulsory passages for translation and for comment will be set from *Wasps* and from *Lysistrata* 387–613 and 980–1220. Candidates will also be expected to be familiar with the 'Old Oligarch'.

D.   5

1. *Cicero and Catiline*

The prescribed texts are: Sallust, *Catiline*; Cicero, *In Catilinam* I–IV, *Pro Sulla*; Asconius, *In orationem in toga candida*. Compulsory passages for translation and comment will be set from these.

2. *Tacitus and Tiberius*   10

The prescribed text is Tacitus, *Annals* I and III. Compulsory passages for translation and comment will be set from these books. Candidates will also be expected to be familiar with *Annals* II and IV–VI.

E.

1. *Homeric Archaeology and Early Greece from 1550 BC to 700 BC*   15

Evidence on the composition and history of the poems provided by extant archaeological remains, with special emphasis on burial practices, architecture, metals, and the world outside the Aegean. An overall knowledge will be required of the archaeological evidence for the Late Bronze Age and Early Iron Age of the Aegean from 1550 BC to 700 BC. The examination will consist of one picture question and three essay questions.   20

2. *Greek Vases*

The study of the general history of Greek decorated pottery from *c.* 800 BC to *c.* 300 BC, including study of the Attic black-figure and red-figure styles and of South Italian Greek vase painting. Knowledge will be required of the techniques used in making Greek pottery and in drawing on vases, and also of the ancient names for vases and the   25 shapes to which they refer. Candidates should in addition study the subjects of the paintings and their treatment by painters as compared with their treatment by writers and should be familiar with actual vases, for example those in the Ashmolean Museum. The examination will consist of one picture question and three essay questions.

3. *Greek Sculpture*, c. *600–300 BC*   30

The major monuments of archaic and classical Greek sculpture—their context and purpose as well as their subjects, styles, and techniques. Candidates will be expected to have some knowledge of the external documentary evidence, such as literary and epigraphic texts, on which the framework of the subject depends, and to be acquainted with the major sculptures of the period represented in the Ashmolean Cast Gallery.   35 The examination will consist of one picture question and three essay questions.

4. *Roman Architecture*

The subject comprises the study of Roman Architecture from the Republic to the Tetrarchy in Italy and in the provinces, with particular reference to form, materials, technology, and function, and the movement of both materials and ideas. The exam-   40 ination will consist of one picture question and three essay questions.

F.

1. *Historical Linguistics and Comparative Philology*

The subject includes an introduction to the methods and aims of historical and comparative linguistics, the reconstruction of the Indo-European protolanguage and   45 its development into Latin and Greek. The questions set will require specific competence in one of the two classical languages but not necessarily in both. An opportunity will be given for (optional) commentary on Greek or Latin texts.

VII. UNPREPARED TRANSLATION FROM GREEK

One paper (3 hours).   50

VIII. Unprepared Translation from Latin

One paper (3 hours).

IX. Greek Language

One paper (3 hours). The paper will be divided into two main sections.

Candidates are required to offer *either* (*a*) *or* (*b*):

(*a*) a selection of passages from D. A. Russell, *An Anthology of Greek Prose* (OUP, 1991), on which questions on accidence, syntax, and style will be set (for the prescribed passages see the Mods Handbook) AND a short passage for translation into Greek prose;

(*b*) a passage for translation into Greek prose.

X. Latin Language

One paper (3 hours). The paper will be divided into two main sections.

Candidates are required to offer *either* (*a*) *or* (*b*):

(*a*) a selection of passages from D. A. Russell, *An Anthology of Latin Prose* (OUP, 1990), on which questions on accidence, syntax, and style will be set (for the prescribed passages see the Mods Handbook) AND a short passage for translation into Latin prose;

(*b*) a passage for translation into Latin prose.

XI. (Optional Paper) Verse Composition *or* Additional Translation *or* Additional Translation and Metre

This paper (3 hours) will consist of the following:

(*a*) passages for translation into Greek iambics and Latin elegiacs and hexameters, of which candidates will be required to translate one;

(*b*) passages for translation into English from each of the following ten books below, and a question on metre; candidates will be required to attempt *either* (i) three passages *or* (ii) two passages and the question on metre.

   1. Archilochus 3, 60, 79a, frr. 231and 196A1West; Mimnermus 1, 2, 5, 13; Solon 3, 5, 23, 24; Sappho 1, 2, 16, 31, 81b, 94, 96, 130; Alcaeus 38a, 129, 130, 332, 333, 335, 338, 362; Ibycus 286, 287, 288; Anacreon 356, 358, 359, 360, 376, 388, 395, 396, 398, 417; Xenophanes 1, 3; Theognis as in D.A. Campbell, *Greek Lyric Poetry*; Simonides 542, fr. 22 West1; Scolia 884, 889, 890, 892, 893, 900, 901, 902, 903, 907; Bacchylides fr. 20B; Pindar frr. 1231, 124a1.b1, 1271, 1281Maehler

   2. Sophocles, *Antigone*

   3. Demosthenes 54 [*Against Conon*], 59 [*Against Neaera*]

   4. Plato, *Symposium* 172a–178a5, 188e2–223d

   5. Plutarch, *Antony* 1–9, 23–36, 53–87

   6. Plautus, *Menaechmi*

   7. Horace, *Epistles* 1

   8. Livy 30

   9. Ovid, *Metamorphoses* 7.661–8.884

   10. Apuleius, *Cupid and Psyche* (*Metamorphoses* 4.28–6.24)

Candidates will be required to offer *either (a) or (b)*.

Course IB

The examination will consist of the following papers.

I. HOMER, *ILIAD*

One paper (3 hours) of translation and questions. Compulsory passages for translation and commentary will be set from *Iliad* I, IX, XXII, XXIV. Candidates will be expected to have knowledge of the whole poem. They will also be required to scan a short passage.

II. VIRGIL, *AENEID* [COURSE IA PAPER II]   5

III, IV. TEXTS AND CONTEXTS

An essay paper and a translation paper (each 3 hours). Candidates are expected to have considered the general topics as well as the particular texts and archaeological material specified. In the essay paper they will be required to answer a compulsory picture question, and three essay questions. A syllabus of images from which items will   10
be selected for the picture question will be posted on WebLearn under "Texts and Contexts". In the translation paper candidates will be required to translate six passages, three Greek and three Latin, set from the texts listed under α for each topic.

1. *The Persian Wars and Cultural Identities*
   α Herodotus 8.56–110   15
   β Aeschylus, *Persians*
       Herodotus 1.1–32, 131–40; 3.61–88, 150–160; 7.1–239; 8.1–55
       Bisitun Inscription of Darius 1–15, 51–76
   Archaeological material: Identities in Greek and Persian art

2. *Dionysus, Drama, and Athens*   20
   α Euripides, *Bacchae* 1–169, 370–518, 643–976
       Aristophanes, *Frogs* 1–459, 1004–98, 1378–1481
   β Remainder of *Bacchae*
       Remainder of *Frogs*
   Archaeological material: Theatres, theatre images, and Dionysian iconography   25

3. *Love and Luxury*
   α Cicero, *pro Caelio* 17–53 (*...dedisti.*)
       Catullus 1–16, 31–7, 42–5, 48–51, 53, 69–70, 75–6, 79, 83–6, 95, 99–101, 116
       Propertius 1.1–3, 6, 11, 14
   β Remainder of *pro Caelio*   30
       Catullus 64.31–266
       Remainder of Propertius 1
   Archaeological material: Love pictures and Vesuvian villas

4. *Class*
   α Petronius, *Cena Trimalchionis* 26.7–36, 47–78   35
       Juvenal 3, 5
   β Remainder of *Cena Trimalchionis*
       Juvenal 1, 4, 6, 7, 9
       Pliny, *Epistulae* 7.29, 8.6
       Tacitus, *Annals* 14.42–5   40
   Archaeological material: Houses, tombs, and the archaeology of public entertainment.

V PHILOSOPHY SPECIAL SUBJECT

All candidates must offer one Philosophy Special Subject chosen from either Group A or Group B. Candidates may not combine a subject from Group B with a Classical Special Subject (VI) from Group E. One three-hour paper will be set in each subject.   45

A.

1. *Early Greek Philosophy*

Candidates will be expected to have studied:

(*a*) Heraclitus, Parmenides, Empedocles, and Anaxagoras; and **any one** of the following:

(*b*) Early Ionian Philosophy;

(*c*) Zeno;

(*d*) Early Atomism.

A general knowledge of pre-Socratic philosophy will also be expected. The subject shall be studied in (i) Aristotle, *Metaphysics* A 1–8; (ii) G.S. Kirk, J.E. Raven, and M. Schofield, *The Presocratic Philosophers* (second edition, Cambridge, 1981); and (iii) a Faculty Supplement (available on WebLearn).

The prescribed texts under (ii) and (iii) are as follows:

(*a*) Heraclitus Diels–Kranz B 1, 2, 10, 12, 17, 18, 21, 26, 28–32, 40, 41, 45, 50–62, 64, 67, 78–80, 88, 90, 93, 94, 101, 101a, 102, 103, 107, 108, 111, 113–15, 117–19, 123–6, and the first part of A 22 (Aristotle *Eudemian Ethics* 1235^{a}25–7); Parmenides Diels–Kranz B 1–9, 19; Empedocles Diels–Kranz B 6, 8, 11–13, 17, 28–30, 35, 112, 115, 117, 134, 146; Anaxagoras Diels–Kranz B 1–17, 21, 21a;

(*b*) Early Ionian philosophy: Anaximander Diels–Kranz A 9 and B 1; Anaximenes Diels–Kranz B 2; Aristotle *Metaphysics* A 3.983^{a}24–984^{a}18, *Physics* III 4.203^{a}16–18 and 203^{b}3–15; Xenophanes Diels–Kranz B 1, 7, 10–12, 14–16, 18, 23–9, 32, 34–6, 38; Aristotle *Metaphysics* A 5.986^{b}10–27;

(*c*) Zeno: Zeno Diels–Kranz B 1–4; Plato *Parmenides* 127a7–128e4; Aristotle *Physics* VI 2.233^{a}21–31 and 9.239^{b}5–240^{a}18;

(*d*) Early Atomism: Leucippus Diels–Kranz B 2; Democritus Diels–Kranz B 4, 6–8, 9, 10, 11, 117, 118, 125, 156, 164, 167; Aristotle *De Generatione et Corruptione* I 8.324^{b}35–325^{a}36, *Metaphysics* A 4.985^{b}3–22.

There will be a compulsory question containing passages for translation and comment from Aristotle, *Metaphysics* A 1–8. A second compulsory question will contain passages for comment (not for translation). At least one passage will be taken from (*a*), and at least one from each of (*b*)–(*d*); all the passages for this question will be accompanied by a translation (to be taken from Kirk, Raven, and Schofield (eds), and/or the Faculty Supplement). Essay questions will also be set which will include questions on (*a*) and on each of (*b*)–(*d*).

2. Plato, *Euthyphro* and *Meno*

The paper will include questions on the philosophical topics discussed in the dialogues. Candidates will be expected to have read *Meno* 70a–86d2 in Greek and the rest of *Meno* and *Euthyphro* in English. There will be a compulsory question containing passages for translation and comment from *Meno*; any passages for comment from *Euthyphro* and the other parts of *Meno* will be accompanied by a translation (to be taken from *Euthyphro* in *The Last Days of Socrates*, tr. Tredennick & Tarrant (Penguin, revised 1993) and *Meno*, tr. Sharples (Aris & Phillips)).

3. Lucretius, *De Rerum Natura* IV

There will be a compulsory question containing passages for translation and comment from the prescribed book.

The paper will also include questions on the philosophical topics examined in that book, together with some questions of a more general character on Epicurean philosophy as expressed in *De Rerum Natura* as a whole.

B.
1. *General Philosophy* [Course IA, paper V B(1)]
2. *Moral Philosophy* [Course IA, paper V B(2)]
3. *Introduction to Logic* [Course IA, paper V B(3)]

VI. CLASSICAL SPECIAL SUBJECT   5

All candidates must offer one Classical Special Subject, chosen from one of the groups C–F. Candidates may not combine a subject from Group E with a Philosophy Special Subject (V) from Group B. One three-hour paper will be set in each subject.

C.
1. *Thucydides and the West*   10

The prescribed text is Thucydides VI. Compulsory passages for translation will be set only from chapters 1–61. Compulsory passages for comment will be set from the whole book; passages set from 62–105 will be accompanied by the English translation of M. Hammond (World's Classics, OUP, 2009). Candidates will also be expected to be familiar with Thucydides VII and Plutarch, *Nicias*.   15

2. *Aristophanes' Political Comedy*

The prescribed plays are *Knights, Wasps,* and *Lysistrata*. Compulsory passages for translation will be set from *Wasps* 1–728 and from *Lysistrata* 980–1220. Compulsory passages for commentary will be set from *Wasps* and from *Lysistrata* 387–613 and 980–1220; those from *Wasps* 729–1537 and *Lysistrata* 387–613 will be accompanied   20
by the English translation of A.H. Sommerstein (Aris & Phillips). Candidates will also be expected to be familiar with the 'Old Oligarch'.

D.
1. *Cicero and Catiline* [Course IA, paper VI D(1)]
2. *Tacitus and Tiberius* [Course IA, paper VI D(2)]   25

E.
1. *Homeric Archaeology and Early Greece from 1550 BC to 700 BC* [Course IA, paper VI E(1)]
2. *Greek Vases* [Course IA, paper VI E(2)]
3. *Greek Sculpture* [Course IA, paper VI E(3)]   30
4. *Roman Architecture* [Course IA, paper VI E(4)]

F.
1. *Historical Linguistics and Comparative Philology* [Course IA, paper VI F(1)]

VII. UNPREPARED TRANSLATION FROM GREEK
One paper (3 hours).   35

VIII. UNPREPARED TRANSLATION FROM LATIN [Course IA, Paper VIII]

IX. GREEK LANGUAGE
One paper (3 hours). The paper will be divided into two main sections.
Candidates are required to offer *either* (*a*) *or* (*b*):
(*a*) a selection of passages from D. A Russell, *An Anthology of Greek Prose* (OUP,   40
1991), on which questions on accidence, syntax and style will be set (for the prescribed passages see the Mods Handbook) AND a short passage for translation into Greek prose;
(*b*) a passage for translation into Greek prose.

X. LATIN LANGUAGE [Course IA, paper X].   45

XI. (OPTIONAL PAPER) VERSE COMPOSITION *OR* ADDITIONAL TRANSLATION *OR* A TRANSLATION AND METRE (Course IA, Paper XI).

Course IC

The examination will consist of the following papers.

I. HOMER, *ILIAD* [Course IA, Paper I].   5

II. VIRGIL, *AENEID*

One paper (3 hours) of translation and questions. Compulsory passages for translation and commentary will be set from *Aeneid* I, IV and VI. Candidates will be expected to have knowledge of the whole poem. They will also be required to scan a short passage.   10

III, IV. TEXTS AND CONTEXTS

An essay paper and a translation paper (each 3 hours). Candidates are expected to have considered the general topics as well as the particular texts and archaeological material specified. In the essay paper they will be required to answer a compulsory picture question, and three essay questions. A syllabus of images from which items will   15 be selected for the picture question will be posted on WebLearn under 'Texts and Contexts'. In the translation paper candidates will be required to translate six passages, three Greek and three Latin, set from the texts listed under α for each topic.

1. *The Persian Wars and Cultural Identities*
   α Herodotus 7.1–53; 8.56–110   20
   β Aeschylus, *Persians*
   Herodotus 1.1–32, 131–40; 3.61–88, 150–160; 7.54–239; 8.1–55
   Bisitun Inscription of Darius 1–15, 51–76
   Archaeological material: Identities in Greek and Persian art

2. *Dionysus, Drama, and Athens*   25
   α Euripides, *Bacchae* 1–1167
   Aristophanes, *Frogs* 1–459, 830–1533
   β Remainder of *Bacchae*
   Remainder of *Frogs*
   Archaeological material: Theatres, theatre images, and Dionysian iconography   30

3. *Love and Luxury*
   α Cicero, *pro Caelio* 30 (*sunt autem*)-50
   Catullus 1–8, 10–13, 31, 34, 36, 44–5, 48–51, 69–70, 76, 79, 85, 95, 101
   Propertius 1.1, 3, 6, 14
   β Remainder of *pro Caelio*   35
   Catullus 9, 14–16, 32–3, 35, 37, 42–3, 53, 64.31–266, 75, 83–4, 86, 99–100, 116
   Remainder of Propertius 1
   Archaeological material: Love pictures and Vesuvian villas

4. *Class*
   α Petronius, *Cena Trimalchionis* 26.7–36, 64.2–67, 74.6–78   40
   Juvenal 3
   β Remainder of *Cena Trimalchionis*
   Juvenal 1, 4, 5, 6, 7, 9
   Pliny, *Epistulae* 7.29, 8.6
   Tacitus, *Annals* 14.42–5   45

Archaeological material: Houses, tombs, and the archaeology of public entertainment.

V. PHILOSOPHY SPECIAL SUBJECT

All candidates must offer one Philosophy Special Subject, chosen from either Group A or Group B. Candidates may not combine a subject from Group B with a Classical Special Subject (VI) from Group E. One three-hour paper will be set in each subject.

A.
1. *Early Greek Philosophy* [Course IA, paper V A(1)]
2. Plato, *Meno* and *Euthyphro* [Course IA, paper V A(2)]
3. Lucretius, *De Rerum Natura* IV [Course IB, paper V A(3)]

B.
1. *General Philosophy* [Course IA, paper V B(1)]
2. *Moral Philosophy* [Course IA, paper V B(2)]
3. *Introduction to Logic* [Course IA, paper V B(3)]

VI. CLASSICAL SPECIAL SUBJECT

All candidates must offer one Classical Special Subject, chosen from one of the groups C-F. Candidates may not combine a subject from Group E with a Philosophy Special Subject (V) from Group B. One three-hour paper will be set in each subject.

C.
1. *Thucydides and the West* [Course IA, paper VI C(1)]
2. *Aristophanes' Political Comedy* [Course IA, paper VI C(2)]

D.
1. *Cicero and Catiline* [Course IIA, paper V D(1)]
2. *Tacitus and Tiberius* [Course IIA, paper V D(2)]

E.
1. *Homeric Archaeology and Early Greece from 1550 BC to 700 BC* [Course IA, paper VI E(1)]
2. *Greek Vases* [Course IA, paper VI E(2)]
3. *Greek Sculpture* [Course IA, paper VI E(3)]
4. *Roman Architecture* [Course IA, paper VI E(4)]

F.
1. *Historical Linguistics and Comparative Philology* [Course IA, paper VI F(I)]

VII. UNPREPARED TRANSLATION FROM GREEK [Course IA, paper VII]

VIII. UNPREPARED TRANSLATION FROM LATIN [Course IIA, paper VI]

IX. GREEK LANGUAGE [Course IA, paper IX]

X. LATIN LANGUAGE [Course IIA, paper VII]

XI. (OPTIONAL PAPER) VERSE COMPOSITION *OR* ADDITIONAL TRANSLATION *OR* ADDITIONAL TRANSLATION AND METRE [Course IA, paper XI]

Course IIA

The examination will consist of the following papers.

I. VIRGIL, *AENEID*

One paper (3 hours) of translation and questions. Compulsory passages for translation and commentary will be set from *Aeneid* I, II, IV, VI, and XII. Candidates will be expected to have knowledge of the whole poem. They will also be required to scan a short passage.

II, III. TEXTS AND CONTEXTS

An essay paper and a translation paper (each 3 hours). Candidates are expected to have considered the general topics as well as the particular texts and archaeological material specified. In the essay paper they will be required to answer a compulsory picture question, and three essay questions. A syllabus of images from which items will   5
be selected for the picture question will be posted on WebLearn under 'Texts and Contexts'. In the translation paper candidates will be required to translate six passages, set from the Latin texts listed under α for topics 3 and 4.

1. *The Persian Wars and Cultural Identities*
   β Aeschylus, *Persians*   10
      Herodotus 1.1–32, 131–40; 3.61–88, 150–160; 7.1–239; 8.1–110
      Bisitun Inscription of Darius 1–15, 51–76
   Archaeological material: Identities in Greek and Persian art

2. *Dionysus, Drama, and Athens*
   β Euripides, *Bacchae*   15
      Aristophanes, *Frogs*
   Archaeological material: Theatres, theatre images, and Dionysian iconography

3. *Love and Luxury*
   α Cicero, *pro Caelio* 30 (*sunt autem*)-50
      Catullus 1–8, 10–13, 31, 34, 36, 44–5, 48–51, 69–70, 76, 79, 85, 95, 101   20
      Propertius 1.1, 3, 6, 14
   β Remainder of *pro Caelio*
      Catullus 9, 14–16, 32–3, 35, 37, 42–3, 53, 64.31–266, 75, 83–4, 86, 99–100, 116
      Remainder of Propertius 1
   Archaeological material: Love pictures and Vesuvian villas   25

4. *Class*
   α Petronius, *Cena Trimalchionis* 26.7–36, 64.2–67, 74.6–78
      Juvenal 3
   β Remainder of *Cena Trimalchionis*
      Juvenal 1, 4, 5, 6, 7, 9   30
      Pliny, *Epistulae* 7.29, 8.6
      Tacitus, *Annals* 14.42–5
   Archaeological material: Houses, tombs, and the archaeology of public entertainment.

IV. PHILOSOPHY SPECIAL SUBJECT   35

All candidates must offer one Philosophy Special Subject. One three-hour paper will be set in each subject.

   1. Lucretius, *De Rerum Natura* IV [Course IB paper V A(3)]

   2. *Early Greek Philosophy*

Candidates will be expected to have studied: 40

   (*a*) Heraclitus, Parmenides, Empedocles, and Anaxagoras; and **any one** of the following:

   (*b*) Early Ionian Philosophy;

   (*c*) Zeno;

   (*d*) Early Atomism.   45

A general knowledge of pre-Socratic philosophy will also be expected.

This subject shall be studied in (i) Aristotle, *Metaphysics* A 1–8; (ii) G.S. Kirk, J.E. Raven, and M. Schofield, *The Presocratic Philosophers* (second edition, Cambridge,

1981); and (iii) a Faculty Supplement (available on WebLearn). The prescribed texts under (ii) and (iii) are as follows:

(*a*) Heraclitus Diels–Kranz B 1, 2, 10, 12, 17, 18, 21, 26, 28–32, 40, 41, 45, 50–62, 64, 67, 78–80, 88, 90, 93, 94, 101, 101a, 102, 103, 107, 108, 111, 113–15, 117–19, 123–6, and the first part of A 22 (Aristotle *Eudemian Ethics* 1235ᵃ25–7); Parmenides Diels–Kranz B 1–9, 19; Empedocles Diels–Kranz B 6, 8, 11–13, 17, 28–30, 35, 112, 115, 117, 134, 146; Anaxagoras Diels–Kranz B 1–17, 21, 21a;

(*b*) early Ionian philosophy: Anaximander Diels–Kranz A 9 and B 1; Anaximenes Diels–Kranz B 2; Aristotle *Metaphysics* A 3.983ᵃ24–984ᵃ18, *Physics* III 4.203ᵃ16–18 and 203ᵇ3–15; Xenophanes Diels–Kranz B 1, 7, 10–12, 14–16, 18, 23–9, 32, 34–6, 38; Aristotle *Metaphysics* A 5.986ᵇ10–27;

(2) Zeno: Zeno Diels–Kranz B 1–4; Plato *Parmenides* 127a7–128e4; Aristotle *Physics* VI 2.233ᵃ21–31 and 9.239ᵇ5–240ᵃ18;

(3) early atomists: Leucippus Diels–Kranz B 2; Democritus Diels–Kranz B 4, 6–8, 9, 10, 11, 117, 118, 125, 156, 164, 167; Aristotle *De Generatione et Corruptione* I 8.324ᵇ35–325ᵃ36, Metaphysics A 4.985ᵇ3–22.

There will be a compulsory question containing passages for comment from Aristotle, *Metaphysics* A 1–8. The passages will be given in translation (to be taken from J. Barnes (ed.), *The Complete Works of Aristotle: The Revised Oxford Translation*, Volume II (Princeton NJ, 1984). A second compulsory question will contain passages for comment. At least one passage will be taken from (*a*), and at least one from each of (*b*)–(*d*); all the passages for this question will be given in translation (to be taken from Kirk, Raven, and Schofield (eds), and/or the Faculty Supplement). Essay questions will also be set which will include questions on (*a*) and on each of (*b*)–(*d*).

3. Plato, *Euthyphro* and *Meno*

To be studied in *The Last Days of Socrates*, tr. Tredennick & Tarrant (Penguin, revised 1993) and *Meno*, tr. Sharples (Aris & Phillips). The paper will include questions on the philosophical topics discussed in the dialogues. There will be a compulsory question containing passages for comment.

4. *General Philosophy* [Course IA, paper V B(1)]

5. *Moral Philosophy* [Course IA, paper V B(2)]

6. *Introduction to Logic* [Course IA, paper V B(3)]

V. CLASSICAL SPECIAL SUBJECT

All candidates must offer one Classical Special Subject, chosen from Group D, E, or F. One three-hour paper will be set in each subject.

D.

1. *Cicero and Catiline*

The prescribed texts, from which compulsory passages for comment will be set, are Sallust, *Catiline*; Cicero, *In Catilinam* I–IV, *Pro Sulla*; Asconius, *In orationem in toga candida*. Compulsory passages for translation will be set only from Sallust, *Catiline* and Cicero, *In Catilinam* IV. Passages for comment from Cicero, *In Catilinam* I–III and *Pro Sulla* will be accompanied by the English translation of C. Macdonald (Loeb, 1977) and from Asconius, *In orationem in toga candida* by the English translation of R.G. Lewis (ed.), *Asconius: Commentaries on Speeches by Cicero* (Oxford, 2006).

2. *Tacitus and Tiberius*

The prescribed text is Tacitus, *Annals* I and III. Compulsory passages for translation will be set only from *Annals* I. Compulsory passages for comment will be set from

Annals I and III; passages set from *Annals* III will be accompanied by the English translation of A.J. Woodman, *Tacitus Annals*, (Indianapolis, Hackett, 2004). Candidates will also be expected to be familiar with *Annals* II and IV–VI.

E.
1. *Homeric Archaeology and Early Greece from 1550 BC to 700 BC* [Course IA, paper VI E(1)]
2. *Greek Vases* [Course IA, paper VI E(2)]
3. *Greek Sculpture* [Course IA, paper VI E(3)]
4. *Roman Architecture* [Course IA, paper VI E(4)]

F.
1. *Historical Linguistics and Comparative Philology* [Course IA, paper VI F(1)]

VI. UNPREPARED TRANSLATION FROM LATIN
One paper (3 hours).

VII. LATIN LANGUAGE
One paper (3 hours). The paper will be divided into two main sections.
Candidates are required to offer *either* (*a*) *or* (*b*):

(*a*) a selection of passages from D. A Russell, *An Anthology of Latin Prose* (OUP, 1990), on which questions on accidence, syntax and style will be set (for the prescribed passages see the Mods Handbook) AND a short passage for translation into Latin prose;

(*b*) a passage for translation into Latin prose.

VIII. (OPTIONAL PAPER) VERSE COMPOSITION *OR* ADDITIONAL TRANSLATION *OR* ADDITIONAL TRANSLATION AND METRE [Course IA, paper XI]

Course IIB
The examination will consist of the following papers.

I. HOMER, *ILIAD*
One paper (3 hours) of translation and questions. Compulsory passages for translation and commentary will be set from *Iliad* I, VI, IX, XXII, XXIV. Candidates will be expected to have knowledge of the whole poem. They will also be required to scan a short passage.

II, III. TEXTS AND CONTEXTS
An essay paper and a translation paper (each 3 hours). Candidates are expected to have considered the general topics as well as the particular texts and archaeological material specified. In the essay paper they will be required to answer a compulsory picture question, and three essay questions. A syllabus of images from which items will be selected for the picture question will be posted on WebLearn under 'Texts and Contexts'. In the translation paper candidates will be required to translate six passages, set from the Greek texts listed under α for topics 1 and 2.

1. *The Persian Wars and Cultural Identities*
   α Herodotus 8.56–110
   β Aeschylus, *Persians*
   Herodotus 1.1–32, 131–40; 3.61–88, 150–160; 7.1–239; 8.1–55
   Bisitun Inscription of Darius 1–15, 51–76
   Archaeological material: Identities in Greek and Persian art

2. *Dionysus, Drama, and Athens*
   α Euripides, *Bacchae* 1–169, 370–518, 643–976
   Aristophanes, *Frogs* 1–459, 1004–98, 1378–1481
   β Remainder of *Bacchae*

Remainder of *Frogs*
Archaeological material: Theatres, theatre images, and Dionysian iconography

3. *Love and Luxury*
  β Cicero, *pro Caelio*
    Catullus 1–16, 31–7, 42–5, 48–51, 53, 64.31–266, 69–70, 75–6, 79, 83–6, 95, 99–101, 116   5
    Propertius 1
  Archaeological material: Love pictures and Vesuvian villas

4. *Class*
  β Petronius, *Cena Trimalchionis*
    Juvenal 1, 3, 4, 5, 6, 7, 9   10
    Pliny, *Epistulae* 7.29, 8.6
    Tacitus, *Annals* 14.42–5
  Archaeological material: Houses, tombs, and the archaeology of public entertainment.

IV. PHILOSOPHY SPECIAL SUBJECT   15

All candidates must offer one Philosophy Special Subject. One three-hour paper will be set in each subject.

  1. *Early Greek Philosophy* [Course IB, Paper V A(1)]
  2. *Plato, Meno and Euthyphro* [Course IB, Paper V A(2)]
  3. *General Philosophy* [Course IA, Paper V B(1)]   20
  4. *Moral Philosophy* [Course IA, Paper V B(2)]
  5. *Introduction to Logic* [Course IA, Paper V B(3)]

V. CLASSICAL SPECIAL SUBJECT

All candidates must offer one Classical Special Subject, chosen from Group C, E, or F. One three-hour paper will be set in each subject.   25

C.
1. *Thucydides and the West* [Course IB, paper VI C(1)]
2. *Aristophanes' Political Comedy* [Course IB, paper VI C(2)]

E.
1. *Homeric Archaeology and Early Greece from 1550 BC to 700 BC* [Course IA, paper   30
   VI E(1)]
2. *Greek Vases* [Course IA, paper VI E(2)]
3. *Greek Sculpture* [Course IA, paper VI E(3)]
4. *Roman Architecture* [Course IA, paper VI E(4)]

F.   35
1. *Historical Linguistics and Comparative Philology* [Course IA, paper VI F(1)]

VI. UNPREPARED TRANSLATION FROM GREEK [Course IB, paper VII]

VII. GREEK LANGUAGE

One paper (3 hours). The paper will be divided into two main sections.

Candidates are required to offer *either* (*a*) *or* (*b*):   40

  (*a*) a selection of passages from D. A Russell, *An Anthology of Greek Prose* (OUP, 1991), on which questions on accidence, syntax and style will be set (for the prescribed passages see the Honour Moderations Handbook) AND a short passage for translation into Greek prose;

  (*b*) a passage for translation into Greek prose.   45

VIII. (Optional Paper) Verse Composition *or* Additional Translation *or* Additional Translation and Metre [Course IA, paper XI]

N.B. For prescribed editions in all forms of Classics Moderations, see Mods Handbook.]

[For students starting from MT 2015: Candidates shall take one of the following courses: IA, IB, IC, IIA, IIB.

Each paper will be assessed by means of a three-hour written examination. Texts and Contexts will comprise two papers, a three-hour essay paper and a three-hour translation paper.

The papers in *General Philosophy, Moral Philosophy,* and *Introduction to Logic* will be examined in accordance with the regulations for sections I, II and III respectively of *Introduction to Philosophy* in the Preliminary Examination for Philosophy, Politics and Economics.

Detailed syllabuses for all other papers, including prescribed texts and editions where applicable, will be published in the Mods Handbook for the relevant year of examination. This will be published no later than Monday of Week 0 of Michaelmas Term in the academic year preceding that of the examination.

Any candidate whose native language is not English may bring a bilingual (native language to English) dictionary for use in any examination paper where candidates are required to translate Ancient Greek and/or Latin texts into English.

Course IA
The examination will consist of the following papers.
I. HOMER, *ILIAD*
II. VIRGIL, *AENEID*
III, IV. TEXTS AND CONTEXTS
V. PHILOSOPHY SPECIAL SUBJECT
All candidates must offer one Philosophy Special Subject, chosen from either Group A or Group B. Candidates may not combine a subject from Group B with a Classical Special Subject (VI) from Group E.

A.
1. *Early Greek Philosophy*
2. *Plato*, Euthyphro and Meno

B.
1. *General Philosophy*
2. *Moral Philosophy*
3. *Introduction to Logic*

VI. CLASSICAL SPECIAL SUBJECT
All candidates must offer one Classical Special Subject, chosen from one of the groups C–F. Candidates must not combine a subject from Group E with a Philosophy Special Subject (V) from Group B.

C.
1. *Thucydides and the West*
2. *Aristophanes' Political Comedy*

D.
1. *Cicero and Catiline*
2. *Tacitus and Tiberius*

E.
1. *Homeric Archaeology and Early Greece from 1550 BC to 700 BC*
2. *Greek Vases*
3. *Greek Sculpture, c. 600–300 BC*
4. *Roman Architecture*

F.
1. *Historical Linguistics and Comparative Philology*
VII. UNPREPARED TRANSLATION FROM GREEK
VIII. UNPREPARED TRANSLATION FROM LATIN
IX. GREEK LANGUAGE
X. LATIN LANGUAGE
XI. (OPTIONAL PAPER) VERSE COMPOSITION OR ADDITIONAL TRANSLATION OR ADDITIONAL TRANSLATION AND METRE

Course IB
The examination will consist of the following papers.
I. HOMER, *ILIAD*
II. VIRGIL, *AENEID*
III, IV. TEXTS AND CONTEXTS
V. PHILOSOPHY SPECIAL SUBJECT
All candidates must offer one Philosophy Special Subject chosen from either Group A or Group B. Candidates may not combine a subject from Group B with a Classical Special Subject (VI) from Group E.

A.
1. *Early Greek Philosophy*
2. *Plato*, Euthyphro *and* Meno
3. *Lucretius*, De Rerum Natura *IV*

B.
1. *General Philosophy*
2. *Moral Philosophy*
3. *Introduction to Logic*

VI. CLASSICAL SPECIAL SUBJECT
All candidates must offer one Classical Special Subject, chosen from one of the groups C–F. Candidates may not combine a subject from Group E with a Philosophy Special Subject (V) from Group B.

C.
1. *Thucydides and the West*
2. *Aristophanes' Political Comedy*

D.
1. *Cicero and Catiline*
2. *Tacitus and Tiberius*

E.
1. *Homeric Archaeology and Early Greece from 1550 BC to 700 BC*
2. *Greek Vases*
3. *Greek Sculpture, c.600–300 BC*
4. *Roman Architecture*

F.
1. *Historical Linguistics and Comparative Philology*
VII. UNPREPARED TRANSLATION FROM GREEK
VIII. UNPREPARED TRANSLATION FROM LATIN
IX. GREEK LANGUAGE
X. LATIN LANGUAGE
XI. (OPTIONAL PAPER) VERSE COMPOSITION OR ADDITIONAL TRANSLATION OR ADDITIONAL TRANSLATION AND METRE.

Course IC

The examination will consist of the following papers.

I. HOMER, *ILIAD*
II. VIRGIL, *AENEID*
III, IV. TEXTS AND CONTEXTS   5
V. PHILOSOPHY SPECIAL SUBJECT

All candidates must offer one Philosophy Special Subject, chosen from either Group A or Group B. Candidates may not combine a subject from Group B with a Classical Special Subject (VI) from Group E.

A.   10
1. *Early Greek Philosophy*
2. *Plato, Euthyphro and Meno*
3. *Lucretius*, De Rerum Natura *IV*

B.
1. *General Philosophy*   15
2. *Moral Philosophy*
3. *Introduction to Logic*

VI. CLASSICAL SPECIAL SUBJECT

All candidates must offer one Classical Special Subject, chosen from one of the groups C–F. Candidates may not combine a subject from Group E with a Philosophy Special   20
Subject (V) from Group B.

C.
1. *Thucydides and the West*
2. *Aristophanes' Political Comedy*

D.   25
1. *Cicero and Catiline*
2. *Tacitus and Tiberius*

E.
1. *Homeric Archaeology and Early Greece from 1550 bc to 700 bc*
2. *Greek Vases*   30
3. *Greek Sculpture, c.600–300 bc*
4. *Roman Architecture*

F.
1. *Historical Linguistics and Comparative Philology*

VII. UNPREPARED TRANSLATION FROM GREEK   35
VIII. UNPREPARED TRANSLATION FROM LATIN
IX. GREEK LANGUAGE
X. LATIN LANGUAGE
XI. (OPTIONAL PAPER) VERSE COMPOSITION OR ADDITIONAL
TRANSLATION OR ADDITIONAL TRANSLATION AND METRE   40

Course IIA

The examination will consist of the following papers.
I. VIRGIL, *AENEID*
II, III. TEXTS AND CONTEXTS
IV. PHILOSOPHY SPECIAL SUBJECT   45
All candidates must offer one Philosophy Special Subject.
1. *Lucretius*, De Rerum Natura *IV*
2. *Early Greek Philosophy*
3. *Plato*, Euthyphro *and* Meno
4. *General Philosophy*   50
5. *Moral Philosophy*
6. *Introduction to Logic*

V. CLASSICAL SPECIAL SUBJECT
All candidates must offer one Classical Special Subject, chosen from Group
D, E, or F.

D.
1. *Cicero and Catiline*   5
2. *Tacitus and Tiberius*

E.
1. *Homeric Archaeology and Early Greece from 1550 BC to 700 BC*
2. *Greek Vases*
3. *Greek Sculpture, c.600–300 BC*   10
4. *Roman Architecture*

F.
1. *Historical Linguistics and Comparative Philology*

VI. UNPREPARED TRANSLATION FROM LATIN
VII. LATIN LANGUAGE   15
VIII. (OPTIONAL PAPER) VERSE COMPOSITION OR ADDITIONAL
TRANSLATION OR ADDITIONAL TRANSLATION AND METRE

Course IIB
The examination will consist of the following papers.
I. HOMER, *ILIAD*   20
II, III. TEXTS AND CONTEXTS
IV. PHILOSOPHY SPECIAL SUBJECT
All candidates must offer one Philosophy Special Subject.
1. *Early Greek Philosophy*
2. *Plato*, Euthyphro *and* Meno   25
3. *General Philosophy*
4. *Moral Philosophy*
5. *Introduction to Logic*

V. CLASSICAL SPECIAL SUBJECT
All candidates must offer one Classical Special Subject, chosen from Group   30
C, E, or F.

C.
1. *Thucydides and the West*
2. *Aristophanes' Political Comedy*

E.   35
1. *Homeric Archaeology and Early Greece from 1550 BC to 700 BC*
2. *Greek Vases*
3. *Greek Sculpture, c.600–300 BC*
4. *Roman Architecture*

F.   40
1. *Historical Linguistics and Comparative Philology*
VI. UNPREPARED TRANSLATION FROM GREEK
VII. GREEK LANGUAGE
VIII. (OPTIONAL PAPER) VERSE COMPOSITION OR ADDITIONAL
TRANSLATION OR ADDITIONAL TRANSLATION AND METRE]   45

Law Moderations

A

1. The subjects of Law Moderations shall be:
    (1) A Roman Introduction to Private Law.
    (2) Criminal Law.
    (3) Constitutional Law.

2. Every candidate who has passed in three subjects shall be deemed to have satisfied the Moderators, provided that
    (*a*) he or she shall have passed in not less than two subjects at one and the same time, and
    (*b*) he or she shall not be permitted to count any pass obtained in any subject before he or she satisfied the provision in (*a*).

3. Any candidate may offer himself or herself for examination in one, two, or three subjects. Except as provided in clause 2 hereof, a candidate who has passed a subject in one examination may not offer himself or herself for that subject again in a later examination. No candidate may re-enter the examination on more than one occasion after their first attempt, other than in exceptional circumstances and with the permission of the University Education Committee.

4. The Moderators may award a Distinction to any candidate of special merit who passes in three subjects at any one examination.

B

Every candidate who wishes to pass Law Moderations must offer Criminal Law and Constitutional Law and A Roman Introduction to Private Law.

The individual specifications for Law Moderations subjects will be published in the Law Faculty Student Handbook for the academic year ahead by Monday of noughth week of Michaelmas Term each year.

Statutes and other source material
Details of the statutes and other sources of material which will be available to candidates in the examination room will be notified to candidates in Michaelmas Term, and any subsequent changes notified in the moderators' edict.

Preliminary Examination in Ancient and Modern History

A

The Preliminary Examination in Ancient and Modern History shall be under the joint supervision of the Boards of the Faculties of Classics and History and shall consist of such subjects as they shall jointly by regulation prescribe.

B

Every candidate shall offer four papers, as follows:

1. General History: any one of the following period papers I: 370–900 (*The Transformation of the Ancient World*), II: 1000–1300 (*Medieval Christendom and its neighbours*); III: 1400–1650 (*Renaissance, Recovery, and Reform*), and IV: 1815–1914 (*Society, Nation, and Empire*).

2. *Either* Greek History 650–479 BC: The Archaic Greek World *or* Roman History 241–146 BC: Rome and the Mediterranean.

3. *Either The World of Homer and Hesiod* (Homer, *Iliad, Odyssey* (tr. Lattimore); Hesiod, *Works and Days* (tr. M. L. West, Oxford 1988); *or Augustan Rome* (as

specified in the Handbook for the Preliminary Examination in History); *or* any other Optional Subject specified for the Preliminary Examination in History.

4. *Either* Approaches to History, as specified for the Preliminary Examination in History; *or* Historiography: Tacitus to Weber, as specified for the Preliminary Examination in History; *or* Herodotus, V. 26–VI. 131, to be read in Greek, ed. 5 C. Hude (Oxford Classical Texts, 3rd edn., 1927); *or* Sallust, *Jugurtha,* to be read in Latin, ed. L. Reynolds (OCT, 1991) (for Herodotus and Sallust, candidates will be required to illustrate their answers by reference to the specified texts); *or* Beginning Ancient Greek *or* Beginning Latin *or* Intermediate Ancient Greek *or* Intermediate Latin *or* Advanced Ancient Greek or Advanced Latin. 10

Any candidate whose native language is not English may bring a bilingual (native language to English) dictionary for use in any examination paper where candidates are required to translate Ancient Greek and/or Latin texts into English.

The individual specifications and prescribed texts for Optional Subjects, Approaches to History, and Historiography: Tacitus to Weber as specified for the 15 Preliminary Examination in History will be published for candidates in the Handbook for the Preliminary Examination in History by Monday of Week Nought of Michaelmas Term each year for the academic year ahead. The individual specifications and prescribed texts for the Optional Subject *Augustan Rome* will be published for candidates in the Handbook for the Preliminary Examination in History by 20 Monday of Week Nought of Michaelmas Term each year for the academic year ahead. Depending on the availability of teaching resources, with the exception of Optional Subject 1, not all the Optional Subjects listed in the Handbook will be available to candidates in any given year. Candidates may obtain details of the choice for that year by consulting the Definitive List of Optional Subjects posted at the 25 beginning of the first week of Michaelmas Full Term in the History Faculty and circulated to Ancient and Modern History Tutors. The individual specifications and prescribed texts for Beginning Ancient Greek, Beginning Latin, *Intermediate Ancient Greek, Intermediate Latin, Advanced Ancient Greek and Advanced Latin* will be published for candidates in the Ancient and Modern History Handbook by Monday 30 of Week Nought of Michaelmas Term each year for the academic year ahead.

Candidates who fail one or more of papers 1, 2, 3, or 4 above may resit that subject or subjects at a subsequent examination.

Preliminary Examination in Archaeology and Anthropology

A   35

1. The Preliminary Examination in Archaeology and Anthropology shall be under the supervision of the Social Sciences Board, and shall consist of such subjects as it shall by regulation prescribe.

2. The Chair of the Moderators for the Honour Moderations in Archaeology and Anthropology shall designate such of their number as may be required for the 40 Preliminary Examination in Archaeology and Anthropology.

B

Paper (1) Introduction to world archaeology;
Paper (2) Introduction to anthropological theory;
Paper (3) Perspectives of human evolution;   45
Paper (4) The nature of the archaeological enquiry.

Preliminary Examination in Biological Sciences

A

The subjects of the Preliminary Examination in Biological Sciences, the examination, the syllabus, and the number of papers shall be as prescribed by regulation from time to time by the Mathematical, Physical and Life Sciences Board.   5

B

1. The Biological Sciences Steering Committee shall publish the First Year Biology Handbook not later than the beginning of Michaelmas Full Term before the examination in the following Trinity Term. Further details of the papers, data handling course, and practical requirements shall be set out in that Handbook.   10

2. Candidates will be required to offer three papers, each lasting three hours, as follows:

Paper 1: Organisms
Paper 2: Cells and Genes
Paper 3: Ecology and Evolution   15

3. All candidates will be required to undertake a course of practical work, including laboratory exercises and the first year field course. Practical Class co-ordinators and the convenor for the field course shall make available to the chairman of the examiners records showing the extent to which each candidate has pursued an adequate course of practical work. The Moderators may request coursework from any candidate; such   20
candidates will be named in a list posted one week before the day of the first written paper. Each notebook submitted shall be accompanied by a certificate signed by the candidate indicating that the notebook is the candidate's own work. Failure to complete the coursework to the satisfaction of the Moderators, in the absence of appropriate documentary evidence, will normally constitute failure of the Preliminary   25
Examination. Coursework cannot normally be retaken. Exceptionally a candidate who has failed the coursework may be permitted jointly by the Moderators and the candidate's college to retake the entire academic year.

4. Candidates shall be deemed to have passed the examination if they have satisfied the Moderators in all three papers detailed in clause 2, and in the practical work   30
requirements as outlined in clause 3, either at a single examination, or at two examinations, as set out in clause 5.

5. A candidate who fails in any one of the papers listed in clause 2 must re-sit that paper at one, and only one, subsequent examination. A candidate who fails two or more papers listed in clause 2 must re-sit all three papers at one, and only one,   35
subsequent examination.

6. The Moderators will not provide calculators, but will permit the use of any handheld calculator subject to the conditions set out under the heading 'Use of calculators in examinations' in the *Regulations for the Conduct of University Examinations.*   40

Preliminary Examination in Biomedical Sciences

A

1. The subjects of the Preliminary Examination in Biomedical Sciences shall be:

(1) Body, Brain and Behaviour: Papers 1A and 1B
(2) Cells, Molecules and Genes: Papers 2A and 2B   45

(3) Introduction to Probability Theory and Statistics (as specified for the Preliminary Examination in Psychology, Philosophy, and Linguistics)

2. Candidates shall be deemed to have passed the examination if they satisfy the Moderators in all three subjects.

3. Candidates must offer all three subjects at their first examination attempt.

4. A candidate who fails one or two of the five papers comprising subjects 1–3 will be permitted one further attempt at the failed paper or papers, at the first available opportunity.

5. A candidate who fails three or more of the five papers comprising subjects 1–3 shall be deemed to have failed the examination. He or she will be permitted one further attempt at the whole examination, at the first available opportunity.

6. The Moderators may award a Distinction to candidates of special merit who satisfy them in all three subjects at their first examination attempt.

B

For each of subjects 1 and 2, two written papers will be set, each of one hour and thirty minutes' duration. For subject 3, one written paper will be set, as specified for the Preliminary Examination in Psychology, Philosophy, and Linguistics.

The Moderators will permit the use of hand-held pocket calculators subject to the conditions set out under the heading 'Use of calculators' in the *Regulations for the Conduct of University Examinations*. The letter sent to all candidates by the Chairman of Moderators will specify in which papers the use of calculators is permitted, and which calculators candidates will be permitted to use.

All candidates shall be assessed as to their practical ability in coursework under the following provisions:

(*a*) The Course Director, or a deputy, shall make available to the Moderators, at the end of the fifth week of the term in which the examinations are held, records showing the extent and the standard to which each candidate has completed the prescribed coursework. The Moderators may request practical notebooks from any candidate; such candidates will be named in a list posted in the foyer of the Medical Sciences Teaching Centre one week before the day of the first written paper. Each notebook submitted shall be accompanied by a statement signed by the candidate indicating that the notebook is the candidate's own work.

(*b*) Failure to complete the coursework to the satisfaction of the Moderators, in the absence of appropriate extenuating documentary evidence, will normally result in the candidate being required by the Moderators to submit to further examination. Failure of that examination will normally constitute failure of the Preliminary Examination. Coursework cannot normally be re-taken.

Schedule

1. Body, Brain and Behaviour
   a. Body: cardiovascular; respiratory; renal and gastrointestinal systems
   b. Brain: introduction to neuroscience; neuroanatomy overview; sensory; motor; neural development; learning and memory; sleep, dreams, and consciousness
   c. Behaviour: memory; language; awareness and attention; decision-making and rationality; disorders; social; genetics of diseases

2. Cells, Molecules and Genes
   a. Cells: cell division and cell cycle; inter- and intra-cellular signalling; excitable tissues; membrane transport; general principles of pharmacology
   b. Molecules: DNA/RNA structure; protein structure; lipids and membrane structure; energy metabolism
   c. Genes: fundamentals of genes; molecular biology techniques

3. Introduction to Probability Theory and Statistics (as specified for the Preliminary Examination in Psychology, Philosophy, and Linguistics)

Preliminary Examination in Chemistry

A

1. The subjects of the Preliminary Examination in Chemistry shall be Chemistry   5
(comprising Inorganic, Organic, and Physical Chemistry) and Mathematics for Chemistry.

2. The number of papers and other general requirements of the Preliminary Examination in Chemistry shall be prescribed by regulation from time to time by the Mathematical, Physical and Life Sciences Board.   10

B

1. Candidates in the Preliminary Examination in Chemistry must offer four subjects at one examination, provided that a candidate who has failed in one or two subjects may offer that number of subjects at a subsequent examination.

2. The subjects shall be as follows: 15

    (1) Inorganic Chemistry
    (2) Organic Chemistry
    (3) Physical Chemistry
    (4) Mathematics for Chemistry

One two-and-a-half-hour paper will be set for each of subjects (1), (3), and (4); one   20
three-hour paper will be set for subject (2).

3. Candidates shall be deemed to have passed the examination if they have satisfied the Moderators in all four subjects *either* at a single examination *or* at two examinations in accordance with the proviso to clause 1, and provided further that the same subjects as were failed at the first sitting have been passed at the same attempt at a   25
subsequent examination.

4. The Moderators may award a distinction to candidates of special merit who have satisfied them in all four subjects at a single examination.

5. The Moderators will not provide calculators but unless otherwise specified will permit the use of any hand-held pocket calculator subject to the conditions set out   30
under the heading 'Use of calculators in examinations' in the *Regulations for the Conduct of University Examinations* and further elaborated in the Course Handbook.

6. Candidates are required to complete an adequate course of laboratory work as specified in the Course Handbook. Heads of laboratories, or their deputies, and the IT Training Officer, shall make available to the Moderators records showing the extent to   35
which each candidate has pursued an adequate course of laboratory work. Only work completed and marked by 5 p.m. on the Friday of the sixth week of Trinity Term will be taken into account.

Preliminary Examination in Classical Archaeology and Ancient History   40

A

The subjects of the examination shall be under the supervision of the Board of the Faculty of Classics.

B

Every candidate shall offer four papers, as follows:

    I. *Aristocracy and democracy in the Greek world, 550–450 BC*

    II. *Republic to Empire: Rome, 50 BC to AD 50*

    III, IV. Two papers chosen from the following groups. No more than one paper may be chosen from each of groups A, B, and C.

    A. Special subjects in archaeology:

1. *Homeric archaeology and early Greece, 1550–700 BC* 2. *Greek vases* 3. *Greek sculpture, c.600–300 BC* 4. *Roman architecture*

    B. Special subjects in Ancient History:

1. *Thucydides and the west* 2. *Aristophanes' political comedy* 3. *Cicero and Catiline* 4. *Tacitus and Tiberius*

    C. Ancient languages:

1. *Beginning Ancient Greek* (not available to candidates with a qualification in ancient Greek above GCSE or equivalent)

2. *Beginning Latin* (not available to candidates with a qualification in Latin above GCSE or equivalent)

3. *Intermediate Ancient Greek* (not available to candidates with a qualification in ancient Greek above AS level or equivalent)

4. *Intermediate Latin* (not available to candidates with a qualification in Latin above AS level or equivalent)

5. *Advanced Ancient Greek*

6. *Advanced Latin*

    Each paper will be assessed by means of a three-hour written examination. Detailed specifications for each paper, including prescribed texts where applicable, will be published in the CAAH Prelims course handbook no later than Monday of Week 0 of Michaelmas Term in the calendar year preceding the examination.

    The Examiners may award a distinction to any candidate of special merit who has satisfied the Examiners in all papers at a single examination.

    Candidates who fail one or two of papers I, II, III, and IV above may resit only that subject or subjects at a subsequent examination; candidates who fail three or four papers will be required to resit all four papers at a subsequent examination.

Preliminary Examination in Classics

A

    1. The subjects of the examination shall be as prescribed by regulation from time to time by the Board of the Faculty of Classics and the Board of the Faculty of Philosophy.

    2. A candidate shall be deemed to have passed the examination if he or she shall have satisfied the Moderators in all four subjects: provided that he or she shall have passed in not less than three of the four subjects at one and the same examination.

    3. A candidate shall be allowed to offer himself or herself for examination in one or four subjects: provided that no candidate may offer a single subject unless he or she has already satisfied the Moderators in three subjects.

    4. The Moderators shall not publish the name of any candidate as having satisfied them in only one subject, unless that subject shall have been offered by the candidate as a single subject.

5. In the case of candidates who have satisfied the Moderators in four subjects at a single examination, the Moderators may award a Distinction to those of special merit.

B

Any candidate whose native language is not English may bring a bilingual (native language to English) dictionary for use in any examination paper where candidates are required to translate Ancient Greek and/or Latin texts into English.   5

Candidates shall take one of the following courses: IA, IB, IC, IIA, IIB.

Course IA
The examination will consist of the following papers.

I–II. *Texts and Contexts*   10

All candidates must offer 'Texts and Contexts' listed under Honour Moderations in Classics Course IA, papers III and IV.

III. *Special Subject*

All candidates must offer one of the Special Subjects listed under Honour Moderations in Classics Course IA, papers V and VI.   15

IV. *Unprepared Translation from Greek and Latin*

One paper (3 hours).

Course IB
The examination will consist of the following papers.

I–II. *Text and Contexts*   20

All candidates must offer 'Texts and Contexts' listed under Honour Moderations in Classics Course IB, papers III and IV.

III. *Special Subject*

All candidates must offer one of the Special Subjects listed under Honour Moderations in Classics Course IB, papers V and VI.   25

IV. *Unprepared Translation from Latin, with simpler Unprepared Translation from Greek*

One paper (3 hours).

Course IC
The examination will consist of the following papers.   30

I–II. *Text and Contexts*

All candidates must offer 'Texts and Contexts' listed under Honour Moderations in Classics Course IC, papers III and IV.

III. *Special Subject*

All candidates must offer one of the Special Subjects listed under Honour   35
Moderations in Classics Course IC, papers V and VI.

IV. *Unprepared Translation from Greek, with simpler Unprepared Translation from Latin*

One paper (3 hours).

Course IIA   40
The examination will consist of the following papers.

I–II. *Texts and Contexts*

All candidates must offer 'Texts and Contexts' listed under Honour Moderations in Classics Course IIA, papers II and III.

III. *Special Subject*

All candidates must offer one of the Special Subjects listed under Honour Moderations in Classics Course IIA, papers IV and V.

IV. *Unprepared Translation from Latin*

One paper (3 hours), as specified for Honour Moderations in Classics Course IIA, paper VI.

Course IIB
The examination will consist of the following papers.

I–II. *Text and Contexts*

All candidates must offer 'Texts and Contexts' listed under Honour Moderations in Classics Course IIB, papers II and III.

III. *Special Subject*

All candidates must offer one of the Special Subjects listed under Honour Moderations in Classics Course IIB, papers IV and V.

IV. *Unprepared Translation from Greek*

One paper (3 hours), as specified for Honour Moderations in Classics Course IB, paper VII.

Preliminary Examination in Classics and English

A

1. The Preliminary Examination in Classics and English shall be under the joint supervision of the Boards of the Faculties of Classics and English Language and Literature and shall consist of such subjects as they shall jointly by regulation prescribe.

2. The Chair of Examiners for the Preliminary Examination in English Language and Literature shall designate such of the number of examiners as may be required for the English subjects of the examination for the Preliminary Examination in Classics and English, and the nominating committee for examiners appointed by the Board of the Faculty of Classics shall nominate such of the number of examiners as may be required for the Classics subjects of the examination. When these appointments shall have been made the number of examiners shall be deemed to be complete.

3. Candidates must offer all the papers at a single examination, provided that: (i) a candidate who fails to satisfy the Examiners in one or two papers may offer those subjects at one subsequent examination, and (ii) a candidate who fails to satisfy the Examiners in three or more papers must offer all five subjects at one subsequent examination.

B

The committee appointed by the Boards of the Faculties of English Language and Literature and Classics to advise on the examination for the Honour School of Classics and English shall make proposals to the two boards for regulations for this examination.

Any candidate whose native language is not English may bring a bilingual (native language to English) dictionary for use in any examination paper where candidates are required to translate Ancient Greek and/or Latin texts into English.

Candidates shall take one of the following courses:

I. *Course I*

Each candidate shall offer five papers, each of three hours duration except where specified, as follows:

1. *Introduction to English Language and Literature* (a portfolio submitted in Trinity Term year 1)

The paper will be examined by a portfolio of work, comprising one commentary answer and one discursive essay, of not fewer than 1,500 and not more than 2,000 words each. Footnotes will be included in the total word count, but bibliographies do not count towards the limit. The list of questions for this paper will be divided into Section A (Language) and B (Literature) and will be published on Monday of the fourth week of the Trinity Term of the first year. Candidates must select one question from Section A and one question from section B.

Questions in Section A (Language) invite candidates to make their own selection of texts or passages of texts for commentary, in accordance with the terms of the particular question chosen. Copies of the texts or passages used must be included as an appendix to the portfolio. The combined length of all texts or passages chosen must not exceed 70 lines. The texts or passages used will not count towards the word limit for the commentary answer.

Two typed copies of the portfolio must be delivered to the Chair of Examiners for the Preliminary Examinations in English Language and Literature, Examination Schools, High Street, by noon on Thursday of the fifth week of the same Trinity Term. A certificate, signed by the candidate to the effect that each answer is the candidate's own work, and that the candidate has read the Faculty guidelines on plagiarism, must be presented together with each portfolio.

Following the publication of themes for this subject on Monday of the fourth week of Trinity Term, the candidate must neither discuss his or her choice of themes nor the method of handling them with any tutor. Every portfolio must be the work of the candidate alone, but he or she may discuss with his or her tutor the subjects and approach to the essays up until the stated publication date of the portfolio themes.

Portfolios previously submitted for the First Public Examination in English Language and Literature may be resubmitted. No answer will be accepted that has already been submitted, wholly or substantially, for a final honour school or any other degree of this University, or degree of any other institution.

Work deemed to be either too short or of excessive length may be penalised.

Candidates must avoid duplicating material used in this paper when answering other papers. In addition, candidates are not permitted to duplicate material between Section A and Section B of the portfolio.

2. *Literature in English 1550–1660* (excluding the plays of Shakespeare)

3. *Unseen translation from Greek and Latin*

Candidates may offer either Latin or Greek or both. Two passages must be offered and in each language one prose passage and one verse passage will be set.

4, 5. *Greek and Latin Literature*

Candidates must offer two of the following.

They must offer either (*a*) or (*b*), but may not offer both.

    (*a*) Homer, *Iliad*, I, VI, IX, XVI, XVIII, XXII–XXIV;*

    (*b*) Virgil, *Aeneid*, I, II, IV, VI;*

    (*c*) Euripides, *Bacchae* 1–1167; Aristophanes, *Frogs* 1–459, 830–1533; Herodotus 7.1–53; 8.56–110;**

(*d*) Cicero, *Pro Caelio* 17–53 (*...dedisti.*); Catullus 1–16, 31–7, 42–5, 48–51, 53, 69–70, 75–6, 79, 83–6, 95, 99–101, 116; Propertius I.1–3, 6, 11, 14; Petronius, *Cena Trimalchionis* 26.7–36, 47–78; Juvenal 3, 5.***

Paper 4 will consist of essay questions; all candidates will be required to answer questions on each of: Homer or Virgil; other texts; general topics. Paper 5 will comprise passages for translation and comment; all candidates will be required to answer on three passages, at least one passage of Homer or Virgil and at least one from the other texts.

The Examiners shall publish the names of candidates who have satisfied them in all five papers, or all of papers 1 and 2 or all of papers 3, 4 and 5.

N.B For prescribed editions, see the Classics and English handbook.

* For the purposes of the essay paper (paper 4), candidates who offer these texts will be expected to have knowledge of the whole work and not merely the prescribed portions.

** For the purposes of the essay paper (paper 4), candidates who offer these texts will be expected to have knowledge of the whole of *Bacchae, Frogs*, and Herodotus 7–8 and not merely the prescribed portions.

*** For the purposes of the essay paper (paper 4), candidates who offer these texts will be expected to have knowledge of the whole of *Pro Caelio*, Propertius I, and the *Cena Trimalchionis* and not merely the prescribed portions.

II. *Course II*

Candidates for Course II shall be required:

(*a*) during their first year of study to have passed an examination under the auspices of the Board of the Faculty of Classics during the Trinity Term. This examination is also available for appropriate candidates intending to offer papers in the Preliminary Examination for Modern Languages in their second year of study. Candidates who fail to satisfy the examiners shall be permitted to offer themselves for re-examination during the following September. Each candidate shall offer two papers, each of three hours' duration, as follows:

1. Greek or Latin texts. Candidates must offer either (*a*) or (*b*):

   (*a*) Homer, *Iliad* 24; Lysias 1 and 3; Euripides, *Bacchae* 1–63, 180–369, 434–518.

   (*b*) Virgil, *Aeneid* 6; Seneca, *Epistles* 54, 57, 79, 114 and 122; Catullus 1–16, 31–4.

For a list of prescribed texts, see the Classics and English handbook. The paper will comprise passages from these texts for translation and comment.

2. Greek or Latin Language. The paper will consist of passages for unseen translation out of Greek or Latin and sentences for translation from English into Latin or Greek.

   (*b*) during their second year of study, to offer papers as for Course I.

Preliminary Examination in Computer Science

A

1. The subject of the examination shall be Computer Science.

2. The syllabus and number of papers shall be prescribed by regulation from time to time by the Mathematical, Physical and Life Sciences Board.

B

1. The Preliminary Examination in Computer Science shall comprise four compulsory written papers plus compulsory Computer Science practicals equivalent to one written paper:

CS1 Functional Programming, and Design and Analysis of Algorithms   5
CS2 Imperative Programming
CS3 Discrete Mathematics, Probability and Continuous Mathematics
CS4 Digital Systems, Linear Algebra, and Introduction to Formal Proof
Computer Science Practicals

2. The syllabus for each paper will be published by the Department of Computer   10
Science in a handbook for candidates by the beginning of the Michaelmas Full Term
in the academic year of the examination, after consultation with the Faculty of
Computer Science (for papers CS1, CS2, CS3, and CS4) and the Faculty of
Mathematics (for paper CS3). Each paper will contain questions of a straightforward
character.   15

3. All candidates will be assessed as to their practical ability under the following
provisions:

(*a*) The Head of the Department of Computer Science, or a deputy, shall make
    available to the examiners evidence showing the extent to which each
    candidate has pursued an adequate course of practical work. Only that   20
    work completed and marked by noon on Monday of the sixth week of the
    Trinity Term in which the candidate takes the examination shall be included
    in these records.

(*b*) Candidates shall submit to the Chair of the Moderators for the Preliminary
    Examination in Computer Science, c/o the Academic Administrator, Oxford   25
    University Department of Computer Science, Oxford, by noon on Monday
    of the sixth week of the Trinity Term in which the examination is being held,
    their reports of practical exercises completed during their course of study.
    For a report on a practical exercise to be considered by the moderators, it
    must have been marked by a demonstrator and must be accompanied by   30
    a statement that it is the candidate's own work except where otherwise
    indicated.

(*c*) The moderators shall take the evidence (*a*) and the reports (*b*) into account in
    assessing a candidate's performance.

(*d*) Candidates whose overall performance on practical work is not satisfactory   35
    may be deemed to have failed the examination.

4. Candidates shall be deemed to have passed the examination if they have satisfied
the Moderators in the five papers in clause 1 either at a single examination or at two
examinations in accordance with clause 6 or clause 7.

5. The Moderators may award a distinction to candidates of special merit who have   40
satisfied them in all five papers in clause 1 in one examination.

6. Candidates who fail one or two written papers listed in clause 1 may offer those
papers at one, but no more than one, subsequent examination.

7. Candidates who fail three or more written papers may enter the written part of
the examination on one, but no more than one, subsequent examination.   45

8. The use of calculators is generally not permitted but certain kinds may be
allowed for certain papers. Specifications of which papers and which types of calculators
are permitted for those exceptional papers will be announced by the examiners
in the Hilary Term preceding the examination.

Preliminary Examination in Computer Science and Philosophy

A

1. The subject of the examination shall be (a) Computer Science and (b) Philosophy.

2. All candidates must offer both (a) and (b).

3. The Examinations shall be under the joint supervision of the Divisional Board of Mathematical, Physical and Life Sciences and the Board of the Faculty of Philosophy, which shall appoint a joint supervisory committee to make regulations concerning it, subject always to the preceding clauses of this subsection.

B

1. The Preliminary Examination in Computer Science and Philosophy shall comprise five compulsory written papers plus compulsory Computer Science practicals equivalent to one written paper:

CS1 Functional Programming, and Design and Analysis of Algorithms
CS2 Imperative Programming
CSP3 Discrete Mathematics and Probability
P1 Introduction to Philosophy
P2 Elements of Deductive Logic
Computer Science Practicals

2. The syllabus for papers CS1, CS2, and CSP3 will be published by the Joint Supervisory Committee in a handbook for candidates by the beginning of the Michaelmas Full Term in the academic year of the examination, after consultation with the Faculty of Computer Science (for papers CS1, CS2, and CSP3) and the Faculty of Mathematics (for paper CSP3). The syllabus for paper P1 will be as stated below. The syllabus for paper P2 will be as stated for the Elements of Deductive Logic paper in the regulations for the Preliminary Examination in Mathematics and Philosophy.

3. Papers CS1, CS2, and CSP3 will contain questions of a straightforward character.

4. All candidates will be assessed as to their practical ability in Computer Science under the following provisions:

(*a*) The Head of the Department of Computer Science, or a deputy, shall make available to the examiners evidence showing the extent to which each candidate has pursued an adequate course of practical work. Only that work completed and marked by noon on Monday of the sixth week of the Trinity Term in which the candidate takes the examination shall be included in these records.

(*b*) Candidates shall submit to the Chairman of the Moderators for the Preliminary Examination in Computer Science and Philosophy, c/o the Academic Administrator, Oxford University Department of Computer Science, Oxford, by noon on Monday of the sixth week of the Trinity Term in which the examination is being held, their reports of practical exercises completed during their course of study. For a report on a practical exercise to be considered by the Moderators, it must have been marked by a demonstrator and must be accompanied by a statement that it is the candidate's own work except where otherwise indicated.

(*c*) The Moderators shall take the evidence (*a*) and the reports (*b*) into account in assessing a candidate's performance.

(*d*) Candidates whose overall performance on practical work is not satisfactory may be deemed to have failed the examination.

5. Candidates shall be deemed to have passed the examination if they have satisfied the Moderators in all six papers in clause 1 either at a single examination or at two examinations in accordance with clause 7 or clause 8.

6. The Moderators may award a distinction to candidates of special merit who have satisfied them in all six papers in clause 1 in one examination.   5

7. Candidates who fail one or two written papers listed in clause 1 may offer those papers at one, but no more than one, subsequent examination.

8. Candidates who fail three or more papers may enter the written part of the examination on one, but no more than one, subsequent examination.

9. The use of calculators is generally not permitted but certain kinds may be   10
allowed for certain papers. Specifications of which papers and which types of calculators are permitted for those exceptional papers will be announced by the examiners in the Hilary Term preceding the examination.

Paper P1, Introduction to Philosophy
The paper shall consist of two parts: 15

A. *General Philosophy* as stated in the regulations for the Preliminary Examination in Mathematics and Philosophy.

B. *Turing: Computability and Intelligence* This section shall be studied in connection with Alan Turing's papers 'On Computable Numbers, with an Application to the *Entscheidungsproblem*' (reprinted and explained in Charles   20
Petzold's *The Annotated Turing*, Wiley, 2008) and 'Computing Machinery and Intelligence' (*Mind*, 1950). While not being confined to Turing's views, these questions will be satisfactorily answerable by a candidate who has made a critical study of the texts. There will not be a compulsory question containing passages for comment.   25

Candidates will be required to attempt four questions, including at least one question from Part A and at least one question from Part B.

Preliminary Examination in Earth Sciences

A

1. The subject of the Preliminary Examination in Earth Sciences shall be Earth   30
Sciences, including supporting practical techniques and physics, chemistry, mathematics and biology.

2. The number of papers and other general requirements of the Preliminary Examination in Earth Sciences shall be prescribed by regulation from time to time by the Mathematical, Physical and Life Sciences Board.   35

B

1. The Preliminary Examination in Earth Sciences shall consist of 5 compulsory papers taken at one examination, subject to the conditions of clause 5 below:
  (*a*) Paper 1: Planet Earth
  (*b*) Paper 2: Fundamentals of Geology (Theory)   40
  (*c*) Paper 3: Fundamentals of Geology (Practical)
  (*d*) Paper 4: Chemistry, Physics and Biology for Earth Sciences
  (*e*) Paper 5: an approved paper in Mathematics

The syllabus for these papers shall be published annually in the course handbook, not later than the beginning of Michaelmas Full Term for examination three terms thence.

2. In addition to the above five papers a candidate in Earth Sciences shall be required to submit to the examiners such evidence as they require of the successful 5 completion of field work normally pursued during the three terms preceding the examination. Candidates who fail to satisfy the examiners in this regard will be required to sit a further paper, which may only be taken once.

3. Candidates shall be deemed to have passed the examination if they have:

   (*a*) satisfied the Examiners in the five papers in clause 1 either at a single 10 examination or at two examinations in accordance with clause 5, and

   (*b*) satisfied the additional requirements in clause 2.

4. The Examiners may award a distinction to candidates of special merit who have satisfied them in all five papers in clause 1 in one examination and in the requirements of clause 2. 15

5. Candidates who fail in one or two papers listed in clause 1 may offer that number of papers at a subsequent examination. Candidates who fail more than two papers must resit all five papers at a subsequent examination.

6. The examination conventions of each examination paper listed in clause 1 will be published annually in the course handbook. 20

Preliminary Examination in Economics and Management

A

1. The subjects of the Preliminary Examination in Economics and Management shall be:

   (1) Introductory Economics 25
   (2) Financial Management
   (3) General Management.

2. A candidate shall be allowed to offer himself or herself for examination in one, two, or three subjects.

3. A candidate shall be deemed to have passed the examination if he or she shall 30 have satisfied the Moderators in three subjects.

4. The Moderators may award a distinction to candidates of special merit who have passed all three subjects at a single examination.

B

Three three-hour papers will be set as follows: 35

Introductory Economics

As specified in the regulation relating to the Introductory Economics paper of the Philosophy, Politics, and Economics Preliminary Examination.

Financial Management

Financial reporting and analysis of company accounts; management accounting, 40 including cost behaviours, capital budgeting, budgetary planning and control; discounting and net present value; internal rates of return; measurement and evaluation of risk; capital asset pricing; investment appraisal; sources of funds; capital budgeting and implementation.

General Management

Historical context; organisational behaviour; human resources; strategic management; technology and operations management; marketing; international business.

Preliminary Examination in Engineering Science

A

The subjects of the examination, the syllabus, and the number of papers shall be as prescribed by regulation from time to time by the Divisional Board of Mathematical, Physical and Life Sciences.

B

1. Candidates shall take four written papers of three hours each:

Paper P1 Mathematics
Paper P2 Electronic and Information Engineering
Paper P3 Structures and Mechanics
Paper P4 Energy

The syllabus for Papers P1-P4 will be published annually by the Faculty of Engineering Science in the Engineering Science Undergraduate Course Handbook.

In addition Engineering Coursework (P5) shall be considered by the Moderators as equivalent to half of a three hour written paper.

2. Candidates must offer all subjects at one examination provided that: (i) a candidate who fails in one or two written papers may offer those written subjects at one subsequent examination; (ii) a candidate who fails three or four written papers must offer all four written subjects at one subsequent examination.

3. Candidates shall be deemed to have passed the examination if they shall have satisfied the Moderators in all four written papers and in the engineering coursework either at a single examination or at two examinations in accordance with the proviso to clause 2. Any written subjects retaken must be passed at the same attempt at a subsequent examination.

4. All candidates shall be assessed as to their practical ability in engineering coursework under the following provisions:

(*a*) The Chairman of the Faculty, or a deputy, shall make available to the Moderators, by the date of the first written paper, evidence showing the extent to which each candidate has completed coursework.

(*b*) Candidates will not normally be required to submit their coursework. The Moderators may request coursework from some candidates. Such candidates will be named in a list posted by the day of the last written examination.

(*c*) Engineering coursework cannot be retaken. Failure of coursework will normally constitute failure of the examination.

5. In the case of candidates who offer all four written papers, the Moderators shall publish the name of candidates who have satisfied them either in the whole examination or in any written paper. In the case of candidates who, in accordance with the proviso of clause 2, offer one, two, or four written papers at the second attempt, the Moderators shall publish the names only of those candidates who have satisfied them in each of the papers offered.

6. The Moderators may award a distinction to candidates of special merit who have passed all four written subjects and the engineering coursework at a single examination.

7. The Moderators will not provide calculators, but will permit the use of one hand-held pocket calculator from a list of permitted calculators published by the Chairman of the Faculty not later than the end of the fourth week of the Trinity Full Term in the academic year preceding the examination.

Preliminary Examination in English and Modern Languages   5

A

1. Candidates in this Preliminary Examination shall be examined in English and one Modern Language. The modern languages that may be offered shall be those which may be offered in the Honour School of Modern Languages.

2. The subjects of the examination, the syllabus, and the number of papers shall be   10
as prescribed by regulation from time to time by the Boards of the Faculties of English Language and Literature and Medieval and Modern Languages.

3. It shall be the duty (a) of the Chair of the Examiners for the Preliminary Examination in English Language and Literature to designate such of their number as may be required for English in the Preliminary Examination in English and Modern   15
Languages, and when this has been done the number of examiners in English shall be deemed to be complete; and (b) of the Chair of the Examiners for the Preliminary Examination for Modern Languages to designate such of their number as may be required for Modern Languages in the Preliminary Examination in English and Modern   20
Languages, and when this has been done, the number of examiners in Modern Languages shall be deemed to be complete.

B

The Boards of the Faculties of English Language and Literature and of Medieval and Modern Languages shall appoint a joint standing committee to make, and to submit to the two faculty boards, proposals for regulations for this examination.   25

A candidate shall be deemed to have passed the examination if he or she shall have satisfied the Examiners in Part 1 (a Modern Language) and Part 2 (English).

The examiners may award distinctions in Part 1 or in Part 2 or in both to candidates who have done work of special merit in the part or parts concerned.

A candidate who has failed a subject or both the subjects in Part 1 will be allowed to   30
resit the subject or subjects in which he or she has failed at a subsequent examination in accordance with the regulations for the Preliminary Examination for Modern Languages. A candidate who has failed one or both of the papers in Part 2 will be allowed to resit the paper or papers in accordance with the appropriate regulations for the First Public Examinations in English Language and Literature.   35

Part 1: A Modern Language
Each candidate shall offer the following two subjects in the modern language:

(1) Language papers (one paper of three hours and two papers each of one-and-a-half hours including in French certification of attendance and participation in oral classes, as specified for the Preliminary Examination in Modern Languages). As   40
specified for papers I, IIA, and IIB in the regulations for the Preliminary Examination for Modern Languages.

(2) Literature papers (two papers, each of three hours). As specified for papers III and IV in the regulations for the Preliminary Examination for Modern Languages.

Part 2: English   45
Each candidate shall offer the following papers, as specified in the regulations for subjects 1 to 4 of the Preliminary Examination in English Language and Literature:

(1) Introduction to English Language and Literature [as specified for the Preliminary Examination in English Language and Literature, subject 1].

(2) *Either* (*a*) Literature in English 650–1350 [as specified for the Preliminary Examination in English Language and Literature, subject 2].

or (*b*) Literature in English 1830–1910 [as specified for the Preliminary Examination in English Language and Literature, subject 3].

or (*c*) Literature in English 1910–present day [as specified for the Preliminary Examination in English Language and Literature, subject 4].

Preliminary Examination in English Language and Literature

A

1. The subjects of the examination, the syllabus, and the number of papers shall be as prescribed by regulation from time to time by the Board of the Faculty of English Language and Literature.

2. A Candidate shall be deemed to have passed the examination when he or she shall have satisfied the Examiners in all the papers specified in the regulations.

3. Candidates must offer all the papers at a single examination, provided that: (i) a candidate who fails to satisfy the Examiners in one or two papers may offer those subjects at one subsequent examination, and (ii) a candidate who fails to satisfy the Examiners in three or four papers must offer all four subjects at one subsequent examination.

4. The Examiners may award a distinction to any candidate of special merit who has satisfied the Examiners in all the papers at a single examination.

B

Each candidate shall offer four papers, as set out below. Paper 1 shall be examined by portfolio submission in the third term. Papers 2, 3, and 4 shall be examined by written examinations of three hours' duration.

1. *Introduction to English Language and Literature*

The paper will be examined by a portfolio of work, comprising one commentary answer and one discursive essay, of not fewer than 1,500 and not more than 2,000 words each. Footnotes will be included in the total word count, but bibliographies do not count towards the limit. The list of questions for this paper will be divided into Section A (Language) and B (Literature) and will be published on Monday of the fourth week of the Trinity Term of the first year. Candidates must select one question from Section A and one question from Section B.

Questions in Section A (Language) invite candidates to make their own selection of texts or passages of texts for commentary, in accordance with the terms of the particular question chosen. Copies of the texts or passages used must be included as an appendix to the portfolio. The combined length of all texts or passages chosen must not exceed 70 lines. The texts or passages used will not count towards the word limit for the commentary answer.

Two typed copies of the portfolio must be delivered to the Chair of Examiners for the Preliminary Examination in English Language and Literature, Examination Schools, High Street, by noon on Thursday of the fifth week of the same Trinity Term. A certificate, signed by the candidate to the effect that each answer is the candidate's own work, and that the candidate has read the Faculty guidelines on plagiarism, must be presented together with each portfolio.

Following the publication of themes for this subject on Monday of the fourth week of Trinity Term, the candidate must neither discuss his or her choice of themes nor the method of handling them with any tutor. Every portfolio must be the work of the candidate alone, but he or she may discuss with his or her tutor the subjects and approach to the essays up until the stated publication date of the portfolio themes.

Portfolios previously submitted for the First Public Examination in English Language and Literature may be resubmitted. No answer will be accepted that has   5
already been submitted, wholly or substantially, for a final honour school or any other degree of this University, or degree of any other institution.

Work deemed to be either too short or of excessive length may be penalised.

Candidates must avoid duplicating material used in this paper when answering other papers. In addition, candidates are not permitted to duplicate material between   10
Section A and Section B of the portfolio.

2. *Early Medieval Literature 650–1350*

The examination for paper 2 will be divided into Section A and Section B.

    (*a*) Section A will consist of four passages for critical commentary: two passages from Old English texts and two passages from Early Middle English texts.   15
Candidates should write on *one* passage only.

Passages will be set from texts specified in the English Preliminary Examination Handbook for the year of examination.

    (*b*) Section B will consist of essay questions that are thematic in nature and may be applied to any texts from the period. Candidates should answer *two*   20
questions from section B.

3. *Literature in English 1830–1910*

4. *Literature in English 1910–present day*

Preliminary Examination in European and   25
Middle Eastern Languages

A

1. The Preliminary Examination in European and Middle Eastern Languages shall be under the joint supervision of the Boards of the Faculties of Medieval and Modern Languages and Oriental Studies and shall consist of such subjects as they shall jointly   30
by regulation prescribe.

2. Candidates in this Preliminary Examination shall be examined (*a*) in one language from among those which may be offered in the Honour School of Modern Languages, and (*b*) in Arabic or in Hebrew or in Persian or in Turkish.

3. It shall be the duty (*a*) of the Chairman of the Examiners for the Preliminary   35
Examination for Modern Languages to designate such of their number as may be required for European Languages in the Preliminary Examination in European and Middle Eastern Languages, and when this has been done the number of examiners in European Languages shall be deemed to be complete; and (*b*) of the Chairman of the Moderators for the Preliminary Examination in Oriental Studies to designate such of   40
their number as may be required for Arabic, Hebrew, Persian, and Turkish in the Preliminary Examination in European and Middle Eastern Languages, and when this has been done the number of examiners in Middle Eastern Languages shall be deemed to be complete.

B

There shall be two subjects in the examination.

(1) *The European Language*

Candidates will be required to offer:

(i) Language papers in the European Language (one paper of three hours and two papers each of one-and-a-half hours including in French certification of attendance and participation in oral classes, as specified for the Preliminary Examination in Modern Languages).

As specified for Papers I, IIA, and IIB in the regulations for the Preliminary Examination for Modern Languages.

(ii) Literature paper in the European Language (one paper of three hours).

As specified *either* for Paper III *or* for Paper IV in the regulations for the Preliminary Examination in Modern Languages (Candidates offering French *must* offer Paper IV).

(2) *Language papers in the Middle Eastern Language*

Candidates will be required to offer two three-hour papers and, in the case of Arabic, an oral/aural examination.

Arabic
   (i) Translation and precis into English.
   (ii) Comprehension, composition, and grammar.
   (iii) Oral/aural examination.

Hebrew
   (i) Biblical and Modern Texts (copies of texts available from the Oriental Institute).
   (ii) Grammar and Translation into Hebrew.

Persian
   (i) Translation from Persian and reading comprehension.
   (ii) Translation into Persian and essay.

Turkish
   (i) Prepared texts and unseen translation from Turkish. (The list of texts to be prepared is published in the current issue of the Islamic Studies handbook.)
   (ii) Turkish grammar and translation into Turkish.

Candidates shall be deemed to have passed the examination if they shall have satisfied the examiners in subject (1) (The European Language) and subject (2) (Language papers in the Middle Eastern Language).

The examiners may award distinctions in either or both subjects to candidates who have done work of special merit in the subject or subjects concerned.

A candidate who has failed (i) or (ii) of subject (1) may resit the paper or papers at a subsequent examination in accordance with the regulations for the Preliminary Examination in Modern Languages. A candidate who has failed a paper or papers in subject (2) may resit that paper or papers at a subsequent examination.

Preliminary Examination in Fine Art

A

1. No person who is not a member of the University may be admitted to the Preliminary Examination in Fine Art.

2. A candidate may enter his or her name for the examination not earlier than the third term from his matriculation.

3. The subjects of the examination shall be

(1) Art Work: exhibition and folio/documentation of supporting or related work;

(2) History and Theory of Visual Culture;

(3) Human Anatomy;

4. Candidates must offer all four subjects of the examination at the same time, provided that a candidate who has passed in at least two of the subjects but failed in the other subjects (or subject) of the examination may offer at a subsequent examination the subjects (or subject) in which he or she has failed.

5. The examination shall be under the supervision of the Committee for the Ruskin School of Art, which shall make regulations for the examination.

6. The examiners may award a distinction in the examination to any candidate.

B

1. The examination shall include both practical and written work.

2. Every candidate will be required in respect of:

(1) *Art Work*

    (*a*) to produce an exhibition/presentation of current art work in any medium or media agreed by the candidate and their tutor; and

    (*b*) to submit an edited selection of art work made during the course preceding the examination in any medium or media agreed by the candidate and their tutor. This selection should provide context to the exhibition described above, demonstrating artistic processes or strategies engaged in and the development of ideas throughout the course.

Candidates may submit a combination of physical and digital portfolio but in any instance the total portfolio submission should include no more than 25 separate items. 2D works and sketch/notebooks may be submitted as part of a physical portfolio where they are under A1 size. Larger 2D, 3D, or performance works should be documented using photography and video as appropriate. In the case of time-based work, the total duration of artworks, excerpts of artworks or documentation should not exceed 10 minutes. Any digital moving image and photographic works should be submitted in universal file formats.

(2) *History and Theory of Visual Culture*

    (*a*) to submit three essays of no more than 2,000 words each (including footnotes) on aspects of the history and theory of visual culture in accordance with the provisions of clause 3 of these regulations;

    (*b*) to offer a paper on history and theory of visual culture;

(3) *Human Anatomy*

    (*a*) to offer a paper on form and function in human anatomy.

    (*b*) to submit notebooks and a portfolio of not less than six and no more than twenty examples of supporting visual material on the candidate's work in human anatomy.

The work required by (1) and (3)(*b*) above must be submitted to the Chair of Examiners, Preliminary Examination in Fine Art, Ruskin School of Art, 74 High Street, in the case of the examination held in Trinity Term not later than noon on Thursday of the sixth week of that term, and in the case of the examination held in the vacation preceding Michaelmas Term not later than noon on Wednesday in the week before Michaelmas Full Term.

3. Of the essays required by the provisions of clause (2)(*a*) of these regulations, one must be submitted not later than noon on the Friday of the ninth week of the Michaelmas Full Term preceding the examination, one must be submitted not later

than noon on the Monday of the first week of Hilary Full Term preceding the examination and one must be submitted not later than noon on the Friday of the ninth week of the Hilary Full Term preceding the examination. One copy of these essays, which may be either typed or in manuscript, must be delivered to the Chair of Examiners, Preliminary Examination in Fine Art, Examination Schools. Each essay   5
must be accompanied by a certificate signed by the candidate that the essay has not been submitted for any previous examination, and that the essay is the candidate's own unaided work save for advice on the choice and scope of the subject, the provision of a reading list, and guidance on matters of presentation. This certificate must be submitted separately in a sealed envelope addressed to the chair of examiners. The   10
chair of the examiners will announce the list of subjects on which the essays may be submitted by the end of the first week of the Michaelmas Full Term preceding the examination.

Preliminary Examination in Geography

A   15

The Preliminary Examination in Geography shall be under the supervision of the Divisional Board of Social Sciences and shall consist of such subjects as it shall prescribe by regulation.

B

1. Each candidate shall offer four papers as follows: 20
   * Earth Systems Processes
   * Human Geography
   * Geographical Techniques
   * Geographical Controversies

Each paper will be of three hours' duration.   25

2. All candidates will be assessed as to their practical ability under the following provisions:

   (*a*) Fieldwork. Candidates shall submit to the Chair of Moderators not later than noon on the Monday of the sixth week of Trinity Full Term a fieldwork folder containing accounts of fieldwork exercises. The requirements for this   30
   folder will be published by the Geography Undergraduate Teaching and Examining Committee at the beginning of the Michaelmas Full Term in the academic year of the examination.

   (*b*) Geographical Techniques. The Chairman of the Undergraduate Teaching and Examining Committee, or a deputy, shall make available to the   35
   Moderators, by the date of the first written paper, evidence showing the extent to which each candidate has pursued an adequate course of practical work for Geographical Techniques.

   (*c*) Geographical Controversies. Candidates shall submit to the Chair of Moderators not later than noon on the Monday of the sixth week of Trinity   40
   Full Term a folder of practical work for the Geographical Controversies paper. The requirements for this folder will be published by the Geography Undergraduate Teaching and Examining Committee at the beginning of the Michaelmas Full Term in the academic year of the examination.

In assessing the candidate's performance in the examination, the moderators shall   45
take this evidence into account.

3. Candidates shall be deemed to have passed if they have satisfied the examiners in all four subjects and in the practical work requirements as outlined in section 2.

4. A candidate who fails in one or more subjects may offer that subject or subjects at one, and only one, subsequent examination. A candidate who fails in three or four subjects is required to re-sit all four papers. A candidate who fails to satisfy the practical requirements as outlined in section 2 will be allowed one opportunity to resubmit this work.

5. Examiners may award a distinction to candidates of special merit who have passed all four subjects and satisfied the requirements for practical work outlined in section 2.

6. The examiners will not provide calculators but will permit the use of any handheld calculator subject to the conditions set out under the heading 'Use of calculators in examinations' in the Regulations for the Conduct of University examinations.

Papers for the Preliminary Examination in Geography

1. *Earth Systems Processes*

The paper will require an understanding of the physical geography of the Earth, based around core concepts and principles. Candidates should be able to display familiarity with mechanisms and processes under the headings of Geomorphology, Climatology, and Ecology of the biosphere and a grasp of linkages between topics taught under these headings.

2. *Human Geography*

The paper will examine the following themes and the relationships between them at a variety of scales Economy and Transformation, Territories and Identities, Culture and Society.

3. *Geographical Controversies*

The paper will require an understanding of geographical controversies past and present. Candidates will be expected to demonstrate critical understanding of the use of evidence and data in geographical argument. Details of the materials to be covered for this course will be published by the Geography Undergraduate Teaching and Examining Committee at the beginning of the Michaelmas Full Term in the academic year of the examination

4. *Geographical Techniques*

The subject will comprise theoretical and practical aspects of geographical techniques. Candidates will be expected to be conversant with problem-solving in both human and physical branches of the discipline. Details of the areas to be covered will be published by the Geography Undergraduate Teaching and Examining Committee at the beginning of the Michaelmas Full Term in the academic year of the examination.

Preliminary Examination in History

A

The subjects of the examination, the syllabus, and the number of papers shall be as prescribed by regulation from time to time by the Board of the Faculty of History.

B

Each candidate shall offer four papers, as follows:

1. History of the British Isles: any one of the following periods:.

(I) *c*.300–1087; (II) 1042–1330; (III) 1330–1550; (IV) 1500–1700; (V) 1685–1830; (VI) 1815–1924; (VII) since 1900.

2. General History: any one of the period papers I: 370–900 (*The Transformation of the Ancient World*), II: 1000–1300 (*Medieval Christendom and its neighbours*), III: 1400–1650 (*Renaissance, Recovery, and Reform*), and IV: 1815–1914 (*Society, Nation,*

and Empire). Candidates will be given a wide choice of questions relating to themes in the history of the period and they are advised not to concentrate narrowly on a particular period or topic.

3. Optional Subject: any one of an approved list of subjects, examples of which are given below. A detailed list of Optional Subjects, including the prescribed texts, will be published in the Handbook for Preliminary Examination in History by the Board of the Faculty of History by Monday of noughth week of Michaelmas Term each year for the academic year ahead. Depending on the availability of teaching resources, with the exception of Optional Subject 1, not all the Optional Subjects listed in the Handbook will be available to all candidates in any given year. Candidates may obtain details of the choice of options for that year by consulting the Definitive List of Optional Subjects posted at the beginning of the first week of Michaelmas Full Term in the History Faculty and circulated to History Tutors.

1. Theories of the State (Aristotle, Hobbes, Rousseau, Marx).
2. The Age of Bede *c.* 660–*c.*740.
3. Early Gothic France *c.* 1100–*c.*1150.
4. Conquest and Frontiers: England and the Celtic Peoples 1150–1220.
5. English Chivalry and the French War *c.* 1330–*c.*1400.
6. Nature and Art in the Renaissance.
7. Witch-craft and witch-hunting in early modern Europe.
8. Nobility and Gentry in England 1560–1660.
9. Conquest and Colonization: Spain and America in the Sixteenth Century.
10. Revolution and Empire in France 1789–1815.
11. Women, Gender and the Nation: Britain, 1789–1825.
12. The Romance of the People: The Folk Revival from 1760 to 1914.
13. The American Empire: 1823–1904.
14. The Rise and Crises of European Socialisms: 1881–1921.
15. Theories of War and Peace in Europe 1890–1914.
16. Working-Class Life and Industrial Work in Britain 1870–1914.
17. The World of Homer and Hesiod, as specified for Preliminary Examination in Ancient and Modern History.
18. Augustan Rome, as specified for Preliminary Examination in Ancient and Modern History.

4. *Either* (*a*) Approaches to History *or* (*b*) Historiography: Tacitus to Weber *or* (*c*) Foreign Texts *or* (*d*) Quantification in History, as specified in the Handbook for the Preliminary Examination in History.

Candidates who fail one or more of papers 1, 2, 3, or 4 above may resit that subject or subjects at a subsequent examination.

Preliminary Examination in History and Economics

A

The Preliminary Examination in History and Economics shall be under the joint supervision of the Divisional Board of Social Studies, and the Board of the Faculty of History and shall consist of such subjects as they shall jointly by regulation prescribe.

B

Every candidate shall offer four papers, as follows:
1. Introductory Economics, as specified for the Preliminary Examination in Philosophy, Politics, and Economics.

2. General History: any one of the periods specified for the Preliminary Examination in History.

3. Optional Subject: any one of an approved list of subjects, as specified for the Preliminary Examination in History.

or 5

Industrialization in Britain and France 1750–1870, which is available only for candidates for this examination.

4. *Either* (*a*) Approaches to History *or* (*b*) Historiography: Tacitus to Weber *or* (*c*) Foreign Texts, as specified for the Preliminary Examination in History.

The individual specifications and prescribed texts for papers 3 and 4 above will be 10 published in the Handbook for the Preliminary Examination in History by Monday of noughth week of Michaelmas Term each year for the academic year ahead. Depending on the availability of teaching resources, with the exception of Optional Subject 1, not all the Optional Subjects listed in the Handbook will be available to candidates in any given year. Candidates may obtain details of the choice of options 15 for that year by consulting the Definitive List of Optional Subjects posted at the beginning of the first week of Michaelmas Full Term in the History Faculty and circulated to tutors.

Schedule

Note. The letter c against a text indicates that it is available as a photocopy from the 20 History Faculty Library. The letter т against a text indicates that it is to be read in specially prepared translation.

INDUSTRIALIZATION IN BRITAIN AND FRANCE 1750–1870

This is a paper in comparative economic history and is concerned with the main relationships involved in the industrialization of these two countries. 25

The texts have been selected to exemplify British commentaries on economic developments in France and French perceptions of Britain's economic progress from 1750 to 1870.

A. Texts by British Authors:

A. Young, *Travels in France During the Years 1787, 1788 and 1789,* ed. Constantia 30 Maxwell (Cambridge, 1950), pp. 279–300, 312–13. (Available in the History Faculty Library.)

c M. Birkbeck, *Notes on a Journey Through France in 1814,* 3rd edn. (London, 1815), pp. 99–115. (Bodleian reference 8θ R 88 BS.)

E. Baines, *History of the Cotton Manufacture in Great Britain* (London, 1835), 35 pp. 512–26. (Bodleian reference 35. 734.)

c H. Colman, *The Agricultural and Rural Economy of France, Belgium, Holland and Switzerland* (London, 1848), pp. 20–40. (Bodleian reference 48. 105.)

c Great Exhibition, *The Industry of Nations as Exemplified in the Great Exhibition of 1851* (London, 1852), pp. 223–7. (Bodleian reference 177e. 15.) 40

c A. B. Reach, *Claret and Olives* (London, 1852), pp. 256–63. (Bodleian reference 203. b. 301.)

c F. Marshall, *Population and Trade in France in 1861–2* (London, 1862), pp. 156–207. (Bodleian reference 232. b. 61.)

T. E. Cliffe Leslie, 'The Land System in France', in *Systems of Land Tenure in* 45 *Various Countries* (London, 1881), ed. J. W. Probyn, pp. 291–312. (Bodleian reference 24754. e. 174.)

B. Texts by French Authors (translated into English):

Leon Faucher, *Manchester in 1844: Its Present Condition and Future Prospects* (London, 1844), pp. 1–20 and 85–152. (Bodleian reference Gough Adds. Lancs., 817.) 50

c A. P. A. Ledru-Rollin, *The Decline of England* (London, 1850), pp. 19–27, 27–32, 189–225, 249–62, 282–91, 328–47. (Bodleian reference 24712 f.43 [R].)

c H. A. Taine, *Notes on England* (London, 1872), pp. 153–75 and 272–99. (Bodleian reference 226. j. 172.)

c La Rochefoucauld, F. de, *A Frenchman in England* (Cambridge, 1933), pp. 157–242.   5

c Nickolls, Sir J., pseud. (i.e. R. B. Plumard de Danguel), *Remarks on the advantages and disadvantages of France and of Great Britain* (London, 1754), pp. 1–48.

c t F. Chaumont, *Mémoire sur la France et l'Angleterre* (1769).

D'Eichthal, G., *A French sociologist looks at Britain,* tr. and ed. B. M. Ratcliffe and W. H. Chaloner (Manchester, 1977), pp. 13–108.   10

Candidates who fail one or more of papers 1, 2, 3, or 4 above may resit that subject or subjects at a subsequent examination.

Preliminary Examination in History and English

A

1. The Preliminary Examination in History and English shall be under the joint   15
supervision of the Boards of the Faculties of History and English Language and Literature and shall consist of such subjects as they shall jointly by regulation prescribe.

2. The Chairs of the Examiners for the Preliminary Examination in History and of the Examiners for the Preliminary Examination in English Language and Literature   20
shall consult together and designate such of their number as may be required for the examination for the Preliminary Examination in History and English, whereupon the number of examiners shall be deemed to be complete.

B

Each candidate shall offer four papers as set out below. The papers will be of three   25
hours' duration, except where otherwise specified. The Examiners shall publish the names of candidates who have satisfied them in the whole of the examination, or in papers 1 and 2 only, or in papers 3 and 4 only.

1. *The History of the British Isles* (any one of the periods specified for the Preliminary Examination in History).   30

2. *One* of the following:

   (*a*) One of the Optional Subjects as specified for the Preliminary Examination in History.

   (*b*) *Approaches to History* (as specified for the Preliminary Examination in History).   35

   (*c*) *Historiography: Tacitus to Weber* (as specified for the Preliminary Examination in History).

The individual specifications and prescribed texts for these papers will be published in the Handbook for the Preliminary Examination in History by Monday of noughth week of Michaelmas Term each year for the academic year ahead. Depending on the   40
availability of teaching resources, with the exception of Optional Subject 1, not all the Optional Subjects listed in the Handbook will be available to candidates in any given year. Candidates may obtain details of the choice of options for that year by consulting the Definitive List of Optional Subjects posted at the beginning of the first week of Michaelmas Full Term in the History Faculty and circulated to tutors.   45

3. *Introduction to English Language and Literature.*

The paper will be examined by a portfolio of work, comprising one commentary answer and one discursive essay, of not fewer than 1,500 and not more than 2,000 words each. Footnotes will be included in the total word count, but bibliographies do not count towards the limit. The list of questions for this paper will be divided into Section A (Language) and B (Literature) and will be published on Monday of the fourth week of the Trinity Term of the first year. Candidates must select one question from Section A and one question from Section B. 5

Questions in Section A (Language) invite candidates to make their own selection of texts or passages of texts for commentary, in accordance with the terms of the particular question chosen. Copies of the texts or passages used must be included as an appendix to the portfolio. The combined length of all texts or passages chosen must not exceed 70 lines. The texts or passages used will not count towards the word limit 10 for the commentary answer.

Two typed copies of the portfolio must be delivered to the Chair of the Examiners for the Preliminary Examination in English Language and Literature, Examination Schools, High Street, by noon on Wednesday of the sixth week of the same Trinity Term. A certificate, signed by the candidate to the effect that each answer is the 15 candidate's own work, and that the candidate has read the Faculty guidelines on plagiarism, must be presented together with each portfolio.

Following the publication of themes for this subject on Monday of the fourth week of Trinity Term, the candidate must neither discuss his or her choice of themes nor the method of handling them with any tutor. Every portfolio must be the work of the 20 candidate alone, but he or she may discuss with his or her tutor the subjects and approach to the essays up until the stated publication date of the portfolio themes.

Portfolios previously submitted for the First Public Examination in English Language and Literature may be resubmitted. No answer will be accepted that has already been submitted, wholly or substantially, for a final honour school or any other 25 degree of this University, or degree of any other institution.

Work deemed to be either too short or of excessive length may be penalised.

Candidates must avoid duplicating material used in this paper when answering other papers. In addition, candidates are not permitted to duplicate material between Section A and Section B of the portfolio. 30

4. *One* of the following:

    (*a*) *Literature in English 650–1350* (as specified in the regulations for the Preliminary Examination in English Language and Literature, subject 2).

    (*b*) *Literature in English 1830–1910* (as specified in the regulations for the Preliminary Examination in English Language and Literature, subject 3). 35

    (*c*) *Literature in English 1910–present day* (as specified in the regulations for the Preliminary Examination in English Language and Literature, subject 4).

Candidates who fail one or more of papers 1, 2, 3, or 4 above may resit that subject or subjects at a subsequent examination.

Preliminary Examination in History and Modern Languages 40

A

1. The Preliminary Examination in History and Modern Languages shall be under the joint supervision of the Boards of the Faculties of History and Medieval and Modern Languages and shall consist of such subjects as they shall jointly by regulation prescribe.

2. The chairs of the examiners for the Preliminary Examination in History and for 45 the Preliminary Examination in Modern Languages shall respectively designate such of their number as may be required for History and for Modern Languages in this examination.

B

Candidates are required to offer History and any one of the languages that may be offered in the Honour School of Modern Languages. The examination shall be in two parts, as follows:

Part 1   5

Each candidate shall offer the following two subjects in the language:

1. *Language papers* (one paper of three hours and two papers each of one and a half hours including in French certification of attendance and participation in oral classes, as specified for the Preliminary Examination in Modern Languages).

As specified for papers I, IIA, and IIB in the regulations for the Preliminary   10
Examination for Modern Languages.

2. *Literature papers* (two papers, each of three hours).

As specified for papers III and IV in the regulations for the Preliminary Examination in Modern Languages.

Part 2   15

Each candidate shall offer subject 3 and any one of the subdivisions of subject 4.

3. General History: any one of the periods specified for the Preliminary Examination in History.

4. (*a*) A period of The History of the British Isles as specified for the Preliminary
    Examination in History;   20
  (*b*) An Optional Subject as specified for the Preliminary Examination in History;
  (*c*) Approaches to History *or* Historiography: Tacitus to Weber *or* Foreign
    Texts as specified for the Preliminary Examination in History.

The individual specifications and prescribed texts for (*b*) and (*c*) above will be published in the Handbook for the Preliminary Examination in History by Monday of nought   25
week of Michaelmas Term each year for the academic year ahead. Depending on the availability of teaching resources, with the exception of Optional Subject 1, not all the Optional Subjects listed in the Handbook will be available to candidates in any given year. Candidates may obtain details of the choice of options for that year by consulting the Definitive List of Optional Subjects posted at the beginning of the first week of   30
Michaelmas Full Term in the History Faculty and circulated to tutors.

Candidates who have satisfied the Examiners in both parts shall be deemed to have passed the examination. The Examiners may award distinctions in either or both parts to candidates who have done work of special merit in the part or parts concerned.

Candidates who fail one or both subjects of part 1 may resit that subject or those   35
subjects at a subsequent examination. Candidates who fail one or two subjects of part 2 may resit that subject or subjects at a subsequent examination.

Preliminary Examination in History and Politics

A

1. The Preliminary Examination in History and Politics shall be under the joint   40
supervision of the Board of the Faculty of History and the Social Sciences Board and shall consist of such subjects as they shall jointly prescribe.

2. The Chair of the Examiners for the Preliminary Examination in History and the Chair of the Examiners for the Preliminary Examination in Philosophy, Politics, and Economics shall consult together and designate such of their number as may be   45
required for the examination for the Preliminary Examination in History and Politics, whereupon the number of examiners shall be deemed to be complete.

B

Every candidate shall offer four papers as follows:

1. *Either* (a) any one of the periods in the History of the British Isles specified for the Preliminary Examination in History *or* (b) any one of the four periods in General History specified for the Preliminary Examination in History. For the First or Second Public Examination candidates are required to choose *at least one* paper—whether in General History or the History of the British Isles—covering a period before the nineteenth century. The list of papers satisfying this provision is given in the Handbook for History and Politics. Candidates who take British History paper VII for the Preliminary Examination or the Final Honour School may not also take Politics core paper 202 for the Final Honour School.

2. An Introduction to the Theory of Politics, as specified in section (a) of Introduction to the Theory and Practice of Politics for the Preliminary Examination for Philosophy, Politics, and Economics.

OR candidates may substitute Optional Subject 1, 'Theories of the State (Aristotle, Hobbes, Rousseau, Marx)' as specified for the Preliminary Examination in History.

3. Any *one* of the following, as specified for the Preliminary Examination in History: (a) Quantification in History *or* (b) any of the Optional Subjects except No. 1 (Theories of the State), *or* (c) Approaches to History, *or* (d) Historiography: Tacitus to Weber, *or* (e) any one of the seven Foreign Texts.

4. *Introduction to the Practice of Politics*

Candidates are required to answer three questions

Questions will be set on the following topics: (i) regime types; definition and measurement of variations between types of democracy; (ii) political institutions and practice outside the advanced industrial democracies; stability, state capacity and state formation; (iii) the state and its institutions (executives, legislatures, parties and party systems, electoral systems, courts, constitutions and centre-periphery relations); (iv) parties and party systems; political values and identity politics.

The individual specifications and prescribed texts for papers 2 and 3 above will be published in the Handbook for the Preliminary Examination in History by Monday of noughth week of Michaelmas Term each year for the academic year ahead. Depending on the availability of teaching resources, with the exception of the Optional Subject 1, not all the Optional Subjects listed in the Handbook will be available to candidates in any given year. Candidates may obtain details of the choice of options for that year by consulting the Definitive List of Optional Subjects posted at the beginning of the first week of Michaelmas Full Term in the History Faculty and circulated to tutors.

Candidates who fail one or more of papers 1, 2, 3, or 4 above may resit that subject or subjects at a subsequent examination.

Preliminary Examination in History of Art

A

The Preliminary Examination in History of Art shall be under the supervision of the Board of the Faculty of History. The subjects of the examination, the syllabus, and the number of papers shall be as prescribed by regulation from time to time by the Board of the Faculty of History.

B

The History Faculty Board shall issue annually the Handbook for the Preliminary Examination in History of Art by Monday of noughth week of Michaelmas Term for the academic year ahead.

Each candidate shall offer four papers as follows:
I. *Introduction to the History of Art*
   Candidates will be examined by three-hour unseen examination.
II. *Antiquity after Antiquity*
   Candidates will be examined by three-hour unseen examination.
III. *European Art 1400–1900:* Meaning and Interpretation
   Candidates will be examined by three-hour unseen examination.
IV. *Objects, Images and Buildings in Oxford*

Candidates will be examined by a 5,000 word extended essay, including footnotes but excluding bibliography. A candidate may propose to study any object, but this object must be approved by the appointed extended essay adviser, and the Preliminary Extended Essay Co-ordinator. Approval will depend on the object's accessibility and the availability of source material and curatorial expertise. Candidates will have no more than the equivalent of five one-hour meetings with their assigned extended essay advisor. A first draft of the extended essay may be commented on by the extended essay adviser during one of these meetings. Candidates must submit the title of the extended essay to the Chair of Examiners, Preliminary Examination in History of Art, Department of History of Art, Littlegate House, St. Ebbes, Oxford, by midday on Monday of the fifth week of the Hilary Term preceding the examination. Any subsequent changes to title require formal application to the Chair of Examiners not later than noon on Monday of second week of the Trinity term preceding the examination and subsequent approval. Essays should be typed or word-processed in double spacing and should conform to the standards of academic presentation prescribed in the course handbook. Essays must be delivered by hand to the Examination Schools (addressed to the Chair of Examiners, Preliminary Examination in History of Art, Examination Schools, Oxford) not later than noon on Monday of sixth week of the Trinity Term in the academic year in which the candidate is presenting himself or herself for examination. Candidates delivering essays will be required to complete a receipt form, which will only be accepted as proof of receipt if it is counter-signed by a member of the Examination Schools staff. Each essay must be accompanied by a sealed envelope (bearing only the candidate's examination number) containing a formal declaration signed by the candidate that the essay is his or her own work. The University's regulations on *Late Entries* will apply.

The Examiners may award a distinction in the examination to any candidate, according to the published classification conventions.

Candidates who fail one or two of papers I, II, III, or IV above may resit only that paper or papers at a subsequent examination. Candidates who fail three of papers I, II, III, or IV above will be asked to resit all papers, including the one they passed, unless the paper they passed is the essay, in which case they will resit only the three written examination papers. Candidates who fail all four of papers I, II, III, and IV will be required to resit all four at a subsequent examination. In the case of failure to reach the required standard in the Preliminary Extended Essay, candidates must resubmit the essay by Monday of noughth week of Michaelmas Term of the second year. Candidates are entitled to one further meeting with their extended essay adviser.

Preliminary Examination in Human Sciences

A

The examination shall be under the supervision of the Social Sciences Board in accordance with the same arrangements as those established under clause 3 of the decree concerning the Honour School of Human Sciences.

B

1. The subjects of the examination shall be the five subjects listed below.

2. All candidates must offer all five subjects at one examination:

Provided that a candidate who has passed in two (or more) subjects but failed in the other subject (or subjects) may offer at a subsequent examination the subjects (or subject) in which he or she has failed.

3. A candidate shall be deemed to have passed the examination if he or she shall have satisfied the Moderators in all five subjects *either* at one and the same examination *or* at two examinations in accordance with the proviso to clause 2.

4. In the case of candidates who have satisfied the Moderators in all five subjects in a single examination, the Moderators may award a distinction to those of special merit.

5. The examiners will permit the use of any hand-held pocket calculator subject to the conditions set out under the heading 'Use of calculators in examinations' in the *Special Regulations concerning Examinations.*

Subject 1. *The Biology of Organisms including Humans*

Principles of mammalian physiology: the cell, body fluids, the cardiovascular and respiratory systems, reproduction, hunger and thirst, movement, the senses, and the integrative organization of the central nervous system.

Principles of ecology: ecosystems, plant and animal communities and numbers, biotic interaction, the impact of man on the environment.

One three-hour paper will be set.

Subject 2. *Genetics and Evolution*

Principles of genetics and evolution illustrated by examples from human and other organisms.

Mechanisms of evolutionary change: selection and adaptation, evolution of sex, altruism, kin selection and co-operation. Alternative models of evolution.

The genetic material—its nature, mode of action, and manipulation: the chromosomal basis of heredity; molecular genetics; mapping the human genome; sex determination; mutation at the level of the gene and the chromosome.

Mendelian inheritance; genetic variation in populations and its maintenance; quantitative variation and its genetic basis.

One three-hour paper will be set. Candidates shall submit notebooks containing reports, initialled by the demonstrators, of practical work completed during their course of study. These notebooks shall be available to the examiners at any time after the end of the first week of the term in which the examination is held, and shall be taken into consideration by the examiners. A practical examination may be set for candidates whose record of practical work is not satisfactory.

Subject 3. *Society, Culture, and Environment*

Social and Cultural Anthropology: the comparative study of the world's civilisations and peoples, including cross-cultural, power-based, and gender perspectives upon social practice and theories of human life. Specific topics will include production and consumption; transactions and modes of exchange; elementary aspects of kinship and marriage; belief systems and social control; political and social organization; classification; technology and social change; material culture and ethnographic resources; the impact of colonialism; space, place and culture; environment and cultural landscapes in transition; land and property rights. Candidates will be expected to be familiar with appropriate ethnographic monographs.

Human Geography: Approaches to understanding contemporary international migration—from neo-classical to post-structuralist; forced migration, changing international, regional and national legislation and policy; diasporas and transnationalism, especially issues of identity, home and belonging; social divisions and the experience of migration and integration addressing gender, class and ethnicity; cosmopolitan or 'superdiverse' cities; and state policy and the influence of nationalism, xenophobia, economics, and ethics.

One three-hour paper will be set, on which candidates will be required to answer four questions. The paper will be divided into two sections: (A) Social and Cultural Anthropology, and (B) Human Geography. Candidates will be required to display knowledge of both sections, and will be required to answer at least two questions from section (A) and at least one question from section (B).

Subject 4. *Sociology and Demography*

Sociology: Current and classic discussions of explanatory strategies and social mechanisms, models of individual action and the consequences of aggregation. Empirical research involving these approaches in areas of substantive sociological interest such as social class, ethnicity, religion, the family, politics.

Demography: Elementary aspects of population analysis. Comparative study of fertility, mortality and family systems in selected human societies. The long-term development of human population and its relation to habitat and resources. The demographic transition.

One three hour paper will be set. The paper will be divided into two sections: (A) Sociology and (B) Demography. Candidates will be required to display knowledge of both sections.

Subject 5. *Quantitative Methods for the Human Sciences*

The use and importance of statistics and quantitative methods in the human sciences. Graphs, scales, indices, and transformations. Frequency distributions and their parameters, including the binomial, normal, and Poisson distributions. Notions of probability and risk. Problems of sampling. Tests of statistical significance including t-tests, χ^2, and confidence intervals. Elementary analysis of variance, correlation, and regression.

One three-hour paper will be set, consisting mostly of examples taken from the human sciences. Graded questions will be set, not all of which will require numerical answers.

Preliminary Examination in Materials Science

A

1. The subject of the Preliminary Examination in Materials Science shall be Materials Science, including basic practical and mathematical techniques.

2. The number of papers and other general requirements of the examination shall be as prescribed by regulation from time to time by the Mathematical, Physical and Life Sciences Board.

B

In the following, 'the Course Handbook' refers to the Materials Science 'Prelims Course Handbook', published annually at the start of Michaelmas Term by the Faculty of Materials, and also posted on the website at: www.materials.ox.ac.uk/teaching/ug/ughandbooks.html.

1. The Preliminary Examination in Materials Science shall comprise four compulsory written examination papers plus compulsory Materials coursework equivalent to one written examination paper:

(*a*) Materials Science 1: Structure of Materials

(*b*) Materials Science 2: Properties of Materials

(*c*) Materials Science 3: Transforming Materials
(*d*) Mathematics for Materials
(*e*) Materials Coursework

The syllabuses for the written papers shall be published annually in the Course Handbook, not later than the beginning of Michaelmas Full Term for examination in the Trinity Term immediately following this. 5

2. In the assessment of the Materials coursework, the Moderators shall take into consideration the requirement for a candidate to complete the coursework to a satisfactory level as defined from time to time by the Faculty of Materials and published in the Course Handbook. Materials Science Coursework shall comprise 10 practical work and work carried out in crystallography classes, as described in the Course Handbook, and it shall be assessed under the following provisions:

(*a*) Candidates will be required to submit the Materials Practical Class reports to the Chair of the Moderators in the Preliminary Examination in Materials Science, c/o the Deputy Administrator (Academic) in the Department of 15 Materials, not later than 10 a.m. on Friday of the sixth week of Trinity Full Term.

(*b*) The Chair of Faculty, or deputy, shall make available to the Moderators, not later than the end of the first week of Trinity Full Term, evidence showing the extent to which each candidate has completed the Crystallography coursework 20 normally pursued during the first two terms preceding the examination.

(*c*) Failure of the coursework normally will constitute failure of the Preliminary Examination. Materials Coursework normally cannot be retaken. Exceptionally a candidate who has failed the coursework may be permitted jointly by the Moderators and the candidate's college to retake the entire 25 academic year.

3. Candidates shall be deemed to have passed the examination if they have satisfied the Moderators in the five papers in clause 1 either at a single examination or at two examinations in accordance with either clause 5 or clause 6, and provided further that the same number of papers as were failed in the first sitting have been passed at the 30 same attempt at a subsequent examination. The Moderators will be guided by the provisions of clause 2 when considering the Materials Coursework paper.

4. The Moderators may award a distinction to candidates of special merit who have satisfied them in all five papers in clause 1 in one examination.

5. Candidates who have passed the coursework paper and fail one or two written 35 papers listed in clause 1 may offer that number of papers at one, but no more than one, subsequent examination.

6. In the case of candidates who offer all four written papers of clause 1, the Moderators shall publish the names only of those who have satisfied them in the coursework paper and in two or more written papers. Candidates whose names do not 40 appear on the Results List but who have passed the coursework paper may enter the written part of the examination on one, but no more than one, subsequent occasion: such candidates must resit all four written papers of clause 1. In the case of candidates who, in accordance with clause 5, offer one or two written papers, the Moderators shall publish the names of only those who have satisfied them in each of the written 45 papers offered.

7. The use of calculators in the papers listed in clause 1 is restricted to those models published annually in the Course Handbook.

8. The examination conventions for the written papers and the coursework listed in clause 1 shall be published annually in the Course Handbook and posted online at the following website: www.materials.ox.ac.uk/teaching/ug/ugexamconventions.html.

Preliminary Examination in Mathematics

A

The subject of the examination shall be mathematics and its applications. The syllabus and number of papers shall be prescribed by regulation from time to time by the Mathematical, Physical and Life Sciences Board.

B

1. Candidates shall take five written papers. The titles of the papers shall be:

A. Mathematics I

B. Mathematics II

C. Mathematics III

D. Mathematics IV

E. Mathematics V

2. In addition to the five papers in clause 1, a candidate must also offer a practical work assessment.

3. Candidates shall be deemed to have passed the examination if they have satisfied the Moderators in all five papers and the practical assessment at a single examination or passed all five papers and the practical assessment in accordance with the proviso of clause 4.

4. A candidate who fails to satisfy the Moderators in one or two of papers A–E may offer those papers on one subsequent occasion; a candidate who fails to satisfy the Moderators in three or more of papers A–E may offer all five papers on one subsequent occasion; a candidate who fails to satisfy the Moderators in the practical work assessment may also offer the assessment on one subsequent occasion.

5. The Moderators may award a distinction to candidates of special merit who have passed all five written papers and the practical work assessment at a single examination.

6. The syllabus for each paper shall be published by the Mathematical Institute in a handbook for candidates by the beginning of the Michaelmas Full Term in the academic year of the examination, after consultation with the Mathematics Teaching Committee. Each paper will contain questions of a straightforward character.

7. The Chair of Mathematics, or a deputy, shall make available to the Moderators evidence showing the extent to which each candidate has pursued an adequate course of practical work. In assessing a candidate's performance in the examination the Moderators shall take this evidence into account. Deadlines for handing in practical work will be published in a handbook for candidates by the beginning of Michaelmas Full Term in the academic year of the examination.

Candidates are usually required to submit such practical work electronically; details shall be given in the handbook for the practical course. Any candidate who is unable for some reason to submit work electronically must apply to the Academic Administrator, Mathematical Institute, for permission to submit the work in paper form. Such applications must reach the Academic Administrator two weeks before the deadline for submitting the practical work.

8. The use of hand held pocket calculators is generally not permitted but certain kinds may be permitted for some papers. Specifications of which papers and which types of calculator are permitted for those exceptional papers will be announced by the Moderators in the Hilary Term preceding the examination.

Preliminary Examination in Mathematics and Computer Science   5

A

The subject of the examination shall be Mathematics and Computer Science. The syllabus and number of papers shall be prescribed by regulation from time to time by the Mathematical, Physical and Life Sciences Board.

B   10

1. The Preliminary Examination in Mathematics and Computer Science shall comprise five compulsory written papers plus compulsory Computer Science practicals equivalent to one written paper:

CS1   Functional Programming, and Design and Analysis of Algorithms
CS2   Imperative Programming   15
MCS3 Continuous Mathematics and Probability
M1   Mathematics I (as specified for the Preliminary Examination in Mathematics)
M2   Mathematics II (as specified for the Preliminary Examination in Mathematics)
Computer Science Practicals

2. The syllabus for each paper will be published by the Department of Computer   20
Science in a handbook for candidates by the beginning of the Michaelmas Full Term in the academic year of the examination, after consultation with the Faculty of Computer Science (for papers CS1, CS2 and MCS3) and the Faculty of Mathematics (for papers M1, M2 and MCS3). Each paper will contain questions of a straightforward character.   25

3. All candidates will be assessed as to their practical ability in Computer Science under the following provisions:

(*a*) The Head of the Department of Computer Science, or a deputy, shall make available to the examiners evidence showing the extent to which each candidate has pursued an adequate course of practical work. Only that   30
work completed and marked by noon on Monday of the sixth week of the Trinity Term in which the candidate takes the examination shall be included in these records.

(*b*) Candidates shall submit to the Chair of the Moderators for the Preliminary Examination in Mathematics and Computer Science, c/o the Academic   35
Administrator, Oxford University Department of Computer Science, Oxford, by noon on Monday of the sixth week of the Trinity Term in which the examination is being held, their reports of practical exercises completed during their course of study. For a report on a practical exercise to be considered by the moderators, it must have been marked by a demon-   40
strator and must be accompanied by a statement that it is the candidate's own work except where otherwise indicated.

(*c*) The moderators shall take the evidence (*a*) and the reports (*b*) into account in assessing a candidate's performance.

(*d*) Candidates whose overall performance on practical work is not satisfactory   45
may be deemed to have failed the examination.

4. Candidates shall be deemed to have passed the examination if they have satisfied the Moderators in the six papers in clause 1 either at a single examination or at two examinations in accordance with clause 6 or clause 7.

5. The Moderators may award a distinction to candidates of special merit who have satisfied them in all six papers in clause 1 in one examination.   5

6. Candidates who fail one or two written papers listed in clause 1 may offer those papers at one, but no more than one, subsequent examination.

7. Candidates who fail three or more papers may enter the written part of the examination on one, but no more than one, subsequent examination.

8. The use of calculators is generally not permitted but certain kinds may be   10
allowed for certain papers. Specifications of which papers and which types of calculators are permitted for those exceptional papers will be announced by the examiners in the Hilary Term preceding the examination.

Preliminary Examination in Mathematics and Philosophy

A   15

1. The subject of the examination shall be (a) Mathematics, and (b) Philosophy. The syllabus and number of papers shall be prescribed by regulation from time to time by the Mathematical, Physical and Life Sciences Board and the Board of the Faculty of Philosophy.

2. A candidate shall offer both subjects for examination.   20

3. The Moderators for Mathematics shall include at least two of the Moderators for the Preliminary Examination in Mathematics; the Moderators for Philosophy shall include at least two Moderators nominated by a committee of the Faculty of Philosophy.

4. It shall be the duty of the Chair of Moderators for the Preliminary Examination   25
in Mathematics to nominate such of their number as shall be required to act as Moderators for the Preliminary Examination in Mathematics and Philosophy.

B

1. Candidates shall take five written papers. The titles of the papers shall be:

A. Mathematics I (as specified by the Preliminary Examination in Mathematics)   30

B. Mathematics II (as specified by the Preliminary Examination in Mathematics)

C. Mathematics III(P)

D. Elements of Deductive Logic

Subjects to be studied include: propositional and predicate languages; truth tables; Natural Deduction; relations; the critical application of formal logic to the analysis   35
of English sentences and inferences (problems of symbolization; scope, truth-functionality, quantification, identity, descriptions); elementary metatheorems about propositional calculus (including the following topics: expressive adequacy, duality, substitution, interpolation, compactness, consistency, soundness and completeness). Some questions of a mathematical nature will be set.   40

These subjects shall be studied in conjunction with Volker Halbach's *Introduction to Logic* manual, published by Oxford University Press. The logical symbols to be used are those found in this publication. Philosophical questions about logic may be studied by reading Mark Sainsbury, *Logical Forms,* 1st or 2nd edition (Blackwell), Chapters 1–2.   45

E. Introduction to Philosophy

The paper shall consist of two parts:

    1. *General Philosophy* Subjects to be studied include: knowledge and scepticism, induction, mind and body, personal identity, free will, and God and evil. Candidates will have the opportunity, but will not be required, to show first-hand knowledge of Descartes' *Meditations* and Hume's *An Enquiry concerning Human Understanding.*

    2. *Frege* This section shall be studied in connection with Frege *Foundations of Arithmetic*, trans. J. L. Austin, Blackwell, 1980. This section, while not being confined to the detailed views of the author of the set text, will be satisfactorily answerable by a candidate who has made a critical study of the text. There will not be a compulsory question containing passages for comment.

    Candidates will be required to attempt four questions, and answer at least one question from Part 1 and at least one question from Part 2.

2. Candidates shall be deemed to have passed the examination if they have satisfied the Moderators in all five papers A–E *either* at a single examination *or* at two examinations in accordance with the proviso of cl 3.

3. A candidate who fails to satisfy the Moderators in one or two of papers A–E may offer the papers failed on one, and only one, subsequent occasion. A candidate who fails to satisfy the Moderators in three or more of papers A-E may offer all five papers on one, and only one, subsequent occasion, *except that* a candidate who fails to satisfy the Moderators in all of papers A–C, but who has satisfied the Moderators in papers D and E, may offer papers A–C only on one, and only one, subsequent occasion.

4. The Moderators may award a distinction to candidates of special merit who have passed all five written papers at a single examination.

5. The syllabus for each paper in Mathematics shall be published by the Mathematical Institute in a handbook for candidates by the beginning of the Michaelmas Full Term in the academic year of the examination, after consultation with the Mathematics Teaching Committee.

6. The use of hand held pocket calculators is generally not permitted but certain kinds may be permitted for some papers. Specifications of which papers and which types of calculator are permitted for those papers will be announced by the Moderators in the Hilary Term preceding the examination.

Preliminary Examination in Modern Languages

A

The languages, subjects, and papers in the examination shall be as prescribed by regulation from time to time by the Board of the Faculty of Medieval and Modern Languages.

B

Not more than two languages may be offered.

1. The languages which may be offered shall be Latin and Greek and those languages which may be offered in the Final Honour School of Modern Languages.[1] **Candidates who offer both Latin and Ancient Greek shall be deemed to be offering one ancient language. Candidates for whom it is appropriate shall pass at the end of their first year of study the examination in Greek or Latin prescribed for first-year candidates in Course**

---

  [1] Czech (with Slovak) and Celtic may not be available in given years. Notice that these subjects will not be available will be given in the *Gazette* in the Trinity Term but one before the examination concerned.

II of Honour Moderations in Classics and English, before proceeding to offer papers in the Preliminary Examination for Modern Languages in accordance with the following regulations in their second year of study.

2. The subjects of the examination shall be:

   (*a*) Language papers (including in French certification of attendance and participation in oral classes[1]);

   (*b*) Literature papers;

   (*c*) Classics and Modern Languages

   (*d*) Linguistics;

   (*e*) Further Topics (for candidates taking French sole or German sole only);

   (*f*) Russian Course B (*ab initio*).

3. A candidate shall be deemed to have passed the examination if he or she shall have satisfied the Examiners

   either (i) in all papers in both subjects (*a*) Language and (*b*) Literature in each of two languages, at least one of the languages being modern;

   or (ii) in all papers in both subjects (*a*) Language and (*b*) Literature in one modern language (other than Czech (with Slovak) or Celtic) and in all papers in subject (*d*) Linguistics;

   or (iii) in all papers in both subjects (*a*) Language and (*b*) Literature in *either* French or German and in all three papers in subject (*e*) Further Topics in the same language;

   or (iv) in all papers in both subjects (*a*) Language and (*b*) Literature in one modern language and in all papers in subject (*f*) Russian Course B (*ab initio*).

Candidates must offer all the papers at one examination, provided that a candidate who has previously failed to satisfy the examiners in any paper or papers shall not be required to resit any paper or papers in which he or she has already satisfied the examiners. The pair of papers IIA and IIB (and BIIA and BIIB) counts as a single paper.

4. To a candidate who has done work of special merit in the papers concerned, the Moderators may award a mark of distinction in a language, and in Further Topics, and in Linguistics. A candidate may be awarded either one or two distinctions.

5. Candidates must offer:

Either: I, IIA, IIB, III, IV in two modern languages:

Or: I, IIA, IIB, III, IV in a modern language together with V, VI, and VII in Latin and/or Ancient Greek;

Or: I, IIA, IIB, III, IV in a modern language together with VIII, IX, and X in Linguistics.

Or: I, IIA, IIB, III, IV in either French or German together with XI, XII, and XIII in the same language. (For candidates offering French sole or German sole.)

Or: I, IIA, IIB, III, IV in a modern language together with BI, BIIA, BIIB, BIII; and BIV Oral Test (for candidates admitted to Russian Course B).

---

[1] Colleges will submit to the Examiners via the Examination Schools by noon on Friday of Week 5 of Trinity Term a certificate stating that their candidates have attended and participated in at least eight oral classes, consisting of reading aloud in French with attention to pronunciation and intonation, and discussion in French of passages dealing with issues in French contemporary culture.

6. *a. Language papers*
I. Language I. 3 hours.

French:	The paper will consist of: (*a*) French grammar (20 short sentences for translation into French); (*b*) A prose passage for translation into French; (*c*) A summary in French of a passage of analytical or critical writing in French.
German:	'Deutsche Gesellschaft und Kultur seit 1890.' Reading comprehension (in German) on a passage which relates to the theme of the paper. One essay in German on a topic relating to the theme of the paper.
Italian:	The paper will consist of: (*a*) audio or video listening comprehension exercises; (*b*) reading comprehension exercises; (*c*) one guided essay in Italian.
Spanish:	The paper will consist of: (*a*) translation into Spanish: a set of grammatical sentences. 1½ hours will be allowed for each part.
Portuguese:	The paper will consist of: (*a*) audio or visual listening comprehension exercises; (*b*) translation into Portuguese; (*c*) a guided composition; (*d*) linguistic tests.
Russian:	Translation into Russian and/or exercises in Russian.
Modern Greek:	Translation into Modern Greek and exercises in Modern Greek.
Czech (with Slovak):	(*a*) a modern English prose passage; and (*b*) English sentences testing basic grammar, both to be translated into *either* Czech *or* Slovak.
Celtic:	(*a*) a modern English prose passage; and (*b*) English sentences testing basic grammar, both to be translated into Welsh.

II. Language II. The paper will be in two parts of 1½ hours each.

French:	Unprepared translation: Translation into English of a prose passage in French.
	Prepared translation: Translation into English of a passage from one of the texts prescribed for French paper IV, excluding *La Chastelaine de Vergi.*
German:	IIA. Translation into German of a prose passage.
	IIB. Translation from German of a prose passage in a modern literary register.
Italian:	IIA. Translation into Italian of a prose passage *or* sentences.
	IIB. Translation from Italian. A passage of modern prose will be set.
Spanish:	IIA. Translation from Spanish of a prose passage in a modern literary register.
	IIB. Translation from Spanish of a prose passage in an informal register such as journalism.
Portuguese:	IIA. Translation from Portuguese of a prose passage in a modern literary register.
	IIB. Translation from Portuguese of a prose passage in an informal register such as journalism, and an exercise or exercises in reading comprehension.

Line numbers in right margin: 5, 10, 15, 20, 25, 30, 35, 40, 45

Russian:	IIA. Translation from Russian. A passage of modern prose will be set.
	IIB. Comprehension exercise. A modern passage in the language will be set to test comprehension. All answers in this paper will be in English.
Modern Greek:	IIA. Translation from Modern Greek. A passage of modern prose will be set.
	IIB. Comprehension exercises. A modern passage or passages in the language will be set to test comprehension. All answers in this paper will be in English.
Czech (with Slovak):	IIA and IIB. One passage of modern prose in each paper for translation from Czech into English.
Celtic:	IIA. A passage of Middle Welsh prose to be translated into English.
	IIB. A passage of Old Irish prose *or* a passage of Modern Welsh prose to be translated into English.

b. *Literature papers*

III. Literature I. 3 hours.

French:	Short texts. Candidates will be required to study six brief but self-contained works arranged in three contrasting pairs:
	Montaigne, 'Des Cannibales' from *Essais I*
	Diderot, *Supplément au Voyage à Bougainville*.
	B Baudelaire, *'Spleen et Idéal'* from *Les Fleurs du Mal*, with 30 poems to be identified for detailed study
	Aimé Césaire, *Cahier d'un retour au pays natal*
	C Racine, *Phèdre*
	Beckett, *En attendant Godot*
	The paper will be examined by commentary only, with all texts set, and candidates required to offer three passages, one from each of sections A, B, and C.
German:	Commentary. Two commentaries on a choice of poems taken from an anthology, which will include some medieval poems. One commentary on an extract from one of the set texts listed under paper IV. Each year two such texts will be designated as the ones from which an extract for commentary may be taken. Texts to be studied for commentary in any given year will be published in the *University Gazette* during noughth week of Michaelmas Term each year.
Italian:	Aspects of Italian lyric poetry. Compulsory passages for explanation and detailed comment will be set.
	The sonnet from the Middle Ages to the present. (Copies of the list of sonnets for the examinations in the academic year concerned will be available in the Modern Languages Faculty Office, 41 Wellington Square, from the beginning of the Michaelmas Full Term of the year.)
	Ungaretti, Selections from *L'Allegria* and *Sentimento del tempo* (in Giuseppe Ungaretti, *Vita d'un uomo, 106 poesie 1914-1960*, Mondadori Oscar).

Spanish:

Prescribed texts to be studied in relation to various possible approaches to literature. One compulsory passage will be set for translation into English and one for commentary. Candidates will also be required to undertake two essays, to be written on texts other than the one from which the passage chosen for commentary was taken.

M. Vargas Llosa, *La fiesta del Chivo*.

Antonio Machado, *Campos de Castilla* (excluding 'La tierra de Alvargonzález', but including 'Elogios': in *Poesías completas*, Selecciones Austral).

Calderón de la Barca, *El médico du su honra* (ed. D. W. Cruickshank, Clásicos Castalia).

Cervantes, 'Rinconete y Cortadillo', from vol. 1 of *Novelas ejemplares*, ed. H. Sieber, 2 vols. (Madrid: Cátedra, 1989).

Portuguese:

Prescribed texts to be studied in relation to various possible approaches to literature. Compulsory passages for explanation and detailed comment will be set. There will be a compulsory essay or commentary question on each of the set texts.

Lídia Jorge, *O vale da paixão*

Pepetela, *O Desejo de Kianda*

Manuel Bandeira, *Libertinagem* and *Estrela da manhã*

Russian:

Poetry. The examination will consist of three commentaries, each on a different author, on the set works by five authors detailed below. One commentary passage will be compulsory.

Derzhavin, *Felitsa*

Pushkin, *Mednyi vsadnik*

Lermontov, *Mtsyri*

Blok, *Na pole Kulikovom* and *Dvenadtsat'*

Akhmatova, *Rekviem*

Examiners may give some guidance to candidates about how to approach the passages set for commentary; they may also require candidates to translate some portion of the passages set for commentary into English.

Modern Greek:

Modern Greek poetry and prose. Compulsory passages for explanation and detailed comment will be set. The syllabus will consist of a selection of poems and short stories by a variety of authors. (A list of the selection for the examinations in the academic year concerned will be available in the Modern Languages Faculty Office, 41 Wellington Square, from the beginning of the Michaelmas Full Term of that year).

The examination paper will be divided into two sections. Section A will consist of two compulsory commentary passages from prescribed texts (one poetry passage and one prose passage). Section B will consist of a choice of essay questions, from which each candidate must choose one.

Czech (with Slovak):

Prescribed texts to be studied as literature. Three compulsory passages for commentary will be set.

Short stories:
Milan Kundera, *Falešný autostop*
Karel Čapek, *Šlépěj*
Egon Hostovský, *Závrať*
Jan Neruda, *Doktor Kazisvět*   5
Jan Neruda, *Pan Ryšánek a pan chlegel*

Celtic: Prescribed texts to be studied as literature. Commentary.
One commentary on a poem taken from an anthology.
Poems will be set from:
Oxford Book of Welsh Verse, ed. T. Parry (Oxford: 10
Oxford University Press, 1962), nos. 31, 40, 78, 298,
318.
Early Irish Lyrics, ed. G. Murphy (Oxford: Oxford
University Press, 1956; repr. Dublin: Four Courts
Press, 1998), nos. 5, 7, 11, 35, 36.   15
and Two commentaries on extracts from the texts listed
under paper IV.

IV. Literature II: Prescribed texts. 3 hours.

French: French narrative fiction:
La Chastelaine de Vergi   20
Laclos, *Les Liaisons dangereuses*
Sand, *Indiana*
Proust, *Combray*
The paper will be examined entirely by essay, with can-
didates required to answer on *three* texts. There will be   25
a choice of questions on each text.

German: Three essays from a choice of questions on the set texts
covering genre, themes, and period:
Prose:
Fontane, *Effi Briest*   30
Kafka, *Die Verwandlung*
Thomas Mann, *Mario und der Zauberer*
Remarque, *Im Westen nichts Neues*
Drama:
Wedekind, *Frühlings Erwachen*   35
Schnitzler, *Leibelei*
Kaiser, *Von morgens bis mitternachts*
Brecht, *Die Maßnahme*, edition suhrkamp 2058
(Frankfurt a. M.: Suhrkamp, 1998), in the version of
1931   40

Italian: Candidates will be expected to show knowledge of three
of the five works listed below. Candidates will be expected to have such knowledge of the literary, intellectual, and historical background as is necessary for the
understanding of these texts. Compulsory passages for   45
commentary will not be set in the examination.
Modern Italian Narrative and Cinema
Primo Levi, *Se questo è un uomo*
Italo Calvino, *Il barone rampante*
Anna Maria Ortese, *Il mare non bagna Napoli*   50

Natalia Ginzburg, *Lessico famigliare*

Spanish: Prescribed texts to be studied in relation to general trends in literature or thought or to historical background. Compulsory passages for explanation and detailed comment will *not* be set. 5

The Spanish Ballad Tradition:

Traditional romances:

El romancero viejo (ed. M. Díaz Roig, Cátedra, Madrid, 1979), poems Nos. 1–3, 5–6, 8–9, 11, 13–14, 23–4, 29–32, 38–59, 63–6, 68, 71–3, 76, 78, 83, 85–6, 88, 10 91, 94, 96–9, 101, 104, 111, 115–9, 121, 125–8.

Golden Age:

Lope de Vega, *Lírica* (ed. J. M. Blecua, Clásicos Castalia), poems Nos. 1–2, 6–10, 125, and 126.

Góngora, *Romances* (ed. Antonio Carreño, Cátedra, 15 Madrid, 1982), poems Nos. 3, 10–11, 15–16, 18, 23, 27, 48, 52, 58, and 79.

Francisco de Quevedo, *Poemas escogidos* (ed. J. M. Blecua, Clásicos Castallia, Madrid), poems Nos. 155, 160, 165, 167, and 172. 20

Nineteenth and Twentieth Centuries:

Duque de Rivas, *El conde de Villamediana; El Alcázar de Sevilla; El fratricidio; Bailén* (from *Romances históricos,* ed. S. García, Cátedra).

Antonio Machado, 'La tierra de Alvargonzález' (from 25 *Poesías completas,* Selecciones Austral).

F. García Lorca, *Romancero gitano* (ed. Mario Hernández, Alianza).

Portuguese: The examination will consist of:

(*a*) a commentary on passages chosen from two of the set 30 texts given below; (*b*) an essay, on one of the remaining three texts; (*c*) an essay on the historical development of the *auto*. Candidates will be expected to show knowledge of at least one text from each of groups A, B, and C below. 35

A Gil Vicente *Auto da Barca do Inferno*

Auto da India

B Ana Luísa Amaral, *Próspero Morreu*

C Suassuna *Auto da Compadecida*

Cabral de Melo Neto *Vida e Morte Severina* 40

Russian: The paper will consist of: (*a*) one compulsory commentary; and (*b*) two essays each from a choice of two covering the other two set authors. Examiners may give some guidance to candidates about how to approach the passage set for commentary; they may also 45 require candidates to translate some portion of the passage set for commentary into English.

Pushkin, *Pikovaya dama*

Chekhov, *Sluchai iz praktiki; Anna na shee; Dom s mezoninom* 50

Dovlatov, *Chemodan*

Modern Greek: Twentieth-century Greek prose in context. Candidates will be expected to have and to be able to demonstrate such knowledge of the literary, intellectual, cultural and historical background as is necessary for the understanding of these texts. Compulsory passages for commentary will not be set in the examination. Angelopoulos's *Ο Θίασος* will be taught with an emphasis on the script, but aspects of the film will also be discussed.Candidates will be encouraged to make connections and comparisons between texts where appropriate.

Prescribed texts   10

Στρατής Δούκας, Ιστορία ενός αιχμαλώτου

Δημήτρης Χατζής, Το τέλος της μικρής μας πόλης

Κώστας Ταχτσής, Το τρίτο στεφάνι

Θόδωρος Αγγελόπουλος, Ο Θίασος

Παύλος Μάτεσις, Η μητέρα του σκύλου   15

Αλέξανδρος Κοτζιάς, Ιαγουάρος'

Czech (with Slovak):   Prescribed texts to be studied as literature. Essay-type questions will be set on the plays, and a compulsory passage for commentary from the poem. Candidates will be required to answer on all three texts.   20

Karel Čapek, *R.U.R.*

Jiří Wolker: *Svatý kopeček*

Karel Jaromír Erben: *Kytice*

Celtic: Prescribed texts. Three essays from a choice of questions on the following set texts: 25

Pwyll Pendefig Dyfed, ed. R. L. Thomson (Dublin, 1957);

Branwen ferch Lyr, ed. D. Thomson (Dublin, 1961);

Saunders Lewis, *Brandwen*, in Saunders Lewis, *Dramâu'r Parlwr: Branwen a Dwy Briodas Ann* (Llandybïe: 30 Christopher Davies, 1975);

Poems of the Cywyddwyr, ed. E. I. Rowlands (Dublin, 1976);

Scéla Muicce Meic Dathó, ed. R. Thurneysen (Dublin, 1976), pp. 33–41;   35

Longes Mac n-Uislenn, ed. V. Hull (New York: Modern Language Association of America, 1949).

c. *Classics and Modern Languages paper*

Latin and Ancient Greek

Any candidate whose native language is not English may bring a bilingual (native   40 language to English) dictionary for use in any examination paper where candidates are required to translate Ancient Greek and/or Latin texts into English.

1. *Course I.*

Papers V, VI and VII: Candidates will be required to take papers identical with papers 3, 4, and 5 for the Preliminary Examination in Classics and English, *Course I.*   45

For prescribed editions of texts, see the Classics and Modern Languages Handbook.

2. *Course II.*

Candidates for Course II shall be required:

(a) to pass at the end of their first year of study the examination in Greek and Latin prescribed for first-year candidates in Course II of the Preliminary Examination   50 in Classics and English.

(b) during their second year of study, to offer papers as for Course I.

d. Linguistics

VIII. General Linguistics. 3 hours.

Candidates will be expected to be familiar with the development of contemporary
linguistic theory, both synchronic and historical, and be able to discuss problems and   5
issues in areas including semantics, pragmatics, sociolinguistics, psycholinguistics,
language acquisition and language change.

IX. Phonetics and Phonology. 3 hours.

Candidates will be expected to be familiar with principles and practice in the
analysis, classification, and transcription of speech, as applied to languages in general,   10
but with an emphasis on European languages.

X. Grammatical Analysis. 3 hours.

Candidates will be expected to be familiar with modern grammatical theory, in
particular as applied to the analysis of European languages.

e. Further Topics   15

XI. Further Topics I:

French: Introduction to French Film Studies:

Candidates must write three essays, each on a different film. There will be a choice
of two questions on each film.

Henri-Georges Clouzot: Le Corbeau (1942)   20
Jean-Luc Godard: Vivre sa vie (1962)
Agnès Varda: Les Glaneurs et la glaneuse (2000)
Bertrand Blier: Les valseuses (1974)

German: Introduction to German Film Studies:

The paper will consist of one commentary and two essays from a choice of ques-   25
tions. The commentary will be on a set of stills from one of the films.

Metropolis (dir. Fritz Lang, 1925/26. Eureka edition EKA40321)

Die Abenteuer des Prinzen Achmed (dir. Lotte Reiniger, 1923/26)

Der blaue Engel (dir. Josef von Sternberg, 1929/1930)

Kameradschaft (dir. G. W. Pabst, 1931)   30

XII. Further Topics II:

French: Introduction to French Literary Theory:

Candidates must write three essays, each on a different author. There will be a
choice of two questions on each author.

Valéry, 'Questions de poésie' and 'Poésie et pensée abstraite', in *Théorie poétique et*   35
esthétique, in *Oeuvres*, I, ed. J. Hytier, Bibliothèque de la Pléiade (Gallimard, 1957),
pp. 1280–94; pp. 1314–39

Sartre, *Qu'est-ce que la littérature?* (Folio) [Sections I and II only]
Barthes, *Critique et vérité* (Seuil)
Todorov, 'La notion de littérature', 'L'origine des genres', 'Les deux principes du   40
récit', 'Introduction au vraisemblable' in *La notion de littérature et autres essais* (Seuil)

German: Introduction to German Medieval Studies:

The paper will consist of one commentary, one question consisting of several
questions on a passage, and one essay from a choice of questions.

Close study of a single text: Hartmann von Aue, *Gregorius* (Reclam edition Middle   45
High German text with a facing page translation in modern German).

XIII. Further Topics III:

French: Key Texts in French Thought:

Candidates must answer three questions (one commentary and two essays), each on a different text. There will be a choice of one commentary passage and one essay question on each text. 5

Descartes, *Discours de la méthode* (Garnier-Flammarion)

Rousseau, *Discours sur l'inégalité* (Folio)

Bergson, *Essai sur les données immédiates de la conscience* (PUF) [Chapters I and II only]

Beauvoir, *Le Deuxième Sexe* (Folio). I: Introduction, 'Mythes'; II: 'La femme 10 mariée', 'La mère'

German: Key Texts in German Thought:

Kant, *Idee zu einer allgemeinen Geschichte in weltbürgerlicher Absicht*

Marx und Engels, *Das kommunistische Manifest*

Nietzsche, 'Zur Naturgeschichte der Moral' in *Jenseits vom Gut und Böse* 15

Freud, *Warum Krieg?*

Candidates will be permitted to use translations alongside, but not instead of, the original texts.

f. *Russian Course B: for students who enter Oxford without A level or equivalent level knowledge of Russian* 20

BI   Translation from English into Russian and Russian grammar exercises.

BIIA   Translation from Russian into English.

BIIB   Comprehension of a passage of written Russian.

BIII   Dictation and Aural Comprehension.

BIV   Oral Test. 25

Preliminary Examination in Molecular and Cellular Biochemistry

A

1. The subjects of the Preliminary Examination in Molecular and Cellular Biochemistry shall be: 30

(1) Molecular Cell Biology

(2) Biological Chemistry

(3) Biophysical Chemistry

(4) Organic Chemistry

(5) Mathematics and Statistics for Biochemists. 35

2. Candidates shall be deemed to have passed the examination if they satisfy the Moderators in all five subjects.

3. Candidates must offer all five subjects at their first examination attempt.

4. A candidate who fails one or two subjects will be permitted one further attempt at the failed subject/s, at the first available opportunity. 40

5. A candidate who fails three or more subjects shall be deemed to have failed the examination. He or she will be permitted one further attempt at the whole examination, at the first available opportunity.

6. The Moderators may award a Distinction to candidates of special merit who satisfy them in all five subjects at their first examination attempt. 45

B

One written paper will be set in each subject. The duration of the written papers will be three hours for subjects 1, 2, and 3, and two hours for subjects 4 and 5. The syllabus for each subject will be that set out in the schedule below.

The Moderators will permit the use of hand-held pocket calculators subject to the conditions set out under the heading 'Use of Calculators in examinations' in the *Regulations for the Conduct of University Examinations*. A list of recommended calculators will be provided by the Chair of the Moderators not later than the Wednesday of the fourth week of the Michaelmas Full Term preceding the examination. The use of calculators may not be permitted in certain papers.

All candidates shall be assessed as to their practical ability in coursework under the following provisions:

(*a*) The Chair of the Teaching Committee, or a deputy, shall make available to the Moderators, at the end of the fifth week of the term in which the examinations are first held, evidence showing the extent to which each candidate has completed the prescribed coursework.

(*b*) The Moderators may request coursework from any candidate. Such candidates will be named in a list posted by the day of the first written paper.

(*c*) Coursework cannot normally be retaken. Failure to complete the coursework to the satisfaction of the Moderators, in the absence of appropriate documentary evidence (e.g. a signed medical certificate), will normally constitute failure of the examination.

SCHEDULE

(1) *Molecular Cell Biology*

Classification, evolution and structure of bacterial, archeal, and eukaryotic cells; structure of subcellular organelles and the cytoskeleton of eukaryotes. Multicellularity and cell specialization. Differences between plant and animal cells. Nuclear and cell division in plants, animals, and bacteria. Intra- and intercellular signalling.

Chromosomes and genes. Transmission of information between generations. Mitosis and meiosis. Evidence for DNA as the genetic material. The nature of the gene. Organisation and expression of genetic information: mechanism of DNA replication; mechanism and control of transcription; mechanisms and structures involved in protein synthesis; the genetic code; phages, plasmids, and hosts. Gene cloning and mapping techniques.

Major metabolic pathways—chemical and thermodynamic principles. ATP. Oxidation of fuels: glycogen, sugars, amino acids, fats. The TCA cycle. Synthesis of carbohydrates and fats. The glyoxylate cycle. Photosynthesis. Urea cycle.

Structure and properties of biological membranes. Membrane potentials and ion channels. Membrane transport; biological pumps. Bioenergetics; electron transfer, oxidative and photophosphorylation.

(2) *Biological Chemistry*

Chemical constraints on biology. Energy transformations. Biological polymers. Polysaccharides: amylose and cellulose. Membranes. Lipid and protein components of membranes.

Structure and properties of proteins: amino acids, peptide bonds, conformational preferences, α-helices, β-sheets, stabilisation by non-covalent interactions; protein sequences and amino acid modification; glycoproteins.

Tertiary structure and protein folding. Structural proteins. Myoglobin and haemoglobin.

Principles of enzyme catalysis - acid-base and nucleophilic catalysis. Proteases and other enzymes.

Organic chemistry of enzyme reactions, particularly those in glycolysis.

Biological aspects of sulphur, iron, and phosphorus chemistry.

Organic chemistry of sugars and other heterocyclic compounds.   5

Structure and properties of nucleic acids; ribose and deoxyribose, keto-enol tautomerism and H-bonding in purines and pyrimidines, phosphate as linking group; nucleotides; polymeric chains of nucleotides; differences in stability between RNA and DNA; the double helix; DNA damage and mutation.

Techniques in molecular biology: purification of DNA and proteins.   10
Electrophoresis. DNA sequencing, cloning, blotting.

(3) *Biophysical Chemistry*

Principles of Newtonian mechanics and electrostatics. Quantum theory: concepts of quantum mechanics in terms of energy levels. Boltzmann distribution. Atomic and molecular structure, atomic orbitals: crystal field theory; LCAO approach to molecular orbitals.   15

Electromagnetic radiation and its interaction with matter. Light absorption. Spectroscopy, Beer's Law. Diffraction; Bragg's Law. X-ray diffraction by crystals. Modern optical microscopy. Electron microscopy.

Thermodynamics of solutions: introduction to First and Second Laws. Gibbs   20
function, chemical potential and electrochemical potential. Osmotic equilibria; chemical equilibria; redox equilibria. Buffer solutions and pH. Non-ideal solutions: activity co-efficients. Debye-Huckel theory. Solubility of proteins and other compounds.

Kinetics: order and molecularity; first, second, and pseudo-first order kinetics,   25
steady state. Half lives. Theories of reaction rates; collision theory, transition state theory. Activation energy and the Arrhenius equation. Isotope effects, acid-base catalysis. Radioactive decay as a first order process. Biological effects of radiation. Enzyme kinetics, Michaelis-Menten equation and the steady state derivation. Irreversible and reversible inhibitors of enzymes. Classification of reversible inhibitors.   30
Allostery.

Non-covalent interactions. Electrostatic forces and dipoles. Electronegativity. Lennard-Jones potential and van der Waal's radii. Hydrogen bonding in proteins, DNA and oligosaccharides. The hydrophobic effect; role of entropy. Accessible surface area and solubility. Protein folding—thermodynamic and kinetic aspects. Co-   35
operativity of folding. Protein denaturation and misfolding.

(4) *Organic Chemistry*

Structure: Elementary atomic and molecular orbital theory. Bonding and molecular geometry. Methods for structure determination (e.g. spectroscopy, mass spectrometry, nmr). Stereochemistry: Absolute configuration. Cis-trans and other isomerisations.   40

Reactivity: Electronegativity; inductive, mesomeric and stereoelectronic effects. Lowry-Bronsted acidity and basicity of organic compounds. Nucleophilicity and electrophilicity. Simple molecular orbital theory as unifying concept.

Mechanism: Classification of reactions proceeding via intermediates and transition states. Substitution, elimination and addition processes. Rate determining steps;   45
kinetic and thermodynamic control. Carbocation, carbanion, carbene and radical intermediates.

Functional group chemistry: Characteristic chemistry of carbonyl groups. Structure, properties and reactions of carbonyls.

(5) *Mathematics and Statistics for Biochemists*

An elementary treatment of the following topics will be expected:

Mathematics

Indices, logarithms, and exponential functions. Graphs and graphical representation of simple equations, slopes, inflexion points. Partial fractions. Basic trigonometric functions: sine and cosine functions, representation of waves. Differentiation: maxima and minima; rates of progress, use of Product and Chain rules. Partial differentiation. Integration: of powers of x including x^{-1}; by substitution, by parts and using partial fractions. Introduction to Complex numbers. Simple separable differential equations and their solution. Zeroth, first and second order processes. Permutations and combinations. Factorials and the Binomial Theorem. Binomial and Poisson distributions.

Statistics

Mean, median, and mode—measures of central tendency. Normal, unimodal, and bimodal distributions. Standard deviation, standard error, and coefficient of variance. Confidence limits. Experimental errors and biological variation. Relationships between variables—line fitting. Accuracy and precision. Experimental design. Significance testing; t-tests and non-parametric tests. Conditional probabilities and expectation.

Preliminary Examination in Music

A

1. The subjects of the examination and the number of papers shall be as prescribed by regulation from time to time by the Board of the Faculty of Music.

2. In the case of candidates who have satisfied the Moderators in all the written and practical subjects, the Moderators may award a distinction to those of special merit.

B

Each candidate will be required to offer papers 1–3 and two of the options in paper 4.

1. *Special Topics*

A three-hour paper in which candidates should attempt to answer three questions.

2. *Musical Analysis*

A three-hour paper in which candidates should attempt to answer one question from a choice of two.

3. *Techniques of Composition and Keyboard Skills*

The paper shall consist of two parts:

A. Techniques of Composition: Studies in Harmony and Counterpoint

A seven-day take-away paper in which candidates should attempt three questions: the two compulsory questions and one other. The examination paper will be available for collection in the Music Faculty Library from noon on Tuesday of the fifth week in the Trinity Term in which candidates are presenting themselves for examination. Completed papers must be submitted to the Chair of Moderators in Music, Examination Schools, High Street, Oxford, not later than noon on Tuesday of the sixth week of the same term. Each paper must be accompanied by a declaration, in a sealed envelope bearing the candidate's examination number, in the form prescribed for the portfolio of compositions and the extended essay.

B. Keyboard Skills

A practical examination in which candidates will be asked to: (a) realise a figured bass line at the keyboard or, where appropriate, on another continuo instrument (e.g.

lute); (b) read at the keyboard three- or four-part writing in three different clefs. Preparation time for candidates in the examination will be 30 minutes.

4. *Options*

Candidates must choose two from the following:

(*a*) *Issues in the Study of Music* 5

A two-hour paper in which candidates should attempt to answer two questions.

(*b*) *Composition*

Candidates will be required to submit a portfolio of compositions and to take a listening examination. The specifications for the portfolio are as published in the Faculty Undergraduate Handbook relating to the examination. 10

(*c*) *Performance*

A solo performance, vocal or instrumental, of some 10–12 minutes in length. Instrumental candidates may choose to perform a single work, a movement from a longer work, or two pieces in contrasting style. The choice of instrument is limited to related families of instruments. Singers may choose to perform up to four pieces. 15 Programmes must be submitted to the Chair of Moderators in Music, Faculty of Music, St Aldate's, not later than noon on Friday of the sixth week in the Hilary Term of the academic year in which the candidates are presenting themselves for examination.

(*d*) *Extended Essay* 20

An essay of 4,000–5,000 words on a subject to be chosen in consultation with the candidate's tutor.

Each portfolio submitted for the subjects of Portfolio of Compositions and Extended Essay must be accompanied by a declaration placed in a sealed envelope bearing the candidate's examination number and in the following prescribed form. 25

Form of Declaration

I, ..., hereby declare that this submission is my own work, except where otherwise stated, and that it has not previously been submitted, either wholly or in part, for any other examination.

Signed.. 30

.... College

Date..

Candidates who fail one or two of papers 1, 2, 3, or 4 above may resit only that paper or papers at a subsequent examination; candidates who fail three or four papers will be required to resit all four papers at a subsequent examination. 35

Preliminary Examination in Oriental Studies

A

1. The languages, subjects, and papers in the examination shall be as prescribed by regulation from time to time by the Board of the Faculty of Oriental Studies.

2. A candidate shall be deemed to have passed the examination when he or she shall 40 have satisfied the Moderators in all the papers associated with one of the languages specified in the regulations.

3. Candidates must offer all subjects at one examination provided that: (i) in languages for which four papers are required, a candidate who fails in one or two papers may offer those subjects at one subsequent examination, and a candidate who 45 fails three or four papers must offer all four subjects at one subsequent examination; and (ii) in languages for which three papers are required, a candidate who fails in one

paper may offer that subject at one subsequent examination, and a candidate who fails two or three papers must offer all three subjects at one subsequent examination.

4. In the case of candidates who have satisfied the Moderators in all the papers at a single examination, the Moderators may award a distinction to those of special merit.

B   5

The languages which may be offered shall be Arabic, Chinese, Egyptology and Ancient Near Eastern Studies, Hebrew, Japanese, Persian, Sanskrit, and Turkish.

Arabic

Candidates will be required to offer three three-hour papers (papers (i), (ii), and (iv) below), plus an oral/aural examination as specified under (iii) below.   10

(i) Translation and precis into English.

(ii) Comprehension, composition, and grammar.

(iii) Oral/aural examination (to be done at the Oriental Institute)[1]

(iv) Islamic history and culture.

Chinese   15

Candidates will be required to offer three three-hour papers.

(i) Modern.

(ii) Classical.

(iii) East Asia Survey: China.

Egyptology and Ancient Near Eastern Studies   20

Candidates offering Egyptology and Ancient Near Eastern Studies are required to offer four three-hour papers:

1, 2   *Either* Akkadian texts. (Lists are available from the Oriental Institute)

and

Akkadian grammar and unprepared translation.   25

Or

Egyptian texts: *Middle Egyptian texts*, ed. Baines and Smith. (Copies are available from the Oriental Institute)

and

Middle Egyptian grammar and unprepared translation.   30

3. Civilizations of the Ancient Near East.

4. History of the Ancient Near East to 30 BCE.

Hebrew and Jewish Studies

Candidates will be required to offer four three-hour papers.

(i) Hebrew Texts I: Biblical and Rabbinic Hebrew.   35

(ii) Hebrew Texts II: Medieval and Modern Hebrew.

Copies of texts for papers (i) and (ii) are available from the Oriental Institute.

(iii) Grammar and Translation into Hebrew.

(iv) General Paper.

Japanese   40

Candidates will be required to offer three three-hour papers.

(i) Modern Japanese I.

(ii) Modern Japanese II.

(iii) East Asia Survey: Japan.

---

[1] Details of the areas in which candidates will be expected to show competence are provided in the examination conventions and in the handbook.

Persian
  Candidates will be required to offer three three-hour papers.
  (i) Translation from Persian and reading comprehension.
  (ii) Translation into Persian and essay.
  (iii) Islamic History and Culture.   5

Sanskrit
  Candidates will be required to offer three three-hour papers.
  (i) Texts: C. R. Lanman, *Sanskrit Reader,* pp. 1–34, l. 11. *Bhagavad-Gītā*
      (ed. Belvalkar), Books II, IV, VI, and XI.
  (ii) Grammar: the subject will be studied from M. A. Coulson, *Teach Yourself*   10
      Sanskrit ; A. A. Macdonell, *Sanskrit Grammar for Students.*
  (iii) General paper.

Turkish
  Candidates will be required to offer three three-hour papers.
  (i) Prepared texts and unseen translation from Turkish. (The list of texts to be   15
      prepared is published in the current issue of the Islamic Studies handbook.)
  (ii) Turkish grammar and translation into Turkish.
  (iii) Islamic history and culture.

Preliminary Examination in Philosophy
and Modern Languages   20

A

1. Candidates in this Preliminary Examination shall be examined in Philosophy
and one Modern Language. The languages that may be offered shall be those
languages which may be offered in the Final Honour School of Modern Languages.

2. The subjects of the examination shall be: 25
In Philosophy,
  (1) Introduction to Philosophy
and, in the Modern Language offered
  (2) Language papers
  (3) Literature papers.   30

3. Candidates must offer all three subjects at one examination provided that

  (*a*) a candidate who fails in either two subjects or one subject may in a subsequent
      examination offer the two subjects or the one subject only;

  (*b*) a candidate who has offered two subjects at a subsequent examination under (*a*)
      above and has failed in one subject may offer in a subsequent examination that   35
      subject only.

Provided that a candidate who fails one only of the papers in 2(1) above may offer,
in a subsequent examination or subsequent examinations, the paper in which he or she
has failed.

4. A candidate shall be deemed to have passed the examination if he shall have   40
satisfied the Examiners in all three subjects.

5. In the case of candidates who have satisfied the Examiners in three subjects at a
single examination the Examiners may award a distinction either in Philosophy or in
the Modern Language or in both to those who have done work of special merit.

6. This Preliminary Examination shall be under the joint supervision of the Boards of the Faculties of Philosophy and of Medieval and Modern European Languages and Literature, which shall appoint a standing joint committee to make regulations concerning it, subject always to the preceding clauses of this subsection.

7. It shall be the duty of the Chair of the Examiners for the Preliminary Examination for Modern Languages to designate such of their number as may be required for Modern Languages in the Preliminary Examination in Philosophy and Modern Languages, and when this has been done and the Examiner for Philosophy has been nominated, the number of the examiners in Philosophy and Modern Languages shall be deemed to be complete.

B

There shall be three subjects in the examination.

(1) *Introduction to Philosophy* (two papers of three hours each).

I. *General Philosophy*

As defined in the regulations for Preliminary Examination in Philosophy, Politics, and Economics. Candidates will be required to answer four questions.

II. (*a*) *Moral Philosophy* and (*b*) *Logic*

As defined in the regulations for the Preliminary Examination in Philosophy, Politics, and Economics. Candidates will be required to answer four questions, including at least one from each section.

(2) *Language papers* (one paper of three hours and two papers each of one and a half hours including in French certification of attendance and participation in oral classes, as specified for the Preliminary Examination in Modern Languages).

As specified for Papers I, IIA, and IIB in the regulations for the Preliminary Examination for Modern Languages.

(3) *Literature papers* (two papers, each of three hours).

As specified for Papers III and IV in the regulations for the Preliminary Examination for Modern Languages.

Preliminary Examination in Philosophy, Politics, and Economics

A

1. The subjects of the Preliminary Examination for Philosophy, Politics, and Economics shall be:

(1) Introductory Economics

(2) Introduction to Philosophy

(3) Introduction to the Theory and Practice of Politics.

2. A candidate shall be allowed to offer himself or herself for examination in one, two, or three subjects.

3. A candidate shall be deemed to have passed the examination if he or she shall have satisfied the Moderators in three subjects.

4. The Moderators may award a distinction to candidates of special merit who have passed all three subjects at a single examination.

B

Three three-hour papers will be set as follows.

Introductory Economics

Elementary economics including: consumer theory; producer theory; market equilibrium with perfect competition, monopoly and imperfect competition; factor markets; partial equilibrium analysis of welfare, market failure and externalities; national income accounting; the determination of national income and employment; monetary   5
institutions and the money supply; inflation; balance of payments and exchange rates; the determinants of long-run economic growth. Elementary mathematical economics; application of functions and graphs, differentiation, partial differentiation, maxima and minima, optimization subject to constraints.

Calculators may be used in the examination room subject to the conditions set out   10
under the heading 'Use of calculators in examinations' in the *Special Regulations concerning Examinations.*

Introduction to Philosophy

The paper shall consist of three sections: (I) General Philosophy, (II) Moral Philosophy, (III) Logic. Each candidate will be required to show adequate knowledge   15
in each of the three sections.

I. *General Philosophy*

Subjects to be studied include: knowledge and scepticism, induction, mind and body, personal identity, free will, and God and evil. Candidates will have the opportunity, but will not be required, to show first-hand knowledge of Descartes'   20
Meditations and Hume's *An Enquiry concerning Human Understanding.*

II. *Moral Philosophy*

This section shall be studied in connection with Mill's *Utilitarianism*. While not being confined to the detailed views of the author of the set text, the section will be satisfactorily answerable by a candidate who has made a critical study of the text.   25
Questions will normally be set on the following topics: pleasure, happiness and well-being; forms of consequentialism; alternatives to consequentialism; ethical truth, ethical realism and the 'Proof' of Utilitarianism; justice and rights; virtue, character, and integrity.

III. *Logic*   30

Subjects to be studied include: syntax and semantics of propositional and predicate logic, identity and definite descriptions, proofs in Natural Deduction, and the critical application of formal logic to the analysis of English sentences and arguments.

These topics shall be studied in conjunction with Volker Halbach's *Introduction to Logic* manual, published by Oxford University Press. The logical symbols to be used   35
are those found in this publication. The first question in this section of the paper will be a question of an elementary and straightforward nature.

Introduction to the Theory and Practice of Politics

The paper will be divided into two sections. Candidates are required to answer *four* questions, of which at least one must be from section (*a*) and two from section (*b*).   40

(a) *The Theory of Politics*

Questions will be set on the following topics: (i) the nature and the grounds of rights; (ii) the nature and grounds of democracy; (iii) the role of civil society; (iv) power in the democratic state; (v) the nature and grounds of liberty; (vi) state paternalism; and (vii) free speech. Questions will also be set on the following texts: (i) John Locke, *Second*   45
Treatise on Government; (ii) Jean-Jacques Rousseau, *Social Contract*; (iii) Alexis de Toqueville, *Democracy in America*; (iv) Karl Marx and Friedrich Engels, *The Communist Manifesto*; (v) John Stuart Mill, *On Liberty.*

(*b*) *The Practice of Politics*

Questions will be set on the following topics: (i) regime types; definition and measurement of variations between types of democracy; (ii) political institutions and practice outside the advanced industrial democracies; stability, state capacity and state formation; (iii) the state and its institutions (executives, legislatures, parties and party systems, electoral systems, courts, constitutions and centre-periphery relations); (iv) parties and party systems; political values and identity politics.

Preliminary Examination in Physics

A

1. The subject of the Preliminary Examination in Physics shall be Physics, including basic practical and mathematical techniques.

2. The number of papers and other general requirements of the Preliminary Examination in Physics shall be as prescribed by regulation from time to time by the Mathematical, Physical and Life Sciences Board.

B

1. Candidates in Physics must offer four Compulsory Papers at one examination, provided that a candidate who has failed in one or two papers may offer that number of papers at a subsequent examination. The titles of the papers shall be:

CP1: Physics 1
CP2: Physics 2
CP3: Mathematical Methods 1
CP4: Mathematical Methods 2.

Their syllabuses shall be approved by the Faculty of Physics and shall be published in the Physics Course Handbook by the Faculty of Physics not later than the beginning of Michaelmas Full Term for examination three terms thence.

2. In addition to the four papers of clause 1, a candidate in Physics shall be required

(i) to submit to the Moderators such evidence as they require of the successful completion of practical work normally pursued during the three terms preceding the examination, *and*

(ii) to offer a written paper on one Short Option.

3. Candidates shall be deemed to have passed the examination if they have satisfied the Moderators in the four compulsory papers either at a single examination or at two examinations in accordance with the proviso to clause 1, and provided further that the same number of papers as were failed at the first sitting have been passed at the same attempt at a subsequent examination.

4. In the case of candidates who offer all four papers of clause 1, the Moderators shall publish the names only of those who have satisfied them in two or more papers. Candidates whose names do not appear on the pass list must offer four papers at a subsequent examination. In the case of candidates who, in accordance with the proviso to clause 1, offer one or two papers, the Moderators shall publish the names only to those who have satisfied them in each of the papers offered.

5. The Moderators may award a distinction to candidates of special merit who have satisfied them in all four papers of clause 1 at the single examination and in the requirements of clause 2.

6. Failure to complete practical work under clause 2(i), without good reason, will be deemed by the Moderators as failure in the Preliminary Examination and the candidate will be required to complete the outstanding practicals either by examination or by completing them alongside second year study, before entry to the Part A

examination will be permitted. In these circumstances, distinction at the Preliminary Examination will not be possible.

7. The list of Short Option subjects in clause 2(ii) and their syllabuses shall be approved by the Faculty of Physics and shall be published in the Physics Course Handbook by the Faculty of Physics not later than the beginning of Michaelmas Full Term for examination three terms thence.

8. With respect to subjects under clause 2(ii) a candidate may propose to the Head of the Teaching Faculty of Physics or deputy, not later than the last week of Michaelmas Full Term preceding the examination, another subject paper. Candidates shall be advised of the decision by the end of the first week of the subsequent Hilary Full Term.

9. Except for papers for which their use is forbidden, the Moderators will permit the use of any hand-held calculator subject to the conditions set out under the heading 'Use of calculators in examinations' in the *Regulations for the Conduct of University Examinations* and further elaborated in the Course Handbook.

Preliminary Examination in Physics and Philosophy

A

1. The subjects of the Examination shall be (a) Physics and Mathematics, (b) Philosophy.

2. All candidates must offer both (a) and (b).

3. The Examiners shall indicate on the pass list each candidate who has not passed the examination, but who has passed in one subject, and shall indicate in which subject the candidate has passed.

4. The Examination shall be under the joint supervision of the Board of the Faculty of Philosophy and the Mathematical, Physical and Life Sciences Board, which shall appoint a standing joint committee to make regulations concerning it, subject always to the preceding clauses of this sub-section.

5. (i) The Examiners for Physics and Mathematics shall be such of the Examiners in the Preliminary Examination in Physics as may be designated by the Chair of Examiners for the Preliminary Examination in Physics.

   (ii) The Examiners for Philosophy shall be nominated by a committee of which the three elected members shall be appointed by the Board of the Faculty of Philosophy.

6. Candidates who do not pass the examination at their first sitting may re-enter on one subsequent occasion as follows:

   (i) Candidates must re-take any papers failed at the first attempt, and

   (ii) Candidates who fail two or more papers in Physics and Mathematics must retake all the papers in that subject.

B

Distinction can be obtained by excellence either in Physics and Mathematics or in Philosophy provided that adequate knowledge is shown in the other subject of the examination.

Candidates will be required to take five papers, as follows:

(*a*) three papers in Physics and Mathematics;

(*b*) two papers in Philosophy.

(*a*) *Physics and Mathematics*

Candidates will be required to take the following three papers:

(1) CP1 Physics 1

(2) CP3 Mathematical Methods 1

(3) CP4 Mathematical Methods 2. 5

Their syllabuses shall be approved by the Faculty of Physics and published in the Physics Course Handbook not later than the beginning of Michaelmas Full Term for examination three terms thence. Except for papers for which their use is forbidden, the Moderators will permit the use of any hand-held calculator subject to the conditions set out under the heading 'Use of calculators in examinations' in the Regulations for the Conduct of 10 University Examinations and further elaborated in the Physics Course Handbook.

(*b*) *Philosophy*

Candidates will be required to take two papers:

(1) *Elements of Deductive Logic*

As specified for the Preliminary Examination in Mathematics and Philosophy. 15

(2) *Introduction to Philosophy*

The paper shall consist of two parts:

    A. *General Philosophy*

As specified for the Preliminary Examination in Mathematics and Philosophy.

    B. *Leibniz-Clarke* 20

This section shall be studied principally as an introduction to the philosophy of space and time in connection with *The Leibniz-Clarke Correspondence*, ed. H. G. Alexander, Manchester University Press, 1956. This section, while not being confined to the detailed views of the author of the set text, will be satisfactorily answerable by a candidate who has made a critical study of the text. There will not be a compulsory 25 question containing passages for comment.

Candidates will be required to attempt four questions, and answer at least one question from Part A and at least one question from Part B.

Preliminary Examination in Psychology, Philosophy, and Linguistics
30

A

1. The subjects of the examination shall be:

    (1) Introduction to Psychology

    (2) Introduction to Philosophy

    (3) Introduction to Linguistics 35

    (4) Introduction to Neurophysiology

    (5) Introduction to Probability Theory and Statistics

2. Candidates shall be deemed to have passed the examination if they satisfy the Moderators in three subjects.

3. Candidates must offer three subjects at their first examination attempt. 40

4. A candidate who fails one subject will be permitted one further attempt at this failed subject, at the first available opportunity.

5. A candidate who fails two or three subjects shall be deemed to have failed the examination. He or she will be permitted one further attempt at the whole examination, at the first available opportunity. 45

6. The Moderators may award a Distinction to candidates of special merit who satisfy them in three subjects at their first examination attempt.

B

(1) *Introduction to Psychology*
Methods and topics in: development; individual differences; social behaviour; animal behaviour; the neural basis of behaviour; perception; learning; memory; language; cognition; skills; abnormal behaviour.
One three-hour paper will be set.

(2) *Introduction to Philosophy*
As specified for the Preliminary Examination for Philosophy, Politics, and Economics.

(3) *Introduction to Linguistics*
Provides a foundation in phonetics, phonology, morphology, syntax, and semantics, with an introduction to linguistic theory and the connections between linguistics and other subjects such as philosophy of language, sociology and psychology.
One three-hour paper will be set.

(4) *Introduction to Neurophysiology*
Excitable Tissues. Membrane potential, ion pumps. Action potential, refractory period. Receptor potentials. Neuromuscular transmission. Synaptic mechanisms.
Chemical Transmitters. Storage and release of transmitter. Removal and synthesis of transmitter. Selected drugs acting on the nervous system.
Efferent Mechanisms. Muscle contraction. Muscle receptors. Spinal reflexes. Higher motor centres. Autonomic nervous system.
Afferent Mechanisms. Hearing. Vision. Somaesthetic system, including pain.
One three-hour paper will be set.

(5) *Introduction to Probability Theory and Statistics*
This examination is intended to test the candidate's understanding of the elements of probability theory and of the principles of statistics as applied to the design and analysis of surveys and experiments and to the interpretation of the results of such investigations. The topics below are more fully detailed in *Definitions and Formulae with Statistical Tables for Elementary Statistics and Quantitative Methods Courses*, which is prepared by the Department of Statistics. Copies of this will be available at the examination.
Descriptive statistics and statistical presentation using graphs and simple measures of central tendency and dispersion. Frequency distributions. Samples and populations. The addition and multiplication laws of probability; conditional probability and Bayes' Rule. The binomial, Poisson and normal distributions: their properties and uses and the relationships between them. Statistical inference using sampling distributions, standard errors and confidence limits. Common uses of z, t, chi-square and F tests and nonparametric tests including tests of hypothesis for the mean, median or proportion of a single population or for the difference between two or more populations, goodness-of-fit tests and tests of difference between two population distributions.
Parametric one-way Analysis of variance. Kruskal-Wallis non-Parametric analysis of variance. The analysis of 2-way contingency tables using chi-square tests. Linear regression and correlation.
A comprehensive list of formulae together with statistical tables will be available at the examination.
One three-hour paper will be set.
For papers (1) and (5) only, examiners will permit the use of any hand-held pocket calculator subject to the conditions set out under the heading 'Use of calculators' in the *Regulations for the Conduct of University Examinations*.

Preliminary Examination in Theology and Religion

A

1. The subjects of the Preliminary Examination for Theology and Religion shall be:
   (1) The Christian Doctrine of Creation
   (2) The Study of Old Testament set texts
   (3) Introducing the New Testament with special reference to the Gospel of Mark
   (4) The History of the Church from Nero to Constantine
   (5) Introduction to the Study of Religions
   (6) Introduction to Philosophy
   (7) New Testament Greek
   (8) Biblical Hebrew
   (9) Classical Arabic
   (10) Pali
   (11) Sanskrit.

2. Candidates must offer at least one from amongst papers (6), (7), (8), (9), (10), and (11).

3. Candidates intending to progress to the Honour School of Theology and Religion must satisfy a language requirement for the degree via his or her Preliminary Examination, or will be required to indicate how he or she will attempt to do so via his or her Second Public Examination. Candidates in the Honour School of Theology and Religion will be deemed to have satisfied a language requirement for their degree if they have passed one of Papers 7 (New Testament Greek), 8 (Biblical Hebrew), 9 (Classical Arabic), 10 (Pali), or 11 (Sanskrit) in their Preliminary Examination.

4. A candidate shall be deemed to have passed the examination if he shall have satisfied the Moderators in three of the subjects from the Preliminary Examination:

Provided that he shall have passed in not less than two subjects at one and the same examination and in the third subject at that or a subsequent examination.

5. Candidates may offer an additional subject if they so wish.

6. All candidates must offer at least three subjects in one examination:

Provided that a candidate who has failed in one subject (or in two subjects if he has offered four) but has passed in the other subjects offered may offer at a subsequent examination the subject or subjects in which he or she failed.

7. In the case of candidates who have satisfied the Moderators in at least three subjects in a single examination, the Moderators may award a mark of distinction to those of special merit.

B

Candidates must offer at least one from amongst papers 6, 7, 8, 9, 10, or 11.

1. *The Christian Doctrine of Creation*

This paper will serve as an introduction to Systematic Theology through the critical examination of different aspects of one basic Christian doctrine, the doctrine of Creation.

2. *The Study of Old Testament set texts: Genesis 1–11 and Amos*

Candidates will be expected to comment on passages from the set texts and will be expected to show a general knowledge of their historical, literary, and theological background.[1]

3. *Introducing the New Testament with special reference to the Gospel of Mark*

Candidates will be expected to show a general knowledge of the contents and background of the New Testament and to answer questions on historical and theological issues which are raised by the Gospel of Mark.

4. *The History of the Church from Nero to Constantine*

Candidates will be expected to show a general knowledge of the history of the Church, and its relations to the Roman empire, from the late first century to the death of Constantine in 337 AD. Questions will be set on some but not necessarily all of the following topics: the growth of the church and the meaning of conversion; the causes, scope, and effects of persecution; patterns of ministry and the threefold hierarchy; ecclesiastical discipline and the beginnings of monasticism; schisms caused by Judaizers, Gnostics, Montanists, Novatianists, and Donatists; the development of orthodoxy and synodical government; the evolution of the Biblical canon; the role of Christianity in the Constantinian Empire.

5. *Introduction to the Study of Religions*

The principal aim of this paper is to introduce the Study of Religions through the critical study of some different approaches. Candidates will be expected to understand the main attempts to define 'religion' and the problems associated with such definitions, and to have acquired a preliminary insight into the variety of religions, both those that are traditional and new religious movements through the world.

6. *Introduction to Philosophy*

As specified for the Preliminary Examination for Philosophy, Politics, and Economics.

7. *New Testament Greek*[2]

Candidates will be expected to show a knowledge of Greek grammar, syntax, and vocabulary (as set out in J. Duff, *The Elements of New Testament Greek*) and its importance for the exegesis of the New Testament, with particular reference to Mark 14:1–16:8 and John 6 and 9, from which passages will be chosen for translation and grammatical comment.

8. *Biblical Hebrew*[3]

The paper will include questions on elementary Hebrew grammar (to include only the topics covered in J. Weingreen, *Practical Grammar of Classical Hebrew*, 2nd edn., pp. 1–123), and short passages will be set for translation and grammatical comment from Genesis 1–2.

9. *Qur'ānic Arabic*

Candidates will be expected to show elementary knowledge of Qur'ānic Arabic grammar, syntax and vocabulary (to include only the topics covered in Alan Jones, *Arabic Through the Qur'ān*, pp. 1–104). Short passages from the Qur'ān will be chosen for translation and grammatical comment.

10. *Pali*

Candidates will be expected to show knowledge of Pali grammar, syntax and vocabulary (as set out in A. K. Warder: *Introduction to Pali*). Passages from the Pali Canon will be chosen for translation and grammatical comment.

---

[1] The texts will be studied in English in the New Revised Standard Version.

[2] The Greek text will be the text of the United Bible Societies, 4th edition.

[3] The Hebrew text will be the *Biblia Hebraica Stuttgartensia* (Stuttgart, 1977).

11. *Sanskrit*

Candidates will be expected to show knowledge of basic Sanskrit grammar, syntax, and vocabulary. The course book will be Walter Maurer's *The Sanskrit Language* and the texts for study will be *Bhagabad Gita* chapter 2 and *Nala* chapter 1. Passages from these texts will be chosen for translation and grammatical comment.   5

HONOUR SCHOOL OF ANCIENT AND MODERN HISTORY

A

1. The examination in the Honour School of Ancient and Modern History shall consist of such subjects in Ancient and Modern History as the Boards of the Faculties of Classics and History from time to time shall in consultation prescribe by regulation.

2. No candidate shall be admitted to the examination in this school unless he or she has either passed or been exempted from the First Public Examination.

3. The examination shall be under the joint supervision of the Boards of the Faculties of Classics and History. They shall appoint a standing joint committee to consider any matters concerning the examination which cannot expeditiously be settled by direct consultation between them. Whenever any matter cannot otherwise be resolved they shall themselves hold a joint meeting and resolve it by majority vote.

B

Each candidate shall offer the following subjects:

I. A PERIOD OF ANCIENT HISTORY (ONE PAPER).

One of the following:

[For students starting before MT 2015: (*a*) Greek History 478–403 BC;

(*b*) Greek History 403–336 BC;

(*c*) Roman History 146–46 BC;

(*d*) Roman History 46 BC–AD 54.]

[For students starting from MT 2015: 452: Greek History 478–403 BC

453: Greek History 403–336 BC

455: Roman History 146–46 BC

456: Roman History 46 BC–AD 54]

II. A PERIOD OF MODERN HISTORY (ONE PAPER).

Either

(*a*) Any one of the periods of General History specified for the Honour School of History;

or:

(*b*) Any one of the periods of the History of the British Isles specified for the Honour School of History except any such period that has already been offered on passing the First Public Examination.

Students participating in the academic exchange scheme with Princeton University will substitute the courses taken at Princeton for either a General History or History of the British Isles paper. The Princeton courses will be examined at Princeton, and the grades awarded will be reviewed and moderated by the Examiners to produce a single University standard mark, according to procedures laid down in the Handbook and Examining Conventions.

III. FURTHER SUBJECTS

Either, (*a*) (i) any one of the Further Subjects as specified for the Honour School of History (one paper);

or, (*b*) any one of the following Further Subjects in Ancient History (one paper) provided that any candidate who offers alternative IV (*a*) below may only offer alternative III (*b*):

[For students starting before MT 2015: (i) *Athenian democracy in the Classical Age* (as specified for the Honour School of Literae Humaniores I. 7).

   (ii) *Politics, Society and Culture from Nero to Hadrian* (as specified for the Honour   5
School of Literae Humaniores I. 11).

   (iii) *Religions in the Greek and Roman World, c* .31 BC–AD 312 (as specified for the Honour School of Literae Humaniores I. 12).

   (iv) *The Greeks and the Mediterranean World 950–500* BC, (IV.1 as specified for the Honour School of Literae Humaniores).   10

   (v) *Art under the Roman Empire, AD 14–337*, (IV.4 as specified for the Honour School of Literae Humaniores).

   (vi) Hellenistic Art and Archaeology, 330–30 BC (as specified for the Honour School of Literae Humaniores IV.3).

   (vii) The Hellenistic World: societies and cultures, c.300 BC–c.100 BC (as specified   15
for the Honour School of Literae Humaniores I.9).]

[For students starting from MT 2015: 409: *The Hellenistic World: societies and cultures, c.300 BC–100 BC*

   411: *Politics, Society and Culture from Nero to Hadrian*
   412: *Religions in the Greek and Roman World, c.31 BC–AD 312*   20
   457: *Athenian democracy in the Classical Age*
   601: *The Greeks and the Mediterranean World c.950–500 BC*
   603: *Hellenistic Art and Archaeology, 330–30 BC*
   604: *Art under the Roman Empire, AD 14–337*

The individual specification and prescribed texts for subject 457 will be pub-   25
lished for candidates in the Ancient and Modern History Handbook by Monday of Week 0 of Michaelmas Term each year for the academic year ahead. All other subjects under III(b) will be as specified for the Honour School of Literae Humaniores.]

IV. SPECIAL SUBJECTS   30
[For students starting before MT 2015: *Either,* (*a*) any one of the Special Subjects as specified for the Honour School of History (one paper and one extended essay);

or, (*b*) any one of the following Special Subjects in Ancient History (two papers), provided that any candidate who offers alternative III (*a*) above may only offer alternative IV (*b*)   35

   (i) *Alexander the Great and his Early Successors (336–302 BC)* (as specified for the Honour School of Literae Humaniores I. 8).

   (ii) *Cicero: Politics and Thought in the Late Republic* (as specified for the Honour School of Literae Humaniores I. 9).

The individual detailed specifications and prescribed texts for the Further and   40
Special subjects as specified for the Honour School of History will be given in the Handbook for the Honour School of History. This will be published by the History Board by Monday of Week 1 of the first Michaelmas Full Term of candidates' work for the Honour School.]

[For students starting from MT 2015: *Either,* (*a*) any one of the Special Subjects as   45
specified for the Honour School of History (one paper and one extended essay);

or, (*b*) any one of the following Special Subjects in Ancient History, provided that any candidate who offers alternative III (*a*) above may only offer alternative IV (*b*)

458: *Alexander the Great and his Early Successors (336–302 bc) (two papers)*
460: *Cicero: Politics and Thought in the Late Republic (two papers)*
461: *The Greek City in the Roman World from Dio Chrysostom to John Chrysostom.*
This option will be examined by a 3-hour commentary paper and an extended essay of between 5,000 and 6,000 words (including footnotes but excluding bibliography). The essay shall be on a topic or theme selected by the candidate from a question paper published by the examiners on Friday of Week 4 of Michaelmas Term in the year of examination. The candidate must deliver two copies of the essay by hand to the Examination Schools (addressed to the Chair of Examiners, Honour School of Ancient and Modern History, Examination Schools, High Street, Oxford) not later than 12 noon on Friday of Week 0 of Hilary Term of the year of examination. A certificate, signed by the candidate to the effect that each essay is the candidate's own work, and that the candidate has read the Faculty's guidelines on plagiarism, must be presented together with the submission. The University's regulations on Late Submission of Work will apply.

Detailed specifications and prescribed texts for subjects 458, 460, and 461 above will be given in the Handbook for the Honour School of Ancient and Modern History. The individual detailed specifications and prescribed texts for the Further and Special subjects as specified for the Honour School of History will be given in the Handbook for the Honour School of History. Both handbooks will be published by the History Board by Monday of Week 1 of the first Michaelmas Full Term of candidates' work for the Honour School.]

Depending on the availability of teaching resources, not all Further and Special Subjects will be available to all candidates in every year. Candidates and Ancient and Modern History tutors will be circulated by the beginning of the fourth week of the first Hilary Full Term of their work for the Honour School with (i) details of any Further and Special Subjects which will not be available for the following year, (ii) the supplement to the Handbook for the Honour School of History. This book will contain full specifications and prescribed texts for any Further or Special Subjects specified for Modern History introduced for the following year, and any amendments to the specifications and prescribed texts for existing Further and Special Subjects approved by the History Board by its first meeting of the preceding Hilary Term.

V. DISCIPLINES OF HISTORY

Each candidate shall be examined in the *Disciplines of History* in accordance with regulation V of the Honour School of History.

VI. A THESIS FROM ORIGINAL RESEARCH

Regulation VI of the Honour School of History applies with the following modifications:

Cl. 3.(a) (For the avoidance of doubt) the Arnold Ancient History Prize and the Barclay Head Prize in Numismatics are to be read with the schedule.

Cl. 5. For 'Honour School of History' read 'Honour School of Ancient and Modern History'. For theses concerning the years before AD 285 read 'Chair of Examiners, Honour School of Ancient and Modern History' for 'Chair of the Examiners, Honour School of History'.

Cl. 8. For 'Chair of Examiners, Honour School of History' read 'Chair of Examiners, Honour School of Ancient and Modern History'.

VII. AN OPTIONAL ADDITIONAL THESIS

Regulation VII *An Optional Additional Thesis* of the Honour School of History shall apply with the following modifications:

Cl. 4. For dissertations concerning the years before AD 285 read 'Chair of Examiners, Honour School of Ancient and Modern History' for 'Chair of the Examiners, Honour School of History'.

Cl. 7. For 'Chair of Examiners, Honour School of History' read 'Chair of Examiners, Honours School of Ancient and Modern History'.

VIII. AN OPTIONAL LANGUAGE PAPER

[**For students starting before MT 2015:** Intermediate Ancient Greek *or* Intermediate Latin or Advanced Ancient Greek or Advanced Latin.   5

The individual specifications and prescribed texts for *Intermediate Ancient Greek, Intermediate Latin, Advanced Ancient Greek and Advanced Latin* will be published for candidates in the Ancient and Modern History Handbook by Monday of Week 0 of Michaelmas Term each year for the academic year ahead.]

[**For students starting from MT 2015:** 571: Intermediate Ancient Greek or 572:   10
Intermediate Latin or 573: Advanced Ancient Greek or 574: Advanced Latin.

The individual specifications and prescribed texts for subjects 571–574 will be published for candidates in the Ancient and Modern History Handbook by Monday of Week 0 of Michaelmas Term each year for the academic year ahead.]

Any candidate whose native language is not English may bring a bilingual (native   15
language to English) dictionary for use in any of the language papers offered under regulation VIII.

HONOUR SCHOOL OF ARCHAEOLOGY AND ANTHROPOLOGY

A

1. The examination in the Honour School of Archaeology and Anthropology shall consist of such subjects in Archaeology and Anthropology as the Social Sciences   5
Board shall prescribe by regulation from time to time.

2. No candidate shall be admitted to the examination in this school unless he or she has either passed or been exempted from the First Public Examination.

3. The examination shall be under the supervision of the Social Sciences Board. Under the overall direction of the board, the examination shall be administered by the   10
School of Archaeology and the School of Anthropology, which shall jointly appoint a standing committee to advise the board as necessary in respect of this examination, and of Honour Moderations and the Preliminary Examination in Archaeology and Anthropology.

4. Candidates will be required to take part in approved fieldwork as an integral part   15
of their course. The fieldwork requirement will normally have been discharged before the Long Vacation of the second year of the course.

B

Candidates are required to offer the following subjects:
1. Social analysis and interpretation.   20
2. Cultural representations, beliefs, and practices.
3. Landscape and Ecology.
4. Urbanisation and change in complex societies: comparative approaches.
5., 6., and 7. An approved combination of three optional subjects, from Schedule A (Anthropology) and Schedule B (Archaeology) [see below] or any other optional   25
subject approved by the Committee for the School of Archaeology or the Committee for the School of Anthropology. To encourage a wide-ranging understanding of archaeology and anthropology, options shall be chosen in such a way that they constitute three independent, non-overlapping subjects.
8. A thesis, of not more than 15,000 words, which may be based on research in   30
either archaeology or anthropology or on an interdisciplinary topic.

Candidates may be examined *viva voce*.

Schedule A (Anthropology)

(*a*) Culture and Society of West Africa
(*b*) South Asia   35
(*c*) Lowland South America
(*d*) Gender theories and realities cross cultural perspectives
(*e*) Understanding Museums and Collections
(*f*) Japanese society
(*g*) **[For students starting before MT 2015:** The anthropology of medicine]   40
[For students starting from MT 2015: Medical Anthropology]
(*h*) Anthropology of Europe

Schedule B (Archaeology)

(*a*) The Later Prehistory of Europe
(*b*) Archaeology of Southern African Hunter-Gatherers   45
(*c*) Farming and early states in Sub-Saharan Africa

(*d*) Mesopotamia and Egypt from the emergence of complex society to *c*.2000 BC
(*e*) Mesopotamia and Egypt 1000–500 BC
(*f*) The Late Bronze Age and Early Iron Age Aegean
(*g*) The Greeks and the Mediterranean World *c*.950–500 BC
(*h*) Greek archaeology and art *c*.500–323 BC   5
(*i*) Roman Archaeology: Cities and settlement under the Empire
(*j*) Art under the Roman Empire, AD 14–336
(*k*) The emergence of Medieval Europe AD 400–900
(*l*) Byzantium: the transition from Antiquity to the Middle Ages, AD 500–1100
(*m*) Science-based methods in Archaeology   10
(*n*) Archaeology of Modern Human Origins
(*o*) Anglo-Saxon Society and Economy in the Early Christian Period
(*p*) Archaeology and Geographical Information Systems
(*q*) Landscape Archaeology
(*r*) Biological Techniques in Environmental Archaeology   15
(*s*) From hunting and gathering to states and empires in South-west Asia
(*t*) Physical Anthropology and Human Osteoarchaeology
(*u*) The Archaeology of Minoan Crete 3200–10000 BC
(*v*) Hellenistic Archaeology, 330–30 BC

Because of the potential overlap in subject matter, approval will not be given to   20
candidates who wish to select from Schedule B (Archaeology) either two of papers
(*f*), (*g*), or (*j*), or both papers (*k*) and (*l*).

Some options may not be available in every year. Candidates will be circulated a list
of options offered for examination in the following two years of study by Friday of the
eighth week of the Michaelmas Full Term.   25

Notice of the options to be offered by candidates must be submitted not later than
the Friday in the fourth week of the Michaelmas Full Term immediately preceding the
examination.

Thesis

1. (*a*) The subject of every thesis shall to the satisfaction of the regulating authority   30
           concerned fall within the field of Archaeology or Anthropology or both.
    (*b*) The subject of the thesis may, but need not, overlap a subject or period on
           which the candidate offers papers. Candidates are warned, however, that
           they must avoid repetition in the papers of material used in their thesis, and
           that they will not be given credit for material extensively repeated.   35
    (*c*) Candidates must submit through their college, to the Chair of the Standing
           Committee for the Undergraduate Degree in Archaeology and Anthropology
           (c/o the Secretary of the Standing Committee, Institute of Archaeology,
           Beaumont Street), the title of the proposed thesis, together with (*a*) a synopsis
           of the subject in about 100 words; and (*b*) a letter of support from the tutor   40
           who will supervise the thesis, not later than Monday of the noughth week of
           the Trinity Full Term preceding that in which the examination is held.
    (*d*) The Standing Committee for the Undergraduate Degree in Archaeology and
           Anthropology will decide as soon as possible, and in every case by the end of
           the fifth week of the Michaelmas Full Term preceding the examination,   45
           whether or not to approve the title, and will advise candidates of its decision
           forthwith.

2. Every thesis must be the candidate's own work, although it is expected that
tutors will discuss with candidates the proposed field of study, the sources available,
and the method of presentation. Tutors may also read and comment on a first draft.   50

Candidates must sign a certificate stating that the thesis is their own work, and their
tutors shall countersign the certificate affirming that they have assisted the candidate

no more than these regulations allow. This certificate must be presented at the same time that the thesis is submitted, but in a separate sealed envelope addressed to the Chair of the Examiners.

3. Theses previously submitted for the Honour School of Archaeology and Anthropology may be resubmitted. No thesis will be accepted if it has already been submitted, wholly or substantially, for another final honour school or degree of this University or a degree of any other institution. The certificate must also contain confirmation that the thesis has not already been so submitted.

4. No thesis shall be ineligible because it has been submitted, in whole or in part, for any scholarship or prize of this University advertised in the *Oxford University Gazette*.

5. No thesis shall exceed 15,000 words in length, that limit to include all notes but not bibliographies, catalogues of material evidence, gazetteers, or technical appendices.

All theses must be typed in double-spacing on one side of A4 paper, and must be bound or held firmly in a stiff cover. Two copies must be submitted to the chair of the examiners, and a third copy must be retained by the candidate. All copies must bear the candidate's examination number but not his or her name.

6. The thesis must be sent, not later than noon on Friday of the ninth week of Hilary Full Term preceding the examination, to the Chair of the Examiners, Honour School of Archaeology and Anthropology, Examination Schools, High Street, Oxford.

Candidates may be examined viva voce.

HONOUR SCHOOL OF BIOLOGICAL SCIENCES

A

1. The subject of the Honour School of Biological Sciences shall be the study of Biological Sciences.

2. No candidate shall be admitted to examination in this school unless he or she has either passed or been exempted from the First Public Examination.

3. The examination in this school shall be under the supervision of the Mathematical, Physical and Life Sciences Board, which shall prescribe the necessary regulations.

4. The examination in Biological Sciences shall consist of Part I (taken at a time not less than two terms after passing the First Public Examination) and Part II (taken at a time not less than five terms after passing the First Public Examination).

5. The name of a candidate shall not be published in a Results List until he or she has completed all parts of the examination. The examiners shall give due consideration to the performance in all parts of the respective examinations.

6. Candidates will be expected to show knowledge based on practical work. This requirement shall normally be satisfied by the examiners' assessment of the practical laboratory work and Quantitative Methods classes work done by candidates in Part I based on attendance records and/or marks awarded.

7. Exceptionally, the examiners may require a candidate to submit all their practical notebooks.

8. Candidates whose overall practical performance is not deemed satisfactory by the examiners may have their degree class reduced. If the work is judged by the examiners to be insufficient to warrant the award of Honours they may either be deemed to have failed the examination, or may, at the discretion of the examiners, be awarded a Pass.

B

1. The subjects of the examination shall be those prescribed in the Regulations for Parts I and II.

2. The examiners will permit the use of any hand-held calculator subject to the conditions set out under the heading 'Use of calculators in examinations' in the Regulations for the Conduct of University Examinations.

3. *Supplementary Subjects*

    (*a*) In addition, candidates may offer themselves for examination in one or more Supplementary Subjects.

    (*b*) Candidates for Supplementary Subjects may offer themselves for examination in the academic year preceding that in which they take the Part II written examinations of the Final Honour School.

    (*c*) Candidates awarded a pass in a Supplementary Subject examination may not retake the same Supplementary Subject examination.

    (*d*) The Supplementary Subjects available in any year will be published, together with the term in which each subject will be examined, in the Final Honour School Handbook (Section 1) at the start of Michaelmas Term of the academic year in which the Supplementary Subjects may be taken.

PART I

1. The examination for Part I shall normally be taken at the start of Trinity Term of the candidate's second year.

2. Further details of the requirements for Part I shall be set out in the Final Honour School Handbook (Section 1), which is published annually at the start of Michaelmas Term of the candidate's second year.

3. *Written papers*

Assessment in Part I will consist of three written papers as follows. Knowledge of first year coursework will be assumed.

Paper 1: Evolution
Paper 2: Quantitative Methods
Paper 3: Essay Paper

In Paper 3, candidates will be required to answer four questions, with no more than one from each of the following themes: (i) Animal Behaviour; (ii) Adaptations to the Environment; (iii) Cell and Developmental Biology; (iv) Disease; (v) Ecology; (vi) Plants and People.

The written papers for Part I may be taken only once.

4. *Practical Coursework*

All candidates shall be assessed as to their practical ability through their performance in three practical blocks and in Quantitative Methods classes. The following provisions apply:

(a) The Chair of the Biological Sciences Steering Committee, or a deputy, shall make available to the examiners, at the end of the term in which the written examinations in Part II are held, records showing the extent to which each candidate has completed the prescribed coursework to a satisfactory standard.

(b) The examiners may require a candidate to submit all their practical notebooks. Such candidates will be named in a list posted by the day of the first written paper in Part II of the examination. Each notebook submitted shall be accompanied by a certificate signed by the candidate indicating that the notebook is the candidate's own work.

(c) In assessing the record of coursework undertaken, the examiners shall have regard to the attendance record of the candidates at the classes provided, and to the marks awarded for the classes provided.

5. The examiners will issue a list of candidates deemed to have completed Part I of the examination, in the form of the completion of the three written papers, and satisfactory performance in the three practical blocks and Quantitative Methods classes.

6. Under exceptional circumstances, candidates who have not been able to complete sufficient practicals may be allowed to fulfil the practical requirement in their third year.

PART II

1. The examination for Part II shall normally be taken during Trinity Term of the candidate's third year.

2. In Part II, a candidate who obtains only a pass, or fails to satisfy the examiners, may enter again for Part II of the examination on one, but no more than one, subsequent occasion.

3. Further details of the requirements for Part II shall be set out in the Guidelines on Projects and Course Assignments and in the Final Honour School Handbook

(Section 2). The Guidelines on Projects and Course Assignments are published annually at the end of Hilary Term of the candidate's second year. The Final Honour School Handbook (Section 2) is published annually at the end of Hilary Term of the candidate's second year.

4. In Part II, candidates will select from a number of Options, and complete a   5
Research Project and two Course Assignments. The Options may be varied from time
to time by the Biological Sciences Steering Committee, and such variations shall be
notified by publication in the Final Honour School Handbook (Section 2) by the end
of Week 8 of Hilary Term of the academic year preceding the first examination of the
changed options. Each candidate will be expected to have studied at least six Options   10
in order to address the requirements of Paper 6, and to have prepared sufficient of
those Options in depth to be able to address the requirements of Papers 5 and 7.

5. Assessment in Part II will consist of four written papers, each of three hours'
duration, submission of a Research Project dissertation, and two Course Assignments,
one of which will be examined as an Oral Presentation.   15

6. *Written papers*

Four written papers, each of three hours, will be set during Trinity Term of the third
year. The papers will be as follows:

Paper 4: General Paper
Paper 5: Long Essay Paper   20
Paper 6: Short Essay Paper
Paper 7: Data Interpretation Paper

In the General Paper, candidates will be required to answer two questions and will
be expected to bring together knowledge of different areas of Biology covered in the
Course. In the Long Essay Paper, candidates will be required to answer three ques-   25
tions, with no more than one from any specific Option. In the Short Essay Paper,
candidates will be required to answer six questions, with no more than one from any
specific Option. In the Data Interpretation Paper, candidates will be required to
answer four questions.

7. *Project dissertation*   30

(i) *Form and subject of the project*

The project shall consist of original experiments, fieldwork or computer-based
Research Project in any area of biology done by the candidate alone or in collaboration with others (where such collaboration is, for instance, needed to produce results in
the time available). When choosing a Research Project, candidates must bear in mind   35
the prohibition on duplicating material in different parts of the examination.

(ii) *Registration*

Candidates must register the provisional title of their project and the name of their
supervisor to the Examinations Co-ordinator no later than noon on Friday of Week 8
of Hilary Term of their second year. Candidates must submit their completed safety   40
registration form to the appropriate Departmental Safety Officer by the same deadline.

(iii) *Residence*

Candidates undertaking project work outside of Oxford will be permitted by the
Director of Undergraduate Teaching for Biological Sciences, subject to the written   45
approval also of the Senior Tutor of the candidate's college, to spend a maximum of
two weeks outside of Oxford during Trinity Term of their second year working at a
supervised field site or another university/institution in the UK or overseas, in accordance with clause 2.8 of the General Regulations for the First and Second Public

Examination regulations pertaining to residence. Candidates will still be liable for their College battels, if applicable, during this time.

(iv) *Examination*

Candidates shall submit to the examiners a dissertation based on their project according to guidelines that will be published in the Guidelines on Projects and Course Assignments in the academic year preceding the examination. The project dissertation shall be of not more than 7,000 words, excluding any tables, figures, or references, and must be prefaced by an Abstract of not more than 250 words, to be included within the word limit.

(v) *Submission and assessment of project-based written work*

The project report (two copies) must be legibly typed or word-processed (double line spacing to be used throughout) on one side only of A4 paper, held firmly in a stiff cover, and submitted on or before 12 noon on the Monday of Week 2 of Hilary Full Term of the academic year in which Part II of the examination is taken. It must be addressed to the Examination Schools, High Street, Oxford, for the Chair of Examiners for the Final Honour School of Biological Sciences. Each project report shall be accompanied by a certificate signed by the candidate indicating that the project report is the candidate's own work. This certificate shall be submitted separately in a sealed envelope addressed to the Chair of Examiners. No report will be accepted if it has already been submitted, wholly or substantially, for another Honour School or degree of this University, or for a degree of any other institution.

In all cases, the examiners shall obtain and consider a written report from each supervisor indicating the extent of the input made by the candidate to the outcome of the project and also any unforeseen difficulties associated with the project (e.g. unexpected technical issues or problems in the availability of materials, equipment, or literature or other published data). Material in a candidate's dissertation must not duplicate material that has been included in the submitted Course Assignments.

8. Course Assignments

(i) *Form and subject of the Course Assignments*

Each candidate must complete two Course Assignments. One assignment shall be examined by means of a written essay, and one shall be examined by means of an Oral Presentation as set out below. The precise format of the Course Assignment may vary between Options and will be specified by the Biological Sciences Steering Committee.

The written essay shall be of not more than 3,000 words, excluding any tables, figures, or references, and must be prefaced by an Abstract of not more than 250 words, to be included within the word limit. All sources used in the essay must be fully documented. The written essay (two copies) must be legibly typed or word-processed on one side only of A4 paper, held firmly in a stiff cover. The Oral Presentation shall be a maximum of fifteen minutes in duration, followed by ten minutes of questions. The Oral Presentation should use appropriate audio-visual aids as specified in the Guidelines on Projects and Course Assignments. Candidates shall also submit an Abstract of the Oral Presentation of not more than 500 words. The Abstract (two copies) must be legibly typed or word-processed on one side only of A4 paper.

Candidates may discuss the proposed topic for both the written essay and the Oral Presentation, the sources available, and the method of presentation with an adviser. The adviser for the written essay may also read and comment on a first draft. Candidates shall not deal with substantially the same material in their Course Assignments as is covered in their project report.

(ii) *Registration*

Each assignment will be on a topic proposed by the student and approved by the Chair of the Biological Sciences Steering Committee. The approval of assignments shall be given not later than Friday of the seventh week of the Michaelmas Full Term of the academic year in which the examination is taken.

(iii) *Authorship*

For each assignment, candidates must sign a certificate stating that the assignment is their own work. This certificate must be submitted at the same time as the essay and Abstract in a sealed envelope addressed to the Chair of Examiners. 5

(iv) *Submission*

The written Course Assignment (two copies), the Abstract for the Oral Presentation (two copies) and the sealed envelope containing the certificate of authorship, should be submitted in an envelope clearly labelled with the candidate's number 10 by noon on Friday of 0th week of the Trinity Term of the academic year in which the examination is taken. The envelope should be addressed to the Examination Schools, High Street, Oxford for the Chair of the Examiners in the Final Honour School of Biological Sciences. Assignments previously submitted for the Honour School of Biological Sciences may be resubmitted. No assignment will be accepted if it has 15 already been submitted, wholly or substantially, for another degree in the University or elsewhere; and each certificate must also contain a confirmation that the assignment has not already been so submitted. Each essay and each Abstract shall clearly indicate on the first page the part of the examination and the subject under which the assignment is submitted. Further guidance on the essay and Oral Presentation will be 20 published in the Guidelines on Projects and Course Assignments.

HONOUR SCHOOL OF CELL AND SYSTEMS BIOLOGY

A

1. The subject of the Honour School of Cell and Systems Biology shall be all aspects of the scientific study of the development and functioning of living organisms with particular but not exclusive reference to mammals.

2. No candidate shall be admitted to examination in this school unless he or she has either passed or been exempted from the First Public Examination.

3. The examination in this school shall be under the supervision of the Medical Sciences Board, which shall make regulations concerning it.

4. The examination in Cell and Systems Biology shall consist of two parts: Part I and Part II.

5. No candidate shall be admitted to the Part II examination in this school unless he or she has completed the Part I examination in this school.

6. The examination for Part I will take place during Week 0 or 1 in Trinity Term of the candidate's second year. The examination for Part II will take place during Trinity Term of the candidate's third year.

7. For the Part I options provided by the Department of Experimental Psychology, candidates shall be examined by such of the Public Examiners in the Honour School of Experimental Psychology as may be required. For the written papers in Part II which are as specified for the Honour School of Medical Sciences, and the Research Project, candidates shall be examined by such of the Public Examiners in the Honour School of Medical Sciences as may be required.

8. In addition to the form of examination prescribed below, candidates may be examined viva voce in either part of the examination.

9. Candidates for Part I and Part II may offer themselves for examination in one or more of the *Supplementary Subjects*. The *Supplementary Subjects* available in any year will be notified to students annually during Trinity Term. Account shall be taken of a candidate's results in any such subject in the candidate's overall classification in the Honour School of Cell and Systems Biology. Candidates awarded a pass in a Supplementary Subject examination may not retake the same Supplementary Subject examination.

B

PART I

1. Candidates will attend lectures and practicals in options selected from a list published to students by the end of Week 8 of Hilary Term in the year preceding the examination. Each option will have a number of units ascribed to it. Candidates will be required to study options totalling ten units. The handbook for the course will specify how many units are assigned to each option, and which options are recommended to proceed to particular advanced options in Part II.

2. Two written papers will be set:

    (i) Paper I will be a three-hour examination comprising a selection of questions requiring short answers. Candidates will be required to answer those questions relating to their chosen options.

(ii) Paper II will be a two-hour essay paper. Candidates will be required to answer questions from a selection relating to the different options that they have studied.

3. If, in Paper II of the Part I Examination, a candidate presents essentially the same information on more than one occasion, then credit will be given in only the first 5 instance.

4. Candidates will be required to undertake practical work and submit written reports as specified in the course handbook which will constitute part of the examination. On the basis of attendance records and the submitted reports, the Course Director, or a deputy, shall make available to the Examiners, at the end of Week 0 10 of Trinity Term in which the examinations are held, evidence showing the extent and the standard to which each candidate has completed the prescribed practical work. Practical work cannot normally be retaken. Candidates whose attendance or performance is deemed unsatisfactory will forfeit one quarter of the marks in the Part I examination, the outcome of which will be carried forward to the Part II 15 Examination.

Part II

1. Each candidate must offer timed written examination papers and a project report based on a research project.

2. The options of the school shall be: 20

A Neuroscience
B Molecular Medicine
C Cardiovascular, Renal, and Respiratory Biology
D Infection and Immunity
E Cellular Physiology and Pharmacology 25

as specified for the Honour School of Medical Sciences.

3. Each candidate must offer four written papers: Paper 1 for *two* chosen options, Paper 2, and Paper 3 as specified for the Honour School of Medical Sciences, except that Paper 1 for the second chosen option will require candidates to answer two questions in two hours. 30

4. The Research Project

The research project will normally be carried out in the Trinity Term of the candidate's second year and the Michaelmas Term of the candidate's third year.

(i) *Form, subject, and approval of the project*

The project shall consist of original experiments carried out by the candidate alone 35 or in collaboration with others (where such collaboration is, for instance, needed to produce results in the time available).

Each project shall be supervised, and the topic and supervisor shall be approved on behalf of the Medical Sciences Board by the Course Director, or a deputy. A list of approved project titles and their supervisors shall be published no later than Friday of 40 Week 1 of Hilary Term in the academic year preceding the examination, and allocation of these projects to candidates shall be carried out through the Faculty of Physiological Sciences Undergraduate Studies Office no later than the end of Week 8 of that term.

As an alternative to the allocation process, a candidate may apply to undertake a 45 project that is not on the approved list. Such application must be made no later than Friday of Week 4 of Hilary Term in the academic year preceding the examination. The candidate must submit the title of their proposed research project, provide a brief outline of the subject matter and supply details of supervision arrangements. The decision on the application shall be made by the Course Director, or a deputy, and shall be communicated to the candidate as soon as possible, and work should not start on the project until approval has been given. Candidates should allow at least one week for the process of approval, and should bear in mind that an application may be referred for clarification or may be refused.

(ii) *Submission of the Project Report*

The length and format of the Project Report based on the project shall be according to guidelines published by the Medical Sciences Board in Week 8 of Hilary Term of the academic year preceding the year of examination. Material in a candidate's Project Report must not be duplicated in any answer given in a written examination paper. Project Reports previously submitted for the Honour School of Cell and Systems Biology may be resubmitted. No Project Report will be accepted if it has already been submitted, wholly or substantially, for another Honour School or degree of this University or for a degree of any other institution.

Project Reports (three copies) must be sent to the Chair of Examiners, Honour School of Cell and Systems Biology, Examination Schools, High Street, Oxford, not later than noon on the Friday of Week 8 of Hilary Term in the academic year in which the candidate intends to take the examination. The copies shall be accompanied (in a separate sealed envelope) by a certificate signed by each candidate indicating that the research project is the candidate's own work and that the supervisor has commented on at least one draft of the Project Report. In the case of work that has been produced in collaboration, the certificate shall indicate the extent of the candidate's own contribution. Each candidate will be required to submit a draft of their Project Report to their supervisor no later than two weeks before the specified deadline for submission to Schools.

In exceptional cases, where through unforeseen circumstances a research project produces no useable results (i.e. not even negative or ambiguous results), the candidate may apply through his or her college to the Course Director, or a deputy, for permission to submit a concise review of the scientific context and the aims of the work that was attempted, in place of the normal Project Report. Such an application must be accompanied by supporting evidence from the supervisor of the project. The concise review to be submitted in such circumstances should be comparable in length to the Report of a successful research project, will be presented orally to the examiners, and will be examined *viva voce* in the usual way for a research project. The examiners will be advised that substantive results could not be produced.

The examiners shall obtain and consider a written report from each supervisor indicating the extent of the input made by the candidate to the outcome of the project and also any unforeseen difficulties associated with the project (e.g. unexpected technical issues or problems in the availability of materials, equipment, or literature or other published data).

(iii) *Oral Assessment of Project-based Written Work*

In addition, each candidate shall make a brief oral presentation of their project to a group of two examiners (or examiners and assessors appointed to ensure an adequate representation of expertise), after which, the candidate shall be examined *viva voce* on the project. The form of the presentation to the examiners shall be specified in guidelines published by the Medical Sciences Board.

5. If, in the Part II Examination, a candidate presents essentially the same information on more than one occasion, then credit will be given in only the first instance.

6. The weighting of marks for the five exercises required of each candidate shall be 25 per cent for the Project Report based on the research project, 15 per cent for each of Papers 1, 2, and 3, except that Paper 1 for the second chosen option will carry 10 per cent of the marks. Marks carried forward from the Part I examination will account for the remaining 20 per cent of the candidate's overall result for the Honour School of Cell and Systems Biology.

5

HONOUR SCHOOL OF CHEMISTRY

A

1. The subject of the Honour School of Chemistry shall be the study of Chemistry.

2. No candidate shall be admitted to examination in this school unless he or she has either passed or been exempted from the First Public Examination.

3. The examination in this school shall be under the supervision of the Mathematical, Physical and Life Sciences Board, which shall prescribe the necessary regulations.

4. The examination in Chemistry shall consist of three parts: IA, IB, II.

5. A candidate shall not be awarded a classified degree until he or she has completed all parts of the examinations, and has been adjudged worthy of honours by the examiners in Part I (Part IA and Part IB) and Part II of the examination in consecutive years. The Examiners shall give due consideration to the performance in all parts of the respective examinations.

6. The examiners shall be entitled to award a Pass to candidates in Part I (Part IA and Part IB) who have reached a standard considered adequate but who have not been adjudged worthy of honours.

7. A candidate adjudged worthy of Honours in Part I (Parts IA and IB) and worthy of Honours in Part II may supplicate for the Degree of Master of Chemistry, provided that the candidate has fulfilled all the conditions for admission to a degree of the University.

8. A candidate who passes Part I (Parts IA and IB) or who is adjudged worthy of Honours in Part I (Parts IA and IB), but who does not enter Part II, or fails to obtain Honours in Part II, is permitted to supplicate for the degree of Bachelor of Arts in Chemistry (pass or unclassified Honours, as appropriate); provided that no such candidate may later enter or re-enter the Part II year or supplicate for the degree of Master of Chemistry; and provided in each case that the candidate has fulfilled all the conditions for admission to a degree of the University.

9. Candidates will be required to complete a core practical requirement: provided that this requirement may be reduced for candidates who have passed one or more supplementary subjects. Details of the requirements and the eligible Supplementary Subjects shall be prescribed in the Course Handbook. Exceptionally, the examiners may require a candidate to take a practical examination.

B

1. In the following, 'the Course Handbook' refers to the Chemistry Undergraduate Course Handbook, posted annually at the start of Michaelmas Term by the Faculty of Chemistry.

2. The examiners will permit the use of any hand-held calculator subject to the conditions set out under the heading 'Use of calculators in examinations' in the Regulations for the Conduct of University Examinations and further elaborated in the Course Handbook.

3. The syllabus for Parts IA and IB shall be published in the Course Handbook.

4. Supplementary Subjects.

(i) Candidates may offer themselves for examination in one or more Supplementary Subjects, provided that no more than three Supplementary Subjects may be offered in total.

(ii) Candidates awarded a pass in a Supplementary Subject examination may not retake the same Supplementary Subject examination.

(iii) Supplementary Subjects may be offered in all or any of the years in which candidates take any Part of the Second Public Examination.

(iv) The Supplementary Subjects available in any year will be published, together with the term in which each subject will be examined, in the Course Handbook in the academic year in which the courses are delivered. Regulations governing the use of calculators in individual Supplementary Subjects will be notified in the Course Handbook.

(v) Where a Language Supplementary Subject is available, entry of candidates for examination in Language Supplementary Subjects shall require the approval of the Chair of the Chemistry Academic Board and the Director of the Language Centre or their deputies. Approval shall not be given to candidates who have, at the start of the course, already acquired demonstrable skills exceeding the target learning outcomes in the chosen language.

(vi) In determining the place of candidates in the Results List the Examiners shall take account of performance in any Supplementary Subjects which have been offered.

Part IA

Candidates are not permitted to enter their names for examination in Part IA until they have entered upon the fifth term from their matriculation.

Part IA shall be entered on one occasion only.

In the Part IA examination, one compulsory paper will be set in each of Inorganic, Organic, and Physical Chemistry, covering the fundamental aspects of material from Years 1 and 2.

Candidates may not be examined viva voce in Part IA.

Marks obtained at Part IA will be carried over to Part IB.

Part IB

Candidates are not permitted to enter their names for examination in Part IB until they have entered upon the eighth term from their matriculation, or before sitting all the papers set for Part IA in a previous year.

In the Part IB examination, there will be two compulsory papers in each of Inorganic, Organic, and Physical Chemistry, covering material in the core courses of Years 1–3. In addition, there will be one Option Paper, which will examine the content of the Option courses, but will also require knowledge of core course material. The Option Paper will offer a choice of three questions from at least twelve, and ten minutes reading time will be allowed.

Heads of the three main Sections of the Chemistry Department, or their deputies, and the IT Training Officer, shall make available to the Examiners records showing the extent to which each candidate has pursued an adequate course in laboratory work and in IT. Only that work completed and marked by 5 p.m. of the Friday of the fourth week of the Trinity Term in which the candidate takes Part IB shall be included in these records. The Examiners will require evidence of satisfactory completion of the core practical requirement, or the reduced requirement in the case of candidates who have passed one or more Supplementary Subjects. In determining the place of candidates in the Results List the Examiners shall take account of the marks reported for the core practical requirement.

Satisfactory completion of the prescribed core practical requirement, (or of a reduced core requirement if a Supplementary Subject is passed), is an absolute requirement for the award of Honours at Part IB and for progression to Part II. Satisfactory completion of a smaller core practical requirement will be required for the award of a Pass degree at Part I. The details of these threshold requirements shall be   5
published in the Course Handbook.

Candidates may be examined viva voce at the Examiners' discretion in Part IB.

A candidate who in Part I (i.e. Part IA and Part IB together) obtains only a pass, or fails to satisfy the examiners, may enter again for Part IB of the examination on one, but no more than one, subsequent occasion subject to the following limitations. Part   10
IB consists of two parts, a set of written examinations and the practical course. A candidate may fail to be awarded honours at Part I for any of the following reasons. The precise circumstances will determine which parts of Part IB may be re-taken/re-entered for.

   (i) The overall mark at Part I is insufficient for honours, but the honours practical   15
       requirement set out in cl. A.9 above is complete and the practical mark is
       sufficient for honours. In this case the candidate will only be permitted to re-
       enter the Part IB written examinations, and the Practical mark will be carried
       forward.
  (ii) The overall mark at Part I is insufficient for honours, and although the marks   20
       for the Part I written examination are sufficient for honours and sufficient
       practicals have been completed to fulfil the requirement set out in cl. A.9
       above, the marks for the practical course are not sufficient for honours. In
       this case the candidate will only be permitted to re-enter to complete the
       practical course to honours standard. The marks for the written examination   25
       will be carried forward.
 (iii) The overall mark at Part I is insufficient for honours, and although sufficient
       practicals have been completed to fulfil the requirement set out in cl. A.9
       above, the marks for both the written examination and the practical course
       are insufficient for honours. In this case, the candidate shall be permitted both   30
       to re-enter the Part IB written examinations and to complete the practical
       course to honours standard.
  (iv) The practical requirement set out in cl. A.9 above is incomplete, but the marks
       in the Part I written examination are sufficient for honours. In this case the
       candidate will only be permitted to re-enter to complete the practical require-   35
       ment to honours standard. The written examination marks will be carried
       forward.
   (v) The practical requirement set out in cl. A.9 above is incomplete and the overall
       mark obtained in Part I is insufficient for honours. In this case the candidate
       shall be permitted both to re-enter the Part IB examination and to complete the   40
       practical requirement to honours standard.

Part II

No candidate may present him or herself for examination in Part II unless he or she has been adjudged worthy of honours by the examiners in Part I (Part IA and Part IB). Part II shall be entered on one occasion only.   45

Candidates, who must have been judged worthy of Honours by the Examiners in Part I (Part IA and Part IB) in a previous year, must present a record of investigations carried out under the supervision of one of the following:

   (i) any professor, reader, university lecturer, departmental demonstrator, or senior
       research officer who is also an official member of the Faculty of Chemistry;   50
  (ii) any other person approved by the Chemistry Academic Board.

In case (ii), a co-supervisor as defined under (i) must also be approved, and so must the proposed project. Applications for project approval, including the names of the supervisor and a co-supervisor and a short project summary (not more than 250 words), should be sent by the student to the Chemistry Academic Board, c/o Chemistry Faculty Office, Inorganic Chemistry Laboratory, South Parks Road, by   5
Friday of the first week of Hilary Full Term preceding the intended Part II year. Students who are uncertain whether their intended Part II supervision is in category (ii) above should consult their College Tutor or the Chemistry Faculty Office.

Candidates shall be examined viva voce, and, if the Examiners think fit, in writing, on their investigations and matters relevant thereto. The Examiners may obtain a   10
report on the work of each candidate from the supervisor concerned.

Heads of the three main Sections of the Chemistry Department, or their deputies, shall make available to the Chemistry Faculty office not later than the Friday of the fourth week of the Hilary Full Term records giving notice of the subject of investigations for each candidate working in their section, together with evidence (a) that the   15
subject has been approved by the candidate's supervisor and (b), if it is to be carried out in a laboratory, that the person in charge of the laboratory considers that it is suitable for investigation in that laboratory. Candidates doing their project outside the Chemistry Department are responsible for ensuring that the subject of their investigations is submitted to the Chemistry Faculty office not later than the Friday of the   20
fourth week of the Hilary Full Term.

A candidate for Part II is required to send in, not later than noon on the Friday of the seventh week of the Trinity Full Term, a record of the investigations which he or she has carried out under the direction of his or her supervisor. Such record, which should conform in length and format with guidance which the examiners may give,   25
should be addressed 'The Examination Schools, Oxford, for the Chair of the Examiners in Part II of the Final Honour School of Chemistry' and should have included a Declaration of Authorship signed by the candidate that it is his or her own work.

Candidates for Part II are required to keep statutory residence and pursue their   30
studies at Oxford during a period of at least 38 weeks in three terms for the dates shown at: http://www.ox.ac.uk/about_the_university/university_year/dates_of_term.html.

HONOUR SCHOOL OF CLASSICAL ARCHAEOLOGY AND ANCIENT HISTORY

A

1. The Honour School of Classical Archaeology and Ancient History shall consist of such subjects as the Board of the Faculty of Classics shall prescribe by regulation from time to time.

2. No candidate shall be admitted to the examination in this school without either having passed, or having been exempted from, the First Public Examination.

3. The examination shall be under the supervision of the Board of the Faculty of Classics, which shall appoint a standing committee to consider matters relating to the examination and to the Preliminary Examination in Classical Archaeology and Ancient History.

4. Candidates shall be required to take part in approved fieldwork as an integral part of the course. The fieldwork requirement shall normally have been discharged before the **[For students starting before MT 2015:** Long Vacation following the second year of the course] **[For students starting from MT 2015:** beginning of Michaelmas Term in the candidate's second year].

Note: It cannot be guaranteed that university lectures or classes or college teaching will be available in all subjects in every academic year. Candidates are advised to consult their tutors about the availability of teaching when selecting their subjects.

B

1. Each candidate shall offer the following elements:

I–VI Six papers from the following options, of which at least one must be taken from each of A, B and C, and no more than one from F. At least two of the six papers must be archaeological (from B and D), and at least two must be historical (from C and E), unless a language paper is taken, as this can replace one of the archaeological or historical requirements.

[For students starting from MT 2015: Subjects 407–13 and 601–5 below will be examined in accordance with the regulations for the Honour School of Literae Humaniores. For each of these subjects, a detailed specification will be given in the Greats Handbook applicable to the relevant year of examination. Detailed specifications for all other subjects in the Honour School will be given in the CAAH Finals Handbook applicable to the relevant year of examination. Both handbooks will be published by Monday of Week 5 of Hilary Term two years preceding the examination.]

Any candidate whose native language is not English may bring a bilingual (native language to English) dictionary for use in any examination paper where candidates are required to translate Ancient Greek and/or Latin texts into English.

A. Integrated Classes

[For students starting before MT 2015: i. *Rome, Italy and the Hellenistic East c.300–100 BC: archaeology and history*

The course studies the political and cultural interaction and conflict between the Hellenistic East and Roman Italy. Candidates will be expected to show knowledge of the material, visual, and written evidence of the period and to show ability in interpreting it in its archaeological and historical contexts. Candidates should be familiar with the relevant archaeology of the following cities and sites: Pella, Alexandria, Pergamon, Ai Khanoum, Athens, Priene, Delos, Praeneste, Pompeii, Rome.

ii. *Imperial Culture and Society, c. AD 50–150: archaeology and history*

The course studies the complex social history and political culture of Rome and leading cities under the Empire, from the last Julio-Claudians to the Antonines, through the rich and diverse body of written and material evidence that survives from this period – monuments, art, inscriptions, and literary texts from a wide variety of genres.

Candidates should be familiar with the archaeology and major monuments of the period at the following sites and cities: Rome, Pompeii, Ostia, Beneventum, Tivoli; Fishbourne, Vindolanda, Hadrian's Wall; Timgad, Djemila; Athens, Aphrodisias, Ephesos, Masada. They should also show knowledge of written texts as specified for this course in the handbook for the Honour School of Classical Archaeology and Ancient History.]

[**For students starting from MT 2015:** 621: *Rome, Italy and the Hellenistic East c.300–100 BC: archaeology and history*

622: *Imperial Culture and Society, c. AD 50–150: archaeology and history*]

B. Core Papers: Classical Archaeology

[**For students starting before MT 2015:** i. *The Greeks and the Mediterranean World, c. 950–500 BC*

As specified for the Honour School of Literae Humaniores, subject IV.1.

ii. *Greek Art and Archaeology c.500–300 BC*

As specified for the Honour School of Literae Humaniores, subject IV.2.

iii. *Cities and Settlement under the Empire*

As specified for the Honour School of Literae Humaniores, subject IV.4.

iv. *Art under the Roman Empire, 14–337*

As specified for the Honour School of Literae Humaniores, subject IV.4.]

[**For students starting from MT 2015:** 601: *The Greeks and the Mediterranean World, c.950–500 BC*

602: *Greek Art and Archaeology c.500–300 BC*

604: *Art under the Roman Empire, AD 14–337*

605: *Roman Archaeology: Cities and Settlement under the Empire*]

C. Core Papers: Ancient History

[**For students starting before MT 2015:** i. *Thucydides and the Greek World 479–403 BC*

As specified for the Honour School of Literae Humaniores, subject 1.2, except that candidates in Classical Archaeology and Ancient History will answer four questions.

ii. *Alexander the Great and his Early Successors*

As specified for the Honour School of Literae Humaniores, subject I. 8.

iii. *Roman History 146–46 BC*

As specified for the Honour School of Literae Humaniores, subject I.5; candidates in Classical Archaeology and Ancient History will answer four questions.]

[**For students starting from MT 2015:** 408: *Alexander the Great and his Early Successors (336 BC–302 BC)*

471: *The Greek City in the Roman World from Dio Chrysostom to John Chrysostom*

482: *Thucydides and the Greek World 479–403 BC*

485: *Republic in Crisis: 146–46 BC Roman History 146–46 BC*]

D. Further Papers: Classical Archaeology

[For students starting before MT 2015: i. *Egyptian Art and Architecture*
ii. *The Archaeology of Minoan Crete, 3200–1000 BC*
iii. *Etruscan Italy, 900–300 BC*

Candidates should be familiar with the relevant archaeology of the following cities   5
and sites: Tarquinia, Caere, Veii, Vulci, Rome, Marzabotto, Populonia, Pyrgi,
Gravisca, Orvieto, Cortona, and Acquarossa.

iv. *Science-Based Methods in Archaeology*
v. *Greek and Roman Coins*

Candidates will be expected to show knowledge of the principal developments in   10
coinage from its beginnings c.600 BC until the reign of Diocletian (AD 284–305).
Emphasis will be placed on the ways in which numismatic evidence may be used to
address questions of historical and archaeological interest.

vi. *Mediterranean Maritime Archaeology*
vii. *The Archaeology of the Late Roman Empire, AD 284–641*   15

The paper studies the archaeology and art of the Roman Empire from Diocletian
through the death of Heraclius. Subjects include urban change; development of the
countryside in the east; industry; patterns of trade; persistence of pagan art; and the
impact of Christianity (church building, pilgrimage, monasticism) on architecture and
art. The main sites to be studied are Rome, Constantinople, Trier, Verulamium,   20
Ravenna, Justiniana Prima, Caesarea Maritima, Scythopolis, Jerusalem and sites in
the Roman provinces of Syria and Palestine.**]**

[For students starting from MT 2015: 631: *Egyptian Art and Architecture*
632: *The Archaeology of Minoan Crete, 3200–1000 BC*
633: *Etruscan Italy, 900–300 BC*   25
634: *Science-Based Methods in Archaeology*
635: *Greek and Roman Coins*
636: *Mediterranean Maritime Archaeology*
637: *The Archaeology of the Late Roman Empire, AD 284–641*]

E. Further Papers: Ancient History   30

[For students starting before MT 2015: i. *Epigraphy of the Greek and/or Roman
World*

The course focuses on the inscribed text, mainly on stone and bronze, as monu-
ment, physical object and medium of information, and it explores the evidence of
particular inscriptions, or groups of inscriptions, for the political, social, and economic   35
history of communities in the ancient world. Candidates may show knowledge of
either Archaic-Classical Greek, or Hellenistic, or Republican Roman or Imperial
Roman inscriptions. They will be expected to show knowledge of epigraphic texts in
Greek and/or in Latin (though all texts will be accompanied by translations).

ii. *Athenian Democracy in the Classical Age*   40
As specified for the Honour School of Literae Humaniores, subject I. 7.

iii. *Sexuality and Gender in Greece and Rome*
As specified for the Honour School of Literae Humaniores, subject I. 13.

iv. *Cicero: Politics and Thought in the Late Republic*
As specified for the Honour School of Literae Humaniores, subject I. 10.   45

v. *Religions in the Greek and Roman World, 31 BC–AD 312*
As specified for the Honour School of Literae Humaniores, subject I.12.

vi. *St Augustine and the Last Days of Rome, 370–430*

Examined by a single 3-hour written paper combining passages for comment and essay questions.

Augustine, *Against the Academics* 2.2.4–6, 3.18–19, tr. J. O'Meara, *Ancient Christian Writers* 23 (Washington, DC, 1951).

Confessions, Books I–X, tr. H. Chadwick (Oxford, 1991), pp. 1–220 (recommended to buy)

City of God, Books XIV, XIX tr. H. Bettenson (Harmondsworth, 1972), pp. 547–94; 842–94

Letters 10, 15, 16, 17, 188, 209, 262, tr. E. Hill *The Works of St Augustine* (New York, 2003–04), II/1, 33–5, 45–50; II/3, 252–59, 394–97; II/4, 203–09

Letters 10*, 12*, 20*, 24*, tr. R. Eno, *Saint Augustine: Letters 1*–29** (Washington, DC, 1989), pp. 75–80, 100–08, 133–49, 172–4 (Also online via Questia)

Sermons 198 (Dolbeau 26), 355, 356, tr. E. Hill (New York, 1997) III/11, 180–228, III/10, 166–84

Sermon on the Sack of Rome, tr. M. O'Reilly (Washington, DC 1955)

Ammianus Marcellinus, *The Later Roman Empire* [*Res Gestae*], Book 14.6; 27.3, 6–7, 9, 11; 28.1, 4; 29. 2; 30. 5–9, 31.1–2, 12–14, tr. J. C. Rolfe, Loeb Classical Library 3 vols. (Cambridge, MA, 1935). I, 35–53, III, 13–21, 45–51, 57–63, 73–77, 87–123, 137–61, 215–33, 335–73, 377–409, 463–89 (Also online at http://penelope.uchicago.edu)

Ausonius, *The Professors of Bordeaux*, tr. H.G. Evelyn White, Loeb Classical Library 2 vols. (Cambridge Mass., 1921), I, 97–139.

Letters 12 and 22, tr. White, II, 33–41, 71–8 (Also online at http://www.archive.org)

Symmachus, *Letters*, Book I. 3, 10, 12, 14, 20, 23, 32, 43, 47–9, 51–3, 58–9, 61, 99; Book III. 36; Book VI. 67 (special translation)

Relatio 3, tr. B. Croke & J. Harries, *Religious Conflict in Fourth-Century Rome* (Sydney, 1982), Document 40, pp. 35–40

Relationes 10–12, tr. R.H. Barrow, *Prefect and Emperor* (Oxford, 1973), pp. 73–81

Ambrose, *Letters* 17 and 18 (now known as 72 and 73), tr. Croke & Harries, *Religious Conflict*, Documents 39 and 41, pp. 30–35, 40–50

Letters 75, 75a, 76, 77, tr. W. Liebeschuetz *Ambrose of Milan : political letters and speeches* (Liverpool, 2005/2010), pp. 124–73

Jerome, Letters 22, 45, 107, tr. F.A. Wright, *Jerome: Select Letters* Loeb Classical Library (London, 1933), pp. 531–59, 177–79, 229–65 (online at http://www.archive.org)

Letter 130, tr. *Nicene and Post Nicene* Fathers, II.6, 261–272 (Online at http://www.ccel.org)

Pelagius, *Letter to Demetrias*, tr. B. R. Rees (Woodbridge, 1991), pp. 29–70

The Life of Melania the Younger, tr. E. Clark (Lewiston, NY, 1984), pp. 25–82

The Theodosian Code, tr. C. Pharr (Princeton, 1952), Book IX. Title 16. paras 4–11; IX. 17.6–7; XII.1 56, 63, 77, 87, 98, 104, 110, 112, 116, 122; XIII. 3, 6–12; XIV. 9.1; XVI. 1.2, 4; XVI. 2.20; XVI. 5.3, 6–7, 9; XVI. 10.4–13

Dessau, *Inscriptiones Latinae Selectae*, nos. 754, 1256, 1258–61, 1265, 294–67, 2951

Diehl, *Inscriptiones Latinae Christianae Veteres*, nos. 63, 104, and 1700

Monica's epitaph]

[**For students starting from MT 2015:** 407: *Athenian Democracy in the Classical Age*
410: *Cicero: Politics and Thought in the Late Republic*
412: *Religions in the Greek and Roman World, c.31 BC–AD 312*
413: *Sexuality and Gender in Greece and Rome*
472: *St Augustine and the Last Days of Rome, 370–430*
473: *Epigraphy of the Greek and/or Roman World*]

F. Classical Languages

[**For students starting before MT 2015:** i. *Intermediate Ancient Greek*

(This paper is available only to those undergraduates who offered Prelims paper C. I and, with the permission of the Standing Committee, to others with equivalent knowledge of Ancient Greek. It is not normally available to candidates with a qualification in Ancient Greek above AS-level or equivalent, nor to those who took paper C.3 Intermediate Greek in the preliminary examination.)

A detailed specification and prescribed texts for the paper will be published in the Classical Archaeology and Ancient History FHS handbook not later than Monday of Week 0 of the Michaelmas Term preceding the examination.

ii. *Intermediate Latin*

(This paper is available only to those undergraduates who offered Prelims paper C.2 and, with the permission of the Standing Committee, to others with equivalent knowledge of Latin. It is not normally available to candidates with a qualification in Latin above AS-level or equivalent, nor to those who took paper C.4 Intermediate Latin in the preliminary examination.)

A detailed specification and prescribed texts for the paper will be published in the Classical Archaeology and Ancient History FHS handbook not later than Monday of Week 0 of the Michaelmas Term preceding the examination.

iii. *Advanced Ancient Greek*

This paper is designed for those with AS or A2 level Greek. Candidates will be expected to show an advanced level of knowledge of Greek grammar and vocabulary (including all syntax and morphology, as laid out in Abbot and Mansfield, Primer of Greek Accidence).

There will be one three-hour paper comprising passages for translation from set texts, grammatical questions on the prepared texts and unseen translation. A detailed specification and prescribed texts for the paper will be published in the Classical Archaeology and Ancient History FHS course handbook not later than Monday of Week 0 of the Michaelmas Term preceding the examination.

iv. *Advanced Latin*

This paper is designed for those with AS or A2 level Latin. Candidates will be expected to show an advanced level of knowledge of Latin grammar and vocabulary (including all syntax and morphology, as laid out in Kennedy's Revised Latin Primer).

There will be one three-hour paper comprising passages for translation from set texts, grammatical questions on the prepared texts and unseen translation. A detailed specification and prescribed texts for the paper will be published in the Classical Archaeology and Ancient History FHS course handbook not later than Monday of Week 0 of the Michaelmas Term preceding the examination.]

[**For students starting from MT 2015:** Each subject will be examined in one paper of three hours. Detailed specifications and prescribed texts for subjects 571–574 will be published in the CAAH Finals handbook not later than Monday of Week 5 of Hilary Term two years preceding the examination.

571: *Intermediate Ancient Greek* This paper is available only to those undergraduates who offered Prelims paper C.1 and, with the permission of the Standing Committee, to others with equivalent knowledge of Ancient Greek. It is not normally available to candidates with a qualification in Ancient Greek above AS-level or equivalent, nor to those who took paper C.3 Intermediate Greek in the preliminary examination.

572: *Intermediate Latin* This paper is available only to those undergraduates who offered Prelims paper C.2 and, with the permission of the Standing Committee, to others with equivalent knowledge of Latin. It is not normally available to candidates with a qualification in Latin above AS-level or equivalent, nor to those who took paper C.4 Intermediate Latin in the preliminary examination.

573: *Advanced Ancient Greek* This paper is designed for those with AS or A2 level Greek.

574: *Advanced Latin* This paper is designed for those with AS or A2 level Latin.]

VII *A Site or Museum report*, prepared in accordance with Regulation 3 below. The report must be on

Either

A. an excavation or archaeological site, based as far as possible on participation or autopsy and on a consideration of all relevant historical and archaeological sources;

Or

B. a coherent body of finds from one site or of one category, based as far as possible on autopsy and on a consideration of all relevant historical and archaeological sources.

VIII An optional *Additional Thesis*, prepared in accordance with Regulation 3 below.

2. Candidates may also be examined viva voce.

[For students starting before MT 2015: 3. Theses.

(*a*) This regulation governs theses submitted under Regulation 1.VIII, and the Site or Museum report submitted under 1.VII.

(*b*) The subjects for all theses and for the Site or Museum report must, to the satisfaction of the Standing Committee, fall within the scope of the Honour School of Classical Archaeology and Ancient History. The subject may, but need not, overlap any subject on which the candidate offers papers. Candidates are warned that they should avoid repetition in papers of materials used in their theses, and that substantial repetition may be penalised.

(*c*) Candidates proposing to offer a thesis must submit the following through their college, to the Secretary of the Standing Committee not later than the Friday of the second week of Trinity Full Term preceding the year of the final examination: (i) the title of the proposed thesis or report, together with (ii) a synopsis of the subject in about 100 words and (iii) a letter of approval from their tutor. The Standing Committee shall decide as soon as possible whether or not to approve the title and shall advise the candidate immediately. No decision shall be deferred beyond the end of the sixth week of the Trinity Full Term preceding the year of the final examination

(*d*) Every thesis or report shall be the candidate's own work. Tutors may, however, discuss with candidates the field of study, the sources available, and the method of presentation, and may also read and comment on a first draft. The amount of assistance a candidate may receive shall not exceed an amount equivalent to the teaching of a normal paper. Candidates shall make a declaration that the thesis or report is their own work, and their tutors shall countersign the declaration confirming that, to the best of their knowledge and belief, this is so. This declaration must be placed in a sealed envelope bearing the candidate's examination number and presented together with the thesis or report.

(*e*) Theses and reports previously submitted for the Honour School of Classical Archaeology and Ancient History may be resubmitted. No thesis or report shall   5
be accepted which has already been submitted, wholly or substantially, for another Honour School or degree of this or any other institution, and the certificate shall also state that the thesis or report has not been so submitted. No thesis or report shall, however, be ineligible because it has been or is being submitted for any prize of this university.   10

(*f*) Candidates should aim at a length of 10,000 words but must not exceed 15,000 words (both figures inclusive of notes and appendices but excluding bibliography). No person or body shall have authority to permit the limit of 15,000 words to be exceeded. Where appropriate, there shall be a select bibliography and a list of sources.   15

(*g*) All theses and reports must be typed in double spacing on one side only of quarto or A4 paper with any notes and references at the foot of each page, and must be bound or held firmly in a stiff cover and identified by the candidate's examination number only. Two copies of each thesis or report shall be submitted to the examiners. Any candidate wishing to have one copy of his or her   20
thesis or report returned must enclose with it, in an envelope bearing only his or her candidate number, a self-addressed sticky label.

(*h*) Candidates wishing to change the title of a thesis or report after it has been approved may apply for permission for the change to be granted by the Chair of the Standing Committee (if the application is made before the first day of Hilary   25
Full Term preceding the examination) or (if later) the Chair of the Examiners, Honour School of Classical Archaeology and Ancient History.

(*i*) Candidates shall submit any thesis or report, identified by the candidates' examination number only, not later than noon on Friday of the week after the Hilary Full Term preceding the examination to the Examination Schools, High   30
Street, Oxford, addressed to the Chair of the Examiners, Honour School of Classical Archaeology and Ancient History.]

[For students staring from MT 2015: 3. Theses and Site or Museum reports.

(*a*) This regulation governs theses submitted under Regulation 1.VIII, and the Site or Museum report submitted under 1.VII.   35

(*b*) The subjects for all theses and for the Site or Museum report must, to the satisfaction of the Standing Committee, fall within the scope of the Honour School of Classical Archaeology and Ancient History. The subject may, but need not, overlap any subject on which the candidate offers papers. Candidates should avoid repetition in papers of materials used in their theses, and may be   40
penalised for substantial repetition.

(*c*) Candidates must submit the following to the Academic Support Officer, loannou Centre, 66 St Giles', not later than the Friday of Week 1 of Trinity Full Term in their second year: (i) the title of the proposed thesis or report, together with (ii) a synopsis of the subject in about 100 words. The Standing Committee   45
shall decide whether or not to approve the title and shall advise the candidate as soon as possible.

(*d*) Every thesis or report shall be the candidate's own work. Tutors may, however, discuss with candidates the field of study, the sources available, and the method of presentation, and may also read and comment on a first draft. The amount of   50 assistance a candidate may receive shall not exceed an amount equivalent to the teaching of a normal paper. Candidates must submit a signed declaration that the thesis or report is their own work.

(*e*) Theses and reports previously submitted for the Honour School of Classical Archaeology and Ancient History may be resubmitted. No thesis or report shall 5 be accepted which has already been submitted, wholly or substantially, for another Honour School or degree of this or any other institution. No thesis or report shall, however, be ineligible because it has been or is being submitted for any prize of this university.

(*f*) Candidates should aim at a length of 10,000 words but must not exceed 15,000 10 words (both figures inclusive of notes and appendices but excluding bibliography). No person or body shall have authority to permit the limit of 15,000 words to be exceeded. Where appropriate, there shall be a select bibliography and a list of sources.

(*g*) All theses and reports must be typed in double spacing and printed on one side 15 only with any notes and references at the foot of each page.

(*h*) Candidates wishing to change the title of a thesis or report after it has been approved may apply for permission for the change to be granted by the Chair of the Standing Committee (if the application is made before the first day of Hilary Full Term preceding the examination) or (if later) the Chair of the Examiners, 20 Honour School of Classical Archaeology and Ancient History.

(*i*) Candidates shall submit two copies of any thesis or report, identified by their candidate number only, not later than noon on Friday of Week 9 of the Hilary Full Term preceding the examination to the Examination Schools, High Street, Oxford, addressed to the Chair of the Examiners, Honour School of Classical 25 Archaeology and Ancient History.]

HONOUR SCHOOL OF CLASSICS
AND ENGLISH

A

1. The Honour School of Classics and English shall be under the joint supervision of the Boards of the Faculties of Classics and English Language and Literature, and shall consist of such subjects as they shall jointly by regulation prescribe. The boards shall establish a joint committee consisting of three representatives of each faculty, of whom at least one on each side shall be a member of the respective faculty board, to advise them as necessary in respect of the examination and of the First Public Examination in Classics and English.

2. No candidate shall be admitted to the examination in this school unless he or she has either passed or been exempted from the First Public Examination.

3. No candidate shall be permitted to enter his or her name for the examination who has been adjudged worthy of Honours in Honour Moderations in Classics, or who has there satisfied the Moderators.

4. The Chair of Examiners for the Honour School of English Language and Literature shall designate such of the number of the examiners as may be required for the English subjects of the examination for the Honour School of Classics and English, and the nominating committee for examiners appointed by the Board of the Faculty of Classics shall nominate such of the number of examiners as may be required for the Classics subjects of the examination. When these appointments have been made the number of examiners shall be deemed to be complete.

B

[For students starting before MT 2015: All candidates must take seven subjects. All candidates not taking subject 4(xx), Second Classical Language, must offer A, two subjects in English, B, two subjects in Classics, C, two subjects linking both sides of the school, and D, a dissertation. The dissertation may be concentrated on English or on Classics, or may link both sides of the school.

Candidates who under B take 3 (*a*) or (*b*) (Greek or Latin Core) and 4(xx) (Second Classical Language) will under C take only one subject, either subject 5 or one of the subjects under 6. The subjects will be examined by written examinations of three hours' duration, unless otherwise specified.

The texts of Greek and Latin works used in the examination will be as specified each year in the Handbook for the Honour School of Classics and English.

A: ENGLISH

1. One of the following periods of English literature:

    (*a*) Literature in English 1350–1550 (one paper) [As specified for the Honour School of English Language and Literature Course I Subject 2]

    (*b*) Literature in English 1660–1760 (one paper) [As specified for the Honour School of English Language and Literature Course I Subject 4]

    (*c*) Literature in English 1760–1830 (one paper) [As specified for the Honour School of English Language and Literature Course I Subject 5]

2. One of the following as specified for the Honour School of English Language and Literature:

(*a*) a second of the periods specified in 1 above;

(*b*) Shakespeare (portfolio) [As specified for the Honour School of English Language and Literature Course I, Subject 1];

(*c*) The Material Text (portfolio) [As specified for the Honour School of English Language and Literature Course II, Subject 5(a)];

(*d*) any of the Special Options subjects from the list for the year concerned, which will be published by the English Faculty Office in the year preceding the examination (extended essay) [As specified for the Honour School of English Language and Literature Course I, Subject 6];

(*e*) any of the Special Options subjects for English Course II, Medieval Literature and Language, from the list for the year concerned [As specified for the Honour School of English Language and Literature Course II, Subject 6];

provided that candidates who offer (*b*), (*c*), (*d*), and (*e*) avoid duplicating, in their answers to one paper, material that they have already used in answering another paper.

B: CLASSICS

Any candidate whose native language is not English may bring a bilingual (native language to English) dictionary for use in any examination paper where candidates are required to translate Ancient Greek and/or Latin texts into English.

3. *Either* (*a*) Greek Literature of the Fifth Century BC (one paper of three hours (commentary and essay) with an additional paper (one-and-a-half hours) of translation) [Honour School of Literae Humaniores, subject III.1(a)].

or (*b*) Latin Literature of the First Century BC (one paper of three hours (commentary and essay) with an additional paper (one-and-a-half hours) of translation) [Honour School of Literae Humaniores, subject III.2(a)].

4. One of the following. *Note*: (*a*) Subject (xxi), Second Classical Language, counts as two subjects; hence candidates offering it should offer only one subject under section C. *Note*: (*b*) Each of the subjects (ii) Historiography, (iii) Lyric Poetry, and (vi) Comedy will be examined by an extended essay of 5,000–6,000 words and a one-and-a-half-hour translation paper, as specified in the Regulations for the Honour School of Literae Humaniores. *Note*: (*c*) It cannot be guaranteed that university lectures or classes or college teaching will be available on all subjects in every academic year. Candidates are advised to consult their tutors about the availability of teaching when selecting their subjects.

(i) *Either* (*a*) Greek Literature of the Fifth Century BC

    or   (*b*) Latin Literature of the First Century BC (whichever is not offered under 3 above).

(ii) [Honour School of Literae Humaniores, subject III.3] *Historiography*

(iii) [Honour School of Literae Humaniores, subject III.4] *Lyric Poetry*

(iv) [Honour School of Literae Humaniores, subject III.6] *Greek Tragedy*

(v) [Honour School of Literae Humaniores, subject III.7] *Comedy*

(vi) [Honour School of Literae Humaniores, subject III.8] *Hellenistic Poetry*

(vii) [Honour School of Literae Humaniores, subject III.9] *Cicero*

(viii) [Honour School of Literae Humaniores, subject III.10] *Ovid*

(ix) [Honour School of Literae Humaniores, subject III.11] *Latin Didactic*

(x) [Honour School of Literae Humaniores, subject III.12] *Neronian Literature*

(xi) [Honour School of Literae Humaniores, subject III.13] *Euripides, Orestes: papyri, manuscripts, text*

(xii) [Honour School of Literae Humaniores, subject III.14]

Either (*a*) *Seneca,* Agamemnon: *manuscripts, text, interpretation*

or   (*b*) *Catullus: manuscripts, text, interpretation.*

Note: University classes will be given for only one of these options each year.

(xiii) [Honour School of Literae Humaniores, subject III.15]

One of the following:

  (*a*) *The Conversion of Augustine*
  (*b*) *Byzantine Literature*
  (*c*) *Modern Greek Poetry*

(xiv) [Honour School of Literae Humaniores, subject III.16] Thesis in Literature

 (xv) Greek Historical Linguistics [Honour School of Literae Humaniores, subject V.1]

(xvi) Latin Historical Linguistics [Honour School of Literae Humaniores, subject V.2]

(xvii) Comparative Philology: Indo-European, Greek and Latin [Honour School of Literae Humaniores, subject V.4]

(xviii) General Linguistics and Comparative Philology [Honour School of Literae Humaniores, subject V.3].

 (xix) Ancient and Medieval Philosophy. Any one of subjects 110 (Aquinas), 111 (Duns Scotus, Ockham), 115 (Plato, *Republic*, in translation), 116 (Aristotle, *Nicomachean Ethics*, in translation), 130 (Plato, *Republic*, in Greek), 131 (Plato, *Theaetetus* and *Sophist*), 132 (Aristotle, *Nicomachean Ethics*, in Greek), 133 (Aristotle, *Physics*), 134 (Sextus Empiricus, *Outlines of Pyrrhonism*), 135 (Latin Philosophy), as specified in Regulations for Philosophy in all Honour Schools including Philosophy.

 (xx) *Either*

    (*a*) The Early Greek World and Herodotus' *Histories*: 650 to 479 BC [Honour School of Literae Humaniores, subject I. 1]

  or   (*b*) Thucydides and the Greek World: 479 to 403 BC [Honour School of Literae Humaniores, subject I. 2]

  or   (*c*) The End of the Peloponnesian War to the Death of Philip II of Macedon: 403 to 336 BC [Honour School of Literae Humaniores, subject I. 3]

  or   (*d*) Polybius, Rome and the Mediterranean: 241–146 BC [Honour School of Literae Humaniores, subject I. 4]

  or   (*e*) Republic in Crisis: 146–46 BC [Honour School of Literae Humaniores, subject I. 5]

  or   (*f*) Rome, Italy and Empire from Caesar to Claudius: 46 BC to AD 54 [Honour School of Literae Humaniores, subject I. 6]

  or   (*g*) Athenian Democracy in the Classical Age [Honour School of Literae Humaniores, subject I. 7]

  or   (*h*) Alexander the Great and his Early Successors [Honour School of Literae Humaniores, subject I. 8]

  or   (*i*) The Hellenistic World: Societies and Cultures c.300–100 BC [Honour School of Literae Humaniores, subject I. 9]

  or   (*j*) Cicero: Politics and Thought in the Late Republic [Honour School of Literae Humaniores, subject I. 10; may not be combined with (vii) Cicero above]

or   (*k*) Politics, Society and Culture from Nero to Hadrian [Honour
School of Literae Humaniores, subject I. 11]

or   (*l*) Religions in the Greek and Roman World, c.31 BC–AD 312
[Honour School of Literae Humaniores, subject I. 12]

or   (*m*) Sexuality and Gender in Greece and Rome [Honour School of   5
Literae Humaniores, subject I. 13]

Note: Candidates offering any of subjects (xix) (*a*)–(*f*) must also offer the associated
translation paper set in the Honour School of Literae Humaniores.

(xxi) Second Classical Language.
As specified for the Honour School of Literae Humaniores (VI).   10
Candidates who offer a Second Classical Language must offer *either* both subjects in
Greek *or both* subjects in Latin, and may not offer either subject in a language in
which they satisfied the Moderators in Honour Moderations in Classics and English
or the Preliminary Examination in Classics and English.

C. LINK PAPERS   15
For Paper 5 *Epic* and Paper 6 (*a*) *Tragedy* and (*b*) *Comedy*: while candidates will be
expected to be familiar with the texts specified, opportunities will be given to show
knowledge of authors and texts beyond those prescribed. Candidates must answer at
least one question that relates Classical and English Literature.

5. *Epic* (one paper of three hours plus 15 minutes' reading time)   20
With special reference to Homer, Virgil, Lucan, Milton, Dryden, Pope.

There will be a compulsory question requiring candidates to comment on and bring
out points of comparison between *either* (*a*) a passage of Homer and one or more
English translations *or* (*b*) a passage of Virgil and one or more English translations.
The passages will be drawn from (*a*) *Odyssey*, Books 6 and 9–12, (*b*) *Aeneid*, Books 7,   25
8 and 12. There will also be a passage for compulsory comment from Milton, *Paradise
Lost*.

6. One of the following:

(*a*) *Tragedy* [Candidates who offer paper B. 4 (iv) *Greek Tragedy* may not also
offer this paper].   30

With special reference to:
Aeschylus, *Agamemnon*.
Sophocles, *Oedipus the King*.
Euripides, *Medea, Hecuba*.
Seneca, *Medea, Thyestes*.   35
Kyd, *The Spanish Tragedy*.
Marlowe, *Tamburlaine the Great* (Parts I and II).
Edward II, Dr Faustus, Dido Queen of Carthage.
Shakespeare.
Jonson, *Sejanus, Catiline*.   40
Webster, *The White Devil, The Duchess of Malfi*.
Middleton, *The Changeling, Women Beware Women*.
Ford, *'Tis Pity She's a Whore*.
Milton, *Samson Agonistes*.
There will be an optional commentary question with passages drawn from   45
Aeschylus, *Agamemnon*, and Seneca, *Medea*.

(*b*) *Comedy* [Candidates who offer paper B. 4 (v) Comedy may not also offer
this paper].

With special reference to:
Aristophanes, *Birds*.   50

Menander, *Dyscolus.*
Plautus, *Amphitryo* and *Menaechmi.*
Terence, *Adelphoe.*
Gascoigne, *Supposes.*
Lyly, *Campaspe, Mother Bombie.*   5
Shakespeare.
Jonson, *Every Man in his Humour, Volpone, Epicoene, The Alchemist, Bartholomew Fair.*
Wycherley, *The Country Wife.*
Vanbrugh, *The Relapse.* Congreve, *The Double Dealer, The Way of the World.*   10
Sheridan, *The Rivals, The School for Scandal, The Critic.*
There will be an optional commentary question with passages drawn from Aristophanes, *Birds*, and Terence, *Adelphoe.*

(c) *The Reception of Classical Literature in Poetry in English since 1900*
Authors in English for study will include Auden, H. D., Eliot, Frost, Longley, Lowell,   15
MacNeice, Carson, Harrison, Heaney, Hughes and Walcott. This paper will be
examined by an extended essay of 5,000–6,000 words. Essay topics set by the examiners will be released on Monday of Week 6 of the Hilary Term preceding the final
examination and essays should be submitted by Monday of Week 10 of the same term
(12 noon) to the Examination Schools, High Street. Candidates will be required to use   20
at least three authors in their essays, at least one of whom must be a classical author.

This subject may NOT be combined with options in Classics examined by extended
essay (4 (ii), (iii), (v)). Candidates must avoid repetition in this paper of material used
in Paper 2(*d*).

D: Dissertation   25
1. All candidates for the Honour School of Classics and English must offer a
dissertation.

    (i) The subject of the dissertation must be substantially connected with any
        subject area in Literae Humaniores and English Language and Literature.
    (ii) The subject of the dissertation may, but need not, overlap any subject or   30
        period on which the candidate offers papers. Candidates are warned, how-
        ever, that they must avoid repetition in their papers of materials used in
        their dissertation, and that they will not be given credit for material exten-
        sively repeated.
    (iii) Candidates must submit a dissertation abstract of no more than 100 words,   35
        to the Chair of Examiners in Classics and English, care of the English
        Faculty Office, by 5pm on Thursday of the eighth week of the Michaelmas
        term preceding the examination.
    (iv) The Chair of Examiners in Classics and English will decide as soon as
        possible, and in every case by Thursday of the first week of the Hilary   40
        Term preceding the examination, whether or not to approve the abstract,
        and will advise candidates of the decision forthwith.

2. The candidate may not discuss with any tutor either his or her choice of content
or the method of handling it after Friday of the sixth week of the Hilary Term
preceding the examination.   45

Candidates must sign a certificate stating that the dissertation is their own work,
and that they have read the Joint School guidelines on plagiarism (see also 3 below).
This certificate must be placed in a sealed envelope bearing the candidate's examination number and presented together with the dissertation.

3. Dissertations previously submitted for the Honour School of Classics and English may be re-submitted. No dissertation will be accepted if it has already been submitted, wholly or substantially, for any other degree of this or any other university; and the certificate must also contain confirmation that the dissertation has not already been so submitted.

4. No dissertation shall be ineligible because it has been submitted, in whole or in part, for any scholarship or prize of this University advertised in the *University Gazette*.

5. The dissertation shall be of 7,000–8,000 words; failure to keep to these limits is liable to be penalized. In the case of a commentary on a text, and at the discretion of the Chair of the Examiners, any substantial quoting of that text need not be included in the word-count. There must be a select bibliography and, if appropriate, list of sources.

6. Two typed copies of the dissertation must be delivered to the Chair of Examiners, Honour School of Classics and English, Examination Schools, High Street, by noon on Tuesday of the ninth week of Hilary Term preceding the examination.]

[For students starting from MT 2015: All candidates must take seven subjects. All candidates not taking subject 4(e), Second Classical Language, must offer A, two subjects in English, B, two subjects in Classics, C, two subjects linking both sides of the school, and D, a dissertation. The dissertation may be concentrated on English or on Classics, or may link both sides of the school.

Candidates who take 4(e), Second Classical Language will under C take only one subject, either subject 5 or one of the subjects under 6. The subjects will be examined by written examinations of three hours' duration, unless otherwise specified.

A: ENGLISH
1. One of the following periods of English literature:
    (*a*) Literature in English 1350–1550 (one paper) [As specified for the Honour School of English Language and Literature Course I Subject 2];
    (*b*) Literature in English 1660–1760 (one paper) [As specified for the Honour School of English Language and Literature Course I Subject 4];
    (*c*) Literature in English 1760–1830 (one paper) [As specified for the Honour School of English Language and Literature Course I Subject 5].

2. One of the following:
    (*a*) a second of the periods specified in 1 above;
    (*b*) Shakespeare (portfolio) [As specified for the Honour School of English Language and Literature Course I, Subject 1];
    (*c*) The Material Text (portfolio) [As specified for the Honour School of English Language and Literature Course II, Subject 5(a)];
    (*d*) any of the Special Options subjects from the list for the year concerned, which will be published by the English Faculty Office in the year preceding the examination (extended essay) [As specified for the Honour School of English Language and Literature Course I, Subject 6];
    (*e*) any of the Special Options subjects for English Course II, Medieval Literature and Language, from the list for the year concerned [As specified for the Honour School of English Language and Literature Course II, Subject 6];
provided that candidates who offer (*b*), (*c*), (*d*), and (*e*) avoid duplicating, in their answers to one paper, material that they have already used in answering another paper.

B: CLASSICS

Subjects **[For students starting before MT 2016:** 401–13] **[For students starting from MT 2016:** 401–14], 501–54 and 566–9 below will be set in accordance with the regulations for the Honour School of Literae Humaniores. For each subject, a detailed specification and prescribed texts will be given in the Greats Handbook applicable to the relevant year of examination. The handbook will be published by Monday of Week 5 of Hilary Term two years preceding the examination.

Any candidate whose native language is not English may bring a bilingual (native language to English) dictionary for use in any examination paper where candidates are required to translate Ancient Greek and/or Latin texts into English.

3. *Either* 501: *Greek Core* (one paper of three hours (commentary and essay) with an additional paper (one-and-a-half hours) of translation);

or 502: *Latin Core* (one paper of three hours (commentary and essay) with an additional paper (one-and-a-half hours) of translation).

4. One subject from (a)–(e) below.

Notes:

   (*i*) Subject (e), *Second Classical Language*, counts as two subjects; hence candidates offering it should offer only one subject under section C.

   (*ii*) Each of the subjects 503: *Historiography*, 504: *Lyric Poetry* and 507: *Comedy* will be examined by an extended essay of 5,000–6,000 words and a one-and-a-half-hour translation paper, as specified in the Regulations for the Honour School of Literae Humaniores.

   (*iii*) University classes will be given for only one of options **[For students starting before MT 2016:** 514 and 515] **[For students starting from MT 2016:** 515 and 524] each year.

   (*iv*) It cannot be guaranteed that university lectures or classes or college teaching will be available on all subjects in every academic year. Candidates are advised to consult their tutors about the availability of teaching when selecting their subjects.

(a) Greek and Latin Literature

   Either 501: *Greek Core* or 502: *Latin Core* (whichever is not offered under 3 above).

   503: *Historiography*
   504: *Lyric Poetry*
   506: *Greek Tragedy*
   507: *Comedy*
   508: *Hellenistic Poetry*
   509: *Cicero*
   510: *Ovid*
   511: *Latin Didactic*
   512: *Neronian Literature*
   513: *Euripides*, Orestes: *papyri, manuscripts, text*

   [For students starting before MT 2016: 514: *Seneca*, Agamemnon: *manuscripts, text, interpretation*]

   515: *Catullus: manuscripts, text, interpretation*

   [For students starting before MT 2016: 516: *The Conversion of Augustine*]

   517: *Byzantine Literature*
   518: *Modern Greek Poetry*

   [For students starting from MT 2016: 524: *Seneca*, Medea: manuscripts, text, interpretation]

   599: *Thesis in Literature*

(b) Philology and Linguistics

   551: *Greek Historical Linguistics*
   552: *Latin Historical Linguistics*
   553: *General Linguistics and Comparative Philology*
   554: *Comparative Philology: Indo-European, Greek and Latin*   5

(c) Ancient and Medieval Philosophy, as specified in the Regulations for Philosophy in all Honour Schools including Philosophy.

   110: *Aquinas*
   111: *Duns Scotus, Ockham*
   115: *Plato*, Republic, *in translation*   10
   116: *Aristotle*, Nicomachean Ethics, *in translation*
   130: *Plato*, Republic, *in Greek*
   131: *Plato*, Theaetetus *and* Sophist
   132: *Aristotle*, Nicomachean Ethics, *in Greek*
   133: *Aristotle*, Physics   15
   134: *Sextus Empiricus*, Outlines of Pyrrhonism
   135: *Latin Philosophy*

(d) Greek and Roman History

   401: *The Early Greek World and Herodotus' Histories: 650 to 479 BC*
   402: *Thucydides and the Greek World: 479 to 403 BC*   20
   403: *The End of the Peloponnesian War to the Death of Philip II of Macedon: 403 to 336 BC*
   404: *Polybius, Rome and the Mediterranean: 241–146 BC*
   405: *Republic in Crisis: 146–46 BC*
   406: *Rome, Italy and Empire from Caesar to Claudius: 46 BC to AD 54*   25
   407: *Athenian Democracy in the Classical Age*
   408: *Alexander the Great and his Early Successors*
   409: *The Hellenistic World: Societies and Cultures c.300–100*
   410: *Cicero: Politics and Thought in the Late Republic.* This subject may not be
        combined with 509: *Cicero*   30
   411: *Politics, Society and Culture from Nero to Hadrian*
   412: *Religions in the Greek and Roman World, c.31 BC–AD 312*
   413: *Sexuality and Gender in Greece and Rome*

   [For students starting from MT 2016: 414: The Conversion of Augustine]

Note: Candidates offering any of subjects 401–406 must also offer the associated   35
translation paper set in the Honour School of Literae Humaniores.

(e) *Second Classical Language.* As specified for the Honour School of Literae Humaniores (VI). Candidates who offer a *Second Classical Language* must offer *either* both subjects in Greek (566/568) *or both* subjects in Latin (567/569), and may not offer either subject in a language in which they satisfied the Examiners in the Preliminary   40
Examination in Classics and English.

C. LINK PAPERS
Detailed prescriptions and set texts for link papers will be provided in the Classics and English FHS handbook for the relevant year of examination.

   5. *Epic* (one paper of three hours plus 15 minutes' reading time)   45
   6. One of the following:

      (*a*) *Tragedy.* This subject may not be combined with 506: *Greek Tragedy.*
      (*b*) *Comedy.* This subject may not be combined with 507: *Comedy.*
      (*c*) *The Reception of Classical Literature in Poetry in English since 1900*

This paper will be examined by an extended essay of 5,000–6,000 words. Essay topics set by the examiners will be released on Monday of Week 6 of the Hilary Term preceding the final examination and essays should be submitted by Monday of Week 10 of the same term (12 noon) to the Examination Schools, High Street. Candidates will be required to use at least three authors in their essays, at least one of whom must be a classical author. This subject may NOT be combined with subjects 503, 504, or 507. Candidates must avoid repetition in this paper of material used in Paper 2(*d*).

D: Dissertation

1. All candidates for the Honour School of Classics and English must offer a dissertation.

    (i) The subject of the dissertation must be substantially connected with any subject area in Literae Humaniores and/or English Language and Literature.

    (ii) The subject of the dissertation may, but need not, overlap any subject or period on which the candidate offers papers. Candidates are warned, however, that they must avoid repetition in their papers of materials used in their dissertation, and that they will not be given credit for material extensively repeated.

    (iii) Candidates must submit a dissertation abstract of no more than 100 words, to the Chair of Examiners in Classics and English, care of the English Faculty Office, by 5 p.m. on Thursday of the eighth week of the Michaelmas term preceding the examination.

    (iv) The Chair of Examiners in Classics and English will decide as soon as possible, and in every case by Thursday of the first week of the Hilary Term preceding the examination, whether or not to approve the abstract, and will advise candidates of the decision forthwith.

2. The candidate may not discuss with any tutor either his or her choice of content or the method of handling it after Friday of the sixth week of the Hilary Term preceding the examination.

Candidates must sign a certificate stating that the dissertation is their own work, and that they have read the Joint School guidelines on plagiarism (see also 3 below). This certificate must be placed in a sealed envelope bearing the candidate's examination number and presented together with the dissertation.

3. Dissertations previously submitted for the Honour School of Classics and English may be re-submitted. No dissertation will be accepted if it has already been submitted, wholly or substantially, for any other degree of this or any other university; and the certificate must also contain confirmation that the dissertation has not already been so submitted.

4. No dissertation shall be ineligible because it has been submitted, in whole or in part, for any scholarship or prize of this University advertised in the University Gazette.

5. The dissertation shall be of 7,000–8,000 words; failure to keep to these limits is liable to be penalized. In the case of a commentary on a text, and at the discretion of the Chair of the Examiners, any substantial quoting of that text need not be included in the word-count. There must be a select bibliography and, if appropriate, list of sources.

6. Two typed copies of the dissertation must be delivered to the Chair of Examiners, Honour School of Classics and English, Examination Schools, High Street, by noon on Tuesday of the ninth week of Hilary Term preceding the examination.]

HONOUR SCHOOL OF CLASSICS AND MODERN LANGUAGES

A

1. The subjects of the examination in the Honour School of Classics and Modern Languages shall be (*a*) the Greek and Latin languages and literatures and the thought and civilisation of the Ancient World and (*b*) those modern European languages and literatures studied in the Honour School of Modern Languages.

2. No candidate shall be admitted to the examination in this School unless he or she has either passed or been exempted from the First Public Examination.

3. The examiners shall indicate in the lists issued by them the language offered by each candidate obtaining honours or satisfying the examiners under the appropriate regulation.

4. The examination in the Honour School shall be under the joint supervision of the Boards of the Faculties of Classics and of Modern Languages, which shall appoint a standing joint committee to make, and to submit to the two boards, proposals for regulations concerning the examination.

5. (i) The Public Examiners for Classics in this school shall be such of the Public Examiners in the Honour School of Literae Humaniores as may be required, together with one or two additional examiners, if required, who shall be nominated by the committee for the nomination of Public Examiners in the Honour School of Literae Humaniores; those for Modern Languages shall be such of the Public Examiners in the Honour School of Modern Languages as shall be required.

(ii) It shall be the duty of the chair of the Public Examiners in the Honour School of Modern Languages to designate such of their number as may be required for Modern Languages in the Honour School of Classics and Modern Languages, and when this has been done, and the examiners for Classics have been nominated, the number of the examiners in Classics and Modern Languages shall be deemed to be complete.

B

Candidates will be examined in accordance with the examination regulations set out below.

They will also be required to spend, after their matriculation, a year of residence in an appropriate country or countries, and to provide on their entry form for the examination a certificate that they have done this, signed by the Head or by a tutor of their society. Candidates wishing to be dispensed from the requirement to undertake a year of residence abroad must apply in writing to the Chair of the Medieval and Modern Languages Board, 41 Wellington Square, Oxford, OX1 2JF, stating their reasons for requesting dispensation and enclosing a letter of support from their society.

Candidates will be expected to carry out during this year abroad such work as their society may require. It is strongly recommended that candidates should apply through the Central Bureau for Educational Visits and Exchanges for an Assistantship, where these are available, and should accept one if offered. Candidates who are not able to obtain an Assistantship should during their year abroad follow a course or courses in an institution or institutions approved by their society, or should spend their time in such other circumstances as are acceptable to their society. Candidates will agree with their College Tutor in advance of their year abroad an independent course of study to be followed during that period.

Except in a Special Subject or an alternative to a Special Subject, a candidate shall offer one modern language and its literature only except that candidates offering Ancient Greek may offer the subject Modern Greek Poetry, and all candidates may offer the subject Byzantine Literature as specified in the regulations below, if and only if they are not offering Medieval and Modern Greek as their modern language.   5

Any candidate may be examined viva voce.

Oral Examination: as specified for the Honour School of Modern Languages.

In every case where, under the regulations for the school, candidates have any choice between one or more papers or subjects, every candidate shall give notice to the Registrar not later than the Friday in the fourth week of Michaelmas Full Term   10 preceding the examination of all the papers and subjects being so offered.

Candidates offering two papers both of which involve the study of the same author or authors, may not make the same text or texts the principal subject of an answer in both the papers.

All candidates must offer eight subjects as specified below and may also offer an   15 Additional Subject as specified at no.9.

Subjects 401–14, 501–69 and 601–5 will be set in accordance with the regulations for the Honour School of Literae Humaniores. For each subject, a detailed specification and prescribed texts will be given in the Greats Handbook applicable to the relevant year of examination. The handbook will be published by Monday of Week 5 of Hilary   20 Term two years preceding the examination.

1. Honour School of Modern Languages, Paper I.

Any candidate whose native language is not English may bring a bilingual (native language to English) dictionary for use in any examination paper where candidates are required to translate Ancient Greek and/or Latin texts into English.   25

2. Honour School of Modern Languages, Papers IIA and IIB.

3. Honour School of Modern Languages, *one* paper chosen from Papers VI, VII, or VIII.

4. Honour School of Modern Languages, *one* paper chosen from Papers IV, V, IX, X, XI, or XII.   30

5. *Either* (*a*) 501: *Greek Core*. One paper of three hours (commentary and essay) with an additional paper (one-and-a-half hours) of translation.

  or   (*b*) 502: *Latin Core*. One paper of three hours (commentary and essay) with an additional paper (one-and-a-half hours) of translation.

6., 7. Two of the following subjects. Candidates not offering Second Classical   35 Language must include at least one of the subjects from (a)–(n).

Note: (*i*) *Second Classical Language* counts as two subjects (566/568 in Greek; 567/ 569 in Latin). It may not be offered by candidates who have satisfied the Moderators in Course IA, IB, or IC of Honour Moderations in Classics or of the Preliminary Examination in Classics, or who offered both Greek and Latin in the Preliminary   40 Examination for Modern Languages. Candidates offering it must also offer at least one of the subjects from (a)–(s) under 8 or 9 below. If they offer *Second Classical Language* in Greek they may if they wish offer Literae Humaniores subject 521 at this point; if they offer it in Latin they may offer Literae Humaniores subject 522.

Note: (*ii*) Each of subjects 503: *Historiography*, 504: *Lyric Poetry* and 507:   45 *Comedy* (of which candidates may offer only one) will be examined by an extended essay of up to 6,000 words and a one-and-a-half-hour translation paper, as specified in the Regulations for the Honour School of Literae Humaniores. For each of subjects 503, 504 and 507, version (a) (as specified for the Honour School of Literae Humaniores) is the only version available to candidates who have satisfied the   50 Moderators in Course IA, IB, or IC of Honour Moderations in Classics or of the

Preliminary Examination in Classics, or who offered both Ancient Greek and Latin in the Preliminary Examination for Modern Languages.

Note: (iii) It cannot be guaranteed that university lectures or classes or college teaching will be available on all subjects in every academic year. Candidates are advised to consult their tutors about the availability of teaching when selecting their   5
subjects.

(a) Either 501: *Greek Core* or 502: *Latin Core* (whichever is not offered under 5 above).

(b) *One of the following subjects (see introductory note 6, 7 (ii) above):*
   503: *Historiography*   10
   504: *Lyric Poetry*
   507: *Comedy*

(c) 505: *Early Greek Hexameter Poetry*

(d) 506: *Greek Tragedy.* This subject may not be combined with subjects 582 *Ancient and French Classical Tragedy* or 583 *The Creative Reception of*   15 *Greek Tragedy in German.*

(e) 508: *Hellenistic Poetry*

(f) 509: *Cicero.* This subject may not be combined with 410.

(g) 510: *Ovid*

(h) 511: *Latin Didactic*   20

(i) 512: *Neronian Literature*

(j) 513: *Euripides,* Orestes: *papyri, manuscripts, text*

(k) *Either* 515: *Catullus: manuscripts, text, interpretation*

   or **[For students starting before TT 2016:** 514: *Seneca,* Agamemnon: *manuscripts, text, interpretation]*   25
   [For students staring from TT 2016: 524: *Seneca,* Medea: *manuscripts, text, interpretation]*

Note: University classes will be given for only one of these options each year.

(l) *One of the following subjects:*
   [For students starting before TT 2016: 516: The conversion of Augustine]   30
   517: *Byzantine Literature.* This subject is not available to candidates offering Medieval and Modern Greek as their modern language.
   581: *The Latin Works of Petrarch,* with special study of *Africa* (ed. N. Festa, Florence, 1926), Books, I, II, V, VII, IX. Candidates will also be expected to have read *Vita Scipionis* (in *La vita di Scipione l'Africano,*   35 ed. G. Martellotti, Milano-Napoli, 1954), and to show acquaintance with Petrarch's major Latin works (e.g. *Rerum memorandarum libri* (ed. G. Billanovich, Florence, 1945), *De secreto conflictu curarum mearum, De vita solitaria, Epistolae familiares* (in F. Petrarca, *Prose,* ed. G. Martellotti, P.G. Ricci, E. Carrara, E. Bianchi, Milano-Napoli, 1955)).   40

(m) 551: *Greek Historical Linguistics.* This subject may be combined with one but not more than one of 552, 553, and 554.

(n) 552: *Latin Historical Linguistics.* This subject may be combined with one but not more than one of 551, 553, and 554.

(o) 553: *General Linguistics and Comparative Philology.* This subject may be   45 combined with one but not more than one of 551, 552, and 554. Candidates offering section (a), General Linguistics, may not also offer the Modern Languages Special Subject General Linguistics.

(p) 554: *Comparative Philology: Indo-European, Greek and Latin.* This subject may not be offered by candidates who offered the paper VI F(1) *Historical*   50 *Linguistics and Comparative Philology* in Honour Moderations in Classics or in the Preliminary Examination in Classics. It may be combined with one but not more than one of 551, 552, and 553.

(q) *One of the following subjects*:

401: *The Early Greek World and Herodotus' Histories: 650 to 479 BC*
402: *Thucydides and the Greek World: 479 to 403 BC*
403: *The End of the Peloponnesian War to the Death of Philip II of Macedon:*
  403 to 336 BC   5
404: *Polybius, Rome and the Mediterranean: 241–146 BC*
405: *Republic in Crisis: 146–46 BC*
406: *Rome, Italy and Empire from Caesar to Claudius: 46 BC to AD 54*
407: *Athenian Democracy in the Classical Age*
408: *Alexander the Great and his Early Successors (336 BC–302 BC)*   10
409: *The Hellenistic World: Societies and Cultures c.300–100 BC*
410: *Cicero: Politics and Thought in the Late Republic.* This subject may not
  be combined with 509.
411: *Politics, Society and Culture from Nero to Hadrian*
412: *Religions in the Greek and Roman World, c.31 BC–AD 312*   15
413: *Sexuality and Gender in Greece and Rome*
414: *The Conversion of Augustine*

Note: Candidates offering any of subjects 401–406 must also offer the associated translation paper set in the Honour School of Literae Humaniores.

(r) *One of the following subjects*:   20

601: *The Greeks and the Mediterranean World c.950–500 BC*
602: *Greek Art and Archaeology c.500–300 BC*
603: *Hellenistic Art and Archaeology, 330–30 BC*
604: *Art under the Roman Empire, AD 14–337*
605: *Roman Archaeology: Cities and Settlement under the Empire*   25

(s) Ancient and Medieval Philosophy. Any one of the following subjects, as specified in the Regulations for Philosophy in all Honour Schools including Philosophy:

110: *Aquinas*
111: *Duns Scotus, Ockham*   30
115: *Plato*, Republic, *in translation*
116: *Aristotle*, Nicomachean Ethics, *in translation*
130: *Plato*, Republic, *in Greek*
131: *Plato*, Theaetetus *and* Sophist
132: *Aristotle*, Nicomachean Ethics, *in Greek*   35
133: *Aristotle*, Physics
134: *Sextus Empiricus*, Outlines of Pyrrhonism
135: *Latin Philosophy*

(t) 518: *Modern Greek Poetry.* This subject is available only to candidates offering Greek Core under 5 above who are neither offering Medieval and   40
Modern Greek as their modern language nor offering subject 517: *Byzantine Literature* nor *Second Classical Language*.

(u) Thesis. Any candidate may offer a thesis in Classics, or in a subject linking Classics and Modern Languages, in accordance with the Regulation on Theses in the regulations for the Honour School of Literae Humaniores.   45

(v) *Second Classical Language.* See introductory note 6, 7 (i) above. Candidates who offer Second Classical Language must offer either both subjects in Greek (566/568) or both subjects in Latin (567/569), and may not offer either subject in the same language as they offered in Course IIA or IIB of Honour Moderations or the Preliminary Examination in Classics or in the   50
Preliminary Examination for Modern Languages.

8. One of the following:

    (i) A second subject chosen from those listed under 4 above.

    (ii) A third subject chosen from those listed under 6, 7 above, subject to the groupings there set out and the restrictions there placed upon choice of subjects.   5

    (iii) 582: *Ancient and French Classical Tragedy* (not to be offered in combination with any of the following: 506: *Greek Tragedy; Racine* [Honour School of Modern Languages, paper X(5)]; *Dramatic Theory and Practice in France 1605–60 with special reference to Corneille* [Honour School of Modern Languages, paper XII Special Subject]).   10

Candidates must make a special study of either of the following pairs of texts, on which a compulsory comparative commentary question will be set: *either (a) Seneca, Phaedra* and Racine, *Phèdre*, or (b) Euripides, *Medea* and Corneille, *Médée.* In addition, essay questions will be set with special reference to the following texts:

Aeschylus, *Agamemnon*   15
Sophocles, *Oedipus the King*
Euripides, *Hippolytus, Andromache, The Phoenician Women, Iphigenia at Aulis*
Seneca, *Medea*
Corneille, *Discours, Horace, Oedipe, Suréna*
Racine, *La Thébaïde, Andromaque, Iphigénie.*   20

Candidates will be required to answer two essay questions, one from a choice of questions specifically on the authors and texts prescribed above, the other from a choice of questions requiring a comparative or generic approach. The following editions will be used in the case of the texts prescribed for commentary: Euripides, J. Diggle (Oxford Classical Text); Seneca, Phaedra, M. Coffey and R. Mayer   25 (Cambridge University Press); Corneille, A. Stegmann (L'Intégrale); Racine, J. Morela and A. Viala (Classiques Garnier).

    (iv) 583: *The Creative Reception of Greek Tragedy in German*

Candidates must make a special study of Sophocles, *Antigone* and Hölderlin, *Antigone*, on which a compulsory comparative commentary question will be set. In   30 addition, they will be required to answer two essay questions, one from a choice of questions specifically on the authors and texts listed below, the other from a choice of questions requiring a comparative or generic approach.

Sophocles, *Oedipus Tyrannus*
Euripides, *Medea, Iphigenia in Tauris*   35
Plato, *Republic* II, III, X
Aristotle, *Poetics*
Goethe, *Iphigenie auf Tauris*
Kleist, *Penthesilea*
Nietzsche, *Die Geburt der Tragödie*   40
Brecht, *Antigone*
Christa Wolf, *Medea: Stimmen*

The following editions will be used in the case of the texts prescribed for commentary: Sophocles, Lloyd-Jones and Wilson (Oxford Classical Text); Hölderlin, Frankfurt edition.   45

9. Additional Subject.

Good performance in such subjects will be taken in account in allocating all classes. Candidates wishing to offer an Additional Subject may offer one of the following.

- (i) A further subject chosen from the list prescribed under 4 above.
- (ii) A further subject chosen from the list prescribed under 6, 7 (a–t) above, subject to the groupings there set out and the restrictions there placed upon choice of subjects.
- (iii) 584: Greek Prose Composition. This subject may not be offered by candidates who have satisfied the Moderators in Course IA or IC of Honour Moderations in Classics.
- (iv) 585: Latin Prose Composition. This subject may not be offered by candidates who have satisfied the Moderators in Course IA or IB of Honour Moderations in Classics.
- (v) An extended essay on a topic in the modern language or combining the modern language and Classics (to be examined under the regulations for the Honour School of Modern Languages).
- (vi) A Special Thesis on a topic in Classics (to be examined under the regulations for the Honour School of Literae Humaniores).

Candidates shall submit two copies of their thesis not later than noon on Friday of the week before the Trinity Full Term of the examination to the Examination Schools, High Street, Oxford, addressed to the Chair of the Examiners, Honour School of Literae Humaniores.

HONOUR SCHOOL OF CLASSICS AND ORIENTAL STUDIES

A

1. The Honour School of Classics and Oriental Studies shall be under the joint supervision of the Boards of the Faculties of Classics and of Oriental Studies, which shall appoint a standing joint committee to make, and to submit to the two boards, proposals for regulations concerning the examination.

2. No candidate shall be admitted to the examination in this School unless he or she has either passed or been exempted from the First Public Examination.

3. The Public Examiners in this School shall be such of the Public Examiners in the Honour Schools of Literae Humaniores and of Oriental Studies as may be required, together with any additional examiners who may be required who shall be nominated by the committee for the nomination of Public Examiners in one or both of those Honour Schools as appropriate.

4. In the Class List issued by the examiners the Main Subject and Subsidiary Language offered by each candidate shall be indicated.

B

Candidates must offer one Main Subject and one Subsidiary Language, of which one must be Classics and the other a subject or language in Oriental Studies as specified below. In addition they may offer, but are not required to offer, a Special Thesis in Classics, or in Oriental Studies, or in a subject linking Classics and Oriental Studies, in accordance with the Regulation on Theses in the Regulations for the Honour School of Literae Humaniores, save that references there to the Honour School of Literae Humaniores shall be deemed to be references to the Honour School of Classics and Oriental Studies, the competent authority for dealing with proposals shall be the Joint Standing Committee for Classics and Oriental Studies, and proposals should be submitted to the chair of that committee. Candidates offering a Special Thesis may not also offer an additional optional special subject where that is allowed under the Regulations for Oriental Studies.

Classics may be offered either as a Main Subject or as a Subsidiary Language, save that those who have satisfied the Moderators in Honour Moderations or the Preliminary Examination in Classics may not offer Classics as a Subsidiary Language without permission from the Joint Standing Committee for Classics and Oriental Studies; such permission must be sought as early as possible, and in any case no later than noon on the Friday of the first week of Michaelmas Term before the examination.

In Oriental Studies, the following may be offered either as a Main Subject or as a Subsidiary Language: Arabic, Hebrew, Persian, Sanskrit, Turkish.

Egyptology and Ancient Near Eastern Studies may be offered only as a Main Subject.

Any candidate whose native language is not English may bring a bilingual (native language to English) dictionary for use in any examination paper where candidates are required to translate Ancient Greek and/or Latin texts into English.

The following may be offered only as a Subsidiary Language: Akkadian, Aramaic and Syriac, Armenian, Coptic, Egyptology, Old Iranian, Pali.

All Subjects and Languages other than Classics will be examined in accordance with the Regulations for the Honour School of Oriental Studies.

The subjects available in Classics are listed below. Those offering Classics as their Main Subject must offer **five** of these, of which at least two (or, in the case of those offering *Greek* or *Latin for Beginners*, at least one) must be drawn from 130–5, 401–6,   5
501–18, **[For students starting from TT 2016:** 524,**]** 541–2, 551–2, and 581; those offering Classics as their Subsidiary Language must offer **three**, of which at least one must be drawn from 130–5, 401–6, 501–18, **[For students starting from TT 2016:** 524,**]** 541–2, 551–2, 581 or *Greek* or *Latin for Beginners* (see note (i) below).

[For students starting before TT 2016: Subjects 401–13, 501–18, 551–4, and 601–5   10
below**] [For students starting from TT 2016:** Subjects 401–14, 501–18, 524, 551–4, and 601–5 below**]** will be set in accordance with the regulations for the Honour School of Literae Humaniores. For each subject, a detailed specification and (where applicable) prescribed texts will be given in the Greats Handbook applicable to the relevant year of examination. The handbook will be published by Monday of Week 5 of Hilary   15
Term two years preceding the examination.

NOTE: (i) *Greek* or *Latin for Beginners* counts as *two* subjects. It may not be offered by candidates who have satisfied the Moderators in Course IA, IB, or IC of Honour Moderations in Classics or of the Preliminary Examination in Classics. Candidates who offer *Greek or Latin for Beginners* must offer *either* both subjects in Greek   20
(566/568) *or* both subjects in Latin (567/569), and may not offer either subject in the same language as they offered in Course IIA or IIB of Honour Moderations or the Preliminary Examination in Classics, if they sat either of those examinations. If they offer *Greek for Beginners* they may, if they wish, offer *Greek Core* as non-text-based (521); in that case, they must also offer at least one of subjects 130–5, 401–6, 502–18,   25
[For students starting from TT 2016: 524,**]** 541–2, 551–2, or 581 if they are offering Classics as their main subject. If they offer *Latin for Beginners* they may if they wish offer *Latin Core* as non-text-based (522); in that case, they must also offer at least one of subjects 130–5, 401–6, 501, 503–18, **[For students starting from TT 2016:** 524,**]** 541–2, 551–2, or 581 if they are offering Classics as their main subject.   30

NOTE: (ii) It cannot be guaranteed that university lectures or classes or college teaching will be available on all subjects in every academic year. Candidates are advised to consult their tutors about the availability of teaching when selecting their subjects.

A. Subjects in Greek and Latin Literature   35

Candidates offering more than one of these subjects must offer 501 or 502, and may offer both.

The following restrictions on combinations of subjects will apply:

(1) Only one of subjects 503, 504, and 507 may be taken.

(2) Only one of subjects 505 and 541 may be taken.   40

(3) Only one of subjects **[For students starting before TT 2016:** 514 and 515**] [For students starting from TT 2016:** 515 and 524**]** may be taken. Note: University classes will be given for only one of these subjects each year.

(4) Only one of subjects **[For students starting before TT 2016:** 516,**]** 517, 518, and 581 may be taken.   45

Each of subjects 503: *Historiography*, 504: *Lyric Poetry* and 507: *Comedy* will be examined by an extended essay of up to 6,000 words and a one-and-a-half hour translation paper. For each of these subjects, version (a) as specified for the Honour School of Literae Humaniores is the only version available to candidates who have satisfied the Moderators in Course IA, IB, or IC of Honour Moderations in Classics or   50
of the Preliminary Examination in Classics. **Candidates offering one of these subjects who are also offering a dissertation on a topic in their Oriental language should consult**

the chair of the standing joint committee for Classics and Oriental Studies about the timing of submission of the dissertation.

501: *Greek Core.* One paper of three hours (commentary and essay) with an additional paper (one-and-a-half hours) of translation.

502: *Latin Core.* One paper of three hours (commentary and essay) with an additional paper (one-and-a-half hours) of translation.

503: *Historiography.* This subject may not be combined with 504 or 507.

504: *Lyric Poetry.* This subject may not be combined with 503 or 507.

505: *Early Greek Hexameter Poetry.* This subject may not be combined with 541.

506: *Greek Tragedy.*

507: *Comedy.* This subject may not be combined with 503 or 504.

508: *Hellenistic Poetry.*

509: *Cicero.* This subject may not be combined with 410.

510: *Ovid.*

511: *Latin Didactic.*

512: *Neronian Literature.*

513: *Euripides,* Orestes: *papyri, manuscripts, text.*

[For students starting before TT 2016: 514: *Seneca,* Agamemnon: *manuscripts, text, interpretation.* This subject may not be combined with 515.**]**

515: *Catullus: manuscripts, text, interpretation.* This subject may not be combined with **[For students starting before TT 2016:** 514**] [For students starting from TT 2016:** 524**]**.

[For students starting before TT 2016: 516: *The Conversion of Augustine.* This subject may not be combined with 517, 518 or 581.**]**

517: *Byzantine Literature.* This subject may not be combined with **[For students starting before TT 2016:** 516,**]** 518 or 581.

518: *Modern Greek Poetry.* This subject is available only to candidates offering 501 Greek Core who are not offering Greek or Latin for Beginners. It may not be combined with **[For students starting before TT 2016:** 516,**]** 517 or 581.

[For students starting from TT 2016: 524: *Seneca,* Medea: *manuscripts, text, interpretation.* This subject may not be combined with 515.**]**

541: *Homer,* Iliad [Honour Moderations in Classics, Course 1A, paper 1]. This option may not be offered by candidates who have satisfied the Moderators in Course IA, IB, IC, or IIB of Honour Moderations in Classics. It may not be combined with 505.

542: *Virgil,* Aeneid [Honour Moderations in Classics, Course 1A, paper 2]. This option may not be offered by candidates who have satisfied the Moderators in Course IA, IB, IC, or IIA of Honour Moderations in Classics.

581: *The Latin Works of Petrarch.* [Honour School of Classics and Modern Languages, subject 6, 7 (xiv) (*d*)]. This subject may not be combined with **[For students starting before TT 2016:** 516,**]** 517 or 518.

B. Subjects in Greek and Roman History

Candidates offering more than one of these subjects must offer at least one of 401–6; those offering more than three of these subjects must offer at least two of 401–6 and may not offer more than two of **[For students starting before TT 2016:** 407–13**] [For students starting from TT 2016:** 407–14**]**. Candidates offering any of subjects 401–6 must also offer the associated translation paper(s) set in the Honour School of Literae Humaniores, though candidates without competence in the relevant language may apply to the chair of the Joint Standing Committee for dispensation from this requirement by noon on the Friday of the first week of Michaelmas Term before the examination, setting out the full range of their intended options and stating why they think it educationally desirable to offer them.

401: *The Early Greek World and Herodotus' Histories: 650 to 479 BC*

402: *Thucydides and the Greek World: 479 to 403 BC*

403: *The End of the Peloponnesian War to the Death of Philip II of Macedon: 403 to 336 BC*

404: *Polybius, Rome and the Mediterranean: 241–146 BC*

405: *Republic in Crisis: 146–46 BC*

406: *Rome, Italy and Empire from Caesar to Claudius: 46 BC to AD 54*   5

407: *Athenian Democracy in the Classical Age*

408: *Alexander the Great and his Early Successors (336 BC–302 BC)*

409: *The Hellenistic World: Societies and Cultures c.300–100 BC*

410: *Cicero: Politics and Thought in the Late Republic*

411: *Politics, Society and Culture from Nero to Hadrian*   10

412: *Religions in the Greek and Roman World (c.31 BC–AD 312)*

413: *Sexuality and Gender in Greece and Rome*

[For students starting from TT 2016: 414: *The Conversion of Augustine*]

C. Subjects in Philology and Linguistics   15
Candidates may not offer more than two of these subjects.

551: *Greek Historical Linguistics*

552: *Latin Historical Linguistics*

553: *General Linguistics and Comparative Philology*

554: *Comparative Philology: Indo–European, Greek and Latin.* This subject may   20
not be offered by candidates who offered the paper *Historical Linguistics and Comparative Philology* (paper VI. F. 1 under Honour Moderation in Classics, Course IA) for their First Public Examination.)

D. Subjects in Greek and Roman Archaeology   25
Candidates may not offer more than two of these subjects.

601: *The Greeks and the Mediterranean World c.950 BC–500 BC*

602: *Greek Art and Archaeology, c.500–300 BC*

603: *Hellenistic Art and Archaeology, 330–30 BC*

604: *Art under the Roman Empire, AD 14–337*   30

605: *Roman Archaeology: Cities and Settlement under the Empire*

E. Subjects in Ancient and Medieval Philosophy
These subjects are specified in Regulations for Philosophy in all Honour Schools including Philosophy. One or two subjects may be offered. 110 may not be combined   35
with 111. 115 may not be combined with 130. 116 may not be combined with 132.

110: *Aquinas*

111: *Duns Scotus, Ockham*

115: *Plato,* Republic, *in translation*

116: *Aristotle,* Nicomachean Ethics, *in translation*   40

130: *Plato,* Republic, *in Greek*

131: *Plato,* Theaetetus *and* Sophist

132: *Aristotle,* Nicomachean Ethics, *in Greek*

133: *Aristotle,* Physics

134: *Sextus Empiricus,* Outlines of Pyrrhonism   45

135: *Latin Philosophy*

F. Other subjects

(a) *Greek* or *Latin for Beginners* [Honour School of Literae Humaniores, subject VI, *Second Classical Language*] **(see note (*i*) above)**.

(b) *Thesis.* Any candidate may offer a thesis in Classics, or in a subject linking Classics and their Main Subject or Subsidiary Language, in accordance with the   5
Regulation on Theses in the Regulations for the Honour School of Literae Humaniores, save that references there to the Honour School of Literae Humaniores shall be deemed to be references to the Honour School of Classics and Oriental Studies, the competent authority for dealing with proposals shall be the standing joint committee for Classics and Oriental Studies, and proposals should be   10
submitted to the chair of that committee.

HONOUR SCHOOL OF COMPUTER SCIENCE

A

In the following, 'the Course Handbook' refers to the Computer Science Undergraduate Course Handbook and supplements to this published by the Computer Science Teaching Committee and also posted on the website at http:// 5
www.cs.ox.ac.uk/currentstudents/.

1. The subject of the Honour School of Computer Science shall be the theory and practice of Computer Science.

2. No candidate shall be admitted to examination in this School unless he or she has either passed or been exempted from the First Public Examination. 10

3. The Examination in Computer Science shall be under the supervision of the Mathematical, Physical and Life Sciences Board. The Board shall have the power from time to time to frame and vary regulations for the different parts and subjects of the examination.

4. (*a*) The examination in Computer Science shall consist of three parts (A, B, C) 15
for the four-year course, and of two parts (A, B) for the three-year course.

(*b*) Parts A, B, and C shall be taken at times not less than three, six, and nine terms, respectively, after passing or being exempted from the First Public Examination.

5. The Examiners shall classify and publish the combined results of the examina- 20
tions in Part A and Part B, and in respect of candidates taking the four-year course shall separately classify and publish results in Part C.

6. (*a*) Part A shall be taken on one occasion only. No candidate shall enter for Part B until he or she has completed Part A of the examination.

(*b*) In order to proceed to Part C, a candidate must achieve upper second class 25
Honours or higher in Parts A & B together.

(*c*) A candidate who obtains only a pass or fails to satisfy the Examiners in Part B may retake Part B on at most one subsequent occasion; a candidate who fails to satisfy the Examiners in Part C may retake Part C on at most one subsequent occasion. Part B shall be taken on one occasion only by candi- 30
dates continuing to Part C.

7. A candidate adjudged worthy of Honours on both Parts A and B together, and on Part C may supplicate for the degree of Master of Computer Science provided that the candidate has fulfilled all the conditions for admission to a degree of the University. 35

8. A candidate in the final year of the four-year course, adjudged worthy of Honours in both Parts A and B together, but who does not enter Part C, or who fails to obtain Honours in Part C, is permitted to supplicate for the Honours degree of Bachelor of Arts in Computer Science with the classification obtained in Parts A and B together; provided that no such candidate may later enter or re-enter the Part C year 40
or supplicate for the degree of Master of Computer Science; and provided in each case that the candidate has fulfilled all the conditions for admission to a degree of the University.

9. All candidates will be assessed as to their practical ability under the following provisions: 45

(*a*) The Head of the Department of Computer Science, or a deputy, shall make available to the examiners evidence showing the extent to which each candidate has pursued an adequate course of practical work. Only that work completed and marked by noon on Monday of the sixth week of the Trinity Term in which the candidate takes the examination shall be included in these records.

(*b*) Candidates for each part of the examination shall submit to the Chair of the Examiners, Honour School of Computer Science, c/o the Academic Administrator, Oxford University Department of Computer Science, Oxford, by noon on Monday of the sixth week of the Trinity Term in which the examination is being held, their reports of practical exercises completed during their course of study. For a report on a practical exercise to be considered by the examiners, it must have been marked by a demonstrator and must be accompanied by a statement that it is the candidate's own work except where otherwise indicated.

(*c*) The examiners shall take the evidence (a) and the report (b) into account in assessing a candidate's performance.

(*d*) Candidates whose overall performance on practical work is not satisfactory may be deemed to have failed the examination or may have their overall classification reduced.

B

The syllabus for each of Parts A, B, and C will be published by the Department of Computer Science in a handbook for candidates by the beginning of Michaelmas Full Term in the academic year of the examination concerned. The duration of each optional paper will be specified in the Course Handbook.

The use of calculators is generally not permitted but certain kinds may be allowed for certain papers. Specifications of which papers and which types of calculators are permitted for those exceptional papers will be announced by the examiners in the Hilary Term preceding the examination.

The schedules of core and optional subjects for Parts A, B, and C of the examination shall be approved by the Faculty of Computer Science, and shall be published in the Course Handbook.

The examiners shall have the power to combine two papers on related optional subjects into a single paper for those candidates who offer both the optional subjects concerned.

Part A

In Part A of the examination, candidates shall be required to offer four core subjects and four optional subjects from Schedule A in the Course Handbook. Each subject shall be examined by means of a written examination with the exception of Object Oriented Programming, which shall be examined by means of a mini project or a written examination, or both, the details of which are set out in the Course Handbook.

Part B

In Part B of the examination, each candidate shall be required to offer six optional subjects from Schedules B1, B2, and B4 in the Course Handbook, subject to the conditions that

(*a*) no candidate shall offer any subject from Schedule B1 that he or she has already offered in Part A of the examination.

(*b*) each candidate shall offer no more than two subjects from Schedule B1.

(*c*) each candidate shall offer no more than two subjects from Schedule B4.

Each optional subject shall be examined by a written paper or by a mini-project. In addition, each candidate in Part B of the examination shall also submit a project report.

Each candidate shall carry out a project on a topic in Computer Science approved   5
by the Teaching Committee of the Department of Computer Science. Each project will be supervised by a member of the Faculty of Computer Science, the Faculty of Mathematics or the Faculty of Engineering Science, or by some other person of equivalent seniority approved by the Teaching Committee. Two copies of a report of the project shall be submitted to the Chair of the Examiners, Honour School of   10
Computer Science, c/o the Examination Schools, Oxford, by noon on Monday of the fifth week of the Trinity Term in which Part B of the examination is held. The report must not exceed 10,000 words plus forty pages of additional material (e.g. diagrams, program text). In retaking Part B of the examination, a project previously submitted for Part B may be resubmitted. No project may be resubmitted if it has already been   15
submitted, wholly or substantially, for another honour school or degree of the University, or of any other institution, or for any other Part of the examination.

Part C

In Part C of the examination, each candidate shall be required to offer five optional subjects from Schedule C1 in the Course Handbook, subject to the condition that no   20
candidate shall offer any subject that he or she has already offered in Part B of the examination. Each optional subject shall be examined by a written paper or by a mini-project. In addition, each candidate in Part C of the examination shall submit a project report.

Each candidate shall carry out a project on a topic in Computer Science approved   25
by the Teaching Committee of the Department of Computer Science. Each project will be supervised by a member of the Faculty of Computer Science, the Faculty of Mathematics or the Faculty of Engineering Science, or by some other person of equivalent seniority approved by the Teaching Committee. Two copies of a report of the project shall be submitted to the Chair of the Examiners, Honour School of   30
Computer Science, c/o the Examination Schools, Oxford, by noon on Monday of the fifth week of the Trinity Term in which Part C of the examination is held. The report must not exceed 10,000 words plus forty pages of additional material (e.g. diagrams, program text). In retaking Part C of the examination, a project previously submitted for Part C may be resubmitted. No project may be resubmitted if it has already been   35
submitted, wholly or substantially, for another honour school or degree of the University, or of any other institution, or for any other Part of the examination.

HONOUR SCHOOL OF COMPUTER SCIENCE AND PHILOSOPHY

A

In the following, 'the Course Handbook' refers to the Computer Science and Philosophy Undergraduate Course Handbook and supplements to this published by the joint supervisory committee and also posted on the website at http://www.cs.ox.ac.uk/teaching/csp.

1. All candidates shall be examined in Computer Science and in Philosophy.

2. No candidate shall be admitted to the examination in this School unless he or she has either passed or been exempted from the First Public Examination.

3. The examinations in this school shall be under the joint supervision of the Divisional Board of Mathematical, Physical and Life Sciences and the Board of the Faculty of Philosophy, which shall appoint a joint supervisory committee to make regulations concerning it, subject in all cases to the preceding clauses of this subsection.

4. (*a*) The examination in Computer Science and Philosophy shall consist of three parts (A, B, C) for the four-year course, and of two parts (A, B) for the three-year course.

   (*b*) Parts A, B and C shall be taken at times not less than three, six, and nine terms, respectively, after passing or being exempted from the First Public Examination.

5. The Examiners shall classify and publish the combined results of the examinations in Part A and Part B, and in respect of candidates taking the four-year course shall separately classify and publish results in Part C.

6. (*a*) Part A shall be taken on one occasion only. No candidate shall enter for Part B until he or she has completed Part A of the examination.

   (*b*) In order to proceed to Part C, a candidate must achieve upper second class Honours or higher in Parts A and B together.

   (*c*) A candidate who obtains only a pass or fails to satisfy the Examiners in Part B may retake Part B on at most one subsequent occasion; a candidate who fails to satisfy the Examiners in Part C may retake Part C on at most one subsequent occasion. Part B shall be taken on one occasion only by candidates continuing to Part C.

7. A candidate adjudged worthy of Honours on both Parts A and B together, and on Part C may supplicate for the degree of Master of Computer Science and Philosophy provided that the candidate has fulfilled all the conditions for admission to a degree of the University.

8. A candidate in the final year of the four-year course, adjudged worthy of Honours in both Parts A and B together, but who does not enter Part C, or who fails to obtain Honours in Part C, is permitted to supplicate for the Honours degree of Bachelor of Arts in Computer Science and Philosophy with the classification obtained in Parts A and B together; provided that no such candidate may later enter or re-enter the Part C year or supplicate for the degree of Master of Computer Science and Philosophy; and provided in each case that the candidate has fulfilled all the conditions for admission to a degree of the University.

B

1. All candidates will be assessed as to their practical ability in Computer Science under the following provisions:

(*a*) The Head of the Department of Computer Science, or a deputy, shall make available to the Examiners evidence showing the extent to which each candidate has pursued an adequate course of practical work. Only that work completed and marked by noon on Monday of the sixth week of the Trinity Term in which the candidate takes the examination shall be included in these records.

(*b*) Candidates for each part of the examination shall submit to the Chair of Examiners, Honour School of Computer Science and Philosophy, c/o the Academic Administrator, Oxford University Department of Computer Science, Oxford, by noon on Monday of the sixth week of the Trinity Term in which the examination is being held, their reports of practical exercises completed during their course of study. For a report on a practical exercise to be considered by the Examiners, it must have been marked by a demonstrator and must be accompanied by a statement that it is the candidate's own work except where otherwise indicated.

(*c*) The Examiners shall take the evidence (a) and the report (b) into account in assessing a candidate's performance. Candidates whose overall performance on practical work is not satisfactory may be deemed to have failed the examination or may have their overall classification reduced.

2. The use of calculators is generally not permitted but certain kinds may be allowed for certain papers. Specifications of which papers and which types of calculators are permitted for those exceptional papers will be announced by the Examiners in the Hilary Term preceding the examination.

PART A

In Part A of the examination, candidates shall be required to offer four Computer Science subjects from Schedule A(CS&P) in the Course Handbook, to include Models of Computation. The manner of examining the subjects in Schedule A(CS&P) shall be the same as that prescribed for the same subject in the Honour School of Computer Science.

PART B

The examination for Part B shall consist of subjects in Computer Science and Philosophy. The subjects in Computer Science shall be published in three schedules, B1(CS&P), B2(CS&P), and B4(CS&P), in a supplement to the Course Handbook by the beginning of the Michaelmas Full Term in the academic year of the examination concerned. Each Computer Science subject shall be examined by a written paper or by a mini-project. The subjects in Philosophy shall be subjects 101–118, 120, 122, 124, 125 and 127 from the list given in Special Regulations for All Honour Schools Including Philosophy, and subject to the regulations therein. Each subject in Philosophy shall be assessed by a 3-hour written examination. Each candidate shall offer:

(*a*) two, four, or six Computer Science subjects, and

(*b*) five, four, or three Philosophy subjects, respectively,

subject to the following constraints:

(i) No candidate shall offer any subject from Schedule B1(CS&P) that he or she has already offered in Part A(CS&P) of the examination;

(ii) Each candidate shall offer no more than two subjects from Schedule B1 (CS&P);

(iii) Each candidate shall offer no more than two subjects from Schedule B4 (CS&P);

(iv) Each candidate shall offer at least two Philosophy subjects from 101, 102, 104, 108, 122, 124, 125, and 127.

PART C

In Part C each candidate shall offer a total of between 24 and 26 units chosen in any combination from the lists of taught courses for Computer Science and for Philosophy, a Computer Science project or a Philosophy thesis subject to the following constraints:

• No candidate may take more than six Computer Science taught subjects;
• No candidate may offer both a Computer Science project and a Philosophy thesis.

The taught subjects in Computer Science shall be published in a schedule, C(CS&P), in a supplement to the Course Handbook by the beginning of the Michaelmas Full Term in the academic year of the examination concerned. Each such subject shall be examined by a written paper or by a mini-project and shall count as three units. Each taught Philosophy subject shall be one of the subjects 101–120, 122, 124, 125, 127, and 180 from the list given in Special Regulations for All Honour Schools Including Philosophy, and subject to the regulations therein. Each such subject shall be assessed by a 3-hour written examination together with an essay of at most 5,000 words, conforming to the rules given in the Course Handbook. Each such subject shall count as eight units. No candidate shall offer any taught subject that he or she has already offered in Part B of the examination. A Computer Science project shall be as specified for the Honour School of Computer Science, and shall count as nine units. A Philosophy thesis shall be as specified in the Regulations for Philosophy in all Honour Schools including Philosophy (subject 199) except that the thesis shall not exceed 20,000 words, and shall count as eight units.

HONOUR SCHOOL OF ECONOMICS AND MANAGEMENT

A

1. The examination in the Honour School of Economics and Management shall include, as stated subjects to be offered by all candidates: 5

(i) Macroeconomics

(ii) Microeconomics

(iii) Quantitative Economics

2. Candidates shall be required to offer, in addition to the above subjects, at least two subjects from Schedule A and a further three subjects from Schedules A and B.   10

3. No candidate shall be admitted to examination in this school unless he or she has either passed or been exempted from the First Public Examination.

4. The examination in this school shall be under the supervision of the Social Sciences Board, which shall appoint a standing committee to make regulations concerning it, subject always to the preceding clauses of this sub-section.   15

B

All candidates will be required to take *eight* subjects in all.

On entering his or her name for the examination by the date prescribed, each candidate must give notice to the Registrar of the papers being offered.

Candidates are permitted the use of one hand-held pocket calculator from a list of   20
permitted calculators published by the Department of Economics on its Undergraduate website, which will be updated annually in the week prior to the first full week of Michaelmas Term.

All candidates will be required to offer the following subjects:

(i) *Macroeconomics*   25

As specified for the Honour School of Philosophy, Politics, and Economics.

(ii) *Microeconomics*

As specified for the Honour School of Philosophy, Politics, and Economics.

(iii) *Quantitative Economics*

As specified for the Honour School of Philosophy, Politics, and Economics.   30

(iv) *Two* subjects selected from Schedule A.

(v) *Three* optional subjects selected from Schedule A, except that a candidate cannot offer a subject selected from Schedule A offered under (iv), and Schedule B.

Depending on the availability of teaching resources, not all Management Options will be available to all candidates in every year. Candidates and Management tutors   35
will be circulated in Trinity Term with details of all Options which will be available for the following year. The list, from which papers in Schedule A may be selected, and the syllabus for each, shall be approved by the Faculty of Management Studies and published on the Saïd Business School Undergraduate website by the Chair of the Standing Committee not later than the end of the Trinity Full Term of the academic   40
year preceding the year of the examination.

Not all Economics subjects may be available in any particular year. There may also be restrictions on numbers permitted to offer some Economics subjects in any particular year.

Economics subjects available to candidates in any particular year will depend on the availability of teaching resources. Details of the choices available for the following year will be announced at the Economics Department's 'Option Fair' at the beginning of the fourth week of the first Hilary Full Term of candidates' work for the Honour School, and will be posted on the Department's Undergraduate website at the same time.

Schedule A

(1) *Accounting*

Nature and regulation of financial reporting, analysis of company accounts. Nature of management accounting, including: cost behaviour, budgetary planning and control, capital budgeting, divisional performance.

(2) *Organisational Behaviour and Analysis*

The individual in the organisation; motivation and job satisfaction; groups at work; decision making; gender; organisational strategy and structure; the organisational environment; managerial work and behaviour; leadership; culture; power, conflict and change; contemporary and comparative approaches.

(3) *Employment Relations*

The structure and management of the employment relationship, including its environment, and economic and social consequences; human resource strategy and style; systems of collective representation; trade union objectives and organisation; pay systems and performance appraisal; explicit and psychological contracts; the management of co-operation and conflict; employee involvement, participation and team working; technology, work design and work organisation; job regulation; the utilisation of human resources; training and performance; contemporary and comparative approaches to the management of employees.

(4) *Finance*

Investment appraisal under conditions of certainty/uncertainty. Portfolio theory and capital asset pricing model. Sources of finance, debt capacity, dividends, and cost of capital. Financial market efficiency. Emerging issues in finance. Takeovers and mergers.

(5) *Strategic Management*

Theoretical foundations of strategic management. Structural analysis of industries and industry dynamics. The resource and capability based view of the firm. Strategy and Organization. Nature and sources of competitive advantage and patterns of competition. Competitive and co-operative strategies. Corporate strategy and competitive advantage. International strategy. Strategic management in the public sector and not-for-profit organisations. Current issues in strategic management.

(6) *Marketing*

Exchange in a modern economy. The marketing concept; the marketing mix, its formulation and common components; the product life-cycle and new product development; segmentation and positioning. Buyer behaviour. Marketing information and the analysis of markets and competitors. Marketing planning and marketing strategies. Models for evaluating strategic marketing opportunities.

(7) *Technology and Operations Management*

Goods and service operations. Vertical integration, facilities location and capacity, volume/mix and process relationships, scale economies, automation. Goods/service design, facilities, process planning, aggregate capacity decisions, resource scheduling. Product/service quality assurance, facilities maintenance.

(8) *International Business*

Theoretical foundations of international business strategy. Definition and historical underpinnings of globalisation. Global value chains. Market entry strategies. Institutional analysis and economic theory. Institutional voids. Theories of competitive and comparative advantage. Global culture and marketing. Ethical supply chains. Contemporary theories and controversies in international business.

Schedule B

Subjects (1) to (15) are as specified in the Honour School of Philosophy, Politics, and Economics.

(1) *Microeconomic Theory*
(2) *Money and Banking*
(3) *Public Economics*
(4) *Economics of Industry*
(5) *Labour Economics and Industrial Relations (222)*
(6) *International Economics*
(7) *Command and Transitional Economies*
(8) *Economics of Developing Countries*
(9) *British Economic History since 1870*
(10) *Econometrics*
(11) *Comparative Demographic Systems*
(12) *Economics of OECD Countries*
(13) *Economic Decisions within the Firm*
(14) *Game Theory*
(15) *Mathematical Methods*

(v) *Thesis*

Any candidate may offer a thesis instead of a subject from Schedule A or Schedule B under (v) above, subject to the following provisions:

(*a*) *Subject*

The subject of every thesis should fall within the scope of the honour school. The subject may, but need not, overlap any subject on which the candidate offers papers. Candidates are warned that they should avoid repetition in papers of materials used in their theses and that substantial repetition may be penalised.

Every candidate shall submit through his or her college for approval to the Chair of the Standing Committee for Economics and Management the title he or she proposes together with

(i) an indication as to the branch of the school in which the subject falls, i.e. Economics or Management;

(ii) an explanation of the subject in about 100 words;

(iii) a letter of approval from his or her tutor,

not earlier than the first day of the Trinity Full Term of the year before that in which he or she is to be examined and not later than the date prescribed for entry to the examination. The standing committee shall decide as soon as possible whether or not to approve the title and shall advise the candidate immediately. No decision shall be deferred beyond the end of the fifth week of Michaelmas Full Term.

(*b*) *Authorship and origin*

Every thesis shall be the candidate's own work. His or her tutor may, however, discuss with him or her the field of study, the sources available, and the method of presentation; the tutor may also read and comment on a first draft. Theses previously submitted for the Honour School of Economics and Management may be resubmitted. No thesis will be accepted if it has already been submitted, wholly or substantially, for another Honour School or degree of this University, or for a degree of any other institution. Every candidate shall sign a certificate to the effect that the thesis is his or her own work and that it has not already been submitted for a degree of this or any other university and his or her tutor shall countersign the certificate confirming that, to the best of his or her knowledge and belief, these statements are true. This certificate shall be submitted separately in a sealed envelope addressed to the chair of examiners. No thesis shall, however, be ineligible because it has been or is being submitted for any prize of this University.

(*c*) *Length and format*

No thesis shall exceed 15,000 words, the limit to include all notes, appendices, but not bibliographies; no person or body shall have authority to permit any excess. There shall be a select bibliography or a list of sources. All theses must be typed in double spacing on one side of quarto or A4 paper. Any notes and references may be placed *either* at the bottom of the relevant pages *or* all together at the end of the thesis, but in the latter case two loose copies of the notes and references must be supplied. The thesis must be bound or held firmly in a stiff cover. *Two* copies shall be submitted to the examiners; they shall be returned to the Saïd Business School library after the examination.

(*d*) *Submission of thesis*

Every candidate who wishes to submit a thesis shall give notice of his or her intention to do so on his or her examination entry form (in addition to seeking approval of the subject from the Chair of the Standing Committee for Economics and Management under (*a*) above); and shall submit his or her thesis not later than noon on Monday of the first week of the Trinity Full Term of the examination to the Chair of the Examiners, Honour School of Economics and Management, Examination Schools, High Street, Oxford.

HONOUR SCHOOL OF ENGINEERING SCIENCE

A

1. No candidate shall be admitted to the examination in this school unless he or she has either passed or been exempted from the First Public Examination.

2. The subject of the examination shall be Engineering Science.

3. The examination in this school shall be under the supervision of the Divisional Board of Mathematical, Physical and Life Sciences, which shall make regulations concerning it, subject always to the provisions of this subsection.

4. (*a*) The examination shall consist of three parts (A, B, C).

    (*b*) Parts A, B and C shall be taken at times not less than three, six, and nine terms, respectively, after passing or being exempted from the First Public Examination.

    (*c*) Parts B and C shall be taken in consecutive years save where approval has been given by the Board for an intercalated year of study or industrial attachment between Parts B and C.

5. (*a*) A candidate adjudged worthy of at least second class honours in Parts A and B together at the first attempt and worthy of Honours in Part C in Engineering Science may supplicate for the Degree of Master of Engineering in Engineering Science provided that the candidate has fulfilled all the conditions for admission to a degree of the University.

    (*b*) A candidate who passes Parts A and B together but fails to be adjudged worthy of at least second class honours at the first attempt, or who is adjudged worthy of at least second class honours in Parts A and B together, but who does not enter, or withdraws from, Part C, is permitted to supplicate for the Degree of Bachelor of Arts in Engineering Science (Pass, or Honours with the classification obtained in Parts A and B together, as appropriate); provided that no such candidate may later enter or re-enter the Part C year or supplicate for the degree of Master of Engineering in Engineering Science; and provided in each case that the candidate has fulfilled all the conditions for admission to a degree of the University.

    (*c*) The Examiners shall give due consideration to the performance in all parts of the respective examinations.

6. The name of a candidate shall not be published in a results list until he or she has completed all parts of the respective examination (Parts A, B, and C for the Master of Engineering in Engineering Science or Parts A and B for students exiting with a Bachelor of Arts in Engineering Science) in accordance with cl. 6 above.

B

1. The examiners will not provide calculators, but will permit the use of one hand-held pocket calculator from a list of permitted calculators published by the Chair of the Faculty not later than the end of the Trinity Full Term in the academic year preceding the examination.

2. Candidates may be examined viva voce at the examiners' discretion.

PART A

1. Part A shall be entered on one occasion only.

2. The Syllabus for Part A will be published in the Course Handbook, together with the relative weighting of each paper and the duration of all written papers. (The 'Course Handbook' refers to the Engineering Science Undergraduate Course Handbook, published annually at the start of Michaelmas Term by the Faculty of Engineering Science.)

3. Each candidate will be required to take four written papers, as follows:
   A1 Mathematics
   A2 Electronic and Information Engineering
   A3 Structures, Materials and Dynamics
   A4 Energy Systems

In addition, they will be required to take Paper A5 Engineering Practical Work, which will be examined by continuous assessment. Candidates will not normally be required to submit their Engineering Practical Work. However, the examiners may request practical work from some candidates. Such candidates will be named in a list posted by the day of the last written examination.

PART B

1. A candidate who obtains only a pass, or fails to satisfy the examiners, may enter again for Part B of the examination on one, but no more than one, subsequent occasion.

2. The Syllabus for Part B will be published annually by the Faculty of Engineering Science on the Course Weblearn site at the start of Michaelmas Term, together with the relative weighting of each paper and the duration of all written papers.

3. Each candidate will be required to take five optional written papers from Schedule B papers published on the Course Weblearn site and, in addition, Paper B2 Engineering in Society.

Candidates will also be required to take three coursework subjects, as follows:

B1 Engineering Computation
B3 Group Design Project
B4 Engineering Practical Work

Paper B4 will be examined through continuous assessment. Candidates will not normally be required to submit their Engineering Practical Work. However, the examiners may request practical work from some candidates. Such candidates will be named in a list posted by the day of the last written examination.

4. Candidates shall submit to the examiners reports on the Group Design Project (Paper B3) completed as a part of their course of study. The subject of the project shall be approved by the Projects Committee of the Faculty of Engineering Science and three copies of the report shall be submitted to the Chair of the Examiners, Honour School of Engineering Science, c/o Examination Schools, High Street, Oxford, by noon on Wednesday of the fourth week of Trinity Term in the year of the Part B examination. The project report must not exceed thirty pages (including all diagrams, photographs, references, and appendices). All pages must be numbered, have margins of not less than 20mm all round and type face of Arial 11 pt font with double-line spacing. The report must be the candidate's own work and should include a signed statement to this effect. Project reports previously submitted for the Honour School of Engineering Science may be resubmitted. No project report will be accepted if it has already been submitted wholly or substantially for another honour school or degree of

this University, or for a degree at any other institution. Resubmitted work must be physically presented at the time and in the manner prescribed for submission

PART C

1. Part C shall be entered on one occasion only.

2. No candidate may present him or herself for examination in Part C unless he or she has been adjudged worthy of at least second class honours by the examiners in Parts A and B together at the first attempt.

3. The Syllabus for Part C will be published annually by the Faculty of Engineering Science on the Course Weblearn site at the start of Michaelmas Term, together with the relative weighting of each paper and the duration of all written papers.

4. Each candidate shall be required to offer six written papers from Schedule C published on the Course Weblearn site or an equivalent approved collection of course options if taking part in an exchange scheme. Candidates taking part in an exchange scheme shall have the proposed set of papers to be taken in the host institution approved by the faculty by the end of Trinity full term before going on the exchange.

5. Each candidate shall carry out a project on a topic of Engineering Science approved by the Projects Committee of the Faculty of Engineering Science. Each candidate shall submit three copies of his or her own report of the project to the Chair of the Examiners, Honour School of Engineering Science, c/o Examination Schools, High Street, Oxford, by noon on Wednesday of the fourth week of Trinity Term. The report must not exceed fifty pages (including all diagrams, photographs, references and appendices). All pages must be numbered, have margins of not less than 20mm all round, and type face of Arial 11 pt font with double-line spacing. The report must be the candidate's own work and should include a signed statement to this effect. Reports previously submitted for Part C for the Honour School of Engineering Science may be resubmitted. No work will be accepted if it has already been submitted, wholly or substantially, for Part B or for another honour school or degree of this University, or for a degree of any other institution. Resubmitted work must be physically presented at the time and in the manner prescribed for submission.

6. Each individual candidate taking part in a full year exchange at a host institution approved by the University will provide a collated set of coursework to the Exchange Coordinator of the Faculty of Engineering Science. The Exchange Coordinator will ensure that the host institution forwards a full transcript of the courses taken certified by the host institution. The Exchange Coordinator will also ensure that the host institution retains the examination papers for the approved courses undertaken and that these are submitted under seal, together with the collated coursework and transcript of courses taken, to the Chair of Examiners, Honour School of Engineering Science, c/o Examination Schools, High Street, Oxford by noon on Friday of the sixth week of Trinity Term.

Exceptionally, and with the approval of the Chair of the Faculty of Engineering Science, candidates may undertake their Project during a twenty-four week placement and take a specified equivalent of six papers from Schedule C in the Course Handbook. The placement shall always include the period from the fifth Friday before to the first Saturday after the end of Michaelmas Full Term. External project reports must be submitted by noon on Friday of the week before the start of Hilary Full Term in the year in which the Part C examination is held.

HONOUR SCHOOL OF ENGINEERING, ECONOMICS, AND MANAGEMENT

For students commencing the Honour School on or before 1 October 2014 only.

A

1. No candidate shall be admitted to examination in this school unless he or she has either passed or been exempted from the First Public Examination.

2. The examination in this school shall be under the joint supervision of the Mathematical, Physical and Life Sciences Board and the Social Sciences Board, which shall appoint a standing joint committee to make regulations concerning it, subject always to the preceding clauses of this subsection.

3. (*a*) The examination shall consist of three parts: A, B, and C.
   (*b*) Parts A, B, and C shall be taken at times not less than three, six and nine terms, respectively, after passing or being exempted from the First Public Examination.
   (*c*) Parts B and C shall be taken in consecutive years, save where approval has been given by the committee for an intercalated year of study or industrial attachment between Parts B and C.

4. The name of a candidate shall not be published in a results list until he or she has completed all parts of the examination, and has been adjudged worthy of Honours by the examiners in Parts A, B, and C of the examination. The Examiners shall give due consideration to the performance in all parts of the respective examinations.

5. The examiners shall be entitled to award a Pass to candidates on Parts A and B who have reached a standard considered adequate but who have not been adjudged worthy of Honours.

6. A candidate adjudged worthy of Honours on both Parts A and B together, and on Part C may supplicate for the Degree of Master of Engineering in Engineering, Economics, and Management, provided he or she has fulfilled all the conditions for admission to a degree of the University.

7. A candidate who passes both Parts A and B or who is adjudged worthy of Honours in Parts A and B together, but who does not enter Part C, or fails to obtain classified Honours in Part C, may be permitted to supplicate for the degree of Bachelor of Arts in Engineering, Economics, and Management (pass or unclassified Honours, as appropriate); provided that no such candidate may later enter or re-enter the Part C year or supplicate for the degree of Master of Engineering in Engineering, Economics, and Management; and provided in each case that the candidate has fulfilled all the conditions for admission to a degree of the University.

8. The examiners for Engineering Science shall be appointed by the committee for the nomination of examiners in Engineering Science; those for Economics shall be appointed by the committee for the nomination of examiners in Economics in the Honour School of Philosophy, Politics, and Economics; those for Management shall be appointed by the committee for the nomination of examiners in Management Studies.

B

1. The examiners will not provide calculators, but will permit the use of one hand-held pocket calculator as specified in the Honour School of Engineering Science.

2. Candidates may be examined viva voce on any part of their course of study, including their industrial project.

PART A

1. Part A shall be entered on one occasion only.

2. The Syllabus for Part A will be published in the Course Handbook, together with the relative weighting of each paper and the duration of all written papers. (The 'Course Handbook' refers to the Engineering, Economics, and Management Undergraduate Course Handbook, published annually at the start of Michaelmas Term by the Faculty of Engineering Science.)

3. Each candidate will be required to take four written papers:
Paper A1 Mathematics (as specified in the Honour School of Engineering Science)
Paper M1 General Management (as specified in the regulation relating to the General Management paper of the Economics and Management Preliminary Examination).

Two papers from:
Paper A2 Electronic and Information Engineering (as specified in the Honour School of Engineering Science)
Paper A3 Structures, Materials and Dynamics (as specified in the Honour School of Engineering Science)
Paper A4 Energy Systems (as specified in the Honour School of Engineering Science).

In addition, they will be required to take Paper A5E Engineering Practical Work (a shortened version of the Honour School of Engineering Science Paper A5), which will be examined by continuous assessment of practical work. Candidates will not normally be required to submit their Engineering Practical Work. However, the examiners may request practical work from some candidates. Such candidates will be named in a list posted by the day of the last written examination.

PART B

1. A candidate who obtains only a pass, or fails to satisfy the examiners, may enter again for Part B of the examination on one, but no more than one, subsequent occasion.

2. The Syllabus for Part B will be published annually by the Faculty of Engineering Science on the Course Weblearn site at the start of Michaelmas Term, together with the relative weighting of each paper and the duration of all written papers.

3. Each candidate will be required to take:
Three optional Engineering written papers from Schedule B of the Honour School of Engineering Science.
Paper B2 Engineering in Society (as specified in the Honour School of Engineering Science)
Paper Ec1 Introductory Economics (as specified in the regulation relating to the Introductory Economics paper of the Economics and Management Preliminary Examination).

Candidates will also be required to take three Engineering coursework subjects:

Paper B1 Engineering Computation (as specified in the Honour School of Engineering Science)

Paper B3 Group Design Project (as specified in the Honour School of Engineering Science)

Paper B4E Engineering Practical Work (a shortened version of the Honour School of Engineering Science Paper B4)

Paper B4E will be examined by continuous assessment. Candidates will not normally be required to submit their Engineering Practical Work. However, the examiners may request practical work from some candidates. Such candidates will be named in a list posted by the day of the last written examination.

4. Candidates shall submit to the examiners reports on the Group Design Project (Paper B3) completed as a part of their course of study. The subject of the project shall be approved by the Projects Committee of the Faculty of Engineering Science and three copies of the report shall be submitted to the Chair of the Examiners, Honour School of Engineering, Economics, and Management, c/o Examination Schools, High Street, Oxford, by noon on Friday of the fourth week of Trinity Term in the year of the Part B examination. The project report must not exceed thirty pages (including all diagrams, photographs, references and appendices); all pages must be numbered, have margins of not less than 20mm all round and type face of Arial 11 pt font with double-line spacing. The report must be the candidate's own work and should include a signed statement to this effect. Project reports previously submitted for the Honour School of Engineering, Economics, and Management may be resubmitted. No project report will be accepted if it has already been submitted wholly or substantially for another honour school or degree of this University, or for a degree at any other institution. Resubmitted work must be physically presented at the time and in the manner prescribed for submission.

PART C

1. Part C shall be entered on one occasion only.

2. No candidate may present him or herself for examination in Part C unless he or she has been adjudged worthy of Honours by the examiners in both Parts A and B together.

3. The Syllabus for Part C will be published annually by the Faculty of Engineering Science on the Course Weblearn site at the start of Michaelmas Term, together with the relative weighting of each paper and the duration of all written papers.

4. Each candidate shall be required to offer:

Two written Engineering papers from Schedule C in the Course Handbook.

Two papers from the list of optional Management and Economics papers published annually.

5. Candidates will also be required to undertake either a twenty-four week external project attached to an industrial firm, or a twenty-four week internal university project. The former will be undertaken between the end of Trinity Full Term in the year in which the Part B examination is held and the beginning of Hilary Full Term in the year in which the Part C examination is held. The latter will run from the beginning of Michaelmas Term to the beginning of Trinity Term in the year in which the Part C examination is held. The project will be carried out under the supervision of a person or persons approved by the Project Co-ordinator in Management or Engineering as appropriate. All projects and industrial attachments will normally be arranged by, and must be approved by, the project co-ordinators in Management and/or Engineering. The report shall be on a topic, approved by the

standing committee, normally in Management or Engineering. Topics in Economics may be approved, but the project co-ordinators cannot undertake to arrange projects in the field of Economics.

Candidates undertaking a management project will be required to keep statutory residence for workshops, as specified by the Course Director, in the year in which the 5 Part B examination is taken in order to prepare for the project to be carried out as part of the Part C examination.

Candidates will be required to present a report on the project carried out during this period. In the case of a management report, the report shall not exceed 20,000 words including appendices and tables, but excluding references. For an engineering project, 10 the report must not exceed fifty pages (including all diagrams, photographs, references and appendices); all pages should be numbered, have margins of not less than 20mm all round, and type face not less than eleven font with line spacing of no less than 8mm.

6. External project reports must be submitted by noon on Wednesday of the week 15 before the start of Hilary Full Term in the year in which the Part C examination is held. Internal projects must be submitted by noon on Wednesday of the fourth week of Trinity Term of the year in which the Part C examination is held. They must be addressed to 'The Examination Schools, High Street, Oxford, OX1 4BG, for the Chair of Examiners in Part C of the examination for the Honour School of Engineering, 20 Economics, and Management'. Reports must be accompanied by a signed statement by the candidate that it is his or her own work. Candidates must submit two copies of each project report. Successful candidates will be required to deposit one of these copies in the library of the Department of Engineering Science and the other in the library of the School of Management. 25

HONOUR SCHOOL OF ENGLISH AND MODERN LANGUAGES

A

1. The subjects of the examination in the Honour School of English and Modern Languages shall be (a) English Language and Literature in English and (b) those modern languages and literatures studied in the Honour School of Modern Languages.

2. All candidates must offer both (a) and one of the languages in (b) with its literature.

3. No candidate shall be admitted to the examination in this school unless he or she has either passed or been exempted from the First Public Examination.

4. The examiners shall indicate in the lists issued by them the language offered by each candidate obtaining honours or satisfying the examiners under the appropriate regulation.

5. The examination in this school shall be under the joint supervision of the Boards of the Faculties of English Language and Literature and of Medieval and Modern Languages, which shall appoint a standing joint committee to make, and to submit to the two faculty boards, proposals for regulations for this examination and for the Preliminary Examination in English and Modern Languages.

6. (i) The examiners in the honour school shall be such of the Public Examiners in the Honour Schools of English and Modern Languages as shall be required.

(ii) It shall be the duty of the chairs of examiners in the Honour School of English and in the Honour School of Modern Languages to consult together and designate such examiners as shall be required for the honour school, whereupon the number of the examiners shall be deemed to be complete.

B

1. The Year Abroad

Candidates will be examined in accordance with the examination regulations set out below. In addition, every candidate shall be required to spend, after their matriculation, a year of residence in an appropriate country or countries, and to provide on their entry form for the examination a certificate confirming that they have done this, signed by the Head or by a tutor of their college or society. Candidates wishing to be dispensed from the requirement to undertake a year of residence abroad must apply in writing to the Chair of the Medieval and Modern Languages Board, 41 Wellington Square, Oxford, OX1 2JF, stating their reasons for requesting dispensation and enclosing a letter of support from their college or society.

Candidates will be expected to carry out during this year abroad such work as their college or society may require. It is strongly recommended that candidates should apply through the Central Bureau for Educational Visits and Exchanges for an Assistantship, where these are available, and should accept one if offered. Candidates who are not able to obtain an Assistantship should during their year abroad follow a course or courses in an institution or institutions approved by their society, or should spend their time in such other circumstances as are acceptable to their society. Candidates will agree with their College Tutor in advance of their year abroad an independent course of study to be followed during that period.

2. English and Modern Languages Papers

Each candidate shall offer Part I, *either* Part II *or* Part III, and Part IV as prescribed below.

Except in a Special Subject or an alternative to a Special Subject, a candidate shall offer (in addition to English) one modern language and its literature only.

Candidates are warned that they must avoid duplicating in their answers to one part of the examination material that they have used in another part of the examination.

Part I

The regulations for these subjects shall be those specified in the regulations for the Honour School of Modern Languages.

1. Honour School of Modern Languages, Paper I.

2. Honour School of Modern Languages, Papers IIA and IIB.

3. Honour School of Modern Languages, one paper chosen from Papers VI, VII, or VIII.

4. Honour School of Modern Languages, one paper chosen from Papers IV, V, IX, X, XI, or XII.

5. Oral examination.

EITHER: *Part II*

6., 7., 8. Three papers chosen from Course I, Subjects 1 to 6 of the Honour School of English Language and Literature. A maximum of two of the three papers may be examined by submission. The papers will be written examinations of three hours' duration, unless otherwise specified. Candidates shall choose three from:

(i) *Shakespeare* (a portfolio of 3 essays, each of not fewer than 1,500 and not more than 2,000 words in length) [as specified for the Honour School of English Language and Literature, Course I, Subject 1]. See in addition the regulations in 3. for 'Submitted work'.

(ii) *Literature in English 1350–1550* [as specified for the Honour School of English Language and Literature, Course I, Subject 2].

(iii) *Literature in English 1550 to 1660* [as specified for the Honour School of English Language and Literature, Course I, Subject 3]. Candidates who have satisfied the Examiners in the Preliminary Examination in Classics and English may not offer this paper.

(iv) *Literature in English 1660 to 1760* [as specified for the Honour School of English Language and Literature, Course I, Subject 4].

(v) *Literature in English 1760 to 1830* [as specified for the Honour School of English Language and Literature, Course I, Subject 5].

(vi) *Special Options* (an extended essay of not fewer than 5,000 and not more than 6,000 words in length) [as specified for the Honour School of English Language and Literature, Course I, Subject 6]. See in addition the regulations in 3. for 'Submitted work'.

OR: *Part III*

6, 7, 8. Three papers chosen from Course II, Subjects 1 to 6 of the Honour School of English Language and Literature. A maximum of two of the three papers may be examined by submission. The papers will be written examinations of three hours' duration, unless otherwise specified. Candidates shall choose three from:

(i) *Literature in English 650–1100* [Honour School of English Language and Literature, Course II, Subject 1].

(ii) *Medieval English and Related Literatures 1066 to 1550* [Honour School of English Language and Literature, Course II, Subject 2].

(iii) *Literature in English 1350–1550* [Honour School of English Language and Literature, Course II, Subject 3].

(iv) *The History of the English Language to c.1800* (a portfolio of two essays of no more than 2,500 words each) [Honour School of English Language and Literature, Course II, Subject 4].

(v) EITHER *The Material Text* (a portfolio of one essay and one commentary, each of not fewer than 2,000 and not more than 2,500 words in length) [Honour School of English Language and Literature, Course II, Subject 5 (a)]. See in addition the introductory regulations for 'Submitted work' for the Honour School of English and Modern Languages. 5

OR *Shakespeare* (a portfolio of three essays, each of not fewer than 1,500 and not more than 2,000 words in length) [Honour School of English Language and Literature, Course I, Subject 1/Course II, Subject 5(b)]. See in addition the regulations in 3. for 'Submitted work'. 10

(vi) *Special Options* (an extended essay of not fewer than 5,000 and not more than 6,000 words in length) [Honour School of English Language and Literature, Course I & II, Subject 6]. See in addition the regulations in 3, for 'Submitted work'. 15

Part IV 9. *Dissertation* (an extended essay of not fewer than 7,000 and not more than 8,000 words in length). See in addition the regulations in 3. for 'Submitted work'. Candidates may offer an extended essay in any subject area of English Language or Literature in English, or combining English and their Modern Language. Candidates should show such historical and/or contextual knowledge as is necessary for the 20 profitable study of the topic concerned. Candidates should submit to the Chair of Examiners, care of the English Faculty Office, by 5 p.m. on Thursday of the eighth week of the Michaelmas Term preceding the examination, an abstract of no more than 100 words, describing their area of study. Confirmation of the abstract will be received from the Chair of Examiners by Thursday of the first week of the Hilary Term 25 preceding the examination. The candidate may not discuss with any tutor either his or her choice of content or the method of handling it after Friday of the sixth week of the Hilary Term preceding the examination. Two typed copies of the essay shall be delivered to the Chair of Examiners, Honour School of English Language and Literature, Examination Schools, High Street, by noon on Tuesday of the ninth 30 week after the commencement of Hilary Full Term. A certificate, signed by the candidate to the effect that each essay is the candidate's own work, and that the candidate has read the Faculty guidelines on plagiarism, must be presented together with the submission (see in addition the regulations in 3. for 'Submitted work').

3. Submitted Work for Parts II, III, and IV 35

(*a*) Two typed copies of each extended essay or portfolio essay must be delivered to the Chair of Examiners, Honour School of English Language and Literature, Examination Schools, High Street, according to the deadlines specified in the regulations for each subject. It is additionally strongly recommended that the candidate keep a third copy of his or her submission. A certificate signed by the candidate to the effect 40 that each extended essay or portfolio is the candidate's own work, and that the candidate has read the Faculty guidelines on plagiarism, must be presented together with each submission (see (*b*) below).

(*b*) Every submission must be the work of the candidate alone, and he or she may not discuss with any tutor either his or her choice of content or the method of handling 45 it after the last date indicated in the regulations for each subject.

(*c*) Essays previously submitted for the Honour School of English and Modern Languages may be re-submitted. No essay will be accepted if it has already been submitted, wholly or substantially, for a final honour school or other degree of this University, or degree of any other institution. 50

(*d*) Essays may be penalised that are deemed to be either too short or of excessive length in relation to the word limits specified in the regulations for each subject.

HONOUR SCHOOL OF ENGLISH LANGUAGE AND LITERATURE

A

1. The subjects of examination in the School of English Language and Literature shall be the English Language and Literature in English, together with such Special Options, texts or authors as may from time to time be prescribed by the Board of the Faculty of English Language and Literature.

2. No candidate shall be admitted to examination in this school unless he or she either (a) has passed or been exempted from the First Public Examination or (b) has successfully completed the Foundation Course in English Language and Literature at the Department for Continuing Education.

3. The Board of the Faculty shall by notice from time to time make regulations respecting the examination, and shall have power:
   (1) To prescribe authors or portions of authors.
   (2) To specify one or more related languages or dialects to be offered either as a necessary or as an optional part of the examination.
   (3) To name periods of the history of English Literature and to fix their limits.
   (4) To issue lists of Special Options in connection either with English Language or with Literature in English, or with both; and to prescribe authors and texts.

B

Candidates shall offer either Course I (a general course in English Language and Literature) or Course II (a special course in English Language and early English Literature). Each course shall consist of seven subjects, as prescribed below.

1. Submitted work

(a) Subjects 1, 6, and 7 in Course I, and Subjects 4, 5, 6, and 7 in Course II, shall be examined by submission.

(b) Two typed copies of each extended essay or portfolio essay must be delivered to the Chair of Examiners, Honour School of English Language and Literature, Examination Schools, High Street, according to the deadlines specified in the regulations for each subject. It is additionally strongly recommended that the candidate keep a third copy of his or her submission. A certificate signed by the candidate to the effect that each extended essay or portfolio is the candidate's own work, and that the candidate has read the Faculty guidelines on plagiarism, and observed the specific requirements in (c) below, must be presented together with each submission.

(c) Every extended essay and portfolio must be the work of the candidate alone, and he or she may not discuss with any tutor either his or her choice of content or the method of handling it after the last date indicated in the regulations for each subject.

(d) Essays previously submitted for the Honour School of English Language and Literature may be re-submitted. No essay will be accepted if it has already been submitted, wholly or substantially, for a final honour school or other degree of this University, or degree of any other institution.

(*e*) Essays may be penalised that are deemed to be either too short or of excessive length in relation to the word limits specified in the regulations for each subject.

2. Course I: General Course in English Language and Literature

Each candidate for Course I shall offer all subjects from the list below. Candidates may not offer any period of English literature in which they have already satisfied Examiners in a First Public Examination in English. The subjects will be examined by written examinations of three hours' duration, unless otherwise specified. Examinations will be held in the Trinity Term of the final year of the Honour School.

Candidates are warned (i) that in the papers for Subjects 1–5 they must not answer questions on any topics of which they offer a special study for Subject 6 or Subject 7 and (ii) that they must avoid duplicating, in their answers to one paper, material that they have already used in answering another paper or in the extended essay under Subject 6 or Subject 7.

1. *Shakespeare* (a portfolio submitted in year 3)

The portfolio will consist of three essays of not fewer than 1,500 and not more than 2000 words each. Footnotes will be included in the total word count, but bibliographies do not count towards the limit. Candidates must address more than one work by Shakespeare in at least two of their portfolio essays.

The three essays may be selected from tutorial work or can be written specially for the portfolio. The candidate may revise tutorial essays for portfolio submission in light of feedback from his or her tutor; however the tutor may not mark or discuss the revised version. If an essay is written specially for the portfolio it will not be read or marked by a tutor prior to submission.

Every portfolio essay produced for the Shakespeare paper must be the work of the candidate alone, but he or she may discuss with his or her tutor the subjects and approach to the essays up until the Friday of the eighth week of the Michaelmas Term preceding the examination.

The candidate must deliver two typed copies of each portfolio essay to the Chair of Examiners, Honour School of English Language and Literature, Examination Schools, High Street by noon on Thursday of the fourth week of the Hilary Term preceding the examination. A certificate, signed by the candidate to the effect that each essay is the candidate's own work, and that the candidate has read the Faculty guidelines on plagiarism, must be presented together with the submission (see the introductory regulations for 'submitted work' for the Honour School of English Language and Literature).

2. *Literature in English from 1350–1550*

Candidates must answer two essay questions and one commentary question, as indicated in the rubric for the examination. Passages for commentary will be taken from Chaucer, *Troilus and Criseyde* (ed. L.D. Benson). The paper will be shared with Course II candidates [see Course II, subject 3 below].

3. *Literature in English from 1550 to 1660, excluding the works of Shakespeare*

Candidates who have satisfied the Examiners in the First Public Examination in Classics and English may not offer this paper, and instead must offer Literature in English 650–1100 [see Course II, subject 1 below].

4. *Literature in English from 1660 to 1760*

5. *Literature in English from 1760 to 1830*

6. *Special Options* (an extended essay of not fewer than 5,000 and not more than 6,000 words) (see the introductory regulations for 'submitted work' for Course I).

All Special Options shall be centrally taught. A list of available Special Options shall be published to candidates by the end of the seventh week of the Hilary Term preceding the year of examination. Enrolment to Special Options will be administered by the English Faculty Office and will take place in the Trinity Term in the first year of the Honour School. Confirmation of the Special Option shall be provided to candidates by the end of the sixth week of the same Trinity Term.

Examination for this paper shall be by an extended essay of not fewer than 5,000 and not more than 6,000 words. Footnotes will be included in the total word count, but bibliographies do not count towards the limit. The theme for the essay shall be formulated by the student in discussion with the option convenors. The candidate may not discuss with any tutor either his or her choice of content or the method of handling it after the conclusion of teaching for the Special Options paper on Friday of the fifth week of the Michaelmas Term preceding the examination.

Two typed copies of the extended essay must be delivered to the Chair of Examiners, Honour School of English Language and Literature, Examination Schools, High Street, by noon on Thursday of the eighth week of Michaelmas Term. A certificate, signed by the candidate to the effect that each essay is the candidate's own work, and that the candidate has read the Faculty guidelines on plagiarism, must be presented together with the submission (see the introductory regulations for 'submitted work' for the Honour School of English Language and Literature).

7. Dissertation (an extended essay of not fewer than 7,000 nor more than 8,000 words) (see the introductory regulations for 'submitted work' for the Honour School of English Language and Literature).

Footnotes will be included in the total word count, but bibliographies do not count towards the limit. Candidates may offer an extended essay in any subject area of English Language or Literature in English. Candidates should show such historical and/or contextual knowledge as is necessary for the profitable study of the topic concerned.

Candidates should submit to the Chair of Examiners, care of the English Faculty Office, by 5p.m. on Thursday of the eighth week of the Michaelmas Term preceding the examination, an abstract of no more than 100 words, describing their area of study. Confirmation of his or her abstract will be received from the Chair of Examiners by Thursday of the first week of the Hilary Term preceding the examination.

The candidate may not discuss with any tutor either his or her choice of content or the method of handling it after Friday of the sixth week of the Hilary Term preceding the examination.

Two typed copies of the essay shall be delivered to the Chair of Examiners, Honour School of English Language and Literature, Examination Schools, High Street, by noon on Tuesday of the ninth week after the commencement of Hilary Full Term. A certificate, signed by the candidate to the effect that each essay is the candidate's own work, and that the candidate has read the Faculty guidelines on plagiarism, must be presented together with the submission (see the introductory regulations for 'submitted work' for the Honour School of English Language and Literature).

3. Course II: Special Course in English Language and Early English Literature

Each candidate shall offer Subjects 1 to 4 and Subjects 6 and 7 below, and may choose between Subject 5 (The Material Text) or Course I Subject 1 (Shakespeare). Candidates may not offer any period of English literature in which they have already satisfied Examiners in a First Public Examination in English. The papers will be written examinations of three hours' duration, unless otherwise specified. Written examinations will be held in the Trinity Term of the final year of the Honour School.

Candidates are warned (i) that in the papers for Subjects 1–5 they must not answer questions on any topics of which they offer a special study for Subject 6 or Subject 7 and (ii) that they must avoid duplicating, in their answers to one paper, material that they have already used in answering another paper or in the extended essay under Subject 6 or Subject 7.

1. *Literature in English 650–1100*

Candidates will be expected to show knowledge of a wide range of Old English literature and should show an awareness of the historical and cultural contexts of the period.

2. *Medieval English and Related Literatures 1066–1550*

A paper on a specified genre or theme. The paper shall be examined by a written examination of three hours' duration, in which candidates shall write two essays of equal weighting. Across the paper as a whole, candidates must demonstrate (a) knowledge of literature written before 1350; and (b) knowledge of writing in insular or European languages other than English, which are expected to have been studied in translation.

The genre or theme for the paper shall be published in the Handbook for the Honour School of English Language and Literature by noughth week of Michaelmas Full Term in the first year of study for the Honour School. The specified genre or theme may be subject to periodic review.

3. *Literature in English 1350–1550* (shared with Course I) [as specified for the Honour School of English Language and Literature, Course I, Subject 2].

4. *The History of the English Language to c.1800*

This paper will cover the development of the written language from the earliest records to c.1800, with particular attention to the emergence of a standard form. The paper will be examined on a portfolio of work, comprising two essays of no more than 2,500 words each. Footnotes will be included in the total word count, but bibliographies do not count towards the limit. The list of themes for these essays will be divided into Section A and B and will be published on Tuesday of the seventh week of the Trinity Term preceding the examination. Candidates may not consult tutors after the list of themes has been circulated.

Candidates will be required to submit two pieces of work, each one of between 2,000–2,500 words. They will be required to submit one piece of work in response to discursive essay questions (Section A) and one piece of close commentary work in response to directed questions (Section B). The commentary questions in Section B will require students to find their own passages for analysis. Passages must not exceed 100 lines in total (i.e. 100 lines altogether, not separately). Copies of the texts or passages used in Section B must be included as an appendix to the portfolio.

Two typed copies of the portfolio must be delivered to the Chair of Examiners, Honour School of English Language and Literature, Examination Schools, High Street, by noon on Thursday of the ninth week of the same Trinity Term. A certificate, signed by the candidate to the effect that each essay is the candidate's own work, and that the candidate has read the Faculty guidelines on plagiarism, must be presented together with the submission (see the introductory regulations for 'submitted work' for the Honour School of English Language and Literature).

Once submitted, the essays will then be held over until the following Trinity Term, when they will be examined at the same time as papers for Course II subjects 1–3 and 5–7.

5. *One* of the following:

(*a*) *The Material Text* (a portfolio submitted in year three)

Candidates will study Old and Middle English texts in their original manuscript context.

The portfolio will consist of one commentary answer and one essay, of not fewer than 2,000 and not more than 2,500 words each. Footnotes will be included in the total word count, but bibliographies do not count towards the limit. Themes for the portfolio commentary and essay will be published on Monday of the second week of the Hilary Term preceding the examination. Following their publication, the candidate must not discuss his or her choice of themes with any tutor, nor the method of handling the themes. Every portfolio commentary and essay produced for the Material Text paper must be the work of the candidate alone, but he or she may discuss with his or her tutor the subjects and approach to the essays up until the stated publication date of the portfolio themes.

The candidate must deliver two typed copies of the portfolio to the Chair of Examiners, Honour School of English Language and Literature, Examination Schools, High Street, by noon on Thursday of the fourth week of the Hilary Term preceding the examination. A certificate, signed by the candidate to the effect that each essay is the candidate's own work, and that the candidate has read the Faculty guidelines on plagiarism, must be presented together with the submission (see the introductory regulations for 'submitted work' for the Honour School of English Language and Literature).

(*b*) *Shakespeare* (a portfolio submitted in year three) [as specified for the Honour School of English Language and Literature, Course I, Subject 1].

6. *Special Options*

For this paper Course II candidates may choose ONE of the following:

(*a*) Literature in English 1550–1660 [as specified for the Honour School of English Language and Literature, Course I, Subject 3];

(*b*) any Special Option from the list published for Course I candidates [as specified for the Honour School of English Language and Literature, Course I, Subject 6];

(*c*) any Special Option from the list published for Course II candidates.

Option (*a*) will be examined by an examination of three hours' duration in Trinity Term of the final year.

A list of available Special Options for (*b*) and (*c*) shall be published to Course II candidates by the end of the seventh week of the Hilary Term in the first year of the Honour School. Enrolment to Special Options will be administered by the English Faculty Office and will take place in the Trinity Term in the first year of the Honour School. Confirmation of the Special Option shall be provided to candidates by the end of the sixth week of the same Trinity Term.

Examination for options (*b*) and (*c*) shall be by an extended essay of not fewer than 5,000 and not more than 6,000 words, except where specified in the published list of options. Footnotes will be included in the total word count, but bibliographies do not count towards the limit. The theme for the essay shall be formulated by the student in discussion with the option convenors. The candidate may not discuss with any tutor either his or her choice of content or the method of handling it after the conclusion of teaching for the Special Options paper on Friday of the fifth week of the Michaelmas Term preceding the examination.

Two typed copies of the extended essay must be delivered to the Chair of Examiners, Honour School of English Language and Literature, Examination

Schools, High Street, by noon on Thursday of the eighth week of Michaelmas Term preceding the examination. A certificate, signed by the candidate to the effect that each essay is the candidate's own work, and that the candidate has read the Faculty guidelines on plagiarism, must be presented together with the submission (see the introductory regulations for 'submitted work' for the Honour School of English   5 Language and Literature).

7. *Dissertation* (an extended essay of not fewer than 7,000 nor more than 8,000 words) [as specified for the Honour School of English Language and Literature, Course I, Subject 7].

HONOUR SCHOOL OF EUROPEAN AND MIDDLE EASTERN LANGUAGES

A

1. The subjects of the examination in the Honour School of European and Middle Eastern Languages shall be (*a*) those modern languages and literatures studied in the Honour School of Modern Languages, and (*b*) Arabic, Hebrew, Persian, and Turkish.

2. All candidates must offer (*a*) one of the languages which may be studied in the Honour School of Modern Languages, with its literature, and (*b*) one of the languages specified in clause 1(*b*) above.

3. No candidate shall be admitted to the examination in this school unless he or she has either passed or been exempted from the first Public Examination.

4. The examiners shall indicate in the lists issued by them the languages offered by each candidate obtaining Honours or satisfying the examiners under the appropriate regulation.

5. The examination in this school shall be under the joint supervision of the Boards of the Faculties of Medieval and Modern Languages and Oriental Studies, which shall appoint a standing joint committee to make, and to submit to the two faculty boards, proposals for regulations for this examination and for the Preliminary Examination in European and Middle Eastern Languages.

6. (i) The examiners in the Honour School shall be such of the Public Examiners in the Honour Schools of Modern Languages and Oriental Studies as shall be required.

   (ii) It shall be the duty of the Chair of Examiners in the Honour School of Modern Languages and in the Honour School of Oriental Studies to consult together and designate such examiners as shall be required for the Honour School, whereupon the number of the examiners shall be deemed to be complete.

B

Candidates will be examined in accordance with the examination regulations set out below.

They will also be required to spend, after their matriculation, a year of residence in an appropriate country or countries, and to provide on their entry form for the examination a certificate that they have done this, signed by the Head or by a tutor of their society. Candidates wishing to be dispensed from the requirement to undertake a year of residence abroad must apply in writing to the Chair of the Medieval and Modern Languages Board, 41 Wellington Square, Oxford, OX1 2JF, stating their reasons for requesting dispensation and enclosing a letter of support from their society.

Candidates will be expected to carry out during this year abroad such work as their society may require. Candidates will agree with their College Tutor in advance of their year abroad an independent course of study to be followed during that period.

Each candidate shall offer the oral examination in the European language.

Except in a Special Subject or an alternative to a Special Subject, a candidate shall offer one European language and its literature only.

In every case where, under the regulations for the school, candidates have a choice between one or more papers or subjects, every candidate shall give notice to the Registrar not later than Friday in the fourth week of the Michaelmas Full Term preceding the examination of all the papers and subjects being so offered.

Candidates are warned that they must avoid duplicating in their answers to one part 5 of the examination material that they have used in another part of the examination.

For those papers in the Middle Eastern language where a selection of unspecified texts is to be examined, the selection of texts will be determined by the Oriental Studies Board in Hilary Term for the examination in the next academic year, and copies of the list of selected texts will be available for candidates no later than Friday of the third 10 week of the same term.

Oral examination in the European language

As specified for the Honour School of Modern Languages.

1. Honour School of Modern Languages, Paper I.
2. Honour School of Modern Languages, Papers IIA and IIB. 15
3. Honour School of Modern Languages, *one* paper chosen from Papers VI, VII, or VIII.
4. Honour School of Modern Languages, *one* paper chosen from IV, V, IX, X, XI, or XII.
5. An extended essay on a topic bridging the European and the Middle Eastern 20 language.

Arabic

6A. Arabic unprepared translation into English (half paper) and 6B. Prose composition in Arabic (half paper).

   7. Spoken Arabic. 25

   8. Arabic literature.

   9. Islamic religion.

  10. One of the following:

     (i) Islamic history, AD 570–1500.

     (ii) Classical Arabic literary texts. 30

     (iii) Modern Arabic literature.

     (iv) Arabic vernacular literature AD 1900 to the present day.

     (v) The Middle East in the Age of the Empire, 1830–1971.

     (vi) A modern Islamic thinker (e.g. Sayyid Qutb, Mohamed Talbi, Rashid Rida). 35

     (vii) Society and Culture in the Modern Arab World.

     (viii) A short-term Further Subject, as approved by the Board of the Faculty of Oriental Studies and publicised in the Arabic Handbook.

Paper 6A. is identical with the first half of paper 1 for Arabic and Islamic Studies, and paper 6B. is identical with the first half of paper 2 for Arabic and Islamic Studies 40 in the Final Honour School of Oriental Studies. Papers 7–9 are identical with papers of the same title for Arabic and Islamic Studies in the same degree. The options under paper 10 are also identical with papers and options of the same titles for Arabic and Islamic Studies. The set texts will be those specified in the Arabic Handbook, available from the Oriental Institute. 45

Hebrew

Candidates must take paper 6. and paper 10. and two of papers 7., 8., and 9.

   6. Hebrew composition and unprepared translation.

   7. Prepared texts I: Biblical texts:

     the texts will be those specified for Hebrew only, paper 2. 50

   8. Prepared texts II: Rabbinic and Medieval Hebrew Texts:
the texts will be those specified for Hebrew only, paper 3.

   9. Prepared texts III: Modern Hebrew literature:
the texts will be those specified for Hebrew only, paper 4.

  10. General paper: language, history, religion, and culture or one of the papers in
Jewish Studies Paper b.

Persian

   6. Unprepared translation from Persian

   7. Translation into Persian and essay

   8. and 9. Two papers from the following:
     (*a*) Persian literature: 1000–1400
     (*b*) Persian literature: 1400–1900
     (*c*) Persian literature: 1900–the present

  10. Spoken Persian (as specified for the Honour School of Oriental Studies).

Turkish

  6A. Unprepared translation from modern Turkish (*half paper*) and 6B. Translation
into Turkish (*half paper*).

[For students starting before MT 2015: 7. Spoken Turkish.

   8. Turkish political and cultural texts, 1860 to the present.

   9. Modern Turkish literary texts.

  10. One of the following:
     (*a*) Ottoman historical texts.
     (*b*) Turkish and Ottoman literary texts, 1300–1900.
     (*c*) Turkish language reform and language politics from 1850 to the present
       day.
     (*d*) The Ottoman Empire and the Republic of Turkey, 1807–1980.

Papers 7–9 are identical with papers 3, 5, and 6 for Turkish in the Honour School of
Oriental Studies. The options under paper 10 are identical with papers 4, 7(*a*), 7(*c*) and
7(*g*) of the same degree. The set texts will be those specified in the Turkish Handbook,
available on the Web site of the Faculty of Oriental Studies.]

[For students starting from MT 2015: 7. Oral

   8. Turkish political and cultural texts, 1860 to the present.

   9. Modern Turkish literary texts.

  10. One paper from a list of options listed in the course handbook.

Papers 7–9 are identical with papers 3, 5, and 6 for Turkish in the Honour School of
Oriental Studies. The options under paper 10 are identical with papers of the same
degree. The set texts will be those specified in the Turkish Handbook, available on the
Web site of the Faculty of Oriental Studies.]

Extended Essay

   1. The Extended Essay shall be subject to the following provisions:

    (i) The subject of every essay shall, to the satisfaction of the boards of the
faculties, fall within the scope of the Honour Schools of Modern Languages
and of Oriental Studies.

   (ii) Candidates proposing to offer an essay must submit, through their college, to
the Chair of the Board of the Faculty of Medieval and Modern Languages (on
a form obtainable from the Modern Languages Faculty Office, 41 Wellington
Square) a statement of their name, college, the academic year in which they

intend to take the examination, and the title of the proposed essay together with (*a*) a statement in about fifty words of how the subject is to be treated, (*b*) a statement signed by a supervisor or tutor, that he or she considers the subject suitable, and suggesting a person or persons who might be invited to be an examiner or assessor (the boards will not approve the title unless they are   5
satisfied that a suitably qualified examiner or assessor based in Oxford will be available), and (*c*) a statement by a college tutor that he or she approves the candidate's application, not later than the Wednesday of the second week of the Michaelmas Full Term preceding the examination.

(iii) The faculty boards will decide by the end of the third week of the Michaelmas   10
Full Term preceding the examination whether the proposed essay title is approved. Approval may be granted on condition that the candidate agrees to amend details of the title to the satisfaction of the boards and submits the required amendments to the Modern Languages Faculty Office by the Friday of sixth week of the Michaelmas Full Term preceding the examination.   15

(iv) A candidate may seek approval after Friday of sixth week of the Michaelmas Full Term preceding the examination for an amendment of detail in an approved title, by application to the Modern Languages Faculty Office. The Chair of Examiners and the chairs of the boards, acting together, will decide whether or not a proposed amendment shall be approved.   20

2. While the topic of the essay may be taught by a series of tutorials, candidates will be solely responsible for the final draft, which will not be read by the supervisor or tutor. Candidates must sign a certificate stating that the essay is their own work and that it has not already been submitted, wholly or substantially, for any honour school or degree of this university or a degree of any other institution. This certificate must be   25
sent at the same time as the essay, but under separate cover, addressed to the chair of examiners.

3. No essay shall exceed 10,000 words, exclusive of notes, appendices, and biblio-graphies. The examiners will not take account of such parts of the essay as are beyond this limit. When appropriate, there must be a select bibliography and a list of sources.   30

Essays must be typed in double-spacing on one side only of quarto or A4 paper, and must be firmly held in a stiff cover. Two copies must be submitted to the chair of examiners, and a third copy should be kept by the candidate.

4. The two copies of the essay must be sent, not later than noon on Monday of Week 11 of Hilary Term of the year in which the examination will be held, to the   35
Chair of Examiners, Honour School of European and Middle Eastern Languages, Examination Schools, High Street, Oxford.

HONOUR SCHOOL OF EXPERIMENTAL PSYCHOLOGY

A

1. The subject of the Honour School of Experimental Psychology shall be the study of psychology as an experimental science. 5

2. The examination in Experimental Psychology shall consist of two parts. In Part I candidates shall be examined in the subjects prescribed by the Medical Sciences Board. In Part II candidates shall be examined in the subjects prescribed by the Medical Sciences Board and shall also present, as part of the examination, a project report based on work carried out under supervision prescribed by the Board. 10

3. No candidate shall be admitted for the Part I examination in this school unless he or she has either passed or been exempted from the First Public Examination.

4. No candidate shall be admitted for the Part II examination in this school unless

(*a*) he or she has passed the Part I examination for Experimental Psychology; and

(*b*) he or she has satisfied the Moderators for the Preliminary Examination in 15 Psychology, Philosophy, and Linguistics in the subject *Introduction to Probability Theory and Statistics* or has passed the Qualifying Examination in Statistics for this School.

The Head of the Department of Experimental Psychology or deputy may dispense a candidate from the Qualifying Examination in Statistics in cases where it is clear that 20 the candidate has reached an adequate standard in Statistics by virtue of previous study and qualification.

5. The examinations in the school shall be under the supervision of the Medical Sciences Board, which shall make regulations concerning them, subject always to the preceding clauses of this sub-section. 25

B

1. GENERAL

Decree (7) of 3 June 1947 permits the number of candidates offering Psychology to be limited, if necessary.

2. The subjects of the examination shall be those prescribed in Parts I and II below. 30

3. The examination for Part I shall be taken during Week 0 and 1 of Trinity Term of the candidate's second year. The examination for Part II shall be taken during Trinity Term of the candidate's third year. The dates of submission for the Part I practical work and Part II project work and library dissertation are those prescribed in Parts I and II below. 35

4. Every candidate shall give notice of all papers being offered not later than Friday in the eighth week of Michaelmas Full Term preceding the examination.

PART I

1. Five written papers will be set:

Paper I Biological Bases of Behaviour. 40

Components: (i) Cognitive Neuroscience, (ii) Behavioural Neuroscience.

Paper II Human Experimental Psychology 1.

Components: (i) Perception, (ii) Memory, Attention, and Information Processing.

Paper III Human Experimental Psychology 2.

Components: (i) Language and Cognition, (ii) Developmental Psychology.

Paper IV Social Psychology, and Personality, Individual Differences and Psychological Disorders.

Components: (i) Social Psychology, (ii) Personality, Individual Differences and Psychological Disorders.

In papers I–IV candidates will be required to answer essay and short answer questions from each of the components.

Paper V Experimental Design and Statistics.

2. Candidates will be required to undertake practical work, as specified by the Head of Department of Experimental Psychology or deputy, and this will constitute a part of the examination. In exceptional circumstances, the Proctors may dispense a candidate from the specified requirements on the recommendation of the Head of Department or deputy.

3. Reports of practical work completed during the course of study for Part I and submitted for marking shall constitute a portfolio which shall be available to examiners as part of the examination. Every report submitted for marking must be accompanied by a statement indicating that the work submitted is the candidate's own work. Where the work submitted has been produced in collaboration the candidates shall indicate the extent of their own contributions. Reports of practical work previously submitted for the Honour School of Experimental Psychology may be resubmitted, but reports will not, be accepted if they have already been submitted, wholly or substantially, for another Honour School or degree of this University, or for a degree of any other institution. The Head of Department or deputy shall inform the examiners by the end of Week 0 of the Trinity Term in which the Part I examination is to be held as to which candidates have (a) failed to satisfy the requirement to undertake practical work or (b) failed to submit a portfolio. Candidates in category (a) will be deemed to have failed Paper V. Candidates in category (b) will be deemed to have failed the entire Part I examination. The Head of Department or deputy shall also make available to the examiners records showing the extent to which each candidate has adequately pursued a course of practical work. The examiners shall take this evidence into consideration along with evidence of unsatisfactory or distinguished performance in each portfolio of practical work.

For all papers in Psychology and for the Qualifying Examination in Statistics but not for papers taken from the Honour School of Medical Sciences, the examiners will permit the use of any hand-held pocket calculators subject to the conditions set out under the heading *Regulations for the Conduct of University Examinations*, Part 10.

4. A candidate who fails the Part I examination may retake the examination once only, in the Long Vacation of the same academic year as the original examination. The highest mark that can be awarded to a candidate retaking the examination is a Pass.

Part II

Part II will consist of a research project and *either* three written papers each of 3 hours duration, *or* two written papers, each of 3 hours duration, and a Library Dissertation.

The written papers will be selected from the list of at least 12 options approved by the Medical Sciences Board and published by the Department of Experimental Psychology. A list of options will be posted in the Department of Experimental Psychology not later than noon on Friday of the fifth week of Hilary Term in the year preceding that in which the examination is taken.

If a Library Dissertation is not chosen, candidates may substitute either one or two papers from the list below in place of one or two of the Psychology Advanced Options. If a Library Dissertation is chosen, candidates may substitute one paper from the list below in place of one of the Psychology Advanced Options:

General Linguistics   5
Phonetics and Phonology

A Paper 1 in the Honour School of Medical Sciences
One or two papers in Philosophy.

1. *Research Project and Library Dissertation*
Whether undertaking the research project, or the research project and the library   10
dissertation, such work will normally be carried out in the Trinity Term and the following Michaelmas Term in the year preceding the Part II examinations.

Candidates will be required to undertake such work under the supervision of one of the following:

(i) any member of the Faculty of Psychological Studies.   15

(ii) any other person approved by the Divisional Board provided that such approval shall be applied for not later than Friday of fourth week of Michaelmas Full Term in the year preceding the Part II examinations.

The subject of the library dissertation and the research project should not overlap to the extent that they should not draw on substantially the same literature. Candidates   20
are warned that they should avoid repetition in examination papers of material used in the research project or library dissertation and that substantial repetition may be penalised.

All proposed research projects or library dissertations must be approved in advance by the Head of the Department of Experimental Psychology or deputy. The proce-   25
dures for obtaining this approval will be notified to students by the Head of Department of Experimental Psychology or deputy.

Two bound copies and one electronic copy of completed research projects and library dissertations must be submitted to the Chair of Examiners, Honour School of Experimental Psychology, Examination Schools, Oxford, not later than noon on   30
Monday of the ninth week and Monday of the eleventh week of Hilary Term respectively, in the year of the examination. A certificate signed by the candidate indicating that the work submitted is the candidate's own work, and a statement of the number of words in the research project or library dissertation, must be submitted separately in respect of each research project and library dissertation in a sealed   35
envelope addressed to the Chair of Examiners. Research projects and library disserta-tions previously submitted for the Honour School of Experimental Psychology may be resubmitted. No research project or library dissertation will be accepted if it has already been submitted wholly or substantially, for another Honour School or degree of this University, or for a degree of any other institution.   40

2. Candidates will be required to undertake practical work, as specified by the Head of Department of Experimental Psychology or deputy, and this will constitute a part of the examination. In exceptional circumstances the Proctors may exempt a candi-date from the specified requirements on the recommendation of the Head of Department or deputy.   45

3. Reports of practical work completed during the course of study for Part II and submitted for marking shall constitute a portfolio which shall be available to exam-iners as part of the examination. Every report submitted for marking must be accom-panied by a statement indicating that the work submitted is the candidate's own work. Reports of practical work previously submitted for the Honour School of   50
Experimental Psychology may be resubmitted but reports will not be accepted if they have been submitted, wholly or substantially, for another Honour School or degree of this University, or for a degree of any other institution. The Head of

Department or deputy shall inform the examiners by the end of Week 0 of the Trinity Term in which the Part II examination is to be held as to which candidates have failed to satisfy the requirement to undertake practical work. Failure to satisfy the requirement to undertake practical work will result in the candidate's final degree classification being lowered by one class. Candidates who fail to submit a portfolio will be 5 deemed to have failed the entire Part II examination. The Head of Department, or deputy, shall make available to the examiners records showing the extent to which candidates have adequately pursued a course of practical work. The examiners shall take this evidence into consideration along with evidence of unsatisfactory or distinguished performance in each portfolio of practical work. 10

HONOUR SCHOOL OF FINE ART

A

1. No person who is not a member of the University may be admitted to the Final Examination in Fine Art.

2. No member of the University shall be admitted to the Final Examination in Fine Art unless they have either passed or been exempted from the Preliminary Examination in Fine Art.

3. (*a*) No one shall be admitted as a candidate for the examination unless by the end of the term in which the examination is held they shall have kept statutable residence for nine terms, except that a candidate who is a Senior Student may be admitted as a candidate if by the end of the term in which the examination is held they shall have kept statutable residence for six terms.

(*b*) Time spent outside Oxford as part of an academic programme approved by Council shall count towards residence for the purposes of this clause.

(*c*) The Proctors shall have power to excuse from one term of statutable residence any member of the University who shall have been duly certified by them to have been prevented by illness or other reasonable cause from keeping such residence for one or more terms, subject to the conditions set out in the appropriate regulation. Application shall be made through the college or other society or approved institution to which the member belongs. The student, or his or her society, may within fourteen days of the date of the Proctors' decision appeal in writing to the Chair of the Education Committee (who may nominate another member of the committee, other than one of the Proctors, to adjudicate the appeal).

(*d*) The Proctors shall have power to dispense, subject to such conditions as it may from time to time determine, from up to three terms of statutable residence any member of the University who has not completed such residence for any reason which the Proctors shall judge to be sufficient. Application shall be made through the college or other society or approved institution to which the member belongs. The student, or his or her society, may within fourteen days of the date of the Proctors' decision appeal in writing to the Chair of the Education Committee (who may nominate another member of the committee, other than one of the Proctors, to adjudicate the appeal).

(*e*) The candidate's college or other society or approved institution shall be required to certify on the entry form, by the time determined for entry, whether or not the candidate will have met the requirement for statutable residence by the end of the term in which the examination is held, and to notify the University of any change in the candidate's status in this respect between entry and the date of the examination.

(*f*) Nothing in this clause shall affect the conditions required for admission to degrees set out in the appropriate regulations.

4. No one shall be admitted as a candidate for the examination after the lapse of twelve terms from the term of their matriculation inclusively, except that a candidate who has been prevented by urgent cause from offering himself or herself for examination may offer himself or herself as a candidate at the next ensuing examination provided that he or she has satisfied the conditions of the relevant regulations.

5. The examination shall be under the supervision of the Committee for the Ruskin School of Art, which shall make regulations for the examination.

B

1. The examination shall include both practical and written work. Candidates will also be examined viva voce, except that the examiners may dispense from the viva voce examination any candidate concerning whom they shall have decided that performance in the viva voce examination could not properly be allowed to affect the result.

2. Every candidate will be required to

(a) Produce a selection of work completed throughout the course preceding the examination in each of the categories scheduled below:

   (i) An exhibition of current work or work constructed especially for assessment.

   (ii) A portfolio of work made during the course preceding the examination in any medium or media agreed by the candidate and their tutor. This should include at least twelve original works; in the case of time-based work, candidates should make a submission of works, or excerpts of works, of no more than a total of twenty minutes' duration. Work which, in the judgement of the candidate's tutor, cannot be submitted for examination for practical reasons, may be represented by documentation.

(b) Submit an essay of no more than 6,000 words (including footnotes), which shall normally be on some aspect of visual culture since 1900, in accordance with the provisions of clause 3 of these regulations.

(c) Satisfy the examiners in a paper on the history and theory of visual culture since 1900.

3. (a) The work required by the provisions of clause 2 must be submitted to the Chair of Examiners, Final Examination in Fine Art, Ruskin School of Art, 74 High Street, Oxford by noon on Tuesday in the eighth week of Trinity Full Term in which the examination is taken.

(b) A candidate submitting an essay in accordance with the provisions of clause 2 (b) of these regulations must apply for the approval of the Head of School not later than Friday in the fourth week of the Michaelmas Full Term preceding the examination. Such application shall include the title of the proposed essay and a synopsis of not more than 100 words setting out the manner in which it is proposed to treat the subject. One typed copy of the essay must be delivered to the Chair of Examiners, Final Examination in Fine Art, Examination Schools not later than noon on the Monday of the eighth week of the Hilary Full Term preceding the examination. Each essay must be accompanied by a certificate signed by the candidate that the essay has not been submitted for any previous examination, and that the essay is his or her own unaided work. Tutors may provide advice on the choice and scope of the subject, the sources available, and the method of presentation. They may also read and comment on a first draft of the essay. This certificate must be submitted separately in a sealed envelope addressed to the Chair of Examiners.

HONOUR SCHOOL OF GEOGRAPHY

A

1. The examination in the Honour School of Geography shall always include, as stated subjects to be offered by all candidates:

Geographical Research   5

2. Candidates shall be required to offer, in addition to the above subject, two foundational courses chosen from the following list:

(i) Earth System Dynamics

(ii) Space, Place and Society

(iii) Environmental Geography   10

3. Candidates shall be required to offer, in addition to the above subjects, and after giving due notice of the subjects they select, three Optional Subjects chosen under arrangements determined by the board by regulation.

4. The examination shall be partly practical.

5. No candidate shall be admitted to the examination in the Honour School unless   15
either

(*a*) he or she is a Senior Student, *or*

(*b*) he or she has passed or been exempted from the First Public Examination.

6. The examination in the Honour School shall be under the supervision of the Social Sciences Board.   20

B

1. All candidates will be required to offer the following subjects:

    i. Geographical Research

    ii. Two foundational courses chosen from the following list: Earth System Dynamics; Space, Place and Society; Environmental Geography   25

    iii. Three Optional Subjects to be chosen from a list published by the department (3 papers). Submitted work will also be required in three subjects.

    iv. A Geographical Dissertation in accordance with the detailed regulations given below. The Dissertation will be treated as the equivalent of two papers.

    v. A fieldwork report in accordance with the detailed regulations below.   30

2. Candidates are required to have undertaken field-work as an integral part of their course. Candidates may be examined viva voce.

Theses, practical notebooks or extended essays previously submitted for the Honour School of Geography may be resubmitted. No thesis, practical notebook or extended essay will be accepted if it has already been submitted, wholly or substan-   35
tially, for another final honour school or degree of this University, or a degree of any other institution.

3. The requirements for each subject are as follows:

    I. *Geographical Research:* A course on the practice of human, physical, and environmental geographical research. Emphasis will be placed on the provi-   40
    sion of research skills and the relation between conceptual and methodolo-
    gical issues and the practice of research.

II. *Earth System Dynamics:* The dynamics of climatic, ecological and geomorphological systems, studied over a wide range of timescales and covering past, present and future changes. Emphasis will also be given to interactions between these components of the earth's system.

III. *Space, Place and Society:* A human geographical perspective on space, place and society, taking account of relevant and major concepts in geographical thought, and acknowledging differing theoretical approaches. Specific cases and practices will be introduced at a range of geographical scales.

IV. *Environmental Geography:* The nature of environmental issues, their causes and consequences, and the development of policies to manage the environment. A range of case studies will be used across various geographical scales.

V. Candidates must offer three Optional Subjects to be chosen from a list to be published by the Head of School not later than the end of the Trinity Full Term preceding the candidate's admission to the Final Honour School. One paper of three hours will be set on each subject. Each candidate must also submit an individual piece of work (as specified on the rubrics for each optional subject) for all three Optional Subjects to the Chair of Examiners in the Final Honour School of Geography, c/o the Examination Schools, High Street not later than 12 noon on the Monday of the first week of the Trinity Term in which they present themselves for examination. The submitted work should not duplicate material in the candidate's dissertation. Instructions for the submitted work will be published by the Chair of the Undergraduate Teaching and Examination Committee not later than the end of the Trinity Full Term preceding the candidate's admission to the Final Honour School. Information about the Optional Subjects and submitted work will be published on the departmental website by early October.

Each candidate will submit

1. A fieldwork report of 4,500 words based on research undertaken as part of the field trip during Trinity Term of the year in which a candidate is admitted to the Honour School. The requirements for the fieldwork report will be published on the departmental website at the beginning of Michaelmas Full Term in the year in which the candidate is admitted to the Honour School. The fieldwork report must be submitted no later than 12 noon on the Friday in the eighth week of Trinity Term in the year preceding that in which they propose to take the examination.

2. A Geographical Dissertation on a Selected Topic.

The Dissertation, exclusive of bibliography, maps, and statistical appendices, must not be more than 12,000 words. The attention of candidates is drawn to the fact that limited rather than large areas are more likely to allow for adequate depth of study. The Dissertation should embody original practical work based on primary data (e.g. data collected in the field, archival materials, census data, etc.), and not be based on secondary material (e.g. text books, published local histories, published papers in learned journals, government or local government reports).

Candidates having first secured the approval of their tutors are required to submit to the Head of the School for approval, not later than noon on Friday at the end of the fourth week of the Trinity Full Term in the year preceding that in which they propose to take the examination, an outline of approximately 500 words of the proposed Dissertation. Special permission must also be sought from the Head of School for any substantive change in the original proposal.

The Dissertation must be firmly bound. It must be the work of the author alone and aid from others must be limited to prior discussion as to the subject and sources and advice on presentation. Every candidate shall sign a declaration of originality to the effect that the Dissertation is his or her own work, and this declaration shall be presented with the Dissertation.

Candidates must submit two copies of their Dissertation not later than 12 noon on the Monday in the first week of the following Hilary Term, to the Chair of Examiners in the Final Honour School of Geography c/o Examination Schools, High Street, Oxford, OX1 4BG.

5

HONOUR SCHOOL OF EARTH SCIENCES

A

1. The subject of the Honour School of Geology/Earth Sciences shall be the study of the natural science of the Earth in space and time.

2. No candidate shall be admitted to examination in this school unless he or she has either passed or been exempted from the First Public Examination.

3. The examination in this school shall be under the supervision of the Mathematical, Physical and Life Sciences Board, which shall prescribe the necessary regulations. Details of the conventions used by the examiners can be found in the Undergraduate Course Handbook (see B1 below).

4. The examination shall consist of one part for the three-year course in Geology (Part A) and two parts for the four-year course in Earth Sciences (A, B). Part A shall be subdivided into Part A1 (examinations taking place three terms after the candidate has passed the First Public Examination) and Part A2 (examinations taking place six terms after the candidate has passed the First Public Examination).

5. No candidate may present him or herself for examination in Part B unless he or she has been adjudged worthy of at least second class honours by the examiners in Part A.

6. The name of a candidate in either the three-year course or the four-year course shall not be published in a class list until he or she has completed all parts of the respective examination; and in the case of the four-year course, has been adjudged worthy of honours by the examiners in Part A and Part B of the examination. The Examiners shall give due consideration to the performance in all parts of the respective examinations.

7. Part A1 may only be taken once, but no candidate shall be deemed to have failed. The second year mapping project should be submitted at the beginning of the fifth term after the candidate has passed the First Public Examination, and may not subsequently be modified. A candidate who obtains only a pass, or fails to satisfy the examiners in Part A, may enter again for Part A2 of the examination on one, but no more than one, subsequent occasion. Where a candidate retakes the whole year, the candidate will submit a new third-year essay on a subject approved by the Chair of the Faculty of Earth Sciences or deputy as set out in section B, Geology (three year course), (ii), below. Where a candidate resits only the examinations, the third-year essay may be resubmitted by the deadline given in the Undergraduate Course Handbook. A candidate who fails to satisfy the examiners in Part A who subsequently enters a second time may not proceed to the fourth year. The fourth-year project should be submitted in the ninth term after the candidate has passed the First Public Examination, and may not subsequently be modified. The rules for handling the fourth-year project are to be found in the departmental Undergraduate Course Handbook. A candidate who obtains only a pass, or fails to satisfy the examiners in Part B, may not enter again for Part B.

8. A candidate adjudged worthy of Honours in the Second Public Examination for the four-year course may supplicate for the Degree of Master of Earth Sciences, provided that the candidate has fulfilled all the conditions for admission to a degree of the University.

9. A candidate in the final year of the four-year course, adjudged worthy of Honours in Part A, but who does not enter Part B, or who fails to obtain Honours

in Part B, is permitted to supplicate for the Honours degree of Bachelor of Arts in Geology with the classification obtained in Part A; provided that no such candidate may later enter or re-enter the Part B year or supplicate for the degree of Master of Earth Sciences; and provided in each case that the candidate has fulfilled all the conditions for admission to a degree of the University.

10. Candidates will be expected to show skills and knowledge based upon practical work. The examiners will assess practical skills and knowledge by means of practical examinations, and by assessment of practical work done by candidates during their course of study.

B

1. In the following, 'the Course Handbook' refers to the Geology/Earth Sciences Undergraduate Course Handbook, published annually at the start of Michaelmas Term by the Faculty of Earth Sciences and also posted on the website at www.earth. ox.ac.uk/undergraduate_course.

2. The examiners will permit the use of any hand-held calculator, subject to the conditions set out under the heading 'Use of calculators in examinations' in the Regulations for the Conduct of University Examinations and further elaborated in the Course Handbook.

PART A1

A candidate shall be required to offer:

(i) Three papers (Part A1), including practical elements, to be taken in Trinity Term, in the third term after the candidate has passed the First Public Examination.

The list of subjects and syllabuses available will be published in the Course Handbook.

PART A2

A candidate shall be required to offer:

(i) a report on an individual mapping or practical project, prepared according to the guidelines set out in the Course Handbook, the report to be submitted by Thursday of Week 0 of Hilary Term in the fifth term after the candidate has passed the First Public Examination; and

(ii) an extended essay, prepared according to the guidelines set out in the Course Handbook, the work to be undertaken in Hilary Term in the fifth term after the candidate has passed the First Public Examination, and the essay to be submitted by the Thursday of Week 0 of Trinity Term in the sixth term after the candidate has passed the First Public Examination. The subject of the essay must have been approved by the Chair of the Faculty of Earth Sciences or deputy no later than the end of Michaelmas Full Term in the fourth term after the candidate has passed the First Public Examination; and

(iii) seven papers, including practical elements, to be taken in Week 5 of Trinity Term in the sixth term after the candidate has passed the First Public Examination.

The list of subjects and syllabuses available will be published in the Course Handbook.

The Head of Department of Earth Sciences or deputy shall provide the examiners with information showing the extent to which each candidate has satisfactorily completed the practicals and field courses. In addition, practical notebooks containing records of both field and laboratory courses must also be made available to the examiners.

Examiners may take into account these records of practical and fieldwork, in particular with regard to the attendance record of the candidates, and to any marks awarded for assignments, when awarding classes. Material handed in from practical   5
classes will be taken as evidence of attendance.

For candidates whose attendance record is deemed unsatisfactory, the examiners have the discretion to reduce the final degree class of the candidate. Examiners may also take into account evidence of excellent performance in field or practical work when drawing up class boundaries.   10

Candidates may be examined viva voce at the examiners' discretion.

Part B

Part B of the examination shall be taken at a time not less than three terms after Part A. In Part B a candidate shall be required to offer:

  (i) written papers on four subjects, chosen from a list published by the Faculty of   15
      Earth Sciences as set out in (4) below, for examination in Trinity Term in the
      ninth term after the candidate has passed the First Public Examination, and

 (ii) either an extended essay, or a report on an advanced practical project or
      other advanced work, prepared according to the guidelines set out in the
      Course Handbook, the work to be undertaken in Michaelmas, Hilary,   20
      and Trinity Terms in the seventh, eighth and ninth terms respectively
      after the candidate has passed the First Public Examination, and the
      essay or report to be submitted by Thursday of Week 3 of Trinity Term
      in the ninth term after the candidate has passed the First Public
      Examination. The proposed nature and duration of the practical or other   25
      advanced work shall be submitted for approval, by no later than the end of
      Trinity Full Term in the sixth term after the candidate has passed the First
      Public Examination, to the Chair of the Faculty of Earth Sciences or
      deputy with the agreement of the Head of the Department of Earth
      Sciences or deputy.   30

The list of subjects and syllabuses for the written papers in 1(i) will be published in the Course Handbook for the academic year in which they are examined. The subjects and syllabuses shall be approved by the Faculty of Earth Sciences with the agreement of the Head of the Department of Earth Sciences or deputy.

Candidates may be examined viva voce at the examiners' discretion.   35

HONOUR SCHOOL OF HISTORY

A

1. The examination in the School of History shall be under the supervision of the Board of the Faculty of History, and shall always include:

(1) The History of the British Isles (including the History of Scotland, Ireland, and   5
Wales; and of British India and of British Colonies and Dependencies as far as they are connected with the History of the British Isles);

(2) General History during some period, selected by the candidate from periods to be named from time to time by the Board of the Faculty;

(3) A Special Historical subject, studied with reference to original authorities.   10

2. No candidate shall be admitted to examination in this school unless he or she has *either* passed or been exempted from the First Public Examination *or* has successfully completed the Foundation Course in History at the Department for Continuing Education.

3. The Board of the Faculty of History shall, by notice from time to time, make   15
regulations respecting the above-named branches of examination, and shall have power

(1) To name certain periods of General History, and to fix their limits;

(2) To issue lists of Special Historical subjects, prescribing particular authorities where they think it desirable.   20

[For students starting before MT 2015: 4. The examination in the Special Historical subject may be omitted by candidates, but such candidates shall not be placed in the Results List.

5. The Board of the Faculty may include in the examination, either as necessary or as optional, other subjects which they may deem suitable to be studied in connection   25
with History, including translation from foreign languages of passages not specially prepared, and may prescribe books or portions of books in any language.]

[For students starting from MT 2015: 4. The Board of the Faculty may include in the examination, either as necessary or as optional, other subjects which they may deem suitable to be studied in connection with History, including translation from   30
foreign languages of passages not specially prepared, and may prescribe books or portions of books in any language.]

B

The History Board shall issue annually the Handbook for the Honour School of History by Monday of Week 1 of the first Michaelmas Full Term of candidates' work   35
for the Honour School. A supplement to the handbook shall be issued to candidates at the beginning of Week 4 of the first Hilary Full Term of their work for the Honour School, and posted in the History Faculty Building and circulated to tutors.

All candidates are required to offer Subjects I, II, III, V, and VI, below. No candidate may be placed in the Class List unless he or she also offers Special   40
Subject IV, below.

Candidates who have taken the Foundation Course in History rather than the Preliminary Examination are required to offer at least one paper from either Subject I or Subject II which relates to a period between 285 and 1550 (this may be taken to include Periods (I), (II), or (III) of the History of the British Isles, or Periods (i), (ii), (iii), (iv), (v), (vi), or (vii) of General History).

Students participating in the academic exchange scheme with Princeton University will substitute the courses taken at Princeton for either a General History or History of the British Isles paper. The Princeton courses will be examined at Princeton, and the grades awarded will be reviewed and moderated by the Examiners to produce a single University standard mark, according to procedures laid down in the Handbook and Examining Conventions.

I. History of the British Isles: any one of the following periods:

   (I) *c.*300–1087;

   (II) 1042–1330;

   (III) 1330–1550;

   (IV) 1500–1700;

   (V) 1685–1830;

   (VI) 1815–1924;

   (VII) since 1900.

No candidate may offer a period offered when passing the First Public Examination.

The History of the British Isles is taken to include the history of the Irish Republic in the twentieth century, and of British India and British Colonies and Dependencies as far as they are connected with the History of Britain.

II. General History: any one of the listed periods:

   (i) 285–476; (ii) 476–750; (iii) 700–900; (iv) 900–1150 and (v) 1100–1273; (vi) 1273–1409; (vii) 1409–1525; (viii) 1500–1618; (ix) 1618–1715; (x) 1715–1799; (xi) 1789–1871; (xii) 1856–1914; (xiii) 1914–1945; (xiv) 1941–1973; (xv) Britain's North American Colonies: from settlement to independence, 1600–1812, (xvi) From Colonies to Nation: the History of the United States 1776–1877, (xvii) The History of the United States since 1863, (xviii) Eurasian Empires 1450–1800; (xix) Imperial and Global History, 1750–1914.

The four periods of British and General History offered by a candidate in the First Public Examination and the Honour School must include at least one from the following groups:

1. Medieval History

   (I) c.300–1087; (II) 1042–1330; General History (taken in the First Public Examination): I: 370–900, II: 1000–1300; (taken in the Final Honour School). (i) 285–476, (ii) 476–750, (iii) 700–900, (iv) 900–1150 and (v) 1100–1273, (vi) 1273–1409.

2. Early Modern History

   (III) 1330–1550, (IV) 1500–1700; General History (taken in the First Public Examination): III: 1400–1650; (taken in the Final Honour School): (vii) 1409–1525; (viii) 1500–1618; (ix) 1618–1715. (xviii) Eurasian Empires 1450–1800.

3. Modern History

   (V) British History 1685–1830; (VI) 1815–1924; (VII) since 1900, General History (taken in the First Public Examination): IV: 1815–1914; (taken in the Final Honour School): (x) 1715–1799; (xi) 1789–1871; (xii) 1856–1914; (xiii) 1914–1945; (xiv) 1941–1973; (xv) Britain's North American Colonies: from settlement to independence, 1600–1812; (xvi) From Colonies to Nation: the History of the United States 1776–1877; (xvii) The History of the United States since 1863; (xix) Imperial and Global History 1750–1914.

Candidates with Senior Student status, and candidates who have passed the First Public Examination in a course other than Modern History are required to offer one paper in British History and one in General History, to be taken from two out of the three period groups (1. Medieval History, 2. Early Modern History, 3. Modern History).

Candidates who participate in the Princeton Exchange are required to offer one period in the History of the British Isles or General History, so chosen that the periods offered in the First Public Examination and the Honour School are taken from at least two out of the three period groups. This requirement shall also apply to candidates who participate in the Princeton Exchange having taken the First Public Examination in a joint school involving History papers.

III. Further Subject: any one of an approved list of Further Subjects, as detailed in the Handbook for the Final Honour School in History published by the Board of the Faculty of History by Monday of first week of Michaelmas Term each year for the academic year ahead.

Candidates who have taken or are taking the Further Subject 'The Soviet Union 1924–1941' cannot also take the Special Subject 'Terror and Forced Labour in Stalin's Russia'.

Candidates will be examined by means of a timed paper, except in the following case(s):

Further Subject, 'Britain at the Movies: Film and National Identity since 1914'.

Candidates taking the Further Subject paper(s) listed above will be examined by means of an essay, which shall not exceed 5,000 words (including footnotes but excluding bibliography), and shall be on a topic or theme selected by the candidate from a question paper published by the examiners on the Monday of the seventh week of Hilary Term in the year preceding final examination. Essays should be typed or word-processed in double spacing and should conform to the standards of academic presentation prescribed in the course handbook. Essays (two copies) will be completed during the eighth week of the Hilary Term in the year preceding final examination, and must be delivered by hand to the Examination Schools (addressed to the Chair of Examiners, Honour School of History, Examination Schools, High Street, Oxford) not later than 12 noon on the Friday of the eighth week of the Hilary Term of the year preceding final examination. Candidates delivering essays will be required to complete a receipt form, which will only be accepted as proof of receipt if it is counter-signed by a member of the Examination Schools staff. Each essay must be accompanied by a sealed envelope (bearing only the candidate's examination number) containing a formal declaration signed by the candidate that the essay is his or her own work. The University's regulations on Late Submission of Work will apply.

Further Subjects 'Representing the City 1558–1640' and 'Post-Colonial Historiography: writing the Indian nation'.

Candidates taking the Further Subject paper(s) listed above will be examined by means of an essay, which shall be between 5,000 and 6,000 words (including footnotes but excluding bibliography), and shall be on an interdisciplinary topic relevant to the Further Subject concerned. Candidates must submit their proposed essay title to the Chair of Examiners for History, care of the History Faculty Office, not later than Friday of the eighth week of Hilary Term in the first year of study for the Honour School. Approval of the title may be assumed unless the Chair of Examiners contacts a candidate's tutor by Monday of the second week of the Trinity Term.

The candidate must deliver two copies of the essay by hand to the Examination Schools (addressed to the Chair of Examiners, Honour School of History, Examination Schools, High Street, Oxford) not later than 12 noon on the Thursday of the eighth week of Trinity Term in the first year of study for the Honour School. A certificate, signed by the candidate to the effect that each essay is the candidate's own work, and that the candidate has read the Faculty's guidelines on plagiarism, must be presented together with the submission. Candidates delivering essays will be required to complete a receipt form, which will only be accepted as proof of receipt if it is counter-signed by a member of the Examination Schools staff. The University's regulations on *Late Submission of Work* will apply.

IV. The Special Subjects available in any given year, as approved by the Board of the Faculty of History, will be publicised in the list posted by the Faculty of History in the Hilary Term of the preceding year.

Candidates will be examined by means of a timed paper including compulsory passages for comment, and by means of an extended essay, which shall not exceed 6,000 words (including footnotes but excluding bibliography), and shall be on a topic or theme selected by the candidate from a question paper published by the examiners on the Friday of the fourth week of Michaelmas Term in the year of examination.

Essays should be typed or word-processed in double spacing and should conform to the standards of academic presentation prescribed in the course handbook.

Essays (two copies) shall normally be written during the Michaelmas Term in the year of examination and must be delivered by hand to the Examination Schools (addressed to the Chair of Examiners, Honour School of History, Examination Schools, High Street, Oxford) not later than 12 noon on the Friday before the beginning of Hilary Full Term of the year of examination. Candidates delivering essays will be required to complete a receipt form, which will only be accepted as proof of receipt if it is counter-signed by a member of the Examination Schools staff. Each essay must be accompanied by a sealed envelope (bearing only the candidate's examination number) containing a formal declaration signed by the candidate that the essay is his or her own work. The University's regulations on *Late Submission of Work* will apply.

Depending on the availability of teaching resources, not all Further and Special Subjects will be available to all candidates in every year. Candidates may obtain details of the choice of options for the following year by consulting lists posted at the beginning of the Week Four of Hilary Full Term in the History Faculty, on Weblearn and circulated to History Tutors.

V. *Disciplines of History*

Candidates will be expected to answer two examination questions selected from a paper divided into two sections. One question should be answered from each section.

The sections are:
1. Making Historical Comparisons;
2. Making Historical Arguments.

VI. *A thesis from original research*

1. Candidates must submit a thesis as part of the fulfilment of their final examination.

2. Theses shall normally be written during the Hilary Term of the final year. All theses must be submitted not later than noon on Friday of eighth week of the Hilary Term of the final year.

3. A candidate may submit
   (*a*) any essay or part of any essay which the candidate has submitted or intends to submit for any university essay prize; or
   (*b*) any other work

provided in either case that (i) no thesis will be accepted if it has already been submitted, wholly or substantially, for a final honour school other than one involving History, or another degree of this University, or a degree of any other university, and (ii) the candidate submits a statement to that effect, and (iii) the subject is approved by the Chair of the Examiners for the Honour School of History.

4. The provisos in cl. 3 above shall not debar any candidate from submitting work based on a previous submission towards the requirements for a degree of any other university provided that:

    (i) the work is substantially new;

    (ii) the candidate also submits both the original work itself and a statement specifying the extent of what is new. The examiners shall have sole authority to decide in every case whether proviso (i) to this clause has been met.

5. Every candidate must submit the title proposed together with a typed synopsis of the thesis topic and proposed method of investigation (no more than 250 words) and the written approval of their College History Tutor to the Chair of the Examiners for the Honour School of History, the History Faculty, George Street, Oxford, not earlier than the beginning of Trinity Full Term in the year preceding that in which the candidate takes the examination and not later than the Friday of sixth week of Michaelmas Term in the final year. If no notification is received from the Chair of Examiners by the first Monday of Hilary Full Term of the final year, the title shall be deemed to be approved. Any subsequent changes to title require formal application to the Chair of Examiners by the Friday of Week 4 of the Hilary Term of the final year and subsequent approval.

6. Theses should normally include an investigation of relevant printed or unprinted primary historical sources, and must include proper footnotes and a bibliography. They must be the work of the author alone. In all cases, the candidate's tutor or thesis adviser shall discuss with the candidate the field of study, the sources available, and the methods of presentation. Candidates shall be expected to have had a formal meeting or meetings with their College History Tutor, and, if necessary, an additional meeting or meetings with a specialised thesis adviser in the Trinity Term of their second year, as well as a second formal meeting or meetings with their thesis adviser in the Michaelmas Term of their final year, prior to submitting the title of their thesis. While writing the thesis, candidates are permitted to have further advisory sessions at which bibliographical, structural, and other problems can be discussed. The total time spent in all meetings with the College History Tutor and/or the specialised thesis adviser must not exceed five hours. A first draft of the thesis may be commented on, but not corrected in matters of detail and presentation, by the thesis adviser.

7. No thesis shall exceed 12,000 words in length (including footnotes, but excluding bibliography and, in cases for which specific permission has been obtained from the Chair of Examiners, appendices), except in the case that a candidate is submitting a thesis as a critical edition of a text, in which case the regulations on word length in VI 10, sections iii and x, below, apply. The thesis should conform to the standards of academic presentation prescribed in the course handbook. Failure to conform to such standards may incur penalties as outlined in the course handbook.

8. All candidates must submit two copies of their thesis, addressed to the Chair of Examiners, Honour School of History, Examination Schools, High Street, Oxford, not later than noon on Friday of eighth week of the Hilary Term of the year in which they are presenting themselves for examination. The University's regulations on *Late Submission of Work* will apply. Every candidate shall present a certificate, signed by him or herself, in a separate envelope bearing the candidate's examination number, addressed to the Chair of Examiners. The certificate (forms are available from the History Faculty Office) should declare that (*a*) the thesis is the candidate's own work,

(*b*) that no substantial portion of it has been presented for any other degree course or examination, (*c*) that is does not exceed 12,000 words in length, except in the case that a candidate is submitting a thesis as a critical edition of a text, in which case the regulations on word length in VI 10, sections iii and x, below, apply, (*d*) that no more than five hours have been spent in preparatory or advisory meetings between the candidate and his or her College History Tutor or thesis adviser, and (*e*) that only the first draft of the thesis has been seen by the thesis adviser. Candidates delivering theses will be required to complete a receipt form, which will only be accepted as proof of receipt if it is countersigned by a member of the Examination Schools staff.

9. Candidates shall not answer in any other paper, with the exception of Disciplines of History (V), questions which fall very largely within the scope of their thesis. Candidates should not choose a thesis that substantially reworks material studied in the Further or Special Subjects, and should demonstrate familiarity with and use of substantially different and additional primary sources.

10. As an alternative route to fulfilling the requirement for the compulsory thesis, or to submitting an optional one, a candidate may prepare an edition of a short historical text with appropriate textual apparatus, historical annotation and introduction. This exercise, which is different in kind from the writing of a normal dissertation, is governed by the following additional regulations:

i. The original work selected for editing may be a narrative, literary, or archival text of any kind, and may be of any period and in any language. It must be susceptible to historical analysis and commentary, and of a kind that requires the application of editorial and historical skills and techniques, including linguistic and palaeographical skills where appropriate.

ii. The choice of text must be approved by the submission to the Chair of the FHS in History, with the support of a supervisor, of a 250-word outline of the text and its context, and specifying its length. This submission must be made by Friday of noughth week of the Michaelmas Term of the candidate's final year, but candidates are advised to seek permission well before this. The Chair must consult appropriate colleagues before approving the project: they will need to be satisfied that it provides scope for displaying appropriate levels of knowledge and expertise.

iii. The length of the chosen text will depend upon the linguistic and technical challenges which it poses, and the scope it offers for historical analysis and commentary; the advice of the supervisor will be essential. A complex text in a difficult language may only run to a few thousand words. The absolute maxima are 15,000 words for a non-English text, and 30,000 for one in English; but these are not norms or targets. An extract from a longer text is permissible, so long as the selection is rationally justified, and the extract can stand on its own for purposes of historical commentary.

iv. A text in a language other than English must be accompanied by an English translation.

v. The examiners must be provided with a facsimile of no less than 30 per cent of the text in its primary manuscript or printed form. Where there are several versions, the most important should be chosen.

vi. A textual introduction should state how many versions (whether manuscript or printed) there are to the text, how they relate to each other, and what editorial principles have been employed.

vii. A textual apparatus should list variant readings, emendations and textual problems in accordance with normal editorial practice.

viii. Historical notes to the text should comment as appropriate on people, places, events and other references, and should draw out points of wider historical interest.   5

ix. A historical introduction should discuss the immediate context of the work, including its author or the record-creating system that produced it, and should explain its wider historical context and significance.

x. The textual and historical introductions and the historical notes should not exceed 8,000 words (for an English text) or 6,000 (for a translated one).   10

xi. The dissertation should be arranged and bound in the following order: historical introduction; textual introduction; text, with textual notes (keyed to the text in the sequence *a, b, c,* etc.) at the foot of the page; historical notes (keyed to the text in the sequence 1, 2, 3, etc.) on separate pages; sample facsimile.   15

VII. *An optional additional thesis*

1. Any candidate may offer an optional additional thesis.

2. Regulation VI 3. above applies.

3. Regulation VI 4. above applies.

4. Every candidate intending to offer an optional thesis except as defined in VI 3(*a*)   20
above must submit the title proposed together with the written approval of a thesis adviser or College History Tutor to the Chair of the Examiners for the Honour School of History, the History Faculty, George Street, Oxford, not earlier than the beginning of Trinity Full Term in the year preceding that in which the candidate takes the examination and not later than Friday of the first week of the following Hilary Full   25
Term. The Chair shall decide whether or not to approve the title, consulting the Faculty Board if so desired, and shall advise the candidate as soon as possible.

5. Optional additional theses should normally include an investigation of relevant printed or unprinted historical sources, and must include proper footnotes and a bibliography. They must be the work of the author alone. In all cases, the candidate's   30
College History Tutor or thesis adviser shall discuss with the candidate the field of study, the sources available, and the methods of presentation (which should conform to the standards of academic presentation described in the course handbook). The College History Tutor or thesis adviser may comment on the first draft.

6. No optional additional thesis shall exceed 12,000 words in length (including   35
footnotes but excluding bibliographies), except in the case that a candidate is submitting a thesis as a critical edition of a text, in which case the regulations on word length in regulation VI 10, sections iii and x, above, apply. All theses must be typed or word-processed in double spacing on one side of A4 paper with the notes and references at the foot of each page, with a left-hand margin of one-and-a-half inches and all other   40
margins of at least one inch.

7. Candidates must submit two copies of their theses, addressed to the Chair of Examiners, Honour School of History, Examination Schools, High Street, Oxford, not later than noon on Monday of first week of the Trinity Term of the year in which they are presenting themselves for examination. Every candidate shall present a   45
certificate signed by him or herself and by a College History Tutor or thesis adviser, in a separate envelope bearing the candidate's examination number, addressed to the Chair of Examiners. The certificate (forms are available from the Faculty Office) should declare that (*a*) the thesis is the candidate's own work, (*b*) that no substantial

portion of it has been presented for any other degree course or examination, (*c*) that is does not exceed 12,000 words in length.

8. Candidates shall not answer in any other paper, with the exception of Disciplines of History (V), questions which fall very largely within the scope of their optional additional thesis.   5

9. Candidates may submit an optional additional thesis in the form of an edition of a short historical text with accompanying scholarly apparatus, in which case the requirements detailed in regulation VI 10, above, apply.

10. The Final Honour School Examiners will arrive at a formal degree result for candidates who submit an Optional Additional Thesis by inclusion of the 7 highest   10
marks awarded for the 8 papers submitted, except that the mark awarded for the Optional Additional Thesis may not substitute for a mark lower than 50. Thus, the papers to be included are determined by the following procedures:

 (i) In the event that the Optional Additional Thesis is awarded a mark below 50, it
      will be disregarded and the formal degree result will be determined solely by the   15
      marks awarded for the compulsory papers.

 (ii) In the event that the Optional Additional Thesis is awarded a mark of 50 or
      above, the paper awarded the lowest mark of 50 or above (which may be the
      Optional Additional Thesis) will be disregarded. All other papers awarded a
      mark of 50 or above, and all papers awarded a mark below 50 will be included.   20

HONOUR SCHOOL OF HISTORY AND ECONOMICS

A

1. The examination in the Honour School of History and Economics shall consist of such subjects in History and Economics as the Board of the Faculty of History and Division of Social Sciences from time to time shall in consultation prescribe by regulation.

2. No candidate shall be admitted to examination in this School unless he or she has either passed or been exempted from the First Public Examination.

3. The examination in the Honour School shall be under the joint supervision of the Board of the Faculty of History and the Social Sciences Divisional Board, which shall appoint a standing joint committee to make proposals for regulations concerning the examination. Such proposals shall be submitted to the boards of the two faculties which shall make regulations concerning the examination and which, in the case of difference of opinion, shall hold a joint meeting at which the matter in dispute shall be resolved by the vote of the majority.

4. The Chairs of Examiners for the Honour School of History and for the Honour School of Philosophy, Politics, and Economics shall consult together and designate such of their number as may be required for the examination for the Honour School of History and Economics, whereupon the number of examiners shall be deemed to be complete.

B

Each candidate shall offer:

1. *Macroeconomics.*

   As specified for the Honour School of Philosophy, Politics, and Economics.

2. *Microeconomics.*

   As specified for the Honour School of Philosophy, Politics, and Economics.

3. *Quantitative Economics.*

   As specified for the Honour School of Philosophy, Politics, and Economics.

4. *British Economic History since 1870.*

   As specified for the Honour School of Philosophy, Politics, and Economics.

5. *Either* one period of General History *or* one period of The History of the British Isles.

6. *Either*

   (*a*) two Further Subjects in History;

   or

   (*b*) two Further subjects in Economics;

   or

   (*c*) (i) one Further Subject in History and (ii) either one period of General History or one period of The History of the British Isles, except any such period offered under paper 5, above.

   (*d*) (i) one Further Subject in History and (ii) one Further Subject in Economics.

7. *A thesis from original research*

Regulation VI of the Honour School of History applies with the following modifications:

Cl. 1 For 'Candidates must submit a thesis as part of the fulfilment of their final examination' read 'Candidates must submit a thesis—normally, but not necessarily in economic history—as part of the fulfilment of their final examination'.

Cl. 2 For 'Theses shall normally be written during the Hilary Term of the final year' read 'Theses shall normally be written during the Michaelmas and/or Hilary Term of the final year'.

Cl. 3(b) (iii) For 'Chair of the Examiners for the Honour School of History' read 'Chair of the Examiners, Honour School of History and Economics'.

Cl. 5 For 'Honour School of History' read 'Honour School of History and Economics'.

Cl. 6 For 'primary historical sources' read 'primary historical sources or economic data'; for 'College History Tutor' read 'College History Tutor' or Economics Tutor'.

Cl. 8 For 'Chair of Examiners, Honour School of History' read 'Chair of Examiners, Honour School of History and Economics'.

Cl. 9 For 'Candidates shall not answer in any other paper, with the exception of Disciplines of History (V), questions which fall very largely within the scope of their thesis' read 'Candidates shall not answer in any other paper questions which fall very largely within the scope of their thesis.'

Cl. 10ii For 'Chair of the FHS in History' read 'Chair of the FHS in History and Economics'.

The syllabus for sections 1–4, 6(*b*), and 6(*c*) (ii) is as specified in the Honour School of Philosophy, Politics, and Economics and for sections 5, 6(*a*), and 6(*c*) (i) as specified for the Honour School of History.

The individual detailed specifications and prescribed texts for the Further Subjects as specified for the Honour School of History will be given in the Handbook for the Honour School of History. This will be published by the History Board by Monday of Week 1 of the first Michaelmas Full Term of candidates' work for the Honour School.

Depending on the availability of teaching resources, not all Further Subjects will be available to all candidates in every year. Candidates may obtain details of the choice of Further Subjects in History available for the following year by consulting the supplement to the Handbook for the Honour School of History. This will be issued by the beginning of the fourth week of the first Hilary Full Term of candidates' work for the Honour School and will contain full specifications and prescribed texts for any Further Subjects specified for History introduced for the following year, and any amendments to the specifications and prescribed texts of existing Further Subjects approved by the History Board by its first meeting of the preceding Hilary Term.

Not all Economics subjects may be offered in any particular year. There may also be restrictions on numbers permitted to offer some Economics subjects in any particular year.

Economics subjects available to candidates in any particular year will depend on the availability of teaching resources. Details of the choices available for the following year will be announced at the Economics Department's 'Options Fair' at the beginning of the fourth week of this first Hilary Term of the candidates' work for the Honour School, and will be posted on the Department's undergraduate WebLearn site at the same time.

No candidate may offer the same subject twice.

For all Economics papers (which shall be taken to include British Economic History since 1870 but not other papers in Economic History) candidates are permitted the use of one hand-held pocket calculator from a list of permitted calculators published annually by the Department of Economics on its Undergraduate website, which will   5
be updated annually in the week prior to the first full week of Michaelmas Term.

In every case where, under the regulations for this Honour School, candidates have any choice between one or more papers or subjects, every candidate shall give notice not later than Friday in the fourth week of Michaelmas Full Term preceding the examination of all the papers and subjects being so offered.   10

A second thesis, in addition to the papers listed under sections 1 to 6 may be offered in accordance with the Regulation VII. *An Optional Additional Thesis* of the Honour School of History, q. v. modified as follows:

(*a*) the subject shall, to the satisfaction of the examiners, fall within the scope of the Honour School of History and Economics; or   15

(*b*) the prizes listed in that regulation with the addition of the Webb Medley Essay Prize and the Sir John Rhys Prize;

(*c*) theses must be submitted to the Chair of the Examiners, Honour School of History and Economics, Examination Schools, High Street, Oxford. In the assignment of honours, attention will be paid to the merits of any such thesis;   20

(*d*) not more than two theses may be offered.

(*e*) Cl.10 For 'The Final Honour School Examiners will arrive at a formal degree result for candidates who submit an Optional Additional Thesis by taking the highest seven marks of 50 or above, out of the eight papers submitted, except that the Optional Additional Thesis may not substitute for any paper awarded a   25
mark below 50' read 'The Final Honour School Examiners will arrive at a formal degree result for candidates who submit an Optional Additional Thesis by taking the highest eight marks of 50 or above, out of the nine papers submitted, except that the Optional Additional Thesis may not substitute for any paper awarded a mark below 50'.   30

HONOUR SCHOOL OF HISTORY AND ENGLISH

A

1. The Honour School of History and English shall be under the joint supervision of the Boards of the Faculties of History and English Language and Literature and shall consist of such subjects as they shall jointly by regulation prescribe. The boards shall establish a joint committee consisting of three representatives of each faculty, of whom at least one of each side shall be a member of the respective faculty board, to advise them as necessary in respect of the Honour School and of the Preliminary Examination in History and English.

2. No candidate shall be admitted to the examination in this school unless he or she has either passed or been exempted from the First Public Examination.

3. The Chairs of Examiners for the Honour School of History and for the Honour School of English Language and Literature shall consult together and designate such of their number as may be required for the examination for the Honour School of History and English, whereupon the number of examiners shall be deemed to be complete.

B

Each candidate shall offer seven subjects as set out below. The subjects will be examined by written examinations of three hours' duration, unless otherwise specified.

1. Submitted work

(*a*) Candidates should note that no more than four out of the total of seven Final Honour School papers can be examined by submission. Candidates should also note that some English and History papers are examined only by submission and should bear this restriction in mind when making their choices.

(*b*) Two typed copies of each extended essay or portfolio must be delivered by hand to the relevant Chair of Examiners, Examination Schools, High Street, according to the deadlines specified in the regulations for each subject. It is additionally strongly recommended that the candidate keep a third copy of his or her submission. A certificate signed by the candidate to the effect that each extended essay or portfolio is the candidate's own work, and that the candidate has read the History Faculty and English Language and Literature Faculty guidelines on plagiarism, must be presented together with each submission (see (*d*) below). Certificates will be circulated to candidates for completion by the History Faculty Office and the English Faculty Office.

(*c*) Every submission must be the work of the candidate alone, and he or she may not discuss with any tutor either his or her choice of content or the method of handling it after the last date indicated in the regulations for each subject.

(*d*) Essays previously submitted for the Honour School of History and English may be re-submitted. No essay will be accepted if it has already been submitted, wholly or substantially, for a final honour school or other degree of this University, or degree of any other institution.

(*e*) Essays may be penalised that are deemed to be either too short or of excessive length in relation to the word limits specified in the regulations for each subject.

2. History and English papers

(i) One compulsory interdisciplinary bridge paper, which shall be examined by an extended essay of between 5,000 and 6,000 words, including footnotes and notes but excluding bibliography. The list of topics for this paper shall be published to candidates by the beginning of the first week of the Michaelmas Term in the year preceding   5
the final examination, and shall be available thereafter from the English Faculty Office and the History Faculty Office.

Candidates must obtain written approval from the Chair of Examiners for the Honour School of History and English for the proposed essay title, not later than Friday of the eighth week of the Hilary Term in the year preceding the final examination.   10

The candidate must deliver two typed copies of the bridge paper essay by hand to the Chair of Examiners for the Joint School of History and English, at the Examination Schools, High Street, by noon on Thursday of the eighth week of the Trinity Term in the final year preceding the final examination. A certificate, signed by the candidate to the effect that each essay is the candidate's own work, and that the   15
candidate has read the History Faculty and English Language and Literature Faculty guidelines on plagiarism, must be presented together with the submission (see the introductory regulations for 'submitted work' for the Honour School of History and English).

(ii) One period of British History not taken in the First Public Examination (as   20
specified in the regulations for History).

(iii) and (iv) Two subjects chosen from subjects 1 to 6 of Course I or two subjects chosen from subjects 1 to 6 of Course II of the Honour School of English Language and Literature (as specified in the regulations for the Honour School of English Language and Literature).   25

(v) and (vi) Two subjects from the Honour School of History, consisting of either (a) Special Subject (which comprises a three hour paper and an extended essay, constituting two papers), or (b) Two of the following:

1. One General History paper from the Honour School of History;
2. One Further Subject from the Honour School of History;   30
3. One additional British History period not taken in the First Public Examination;
4. One additional subject chosen from papers 1 to 6 of Course I or Course II of the Honour School of English Language and Literature. Candidates must offer all Course I or all Course II English subjects.

See the regulations for History and for English Language and Literature. The   35
individual detailed specifications and prescribed texts for the Further and Special Subjects as specified for the Honour School of History will be given in the Handbook for the Honour School of History. This will be published by the History Board by Monday of Week 1 of the first Michaelmas Full Term of candidates' work for the Honour School.   40

Depending on the availability of teaching resources, not all Further and Special Subjects will be available to all candidates in every year. Candidates may obtain details of the choice of Further and Special Subjects available for the following year by consulting the supplement to the Handbook for the Honour School of History. This will be issued by the beginning of the fourth week of the first Hilary Full Term of   45
candidates' work for the Honour School and will contain full specifications and prescribed texts for any Further or Special Subjects specified for History introduced for the following year, and any amendments to the specifications and prescribed texts of existing Further and Special Subjects approved by the History Board.

(vii) One compulsory interdisciplinary dissertation, which shall be examined by an extended essay of not more than 10,000 words, including notes and source material but excluding bibliography.

Candidates must submit to the Chair of Examiners for the Joint School of History and English, care of the History Faculty Office, not later than 5pm. on Friday of the sixth week of the Michaelmas Term preceding the examination, a title and abstract of not more than 200 words detailing the proposed dissertation topic.

The candidate must deliver two typed copies of the dissertation by hand to the Chair of Examiners for the Joint School of History and English, at the Examination Schools, High Street, by noon on Thursday of the eighth week of the Hilary Term preceding the examination. A certificate, signed by the candidate to the effect that each essay is the candidate's own work, and that the candidate has read the History Faculty and English Language and Literature Faculty guidelines on plagiarism, must be presented together with the submission (see the introductory regulations for 'submitted work' for the Honour School of History and English).

HONOUR SCHOOL OF HISTORY AND MODERN LANGUAGES

A

1. The subjects of the examination in the Honour School of History and Modern Languages shall be (*a*) History, and (*b*) those modern European languages and literatures studied in the Honour School of Modern Languages.

2. All candidates must offer both (*a*) and one of the languages in (*b*) with its literature.

3. No candidate shall be admitted to examination in the School unless he or she has either passed or been exempted from the First Public Examination.

4. The examination shall always include a period of General History selected by the candidate from periods to be named from time to time in the Regulations of the Honour School.

5. The examiners shall indicate in the lists issued by them the language offered by each candidate obtaining Honours or satisfying the examiners under the appropriate regulation.

6. The examiners in the Honour School shall be under the joint supervision of the Boards of the Faculties of History and Modern Languages, which shall appoint a standing joint committee to make proposals for regulations concerning the examination. Such proposals shall be submitted to the boards of the two faculties which shall make regulations concerning the examination and which, in case of difference of opinion, shall hold a joint meeting at which the matter in dispute shall be resolved by the vote of the majority.

7. (i) The examiners in the Honour School shall be such of the Public Examiners in the Honour Schools of History and Modern Languages as shall be required.

   (ii) It shall be the duty of the Chair of Examiners in the Honour Schools of History and Modern Languages to consult together and designate such examiners as shall be required for the Honour School, whereupon the number of examiners shall be deemed to be complete.

B

Candidates will be examined in accordance with the examination regulations set out below.

They will also be required to spend, after their matriculation, a year of residence in an appropriate country or countries, and to provide on their entry form for the examination a certificate that they have done this, signed by the Head or by a tutor of their society. Candidates wishing to be dispensed from the requirement to undertake a year of residence abroad must apply in writing to the Chair of the Medieval and Modern Languages Board, 41 Wellington Square, Oxford, OX1 2JF, stating their reasons for requesting dispensation and enclosing a letter of support from their society.

Candidates will be expected to carry out during this year abroad such work as their society may require. It is strongly recommended that candidates should apply through the Central Bureau for Educational Visits and Exchanges for an Assistantship, where these are available, and should accept one if offered. Candidates who are not able to obtain an Assistantship should during their year abroad follow a course or courses in an institution or institutions approved by their society, or should spend their time in such other circumstances as are acceptable to their society. Candidates will agree with their College Tutor in advance of their year abroad an independent course of study to be followed during that period.

Save in a Special Subject, each candidate shall offer in his or her language and literature papers one language and literature only.

Oral Examination: as specified for the Honour School of Modern Languages.

Candidates are advised, where possible, to ensure that their choice of options provides some chronological overlap between their history and literature papers.

In addition to the compulsory papers listed below, candidates who so desire may offer an optional additional thesis in accordance with Regulation VII. *An Optional Additional Thesis* of the Honour School of History *q.v.*, modified as follows:

(*a*) the subject shall, to the satisfaction of the examiners, fall within the scope of the Honour School of History and Modern Languages; or

(*b*) the prizes listed in that regulation with the addition of the Sir John Rhys Prize;

(*c*) theses must be submitted to the Chair of the Examiners, Honour School of History and Modern Languages, Examination Schools, High Street, Oxford.

(*d*) Cl.10 For 10. The Final Honour School Examiners will arrive at a formal degree result [...] all papers awarded a mark below 50 will be included.' read 'The Final Honour School Examiners will arrive at a formal degree result for candidates who submit an Optional Additional Thesis by taking the marks awarded for the 2 language papers and the oral examination, together with the highest seven marks out of the eight content papers submitted, except that the Optional Additional Thesis may not substitute for a mark lower than 50. Thus, the papers to be included are determined by the following procedures:

(i) In the event that the Optional Additional Thesis is awarded a mark below 50, it will be disregarded and the formal degree result will be determined solely by the marks awarded for the compulsory papers.

(ii) In the event that the Optional Additional Thesis is awarded a mark of 50 or above, the content paper awarded the lowest mark of 50 or above (which may be the Optional Additional Thesis) will be disregarded. All other content papers awarded a mark of 50 or above, and all content papers awarded a mark below 50, together with the marks awarded for the 2 language papers and the oral examination, will be included.

Every candidate shall offer:

1. One period of General History as specified for the Honour School of History (except for candidates offering Celtic, who shall offer one period of The History of the British Isles as specified for the Honour School of History).

[**For students starting before MT 2014:** 2. A bridge essay of 7,500 words on an interdisciplinary topic, designed to draw together interests and develop skills from both sides of the course. The limit of 7,500 words includes footnotes, but excludes bibliography, and, in cases for which specific permission has been obtained from the convenor of the joint school, appendices. Candidates must follow the guidelines on word count, presentation and referencing as outlined in the course handbook.

The candidate will submit a title and short statement of up to fifty words on the manner in which he/she proposes to treat the topic, together with a note from his/her tutor approving the topic, addressed to the convener of the Joint School of History and Modern Languages, c/o the History Faculty, no later than Monday of sixth week of Trinity Term of his/her second year. Titles will be approved by the convener and one other member of the Standing Committee of the Joint School of History and Modern Languages. Notification of whether or not approval is forthcoming will be given by eighth week of Trinity Term.

Changes to the title must be submitted to the convener of the joint school at the latest by the Friday of second week of the Michaelmas Term of the candidate's final year. Notification of whether or not approval is forthcoming will be given no later

than fourth week of the Michaelmas Term of the candidate's final year. Bridge essays on approved titles should be submitted to the Chair of the Examiners for the Joint School of History and Modern Languages at the Examination Schools, High Street, Oxford, by noon on the Friday of noughth week in the Hilary Term preceding the examination. Every candidate shall present a certificate, signed by him or herself and   5
by his or her College History Tutor, in a separate envelope bearing the candidate's examination number. The certificate should declare (using a specified form available from the History Faculty Office and Faculty website) that (a) the bridge essay is the candidate's own work, (b) that it does not exceed 7,500 words in length (including footnotes but not including bibliography and translations from quotations), (c) that   10
no more than the specified maximum amount of advice and assistance (no more than three hours of preparatory or advisory meetings and/or email consultations) from college or external advisers has been received. In the rare cases when a candidate is dispensed from the requirement to spend a year abroad after their second year, that candidate shall not be required to submit their Bridge Essay until noon on Friday of   15
eighth week of the Hilary Term preceding the examination. Any changes in title for such candidates should be submitted to the convenor of the joint school by the second week of Hilary Term of the final year. Notification of whether approval is forthcoming will be given no later than sixth week of Hilary Term of the final year.

A first draft of the bridge essay may be read and commented on, but not corrected   20
in matters of detail and presentation, by the bridge essay adviser.]

[For students starting from MT 2014: 2. A bridge essay of between 8,000 and 10,000 words on an interdisciplinary topic, designed to draw together interests and develop skills from both sides of the course. The limit of 10,000 words includes footnotes, but excludes bibliography, and, in cases for which specific permission has been obtained   25
from the convenor of the joint school, appendices. Candidates must follow the guidelines on word count, presentation, and referencing as outlined in the course handbook.

The candidate will submit a title and short statement of up to fifty words on the manner in which he/she proposes to treat the topic, together with a note from his/her tutor approving the topic, addressed to the convener of the Joint School of History   30
and Modern Languages, c/o the History Faculty, no later than Monday of sixth week of Trinity Term of his/her second year. Titles will be approved by the convener and one other member of the Standing Committee of the Joint School of History and Modern Languages. Notification of whether or not approval is forthcoming will be given by eighth week of Trinity Term.   35

Changes to the title must be submitted to the convener of the joint school at the latest by the Friday of fourth week of the Hilary Term of the candidate's final year. Notification of whether or not approval is forthcoming will be given no later than fourth week of the Hilary Term of the candidate's final year. Bridge essays on approved titles should be submitted to the Chair of the Examiners for the Joint   40
School of History and Modern Languages at the Examination Schools, High Street, Oxford, by noon on the Tuesday of ninth week in the Hilary Term preceding the examination. Every candidate shall present a certificate, signed by him or herself and by his or her College History Tutor, in a separate envelope bearing the candidate's examination number. The certificate should declare (using a specified form available   45
from the History Faculty Office and Faculty website) that (a) the bridge essay is the candidate's own work, (b) that it does not exceed 10,000 words in length (including footnotes but not including bibliography and translations from quotations), (c) that no more than the specified maximum amount of advice and assistance (no more than five hours of preparatory or advisory meetings and/or email consultations) from   50
college or external advisers has been received. In the rare cases when a candidate is dispensed from the requirement to spend a year abroad after their second year, that candidate shall not be required to submit their Bridge Essay until noon on Friday of noughth week of the Trinity Term preceding the examination. Any changes in title for

such candidates should be submitted to the convenor of the joint school by the fourth week of Hilary Term of the final year. Notification of whether approval is forthcoming will be given no later than sixth week of Hilary Term of the final year.

A first draft of the bridge essay may be read and commented on, but not corrected in matters of detail and presentation, by the bridge essay adviser.] 5

3. Honour School of Modern Languages, Paper I.

4. Honour School of Modern Languages, Papers IIA and IIB.

5. Honour School of Modern Languages, *one* paper chosen from Papers VI, VII, or VIII.

6. Honour School of Modern Languages, *one* paper chosen from Papers IV, V, IX, 10
X, XI, or XII.

7, 8, 9. *Either* (*a*) a Special Subject as specified for the Honour School of History (two papers, paper (*b*) of which shall be by extended essay) and one of the items (*b*), (i), (ii), (iii), or (iv) below.

or (*b*) any three of the following four items: 15

    (i) Any period of The History of the British Isles as specified for the Honour School of History; (except for candidates offering Celtic, who may offer one period of General History as specified for the Honour School of History)

    (ii) A Further Subject as specified for the Honour School of History;

    (iii) Any one of the Papers IV, V, IX, X, XI, XII not already offered, as specified 20 for the Honour School of Modern Languages;

    (iv) An Extended Essay as specified for the Honour School of Modern Languages *or* a thesis based on original research as specified in Regulation VI for the Honour School of History, *except* Cl. 5. of that regulation should read 'beginning of Trinity Full Term of the academic year preceding that in 25 which the candidate spends a year abroad'.

The individual detailed specifications and prescribed texts for the Further and Special Subjects as specified for the Honour School of History will be given in the Handbook for the Honour School of History. This will be published by the History Board by Monday of Week 1 of the first Michaelmas Full Term of candidates' work 30 for the Honour School.

Depending on the availability of teaching resources, not all Further and Special Subjects will be available to all candidates in every year. Candidates may obtain details of the choice of Further and Special Subjects available for the following year by consulting the supplement to the Handbook for the Honour School of History. 35 This will be issued by the beginning of the fourth week of the first Hilary Full Term of candidates' work for the Honour School and will contain full specifications and prescribed texts for any Further or Special Subjects specified for History introduced for the following year, and any amendments to the specifications and prescribed texts of existing Further and Special Subjects approved by the History Board by its first 40 meeting of the preceding Hilary Term.

Mutual exclusions and other restrictions

No candidate may offer a period of British History which he or she has offered as a successful candidate in the First Public Examination.

Candidates may offer both the History Further Subject *Culture and Society in Early* 45
Renaissance Italy 1290–1348 and the Modern Languages Early Texts paper in Italian. Where candidates offer both the Further Subject and Early Texts papers, they may not answer on Dante in the Further Subject paper.

Candidates offering a paper from the Honour School of Modern Languages and a paper from the Honour School of History, both of which involve the study of the same 50 author or authors, may not make the same text or texts the principal subject of an answer in both the papers. The same regulation applies to the use of material in the Bridge essay and any other papers.

HONOUR SCHOOL OF HISTORY AND POLITICS

A

1. The examination in the Honour School of History and Politics shall consist of such subjects in History and Politics as the Board of the Faculty of History and the Social Sciences Board shall from time to time in consultation prescribe by regulation.

2. No candidate shall be admitted to examination in this School unless he or she has either passed or been exempted from the First Public Examination.

3. The examination in the Honour School shall be under the joint supervision of the Board of the Faculty of History and the Social Sciences Board, which shall appoint a standing joint committee to make proposals for regulations concerning the examination. Such proposals shall be submitted to the boards which shall make regulations concerning the examination and which, in the case of difference of opinion, shall hold a joint meeting at which the matter in dispute shall be resolved by the vote of the majority.

4. The Chairs of Examiners for the Honour School of History and for the Honour School of Philosophy, Politics, and Economics shall consult together and designate such of their number as may be required for the examination for the Honour School of History and Politics, whereupon the number of examiners shall be deemed to be complete.

B

1. Except where indicated a paper cannot be substituted. Candidates shall offer seven papers from the following options, which must include the compulsory substitute thesis based on original research, as specified under Regulation 6 below.

Candidates shall offer either one British History paper and one General History paper as specified under sections 2 and 3, or two British History papers or two General History papers.

2. Paper 1. Each candidate may offer one or two papers in a period of the *History of the British Isles*, as specified for the Honour School of History, provided that:
   (a) one paper may be replaced by a compulsory thesis in History;
   (b) no candidate may offer a period of British History already offered in the First Public Examination;
   (c) candidates who have not offered a period of British or General History before the nineteenth century in the First Public Examination are required to choose at least one such period in the Honour School of History and Politics. The list of papers satisfying this provision is given in the Handbook for History and Politics;
   (d) candidates who have taken or are taking British History VII (since 1900) cannot also take Politics paper 202 (British Politics and Government since 1900); and candidates taking British History VI (1815–1924) in the Honour School of History and Politics and who are also taking Politics Paper 202 must not substantially duplicate material in the two papers.

3. Paper 2. Each candidate may offer one or two papers in a period of General History, as specified for the Honour School of History, provided that:

(*a*) one paper may be replaced by a compulsory thesis in History;

(*b*) candidates who have not offered a period of British or General History before the nineteenth century in the First Public Examination are required to choose at least one such period in the Honour School of History and Politics. The list of papers satisfying this provision is given in the Handbook for History and Politics;

(*c*) candidates taking Politics Paper 212 (International Relations in the era of the Two World Wars) cannot also take General History XIII (1914–45); candidates taking Politics Paper 213 (International Relations in the era of the Cold War) cannot also take General History XIV (1945–73).

4. Papers 3 and 4. Each candidate shall offer any two of the five 'core subjects' in Politics, as specified for the Honour School of Philosophy, Politics and Economics (i.e. 201, 202, 203, 214, and 220). A thesis as specified in Regulation 6 below may not be substituted for a Politics core subject.

5. Papers 5, 6, and 7. Each candidate shall offer one of the following combinations:

   (i) one Special Subject in History (examined in two papers) and one of subjects 201–228 in Politics which is not offered under Regulation 4 above;

   (ii) one Further Subject in History and two of subjects 201–228 in Politics which are not offered under Regulation 4 above;

   (iii) one Further Subject in History, one of subjects 201–228 in Politics which are not offered under Regulation 4 above, and one Special Subject in Politics.

Provided that:

   (*a*) one of the optional papers in Politics in any of these combinations may be substituted by a compulsory thesis from the Honour School of Philosophy, Politics, and Economics;

   (*b*) Candidates who choose Politics Further Subject 215 (Political Thought: Plato to Rousseau) cannot also take History Further Subjects *Scholasticism and Humanism* and *The Science of Society*. Candidates who choose Politics Further Subject 216 (Political Thought: Bentham to Weber) cannot also take History Further Subject *Political Theory and Social Science*. Candidates who choose the Politics Further Subject 221 (British Society in the Twentieth Century) cannot also take the History Further Subject British Society in the 20th Century.

6. Paper 8. Each candidate must offer a thesis, which must be offered in place of either a period of the *History of the British Isles*, as specified under Regulation 2 above, or a period of *General History*, as specified under Regulation 3 above, or a Politics option in any of the combinations as specified under Regulation 5 above. A thesis offered in place of a Politics optional paper shall be either a substitute thesis or a supervised dissertation submitted in accordance with the regulations prescribed for Politics in the Honour School of Philosophy, Politics, and Economics.

   (*a*) A thesis in History submitted in accordance with the Regulation VI, *A thesis based on original research*, for the Final Honour School of History may be offered in place of a paper in the History of the British Isles or General History and the candidate (unless he or she is a Senior Student, as defined by decree of Council, or has passed the First Public Examination in a course other than History and Politics, History, or any other joint school with History) must also offer a paper satisfying those requirements specified in Regulations 1(c) above which have not been satisfied in the First Public Examination.

   (*b*) A thesis or supervised dissertation in Politics submitted in accordance with the regulations prescribed for Politics in the Honour School of Philosophy, Politics, and Economics may be offered in place of any one of subjects 201–228 in Politics (as specified for the Honour School of Philosophy, Politics, and Economics) which is not offered under Regulation 4 above.

7. All candidates must offer a substitute thesis or supervised dissertation, but may not offer more than one substitute thesis or supervised dissertation in place of a paper.   5

8. In every case where, under the regulations for this honour school, candidates have any choice between one or more papers or subjects, every candidate shall give notice to the Registrar not later than Friday in the fourth week of Michaelmas Full Term preceding the examination of all the papers and subjects being offered.

HONOUR SCHOOL OF HISTORY OF ART

A

1. The examination in the School of History of Art shall be under the supervision of the Board of the Faculty of History.

2. No candidate shall be admitted to the examination in this school unless he or she has passed or been exempted from the First Public Examination.

3. The Board of the Faculty of History shall, by notice from time to time, make regulations respecting the examination.

4. The Board of the Faculty of History may include in the examination, either as necessary or optional, other subjects which they may deem suitable to be studied in connection with History of Art.

B

The History Board shall issue annually the Handbook for the Honour School of History of Art by Monday of first week of the first Michaelmas Full Term of candidates' work for the Honour School.

All candidates are required to offer Subjects I, II, III, IV, V, and VI below.

I. *Approaches to the History of Art*

II. *A Further Subject in Art History*

Any one of the Further Subjects listed below, as specified for the Honour School of History:

1. Anglo-Saxon Archaeology **[For students starting before MT 2015:** of the Early Christian Period] **[For students starting from MT 2015:** c. 600–750: Society and economy in the Early Christian Period]

2. The Carolingian Renaissance

3. Northern European Portraiture 1400–1800

4. Culture and Society in Early Renaissance Italy 1290–1348

5. Flanders and Italy in the Quattrocento 1420–1480

6. Court Culture and Art in Early Modern Europe

7. Intellect and Culture in Victorian Britain

III. *Classical, Pre-Modern or Non-Western Art Option*

Any one of the options below:

1. Greek Art and Archaeology *c*.500–300 BC (as specified for the Honour School of Literae Humaniores, Greek and Roman Archaeology).

2. Art under the Roman Empire AD 14–337 (as specified for the Honour School of Literae Humaniores, Greek and Roman Archaeology).

3. Hellenistic Art and Archaeology, 330–30 BC.

[For students starting before MT 2015: 4. The formation of the Islamic World, AD 550–950 (as specified for the Honour Schools of Archaeology and Anthropology, and of Classical Archaeology and Ancient History).

5. Byzantine Art: the transition from Antiquity to the Middle Ages, AD 500–1100.

6. Gothic Art through Medieval Eyes.

7. Art in China since 1911.

8. Understanding Museums and Collections (as specified for the Honour School of Archaeology and Anthropology), if not taken under IV below.

9. Egyptian Art and Architecture (as specified for the Honour School of Oriental Studies, Egyptology and Ancient Near Eastern Studies with Archaeology and Anthropology).]   5

[For students starting from MT 2015: 4. Byzantine Art: the transition from Antiquity to the Middle Ages, AD 500–1100.

5. Gothic Art through Medieval Eyes.

6. Art in China since 1911.

7. Understanding Museums and Collections (as specified for the Honour School of   10
Archaeology and Anthropology), if not taken under IV below.

8. Egyptian Art and Architecture (as specified for the Honour School of Oriental Studies, Egyptology and Ancient Near Eastern Studies with Archaeology and Anthropology).]

IV. *Modern Art Option*   15
Any one of the options below:

1. Literature and the Visual Arts in France (as specified for the Honour School of Modern Languages, Special Subjects).

2. German Expressionism in literature and the visual arts (as specified for the Honour School of Modern Languages, Special Subjects).   20

3. European Cinema (as specified for the Honour School of Modern Languages, Special Subjects).

4. Modernism and After (as specified for the Final Examination in Fine Art; paper on the history and theory of visual culture since 1900 (Modernism and After)).

5. Understanding Museums and Collections (as specified for the Honour School of   25
Archaeology and Anthropology), if not taken under III above.

6. The Experience of Modernity: Visual Culture, 1880–1925

7. Art in China since 1911, if not taken under III above.

In the case of Modern Art options 1–3 above, the relevant regulation for the Honour School of Modern Languages, XII Special Subjects, Section B, is modified   30
(modification in italics) for History of Art students to read: An essay or portfolio of essays (the number of essays to be shown in parentheses) aggregating to about 6,000 words and not exceeding 8,000 words, to be submitted by hand to the Examination Schools, High Street, Oxford by noon on the Friday of ninth week of the Hilary Term in *the year prior to examination (i.e. the student's second year of study)*, together with a   35
statement certifying that the essay(s) are the candidate's own work and that they have not already been submitted, either wholly or substantially, for a degree in this university or elsewhere.

In the case of Modern Art option 4, History of Art students are assessed based on an examination taken in Week 9 of the Michaelmas Term of their final year.   40

V. *Special Subject in Art History*, consisting of
(*a*) a paper including compulsory passages and/or images for comment; (*b*) an extended essay.

Any one of the Special Subjects listed below, as specified for the Honour School of History: 45

[For students starting before MT 2015: 1. Royal Art and Architecture in Norman Sicily, 1130–1194.

2. Painting and Culture in Ming China.

3. Politics, Art and Culture in the Italian Renaissance: Venice and Florence, *c*.1475–1525.   50

4. The Dutch Golden Age: 1618–1672.

5. English Architecture 1660–1720.

6. Art and its Public in France 1815–67.]

[For students starting from MT 2015: 1. Painting and Culture in Ming China.

2. Politics, Art and Culture in the Italian Renaissance: Venice and Florence, c.1475–1525.

3. The Dutch Golden Age: 1618–1672.

4. English Architecture 1660–1720.

5. Art and its Public in France 1815–67.]

Depending on the availability of teaching resources in the different Faculties, not all of the options listed under II, III, IV and V will be available to all candidates in every year. Candidates should refer to the course handbook for details about availability and registration for individual options.

VI. *A thesis from original research*

1. Candidates must submit a thesis as part of the fulfilment of their Final Examination.

2. Theses shall normally be written during the Hilary Term of the final year. All theses must be submitted not later than noon on Friday of eighth week of the Hilary Term of the academic year in which the candidate is presenting himself or herself for examination.

3. A candidate may submit:

(*a*) any essay or part of any essay which he or she has submitted or intends to submit for any university essay prize; or

(*b*) any other work provided in either case that (i) no thesis will be accepted if it has already been submitted, wholly or substantially, for a final honour school other than one involving Modern History or History of Art, or another degree of this University, or a degree of any other university, and (ii) the candidate submits a statement to that effect, and (iii) the subject is approved by the Chair of the Examiners for the Honour School of History of Art.

4. The provisos in cl. 3 above shall not debar any candidate from submitting work based on a previous submission towards the requirements for a degree of any other university provided that

(i) the work is substantially new;

(ii) the candidate also submits both the original work itself and a statement specifying the extent of what is new. The examiners shall have sole authority to decide in every case whether proviso (i) has been met.

5. Every candidate except when offering a thesis as defined in cl. 3 (*a*) must submit a proposed preliminary title to the Department of History of Art, St Ebbes, Oxford together with a typed synopsis of the thesis topic and proposed method of investigation (no more than 250 words) and the written approval of their College History of Art Co-ordinator, not later than Friday of eighth week of Michaelmas Term in the year of the examination. The Chair of Examiners shall give notification whether or not the title is approved by the first Monday of Hilary Full Term of the same year. Any subsequent changes to title require formal application to the Chair of Examiners by the Friday of Week 4 of the Hilary Term of the final year and subsequent approval.

6. Theses should normally include an investigation of visual and material culture (broadly defined), with references made to relevant images and printed and/or unprinted primary written sources, and must include proper footnotes and a bibliography. They must be the work of the author alone. In all cases, the candidate's Undergraduate Thesis

Adviser shall discuss with the candidate the field of study, the sources available, and the methods of presentation. Candidates shall be expected to have attended a class on choosing a thesis topic, led by the Undergraduate Thesis Co-ordinator, and to have discussed their choice of topic with their College History of Art Co-ordinator during the Trinity Term of the year prior to examination and Michaelmas Term of the year of examination. Details of arrangements are given in the course handbook. The Undergraduate Thesis Co-ordinator will appoint an appropriate expert thesis adviser for each candidate. Candidates shall have meetings with their Undergraduate Thesis Adviser lasting no more than five hours in total. These hours of meetings shall be normally distributed as follows: one hour in total in Trinity Term of the year prior to the examination; one hour in total in the Michaelmas Term of the year of examination; three hours in total in Hilary Term of the year of examination. A first draft of the thesis may be commented on, but not corrected in matters of detail and presentation, by the Undergraduate Thesis Adviser.

7. No thesis shall exceed 12,000 words in length (including footnotes, but excluding bibliography, and, in cases for which specific permission has been obtained from the Chair of Examiners, appendices). All theses must be typed or word-processed in double spacing on one side of A4 paper with the notes and references at the foot of each page, with a left-hand margin of one-and-a-half inches and all other margins of at least one inch. The thesis should conform to the standards of academic presentation prescribed in the course handbook. Failure to conform to such standards may incur penalties as outlined in the course handbook.

8. All candidates must submit two copies of their thesis, addressed to the Chair of Examiners, Honour School of History of Art, Examination Schools, High Street, Oxford, not later than noon on Friday of eighth week of the Hilary Term of the year in which they are presenting themselves for examination. The University's regulations on late submission of work will apply. Every candidate shall present a certificate, signed by him or herself and by his or her College History of Art Co-ordinator in a separate envelope bearing the candidate's examination number, addressed to the Chair of Examiners. The certificate (forms are available from the History of Art Department) should declare that (*a*) the thesis is the candidate's own work, (*b*) that no substantial portion of it has been presented for any other degree course or examination, (*c*) that it does not exceed 12,000 words in length, (*d*) that no more than five hours have been spent in preparatory or advisory meetings between the candidate and his or her Undergraduate Thesis Adviser, and (*e*) that only the first draft of the thesis has been seen by the Undergraduate Thesis Adviser. Candidates delivering theses will be required to complete a receipt form, which will only be accepted as proof of receipt if it is countersigned by a member of the Examination Schools staff.

9. Candidates shall not answer in any other paper questions which fall very largely within the scope of their thesis nor choose a Special Subject extended essay topic related to their thesis. Candidates should not choose a thesis that only substantially reworks material studied in the Further Subject in Art History, in the Classical, Pre-Modern or non-Western art option, in the Modern art option, or in the Special Subject, and should demonstrate familiarity with and use of substantially different and additional primary sources and visual material.

HONOUR SCHOOL OF HUMAN SCIENCES

A

1. The subject of the Honour School of Human Sciences shall be the biological and social aspects of the study of human beings.

2. No candidate shall be admitted for examination in this school unless he or she has either passed or been exempted from the First Public Examination.

3. The examination shall be under the supervision of the Social Sciences Board, which shall appoint a Teaching Committee for Human Sciences to supervise the arrangements for this examination and the Preliminary Examination in Human Sciences, to consult as necessary with contributing teachers and others; and to carry out such other functions as may be laid down by the Divisional Board by standing order. The committee shall be recognised as having an interest in appointments specifically concerned with the Honour School, and the bodies responsible for such appointments shall ensure that the selection committees for such posts include at least one member appointed in consultation with the committee. It shall be responsible for such funds as the Divisional Board may place at its disposal for general purposes connected with Human Sciences.

B

[For students starting before MT 2015: The Honour School is divided into two sections. All candidates will be required to offer papers: 1, 2, 3, 4, 5(*a*), or 5(*b*), and a dissertation (paper 6)] **[For students starting from MT 2015:** The Honour School is divided into two sections. All candidates will be required to offer papers: 1, 2, 3 (examined by extended essay and a presentation), 4, 5(a), or 5(b), a dissertation (paper 6) and two option papers (7 and 8)]:

1. Behaviour and its Evolution: Animal and Human
2. Human Genetics and Evolution
3. Human Ecology
4. Demography and Population The examiners will permit the use of any hand-held pocket calculator subject to the conditions set out under the heading 'Use of calculators in examinations' in the Special Regulations concerning Examinations.

5(*a*). Anthropological analysis and Interpretation *or* 5(*b*). Sociological Theory
The date by which students must make their choice will be stated in the course handbook.

6. Dissertation

7. and 8. Candidates will also be required to offer any two optional subjects from a list posted in the Human Sciences Centre at the beginning of the first week of Hilary Full Term in the year preceding the final examination. These lists will also be circulated to College Tutors. The date by which students must make their choice will be stated in the course handbook.

Schedule of Subjects

1. *Behaviour and its Evolution: Animal and Human*

Introduction to the study of behaviour including the evolution of behavioural interactions within groups. Behavioural strategies that have evolved in humans and other animals. The use of models to understand complex behaviour. Advanced ethology and cognition, including learning. Perception and decision-making. Primate behaviour and evolutionary ecology, including the development of primate social systems and the evolution of cognition. This paper will be examined by an unseen written examination paper.

2. *Human Genetics and Evolution*

The nature and structure of the human genome, including single gene traits, gene function, and assessment of social implications. Population genetics of humans and primates. Quantitative genetics and complex trait analysis in humans. Genomic complexity as illustrated by the genetic basis for immune response. Molecular evolution, human genetic diversity and the genetic basis of human evolution. Genetic basis of common complex diseases. Human behaviour, cognition and cultural transmission in the context of six million years of physiological evolution and ecological change. This paper will be examined by an unseen written examination paper.

3. *Human Ecology*

[For students starting before MT 2015: Human ecology of disease, emphasising diseases that significantly contribute to the global burden of mortality and cultural change. Diet and nutrition anthropology of human societies. Socio-cultural systems in their environmental context, including philosophical and religious values, differences in ecological perception, and the development of viable conservation strategies, including the impact of humans on other species, the biosphere and climate. Ecology of human reproduction, including cultural differences in reproductive strategies.] [For students starting from MT 2015: Human ecology of disease, emphasising diseases that significantly contribute to the global burden of mortality and cultural change. Diet and nutrition anthropology of human societies. Ethno-biology and its cultural, onto-logical and epistemological contextualization, including Traditional Ecological Knowledge (TEK), Ethno-linguistics and the principles of folk-naming and folk-taxonomy of organisms, Local Ecological Knowledge (LEK) and the significance of place, and practical applications of ethnobiology including biological conservation. Ecology of human reproduction, including cultural differences in re-productive strategies.

This paper will be examined by an extended essay not exceeding 5,000 words (including references and footnotes but excluding bibliography) and a presentation. The essay will be chosen from a list of titles published by the Examiners on Monday of Week 1 of Trinity Term of their second year. Essays should be word-processed in double-line spacing and should conform to the standards of academic presentation prescribed in the course handbook. Two copies of the essay must be delivered to the Examination Schools (addressed to the Chair of Examiners of the Final Honour School of Human Sciences, High Street, Oxford) not later than 12 noon on Friday of Week 6 of Trinity Term of their second year. Candidates will be required to give a short presentation on the topic of the extended essay in Michaelmas Term of their Final year. The exact date of the presentation will be notified to students by Week 1 of Michaelmas Term. The presentation will be assessed for clarity and engagement and contributes 5% of the final mark for the extended essay.]

4. *Demography and Population*

Candidates will be expected to show knowledge of the major features of past and present population trends, the socio-economic, environmental and biomedical factors affecting fertility, mortality and migration; the social, economic and political conse-quences of population growth, decline and ageing; and major controversies in demo-graphic theory.

Specific topics will include traditional and transitional population systems in histor-ical and contemporary societies; demographic transitions and their interpretation;

demographic processes in post-transitional societies (modern Europe and other industrial areas) including very low fertility, longer life, international migration and new
patterns of marriage and family; the changing position of women in the workforce;
ethnic dimensions of demographic change; and policy interventions.

The paper will also test knowledge of demographic analysis and techniques includ-   5
ing data sources, the quantitative analysis of fertility and mortality, the life table, the
stable population and other population models, population dynamics and projections,
and limits to fertility and the lifespan. The paper will comprise two sections. Section 1
will test the candidate's knowledge of substantive trends and their explanation.
Section 2 will test the candidate's ability to interpret quantitative results and the   10
methods of demographic analysis. Candidates will be required to answer three questions, two from Section 1 and one from Section 2.

5(*a*). *Anthropological analysis and interpretation*

The comparative study of social and cultural forms in the global context: to include
economics and exchange, domestic structures and their reproduction, personal   15
and collective identity, language and religion, states and conflict, understanding
of biology and environment, historical perspectives on the social world and upon
practice in anthropology. This paper will be examined by an unseen written examination paper.

5(*b*). *Sociological Theory*   20

Theoretical perspectives including rational choice; evolutionary psychology; interpersonal interaction; social integration and networks; functionalism. Substantive
problems including stratification; gender; race and ethnicity; collective action;
norms; ideology. Candidates will be expected to use theories to explain substantive
problems. This paper will be examined by an unseen written examination paper.   25

6. *Dissertation*

(*a*) *Subject*

In the dissertation the candidate will be required to focus on material from within
the Honour School, and must show knowledge of more than one of the basic
approaches to the study of Human Sciences. The subject may, but need not, overlap   30
any subject on which the candidate offers papers. Candidates are warned that they
should avoid repetition in papers of material used in their dissertation and that
substantial repetition may be penalised.

Every candidate shall deliver for approval to the Chair of the Human Sciences
Teaching Committee c/o the Academic Administrator, Institute of Human Sciences,   35
The Pauling Centre, 58a Banbury Road, the title he or she proposes together with:

(i) an explanation of the subject in about 100 words explicitly mentioning the two
    or more basic approaches to the study of Human Sciences that will be incorpo-
    rated in the dissertation.

(ii) a letter of approval from his or her tutor **and** the name(s) of the advisor(s) who   40
     will supervise the dissertation.

This should not be earlier than the first day of Trinity Full Term of the year before
that in which the candidate is to be examined and not later than 12 midday on Friday
of the fifth week of the same term.

The Chair of the Teaching Committee, in consultation with the Chair of Examiners   45
and other Senior Members if necessary, shall as soon as possible decide whether or not
to approve the title and shall advise the candidate through his or her college. No
decision shall normally be deferred beyond the end of the eighth week of the relevant
Trinity Term.

Proposals to change the title of the dissertation may be made in exceptional   50
circumstances and will be considered by the Chair of the Teaching Committee until

the first day of Hilary Full Term of the year in which the student is to be examined, or only by the Chair of Examiners thereafter, but not later than the last day of the same term. Proposals to change the title of the dissertation should be made through the candidate's college via the Academic Administrator, Institute of Human Sciences, The Pauling Centre, 58a Banbury Road.   5

(*b*) *Authorship and origin*

The dissertation must be the candidates' own work. Tutors may, however, discuss with candidates the proposed field of study, the sources available and the method of presentation. They may also read and comment on a first draft. Every candidate shall sign a certificate to the effect that the thesis is his or her own work and that it has not   10
already been submitted, wholly or substantially, for another Honour School or degree of this University, or for a degree of any other institution. This certificate shall be submitted separately in a sealed envelope addressed to the chair of examiners. No dissertation shall, however, be ineligible because it has been or is being submitted for any prize of this University.   15

(*c*) *Length and format*

No dissertation shall be less than 5,000 words nor exceed 10,000 words; no person or body shall have authority to permit any excess. Candidates may include appendices which will not count towards the word limit. However the examiners are not bound to read the appendices and they shall not be taken into consideration when marking the   20
dissertation. There shall be a select bibliography or a list of sources; this shall not be included in the word count. Each dissertation shall be prefaced by an abstract of not more than 350 words which shall not be included in the overall word count. All dissertations must be typed on A4 paper and be held firmly in a cover. Two copies of the dissertation shall be submitted to the examiners.   25

(*d*) *Submissions of dissertation*

Every candidate shall deliver two copies of the dissertation to the Chair of Examiners, Honour School of Human Sciences, Examination Schools, High Street, Oxford, not later than noon on Friday of the week preceding Trinity Full Term in the year of the examination.   30

(*e*) *Resubmission of dissertation*

Dissertations previously submitted for the Honour School of Human Sciences may be resubmitted. No dissertation will be accepted if it has already been submitted, wholly or substantially, for another Honour School or degree of this University, or for a degree of any other institution.   35

HONOUR SCHOOL OF JURISPRUDENCE

A

1. Candidates in the School of Jurisprudence shall be examined in subjects from such branches of the law and of philosophy as may be prescribed by regulation.

2. No candidate shall be admitted to examination in this school unless he has either passed or been exempted from the First Public Examination.

3. The examination in this school shall be under the supervision of the Board of the Faculty of Law, which shall make regulations concerning it, subject always to the preceding clauses of this sub-section and to the concurrence of the Divisional Board of Humanities in respect of regulations concerning philosophy.

Candidates shall take one of the following courses.

Course 1. Candidates shall be examined in nine standard subjects. Candidates will be examined in accordance with the Examination Regulations set out below.

Course 2. Candidates shall be examined in nine standard subjects. Candidates will be examined in accordance with the Examination Regulations set out below. They will also be required to spend, after their matriculation, an academic year of residence in a European university approved in accordance with these regulations, and to have attended such courses at the approved university as are approved in accordance with these regulations, and to have completed such examinations at the approved university as the faculty board may specify.

B

Regulations applying to Course 2

1. The Law Board will approve courses at certain European universities. The list of approved courses will be available at the Institute of European and Comparative Law, St Cross Building, Manor Road.

2. Candidates may proceed to an academic year of residence at an approved university only if so permitted by the Board of the Faculty of Law. The board shall not give such permission unless the candidate presents (*a*) a certificate of linguistic competence relevant to the proposed year of residence and (*b*) a certificate from his or her society stating that he or she will have resided in Oxford for six terms (or three terms in the case of an applicant with senior status) since matriculation before proceeding to such residence, and (*c*) a statement in support from the head or a tutor of the candidate's society.

3. The certificate of linguistic competence may be provided only by a member of the University approved by the board.

4. Candidates will be required to take certain examinations at the approved universities. Details will be available from the Institute of European and Comparative Law.

5. The Institute of European and Comparative Law will certify to the chair of the examiners for the Honour School of Jurisprudence the names of candidates who have satisfied the requirements for the year abroad.

6. The board may amend or add to any provision in Regulations 1, 4, and 5 by regulation published in the *Gazette* at any time before the commencement of the academic year to which such addition or amendment applies.

Regulations applying to both Course 1 and Course 2:

Candidates shall be examined in the following seven standard subjects

1. Jurisprudence
2. Contract
3. Tort
4. Land Law
5. European Union Law
6. Trusts
7. Administrative Law

and in two further standard optional subjects, and must have satisfactorily completed the Legal Research and Mooting Skills Programme. A list of standard optional subjects approved by the Board of the Faculty of Law for the following academic year shall be posted in the Law Faculty Office and sent to college tutors, together with individual specifications and examination methods, not later than the beginning of the fifth week of the Hilary Term in the year before the Honour School examination will be held. Depending on the availability of teaching resources, not all standard optional subjects will be available to all candidates in every given year. If any such subject has to be withdrawn after it has appeared on the lists approved by the Board of the Faculty of Law, notice will be given in the Law Faculty Handbook for Undergraduate Students for the relevant year, which will be published and made available on the Faculty website by Monday of noughth week of Michaelmas Term that year.

Candidates who have been awarded the Diploma in Legal Studies shall be examined in the same number of subjects as other candidates but shall not be required to repeat in the Final Honour School papers taken for the Diploma which would otherwise be compulsory.

The following further regulations shall apply to the undermentioned Standard Subjects:

1. JURISPRUDENCE

Candidates offering Jurisprudence will be examined in that subject by:

(a) a two hour closed book examination at the end of a student's final year of the Final Honours School, in which students answer two questions from a selection of ten, and

(b) a single essay of 3,000–4,000 words to be written during the summer vacation between the end of Year 2 and commencement of Year 3 of the Final Honour School. Essay questions will be published by the Board of Examiners at noon on the Friday of the seventh week of the Trinity Term preceding the examination. Candidates will be contacted with details of how to collect or access the questions. Two copies of each essay submitted must be delivered to the Chair of the BA Jurisprudence Final Honours School Examiners, Examination Schools, High Street, Oxford, OX1 4BG, by noon on the Friday of noughth week preceding the beginning of the Michaelmas Full Term immediately following. The essays must bear the candidate's examination number, but not his or her name or the name of his or her college. Every candidate shall sign a Declaration of Authorship to the effect that the essay is his or her own work. Candidates shall further state the total number of words used in their essays. This certificate shall be presented together with the essays. To ensure anonymity the certificate must be placed in a sealed envelope.

2. CONTRACT

Candidates will be required to show a knowledge of such parts of the law of restitution as are directly relevant to the law of contract. Questions may be set in this paper requiring knowledge of the law of tort.

3. TORT

Questions may be set in this paper requiring knowledge of the law of contract.

4. LAND LAW

5. EUROPEAN UNION LAW

Comprises: 5

A. The basic structure and functions of the institutions; the aims of the EU; law-making; the composition and jurisdiction of the Court of Justice; the penetration of EU law into national legal orders.

B. Free movement of persons and services.

C. Free movement of goods. 10

6. TRUSTS

7. ADMINISTRATIVE LAW

Questions will not be set on the law of local government or of public corporations except as illustrating general principles of administrative law.

Candidates will be required to show a sufficient knowledge of such parts of the 15 general law of the constitution as are necessary for a proper understanding of this subject.

Statutes and other source material

Details of the statutes and other sources of material which will be available to candidates in the examination room for certain papers will be given in the teaching 20 conventions and in examiners' edicts circulated to candidates.

Legal Research and Mooting Skills Programme

The Law Board offers a Legal Research and Mooting Skills Programme, which provides training in the use of legal information resources (both paper and electronic), legal research, and team-working. The programme will also check students' compe- 25 tence in the use of Information Technology. Students are required to undertake this programme and to complete the assessments which form part of it, to the satisfaction of the Programme Co-ordinator appointed by the Law Board. The Programme Co-ordinator will certify to the Chair of Examiners for the Honour School of Jurisprudence the names of those students who have done so. 30

LINGUISTICS IN ALL HONOUR SCHOOLS INCLUDING LINGUISTICS

Candidates offering Linguistics papers in any Honour School must conform to the General Regulations below, and to those for their particular school, as specified elsewhere.   5

Subjects in Linguistics

The subjects in Linguistics are specified below. Paper A will be examined by three-hour examination. The mode of assessment for B1–6 and F will be specified in the Faculty Handbook.

A General Linguistics   10
B1 Phonetics and Phonology
B2 Syntax
B3 Semantics
B4 Psycholinguistics
B5 Sociolinguistics   15
B6 Historical Linguistics
C Linguistic Project
D Thesis
E1 Linguistic Studies I (=Paper IV of the Honour School of Modern Languages)
E2 Linguistic Studies II (=Paper V of the Honour School of Modern Languages)   20
F A Special Subject in Linguistics

Linguistic Project

The Linguistic Project will consist of a project report of between 8,000 and 10,000 words. Two copies of the project should be submitted by hand to the Examination Schools and addressed to the Chair of Examiners in the candidate's Honour School,   25
by noon on the Friday of the ninth week of Hilary Term in the year of the examination, together with a statement, sent under separate cover, certifying that the project is the candidate's own work and has not already been submitted, either wholly or substantially, for a degree in this university or elsewhere. A third copy must be retained by the candidate.   30

Not later than the Wednesday of the second week of the Michaelmas Full Term preceding the examination, candidates proposing to offer a Linguistic Project must submit, through their college, to the Director of Undergraduate Studies of the Faculty of Linguistics, Philology and Phonetics (on a form obtainable from the Linguistics Faculty Office) a statement of their name, college, the Honour School they intend to   35
offer, the academic year in which they intend to take the examination, and the title of the proposed project together with:

(*a*) a statement of approximately fifty words of how the subject is to be treated,

(*b*) a statement signed by a supervisor or tutor that he or she considers the subject suitable, and suggesting a person or persons who might be invited to be an examiner or   40
an assessor (the Board will not approve a title unless it is satisfied that a suitably qualified examiner or assessor based in Oxford will be available),

(*c*) a statement by a college tutor that he or she approves the candidate's application, and

(*d*) confirmation that relevant CUREC approval was or will be obtained before work with human subjects has begun.

One complete draft of the Linguistic Project may be read and commented on by the supervisor.

The Linguistic Project must be typed in double-spacing on A4 paper, and must be bound or held firmly in a stiff cover. All quotations, whether direct or indirect, from primary or secondary sources must be explicitly acknowledged. The use of unacknowledged quotations will be penalized. The word count is exclusive of the footnotes and the bibliography. Extensive textual material may be placed in an appendix and need not be included in the word limit. An abstract or summary need not be included.

Thesis

1. Candidates may offer a Thesis, subject to the following provisions:

   (i) The subject of every thesis shall, to the satisfaction of the Board of the Faculty, fall within the scope of Linguistics.

   (ii) The subject of a thesis may, but need not, overlap any subject on which the candidate offers a paper, but candidates should avoid repetition of material presented in the extended essay in other parts of the examination.

   (iii) Not later than the Wednesday of the second week of the Michaelmas Full Term preceding the examination, candidates proposing to offer a thesis must submit, through their college, to the Director of Undergraduate Studies of the Faculty of Linguistics, Philology and Phonetics (on a form obtainable from the Linguistics Faculty Office) a statement of their name, college, the Honour School they intend to offer, the academic year in which they intend to take the examination, and the title of the proposed thesis together with

   (*a*) a statement of approximately fifty words of how the subject is to be treated,

   (*b*) a statement signed by a supervisor or tutor, preferably in the field of study with which the thesis is concerned, that he or she considers the subject suitable, and suggesting a person or persons who might be invited to be an examiner or an assessor (the Board will not approve a title unless it is satisfied that a suitably qualified examiner or assessor based in Oxford will be available),

   (*c*) a statement by a college tutor that he or she approves the candidate's application, and

   (*d*) confirmation that relevant CUREC approval, if necessary, was or will have been obtained before work with human subjects has begun.

   (iv) The Board of the Faculty will decide by the end of the third week of the Michaelmas Full Term preceding the examination whether the candidate has permission to offer a thesis. Permission may be granted on the condition that the candidate agrees to amend details of the title to the satisfaction of the Board, and submits the required amendments to the Faculty Office for the Board's approval by Friday of the sixth week of the Michaelmas Full Term preceding the examination. If the proposed title is approved, this will be notified by the Administration and Faculty Office, together with any conditions attached to the approval, to the candidate and to the Chair of the Examiners for the candidate's Honour School.

   (v) A candidate may seek approval after Friday of the sixth week of the Michaelmas Full Term preceding the examination for an amendment of detail in an approved title, by application to the Faculty Office. The Chair of the Examiners and the Chair of the Board, acting together, will decide whether or not a proposed amendment shall be approved.

2. Every thesis must be the candidate's own work. Tutors may, however, discuss with candidates the proposed field of study, the sources available, and the method of presentation. Tutors may also read and comment on a first draft. All quotations, whether direct or indirect, from primary or secondary sources must be explicitly acknowledged. The use of unacknowledged quotations will be penalized. Candidates   5
must sign a certificate stating that the thesis is their own work and this certificate must be sent at the same time as the thesis, but under separate cover, to the Examination Schools, Oxford, addressed to the Chair of the Examiners in the candidate's Honour School.

3. No thesis shall be ineligible because it has been submitted, in whole or in part, for   10
any scholarship or prize in this university.

4. Candidates shall present a one-page summary of the arguments at the beginning of their thesis. Theses shall be in the range 10,000–12,000 words (exclusive of the footnotes, the bibliography, any appendices, and summary). No person or body shall have authority to permit the limit of 12,000 words to be exceeded, except that, in the   15
case of a commentary on a text, and at the discretion of the Chair of the Examiners, any substantial quoting of that text need not be included in the word limit. The examiners will not take account of such parts of an essay as are beyond these limits. There must be a select bibliography, listing all primary and secondary sources cited in the thesis, and full details must be given of all citations at the end of the thesis. All   20
theses must be typed in double-spacing on A4 paper, and must be bound or held firmly in a stiff cover. Two copies must be submitted to the Chair of the Examiners, and a third copy must be retained by the candidate.

5. The candidate shall submit two copies of the thesis, identified by the candidate's examination number only, not later than noon on Friday of the week before the   25
Trinity Full Term of the examination, to the Examination Schools, Oxford, addressed to the Chair of the Examiners in the candidate's Honour School.

Special Subjects

Special Subjects available in Linguistics will be published in the *Gazette* and on-line by the beginning of the fifth week of the Trinity Term preceding the year of examina-   30
tion. Candidates in the Joint Schools involving Linguistics may offer any of the special subjects for paper XII in the Honour School of Modern Languages, provided they are marked with the Linguistics identifier L.

The method of assessment for each subject will be published in the *Gazette* and on-line by the beginning of the fifth week of the Trinity Term preceding the year of   35
examination, according to the following key:

A: Three-hour unseen written paper. N.B. For the option paper in Phonetics and Phonology, candidates must also offer either a 30 minute Phonetics Transcription aural test or a Laboratory Report of a Phonetics experiment.

B: An essay or portfolio of essays (the number of essays required to be shown in   40
parentheses) aggregating to approximately 6,000 words and not exceeding 8,000 words, to be submitted by hand to the Examinations Schools, High Street, Oxford by noon on the Friday of the ninth week of Hilary Term in the year of the examination, together with a statement certifying that the essay(s) are the candidate's own work and that they have not already been submitted, either wholly or substantially, for   45
a degree in this university or elsewhere.

C: An essay or portfolio of essays (the number of essays required to be shown in parentheses) aggregating to approximately 6,000 words and not exceeding 8,000 words written as answers to an examination paper to be collected from the Examination Schools, and signed for by candidates, on the Friday of the fifth week   50
of the Hilary Term before the examination. Completed essay(s) should be submitted by hand to the Examination Schools by noon on the Friday of the ninth week of

Hilary Term in the year of the examination, together with a statement certifying that the essay(s) are the candidate's own work and that they have not already been submitted, either wholly or substantially, for a degree in this university or elsewhere.

General Regulations

Candidates in the Honour School of Psychology, Philosophy, and Linguistics may offer paper E1 or E2 only with the agreement of the Board of the Faculty of Linguistics, Philology, and Phonetics.

No candidate may offer more than one special subject F. Candidates may not be permitted to offer certain special subjects in combination with certain other subjects, or may be permitted to do so only on condition that in the papers on the other subjects they will not be permitted to answer certain questions.

Regulations for Particular Honour Schools

Psychology, Philosophy, and Linguistics

Candidates may take at most five subjects in Linguistics. All candidates must take eight subjects in total. Candidates may only take subjects in Psychology if they offer Psychology Parts I and II.

Candidates may take no more than one paper from group F.

All candidates in Linguistics must take paper A.

Candidates who take **two** subjects in Linguistics must take paper A and one of papers B1–B6.

Candidates who take **three** subjects in Linguistics must take (1) paper A, (2) one of papers B1, B2, B3, and (3) one of papers B1–6, C, D, F.

Candidates who take **four** subjects in Linguistics must take (1) paper A, (2) one of papers B1, B2, B3, and (3) two of papers B1–6, C *or* D, E1 *or* E2, F.

Candidates who take **five** subjects in Linguistics must take (1) paper A, (2) one of papers B1, B2, B3, and (3) three of papers B1–6, C, D, E1 *or* E2, F.

HONOUR SCHOOL OF LITERAE HUMANIORES

A

1. The Branches of the Honour School of Literae Humaniores shall be (I) Greek and Roman History, (II) Philosophy, (III) Greek and Latin Literature, (IV) Greek and Roman Archaeology, (V) Philology and Linguistics, (VI) Second Classical Language.

2. Each candidate must offer at least two of Branches (I)–(V).

3. No candidate shall be admitted to the examination in this school unless he or she has either passed or been exempted from the First Public Examination.

4. The examination in this school shall be under the joint supervision of the Boards of the Faculties of Classics and Philosophy, which shall appoint a joint standing committee to make regulations concerning it and review its operation, subject always to the preceding clauses of this subsection.

B

1. Candidates shall take either Course I or Course II. Persons who have satisfied the Moderators in Course IA, IB, or IC of Honour Moderations in Classics or of the Preliminary Examination in Classics may not enter for the Honour School of Literae Humaniores Course II without permission from the Board of the Faculty of Classics after consultation where appropriate with the Board of the Faculty of Philosophy. Such permission, which will be given only for special reasons, must be sought as early as possible, and in no case later than noon on the Friday of the first week of Michaelmas Term before the examination, by writing to the Chair of the Board of the Faculty of Classics, c/o 66 St Giles'. Applications must be accompanied by a letter of support from the applicant's society.

2. Candidates must offer eight subjects (and any associated papers of translation), which may include: up to five subjects in Greek and Roman History; up to five subjects in Philosophy; up to five subjects in Greek and Latin Literature; up to two subjects (or up to three, if one is a thesis [699]) in Greek and Roman Archaeology; up to two subjects (or up to three, if one is a thesis [598]) in Philology and Linguistics; two subjects in Second Classical Language; except that (i) candidates in Course I may not offer Second Classical Language and (ii) candidates in Course II who offer Second Classical Language may not offer more than four subjects in any one of Greek and Roman History, Philosophy, and Greek and Latin Literature. The combinations of subjects permitted are set out in I–VI below. Candidates may offer a thesis as one of their subjects, with the proviso that those offering a thesis in Philosophy must offer at least three other subjects in Philosophy. No candidate may offer more than one thesis, except that a Special Thesis may be offered in addition to one other thesis.

3. All candidates must offer at least four text-based subjects, except that candidates in Course II who offer Second Classical Language must offer at least three text-based subjects. All candidates in Course I must offer at least one text-based subject in each of (1) Greek and (2) Latin. Some subjects (503, 504, 507) may count as text-based subjects in either Greek or Latin. The text-based subjects are as follows:

(1) in Greek

    130: Plato, *Republic*
    131: Plato, *Theaetetus* and *Sophist*
    132: Aristotle, *Nicomachean Ethics*
    133: Aristotle, *Physics*   5
    134: Sextus Empiricus
    401: Greek History 1
    402: Greek History 2
    403: Greek History 3
    404: Roman History 4   10
    501: Greek Core, if offered in version (a)
    503: Historiography, if offered in version (a) or (b)
    504: Lyric Poetry, if offered in version (a) or (b)
    505: Early Greek Hexameter Poetry
    506: Greek Tragedy   15
    507: Comedy, if offered in version (a) or (b)
    508: Hellenistic Poetry
    513: Euripides, *Orestes*
    517: Byzantine Literature
    518: Modern Greek Poetry   20
    551: Greek Historical Linguistics

(2) in Latin

    135: Latin Philosophy
    405: Roman History 5
    406: Roman History 6   25
    [For students starting from TT 2016: 414: The Conversion of Augustine**]**
    502: Latin Core, if offered in version (a)
    503: Historiography, if offered in version (a) or (c)
    504: Lyric Poetry, if offered in version (a) or (c)
    507: Comedy if offered in version (a) or (c)   30
    509: Cicero
    510: Ovid
    511: Latin Didactic
    512: Neronian Literature
    [For students starting before TT 2016: 514: Seneca, *Agamemnon***]**   35
    515: Catullus
    [For students starting before TT 2016: 516: The Conversion of Augustine**]**
    [For students starting from TT 2016: 524: Seneca, *Medea***]**
    552: Latin Historical Linguistics

4. In the assignment of honours all eight subjects offered by a candidate shall count   40
equally. In assessing a candidate's performance in a subject, the examiners shall have
regard to performance in any associated translation papers.

5. In addition to their eight subjects candidates may also offer, but are not required
to offer, a Special Thesis in accordance with VII below.

6. Any candidate whose native language is not English may bring a bilingual   45
(native language to English) dictionary for use in any examination paper where
candidates are required to translate Ancient Greek and/or Latin texts into English.

7. For each subject in I, III, IV, V and VI below, a detailed specification and (where
applicable) prescribed texts will be given in the Greats Handbook applicable to the

relevant year of examination. The handbook will be published no later than Monday of Week 5 of Hilary Term two years preceding the examination.

I. *Greek and Roman History*

Candidates may offer up to five subjects (or up to four if they are offering Second Classical Language in Course II). If they offer more than one subject, at least one must   5
be taken from A below; if they offer more than three subjects, at least two must be taken from A; if they offer five subjects, at least three must be taken from A.

One three-hour paper will be set on each subject except 499. For all of the period subjects which they offer under A as text-based (401–6), candidates will be required to sit an associated paper (one-and-a-half hours) comprising translation from the pre-   10
scribed texts.

A. GREEK AND ROMAN HISTORY PERIODS

In Course I all period subjects must be offered as text-based. Course II candidates who are taking period subjects must offer at least one as text-based, and may not offer more than one as non-text-based. Course IIA candidates taking Roman History 5 and   15
6 must offer them as text-based papers; Course IIB candidates taking Greek History 1–3 and Roman History 4 must offer them as text-based papers.

Greek History 1 (401 text-based; 421 non text-based): *The Early Greek World and Herodotus' Histories: 650 to 479 BC*

Greek History 2 (402 text-based; 422 non text-based: *Thucydides and the Greek*   20
World: 479 to 403 BC

Greek History 3 (403 text-based; 423 non text-based): *The End of the Peloponnesian War to the Death of Philip II of Macedon: 403 to 336 BC*

Roman History 4 (404 text-based; 424 non text-based): *Polybius, Rome and the Mediterranean: 241–146 BC*   25

Roman History 5 (405 text-based; 425 non text-based): *Republic in Crisis: 146–46 BC*

Roman History 6 (406 text-based; 426 non text-based): *Rome, Italy and Empire from Caesar to Claudius: 46 BC to AD 54*

B. GREEK AND ROMAN HISTORY TOPICS

Note: It cannot be guaranteed that university lectures or classes or college teaching   30
will be available in all subjects in this section in every academic year. Candidates are advised to consult their tutors about the availability of teaching when selecting their subjects.

407: *Athenian Democracy in the Classical Age*

408: *Alexander the Great and his Early Successors* (336 BC–302 BC)   35

409: *The Hellenistic World: Societies and Cultures* (c.300–100 BC)

410: *Cicero: Politics and Thought in the Late Republic.* This subject may not be combined with subject 509 *Cicero.*

411: *Politics, Society and Culture from Nero to Hadrian*

412: *Religions in the Greek and Roman World* (c.31 BC–AD 312)   40

413: *Sexuality and Gender in Greece and Rome*

[For students starting from TT 2016: 414: *The Conversion of Augustine*]

C.

499: *Thesis in Ancient History*

Any candidate who is not offering a thesis in any other branch of the examination   45
may offer a thesis in Ancient History in accordance with the Regulations on Theses below.

II. *Philosophy*

Candidates may offer up to five subjects in Philosophy, from the list below. Candidates offering one Philosophy subject only may offer any of the subjects listed below except 199. Those offering at least two Philosophy subjects must select at least one subject in ancient philosophy, i.e. one of 115, 116, 130, 131, 132, 133, 134 and 135. Those offering three or more subjects must also select one subject from 101, 102, 103 and 108. Candidates offering subject 199 (Thesis in Philosophy) must offer at least three other subjects in Philosophy. The syllabus for each subject, including thesis regulations, is specified in **Regulations for Philosophy in all Honour Schools including Philosophy**. In the list below, numbers in parenthesis after a subject's title indicate other subjects with which it may not be combined.

101 Early Modern Philosophy
102 Knowledge and Reality
103 Ethics
104 Philosophy of Mind
106 Philosophy of Science and Social Science (**124**)
107 Philosophy of Religion
108 The Philosophy of Logic and Language
109 Aesthetics and the Philosophy of Criticism
110 Medieval Philosophy: Aquinas (**111**)
111 Medieval Philosophy: Duns Scotus, Ockham (**110**)
112 The Philosophy of Kant
113 Post-Kantian Philosophy
114 Theory of Politics
115 Plato: *Republic* (in translation) (**130**)
116 Aristotle: *Nicomachean Ethics* (in translation) (**132**)
117 Frege, Russell, and Wittgenstein (**118**)
118 The Later Philosophy of Wittgenstein (**117**)
120 Intermediate Philosophy of Physics
122 Philosophy of Mathematics
124 Philosophy of Science (**106**)
125 Philosophy of Cognitive Science
127 Philosophical Logic
130 Plato: *Republic* (in Greek) (**115**)
131 Plato: *Theaetetus* and *Sophist* (in Greek)
132 Aristotle: *Nicomachean Ethics* (in Greek) (**116**)
133 Aristotle: *Physics* (in Greek)
134 Sextus Empiricus: *Outlines of Pyrrhonism* (in Greek)
135 Latin Philosophy (in Latin)
199 Thesis in Philosophy (**499, 598, 599, 699**)

III. *Greek and Latin Literature*

Course I candidates may offer up to a maximum of five subjects from **[For students starting before TT 2016: 501–522] [For students starting from TT 2016: 501–524]** and 599 below. *Course II* candidates may offer up to a maximum of five subjects, or four if they take VI, Second Classical Language. Candidates offering three or more subjects must offer at least one of Greek Core (501 or 521) and Latin Core (502 or 522).

The following restrictions on combinations of literature subjects apply to both Course I and Course II candidates:

(1) Subject 521 may only be offered by Course II students taking Second Classical Language in Greek. Subject 522 may only be offered by Course II students taking Second Classical Language in Latin.

(2) Only one of subjects 503, 504, 507, and 519 may be offered.

(3) **[For students starting before TT 2016:** Only one of subjects 514 and 515 may be offered.] **[For students starting from TT 2016:** Only one of subjects 515 and 524 may be offered.]

(4) Only one of subjects **[For students starting before TT 2016:** 516,] 517, 518 and 519 may be offered.

One three-hour paper will be set on each subject except 503, 504, 507, 519 and 599. Additional translation papers (one-and-a-half hours each) will be set on 501 and 502.

Note 1: Each of subjects 503, 504 and 507 will be examined by a one-and-a-half hour translation paper on the prescribed texts and an extended essay of up to 6,000 words. Each of these subjects is available in three versions:

(*a*) Greek and Latin, for Course I candidates.

(*b*) Greek only, for Course II candidates or single-language candidates in Classics & English, Classics & Modern Languages, or Classics & Oriental Studies offering Greek.

(*c*) Latin only, for Course II candidates or single-language candidates in Classics & English, Classics & Modern Languages, or Classics & Oriental Studies offering Latin.

Essay topics set by the examiners will be released on Monday of Week 6 of Hilary Term immediately preceding the examination and essays should be submitted to the Examination Schools by 12 noon on Monday of Week 10 of the same term; at the same time candidates should email a searchable electronic version to undergraduate@classics.ox.ac.uk. Every extended essay must be the work of the candidate alone, and he or she must not discuss with any tutor either his or her choice of theme or the method of handling it.

Note 2: In all subjects credit will be given for showing wider knowledge of Greek and Roman culture.

Note 3: It cannot be guaranteed that university lectures or classes or college teaching will be available in all subjects in every academic year. Candidates are advised to consult their tutors about the availability of teaching when selecting their subjects.

501/521: *Greek Core*
Either:
(a) 501: One paper of three hours (commentary and essay) with an additional paper (one-and-a-half hours) of translation.
or
(b) 521: One paper of three hours (commentary and essay). Translations of the passages set for commentary will be provided. **This version of the subject is only available to those taking VI. Second Classical Language in Greek and will not count as text-based.**

502/522: *Latin Core*
Either:
(a) 502: One paper of three hours (commentary and essay) with an additional paper (one-and-a-half-hours) of translation.
or:
(b) 522: One paper of three hours (commentary and essay). Translations of the passages set for commentary will be provided. **This version of the subject is only available to those taking VI. Second Classical Language in Latin and will not count as text-based.**

503: *Historiography*
One of the following (*see Note 1 above*):
(a) Greek and Latin version
(b) Greek only version
(c) Latin only version
This subject may not be combined with 504, 507, or 519.

504: *Lyric Poetry*
One of the following (*see Note 1 above*):
(a) Greek and Latin version
(b) Greek only version
(c) Latin only version   5
This subject may not be combined with 503, 507, or 519.
505: *Early Greek Hexameter Poetry*
506: *Greek Tragedy*
507: *Comedy*
One of the following (*see Note 1 above*):   10
(a) Greek and Latin version
(b) Greek only version
(c) Latin only version
This subject may not be combined with 503, 504, or 519.
508: *Hellenistic Poetry*   15
509: *Cicero*
This subject may not be combined with 410, *Cicero: Politics and Thought in the Late Republic.*
510: *Ovid*
511: *Latin Didactic*   20
512: *Neronian Literature*
513: *Euripides*, Orestes: *papyri, manuscripts, text*
[For students starting before TT 2016: 514: *Seneca*, Agamemnon: *manuscripts, text, interpretation*
This subject may not be combined with 515.**]**   25
515: Catullus:*manuscripts, text, interpretation*
This subject may not be combined with **[For students starting before TT 2016:** 514**]** **[For students starting from TT 2016:** 524**]**.
[For students starting before TT 2016: 516: *The Conversion of Augustine*
This subject may not be combined with 517, 518, or 519.**]**   30
517: *Byzantine Literature*
This subject may not be combined with **[For students starting before TT 2016:** 516,**]** 518, or 519.
518: *Modern Greek Poetry*
This subject may not be combined with **[For students starting before TT 2016:** 516,**]** 35
517, or 519.
519: *The Reception of Classical Literature in Poetry in English since 1900*
This paper will be examined only by extended essay of up to 6,000 words. Essay topics set by the examiners will be released on Monday of Week 6 of Hilary Term and essays should be submitted by 12 noon on Monday of Week 10 of the same term to the   40
Examination Schools; at the same time candidates should email a searchable electronic version to undergraduate@classics.ox.ac.uk. Candidates will be required to use at least three authors in their essays, at least one of which must be a classical author. Every extended essay must be the work of the candidate alone, and he or she must not discuss with any tutor either his or her choice of theme or the method of handling it.   45
This subject may not be combined with 503, 504, 507, **[For students starting before TT 2016:** 516,**]** 517, or 518.
[For students starting from TT 2016: 524: *Seneca*, Medea: *manuscripts, text, interpretation.*
This subject may not be combined with 515.**]**   50
599: Thesis in Literature

Any candidate may offer a thesis in Greek and Latin Literature in accordance with the Regulation on Theses below. This subject may not be combined with any of 199, 499, 598, or 699.

IV. *Greek and Roman Archaeology*

Course I and *Course II*: Candidates may offer *one* or *two* of the following subjects   5
601–605, and may, if they wish, offer subject 699 as well. They may also offer subject
699 as their sole Archaeology subject.

Each of subjects 601–605 will be examined in one paper (3 hours).

601: *The Greeks and the Mediterranean World* c.*950 BC–500 BC*
602: *Greek Art and Archaeology,* c.*500–300 BC*   10
603: *Hellenistic Art and Archaeology, 330–30 BC*
604: *Art under the Roman Empire AD 14–337*
605: *Roman Archaeology: Cities and Settlement under the Empire*
699: *Thesis in Greek and Roman Archaeology*

Any candidate may offer a thesis in Greek or Roman Archaeology in accordance   15
with the Regulation on Theses below. This subject may not be combined with any of
199, 499, 598, or 599.

V. *Philology and Linguistics*

Course I and *Course II*: Candidates may offer *one* or *two* of subjects 551–554, and may
if they wish offer subject 598 as well. They may also offer subject 598 as their sole   20
Philology and Linguistics subject.

Each of subjects 551–554 will be examined in one paper (3 hours).

551: *Greek Historical Linguistics*
552: *Latin Historical Linguistics*
553: *General Linguistics and Comparative Philology*   25
554: *Comparative Philology: Indo-European, Greek and Latin*

This subject may not be offered by any candidate who offered the Special Subject
Historical Linguistics and Comparative Philology in Honour Moderations in Classics
or in the Preliminary Examination in Classics.

598: *Thesis in Philology and Linguistics*   30

Any candidate may offer a thesis in Philology and Linguistics in accordance with
the Regulation on Theses below. This subject may not be combined with any of 199,
499, 599, or 699.

VI. *Second Classical Language*

Second Classical Language is available only in Course II. Candidates offering Second   35
Classical Language who satisfied the Moderators in Course IIA of Honour
Moderations in Classics or of Preliminary Examination in Classics must offer
566 and 568. Candidates offering Second Classical Language who satisfied the
Moderators in Course IIB of Honour Moderations in Classics or of Preliminary
Examination in Classics must offer 567 and 569. Each subject will be examined in   40
one three-hour paper.

566: *Greek Verse*
567: *Latin Verse*
568: *Greek Prose*
569: *Latin Prose*   45

VII. *Special Theses*

Candidates may offer, but are not required to offer, a Special Thesis in addition to the eight subjects required above, in accordance with the Regulations on Theses below.
Regulation on Theses

1. This regulation governs theses in Ancient History (subject 499), Literature (599), 5
Archaeology (699), Philology and Linguistics (598), and Special Thesis (VII), with the exception of Special Theses on subjects relating to Philosophy. For theses in Philosophy (199) and Special Theses (VII) on Philosophy subjects, see **Regulations for Philosophy in all Honour Schools including Philosophy.**

2. The subject of every thesis shall, to the satisfaction of the Standing Committee 10
for Mods and Greats, fall within the scope of the Honour School of Literae Humaniores. The subject may but need not overlap any subject or period on which the candidate offers papers. Candidates should avoid repetition in examination essays of material used in their theses and may be penalised for substantial repetition. Candidates who offer a Special Thesis and another thesis must avoid all overlap 15
between them.

3. Candidates proposing to offer a thesis must submit to the Academic Administrative Officer of the Faculty of Classics, on a form obtainable from the Classics Office which must be countersigned by their tutor and (if different) by their proposed supervisor, the title of the proposed thesis, together with a synopsis of the 20
subject in about 100 words, not later than the Wednesday of the first week of the Michaelmas Full Term preceding the examination. The Standing Committee for Mods and Greats shall decide whether or not to approve the title and shall advise the candidate as soon as possible.

4. Every thesis shall be the candidate's own work. Tutors may, however, assist 25
candidates by discussing with them, for example, the field of study, the sources available, bibliography, and the method of presentation, and may also read and comment on drafts. The amount of assistance a candidate may receive shall not exceed an amount equivalent to the teaching of a normal paper. All quotations from primary or secondary sources, and all reporting or appropriation of material 30
from those sources, must be explicitly acknowledged. Candidates must submit a signed declaration that the thesis is their own work.

5. Theses previously submitted for the Honour School of Literae Humaniores may be resubmitted. No thesis shall be accepted which has already been submitted, wholly or substantially, for another Honour School or degree of this or any other institution, 35
and the certificate shall also state that the thesis has not been so submitted. No thesis shall, however, be ineligible because it has been or is being submitted for any prize of this university.

6. No thesis shall exceed 10,000 words (the limit to include all notes and appendices but not including the bibliography). No person or body shall have authority to permit 40
the limit of 10,000 words to be exceeded, except that, in the case of a commentary on a text and at the discretion of the chair of examiners, any substantial quoting of that text or of any translation of that text need not be included in the word limit. Where appropriate, there shall be a select bibliography and a list of sources.

7. All theses must be typed in double spacing on one side only, with any notes and 45
references at the foot of each page.

8. Candidates wishing to change the title of their thesis after it has been approved may apply for permission for the change to be granted by the Chair of the Standing Committee for Mods and Greats (if the application is made before the first day of Hilary Full Term preceding the examination) or (if later) the Chair of the Examiners, 50
Honour School of Literae Humaniores.

9. Candidates shall submit two copies of their thesis, identified by their candidate number only, not later than noon on Friday of Week 0 of the Trinity Full Term of the examination to the Examination Schools, High Street, Oxford, addressed to the Chair of the Examiners, Honour School of Literae Humaniores. At the same time they shall submit a searchable electronic version to undergraduate@classics.ox.ac.uk.   5

N.B. For prescribed editions in all forms of the Honour School of Literae Humaniores, see the Greats Handbook

HONOUR SCHOOL OF MATERIALS SCIENCE

A

1. The subject of the Honour School of Materials Science shall be the study of Materials Science.

2. No candidate shall be admitted to the examination in this school unless he or she has either passed or been exempted from the First Public Examination.

3. The examination in this school shall be under the supervision of the Mathematical, Physical and Life Sciences Board, which shall prescribe the necessary regulations.

4. A candidate registered on the four year Master of Engineering in Materials Science degree programme is permitted, at a date no later than Friday of the 3rd week of Michaelmas Term in the year of Part I of the Second Public Examination, to transfer to the three year Bachelor of Arts in Materials Science programme, provided no such candidate may later enter the Part II year or supplicate for the degree of Master of Engineering in Materials Science.

5. Following Friday of the 3rd week of Michaelmas Term in the year of Part I of the Second Public Examination a candidate registered on the four year Master of Engineering in Materials Science degree programme is permitted, at a date no later than Friday of the 8th week of Trinity Term in the year of Part I of the Second Public Examination, to transfer to the three year Bachelor of Arts in Materials Science Programme, provided no such candidate may later enter the Part II year or supplicate for the degree of Master of Engineering in Materials Science. In such cases the candidate will complete the Part I Examination as specified for the Master of Engineering programme and will in addition be required to complete during a specified period of the Long Vacation immediately following Trinity Term of the year of Part I of the Second Public Examination the extended essay specified in the programme for the degree of Bachelor of Arts in Materials Science. The Examiners will consider the outcome for such a candidate at the classification meeting held soon after the end of Trinity full term in the year following that of Part I of the Second Public Examination.

6. The examination for the Master of Engineering degree in Materials Science shall consist of Part I and Part II, and shall be partly of a practical nature. Candidates will be expected to show knowledge based on practical work: normally this requirement shall be satisfied by the Examiners' assessment of the practical work done by candidates during their course of study.

7. The examination for the Bachelor of Arts degree in Materials Science shall consist of one Part only, and shall be partly of a practical nature. Candidates will be expected to show knowledge based on practical work: normally this requirement shall be satisfied by the Examiners' assessment of the practical work done by candidates during their course of study.

8. No candidate for the degree of Master of Engineering in Materials Science may present him or herself for examination in Part II unless he or she has (a) been adjudged worthy of Honours by the Examiners in Part I and (b) normally obtained a minimum mark of 50% averaged over all elements of assessment for the Part I Examination.

9. The name of a candidate for the degree of Master of Engineering in Materials Science shall not be published in a class list until he or she has completed all parts of the examination and has been adjudged worthy of Honours by the Examiners in Part I

and Part II of the examination in consecutive years. The Examiners shall give due consideration to the performance in all elements of the respective examinations.

10. The name of a candidate for the degree of Bachelor of Arts in Materials Science shall not be published in a class list until he or she has completed the examination and has been adjudged worthy of Honours by the Examiners. The Examiners shall give   5
due consideration to the performance in all elements of the examination.

11. For candidates for the degree of Master of Engineering in Materials Science the Examiners shall be entitled to award (i) unclassified Honours to candidates in Part I who have been adjudged worthy of Honours but have obtained a mark of less than 50% averaged over all elements of assessment for the Part I Examination or (ii) a pass to   10
candidates in Part I who have reached a standard considered adequate but who have not been adjudged worthy of Honours. To achieve Honours at Part I normally a candidate must fulfil all of the requirements under (a), (b), & (c) of this clause. (a) Obtain a minimum mark of 40% averaged over all elements of assessment for the Part I Examination, (b) obtain a minimum mark of 40% in each of at least four of the six written papers sat in   15
Trinity Term of the year of Part I of the Second Public Examination, and (c) satisfy the coursework requirements set out in Section B, Part I below.

12. For candidates for the degree of Bachelor of Arts in Materials Science the Examiners shall be entitled to award a pass to candidates who have reached a standard considered adequate but who have not been adjudged worthy of Honours.   20
To achieve Honours normally a candidate must fulfil all of the requirements under (a), (b), & (c) of this clause. (a) Obtain a minimum mark of 40% averaged over all elements of assessment for the Examination, (b) obtain a minimum mark of 40% in each of at least four of the six written papers sat in Trinity Term of the year of the Second Public Examination, and (c) satisfy the coursework requirements set out in Section B, below.   25

13. A candidate for the degree of Master of Engineering in Materials Science who obtains a mark of less than 50% averaged over all elements of assessment for the Part I Examination or who fails to satisfy the Examiners may enter again for the whole of Part I of the examination on one, but no more than one, subsequent occasion. Normally (i) this subsequent occasion shall be during the academic year immediately   30
following the first decision of the Examiners and (ii) the examination will be identical to that taken by the other Part I candidates in said academic year. A candidate who is adjudged worthy of Honours and obtains a mark of 50% or more averaged over all elements of assessment on the occasion of this resit may progress to Part II in the academic year following that of the resit examination; such a candidate will carry   35
forward a Part I mark of 50% only. Part II shall be entered on one occasion only.

14. A candidate for the degree of Bachelor of Arts in Materials Science who obtains only a pass, or fails to satisfy the Examiners may enter again for the examination on one, but no more than one, subsequent occasion. Normally (i) this subsequent occasion shall be during the academic year immediately following the first decision of the   40
Examiners and (ii) the examination will be identical to that taken by the other candidates for the BA in Materials Science in said academic year. The Examiners shall be entitled to award a 3rd class Honours classification to a candidate who is adjudged worthy of Honours and obtains a mark of 40% or more averaged over all elements of assessment on the occasion of this resit. The Examiners shall be entitled to   45
award a Pass to a candidate who has reached a standard considered adequate but who has not been adjudged worthy of Honours on the occasion of this resit.

15. A candidate for the degree of Master of Engineering in Materials Science adjudged worthy of Honours in Part I and worthy of Honours in Part II may supplicate for the Degree of Master of Engineering in Materials Science, provided   50
that the candidate has fulfilled all the conditions for admission to a degree of the University.

16. A candidate for the degree of Bachelor of Arts in Materials Science adjudged worthy of Honours may supplicate for the Degree of Bachelor of Arts in Material Science, provided that the candidate has fulfilled all the conditions for admission to a degree of the University.

17. A candidate for the degree of Master of Engineering in Materials Science who fails to obtain Honours in Part II, or who is adjudged worthy of Honours in Part I and who obtains a minimum mark of 50% averaged over all elements of assessment for the Part I Examination but who does not enter Part II, or who is adjudged worthy of Honours in Part I but who obtains a mark of less than 50% averaged over all elements of assessment for the Part I Examination, or who passes Part I, is permitted to supplicate for the degree of Bachelor of Arts in Materials Science (unclassified Honours or pass, as appropriate); provided that no such candidate may later enter or re-enter the Part II year or supplicate for the degree of Master of Engineering in Materials Science or supplicate for the degree of Bachelor of Arts in Materials Science (classified Honours); and provided in each case that the candidate has fulfilled all the conditions for admission to a degree of the University.

18. A candidate for the degree of Bachelor of Arts in Materials Science who passes the Second Public Examination but is not adjudged worthy of Honours is permitted to supplicate for the degree of Bachelor of Arts in Materials Science (pass); provided that no such candidate may later supplicate for the degree of Bachelor of Arts (classified or unclassified Honours) in Materials Science; and provided in each case that the candidate has fulfilled all the conditions for admission to a degree of the University.

B

1. In the following, 'the Course Handbook' refers to the Materials Science and Materials, Economics & Management Final Honours School Course Handbook, published annually at the start of Michaelmas Term by the Faculty of Materials and also posted on the website at: http://www.materials.ox.ac.uk/teaching/ug/ughandbooks.html.

2. Candidates are restricted to models of calculators included in the Course Handbook published in the academic year preceding either Part I of the Second Public Examination for the degree of Master of Engineering in Materials Science or the Second Public Examination for the degree of Bachelor of Arts in Materials Science.

3. Supplementary subjects or the completion of an approved course of instruction in a foreign language:

(*a*) As an alternative to offering Engineering and Society coursework, candidates may either offer themselves for examination in a Supplementary Subject or complete an approved, assessed course of instruction in a foreign language, as permitted under clause 3.(*c*) of the regulations for Materials Science Part I. A candidate who wishes to offer a Supplementary Subject must have the proposal approved by the Chair of the Faculty of Materials or deputy. Where an approved course of instruction in a foreign language is available (including a Supplementary Subject in a foreign language), entry of candidates for such examinations shall require the approval of the Chair of the Faculty of Materials and the Director of the Language Centre or their deputies. Approval shall not be given to candidates who have, at the start of the course, already acquired demonstrable skills exceeding the target learning outcomes in the chosen language.

(*b*) Candidates for Supplementary Subjects or a Foreign Language course may offer themselves for examination in the academic year preceding that in which they take either Part I of the Second Public Examination for the degree of Master of Engineering in Materials Science or the Second Public Examination for the degree of Bachelor of Arts in Materials Science.

(c) The Supplementary Subjects available in any year will be published, together with the term in which each subject will be examined, in the Course Handbook in the academic year in which the courses are delivered. Regulations governing the use of calculators in individual Supplementary Subjects will be notified when the availability of these subjects is published in the Course Handbook.

PART I OF THE EXAMINATION FOR THE DEGREE OF MASTER OF ENGINEERING IN MATERIALS SCIENCE

The examination will consist of:

1. Four general papers of three hours each on the fundamental principles and engineering applications of the subject in accordance with the schedule below. The questions set in these papers normally will be such that candidates may reasonably be expected to answer a high proportion of them.

2. Two Materials Options papers, each of three hours, containing a wide choice of questions in accordance with the schedule below.

3. In addition to the written papers, the Examiners shall require evidence of satisfactory completion, over a period of five terms subsequent to the sitting of the First Public Examination, of each *element* of coursework in Materials, as detailed below. In the assessment of the Materials coursework, the Examiners shall take into consideration the requirement for a candidate to complete satisfactorily the coursework to a level prescribed from time to time by the Faculty of Materials and published in the Course Handbook. Normally, failure to complete satisfactorily all five elements of Materials Coursework will constitute failure of Part I of the Second Public Examination. The coursework *elements* shall be:

(a) *Materials Practical Classes*

Candidates shall be required to submit a set of detailed reports of the practical work completed over a period of three terms subsequent to the sitting of the First Public Examination. Such reports should be delivered to the Chair of the Examiners in the Honour School of Materials Science, c/o the Deputy Administrator (Academic) in the Department of Materials (or their deputy as nominated in the Course Handbook), not later than noon on Tuesday of the second week of Michaelmas Full Term in the year of Part I of the Second Public Examination. The Examiners shall have the power to require a practical examination of any candidate or to require further evidence, of any kind that they deem appropriate, of a candidate's practical work and ability.

(b) *Reports on Industrial Visits*

Candidates shall be required to submit to the Department (to the person specified in the Course Handbook) reports on a number of industrial visits normally undertaken over a period of five terms subsequent to the sitting of the First Public Examination. The required number of visits, types of visits allowed, the nature of the reports, and deadlines for submission shall be specified in the Course Handbook.

(c) *Engineering and Society Coursework*

Candidates shall be required to submit one piece of Engineering and Society Coursework, the details of which shall be stated in the Course Handbook. Three copies of the coursework shall be submitted to the Chair of Examiners in the Honour School of Materials Science, c/o Examination Schools, High Street, Oxford, not later than noon on the Monday following the end of Hilary Full Term in the year preceding the Part I examination. The work must be the candidate's own and the candidate shall sign and present with the work a detachable certificate to this effect. As an alternative to offering Engineering and Society coursework, candidates may either offer themselves for examination in a Supplementary Subject or complete an approved, assessed course of instruction in a foreign language.   5

(*d*) *Team Design Project*

Candidates shall be required to complete a team design project in the first two weeks of Michaelmas Full Term in the year of the Second Public Examination, and subsequently (i) to submit to the Chair of the Examiners in the Honour School of Materials Science, c/o the Deputy Administrator (Academic) in the Department of Materials (or   10 their deputy as nominated in the Course Handbook), three copies of a report on the project and (ii) to deliver to the Examiners an oral presentation on the project, both as detailed in the Course Handbook. The work must be the candidate's own and the candidate shall sign and present with the written report a detachable certificate to that effect.   15

(*e*) *Characterisation of Materials Coursework or Introduction to Modelling in Materials Coursework*

Candidates shall be required to complete **either** a Characterisation of Materials course **or** an Introduction to Modelling in Materials course in the first two weeks of Hilary Full Term in the year of the Second Public Examination, and subsequently to   20 submit to the Chair of the Examiners in the Honour School of Materials Science, c/o the Deputy Administrator (Academic) in the Department of Materials (or their deputy as nominated in the Course Handbook), three copies of a portfolio of work from the course, as detailed in the Course Handbook. The work must be the candidate's own and the candidate shall sign and present with the written report a detachable certificate   25 to that effect.

Elements of coursework previously submitted for the Honour School of Materials Science may be resubmitted. No essay or report will be accepted if it has already been submitted wholly or substantially for another honour school or degree of this University, or for a degree at any other institution. Resubmitted work must be   30 physically presented at the time and in the manner prescribed for submission.

EXAMINATION FOR THE DEGREE OF BACHELOR OF ARTS IN MATERIALS SCIENCE

For a candidate under clause (4) of Part A of the special regulations for the Honour School of Materials Science the examination will consist of: 35

All elements described in clauses one, two, and three under Part I of the Examination for the degree of Master of Engineering in Materials Science, excepting that:

1. The two Materials Options papers of clause two will be each of 1.5 hours duration.   40

2. An additional element of coursework is included under clause three:

(*f*) *An Extended Essay on an approved topic in Materials Science*

Candidates shall be required to complete an extended essay, as detailed in the Course Handbook, in the year of the Second Public Examination, under the guidance of an advisor appointed by the Chair of Faculty or his/her deputy. Every candidate is   45 required to submit three copies of their essay. The Examiners shall obtain a report on the work of each candidate from the advisor concerned. The essay shall also include an abstract and should be accompanied by a signed statement by the candidate that it is his or her own work. The copies should be handed in to the Chair of the Examiners in the Honour School of Materials Science, c/o Examination Schools, High Street, Oxford, not later than noon on the third Monday following the end of Hilary Full Term. The essay shall be word-processed or typewritten on A4 paper (within a page area of 247 mm × 160 mm, using double line-spaced type of at least 11pt font size, printed on one side only of each sheet, with a left hand margin of at least 30mm) and presented in a binder. The essay should not exceed 4,000 words. This word count excludes references, title page, acknowledgements and table of contents. All other text is included in the word count, including the abstract, tables and the figure captions.

Elements of coursework submitted for the Honour School of Materials Science may be resubmitted. No essay or report will be accepted if it has already been submitted wholly or substantially for another honour school or degree of this University, or for a degree at any other institution. Resubmitted work must be physically presented at the time and in the manner prescribed for submission.

For a candidate under clause (5) of Part A of the special regulations for the Honour School of Materials Science the examination will consist of:

All elements described in clauses one, two, and three under Part I of the Examination for the degree of Master of Engineering in Materials Science, excepting that:

1. An additional element of coursework is included under clause three:

(f) An Extended Essay on an approved topic in Materials Science

As for a candidate under clause (4) of Part A of the special regulations for the Honour School of Materials Science excepting that, as specified in the Course Handbook, (i) candidates shall be required to complete the extended essay during the Long Vacation immediately following the year of the Second Public Examination and (ii) submission to the Chair of the Examiners in the Honour School of Materials Science, c/o Examination Schools, High Street, Oxford, shall be no later than noon on a day to be specified by the Chair of Faculty or his/her deputy and in any case shall be no later than the last Friday of the Long Vacation immediately following the year of the Second Public Examination.

Schedule

(*a*) *General papers*

All candidates will be expected to have such knowledge of mathematics as is required for the study of the subjects of the examination.

General Paper 1: Structure and Transformations
General Paper 2: Electronic Properties of Materials
General Paper 3: Mechanical Properties
General Paper 4: Engineering Applications of Materials

(*b*) *Materials Options Papers 1 and 2*

The subjects for these papers will be published annually in the Course Handbook.

PART II OF THE EXAMINATION FOR THE DEGREE OF MASTER OF ENGINEERING IN MATERIALS SCIENCE

Candidates offering Part II of the examination will be expected to carry out investigations in Materials Science or in related subjects under the supervision of one of the following:

(i) any professor who is a member of one of the Faculties in the Physical Sciences;

(ii) a reader or university lecturer or senior research officer who is a member of one of the Faculties of Physical Sciences;

(iii) a tutor or lecturer in any society who is a member of one of the Faculties of Physical Sciences;

(iv) any other person listed in a Register of Part II Supervisors to be maintained by the Faculty of Materials.

Each candidate shall be examined viva voce, and, if the Examiners think fit, in writing, on the subject of his or her work and on matters relevant thereto. The Examiners shall obtain a report on the work of each candidate from the supervisor concerned.

A candidate intending to offer Part II shall give notice to the Registrar not later than Friday in the fourth week of Michaelmas Full Term in the calendar year in which he or she satisfied the Examiners in Part I. Such notice must be given on a form to be obtained from the Registrar, University Offices.

Every candidate for Part II is required to submit three copies of a report on the investigations which he or she has carried out under the direction of his or her supervisor. The report on the investigations shall also include an abstract, a literature survey, a brief account of the project management aspects of the investigation, and a description of the engineering context of the investigation and should be accompanied by a signed statement by the candidate that it is his or her own work. The copies should be handed in to the Chair of the Examiners in the Honour School of Materials Science, c/o Examination Schools, High Street, Oxford, not later than noon on the Wednesday of the seventh week of Trinity Full Term. The report shall be word-processed or typewritten on A4 paper (within a page area of 247 mm × 160 mm, using double line-spaced type of at least 11pt font size, printed on one side only of each sheet, with a left hand margin of at least 30mm) and presented in a binder. The main report should not normally exceed **12,000 words** together with a maximum of a further **1,500** words for the reflective account of the project management aspects of the investigation that must be included in the final chapter. These word counts exclude references, title page, acknowledgements, table of contents and the three Project Management Forms. All other text is included in the word count, including the abstract, tables and the figure captions. Additionally, the main report should not normally exceed **100 pages** in length (including an abstract, the text as defined above for the word limits, the three Project Management Forms, computer programs, graphs, diagrams, photographs, tables, and similar material). All pages of the report should be numbered sequentially. The report must be accompanied by a signed declaration that it is within the allowed word and page limits. Candidates seeking permission to exceed the word and/or page limits should apply to the Chair of Examiners at an early stage. Further detailed data, computer programs and similar material may be included in one or more appendices at the end of the main report, but appendices are not included within the limits of the word or page counts of the thesis and, entirely at the discretion of the Examiners for each report, may or may not be read.

Candidates for Part II will be required to keep statutory residence and pursue their investigations at Oxford during a period thirty-seven weeks between the dates specified below, except that the Divisional Board of Mathematical, Physical and Life Sciences shall have power to permit candidates to vary the period of their residence so long as the overall programme requirement is met. The Divisional Board may, on the recommendation of the Department of Materials, permit candidates to carry out their investigations for the required period at an approved institution outside Oxford; the Board shall determine the conditions upon which applications for such permission may be approved and will require to be satisfied in each case (a) that adequate arrangements are made for the candidate's supervision and (b) that the proposals for the investigations are agreed in advance between the Department of Materials and the host institution.

Periods of required residence for Part II

From the fifth Friday before to the first Saturday following Michaelmas Full Term.

From the second Friday before Hilary Full Term to the Saturday before Palm Sunday.

From the Friday following Easter to the second Saturday following Trinity Full Term.

HONOUR SCHOOL OF MATERIALS, ECONOMICS, AND MANAGEMENT

[For students starting before MT 2015:

A

1. The subjects of the Honour School shall be (*a*) Materials, (*b*) Economics, and (*c*)   5
Management.

2. All candidates must offer (*a*), (*b*), and (*c*). The examination in all three subjects
may be partly practical.

3. No candidate shall be admitted to examination in this school unless he or she has
either passed or been exempted from the First Public Examination.   10

4. The examination in this school shall be under the joint supervision of the
Mathematical, Physical and Life Sciences Board and the Social Sciences Board.
The standing joint committee set up in accordance with the sub-section relating to
the Honour School of Engineering, Economics, and Management shall have power
to make regulations concerning this school, subject always to the preceding clauses of   15
this sub-section.

5. The examination shall consist of Part I and Part II. In both parts candidates shall
be examined in the subjects prescribed by the committee set up in accordance with the
provisions of clause 4 above. In Part II candidates shall also present, as part of the
examination, a report on either a project carried out during a period of attachment to   20
an industrial firm, or an industrially-related internal university project.

6. The name of a candidate in this school shall not be published in a class list unless
he or she has been adjudged worthy of Honours by the Examiners in Part I and in Part
II of the respective examinations in consecutive years, and no candidate may present
himself or herself for examination in Part II unless he or she has been adjudged worthy   25
of Honours by the Examiners in Part I.

7. The Examiners shall be entitled to award a pass to candidates in Part I who have
reached a standard considered adequate but who have not been adjudged worthy of
Honours. To achieve Honours at Part I normally a candidate must fulfil all of the
requirements under (a), (b) & (c) of this clause. (a) Obtain a minimum mark of 40%   30
averaged over all elements of assessment for the Part I Examination, (b) obtain a
minimum mark of 40% in each of at least four of the six written papers sat in Trinity
Term of the year of Part I of the Second Public Examination, and (c) satisfy the
coursework requirements set out in Section B, Part I below.

8. A candidate who obtains only a pass, or fails to satisfy the Examiners, may enter   35
again for Part I of the examination on one, but no more than one, subsequent
occasion. Part II shall be entered on one occasion only.

9. A candidate adjudged worthy of Honours in Part I and Part II may supplicate
for the Degree of Master of Engineering in Materials, Economics, and Management
provided that the candidate has fulfilled all the conditions for admission to a degree of   40
the University.

10. A candidate who passes Part I or who is adjudged worthy of Honours in Part I,
but who does not enter Part II, or fails to obtain Honours in Part II, is permitted to
supplicate for the degree of Bachelor of Arts in Materials, Economics, and
Management (pass or unclassified Honours, as appropriate); provided that no such   45
candidate may later enter or re-enter the Part II year or supplicate for the degree of
Master of Engineering in Materials, Economics, and Management; and provided in

each case that the candidate has fulfilled all the conditions for admission to a degree of the University.

11. The examiners for Materials shall be appointed by the committee for the nomination of Public Examiners in Materials Science in the Honour School of Materials; those for Economics shall be appointed by the committee for the nomination of examiners in Economics in the Honour School of Philosophy, Politics, and Economics; those for Management shall be appointed by the committee for the nomination of examiners in Management Studies for the Degree of Master of Philosophy.

B

1. In the following, 'the Course Handbook' refers to the Materials Science and Materials, Economics & Management Final Honours School Course Handbook, published annually at the start of Michaelmas Term by the Faculty of Materials and also posted on the website.

2. For all written papers, candidates are restricted to models of hand-held calculators as specified for the Honour School of Materials and published in the Course Handbook.

3. Periods of required residence in addition to full term

(*a*) For the purpose of sitting the written examination paper Ec1—Introductory Economics. In the academic year preceding Part I of the Second Public Examination, from the first Monday following Trinity Full Term to the first Saturday following Trinity Full Term.

(*b*) For the purpose of sitting the written examination paper General Management. In the academic year of Part I of the Second Public Examination, from the first Monday following Trinity Full Term to the first Saturday following Trinity Full Term.

(*c*) Candidates undertaking management projects will be required to keep statutory residence for workshops, as specified by the Course Director, in the year in which the Part I examination is taken in order to prepare for the projects to be carried out as part of the Part II examination.

PART I

Candidates will be required to take seven papers as follows:

(*a*) *Materials*

The four general papers of three hours each on the fundamental principles and engineering applications of the subject as specified for Part I of the Honour School of Materials Science.

(*b*) *Economics*

Two papers: Ec1—Introductory Economics (as specified in the regulation relating to the Introductory Economics paper of the Economics and Management Preliminary Examination). Microeconomics (as specified for the Honour School of Philosophy, Politics, and Economics).

(*c*) *Management*

One paper: M1—General Management (as specified in the regulation relating to the General Management paper of the Economics and Management Preliminary Examination).

Candidates will take paper Ec1 in the third term after passing the First Public Examination and the remaining papers in the sixth term after passing the First Public Examination.

In addition to the written papers, the Examiners shall require evidence of satisfactory completion, over a period of five terms subsequent to the sitting of the First Public Examination, of each *element* of coursework in Materials, as detailed below. In the assessment of the Materials coursework, the Examiners shall take into consideration the requirement for a candidate to complete satisfactorily the coursework to   5
a level prescribed from time to time by the Faculty of Materials and published in the Course Handbook. Normally, failure to complete satisfactorily all three elements of Materials coursework will constitute failure of Part I of the Second Public Examination.

The coursework *elements* shall be: 10

(*a*) *Materials Practical Classes*

Candidates shall be required to submit a set of detailed reports of the practical work completed over a period of five terms subsequent to the sitting of the First Public Examination. Such reports should be handed in to the Chair of the Examiners in the Honour School of Materials Science, c/o the Deputy Administrator (Academic) in the   15
Department of Materials (or their deputy as nominated in the Course Handbook), not later than noon on Tuesday of the second week of Trinity Full Term in the year of Part I of the Second Public Examination. The Examiners shall have the power to require a practical examination of any candidate or to require further evidence, of any kind that they deem appropriate, of a candidate's practical work and ability.   20

(*b*) *Reports on Industrial Visits*

Candidates shall be required to submit to the Department (to the person specified in the Course Handbook) reports on a number of industrial visits undertaken over a period of five terms subsequent to the sitting of the First Public Examination. The required number of visits, types of visits allowed, the nature of the reports, and   25
deadlines for submission shall be specified in the Course Handbook.

(*c*) *Team Design Project*

Candidates shall be required to complete a team design project in the first two weeks of Michaelmas Full Term in the year of the Second Public Examination, and subsequently (i) to submit to the Chair of the Examiners in the Honour School of Materials   30
Science, c/o the Deputy Administrator (Academic) in the Department of Materials (or their deputy as nominated in the Course Handbook), three copies of a report on the project and (ii) to deliver to the Examiners an oral presentation on the project, both as detailed in the Course Handbook. The work must be the candidate's own and the candidate shall sign and present with the written report a detachable certificate to that   35
effect.

Elements of coursework previously submitted for the Honour School of Materials, Economics, and Management may be resubmitted. No report will be accepted if it has already been submitted wholly or substantially for another honour school or degree of this University, or for a degree at any other institution. Resubmitted work must be   40
physically presented at the time and in the manner prescribed for submission.

Schedule

Part II

Candidates will be required to present a report on either a project carried out during a twenty-four week period of attachment to an industrial firm, or an industrially-   45
related internal university project, and to take two papers. Normally the project will be a Management Project. One paper must be from (*a*), and the other may be from (*b*) or (*c*). The papers are described as:

(*a*) *Materials*

Materials Options Paper 2, as specified for Part I of the Honour School of Materials   50
Science. The subjects for this paper will be published annually in the Course Handbook.

(*b*) *Economics*
(*c*) *Management*
Optional papers:
    The list from which papers in (b) may be selected shall be published annually by the
Faculty of Economics no later than the end of Trinity Full Term of the academic year   5
preceding the Part II examination. The list from which papers in (c) may be selected
shall be published annually by the Faculty of Management Studies no later than the
end of Trinity Full Term of the academic year preceding the Part II examination.
    Candidates will be required to undertake either a twenty-four week period attached
to an industrial firm, or a twenty-four week internal university project. The former will   10
be undertaken between the end of the Trinity Full Term in the academic year in which
the Part I examination is held and the beginning of Hilary Full Term in the year in
which the Part II examination is held. The latter will run from the beginning of
Michaelmas Term to the beginning of Trinity Term in the academic year in which
the Part II examination is held. Candidates will be required to present, as part of the   15
Part II examination, a report on a project carried out during this period under the
supervision of a person approved by the standing committee for the school.
    The industrial attachment and associated Management Project or the industrially-
related internal University project required for the course normally will be arranged
by, and must be approved by, the Management Project Co-ordinator.   20
    The report shall not exceed 20,000 words.
    Two copies of External project reports must be submitted by noon on the Friday of
the week before the start of Hilary Full Term in the year following the year in which
the Part I examination is held. Two copies of Internal project reports must be
submitted by noon on Friday of the fourth week of Trinity Term of that year.   25
Reports must be addressed 'Examination Schools, High Street, Oxford, OX1 4BG,
for the Chair of the Examiners in the Honour School of Materials, Economics, and
Management', and should be accompanied by a signed statement by the candidate
that it is his or her own work. Successful candidates will be required to deposit one
copy of the report in the library of the Department of Materials and the other in the   30
library of the Business School. Project reports previously submitted for the Honour
School of Materials, Economics, and Management may be resubmitted. No project
report will be accepted if it has already been submitted, wholly or substantially, for
another Honour School or degree of this University, or for a degree of any other
institution.]   35

HONOUR SCHOOL OF MATHEMATICS

A

In the following 'the Course Handbook' refers to the Mathematics Undergraduate Handbook and supplements to this published by the Mathematics Teaching Committee.

1. The subject of the Honour School of Mathematics shall be Mathematics, its applications and related subjects.

2. No candidate shall be admitted to examination in this School unless he or she has either passed or been exempted from the First Public Examination.

3. The Examination in Mathematics shall be under the supervision of the Mathematical, Physical and Life Sciences Board. The Board shall have the power, subject to this decree, from time to time to frame and vary regulations for the different parts and subjects of the examination.

4. (*a*) The examination in Mathematics shall consist of three parts (A, B, C) for the four-year course, and of two parts (A, B) for the three-year course.

   (*b*) Parts A, B, and C shall be taken at times not less than three, six, and nine terms, respectively, after passing or being exempted from the First Public Examination.

5. The Examiners shall classify and publish the combined results of the examinations in Part A and Part B, and in respect of candidates taking the four-year course shall separately classify and publish results in Part C.

6. (*a*) Part A shall be taken on one occasion only. No candidate shall enter for Part B until he or she has completed Part A of the examination.

   (*b*) In order to proceed to Part C, a candidate must achieve upper second class Honours or higher in Parts A and B together.

   (*c*) A candidate who obtains only a pass or fails to satisfy the Examiners in Parts A and B together may retake Part B on at most one subsequent occasion; a candidate who fails to satisfy the Examiners in Part C may retake Part C on at most one subsequent occasion. Part B shall be taken on one occasion only by candidates continuing to Part C.

7. A candidate on the three-year course adjudged worthy of Honours on both Parts A and B together may supplicate for the degree of BA in Mathematics provided that the candidate has fulfilled all conditions for admission to a degree of the University.

8. A candidate on the four-year course adjudged worthy of Honours on both Parts A and B together, and on Part C may supplicate for the degree of Master of Mathematics provided that the candidate has fulfilled all the conditions for admission to a degree of the University.

9. A candidate in the final year of the four-year course, adjudged worthy of Honours in both Parts A and B together, but who does not enter Part C, or who fails to obtain Honours in Part C, is permitted to supplicate for the Honours degree of Bachelor of Arts in Mathematics with the classification obtained in Parts A and B together; provided that no such candidate may later enter or re-enter the Part C year or supplicate for the degree of Master of Mathematics; and provided in each case that the candidate has fulfilled all the conditions for admission to a degree of the University.

10. The use of calculators is generally not permitted for written papers. However, their use may be permitted for certain exceptional examinations. The specification of calculators permitted for these exceptional examinations will be announced by the Examiners in the Hilary Term preceding the examination.

Transfer to the Honour School of Mathematical and Theoretical Physics

11. Subject to the regulations for the Honour School in Mathematical and Theoretical Physics, candidates on the four-year course in Mathematics may apply to the Supervisory Committee for Mathematics and Physics to transfer, after their Part B examination, to the Honour School of Mathematical and Theoretical Physics for their Part C examination. Such a candidate will need to achieve at least an upper second class or higher at the end of Part B, and be accepted by the Supervisory Committee for Mathematics and Physics under the procedures referred to in the regulations for the Master of Mathematical and Theoretical Physics and set out in the course handbook for that degree. Acceptance is not automatic. As specified in the regulations for that degree, Part C in Mathematical and Theoretical Physics must be taken in the academic year following the candidate's Part B examination, and on successful completion of Part C of the Honour School of Mathematical and Theoretical Physics candidates will be awarded the Master of Mathematics and Physics in Mathematical and Theoretical Physics.

12. The Handbook for Mathematical and Theoretical Physics shall set out the options that candidates should follow to maximize their chances of being accepted for transfer to Mathematical and Theoretical Physics for their Part C examination. This Handbook shall be available by the start of Michaelmas Term in the year in which a candidate starts Part A in Mathematics.

13. A candidate who has transferred from the Honour School of Mathematics to the Honour School of Mathematical and Theoretical Physics for their Part C examination in accordance with cl.9 above is permitted transfer to the Honour School of Mathematics for their Part C examination up to the end of Week 4 of the Michaelmas Term in which he or she first registered for Part C in the Honour School of Mathematical and Theoretical Physics, so long as that candidate has not opted to supplicate for the degree of Bachelor of Arts in Mathematics under the regulations for the Honour School of Mathematical and Theoretical Physics.

14. The regulations for the Honour School of Mathematical and Theoretical Physics set out how the results obtained in Parts A and B in the Honour School of Mathematics are published for candidates who transfer to the Honour School of Mathematical and Theoretical Physics for their Part C examination.

PART A

In Part A each candidate shall be required to offer A1, A2, ASO, and five or six papers from A3–A11 from the schedule of papers for Part A.

Schedule of Papers in Part A

A0 Linear Algebra
A1 Differential Equations 1
A2 Metric Spaces and Complex Analysis
A3 Rings and Modules
A4 Integration
A5 Topology
A6 Differential Equations 2
A7 Numerical Analysis
A8 Probability
A9 Statistics

A10 Fluids and Waves
A11 Quantum Theory
ASO Short Options

Syllabus details will be published in the Course Handbook by the beginning of the Michaelmas Full Term in the academic year of the examination for Part A.   5

PART B

In Part B each candidate shall offer a total of eight units from the schedule of units for Part B (see below).

(*a*) A total of at least four units offered should be from the schedule of Mathematics Department units.   10

(*b*) A candidate may offer up to four units from:
   (i) the schedule of Statistics options
   (ii) the schedule of Computer Science options
   (iii) the schedule of Other options
but may offer no more than two units from each of the above schedules.   15

(*c*) Candidates may offer a double unit which is an Extended Essay or a Structured Project.

Schedule of Units for Part B

The final list of units will be published in the Course Handbook by the beginning of the Michaelmas Full Term in the academic year of the examination concerned,   20
together with the following details.

1. Designation as either 'H' level or 'M' level.

2. 'Weight' as either a unit or double unit.

3. Method of assessment. Details of methods of assessment for Other Mathematics or Other Non-Mathematical units will be given elsewhere. Some options may require   25
assessment by oral presentation. The Course handbook will indicate where such details will be specified.

4. Rules governing submission of any extended essay, dissertation or mini-project, including deadlines, provided that these shall always be submitted to the Chair of Examiners, Honour School of Mathematics, c/o Examination Schools, High Street,   30
Oxford. In addition an electronic copy must be submitted to the Mathematical Institute's website, details will be included in the relevant Notice to Candidates. No part of any extended essay, dissertation or mini-project submitted may include work previously submitted for this or any other degree.

5. Syllabus content.   35

6. Whether there is a requirement to register or apply for a place to take a unit, and details of any registration or application procedure.

PART C

In Part C each candidate shall offer a total of eight units from the schedule of units for Part C (see below).   40

(*a*) All eight units offered should be from those designated as M level.

(*b*) A total of at least four of the units offered should be from the schedule of Mathematics Department units.

(c) A candidate may offer up to four units from:

(i) the schedule of Statistics options

(ii) the schedule of Computer Science options

(iii) the schedule of Other options

but may offer no more than two units from each of the above schedules.

(*d*) Candidates may offer a double unit which is a Dissertation. If the Dissertation is   5
a mathematical topic this would be offered under the schedule of Mathematics
Department units. If the Dissertation is on a mathematics-related topic, this would
be offered under the schedule of 'other options'.

No candidate shall offer any unit for Part C that he or she has also offered in Part B.

Schedule of Units for Part C   10

The final list of units will be published in the Course Handbook by the beginning of
the Michaelmas Full Term in the academic year of the examination concerned,
together with the following details.

1. Designation as either 'H' level or 'M' level.

2. 'Weight' as either a unit or double unit.   15

3. Method of assessment. Details of methods of assessment for Other Mathematics
or Other Non-Mathematical units will be given elsewhere. Some options may require
assessment by oral presentation. The Course handbook will indicate where such
details will be specified.

4. Rules governing submission of any extended essay, dissertation or mini-project, in-   20
cluding deadlines, provided that these shall always be submitted to the Chair of Examiners,
Honour School of Mathematics, c/o Examination Schools, High Street, Oxford. In addition
an electronic copy must be submitted to the Mathematical Institute's website, details will be
included in the relevant Notice to Candidates. No part of any extended essay, dissertation or
mini-project submitted may include work previously submitted for this or any other degree.   25

5. Syllabus content.

6. Whether there is a requirement to register or apply for a place to take a unit, and
details of any registration or application procedure.

HONOUR SCHOOL OF MATHEMATICS AND COMPUTER SCIENCE

A

In the following, 'the Course Handbook' refers to the Mathematics and Computer Science Undergraduate Course Handbook and supplements to this published by the Teaching Committee and also posted on the website at: http://www.cs.ox.ac.uk/currentstudents/.

1. The subject of the Honour School of Mathematics and Computer Science shall be Mathematics and the theory and practice of Computer Science.

2. No candidate shall be admitted to examination in this School unless he or she has either passed or been exempted from the First Public Examination.

3. The Examination in Mathematics and Computer Science shall be under the supervision of the Mathematical, Physical and Life Sciences Board. The Board shall have the power from time to time to frame and vary regulations for the different parts and subjects of the examination.

4. (*a*) The examination in Mathematics and Computer Science shall consist of three parts (A, B, C) for the four-year course, and of two parts (A, B) for the three-year course.

   (*b*) Parts A, B, and C shall be taken at times not less than three, six, and nine terms, respectively, after passing or being exempted from the First Public Examination.

5. The Examiners shall classify and publish the combined results of the examinations in Part A and Part B, and in respect of candidates taking the four-year course shall separately classify and publish results in Part C.

6. (*a*) Part A shall be taken on one occasion only. No candidate shall enter for Part B until he or she has completed Part A of the examination.

   (*b*) In order to proceed to Part C, a candidate must achieve upper second class Honours or higher in Parts A and B together.

   (*c*) A candidate who obtains only a pass or fails to satisfy the Examiners in Part B may retake Part B on at most one subsequent occasion; a candidate who fails to satisfy the Examiners in Part C may retake Part C on at most one subsequent occasion. Part B shall be taken on one occasion only by candidates continuing to Part C.

7. A candidate adjudged worthy of Honours on both Parts A and B together, and on Part C may supplicate for the degree of Master of Mathematics and Computer Science provided that the candidate has fulfilled all the conditions for admission to a degree of the University.

8. A candidate in the final year of the four-year course, adjudged worthy of Honours in both Parts A and B together, but who does not enter Part C, or who fails to obtain Honours in Part C, is permitted to supplicate for the Honours degree of Bachelor of Arts in Mathematics and Computer Science with the classification obtained in Parts A and B together; provided that no such candidate may later enter or re-enter the Part C year or supplicate for the degree of Master of Mathematics and Computer Science; and provided in each case that the candidate has fulfilled all the conditions for admission to a degree of the University.

9. All candidates will be assessed as to their practical ability under the following provisions:

(*a*) The Head of the Department of Computer Science, or a deputy, shall make available to the examiners evidence showing the extent to which each candidate has pursued an adequate course of practical work. Only that work completed and marked by noon on Monday of the sixth week of the Trinity Term in which the candidate takes the examination shall be included in these records.

(*b*) Candidates for each part of the examination shall submit to the Chair of the Examiners, Honour School of Mathematics and Computer Science, c/o the Academic Administrator, Oxford University Department of Computer Science, Oxford, by noon on Monday of the sixth week of the Trinity Term in which the examination is being held, their reports of practical exercises completed during their course of study. For a report on a practical exercise to be considered by the examiners, it must have been marked by a demonstrator and must be accompanied by a statement that it is the candidate's own work except where otherwise indicated.

(*c*) The examiners shall take the evidence (a) and the report (b) into account in assessing a candidate's performance.

(*d*) Candidates whose overall performance on practical work is not satisfactory may be deemed to have failed the examination or may have their overall classification reduced.

B

The syllabus for each of Parts A, B, and C will be published by the Department of Computer Science in a handbook for candidates by the beginning of Michaelmas Full Term in the academic year of the examination concerned. The duration of each optional paper will be specified in the Course Handbook.

The use of calculators is generally not permitted but certain kinds may be allowed for certain papers. Specifications of which papers and which types of calculators are permitted for those exceptional papers will be announced by the examiners in the Hilary Term preceding the examination.

The schedules of optional subjects for Parts A, B, and C of the examination shall be approved by the Faculty of Mathematics and the Faculty of Computer Science, and shall be published in the Course Handbook.

The examiners shall have power to combine two papers on related optional subjects into a single paper for those candidates who offer both the optional subjects concerned.

PART A

In Part A of the examination, candidates shall be required to offer, from the Mathematics Schedule, papers A1(CP), A2, and either two papers from papers A3–A5, A7–A11 or one paper from A3–A5, A7–A11 and paper ASO:

A1 (CP) Algebra 1
A2 Metric Spaces and Complex Analysis
A3 Algebra 2
A4 Integration
A5 Topology
A7 Numerical Analysis
A8 Probability
A9 Statistics

A10 Waves and Fluids
A11 Quantum Theory
ASO Short Options

Candidates shall also be required to offer four subjects from Schedule A (MC) in the Course Handbook. The manner of examining the subjects in Schedule A (MC) shall   5
be the same as that prescribed for the same subject in the Honour School of Computer Science.

PART B

In Part B of the examination, each candidate shall be required to offer eight optional subjects from Schedules B1-B5 in the Course Handbook, subject to the   10
conditions that:

(*a*) no candidate shall offer any subject from Schedule B1 that he or she has already offered in Part A of the examination.

(*b*) each candidate shall offer no more than two subjects from Schedule B1.

(*c*) each candidate shall offer no more than two subjects from Schedules B4 and B5.   15

(*d*) each candidate shall offer at least two subjects from Schedules B1 and B2.

(*e*) each candidate shall offer at least two subjects from Schedule B3.

Each optional subject in Schedules B1, B2, and B4 shall be examined by a written paper or by a mini-project. The manner of examining each subject in Schedules B3 and B5 shall be the same as that prescribed for the same subject in the Honour School of   20
Mathematics. Each 'unit' in schedules B3 and B5 shall be regarded as equivalent to one subject in the examination, and each 'double unit' shall be regarded as equivalent to two subjects.

PART C

In Part C of the examination, each candidate shall be required to either offer six   25
optional subjects from Schedules C1 and C2 in the Course Handbook and submit a Mathematics dissertation, or offer five optional subjects from Schedules C1 and C2 in the Course Handbook and submit a report on a Computer Science project, subject to the condition that no candidate shall offer any subject that he or she has already offered in Part B of the examination. Each optional subject in Schedule C1 shall be   30
examined by a written paper or by a mini-project. The manner of examining each subject in Schedule C2 shall be the same as that prescribed for the same subject in the Honour School of Mathematics. Each 'unit' in schedule C2 shall be regarded as equivalent to one subject in the examination, and each 'double unit' shall be regarded as equivalent to two subjects.   35

Each candidate shall carry out a Computer Science project or a Mathematics dissertation on a topic approved by the Teaching Committee. Each project or dissertation will be supervised by a member of the Faculty of Computer Science, the Faculty of Mathematics or the Faculty of Engineering Science, or by some other person of equivalent seniority approved by the Teaching Committee. Two copies of a   40
report of the project or dissertation shall be submitted to the Chair of the Examiners, Honour School of Mathematics and Computer Science, c/o Examination Schools, High Street, Oxford, by the date given in the Course Handbook. Rules concerning the form of the report will be published in the Course Handbook. In addition for the Mathematics dissertations an electronic copy must be submitted to the Mathematical   45
Institute's website, details will be included in the relevant Notice to Candidates.

In retaking Part C of the examination, projects or dissertations previously submitted for the examination may be resubmitted. No project or dissertation may be resubmitted if it has already been submitted, wholly or substantially, for another honour school or degree of the University, or of any other institution.   50

HONOUR SCHOOL OF MATHEMATICS AND PHILOSOPHY

A

In the following 'the Mathematics Course Handbook' refers to the Mathematics Undergraduate Handbook and supplements to this published by the Teaching Committee of the Department of Mathematics.

1. All candidates shall be examined in Mathematics and in Philosophy.

2. No candidate shall be admitted to the examination in this School unless he or she has either passed or been exempted from the First Public Examination.

3. (*a*) The examination in Mathematics and Philosophy shall consist of three parts: Part A, Part B and Part C.

    (*b*) Parts A, B and C shall be taken at times not less than three, six, and nine terms, respectively, after passing or being exempted from the First Public Examination.

    (*c*) Part A shall be taken on one occasion only. No candidate shall enter for Part B until he or she has completed Part A of the examination.

4. (*a*) In order to proceed to Part C, a candidate must achieve upper second class Honours or higher in Parts A and B together.

    (*b*) A candidate who obtains only a pass or fails to satisfy the Examiners in Parts A and B together may retake Part B on at most one subsequent occasion; a candidate who fails to satisfy the Examiners in Part C may retake Part C on at most one subsequent occasion. Candidates who retake Part B are not allowed to go on to Part C.

    (*c*) A candidate who has obtained Honours in Parts A and B together or has satisfied the examiners but has not obtained Honours in Parts A and B together is permitted to supplicate for the degree of Bachelor of Arts in Mathematics and Philosophy. A candidate who has achieved upper second class Honours or higher in Parts A and B together and who takes the examination in Part C and fails to obtain Honours in Part C, is permitted to supplicate for the Honours degree of Bachelor of Arts in Mathematics and Philosophy with the classification obtained in Parts A and B together; provided that no such candidate may later enter or re-enter the Part C year or supplicate for the degree of Master of Mathematics and Philosophy; and provided in each case that the candidate has fulfilled all the conditions for admission to a degree of the University.

    (*d*) A candidate who has achieved upper second class Honours or higher in Parts A and B together, and achieves Honours in Part C may supplicate for the degree of Master of Mathematics and Philosophy provided that the candidate has fulfilled all the conditions for admission to a degree of the University.

5. The Examiners shall classify and publish the combined results of the examinations in Part A and Part B, and in respect of candidates taking the four-year course shall separately classify and publish results in Part C.

6. The examinations in this school shall be under the joint supervision of the Divisional Board of Mathematical, Physical and Life Sciences and the Board of the

Faculty of Philosophy, which shall appoint a standing joint committee to make regulations concerning it, subject in all cases to clauses 1–4 above.

7. (*a*) The Public Examiners for Mathematics in this school shall be such of the Public Examiners in the Honour School of Mathematics as may be required, not being less than three; those for Philosophy shall be appointed by a committee whose three elected members shall be appointed by the Board of the Faculty of Philosophy.

(*b*) It shall be the duty of the chairs of the Public Examiners in Parts A, B and C of the Honour School of Mathematics to designate such of their number as may be required for Mathematics in the Honour School of Mathematics and Philosophy, and when this has been done and the examiners for Philosophy have been nominated, the number of the examiners in Mathematics and Philosophy shall be deemed to be complete. No examiners for Philosophy will be required in Part A of the examination.

8. The highest honours can be obtained by excellence either in Mathematics or in Philosophy provided that adequate knowledge is shown in the other subject of the examination.

9. The use of calculators is generally not permitted for written papers. However, their use may be permitted for certain exceptional examinations. The specification of calculators permitted for these exceptional examinations will be announced by the Examiners in the Hilary Term preceding the examination.

Part A

In Part A, each candidate shall be required to offer, from the Mathematics Part A Schedule (see below), papers A0, A2, and either two papers from papers A3, A4, A5, A8 or one paper from papers A3, A4, A5, A8, and paper ASO.

A candidate may, with the support of his or her Mathematics tutor, apply to the Chair of the Joint Committee for Mathematics and Philosophy for approval of one or more other options from the list of Mathematics Department units for Part A which can be found in the Supplement to the Mathematics Course Handbook for courses in Mathematics Part A. Applications for special approval must be made through the candidate's college and sent to the Chair of the Joint Committee for Mathematics and Philosophy, c/o Academic Administrator, Mathematical Institute, to arrive by Friday of Week 2 of Hilary Term in the academic year of the examination for Part A.

Schedule of Papers in Part A
A0 Linear Algebra
A2 Metric Spaces and Complex Analysis
A3 Rings and Modules
A4 Integration
A5 Topology
A8 Probability
ASO Short Options

Syllabus details will be published in the Mathematics Course Handbook by the beginning of the Michaelmas Full Term in the academic year of the examination for Part A.

Part B

The examination for Part B shall consist of units in Mathematics and subjects in Philosophy. The schedule of units in *Mathematics* shall be published in Mathematics and Philosophy Synopses of lecture courses supplement to the Mathematics Course

Handbook by the beginning of the Michaelmas Full Term in the academic year of the examination concerned. The schedule shall be in two parts: Schedule 1 (standard units) and Schedule 2 (additional units). A candidate may, with the support of his or her Mathematics tutor, apply to the Chair of the Joint Committee for Mathematics and Philosophy for approval of one or more other options from the list of Mathematics Department units for Part B which can be found in the Supplement to the Mathematics Course Handbook for courses in Mathematics Part B. Applications for special approval must be made through the candidate's college and sent to the Chair of the Joint Committee for Mathematics and Philosophy, c/o Academic Administrator, Mathematical Institute, to arrive by Friday of Week 5 of Michaelmas Term in the academic year of the examination for Part B. In Philosophy the subjects shall be subjects 101–118, 120, 122, 124, 125, 127, and 199 from the list given in *Special Regulations for All Honour Schools Including Philosophy*. Each subject in Philosophy other than a Thesis shall be examined in one 3-hour paper. Each candidate shall offer:

(i) Four units of *Mathematics* from Schedule 1, two of which shall be B1.1 *Logic* and B.1.2 *Set Theory*.

(ii) Three subjects in *Philosophy* from 101–118, 120, 122, 124, 125, and 127, of which two must be 122 and **either** 101 **or** 102, and

(iii) **Either** two further units in *Mathematics* drawn from Schedule 1 and 2 combined **or** one further subject in *Philosophy* from subjects 101–118, 120, 124, 125, 127 and 199: *Thesis*.

Schedule of Units in Mathematics for Part B
The list of units and double units along with synopses and other details, will be approved by the Mathematics Teaching Committee and published in the Mathematics Course Handbook by the beginning of Michaelmas Full Term in the academic year of the examination concerned.

The list of units for Part C shall include units in Mathematical Logic as specified by the Joint Committee for Mathematics and Philosophy.

PART C
In Part C each candidate shall offer one of the following:
  (i) Eight units in Mathematics;
  (ii) Six units in Mathematics and one unit in Philosophy;
  (iii) Three units in Mathematics and two units in Philosophy;
  (iv) Three units in Philosophy;

from the lists for Mathematics and for Philosophy.

The schedule of units in Mathematics shall be published in the Mathematics and Philosophy Synopses of lecture courses supplement to the Mathematics Course Handbook by the beginning of the Michaelmas Full Term in the academic year of the examination concerned.

A candidate may, with the support of his or her Mathematics tutor, apply to the Chair of the Joint Committee for Mathematics and Philosophy for approval of one or more other options from the list of Mathematics Department units for Part C which can be found in the Supplement to the Mathematics Course Handbook for courses in Mathematics Part C. Applications for special approval must be made through the candidate's college and sent to the Chair of the Joint Committee for Mathematics and Philosophy, c/o Academic Administrator, Mathematical Institute, to arrive by Friday of Week 5 of Michaelmas Term in the academic year of the examination for Part C.

No unit in Mathematics, and no subject in Philosophy, may be offered in both Part B and Part C. A unit in Philosophy consists of one of the subjects 101–118, 120, 124,

125, 127, and 180 as specified in the Regulations for Philosophy in all Honour Schools including Philosophy, or a Special Subject in Philosophy as approved by the Joint Committee for Mathematics and Philosophy by regulations published in the University Gazette and communicated to college tutors by the end of the fifth week of Trinity Term in the year before the Part C examination in which it will be   5
examined, or a Thesis as specified below. No candidate may offer more than one Special Subject in Philosophy in Part C. In approving a Special Subject in Philosophy for Part C, the Joint Committee for Mathematics and Philosophy may specify that candidates will not be permitted to offer certain special subjects in combination with certain other subjects, or will be permitted to do so only on condition that in the   10
papers on the other subjects they will not be permitted to answer certain questions. Subject to these qualifications, any candidate may offer any special subject. Each unit in Philosophy other than a Thesis shall be examined by a three-hour written paper together with an essay of at most 5,000 words. The relative weight of the essay to the three-hour exam shall be 1 to 3, i.e. the essay shall count for 25% of the mark in that   15
subject. No essay shall exceed this word limit, which includes all notes and appendices, but not the bibliography. The word count should be indicated on the front of the essay. There shall be a select bibliography or a list of sources. All essays must be typed in double spacing on one side of quarto or A4 paper, with footnotes rather than endnotes. Candidates should avoid any substantial repetition of material between   20
examination scripts and examination essays.The topic for a Philosophy examination essay in a given subject can be any question set for the most recent examination of that subject in Honour Schools with Philosophy, with the exception of questions for Plato Republic (115) and Aristotle Nicomachean Ethics (116) consisting of multiple passages for comment, and the questions for Philosophical Logic (127) consisting of   25
formal exercises. Candidates may apply for approval of other essay topics by writing to the Chair of the Board, c/o the Administrator, Philosophy Centre, Radcliffe Humanities Building, Woodstock Road, giving the title he or she proposes, together with an explanation of the subject in about 100 words and enclosing a letter from their tutor attesting to the suitability of this topic for the candidate. Any such application   30
must be received no later than Friday of the sixth week of the Hilary Term preceding the Part C examination for which the essay is to be submitted. Late applications will not be considered. Any such application shall be accepted or rejected by the Board within two weeks of its being received.

Each essay shall be the candidate's own work, though it should show knowledge of   35
relevant literature in the subject and may include passages of quotation or paraphrase so long as these passages are clearly indicated as such and the source properly attributed. The candidate may discuss a first draft of the essay with his or her tutor for that subject. The amount of assistance the tutor may give shall be limited to what can be provided in one of the candidate's tutorials for their study of that subject. For   40
each essay the candidate shall sign a statement to the effect that the essay is his or her own work and the tutor shall also sign a statement confirming that, to the best of his or her knowledge and belief, this is so. These statements shall be placed in a sealed envelope bearing the candidate's examination number and the name of the subject for which the essay has been written and presented with two copies of each essay. Each   45
copy of an essay shall be identified only by the candidate's examination number and bear the name of the Philosophy subject for which the essay is being submitted and must be submitted not later than noon on Friday of the first week of the Trinity Full Term of the examination to the Examination Schools, High Street, Oxford, addressed to the Chair of the Examiners for Part C of the Final Honour School of Mathematics   50
and Philosophy.

Philosophy Thesis

1. *Subject*

The subject of every thesis should fall within the scope of philosophy. The subject may but need not overlap any subject on which the candidate offers papers. Candidates should avoid substantial repetition in examination scripts or examination essays of material from their theses. No part of a Philosophy thesis submitted for Part C may include work submitted for this or any other degree. Every candidate shall submit through his or her college for approval by the Board of the Faculty of Philosophy the title he or she proposes, together with an explanation of the subject in about 100 words; and a letter of approval from his or her tutor, not earlier than the first day of Trinity Full Term of the year before that in which he or she is to be examined and not later than Friday of the fourth week of the Michaelmas Full Term preceding his or her examination. Applications for approval of subject should be directed to the Chair of the Board, c/o The Administrator, Philosophy Centre, Radcliffe Humanities Building, Woodstock Road. The Board shall decide as soon as possible whether or not to approve the title and shall advise the candidate immediately. No decision shall be deferred beyond the end of the fifth week of Michaelmas Full Term. If a candidate wishes to change the title of his or her thesis after a title has already been approved by the Board, he or she may apply for such permission to be granted by the Board. Applications should be directed to the Chair of the Board (if the application is made before the first day of Hilary Full Term preceding the examination). If later than the first day of Hilary Full Term preceding the examination application for change of title should be made to the Chair of Examiners for Part C of the Final Honour School of Mathematics and Philosophy.

2. *Authorship and origin*

Every thesis shall be the candidate's own work. A candidate's tutor may, however, discuss with the candidate the field of study, the sources available, and the method of presentation; the tutor may also read and comment on drafts. The amount of assistance the tutor may give is equivalent to the teaching of a normal paper. Every candidate shall sign a certificate to the effect that the thesis is his or her own work and the tutor shall countersign the certificate confirming, to the best of his or her knowledge and belief, that this is so. This certificate shall be placed in a sealed envelope bearing the candidate's examination number presented together with the thesis. No thesis shall be accepted which has already been submitted for a degree of this or any other university, and the certificate shall also state that the thesis has not been so submitted. No thesis shall, however, be ineligible because it has been or is being submitted for any prize of this university.

3. *Length and format*

No thesis shall exceed 20,000 words, the limit to include all notes and appendices, but not including the bibliography; no person or body shall have authority to permit any excess. The word count should be indicated on the front of the thesis. There shall be a select bibliography or a list of sources. All theses must be typed in double spacing on one side of quarto or A4 paper, with any notes and references at the foot of each page. Two copies of the thesis shall be submitted to the examiners.

4. *Submission of thesis*

Every candidate shall submit two copies of their thesis, identified by the candidate's examination number only, not later than noon on Friday of the week before the Trinity Full Term of the examination to the Examination Schools, High Street, Oxford, addressed to the Chair of the Examiners for Part C of the Final Honour School of Mathematics and Philosophy.

Schedule of Units in Mathematics for Part C

The list of units and double units along with synopses and other details, will be approved by the Mathematics Teaching Committee and published in the Mathematics Course Handbook by the beginning of Michaelmas Full Term in the academic year of the examination concerned.   5

The list of units for Part C shall include units in Mathematical Logic as specified by the Joint Committee for Mathematics and Philosophy.

HONOUR SCHOOL OF MATHEMATICAL AND THEORETICAL PHYSICS

A

In the following 'the Course Handbook' refers to the Mathematical and Theoretical Physics Handbook and supplements to this published by the Joint Supervisory Committee for Mathematical and Theoretical Physics.

The Divisional Board of Mathematical, Physical and Life Sciences shall appoint for the supervision of the course a supervisory committee, which shall have the power to approve lectures and other instruction. The committee shall appoint a Director of Studies who will be responsible for ensuring that the programme is set up and the decisions of the committee are carried out.

1. The subject of Honour School of Mathematical and Theoretical Physics shall be Mathematical and Theoretical Physics and related subjects.

2. The Examination in the Honour School of Mathematical and Theoretical Physics shall be under the supervision of the Mathematical, Physical and Life Sciences Board. The Board shall have power from time to time to frame and vary regulations for different parts and subjects of the examination.

3. The examination in the Honour School of Mathematical and Theoretical Physics shall consist of one Part only, namely Part C, and each candidate shall follow a course of study in Mathematical and Theoretical Physics for three terms.

4. A candidate may only be admitted to the examination in this School if he or she:

   (a) was, at the time of taking their Part B examinations, registered for the four year course in one of the following Honour Schools: Mathematics, Physics, or Physics and Philosophy;

   (b) has achieved an upper second class Honours or higher in their Part B examinations referred to in (a) above;

   (c) has applied for and been accepted for entry to Part C in Mathematical and Theoretical Physics in accordance with the procedure set out in the Handbook for Mathematical and Theoretical Physics;

   (d) enters the Mathematical and Theoretical Physics Part C examinations in the academic year after taking their Part B examinations.

(a) and (b) above are necessary minimum conditions of eligibility to transfer to Part C in Mathematical and Theoretical Physics after the Part B examinations. Candidates wishing to transfer will also have to apply to transfer as stated in (c) above by the end of week 1 of Hilary Term of their third year. To be accepted they will have to satisfy the other requirements set out in the Handbook for Mathematical and Theoretical Physics from time to time. These requirements may specify the subject matter of the papers chosen for their Part A and Part B examinations (where relevant), the marks achieved in those papers, the overall mark achieved in their Part A and Part B examinations, and an assessment of their overall aptitude for Mathematical and Theoretical Physics. The Handbook for Mathematical and Theoretical Physics shall set out the subject matter of optional papers that candidates should follow in Part A or Part B to maximize their chances of being accepted for transfer to Mathematical and Theoretical Physics at Part C. For this purpose, this Handbook shall be available by the start of Michaelmas Term in the year in which a candidate starts Part A in Mathematics, Physics, or Physics and Philosophy.

5. A candidate who has transferred to Part C in Mathematical and Theoretical Physics in accordance with cl.4 above is permitted transfer to Part C of the Honour School in which he or she was registered at the time of his or her Part B examination up to the end of Week 4 of the Michaelmas Term in which he or she first registered for Part C in Mathematical and Theoretical Physics, so long as that candidate has not opted to supplicate for the degree of Bachelor of Arts under cl.8 below.

6. The result of the Mathematical and Theoretical Physics Part C examination will be published in terms of Distinction, Pass, or Fail.

7. (*a*) A candidate who obtains a Distinction or Pass in the Mathematical and Theoretical Physics Part C may supplicate for the degree of Master in Mathematical and Theoretical Physics provided that the candidate has fulfilled all the conditions for admission to a degree of the University.

   (*b*) For such a candidate, the Examiners of the Honours School in which the candidate sat Parts A and B shall classify and publish the combined results of the examinations in Part A and Part B, and the examiners for the Honour School of Mathematical and Theoretical Physics shall separately assess and publish the results in Part C.

   (*c*) Such a candidate will receive a classification for Parts A and B in the subject in which he or she sat those Parts, and a separate result for Part C in Mathematical and Theoretical Physics.

8. A candidate in the final year of a four-year course, registered for Part C in Mathematical and Theoretical Physics, but who does not enter Part C, or who fails to obtain a Distinction or Pass in Part C, is permitted to supplicate for the Honours degree in the subject in which he or she sat Parts A and B (namely the Bachelor of Arts in Mathematics, Physics, or Physics and Philosophy respectively), with the classification he or she obtained in Parts A and B together; provided that no such candidate may later enter or re-enter the Part C year or supplicate for the degree of Master of Mathematics, Master of Physics, Master of Physics and Philosophy, or Master of Mathematics and Physics; and provided in each case that the candidate has fulfilled all the conditions for admission to a degree of the University.

9. A candidate on the four-year course who fails to satisfy the Examiners in Part C may retake Part C on at most one subsequent occasion, not later than one year after the initial attempt. In such a case the examiners will specify at the time of failure which components of the examination may or must be redone.

B

1. Candidates will complete and be assessed on the following parts:
   (i) Candidates will offer 10 units with one unit corresponding to a 16 hour lecture course.
   (ii) At least four units will be assessed by written examination.
   (iii) The other units will be assessed by marked course work, takehome papers or mini-projects. The Course Handbook will specify which units will be assessed by each method mentioned above and sets out the rules governing submission of coursework. In addition, for certain courses, and electronic copy may be required. Details of the courses to which this applies, and instructions for the online submission process will be included in the Notice to Candidates that applies to the candidates of the Honour School of Mathematical and Theoretical Physics.
   (iv) Candidates may offer one unit which is a dissertation. The dissertation will follow the guidelines and procedures of the Part C Mathematics

course outlined in the Special Regulations for the Honour School of Mathematics.

(v) Candidates will be required to attend an oral examination at the end of the course of studies.

The examiners may award a distinction for excellence in the whole examination.   5

2. Syllabus and examination details will be published each year in the Course Handbook and on the course web pages by the beginning of Michaelmas Full Term in the academic year of the examination.

HONOUR SCHOOL OF MATHEMATICS AND STATISTICS

A

In the following 'the Course Handbook' refers to the Mathematics and Statistics Undergraduate Handbook and supplements to this published by the Statistics Academic Committee.

1. The subjects of the Honour School of Mathematics and Statistics shall be Mathematics and its applications, and Statistics.

2. No candidate shall be admitted to examination in this School unless he or she has either passed or been exempted from the First Public Examination.

3. The Examinations in Mathematics and Statistics shall be under the supervision of the Mathematical, Physical and Life Sciences Board. The Board shall have the power, subject to this decree, from time to time to frame and vary regulations for the different parts and subjects of the examination.

4. (*a*) The examination in Mathematics and Statistics shall consist of three parts (A, B, C) for the four-year course, and of two parts (A, B) for the three-year course.

   (*b*) Parts A, B, and C shall be taken at times not less than three, six, and nine terms, respectively, after passing or being exempted from the First Public Examination.

5. The Examiners shall classify and publish the combined results of the examinations in Part A and Part B, and in respect of candidates taking the four-year course shall separately classify and publish results in Part C.

6. (*a*) Part A shall be taken on one occasion only. No candidate shall enter for Part B until he or she has completed Part A of the examination.

   (*b*) In order to proceed to Part C, a candidate must achieve upper second class Honours or higher in Parts A and B together.

   (c) A candidate who obtains only a pass or fails to satisfy the Examiners in Parts A and B together may retake Part B on at most one subsequent occasion; a candidate who fails to satisfy the Examiners in Part C may retake Part C on at most one subsequent occasion. Part B shall be taken on one occasion only by candidates continuing to Part C.

7. A candidate on the three-year course adjudged worthy of Honours on both Parts A and B together may supplicate for the degree of BA in Mathematics and Statistics provided that the candidate has fulfilled all conditions for admission to a degree of the University.

8. A candidate on the four-year course adjudged worthy of Honours on both Parts A and B together, and on Part C may supplicate for the degree of Master of Mathematics in Mathematics and Statistics provided that the candidate has fulfilled all the conditions for admission to a degree of the University.

9. A candidate in the final year of the four-year course, adjudged worthy of Honours in both Parts A and B together, but who does not enter Part C, or who fails to obtain Honours in Part C, is permitted to supplicate for the Honours degree of Bachelor of Arts in Mathematics and Statistics with the classification obtained in Parts A and B together; provided that no such candidate may later enter or re-enter the Part C year or supplicate for the degree of Master of Mathematics in Mathematics and

Statistics; and provided in each case that the candidate has fulfilled all the conditions for admission to a degree of the University.

PART A

In Part A each candidate shall be required to offer Papers A0, A1, A2, A8, A9, ASO, and three or four papers from A3–A7 and A10–A12 from the schedule of papers for Part A.

Schedule of Papers in Part A

  A0   Differential Equations 1

  A1   Linear Algebra

  A2   Metric Spaces and Complex Analysis

  A3   Rings and Modules

  A4   Integration

  A5   Topology

  A6   Differential Equations 2

  A7   Numerical Analysis

  A8   Probability

  A9   Statistics

  A10   Fluids and Waves

  A11   Quantum Theory

  A12   Simulation and Statistical Programming

  ASO   Short Options

Syllabus details will be published in the Course Handbook by the beginning of the Michaelmas Full Term in the academic year of the examination for Part A.

PART B

In Part B each candidate shall offer a total of eight units from the schedule of units for Part B (see below).

  (*a*) Each candidate shall offer the double unit SB1.

  (*b*) Each candidate shall offer a total of at least two units from SB2 and SB3.

  (*c*) Each candidate may offer a total of at most two units from SB4 and the schedule of 'Other units':

  (*d*) Each candidate may offer at most one double unit which is an Extended Essay or Structured Project.

Schedule of Units for Part B

The final list of units will be published in the Course Handbook by the beginning of Michaelmas Full Term in the academic year of the examination concerned, together with the following details.

  1. Designation as either 'H' level or 'M' level.

  2. 'Weight' as either a unit or double-unit.

  3. Method of assessment. Details of methods of assessment for units delivered by other departments will be given elsewhere. Some options may require assessment by oral presentation. The Course handbook will indicate where such details will be specified.

  4. Rules governing submission of any extended essay, dissertation or mini-project, including deadlines, provided that these shall always be submitted to the Chair of Examiners, Honour School of Mathematics and Statistics, c/o Examination Schools,

High Street, Oxford. In addition any submission on a mathematical unit must also be submitted to the Mathematical Institute's website, details will be included in the relevant Notice to Candidates.

5. Syllabus content.

6. Whether there is a requirement to register or apply for a place to take a unit or   5
double unit, and details of any registration or application procedure.

Part C

In Part C each candidate shall offer a total of five units from the schedule of units for Part C (see below), and each candidate shall also offer a dissertation on a statistics project.   10

(*a*) The five units offered should be from those designated as M level.

(*b*) At least one unit should be offered from the schedule of 'Statistics' units.

No candidate shall offer any unit for Part C that he or she has also offered in Part B.

The use of calculators is generally not permitted for written papers. However, their use may be permitted for certain exceptional examinations. The specification of   15
calculators permitted for these exceptional examinations will be announced by the Examiners in the Hilary Term preceding the examination.

Schedule of Units for Part C

The final list of units will be published in the Course Handbook by the beginning of Michaelmas Full Term in the academic year of the examination concerned, together   20
with the following details.

1. Designation as either 'H' level or 'M' level.

2. 'Weight' as either a unit or double-unit.

3. Method of assessment. Details of methods of assessment for units delivered by other departments will be given elsewhere. Some options may require assessment by oral   25
presentation. The Course handbook will indicate where such details will be specified.

4. Rules governing submission of any extended essay, dissertation or mini-project, including deadlines, provided that these shall always be submitted to the Chair of Examiners, Honour School of Mathematics and Statistics, c/o Examination Schools, High Street, Oxford. When submitting their Part C dissertation, candidates must   30
submit both paper and electronic versions which must be identical. The latter may be used by the examiners to check for plagiarism. See the Course Handbook for further details. In addition any submission on a mathematical unit must also be submitted to the Mathematical Institute's website, details will be included in the relevant Notice to Candidates.   35

5. Syllabus content.

6. Whether there is a requirement to register or apply for a place to take a unit or double unit, and details of any registration or application procedure.

HONOUR SCHOOL OF MEDICAL SCIENCES

A

1. The subject of the Honour School of Medical Sciences shall be the sciences basic to medicine.

2. No candidate shall be admitted for examination in this school unless he or she has passed Part I of the First Examination for the Degree of Bachelor of Medicine.

3. The examination in this school shall be under the supervision of the Medical Sciences Board, which shall prescribe the necessary regulations.

4. Any candidate offering an optional subject based on courses provided within the Honour School of Experimental Psychology shall be examined in that subject by the Public Examiners in Experimental Psychology.

5. Candidates may offer themselves for examination in one or more *Supplementary Subjects*. The Supplementary Subjects available in any year will be notified to students annually during Trinity Term. A candidate's results in any such subject shall be published, and account shall be taken of those results in the production of the class list. Candidates awarded a pass in a Supplementary Subject examination may not retake the same Supplementary Subject examination.

6. Every candidate shall give notice of all papers being offered not later than Friday in the Week 8 of Michaelmas Term in the academic year in which the candidate intends to sit the examination.

B

1. The options of the school shall be:

  A Neuroscience
  B Molecular Medicine
  C Cardiovascular, Renal and Respiratory Biology
  D Infection and immunity
  E Cellular Physiology and Pharmacology

This list may be varied from time to time by the Medical Sciences Board, and such variations shall be published in the *University Gazette* by the end of Week 8 of Trinity Term of the academic year two years preceding the first examination of the changed options.

Minor variations, including changes of nomenclature, and/or changes of content to one or two themes within an option, shall be published by the end of Week 8 of Hilary Term of the academic year preceding the first examination of the changed options.

Each option shall be divided into themes that will be taught starting in Michaelmas Term. The list of themes shall be published no later than Week 0 of Michaelmas Term in the academic year in which the themes will be examined. Most themes will be specific to a single option, but some may be shared. The total number of themes comprising each option shall be at least 8 and no more than 11 (taking account of shared themes). Each candidate will be expected to have studied 8 themes in order to address the synoptic questions of Paper 2, and to have prepared sufficient of those themes in depth to be able to address the requirements of Paper 1 (see paras 2, 3, and 5 below).

2. The following written papers shall be set:

Paper 1 One separate paper for each option (Paper 1A to 1E)
Paper 2 One paper consisting of synoptic questions from each option
Paper 3 Critical reading, data analysis and experimental design

Each Paper 1 shall be of three hours duration and shall contain a choice of questions addressing in-depth knowledge and understanding within individual specified themes of the option. Each Paper 1 will require candidates to answer questions on three different themes.

Paper 2 shall be of three hours duration and shall contain a choice of questions from each option. Each question will require a synoptic approach across several themes of an option. Candidates shall be required to answer any two questions from this paper.

Paper 3 shall be of three hours duration and shall have questions relating to pieces of primary literature relevant to each of the options individually.

3. Each candidate must offer three written papers:

Paper 1 for *one* chosen option, Paper 2, and Paper 3.

In addition, each candidate must both:

(i) undertake and be examined in a research project

and

(ii) either submit an Extended Essay; or offer a fourth written paper based on courses provided within Parts I and II of the Honour School of Experimental Psychology. The subjects of the papers to be available for this purpose shall be published no later than the end of Week 5 of Hilary Term in the academic year preceding that in which the examination is taken.

If, in any part of the examination, a candidate presents essentially the same information on more than one occasion, then credit will be given in only the first instance.

4. Research project

(i) *Form, subject and approval of the project*

The project shall consist of original experiments and/or data analysis carried out by the candidate alone or in collaboration with others (where such collaboration is, for instance, needed to produce results in the time available).

Each project shall be supervised, and the topic and supervisor shall be approved on behalf of the Medical Sciences Board by the Director of Pre-Clinical Studies or his or her deputy. A list of approved project titles and their supervisors shall be published no later than Friday of Week 1 of Hilary Term in the academic year preceding the examination, and allocation of these projects to candidates shall be carried out through the Faculty of Physiological Sciences Undergraduate Studies Office no later than the end of Week 8 of that term.

As an alternative to the allocation process, a candidate may apply to undertake a project that is not on the approved list. Such application must be made no later than Friday of Week 4 of Hilary Term in the academic year preceding the examination. The candidate must submit the title of their proposed research project, provide a brief outline of the subject matter and supply details of supervision arrangements. The decision on the application shall be made by the Director of Preclinical Studies or his or her deputy and shall be communicated to the candidate as soon as possible, and work should not start on the project until approval has been given. Candidates should allow at least one week for the process of approval, and should bear in mind that an application may be referred for clarification or may be refused.

When choosing a research project, candidates must bear in mind the prohibition on duplicating material in different parts of the examination (see para 3).

(ii) *Pre-submission Confirmation*

Candidates must provide final confirmation of the details of their project (including title of project and name of supervisor) to the Examiners through the Faculty of 5 Physiological Sciences Undergraduate Studies Office no later than noon on Friday of Week 8 of Michaelmas Term in the academic year in which they intend taking the examination.

(iii) *Examination*

Candidates shall submit a brief Project Report according to guidelines that will be 10 published by the Medical Sciences Board in Week 8 of Hilary Term in the academic year preceding the examination.

Each candidate shall make a brief oral presentation of their project to a group of two examiners (or examiners and assessors appointed to ensure an adequate representation of expertise), after which, the candidate shall be examined *viva voce* on the 15 project. The form of the presentation to the examiners shall be specified in guidelines published by the Medical Sciences Board in Week 8 of Hilary Term in the academic year preceding the examination.

(iv) *Submission and assessment of project-based written work*

Project Reports (three copies) must be sent to the Chair of Examiners in Medical 20 Sciences, c/o Examination Schools, High Street, Oxford, not later than noon on the Friday of Week 8 in Hilary Term in the academic year in which the candidate intends to take the examination. The copies shall be accompanied (in a separate sealed envelope) by a certificate signed by each candidate indicating that the research project is the candidate's own work. The certificate shall certify that the supervisor has 25 commented on at least one draft of the written submission. Where work has been produced in collaboration, the certificate shall indicate the extent of the candidate's own contribution. Each candidate will be required to submit a draft of their Project Report to their supervisor no later than Friday of Week 6 (two weeks before submission to Schools). 30

The examiners shall obtain and consider a written report from each supervisor indicating the extent of the input made by the candidate to the outcome of the project and also any unforeseen difficulties associated with the project (e.g. unexpected technical issues or problems in the availability of materials, equipment, or literature or other published data). 35

In exceptional cases, where through unforeseen circumstances a research project produces no useable results (i.e. not even negative or ambiguous results), the candidate may apply through his or her college to the Director of Preclinical Studies or his or her deputy for permission to submit a concise review of the scientific context and the aims of the work that was attempted, in place of the normal Project Report. Such an 40 application must be accompanied by supporting evidence from the supervisor of the project. The concise review to be submitted in such circumstances should be comparable in length to the Report of a successful research project, will be presented orally to the examiners and will be examined *viva voce* in the usual way for a research project. The examiners will be advised that substantive results could not be produced. 45

When submitting a Project Report, candidates must bear in mind the prohibition on duplicating material in different parts of the examination (see para 3).

Project Reports previously submitted for the Honour School of Medical Sciences may be resubmitted. No Project Report will be accepted if it has already been submitted, wholly or substantially, for another Honour School or degree of this 50 University, or for a degree of any other institution.

5. The Extended Essay

(i) *Form and subject of the essay*

The Extended Essay shall be not more than 3,000 words, including figure legends but excluding references. It must be typed and bound according to guidelines that will be published by the Medical Sciences Board in Week 5 of Trinity Term in the academic year preceding the examination.

The subject matter of a candidate's essay shall be within the scope of the school. The essay may relate to any of the themes taught in the options of the school, regardless of the candidate's chosen option for Paper 1. However, when choosing an Extended Essay topic, candidates must bear in mind the prohibition on duplicating material in different parts of the examination (see para 3).

A list of essay titles registered by students in previous academic years will be made available by Week 5 of the Trinity Term of the academic year preceding that of the examination, to assist candidates in the choice of topic or general field for the essay.

(ii) *Registration*

No later than Friday of Week 8 of Michaelmas Term in the academic year of the examination, every candidate must register through the Faculty of Physiological Sciences Undergraduate Studies Office the title of their essay, provide a brief outline of the subject matter, and confirm the main themes to which it relates. A decision on the application shall be made by the Director of Preclinical Studies or his or her deputy and shall be communicated to the candidate not later than Week 4 of Hilary Term in the academic year of the examination.

(iii) *Authorship*

The essay must be the candidate's own work. Candidates' tutors, or their deputies nominated to act as advisors, may discuss with candidates the proposed field of study, the sources available, and the method of treatment, but on no account may they read or comment on any written draft. Every candidate shall sign a certificate to the effect that this rule has been observed and that the essay is their own work; and the candidate's tutor or adviser shall countersign the certificate confirming that, to the best of their knowledge and belief, this is so.

(iv) *Submission*

Essays (two copies) must be submitted to the Chair of Examiners in Medical Sciences, c/o Examination Schools, High Street, Oxford, not later than noon on the Friday of Week 0 of the Trinity Term in which the candidate intends to take the examination. Each essay shall be accompanied (in a separate sealed envelope addressed to the Chair of Examiners) by a certificate of authorship as specified in the preceding paragraph and an electronic copy of the text of the essay.

6. Should any one option of the school be oversubscribed and the supply of suitable teaching in that option is unable to meet the demand, then the Medical Sciences Board may impose a limit on the number of candidates that may enter for that option. Such regulation of numbers may be achieved by the allocation of places in the option to specified students provided that these allocations are published by 0th week of Michaelmas Term of the academic year in which the candidates are to sit the examination. The board shall make arrangements to allow subsequently for regulated migration between options on receipt of written applications from candidates to the Director of Preclinical Studies or his or her deputy. Such migration will be permitted provided a sufficient supply of suitable teaching can be maintained.

7. Candidates may be examined *viva voce*, the topics may include the subject of any written paper taken by the candidate, or the research project or Extended Essay.

HONOUR SCHOOL OF MODERN LANGUAGES

A

1. The subjects of examination in the Honour School of Modern Languages shall be the French, German, Italian, Spanish, Portuguese, Russian, Medieval and Modern Greek, Czech (with Slovak),[1] and Celtic[1] languages and the literatures associated with them, and Linguistics. Save in the case of the subjects Czech (with Slovak) and Celtic, which may be offered only with another of the languages, a candidate may offer one or two languages, or one language and Linguistics. The standard of competence required of a candidate shall be the same in any language which he or she offers whether it be his or her sole language or one of two languages.

2. Every candidate shall be required to show, in the case of any language which he or she offers, a competent knowledge

   (1) of the language as it is spoken and written at the present day, such knowledge to be tested by oral and written examination;

   (2) of at least one specified period in its literature;

   (3) of the history, thought, and civilization of the country necessary for the understanding of the language and literature.

3. A candidate offering one language shall be required to show a competent philological knowledge of the language he or she is offering. A candidate offering two languages shall be permitted to offer a paper or papers on philological topics.

4. Candidates offering the subject Linguistics shall be required to show a competent knowledge of analytical techniques and problems in descriptive and theoretical linguistics and the application of these to the language they are offering.

5. No candidate shall be admitted to examination in this School unless he or she has either passed or been exempted from the First Public Examination.

6. The examiners shall indicate in the lists issued by them the subject or subjects offered by each candidate obtaining honours or satisfying the examiners under the appropriate regulation. In drawing up the Class List the examiners shall satisfy themselves that each candidate has shown an appropriate level of competence both in literature (and linguistic studies where this applies) and in language.

7. The board of the faculty shall by notice from time to time make regulations concerning the examination; and shall have power in respect of each subject included in the examination

   (1) to determine, within the limits of this decree, the form and content of the individual papers of the examination, and

   (2) to issue a list of Special Subjects, prescribing books or authorities where they think it desirable. Such books or authorities may be in other languages than that to which the Special Subject is related. A Special Subject may be concerned with a language or literature not specified in clause 1 of this Regulation.

---

[1] Czech (with Slovak) and Celtic may not be available in every year. Notice that these subjects, or a particular paper or particular papers, will not be available in a given year will be published in the *University Gazette* in the Trinity Term three years before the examination concerned.

8. A candidate whose name has been placed in the Class List upon the result of the examination in any one or more of the subjects included in the examination shall be permitted to offer himself or herself for examination in any of the other subjects so included at the examination in either the next year or the next year but one, provided that no such candidate shall offer any of the languages or subjects already offered by   5
him or her in the Honour School of Modern Languages or in the Honour Schools of History and Modern Languages, Philosophy and Modern Languages, Classics and Modern Languages, or English and Modern Languages, or European and Middle Eastern Languages, and provided always that he or she has not exceeded six terms from the date on which he or she first obtained Honours in a Final Honour School.   10

B

Candidates will be examined in accordance with the examination regulations set out below.

They will also be required to spend, after their matriculation, a year of residence in an appropriate country or countries, and to provide on their entry form for the examina-   15
tion a certificate that they have done this, signed by the Head or by a tutor of their society. Candidates wishing to be dispensed from the requirement to undertake a year of residence abroad must apply in writing to the Chair of the Medieval and Modern Languages Board, 41 Wellington Square, Oxford, OX1 2JF, stating their reasons for requesting dispensation and enclosing a letter of support from their society.   20

Candidates will be expected to carry out during this year abroad such work as their society may require. It is strongly recommended that candidates should apply through the Central Bureau for Educational Visits and Exchanges for an Assistantship, where these are available, and should accept one if offered. Candidates who are not able to obtain an Assistantship should during their year abroad follow a course or courses in   25
an institution or institutions approved by their society, or should spend their time in such other circumstances as are acceptable to their society. Candidates will agree with their College Tutor in advance of their year abroad an independent course of study to be followed during that period.

It is strongly recommended that candidates offering two languages who spend their   30
year abroad in a country or countries of one of the languages only should in addition spend between their matriculation and examination at least four weeks in a country of the other language.

Candidates may offer either one or two languages. The standard of competence shall be as high for candidates who offer two languages as for those who offer only   35
one. A candidate offering one language may also offer Linguistics. The papers and choices of options available to candidates for each of the two courses will be the same.

Candidates may additionally offer an Extended Essay, good performance in which will be taken into account in allocating all classes.

The following is the general scheme of papers in Modern Languages: 40

I, II, III	Language papers
IV, V	Linguistic Studies
VI, VII, VIII	Period of Literature or Period Topics
IX	Early Texts
X, XI	Prescribed Authors (German XI: Early Modern Texts or Goethe) 45
XII	Special Subjects
XIII	General Linguistics
XIV	Extended Essay

Candidates must take one of the schedules of papers listed in 1 below, subject to the general and specific conditions listed in 2, and the special regulations concerning Paper   50
XII Special Subjects listed in 3.

1. Combinations of Papers

I. A candidate who offers two languages must take the written papers listed below, and oral examinations in both languages:

Five papers in language A

> *Two* language papers I, II(A+B)   5
> *One* of VI, VII, VIII
> *Two* of IV, V, IX, X, XI, XII

Four papers in language B

> *Two* language papers I, II(A+B)
> *One* of VI, VII, VIII   10
> *One* of IV, V, IX, X, XI, XII

Optionally, XIV Extended Essay

II. A candidate who offers one language only must take the written papers listed below, and the oral examination in the language:

(*a*) French: 15

> *Three* language papers I, II(A+B), III
> *One* of VI, VII, VIII
> *Five* of IV, V, VI, VII, VIII, IX, X, XI, XII, XIII
> Optionally, XIV Extended Essay

(*b*) Spanish: 20

> *Three* language papers I, II(A+B), III
> Paper IX
> *Two* of VI, VII, VIII, XIII
> *Three* of IV, V, X, XI, XII, XII (Modern Galician *or* Modern Catalan) of which *at least one* must be IV or V   25
> Optionally, XIV Extended Essay

(*c*) All other languages:

> *Three* language papers I, II(A+B), III
> Paper IX
> *Two* of VI, VII, VIII, XIII   30
> *Three* of IV, V, X, XI, XII, of which at least one must be IV or V
> Optionally, XIV Extended Essay

III. Candidates offering one language and Linguistics must take eight papers as listed below, and the oral examination in the language.

Three papers in the language: 35

> Two language papers I, II(A+B)
> *One* of VI, VII, VIII

Four papers in Linguistics:

> IV and V (in the language)
> XII (drawn from Special Subjects bearing the Linguistics identifier)   40
> XIII
> One paper, from IX, X, XI, or XII (whether in the language or Linguistics)
> Optionally, XIV Extended Essay

Candidates must avoid substantial overlap between Paper XII Special Subjects and other Linguistics Papers.

IV. Candidates offering one language with Polish must offer:

Three papers in Polish: II(A+B), IV *or* V, VIII
Six papers in the other language, as specified below   5
Oral examination in the other language
Optionally, XIV Extended Essay

In French

Two language papers I, II(A+B)
One of VI,VII,VIII   10
Three of IV, V, VI, VII, VIII, IX, X, XI, XII, XIII

In German

Two language papers I, II(A+B)
One of VI, VII, VIII, XIII
Three of IV, V, VI, VII, VIII, IX, X, XI, XII (provided that no more than two of IV,   15
V, IX are taken)

In Italian

Two language papers I, II(A+B)
One of VI, VII, VIII
One of IV, V   20
Paper IX
One of IV *or* V, VI, VII, VIII, X, XI, XII, XIII

In Spanish

Two language papers I, II(A+B)
One of VI, VII, VIII, XIII   25
Paper IX
Two of IV *or* V, VI, VII, VIII, X, XI, XII, XII (Modern Galician *or* Modern Catalan)

In Russian

Two language papers I, II(A+B)
One of VII, VIII   30
Paper IX
Two of IV *or* V, VI, VII, VIII, X, XI, XII, XIII

In Portuguese

Two language papers I, II(A+B)
One of Papers VI, VII, VIII   35
Three of IV *or* V, VI, VII, VIII, IX, X, XI, XII

In Medieval and Modern Greek

Two language papers I, II(A+B)
Two of VI, VII, VIII, XIII
Two of IX, X, XI, XII   40

Examination answers must be written in English, except when directions are given to the contrary.

Candidates will be required to attend for an oral examination in each language they offer. A candidate failing to appear for the oral examination, without good cause shown, will be deemed to have withdrawn from the whole examination.   45

In the oral examination a candidate will be required to show in each language he offers competence in the following:
   (i) Comprehension of a passage or passages of text;
   (ii) A short discourse;
   (iii) Conversation. Reading aloud may be required of candidates as a further test of their pronunciation.

2. Special Provisions

   i. All candidates offering Italian must offer at least one of IV, V, IX in Italian

   ii. A candidate offering two languages is required to offer, in one language,

   either at least one of papers IV, V

   or at least one pre-Modern paper as designated below:

   French VI, VII, IX, X
   German VI, VII, IX, XI(A)
   Italian VI, VII, IX, X
   Spanish VI, VII, IX, X
   Portuguese VI, VII, IX, X
   Russian VI, VII, IX
   Medieval and Modern Greek VI, VII, IX, X
   Celtic VI, IX, X
   Czech IX

   or one Paper XII designated as pre-Modern.

   Details of Paper XII Special Subjects which have been designated as pre-Modern will be provided in the list of Special Subjects published by the Faculty by the beginning of the fifth week of the Trinity Term one year before the examination.

3. Paper XII Special Subjects

   Candidates may offer only one Paper XII, with the following exceptions:
   (*a*) Candidates offering Spanish as a sole language or as one of two languages may offer two Paper XII Special Subjects in total, provided that one is either Modern Catalan or Modern Galician;
   (*b*) Candidates offering Linguistics may offer either one or two Paper XII Special Subjects. Where one Special Subject is offered, it must bear the appropriate Linguistics identifier. Where two Special Subjects are offered, one must bear the appropriate Linguistics identifier.

   Candidates offering a Paper XII Special Subject in the second of two languages (Language B) may choose only a Special Subject bearing the appropriate language identifier.

   Candidates offering Spanish as a sole language or in combination with any language other than Portuguese may offer one of the following papers in Portuguese as a Paper XII Special Subject: Paper X, Paper XI, half of the period covered in Paper VII or Paper VIII.

4. Detailed specifications of papers I to XIV
I, II, III Language Papers

French

I	Essay in French
IIA	Translation from Modern French
IIB	Translation into Modern French
III	Translation from pre-Modern French

German

I	Translation into German and Essay in German
IIA	Translation from Modern German
IIB	Translation from Modern German
III	Translation from pre-Modern German

Italian

I	Essay in Italian
IIA	Translation from Italian
IIB	Translation into Italian
III	Translation from pre-Modern Italian

Spanish

I	Prose translation from English into Spanish and an essay in Spanish
IIA	Translation from Modern Spanish
IIB	Translation from Modern Spanish
III	Prose translation from English into Spanish and a translation from Spanish into English (medieval or golden age)

Portuguese

I	Prose composition and essay
IIA	Translation from Modern Portuguese (European)
IIB	Translation from Modern Portuguese (Brazilian)
III	(A) Translation from pre-Modern Portuguese and (B) a Year Abroad Essay

Russian

I	Translation into Russian and essay in Russian with further specifications
IIA	Translation from Modern Russian
IIB	Translation from Modern Russian
III	Translation from pre-Modern Russian with further specifications

Czech (with Slovak)

I	Translation into Czech or Slovak and essay in Czech or Slovak
IIA	Translation from Modern Czech
IIB	Translation from Modern Slovak

Medieval and Modern Greek

I	Translation into Modern Greek and essay in Modern Greek
IIA	Translation from Modern Greek
IIB	Translation from Modern Greek
III	Translation of a prose text in kathareuousa into English

Polish

| IIA | Translation from Modern Polish |
| IIB | Translation into Modern Polish |

Celtic

I	Translation into Irish or Welsh and essay in Irish or Welsh
IIA	Translation from Modern Irish or Modern Welsh
IIB	Translation from Irish from the period up to 1200 or Welsh from the period up to 1400.

IV. Linguistic Studies I.

French:

The History of the French language up to the mid-twentieth century. The paper will consist of two sections as follows. Candidates must answer questions from both sections.

(1) The history of the language (phonetics, phonology, grammar, vocabulary, semantics, sociolinguistics, external history).

(2) The description of the language of literary and non-literary texts from past periods. Candidates may confine their answer(s) to *one* of the following sub-sections:

(*a*) From Latin to Early Old French: Before 1150;

(*b*) Old and Middle French: 1100–1530;

(*c*) Renaissance and Classical French: 1530–1715;

(*d*) Into Modern French: 1715–1940.

Optional passages from texts for linguistic and stylistic commentary will be set for each period. The following are suggested as illustrative texts:

(*a*) Studer and Waters, *Historical French Reader,* 1, 6, 7, 10, 11, 13.

(*b*) Studer and Waters, *Historical French Reader,* 20, 26, 34, 40, 41, 45, 46, 47, 65.

Passages for commentary will be selected from the texts listed above.

In (*c*) and (*d*) the texts will be selected from appropriate literary and non-literary works.

German:

The development of the German language from 1170 to the present, with a special study of:

Werner der Gärtner, *Helmbrecht* (Reclam edn.).

Martin Luther, *Sendbrief vom Dolmetschen,* ed. K. Bischoff, pp. 6/7–28, l. 21/29, l. 22, and pp. 36–57.

Italian:

The history of the Italian language from the earliest times to the twentieth century.

Spanish:

The history of the Spanish language to 1700. The paper will be divided into three sections, and candidates must answer from two: (*a*) to 1250; (*b*) 1250–1500; (*c*) 1500–1700.

Portuguese:

The history and structure of the Portuguese language. Candidates will be required to show knowledge of the descriptive analysis of the contemporary language, as used in Portugal and Brazil, and of its historical development.

Russian:

The history of the Russian language with the following texts prescribed:

(1) for linguistic comment:

(*a*) Marginalia to Novgorod service books (V. V. Ivanov *et al., Khrestomatiya po istorii russkogo yazyka,* Moscow, 1990, pp. 26–7).

Novgorod birchbark texts, nos. 247, 752, 644, 605, 424, 776, 724, 717, 725, 531, 705, 765, 142, 370, 363, 364, 361, 43, 49, 154 (A. A. Zaliznyak, *Drevnenovgorodskii dialekt,* Moscow, 2004, pp. 239–40, 249–54, 267–8, 271–2, 307–9, 350–4, 396–7, 415–20, 422–4, 480–1, 536–8, 588–90, 606–7, 614, 651–2, 672–3).

Vkladnaya Varlaama (Zaliznyak, pp. 458–60).

Treaty of Alexander Nevsky and Novgorod with the Germans, 1262–3 (S. P. Obnorsky and S. G. Barkhudarov, *Khrestomatiya po istorii russkogo yazyka,* part 1, 2nd edn., Moscow, 1952, pp. 51–2).

Novgorod First Chronicle, *s.a.* 6738–9 (ed. A. N. Nasonov, *Novgorodskaya Pervaya letopis' starshego i mladshego izvoda*, Moscow-Leningrad, 1950, pp. 69–71).

(*b*) Afanasy Nikitin, *Khozhenie za tri morya* (Ivanov *et al.*, pp. 322–5). *Dukhovnaya gramota I. Yu. Gryaznogo* (Ivanov *et al.*, pp. 279–80). Letter of T. I. Golitsyna to V. V. Golitsyn (S. I. Kotkov *et al.*, *Moskovskaya*   5 *delovaya i bytovaya pis'mennost' XVII veka*, Moscow, 1968, p. 20). Letters of D. V. Mikhalkov to M. I. Mikhalkova and P. D. Mikhalkov (Kotkov *et al.*, pp. 39–40 (17b-v), 41 (18b)). Letters of U. S. Pazukhina to S. I. Pazukhin and E. Klement'ev to F. M. Chelishchev (S. I. Kotkov and N. P. Pankratova, *istochniki po istorii narodno-razgo-*   10 *vornogo yazyka XVII-nachala XVIII veka*, Moscow, 1964, pp. 169–70, 233).

Letters of Peter I to Tsaritsa Natal'ya Kirillovna, to F. M. Apraksin, to B. P. Sheremetev (*Pis'ma i bumagi Petra Velikago*, vol. 1 (1688–1701), St Petersburg, 1887, No. 6, p. 11, No. 14, pp. 15–16; vol. 5 (1707), St Petersburg, 1907, No. 1695, pp. 221–2; vol. 7(i) (1708), St Petersburg, 1918, No. 2186, pp. 35–6).   15

Evidence of A. Turcheninov on fire of 29 May 1737 (A. I. Sumkina and S. I. Kotkov, *Pamyatniki moskovskoi delovoi pis'mennosti XVIII veka*, Moscow, 1981, pp. 159–60).

Letters of V. B. Golitsyn to Vl. B. Golitsyn, M. D. Kurakina to B. I. Kurakin, M. M. Shcherbatov to D. M. Shcherbatov (Sumkina and Kotkov, pp. 24–6, 49–50   20 (50), 73–4).

(2) for translation and linguistic comment:

(*a*) Colophon to Ostromir Codex (Ivanov *et al.*, pp. 15–16).

Mstislavova gramota (Ivanov *et al.*, pp. 39–41). Colophon to Mstislav's Gospel Book (Ivanov *et al.*, pp. 49–50).   25

Spisok ubytkov novgorodtsev, 1412 (Zaliznyak, pp. 686–692).

Russkaya Pravda (Ivanov, *et al.*, pp. 67–73).

Novgorod First Chronicle, *s.a.* 6633–8, 6675–7, 6700, 6712, 6777–80 (Nasonov, pp. 21–2, 32–3, 40, 46–9, 87–90).

(*b*) *Statejnyi spisok G. I. Mikulina* (D. S. Likhachev, *Puteshestviya russkikh poslov*   30 *XVI–XVII vv.*, Moscow – Leningrad, 1954, p. 178, 4th paragraph – p. 181, 2nd paragraph).

Domostroi (Obnorsky and Barkhudarov, part I, pp. 236–241).

Ulozhenie Alekseya Mikhailovicha, Chapter 10 (Ivanov *et al.*, pp. 380–1).

G. Kotoshikhin, O Rossii v tsarstvovanie Alekseya Mikhailovicha, Chapter 4,   35 Section 24, Chapter 13, Sections 1–4 (ed. A. E. Pennington, Oxford, 1980, pp. 65–7, 159–63).

Stateinyi spisok P. A. Tolstogo (Obnorsky and Barkhudarov, part 2:1, 1949, pp. 72–5).

Candidates will be required to show knowledge *either* of the texts listed under (1) (*a*)–(*b*), *of* those listed under (1) (*a*) and (2) (*a*), *or* of those listed under (1) (*b*)   40 and (2) (*b*).

Medieval and Modern Greek:
The History of Modern Greek Language. The paper will study the development of Greek language from Koine to Standard Modern Greek. A discussion of the Language Debate will be included in this paper.   45
Czech (with Slovak):
The history of Czech and Slovak. Passages for commentary and translation will be taken from Porák, *Chrestomatie k vývoji českého jazyka* (1979), pp. 31–40, 54–64,

72–88, 115–18, 126–31, 383–7. Candidates will be required to write one translation, one commentary, and two essay-type questions.
Polish:
  The History of the Polish Language
Celtic: 5
  Comparative and Historic Celtic Linguistics. Passages will be set for linguistic commentary on *one* of *(a)* The history of Welsh *or* of Irish and Scottish Gaelic *or* *(b)* Comparative Celtic Linguistics[1]

V. Linguistic Studies II.
French: 10
  Modern French. Candidates will be required to show knowledge of the descriptive analysis of the contemporary language, and will have the opportunity of discussing the historical development of the language where this illuminates present-day usage. The paper will contain optional questions on the principles of descriptive linguistics to be answered with particular reference to French.   15
German:
  Either (1) Old High German, with the following texts prescribed for study: W. Braune, *Althochdeutsches Lesebuch* (17th edn., by E. A. Ebbinghaus): V *Gespräche*; VIII Isidor, cap. iii; XX Tatian, subsections 2, 4, and 7; XXIII Notker, subsections 1 and 13; XXVIII *Hildebrandslied*; XXIX *Wessobrunner Gebet*; XXX *Muspilli*; XXXII   20
  Otfrid, subsections 7 (*Missus est Gabrihel angelus*) and 21 (*De die judicii*); XXXVI *Ludwigslied*; XLIII *Ezzos Gesang,* Strasbourg version only.

  Or

  (2) Descriptive analysis of German as spoken and written at the present day (phonetics, phonology, grammar, vocabulary, semantics, style). The paper will con-   25
  tain optional questions on the principles of descriptive linguistics to be answered with particular reference to German.

Italian:
  Modern Italian. Candidates will be required to show knowledge of the descriptive analysis of the contemporary language, and will have the opportunity of discussing the   30
  historical development of the language where this illuminates present-day usage. The paper will contain optional questions on the principles of descriptive linguistics to be answered with particular reference to Italian.
Spanish:
  Modern Spanish. Candidates will be required to show knowledge of the descriptive   35
  analysis of the structure of the contemporary language, as used in Spain and in the Americas.
Portuguese:
  Varieties of Portuguese. Candidates will be required to apply the principles of descriptive linguistics to the analysis of regional and social varieties of the   40
  Portuguese of Portugal, Brazil, and Africa, and to Portuguese-based creoles. This paper will include commentaries on linguistic samples.

---

[1] It is possible to do this paper with a knowledge of either Irish (with Scottish Gaelic) or Welsh, together with some Continental Celtic, or with a knowledge of both Irish and Welsh. Details of the passages for translation and comment are available from the Modern Languages Faculty Office.

Russian:
Either
(1) The development of the Church Slavonic language, with the following texts prescribed:

(*a*) for linguistic comment: 5

Kiev Missal and *Euchologium Sinaticum* (R. Auty, *Handbook of Old Church Slavonic*, London, 1968 and subsequent reprints, Pt. ii, Texts and Glossary, passages IV, pp. 52–7, and VI, pp. 64–9).

Luke x: 25–37 (Auty, passage XIV, pp. 97–106: ed. L. P. Zhukovskaya *et al.*, *Aprakos Mstislava Velikogo*, Moscow, 1983, p. 131).   10

Psalm liv (ed. S. Sever'yanov, *Sinaiskaya Psaltyr'*, Petrograd, 1922, pp. 67–9; ed. E. V. Cheshko *et al.*, *Norovskaya psaltyr'*. *Srednebolgarskaya rukopis' XIV veka*, Sofia, 1989, Pt. ii, pp. 387–91; *Psaltir s posljedovanjem Đurđ~a Crnojevića 1494*, reprinted Cetinje, 1986; the Synodal Bible of 1751 and subsequent editions, e.g. Moscow, 1815, St Petersburg, 1820).   15

(*b*) for translation and linguistic comment:

Vita Constantini, xiv–xv, xvii–xviii, *Vita Methodii*, v–xvii, the Treatise on Letters, the Acrostich Prayer (A. Vaillant, *Textes vieux-slaves*, Paris, 1968, Pt. i, Textes et glossaire, passages I, pp. 30–3, 37–40, II, pp. 46–55, III, pp. 57–61, IV C. pp. 68–70).

Povest' vremennykh let, s.a. 6406 (D. S. Likhachev, *Povest' vremennykh let*, part I,   20
Moscow–Leningrad, 1950, pp. 21–23).

Zhitie sv. Stefana episkopa Permskogo (ed. V. Druzhinin, St Petersburg, 1897, reprinted The Hague, 1959, pp. 69–74).

V. F. Burstov's *Bukvar'* (V. V. Ivanov *et al.*, *Khrestomatiya po istorii russkogo yazyka*, Moscow, 1990, pp. 369–74).   25

Candidates will be required to show knowledge of the texts listed under (1) (*a*) and (1) (*b*).

Or

(2) Descriptive analysis of Russian as spoken and written at the present day (phonetics, phonology, grammar, vocabulary, semantics, style). The paper will con-   30
tain optional questions on the principles of descriptive linguistics to be answered with particular reference to Russian.

Medieval and Modern Greek:
The structure of the standard language as spoken and written at the present day (phonetics, phonology, grammar, vocabulary, semantics, style). The paper will con-   35
tain optional questions on the principles of descriptive linguistics to be answered with particular reference to Modern Greek.

Polish:
Descriptive analysis of Polish as spoken and written at the present day.

VI. Topics in the period of literature (*French only*) *or* Period of literature (i):   40
French: to 1530.
German: Medieval German Culture (to 1450): Texts, Contexts, and Issues.
Italian: 1220–1430.
Spanish: to 1499.
Portuguese: to 1540.[1]   45
Medieval and Modern Greek: Byzantine Greek to 1453.

---

[1] Candidates offering both Portuguese paper VI and Portuguese paper VII may answer questions on the period 1500–40 in one of the two papers only. In papers VI and VII the questions affected by this provision will be indicated by an asterisk.

Celtic: Medieval Irish up to 1600 and Medieval Welsh up to 1500. [Candidates will be able to confine their answers to questions on *either* Irish *or* Welsh topics.]

VII. Topics in the period of literature (*French only*) *or* Period of literature (ii):
French: 1530–1800[1]
German: Early Modern German Culture (1450–1730): Texts, Contexts, and Issues.   5
Italian: 1430–1635
Spanish: 1543–1695
Portuguese: 1500–1697[2]
Russian: 1100–1700
Medieval and Modern Greek: Medieval Greek to 1669   10

VIII. Topics in the period of literature (*French only*) *or* Period of literature (iii):
French: 1715 to the present.[3]
German: Modern German Literature (1730 to the present): Texts, Contexts, and Issues.
Italian: Modern Italian Literature (1750 to the present) and Cinema   15
Spanish: The literature of Spain and of Spanish America: 1811 to the present.
Candidates may offer themselves for examination *either* in the literature of both Spain and Spanish America, *or* in the literature of Spain only, *or* in the literature of Spanish America only.
Portuguese: The literature of Portugal and Brazil: 1761 to the present.   20
Candidates may offer themselves for examination *either* in the literature of both Portugal and Brazil, *or* in the literature of Portugal only, *or* in the literature of Brazil only.
Russian: **[For students starting before MT 2015: 1820–1953] [For students starting from MT 2015: 1820–present]**   25
Medieval and Modern Greek: Modern Greek, 1821 to the present.
Czech (with Slovak): Czech and Slovak literature, 1774 to the present.
Polish: Polish literature from the late 18th century to the 20th century.
Candidates will be required to answer three questions.

[3]**IX. Enlightenment Texts (Russian only) or Early texts prescribed for study as examples**   30
of literature:
French:
In French paper IX, the commentary section of the paper will include compulsory passages for translation.
La Chanson de Roland, ed. Whitehead (Blackwell).   35
Béroul, *The Romance of Tristran,* ed. Ewert (Blackwell).

---

[1] (*a*) Candidates offering both French paper VII and French paper VIII may answer questions on the period 1715–1800 in *one* of the two papers only. In both papers, the questions most obviously affected by this provision will be indicated by an asterisk. (*b*) Candidates offering subject 8(iii), Ancient and French Classical Tragedy, in the Honour School of Classics and Modern Languages will not be permitted to discuss the work of Corneille and Racine in French paper VII.

[2] Candidates offering both Portuguese paper VI and Portuguese paper VII may answer questions on the period 1500–40 in one of the two papers only. In papers VI and VII the questions affected by this provision will be indicated by an asterisk.

[3] Each paper will be divided into two sections, one containing questions on the general aspects of the books and authors, and the other containing passages for explanation and comment. Both sections will be compulsory.

Villon, *Œuvres,* ed. Longnon-Foulet, 4th edn., with a special study of *Le Testament,* 1–909, 1660–end, and *Poésies Diverses* IX-XVI.
Candidates will be required to translate from one or more passages set for comment.
German:
Das Nibelungenlied, ed. K. Bartsch *et al.* (Reclam 1997), avent. 1, 14–17, 23–30, 36–9.   5
Wolfram von Eschenbach, *Parzival,* books 3, 5, and 9.
Heinrich von Morungen, *Lieder,* ed. H. Tervooren (Reclam 1986)
Das Osterspiel von Muri and Das Innsbrucker Osterspiel
Italian:
Dante, *La divina commedia,* with a special study of two of the three *Cantiche.*   10
Spanish:
Poema de mio Cid, ed. Michael (Clásicos Castalia).
Juan Ruiz, *Libro de Buen Amor,* ed. Gybbon-Monypenny (Clásicos Castalia).
Comedia o tragicomedia de Calisto y Melibea, ed. P. E. Russell (Clásicos Castalia).
Portuguese: 15
E. Gonçalves and M. A. Ramos, *A Lírica Galego-Portuguesa* (Comunicação).
Alfonso X of Castile, *Cantigas de Santa Maria,* ed. W. Mettmann (Clásicos Castalia, vol. I, 1986).
Fernão Lopes, *Crónica de D. João* I (textos escolhidos), ed. T. Amado (Comunicação).   20
Zurara, *Crónica dos feitos de Guiné* (chs. 1–25). (Candidates are advised also to read Zurara, *Chronique de Guinée,* ed. L. Bourdon (Ifan-Dakar, 1960)).
Russian:
The syllabus will consist of the following texts with passages for commentary eligible to be set from those marked with an*:   25
Avvakum, *Zhitie**
'Povest' o Savve Grudtsyne'; 'Povest' o Frole Skobeeve'; 'Povest' o Bove Koroleviche'
Antiokh Kantemir *Satires* I*, II, IV, VII, IX
Mikhailo Lomonosov: 'Oda na vzyatie Khotina'; 'Pis'mo o pol'ze stekla', 'Oda   30
torzhestvennaya (1747)*; 'Oda torzhestvennaya (1762)*'; 'Utrennee razmyshlenie o bozhiem velichestve'*, 'Vechernee ramyshlenie'*.
Aleksandr Sumarokov, 'Epistola o stikhotvorstve'; 'Lyubovnye elegii' [extracts]*
Denis Fonvizin, *Brigadir, Nedorosl'**;
Vassily Kapnist, *Yabeda*   35
Ippolit Bogdanovich, *Dushen'ka*
N.I. Novikov, *Satiricheskie zhurnaly.* Excerpts.
M. Chulkov, *Prigozhaya povarikha**
Alexander Radishchev, *Puteshestvie iz Peterburga v Moskvu* [3 chapters to be prescribed*]   40
Gavriil Derzhavin: 'Bog'*; 'Pamyatnik geroyu'; 'Vel'mozha'; 'Vlastitelyam i su-d'yam'; 'Russkie devushki'; 'Evgeniyu. Zhizn' zvanskaya'*; 'Solovey vo sne'; 'Na smert' knyazya Meshcherskogo'*, 'Priglashenie k obedu'; 'Pamyatnik'; 'Moi istukan'; 'Reka vremen v svoem stremlenii'.
Nikolai Karamzin, Bednaya Liza*, *Ostrov Borngol'm; Pis'ma russkogo puteshes-*   45
vennika [extracts]
Vassily Zhukovsky, *Svetlana; 'Sel'skoe kladbishche'**
Ivan Krylov, 'Pis'mo o pol'ze zhelanii'; 'Strekoza i muravei', 'Vorona i lisitsa', 'Lebed' rak i shchuka', 'Volk i iagnionok', 'Volk na psarne', 'Kvartet', 'Ryb'i pliaski'
Konstantin Batiushkov, 'Moi Penaty'*; 'Moi genii'; Elegiia; Na razvalnyakh zamke   50
v Shvetsii;
Alexandr Pushkin, *Ruslan i Liudmila;* selected lyrics*

Medieval and Modern Greek:
Candidates may choose one of either A or B:[1]
The commentary section of the paper will include compulsory passages for translation.
A: Byzantine texts:
Paul the Silentiary, *Ekphrasis* of Haghia Sophia (ed. Friedlander).
Christ and Paranikas, *Anthologia graeca carminum Christianorum*, pp. 147–236 and 247–52.
The Life of St Andreas Salos (ed. L. Ryden).
Michael Psellos, *Chronographia*, bk. VI (ed. S. Impellizzeri, vol. 1, pp. 246–320, and vol. 2, pp. 8–152).
B: Medieval vernacular texts:
Digenis Akritis: the Grottaferrata and Escorial Versions (ed. E. M. Jeffreys).
Livistros kai Rodamni (ed. P. A. Agapitos).
Ptochoprodromos (ed. H. Eideneier).
Passages will *not* be set from:
Digenis Akritis, Grottaferrata version, book V.
Ptochoprodromus, poem IV.
Czech (with Slovak):
Dalimilova kronika, chs. 1–32, 41, 66–70, 102–6.
Život svaté Kateřiny.
Tkadleček.
Candidates will be required to answer one question on each of the three texts, including one commentary. They will also be required to translate a passage.
Celtic:
Any four of the following: Early Texts (commentary section of the paper will include compulsory passages for translation).
Togail Bruidne Da Derga, ed. E. Knott (Dublin, 1936).
Fingal Rónáin and Other Stories, ed. D. Greene (Dublin, 1955).
Scéla Cano meic Gartnáin, ed. D. A. Binchy (Dublin, 1963).
Serglige Con Culainn, ed. M. Dillon (Dublin, 1953).
Cath Almaine, ed. P. O. Riain (Dublin, 1978).
The Irish Adam and Eve Story from Saltair na Rann, ed. D. Greene and F. Kelly (Dublin, 1976).
Canu Aneirin, ed. I. Williams (Cardiff, 1938).
Canu Llywarch Hen, ed. I. Williams (Cardiff, 1935).
Armes Prydein, ed. I. Williams (Cardiff, 1955; or Dublin, 1972).
M. Haycock, *Blodeugerdd Barddas o Ganu Crefyddol Cynnar* (Y Bala: Barddas, 1994).
Culhwch ac Olwen, ed. R. Bromwich and D. Simon Evans (Cardiff, 1992).
Selection from the series: R. Geraint Gruffydd (gen. ed.), Cyfres Beirdd y Tywysogion vols. I, II, V–VII (Cardiff, 1991–6).

[2]**X. Modern Prescribed Authors (i):**[3] Passages for explanation and comment will be taken from the works prescribed for special study. Candidates will be expected to have read works by their chosen authors other than those prescribed for special study.

---

[1] Those who offer B may not offer options (1) and (2) in Paper X.
[2] Each paper will be divided into two sections, one containing questions on the general aspects of the books and authors, and the other containing passages for explanation and comment. Both sections will be compulsory.
[3] Except in the case of Medieval and Modern Greek.

French:

Any two of the following:

(1) Rabelais, with a special study of *Gargantua* and *Le Quart Livre.*

(2) Montaigne, with a special study of *Essais,* I. 20 (Que philosopher, c'est apprendre à mourir), I. 23 (De la coutume et de ne changer aisément une loi reçue), I. 26 (De l'institution des enfants), II. 17 (De la praesumption), II. 6 (De l'exercitation), III. 2 (Du repentir), III. 5 (Sur des vers de Virgile), III. 13 (De l'expérience).

(3) Pascal, *Les Provinciales, Pensées et opuscules divers,* éd. G. Ferreyrolles et P. Sellier, in *La Pochothéque* (Livres de poche/Classiques Garnier), with a special study of *Pensées,* 1–414; 419–671; 680–690; 694–695; 697–717; 742–769; *De l'esprit géométrique et de l'art de persuader.*

(4) Molière, with a special study of *L'École des femmes, Les Fourberies de Scapin, Le Tartuffe, Dom Juan, Le Misanthrope, Le Malade Imaginaire.*

(5) Racine, with a special study of: *Andromaque, Britannicus, Bérénice, Bajazet, Iphigénie, Athalie* in *Théâtre complet,* ed. J. Rohou (Pochothèque, Livre de Poche, 1998).

(6) Voltaire, with a special study of *Romans et contes,* ed. E. Guitton (Pochothèque, Livre de Poche, 1994): the following works: *Zadig, Paméla* (pp. 138–96), *Candide, contes de Guillaume Vadé* (pp. 339–453), *La Princesse de Babylone, Les Lettres d'Amabed, Le Taureau blanc; Lettres philosophiques,* ed. F. Deloffre, Folio.

(7) Diderot, with a special study of *Le Rêve d'Alembert,* ed. Chouillet, Livre de Poche, *Jacques le fataliste,* ed. Belaval, Folio *Le Neveu de Rameau,* ed. Varloot, Folio, *Le Salon de 1765,* ed. Bukdahl and Lorenceau, Hermann.

German:

Any two of the following:

(1) Luther, with a special study of *Von der Freyheyt eyniß Christenmenschen* (http://luther.chadwyck.co.uk).

(2) Gryphius, with a special study of Gedichte, ed. Elschenbroich (Reclam). Candidates will further be expected to have studied a representative selection of Gryphius's drama.

(3) Grimmelshausen, with a special study of *Simplicissimus (Teutsch).* Candidates will further be expected to have studied others of the 'Simplizianische Schriften'.

(4) Goethe as dramatist, with a special study of *Faust,* part I. Candidates will further be expected to have studied at least three other dramatic works by Goethe.

(5) Schiller, with a special study of *Wallenstein.* Candidates will further be expected to have studied other works representative of Schiller's development as a dramatist.

(6) Hölderlin, with a special study of Friedrich Hölderlin, *Gedichte,* ed. Gerhard Kurz and Wolfgang Braungart, Reihe Reclam, the poetry 1798–1806.

(7) Kleist, with a special study of *Prinz Friedrich von Homburg.* Candidates will further be expected to have studied a representative selection of Kleist's plays and prose works.

(8) Hoffmann, with a special study of *Der Sandmann* and *Der goldne Topf.* Candidates will further be expected to have studied at least one of the novels and a representative selection of the shorter fiction.

(9) Heine, with a special study of *Atta Troll* and *Deutschland, ein Wintermärchen*. Candidates will further be expected to have studied a representative selection of Heine's poetry and prose, the latter to include the *Reisebilder*.

(10) Rilke, with a special study of *Neue Gedichte*. Candidates will further be expected to have studied a representative selection of Rilke's other writings.

(11) Thomas Mann, with a special study of *Bekenntnisse des Hochstaplers Felix Krull*. Candidates will further be expected to have studied at least one of the novels and a representative selection of the shorter fiction.

(12) Kafka, with a special study of *Der Proceß: Roman in der Fassung der Handschrift*, ed. Malcolm Pasley (Fischer Taschenbuch Verlag, No. 114123). Candidates will further be expected to have studied a representative selection of Kafka's other fiction.

(13) Brecht, with a special study of *Leben des Galilei*. Candidates will further be expected to have studied other works representative of Brecht's development as dramatist and poet.

(14) Grass, with a special study of *Die Blechtrommel*. Candidates will further be expected to have studied a representative selection of Grass's prose fiction.

(15) Christa Wolf, with a special study of *Nachdenken über Christa T.* Candidates will further be expected to have studied a representative selection of Christa Wolf's prose works.

(16) W. G. Sebald, with special study of *Austerlitz*. Candidates will further be expected to have studied a representative selection of Sebald's other works.

(17) Rainer Werner Fassbinder, with special study of the film *Katzelmacher*. Candidates will further be expected to have studied a representative selection of Fassbinder's other films and plays.

(18) Elfriede Jelinek, with special study of *Die Klavierspielerin*. Candidates will further be expected to have studied a representative selection of Jelinek's other works.

Note. The paper will contain questions of a general nature, and questions on specific texts. Candidates will not be allowed to make any one text the principal subject of more than one answer.

Italian:
Any two of the following:

(1) Petrarch, with a special study of the *Canzoniere,* Nos. 1–12; 16–24; 30; 34–7; 50–4; 60–2; 70; 72; 77; 80–1; 90–2; 102; 119; 125–6; 128–9; 132–4; 136; 142; 145; 148; 159–60; 164; 197; 211; 219; 263–4; 268; 272; 279–80; 287–92; 302–4; 310–11; 315; 327; 353; 359–60; 364–6. Candidates will further be expected to have studied a representative selection of Petrarch's other Italian poems and of works originally written in Latin.

(2) Boccaccio, with a special study of the *Decameron,* I. 1–3; II, 2, 5, 10; III, 2; IV, 1, 2, 5, 7, 9; V, 6, 8, 9; VI, 1, 9, 10; VII, 4, 9; VIII, 3, 8; IX, 1, 2; X, 2, 9, 10. Candidates will further be expected to have studied a representative selection of other parts of the *Decameron* and of other works by Boccaccio.

(3) Machiavelli, with a special study of *Il Principe*. Candidates will further be expected to have studied a representative selection of Machiavelli's other works, including *I discorsi* and *La mandragola*.

(4) Ariosto, with a special study of *Orlando Furioso,* cantos I–XIII.45; XVIII.146–XXIV; XXVIII–XXX; XXXIV; XLV–XLVI. Candidates will further be expected to have studied other parts of the *Orlando Furioso* and a selection of the *Satire*.

(5) Tasso, with a special study of *Gerusalemme Liberata*, cantos I–VII, XI–XVI; XIX–XX, and *Aminta*. Candidates will further be expected to have studied other parts of the *Gerusalemme Liberata*.

Spanish:
Any two of the following: 5
   (1) Garcilaso de la Vega, *Obra poética y textos en prosa* (ed. B. Morros, Crítica) (not including the Latin poetry and the prose texts).
   (2) Cervantes, with a special study of *El ingenioso hidalgo don Quijote de la Mancha.* (Passages for commentary will be set from the Second Part only.)
   (3) Góngora, with a special study of *Soledad primera* (from *Soledades*, ed. R.   10 Jammes, Castalia), *Fábula de Polifemo y Galatea* (ed. J. Ponce Cárdenas, Cátedra), *Sonnets* (in *Poems of Góngora*, ed. R. O. Jones, pp. 87–92). Candidates will be expected to have read *Soledad segunda*, but passages for commentary will not be set from it.
   (4) Quevedo, with a special study of 'Infierno', 'El mundo por de dentro', 'Sueño de   15 la muerte', in *Sueños y discursos* (ed. J. O. Crosby, Castalia); *La cuna y la sepultura*, and *España defendida* (Preliminaries and Chapter 5 only), in *Obras completas, I: Prosa* (ed. F. Buendía, Aguilar); *Poesía varia* (ed. J. O. Crosby, Cátedra), nos. 16–30, 35–53, 71–83, 87–106, 128–33, 160–1; *El buscón* (ed. D. Ynduráin, Cátedra).   20
   (5) Calderón, with a special study of *La vida es sueño* (ed. C. Morón, Cátedra) (candidates will be expected to have read the *auto* of the same name, but passages for commentary will be not be set from it). *El pintor de su deshonra* (ed. Ruiz Lagos, Colección Aula Magna), *El mágico prodigioso*, and *El Alcalde de Zalamea* (both Clásicos castellanos), *El gran teatro del mundo* (ed. B. W.   25 Wardropper, Cátedra), *El alcalde de Zalamea* (ed. J. Ma. Díez Borque, Castalia), and *El gran teatro del mundo* (ed. E. Frutos Cortés, Cátedra).

Portuguese:
Any two of the following:
   (1) Gil Vicente, with a special study of *Auto da Alma, Auto da Feira, Farsa de Inês*   30 *Pereira, Farsa dos Almocreves, O Triunfo do Inverno, Dom Duardos.*
   (2) João de Barros, with a special study of *Rópica Pnefma* (ed. I. S. Révah, Lisbon, 1955) and *Décadas*, vol. I (ed. A. Baião, Sá da Costa, Lisbon, 1945).
   (3) Camões, with a special study of *Os Lusíadas* (ed. F. Pierce) and *Líricas* (ed. Rodrigues Lapa, 1970 or later).   35
   (4) Francisco Manuel de Melo, with a special study of *Epanáfora política, Relógiosfalantes, Hospital das Letras, Carta de Guia de Casados, O Fidalgo Aprendiz.*
   (5) António Ferreira, *Bristo, Cioso, Poemas Lusitanos* (including *A Castro*).

Russian: 40
Any two of the following:
   (1) Pushkin, with a special study of *Tsygany, Evgeny Onegin, Povesti Belkina,* Selected lyrics (copies of the list of prescribed poems are available from the Slavonic Library, 47 Wellington Square).
   (2) Gogol, with a special study of *Mirgorod,* (excluding *Taras Bul'ba*) *Shinel',*   45 *Zapiski sumasshedshego, Nevsky Prospekt, Portret, Nos, Mertvye dushi* Part I, *Revizor.*
   (3) Mandel'shtam. Selected lyrics (copies of the prescribed poems are available from the Slavonic Library, 47 Wellington Square). Candidates will also be

expected to have read a representative selection of Mandel'shtam's artistic prose and articles on literary topics.

(4) Mayakovsky, with a special study of *Oblako v shtanakh, Pro eto, Lyublyu, Klop,* and selected lyrics (copies of the prescribed poems are available from the Slavonic Library, 47 Wellington Square). Candidates will also be expected to have read *Kak delat' stikhi* and a representative selection of Mayakovsky's other works.

(5) Bulgakov, with a special study of *Beelaya gvardiya, Sobach'e serdtse, Beg, Master i Margarita.*

Medieval and Modern Greek:
Any two of the following:
  (1) *Digenis Akritis: the Grottaferrata and Escorial Versions* (ed. E. M. Jeffreys).
  (2) The vernacular verse romances.
  (3) Cretan drama, with a special study of Chortatsis' *Erophile, Katzourbos,* and *Panoria* (ed. R. Bancroft-Marcus).
  (4) *Erotokritos.*
  (5) Greek oral poetry.

Czech (with Slovak):
Any three of the following:
  (1) Comenius, with a special study of *Labyrint světa a ráj srdce.*
  (2) Hrabal, with a special study of *Obsluhoval jsem anglického krále.*
  (3) Hodrová, with a special study of *Podobojí.*
  (4) Holan, with a special study of *Terezka Planetová.*
  (5) Johanides, with a special study of *Marek koniar a uhorský pápež.*
  (6) Mitana, with a special study of the volume *Prievan.*
Candidates will be required to answer questions on each of their three authors, including one commentary.

Celtic:
Any two of the following:
  (1) *Gwaith Guto'r Glyn,* ed. I. Williams and J. Llywelyn Williams (Cardiff, 1939).
  (2) *Gwaith Tudur Aled,* ed. T. Gwynn Jones (Cardiff, 1926).
  (3) *Gwaith Iorwerth Fynglwyd,* ed. H. Ll. Jones and E. I. Rowlands (Cardiff, 1973).
  (4) *Gramadegau'r Penceirddiaid,* ed. G. J. Williams and E. J. Jones (Cardiff, 1934), Texts A and C (pp. 1–18, 39–58).
  (5) *Acallam na Senórach* (in the selection ed. M. Dillon, *Stories from the Acallam* [Dublin, 1970]).
  (6) *Caithréim Cellaig,* ed. K. Mulchrone, 2nd edn. (Dublin, 1971).
  (7) *Buile Shuibne,* ed. J. G. O'Keefe (Dublin, 1931).
  (8) *Tóruigheacht Dhiarmada agus Ghráinne,* ed. N. Ní Sheaghdha, Irish Texts Society 48 (Dublin, 1967).
  (9) *Dánta Grádha,* ed. T. F. O'Rahilly, 2nd edn. (Cork: Cork University Press, 1926).

[1]**XI. Early Modern Literary Texts** *or* **Goethe (*German only*) or**
[1]**Modern Prescribed Authors (ii):**

Passages for explanation and comment will be taken from the works prescribed for special study. Candidates will be expected to have read works by their chosen authors other than those prescribed for special study.   5

French:
Any two of the following:
   (1) Stendhal, with a special study of *Le Rouge et le Noir* and *La Chartreuse de Parme.*

   (2) Baudelaire, with a special study of *Les Fleurs du Mal* and the *Petits Poèmes en*   10
   prose.

   (3) Flaubert, with a special study of *Madame Bovary, Trois Contes,* and
   L'Éducation sentimentale.

   (4) Mallarmé, with a special study of *Poésies* (edition Deman), ed. Bertrand
   Marchal (Gallimard, Collection Poésie, 1992, pp. 1–74), and *Igitur,*   15
   Divagations, Un coup de dés, ed. Bertrand Marchal (Gallimard, Collection
   Poésie, 2003), omitting *Igitur, Quelques médaillons et portraits en pied* and
   Pages diverses.

   (5) Gide, with a special study of *L'Immoraliste, La Porte étroite, Si le grain ne*
   meurt, and *Les Faux-Monnayeurs.*   20

   (6) Sartre, with a special study of *La Nausée, Les Mouches, Les Séquestrés*
   d'Altona, and *Les Mots.*

   (7) Duras, with a special study of *Un barrage contre le Pacifique, Le Ravissement de*
   Lol V. Stein, L'Amant, and *Hiroshima, mon amour* (film script).

   (8) Barthes, with a special study of *L'Empire des signes, Le Plaisir du texte, Roland*   25
   Barthes par Roland Barthes, and *La Chambre claire.*

German:
Either A : Early Modern Literary Texts
Any four out of the following six topics:
   (1) Luther: *Von der Freyheyt eyniβ Christenmenschen* and *Von weltlicher Obrigkeit*   30
   (http://luther.chadwyck.co.uk).

   (2) Reformation controversy: Hans Sachs, *Die Wittenbergisch Nachtigall* (Reclam
   edition), and Caritas Pirckheimer, *Denkwürdigkeiten* (http://sophie.byu.edu).

   (3) Religious poetry: Andreas Gryphius, *Gedichte* (Reclam edition) and Catharina
   Regina von Greiffenberg, *Gedichte* (www.wortblume.de).   35

   (4) Secular poetry: Paul Fleming, *Gedichte* (Reclam edition) and Sybille Schwarz,
   Gedichte (www.wortblume.de).

   (5) The novel: *Historia von D. Johann Fausten* (Reclam edition) and
   Grimmelshausen: *Courasche* (Reclam edition).

   (6) Baroque tragedy: Daniel Casper von Lohenstein, *Cleopatra* (Reclam edition)   40
   and *Sophonisbe* (Reclam edition).

Note. This paper will require candidates to attempt a commentary and two essay questions.

---

[1] Each paper will be divided into two sections, one containing questions on the general aspects of the books and authors, and the other containing passages for explanation and comment. Both sections will be compulsory.

Or B: Goethe. Candidates will be required to read a selection of Goethe's works in more than one genre. Candidates for this paper may not offer Goethe as dramatist as one of their authors on Paper X.

Italian:
Any two of the following: 5
 (1) Manzoni, with a special study of *I promessi sposi*. Candidates will further be expected to have studied Manzoni's tragedies and a selection of his other works.

 (2) Leopardi, with a special study of *I Canti*. Candidates will further be expected to have studied the *Operette morali* and a selection of Leopardi's other writings.

 (3) D'Annunzio, with a special study of *Alcyone*. Candidates will further be   10
expected to have studied a selection of D'Annunzio's other works in verse and prose.

 (4) Verga, with a special study of *I Malavoglia* and *Mastro-don Gesualdo*. Candidates will further be expected to have studied a selection of Verga's other fiction.   15

 (5) Pirandello, with a special study of *Il fu Mattia Pascal, Sei personaggi in cerca d'autore*, and *I giganti della montagna*. Candidates will further be expected to have studied a representative selection of Pirandello's drama and prose work.

 (6) Montale, with a special study of 'Ossi di seppia' in *Ossi di seppia*, Section IV of *Le occasioni*, 'Finisterre' in *La bufera e altro* and 'Xenia I' in *Satura*.   20
Candidates will further be expected to have studied a representative selection of Montale's other poems.

 (7) Calvino, with a special study of *Il cavaliere inesistente* and *Se una notte d'inverno un viaggiatore*. Candidates will further be expected to have studied other works representative of Calvino's development as a writer.   25

Spanish:
Any two of the following:
 (1) Pérez Galdós, with a special study of *Juan Martín el Empecinado, El amigo Manso, Miau, Nazarín*. Candidates will further be expected to have studied other works representative of Galdós's development as a writer.   30

 (2) Leopoldo Alas, with a special study of *La Regenta* (ed. Gonzalo Sobejano, Clásicos Castalia), and *Cuentos escogidos* (ed. G. G. Brown, Oxford, 1964).

 (3) Valle-Inclán, with a special study of *Sonatas*; *Divinas palabras*; *Tirano Bandera; Los cuernos de don Friolera* (ed. A. Zamora Vicente, Clásicos castellanos).

 (4) Federico García Lorca, with a special study of *Bodas de sangre, Mariana*   35
Pineda, Poeta en Nueva York (ed. Millán), *El público,* (ed. C. Millán). Candidates will further be expected to have studied other works representative of Lorca's development as a writer.

 (5) Neruda, with a special study of *Veinte poemas de amor y una canción desesper-*
ada (ed. Montes, Clásicos Castalia, Madrid, 1987); *Canto general* (I, II, XIV,   40
XV); *Memorial de Isla Negra* (I, IV) (Seix Barral, Barcelona, 1976); *Pablo Neruda : A Basic Anthology* (ed. Pring-Mill, Dolphin, Oxford, 1975), pp. 8–42 and 80–109, and those poems included in the *Basic Anthology* from the following collections: *Estravagario, Plenos poderes, Jardín de invierno*, and *El mar y las campanas*.   45

 (6) Borges, with a special study of *Ficciones* (ed. either Emecé or Alianza-Emecé); *El aleph*; *El informe de Brodie*; *Obra poética 1923–1976* (ed. Alianza-Emecé, sections entitled *El hacedor* and *El otro, el mismo*).

 (7) Julio Cortázar, with a special study of Bestiario, 'El perseguidor', Rayuela and Todos los fuegos el fuego.   50

(8) Gabriel García Márquez, with a special study of El coronel no tiene quien le escriba and Cien años de soledad.

Portuguese:
Any two of the following:

(1) Almeida Garrett, with a special study of *Frei Luís de Sousa, O Arco de Sant'*   5
Ana, Viagens na Minha Terra, Folhas Caídas.

(2) Eça de Queirós, with a special study of *O Crime do Padre Amaro, Os Maias,* and *A Cidade e as Serras.*

(3) Machado de Assis, with a special study of *Memórias póstumas de Brás Cubas, Dom Casmurro,* and *Quincas Borba.*   10

(4) Fernando Pessoa, with a special study of *Obras completas,* vol. I (Ática) *Mensagem and Poesia de Alvaro de Campos.*

(5) Graciliano Ramos, with a special study of *Caetés.*

(6) Clarice Lispector, with a special study of *Perto do Coração Selvagem, A Paixão segundo G. H., A Hora da Estrela.*   15

(7) Mia Couto, with special study of *Vozes anoitecidas, Terra sonâmbula, A varanda do frangipani.*

(8) Pepetela, with special reference to Yaka, Predadores, and A Gloriosa Famlia.

Russian:
Any two of the following: 20

(1) Dostoevsky, with a special study of *Prestuplenie i nakazanie, Brat'ya Karamazovy, Zapiski iz podpol'ya.*

(2) Tolstoy, with a special study of *Anna Karenina, Voyna i mir.*

(3) Chekhov, with a special study of *Palata No. 6, Poprygun'ya, Moya zhizn, Muzhiki, Dama s sobachkoy, V ovrage, Dushechka, Arkkhierey,* and *Nevesta,*   25
as well as *Chayka, Dyadya Vanya, Tri sestry, Vishnevi sad.*

(4) Solzhenitsyn, with a special study of *Odin den' Ivana Denisovicha, V kruge pervom* (candidates are expected to be familiar with the 96-chapter version of the novel first published in 1978), *Rakovy korpus.*

(5) Nabokov, with a special study of *Otchayanie, Priglashenie na kazn', Dar.*   30

Medieval and Modern Greek:
Any two of the following:

(1) Solomos, with a special study of the poems composed between 1825 and 1849 (*Apanta,* ed. L. Politis (Athens, 1961), pp. 139–255), the *Dialogos,* and the *Gynaika tes Zakythos.*   35

(2) Palamas, with a special study of *O dodekalogos tou Gyftou, Oi khairetismoi tes Eliogennetes* and the following sections of *E asalefte zoe*: *Patrides, Foinikia, Askraios, Alysides.*

(3) Kavafis, with a special study of *Poiemata,* vols. i and ii, ed. G. P. Savidis (Ikaros, Athens, 1963, or later).   40

(4) Seferis, with a special study of *Poiemata* (Athens, 1972, or later).

(5) Tsirkas, with a special study of the trilogy *Akyvernetes politeies (E leskhe, Ariagne,* and *E nykhterida).*

(6) The novels of Kazantzakis, with a special study of *Vios kai politeia tou Alexe Zorba* and *O Khristos xanastavronetai.*   45

(7) Melipoiemene Poiese, with special study of Nikos Gatsos, *Amorgos* and *Collected Versus* (Ikaros); Dionysis Savvopoulos, *He Souma* (Ianos, 2004).

XII. Special Subjects.

1. A candidate may offer one or two (depending on the regulations outlined above) of the Special Subjects from the list circulated in the Trinity Term one year before the examination. The list of options available in that year will be publicised on the Faculty's internal website (and circulated to all students and tutors by e-mail) by the   5
beginning of fifth week of Trinity Term.

Methods of assessment:

The method of assessment for each subject will be published with the list of options by the beginning of the fifth week of the Trinity Term one year before the examination, according to the following key: 10

A: Three-hour unseen written paper.

B: An essay or portfolio of essays (the number of essays required to be shown in parentheses) aggregating to about 6,000 words and not exceeding 8,000 words, to be submitted by hand to the Examinations Schools, High Street, Oxford by noon on the Friday of the ninth week of Hilary Term in the year of the   15
examination, together with a statement certifying that the essay(s) are the candidate's own work and that they have not already been submitted, either wholly or substantially, for a degree in this university or elsewhere.

C: An essay or portfolio of essays (the number of essays required to be shown in parentheses) aggregating to about 6,000 words and not exceeding 8,000 words   20
(except that the Linguistic Project shall be in the range 8,000–10,000 words), written as answers to an examination paper to be downloaded from the Faculty WebLearn website after 10am on the Friday of the fifth week of the Hilary Term next before the examination. Completed essay(s) should be submitted by hand to the Examinations Schools by noon on the Monday of tenth week of   25
Hilary Term in the year of the examination, together with a statement certifying that the essays are the candidate's own work and that they have not already been submitted, either wholly or substantially, for a degree in this university or elsewhere.

2. Candidates may not be permitted to offer certain Special Subjects in combina-   30
tion with certain other papers. Candidates offering a Special Subject and another paper both of which involve the study of the same author or authors, may not make the same texts the principal subject of an answer in both the papers.

3. Instead of a Special Subject from the list for the year concerned, a candidate may follow the directions under **Section 3. Paper XII. Special Subjects**.   35

XIII. General Linguistics.

Candidates will be required to show knowledge of analytic techniques and problems in contemporary syntax and semantic theory, phonetics, and phonology, and their relation to issues of linguistic variation, language acquisition, and language change.

XIV. Extended Essay (*optional*).   40

1. Candidates may offer an Extended Essay, subject to the following provisions:

(i) The subject of every essay shall, to the satisfaction of the board of the faculty, fall within the scope of the Honour School of Modern Languages.

(ii) The subject of an essay may, but need not, overlap any subject or period on which the candidate offers a paper, but candidates should avoid repetition of   45
material presented in the extended essay in other parts of the examination. Candidates should not offer a title involving the reading of works only or mainly in translation from the original.

(iii) Candidates are prohibited from making the same *text or texts* the principal subject of their Special Subject or Extended Essay and of an answer or essay in papers VI-XI but they are *not* prohibited from making an *author* the focus of their Special Subject or Extended Essay on whom they also intend to write in another part of the examination, as long as they make use of different texts and have due regard to the need to avoid repetition of the same material.

(iv) Candidates proposing to offer an essay must submit, through their college, to the Chair of the Board of the Faculty of Medieval and Modern Languages (on a form obtainable from the Modern Languages Administration and Faculty Office, 41 Wellington Square,) a statement of their name, college, the honour school they intend to offer, the academic year in which they intend to take the examination, and the title of the proposed essay together with (*a*) a statement in about fifty words of how the subject is to be treated, (*b*) a statement signed by a supervisor or tutor, preferably in the language or in one of the languages or in the field of study with which the extended essay is concerned, that he or she considers the subject suitable, and suggesting a person or persons who might be invited to be an examiner or an assessor (the board will not approve a title unless it is satisfied that a suitably qualified examiner or assessor based in Oxford will be available), and (*c*) a statement by a college tutor that he or she approves the candidate's application, not later than the Wednesday of the second week of the Michaelmas Full Term preceding the examination.

(v) Subject to the agreement of the faculty board, candidates may offer an essay written in the language or one of the languages they are offering in the Honour School; application, with a letter of support from a college tutor, should be made at the same time as the proposed title of the essay is submitted for approval. (*This provision is not available in the case of Russian*).

(vi) The faculty board will decide by the end of the third week of the Michaelmas Full Term preceding the examination whether the candidate has permission to offer an essay. Permission may be granted on the condition that the candidate agrees to amend details of the title to the satisfaction of the board, and submits the required amendments to the Administration and Faculty Office for the board's approval by Friday of the sixth week of the Michaelmas Full Term preceding the examination. If the proposed title is approved, this will be notified by the Administration and Faculty Office, together with any conditions attached to the approval, to the candidate and to the Chair of the Examiners for the Honour School.

(vii) A candidate may seek approval after Friday of the sixth week of the Michaelmas Full Term preceding the examination for an amendment of detail in an approved title, by application to the Administration and Faculty Office. The Chair of the Examiners and the Chair of the Board, acting together, will decide whether or not a proposed amendment shall be approved.

2. Every essay must be the candidate's own work. Tutors may, however, discuss with candidates the proposed field of study, the sources available, and the method of presentation. Tutors may also read and comment on a first draft.

All quotations, whether direct or indirect, from primary or secondary sources must be explicitly acknowledged. The use of unacknowledged quotations will be penalized.

Candidates must sign a certificate stating that the essay is their own work and this certificate must be sent at the same time as the essay, but under separate cover, addressed to: The Chair of the Examiners, Honour School of Modern Languages, Examination Schools, High Street, Oxford.

3. Essays previously submitted for the Honour School of Modern Languages may be resubmitted. No essay will be accepted if it has already been submitted, wholly or substantially, for another Honour School or degree of this University or a degree of any other institute. The certificate must contain a confirmation that the essay has not already been so submitted. 5

4. No essay shall be ineligible because it has been submitted, in whole or in part, for any scholarship or prize in this university.

5. Candidates shall present a one-page summary of the arguments in English at the beginning of their essay; essays shall be in the range 6,000–8,000 words (exclusive of the footnotes, the bibliography, any appendices, and summary (where this applies)). 10 No person or body shall have authority to permit the limit of 8,000 words to be exceeded, except that, in the case of a commentary on a text, and at the discretion of the chair of the examiners, any substantial quoting of that text need not be included in the word limit. The examiners will not take account of such parts of an essay as are beyond these limits. There must be a select bibliography, listing all primary and 15 secondary sources consulted when writing the essay, and full details must be given of all citations (either in the text, or in footnotes).

All essays must be typed in double-spacing on one side only of A4 paper, and must be bound or held firmly in a stiff cover. Two copies must be submitted to the chair of the examiners, and a third copy must be retained by the candidate. 20

6. The two copies of the essay must be sent, not later than noon on the **[For students starting before MT 2015:** first Friday after the Hilary Full Term**] [For students starting from MT 2015:** Monday of tenth week of Hilary Term**]** of the year in which the examination will be held, to: The Chair of the Examiners, Honour School of Modern Languages, Examination Schools, High Street, Oxford. 25

HONOUR SCHOOL OF MOLECULAR AND CELLULAR BIOCHEMISTRY

A

1. The subject of the Honour School of Molecular and Cellular Biochemistry shall be the study of Molecular and Cellular aspects of the structure and behaviour of biological molecules.

2. No candidate shall be admitted to examination in this school unless he or she has either passed or been exempted from the First Public Examination.

3. The examination in this school shall be under the supervision of the Medical Sciences Board, which shall prescribe the necessary regulations.

4. The examination in Molecular and Cellular Biochemistry shall consist of two parts: Part I and Part II.

5. No candidate may present him or herself for examination in Part II unless he or she has been adjudged worthy of Honours by the examiners in Part I.

6. A candidate will not be classified for Honours until he or she has completed all parts of the examination and has been adjudged worthy of Honours by the examiners in Part I and Part II of the examination in consecutive years. The examiners shall give due consideration to the performance in all parts of the respective examinations.

7. A candidate who obtains only a pass, or fails to satisfy the examiners, may enter again for Part I of the examination on one, but no more than one, subsequent occasion. Part II shall be entered on one occasion only.

8. A candidate adjudged worthy of Honours in Part I and Part II may supplicate for the Degree of Master of Biochemistry, provided he or she has fulfilled all the conditions for admission to a degree of the University.

9. A candidate who passes Part I or who is adjudged worthy of Honours in Part I of the examination, but who does not enter Part II of the examination, or who fails to obtain honours in Part II, may be allowed to supplicate for the degree of Bachelor of Arts (pass or unclassified Honours as appropriate), provided he or she has fulfilled all the conditions for admission to a degree of the University; but such a candidate may not later enter or re-enter Part II or supplicate for the degree of Master of Biochemistry.

10. Candidates will be expected to show knowledge based on practical work. The examination shall be partly practical: this requirement shall normally be satisfied by the examiners' assessment of the practical work done by candidates during their course of study.

B

1. The examiners will permit the use of any hand-held calculator subject to the conditions set out under the heading 'Use of calculators in examinations' in the *Regulations for the Conduct of University Examinations.*

2. *Supplementary Subjects*

(a) Candidates may, in addition to any one or more of the below-mentioned subjects, offer themselves for examination in one or more Supplementary Subjects.

(*b*) Candidates for Supplementary Subjects may offer themselves for examination in the academic year preceding that in which they take the Final Honour School; they may also offer themselves for examination in the year in which they take the Final Honour School, Part I or Part II. No more than one Supplementary Subject may be offered in any one year. 5

(*c*) The Supplementary Subjects available in any year will be published, together with the term in which each subject will be examined, in the *University Gazette* not later than the end of the Trinity Term of the academic year prior to delivery of the courses. Regulations governing the use of calculators in individual Supplementary Subjects will be notified when the availability of these subjects 10 is published in the *Gazette*.

(*d*) In determining the place of candidates in the Class List the examiners shall take account of good performance in any Supplementary Subjects which have been offered.

(*e*) Candidates awarded a pass in a Supplementary Subject examination may not 15 retake the same Supplementary Subject examination.

Part I

Six written papers will be set:
Paper I Structure and Function of Macromolecules;
Paper II Energetics and Metabolic Processes; 20
Paper III Genetics and Molecular Biology;
Paper IV Cell Biology and the Integration of Function;
Paper V General Paper;
Paper VI Data Analysis and Interpretation.

Candidates will be required to show knowledge of the fundamental biochemistry of 25 animals, plants, and micro-organisms. This will include the chemical and physical basis of the subject, its relevance to living systems; structure, function, and metabolism of viruses, cells and subcellular components, organs and organisms; biochemical aspects of nutrition, differentiation, genetics, absorption, secretion, biosynthesis, and maintenance of a dynamic state. In the general paper, candidates will be expected to 30 bring together a knowledge of these disparate areas of Biochemistry. The data analysis and interpretation paper will consist of questions designed to examine candidates' skills in data handling and the interpretation of experimental data; relevant tables and formulae will be supplied.

Except with the express permission of the Head of the Department of Biochemistry, 35 no one shall be admitted to the Final Honour School of Molecular and Cellular Biochemistry course of practical work and exercises in biochemical reasoning who has not passed, or been exempted from, the First Public Examination.

The Director of Teaching, or a deputy, shall make available to the examiners records showing the extent to which each candidate has adequately pursued a course 40 of laboratory work and exercises in biochemical reasoning. In assessing the record of practical work and exercises in data handling, the examiners shall have regard to the attendance record of the candidates at each and every class provided, and to the marks recorded for each and every class provided. Candidates whose overall performance in either the written papers or in practical work and data handling is judged by the 45 examiners to be insufficient to warrant the award of Honours may either be deemed to have failed the examination, or may be awarded a Pass. Candidates in either category will not be allowed to proceed to Part II. The examiners will issue a list of candidates who are allowed to proceed to Part II.

If requested by the examiners, candidates shall submit notebooks containing reports, initialled by the demonstrators, of practical work and exercises in biochemical reasoning completed during their course of study for Part I. These notebooks shall be available to the examiners at any time after the end of the first week of the term in which the examination is held. Each notebook shall be accompanied by a certificate   5
signed by the candidate indicating that the notebook submitted is the candidate's own work.

Candidates may be examined viva voce.

Part II

Part II will consist of project work and assessments based on two options. Each   10
candidate may be examined viva voce on the Part II examination.

Candidates will be required to pursue their investigations during a period of twenty-eight weeks including an extended Michaelmas Term which will begin on the fourth Friday before the stated Full Term and extend until the first Saturday following it, provided that the divisional board shall have power to permit candidates to vary the   15
dates of their residence so long as the overall requirement is met.

Project work: The project will normally be carried out in the extended Michaelmas Term plus the first six weeks in Hilary Term.

Candidates will be required to undertake project work under the supervision of a person approved by the Biochemistry Steering Committee provided that such approval   20
shall be applied for not later than Friday in the second week of Trinity Full Term in the year preceding the Part II examination.

Candidates will be required to present an account of such work in the form of a dissertation (not more than 8,000 words excluding tables, figures, reference list and abstract). Dissertations (two copies) must be legibly typed on one side only of A4   25
paper and must be held in a stiff cover. An electronic copy (ideally on CD) including this, and only this material, should also be provided. Each dissertation must begin with an abstract of not more than 300 words, which should include a brief statement of the aims of the project and a summary of its important findings. The two typed copies, and the electronic copy, of the dissertation must be submitted by noon on Friday of   30
the first week of the Trinity Full Term of the examination, addressed to the Chair of Examiners in the Final Honour School of Molecular and Cellular Biochemistry, Part II, c/o the Examination Schools, High Street, Oxford. Each candidate must submit, together with his or her project, a statement to the effect that the project is the candidate's own work or indicating where the work of others has been used, save   35
that supervisors should give advice on the choice and scope of the project, provide a reading list, and comment on the first draft. This statement must be submitted at the same time as the project in a sealed envelope addressed to the Chair of Examiners. Each project, and the envelope containing the statement, must be clearly labelled with the candidate's number. The name and college of the candidate must not appear on   40
the project or on the envelope. The examiners may obtain a written report on the work of each candidate from the supervisor concerned.

Candidates will be required to present a brief oral report of their research project in the first half of Trinity Full Term, after which the candidate shall be examined viva voce on the project. The form of the presentation to examiners shall be specified in   45
guidelines published by the Department of Biochemistry in Week 8 of Trinity Full Term in the academic year preceding the examination.

No dissertation will be accepted if it has already been submitted, either wholly or substantially, for an Honour School other than Molecular and Cellular Biochemistry, or for another degree of this University, or for a degree of any other institution.   50

Options: Each candidate will undertake and be assessed in two areas of Biochemistry, each selected from options approved by the Biochemistry Steering

Committee, and published by the Department of Biochemistry. Two lists, each consisting of three options, will be published and one option must be chosen from each list. The lists of options will be posted in the Department of Biochemistry and sent to Senior Tutors of all colleges not later than noon on Friday of the eighth week of Trinity Term in the year preceding that in which the examination is taken.

The form of assessment for each option will consist of at least one, and at most two, of the following:

A. an unseen written paper.

B. an oral assessment in the second half of Trinity Full Term, involving a presentation and/or questions.

C. a submitted assignment, based on course work undertaken during the option.

D. an essay, selected from a list of titles provided.

Assessment method B will not be used in isolation; it will always be combined with one of assessment methods A, C or D.

The form of assessment for each Part II option offered in an academic year will be published not later than noon on Friday of the eighth week of Trinity Term in the year preceding that in which the examination is taken, including the duration of unseen written papers and the required length of submitted work. The detailed specifications for each assessment method will be published not later than noon on Friday of the eighth week of Michaelmas Term in the year of the examination. Both the form and the detailed specifications for the assessment of options will have been approved by the Biochemistry Steering Committee, prior to publication by the Department of Biochemistry.

For assessment methods C and D, two hard copies and one electronic copy (ideally on CD) of the work are to be submitted to the Chair of Examiners, Honour School of Molecular and Cellular Biochemistry, Part II, c/o the Examinations Schools, High Street, Oxford by noon on Friday of the seventh week of Trinity Full Term in the year of the examination, together with a statement certifying that the work is the candidate's own work or indicating where the work of others has been used. No work will be accepted if it has already been submitted, either wholly or substantially, for an Honour School other than Molecular and Cellular Biochemistry, or for another degree of this University, or for a degree of any other institution.

HONOUR SCHOOL OF MUSIC

A

1. The subject of the Honour School of Music shall be the study of the history, criticism, theory, composition, performance, and practice of music.

2. No candidate shall be admitted to examination in this school, unless he has   5
either passed or been exempted from the First Public Examination.

3. The examination in this faculty shall be under the supervision of the Board of the Faculty of Music which shall make regulations concerning it subject always to the preceding clauses of this subsection.

B   10

Each candidate will be required to offer papers (1) and (2) from List A, any two of papers (3), (4), and (5) in that list, and four other papers, always provided that of these four at least one is from List B, one is from List C, one is from either List B or C, and one is from List B, C, or D. Candidates may always offer both List A (3) and B (1); but certain other combinations of papers may from time to time be disallowed, always   15
provided that notice of such disallowance be communicated to candidates not later than the third week of Michaelmas Full Term in the academic year preceding that of examination.

Candidates must indicate, not later than Friday of the fourth week of Michaelmas Full Term in the academic year of examination, of the eight papers they propose to offer.   20

Candidates may also be examined viva voce.

List A (core subjects)

(1) Topics in Music History before 1750 (one three-hour paper)

(2) Topics in Music after 1700 (one three-hour paper)

The Board of the Faculty of Music shall approve, and publish each year by notice in   25
the Faculty of Music, not later than the eighth week of Trinity Full Term, a list of specified areas of study in (1) and (2) above for the examination six terms thence.

(3) **Either** *Techniques of Composition I* (one three-hour paper)

Candidates will be required to complete or continue in the appropriate style a piece of music from which at least one part will be given. One question must be answered   30
from four set as follows:

    (*a*) later sixteenth-century continental vocal polyphony in four parts;

    (*b*) aria in three parts (voice, obbligato instrument, and basso continuo) from the period *c.* 1700–*c.* 1760;

    (*c*) four-part texture, of the period *c.* 1760–*c.* 1830;   35

    (*d*) nineteenth-century song accompaniment for piano, in the Austro-Germanic tradition.

Or *Techniques of Composition II* (portfolio submission): see under List B (1)

(4) *Musical Analysis and Criticism* (one three-hour paper)

Analytical and critical comment on one musical work (or movement of a work),   40
normally from the late eighteenth or nineteenth century. The score will be provided but the music will not be heard in performance.

(5) *Musical Thought and Scholarship* (one three-hour paper)

A paper on the history, criticism, and philosophy of music. Candidates may choose to answer either one or two questions.

Lists B, C, and D (optional subjects)
List B (Portfolio and performance options)

(1) *Techniques of Composition II* (portfolio submission)

Candidates will be required to write, at their choice and on material set by the examiners in the eighth week of Hilary Full Term in the academic year of examination, one of the following:

(*a*) a fugue;

(*b*) a sixteenth-century motet or Mass movement in five parts;

(*c*) an eighteenth-century (Baroque style) aria or other ritornello-based movement;

(*d*) a sonata movement (not necessarily the first) from the period from Haydn to Brahms;

(*e*) a movement in a twentieth-century idiom (questions requiring familiarity with indeterminate or electronic techniques will not be set);

(*f*) such other form of music as the examiners may offer,

provided that the examiners shall always offer material on each of (*a*)–(*e*).

Papers will be available for collection in the Music Faculty Library from 12 noon on Tuesday in the eighth week of Hilary Full Term in the academic year of examination. Two copies of the portfolio, accompanied by a form of declaration must be submitted by candidates not later than noon on Friday of the first week of Trinity Full Term in the academic year of examination, to the Chair of the Examiners, Honour School of Music, Examination Schools, High Street, Oxford.

This option may not be selected under List B(1) if it has already been selected under list A(3).

(2) *Orchestration* (portfolio submission)

Candidates will be required to submit two copies of a piece of orchestration, the style and technique of the orchestration being appropriate to the material set. A choice of pieces, taken from the period 1750 to the present day, will be set. Papers will be available for collection in the Music Faculty Library from 12 noon on Tuesday in the seventh week of Hilary Full Term in the academic year of examination. The copies, accompanied by a form of declaration must be submitted by candidates not later than noon on Friday of the third week of Trinity Full Term in the academic year of examination, to the Chair of the Examiners, Honour School of Music, Examination Schools, High Street, Oxford.

(3) *Solo Performance, instrumental or vocal* (practical test)

Candidates shall prepare a programme of works in varying styles and submit it for the approval of the examiners, not later than Friday in the fourth week of Hilary Full Term in the academic year of examination, addressed to the Chair of the Examiners, Honour School of Music, Faculty of Music, St Aldate's. They may indicate a single work or a complete movement which they would like to play in full. The time each piece takes to play must be stated. The programme shall be timed to last between 35–40 minutes, including breaks and pauses. If the programme significantly exceeds 40 minutes the examiners are entitled to curtail or interrupt the performance. Candidates must provide for accompaniment, where required.

Candidates may offer self-accompanied vocal performance, which will be judged on both the singing and playing elements. They may not, however, propose a programme on more than one instrument in turn (such as violin and cello), other than such as might occur in the context of normal recital convention. Any candidate contemplating such a proposal should seek early advice from the Chair of the Faculty Board, whose decision on behalf of the Board will be final.

Candidates are required to provide for the examiners two copies of each piece to be performed, in the edition used. The copies shall be presented to the examiners at the beginning of the examination and collected from them at the end.

(4) *Composition* (portfolio submission)

Candidates will be required to submit two copies of a portfolio of four original compositions as follows:

(*a*) one work (or set of pieces) of approximately 5 minutes duration for one of the following mediums:

    (i) solo piano;

    (ii) solo instrument and piano;

(*b*) and three of the following options (the three pieces to make up a minimum duration of 24 minutes):

    (i) a work of 6–10 minutes duration for orchestra;

    (ii) a work of 6–10 minutes duration for mixed ensemble of between five and fourteen players;

    (iii) a work of 6–10 minutes duration for string quartet;

    (iv) a work of 6–10 minutes duration for SATB chorus in up to eight parts;

    (v) an electroacoustic composition of no more than 6 minutes, submitted alongside the source materials upon which the work is based;

    (vi) a work of the candidate's choice.

Each of these categories may be scored with amplification, live electronics or with an electroacoustic backing track.

Candidates intending to use the electronic studio in connection with this option are required to have attended the preliminary courses offered to undergraduates in their first year. Details relating to submission are given in the general note below.

(5) *Dissertation* (portfolio submission)

Candidates must submit two copies of a dissertation of between 8,000 and 10,000 words (exclusive of bibliography) which has not been previously submitted for a degree of another university. The subject and title must be approved by the Board of the Faculty of Music. Details relating to approval and submission are given in the general note below.

(6) *Edition with commentary* (portfolio submission)

Candidates must submit two copies of an edition with commentary. Editions previously submitted for the Honour School of Music may be resubmitted. No edition will be accepted if it has already been submitted, wholly or substantially, for another Honour School or degree of this University, or a degree of any other institution. The work or works to be edited must be approved by the Board of the Faculty of Music. Details relating to approval and submission are given in the general note below.

(7) *Analysis* (portfolio submission)

Candidates must submit two copies of an analytical study of not more than 10,000 words which has not been previously submitted for a degree of another university. The subject and title must be approved by the Board of the Faculty of Music. Details relating to approval and submission are given in the general note below.

(8) *Music Ethnography* (portfolio submission)

Candidates must submit two copies of a portfolio of essays and ethnographic work to a total of around 10,000 words (or equivalent). This may be submitted in a variety of formats, including recordings with commentary, video, photography, transcription and analysis. The subject and title must be approved by the Board of the Faculty of

Music. Details relating to approval and submission are given in the general note below.

General Note on approval of subjects for List B(5), (6), (7), and (8); and the submission of written work for List B(4)–(8).

(a) *Approval of subjects*   5

Candidates intending to submit any of *B(5), (6), (7),* or *(8)* must obtain prior approval of the subject and title from the Board of the Faculty of Music. They are urged to seek early guidance from their college tutor on whether the subject is likely to be acceptable and must submit the proposed subject and title, together with the signed approval of the tutor, to the Academic Administrator by Friday of the fourth week of   10 Trinity Term in the academic year preceding that of examination. The faculty board shall decide whether or not to approve the subject and title and shall advise the candidate as soon as possible.

(b) *Submission of written work*

Candidates must also submit two copies of the written work related to the exam-   15 ination of subjects B(4)–(8) by noon on Friday of the second week of Trinity Full Term in the academic year of examination. It must be addressed to the Chair of the Examiners, Honour School of Music, Examination Schools, High Street, Oxford. Each submission (but not each copy) must be accompanied by a form of declaration.

Each portfolio submitted for the subjects of Techniques of Composition II and   20 Orchestration must be accompanied by a form of declaration.

List C (three-hour paper options) and *List D* (practical options)

The Board of the Faculty of Music shall approve, and publish each year by notice in the Faculty of Music, not later than the eight week of Trinity Full Term, a list of subjects for the examination six terms hence.   25

List C consists of special topics, each examined by written paper or by a portfolio of coursework, as specified in the Music Faculty Undergraduate Handbook relating to the examination. List D options combine a practical element with an extended essay (two copies of which must be submitted). Approval and submission details for List D are as published within the Faculty Undergraduate Handbook relating to the   30 examination.

HONOUR SCHOOL OF NEUROSCIENCE

A

1. The subject of the Honour School of Neuroscience shall be all aspects of the scientific study of the nervous system.

2. No candidate shall be admitted to examination in this school unless he or she has either passed or been exempted from the First Public Examination.

3. The examination in this school shall be under the supervision of the Medical Sciences Board, which shall make regulations concerning it.

4. The examination in Neuroscience shall consist of two parts: Part I and Part II.

5. No candidate shall be admitted to the Part II examination in this school unless he or she has completed the Part I examination in this school.

6. The examination for Part I will take place during Week 0 or 1 in Trinity Term of the candidate's second year. The examination for Part II will take place during Trinity Term of the candidate's third year.

7. For the Part I options provided by the Department of Experimental Psychology, and the Part II advanced options which are as specified for Part II of the Honour School of Experimental Psychology, candidates shall be examined by such of the Public Examiners in the Honour School of Experimental Psychology as may be required. For the written papers in Part II which are as specified for the Honour School of Medical Sciences, and the Research Project, candidates shall be examined by such of the Public Examiners in the Honour School of Medical Sciences as may be required.

8. In addition to the form of examination prescribed below, candidates may be examined *viva voce* in either part of the examination.

9. Candidates for Part I and Part II may offer themselves for examination in one or more *Supplementary Subjects*. The *Supplementary Subjects* available in any year will be notified to students annually during Trinity Term. Account shall be taken of a candidate's results in any such subject in the candidate's overall classification in the Honour School of Neuroscience. Candidates awarded a pass in a Supplementary Subject examination may not retake the same Supplementary Subject examination.

B

Part I

1. Candidates will attend lectures and practicals in options selected from a list published to students by the end of Week 8 of Hilary Term in the year preceding the examination. Each option will have a number of units ascribed to it. Candidates will be required to study options totalling ten units. The handbook for the course will specify how many units are assigned to each option, and which options are recommended to proceed to particular advanced options in Part II.

2. Two written papers will be set:
   (i) Paper I will be a three-hour examination comprising a selection of questions requiring short answers. Candidates will be required to answer those questions relating to their chosen options.

(ii) Paper II will be a two-hour essay paper. Candidates will be required to answer questions from a selection relating to the different options that they have studied.

3. If, in Paper II of the Part I Examination, a candidate presents essentially the same information on more than one occasion, then credit will be given in only the first instance.

4. Candidates will be required to undertake practical work and submit written reports as specified in the course handbook which will constitute part of the examination. On the basis of attendance records and the submitted reports, the Course Director, or a deputy, shall make available to the Examiners, at the end of Week 0 of Trinity Term in which the examinations are held, evidence showing the extent and the standard to which each candidate has completed the prescribed practical work. Practical work cannot normally be retaken. Candidates whose attendance or performance is deemed unsatisfactory will forfeit one quarter of the marks in the Part I examination, the outcome of which will be carried forward to the Part II Examination.

Part II

1. Each candidate must offer timed written examination papers and a project report based on a research project.

2. Each candidate must offer Paper 1A, Neuroscience, and Paper 2 as specified for the Honour School of Medical Sciences. In addition, each candidate must offer either two advanced options as specified for the Honour School of Experimental Psychology Part II or one advanced option as specified for the Honour School of Experimental Psychology Part II and Paper 3 as specified for the Honour School of Medical Sciences.

3. The Research Project

The research project will normally be carried out in the Trinity Term of the candidate's second year and the Michaelmas Term of the candidate's third year.

(i) *Form, Subject and Approval of the Project*

The project shall consist of original experiments carried out by the candidate alone or in collaboration with others (where such collaboration is, for instance, needed to produce results in the time available).

Each project shall be supervised, and the topic and supervisor shall be approved on behalf of the Medical Sciences Board by the Course Director, or a deputy. A list of approved project titles and their supervisors shall be published no later than Friday of Week 1 of Hilary Term in the academic year preceding the examination, and allocation of these projects to candidates shall be carried out through the Faculty of Physiological Sciences Undergraduate Studies Office no later than the end of Week 8 of that term.

As an alternative to the allocation process, a candidate may apply to undertake a project that is not on the approved list. Such application must be made no later than Friday of Week 4 of Hilary Term in the academic year preceding the examination. The candidate must submit the title of their proposed research project, provide a brief outline of the subject matter and supply details of supervision arrangements. The decision on the application shall be made by the Course Director, or a deputy, and shall be communicated to the candidate as soon as possible, and work should not start on the project until approval has been given. Candidates should allow at least one week for the process of approval, and should bear in mind that an application may be referred for clarification or may be refused.

(ii) *Submission of the Project Report*

The length and format of the Project Report based on the project shall be according to guidelines published by the Medical Sciences Board in Week 8 of Hilary Term of the academic year preceding the year of examination. Material in a candidate's Project Report must not be duplicated in any answer given in a written examination paper. Project Reports previously submitted for the Honour School of Neuroscience may be resubmitted. No Project Report will be accepted if it has already been submitted, wholly or substantially, for another Honour School or degree of this University, or for a degree of any other institution.

Project Reports (three copies) must be sent to the Chair of Examiners, Honour School of Neuroscience, Examination Schools, High Street, Oxford, not later than noon on the Friday of Week 8 of Hilary Term in the academic year in which the candidate intends to take the examination. The copies shall be accompanied (in a separate sealed envelope) by a certificate signed by each candidate indicating that the research project is the candidate's own work and that the supervisor has commented on at least one draft of the Project Report. In the case of work that has been produced in collaboration, the certificate shall indicate the extent of the candidate's own contribution. Each candidate will be required to submit a draft of their Project Report to their supervisor no later than two weeks before the specified deadline for submission to Schools.

In exceptional cases, where through unforeseen circumstances a research project produces no useable results (i.e. not even negative or ambiguous results), the candidate may apply through his or her college to the Course Director, or a deputy, for permission to submit a concise review of the scientific context and the aims of the work that was attempted, in place of the normal Project Report. Such an application must be accompanied by supporting evidence from the supervisor of the project. The concise review to be submitted in such circumstances should be comparable in length to the Report of a successful research project and will be presented orally to the examiners and be examined viva voce in the usual way for a research project. The examiners will be advised that substantive results could not be produced.

The examiners shall obtain and consider a written report from each supervisor indicating the extent of the input made by the candidate to the outcome of the project and also any unforeseen difficulties associated with the project (e.g. unexpected technical issues or problems in the availability of materials, equipment, or literature or other published data).

(iii) *Oral Assessment of Project-based Written Work*

In addition, each candidate shall make a brief oral presentation of their project to a group of two examiners (or examiners and assessors appointed to ensure an adequate representation of expertise), after which, the candidate shall be examined *viva voce* on the project. The form of the presentation to the examiners shall be specified in guidelines published by the Medical Sciences Board.

4. If, in the Part II Examination, a candidate presents essentially the same information on more than one occasion, then credit will be given in only the first instance.

5. The weighting of marks for the five exercises required of each candidate shall be 25 per cent for the Project Report based on the research project and 55 per cent in total for the four written papers. Marks carried forward from the Part I examination will account for the remaining 20 per cent of the candidate's overall result for the Honour School of Neuroscience.

HONOUR SCHOOL OF ORIENTAL STUDIES

A

1. The main subjects of the examination in the Honour School of Oriental Studies shall be Arabic, Chinese, Egyptology and Ancient Near Eastern Studies, Hebrew, Japanese, Jewish Studies, Persian, Sanskrit, and Turkish, together with such other subjects as may be determined by the Board of the Faculty of Oriental Studies.

2. Every candidate in the examination shall be required to offer one of the main subjects listed above: candidates offering one of the above languages shall also be required to show an adequate knowledge of the literature and history of the civilization concerned, and candidates offering a history subject listed above shall also be required to show an adequate knowledge of the language concerned.

3. No candidate shall be admitted to examination in this school unless he or she has either passed or been exempted from the First Public Examination.

4. In the Class List issued by the examiners in the Honour School of Oriental Studies the main subject and (where appropriate) subsidiary language offered by each candidate who obtains Honours shall be indicated.

5. Any candidate whose name has been placed in the Class List, upon the result of the examination in any one of the subjects mentioned in clause 1, shall be permitted to offer himself or herself for examination in any other of the subjects mentioned in the same clause at the examination in either the next year or the next year but one, provided always that he or she has not exceeded six terms from the date on which he or she first obtained Honours in a Final Honour School, and provided that no such candidate shall offer any of the main subjects already offered by him or her in the School of Oriental Studies.

6. The examination in this school shall be under the supervision of the Board of the Faculty of Oriental Studies, which shall make regulations concerning it subject always to the preceding clauses of this sub-section.

B

Candidates, except in the case of Arabic, proposing to offer a Special Subject not included in the lists below must obtain the approval of the board both for their subject and for the treatises or documents (if any) which they propose to offer with it.

Except in the case of Arabic, Chinese and Japanese, if the candidate so desires and the board thinks it appropriate, such a Special Subject may be examined in the form of a dissertation.

All dissertation titles must be approved by the Board of the Faculty of Oriental Studies. Applications for approval must be made by Monday Week 0 of Hilary Term in the year of the exams.

For the submission of all dissertations, two typewritten copies and an electronic copy in PDF format in a memory stick or CD, of the dissertation and a signed declaration form certifying that the dissertation is the candidate's own work must be sent to the Chair of Examiners, Honour School of Oriental Studies, c/o Examination Schools, High Street, Oxford, not later than 12 noon on Friday of the tenth week of the Hilary Term preceding the examination. The dissertation must not bear the candidate's name, but only the examination number. Dissertations previously submitted for the Honour School of Oriental Studies may be resubmitted. No dissertation will be accepted if it has already been submitted, wholly or substantially, for another Honour School or degree of this University, or for a degree of any other institution. The dissertation shall not exceed 15,000 words.

All applications for approval by the board must be sent to the Secretary of the   5
Board of the Faculty of Oriental Studies, Oriental Institute, on the date published in the course handbook and must be accompanied by two copies of a list of the treatises or documents (if any) offered.

All candidates must give notice, on their examination entry forms, of their Special Subjects and choice of books or subjects, where alternatives exist, to the Registrar on or   10 before the Friday in the fourth week of the Michaelmas Full Term preceding the examination. The notice must specify the subject so offered, and, if a subject specially approved by the board, also the treatises or original documents (if any) which it has approved.

Candidates may be examined *viva voce.*   15

The editions of texts specified in the course handbooks are the ones which will be used for the reproduction of material for examination purposes, not necessarily the ones which provide the most useful material for the study of the texts concerned.

For those papers where a selection of unspecified texts is to be examined, the selection of texts will be reported to the Undergraduate Studies Committee of the   20 board at its first meeting in Hilary Term for the examination in the year of the examination, and copies of the lists of selected texts will be available for candidates not later than Friday of the third week of the same term in the course handbook.

Oral examinations for Arabic, Chinese, Hebrew (Course II) Japanese, Persian, and Turkish will be held in the week before Trinity Full Term in the year in which the   25 Honour School examination is taken.

REGULATIONS CONCERNING INDIVIDUAL SUBJECTS

The subjects of the school are arranged below in two sections: (i) main subjects; (ii) subsidiary languages. Within each section subjects are listed in alphabetical order as follows: 30

Main Subjects	*Subsidiary Languages*	
Arabic	Akkadian	Egyptology
Chinese	Arabic	Hebrew
Egyptology and Ancient	Aramaic and Syriac	Hindi
Near Eastern Studies	Armenian	Hittite 35
Hebrew	Chinese	Japanese
Japanese	Coptic	Korean
Jewish Studies	Persian	Old Iranian
Persian	Prakrit	Pali
Sanskrit	Sanskrit	Tibetan 40
Turkish	Sumerian	Turkish

In addition, candidates may offer Classics either as a main subject or as a subsidiary language in the Honour School of Classics and Oriental Studies.

Candidates offering Arabic, Chinese, Hebrew, Japanese, Persian or Turkish as their main subject *may* offer a subsidiary language as specified below; candidates offering   45 Sanskrit *must* offer a subsidiary language as specified below; and candidates offering

Egyptology and Ancient Near Eastern Studies *must* offer either a subsidiary language or Archaeology and Anthropology as specified below.

Candidates offering Arabic or Turkish or Persian as their main subject will be required to spend a period of at least one academic year on an approved course of language study in the Middle East. 5

Candidates offering Chinese or Japanese as their main subject are required to spend a period of at least one academic year on an approved course of language study in East Asia.

Candidates offering Hebrew shall take one of the following courses:

Course I: Candidates will be examined in accordance with the regulations set out 10 below.

Course II: Candidates will be examined in accordance with the regulations set out below. Candidates offering Hebrew **Course II** as their main subject will be required to spend a period of at least one academic year on an approved course of study in Israel.

References to Classics in the following Regulations are to the syllabus in Classics 15 for the Honour School of Classics and Oriental Studies.

Main Subjects

Arabic

Arabic Handbook. The Board of the Faculty of Oriental Studies shall issue annually the Handbook by Monday of Week 1 of the first Hilary Full Term of candidates' work 20 for the Honour Schools. The Handbook will include, amongst other things, lists of set texts.

Choice and availability of options. It cannot be guaranteed that teaching will be available on all Further and Special Subjects in every academic year. Similarly, the choice of subject for the dissertation will necessarily depend upon availability of a 25 suitable supervisor. Candidates should therefore consult with their tutors about the availability of teaching when selecting their optional and dissertation subjects.

Either, for Arabic and Islamic Studies
1. Arabic unprepared translation into English and comprehension.
2. Composition in Arabic. 30
3. Oral.[1]
4. Arabic literature.
5. Islamic history, 570–1500.
6. Islamic religion.
7. A Further Subject, chosen from a list published in the course handbook. 35
8. and 9. A Special Subject (to be examined in two papers), chosen from a list published in the course handbook.

10. Candidates for all Special Subjects will be examined by means of a timed paper, and by means of an extended essay, which shall not exceed 6,000 words (including footnotes but excluding bibliography), and shall be on a topic or theme selected by the 40 candidate from a question paper published by the examiners on the Friday of the fourth week of Michaelmas Term in the year of examination. Candidates will be contacted with details of how to collect or access the question paper. Essays should be typed or word-processed in double-spacing and should conform to the standards of academic presentation prescribed in the 'Guidelines for writers of Theses' in the 45

---

[1] Details of the oral examination and of the areas in which candidates will be expected to show competence are provided in the examination conventions and in the handbook. All Oriental Studies oral examinations in FHS are weighted as a half paper.

course handbook. Essays (two copies) shall normally be written during the Michaelmas Term in the year of examination and must be delivered by hand to the Examination Schools (addressed to the Chair of Examiners, Honour School of Oriental Studies, Examination Schools, High Street, Oxford) not later than 12 noon on the Friday before the beginning of Hilary Full Term of the year of examination. Candidates delivering essays will be required to complete a receipt form, which will only be accepted as proof of receipt if it is countersigned by a member of the Examination Schools staff. Each essay must be accompanied by a sealed envelope (bearing only the candidate's examination number) containing a formal declaration signed by the candidate that the essay is his or her own work. The University's regulations on Late Submission of Work will apply.

11. Any candidate may be examined *viva voce*.

12. A dissertation.[1]

or, for Arabic with a Subsidiary Language, Papers 1–6 above **and** 13, 14, and 15. Three papers from one of the following:

Akkadian.
Aramaic and Syriac.
Armenian.
Classics (in the Honour School of Classics and Oriental Studies).
Hebrew.
Hindi/Urdu.
Persian.
Turkish.

16. An optional dissertation to be approved by the Board. See under Arabic and Islamic Studies above for notes concerning the choice and approval of options and the preparation and submission of theses.

Chinese

The Board of the Faculty of Oriental Studies shall issue the handbook for the Honour School of Oriental Studies (Chinese and Chinese with a subsidiary language) no later than the Monday of first week of the Hilary full-term prior to the year in which candidates shall sit their Final Honour School examinations. The handbook shall include, amongst other information, course details, lists of set texts and regulations regarding the submission of dissertations and long-essays.

All candidates must have fulfilled attendance requirements (as set out in the handbook) on a designated course at Peking University, unless given exemption by the Board of the Faculty.

Either, for Chinese only,

The following papers will be set:

1. Modern Chinese I.
2. Modern Chinese II.
3. Oral.[2]
4. Classical I.
5. Classical II.

---

[1] Refer to Section B, Special Regulations for the Honour School of Oriental Studies

[2] Details of the oral examination and of the areas in which candidates will be expected to show competence are provided in the examination conventions and in the handbook. All Oriental Studies oral examinations in FHS are weighted as a half paper.

6. Modern China.

7. Dissertation on a subject approved by the Board of the Faculty.

8. Special Option I: Texts

The subjects available together with the relevant texts will be set out in the handbook for the year prior to year of the examinations.

9. Special Option II: Essays

These will be in the same area as that chosen under 8.

10. Special Option III: Extended Essay

This will be in the same area as that chosen under 8 and 9 or Linguistics (if available).

Or Chinese with a subsidiary language, Papers 1–7 above and papers 11, 12, and 13 below in Japanese, Korean, or Tibetan.

11. Japanese, Korean, or Tibetan Texts (Subsidiary).

12. Japanese, Korean, or Tibetan History and Culture (Subsidiary).

13. Japanese, Korean, or Tibetan Language (Subsidiary).

Egyptology and Ancient Near Eastern Studies
Either, for Egyptology and Ancient Near Eastern Studies with a subsidiary language
The languages which may be offered shall be:

As first language: Akkadian or Egyptian

One of the following as second language (which must be different from the first language):

Akkadian

Egyptian

Coptic

Hittite (may not be available every year)

Sumerian

will be required to offer the following papers:

1. Translation paper (first language).

2. Translation paper (second language).

3, 4. Literary and historical topics including prepared translation from first language.

5, 6. Literary and historical topics including prepared translation from second language.

For papers 4 and 6, in each case four passages from a list of prescribed texts will be set for examination by essay. For each paper, candidates must present a translation of and essay on one passage. Papers should be typed and provided with proper scholarly apparatus. The passages for paper 4 will be published at 10 a.m. on Monday of Week 1 in Full Term in the term in which the final examination is to be offered, and must be handed in to the Examination Schools, High Street, Oxford no later than 12 noon on Monday of Week 2. A signed statement that the essay is the candidate's own work should be submitted separately in a sealed envelope bearing his or her candidate number, to the Chair of examiners (forms are available from the Faculty Office, Oriental Institute). The passages for paper 6 will be published at 10 a.m. on Monday of Week 3 in Full Term in the term in which the final examination is to be offered, and must be handed in to the Examination Schools, High Street, Oxford no later than 12 noon on Monday of Week 4. Essays should not exceed 3,500 words. A signed statement that the essay is the candidate's own work should be submitted separately in a sealed envelope bearing his or her candidate number, to the Chair of examiners (forms are available from the Faculty Office, Oriental Institute). Candidates will be contacted with details of how to collect or access the papers.

Candidates offering one of the following as the second language in the above papers follow the regulations for 'Subsidary Languages' in the Honour School of Oriental Studies:

Arabic
Aramaic and Syriac   5
Classics (in the Honour School of Classics and Oriental Studies)
Hebrew (Biblical and Rabbinic)
and Old Iranian.

Candidates offering Classics as a subsidiary language in the Honour School of Classics and Oriental Studies must offer in place of papers 2, 5 and 6 three subjects in   10
Classics according to the conditions specified in the syllabus for that School.

7. A field of concentration to be chosen from a list of topics published at the beginning of Michaelmas Term each year by the Oriental Studies Faculty Board for examination in the following academic year. Candidates may propose their own field of concentration. The choice must be approved by the Board in each case.   15

8. Selected Egyptian and/or Ancient Near Eastern artefacts together with essay questions on material culture.

9. General paper, including questions on Egyptology and Ancient Near Eastern Studies today.

10. A dissertation on a topic to be approved by the Faculty Board, of a different   20
character from that chosen for paper 7.[1]

11. Egyptian art and architecture. This paper is optional and may be taken in substitution for 7. or 10. above. Selection of this paper is subject to approval by the Board of the Faculty of Oriental Studies.

Or, for Egyptology and Ancient Near Eastern Studies with Archaeology and   25
Anthropology, candidates will be required to offer papers 1, 3–4, and 7–10 above,
and the following papers:

12. Anthropological theory and archaeological enquiry.

13. Urbanisation and change in complex societies: comparative approaches **or**
From Hunting and Gathering to States and Empires in South-West Asia.   30

14. Social analysis and interpretation **or** Cultural representations, beliefs and practices.

All candidates will be required to undertake a course of practical work, including laboratory work.

Candidates will be assessed, at the end of the sixth term from matriculation, on their   35
practical ability, under the provisions for Honour Moderations in Archaeology and Anthropology.

Candidates will be required to take part in approved fieldwork as an integral part of their course. The fieldwork requirement will normally have been discharged before the Long Vacation of six terms from matriculation.   40

Hebrew
Either, for Hebrew only,
Candidates for **Course I** will be required to offer seven papers and a dissertation.
Candidates for **Course II** will be required to offer seven papers and a dissertation, and

---

[1] Refer to Section B, Special Regulations for the Honour School of Oriental Studies.

an oral examination. They will be expected to carry out during their year abroad such work as the Board of the Faculty of Oriental Studies may require.

1. (for **Course I**): Hebrew composition and unprepared translation.

(for **Course II**): Essay in modern Hebrew and unprepared translation.

2. Prepared texts I: Biblical texts (lists of texts are available in the course handbook).

3. Prepared texts II: Rabbinic and Medieval Hebrew texts (lists of texts are available in the course handbook).

4. Prepared texts III: Modern Hebrew literature (lists of texts are available in the course handbook).

5. General paper; language, history, religion, and culture.

6. Prepared texts IV:

(*a*) Jewish Aramaic and *either* (*b*) Biblical Hebrew *or* (*c*) Rabbinic and Medieval Hebrew *or* (*d*) Modern Hebrew (lists of texts are availablein the course handbook).

7. One of the papers in Jewish Studies paper *b*.

8. Candidates who so desire may offer any special subject as may be approved by the Board of the Faculty of Oriental Studies. Applications for the approval of options must be submitted to the Board not later than Monday of the second week of the Michaelmas Term preceding the examination.

9. (for **Course II**) Spoken Hebrew.[1]

Or, for Hebrew with a subsidiary language, Papers 1–5 above, and three papers from one of the following additional subjects: Akkadian, Arabic, Aramaic and Syriac, Classics (in the Honour School of Classics and Oriental Studies), Egyptology. Candidates who so desire may offer a special subject as specified in 8.

Japanese

The Board of the Faculty of Oriental Studies shall issue the handbook for the Honour School of Oriental Studies (Japanese and Japanese with a subsidiary language) no later than the Monday of first week of the Hilary Full Term prior to the year in which candidates shall sit their Final Honour School examinations. The handbook shall include, amongst other information, course details, lists of set texts and regulations regarding the submission of dissertations and long-essays.

Either, for Japanese only,

The following papers will be set:

1. Modern Japanese I.
2. Modern Japanese II.
3. Oral.[1]
4. Classical Japanese.
5. Dissertation on a subject approved by the Board of the Faculty.[2]
6. Special text option I.[3]
7. Special subject option I.[3]
8. Special text option II.[3]

---

[1] Details of the oral examination and of the areas in which candidates will be expected to show competence are provided in the examination conventions and in the handbook. All Oriental Studies oral examinations in FHS are weighted as a half paper.

[2] Refer to Section B, Special Regulations for the Honour School of Oriental Studies.

[3] List of texts in the course handbook.

9. Special subject option II.[1]

10. Either Special Text option III or Special subject option III.[1]

Or, for Japanese with a subsidiary language, Papers 1–7 above and papers 11, 12, and 13 below in Chinese, Korean, or Tibetan.

11. Chinese, Korean, or Tibetan Texts (Subsidiary).

12. Chinese, Korean, or Tibetan History and Culture (Subsidiary).

13. Chinese, Korean, or Tibetan Language (Subsidiary).

Jewish Studies

The following papers will be set.

a. Jewish History, Religion and Culture

b. Five of the following, of which at least one must be chosen from each of sections I, II, and III. At least two must be chosen from papers which require study of set texts in the original language. Not more than one paper may be chosen from section V.

Section I	(*a*) Biblical History[1]
	(*b*) Biblical Archaeology
	(*c*) Biblical Narrative[1]
	(*d*) Biblical Prophecy[1]
Section II	(*e*) Second Temple Judaism[1]
	(*f*) Second Temple History
	(*g*) History of the Talmudic Period
	(*h*) Medieval Jewish History[1]
	(*i*) Jewish Aramaic Literature[1, 2]
Section III	(*j*) Haskalah[1]
	(*k*) Modern Jewish Society
	(*l*) Israel: History, Politics and Society
	(*m*) Modern Hebrew Literature[1]
	(*n*) Yiddish Literature[1, 2]
Section IV	(*o*) History of Jewish-Christian Relations
	(*p*) History of Jewish-Muslim Relations
	(*q*) History of Jewish Bible Interpretation[1]
	(*r*) Hebrew Texts for Jewish Studies[1]
Section V	(*s*) Biblical Religion
	(*t*) Medieval Jewish Thought[1]
	(*u*) Modern Jewish History
	(*v*) Modern Judaism

Papers in section V will be examined in the form of two essays (one compulsory, the other from a choice of two) not exceeding 5,000 words in total. The subjects will be assigned in the Oriental Institute at 10 a.m. on Monday of second week in the term in which the final examination is to be offered, and must be handed in to the Examination Schools, High Street, Oxford no later than 12 noon on Monday of third week. A signed statement that the essays are the candidate's own work should be submitted separately in a sealed envelope bearing his or her candidate number, to the Chair of Examiners (forms are available from the Faculty Office, Oriental Institute).

---

[1] List of texts in the course handbook.

[2] These courses are available only to students with adequate knowledge of the relevant language.

c. A dissertation (see the regulations for dissertations set out under B, SPECIAL REGULATIONS FOR THE HONOUR SCHOOL OF ORIENTAL STUDIES).

Special subjects may be offered subject to the approval of the Oriental Studies Board.

Some options may not be available in every year.

Candidates may obtain from the Oriental Institute information about which options may be offered for examination the first Monday of Michaelmas Full Term of the academic year preceding that in which the papers will be set.

Applications for the approval of options must be submitted not later than Monday of the second week of the Michaelmas Term preceding the examination.

Persian

The following papers will be set. Candidates will be required to offer ten papers.

Either, for Persian only,

1. Unprepared translation from Persian.
2. Translation into Persian and essay
3. Oral.[1]
4. Persian literature: 1000–1400
5. Persian literature: 1400–1900
6. Persian literature: 1900–the present
7. Themes in Iranian history

8. and 9. Optional subjects in Iranian and Middle Eastern History and Culture. The list of available optional subjects will be available in the Course Handbook

10. Dissertation[2]

or, for Persian with a subsidiary language,

Papers 1., 2., 3., 7., and 10. above *and* 11. and 12.

Two papers from papers 4., 5., and 6 above

13., 14., and 15. Subsidiary language. Three papers on one of the following languages: Arabic, Armenian, Old Iranian, Classics (in the Honour School of Classics and Oriental Studies), Hindi/Urdu, and Turkish.

Applications for the approval of options in papers, 8., 9., 13., 14., and 15. must be submitted to the Faculty Office by the deadline in the Course Handbook.

Sanskrit

The following papers will be set:

1. Sanskrit unprepared translation.
2. Essay questions on the history of classical Indian literature and civilization. This paper may include questions on the visual arts in ancient India.
3. Indian linguistics.

Candidates will be examined on their general knowledge and understanding of *vyākaraṇa a śāstra,* with particular reference to Pāṇ ini, *Aṣṭādhyāyi* (ed. Bhtlingk, 1,1,1–1,3,16; 1,4–2,2 (inclusive); and 3,1,91–132).

---

[1] Details of the oral examination and of the areas in which candidates will be expected to show competence are provided in the examination conventions and in the handbook. All Oriental Studies oral examinations in FHS are weighted as a half paper.

[2] Refer to Section B, Special Regulations for the Honour School of Oriental Studies.

4. For candidates offering Hindi, Old Iranian, Pali, Prakrit, or Tibetan as additional language: The historical philology of Old Indo-Aryan, with particular reference to:

(*a*) Selected *sūktas* from the *Ṛg Veda* (ed. Müller). A list of *sūktas* is available in the course handbook.   5

(*b*) Selected passages of prose from the Yajurveda Samhitā and Brahmanas, and from the early Upanisads. A list of passages is available in the course handbook.

For papers 5 and 6, two papers in a chosen area of Sanskrit studies approved by the Board of the Faculty. Applications for approval must be submitted by the Monday of   10
the sixth week of the Trinity Term of the academic year preceding the examination. (*Note*: These papers are intended to allow candidates to specialise in a particular area of Sanskrit studies such as *kāvya, dharmaśāstra*, philosophy, grammar, or religion.)

5. Unprepared translation from Sanskrit texts.

6. Essay questions on the chosen area.   15

7. A special subject from among the following, or such other special subjects as may be approved by the board of the faculty:

(*a*) Comparative grammar of Sanskrit and Old Iranian.

(*b*) Indian art and archaeology.

(*c*) Composition in Sanskrit prose and/or verse.   20

(*d*) Practical criticism and appreciation, including translation from the Sanskrit.

Either

8. and 9. Two papers on one of the following additional languages: Hindi, Old Iranian, Pali, Prakrit, Tibetan.

Or 8., 9., 10. Three papers on Classics (in the Honour School of Classics and   25
Oriental Studies) as an additional language.

Turkish

Turkish Handbook. The Board of the Faculty of Oriental Studies shall issue annually the Handbook for the Honour Schools of Oriental Studies (Turkish, Turkish with a Subsidiary Language, and Turkish with Islamic Art and   30
Archaeology) by Monday of Week 1 of the first Hilary Term of candidates' work for the Honour School. The Handbook will include, amongst other things, lists of the set texts prescribed for particular papers.

The following papers will be set:

Either, for Turkish only,   35

1. Unprepared translation from Ottoman and modern Turkish.

2. Translation into Turkish and essay in Turkish.

3. Oral.[1]

4. Ottoman historical texts.

5. Turkish political and cultural texts, 1860 to the present.   40

6. Modern Turkish literary texts.

7., 8., 9. Three papers from a list of options published in the course handbook.

10. A dissertation.[2]

or, for Turkish with a subsidiary language, Papers 1–6 above **and**

---

[1] Details of the oral examination and of the areas in which candidates will be expected to show competence are provided in the examination conventions and in the handbook. All Oriental Studies oral examinations in FHS are weighted as a half paper.

[2] Refer to Section B, Special Regulations for the Honour School of Oriental Studies

7., 8., 9. Three papers on one of the following languages: Arabic, Armenian, Classics (in the Honour School of Classics and Oriental Studies), Hindi/Urdu, Persian.

10. An *optional* special subject, to be approved by the Board of the Faculty of Oriental Studies.

SUBSIDIARY LANGUAGES

5

Akkadian (for candidates offering Arabic, Classics (in the Honour School of Classics and Oriental Studies) or Hebrew as main subject).

The following papers will be set:

1, 2, 3 = Papers 2, 5, and 6 as specified for Akkadian in the Honour School of Oriental Studies (Egyptology and Ancient Near Eastern Studies). (Instead of either paper 5 or paper 6, candidates may offer one of papers 7, 9, or 10 as specified for the Honour School of Oriental Studies (Egyptology and Ancient Near Eastern Studies).

10

Arabic (for candidates offering Classics (in the Honour School of Classics and Oriental Studies), Egyptology and Ancient Near Eastern Studies, Hebrew, Persian, or Turkish as main subject).

15

The following papers will be set:

1. Arabic prose composition and unprepared translation.

2. Additional Arabic: literary texts.

Selected classical and modern Arabic prose texts (lists available in the course handbook).

20

3. Additional Arabic: Islamic texts.

Selected Arabic religious texts (list available in the course handbook).

Papers 2 and 3 *may* contain general and linguistic questions.

Aramaic and Syriac (for candidates offering Arabic, Classics (in the Honour School of Classics and Oriental Studies), Egyptology and Ancient Near Eastern Studies, Hebrew or Persian as main subject).

25

The following papers will be set:

1. Syriac prose composition and Aramaic and Syriac unprepared translation.

2. Aramaic prepared texts.[1]

3. Syriac prepared texts.[1]

30

Papers 2 and 3 may contain general and grammatical questions.

Armenian

The following papers will be set:

either

A. Classical Armenian[2]

35

1. Classical Armenian prose composition and unprepared translation.

2. Prepared religious texts.[1]

3. Prepared historical and other texts.[1]

or

B. Modern Armenian[3]

40

1. Modern Armenian prose composition and unprepared translation.

2. Prepared texts from the sixteenth to nineteenth centuries.[1]

3. Prepared texts from the twentieth and twenty-first centuries.[1]

---

[1] Lists of texts are available in the course handbook.

[2] For candidates offering Arabic, Classics (in the Honour School of Classics and Oriental Studies), Persian or Turkish as main subject.

[3] For candidates offering Arabic, Persian or Turkish as main subject.

Papers 2 and 3 will include questions on the subject-matter and grammar of the texts offered, and Paper 3 will also include questions on Armenian language, literature, and history.

Chinese (for candidates offering Japanese as main subject)
The following papers will be set:
1. Chinese Prescribed Texts. (Lists of texts will be available in the course handbook.)
2. *Either* (*a*) Unprepared translation and prose composition, *or* (*b*) Classical Chinese. (Texts will be as prescribed for paper 3, 'Classical texts' of Moderations in Oriental Studies (Chinese).)
3. History and Culture of China.

Coptic (for candidates offering Classics (in the Honour School of Classics and Oriental Studies) or Egyptology as main subject).
The following papers will be set:
1. Coptic unprepared translation and grammar.
2. Prepared texts I[1]
3. Prepared texts II, with general questions[1]

Egyptology (for candidates offering Classics (in the Honour School of Classics and Oriental Studies) or Hebrew as main subject).

The following papers will be set:
1, 2, 3 = Papers 2, 5, and 6 as specified for Egyptian in the Honour School of Oriental Studies (Egyptology and Ancient Near Eastern Studies). (Instead of either paper 5 or paper 6, candidates may offer one of papers 7, 9 or 10 as specified for the Honour School of Oriental Studies (Egyptology and Ancient Near Eastern Studies).

Hebrew (for candidates offering Arabic, Classics (in the Honour School of Classics and Oriental Studies) or Egyptology and Ancient Near Eastern Studies as main subject).
Candidates taking Arabic may offer *either* (*a*) Biblical and Rabbinic *or* (*b*) Medieval *or* (*c*) Modern Hebrew. Candidates taking Classics (in the Honour School of Classics and Oriental Studies) may offer *either* (*a*) Biblical and Rabbinic or (*b*) Medieval Hebrew. Candidates taking Egyptology may offer only Biblical and Rabbinic Hebrew. Biblical texts will be set from *Biblia Hebraica Stuttgartensia* (ed. Elliger and Rudolph).
The following papers will be set:
(*a*) Biblical and Rabbinic Hebrew:
1. Prose composition and unprepared translation.
2. Prepared texts I: Biblical texts[1]
3. Prepared texts II: Biblical and Rabbinic texts[1]

Papers 2 and 3 may contain general and grammatical questions.

(*b*) Medieval Hebrew:
1. Unprepared translation.
2. Prepared texts I[1]
3. Prepared texts II[1]

Papers 2 and 3 may contain general and grammatical questions.

(*c*) Modern Hebrew:
1. Prose composition and unprepared translation.
2. Prepared texts I[1]
3. Prepared texts II[1]

Papers 2 and 3 may contain general and grammatical questions.

---

[1] Lists of texts are available in the course handbook.

Hindi (for candidates offering Sanskrit as main subject)
  The following papers will be set:
  1. Hindi unprepared translation.
  2. Prepared texts, with questions on Hindi language and literature.

Hindi/Urdu (For candidates offering Arabic, Persian, or Turkish as main subject)
  The following papers will be Set:
  1. Hindi and Urdu prose composition and unprepared translation;
  2. Hindi prepared texts with questions on language and literature;
  3. Urdu prepared texts with questions on language and literature.

Japanese (for candidates offering Chinese as main subject)
  The following papers will be set:
  1. Japanese Prescribed Texts.[1]

  2. *Either* Unprepared translation, Prose Composition, and Grammatical Questions, *or* any Special Subject set for paper 8 of the syllabus in Japanese only [see the list of Special Subjects for Paper 8 set out under SPECIAL REGULATIONS FOR THE HONOUR SCHOOL OF ORIENTAL STUDIES, REGULATIONS CONCERNING INDIVIDUAL SUBJECTS, MAIN SUBJECTS, **Japanese, Japanese only**]

  3. Essay questions on Japanese Culture.

Korean (for candidates offering Chinese and Japanese as main subject)
  The following papers will be set:
  1. Korean texts.[1]
  2. Korean History and Culture.
  3. Korean Language.

Old Iranian (for candidates offering Classics (in the Honour School of Classics and Oriental Studies), Egyptology and Ancient Near Eastern Studies or Persian as main subject).
  The following papers will be set:
  1. Avestan Texts[1]
  2. (i) Old Persian texts[1]
    (ii) *either* (*a*) Questions on the content of the Old Persian texts and their historical background *or* (*b*) Questions on the history of the Persian language.
  3. Questions on Avestan and Old Persian language, and on pre-Islamic Iranian history, religion, and literature.

Old Iranian (for candidates offering Sanskrit as main subject).
  The following papers will be set:
  1. Old Persian and Avestan Texts[1]
  2. Questions on Old Persian and Avestan language and literature, and on the religious and historical background to the texts studied for Paper 1.

Pali (for candidates offering Sanskrit as main subject).
  The following papers will be set:
  1. Pali unprepared translation.
  2. Questions on Pali language and literature, on Theravāda Buddhist doctrine, and on the early history of Buddhism in South Asia.

Pali (for candidates offering Classics (in the Honour School of Classics and Oriental Studies) as main subject).

---

[1] Lists of texts are available in the course handbook.

The following papers will be set:
1. Pali unprepared translation.
2. Questions on Pali language and literature, on Theravāda Buddhist doctrine, and on the early history of Buddhism in South Asia.
3. Prepared texts, with questions on contents.   5

Persian (for candidates offering Arabic, Classics (in the Honour School of Classics and Oriental Studies) or Turkish as main subject).
The following papers will be set:
1. Persian Language.
2. Pre-Modern Persian Literature.   10
3. Modern Persian Literature.

Prakrit (for candidates offering Sanskrit as main subject).
The following papers will be set:
1. Prakrit unprepared translation.
2. Questions on Prakrit language and literature and on the doctrine and early   15
history of the Jains.

Sanskrit (for candidates offering Classics (in the Honour School of Classics and Oriental Studies) as main subject.)
The following papers will be set:
1. Sanskrit unprepared translation.   20
2. Questions on Sanskrit language and literature.
3. Prepared texts.

Tibetan (for candidates offering Chinese or Japanese as main subject)
1. Tibetan prose composition and unprepared translation.
2. Prepared texts, with questions.[1]   25
3. Questions on Tibetan culture and history.

Tibetan (for candidates offering Sanskrit as main subject).
The following papers will be set:
1. Tibetan prose composition and unprepared translation.
2. Prepared texts, with questions on Tibetan culture and history.   30

Turkish (for candidates offering Arabic, Classics (in the Honour School of Classics and Oriental Studies) or Persian as main subject).
The following papers will be set:
1. Turkish prose composition and unprepared translation.
2. *Either* (*a*) Additional Turkish: Late Ottoman and modern Turkish literary texts[1]   35
Or (*b*) Additional Turkish: Modern Turkish literary texts:[1]
Either (*a*) Additional Turkish: Political and cultural texts, 1860 to the present.[1]
Or (*b*) Additional Turkish: Political and cultural texts, 1920 to the present.[1]

---

[1] Lists of texts are available in the course handbook.

PHILOSOPHY IN ALL HONOUR SCHOOLS INCLUDING PHILOSOPHY

Candidates offering Philosophy papers[1] in any honour school must conform to the General Regulations below, and to those for their particular school, as specified elsewhere.

Subjects in Philosophy

The syllabuses of the subjects in Philosophy are specified below. A three-hour written examination paper will be set in each subject, except 199, and any other paper where expressly indicated below.

101. *Early Modern Philosophy*
Candidates will be expected to show critical appreciation of the main philosophical ideas of the period. The subject will be studied in connection with the following texts: Descartes, *Meditations, Objections and Replies*; Spinoza, *Ethics*; Leibniz, *Monadology, Discourse on Metaphysics*; Locke, *Essay Concerning Human Understanding*; Berkeley, *Principles of Human Knowledge, Three Dialogues Between Hylas and Philonous*; Hume, *Treatise of Human Nature*. The paper will consist of three sections; Section A will include questions about Descartes, Spinoza, and Leibniz; Section B will include questions about Locke, Berkeley and Hume. Candidates will be required to answer three questions, with at least one question from Section A and at least one question from Section B.

102. *Knowledge and Reality*
Candidates will be expected to show knowledge in some of the following areas: knowledge and justification; perception; memory; induction; other minds; *a priori* knowledge; necessity and possibility; reference; truth; facts and propositions; definition; existence; identity, including personal identity; substances, change, events; properties; causation; space; time; essence; natural kinds; realism and idealism; primary and secondary qualities.

103. *Ethics*
Candidates will be given an opportunity to show some first-hand knowledge of some principal historical writings on this subject, including those of Aristotle, Hume, and Kant, but will not be required to do so. Questions will normally be set on the following topics:
    1. The Metaphysics of Ethics: including the nature of morality and moral properties, the truth-aptness of moral judgements, moral knowledge and moral relativism.
    2. Value and Normativity: including good and right, reasons, rationality, motivation, moral dilemmas.
    3. Self-interest, Altruism, and Amoralism.
    4. Ethical Theories: including consequentialism, utilitarianism, and contractualism.
    5. Specific Moral Concepts: including happiness, well-being, rights, virtue, fairness, equality, and desert.

---

[1] The paper for the supplementary subject "History and Philosophy of Science" is not here counted as a Philosophy paper, since it is a joint paper in both History and Philosophy.

6. Moral Psychology: including conscience, guilt and shame, freedom and responsibility.

7. Applied Ethics, including medical ethics.

104. *Philosophy of Mind*
Topics to be studied include the nature of persons, the relation of mind and body, self-knowledge, knowledge of other persons, consciousness, perception, memory, imagination, thinking, belief, feeling and emotion, desire, action, the explanation of action, subconscious and unconscious mental processes.

106. *Philosophy of Science and Social Science*
The paper will include such topics as:
    Part A: the nature of theories; scientific observation and method; scientific explanation; the interpretation of laws and probability; rationality and scientific change; major schools of philosophy of science.
    Part B: social meaning; individualism; rationality; rational choice theory; prediction and explanation in economics; the explanation of social action; historical explanation, ideology.
    Candidates will be required to answer at least one question from each part of the paper.

107. *Philosophy of Religion*
The subject will include an examination of claims about the existence of God, and God's relation to the world; their meaning, the possibility of their truth, and the kind of justification which can or needs to be provided for them; and the philosophical problems raised by the existence of different religions. One or two questions may also be set on central claims peculiar to Christianity, such as the doctrines of the Trinity, Incarnation, and Atonement.

108. *The Philosophy of Logic and Language*
The subject will include questions on such topics as: meaning, truth, logical form, necessity, existence, entailment, proper and general names, pronouns, definite descriptions, intensional contexts, adjectives and nominalization, adverbs, metaphor, and pragmatics. Some questions will be set which allow candidates to make use of knowledge of linguistics.

109. *Aesthetics and the Philosophy of Criticism*
Candidates will have the opportunity to show first-hand knowledge of some principal authorities on the subject, including Plato, *Ion* and *Republic*; Aristotle, *Poetics*; Hume, *Of the Standard of Taste*; Kant, *Critique of Aesthetic Judgement*. Questions will normally be set on the following topics: the nature of aesthetic value; the definition of art; art, society, and morality; criticism and interpretation; metaphor; expression; pictorial representation.

110. *Medieval Philosophy: Aquinas*
The subject will be studied in the following text (The Fathers of the English Dominican Province edition, 1911, rev. 1920):
    Aquinas, *Summa Theologiae*, Ia, 2–11, 75–89 (God, Metaphysics, and Mind); *or* Aquinas, *Summa Theologiae*, Ia IIae qq. 1–10, 90–97 (Action and Will; Natural Law). This paper will include an optional question containing passages for comment. This subject may not be combined with subject 111.

111. *Medieval Philosophy: Duns Scotus, Ockham*
The subject will be studied in the following texts:
    Duns Scotus, *Philosophical Writings*, tr. Wolter (Hackett) pp. 13–95 (chapters II–IV); Spade, *Five Texts*, pp. 57–113. Ockham, *Philosophical Writings*, tr. Boehner (Hackett), pp. 17–27, 96–126 (chapters II §1–2, chapters VIII–IX); Spade, *Five Texts*,

pp. 114–231. This paper will include an optional question containing passages for comment. This subject may not be combined with subject 110.

112. *The Philosophy of Kant*
Critique of Pure Reason, Groundwork of the Metaphysic of Morals. The editions to be used are *Critique of Pure Reason*, ed. and trans. by P. Guyer and A. Wood   5
(Cambridge University Press, 1998) and *Groundwork of the Metaphysics of Morals*, ed. and trans. by M. Gregor (Cambridge University Press, 1997).
Candidates may answer no more than one question on Kant's moral philosophy.

113. *Post-Kantian Philosophy*
The main developments of philosophy in Continental Europe after Kant, excluding   10
Marxism and analytical philosophy. Questions on the following authors will regularly be set: Hegel, Schopenhauer, Nietzsche, Husserl, Heidegger, Sartre, Merleau-Ponty. There will be some general and/or comparative questions, and questions on other authors may be set from time to time. Candidates will be required to show adequate first-hand knowledge of works of at least two authors (who may be studied in   15
translation).

114. *Theory of Politics*
The critical study of political values and of the concepts used in political analysis: the concept of the political; power, authority, and related concepts; the state; law; liberty and rights; justice and equality; public interest and common good; democracy and   20
representation; political obligation and civil disobedience; ideology; liberalism, socialism, and conservatism.

115. Plato: *Republic*, tr. Grube, revised Reeve (Hackett).
There will be a compulsory question containing passages for comment.

116. Aristotle: *Nicomachean Ethics*, tr. Irwin (Hackett, second edition).   25
There will be a compulsory question containing passages for comment.

117. *Frege, Russell, and Wittgenstein*
Works principally to be studied are:
   Frege, *Foundations of Arithmetic*, trans. Austin; *Begriffsschrift* ch. 1, 'Function and Concept', 'Sense and Meaning', 'Concept and Object', and 'Frege on Russell's   30
Paradox', in Geach and Black, eds. *Translations from the Philosophical Writings of Gottlob Frege*;
   Russell, 'On Denoting', 'Mathematical Logic as Based on the theory of Types', and 'On the Nature of Acquaintance', in Marsh, ed., *Logic and Knowledge*; 'The Ultimate Constituents of Matter', 'The Relation of Sense-Data to Physics', and 'Knowledge by   35
Acquaintance and Knowledge by Description', in *Mysticism and Logic; Our Knowledge of the External World*, chs. I–IV; **either** *Introduction to Mathematical Philosophy*, chs. 1–3 and 12–18, **or** 'The Philosophy of Logical Atomism', in Marsh, ed., *Logic and Knowledge*;
   Wittgenstein, *Tractatus Logico-Philosophicus*.   40
   Candidates will be required to show adequate knowledge of at least two authors.

118. *The Later Philosophy of Wittgenstein*
Works principally to be studied are *Philosophical Investigations* and *The Blue and Brown Books*.

119. *Formal Logic*   45
This paper was examined for the last time in Trinity Term 2014 and will not be available thereafter. Students in all Philosophy Honour Schools except Mathematics and Philosophy, and Computer Science and Philosophy may, after Trinity Term 2014 and until further notice, offer the paper(s) in Set Theory and Logic from part B of the Honour School of Mathematics, which shall count as one Philosophy paper.   50

120. *Intermediate Philosophy of Physics*
The paper will consist of two sections. Section A will include philosophical problems associated with classical physics and some basic philosophical issues raised by the Special Theory of Relativity. Section B will be concerned with introductory philosophical problems related to the interpretation of quantum mechanics. Candidates will be required to answer at least one question from each section.

121. *Advanced Philosophy of Physics*
The subject will include advanced topics in the philosophy of space, time, and relativity and in the philosophical foundations of quantum mechanics. It will also include some philosophical issues raised by thermodynamics and statistical mechanics. This paper will be examined by two submitted essays of 5,000 words each. There will be no written paper in this subject. The submitted essays will be of the kind for Philosophy specified under the regulations for the Honour School of Physics and Philosophy, part C, except that (i) candidates must submit two essays for this subject, rather than one, and (ii) candidates will not select essay titles from past papers but seek approval for their titles in the way set out in the Physics and Philosophy regulations referred to.

122. *Philosophy of Mathematics*
Questions may be set which relate to the following issues: Incommensurables in the development of Greek geometry. Comparisons between geometry and other branches of mathematics. The significance of non-Euclidean geometry. The problem of mathematical rigour in the development of the calculus. The place of intuition in mathematics (Kant, Poincaré). The idea that mathematics needs foundations. The role of logic and set theory (Dedekind, Cantor, Frege, Russell). The claim that mathematics must be constructive (Brouwer). The finitary study of formal systems as a means of justifying infinitary mathematics (Hilbert). Limits to the formalization of mathematics (Gödel). Anti-foundational views of mathematics. Mathematical objects and structures. The nature of infinity. The applicability of mathematics.

124. *Philosophy of Science*
This paper will include such topics as: scientific method, including induction, confirmation, corroboration, and explanation; the structure of scientific theories, including syntactic and semantic approaches, the nature of scientific laws, the theory-observation distinction, inter-theory reduction, theory unification, and emergence; debates over realism, including the aims of science, the under-determination of theory by data, and structuralism; and scientific rationality, including theory change, epistemological naturalism, and Bayesian epistemology. Questions will also be set on historical schools in the philosophy of science, in particular logical positivism and logical empiricism, on aspects of the history of science, and on the philosophy of probability, including the nature of probabilistic laws.

125. *Philosophy of Cognitive Science*
Topics to be studied include: levels of description, including personal and subpersonal levels, and relationships between levels; the nature of cognitive scientific theories; information and representation, including representational format, the language of thought, and connectionist alternatives; information processing, including algorithms, and tacit knowledge of rules; cognitive architecture, including modularity, and homuncular functionalism; explanation in cognitive science, including functional explanation and mechanistic explanation; methods in cognitive science, including cognitive neuropsychology, computational modelling, and experimental cognitive psychology; the scientific study of consciousness, including the status of introspective reports and non-verbal measures, and the notion of a neural and computational correlate of consciousness. Questions will also be set on philosophical issues arising from aspects

of the history of cognitive science and from areas of active research in cognitive science.

126. *The Philosophy and Economics of the Environment*[1]
Philosophical foundations: justice and goodness, theories of value; decision-making under uncertainty. Economic foundations: externalities, public goods, international environmental agreements. Politics and the environment. Intergenerational ethics, discounting. The choice of instruments: taxes, permits and command-and-control; environmental instruments in practice. Valuing human life. Valuing nature. Cost-benefit analysis: foundations and critiques; valuation methods.

127. *Philosophical Logic*
Topics to be studied include: classical and non-classical propositional logic, modal propositional logic, deontic, epistemic and tense logic, counterfactuals, predicate logic and its extensions, and quantified modal logic. These topics shall be studied in conjunction with Theodore Sider's Logic for Philosophy, published by Oxford University Press. The logical symbols to be used are those found in this publication. This subject will be available in all Honour Schools involving Philosophy.

130. Plato, *Republic*
Candidates will be expected to have read books I, IV–VII, X in Greek (Slings Oxford Classical Text), and books II–III, VIII–IX in translation (Grube, revised Reeve, Hackett). There will be a compulsory question containing passages for translation and comment from the books read in Greek; any passages for comment from the remaining books will be accompanied by a translation.

131. Plato, *Theaetetus* and *Sophist*
Candidates will be expected to have read both dialogues in Greek (Duke *et al.*, Oxford Classical Text). There will be a compulsory question containing passages for translation and comment.

132. Aristotle, *Nicomachean Ethics*
Candidates will be expected to have read books I–III, VI–VII, X in Greek (Bywater, Oxford Classical Text), and books IV–V, VIII–IX in translation (Irwin, Hackett second edition). There will be a compulsory question containing passages for translation and comment from the books read in Greek; any passages for comment from the remaining books will be accompanied by a translation.

133. Aristotle, *Physics*
Candidates will be expected to have read books I–IV and VIII in Greek (Ross, Oxford Classical Texts), and books V–VII in translation (in Barnes, ed., *The Complete Works of Aristotle: The Revised Oxford Translation* (Princeton), vol. 1). There will be a compulsory question containing passages for translation and comment from the books read in Greek; any passages for comment from the remaining books will be accompanied by a translation.

134. Sextus Empiricus: *Outlines of Pyrrhonism* (Bury, Loeb)
There will be a compulsory question containing passages for translation and comment.

135. *Latin Philosophy*
Cicero: *De Finibus* III (Reynolds, Oxford Classical Text), *De Officiis* I in translation (Griffin and Atkins, *Cicero, On Duties*, Cambridge); Seneca, *Epistulae Morales* 92, 95, 121, *De Constantia, De Vita Beata* (Reynolds, Oxford Classical Text).

---

[1] This paper is only available in the Honour School of Philosophy, Politics, and Economics (where it can be offered alternatively as Economics paper 321).

There will be a compulsory question containing passages for translation and comment from the texts read in Latin; any passages for comment from Cicero, *De Officiis* I will be accompanied by a translation.

150. *Jurisprudence*

As specified in the regulations for the Honour School of Jurisprudence. This subject may be offered only by candidates in PPE, and cannot be combined with either subject 114 or subject 203. Tutorial provision will be subject to the availability of Law tutors and will normally take place in either Hilary or Trinity Term.

180. *The Rise of Modern Logic*

The original authorities for the Rise of Modern Logic. The period of scientific thought to be covered is from 1879 to 1931 and includes principally the logical and foundational works of Frege, Russell, Hilbert, Brouwer, and Gödel that fall within this period. Questions may also be asked concerning Cantor, Dedekind, Poincaré, Zermelo, Skolem, Wittgenstein (Tractatus only), and Ramsey.

198. *Special Subjects*

From time to time special subjects may be approved by the Undergraduate Studies Committee of the Faculty of Philosophy. Special subjects will be communicated to college tutors and to undergraduates by the end of the fifth week of Hilary Term one year before examination. The Undergraduate Studies Committee will (a) agree the method of assessment for each special subject offered, which may be by written paper, submitted essay and/or other method (b) forbid, where it sees fit, a combination of a special subject with other subjects (c) forbid, where it sees fit, candidates taking any particular special subject to answer certain questions on the papers for other subjects (d) place restrictions, where it sees fit, on the number of candidates that may take any special subject in any year. No candidate may offer more than one special subject. Subject to these qualifications, any candidate may offer any special subject.

199. *Thesis*:

  1. *Subject*

The subject of every thesis should fall within the scope of philosophy. The subject may but need not overlap any subject on which the candidate offers papers. Candidates are warned that they should avoid repetition in papers of material used in their theses and that substantial repetition may be penalised. Every candidate shall submit for approval by the Director of Undergraduate Studies of the Faculty of Philosophy, c/o the Undergraduate Studies Administrator at Philosophy Centre, Radcliffe Humanities Building, Woodstock Road, Oxford OX2 6GG, the title he or she proposes, together with (*a*) an explanation of the subject in about 100 words; and (*b*) a letter of approval from his or her tutor, not earlier than the first day of the Trinity Full Term of the year before that in which he or she is to be examined and not later than Friday of the fourth week of the Michaelmas Full Term preceding his or her examination. (The date before which a proposal cannot be submitted is different in certain circumstances in the case of the Honour School of Philosophy and Modern Languages. See the regulations below for that honour school.) The Director of Undergraduate Studies of the Faculty of Philosophy shall decide as soon as possible whether or not to approve the title and shall advise the candidate immediately. No decision shall be deferred beyond the end of the fifth week of Michaelmas Full Term. If a candidate wishes to change the title, subject or focus of his or her thesis after his or her thesis proposal has already been approved by the body responsible: he or she should write to the Director of Undergraduate Studies of the Faculty of Philosophy, c/o the Undergraduate Studies Administrator, to seek approval. The Undergraduate Studies Administrator will inform the candidate whether the change to the thesis has been approved, and communicate any change, where approved, to the appropriate chair of examiners.

2. *Authorship and origin*

Every thesis shall be the candidate's own work. A candidate's tutor may, however, discuss with the candidate the field of study, the sources available, and the method of presentation; the tutor may also read and comment on drafts. The amount of assistance the tutor may give is equivalent to the teaching of a normal paper. Every candidate shall sign a certificate to the effect that the thesis is his or her own work and the tutor shall countersign the certificate confirming, to the best of his or her knowledge and belief, that this is so. This certificate shall be placed in a sealed envelope bearing the candidate's examination number presented together with the thesis. No thesis shall be accepted which has already been submitted for a degree of this or any other university, and the certificate shall also state that the thesis has not been so submitted. No thesis shall, however, be ineligible because it has been or is being submitted for any prize of this university.

3. *Length and format*

No thesis shall exceed 15,000 words, the limit to include all notes and appendices but not including the bibliography; no person or body shall have authority to permit any excess, except that in Literae Humaniores, in a thesis consisting in commentary on a text, quotation from the text will not be counted towards the word limit. The word count should be indicated at the front of the thesis. There shall be a select bibliography or a list of sources. All theses must be typed in double spacing on one side of quarto or A4 paper with any notes and references at the foot of each page. *Two* copies of the thesis shall be submitted to the examiners.

4. *Submission of thesis*

Every candidate shall submit the thesis, identified by the candidate's examination number only, not later than noon on Friday of the week before the Trinity Full Term of the examination to the Examination Schools, Oxford, addressed to the Chair of the Examiners in the candidate's honour school.

General Regulations

The following restrictions on combinations apply to candidates whatever their honour school:

(i) A candidate may not take both of subjects 106 and 124.
(ii) A candidate may not take both of subjects 115 and 130.
(iii) A candidate may not take both of subjects 116 and 132.
(iv) Both of subjects 117 and 118 may be offered *only* by candidates in *Mathematics and Philosophy* and *Computer Science and Philosophy*.
(v) A candidate may not take subject 199 unless he or she also takes three other philosophy subjects.
(vi) Notwithstanding any contrary indication in these regulations, subjects 130, 131, 132, 133, 134, and 135 may be offered *only* by candidates in *Classics and English, Classics and Modern Languages, Classics and Oriental Studies, Literae Humaniores,* and *Oriental Studies.*
(vii) A candidate may not take both of subjects 110 and 111.
(viii) Jurisprudence (subject 150) may be offered only by candidates in PPE, and cannot be combined with either subject 114 or subject 203.
(ix) The Rise of Modern Logic (180) may only be offered by candidates in Part C of the Honour Schools in Mathematics and Philosophy, Physics and Philosophy, and Computer Science and Philosophy.
(x) Except in the school of Mathematics and Philosophy, and Computer Science and Philosophy, and in part C of the schools of Physics and Philosophy, the paper(s) from part B of the Honour School of Mathematics in Set Theory

and Logic may be taken, and will count as one Philosophy paper.' '(xi) Whenever a new paper is introduced, the Faculty of Philosophy will publish, during the first academic year in which the paper is examined, a list of essay titles which the first cohort of candidates taking the new paper may offer for their extended essay, in those schools where they are required to offer an extended essay in addition to taking the written paper.

Whichever a candidate's honour school, where it is prescribed that he or she must take one or other of certain specified subjects and must take in addition some further subjects, a subject that is not chosen from among the specified ones may be chosen as a further subject.

Regulations for Particular Honour Schools

Computer Science and Philosophy
See SPECIAL REGULATIONS FOR THE HONOUR SCHOOL OF COMPUTER SCIENCE AND PHILOSOPHY.

Literae Humaniores
The Honour School is divided into two Courses; for restrictions on entry to Course II, see the regulations under *Honour School of Literae Humaniores*. Candidates in either Course may offer any number of subjects in Philosophy up to five, or up to four if they are offering Second Classical Language in Course II. Any selection is permitted which conforms to the General Regulations above and also to (i)–(v) following:
  (i) candidates offering one Philosophy subject only may offer any of the subjects listed above except 121 and 199.
  (ii) candidates offering at least two Philosophy subjects must select at least one subject in ancient philosophy, i.e., one of 115, 116, 130, 131, 132, 133, 134, and 135. Those offering three or more subjects must also select one subject from 101, 102, 103, and 108.
  (iii) candidates offering subject 199, Thesis in Philosophy, may not offer any other thesis except a Special Thesis;
  (iv) all candidates must offer at least four text-based subjects, not necessarily in Philosophy (or three if offering Second Classical Language in Course II);
  (v) all candidates in Course I must offer at least one text-based subject in each of classical Greek texts and classical Latin texts, not necessarily in Philosophy.

The text-based subjects in Philosophy are 130 (Greek), 131 (Greek), 132 (Greek), 133 (Greek), 134 (Greek), 135 (Latin).

Candidates may also offer a Special Thesis, which may be in Philosophy, in accordance with the regulations under Honour School of Literae Humaniores.

Mathematics and Philosophy
See SPECIAL REGULATIONS FOR THE HONOUR SCHOOL OF MATHEMATICS AND PHILOSOPHY.

Philosophy and Modern Languages
Candidates are required to take **one** of the following subjects: 101, 115, 116. In addition to this subject, they must take two or three or four further subjects in Philosophy, depending upon whether the number of subjects they take in part II in Modern Languages is three or two or one. Further subjects in Philosophy must be chosen in conformity with the General Regulations.

Where subject 199 is taken, every candidate shall submit his or her application for approval of the subject not earlier than the first day of Trinity Full Term two years before the term of the written examination in the case of candidates planning to spend a year abroad.

Philosophy, Politics, and Economics

Any candidate in this school offers *either* Philosophy Politics and Economics *or* Philosophy and Politics *or* Philosophy and Economics *or* Politics and Economics; and takes eight subjects in all. Subjects in Philosophy must be chosen in conformity with the regulations for the honour school and with the General Regulations above; and subject 114 may not be offered by any candidate who takes subject 203 in Politics.

Candidates offering Philosophy Politics and Economics are required to take (i) *either* subject 101, *or* subject 102, *or* subject 115, *or* subject 116, and (ii) subject 103. In addition to these subjects, they may take one or two further subjects in Philosophy.

Candidates offering Philosophy and Politics are required to take (i) *either* subject 101, *or* subject 102, *or* subject 115, *or* subject 116, and (ii) subject 103. In addition to these two, they must take one, and they may take two or three, further subjects in Philosophy.

Candidates offering Philosophy and Economics are required to take (i) *either* subject 101 , *or* subject 102, *or* subject 115, *or* subject 116, and (ii) subject 103. In addition to these two, they must take one, and they may take two or three, further subjects in Philosophy.

Candidates offering Politics and Economics may take any one subject in Philosophy.

Philosophy and Theology

Candidates are required to take (i) subject 107, (ii) **one** of the subjects 101, 115, and 116, and (iii) *either* subject 102 *or* subject 103. In addition to these three, they may take one or two further subjects in Philosophy, depending upon whether they take five or four or three subjects in all in Theology. Further subjects in Philosophy must be chosen in conformity with the General Regulations.

Candidates taking subject 199 who wish to write their thesis during the Long Vacation may submit titles for approval before noon on Friday of the fourth week of the Trinity Term in the year preceding the examination, and approval will be notified before the end of that term.

Physics and Philosophy

See SPECIAL REGULATIONS FOR THE HONOUR SCHOOL OF PHYSICS AND PHILOSOPHY.

Psychology, Philosophy, and Linguistics

Candidates may take at most five subjects in Philosophy. All candidates must take eight subjects in total. Candidates may only take subjects in Psychology if they offer Psychology Parts I and II.

Candidates who take one subject in Philosophy may take any subject, except 121, in conformity with the General Regulations. Candidates who take two subjects in Philosophy must take at least one of 101, 102, 104, 108, 124 or 125. Those offering three or more Philosophy subjects must choose at least two from the above list. Their further subjects taken in Philosophy must be chosen in conformity with the General Regulations.

HONOUR SCHOOL OF PHILOSOPHY AND MODERN LANGUAGES

A

1. The subjects of the examination in the Honour School of Philosophy and Modern Languages shall be (*a*) Philosophy and (*b*) those modern European languages and literatures studied in the Honour School of Modern Languages.

2. All candidates must offer both (*a*) and one of the languages in (*b*) with its literature.

3. No candidate shall be admitted to examination in this school unless he or she has either passed or been exempted from the First Public Examination.

4. The examiners shall indicate in the lists issued by them the language offered by each candidate obtaining honours or satisfying the examiners under the appropriate regulation.

5. The examination in this school shall be under the joint supervision of the Boards of the Faculties of Philosophy and of Medieval and Modern European Languages and Literature, which shall appoint a standing joint committee to make regulations concerning it, subject always to the preceding clauses of this subsection.

6. The examiners for Philosophy shall be nominated by a committee of which the three elected members shall be appointed by the Board of the Faculty of Philosophy. It shall be the duty of the chair of the examiners for the Honour School of Modern Languages to designate such of their number as may be required for Modern Languages in the Honour School of Philosophy and Modern Languages, and when this has been done and the examiners for Philosophy have been nominated, the number of examiners in Philosophy and Modern Languages shall be deemed to be complete.

B

Candidates will be examined in accordance with the examination regulations set out below.

They will also be required to spend, after their matriculation, an academic year of approved residence in an appropriate country or appropriate countries, and to provide on their entry form for the examination a certificate that they have done this, signed by the Head or by a tutor of their society. Candidates wishing to be dispensed from the requirement to undertake a year of residence abroad must apply in writing to the Chair of the Medieval and Modern Languages Board, 41 Wellington Square, Oxford, OX1 2JF, stating their reasons for requesting dispensation and enclosing a letter of support from their society.

Candidates will be expected to carry out during this year abroad such work as their society may require. It is strongly recommended that candidates should apply through the Central Bureau for Educational Visits and Exchanges for an Assistantship, where these are available, and should accept one if offered. Candidates who are not able to obtain an Assistantship should during their year abroad follow a course or courses in an institution or institutions approved by their society, or should spend their time in such other circumstances as are acceptable to their society. Candidates will agree with their College Tutor in advance of their year abroad an independent course of study to be followed during that period.

A candidate shall offer in his or her language and literature papers one modern language and its literature only, except in a Special Subject or an alternative to a Special Subject (Honour School of Modern Languages, paper XII).

No candidate will be examined viva voce unless the examiners elect to do so and have been given leave by the Proctors to take into account illness or other urgent and reasonable cause that may have affected the candidate's performance in any part of the examination.

Oral Examination: as specified for the Honour School of Modern Languages.

In the assignment of honours, in the case of a candidate who offers four Philosophy subjects, Philosophy shall count for the same as the Modern Language and, in the case of a candidate who offers three or five Philosophy subjects, it shall count for correspondingly less or more, provided in each case that the highest honours can be obtained by marked excellence in either Philosophy or the Modern Language subject to an adequate standard being shown in the other branch.

In every case where, under the regulations for the school, candidates have any choice between one or more papers or subjects, every candidate shall give notice to the Registrar not later than the Friday in the fourth week of Michaelmas Full Term preceding the examination of all the papers and subjects being so offered.

Candidates must take eight subjects in all. They must take three subjects in Philosophy of which one shall be either 101, 115, or 116 and they must take three subjects in Modern Languages of which two must be 1. and 2. prescribed in part I of Modern Languages. Candidates take *either* one subject in part II of Modern Languages and five subjects in all in Philosophy *or* two subjects in part II of Modern Languages and four subjects in all in Philosophy *or* three subjects in part II of Modern Languages and three subjects in all in Philosophy.

Candidates offering a paper from the Honour School of Modern Languages and a paper in Philosophy, both of which involve the study of the same author or authors, may not make the same text or texts the principal subject of an answer in both the papers.

Philosophy

Subjects as specified in **Regulations for Philosophy in all Honour Schools including Philosophy**.

Modern Languages

There are nine subjects in Modern Languages, specified below. They are divided between Part I and Part II. The language papers (*a*) and (*b*) in 1 in Part I constitute one subject. Subject 9 (an extended essay) may not be offered as an additional optional subject.

PART I

1. Three papers as follows:
    (*a*) Honour School of Modern Languages Paper I.
    (*b*) Honour School of Modern Languages, Papers IIA and IIB.
2. Honour School of Modern Languages, *one* paper chosen from VI, VII, or VIII.

PART II

3. Honour School of Modern Languages Paper IV.
4. Honour School of Modern Languages Paper V.

5. Honour School of Modern Languages Paper IX.

6. Honour School of Modern Languages Paper X.

7. Honour School of Modern Languages Paper XI.

8. Honour School of Modern Languages Paper XII.

9. An extended essay as specified for the Honour School of Modern Languages. Candidates may not offer a Special Topic from Course I for the Honour School of English Language and Literature. They also may not offer an extended essay as well as subject 199 in Philosophy.

Candidates who are offering one subject only from Part II may not offer Subject 9 as that subject.

HONOUR SCHOOL OF PHILOSOPHY, POLITICS, AND ECONOMICS

A

1. The subject of the Honour School of Philosophy, Politics, and Economics shall be the study of modern philosophy, and of the political and economic principles and structure of modern society.

2. Candidates must offer Philosophy, Politics, and Economics or such combination of these subjects as may be determined by the Division of Social Sciences.

3. No candidate shall be admitted to examination in this school unless he or she either (*a*) has passed or been exempted from the first Public Examination or (*b*) has successfully completed the Foundation Course in Social and Political Science at the Department for Continuing Education.

4. The examination for this school shall be under the joint supervision of the Social Sciences Board and the Humanities Board which shall appoint a standing joint committee to make regulations concerning it subject always to the preceding clauses of this sub-section.

B

Candidates may offer *either* Philosophy, Politics, and Economics *or* Philosophy and Politics *or* Politics and Economics *or* Philosophy and Economics.

The highest Honours can be obtained by excellence in a minority of subjects offered provided that adequate knowledge is shown throughout the examination.

Candidates must take *eight* subjects in all, and must satisfy requirements of particular branches of the school, including, in Philosophy, those set out in the *Regulations for Philosophy in all Honour Schools including Philosophy*, and, in Politics and Economics, requirements to take core subjects. In Politics, the core subjects are any two of 201, 202, 203, 214, and 220; in Economics the core subjects are 300, 301 and 302. In Politics, any of 201, 202, 203, 214, and 220 which are not offered as core subjects may be offered as further subjects.

On entering his or her name for the examination by the date prescribed, each candidate must give notice to the Registrar of the papers being offered.

For all Economics papers candidates are permitted the use of one hand-held pocket calculator from a list of permitted calculators published annually by the Department of Economics on its undergraduate website, which will be updated annually in the week prior to the first full week of Michaelmas Term.

A. *Philosophy, Politics, and Economics.*

Candidates must take (i) **one** of subjects 101, 102, 115, and 116, and (ii) subject 103, any two of subjects 300, 301, and 302 and any two of 201, 202, 203, 214, and 220.

Their other two subjects may be chosen freely from those listed under Philosophy and under Politics and under Economics, except that (i) if any subjects in Economics are chosen they must include the third core subject; (ii) certain combinations of subjects may not be offered (see List of Subjects below); and (iii) not all Economics subjects may be available in any particular year (see below for details). There may also be restrictions on numbers permitted to offer some Economics subjects in any particular year.

B. *Philosophy and Politics.*

Candidates must take (i) **one** of subjects 101, 102, 115, and 116, and (ii) subject 103, and any two of 201, 202, 203, 214, and 220.

Their other four subjects may be chosen freely from those listed under Philosophy and under Politics, except that (i) at least one must be a subject in Philosophy and the   5
Regulations for Philosophy in all Honour Schools including Philosophy must be adhered to; (ii) at least one must be a further subject in Politics (other than the thesis (or the supervised dissertation) if offered); (iii) certain combinations of subjects may **not** be offered (see List of Subjects below).

C. *Politics and Economics.*   10

Candidates must take subjects 300, 301, and 302 and any two of 201, 202, 203, 214, and 220.

Their other three subjects may be chosen freely from those listed under Politics and under Economics except that (i) at least one must be a further subject in Politics (other than the thesis (or the supervised dissertation) if offered); (ii) one but only one may be   15
a subject in Philosophy; (iii) certain combinations of subjects may **not** be offered (see List of Subjects below); (iv) not all Economics subjects may be available in any particular year (see below for details). There may also be restrictions on numbers permitted to offer some Economics subjects in any particular year.

D. *Philosophy and Economics.*   20

Candidates must take (i) **one** of subjects 101, 102, 115, and 116, and (ii) subjects 103, 300, 301, and 302.

Their other three subjects may be chosen freely from those listed under Philosophy and under Economics, except that (i) at least one must be a subject in Philosophy and the *Regulations for Philosophy in all Honour Schools including Philosophy* must be   25
adhered to; (ii) one but only one may be a subject in Politics, selected from the following list: 201, 202, 214, 215, 216, 220; (iii) certain combinations of subjects may **not** be offered (see List of Subjects below); (iv) not all Economics may be available in any particular year (see below for details). There may also be restrictions on numbers permitted to offer some Economics subjects in any particular year.   30

LIST OF SUBJECTS

Certain combinations of further subjects may not be offered: in parentheses after the title of each further subject is the number of any other subject or subjects with which it may *not* be combined. The syllabuses for the subjects in this List are given in *Regulations for Philosophy in all Honour Schools including Philosophy* or in the schedule below.   35
Philosophy

    101. Early Modern Philosophy
    102. Knowledge and Reality
    103. Ethics
    104. Philosophy of Mind   40
    106. Philosophy of Science and Social Science (105, 124)
    107. Philosophy of Religion
    108. The Philosophy of Logic and Language
    109. Aesthetics and the Philosophy of Criticism
    110. Medieval Philosophy: Aquinas (111)   45
    111. Medieval Philosophy: Duns Scotus, Ockham (110)
    112. The Philosophy of Kant
    113. Post-Kantian Philosophy

114. Theory of Politics (203)
115. Plato *Republic*
116. Aristotle *Nicomachean Ethics*
117. Frege, Russell, and Wittgenstein (118)
118. The Later Philosophy of Wittgenstein (117)   5
120. Intermediate Philosophy of Physics
122. Philosophy of Mathematics
124. Philosophy of Science (105, 106)
125. Philosophy of Cognitive Science
126. The Philosophy and Economics of the Environment (321)   10
127. Philosophical Logic
150. Jurisprudence (*The change to the method of examination by long essay under
(b) as specified in the regulations for the Honour School of Jurisprudence, will apply to
PPE candidates in the following manner:*

    (i) *All Year 2 students in 2013–14 will undertake the long essay in the summer of*   15
        2014;

    (ii) *Year 3 students in 2013–14 will have been taught the traditional Jurisprudence
        course in 2012–13 (Year 2), and will sit an unseen written examination in
        2013–14)* (114, 203).

198. Special Subjects   20
199. Thesis (298, 299, 399)

Politics (including Sociology)
Candidates should note that the Politics subjects available in any particular year
will depend on the availability of teaching resources. Not all subjects will be available
in every year and restrictions may be placed on the number of candidates permitted to   25
offer certain subjects in any particular year.
201. Comparative Government
202. British Politics and Government since 1900
203. Theory of Politics (114)
204. Modern British Government and Politics   30
205. Government and Politics of the United States
206. Politics in Europe
207. Politics in Russia and the Former Soviet Union
208. Politics in Sub-Saharan Africa
209. Politics in Latin America   35
210. Politics in South Asia
211. Politics in the Middle East
212. International Relations in the Era of Two World Wars
213. International Relations in the Era of the Cold War
214. International Relations   40
215. Political Thought: Plato to Rousseau
216. Political Thought: Bentham to Weber
217. Marx and Marxism
218. Sociological Theory
219. The Sociology of Post-Industrial Societies   45
220. Political Sociology
222. Labour Economics and Industrial Relations (307)
223. The Government and Politics of Japan
224. Social Policy
225. Comparative Demographic Systems (315)   50
226. Quantitative Methods in Politics and Sociology (313)
227. Politics in China

228. The Politics of the European Union
297. Special subject in Politics [**For students starting before MT 2015:** (199, 298, 299, 399)]
298. Supervised dissertation [**For students starting before MT 2015:** (199, 297, 299, 399)] [**For students starting from MT 2015:** (199, 299, 399)]   5
299. Thesis (199, 298, 399)

Economics

Not all Economics subjects may be offered in any particular year. There may also be restrictions on numbers permitted to offer some Economics subjects in any particular year.   10

Economics subjects available to candidates in any particular year will depend on the availability of teaching resources. Details of the choices available for the following year will be announced at the Economics Department's 'Options Fair' at the beginning of the fourth week of the first Hilary Full Term of candidates' work for the Honour School, and will be posted on the Department's undergraduate web-site at the same time.   15

300. Quantitative Economics
301. Macroeconomics
302. Microeconomics
303. Microeconomic Theory   20
304. Money and Banking
305. Public Economics
306. Economics of Industry
307. Labour Economics and Industrial Relations (222)
308. International Economics   25
309. Command and Transitional Economies
310. Economics of Developing Countries
311. British Economic History since 1870
314. Econometrics
315. Comparative Demographic Systems (225)   30
316. Economics of OECD Countries
317. Economic Decisions within the Firm
318. Finance
319. Game Theory
320. Mathematical Methods   35
321. The Philosophy and Economics of the Environment (126)
399. Thesis (199, 298, 299)

[**For students starting before MT 2015:** *The Department of Economics should be consulted to confirm numbering and titles in the above list.*]

Schedule   40

The schedule of subjects in Philosophy is given in the *Regulations for Philosophy in all Honour Schools including Philosophy*

201. *Comparative Government*

[**For students starting before MT 2015:** Candidates may be expected to show knowledge of the following topics: political parties and party systems; electoral systems; political executives; legislatures; bureaucracies; federalism and other forms of territorial decentralisation; judiciaries; interest groups; forms of government and the constitutional allocation of power between institutions; democratisation. Questions may be set regarding the nature, origins, and political effects of the individual institutions in the preceding list. Candidates should answer all questions comparatively. They should   50 show knowledge of relevant empirical material, and use evidence, comparative methods, and theoretical perspectives appropriately.] **[For students starting from MT 2015:** Candidates are required to show knowledge of theories and methods of comparison in empirical political analysis, including both quantitative and qualitative approaches, and their application to specific problems. The course will include the study of (i) regimes and states; (ii) institutions; and (iii) political actors. Candidates may select any combination of questions in the examination. Topics in the area of regimes and states will include: state-building; structural and actor-based explanations of democratization processes; institutional and legitimacy-rooted variation across hybrid and autocratic regimes; the outcomes of different regimes. Topics in the area of institutions will include: constitutional design and constitutional practice under different regime styles; executives and legislatures; judiciaries; bureaucracies; structures, purposes and consequences of devolved power; and variations in and consequences of electoral systems. Topics in the area of political actors will include: the origin of parties; the explanation of party-system variation and the causes of party-system change; interest groups and social movements, and their interaction with parties and government; the nature of political activism. Where appropriate, candidates must demonstrate an understanding of casual inference and causal mechanisms, and of associated problems of selection, endogeneity, and interaction effects.]

202. *British Politics and Government since 1900*

British politics (including the major domestic political crises, ideologies and political issues) and the evolution of the British political and constitutional system (including elections and the electoral system, political parties, parliament, the cabinet system, and machinery of government). 'Political issues' will be taken to include the political implications of social and economic development and the domestic implications of foreign and imperial policy. Candidates will be expected to show knowledge of developments both before and since 1951.

203. *Theory of Politics*[1]

The critical study of political values and of the concepts used in political analysis: the concept of the political; power, authority, and related concepts; the state; law; liberty and rights; justice and equality; public interest and common good; democracy and representation; political obligation and civil disobedience; ideology; liberalism, socialism, and conservatism.

204. *Modern British Government and Politics*

A study of the structure, powers, and operations of modern British Government, including its interaction with the European Union: the Crown, Ministers, Parliament, elections, parties and pressure groups, the legislative process; Government departments, agencies, and regulatory bodies; local authorities; administrative jurisdiction and the Courts. Candidates will be expected to show familiarity with certain prescribed documents, a schedule of which may be revised annually. Any revisions to the schedule shall apply only to candidates taking the Final Honour School five terms hence, and if no proposals for revising the schedule have been received by noon on Friday of Week One of Hilary Term, the previous year's list shall stand. The revised schedule will be displayed on the PPE syllabus notice-board at the Department of Politics and International Relations, Manor Road Building, and on the Department's website.

---

[1] May be offered alternatively as a further subject in Philosophy as 114.

205. *Government and Politics of the United States*

The constitution; federalism and separation of powers; the presidency; congress; the federal courts; the federal bureaucracy; parties and the party system; electoral politics; mass media; interest groups; state and local politics; processes of policy-formation and implementation; political culture.   5

206 *Politics in Europe*

This paper is a comparative study of the national party and institutional systems of Europe, and of comparative issues in European politics, including democratisation, institutional relations, political economy and party politics. Candidates are expected to show a broad knowledge of European politics, and may where appropriate include   10
reference to the UK in answers, but should not answer any question mainly or exclusively with reference to the UK.

207. *Politics in Russia and the Former Soviet Union*

Candidates will be required to show knowledge of the transformation of the Soviet system from 1985, and an understanding of the politics of countries of the former   15
Soviet Union with respect to their formation, post-Soviet transitions, regime types, institutional arrangements, party systems, electoral processes, ethnic and clan compo-sition, political economy, corruption, and the influence of external factors.

208. *Politics in Sub-Saharan Africa*

Candidates will be required to show knowledge of the politics of the countries of   20
sub-Saharan Africa with respect to their political institutions, political sociology, and political economy. The following topics may be considered: nationalism; forms of government, civilian and military; parties and elections; conditions for democracy; class, ethnicity, religion, and gender; business, labour, and peasantries; structural adjustment and agricultural policies; the influence of external agencies.   25

209. *Politics in Latin America*

Candidates will be required to show knowledge of politics in Latin America; of the structure of government of the major states of the area; and of their political sociology and political economy. The following topics may be considered: presidential systems; the role of congress; public administration; party and electoral systems; the politics of   30
major groups such as the military, trade unions and business groups, and the churches; political ideologies; political movements; the politics of economic stabilization; the politics of gender; theories of regime breakdown, and of democratic transition and consolidation; the influence of external factors.

210. *Politics in South Asia*   35

Candidates will be expected to show knowledge of political developments in South Asian countries since their independence, with regard to their political institutions, political sociology, and political economy. The following topics may be considered: the nature of the state; government and political institutions; party and electoral systems; politics in the provinces or states of a federation; the evolution of political   40
ideologies; the politics of gender, caste, religion, language, ethnic regionalism, and national integration; the political economy of development, social change, and class relations; 'New' social movements and Left politics; regional conflicts in South Asia and the influence of external factors on South Asian politics. South Asia is taken to include India, Pakistan, Sri Lanka, and Bangladesh.   45

211. *Politics in the Middle East*

Candidates will be expected to show knowledge of the politics of the Middle East with regard to their political institutions, political sociology, and political economy.

The following topics may be considered: the emergence of the state system in the modern Middle East; the influence of colonialism and nationalism in its development; the military in state and politics; party systems and the growth of democratic politics; the politics of religion; women in the political sphere; the influence of major inter-state conflicts and external factors on internal politics. The Middle East is taken to comprise Iran, Israel, Turkey, and the Arab States.

212. *International Relations in the Era of Two World Wars*

The relations between the major powers; the twentieth-century origins of the First World War and the origins of the Second World War; war aims, strategies, and peacemaking; the disintegration of war-time alliances; the League of Nations and the establishment of the United Nations; the impact of major political movements (Communism, Fascism, nationalism) on international society; monetary and economic developments as they affected international politics.

Knowledge of events before 1900 and after 1947 will not be demanded, nor will questions be set on extra-European developments before 1914.

213. *International Relations in the Era of the Cold War*

The relations among the major powers, 1945–91, including domestic and external factors shaping foreign policy; the origins and course of the cold war, including detente and the end of the cold war; East-West relations in Europe with particular reference to the foreign policies of France and the Federal Republic of Germany; European integration; the external relations of China and Japan, particularly with the Soviet Union and the United States; the Soviet Union's relations with Eastern Europe; decolonization and conflict in the developing world.

214. *International Relations*

The primary topics will be: the competing approaches to the study of international relations; global governance and the world economy; and global governance and security. Other topics will include: international law; regional organizations; economic integration; globalization; ethnic, national, and cultural sources of insecurity; power, interdependence, and dependency. Candidates will be required to illustrate their answers with contemporary or historical material. They will be expected to know the major developments in international affairs from 1990 onwards, and to cite these wherever appropriate. They may also be given the opportunity to show knowledge of earlier developments; but questions referring specifically to events before 1990 will not be set.

215. *Political Thought: Plato to Rousseau*

The critical study of political thought from Plato to Rousseau. Candidates will be expected to show knowledge of at least three of the following authors, with a primary though not necessarily exclusive focus on the following texts: Plato, *The Republic*; Aristotle, *Politics*; Aquinas: *Political Writings*, ed. R. W. Dyson 2002; Machiavelli, *The Prince, The Discourses* ed. Plamenatz 1972; Hobbes *Leviathan* Parts I and II; Locke, *Second Treatise of Civil Government*; Montesquieu, *The Spirit of the Laws*, Books I-VIII, XI, XII, XIX; Hume, *Moral and Political Writings* ed. Aiken 1948; Rousseau, *Discourse on the Origin of Inequality, The Social Contract*. Questions will also be set on the following topics: theories of political stability and civic virtue; the relationship between the personal and the political; utopian political thought; theories of natural law and justice. In answering examination questions, candidates are expected to discuss the primary texts identified in this rubric, but may also draw on their knowledge of a range of other primary texts from the canon of political thought to the end of the eighteenth century, as indicated in the bibliography issued by the Department of Politics and International Relations.

216. *Political Thought: Bentham to Weber*

The critical study of political and social thought from Bentham to Weber. Candidates will be expected to show knowledge of at least three of the following authors, with a primary though not necessarily exclusive focus on the following texts: Bentham, *Political Thought* ed. Parekh; J. S. Mill, *On Liberty*, essays 'The Spirit of the   5
Age', 'Civilization', 'Bentham', 'Coleridge'; Hegel, *The Philosophy of Right, Lectures on the Philosophy of World History* (Introduction) (CUP edn.); Saint-Simon, *Selected Writings 1760–1825*, ed. Taylor 1975; Tocqueville, *Democracy in America* - Everyman edition (Vol. I: Introduction, chapters 2–6, the last section of chapter 8, chapters 11, 12, the first section of chapter 13, chapters 14–17; Vol II: Book II, chapters 1–8, 16–20,   10
Book III, chapters 1, 2, 13–21, Book IV, chapters 1–8); Marx, *Selected Writings*, ed. McLellan, nos. 6–8, 13, 14, 18, 19, 22, 23, 25, 30, 32, 37–40; Weber, *From Max Weber*, eds. Gerth and Mills; Durkheim, *The Division of Labour in Society* (Prefaces, Introduction, Book I, chapters 1–3, 7; Book 2, chapters 1, 3; Book 3, chapters 1, 2; Conclusion), *Professional Ethics and Civic Morals*, chapters 4–9. Questions will also   15
be set on the following topics: state, society, and the family; individual and community; history and social change; science and religion. In answering examination questions candidates are expected to discuss the primary texts identified in this rubric, but may also draw on their knowledge of other primary texts from the canon of modern social and political thought, as indicated in the bibliography issued by the Department   20
of Politics and International Relations.

217. *Marx and Marxism*

The study of the ideas of Marx and Engels, of later Marxists and critics of Marxism. Candidates will be expected to study Marxism as an explanatory theory, and also to examine its political consequences. They will be required to show knowledge of the   25
relevant primary texts as specified in the bibliography issued by the Department of Politics and International Relations. Questions will also be set on some later Marxists, as indicated in the bibliography.

218. *Sociological Theory*

Theoretical perspectives including rational choice; evolutionary psychology; inter-   30
personal interaction; social integration and networks; functionalism. Substantive problems including stratification; gender; race and ethnicity; collective action; norms; ideology. Candidates will be expected to use theories to explain substantive problems.

219. *The Sociology of Post-Industrial Societies*   35

Candidates will be expected to show knowledge of the following aspects of the social structure of urban-industrial societies: occupation and economic structure; social stratification and mobility; education; the social significance of gender and ethnicity; demography and the family; the social structure of religion; and the impact on society of the state and politics. They must show knowledge of modern Britain and   40
at least one other industrial society, and of the main general theories of industrial society.

220. *Political Sociology*

The study of the social basis of political competition (including social cleavages and identities), social and political attitudes (including political culture), processes of   45
political engagement and competition (including elections, protest politics, elite formation and the mass media), the social basis for the formation, change, and maintenance of political institutions (including democracy and welfare states).

222. *Labour Economics and Industrial Relations*
As specified for 307 below.

223. *The Government and Politics of Japan*
The constitutional framework and structure of government; parliamentary and local politics; the electoral and party systems; the role of corporate interests and pressure groups; the bureaucracy; foreign policy. Candidates will be expected to show knowledge of Japanese political history since 1945 and of the social context of Japanese political institutions and policy-making.

224. *Social Policy*
The nature and development of social policy and welfare states. Public, private and informal systems of welfare. Alternative definitions and explanations of poverty and deprivation. The sources, growth, organisation and outcomes of British social policy with special reference to health, housing, social security, and education.

225. *Comparative Demographic Systems*
As specified for 315 below.

226. *Quantitative Methods in Politics and Sociology*
Candidates will be expected to show an understanding of applications of quantitative methods in politics and sociology including the following: the principles of research design in social science: data collection, the logic of casual inference, and comparative method; major statistical methods and concepts: types of random variables, independence, correlation and association, sampling theory, hypothesis testing, linear and non-linear regression models, event-history analysis, and time-series. Candidates will also be expected to interpret information and show familiarity with major methodological debates in politics and sociology.

227. *Politics in China*
Candidates will be required to show knowledge of the government and politics of China since 1949, and with particular reference to the period since 1978, with respect to its political institutions, political sociology, and political economy. The following topics may be considered: the Communist party and its structure, urban and rural reform since 1978, foreign relations, nationalism, elite politics, gender, legal culture, and the politics of Hong Kong and Taiwan.

228. *The Politics of the European Union*
This paper focuses on the study of the history, institutions, and policy processes of the European Union. It includes analysis of the history and theories of the European integration process. Candidates are expected to show knowledge of politics of the European Union, including the main institutions of the EU, decision making procedures and specific policies, as well as relations between the EU and the rest of the world. The paper also focuses on democracy in the European Union and the impact of European integration on the domestic politics and policies of the member states.

297. *Special Subject in Politics* [**For students starting before MT 2015:** (199, 298, 299, 399)]
Special Subjects will be examined by examination paper. No candidate may offer more than one Special Subject. [**For students starting before MT 2015:** A Special Subject may not be offered by candidates also offering a thesis (199, 299, 399) or Supervised dissertation (298).] Depending on the availability of teaching resources, not all Special Subjects will be available to all candidates in every year. Candidates may obtain details of the choice of Special Subjects for the following year by consulting lists posted at the beginning of the fourth week of Hilary Term in the Department

of Politics and International Relations and circulated to Politics tutors at colleges admitting undergraduates.

298. *Supervised dissertation*[1]

With the approval of the Politics sub-faculty, members of staff willing to supervise a research topic shall through the Administrator of the Department of Politics and International Relations place on the noticeboard of that Department not later than Friday of fourth week of Hilary Term a short description of an area of politics (including international relations and sociology) in which they have a special interest, a list of possible dissertation topics lying within that area, an introductory reading list, and a time and place at which they will meet those interested in writing a dissertation under their supervision for assessment in the following year's examination. Members of staff agreeing to supervise an undergraduate shall provide him or her with tutorials or intercollegiate classes equivalent to a term's teaching for a normal paper, the cost of such tutorials or classes to be met by the college. They shall notify the colleges of the undergraduates involved and the Administrator of the Department of Politics and International Relations. Candidates offering a thesis (199, 299, or 399) **[For students starting before MT 2015: or a Special Subject in Politics (297)]** may not also offer a supervised dissertation. The regulations governing the length, the format, and the time, date and place of submission of a supervised dissertation shall be the same as those for the thesis. Every candidate who wishes to submit a supervised dissertation shall give notice of his or her intention to do so to the Registrar on his or her examination entry form. Every candidate shall sign a certificate to the effect that the supervised dissertation is his or her own work and that it has not already been submitted, wholly or substantially, for another Honour School of this University or for a degree of any other institution. The supervisor(s) shall countersign the certificate confirming that to the best of his, her or their knowledge and belief these statements are true, and shall also submit a short statement of the supervision provided, together with the original specification of the research topic and any other course material provided. The candidate's certificate and the supervisor's or supervisors' statements shall be presented together with the supervised dissertation. Candidates are warned that they should avoid repetition in papers of material in their supervised dissertation and that substantial repetition may be penalized. Every candidate who wishes to have his or her supervised dissertation returned is required to enclose with the thesis, in an envelope bearing only his or her candidate number, a self-addressed sticky label.

299. *Thesis*

As specified for 399 below.

300. *Quantitative Economics*

Unconditional Modelling: Descriptive statistics, basic statistical distributions and applications to economic data, sampling and hypothesis testing.

Conditional Modelling: Binary data with regressors, regression analysis with two and three variables, testing and interpretation of regression results.

Time series Modelling: introduction to issues of temporal correlation and regression analysis.

Empirical applications in micro and macroeconomics: Interpretation of current literature in two areas of microeconomics and two areas of macroeconomics. Topics will be announced at the beginning of Michaelmas Term for examination in Trinity Term two years later.

The examination will include questions covering theoretical issues and interpretation of econometric results.

---

[1] This option may not be available every year.

301. *Macroeconomics*

Macroeconomic theories and their policy implications; macroeconomic shocks and fluctuations; unemployment and inflation; exchange rates; interest rates and the current account; intertemporal adjustment, growth theory; monetary and fiscal policy.

The paper will be set in two parts. Candidates will be required to answer questions from both parts. Part A will consist of short questions and Part B will consist of longer questions.

302. *Microeconomics*

Risk, expected utility theory; welfare economics and general equilibrium, public goods and externalities; game theory and industrial organisation; information economics; applications of microeconomics.

The paper will be set in two parts. Candidates will be required to answer questions from both parts. Part A will consist of short questions and Part B will consist of longer questions.

303. *Microeconomic Theory*

Rigorous study of core elements of microeconomic theory. Topics may (but not necessarily) include: decision making under risk and uncertainty; theory of search under uncertainty; models of contracting under asymmetric information; theory of general economic equilibrium; theory of social choice. A descriptive list of the topics will be published on the Economics website before the beginning of the year in which the course is taught and examined.

Questions will be set requiring candidates to solve problems and demonstrate conceptual understanding of core elements of microeconomic theory.

304. *Money and Banking*

The role of money in general equilibrium models. Aggregate models of price and output fluctuations. The role of banks and other financial intermediaries. Models of monetary policy. Inflation targeting and other policy regimes. Money and public finance. The transmission of monetary policy to asset prices and exchange rates.

The paper will be set in two parts. Candidates will be required to show knowledge on both parts of the paper. Part A will comprise questions requiring analysis of specific models. Part B will comprise essay questions requiring discussion of the theoretical and empirical literature.

305. *Public Economics*

Welfare measurement and cost-benefit analysis, with applications to healthcare and the environment; taxes and transfers; optimal income and commodity taxation, and intertemporal public finance including pensions provision; government expenditure, including healthcare and education; political economics.

306. *Economics of Industry*

Market structures, costs and scale economies, oligopoly and the theory of games, entry, empirical studies of pricing and profitability, advertising, product differentiation, managerial theories of the firm, mergers and vertical integration, innovation, public policy towards market structure and conduct, regulation.

Candidates will be expected to show knowledge of empirical studies relating to one or more of the advanced industrial economies, but questions relating to specific industrial economies will not be set.

307. *Labour Economics and Industrial Relations*[1]

The analysis of labour markets from both microeconomic and macroeconomic perspectives; collective bargaining and trade unions; personnel economics; the economics of education and human capital; wage determination and inequality.

308. *International Economics*   5

Theories of international trade and factor movements, positive and normative, and their application to economic policy and current problems. Theory and practice of economic integration. Current problems of the international trading system. Methods of balance of payments adjustment and financing; policies for attaining internal and external balance. Behaviour of floating exchange rates: theory and evidence. Optimum   10
Currency Areas and Exchange Rate Regimes. International Policy Co-ordination and the International Monetary System.

309. *Command and Transitional Economies*

This paper covers the traditional command economy, attempts to reform it in the direction of market socialism, and transition to a market economy. Candidates will be   15
expected first to be familiar with the evolution of the command economy in the prewar USSR (War Communism, New Economic Policy, Stalinist central planning) and in the post-war period in the USSR, Eastern Europe and China. But emphasis is placed on knowledge of the features and policies of the main variants of the command system (e.g. central planning, performance of state enterprises, fiscal and monetary   20
policies, foreign trade), rather than of the details of economic history or experiences of countries. The second area includes the 1965 reform and perestroika in the USSR, the New Economic Mechanism in Hungary, self-management in Yugoslavia, and post-1978 reforms in China. The third area comprises the theory of the transition from command to market systems, as well as policies and economic developments in the   25
major countries after 1989. Although most questions will deal with the Soviet Union and Eastern Europe, at least two will relate fully or partially to the economy of China.

310. *Economics of Developing Countries*

Theories of growth and development. Poverty and income distribution. Human resources. Labour markets and employment. Industrialisation and technology.   30
Agriculture and rural development. Monetary and fiscal issues; inflation. Foreign trade and payments. Foreign and domestic capital; economic aid. The role of government in development; the operation of markets.

Where appropriate, candidates will be expected to illustrate their answers with knowledge of actual situations.   35

311. *British Economic History since 1870*

Trends and cycles in national income, factor supplies, and productivity; changes in the structure of output, employment, and capital; management and entrepreneurship; the location of industries, industrial concentration, and the growth of large firms; prices, interest rates, money, and public finance; wages, unemployment, trade unions,   40
and the working of the labour market; the distribution of incomes, poverty, and living standards; foreign trade, tariffs, international capital movements, and sterling; Government economic policy in peace and war.

Questions concerned *exclusively* with the periods before 1900 or after 1973 will not be set.   45

---

[1] May be offered alternatively as a subject in Politics as 222.

314. *Econometrics*

A variety of econometric topics will be covered, drawn from the following list: maximum likelihood, endogeneity and instrumental variables, unit roots and cointegration, limited dependent variable models, duration models and panel data models. Application of the introduced econometric methods to economic problems will also be discussed.

A descriptive list of the topics will be published on the Economics website before the beginning of the year in which the course is taught and examined.

315. *Comparative Demographic Systems*[1]

Candidates will be expected to show knowledge of controversies in demographic theory (Malthus and his critics, Easterlin, Caldwell, the New Home Economics school and others) and to illustrate their answers with varied and specific examples. The paper will comprise two sections. Section 1 will test the candidate's ability to interpret quantitive results and the methods of demographic analysis. Section 2 will test the candidate's knowledge of substantive trends and their explanation. Candidates will be required to answer three questions, one from Section 1 and two from Section 2.

    I Demographic analysis and techniques: data sources, adequacy and remedies. Statistical analysis of fertility, mortality, and other demographic phenomena. The life table, stable population, and other models of population structure and growth. Population dynamics, projections and simulations.

   II Demographic trends and explanations. Limits to fertility and the lifespan. Contrasts between stable and transitional population systems in historical European and current non-European societies: the decline of mortality, fertility patterns in relation to systems of household formation, kin organization and risk environments, marital fertility decline and the current status of transition theory. Social, economic, and political consequences of rapid population growth at the national level and the local level.

Demographic systems in post-transitional societies (modern Europe and other industrial areas): low fertility, trends in health and survival, and age structure change; their economic and social causes and consequences. New patterns of marriage and family, women in the workforce, labour migration and the demography of ethnic minorities, population policies.

316. *Economics of OECD Countries*

Main phases of development since 1945. Institutional framework of policy formation; conduct of demand management policies; the welfare state and public expenditure; experience of policies and strategies. The behaviour of major macroeconomic aggregates; the labour market and industrial relations. Development of external trade and financial relations; competitiveness and exchange rates; economic integration and the international coordination of economic policies.

Questions will be set requiring knowledge of one or more of the following countries: France, Germany, Italy, Japan, UK, and US. Candidates will be expected to answer at least one question (out of three) from Part A.

Part A. Comparative analysis of the OECD countries
Part B. The Major Areas
Section 1: Western Europe
Section 2: the United States
Section 3: Japan.

---

[1] May be offered alternatively as a subject in Politics as 225.

317. *Economic Decisions within the Firm*

Linear economics models, simplex method for linear programming, duality, and sensitivity analysis. Network models, including the transportation and assignment problems, shortest path problems, project scheduling. Dynamic and integer programming. 5

Expected utility theory and decision trees. Markov chain models. Queuing systems. Stochastic dynamic programming. Inventory control. Monte Carlo methods and simulation. Two-person, zero-sum games.

318. *Finance*

As specified in Paper 3, *Finance*, in the Honour School of Economics and 10 Management.

319. *Game Theory*

Strategic-form games and extensive-form games. Solution concepts. Games with incomplete information. Applications and topics which may (but not necessarily) include bargaining, auctions, global games, evolutionary games, co-operative games, 15 learning, games in political science.

The paper will be set in two parts. Candidates will be required to show knowledge on both parts of the paper.

Part A. Questions will be set requiring candidates to solve problems involving the core elements of game theory. 20

Part B. Questions will be set requiring candidates to solve problems in and show knowledge of specific applications and topics in game theory.

320. *Mathematical Methods*

The paper will cover mathematical tools such as Calculus, Linear Algebra, Differential and Difference Equations, Probability and Statistical Inference and 25 their applications to Economics. Applications will not require knowledge of material covered in other optional papers but will assume knowledge of the core first and second year papers. A detailed syllabus will be published every year.

321. *The Philosophy and Economics of the Environment* (126)[1] **[NB: This paper may not be taken by bipartite Politics and Philosophy candidates.]** 30

Philosophical foundations: justice and goodness, theories of value; decision-making under uncertainty. Economics foundations: externalities, public goods, international environmental agreements. Politics and the environment. Inter-generational ethics, discounting. The choice of instruments: taxes, permits and command-and-control; environmental instruments in practice. Valuing human life. Valuing nature. Cost- 35 benefit analysis: foundations and critiques; valuation methods.

399. *Thesis*

(*a*) *Subject*

The subject of every thesis should fall within the scope of the Honour School. The subject may but need not overlap any subject on which the candidate offers papers. 40 Candidates are warned that they should avoid repetition in papers of material used in their theses and that substantial repetition may be penalized.

Every candidate shall submit through his or her college for approval to the Director of Undergraduate Studies for Philosophy, Politics and International Relations, or Economics the title he or she proposes together with 45

---

[1] May be offered alternatively as a subject in Philosophy as 126.

(i) an indication as to the branch of the school in which the subject falls, e.g. Economics;

(ii) an explanation of the subject in about 100 words;

(iii) a letter of approval from his or her thesis tutor;

not earlier than the first day of the Trinity Full Term of the year before that in which   5
he or she is to be examined and not later than the date prescribed for entry to the examination. The relevant chair shall decide as soon as possible whether or not to approve the title and shall advise the candidate immediately. No decision shall be deferred beyond the end of the fifth week of Michaelmas Full Term.

Proposals to change the title of the thesis may be made through the college and will   10
be considered by the chair of the relevant sub-faculty until the first day of the Hilary Full Term of the year in which the student is to be examined, and by the chair of the examiners thereafter.

(*b*) *Authorship and origin*

Every thesis shall be the candidate's own work. His or her thesis tutor may,   15
however, discuss with him or her the field of study, the sources available, and the method of presentation; the thesis tutor may also read and comment on a first draft. The amount of assistance that may be given is equivalent to the teaching of a normal paper. Theses previously submitted for the Honour School of Philosophy, Politics, and Economics may be resubmitted. No thesis will be accepted if it has already been   20
submitted, wholly or substantially, for another Honour School or degree of this University, or for a degree of any other institution. Every candidate shall sign a certificate to the effect that the thesis is his or her own work and that it has not already been submitted, wholly or substantially, for another Honour School or degree of this University, or for a degree of any other institution. This certificate shall be   25
presented together with the thesis. No thesis shall, however, be ineligible because it has been or is being submitted for any prize of this University.

(*c*) *Length and format*

No thesis shall exceed 15,000 words, the limit to include all notes and appendices, but not bibliographies; no person or body shall have authority to permit any excess.   30
There shall be a select bibliography or a list of sources. All theses must be typed in double spacing on one side of quarto or A4 paper. Any notes and references may be placed *either* at the bottom of the relevant pages *or* all together at the end of the thesis, but in the latter case two loose copies of the notes and references must be supplied. The thesis must be bound or held firmly in a stiff cover. Two bound copies shall be   35
submitted to the examiners, along with one electronic copy; they shall be returned to the candidate's college after the examination.

(*d*) *Notice of submission of thesis*

Every candidate who wishes to submit a thesis shall give notice of his or her intention to do so on his or her examination entry form (in addition to seeking   40
approval of the subject from the relevant Chair of the sub-faculty or head of department under (*a*) above); and shall submit his or her thesis not later than noon on Thursday of the week before the Trinity Full Term of the examination to the Chair of the Examiners, Honour School of Philosophy, Politics, and Economics, Examination Schools, High Street, Oxford. Every candidate who wishes to have his or her thesis   45
returned is required to enclose with the thesis, in an envelope bearing only his or her candidate number, a self-addressed sticky label.

HONOUR SCHOOL OF PHILOSOPHY AND THEOLOGY

A

1. The subjects of the Honour School of Philosophy and Theology shall be (*a*) Philosophy and (*b*) Theology.

2. All candidates must offer both (*a*) and (*b*).

3. No candidate shall be admitted to examination in this school unless he or she has either passed or been exempted from the First Public Examination.

4. The examination in this school shall be under the joint supervision of the Boards of the Faculties of Philosophy and Theology and Religion, which shall appoint a standing joint committee to make regulations concerning it, subject always to the preceding clauses of this subsection.

5. (i) The examiners for Philosophy in this school shall be such of the Public Examiners in Philosophy in the Honour School of Psychology, Philosophy, and Physiology, and those for Theology shall be such of the Public Examiners in the Honour School of Theology and Religion, as may in each case be required.

    (ii) It shall be the duty of the chair of the Public Examiners in Psychology, Philosophy, and Physiology to designate such of the examiners in Philosophy as may be required for Philosophy in the Honour School of Philosophy and Theology, and the duty of the chair of the Public Examiners in the Honour School of Theology to designate such of their number as may be required for Theology in the Honour School of Philosophy and Theology, and when this has been done the number of the examiners in Philosophy and Theology shall be deemed to be complete.

B

The highest honours can be obtained by excellence either in Philosophy or in Theology provided that adequate knowledge is shown in the other subject of the examination.

Candidates are required to take *either* four subjects in Philosophy and four in Theology, *or* five in Philosophy and three in Theology, *or* three in Philosophy and five in Theology. A candidate may offer a Philosophy thesis, or a Theology extended essay, but may not offer both. A candidate may offer an extended essay on a topic combining Philosophy and Theology; such an essay is subject to the provisions below regarding the extended essay in Theology, but additionally, approval will be sought by the Faculty of Theology and Religion from the Director of Undergraduate Studies of the Faculty of Philosophy.

(a) Philosophy Subjects as specified in **Regulations for Philosophy in all Honour Schools including Philosophy**

(b) Theology

All candidates must take papers (i) and (ii) below. In addition they must take either (iii) or (iv) below. Candidates may select their remaining papers from the paper not selected from (iii) and (iv), paper (v) below, and any other papers prescribed for the Honour School of Theology.

  (i) *The Gospels and Jesus (with special reference to the gospels of Matthew and John)* (Paper (2) in the Honour School of Theology and Religion).

Questions will be set on the four gospels, their theology and ethics, literary and historical problems associated with the gospels, the historical Jesus, and different approaches to the gospels. Candidates will be required to comment on two passages from Matthew, at least three of which will be printed in English. They will also be required to comment on two passages from John, at least three of which will be printed in English.

(ii) *God, Christ, and Salvation* (Paper (5) in the Honour School of Theology and Religion).

(iii) *The Development of Doctrine in the Early Church to 451* (Paper (4) in the Honour School of Theology and Religion).

(iv) *Christian Moral Reasoning* (Paper (12) in the Honour School of Theology and Religion).

(v) Thesis. A thesis may be offered either in Theology or in Philosophy or in both Philosophy and Theology jointly. A candidate who offers a thesis in Philosophy and Theology cannot also offer any other thesis. The provisions governing theses are the same as those given for theses in Philosophy in this school, as specified in *Regulations for Philosophy in some of the Honour Schools*, except that the provisions in the Regulations for Philosophy for subject 199 that 'The subject of every thesis should fall within the scope of philosophy' does not apply to theses in theology.

Optional translation papers (2 hours each).

The translation components of paper (24), *The Hebrew of the Old Testament*, of the Honour School of Theology and Religion may be offered as an optional extra paper by candidates for the Honour School of Philosophy and Theology. Paper (27), *The New Testament in Greek*, of the Honour School of Theology and Religion may also be offered as an optional extra paper by candidates for the Honour School of Philosophy and Theology.

No candidate may offer both philosophy paper 110: *Medieval Philosophy*, and Aquinas for study as a major theologian for paper (10) *Further Studies in History and Doctrine* as prescribed for the Honour School of Theology and Religion.

HONOUR SCHOOL OF PHYSICS

A

1. (1) The subject of the Honour School in Physics shall be the study of Physics as an experimental science.

(2) *Physics (four year course)*   5

The examination shall be in three parts, A, B, C, taken at times not less than three, six and nine terms, respectively after passing the First Public Examination.

In order to proceed to Parts B and C of the four-year course in physics a minimum standard of achievement in Part A may be required, as determined by the Faculty of Physics from time to time. Any such requirement shall be published in the Course   10 Handbook not later than the beginning of Michaelmas Full Term of the academic year preceding the year of the Part A examination. Names of those satisfying the requirement shall be published by the Examiners.

(3) *Physics (three year course)*

The examination shall be in two parts, A and B, taken at times not less than three   15 and six terms, respectively, after passing the First Public Examination.

2. (1) The name of a candidate in either the three-year course or the four-year course shall not be published in a Class List until he or she has completed all parts of the respective examinations.

    (2) The Examiners in Physics for the three-year course or the four-year course shall   20 be entitled to award a pass or classified Honours to candidates in the Second Public Examination who have reached a standard considered adequate; the Examiners shall give due consideration to the performance in all parts of the respective examinations.

    (3) (*a*) A candidate who obtains only a pass or fails to satisfy the Examiners may   25 enter again for Part B (three-year course) or Part C (four-year course) of the examination on one, but not more than one, subsequent occasion.

        (*b*) Part A (three-year and four-year courses) and Part B (four-year course) shall be entered on one occasion only.

    (4) A candidate adjudged worthy of Honours in the Second Public Examination   30 for the four-year course in Physics may supplicate for the Degree of Master of Physics provided that the candidate has fulfilled all the conditions for admission to a degree of the University.

    (5) A candidate who has satisfied the requirements for Part A and Part B of the four-year course, but who does not start or enter Part C or who fails to obtain   35 Honours in Part C is permitted to supplicate for the Degree of Bachelor of Arts in Physics (Pass, or Honours with the classification obtained in Parts A and B together, as appropriate); provided that no such candidate may later enter or re-enter the Part C year, or supplicate for the degree of Master of Physics; and provided in each case that the candidate has fulfilled all the conditions for   40 admission to a degree of the University.

3. The examination shall be partly practical: this requirement shall normally be satisfied by the Examiners' assessment of the practical work done by candidates during their course of study; exceptionally, the Examiners may require a candidate to take a practical examination.   45

4. No candidate shall be admitted to examination in this school unless he or she has either passed or been exempted from the First Public Examination.

5. (1) The Examination in Physics shall be under the supervision of the Mathematical, Physical and Life Sciences Board.

    (2) The board shall have power, subject to this decree, from time to time to frame and to vary regulations for the different parts and subjects of the examination.

Transfer to the Honour School of Mathematical and Theoretical Physics

6. Subject to the regulations for the Honour School in Mathematical and Theoretical Physics, candidates on the four-year course in Physics may apply to the Supervisory Committee for Mathematics and Physics to transfer, after their Part B examination, to the Honour School of Mathematical and Theoretical Physics for their Part C examination. Such a candidate will need to achieve at least an upper second class or higher at the end of Part B, and be accepted by the Supervisory Committee for Mathematics and Physics under the procedures referred to in the regulations for the Master of Mathematical and Theoretical Physics and set out in the course handbook for that degree. Acceptance is not automatic. As specified in the regulations for that degree, Part C in Mathematical and Theoretical Physics must be taken in the academic year following the candidate's Part B examination, and on successful completion of Part C of the Honour School of Mathematical and Theoretical Physics candidates will be awarded the Master of Mathematics and Physics in Mathematical and Theoretical Physics.

7. The Handbook for Mathematical and Theoretical Physics shall, where relevant, set out the options that candidates should follow to maximize their chances of being accepted for transfer to Mathematical and Theoretical Physics for their Part C examination. This Handbook shall be available by the start of Michaelmas Term in the year in which a candidate starts Part A in Physics.

8. A candidate who has transferred from the Honour School of Physics to the Honour School of Mathematical and Theoretical Physics for their Part C examination in accordance with cl.9 above is permitted transfer to the Honour School of Physics for their Part C examination up to the end of Week 4 of the Michaelmas Term in which he or she first registered for Part C in the Honour School of Mathematical and Theoretical Physics, so long as that candidate has not opted to supplicate for the degree of Bachelor of Arts in Physics under the regulations for the Honour School of Mathematical and Theoretical Physics.

9. The regulations for the Honour School of Mathematical and Theoretical Physics set out how the results obtained in Parts A and B in the Honour School of Physics are published for candidates who transfer to the Honour School of Mathematical and Theoretical Physics for their Part C examination.

B

In the following 'the Course Handbook' refers to the Physics Undergraduate Course Handbook, published annually at the start of Michaelmas Term by the Faculty of Physics.

Candidates will be expected to show knowledge based on practical work.

The Examiners will permit the use of any hand-held calculator subject to the conditions set out under the heading 'Use of calculators in examinations' in the Regulations concerning the Conduct of University Examinations and further elaborated in the Course Handbook.

The various parts of the examinations for the three and four year courses shall take place in Trinity Term of the year in question and, unless otherwise stated, deadlines shall apply to the year in which that part is taken.

PART A – for candidates on both the three-year and the four-year course

1. In Part A   5
   (*a*) the candidate shall be required
      (i) to offer three written papers on the Fundamental Principles of Physics, and
      (ii) to submit to the Examiners such evidence as they require of the successful completion of practical work normally pursued during the three terms preceding the examination, and   10
      (iii) to offer a written paper on one Short Option.
   (*b*) A candidate may also offer a written paper on a second Short Option, in which case the candidate need only submit evidence of the successful completion of practical work normally pursued during one and a half terms of the three terms specified in cl. 1(*a*)(ii).   15

2. The titles of the written papers of cl. 1(*a*)(i) are given in the Schedule below. Their syllabuses shall be approved by the Faculty of Physics and shall be published in the Course Handbook not later than the beginning of Michaelmas Full Term for the examination three terms thence.

3. The list of Short Option subjects in cl. 1(*a*)(iii), 1(*b*), and their syllabuses shall be   20
approved by the Faculty of Physics and shall be published in the Course Handbook not later than the beginning of Michaelmas Full Term for the examination three terms thence.

4. With respect to cl. 1(*a*)(iii) a candidate may take, as alternative to the written examination, an assessed course of instruction in a foreign language. A candidate   25
proposing to take this alternative must have the proposal approved by the Head of the Teaching Faculty of Physics or deputy and by the Director of the Language Centre or deputy, by the end of the first week of Hilary Full Term preceding the examination. Approval shall not be given to candidates who have, at the start of the course, already acquired demonstrable skills exceeding the target learning outcomes in the chosen   30
language.

5. With respect to subjects under cl. 1(*a*)(iii) a candidate may propose to the Head of the Teaching Faculty of Physics or deputy, not later than the fourth week of Michaelmas Full Term preceding the examination, either to offer another subject paper, or to offer instead a written account of extended practical work, in addition to   35
that specified in cl.1(*a*)(ii). Candidates will be advised of the decision by the end of eighth week of that term.

Schedule

Fundamental Principles (Part A)
  A1: Thermal Physics   40
  A2: Electromagnetism and Optics
  A3: Quantum Physics

PART B – for candidates on the three-year course

1. In Part B
   (*a*) the candidate shall be required   45
      (i) to offer four written papers on Physics, and

(ii) to submit to the Examiners such evidence as they require of the successful completion of practical work normally pursued during three terms in the academic year of the examination, and

(iii) to offer a written paper on one Short Option.

(*b*) a candidate may also offer a written paper on a second Short Option, in which case the candidate need only submit evidence of the successful completion of practical work normally pursued during one and a half terms of the three terms specified in cl. 1(*a*)(ii).

(*c*) to offer a project report on practical work or other work undertaken in the academic year in which the examination takes place on a subject approved by the Head of the Teaching Faculty of Physics or deputy.

(*d*) candidates may be examined by viva voce.

2. The titles of the written papers of cl. 1(*a*)(i) are given in the Schedule below. Their syllabuses shall be approved by the Faculty of Physics and shall be published in the Course Handbook not later than the beginning of Michaelmas Full Term for the examination three terms thence. The four papers offered shall include B3, B4 and B6.

3. The list of Short Option subjects in cl. 1(*a*)(iii), cl. 2 and their syllabuses shall be approved by the Faculty of Physics and shall be published in the Course Handbook not later than the beginning of Michaelmas Full Term for the examination three terms thence.

4. In cl. 1(a)(ii), practical work may be replaced by project work, if an appropriate supervisor is available. The subject, duration, and replacement value shall be approved by the Head of the Teaching Faculty of Physics or deputy, by the end of Michaelmas Full Term.

5. With respect to cl. 1(*a*)(iii) a candidate may take, as alternative to the written examination, an assessed course of instruction in a foreign language. A candidate proposing to take this alternative must have the proposal approved by the Head of the Teaching Faculty of Physics or deputy and by the Director of the Language Centre or deputy, by the end of the first week of Hilary Full Term. Approval shall not be given to candidates who have, at the start of the course, already acquired demonstrable skills exceeding the target learning outcomes in the chosen language.

6. With respect to subjects under cl. 1(*a*)(iii) a candidate may propose to the Head of the Teaching Faculty of Physics or deputy, not later than the fourth week of Michaelmas Full Term preceding the examination, another subject paper. Candidates shall be advised of the decision by the end of eighth week of that term.

Schedule

Physics (Part B)

Six papers, B1 to B6 as follows:

B1. Flows, Fluctuations and Complexity
B2. Symmetry and Relativity
B3. Quantum, Atomic and Molecular Physics
B4. Sub-Atomic Physics
B5. General Relativity and Cosmology
B6. Condensed-Matter Physics

PART B – for candidates on the four-year course

1. In Part B

(*a*) the candidate shall be required

   (i) to offer six written papers on Physics, and

   (ii) to submit to the Examiners such evidence as they require of the successful   5
completion of practical work normally pursued during the three terms
preceding the examination, and

   (iii) to submit to the Examiners such evidence as they require of the successful
completion of practical work normally pursued during the three terms
preceding the examination, and (iii) to offer a written paper on one Short   10
Option.

(*b*) A candidate may also offer a written paper on a second Short Option, in which
case the candidate need only submit evidence of the successful completion of
practical work normally pursued during one and a half terms of the three terms
specified in cl. 1(*a*)(ii).   15

2. The titles of the written papers of cl. 1(*a*)(i) are given in the Schedule below.
Their syllabuses shall be approved by the Faculty of Physics and shall be published in
the Course Handbook not later than the beginning of Michaelmas Full Term for the
examination three terms thence.

3. The list of Short Option subjects in cl. 1(*a*)(iii), 1(*b*) and their syllabuses shall be   20
approved by the Faculty of Physics and shall be published in the Course Handbook
not later than the beginning of Michaelmas Full Term for the examination three terms
thence.

4. In cl. 1(*a*)(ii), practical work may be replaced by project work, if an appropriate
supervisor is available. The subject, duration, and replacement value shall be ap-   25
proved by the Head of the Teaching Faculty of Physics or deputy, by the end of
Michaelmas Full Term.

5. With respect to cl. 1(*a*)(iii) a candidate may take, as alternative to the written
examination, an assessed course of instruction in a foreign language. A candidate
proposing to take this alternative must have the proposal approved by the Head of the   30
Teaching Faculty of Physics or deputy and by the Director of the Language Centre or
deputy, by the end of the first week of Hilary Full Term preceding the examination.
Approval shall not be given to candidates who have, at the start of the course, already
acquired demonstrable skills exceeding the target learning outcomes in the chosen
language.   35

6. With respect to subjects under cl. 1(*a*)(iii) a candidate may propose to the Head
of the Teaching Faculty of Physics or deputy, not later than the fourth week of
Michaelmas Full Term preceding the examination, either to offer another subject
paper, or to offer instead a written account of extended practical work, in addition to
that specified in cl.1(a)(ii). Candidates will be advised of the decision by the end of   40
eighth week of that term.

Schedule

Physics (Part B)

Six papers, B1 to B6 as follows:

  B1. Flows, Fluctuations and Complexity   45

  B2. Symmetry and Relativity

  B3. Quantum, Atomic and Molecular Physics

  B4. Sub-Atomic Physics

  B5. General Relativity and Cosmology

  B6. Condensed-Matter Physics   50

PART C

1. In Part C the candidate shall be required to offer

   (a) written papers on each of two Major Options, and

   (b) a project report on either advanced practical work, or other advanced work.

Candidates may also be examined viva voce. 5

2. In cl. 1(a), the Major Options and their syllabuses shall be approved by the Faculty of Physics and the Physics Academic Committee. The titles of the Major Options are given in the Schedule below and the syllabuses shall be published in the Course Handbook not later than the beginning of Michaelmas Full Term for the examination three terms thence. 10

3. With respect to subjects under cl. 1(a) a candidate may propose to the Head of the Teaching Faculty of Physics or deputy, not later than the fourth week of Trinity Full Term in the academic year preceding the examination, another subject paper or papers. Candidates will be advised of the decision by the end of eighth week of that term. 15

4. In cl. 1(b), the proposed nature of the practical or other advanced work and its duration shall be submitted for approval to the Head of the Teaching Faculty of Physics or deputy with the agreement of the Physics Academic Committee.

Schedule

Major Options (Part C) 20
   C1: Astrophysics
   C2: Laser Science and Quantum Information Processing
   C3: Condensed Matter Physics
   C4: Particle Physics
   C5: Physics of Atmospheres and Oceans 25
   C6: Theoretical Physics
   C7: Biological Physics

HONOUR SCHOOL OF PHYSICS AND PHILOSOPHY

A

In the following 'the Physics Course Handbook' refers to the Physics Undergraduate Handbook, published annually at the start of Michaelmas Term by the faculty of Physics. The Physics and Philosophy Course Handbook is published annually at the start of Michaelmas Term by the Faculty of Philosophy.

1. All candidates shall be examined in Physics and in Philosophy.

2. No candidate shall be admitted to examination in this school unless he or she has either passed or been exempted from the First Public Examination.

3. (*a*) The examination in Physics and Philosophy shall consist of three parts: Part A, Part B, and Part C.

   (*b*) Parts A, B, and C shall be taken at times not less than three, six, and nine terms, respectively, after passing or being exempted from the First Public Examination.

4. (*a*) In order to proceed to Part C a minimum standard of achievement in either Part A in physics or in Part B in philosophy may be required, as determined by the Faculty of Physics or the Faculty of Philosophy from time to time. Any such requirement shall be published in the Physics and Philosophy Course Handbook not later than the beginning of the Michaelmas Full Term of the academic year preceding the year of the Part A examination. Names of those satisfying the requirement shall be published by the Examiners.

   (*b*) A candidate who obtains only a Pass or fails to satisfy the Examiners in Part C may enter again for Part C on at most one subsequent occasion; Parts A and B shall be entered on one occasion only.

   (*c*) A candidate in the final year of the four-year course, adjudged worthy of Honours in both Parts A and B together, but who does not enter Part C, or who fails to obtain Honours in Part C, is permitted to supplicate for the Honours degree of Bachelor of Arts in Physics and Philosophy with the classification obtained in Parts A and B together; provided that no such candidate may later enter or re-enter the Part C year or supplicate for the degree of Master of Physics and Philosophy; and provided in each case that the candidate has fulfilled all the conditions for admission to a degree of the University.

   (*d*) A candidate who is adjudged worthy of Honours on Parts A and B together, and on Part C, may supplicate for the degree of Master of Physics and Philosophy provided that the candidate has fulfilled all the conditions for admission to a degree of the University.

5. The examination in this school shall be under the joint supervision of the Board of the Faculty of Philosophy and the Mathematical, Physical and Life Sciences Board, which shall appoint a standing joint committee to make regulations concerning it, subject in all cases to clauses 1–4 above.

6. (*a*) The examiners for Physics shall be such of the Public Examiners in Physics in the Honour School of Physics as may be required; those for Philosophy shall be nominated by a committee of which three elected members shall be appointed by the Board of the Faculty of Philosophy.

(*b*) It shall be the duty of the Chair of the Public Examiners in Physics in the Honour School of Physics to designate such of their number as may be required for Physics and Philosophy, and when this has been done and the Examiners for Philosophy have been nominated, the number of the Examiners in Physics and Philosophy shall be deemed to be complete.

Transfer to the Honour School of Mathematical and Theoretical Physics

7. Subject to the regulations for the Honour School in Mathematical and Theoretical Physics, candidates on the four-year course in Physics and Philosophy may apply to the Supervisory Committee for Mathematics and Physics to transfer, after their Part B examination, to the Honour School of Mathematical and Theoretical Physics for their Part C examination. Such a candidate will need to achieve at least an upper second class or higher at the end of Part B, and be accepted by the Supervisory Committee for Mathematics and Physics under the procedures referred to in the regulations for the Master of Mathematical and Theoretical Physics and set out in the course handbook for that degree. Acceptance is not automatic. As specified in the regulations for that degree, Part C in Mathematical and Theoretical Physics must be taken in the academic year following the candidate's Part B examination, and on successful completion of Part C of the Honour School of Mathematical and Theoretical Physics candidates will be awarded the Master of Mathematics and Physics in Mathematical and Theoretical Physics.

8. The Handbook for Mathematical and Theoretical Physics shall set out the options that candidates should follow to maximize their chances of being accepted for transfer to Mathematical and Theoretical Physics for their Part C examination. This Handbook shall be available by the start of Michaelmas Term in the year in which a candidate starts Part A in Mathematics.

9. A candidate who has transferred from the Honour School of Physics and Philosophy to the Honour School of Mathematical and Theoretical Physics for their Part C examination in accordance with cl.9 above is permitted transfer to the Honour School of Physics and Philosophy for their Part C examination up to the end of Week 4 of the Michaelmas Term in which he or she first registered for Part C in the Honour School of Mathematical and Theoretical Physics, so long as that candidate has not opted to supplicate for the degree of Bachelor of Arts in Physics and Philosophy under the regulations for the Honour School of Mathematical and Theoretical Physics.

10. The regulations for the Honour School of Mathematical and Theoretical Physics set out how the results obtained in Parts A and B in the Honour School of Physics and Philosophy are published for candidates who transfer to the Honour School of Mathematical and Theoretical Physics for their Part C examination.

B

1. For the Physics papers, the Examiners will permit the use of any hand-held calculator subject to the conditions set out under the heading 'Use of calculators in examinations' in the Regulations concerning the Conduct of University Examinations and further elaborated in the Physics Course Handbook, save that candidates taking part in an exchange scheme shall be subject to the provisions of the host institution in this regard.

2. The requirements for Parts A, B, and C are specified in the regulations for Parts A, B, and C.

3. The highest honours can be obtained by excellence either in Physics or Philosophy, providing that adequate knowledge is shown in the other subject areas. An honours classification will be awarded only if performance in both Physics and Philosophy is of honours standard in Parts A and B taken together, or in Part C.

PART A

Physics

Candidates are required to

(i) offer three written papers on Fundamental Principles of Physics, and

(ii) submit to the Examiners such evidence as they require of the successful completion of practical work normally pursued during the three terms preceding the examination.

The titles of the written papers are given below. Their syllabuses shall be approved by the Faculty of Physics and shall be published in the Physics Course Handbook not later than the beginning of Michaelmas Full Term for the examination three terms thence.

Fundamental Principles of Physics:

A1: Thermal Physics

A2P: Electromagnetism

A3: Quantum Physics

Candidates who have successfully completed the First Public Examination in Physics are exempted from Paper A2P: Electromagnetism. Candidates who have successfully completed the practical requirements for the First Public Examination in Physics are deemed to have satisfied the practical requirements given under (ii) above.

PART B

Candidates are required to offer either (a) three subjects in Physics (each having the weight of half a paper) and four subjects in Philosophy (each having the weight of a full paper), or (b) five subjects in Physics (each having the weight of half a paper) and three subjects in Philosophy (each having the weight of a full paper).

Candidates for Part B must give to the Registrar notice of their choice of papers not later than Friday in the eighth week of the Michaelmas Full Term preceding that part of the examination.

Candidates may choose their three or five subjects from the following list:

Paper B1. Flows, Fluctuations and Complexity

Paper B2. Symmetry and Relativity

Paper B3. Quantum, Atomic and Molecular Physics

Paper B4. Sub-Atomic Physics

Paper B5. General Relativity and Cosmology

Paper B6. Condensed-Matter Physics

Paper B7. Classical Mechanics

Candidates must choose at least two of subjects B2, B5, and B7.

The syllabuses for the above Physics subjects shall be approved by the Faculty of Physics and published in the Physics Course Handbook not later than the beginning of the Michaelmas Full Term preceding the examination.

Philosophy

Candidates are required to take (i) subject 101 or 102; (ii) one of subjects 106 and 124; and (iii) subject 120 as specified in the Regulations for Philosophy in all Honour

Schools including Philosophy. Candidates who offer a fourth subject in Philosophy must select one from the list of subjects 101–122, 125, and 127 as specified in the Regulations for Philosophy in all Honour Schools including Philosophy, and in accordance with the General Regulations therein.

PART C

Candidates not on an exchange scheme shall offer a total of three units chosen in any combination from the lists for Physics and for Philosophy, or an approved collection of course options if taking part in an exchange scheme.

Candidates for Part C must give to the Registrar notice of their choice of written papers not later than Friday in the eighth week of the Michaelmas Full Term preceding that part of the examination, or, if taking part in an exchange scheme, shall have the proposed set of papers to be taken in the host institution approved by the standing joint committee by the beginning of the Michaelmas Full Term preceding that part of the examination.

A unit in Physics consists of either a written paper on a Major Option, or a project report on either advanced practical work or other advanced work, as specified for Part C of the Honour School of Physics. Candidates may be examined viva voce. A unit in Philosophy consists of one of the subjects 101–104, 107–122, 125, 127, and 180 as specified in the Regulations for Philosophy in all Honours Schools including Philosophy, or a Thesis as specified below. No subject in Philosophy may be offered in both Part B and Part C.

Each unit in Philosophy other than a Thesis shall be examined by a three-hour written paper together with an essay of at most 5,000 words, except 121 Advanced Philosophy of Physics, which shall be examined by two essays of at most 5,000 words each. No essay shall exceed this word limit, which includes all notes and appendices, but not the bibliography. The word count should be indicated on the front of the essay. There shall be a select bibliography or a list of sources. All essays must be typed in double spacing on one side of quarto or A4 paper, with footnotes rather than endnotes. Candidates should avoid any substantial repetition of material between examination scripts and examination essays. The topic for a Philosophy examination essay in a given subject can be any question set for the most recent examination of that subject in Honour Schools with Philosophy, with the exception of questions for Plato: Republic (115) and Aristotle: Nicomachean Ethics (116) consisting of multiple passages for comment. Candidates offering Advanced Philosophy of Physics should not take essay titles from old papers, but should seek approval for both their essay titles. Candidates may apply for approval of other essay topics by writing to the Chair of the Board, c/o The Administrator, Philosophy Centre, Radcliffe Humanities Building, Woodstock Road, giving the title he or she proposes, together with an explanation of the subject in about 100 words and enclosing a letter from their tutor attesting to the suitability of this topic for the candidate. Any such application must be received no later than Friday of the sixth week of the Hilary Term preceding the Part C examination for which the essay is to be submitted. Late applications will not be considered. Any such application shall be accepted or rejected by the Board within two weeks of its being received.

Each essay shall be the candidate's own work, though it should show knowledge of relevant literature in the subject and may include passages of quotation or paraphrase so long as these passages are clearly indicated as such and the source properly attributed. The candidate may discuss a first draft of the essay with his or her tutor for that subject. The amount of assistance the tutor may give shall be limited to what can be provided in one of the candidate's tutorials for their study of that subject. For each essay the candidate shall sign a statement to the effect that the essay is his or her own work and the tutor shall also sign a statement confirming that, to the best of his or her knowledge and belief, this is so. These statements shall be placed in a sealed envelope bearing the candidate's examination number and the name of the subject for which the essay has been written, and presented with two copies of each essay. Each copy of an essay shall be identified only by the candidate's examination number and bear the name of the Philosophy subject for which the essay is being submitted and must be submitted not later than noon on Friday of the first week of the Trinity Full Term of the examination to the Examination Schools, High Street, Oxford, addressed to the Chair of the Examiners for Part C of the Final Honour School of Physics and Philosophy.

PHILOSOPHY THESIS

(*a*) Subject

The subject of every thesis should fall within the scope of philosophy. The subject may but need not overlap any subject on which the candidate offers papers. Candidates should avoid substantial repetition in examination scripts or examination essays of material from their theses. No part of a Philosophy thesis submitted for Part C may include work submitted for this or any other degree. Every candidate shall submit through his or her college for approval by the Board of the Faculty of Philosophy the title he or she proposes, together with an explanation of the subject in about 100 words; and a letter of approval from his or her tutor, not earlier than the first day of Trinity Full Term of the year before that in which he or she is to be examined and not later than Friday of the fourth week of the Michaelmas Full Term preceding his or her examination. Applications for approval of subject should be directed to the Chair of the Board, c/o The Administrator, Philosophy Centre, Radcliffe Humanities Building, Woodstock Road, Oxford, OX2 6GG. The Board shall decide as soon as possible whether or not to approve the title and shall advise the candidate immediately. No decision shall be deferred beyond the end of the fifth week of Michaelmas Full Term. If a candidate wishes to change the title of his or her thesis after a title has already been approved by the Board, he or she may apply for such permission to be granted by the Board. Applications should be directed to the Chair of the Board (if the application is made before the first day of Hilary Full Term preceding the examination). If later than the first day of Hilary Full Term preceding the examination application for change of title should be made to the Chair of Examiners for Part C of the Final Honour School of Physics and Philosophy.

(*b*) Authorship and origin

Every thesis shall be the candidate's own work. A candidate's tutor may, however, discuss with the candidate the field of study, the sources available, and the method of presentation; the tutor may also read and comment on drafts. The amount of assistance the tutor may give is equivalent to the teaching of a normal paper. Every candidate shall sign a certificate to the effect that the thesis is his or her own work and the tutor shall countersign the certificate confirming, to the best of his or her knowledge and belief, that this is so. This certificate shall be placed in a sealed envelope bearing the candidate's examination number presented together with the thesis. No thesis shall be accepted which has already been submitted for a degree of this or any other university, and the certificate shall also state that the thesis has not been so submitted. No thesis shall, however, be ineligible because it has been or is being submitted for any prize of this university.

(*c*) Length and format

No thesis shall exceed 20,000 words, the limit to include all notes and appendices, but not including the bibliography; no person or body shall have authority to permit any excess. The word count should be indicated on the front of the thesis. There shall be a select bibliography or a list of sources. All theses must be typed in double spacing on one side of quarto or A4 paper, with any notes and references at the foot of each page. Two copies of the thesis shall be submitted to the examiners.

(*d*) Submission of thesis

Every candidate shall submit two copies of their thesis, identified by the candidate's examination number only, not later than noon on Friday of the week before the Trinity Full Term of the examination to the Examination Schools, Oxford, addressed to the Chair of the Examiners for Part C of the Final Honour School of Physics and Philosophy.

EXCHANGE SCHEME

Each individual candidate taking part in a full-year exchange at a host institution approved by the University will provide a collated set of coursework to the standing joint committee. Each individual candidate will ensure that the host institution forwards a full transcript of the courses taken certified by the host institution. Each individual candidate will ensure that the host institution retains the examination papers and scripts for the approved courses undertaken and that these are submitted under seal, together with the collated coursework and transcript of courses taken, to the Chair of Examiners, Honour School of Physics and Philosophy, c/o Examination Schools, High Street, Oxford by noon on Friday of the sixth week of Trinity Term.

HONOUR SCHOOL OF PSYCHOLOGY, PHILOSOPHY, AND LINGUISTICS

A

1. The branches of the Honour School of Psychology, Philosophy, and Linguistics shall be Psychology, Philosophy, and Linguistics. Candidates must offer two or three branches.

2. No candidate shall be admitted to the examination in this school unless he or she has either passed or been exempted from the First Public Examination.

3. For candidates offering Psychology, the examination shall consist of two parts. Part I shall consist of the one subject area, Psychology. Part II shall consist of two or three subject areas: Psychology, and one or both of Philosophy and Linguistics. For candidates not taking Psychology Parts I and II, the examination shall consist only of papers in Philosophy and Linguistics.

4. No candidate who offers Psychology shall be admitted for the Part II examination in this school unless

   (*a*) he or she has passed the Part I examination specified for this school; and

   (*b*) he or she has satisfied the Moderators for the Preliminary Examination for Psychology, Philosophy, and Linguistics, in the subject *Introduction to Probability Theory and Statistics* or has passed the Qualifying Examination in Statistics for this school.

The Head of the Department of Experimental Psychology or deputy may dispense a candidate from the Qualifying Examination in Statistics in cases where it is clear that the candidate has reached an adequate standard in Statistics by virtue of previous study and qualification.

5. Candidates offering Psychology shall be examined by such of the Public Examiners in the Honour School of Experimental Psychology as may be required; candidates offering Philosophy shall be examined by such examiners as are nominated by a committee of which the two elected members shall be appointed by the Board of the Faculty of Philosophy; and candidates offering Linguistics shall be examined by such examiners as are nominated by the Board of the Faculty of Linguistics, Philology and Phonetics.

6. The examinations in this school shall be under the joint supervision of the Medical Sciences Board and the Faculty Boards of Philosophy and of Linguistics, Philology and Phonetics, which shall make regulations concerning them subject always to the preceding clauses of this sub-section.

B

Candidates may offer *either* Psychology, Philosophy, and Linguistics *or* Psychology and Philosophy *or* Psychology and Linguistics *or* Philosophy and Linguistics.

For candidates offering Psychology, the examination shall consist of two parts. The five papers for Psychology Part I shall count as two papers for the Final Honour School. Part II will consist of six papers covering two or three subject areas; Psychology, and one or both of Philosophy and Linguistics.

For candidates not offering Psychology, the examination shall consist of eight papers in Philosophy and Linguistics.

No candidate who offers Psychology shall be admitted for the Part II examination in this school unless he or she has passed the Part I examination specified for this school.

The examination for Psychology Part I shall be taken during Weeks 0 and 1 of Trinity Term of the candidate's second year. The examination for Psychology Part II 5 and for Philosophy and Linguistics shall be held during Trinity Term of the candidate's third year. The dates of submission for assessed work are those prescribed in sections 1–3 below.

The subjects in Psychology shall be those specified in *1. Psychology* below; in Philosophy those listed in the *Special Regulations for Philosophy in all Honour* 10 *Schools including Philosophy*, and in Linguistics those specified in the *Special Regulations for Linguistics in all Honour Schools including Linguistics.*

Candidates may offer *either* a research project or a library dissertation in Psychology, *or* a thesis in Philosophy, *or either* a thesis *or* project in Linguistics.

There are further restrictions on the choice of subjects and requirements to be 15 satisfied within each branch, which are set out below.

The highest honours can be obtained by excellence in any of the branches offered, provided that the candidate has taken sufficient subjects in the branch and that adequate knowledge is shown in the other branch(es) of examination.

Every candidate shall give notice to the Registrar of all papers being offered not 20 later than Friday in Week 8 of Michaelmas Full Term preceding the examination.

1. PSYCHOLOGY

PART I

The five written papers as specified for Part I of the Honour School of Experimental Psychology will be set: 25

Paper I Biological Bases of Behaviour

Component parts: (i) Cognitive Neuroscience, (ii) Behavioural Neuroscience.

Paper II Human Experimental Psychology 1

Component parts: (i) Perception, (ii) Memory, Attention, and Information Processing. 30

Paper III Human Experimental Psychology 2

Component parts: (i) Language and Cognition, (ii) Developmental Psychology.

Paper IV Social Psychology, and Personality, Individual Differences and Psychological Disorders

Component parts: (i) Social Psychology, (ii) Personality, Individual Differences and 35 Psychological Disorders.

Paper V Experimental Design and Statistics

Candidates will be required to answer essays and short answer questions in *four* of the eight components of Papers I–IV. All candidates are required to offer Paper V.

Candidates who wish to be deemed eligible for Graduate Basis for Chartered 40 Membership (GBC) of the British Psychological Society (BPS) must ensure that the components they select provide coverage of all five of the areas defined in the GBC curriculum. In order to achieve this, candidates must offer one component from each of four areas, chosen from the five areas prescribed below:

1. Cognitive Neuroscience or Behavioural Neuroscience from Paper I; 45

2. Perception; *or* Memory, Attention and Information Processing; *or* Language and Cognition from Papers II and III;

3. Developmental Psychology from Paper III;

4. Social Psychology from Paper IV;

5. Personality, Individual Differences, and Psychological Disorders from Paper IV.

In addition, candidates must sit additional short answer questions covering one component from the remaining fifth area.

The other requirements for BPS Graduate Basis for Chartered Membership are set out in Part II below.   5

Qualifying Examination in Statistics

Any candidate who has not satisfied the Moderators for the Preliminary Examination for Psychology, Philosophy, and Linguistics in the subject *Introduction to Probability Theory and Statistics* must pass a Qualifying Examination in Statistics before being admitted for examination in the Honour School. The Head of the   10
Department of Experimental Psychology or deputy shall have the capacity to dispense a candidate from the examination in cases where it is clear that an individual has reached an adequate standard by virtue of previous study and qualification.

The syllabus and paper set for the examination shall be that for the subject *Introduction to Probability Theory and Statistics* in the Preliminary   15
Examination in Psychology, Philosophy, and Linguistics.

For all papers in Psychology and for the Qualifying Examination in Statistics, the examiners will permit the use of any hand-held pocket calculator subject to the conditions set out under the heading 'Use of calculators' in the *Regulations for the Conduct of University Examinations.*   20

Practical work

Candidates will be required to undertake practical work, as specified by the Head of the Department of Experimental Psychology or deputy, and this will constitute a part of the examination. In exceptional circumstances the Proctors may dispense a candidate from the specified requirements on the recommendation of the Head of   25
Department or deputy.

Reports of practical work completed during the course of study for Part I and submitted for marking shall constitute a portfolio which shall be available to examiners as part of the examination. Every report submitted for marking must be accompanied by a statement indicating that the work submitted is the candidate's own work.   30
Where the work submitted has been produced in collaboration the candidates shall indicate the extent of their own contributions. Reports of practical work previously submitted for the Honour School of Psychology, Philosophy, and Linguistics may be resubmitted, but reports will not be accepted if they have already been submitted, wholly or substantially, for another Honour School or degree of this University, or for   35
a degree of any other institution. The Head of Department or deputy shall inform the examiners by the end of Week 0 of the Trinity Term in which the Part I examination is to be held as to which candidates have (a) failed to satisfy the requirement to undertake practical work or (b) failed to submit a portfolio. Candidates in category (a) will be deemed to have failed Paper V. Candidates in category (b) will be deemed to have   40
failed the entire Part I examination. The Head of Department or deputy shall also make available to the examiners records showing the extent to which each candidate has adequately pursued a course of practical work. The examiners shall take this evidence into consideration along with evidence of unsatisfactory or distinguished performance in each portfolio of practical work.   45

A candidate who fails the Part I examination may retake the examination once only, in the Long Vacation of the same academic year as the original examination. The highest mark that can be awarded to a candidate retaking the examination is a Pass.

Part II

Candidates must offer six papers for Part II. At least one and at most three of the   50
papers must be in Psychology, the others to be chosen from those available in

Philosophy and/or Linguistics below. Candidates taking three papers in Psychology may offer a Research Project or a Library Dissertation in place of one of the three Psychology papers.

In order to be deemed eligible for Graduate Basis for Chartered Membership of the British Psychological Society, candidates must take at least two subjects in Part II Psychology.

Written papers, Research Project, and Library Dissertation:

Each candidate will be examined in either one, two or three areas of Psychology by means of one, two or three written papers, each of three hours *or* two written papers, each of three hours, and *either* a Research Project or a Library Dissertation. The written papers will be selected from the list of at least 12 options approved by the Medical Sciences Division and published at the Department of Experimental Psychology. A list of options will be posted in the Department of Experimental Psychology not later than noon on Friday of Week 5 of Hilary Term in the year preceding that in which the examination is taken.

Research Project

As specified for the Honour School of Experimental Psychology.

Library Dissertation

As specified for the Honour School of Experimental Psychology.

Reports of practical work completed during the course of study for Part II and submitted for marking shall constitute a portfolio which shall be available to examiners as part of the examination. Every report submitted for marking must be accompanied by a statement indicating that the work submitted is the candidate's own work. Reports of practical work previously submitted for the Honour School of Psychology, Philosophy, and Linguistics may be resubmitted but reports will not be accepted if they have been submitted, wholly or substantially, for another Honour School or degree of this University, or for a degree of any other institution. The Head of Department or deputy shall inform the examiners by the end of Week 0 of the Trinity Term in which the Part II examination is to be held as to which candidates have failed to satisfy the requirement to undertake practical work. Failure to satisfy the requirement to undertake practical work will result in the candidate's final degree classification being lowered by one class. Candidates who fail to submit a portfolio will be deemed to have failed the entire Part II examination. The Head of Department, or deputy, shall make available to the examiners records showing the extent to which candidates have adequately pursued a course of practical work. The examiners shall take this evidence into consideration along with evidence of unsatisfactory or distinguished performance in each portfolio of practical work.

2. PHILOSOPHY

Candidates must satisfy both the General Regulations, and those relating specifically to Psychology, Philosophy, and Linguistics in the *Special Regulations for Philosophy in all Honour Schools including Philosophy*.

3. LINGUISTICS

Candidates must satisfy both the General Regulations, and those relating specifically to Psychology, Philosophy, and Linguistics in the *Special Regulations for Linguistics in all Honour Schools including Linguistics*.

HONOUR SCHOOL OF THEOLOGY AND RELIGION

A

1. The examination in the Honour School of Theology and Religion shall include:

(1) Biblical Studies including such sections of the New Testament in Greek as the Board of the Faculty of Theology and Religion shall from time to time prescribe by regulation.

(2) Christian Doctrine and its Historical Context.

(3) The study of a variety of religions.

(4) Such other subjects as the Board of the Faculty of Theology and Religion shall from time to time prescribe by regulation.

2. No candidate shall be admitted to examination in this school unless he or she has either passed or been exempted from the First Public Examination.

3. No candidate shall be admitted to examination in this Honour School unless he or she has satisfied a language requirement for the degree.

4. No candidate shall be admitted to examination in this school unless he or she has satisfied a language requirement for the degree via his or her Preliminary Examination or has indicated how he or she will attempt to do so via his or her Second Public Examination.

5. The examination in this school shall be under the supervision of the Board of the Faculty of Theology and Religion, which shall prescribe the necessary regulations.

B

1. All candidates will be required to offer eight papers, as specified below, from the Schedule of Papers. There shall be four compulsory papers, taken by all candidates, covering the Old and New Testaments and the development of Christian Doctrine in its historical context. In addition to these compulsory papers, candidates will be required to offer four further papers chosen according to the schedules in either Track I, Track II, or Track III.

Examination regulations applying to all Tracks

2. With the permission of the Board of the Faculty of Theology and Religion, any candidate may offer an essay *either* in place of one of the eight papers, *or* in addition to the eight required papers. The regulations governing essays are set out below.

3. Candidates not offering the full Hebrew paper (24) as one of their eight papers may, in addition to their eight papers, offer the Hebrew translation component of paper 24 as an optional extra paper. All candidates may, in addition to their eight papers, offer the optional translation paper in New Testament Greek (paper 27). Candidates who so wish may offer both the Hebrew paper (whether as a full paper or as an optional translation paper) and the optional translation paper in New Testament.

4. In papers (7) to (36), teaching may not be available every year on every subject.

5. Any candidate may be examined *viva voce*.

6. Candidates in the Final Honour School of Theology and Religion will be deemed to have satisfied a language requirement for their degree if they have passed one of Papers 7 (New Testament Greek), 8 (Biblical Hebrew), 9 (Qur'ānic Arabic), 10 (Pali), or 11 (Sanskrit) in their Preliminary Examination.

Candidates in the Final Honour School of Theology and Religion who have not passed one of Papers 7, 8, 9, 10, or 11 in their Preliminary Examination can still satisfy a language requirement by demonstrating a familiarity in their Second Public Examination with either Biblical Hebrew in Paper 1 or New Testament Greek in Paper 2.

Candidates on Track I of the Single Honour School of Theology may also satisfy a requirement to be familiar with Biblical Hebrew by passing one of Papers 22, 23, or 24.

7. In the following regulations, the English version of the Bible used will be the New Revised Standard Version. The Greek text used will be the text of the United Bible Societies, 4th edn.

All candidates must offer eight subjects, as specified below, from the Schedule of Papers.

TRACK I
- (i) Paper (1)
- (ii) Paper (2)
- (iii) Paper (3)
- (iv) Paper (4)
- (v) Paper (5)
- (vi) One paper chosen from Papers (22), (23), (24), (25), (26), or (28)
- (vii) One further paper
- (viii) One further paper.

TRACK II
- (i) Paper (1)
- (ii) Paper (2)
- (iii) Paper (4)
- (iv) Paper (5)
- (v) One paper chosen from Papers (7), (8), or (9)
- (vi) Paper (10)
- (vii) One further paper
- (viii) One further paper.

TRACK III
- (i) Paper (1)
- (ii) Paper (2)
- (iii) Paper (4)
- (iv) Paper (5)
- (v) Paper (13)
- (vi) and (vii)
    either Papers (14) and (15) OR Papers (16) and (17) *or* Papers (18) and (19) *or* Papers (20) and (21)
- (viii) One further paper.

Regulations concerning language requirements

Candidates for the Final Honour School of Theology and Religion will be deemed to have satisfied a language requirement for their degree if they have passed one of Papers 7 (New Testament Greek), 8 (Biblical Hebrew), 9 (Qur'ānic Arabic), 10 (Pali), or 11 (Sanskrit) in their Preliminary Examination. Candidates in the Final Honour School of Theology and Religion who have not passed one of Papers 7, 8, 9, 10, or 11 in their Preliminary Examination can still satisfy a language requirement by demonstrating a familiarity in their Second Public Examination with either Biblical Hebrew in Paper 1 or New Testament Greek in Paper 2. Candidates on Track I of the Single Honour School of Theology may also satisfy a requirement to be familiar with Biblical Hebrew by passing one of Papers 22, 23, or 24. Failure to attempt to demonstrate knowledge of a biblical language ('language requirement') in the paper through which a candidate has stated he or she will do so, will result in a failure of the examination. Inadequate demonstration of knowledge or understanding of the language concerned may result in the reduction of the mark for the paper by one class (i.e. normally 10 marks).

Regulations concerning essays

1. Candidates may offer an extended essay *either* in place of the paper to be chosen under clause (viii) of Tracks I–III, *or* in addition to the eight required papers. Candidates should in general aim at a length of 10,000 words, but must not exceed 15,000 words (both figures inclusive of notes and appendices, but excluding bibliography).

2. Prior approval of the subject of the essay must be obtained from the Board of the Faculty of Theology and Religion. Such approval must be sought not later than Friday in the third week of Trinity Full Term in the year preceding the examination. The request for approval should be addressed to the Undergraduate Studies and Examination Assistant, Faculty of Theology and Religion, Faculty Centre, Gibson Building, ROQ, Woodstock Road. The request must be accompanied by a letter from the tutor stating that this subject has his or her approval. The application should include, in about 100 words, an explanation as to how the topic will be treated, and a brief bibliography.

3. The candidate's application for approval of title should be submitted through and with the support of his or her college tutor or the tutor with overall responsibility for his or her studies, from whom he or she should seek guidance on whether the subject is likely to be acceptable to the Board.

4. The candidate is advised to have an initial discussion with his or her supervisor regarding the proposed field of study, the sources available, and the method of presentation. He or she should have further discussions with his or her supervisor during the preparation of the essay. His or her supervisor may read and comment on drafts of the essay.

5. The subject of the essay need not fall within the areas covered by the papers listed in the Honour School of Theology. It may overlap any subject or period on which the candidate offers papers, but the candidate is warned against reproducing the content of his or her essay in any answer to a question in the examination. Subject to the provision of cl. 4 above, every candidate shall sign a letter declaring the essay to be his or her own work and that it has not already been submitted (wholly or substantially) for a final honour school other than one involving Theology, or another degree of this University, or a degree of any other institution. This letter, which can be found in the Handbook or on weblearn shall be presented together with the essay. No essay shall, however, be ineligible because it has been or is being submitted for any prize of this University.

6. The candidate must submit two typed copies of the essay (bound or held firmly in a stiff cover), addressed to the Chair of the Examiners, Honour School of Theology and Religion, Examination Schools, High Street, Oxford not later than noon on the Friday of the eighth week of Hilary Term in the academic year in which he or she is presenting himself or herself for examination. The letter signed by the candidate in accordance with cl. 5 above must be submitted separately in a sealed envelope

addressed to the Chair of the Examiners at the above address at the same time as the copies are submitted.

7. The provisions of clauses 3–4 and clause 6 of these regulations will also apply to candidates submitting an extended essay as part of papers 6 and 34.

Schedule of papers

(1) *God and Israel in the Old Testament*

The paper will include questions on such topics as the origins and purpose of Deuteronomy; the development of Israelite law; the theology and setting of Isaiah of Jerusalem; Deutero-Isaiah; psalmody and the Psalms; worship and festivals; the history of Israel; pentateuchal issues; the covenant; prophecy and particular prophets; wisdom; apocalyptic; the fate of the individual; creation; the Torah in post-exilic Judaism; method in Old Testament study; Old Testament ethics; Israel within its ancient Near Eastern Environment; God in history; king and messiah; divine grace and human freedom; Israel and the nations.

Candidates will be required to comment on passages from the following texts in English:

(*a*) Deuteronomy 5–15; 26–8.
(*b*) Isaiah 1–11; 28–31; 40–5.
(*c*) Psalms 1, 2, 8, 15, 19, 46–9, 51, 72–4, 89, 96–9, 104, and 118.

There will be an opportunity to comment on passages in Hebrew from:

Deuteronomy 5; 12; 26.
Isaiah 1; 6; 40.
Psalms 1, 2, 8, 48, and 96.

Candidates who choose to comment on Hebrew passages must also translate them. Credit will be given to candidates demonstrating competence in Biblical Hebrew.

(2) *The Gospels and Jesus (with special reference to the gospels of Matthew and John)*

Questions will be set on the four gospels, their theology and ethics, literary and historical problems associated with the gospels, the historical Jesus, and different approaches to the gospels.

Candidates will be required to comment on two passages from Matthew, at least three of which will be printed in English. They will also be required to comment on two passages from John, at least three of which will be printed in English.

(3) *Pauline Literature*

Candidates will be expected to show a knowledge of the theological, ethical, literary and historical issues posed by study of the Pauline corpus of letters in the New Testament.

Candidates will be required to comment on two passages from 1 Corinthians, and on two passages from Romans. Candidates for Track 1 will be required to comment on at least one passage from 1 Corinthians in Greek, and at least one passage from Romans in Greek. Of the passages printed in Greek only, at least one will be taken from 1 Corinthians 1–7, 15, and at least one from Romans 3–8. Of the passages printed in English only, at least one will be taken from 1 Corinthians 1–7, 15, and at least one from Romans 3–8; however, candidates from Track I may restrict their comment to texts printed in English if their other papers include translation and/or comment on at least two passages of Hebrew. Candidates for Track II or Track III or for the Joint School of Philosophy and Theology may restrict their comment to passages printed in English.

(4) *The Development of Doctrine in the Early Church to AD 451*

Candidates will be expected to explain how early Christian thinkers undertook to clarify the teachings of the primitive Church and formulate a coherent system of thought in their cultural context. The paper will not only concern itself with formal pronouncements on the doctrines of the Trinity and Incarnation, but also with other controversies and the contributions of particular theologians.

Questions relevant to the Gnostic, Arian, Nestorian and Pelagian controversies will always be set; other questions may relate, wholly or partly, to such topics as anthropology, soteriology, hermeneutics, ecclesiology, political theology, and the doctrine of creation and the fall. Candidates will be required to comment on a passage from one of the following texts or group of texts:

The Nicene Definition, Arius' Letter to Eusebius, Arius' Letter to Alexander (from E. R. Hardy, *Christology of the Later Fathers*, Library of Christian Classics).

Gregory of Nyssa, *That there are not Three Gods* (in Hardy, *op. cit.*).

Cyril's Second Letter to Nestorius (in R. A. Norris, *The Christological Controversy*, Philadelphia: Fortress Press).

The tome of Leo and the Chalcedonian Definition (in Norris *op. cit.*).

Credit will be given to candidates who show knowledge (where appropriate) of the other texts contained in Norris.

(5) *God, Christ, and Salvation*

Candidates will be expected to answer questions on topics in modern theology, from the early twentieth century through to the present, with particular reference to the doctrine of God, Christology, and soteriology. Special emphasis will be placed on the interrelationship between these three topics and on the way in which their treatment is affected by differing understandings of the nature, the sources, and the practice of theology. Candidates will be expected to be aware of the interplay of tradition, innovation and confessional context in the work of major systematic theologians of the twentieth century. All candidates should be able to use prescribed texts in an appropriate manner.

(6) *Further Studies in New Testament and Christian Origins*

Candidates will be expected to study one particular subject area concerned with New Testament texts and/or related literature. In the Michaelmas Term of each year, the Board of the Faculty of Theology will publish a list of options on which teaching will be provided in the following academic year and on which the examination will be based. The options offered may vary from year to year and will be related to the research interests of the teachers concerned.

(7) *The History and Theology of Western Christianity, 1050–1350*

The paper will consist of questions on the thought of the leading theologians (especially Anselm, Peter Abelard, Aquinas, Duns Scotus, and William of Ockham), and of questions on the main developments in the western church. It will be so set that any period of 150 years, with its theological writers, will provide sufficient coverage.

(8) *The History and Theology of Western Christianity, 1500–1648*

The subject includes the work and thought of the leading mainstream Protestant reformers, especially Luther, Zwingli, and Calvin, together with the radicals, and the development of the Reformation in European society. Questions will be set both on renewal in the Roman Catholic Church throughout Europe, the confessional tensions which led to the Thirty Years' War (1618–48) and on religious change in the kingdom of England from the Henrician reforms through to the reign of Charles I and the downfall of his government and Church.

(9) EITHER

A. *Christian Life and Thought in Europe and the English-Speaking World, 1789–1921*

Candidates will be expected to show knowledge of the life and thought of the Christian churches of Europe and North America in their social and political context (with special reference to Britain) and the development and influence of Roman 5
Catholic and Protestant theology in the context of Europe (including Britain) and North America. Candidates may approach the topic through the works of theologically important writers of the period, as well as other historical materials. Such writers might typically include S.T. Coleridge, J.H. Newman, F.D. Maurice, G. Tyrrell, E. Underhill, and P.T. Forsyth in Britain; R.W. Emerson, W. James, H. Bushnell, 10
and W. Rauschenbusch in the USA; and F.D.E. Schleiermacher, G.W.F. Hegel, K. Marx, L. Feuerbach, S. Kierkegaard, F.R. de Lamennais, A. Harnack, A. Loisy, and K. Barth in Europe.

OR

B. *Issues in Theology, 1789–1921* 15

The paper addresses key issues in theological thinking in Britain and Europe during the long nineteenth century. These include biblical interpretation, the nature of authority, reason and faith, ecclesiology, Christology, romanticism, literature and imagination, spirit and history, reductionism, religious experience, and the encounter with world religions. The topics will be addressed through seminal or representative 20
texts. Kant, Hegel, Schleiermacher, Kierkegaard, Nietzsche, Newman and Coleridge are especially significant thinkers whose work or influence will normally be represented in the paper. Four main topics with prescribed texts will be published for each year.

(10) *Further Studies in History and Doctrine* 25

Candidates will be expected to study one major theologian in relation to the situation and problems of the time, with special attention to certain texts. In the Michaelmas Term of the year preceding the year of the examination the Board of the Faculty of Theology and Religion will publish a list of theologians (with texts) on which teaching will be provided in the following academic year and on which the 30
examination will be based. In the event of a candidate's opting to take a year out after having studied a chosen theologian, the examiners will set questions on that theologian in the year of that candidate's examination, even if that theologian is not available for study that year. Texts will be studied in English. One or two optional questions may be set which will require knowledge of the texts in original languages 35
when these are other than English.

A candidate may offer a second major theologian from amongst those available in the year of his or her examination. In the event that a candidate does choose to offer a second major theologian, that candidate will offer paper 10 as two papers. To facilitate this, separate papers (10(*a*), 10(*b*) etc.) will be set for each major theologian. 40

(11) *Philosophy of Religion*

The subject will include an examination of claims about the existence of God, and God's relation to the world: their meaning, the possibility of their truth, and the kind of justification which can or needs to be provided for them, and the philosophical problems raised by the existence of different religions. One or two questions may also 45
be set on central claims peculiar to Christianity, such as the doctrines of the Trinity, Incarnation, and Atonement.

(12) *Christian Moral Reasoning*

Candidates will be expected to elucidate and assess themes in Christian traditions of moral reasoning in relation to major ethical writings and contemporary moral and 50 social debates. The paper will consist of three sections: (A) Christian Moral Concepts; (B) Prescribed Texts; (C) Concrete Moral Issues.

Candidates will be required to answer one question from each section.

A. *Christian Moral Concepts*

Methodological issues such as the moral roles of Scripture, and the relation of Scripture to other moral sources (e.g., reason, theological and philosophical traditions, experience); and basic concepts such as the good, worship, sanctification, freedom, natural law, divine command, discipleship, virtue, love, justice, and double effect.

B. *Prescribed Texts*

Augustine, *On Christian Doctrine*, bk.1 (trans. R.P.H. Green, Oxford University Press)

Thomas Aquinas, *Summa Theologiae*, Ia IIae, pp. 91–4 (trans. Thomas Gilby, Blackfriars ed., vol.28, Eyre & Spottiswood)

Martin Luther, 'The Freedom of a Christian' (trans. W.A. Lambert, Harold J. Grimm, *Luther's Works*, vol.31, Fortress Press)

Dietrich Bonhoeffer, 'Christ, Reality and Good', in *Ethics* (*Works*, vol. 6, ed. C. Green, Fortress Press).

C. *Concrete Moral Issues*

Sexual, medical, and political.

(13) *The Nature of Religion*

This paper will examine students in the main classical and contemporary approaches to the study of religions. It will cover some of the most important thinkers in the humanities and the social sciences who established the study of religion as a field of academic inquiry in the nineteenth and twentieth centuries. Students will be expected to be able to speak to basic questions about the relationship of religion to social change; the paper will focus on the fundamental theoretical questions about the concept of religion and strategies for defining it.

(14) *The Formation of Rabbinic Judaism (Judaism I)*

This paper examines the history of rabbinic Judaism from the first century CE to the Renaissance against the background of the societies in which it flourished. Candidates will be required to comment on passages from the prescribed texts in English, and will be given an opportunity to comment upon the Hebrew text of certain selected passages. Also, discussion of the relation of Judaism to other religious traditions may be included.

(15) *Judaism in History and Society (Judaism II)*

This paper examines the nature of modern Judaism against the background of recent history, including such topics as: the impact on Jewish thought and society of the Enlightenment and the Emancipation; the growth of Hasidism in the eighteenth and Reform in the nineteenth century; responses to the Holocaust, to the establishment of the State of Israel, and to the women's movement. Also, discussion of the relation of Judaism to other religious traditions may be included.

(16) *Islam in the Classical Period (Islam I)*

The paper covers the historical origins and development of the theology, law, and mysticism of Islam, from the seventh to the fifteenth centuries. It will consist of questions on the Prophethood of Muhammad; the Qur'an; the Hadith; Shi'ism; the theologies of the Mu'tazilis, Ash'aris, and Hanbalis; Sufism (*tasawwuf*) and the major Sufi orders; and classical Muslim authorities. Candidates should be aware of the various interpretative methods relating to Muslim Scripture, the main debates and historical controversies of the Islamic tradition, and of contemporary methodologies in philosophy of religion. References to other religious traditions may be included.

(17) *Islam in Contemporary Society (Islam II)*

The paper examines Islam against the background of recent history, including such topics as: Islamic reformism in the nineteenth to the twenty-first centuries; various Islamic movements including the anti-Hadith faction and Wahhabism; women and Islam; democracy and Islam; violence and war in Islam; and various modern Muslim thinkers.

(18) *Foundations of Buddhism (Buddhism I)*

The paper deals with the main teachings and practices of early Buddhism, as reflected by the surviving literature of the various schools, discussing their formation against the background of the main religious movements existing in north-east India around the fifth century BC. Practices include both meditation and monastic life.

(19) *Buddhism in Space and Time (Buddhism II)*

This paper deals with Buddhism as it developed and changed in space and time. The first part of the course will be devoted to the main ideas and schools of Mahāyāna (Great Vehicle) Buddhism. The second part will discuss the transmission and transformation of Buddhism in some of the main areas where it continues to exist in the modern world.

(20) *Hinduism I: Sources and Development*

This paper offers a thematic and historical introduction to the sources and development of "Hindu" traditions from their early formation to the medieval period. It will explore the formation of Hindu traditions through textual sources, such as the Vedas, Upaniṣads and Bhagavad Gītā, along with the practices and social institutions that formed classical Indic religions.

(21) *Hinduism II: Hinduism in History and Society*

Beginning with the early medieval period, this paper traces the development of Hinduism in devotional (bhakti) and tantric traditions. The paper examines the development of Śaiva, Śākta, and Vaiṣṇava traditions along with ideas about liberation, ritual, caste, asceticism, yoga and devotion. Candidates will be encouraged to consider the relations between Hinduism, modernity, and nationalism.

(22) *Selected topics (Old Testament) I*

Candidates will be required to show detailed knowledge of one of the following topics. They will be required to comment on passages from the prescribed texts in English (New Revised Standard Version), and will be given an opportunity to comment upon the Hebrew text of certain specified chapters and sections.

(i) *Prophecy*

1 Samuel 9; 10
2 Samuel 7
1 Kings 13; 18; 22
Isaiah 1; 5–8; 10; 40; 42–4; 49; 51–3; 55
Jeremiah 1–5; 7–9; 11; 12; 26–8; 31
Ezekiel 1–4; 8–11; 14; 18; 20; 23; 36; 37
Amos 1–5; 6–9
Zechariah 1–8; 13

Among these the following may be offered in Hebrew:
1 Kings 13; 18; 22
Isaiah 42–4
Amos 1–5

(ii) *Apocalyptic*
Isaiah 24–7
Daniel
Zechariah

1 Enoch 1–16 (ed. H. F. D. Sparks, *The Apocryphal Old Testament*, OUP, 1984)   5
2 Esdras 3–14
Revelation

Among these the following may be offered in Hebrew:
Isaiah 24–7
Zechariah 9–14   10

(23) *Selected topics (Old Testament) II*

Candidates will be required to show detailed knowledge of one of the following topics. They will be required to comment on passages from the prescribed texts in English (New Revised Standard Version), and will be given an opportunity to comment upon the Hebrew text of certain selected chapters and sections.   15

(1) *Wisdom*
Proverbs 1–9; 22:17–31:31
Job 1–19; 38–42
Ecclesiastes
Wisdom of Solomon 1–9   20
Ecclesiasticus (Sirach) Prologue; 1:1–25:12; 36:18–43:33; 51

Among these the following may be offered in Hebrew:
Proverbs 1–9

(ii) *Worship and Liturgy*
Exodus 12–15; 19; 20; 24   25
Leviticus 1–7; 16
Deuteronomy 12–18
1 Kings 5–8
1 Chronicles 16
Psalms 2; 18; 24; 27; 47–51; 68; 72; 78; 89; 95–100; 110; 113–18; 122; 124; 126;   30
128; 130–2
A. E. Cowley, *Aramaic Papyri of the Fifth Century BC* (OUP, 1923), nos. 21; 30–4

Among these the following may be offered in Hebrew:
Exodus 19; 20; 24
Leviticus 16   35
Psalms 24; 95–100

(24) *The Hebrew of the Old Testament*

Candidates will be required to show a general knowledge of the language, with a special study of the following prose texts from which passages will be set for translation and comment: 40

Genesis 6–9
Deuteronomy 5–6; 12; 26
2 Samuel 11–14
1 Kings 17–19
Jonah   45

Candidates will also be given an opportunity to show knowledge of Hebrew verse, and especially of the following texts, from which passages will be set for translation and comment:

Psalms 1; 2; 8; 45–48; 96
Proverbs 7–9   50

Isaiah 1–2; 6; 40–42

Candidates who do not offer Hebrew verse will not thereby be penalized.

(25) *Archaeology in relation to the Old Testament*

The subject includes the geography of Palestine and of the neighbouring lands; the history of the development of Canaanite, Hebrew, and Jewish social life and culture; the history of places of worship and their furniture; and the general results of recent archaeological research in the Ancient Near East, insofar as they throw light on these subjects.

(26) *Religions and Mythology of the Ancient Near East*

The paper will include a wide range of questions. The following texts are prescribed for special study:

(a) Akkadian Myths and Epics: The Epic of Creation, in B.R. Foster, *Before the Muses: An Anthology of Akkadian Literature* (3rd edition, Bethesda: CDL Press, 2005), pp. 439–85, and The Epic of Gilgamesh (standard version), in A. George, *The Epic of Gilgamesh* (revised edition, London: Penguin, 2003), pp. 1–100, 191–5.

(b) Egyptian Myths, Hymns and Prayers: in M. Lichtheim, *Ancient Egyptian Literature* (Berkeley: University of California Press, 1973–1980; republished 2006), vol. I, pp. 51–7, 131–3; vol. II, pp. 81–132, 197–9, 203–23.

(c) Hittite Myths: The Disappearance of Telipinu (version 1) and The Song of Kumarbi, in H.A. Hoffner, *Hittite Myths* (2nd edition, Atlanta: Scholars Press, 1998), pp. 15–18, 42–5.

(d) Ugaritic Myths: The Baal Cycle, in W.W. Hallo (ed.), *The Context of Scripture* (Leiden: Brill, 1997; republished 2003), vol. I, pp. 243–73, 'The Ba'lu Myth' (trans. D. Pardee).

(e) Philo of Byblos' Phoenician History, in H.W. Attridge and R.A. Oden, *Philo of Byblos: The Phoenician History* (Washington: Catholic Biblical Association of America, 1981), pp. 29–71.

(f) The Sefire Inscriptions, in W.W. Hallo (ed.), *The Context of Scripture* (Leiden: Brill, 2000; republished 2003), vol. II, pp. 213–17, 'The Inscriptions of Bar-Ga'yah and Mati'el from Sefire' (trans. J.A. Fitzmyer).

(27) *The New Testament in Greek*

Candidates will choose passages for translation from amongst a number taken from the Greek New Testament. The text used will be that of the United Bible Societies, 4th edn. The selection of passages will allow candidates to select passages for translation from the following texts and chapters: Acts 20–6, Colossians, 1 and 2 Thessalonians, Hebrews 7–10, James, 1 and 2 Peter, Revelation 1–12. There will also be opportunity to translate passages from outside these specified chapters.

NB. This paper is not available as a full paper but only as an optional extra translation paper.

(28) *Varieties of Judaism 100 BC–AD 100*

The paper will include a number of general questions and the following texts are prescribed for special study:

Set texts in English:

Qumran Community Rule, MMT (Miqsat Ma'ase Ha-Torah) (Some Observances of the Law) and *Commentary on Habakkuk,* in G. Vermes, *The Complete Dead Sea Scrolls in English* (Allen Lane/Penguin, 1997).

Josephus, *Jewish War* II (Loeb, 1956); *Antiquities* XVIII, 1–119 (Loeb, 1965); *Against Apion* II, 145–296 (Loeb, 1956).

IV Ezra, ed. B. M. Metzger, in J. H. Charlesworth, ed., *The Old Testament Pesudepigrapha* (2 vols., DLT, 1983–5).

Wisdom of Solomon (New Revised Standard Version).   5

Philo, *Migration of Abraham; Life of Moses* I, 1–84 (Loeb, 1958).

Mishnah, Berakoth, Bikkurim, and Aboth, chapter 1 (translated Danby, OUP, 1933).

Psalms of Solomon XVII, tr. S. P. Brock, in H. F. D. Sparks, ed., *The Apocryphal Old Testament* (OUP, 1984).   10

I Enoch 92–105, tr. M. A. Knibb, in Sparks, *op. cit.*

Any or all of the following texts may be offered in the original languages. Such questions will only be set when a candidate or candidates have given notice on the entry form of an intention to comment on texts in Hebrew and/or Greek.

Qumran Community Rule 1–4, in E. Lohse (ed.), *Die Texte aus Qumran, Hebräisch*   15 *und Deutsch* (2nd edn., Darmstadt, Wissenschaftliche Buchgesellschaft, 1971).

Qumran Commentary on Habakkuk, ed. E. Lohse, *op. cit.*

Josephus, *Antiquities* XVIII, 1–28, 63–4, 109–19 (Loeb, 1965).

Philo, *Life of Moses* I, 1–44 (Loeb, 1958).

(29) *Christian Liturgy*   20

Candidates will be expected to study the rites of initiation and the eucharist up to AD 451, the relationship between liturgy and theology and the influence of early Christian worship on contemporary liturgical revision.

Candidates will be expected to have studied the following texts. Texts shown in square brackets will not be examined by gobbets.   25

E. C. Whitaker (ed. M. E. Johnson), *Documents of the Baptismal Liturgy* (3rd edn., SPCK, 2003) pp.1–11, [11–13], 14–21, 40–50, 124–7, 176–83.

R. C. D. Jasper and G. J. Cuming, *Prayers of the Eucharist: Early and Reformed* (3rd edn., Pueblo, 1987) pp. 7–12, 20–44, [52–66], 67–81, 88–99, 114–23, 129–37, 143–6, 159–67.   30

E. J. Yarnold, *The Awe-Inspiring Rites of Initiation* (2nd edn., T. & T. Clark. 1994) pp. [70–5], 76–97.

[Church of England, *Common Worship* (Church House Publishing, 2000), Eucharistic Prayers B & F, 188–90, 198–200].

[Church of England, *Common Worship: Initiation Services* (Church House   35 Publishing, 2005)].

[Methodist Church, *Methodist Worship Book* (Methodist Publishing House, 1999), The Baptism of those who are able to answer for themselves, and of Young Children, with Confirmation and Reception into Membership, 62–75; Eucharistic Prayer for Ordinary Seasons (3), 215–17].   40

[Roman Catholic Church, *The Roman Missal* (ICEL, 1973), Eucharistic Prayers 2 & 4]

[Roman Catholic Church, *The Rite of Christian Initiation of Adults* (ICEL, 1985)]

[M. Thurian and G. Wainwright (eds.), *Baptism and Eucharist: Ecumenical Texts in Convergence* (WCC Publications, 1983), Eucharistic Prayer from the Eucharistic Liturgy of Lima, 252–4].   45

(30) *Early Syriac Christianity*

Candidates will be expected to show a general knowledge of symbolism in the theology of the early Syriac Church.

The following texts are prescribed for special study:

Odes of Solomon 6, 11, 17, 19, 21, 24, 30, 36, 42, tr. J. A. Emerton in H. F. D. Sparks. *The Apocryphal Old Testament* (OUP, 1984). 5

Acts of Thomas, secs. 1–29, 108–14, tr. A. F. J. Klijn (E. J. Brill, 1962).

Aphrahat, *Demonstrations* 1, 4, 6, 12 (*Dem.* 1 and 6 tr. in J. Gwynn, ed. S*elect Library of Nicene and Post-Nicene Fathers* II.13 [1898, repr. W. B. Eerdmans, 1956], Dem. 4, tr. S. P. Brock, *The Syriac Fathers on Prayer and the Spiritual Life* [1987], ch. 10 1; *Dem.* 12, tr. in J. Neusner, *Aphrahat and Judaism* [E. J. Brill, 1971]).

Ephrem, *Sermon on Our Lord*, tr. in E. Mathews and J. Amar, *St Ephrem the Syrian. Selected Prose Works* (1994); *Hymns on the Nativity*, nos. 1 and 2, tr. K. McVey, *St Ephrem the Syrian . Hymns* (*Classics of Western Spirituality*, 1989); *Hymns on Faith*, no. 10, *Hymns on the Church*, no. 36, *Hymns on Epiphany*, nos. 1 and 6, tr. S. 15 P. Brock in T. Finn, *Early Christian Baptism and the Catechumenate* (1992). The Hymns, tr. S. P. Brock, *The Harp of the Spirit: Eighteen Poems of St Ephrem* (Fellowship of St Alban and St Sergius, 2nd edn. 1983). *Letter to Publius*, tr. S. P. Brock, Le Muséon (1976) *Book of Steps*, Homily 12, tr. R. Murray, *Symbols of Church and Kingdom* (CUP, 1975). 20

(31) *History and Theology of the Church in the Byzantine Empire from* AD 1000 *to* AD 1453

Candidates will be expected to show knowledge of the constitution and worship of the Church; monasticism; the development of mystical theology; the relations between Church and state and with the Western Church. 25

(32) *Science and Religion*

Candidates will be expected to have an understanding of the richness and diversity of the relations between science and religion as they have been constructed in western cultures. They should be able to analyse the simplistic models of conflict and harmony, which have so often served ideological purposes. Questions will be set on the role of 30 religious belief in the rise of modern science and on the challenge to religious ortho-doxies from new forms of science. There will be questions on the religious beliefs of major scientists, such as Newton and Darwin, on the responses of theologians to major paradigm shifts within the sciences, and on the interplay between natural theol-ogy and the natural sciences. The examination will also provide an opportunity for 35 candidates to discuss current issues such as the most appropriate response theologians might make to contemporary neuroscience and genetic reductionism. Questions may also be set on recurrent issues such as the presumed existence of extraterrestrial life.

(33) *The Sociology of Religion*

The paper will consist of two parts. Candidates will be expected to answer at least 40 one question from each part.

(*a*) *Texts*

Candidates will be expected to know at least one of the following in detail:

   (i) Karl Marx, *Marx on Religion*, ed. John Raines, Temple University Press, 2002 together with *Capital*, chapters 1 and 13 (Penguin Books, 1990). 45

  (ii) E. Durkheim, *The Elementary Forms of the Religious Life* (Allen and Unwin, 1976).

 (iii) M. Weber, *The Protestant Ethic and the Spirit of Capitalism* (Harper Collins, 1991).

(iv) E. Troeltsch, *The Social Teaching of the Christian Churches* (2 vols., J. Knox, 1992).

(v) Talcott Parsons, *Action Theory and the Human Condition* (New York, 1978).

(*b*) *Themes*

Candidates will be expected to show an understanding of some of the following 5 issues in sociology of religion: secularization, fundamentalism, church and sect, new religious movements, civil religion. Questions will also be set on issues relating to class, race, legitimation, power and violence in religion and religious organization; and sociological readings of other parts of the Theology syllabus, including Biblical studies, doctrine and Church history. Familiarity with contemporary sociological 10 discussion will be assumed.

(34) *Mysticism*

Candidates will be expected to show knowledge of theoretical issues relating to the definition and interpretation of mysticism as well as important examples of mystical literature and traditions. The paper will be examined by two 5,000 word essays: one 15 essay, chosen from a list of prescribed titles, will address theoretical issues; the other will relate to a special topic. The subject of the second essay will be chosen by candidates in consultation with tutors. Prior approval of the subject of the second essay must be obtained in advance from the Faculty Board. Titles, abstracts and bibliographies should reach the Faculty Board Secretary not later than the Friday of 20 third week in Trinity Term of the candidate's second year.

Possible subjects for essays include, but will not be limited to: Neoplatonism, hermetic and alchemical speculations, the Origenist tradition in Christianity, the Dionysian tradition, Rhineland mystics, medieval English mystics, Counter-Reformation mystics, Merkabah mysticism, Hekhalot mysticism, Ismaili and Sufi 25 traditions, Upanishadic thought, Vedanta philosophy, Tantric traditions, Buddhist traditions.

(35) *Psychology of Religion*

Psychology of religion is concerned with human experience and behaviour associated with religion in general. Psychological explanations of religion are based on 30 empirical research of human behaviour (cognitive, emotional, and social) through life span and across different cultures.

The paper will cover theories about aspects of behaviour or experiences relevant to religion and the empirical evidence on these theories: psychological research of different aspects of religion such as conversion, prayer, mysticism; cognitive and 35 affective (i.e. psychoanalytic) accounts of religion; origin and development of religious concepts; normal and abnormal religious experience and behaviour; religious and secular moral behaviour; applications of psychology to religious education and health.

(36) *English Church and Mission* 597–754

Candidates will be expected to study the main lines of the history of the English 40 Church in this period, and some aspects of its theology. There will also be an opportunity to study works of art. Candidates will be expected to have studied the texts in Group I, on which alone gobbets will be set, and in at least one of sections (*a*), (*b*), (*c*) in Group II.

Group I   45

(*a*) Bede, *Ecclesiastical History of the English People*, Preface, Books I, 23–26; II; III; IV; V, 9–10, 19 (trans. B. Colgrave, in: *Bede: the Ecclesiastical History of the English People; The Greater Chronicle; Bede's Letter to Egbert*, ed. Judith McClure and Roger Collins, OUP, 1994) pp. 37–41, 63–233, 247–51, 267–74.

(*b*) Bede's *Letter to Egbert*, trans. D. H. Farmer, ibid., pp. 337–51.

(*c*) Bede, *On the Temple*, trans. S. Connolly, in J. O'Reilly (Liverpool University Press: *Translated Texts for Historians* 21, 1995), Prologue and Book I to I, 8.4, pp. 1–33; Book II, 18.8 to 20.9, pp. 76–100.

(*d*) Eddius Stephanus, *Life of Wilfrid in The Age of Bede* (ed. D. H. Farmer, trans. J. Webb, Penguin Classics, 1988) pp. 105–82.

(*e*) 'The Dream of the Rood', in *A Choice of Anglo-Saxon Verse*, ed. and trans. R. Hamer (Faber, 1970), pp. 161–71.

Group II

(*a*) Adomnan of Iona, *Life of St Columba*, ed. and trans. R. Sharpe (Penguin Classics, 1995).

(*b*) Bede, *Life of Cuthbert*, in *The Age of Bede* (Penguin Classics, 1988), pp. 41–102, Bede, *Lives of the Abbots of Wearmouth and Jarrow*, ibid., pp. 185–208.

Bede's *Homily on the Gospel for the Feast of St Benedict Biscop*, in Bede, *Homilies on the Gospels*, trans. L. T. Martin and D. Hurst, Preface by B. Ward (Cistercian Studies Series, 110, 1991), pp. 125–32.

Letters of Aldhelm, in Aldhelm, *The Prose Works*, trans. M. Lapidge and M. Herren (Boydell and Brewer, 1979), pp. 152–70.

(*c*) Willibald's *Life of St Boniface* and *The Correspondence of St Boniface*, in C. H. Talbot, *The Anglo-Saxon Missionaries in Germany* (Stead and Ward, 1954), pp. 25–62, 65–149.

(37) Any other subject that may be approved by the Board of the Faculty of Theology from time to time by regulation published in the Gazette and communicated to college tutors by the end of the first week of the Trinity Full Term in the academic year preceding the examination in which the option will be available.

Optional translation papers (2 hours each)

The translation component of paper (24), *The Hebrew of the Old Testament*, may be offered as an optional extra paper by candidates who are not taking the full paper. Paper (27), *The New Testament in Greek*, may also be offered as an optional extra translation paper.

HONOUR SCHOOL OF THEOLOGY AND ORIENTAL STUDIES

A

1. The subjects of the Honour School of Theology and Oriental Studies shall be 1 Theology and 2 Oriental Studies. All candidates must offer both 1 and 2.

2. The Honour School of Theology and Oriental Studies shall be under the joint supervision of the Boards of the Faculties of Theology and Religion, and of Oriental Studies, which shall appoint a standing joint committee to make, and to submit to the two boards, proposals for regulations concerning the examination.

3. No candidate shall be admitted to the examination in this School unless he or she has either passed or been exempted from the First Public Examination.

4. The Public Examiners in this School shall be such of the Public Examiners in the Honour Schools of Theology and of Oriental Studies as may be required, together with any additional examiners who may be required who shall be nominated by the committee for the nomination of Public Examiners in one or both of those Honour Schools as appropriate.

B

1. In the Honour School candidates will take eight papers, of which at least three and not more than five must be taken in Theology, and at least three and not more than five must be taken in Oriental Studies. One paper will be examined in the form of a dissertation. Completion of an application form will be required for the approval of the subject of the dissertation, indicating the paper for which it is substituting. In all cases the regulations that apply to the dissertation will be the Theology and Religion regulations, except for the date for submission of the title for approval, which will be sixth week in Hilary Term of Year 2. The request for approval should be addressed to the relevant Faculty Board Secretary using the application form available from the relevant Faculty Office. The application should include, in about 100 words, an explanation as to how the topic will be treated, and a brief bibliography.

Candidates should in general aim at a length of 10,000 words, but must not exceed 15,000 words (both figures inclusive of notes and appendices, but excluding bibliography). The candidate is advised to have an initial discussion with his or her supervisor regarding the proposed field of study, the sources available, and the method of presentation. He or she should have further discussions with his or her supervisor during the preparation of the dissertation. His or her supervisor may read and comment on drafts of the dissertation.

Every candidate shall sign a letter declaring the dissertation to be his or her own work and that it has not already been submitted (wholly or substantially) for a final honour school other than one involving Theology or Oriental Studies, or another degree of this University, or a degree of any other institution. This letter, which can be found in the Course Handbook or collected from the relevant Faculty Office, shall be presented together with the dissertation. No dissertation shall, however, be ineligible because it has been or is being submitted for any prize of this University.

The candidate must submit two typed copies of the dissertation (bound or held firmly in a stiff cover), addressed to the Chair of the Examiners, Honour School of Theology and Oriental Studies, Examination Schools, High Street, Oxford not later than noon on the Friday of the eighth week of Hilary Term in the academic year in which he or she is presenting himself or herself for examination. The letter of declaration signed by the candidate must be submitted separately in a sealed envelope addressed to the Chair of the Examiners at the above address at the same time as the copies are submitted. 5

2. Candidates who offer some papers in Oriental Studies will be precluded from taking papers in Theology that have a similar content. A list of combinations of papers that are not permitted will be published in the course handbook two years before the examination.

1. Theology 10

Candidates will be required to offer *either*: God and Israel in the Old Testament (as for the Honour School of Theology Paper 1)

or The Gospels and Jesus (with special reference to the gospels of Matthew and John) (as for the Honour School of Theology Paper 2)

and either: The Development of Doctrine in the Early Church to AD 451 (as for the 15 Honour School of Theology Paper 4)

or God, Christ and Salvation (as for the Honour School of Theology Paper 5) and may take up to three other papers chosen from the Theology FHS.

2. Oriental Studies

The Oriental Studies papers may be chosen from any one of the following sections: 20 1 Buddhism, 2 Eastern Christianity, 3 Hinduism, 4 Islam, and 5 Judaism.

Choice and availability of options. It cannot be guaranteed that teaching will be available on all papers in every academic year. Similarly, the choice of subject for the dissertation will necessarily depend upon availability of a suitable supervisor. Candidates should therefore consult with their tutors about the availability of teaching 25 when selecting their optional and dissertation subjects.

Approval of choice of options. Applications for the approval of all options and papers must be submitted to the Undergraduate Studies Committee of the Faculty Board of Oriental Studies by Monday of the sixth week of Hilary Term in the academic year preceding that in which the examination is taken. 30

1. *Buddhism*

1. Pali, Sanskrit, *or* Tibetan language

either (a) A Buddhist canonical language: Pali

or   *(b)* A Buddhist canonical language: Tibetan

or   *(c)* A Buddhist canonical language: Sanskrit 35

2. Pali texts, Sanskrit texts, *or* second Tibetan language paper

either (a) Set texts in a Buddhist canonical language: Pali

or   *(b)* Set texts in a Buddhist canonical language: Tibetan

or   *(c)* Set texts in a Buddhist canonical language: Sanskrit

3. Foundations of Buddhism (Buddhism I) (as for the Honour School of Theology 40 Paper 18)

4. Buddhism in Space and Time (Buddhism II) (as for the Honour School of Theology Paper 19)

5. Further Buddhist texts

either (a) Further Buddhist texts: Pali 45

or   *(b)* Further Buddhist Texts: Tibetan

or   *(c)* Further Buddhist Texts: Sanskrit

Candidates will be required to take paper 1 and up to four other papers. Students must choose the same language in papers 1, 2, and 5.

2. Eastern Christianity

1. Armenian *or* Syriac language
2. Early Armenian theological and ecclesiastical texts *or* Early Syriac Christianity (Armenian as for the Honour School of Oriental Studies, SUBSIDIARY LANGUAGES, Armenian, A. Classical Armenian, Paper 2. Prepared religions texts; Early Syriac Christianity as for FHS Theology Paper 32)
3. Armenian historical texts *or* Syriac biblical and exegetical texts (Armenian as for FHS Oriental Studies, SUBSIDIARY LANGUAGES, Armenian, A. Classical Armenian, Paper 3. Prepared historical and other texts, but excluding essay questions on literature, etc.)
4. Armenian *or* Syriac poetry (Armenian as for FHS Oriental Studies, SUBSIDIARY LANGUAGES, Armenian, A. Classical Armenian, Paper 3. Prepared historical and other texts, but excluding essay questions on literature, etc.)
5. Armenian Christology and the development of doctrine *or* Syriac theology and mystical texts.

Candidates will be required to take paper 1 and up to four other papers.

3. Hinduism

1. Sanskrit language and texts I
2. Sanskrit language and texts II
3. Hinduism I: Sources and Development (as for the Honour School of Theology Paper 20)
4. Texts on the nature of dharma
5. Vedic religion and Brahmanism
6. Saiva Doctrine and Practice

Candidates will be required to take papers 1, 2 and 3, and up to two other papers.

4. Islam

1. Translation from Classical Arabic
2. Islamic Texts (as for the Honour School of Oriental Studies, SUBSIDIARY LANGUAGES, Arabic Paper 3. Additional Arabic: Islamic texts)
3. Hadith (as for the Honour School of Oriental Studies, Arabic and Islamic Studies, Paper 7. i.)
4. Medieval Sufi thought (as for the Honour School of Oriental Studies, Arabic and Islamic Studies, Paper 7. ix.)
5. A modern Islamic thinker (as for the Honour School of Oriental Studies, Arabic and Islamic Studies, Paper 7. xvi.)
6. Topics in Islamic Law (The Honour School of Oriental Studies, Arabic and Islamic Studies, Paper 9 iv.)

Candidates will be required to take papers 1 and 2 and may take up to three other papers. Teaching may not be available for all of papers 3–6 in every year.

5. Judaism

1. Classical Jewish Texts and Language
2. Second Temple Judaism (as for the Honour School of Oriental Studies, Jewish Studies, b. Section II. (e))

3. The Formation of Rabbinic Judaism (as for the Honour School of Theology, The Formation of Rabbinic Judaism (Judaism 1), Paper 14)

4. History of Jewish-Christian Relations (as for the Honour School of Oriental Studies, Jewish Studies, b. Section IV. (o))

5. History of Jewish-Muslim Relations (as for the Honour School of Oriental Studies, Jewish Studies, b. Section IV. (p))

6. History of Jewish Bible Interpretation (as for the Honour School of Oriental Studies, Jewish Studies, b. Section IV. (q))

7. Modern Judaism (as for the Honour School of Oriental Studies, Jewish Studies, b. Section V. (v)).

Candidates will be required to take paper 1 and up to four other papers. Lists of set texts will be published in the handbook.

NOTES

3

BACHELOR OF THEOLOGY

1. The examination for the Degree of Bachelor of Theology shall be under the supervision of the Board of the Faculty of Theology and Religion which shall have power to make regulations governing the examination.

2. Any person who has been admitted under the provisions of this section as a Student for the Degree of Bachelor of Theology, who has satisfied the conditions prescribed in this section, and who has satisfied the examiners for the degree may supplicate for the Degree of Bachelor of Theology.

3. No full-time student for the Degree of Bachelor of Theology shall be granted leave to supplicate unless, after admission, he or she has kept statutory residence and pursued his or her course of study at Oxford for at least nine terms. Time spent outside Oxford as part of an academic programme approved by the faculty board shall count towards residence for the purposes of this clause.

4. No full-time student for the Degree of Bachelor of Theology shall retain that status for more than twelve terms in all.

5. Part-time students for the Degree of Bachelor of Theology shall in each case be required to pursue their course of study for twice the number of terms required of an equivalent full-time student. A student who takes the degree by two years full-time and the rest part-time shall retain the status of Student for the Degree of Bachelor of Theology for no more than fifteen terms. A student who takes the degree by one year full-time and the rest part-time shall retain that status for no more than eighteen terms. A student who takes the degree wholly part-time shall retain that status for no more than twenty-one terms. A student may transfer from full-time to part-time status or vice-versa with the approval of the B.Th. Supervisory Committee.

6. Part-time students shall not be required to keep statutory residence, but must attend for such instruction at their college for such times during full term as shall be required by the faculty board concerned, and must also attend at least one week's residential course each year, the total hours of attendance in each year of the course being as prescribed by the faculty board concerned.

7. Students for the Degree of Bachelor of Theology may transfer to the Certificate in Theology with the approval of the B.Th. Supervisory Committee.

8. The B.Th. Supervisory Committee will supervise arrangements for the Bachelor of Theology, the Certificate in Theology and the Certificate for Theology Graduates. This committee will elect its Chair, Secretary, and Treasurer. The Chair and Secretary will form a Standing Committee together with the Chair of Examiners for these courses. In addition to these officers, the committee will consist of two representatives of the Board of the Faculty of Theology and one representative of each of the participating institutions. The committee will have such powers and duties as may from time to time be prescribed by the Board of the Faculty of Theology and Religion.

9. Candidates for this degree may be admitted by Blackfriars; Campion Hall; Harris Manchester College; Mansfield College; Regent's Park College; Ripon College, Cuddesdon; St Benet's Hall; St Stephen's House; and Wycliffe Hall.

10. The Registrar shall keep a register of all candidates so admitted.

A. REGULATIONS FOR THE COURSE OF INSTRUCTION AT BLACKFRIARS; CAMPION HALL; HARRIS MANCHESTER COLLEGE; MANSFIELD COLLEGE; REGENT'S PARK COLLEGE; RIPON COLLEGE, CUDDESDON; ST BENET'S HALL; ST STEPHEN'S HOUSE; AND WYCLIFFE HALL.   5

A.1 *Course requirements*

Candidates must take at least *twelve* papers. In Part 1 candidates must take all four papers. In Part 2 they must take at least: one paper from section B; either C1 or C4; and one paper from section D. Candidates, including those who take E9 twice, may take a maximum of four papers from section E. Only one paper may be taken from   10
section F. The B.Th. Supervisory Committee may dispense a candidate from individual compulsory papers on the basis of previous academic work, but not from the total number of papers required.

Details of which subjects may or must be taken by two short essays or one long essay in place of written examination papers are given in the syllabus in section B   15
below.

A.2 *Examinations*

Candidates will be examined at the end of each academic year of their course of study. Examination will be held in April or May, beginning on the Monday of the second week of Trinity Term, and in September or October, at the end of the second   20
week before Michaelmas Full Term.

Every candidate shall complete an entry form, showing the subject he or she intends to take in that year, by noon on Friday of the second week of Hilary Term for the May examination, and by noon on Friday of the seventh week of Trinity Term for the Autumn examination.   25

The examiners may examine the candidate viva voce, no candidate who has passed in a subject may sit that examination again.

A candidate who has failed in more than two subjects in an examination shall be deemed to have failed in all the subjects offered at that examination. A candidate may offer at a subsequent examination a subject or subjects in which he or she has failed.   30
Normally only one resit will be allowed in each subject, provided that the B.Th. Supervisory Committee shall have power in exceptional circumstances and on submission of a case by a candidate's college to approve a second resit.

A.3 *Long Essays*

Approval for the subjects proposed for long essays must be obtained from the B.Th.   35
Supervisory Committee by completing a Long Essay Title Form and submitting it to the Supervisory Committee by noon on the Friday of: Week Four of Michaelmas Term, Week Four of Hilary Term, or Week Six of Trinity Term.

A proposed title must cover a theme within the rubric of the paper **[Until MT 2016:** (For those candidates admitted before 1 October 2012), and the Long Essay Title   40
Form must include a list of four college-assessed pieces of work; together these must adequately cover the syllabus**]**. Candidates are advised to seek approval for titles as early as practicable in advance of the examination. After the Long Essay Title Form is returned with dated approval, it must be retained for submission with the completed work.   45

Long essays must be entirely the candidate's own work. Candidates may receive tutorial guidance in the early stages of composition, and tutors may read and comment on a first draft.

Candidates must submit two copies of each essay (marked A and B), which must be printed on a single side of paper. Each copy must have a standard title sheet,   50 indicating essay title and candidate number (but not name or college) and word count (including footnotes but not bibliography). Candidates must also submit the approved Long Essay Title Form, with its final section now completed to confirm that the essay is entirely the candidate's own work and that **[Until MT 2016:** (For those candidates admitted before 1 October 2012) the college assessed work**]** (For those candidates 5 admitted on or after 1 October 2012) a course of instruction covering the syllabus has been satisfactorily completed. These documents must be placed together in a sealed envelope, marked with the number and title of the paper and the candidate's examination number and addressed to the Chair of Examiners, Bachelor of Theology, Examination Schools, High Street, Oxford OX1 4BG. Long essays must be submitted 10 by noon on the first Monday of Trinity Full Term for the Trinity Term examination, or the second Monday before Michaelmas Full Term for the Long Vacation examination.

Note. All communications for the Supervisory Committee for the Degree of Bachelor of Theology should be addressed to the Secretary of the B.Th. Supervisory 15 Committee, whose address may be obtained from each college's B.Th. course director or from the Theology and Religion Faculty Centre, Gibson Building ROQ, OX2 6GG.

B. THE SYLLABUS

† assessed by three-hour written examination 20

‡ assessed **[Until MT 2016:** (For those candidates admitted before 1 October 2012) by long essay of 4,000–5,000 words in Part 1 or 6,000–7,000 words in Part 2, along with four college-assessed pieces of work. Candidates must submit the titles of each long essay and the attendant college-assessed work**]** (For those candidates admitted on or after 1 October 2012) in Part I by two essays of 2,500 words 25 (± 10%), whose titles are to be drawn from a list agreed by tutors and approved by the Supervisory Committee; and in Part II by a long essay of 5,000 words (± 10%), the title of which must be submitted to the Supervisory Committee for approval. **[Until MT 2016:** (For those candidates admitted before 1 October 2012) Together these must adequately cover**]** (For those candidates admitted on or after 1 October 30 2012) Candidates must sign a declaration supported by their society that they have attended an appropriate course of instruction and have adequately covered the syllabus of the paper or, where specified, of the option(s) selected.

§ assessed by other means, as noted in the rubric.

Note that most papers may be examined by more than one means. 35

Full-time candidates must attempt all Part 1 papers in their first year. They may attempt Part 2 papers at any examination session following the first Trinity Term. Part-time candidates must attempt all Part 1 papers in their first two years. They may attempt Part 2 papers at any examination session after their first year, provided they have completed Part 1 or are completing it in the same session. Any candidate who 40 withdraws from a Part I paper must also withdraw from all Part II papers entered in the same session.

Part 1 papers will be assessed at first year level, and will be given reduced weighting in considering a candidate's degree classification or certificate award.

In all written examinations candidates will be provided with a copy of the New 45 Revised Standard Version with the Apocrypha (Anglicized Edition), except when they are answering questions on Hebrew or Greek texts. Those who wish to answer questions on Hebrew or Greek texts must specify this on their entry forms. The texts used in these cases will be: *The Greek New Testament* (United Bible Societies, 4th edn. 1993); *Biblia Hebraica Stuttgartensia* (Stuttgart, 1977). 50

PART 1

This part addresses fundamental issues of Biblical Study, Christian Thought, and Christian Ministry, laying a foundation for further study.

SECTION A. FOUNDATION STUDIES
†A.1—Old Testament A   5

Candidates will study the Pentateuch and the Prophetic Books, with particular reference to Genesis, Deuteronomy and Isaiah. They will study specific texts: *either* Genesis 1–3, 15–17, Deuteronomy 5–7, 12, 15–16 and Isaiah 5–11, 49–53 in English; *or* Genesis 1–4 or Jonah in Hebrew. Candidates who wish to prepare for assessment in Hebrew must enter for the written examination with texts in Hebrew. However, in the   10
examination itself they may transfer to texts in English without penalty.

† A.2 —New Testament A

Candidates will study Matthew and 1 Corinthians, and may also study Mark, addressing such issues as methodology in New Testament study, the person and ministry of Jesus, the context and theology of the authors, and ecclesiological issues.   15
They will also study in detail *either* Matthew 9–10, 26–8 (with the option of Markan parallels) and 1 Corinthians 7–11 in English, *or* Matthew 9–10 in Greek, *or* 1 Corinthians 7–8 in Greek. Candidates who wish to prepare for assessment in Greek must enter for the written examination with texts in Greek. However, in the examination itself they may transfer to texts in English without penalty.   20

[Until MT 2016: (For those candidates admitted before 1 October 2012) †] ‡ **A.3— Christian Life and Thought**

Foundation studies in this discipline can take different routes:

Either **[Until MT 2016:** (For those candidates admitted before 1 October 2012) †] ‡ **A.3.A—Foundations of Christian Thought**   25

Candidates will study some of the foundational issues involved in the study of Christian theology including faith, revelation, Scripture, authority, tradition, development, religious language, and the relationship of Christian theology to other disciplines.

Or **[Until MT 2016:** (For those candidates admitted before 1 October 2012) †] ‡   30
A.3.B—Development of Christian Life and Thought

Candidates will study the development of Christian life and thought in its cultural and historical context, including issues of authority, spirituality and ministry within Christian communities; and sources and forms of theological reflection and conflict. They should demonstrate some awareness of primary sources (in translation).   35

Candidates will study the following foundational period:

(*a*) First to fifth centuries.

They may also study one of the following periods:

(*b*) Sixth to eleventh centuries;

(*c*) Eleventh to fourteenth centuries;   40

(*d*) Fifteenth and sixteenth centuries.

Candidates must specify **[Until MT 2016:** (For those candidates admitted before 1 October 2012) periods studied] (For those candidates admitted on or after 1 October 2012) the periods within which the subjects of their essays fall on their examination entrance forms; they cannot subsequently be assessed on these periods in Paper C.2.   45

[Until MT 2016: (For those candidates admitted before 1 October 2012) †] ‡ **A.4— Christian Witness and the Contemporary World**

Candidates will study the relationship between Christian faith and contemporary culture, including religious and secular understandings of society, environment, personhood, and faith. Candidates will be expected to reflect on the practice of mission.

PART 2

SECTION B. BIBLICAL STUDIES

†‡ B.1—Old Testament B

Candidates will study the Historical Books (Joshua, Judges, 1 and 2 Samuel, 1 and 2 Kings, 1 and 2 Chronicles, Ezra, Nehemiah) and the other Writings (Psalms, Proverbs, Job, Ecclesiastes, Song of Songs, Lamentations, Ruth, Esther, Daniel).

They will also study at least one of the following set texts:

   (i) 2 Samuel 1–12 or 2 Kings 17–25 in English;

   (ii) Psalms 42–49, 84–89 or Job 1–5, 38–42 in English;

   (iii) 2 Kings 21–23 in Hebrew;

   (iv) Ruth in Hebrew.

Candidates who wish to prepare for assessment in Hebrew must enter for the written examination with texts in Hebrew. However, in the examination itself they may transfer to texts in English without penalty.

†‡ B.2—New Testament B

Candidates will study issues of New Testament theology, ethics and interpretation, and at least two of the following books: John, Romans, Hebrews. They may also study the Pastoral Epistles and Revelation. They will study in detail texts from John 1–6, 9–12, 17–20, Romans 1–12, and Hebrews in English; and they may study John 1–3, 6, 17 *and/or* Romans 5–8 in Greek. Candidates being assessed by long essay may write on any New Testament text (except those texts listed in the rubric for paper A.2), so long as [Until MT 2016: (For those candidates admitted before 1 October 2012) the college-assessed work adequately covers] (For those candidates admitted on or after 1 October 2012) they have adequately covered the syllabus of the paper (For those candidates admitted on or after 1 October 2012) in their course of instruction. Candidates who wish to prepare for assessment in Greek must enter for the written examination with texts in Greek. However, in the examination itself they may transfer to texts in English without penalty.

†‡ B.3—Biblical Interpretation

Candidates will study Part A or Part B or both.

Part A: Candidates will study: central themes in both testaments such as God, creation, the people of God, redemption, messiah, community, worship, hope; and the methodological issues of constructing biblical theology.

Part B: Candidates will study the history and practice of biblical interpretation, including major contemporary trends.

SECTION C. DOCTRINE AND HISTORY

†‡ C.1—Christian Doctrine

Candidates will study the central doctrines of the Christian church, as set out in the historic creeds and formulae, including critical reflection on traditional and recent expositions of these doctrines and engagement with contemporary theological discussion.

†‡ C.2—Church History

Candidates will study the development of Christian life and thought in its cultural and historical context, including issues of authority, spirituality, and ministry within

Christian communities; and sources and forms of theological reflection and conflict. They should demonstrate some awareness of primary sources (in translation).

Candidates must specify one period for assessment by written exam or long essay, which must not be one on which they were assessed in Paper A.3.B:

(*a*) First to fifth centuries;   5

(*b*) Sixth to eleventh centuries;

(*c*) Eleventh to fourteenth centuries;

(*d*) Fifteenth and sixteenth centuries;

(*e*) Seventeenth and eighteenth centuries;

(*f*) Nineteenth and twentieth centuries.   10

†‡ C.3—Ecclesiology

Candidates will study the theology of the church, including ministry and the sacraments, in its historical development and contemporary practice.

†‡ C.4—Study of Theology

(Candidates who have taken A.3.A may not take this paper.)   15

Candidates will study some of the major issues involved in the study of Christian theology, including faith, revelation, reason, Scripture, authority, tradition, development, religious language, and the relationship of Christian thought to other disciplines and other religions.

SECTION D. PRACTICAL THEOLOGY   20
§ D.1—Mission and Ministry

This paper will be assessed by an essay of 5,000 words (± 10%), which must be based on a supervised placement of at least twenty-one days in a church or secular setting in which the candidate shares in the experiences of those involved, and must be accompanied by a declaration supported by the student's society that the placement has been   25
undertaken. The essay may be accompanied by additional documentation on the nature of the placement that would not otherwise be available to the examiner, which must not exceed ten A4 pages in total and must not identify the candidate. The essay should contain theological reflection on the placement with the help of the candidate's study of issues of mission and ministry and, as appropriate, of contribu-   30
tory disciplines.

[**Until MT 2016:** (For those candidates admitted before 1 October 2012) College-assessed work for assessment by long essay may come from any period except the period(s) studied by the candidate in A.3.B.]

§ D.2—Christian Ethics   35

This paper consists of two parts, (*a*) and (*b*):

(*a*) Ethics and Faith (three hour examination or long essay)

Candidates will study the foundations of Christian moral thought and practice; contemporary moral and social problems; and the relation of Christian moral life to faith, witness, and worship. This part of the paper will be assessed either by a long   40
essay of 4,000 words (± 10%), the title of which must be submitted for approval to the Supervisory Committee, or by a three-hour written examination.

(*b*) Ethics and Ministry (two hour examination)

This part of the paper will be assessed by a two-hour written examination. Candidates should demonstrate ethical and pastoral competence in analysis of, reflec-   45
tion on, and response to a particular situation. This will be a situation relating to sexuality, marriage, and the family, unless the Supervisory Committee gives notice otherwise.

†‡ D.3—Christian Worship

Candidates will study the history and theology of Christian initiation, the Eucharist, the daily worship; the place of prayer in worship; non-verbal aspects of liturgy and their cultural factors; relevant insights from the human sciences; word and sacrament, liturgical symbolism, and the place of preaching; worship and the Church's mission; other forms of corporate worship.   5

†‡ D.4—Christian Spirituality

Candidates will study the history and theology of Christian spirituality including major traditions and figures; and the relationship of spirituality to: scripture, liturgy, hymnody, doctrine, and current trends.   10

SECTION E. OTHER SUBJECTS

†‡ E.1—Christian Mission

Candidates will study the following: the biblical and theological foundations of mission; the relationship of the Church to the *missio Dei*; factors in the contemporary world affecting mission, such as industrialisation, urbanisation, secularism, pluralism, and new forms of imperialism. These subjects may be focused through the study of: the history of Christian mission; the distinction between mission and evangelism; the encounter with other faiths; issues of contextualisation; apologetics; liberation movements; and the work of significant missiologists.   15

†‡ E.2—Christian Faith and Other Religions   20

Candidates will study methodology in the study of religion; Christian approaches to other religions; and one religion other than Christianity, chosen from (and to be specified on the entry form): Hinduism, Buddhism, post-Biblical Judaism, Islam, or a religion proposed by the candidate and approved by the Supervisory Committee.

†‡ E.3—Christian Faith and Philosophy   25

Candidates will study the relationship between Christianity and the Western philosophical tradition. They will also study relevant issues including: the relation between reason and revelation; the existence of God; the problem of evil; non-objective theism; religious language; religious experience; resurrection and the immortality of the soul.

†‡ E.4—Christian Faith and Science   30

Candidates will study the relationship between Christian theology and the development of modern science, including: methodology and epistemology in science and theology; the origin of the universe and humanity; the quantum world; the biosphere and ecosystems; and ethical issues of scientific research and development.

†‡ E.5—Christian Faith and Social Sciences   35

Candidates will study the relationship between Christian theology and the social sciences, including such areas as methodology in both disciplines; sociological and anthropological interpretations of religion; theological and sociological understandings of social phenomena; sociological understandings of religious organisation; and theological critiques of social sciences.   40

†‡ E.6—Christian Faith and Psychology

Candidates will study the contribution of psychological theory to pastoral theology and pastoral care, in areas such as: developmental theory and the life cycle; human sexuality; love and attachment; and mental health. They will also study: major psychological theories and their critique of religious systems; the counselling movement; the role of the pastor; the nature of pastoral ministry in relation to birth, marriage, and death.   45

†‡ E.7—Canon Law

Candidates will study the sources, history, and theology of Western canon law or the Eastern canonical tradition or both (to be specified on the entry form); and current systems of canons, e.g. the Roman Catholic *Code of Canon Law* and the *Canons of the Church of England*, including an introduction to comparative issues.

‡ **E.8—Confessional Study**   5

Candidates will study the tradition of a Christian denomination as expressed in its formularies, liturgy, spirituality, and ethics.

[Until MT 2016: (For those candidates admitted before 1 October 2012) § † ‡ **E.9— Special Subject**

Candidates may propose one of the following for approval by the Supervisory   10
Committee:

(*a*) a topic which falls outside the other rubrics, assessed by a long essay of 7,000 words along with four college-assessed pieces of work;

(*b*) a topic involving some research or interdisciplinary study, assessed by a long essay of 10,000 words without any college-assessed work;   15

(*c*) a translation paper, assessed by written examination;

(*d*) a project with suitable assessment.

The proposal should include the title, a brief description of the subject and approach envisa-ged, a preliminary bibliography, and in the case of (*d*) the proposed assessment method. A candidate may offer Paper E.9(*c*) twice, so as to be examined on texts in   20
two different languages.]

(For those candidates admitted on or after 1 October 2012) † **E.10 [E.9]— Translation Paper**

Candidates may propose texts for approval by the Supervisory Committee, from which passages will be set for translation and comment in a three-hour written   25
examination. The texts must be in a language relevant to theological study, such as Biblical Hebrew, New Testament Greek or Ecclesiastical Latin.

A candidate may offer Paper E.9 twice, so as to be examined on texts in two different languages.

SECTION F. DISSERTATION OR PROJECT   30

Candidates may either write a dissertation or undertake a project capable of suitable assessment. In either case, it is expected that no college-assessed formative pieces of work will be required.

§ **F.1—Dissertation**

Candidates may propose a topic for approval by the Supervisory Committee, a   35
topic which will involve some research and/or interdisciplinary study leading to the composition of a dissertation of 10,000 words (± 10%).

The proposal should include the title, a brief description of the subject and approach envisaged, and a preliminary bibliography.

§ **F.2—Project**   40

Candidates may propose a project for approval by the Supervisory Committee.

The proposal should include the title, a brief description of the subject and approach envisaged, a preliminary bibliography and details of the proposed assessment method.

GENERAL REGULATIONS

[new regulations for students entering from 1 October 2014]

1. The examination for the Degree of Bachelor of Theology shall be under the supervision of the Continuing Education Board, which shall have power, subject to the approval of the Education Committee, to make regulations governing the examination.

2. Any person who has been admitted under the provisions of this section as a Student for the Degree of Bachelor of Theology, who has satisfied the conditions prescribed in this section, and who has satisfied the examiners for the degree, may supplicate for the Degree of Bachelor of Theology.

3. No full-time student for the Degree of Bachelor of Theology shall be granted leave to supplicate unless, after admission, he or she has kept statutory residence and pursued his or her course of study at Oxford for at least nine terms. Time spent outside Oxford while registered as a student for the Undergraduate Certificate in Theological Studies or as part of an academic programme approved by the Continuing Education Board shall count towards residence for the purposes of this clause. No full-time student for the Degree of Bachelor of Theology shall retain that status for more than twelve terms in all.

4. A student who takes the degree by two years of full-time study and the remainder by means of part-time study shall retain the status of Student for the Degree of Bachelor of Theology for no more than fifteen terms. A student who takes the degree by one year of full-time study and the remainder by means of part-time study shall retain that status for no more than eighteen terms. A student who takes the degree wholly part-time shall retain that status for no more than twenty-one terms.

5. A student may transfer from full-time to part-time status or vice versa with the approval of the Continuing Education Board.

6. Part-time students shall not be required to keep statutory residence, but must attend for such instruction at their Hall for such times as shall be required by the Continuing Education Board.

7. Candidates for this degree may be admitted by such Permanent Private Halls as have been granted permission to do so.

8. The Registrar shall keep a register of all candidates so admitted.

SPECIAL REGULATIONS

A

1. Candidates may be admitted either onto Part 1 or directly onto Part 2 of the course. Admission directly onto Part 2 is at the discretion of the Continuing Education Board, and candidates so admitted will normally be expected to have satisfactorily completed the Undergraduate Certificate in Theological Studies. Applications for dispensation from this requirement will be considered, in exceptional circumstances only, by the Board. To be dispensed from this requirement, candidates must demonstrate that they have undertaken equivalent study to an equivalent standard. Where candidates are admitted on the basis of having completed the Undergraduate Certificate, work done for the Certificate will be deemed to be work done for the Bachelor of Theology.

2. Part 1 is available on a full time basis over three terms and on a part time basis over six terms. Part 2 is available on a wholly full time basis over six terms and on a wholly part time basis over twelve terms.

3. Candidates may be permitted under certain circumstances to suspend status for a maximum of six terms. Any such period shall not count towards the minimum and maximum periods of registration, and no fee liability will be incurred during such periods.

4. No candidate may attempt Part 2 until he or she has either satisfactorily   5
completed or has been dispensed from Part 1.

5. For any candidate who is successful in the examination for the Degree of Bachelor of Theology, and who has already successfully completed the Undergraduate Certificate in Theological Studies (and for the Bachelor of Theology examination has incorporated the assignments submitted for the Undergraduate   10
Certificate) the Degree will subsume his or her Certificate.

6. In the following regulations, the English version of the Bible used will be the New Revised Standard Version with the Apocrypha (Anglicized Edition). The Greek text used will be the The Greek New Testament (United Bible Societies, 4th edn. 1993). The Hebrew text used will be the Biblia Hebraica Stuttgartensia (Stuttgart,   15
1977).

B

Part 1

7. Every candidate will be required to satisfy the examiners in the following:

(*a*) Attendance at classes and other sessions as indicated in the course handbook   20

(*b*) Written assignments or examination papers, as specified, for six papers to include:

　i. At least one of A1 or A2 from Part 1 of the Schedule;

　ii. At least one of A3 or A4 from the Part 1 Schedule;

　iii. At least one of A5–A10 from the Part 1 Schedule;   25

　iv. Three other papers from the Part 1 Schedule.

The written work under (*b*) will be submitted to the Examiners for the Bachelor of Theology, Examination Schools, High Street, Oxford for consideration by such dates as the examiners shall determine and shall notify candidates.

8. Candidates who fail to satisfy the examiners in the written work or the examina-   30
tions under 7(*b*) may be permitted to resubmit work in respect of part or parts of the examination which they have failed, on not more than one occasion, which shall normally be within one year of the initial failure.

Part 2

9. Every candidate will be required to satisfy the examiners in the following: 35

(*a*) Attendance at classes and other sessions as indicated in the course handbook

(*b*) Written assignments or examination papers, as specified, for a further twelve papers (or eleven see v. below):

　i. At least one paper from section B of the Part 2 Schedule;

　ii. At least one paper from section C of the Part 2 Schedule;   40

　iii. At least one paper from Section D of the Part 2 Schedule;

　iv. At least one paper from Section E of the Part 2 Schedule;

　v. Eight, or seven if paper E2 or E3 is chosen, other papers from any paper listed in i–iii above. Candidates who offered either A11 or A12 for the Undergraduate Certificate may not offer that paper in Part 2.   45

The written work under (*b*) will be submitted to the Examiners for the Bachelor of Theology, Examination Schools, High Street, Oxford, for consideration by such dates as the examiners shall determine and shall notify candidates.

10. All candidates must be assessed by written examinations in at least two modules during the course of their study.   5

11. Candidates who fail to satisfy the examiners in the written work or the examinations under 9(*b*) may be permitted to resubmit work in respect of part or parts of the examination which they have failed, on not more than one occasion, which shall normally be within one year of the initial failure.

12. Candidates may be expected to attend a viva voce examination at the end of the   10 course.

Schedule of Papers

[*Note: Not all options may be available in any one year*]
Part One:
Section A: Introductory papers   15

A1   *Introduction to the Old Testament*
A2   *Introduction to the New Testament*
A3   *The History of the Church*
A4   *Introduction to Christian Doctrine*
A5   *Contemporary Mission and Culture*   20
A6   *Introduction to Spirituality*
A7   *Introduction to Ministry and Worship*
A8   *Introduction to the Study of Religion*
A9   *Introduction to Christian Faith and Philosophy*
A10 *Introduction to Christian Faith and Science*   25
A11 *Elementary Biblical Hebrew*
A12 *Elementary Biblical Greek*

Part Two:
Section B: Biblical Studies

B1 *Studies in the Old Testament*   30
B2 *Studies in the New Testament*
B3 *Biblical Interpretation*
B4 *An Old Testament Book*
B5 *A New Testament Book*
B6 *Advanced New Testament Hebrew*   35
B7 *Advanced New Testament Greek*

Section C: History and Doctrine

C1 *Issues in Church History*
C2 *Issues in Christian Doctrine*
C3 *Ecclesiology*   40
C4 *Theologies of Salvation*
C5 *A Special Theologian*

Section D: Practical Theology and Religious Studies

D1 *Issues in Christian Ministry*
D2 *The Person and Role of an Ordained Minister*   45
D3 *Christian Ethics*
D4 *Issues in Mission*
D5 *Issues in Christian Worship*
D6 *Issues in Christian Spirituality*
D7 *World Religions*   50

D8 *Philosophical Theology*
D9 *Issues in Christian Faith and Science*

Section E: Independent Study

E1 *Theological Reflection*
E2 *Dissertation* (counts as 2 papers)
E3 *Project* (counts as 2 papers)

NOTES

4

MASTER OF ARTS

1. A Bachelor of Arts (other than one covered by the provisions of clause 2 below) or a Bachelor of Fine Art may, with the approval of his or her society, supplicate for the Degree of Master of Arts in or after the twenty-first term from his or her matriculation.   5

2. A Bachelor of Arts whose qualification for admission to a Final Honour School was the successful completion of a Foundation Course at the Department for Continuing Education may, with the approval of his or her society, supplicate for the Degree of Master of Arts in or after the eighteenth term from his or her matriculation.   10

3. A Bachelor of Arts or a Bachelor of Fine Art who has been admitted to the Degree of Doctor of Philosophy may supplicate for admission to the Degree of Master of Arts, provided that he or she has satisfied all other necessary conditions, at any time after his or her admission to the Degree of Doctor of Philosophy.   15

4. If a Bachelor of Civil Law or a Bachelor of Medicine shall first have been admitted to the Degree of Bachelor of Arts, he or she may supplicate for the Degree of Master of Arts with the approval of his or her society in or after the nineteenth term from his or her matriculation, and may retain the Degree of Bachelor of Civil Law or of Medicine, as the case may be.   20

NOTES

5

REGULATIONS FOR HIGHER
DEGREES IN MUSIC

§1. Qualifications of Candidates for the
Degree of Bachelor of Music

Any persons who have been admitted to the Degree of Bachelor of Arts and have been placed in the First or Second Class (Division 1) in the Final Honour School of Music may apply to the Board of the Faculty of Music for the appointment of examiners and for leave to supplicate for the Degree of Bachelor of Music.

§2. Musical Exercise for the Degree
of Bachelor of Music

1. Candidates shall submit to the Board of the Faculty of Music through the Registrar a Musical Exercise of their own unaided composition. The board shall make and publish regulations concerning the type and content of the Exercise.

2. The Exercise shall be accompanied by:

(1) a statement signed by the candidate that the whole of the Exercise is his or her own unaided work and has not been submitted to any other person for advice, assistance, or revision or presented for examination in whole or in part in the Final Honour School of Music;

(2) a certificate signed by an officer of, or person deputed by, the society to which the candidate belongs, showing that the entry is made with the approval of such society and that he or she has paid the fee prescribed in the appropriate regulation (see Appendix I).

3. The Musical Exercise shall be examined by at least two examiners appointed by the Board of the Faculty of Music. The examiners shall report to the board, and it shall be the duty of the board to decide whether leave to supplicate for the degree should be granted to the candidate, provided that such leave shall in no case be granted unless the examiners have reported that the Exercise submitted by the candidate is of a high standard of merit such as to entitle him or her to supplicate for the Degree of Bachelor of Music.

4. Candidates shall not be permitted to submit their Exercise for approval earlier than the third term after that in which they have passed the examination in the Final Honour School of Music.

5. No candidate shall be permitted to supplicate for the Degree of Bachelor of Music who has not delivered his or her Exercise in a form approved by the examiners to the Registrar, who shall deposit it in the Bodleian Library.

§3. Degree of Doctor of Music

1. Any person belonging to one of the following classes may apply to the Board of the Faculty of Music for leave to supplicate for the Degree of Doctor of Music:

(*a*) Persons who have been admitted to the Degree of Bachelor of Music at this University; provided that no Bachelor of Music may submit evidence for approval until he or she has entered upon the ninth term after that in which he or she was admitted to the Degree of Bachelor of Music;

(*b*) Masters of Arts who have incepted in this University and have entered upon the thirtieth term from their matriculation;

(*c*) Masters of Arts of the University of Cambridge or Dublin who have been incorporated in this University and have entered upon the thirtieth term from their matriculation at Cambridge or Dublin;

(*d*) Undergraduates or Bachelors of Arts of the University of Cambridge or Dublin who have been incorporated and have incepted in the Faculty of Arts in this University and have entered upon the thirtieth term from their matriculation at Cambridge or Dublin;

(*e*) Persons on whom the Degree of Master of Arts has been conferred by decree or special resolution, other than a degree *honoris causa,* and who have entered upon the ninth term from their admission to that degree.

Candidates intending to submit for the Degree of Doctor of Music are strongly advised to consult the Chair of the Faculty Board who will arrange, free of charge, for an advisory consultation on one or more of the works intended for submission, prior to their formal submission.

2. A candidate for the Degree of Doctor of Music shall be required to submit through the Registrar two copies of a portfolio for approval by the Board of the Faculty of Music. The portfolio shall normally consist of between five and seven compositions which, taken together, demonstrate originality and high level of technical and aesthetic distinction, significantly in advance of what is required for a D.Phil. in composition. Each portfolio shall include a copy of any recordings of the compositions. The portfolio should demonstrate an ability to handle varied musical forces and large-scale structures. Where the composer is predominantly concerned with acoustic instrumental music, there should be evidence of extended structures such as symphonic work and carefully wrought music such as that associated with the string quartet medium, amongst contrasting work. Where the composer has concentrated on the development of other areas, such as mixed media, studio, ethnic or community approaches, the work should be of comparable quality in its field. No work so submitted shall have previously been submitted for examination purposes, but it may previously have been published in any of the forms indicated in (3) below. The application shall be accompanied by:

(1) evidence that the candidate's application has the approval of his or her society;

(2) the fee prescribed in the appropriate regulation (see Appendix I).

(3) A list of publications where publication is understood to take place by any or all means including public performance, CD recording, broadcast etc. and not solely or necessarily by commercial printing of the score.

(4) A *curriculum vitae* (including main landmarks in career, full list of significant published works with full details of principal performances, esteem indicators such as prizes, bursaries, composer-in-residence posts, honours).

(5) A declaration that the portfolio is the candidate's own unaided work.

3. On receipt of an application under clause 2 above, the Registrar shall submit it to the Board of the Faculty of Music as soon as may be, for approval. The board shall appoint two external assessors to consider the portfolio and present an agreed joint report to the board. The report should be sufficiently comprehensive and detailed to enable the board to assess the work submitted by the candidate, and should make a clear recommendation as to whether the degree is to be awarded. The board shall

decide whether the evidence submitted by the candidate is of sufficient merit to entitle him or her to supplicate for the Degree of Doctor of Music.

4. If the board approves the evidence as of sufficient merit it shall give leave to the candidate to supplicate for the degree, and shall notify its decision in the *University Gazette.* One copy of each musical work so approved shall remain in the possession of   5
the University for deposit in the Bodleian Library.

DEGREE OF BACHELOR OF MUSIC

1. *The Exercise for the Degree of Bachelor of Music*

(*a*) The Exercise shall consist of a portfolio of three or more original musical compositions of varied character, lasting in total at least thirty minutes. Music for   10
any combination of three or more of the categories specified below will be acceptable, provided that the portfolio includes some purely instrumental music and some vocal music with words. Candidates may also submit recordings of any of their works, and shall submit recordings of electro-acoustic compositions and of any pieces whose ordering or content is not fixed by the notation. The categories are (i) music for one   15
or two instruments, or instrument and voice; (ii) music for choral or solo vocal ensemble, accompanied or unaccompanied; (iii) music for chamber ensemble, with or without voice or voices; (iv) music for larger forces than the above; (v) music involving electro-acoustic composition, accompanied by a commentary describing the technical procedures.   20

(*b*) A viva-voce examination may be held unless candidates are individually dispensed by the examiners.

2. *General Regulations about the Exercise*

(*a*) The score of each work must be written out so as to accord with the standards and methods that a professional performer, copyist, or publisher would expect, with   25
rehearsal letters and/or regular bar-numbering. The pages should be numbered consecutively throughout the portfolio.

(*b*) **The Exercise must be accompanied by a declaration on a prescribed form, which must be obtained beforehand by application to the Examination Schools, High Street, Oxford. It must be sent in by the Friday in Trinity Term in the fifth week.**   30

I,..

hereby declare that these compositions are entirely my own unaided work and that no part of them has been presented for examination on any previous occasion.

Signed...   5

.... College,

in the presence of

	....
Witnesses'	....
names and	10
addresses	
in full.	....
Date	....

The Exercise must show the private address as well as the name and college of the composer.   15

It must be strongly bound and paged, and lettered (with clearly stamped lettering) up the spine with title and composer's name, and also on the outside cover with title, name, and college, and the words 'B.Mus. Exercise'.

Any electronic tape submitted in addition to the Exercise must be in a box on which the title, the composer's name and college, and the words 'B.Mus. Exercise' are again   20
clearly shown.

DEGREE OF DOCTOR OF MUSIC

A candidate is required to submit for approval by the board of the faculty a major musical work or works of his own composition and of outstanding merit. Two copies of each work must be submitted   25

Evidence submitted for the Degree of Doctor of Music

The work or works submitted must show the private address as well as the name and college of the composer. The work or works must be strongly bound and paged, and lettered (with clearly stamped lettering) up the spine with title and composer's name, and also on the outside cover with title, name, and college, and the degree for   30
which it was composed.

NOTES

6

REGULATIONS CONCERNING THE STATUS OF GRADUATE TAUGHT STUDENTS

GENERAL REGULATIONS

§1. Registration of Graduate Taught Students

Any person who, in the opinion of the board concerned, is well-qualified and well-fitted to undertake the programme of study for which application is made, may be admitted to the status of Student for the Degree.

§2. Suspension of Status of Graduate Taught Students

If, for good cause, a student is temporarily unable to carry out his or her course-work or research (if applicable), the board concerned may grant his or her request for a temporary suspension of status. Applications for suspension of status should be made to the board concerned, c/o the relevant Graduate Studies Assistant; and should be accompanied by statements of support from the relevant course director (or the student's supervisor, if applicable) and society. No student may be granted more than the number of terms' or months' suspension of status set out below.

§3. Termination of status of a Graduate Taught Student

A student shall cease to hold the status of Student for the Degree through failure to meet the requirements laid down in the regulations governing that degree including failure to meet the requirements within the maximum terms or months permitted for completion.

§4. Reinstatement of status of a Graduate Taught Student

A student who has withdrawn or who has been withdrawn may apply for reinstatement to his or her former status on the Register within two years of his or her status ceasing. Such applications shall be addressed by the former student to the board concerned, and shall be accompanied by written statements commenting on the application from the candidate's society, the course director or Director of Graduate Studies, and former supervisor (if applicable). The board shall reach a decision on such applications and shall determine the date from which any reinstatement granted under these provisions shall be effective. No reinstatement may be granted under these provisions if the student has held the relevant status for the maximum number of terms allowed under the regulations governing that status.

Programme	Duration	Maximum time permitted	Maximum suspensions permitted
B.Phil./M.Phil.	6 terms	12 terms	6 terms
M.St.	3 terms	6 terms	3 terms
M.St. (part time)	6 terms	12 terms	6 terms
M.Sc. (coursework)	3 terms	6 terms	3 terms
M.Sc. (coursework) (part time)	6 terms	12 terms	6 terms
M.Th.	6 terms	12 terms	6 terms
MBA	32 weeks	6 terms	3 terms
MBA (part time)	21 months	48 months	24 months
MFA	40 weeks	2 years	3 terms
MPP	32 weeks	6 terms	3 terms
BCL/M.J.ur	3 terms	6 terms	3 terms

NOTES

7

GENERAL REGULATIONS FOR THE DEGREE OF BACHELOR OF PHILOSOPHY OR MASTER OF PHILOSOPHY

§1. Degrees of Bachelor and Master of Philosophy

1. Any person who has kept six terms of statutory residence after admission as a student for the Degree of Bachelor or Master of Philosophy (or, in the case of a Student for any of the Degrees of Doctor of Philosophy, Master of Science by Research, Master of Letters, Master of Science by Coursework or Master of Studies who has transferred to the Degree of Bachelor or Master of Philosophy, after his or her admission as a Student for one of these degrees), and who has satisfied the examiners in one of the examinations hereinafter provided may supplicate for the Degree of Bachelor or Master of Philosophy as appropriate; provided that the board or other authority specified in cl. 3 of §2 below may dispense a student on application through his or her college and with the support of his or her supervisor from not more than two terms of such statutory residence if he or she has been granted leave to pursue his or her course of study at some other place than Oxford for those terms under the provisions of cl. 2(*c*) of §3 hereof.

2. A Student for the Degree of Bachelor or Master of Philosophy who is not a graduate of the University may wear the same gown as that worn by Students for the Degree of Doctor of Philosophy.

§2. Examinations for the Degrees of Bachelor and Master of Philosophy

1. For the Degree of Bachelor of Philosophy there shall be an examination in Philosophy.

For the Degree of Master of Philosophy there shall be examinations in Archaeology, British and European History, Celtic Studies, Classical Archaeology, Comparative Social Policy, Criminology and Criminal Justice, Development Studies, Eastern Christian Studies, Economic and Social History, Economics, English Studies (Medieval Period), Evidence-Based Social Intervention, General Linguistics and Comparative Philology, Geography and the Environment, Greek and Latin Languages and Literature, Greek and/or Roman History, History of Science, Medicine, and Technology, International Relations, Judaism and Christianity in the Graeco-Roman World, Late Antique and Byzantine Studies, Latin American Studies, Medical Anthropology, Modern British and European History, Modern Japanese Studies, Modern Languages, Music, Oriental Studies, Philosophical Theology, Politics (Comparative Government, Political Theory, European Politics and Society), Russian and East European Studies, Slavonic Studies, Social Anthropology, Sociology, Theology, Visual, Material and Museum Anthropology, and such other subjects as the University may hereafter determine.

2. There shall be a Register of students who are studying for the Degrees of Bachelor and Master of Philosophy which shall be entitled the Register of Bachelor and Master of Philosophy Students and the University may from time to time determine by decree the conditions of admission to the Register.

3. Subject to such regulations as the University may make under the provisions of cl. 2, any person who has obtained permission from the board concerned (or other authority as hereinafter specified) may enter for the examinations as follows. The bodies specified below shall be responsible for the examinations as listed.

Archaeology—Social Sciences

British and European History, from 1500 to the present—History

Celtic Studies—Modern Languages

Classical Archaeology—Social Sciences

Comparative Social Policy—Social Sciences

Criminology and Criminal Justice—Social Sciences

Development Studies—International Development, Queen Elizabeth House

Eastern Christian Studies—Oriental Studies and Theology

Economic and Social History—History

Economics—Social Sciences

English Studies (Medieval Period)—English Language and Literature

Evidence-Based Social Intervention—Social Sciences

General Linguistics and Comparative Philology—Linguistics, Philology
    and Phonetics

Geography and the Environment—Social Sciences

Greek and/or Latin Languages and Literature—Classics

Greek and/or Roman History—Classics

History of Science, Medicine, and Technology—History

International Relations—Social Sciences

Judaism and Christianity in the Graeco-Roman World—Oriental Studies
    and Theology

Late Antique and Byzantine Studies—Classics and History

Latin American Studies—Social Sciences

Law—Law (see SECTION 18 : *Regulations for Degrees in Civil Law and for the Degrees
    of Magister Juris and Master of Philosophy in Law*)

Medical Anthropology—Social Sciences

Modern British and European History—History

Modern Japanese Studies—Social Sciences

Modern Languages—Modern Languages

Music—Music

Oriental Studies—Oriental Studies

Philosophical Theology—Theology

Philosophy (Bachelor of Philosophy)—Philosophy

Politics (Comparative Government, Political Theory, European Politics
    and Society) —Social Sciences

Russian and East European Studies—Social Sciences

Slavonic Studies—Modern Languages

Social Anthropology—Social Sciences

Sociology and Demography—Social Sciences
Theology—Theology
Visual, Material and Museum Anthropology—Social Sciences

The subjects of each examination shall be determined by regulation of the board or other authority concerned, which shall have power to include therein a thesis written   5
by the candidate on a subject approved by the board or other authority or by a person or persons to whom the board or other authority may delegate the function of giving such approval. The thesis submitted shall be wholly or substantially the result of work undertaken while a candidate is studying for the Degree of Bachelor or Master of Philosophy, except that a candidate may make application for dispensation from this   10
requirement to the Education Committee not later than the fourth term after his or her admission to the Register of Bachelor and Master of Philosophy Students.

4. Final examination marks shall be released to candidates at the conclusion of the examination. Exceptions to this may be made where assessment takes place throughout the course. In such cases, examination boards must meet formally, with all   15
members present, at interim points in the year in order to agree final marks for specified assessment components. Marks released as final marks may not subsequently be amended without permission of the Proctors.

5. A candidate who has failed to satisfy the examiners in any one of the examinations for the Degrees of Bachelor or Master of Philosophy may enter again for that   20
examination on one (but not more than one) subsequent occasion.

6. The examiners may award a distinction for excellence in the whole examination. Candidates who have initially failed any element of assessment shall not normally be eligible for the award of distinction.

§3. Admission of Candidates   25

1. The Registrar shall keep a Register of students who are studying for the Degrees of Bachelor or Master of Philosophy. The Register shall be entitled the Register of Bachelor and Master of Philosophy Students.

2. No candidate for the Degree of Bachelor or Master of Philosophy shall be admitted to the examination for the degree unless   30

(*a*) he or she has applied through the Head or a tutor of his or her college to the Registrar to have his or her name entered by the appropriate board or other authority on the Register of Bachelor and Master of Philosophy Students;

(*b*) his or her name shall have been kept on the Register for at least six terms inclusive of the term in which it was placed on the Register;   35

(*c*) he or she shall have pursued his or her course of study at Oxford for not less than six terms, except that the board or other authority concerned may grant him or her leave of absence for up to two of these terms if it is desirable in the interests of his or her work that he or she should be allowed to pursue his or her studies at some other place; time spent outside Oxford during term as part of an   40
academic programme approved by Council shall count towards residence for the purpose of this clause:

Provided that

(i) a graduate may be admitted to the examination after his or her name has been on the Register and he or she has pursued his or her course of study at   45
Oxford for only four or five terms if he or she has been given leave by the appropriate board or other authority to enter for the examination;

(ii) a Student for the Degree of Doctor of Philosophy or Student for the Degree of Master of Letters or Student for the Degree of Master of Studies or a Diploma Student may apply through his or her college to the appropriate board or other authority for the transference of his or her name to the Register of Students for the Degrees of Bachelor and Master of Philosophy   5
and, if it is transferred, the number of terms he or she held the status of Student for the Degree of Doctor of Philosophy or Student for the Degree of Master of Letters or Student for the Degree of Master of Studies or Diploma Student shall be reckoned for the purpose of this clause.

3. No person shall attend seminars or advanced classes for Bachelor or Master of   10
Philosophy Students unless his or her name is on the Register of Bachelor and Master of Philosophy Students; provided that the holder of a seminar or advanced class may give leave to a person who is not studying for the Degree of Bachelor or Master of Philosophy to attend his or her seminar or advanced class.

4. Any person shall be entitled to have his name entered on the Register of Bachelor   15
and Master of Philosophy Students if he or she has obtained permission from the appropriate faculty board or other authority under the provisions of the appropriate regulation, provided he or she has matriculated as a member of the University.

5. The name of any Bachelor and Master of Philosophy Student may be removed from the Register by the body which entered it.   20

6. No name shall remain on the Register for more than twelve terms in all.

7. A Student for the Degree of Master of Philosophy shall cease to hold that status if:

(i) he or she shall have been refused permission to supplicate for the Degree of Master of Philosophy;

(ii) the board concerned shall, in accordance with provisions set down by   25
regulation by the Education Committee, and after consultation with the student's society and supervisor, have deprived the student of such status;

(iii) he or she shall have been transferred under the relevant provisions to another status;

(iv) he or she shall not have entered for the relevant examination within the time   30
specified under this subsection.

§4. Supervision of Students for the Degrees

1. Any board or other authority having power to make regulations for the subjects for the Degrees of Bachelor and Master of Philosophy may place a student for those degrees under the supervision of a graduate member of the University or other   35
competent person selected by it, and it shall have power, for sufficient reason, to change the supervisor of any student. If a student requires special supervision in some branch of his or her studies, the supervisor may give this himself or herself or, with the approval of the board or other authority concerned, arrange for it to be given by some other person or persons.   40

2. A supervisor shall send a report on the progress of a student to the board at the end of each term (excepting the term in which the student is admitted to the examination) and at any other time when the board so requires or he or she deems it expedient. The supervisor shall communicate the contents of the report to the student on each occasion that a report is made, so that the student is aware of the supervisor's   45
assessment of his or her work during the period in question. In addition he or she shall inform the board if he or she is of the opinion that a student is unlikely to reach the standard required for the Degree of Bachelor or Master of Philosophy.

§5. Examination Regulations

1. *Notice of Options*

In the Trinity Full Term preceding the year in which the examination is to be taken, candidates must give notice to the Registrar of all the subjects and options which they intend to offer, together with the subject of their thesis by the following weeks:

B.Phil. in Philosophy	By Friday in the first week

In the Michaelmas Full Term preceding the examination, candidates must give notice to the Registrar of all the subjects and options which they intend to offer, together with the subject of their thesis (if offered) by the following weeks:

M.Phil. in Archaeology and in Classical Archaeology and M.Phil. in Comparative Social Policy, and in Evidence-Based Social Intervention	By Friday in the eighth week
All other M.Phil. courses	By Friday in the second week

2. *Preparation and dispatch of B.Phil. and M.Phil. theses*

The theses (**two copies**) must be typewritten and sent to the Chair of the Examiners for the Degree of B.Phil. [or M.Phil.], c/o the Examination Schools, High Street, Oxford, at least fourteen days before the first day of the examination, **except where stated otherwise in the particular regulations for individual courses in the following pages.**

The parcel should bear the words 'B.PHIL. [or M.PHIL.] THESIS IN [here insert subject]' in **BLOCK CAPITALS** in the bottom left-hand corner. The thesis must be printed or typed with a margin of 3 to 3.5 cms on the left-hand edge of each page (or on the inner edge, whether left-hand or right-hand, in the case of a thesis which is printed on both sides of the paper). Loose-leaf binding is not acceptable.

3. *Deposit of theses or dissertations in a university library*

If the examiners are satisfied that the candidate's thesis or dissertation, as submitted, is of sufficient merit but they consider, nevertheless, that before the thesis is deposited in a university library the candidate should make minor corrections, they may require the candidate to correct the thesis to their satisfaction. The library copy of the thesis must be hard bound.

4. *Submission of theses, dissertations and other material*

Except where otherwise indicated, all material submitted for examination (dissertations, extended essays, etc) shall be accompanied by a statement signed by the candidate indicating that it is the candidate's own work, except where otherwise specified. This statement must be submitted separately in a sealed envelope addressed to the chair of examiners of the degree course in question.

Bachelor of Philosophy

The regulations made by the Board of the Faculty of Philosophy are as follows:

1. Candidates will be required to attend the B.Phil. Pro-seminar in the first year of their studies (i.e. the year in which their names are first entered on the Register of B.Phil. students). In addition, candidates will be required to attend two graduate classes in each of the first four terms of their studies.

2. Candidates will be examined by submitting:

(A) Six essays of no more than 5,000 words each, in conformity with the following distribution requirement. Each essay will be assigned to a subject; the six essays must cover at least five subjects. One essay must be on a subject from Group 1 (Theoretical Philosophy), one on a subject from Group 2 (Practical Philosophy) and two on a subject or subjects from Group 3 (History of Philosophy), of which at least one must be concerned with philosophy written before 1800. The remaining two essays may be assigned to subjects in any of the three Groups, provided that the distribution requirement above is met. The list of approved subjects in each Group will be published at the beginning of each academic year in the Graduate Student Handbook. In exceptional circumstances, students may request to have one or more elements of the distribution requirement waived. Candidates wishing to do this must seek approval from the Graduate Studies Committee in Philosophy *as soon as they decide they would like to do so*, and in any case no later than the Friday of the noughth week of the Michaelmas Term of their second year of study. Any such application must be supported by the relevant B.Phil. Course Coordinator.

(B) A thesis of no more than 30,000 words, exclusive of bibliographical references, on a subject proposed by the candidate in consultation with his or her supervisor, and approved by the Graduate Studies Committee in Philosophy.

3. Topics for the essays will be chosen by the candidates. Candidates may offer up to two essays on at most one subject not included in the list of approved subjects in the Graduate Student Handbook, provided that the distribution requirement above is met. Candidates wishing to offer an essay or essays on a subject not on the prescribed list must seek approval for the proposed subject from the Graduate Studies Committee in Philosophy *as soon as they decide they would like to offer it*, and in any case no later than Friday of the fifth week of the Trinity Term of the first year of their studies. Any such application must be supported by the relevant B.Phil. Course Coordinator. Where a subject is approved by the Graduate Studies Committee in Philosophy, the Committee will assign it to one of Groups 1–3.

4. Candidates must inform the Graduate Studies Committee in Philosophy of their thesis title and abstract as soon as they have made their decisions and in any case no later than Friday of the eighth week of Trinity Term of the first year of their studies. Requests for permission to change the thesis title must be submitted for approval, with the support of the candidate's supervisor, to the Director of Graduate Studies in Philosophy *as soon as the candidate has decided to seek such permission*.

5. Two printed copies of each essay must be delivered to the Examination Schools, High Street, Oxford OX1 4BG, by 10 a.m. on the Wednesdays of the following weeks. In the first year of study two essays are due in noughth week of Trinity Term. In the second year of study, two essays are due in each of the noughth weeks of Michaelmas and Hilary Terms. Candidates must give notice of the subject of each essay and the Group to which it will be assigned in accordance with the procedures and deadlines specified in the Graduate Student Handbook.

6. The thesis must be delivered to the Examination Schools, at the above address, by 10 a.m. on Wednesday of the eighth week of Trinity Term in the second year of

study. The thesis must be accompanied by a brief abstract and a statement of the number of words it contains (exclusive of bibliographical references). A penalty may be imposed on any thesis that exceeds the word limit. Successful candidates will be required to deposit one copy of the thesis in the Bodleian Library.

7. The examiners may award a distinction for excellence in the whole examination. 5

8. Candidates who fail up to two essays will be permitted to resubmit those essays at any of the subsequent essay submission dates during the first or second year of their studies, or at the thesis submission date in their second year. A resubmitted essay may be on a new topic, and may be on a new subject, provided that the distribution requirement is met. Candidates who fail the thesis but who receive passing marks on   10
all their essays will be permitted to resubmit an amended or different thesis by 10 a.m. on Wednesday of noughth week of the Hilary Term of the year following the whole examination. Candidates who fail three or more essays or two or more essays and the thesis will be permitted to resubmit work for the failed elements of the examination in the following academic year (or over four terms for candidates who fail more than five   15
essays or more than four essays and the thesis). Candidates need only resubmit work for those elements of the Examination that they failed, but no resubmitted essay or thesis can receive a mark of more than 60. Candidates who fail to satisfy the examiners a second time in any part of the examination may not resubmit work for any part of the examination on any subsequent occasion.   20

9. Candidates for the M.St. in Philosophy of Physics may apply to transfer to the second year of the B.Phil. in Philosophy. A formal application must be made by Friday of fourth week of the Trinity Term preceding the Michaelmas Term in which they wish to transfer to the B.Phil. Admission of those whose application is approved by the Philosophy Faculty's Graduate Studies Committee shall always be conditional   25
on a level of performance in the examination for the M.St. in Philosophy of Physics, as specified in the Graduate Student Handbook.

10. Candidates for the M.St. in Philosophy of Physics who have successfully transferred to the second year of the B.Phil. in Philosophy shall be deemed to have completed the first year of the B.Phil. in Philosophy and the four essays submitted for   30
their M.St. examination shall be deemed to replace the first four essays required of candidates for the B.Phil. In the second year of study, such candidates will be required to submit two 5,000-word essays by 10 a.m. on Wednesday of noughth week of Hilary Term and a 30,000-word thesis by 10 a.m. on Wednesday of eighth week of Trinity Term, in line with the B.Phil. assessments schedule specified under paragraphs 5. and   35
6. above.

11. Candidates for the M.St. in Philosophy of Physics who have successfully transferred to the second year of the B.Phil. in Philosophy, may apply for the award of M.St. in Philosophy of Physics only if they fail or withdraw from the second year of the B.Phil. in Philosophy.   40

12. Candidates who fail or withdraw from the B.Phil. but have completed the requirements for the M.St. in Philosophy may be permitted to supplicate for that degree.

Master of Philosophy in Archaeology

(*See also the general notice at the commencement of these regulations.*)

Within the Division of Social Sciences, the course shall be administered by the Committee for the School of Archaeology. The regulations made are as follows:

1. Candidates for admission must apply to the Committee for the School of Archaeology. They will be required to produce evidence of their appropriate qualifications for the proposed course including their suitable proficiency in relevant ancient or modern languages.

2. Candidates must follow for six terms a course of instruction in Archaeology.

3. The registration of candidates will lapse from the Register of M.Phil. students on the last day of the Trinity Full Term in the academic year after that in which their name is first entered in it, unless the committee decides otherwise.

4. All candidates are required:

(*a*) to satisfy the examiners in a Qualifying Examination identical with that for the degree of Master of Studies in Archaeology and governed by regulations 5–9 for that degree, in the Trinity Full Term of the academic year in which their name is first entered on the Register for M.Phil. students except that under regulation 5 (*c*) of that degree a 10,000 word dissertation may not normally be offered, and in its place of a second subject should be offered selected from Schedules B–D, examined by two pre-set essays. In the case of failure inone part of the Qualifying Examination, the candidate will have the same rights of resubmission as for the Master of Studies and, if successful, will be granted permission to supplicate for the degree of Master of Studies but will not be permitted to proceed to the second year of the M.Phil. Candidates whose work in the Qualifying Examination is judged by the examiners to be of the standard required for the degree of M.St in Archaeology, but not of the standard required to proceed to the second year of the M.Phil. in Archaeology, will be granted permission to supplicate for the degree of Master of Studies in Archaeology;

(*b*) to deliver to the Examination Schools, High Street, Oxford, not later than noon on the Friday of the sixth week of Trinity Full Term in the academic year after that in which their name is first entered on the Register for M.Phil. students, a thesis of not more than 25,000 words (excluding bibliography and any descriptive catalogue or other factual matter, but including notes and appendices) on the subject approved in accordance with regulations 6 and 10 below;

(*c*) to present themselves for written examination in accordance with regulation 5 below in the Trinity Full Term of the academic year after that in which their name is first entered on the Register for M.Phil. students;

(*d*) to present themselves for an oral examination as required by the examiners.

5. The written examination shall comprise one subject chosen from Schedules A–D for the Master of Studies in Archaeology. [Candidates who offered a subject from Schedule C or D in the Qualifying Examination may not normally offer another subject from the same schedule.] The subjects will be examined by two pre-set essays (each of 5,000 words), except that further subjects from Schedule A in the M.St in Archaeology may also be examined by a written paper, and those from Schedule A of the M.St in Classical Archaeology will only be examined by written paper.

6. The choice of subjects for thesis and examination must be approved by the candidate's supervisor and by the committee, having regard to the candidate's previous experience and to the availability of teaching.

7. Candidates will be expected to show sufficient general knowledge of the appropriate history and geography for a proper understanding of their subjects.

8. The subject for examination and the chosen method of examination must be submitted for approval by the committee in time for its meeting in eighth week of the Trinity Full Term of the academic year in which the candidate's name is first entered on the Register for M.Phil. students. Notice of the subject must be given to the Registrar no later than Friday of the eighth week of the Michaelmas Full Term preceding the examination.

9. Where options are examined by pre-set essays (as specified in 5 above), candidates will normally select essay topics from a list offered by their supervisors. The proposed essay titles, countersigned by the supervisor, must be submitted for approval to the Chair of Examiners by noon on Friday of the seventh week of the Hilary Full Term preceding the examinations. Candidates must submit two copies of their essays by not later than noon on Friday of the sixth week of Trinity Full Term, to the Examination Schools. Essays must be typed or printed.

10. The proposed thesis title must be submitted for approval by the committee in time for its meeting in the eighth week of the Trinity Full Term of the year in which the candidate's name is first entered on the Register for M.Phil. students.

11. Candidates are advised that adequate reading knowledge of an appropriate language or languages (other than English) may be necessary to reach the standard required by the examiners.

12. Candidates will be required to deposit one copy of the thesis with the Examination Schools. Successful candidates will be required to deposit one copy of the thesis in the Sackler Library or the Balfour Library, as directed by the examiners. Such candidates will be required to complete a form stating whether they give permission for their thesis to be consulted.

13. Candidates whose work in the Final Examination is judged by the Examiners not to be of the standard required for the degree of M.Phil. in Archaeology but whose work in the Qualifying Examination nevertheless reached the standard required for the degree of M.St in Archaeology, may be offered the option of resitting the M.Phil. Examination under the General Regulations § 2, cl. 4, or of being granted permission to supplicate for the degree of Master of Studies in Archaeology.

14. The examiners may award a distinction for excellence in the whole examination.

Master of Philosophy in British and European History, from 1500 to the present

(See also the general notice at the commencement of these regulations.)

The regulations of the Board of the Faculty of History are as follows:

1. Candidates for the Master of Philosophy in British and European History, from 1500 to the present, must follow for at least six terms a course of instruction and directed research and must, upon entering the examination, produce from their society a certificate to that effect.

2. Candidates must attend such lectures, seminars and classes as their supervisor shall determine. In addition to the formally examined programme elements described below, each candidate will be expected to attend and complete in-course requirements for a series of skills and specialist options based on a schedule to be published from year to year by the Faculty's Graduate Studies Committee. The candidate's individual programme, agreed with her/his supervisor, will be subject to approval by the Director of Graduate Studies, in consultation with the programme convenor, by Friday of Week One of Michaelmas Term; subsequent changes must be agreed by the Director of Graduate Studies not later than Friday of Week Three of Hilary Term. Class teachers will report to the Chair of Examiners on the candidate's attendance and participation, and, where appropriate, test results, not later than Monday of Week

Nine of Hilary Term, except in the case of three-term language classes where the respective reporting deadline will be Monday of Week Nine of Trinity Term.

3.   The final examination shall comprise (i) one extended essay based on the programme's theory and methods component plus an annotated bibliography based on the sources and resources component, (ii) one extended essay based on an Advanced Option, (iii) one extended essay based on a class on the writing of History, and (iv) one dissertation proposal in the first year of the programme, and (v) one research methodology essay and (vi) a dissertation of not more than 30,000 words in the final year of the programme.

I.   During Michaelmas Term of the first year each candidate will attend core classes on historical theory and methodological approaches as well as a series of classes on sources and resources. The core classes will be assessed by an extended essay of between 4,000 and 5,000 words and the sources and resources component by an annotated bibliography. Two copies of the essay and the annotated bibliography, addressed to the Chair of Examiners for the Master of Philosophy in British and European History, from 1500 to the present, must be submitted to the Examination Schools by 12 noon on Monday of Week One of Hilary Term of the candidate's first year. The assessment of the annotated bibliography will be on a pass/fail basis only, and candidates who fail this element will be given the opportunity to submit a revised version in the first year of the programme.

II. In Hilary Term of the first year candidates must choose one Advanced Option, either from the joint Advanced Options for the Master of Studies and the Master of Philosophy in British and European History, from 1500 to the present, or from the Advanced Options for one of the Faculty of History's other Master's programmes. The choice of Advanced Option will depend on the candidate's training objectives or dissertation project. Details of available Advanced Options are published in course handbooks. Approval of the Advanced Option choice must be obtained from the programme convenor and Director of Graduate Studies by Friday of Week Four of Michaelmas Term. The request for approval must be sent to the History Graduate Office. On recommendation from the candidate's supervisor, the Director of Graduate Studies, in consultation with the programme convenor, may approve relevant taught papers from Master's programmes offered by faculties other than History, provided that the respective faculty's Graduate Studies Committee is satisfied that the candidate has an adequate background in the subject. This part of the programme will be assessed by one extended essay of between 6,500 and 7,500 words. Two copies of the essay, addressed to the Chair of Examiners for the Master of Philosophy in British and European History, from 1500 to the present, must be submitted to the Examination Schools by 12 noon on Monday of Week Nine of Hilary Term of the candidate's first year. Essays should reflect skills and understanding the candidate has developed by following the approved choice of paper. The essay may complement but must not share significant content with the essay submitted under I. above. *Teaching may not be available for all the Advanced Options each year, and restrictions may be imposed on the combination of Advanced Options that may be taken in a particular year.*

III. In Trinity Term candidates take a class on Writing History and finalise a proposal for their dissertation research during the Long Vacation and Michaelmas Term of their second year. The Writing History classes will be assessed by an extended essay of between 4,000 and 5,000 words. The essay may complement but must not share significant content with the essays submitted under I. and II. above. Two copies of the extended essay on Writing History, addressed to the Chair of Examiners for the Master of Philosophy in British and European History, from 1500 to the present, must be submitted to the Examination Schools by 12 noon on Monday of Week Nine of Trinity Term of the candidate's first year.

IV. Candidates must prepare an extended dissertation proposal of between 2,000 and 2,500 words. Two copies of the extended dissertation proposal, addressed to the Chair of Examiners for the Master of Philosophy in British and European History, from 1500 to the present, must be submitted to the Examination Schools by 12 noon on Monday of Week Six of Trinity Term of the candidate's first year.

V. Candidates must prepare one methodological essay (of up to 7,000 words) and a seminar presentation for a class on 'Historical concepts and controversies', to be examined in Trinity Term of the candidate's second year. Students may choose a topic for their essay and presentation in an area proximate to their dissertation subject, but may not replicate any other material submitted for examination. Two typewritten copies of the extended essay, addressed to the Chair of Examiners for the Master of Philosophy in British and European History, from 1500 to the present, must be submitted to the Examination Schools by 12 noon on Monday of first week of Trinity Term of the candidate's second year.

VI. A dissertation of not more than 30,000 words, including footnotes and appendices but excluding bibliography, on a topic approved by the candidate's supervisor and the Programme Convenor of the M.Phil. in British and European History, from 1500 to the present. Candidates must apply in writing to the Programme Convenor for approval of the proposed topic of their dissertation. The application must be submitted to the History Graduate Office by 12 noon on Monday of Week Six of Trinity Term of the candidate's first year. Two copies of the dissertation must be submitted to the Examination Schools by 12 noon on Monday of Week Eight of Trinity Term of the candidate's second year. Dissertations submitted must not exceed the permitted length. If they do the Examiners will reduce the marks awarded. The presentation and footnotes should comply with the requirements specified in the Regulations of the Education Committee for the degrees of M.Litt. and D.Phil. and follow the *Conventions for the presentation of dissertations* and theses of the Faculty of History. Each dissertation must include a short abstract which concisely summarises its scope and principal arguments, in about 300 words. Each copy of the dissertation must be securely and firmly bound in either hard or soft covers. One copy of an M.Phil. dissertation which is approved by the examiners must be deposited in the Bodleian Library. This final copy should incorporate any corrections or amendments which the examiners may have requested. It must be hard bound, in a dark colour, and lettered on the spine with the candidate's name and initials, the degree, and the year of submission.

4. A candidate who, at the end of the first year of the course, is unable to continue on to the second year, may, with the support of his or her college and supervisor, apply to the Director of Graduate Studies in History for permission to transfer to the status of a student for the Master of Studies in British and European History, from 1500 to the present, and to enter that examination in the current year.

5. The examiners may award a distinction to candidates who have performed with special merit in all parts of the examination for the Master of Philosophy in British and European History, from 1500 to the present.

A candidate who fails the examination will be permitted to retake the examination on one further occasion only, not later than one year after the initial attempt. A candidate whose dissertation has been of satisfactory standard will not be required to resubmit the dissertation. A candidate who has reached a satisfactory standard on the extended essays will not be required to retake those papers. If it is the opinion of the   5
examiners that the work done by a candidate, while not of sufficient merit to qualify for the Degree of Master of Philosophy, is nevertheless of sufficient merit to qualify for the Degree of Master of Studies in British and European History, from 1500 to the present, the candidate shall be given the option of resitting the M.Phil. (as provided under the General Regulations § 2, cl. 4, and in accordance with this regulation) or of   10
being granted leave to supplicate for the Degree of Master of Studies.

Master of Philosophy in Celtic Studies

(*See also the general notice at the commencement of these regulations.*)

The regulations made by the Board of the Faculty of Medieval and Modern Languages are as follows: 15

1. All candidates shall be required at the time of admission to satisfy the Board of Faculty of Medieval and Modern Languages (if necessary, by written test) that they possess the appropriate qualifications for the proposed course, including suitable proficiency in relevant languages. Normally the course will be restricted to candidates who have taken a first degree in a relevant subject area.[1]   20

2. All candidates shall be required

   (*a*) To offer themselves for written examination as defined in section 5 below.

   (*b*) To present themselves for viva voce examination at the time appointed by the examiners.

3. The subjects and papers of the examination shall be as follows: 25

   (*a*) Historical and comparative Celtic linguistics.

   (*b*) Irish literature up to the Cromwellian wars. Candidates will be expected to offer nine texts in all, three from each of the three periods, Old Irish, Middle Irish, and Early Modern Irish. The following are the prescribed texts:

Old Irish: 30

Scéla mucce Meic Dathó, ed. R. Thurneysen (Dublin, 1951).

Togail bruidne Dá Derga, ed. E. Knott (Dublin, 1936).

Longes mac n-Uislenn, ed. V. Hull (New York, 1949).

Scéla Cano meic Gartnáin, ed. D. A. Binchy (Dublin, 1963).

Fingal Rónáin and Other Stories, ed. D. Greene (Dublin, 1955).   35

Táin Bó Fraích, ed. W. Meid, rev. edn. (Dublin, 1974).

Selected passages from *Táin Bó Cúailnge*, Recension I, ed. C. O'Rahilly (Dublin, 1976).

Middle Irish:

Stories from the Acallam, ed. M. Dillon (Dublin, 1970).   40

Aislinge meic Conglinne, ed. K. H. Jackson (Dublin, 1990).

Caithreim Cellaig, ed. K. Mulchrone (Dublin, 1933).

---

[1] Even though their first degree is considered to have fitted them to pursue a course of study for an M.Phil. in Celtic Studies candidates may be required to take an intensive course in a Modern Celtic language *either* in the long vacation prior to their admission *or* in the long vacation following the third term of their course of instruction.

Cath Almaine, ed. P. Ó Riain (Dublin, 1978).

The Irish Adam and Eve Story from Saltair na Rann, ed. D. Greene and F. Kelly (Dublin, 1976).

Buile Shuibne, ed. J. G. O'Keeffe (Dublin, 1931).

Selected passages from *Táin Bó Cúalnge from the Book of Leinster*, ed. C. O'Rahilly 5 (Dublin, 1967).

Early Modern Irish:

An introduction to Irish syllabic poetry of the period 1200–1600, ed. E. Knott (2nd edn., Dublin, 1957).

Tóruigheacht Dhiarmada agus Ghráinne, ed. Nessa Ni Shéaghdha (Dublin, 1967). 10

The Bardic poems of Tadhg Dall O Huiginn, ed. E. Knott (2 vols., London, 1922–6).

Sgéalaigheacht Chéitinn, ed. O. Bergin, 3rd edn. (Dublin, 1930).

Cath Muighe Tuireadh, ed. B. Ó Cuív (Dublin, 1945).

Nua-Dhuanaire, vol. 1, ed. P. de Brún, B. Ó Buachalla and Tomás Ó Concheanainn (Dublin, 1975). 15

Dánta Gradha, ed. T. F. O'Rahilly, 2nd edn. (Cork, 1926).

Scottish Poetry from the Book of the Dean of Lismore, ed. W. J. Watson (Edinburgh, 1937).

(*c*) Welsh literature up to the Reformation. Candidates will be expected to offer nine texts in all, three from each of three periods, Old, Middle and Early 20 Modern Welsh. The following are prescribed texts:

Old Welsh:

Canu Taliesin, ed. I. Williams (Cardiff, 1960).

Canu Aneirin, ed. I. Williams (Cardiff, 1938).

Canu Llywarch Hen, ed. I. Williams (Cardiff, 1953). 25

Armes Prydein, ed. I. Williams, Engl. version by R. Bromwich (Dublin, 1972).

M. Haycock, *Blodeugerdd Barddas o Ganu Crefyddol Cynnar* (Y Bala, 1994), Nos. 1–8, 13–14, 16, 18, 21, 30.

Middle Welsh:

Pedeir Keinc y Mabinogi, ed. I. Williams (Cardiff, 1951). 30

Culhwch and Olwen, ed. R. Bromwich and D. Simon Evans (Cardiff, 1992).

Welsh Court Poems, ed. Rhian Andrews (Cardiff: University Wales Press, 2007).

Historia Peredur vab Efrawc (from Llyfr Gwyn Rhydderch: Y Chwedlau a'r Rhamantau, ed. J. Gwenogvryn Evans (Cardiff, 1973).

Brut y Brenhinedd, ed. B. F. Roberts (Dublin, 1971). 35

The following shorter tales: *Breudwyt Ronabwy*, ed. M.Richards (Cardiff, 1948), *Breudwyt Maxen Wledic*, ed. B. F. Roberts (Dublin, 2005), *Cyfranc Lludd a Llefelys*, ed. B. F. Roberts (Dublin, 1975).

Early Modern Welsh:

Cerddi Dafydd ap Gwilym, ed. D. Johnston et al. (Cardiff, 2010). 40

Poems of the Cywyddwyr, ed. E. I. Rowlands (Dublin, 1976).

Rhagymadroddion 1547–1659, ed. Garfield H. Hughes (Cardiff, 1951).

A Welsh Bestiary of Love, ed. G. C. G. Thomas (Dublin, 1988).

Gwaith Tudur Aled, ed. T. Gwynn Jones (Cardiff, 1926).

Gwaith Guto'r Glyn, ed. I. Williams and J. Ll. Williams (Cardiff, 1939). 45

T. Parry, *Detholion o Destament Newydd 1567* (Cardiff, 1967).

Llyvyr Iob: Cyvieithad Dr. Morgan 1588, ed. J. Gwenogvryn Evans (Oxford, 1888).

(*d*) Special Subjects

For the special subjects, each candidate may, with the agreement of his/her supervisor, submit an extended essay not exceeding 8,000 words in lieu of a three-hour examination.

(1) The archaeology of Celtic Society in pre-Christian Europe.
(2) The Latin Literature of the British Isles.
(3) The records of Continental Celtic.
(4) Irish and Welsh origin legends.
(5) The Celtic context of Old and Middle English literature.
(6) The history of Ireland up to 1216.
(7) The history of Scotland up to 1153.
(8) The history of Wales *either* from *c* .550 to 1063 *or* from 1063 to 1415.
(9) The history of the Celtic peoples from *c*.400 to *c*.900.
(10) The Normans and the Celtic peoples 1066–1216.
(11) Early Irish Law.
(12) Medieval Welsh Law.
(13) The Ulster Cycle of tales.
(14) The Classical Irish bardic tradition.
(15) *Echtrai* and *immrama*.
(16) The medieval Welsh Arthurian romances.
(17) Middle Cornish language and literature.
(18) Middle Breton language and literature.
(19) Twentieth-Century Scottish Gaelic literature.
(20) Literature of the modern revival in Irish.
(21) The Welsh literary renaissance of the twentieth century.
(22) Language and society in modern Scotland.
(23) The palaeography of medieval Celtic vernacular manuscripts (candidates may restrict themselves either to Irish or to Welsh manuscripts).
(24) The comparative syntax of modern Celtic languages.
(25) The Celtic inscriptions of the British Isles before 800.
(26) The poetry of Cynddelw.

The Special Subjects listed above are not prescriptive: candidates are allowed to offer a Special Subject or Special Subjects of their own devising, provided that these are similar in character and scope to those listed and that they are approved under the arrangements set out in section 6 below.

(*e*) A thesis of approximately 20,000 words and not more than 25,000 words on a subject approved by the board or by a person or persons to whom the board may delegate this function. When seeking approval for the subject of the thesis, every candidate shall submit with the proposed title a written statement of not more than 500 words explaining the scope of the topic and the manner in which it is proposed to treat it.

4. Candidates shall be required to offer three papers and a thesis, as follows:

(*a*) *Either*

(i) Two papers, one on each of two subjects selected from those described in section 3 (*a*), (*b*), and (*c*) above.

(ii) One paper on a Special Subject as described in Section 3 (*d*) above.

Or

(i) One paper on a subject selected from those described in section 3 (*a*), (*b*), and (*c*) above.

(ii) Two papers, one on each of two Special Subjects as described in section 3 (*d*) above.

(*b*) A thesis as described in section 3 (*e*) above.

5. Candidates shall seek approval (by application to the Modern Languages Graduate Office, 41 Wellington Square, Oxford) for the proposed subject of their thesis by the end of the fourth week of the second term after that in which their names have been placed on the register of M.Phil. Students, i.e. normally by the end of the fourth week of Trinity Term in their first year.

The thesis (*two copies*) must be typewritten and must be delivered to the Examination Schools, High Street, Oxford, not later than Friday of the first week of the Trinity Full Term in which the examination is to be taken.[1]

Successful candidates will be required to deposit one copy of their thesis in the Bodleian Library.[2]

6. Each candidate's choice of papers shall be subject to the approval of the Board of the Faculty of Medieval and Modern Languages or of a person or persons to whom the board may delegate the function of giving such approval. Approval shall be given only if the choice of papers proposed, and any titles of Special Subjects of the candidate's own devising, have the written support of the candidate's supervisor. Approval of the choice of papers proposed will be dependent on the availability of teaching and examining resources at the relevant times. Candidates shall seek approval (by application to the Modern Languages Graduate Office, 41 Wellington Square, Oxford) by the end of the first term after that in which their names have been placed on the register of M.Phil. students, i.e. normally by the end of Hilary Term in their first year.

A proposal for a Special Subject or Special Subjects of the candidate's own devising shall be accompanied by a *brief* statement of the candidate's view of the character and scope of the Special Subject or Special Subjects proposed.

7. If it is the opinion of the examiners that the work done by a candidate while not of sufficient merit to qualify for the degree of M.Phil. is nevertheless of sufficient merit to qualify for the degree of Master of Studies in Celtic Studies, the candidate shall be given the option of resitting the M.Phil. examination under the appropriate regulation or of being granted permission to supplicate for the Degree of Master of Studies.

8. The examiners may award a distinction for excellence in the whole examination.

Master of Philosophy in Classical Archaeology

Within the Division of Social Sciences, the course shall be administered by the Committee for the School of Archaeology. The regulations made are as follows:

1. Candidates for admission must apply to the Committee for the School of Archaeology. They will be required to produce evidence of their appropriate qualifications for the proposed course, including their suitable proficiency in relevant ancient or modern languages.

2. Candidates must follow for six terms a course of instruction in Classical Archaeology.

---

[1] See the general regulation concerning the preparation and dispatch of theses. Candidates are reminded that work submitted for the Degree of M.Phil. may subsequently be incorporated in a thesis submitted for the Degree of D.Phil.

[2] Such candidates will also be required to sign a form stating whether they give permission for their theses to be consulted.

3. The registration of candidates shall lapse from the Register of M.Phil. students on the last day of Trinity Term in the academic year after that in which their name is first entered in it, unless the committee decides otherwise.

4. All candidates are required:

(*a*) to satisfy the examiners in a Qualifying Examination identical with that for the degree of Master of Studies in Classical Archaeology and governed by regulations 5–9 for that degree, in the Trinity Full Term of the academic year in which their name is first entered on the Register of M.Phil. students except that under regulation 5(*b*) of that degree a 10,000 word dissertation may not normally be offered in place of one of the subject options (examined by two pre-set essays). In the case of failure in one part of the qualifying examination, the candidate will have the same rights of resubmission as for the M.St in Classical Archaeology and, if successful, will be granted permission to supplicate for the degree of M.St in Classical Archaeology but will not be permitted to proceed to the second year of the M.Phil. in Classical Archaeology. Candidates whose work in the Qualifying Examination is judged by the examiners to be of the standard required for the degree of M.St. in Classical Archaeology but not of the standard required to proceed to the second year of the M.Phil. in Classical Archaeology, will be granted permission to supplicate for the degree of Master of Studies in Classical Archaeology;

(*b*) to deliver to the Examination Schools, High Street, Oxford, not later than noon on the Friday of the sixth week of Trinity Full Term in the academic year after that in which their name is first entered on the Register for M.Phil. Students, a thesis[1] of not more than 25,000 words (excluding bibliography and any descriptive catalogue or other factual matter, but including notes and appendices) on the subject approved in accordance with regulations 6 and 10 below; the thesis should bear the candidate's examination number but not his or her name.

(*c*) to present themselves for written examination in accordance with regulation 5 below in the Trinity Full Term of the academic year after that in which their name is first entered on the Register for M.Phil. students;

(*d*) to present themselves for an oral examination as required by the examiners.

5. The written examination shall comprise one subject chosen from Schedules A–C for the Master of Studies in Classical Archaeology to be examined by two pre-set essays each of 5,000 words. [Candidates who offered a subject from Schedule C in the qualifying examination may not normally offer another subject from Schedule C.]

6. The choice of subjects for thesis and examination must be approved by the candidate's supervisor and by the committee, having regard to the candidate's previous experience and to the availability of teaching.

7. Candidates will be expected to show sufficient general knowledge of Ancient History and Geography for a proper understanding of their periods and subjects.

---

[1] See the general regulation concerning the preparation and dispatch of theses. Candidates are reminded (i) that two copies are required but that one of these may be a reproduction or carbon copy of the other, provided that any maps, diagrams, or other illustrations in the second copy are adequately reproduced, (ii) that the copy of the thesis deposited in the Ashmolean Library shall be the one containing the original illustrations, and (iii) that work submitted for the Degree of M.Phil. may be subsequently incorporated in a thesis submitted for the Degree of D.Phil.

8. The period or subject for examination must be submitted for approval by the committee in time for its meeting in the eighth week of the Trinity Full Term of the academic year in which the candidate's name is first entered on the Register for M.Phil. students. Notice of the period or subject to be offered by each candidate must be given not later than Friday of the eighth week of the Michaelmas Term preceding the examination. 5

9. [For students starting before MT 2015: Where options are being examined by pre-set essays (as specified in 5 above), candidates will normally select essay topics from a list offered by their supervisors. The proposed essay titles, countersigned by the supervisor, must be submitted for approval to the Chair of Examiners by noon on Friday of the seventh week of the term in which the instruction for that subject is given. Candidates must submit two copies of their essays by not later than noon on the Monday of the second week of the term following that in which the instruction for that subject was given to the Examination Schools, High Street, Oxford. Essays must be typed or printed and should bear the candidate's examination number but not his or her name.] [For students starting from MT 2015: Where options are being examined by pre-set essays (as specified in 5 above), candidates will propose essay topics in consultation with their supervisor or relevant course provider. The proposed essay titles, countersigned by the supervisor, must be submitted for approval to the Chair of Examiners by no later than noon on Friday of the seventh week of the term in which the instruction for that subject is given. Candidates must submit two copies of their essays by no later than noon on the Monday of the first week of the term following that in which the instruction for that subject was given to the Examination Schools, High Street, Oxford. Essays must be typed or printed and should bear the candidate's examination number but not his or her name.] 10 15 20 25

10. The proposed thesis title must be submitted for approval by the committee in time for its meeting in the eighth week of the Trinity Term of the year in which the candidate's name is first entered on the Register for M.Phil. students.

11. Candidates are advised that adequate reading knowledge of an appropriate language or languages (other than English) may be necessary to reach the standard required by the examiners. 30

12. Candidates will be required to deposit one copy of the thesis with the Examination Schools, High Street, Oxford. Successful candidates will be required to deposit one copy of the thesis in the Sackler Library. Such candidates will be required to complete a form stating whether they give permission for their thesis to be consulted. 35

13. In the case of failure in just one part of the final examination, the candidate will be permitted to retake that part of the examination on one further occasion, not later than one year after the initial attempt. Written papers would be retaken the following year. A candidate who is not judged to have reached the standard required for the degree of Master of Philosophy in Classical Archaeology but whose examinations fulfil the requirements of the M.St in Classical Archaeology may be granted permission to supplicate for the degree of M.St in Classical Archaeology. 40

14. The examiners may award a distinction for excellence in the whole examination. 45

Master of Philosophy in Comparative Social Policy

(*See also the general notice at the commencement of these regulations.*)

The regulations made by the Divisional Board of Social Sciences are as follows:

Qualifying Test

Every candidate must pass a qualifying test at the end of the third term from the   5
beginning of the course in the *two* compulsory papers, *Methods of Social Research*,
and *Comparative Social Policy/Welfare States* and *one Optional Paper* from the list of
optional papers, specified by the Department of Social Policy and Intervention. This
will be from a list published annually by Friday of the sixth week of Michaelmas Full
Term in the Department of Social Policy and Intervention. Candidates may, after   10
special permission of the Course Director, offer subjects outside this list. This may also
include papers offered in any other relevant master's degree in the University subject
to the permission of the relevant Course Director as appropriate. The examiners may
examine candidates viva voce. Candidates who fail the qualifying test may, in exceptional circumstances, be allowed to retake the test before the beginning of the first   15
week of the next academic year. The examiners can decide that the retake shall consist
of the whole test or parts thereof.

Final Examination

Every candidate must offer:

1. One further optional paper. This will be from a list published annually by Friday   20
of the sixth week of Michaelmas Full Term in the Department of Social Policy and
Intervention. Candidates may, after special permission of the Course Director, offer
subjects outside this list. This may also include papers offered in any other relevant
master's degree in the University subject to the permission of the relevant Graduate
Studies Committee as appropriate.   25

2. A thesis[1] of not more than 30,000 words to be delivered to the Examination
Schools, High Street, Oxford, by noon on Friday of the sixth week of Trinity Full
Term in which the examination is to be taken. The thesis should employ comparative
method in the study of a social policy topic. This word count applies to the text, but
does not include graphs, tables and charts in the main text, or bibliography. An   30
additional word limit of 6,000 words in total applies to the abstract, footnotes, endnotes and technical appendices (including graphs, tables and charts). Successful
candidates may be required to deposit a copy of their thesis in the Social Science
Library.

The examiners may examine any candidate viva voce.   35

The examiners may award a Distinction for excellence in the whole examination on
the basis of the material submitted to them in both the qualifying and the final
examination.

Compulsory Papers

Methods of Social Research   40

(*a*) A course of practical work in (i) basic principles of statistical inference, and
statistical models for the analysis of quantitative social science data, (ii) the rationale
and techniques of qualitative research appropriate to social policy and related social
enquiry, and (iii) methods of data collection including research and questionnaire
design, interviewing and coding. Such practical course work in social research meth-   45
ods shall be assessed by a series of assignments set during the first two terms of the
course. These shall be listed in the Course Handbook and submission dates set for
each assignment. Each of the two quantitative assignments will be of a maximum
length of 2,500 words. The qualitative assignment will be of a maximum length of

---

[1] See the general regulation concerning the preparation and dispatch of theses.

3,000 words. shall be marked during the course. In the event of any candidate not reaching the pass mark set, one further attempt shall be permitted, though in the event of a successful resubmission only the bare pass mark shall be awarded. The combined set of completed assignments forms the practical research methods workbook. Candidates shall submit this workbook to the Director of Graduate Studies in the 5 Department of Social Policy and Intervention by noon on Friday of the sixth week of the third term of the course, accompanied by a statement that it is the candidate's own work except where otherwise indicated. The practical workbooks shall be available for inspection by the examiners.

(*b*) Candidates are required to produce two essays of up to 2,500 words evaluating 10 the research design, methods of data collection and analysis, and any ethical or philosophical issues that arise in a specified research paper. The Director of Graduate Studies shall publish two lists of research papers not later than noon on Monday of the first week of the second term; candidates will be required to select one from both of these lists of papers as the subject for each essay. Candidates shall submit 15 their essay to the Examination Schools by 12 noon on Monday of the first week of the third term of the course, accompanied by a statement that it is the candidate's own work except where otherwise indicated.

Comparative Social Policy/Welfare States

Concepts and typologies of social policies and welfare states. Approaches to the 20 study of social policy. Theories of the origin and growth of the welfare state. Goals and means in social policy. Effectiveness and efficiency in social policy: unintended side effects. Methodological issues in comparative social research.

Optional Papers

These will be from a list published annually by Friday of the sixth week of 25 Michaelmas Full Term in the Department of Social Policy and Intervention. Candidates may, after special permission of the Course Director, offer subjects outside this list. This may also include papers offered in any other relevant master's degree in the University subject to the permission of the relevant Course Director as appro-priate. 30

Master of Philosophy in Criminology and Criminal Justice

(*See also the general notice at the commencement of these regulations.*)

1. Candidates must follow for at least six terms a course of instruction in Criminology and Criminal Justice.

2. There shall be a Board of Studies for the course, to be chaired by the Director of 35 Graduate Studies for Criminology, and also comprising all the members of the Board of Examiners for the Master of Philosophy in Criminology and Criminal Justice for the current year, the Director or Assistant Director of the Centre for Criminology, and a student representative (the latter for open business only).

3. *Admissions* 40

Candidates may signify their intention to take the M.Phil. in Criminology and Criminal Justice when they apply for the M.Sc. in Criminology and Criminal Justice or after they have been admitted. In either case, a formal application, the form for which is obtainable from the Graduate Studies Office, must then be made by Friday of Week Four of Trinity Term preceding the Michaelmas Term in which they wish to 45 study for the M.Phil. Admission of those whose thesis topics are approved by the Centre for Criminology's Board of Studies and for whom that Committee certifies the availability of supervision will always be conditional on a specified level of perfor-mance in the Part I examination.

4. *Residence*

Candidates must keep six terms statutory residence, which may include periods spent in residence while studying for the M.Sc. in Criminology and Criminal Justice.

5. *Courses and examination*

Candidates for the M.Phil. shall satisfactorily complete Part I and Part 2. Part I and Part 2 shall be taken in that order and shall normally be taken in successive years. A candidate wishing to take Part 2 but not to proceed directly from Part I to Part 2 in successive years must seek permission from the Centre for Criminology's Board of Studies. Part I shall consist of the courses and examinations as specified for the M.Sc. in Criminology and Criminal Justice.

6. (*a*) *Qualifying Test (Part 1)*

Every candidate must pass a qualifying test by the end of the third term from the beginning of the course, which shall consist of the elements as specified in cll. 3–7 of the examination regulations for the M.Sc. in Criminology and Criminal Justice.

Candidates who fail the qualifying test may be allowed to be reassessed, as specified in cl. 10 of the examination regulations for the M.Sc. in Criminology and Criminal Justice.

6. (*b*) *Final examination (Part 2)*

Candidates shall follow a course of instruction in Empirical Research Methods, satisfy the examiners that they have completed to the required standard such tests or exercises in Research Methods as prescribed as part of such a course of instruction, and be examined by thesis which must not exceed 30,000 words and should not normally be less than 25,000 words. Candidates are required to deliver two type-written copies of the thesis to the Examination Schools, High Street, Oxford, by noon on Friday of Week Eight of the Trinity Term in which the examination is to be taken.

The course in Empirical Research Methods shall be Research Design and Data Collection, and Social Explanation and Data Analysis, as specified for the M.Sc. in Criminology and Criminal Justice. Where candidates have already taken these courses as part of either M.Sc., they will not be required to take them a second time. Where a candidate has elected to write a thesis that draws significantly on legal research methods, the Director of Graduate Studies (Research) for Criminology, at the suggestion of the prospective thesis supervisor, may grant the candidate exemption from taking Research Design and Data Collection, and Social Explanation and Data Analysis and instruct the candidate to take the Legal Research Method Course, as specified for the M.Phil. in Law.

7. The examiners may award a distinction for excellence in the whole examination.

8. Arrangements for reassessment shall be as follows:

Candidates who fail, or withdraw from, Social Explanation and Data Analysis may resubmit assessments in line with cl. 10 of the examination regulations for the M.Sc. in Criminology and Criminal Justice. Such candidates who have completed successfully all or part of any of the other components may carry forward the marks gained for the successfully completed parts of the degree.

Candidates who fail, or withdraw from, the Legal Research Method course as specified for the M.Phil. in Law (if they have received permission to take this course instead of Research Design and Data Collection and Social Explanation and Data Analysis), may resit course elements according to the standard arrangements for reassessment for that course. Such candidates who have completed successfully all or part of any of the other components may carry forward the marks gained for the successfully completed parts of the degree.

Candidates who fail, or withdraw from, the M.Phil. thesis may resubmit the thesis to the Examination Schools, High Street, Oxford, by noon on Friday Week 8 of the term following publication of their results. Such candidates who have completed successfully all or part of any of the other components may carry forward the marks gained for the successfully completed parts of the degree.

Master of Philosophy in Development Studies

(*See also the general notice at the commencement of these regulations.*)
The regulations made by the Graduate Studies Committee are as follows:

1. Candidates for admission must apply to the Graduate Studies Committee. They will be required to produce evidence of their appropriate qualifications for the proposed course.

2. Candidates must follow for six terms courses of instruction as laid down for the M.Phil. in Development Studies by the Graduate Studies Committee.

3. Candidates will be admitted to take the examination as defined below in a specific year. In exceptional circumstances candidates may be allowed to take an examination later than the one to which they were admitted. Permission for this must be sought from the Proctors through the candidate's college.

4. The registration of candidates shall lapse from the Register of M.Phil. Students on the last day of Trinity Term of their second academic year.

5. *Qualifying Test*

5.1. Every candidate must pass a qualifying test in two foundation papers to be taken at the start of the Trinity Term of the first year of study.

5.2. The qualifying test will be set and administered by the examiners appointed to examine for the M.Phil. in Development Studies. Candidates must enter themselves for the qualifying test via their Colleges.

5.3. Candidates may select the two foundation papers which they offer from the list set out below except that candidates with a non-economics background are required to include Economics as one of the two papers and candidates are not permitted, except with the permission of the Graduate Studies Committee, to offer a paper in the subject of their bachelor's degree.

(i) *History and Politics*

Topics may include the themes of state formation and development; encounters between different civilisations; colonialism, collaboration, and resistance; nationalism, decolonisation; class formation, gender relations, and the formation of political identities; politics and policy. Students will be expected to show knowledge of developments in countries from more than one of the following regions: Africa, Asia, and Latin America.

(ii) *Economics*

Topics may include the basic elements of macro- and micro-analysis for open, less developed, economies; national income accounting and analysis; macroeconomic policy, theories of inflation and growth; supply and demand; theories of the firm; the functioning of markets, externalities and other market failures; theories of international trade; trade policy, exchange rates, and balance of payments management; the operation of the international monetary system. The emphasis will be on concepts and their application in the context of development.

(iii) *Social Anthropology*

Topics may include the perspectives of anthropology upon social change; personhood and well-being; social and personal agency, authority and responsibility in the field of productive activity; marriage, kinship, family and gender in theory and practice; agencies of managed change and their interaction with local communities.

5.4. A candidate who fails to pass the qualifying test may be permitted to retake the test before the beginning of the first week of the next academic year. Candidates shall retake only the failed component of the qualifying test.

5.5. Only candidates who have passed the qualifying test may proceed to the second year of the course.

6. *Core Course in Development Studies*

Candidates must pursue a core course in development studies which runs throughout the two years of the degree. The core course covers the following three aspects: (i) social theory and development theory, (ii) analysis of major interdisciplinary issues, and (iii) international dimensions of development. Issues which may be included are, under (i) the intellectual origins and legacies of development; under (ii) the agrarian question; industrialisation; urbanisation; gender, ethnicity, culture and development and environmental aspects of development; and under (iii) finance, trade, aid, information technology, the United Nations and global governance.

7. *Final Examination*

7.1. The final examination shall consist of the following:

(*a*) One written paper on *Research Methods* which is taken at the end of the Trinity Term of the first year of study. Questions will be set on: Epistemology of social science, social science paradigms; ethics and values; quantitative methods; the presentation of statistical information, hypothesis testing; research design; sampling theory; questionnaire design; the critical reading of documents; participant observation; action research; rapid research; evaluation research.

A candidate who fails to pass the paper in Research Methods may, at the discretion of the Development Studies Committee, be permitted to retake the paper before the beginning of the first week of the next academic year. Only candidates who have passed the paper in Research Methods may proceed to the second year of the course.

(*b*) One research design essay of 3,000–5,000 words, assessed by the examiners appointed to examine for the M.Phil. in Development Studies. Candidates are required to submit the essay in Trinity Term of the first year of study. In the event of a candidate's failing the essay, it must be rewritten, resubmitted and a pass mark awarded before the candidate may proceed to the second year of the course. The research design essay and the written paper in (a) above shall each constitute 50 per cent of the marks available for the examination of the candidate's knowledge of research methods.

(*c*) Three core course essays assessed by the examiners appointed to examine for the M.Phil. in Development Studies. Candidates are required to submit these essays at specified intervals over the two years of the course. The topics to be covered in these essays must fall within the three themes (one per essay) included in the core course in development studies: social theory and development; major interdisciplinary issues; and the international dimension of development. Candidates must pass all three essays. In the event of a candidate's failing either or both essays submitted in the first year of the course, either or both must be rewritten, resubmitted and a pass mark awarded before the candidate may proceed to the second year of the course. In the event of a candidate's failing the third essay, submitted in the second year of the course, it must be rewritten, resubmitted and a pass-mark awarded before the candidate can be deemed to have successfully completed the course.

(*d*) A thesis of not more than 30,000 words (excluding bibliography but including footnotes and appendices) on a topic approved by the M.Phil. Teaching Committee, to which the Graduate Studies Committee delegates this function. The thesis must be on a topic in the general field of development studies. The topic of the thesis must be chosen in consultation with and with the approval of the candidate's supervisor. If a separate thesis supervisor is required, he or she must have agreed to undertake the supervision prior to the approval of the topic as specified above.

(*e*) One written paper selected from a range of optional papers. Details of the optional papers available will be notified during the first year of the course. Candidates may include subjects offered in other relevant masters degrees in the University, subject to permission from the relevant graduate studies committee and from the M.Phil. Teaching Committee. Applications to do this must normally be made by the first Friday of Trinity Term in the student's first year.

(*f*) One further written paper selected from a range of optional papers, or offered in other relevant masters degrees in the University with the provisos specified in section 7.1 (e) above.

7.2. Theses must be delivered to the Examination Schools, High Street, Oxford not later than the Friday of the first week of the Trinity Full Term in which the examination is to be taken.

7.3. Failure in one or more components of the final examination results in failure of the degree. The examiners may permit candidates to re-take the examination of the failed component(s) in Trinity Term of the following academic year. In the case of a failed dissertation, the dissertation must be re-submitted in Trinity Term of the following year. Viva voce examinations are not used for this course.

7.4. The examiners may award a Distinction for excellence in the whole examination.

Master of Philosophy in Eastern Christian Studies

(*See also the general notice at the commencement of these regulations.*)

The regulations made by the Boards of the Faculties of Oriental Studies and Theology are as follows:

Candidates will be admitted to take the examination as defined below in a specific year. In exceptional circumstances candidates may be allowed to take an examination later than one to which they were admitted. Permission for this must be sought from the faculty board not later than Monday of the week before the first week of the Trinity Term in which the examination was to have been taken. The application must have the support of the candidate's college and be accompanied by a statement from the supervisor.

I. Every candidate shall be required

(*a*) to present himself or herself for a written examination, as prescribed below;

(*b*) to present a thesis of not more than 30,000 words on a subject approved by the faculty boards. Theses should be presented not later than noon on the Friday of the second week of the Trinity Term in which the examination is taken.

Successful candidates may be required to deposit one copy of the thesis in the Bodleian;[1]

(*c*) to present himself or herself for a viva voce examination, unless individually dispensed by the examiners.

II. The written examination shall consist of four papers: 5

(1) A general paper on the development of doctrine and the history of the Church in the Christian East to AD717.

(2), (3), (4) Three papers on one of the following options.

A. *Greek*

    (i) The philosophical background of the Greek Fathers.[2]   1(

    (ii) The history of the Church in the Byzantine Empire, AD 717–886.[2]

    (iii) Byzantine ecclesiastical texts.[2]

The three papers will include passages for comment as well as general questions relating to the set texts.

B. *Armenian with Greek*   1:

    (i) Armenian historical texts.[2]

    (ii) Armenian theological and ecclesiastical texts.[2]

    (iii) A translation paper from Greek ecclesiastical texts. Passages for translation will be set from unspecified texts and set texts.[2]

Papers (i) and (ii) will include passages for translation and comment as well as general   2(
questions relating to the set texts.

C. *Syriac with Greek*

    (i) Syriac historical texts.[2]

    (ii) Syriac theological texts.[2]

    (iii) as Paper B (iii) above.   2:

Papers (i) and (ii) will include passages for translation and comment as well as general questions relating to the set texts.

Teaching in all three options (Greek, Armenian with Greek, Syriac with Greek) may not be available every year, and applicants for admission will be advised whether teaching will be available in the option of their choice.   3(

Note. Candidates with sufficient knowledge of Greek may offer Paper A (i) in place of Paper B (iii)/C (iii). Except in the case of Papers A (i) and B (iii)/C (iii), and subject to the approval of the faculty boards, a candidate may offer texts — or, in the case of Paper A (ii), a period of Greek church history — other than those specified in the regulations.   3!

III. The examiners may award a Distinction for excellence in the whole examination.

Master of Philosophy in Economic and Social History

(*See also the general notice at the commencement of these regulations.*)

The regulations of the Board of the Faculty of History are as follows: 4(

1. Every candidate must follow for at least six terms a course of instruction in Economic and Social History and must upon entering for the examination produce from his or her society a certificate to that effect.

---

[1] Candidates will also be required to sign a form stating whether they give permission for the thesis to be consulted.

[2] Lists of texts are available in the Course Handbook.

2. The examination will consist of the following parts:

Qualifying test

Every candidate must pass a qualifying test. The test shall consist of two courses on

(1) Methodological introduction to research in the social sciences and history.

(2) *Either* Quantitative methods and computer applications for historians

or A paper from another established course within the University where this would provide a more appropriate training for the candidate's dissertation focus. Such a choice will need formal approval from both the Course Director and the Chair of the Graduate Studies Committee of the Board of the Faculty of History.

The methodological introduction course will be assessed by an end of course essay of up to 4,000 words. Two copies of the essay must be submitted by noon on Friday of **[For students starting before MT 2015:** fifth week of Hilary Term**] [For students starting before MT 2015:** Week 10 of Michaelmas Term**]** of the candidate's first year to the Chair of Examiners for the M.Phil. in Economic and Social History, c/o Examination Schools, High Street, Oxford OX1 4BG. A quantitative methods course is assessed by an assignment to be completed over the Christmas Vacation; two typewritten copies of the completed assignment must be submitted by noon on Monday of second week of Hilary Term of the candidate's first year to the Chair of Examiners for the M.Phil. in Economic and Social History at the above address. In addition, convenors of qualifying courses will confirm in writing to the chair of examiners not later than Friday of eighth week of Hilary Term the candidates' satisfactory participation in their classes, including the completion of any assignments for the weekly sessions. Any approved alternative qualifying course will be assessed within the format and timetable of the paper's parent course. No candidate who has failed the qualifying test of two courses will be permitted to supplicate for the degree. Candidates who fail a qualifying course once will be permitted to take it again, not later than one year after the initial attempt.

Final examination

The examination shall consist of four papers and a dissertation.

I. Three advanced papers at least two of which must be selected from Schedule I below (Advanced Papers for the M.Phil. and M.Sc. in Economic and Social History), and not more than one from any other M.Phil. the choice of which must be approved by the chair of the Graduate Studies Committee of the History Board not later than Monday of the fourth week of the second Michaelmas Term of the course.

Candidates must take at least two of their advanced papers as three-hour written examinations. For each of their remaining advanced papers candidates must choose to be assessed either by written examination or by two 5,000 word essays. Essays may be only submitted in lieu of written papers for subjects in Schedule I or for papers from other M.Phil.s where similar provision exists in the regulations for those examinations. The essays must be the work of the candidates alone and they must not consult any other person including their supervisors in any way concerning the method of handling the themes chosen. The themes chosen by the candidate must be submitted for approval by the chair of examiners by the examination entry date. Candidates will be informed within two weeks, by means of a letter directed to their colleges, whether the topics they have submitted have been approved. The finished essays must be delivered by the candidate to the Examination Schools, High Street, Oxford, by noon on Monday of sixth week of Trinity Full Term. The essays must be presented in proper scholarly form, and two typed copies of each must be submitted.

II. *Either*   (i) one paper in a discipline or skill or sources or methods selected from Schedule II below.

    or   (ii) A fourth advanced paper selected from Schedule I or from any additional list of papers for the M.Phil. and M.Sc. in Economic and Social History approved by the Graduate Studies Committee of the Board of the Faculty of History and published in the definitive list of Advanced Papers as set out in Schedule I.

III. A dissertation of not more than 30,000 words, including appendices but excluding bibliography on a topic approved by the candidate's supervisor. The dissertation must be delivered not later than noon on the Monday of the first week of the Trinity Full Term in which the examination is to be taken to the Examination Schools, High Street, Oxford. Dissertations submitted must not exceed the permitted length. If they do the examiners will reduce the marks awarded. The presentation and footnotes should comply with the requirements specified in the Regulations of the Education Committee for the degree of M.Litt. and D.Phil. and follow the *Conventions for the presentation of dissertations and theses* of the Board of the Faculty of History.

Each dissertation must include a short abstract which concisely summarises its scope and principal arguments, in about 300 words.

Candidates must submit by the specified date three copies of their dissertation. These must be securely and firmly bound in either hard or soft covers. One copy of an M.Phil. dissertation which is approved by the examiners must be deposited in the Bodleian Library. This finalised copy should incorporate any corrections or amendments which the examiners may have requested. It must be in a permanently fixed binding, drilled and sewn, in a stiff board case in library buckram, in a dark colour, and lettered on the spine with the candidate's name and initials, the degree, and the year of submission.

3. Candidates may, if they so wish, be examined in up to two of their four papers (or submit essays in lieu of these papers as provided for above) at the end of their first year.

4. The examiners will permit the use of any hand-held pocket calculator subject to the conditions set out under the heading 'Use of calculators in examinations' in the *Regulations for the conduct of University Examinations.*

5. The examiners may award a distinction for excellence in the whole examination.

6. If it is the opinion of the examiners that the work done by a candidate, while not of sufficient merit to qualify for the degree of M.Phil., is nevertheless of sufficient merit to qualify for the degree of Master of Science in Economic and Social History, the candidate shall be given the option of re-sitting the M.Phil. (as provided under the appropriate regulation) or of being granted leave to supplicate for the degree of Master of Science.

7. A candidate who fails the examination will be permitted to re-take it on one further occasion only, not later than one year after the initial attempt.

Such a candidate whose dissertation has been of a satisfactory standard may re-submit the same piece of work, while a candidate who has reached a satisfactory standard on the written papers will not be required to re-take that part of the examination.

Schedule I

Advanced Papers for the M.Phil. and M.Sc. in Economic and Social History

A broad range of the course resources are shared with the corresponding courses in History of Science, Medicine, and Technology, and Advanced Papers are therefore available in the subject areas listed here.

1. Economic and business history
2. History of science and technology
3. Social history
4. Historical demography
5. History of medicine   5

A descriptive list of Advanced Papers will be published by the Board of the Faculty of History in September for the academic year ahead (not all options may be available in every year). The definitive list of the titles of Advanced Papers for any one year will be circulated to candidates and their supervisors and posted on the Faculty notice board not later than Friday of third week of Michaelmas Term of the academic year in   10 which the paper is to be taken.

Schedule II

The paper in a relevant discipline or skill may be:

1. One of the papers from the M.Phil. in Economics.

2. One of the papers from the M.Phil. in Sociology or in Comparative Social   15 Policy.

3. One of the papers from the M.Phil. in Russian and East European Studies.

4. One suitable paper from another Master's degree under the auspices of the Faculty of History approved from time to time by the Graduate Studies Committee of the Board of History.   20

5. One suitable paper from another Master's degree on the recommendation of the candidate's supervisor and endorsed by the Course Director.

Choices under Schedule II have to be approved by the chair of the Graduate Studies Committee of the Board of the Faculty of History not later than Monday of the fourth week of the second Michaelmas Term of the course. Candidates wishing to take a   25 paper under 1, 2, 3, or 5 will also need the approval of the appropriate course convenor and the Graduate Studies Committee of the relevant faculty board or inter-faculty committee who need to be satisfied that each candidate has an adequate background in the subject. Not all options may be available in any one year.

Master of Philosophy in Economics   30

(*See also the general notice at the commencement of these regulations.*)

The regulations made by the Divisional Board of Social Sciences are as follows:

First-year examinations

There will be three compulsory papers to be taken at the end of the first year of the course.   35

(*a*) *Macroeconomics*

(*b*) *Microeconomics*

(*c*) *Econometrics*

Details of the content of the three compulsory papers will be published **[For students starting before MT 2015:** in the Course Booklet distributed to students**] [For students**   40 **starting from MT 2015:** on the Department of Economics WebLearn site**]** at the beginning of Michaelmas Term each year.

[For students starting before MT 2015: The papers shall be set and administered by the examiners appointed to examine the M.Phil. in Economics. Applications must be made by the Friday of eighth week in Michaelmas Full Term. The examination will be   45 held in the eighth week of Trinity Full Term. The examiners may also examine any candidate viva voce.**]** In exceptional circumstances, the Economics Graduate Studies

Committee may give permission for a candidate to defer one of these papers. This paper will then be taken at the same time as the final examination.

Candidates who pass these papers will proceed to the second year of the course and take the Final Examination at the end of the second year. Candidates who fail only one out of the three papers may, by permission of the Economics Graduate Studies Committee, proceed to the second year of the course and resit the one failed paper at the same time as the final examination. Otherwise, candidates who fail the first-year examination will be permitted to resit all three papers at the end of their second year but will not be permitted to enter the final examination at that time. If they then pass the three compulsory papers, they will be permitted to proceed with the course and enter the final examination at the end of their third year. In exceptional cases, the Economics Graduate Studies Committee may permit the deferral of resitting one of the three papers at the end of the second year until the final examination. No candidate will be permitted to resit any of the compulsory papers more than once.

Final Examination

No candidate shall enter the final examination unless he or she has already passed the three compulsory papers in the first-year examinations, save that the Economics Graduate Studies Committee may permit any candidate who has failed one of the compulsory papers to resit that paper at the same time as the final examination.

All candidates must offer five second year papers and submit a thesis.[1]

Candidates must take at least one starred (*) paper (advanced core subject) and at least one non-starred paper (field subject).

Candidates must deliver two copies of the thesis (clearly marked with the candidate's name, college, and the words 'M.Phil. in Economics' and accompanied by a statement signed by the candidate that it is the candidate's own work except where otherwise indicated) to the Examination Schools, High Street, Oxford OX1 4BG, by noon on Wednesday in the third week of Trinity Full Term in which the final examination is to be taken. Successful candidates will have one copy of their thesis deposited in the Economics Library by the Department at the end of the examination.

[For students starting before MT 2015: The Examiners may also examine any candidate viva voce.]

Second year papers for the M.Phil. in Economics

Second year papers may be offered from the following list:

1. Advanced Macroeconomics 1*
2. Advanced Macroeconomics 2*
3. Advanced Microeconomics 1*
4. Advanced Microeconomics 2*
5. Advanced Econometrics 1*
6. Advanced Econometrics 2*
7. Advanced Econometrics 3*
8. Behavioural Economics
9. Development Economics 1
10. Development Economics 2
11. Economic History 1

---

[1] Theses must be of not more than 30,000 words and must be typewritten. The thesis must be accompanied by a statement that it is the candidate's own work except where otherwise indicated. See the general regulation concerning the preparation and dispatch of theses. Candidates are reminded that work submitted for the Degree of M.Phil. may subsequently be incorporated in a thesis submitted for the Degree of D.Phil.

12. Economic History 2
13. Financial Economics 1
14. Financial Economics 2
15. Industrial Organisation 1
16. Industrial Organisation 2   5
17. International Trade 1
18. International Trade 2
19. Labour Economics
20. Public Economics
21. Theory Based Empirical Analysis   10

Not all papers on this list will be available every year. The *definitive list* of second year papers together with information on content and structure will be published **[For students starting before MT 2015:** in the M.Phil. Economics Handbook] **[For students starting from MT 2015:** on the Department of Economics WebLearn site] at the beginning of Michaelmas Term of the year in which the exam is to be taken. The   15 examiners will not provide calculators, but will permit the use of a hand-held pocket calculator in the examination room, both for the first year examinations and for the final examination, subject to the conditions set out under the heading 'Use of calculators in examinations' in the *Regulations for the Conduct of University Examinations*.

A list of permitted calculators will be reviewed annually in the week prior to the first   20 *full week of Michaelmas Term and published by the Department of Economics on its weblearn site.*

Master of Philosophy in English Studies (Medieval Period)

(*See also the general notice at the commencement of these regulations.*)

The regulations made by the Board of the Faculty of English Language and   25 Literature are as follows:

Every candidate must follow for at least six terms a course of study in English.

In the first year candidates must follow the courses and submit the essays and dissertations prescribed for the M.St. in English. Candidates must have achieved a pass mark in the first-year assessments before they are allowed to proceed to the   30 second year.

In the second year candidates must offer three of the following subjects and a dissertation.

Syllabus
1. The History of the Book in Britain before 1550 (Candidates will be required to   35 transcribe from and comment on specimens written in English under examination conditions (1 hour).)

2. Old English
3. The Literature of England after the Norman Conquest
4. The Medieval Drama   40
5. Religious Writing in the Later Middle Ages
6. Medieval Romance
7. Old Norse sagas
8. Old Norse poetry
9. Old Norse special topic (only to be taken by candidates offering either paper 7 or   45 paper 8 or both)

10./11. One or two of the C course special options as on offer in any year, as specified by the M.St. English, provided that they may not re-take any option on which they have submitted examined work as part of their M.St. course.

12./13./14./15. Relevant options offered by other Faculties as agreed with the Course Convenors. The teaching and assessment of these options will follow the   5 provisions and requirements as set by the Faculty offering the option.

Examination

The method of examination for each course will be an essay of 5,000–7,000 words to be submitted to Examination Schools, High Street, Oxford not later than noon on Thursday of the tenth week of Michaelmas Term or Hilary Term (depending on the   10 term in which the course was offered).

Candidates must gain approval of the topic of their essays by writing to the Chair of M.St./M.Phil. Examiners, care of the English Graduate Studies Office, by Friday of the sixth week of Michaelmas Term or Hilary Term (depending on the term in which the course was offered).   15

Two copies of the dissertation (not more than 15,000 words) on a subject related to their subject of study should be delivered to Examination Schools, High Street, Oxford, not later than by noon on Monday of the eighth week of Trinity Term. The dissertation must be presented in proper scholarly form. Candidates must gain approval of the topic of their dissertation by writing to the Chair of M.St./M.Phil.   20 Examiners care of the English Graduate Studies Office, by Friday of sixth week of Hilary Term, providing an outline of the topic of not more than 200 words.

Candidates are warned that they must avoid duplicating in their answers to one part of the examination material that they have used in another part of the examination, but the dissertation may incorporate work submitted for the first year dissertation.   25

No candidate who has failed any of the above subjects will be awarded the degree in that examination. Candidates who fail any one of the three papers or the dissertation may re-submit that element by noon on the last Monday of the Long Vacation; candidates who fail more than one element of the examination (including one element plus the translation paper where applicable) must re-submit those elements (and,   30 where applicable, take the translation paper) according to the timetable for the examination in the following year. A candidate may only resubmit or retake a paper on one occasion.

Master of Philosophy in Evidence-Based Social Intervention and Policy Evaluation (EBSIPE)   35

(*See also the general notice at the commencement of these regulations.*)

1. Candidates must follow for at least six terms a course of instruction in Evidence-Based Social Intervention and Policy Evaluation.

2. *Qualifying Test*

Every candidate must pass a qualifying test at the end of the third term from the   40 beginning of the course in the *two* compulsory papers, *Evidence-Based Social Intervention* **[For students starting before MT 2015: and] [For students starting from MT 2015: or]** *Policy Evaluation* and *Research Methods* and one *Optional Paper* from the list of optional papers specified by the Department of Social Policy and Intervention. This will be from a list published annually by Friday of the sixth week   45 of Michaelmas Full Term in the Department of Social Policy and Intervention. The examiners may examine candidates viva voce. Candidates who fail the qualifying test will be allowed to retake the test before the beginning of the first week of the next academic year. The Social Policy and Intervention Graduate Studies Committee can decide that the retake shall consist of the whole test or parts thereof.   50

3. *Final Examination*

Every candidate must offer:

(i) One further optional paper. This will be from a list published annually by Friday of the sixth week of Michaelmas Full Term in the Department of Social Policy and Intervention.

(ii) A thesis[1] of not more than 30,000 words, on a topic related to, and attentive to the **[For students starting before MT 2015:** evidence-based social intervention and policy evaluation and evaluation methods**] [For students starting from MT 2015:** evidence-based social intervention, policy evaluation or evaluation methods**]**, to be delivered to the Examination Schools, High Street, Oxford, by noon of Friday of the sixth week of Trinity Full Term in which the examination is to be taken. Successful candidates may be required to deposit a copy of their thesis in the Social Science Library.

The examiners may examine any candidate viva voce.

The examiners may award a distinction for excellence in the whole examination on the basis of the material submitted to them in both the qualifying test and the final examination.

Compulsory Papers

Evidence-BasedSocial Intervention and Policy Evaluation. As specified for the M.Sc. in Evidence-Based Social Intervention and Policy Evaluation.

Research Methods. As specified for the M.Sc. in Evidence-Based Social Intervention and Policy Evaluation.

Optional Papers

These will be from a list published annually by Friday of the sixth week of Michaelmas Full Term in the Department of Social Policy and Intervention. Not every option will be offered in any one year, and applicants for admission will be advised of this. Areas from which options may be offered include: promoting the welfare of children and families; multicultural mental health interventions; substance misuse and offending; interventions in relation to HIV and AIDS; community analysis and community-based intervention; refugees and asylum seekers. Certain other options from the M.Sc. in Comparative Social Policy may also be available in any one year.

Master of Philosophy in General Linguistics and Comparative Philology

(*See also the general notice at the commencement of these regulations.*)

The regulations made by the Faculty of Linguistics, Philology and Phonetics are as follows:

1. Candidates shall normally have a degree in a subject which has given them at least some experience of linguistic or philological work. Those intending to offer options chosen from C or D below should normally have, and may be required to demonstrate, some knowledge of the chosen (group of) language(s) and those intending to offer options chosen from C will normally be expected to be able to read secondary literature in French and German.

2. Each candidate is required:

(*a*) to present himself or herself for written examination as defined in regulation 2 below;

---

[1] See the general regulations concerning the preparation and dispatch of theses.

(*b*) to deliver to the Examination Schools, High Street, Oxford, not later than noon on the Friday of the first week of the Trinity Term in the academic year in which he is examined, two copies of a thesis of not more than 25,000 words on the subject approved in accordance with regulation 5 below. The word limit excludes the bibliography, appendices consisting of a catalogue of data, any extensive text which is specifically the object of a commentary or linguistic analysis, and any translation of that text, but includes quotations and footnotes.   5

(*c*) to present himself or herself for an oral examination if and when required by the examiners.

3. The examination shall consist of four parts: 10

(*a*) One general paper as indicated in A.

(*b*) Three papers which must be chosen from those listed in B or must be those listed in C or those listed in D.

A. Linguistic Theory.

B.   (i) Phonetics and Phonology.   15

    (ii) Syntax.

    (iii) Semantics.

    (iv) Historical and comparative linguistics.

    (v) Psycholinguistics and Neurolinguistics.   20

    (vi) History and structure of a language.

    (vii) Experimental Phonetics.

    (viii) Sociolinguistics.

    (ix) Computational Linguistics.

    (x) Any one option from those offered as C options for the M.St. in English   25
    Language.

    (xi) Any other subject which, from time to time, the Faculty of Linguistics, Philology and Phonetics at its own discretion may consider suitable.

C.   (i) The comparative grammar of two Indo-European languages or language   30
    groups.

    (ii) The historical grammar of the languages or language groups selected.

    (iii) Translation from, and linguistic comment upon, texts in the languages selected.

D.   (i) The history of one or two languages.   35

    (ii) The structure of the language or languages selected.

    (iii) *Either* (*a*) Translation from, and/or linguistic comment upon, texts in the language or languages selected, *Or* (*b*) Any paper from B above except B (vi).

4. Paper A must be taken at the end of the first year of study. In addition, a student   40
may take one other module for assessment in the first year, where there are good reasons for doing so. Marks will be moderated by the board of examiners for the relevant year, and then be released as final. A candidate who fails paper A or another module taken in the first year will have the option of sitting the same module(s) again at the end of the second year; modules retaken in the second year shall be subject to   45
the cap on marks for re-examined options (paragraph 11 below). The general paper A and the papers in C and D are each assessed by 3-hour written examination. The papers in B are assessed by one of:

(*a*) 3-hour written examination.

(*b*) An essay of between 5,000 and 7,500 words (these limits to exclude symbols and diacritics, figures, the bibliography, appendices consisting of a catalogue of data, questionnaire, or other research instrument used to gather data, any extensive text which is specifically the object of a commentary or linguistic 5 analysis, and any translation of that text, but include quotations and footnotes). For all B papers except for B(ix) and B(x), the essay (in two typewritten copies) must be sent in a parcel bearing the words 'Essay for the M.St./M.Phil. in General Linguistics and Comparative Philology' to the Chair of Examiners for the Degree of M.St/M.Phil. in General Linguistics, c/o Examination Schools, 10 High Street, Oxford. Work for paper B(ix) is submitted as specified in the regulations for the M.Sc. in Computer Science, and work for papers under B (x) is submitted as specified in the regulations for the M.St. in English Language.

(*c*) A written report of between 5,000 and 7,500 words on the design and execution 15 of an original research project (these limits exclude symbols and diacritics, figures, the bibliography, appendices consisting of a catalogue of data, questionnaire, or other research instrument used to gather data, any extensive text which is specifically the object of a commentary or linguistic analysis, and any translation of that text, but include quotations and footnotes). The research 20 report (in two typewritten copies) must be sent in a parcel bearing the words 'Written work for the M.St./M.Phil. in General Linguistics and Comparative Philology' to the Chair of Examiners for the Degree of M.St./M.Phil. in General Linguistics, c/o Examination Schools, High Street, Oxford.

In addition, the lecturer on the course of instruction may require: 25

(*a*) one or more practical problem set(s), to be completed and submitted at a time specified by the lecturer; and

(*b*) one or more oral presentation(s) in a public forum.

For each paper in B, the lecturer on the course of instruction shall prescribe a suitable combination of these options, and shall make available to the Chair of 30 Examiners evidence showing the extent to which each candidate has pursued an adequate course of work.

5. Of the two languages or language groups selected by the candidates who wish to offer the papers mentioned in C above, one must be studied in greater depth than the other. 35

Combinations previously offered under the auspices of the Faculty of Linguistics, Philology and Phonetics are:

(*a*) Greek with the elements of Sanskrit Philology.

(*b*) Italic with the elements of Old Irish Philology.

(*c*) Germanic with the elements of Greek Philology. 40

(*d*) Greek with the elements of Anatolian Philology.

(*e*) Romance with the elements of Italic Philology.

(*f*) Italic with the elements of Greek Philology.

(*g*) Sanskrit with the elements of Greek Philology.

(*h*) Greek with the elements of Slavonic Philology. 45

(*i*) Celtic with the elements of Italic Philology.

Other combinations will be allowed subject to the approval of the faculty and the availability of teaching.

6. The language or languages selected by the candidates who wish to offer the papers mentioned in D above may be ancient (e.g. Ancient Greek, Latin, Sanskrit, Akkadian, etc.) or modern (e.g. French, Italian, German, English, Turkish, etc.). Only languages for which teaching is available at the time may be offered.

7. The choice of the subjects for the thesis and examination will be subject to the approval of the candidate's supervisor and the faculty, having regard to the candidate's previous experience and to the availability of teaching. Not all options may be offered every year. The subjects which a candidate wishes to offer for examination must be submitted to the faculty for approval not later than Monday of the first week in Michaelmas Term in the academic year in which the candidate is to be examined.

The subject of the thesis must be submitted for approval by the faculty not later than Monday of the first week in Michaelmas Term in the academic year in which the candidate is to be examined.

8. The examiners may require a successful candidate to deposit one of the submitted copies of his thesis in the Bodleian Library. Such a candidate will be required to complete a form stating whether he gives permission for his thesis to be consulted.

Candidates are reminded that work submitted for the degree of M.Phil. may subsequently be incorporated in a thesis submitted for the degree of D.Phil.

9. The Examiners may award a distinction for excellence in the whole examination.

10. If it is the opinion of the examiners that the work done by a candidate is not of sufficient merit to qualify him for the degree of M.Phil. but is nevertheless of sufficient merit to qualify him for the Degree of Master of Studies in General Linguistics and Comparative Philology, the candidate shall be given the option of resitting the M.Phil. examination under the appropriate regulation or of being granted permission to supplicate for the Degree of Master of Studies.

11. Candidates requesting re-examination should be required to resit or resubmit any paper in which they have failed to achieve a pass mark. The highest mark awarded for a re-examined paper should be the pass mark.

Master of Philosophy in Geography and the Environment

1. The Social Sciences Board shall elect for the supervision of the course a Standing Committee. The Course Director will be responsible to the Standing Committee.

2. During the first year, candidates for the M.Phil. will:

(*a*) follow a course of instruction for three terms under the aegis of the School of Geography and the Environment in one of the four M.Sc. programmes, either Nature, Society and Environmental Governance, or Biodiversity, Conservation and Management, or Environmental Change and Management, or Water Science, Policy and Management. They will be assessed in all aspects of the M.Sc. programme, with the exception of the dissertation.

(*b*) develop a thesis topic, the title and proposal for which will be submitted for approval to the Course Director by the end of Hilary Term of the first year, together with the name and approval of a person who has agreed to act as their supervisor during the preparation of the dissertation, on the date specified by the department. Candidates registered for the M.Sc programmes listed in paragraph 2 may request a transfer to the M.Phil. degree by submitting an application by the deadline stipulated by the Standing Committee.

3. Examinations at the end of the first year will serve to qualify for entry into the second year of the M.Phil. course. Candidates who fail one or more papers at the end of the first year will be required to resit and pass the failed paper or papers, normally

when next offered the following year, before being permitted to proceed with the degree.

4. In the second year, candidates for the M.Phil. will:

(*a*) offer a thesis of not more than 30,000 words accompanied by an abstract not exceeding 300 words. **[For students starting before MT 2015:** The maximum word count shall exclude footnotes, appendices, references and the abstract.**] [For students starting from MT 2015:** The maximum word count shall include footnotes, but exclude appendices, references and the abstract.**]** The detailed format and specification of the dissertation shall be approved by the Standing Committee, and be published in the course handbook. Two typewritten copies of the thesis must be submitted to the Examination Schools and addressed to the Chair of Examiners of the M.Phil. in Geography, c/o the Examination Schools, High Street, Oxford, by noon of the first weekday of September at the end of the second year. Successful candidates will be required to deposit one copy of their thesis in the Bodleian Library, and will be required to sign a form stating whether they will permit their thesis to be consulted. The thesis shall be accompanied by a statement certifying that the thesis is the candidate's own work except where otherwise indicated. **[For students starting from MT 2015:** Both copies must bear the candidate's examination number but not his/her name.**]**

(*b*) submit one extended essay based on new work set as part of the assessment of the appropriate SoGE M.Sc elective module not taken in the first year of study. Essays based on an elective taken during Michaelmas Term shall be submitted by noon on the first weekday of Hilary Term. Essays based on an elective taken during Hilary Term, shall be submitted by noon on the first weekday of Trinity Term. Approval for the topic of the essay must have been obtained from the elective leader prior to submission. The extended essay shall be accompanied by a statement certifying that the extended essay is the candidate's own work except where otherwise indicated.

5. Arrangements for reassessment shall be as follows:

Candidates who fail to satisfy the examiners on the thesis and/or the extended essay may resubmit the thesis and/or the extended essay on not more than one occasion, which shall normally be within one year of the original failure.

6. Viva voce examination: Candidates must present themselves for viva voce examination when required to do so by the examiners.

7. The examiners may award a distinction for excellence in the whole examination.

Master of Philosophy in Greek and/or Latin Languages and Literature

(*See also the general notice at the commencement of these regulations.*)

The regulations made by the Board of the Faculty of Classics are as follows:

[For students starting before MT 2015: 1. *Qualifications.* Candidates must satisfy the board that they possess the necessary qualifications in Greek and/or Latin to profit by the course.

2. *Course.* Every candidate must follow for at least six terms a course of instruction in Greek and/or Latin Languages and Literature. Candidates will, when they enter for the examination, be required to produce from their society a certificate that they are following such a course.

3. *Options.* See the schedule below. Candidates are required to offer a thesis (C) and any *two* options chosen from A and B.

4. *Approval of Options*. The choice of options will be subject to the approval of the candidate's supervisor and of the Graduate Studies Committee in Classics, having regard to the candidate's previous experience, the range covered by the proposed options, and the availability of teaching and examining resources.

Not all options may be available in any given year.   5

Candidates must submit their provisional choice of *options* to the Academic Administrative Officers, Ioannou Centre, 66 St. Giles', Oxford OX1 3LU not later than noon on the Monday of the week preceding first week of Hilary Full Term next after the beginning of their course; the proposed *thesis title* not later than Tuesday of first week in the Trinity Full Term next following; and the proposed titles of any *pre-*   10
submitted essays (*see* §§ 5 and 7) as soon as practicable, but in any case no later than noon on the Monday of the week preceding first week of Hilary Full Term of the second year of the course (except that the titles of essays to be examined at the end of the first year of study in accordance with cl. 8 below should be submitted no later than the noon on the Monday of the week preceding first week of Hilary Full Term of the   15
first year of the course).

5. *Examination* . Each option in section A will be examined by (i) a written paper (three hours) of passages for translation and comment, in which the passages for comment will be set only from the books listed under α in each case, while passages for translation will be set from the books listed under both α and β in each case, and (ii)   20
by three presubmitted essays (see § 7 below) which between them display knowledge of more than a narrow range of the topic. For the examinations to be set in the options under Section B, see the detailed schedule in the Student Handbook.

6. Any candidate whose native language is not English may bring a bilingual (native language to English) dictionary for use in any examination paper where   25
candidates are required to translate Ancient Greek and/or Latin texts into English.

7. *Presubmitted essays.* Essays should each be of between 5,000 and 7,500 words (these limits to exclude the bibliography, any text that is being edited or annotated, any translation of that text, and any descriptive catalogue or similar factual matter, but to include quotations, notes and appendices). A note of the word-count must be   30
included.

Supervisors or others are permitted to give bibliographical help with, and to discuss a first draft of, such essays.

The essays (two typewritten or printed copies) must be delivered in a parcel bearing the words 'Essays presubmitted for the M.Phil. in Greek and/or Latin Languages and   35
Literature' to the Examination Schools, High Street, Oxford OX1 4BG, to arrive by noon on Thursday of sixth week in the appropriate Trinity Full Term.

8. One of the two options taken from A and B must be completed by the end of the first year of study. If it is an option to be examined by presubmitted essays, these must be delivered as in § 7 above, but to arrive by noon on the Thursday of sixth week in the   40
Trinity Full Term of the first year of study for the M.Phil.

9. In theses and pre-submitted essays all quotations from primary or secondary sources, and all reporting or appropriation of material from those sources, must be explicitly acknowledged. Each candidate must sign a certificate to the effect that the thesis or pre-submitted essay is the candidate's own work, and that the candidate has   45
read the Faculty's guidelines on plagiarism. This declaration must be placed in a sealed envelope bearing the candidate's examination number and presented together with the thesis or pre-submitted essay.

10. *Oral Examination.* Candidates are required to present themselves for oral examination if summoned by the examiners.   50

11. *Distinction.* The examiners may award a distinction for excellence in the whole examination.

12. A candidate who fails to satisfy the examiners may enter for the examination on one (but not more than one) subsequent occasion (as provided under the appropriate regulation). If it is the opinion of the examiners that the work done by a candidate, while not of sufficient merit to qualify for the degree of M.Phil., is nevertheless of sufficient merit to qualify for the degree of M.St. in Greek and/or Latin Languages and Literature, the candidate shall be given the option of resitting the M.Phil. or of being granted leave to supplicate for the degree of Master of Studies.

5

10

SCHEDULE

Section A

1. Historiography
2. Lyric Poetry
3. Early Greek Hexameter Poetry
4. Greek Tragedy
5. Comedy
6. Hellenistic Poetry
7. Cicero
8. Ovid
9. Latin Didactic
10. Neronian Literature

15

20

The exact prescribed texts for each of options 1–10 will be as listed in the Student Handbook.

11. Medieval and Renaissance Latin Hexameter Poetry

25

α   In Latin:
   1. Walter of Châtillon, *Alexandreis* Book 10;
   2. Petrarch, *Africa* Book 9; *Bucolicum Carmen* 1 and 3;
   3. Vida, *Ars Poetica* Book 3;
   4. Milton, *In Quintum Novembris, Mansus, Epitaphium Damonis.*

β   In translation:
   1. Walter of Châtillon, *Alexandreis* Books 1-9;
   2. Petrarch, *Africa* Books 1-8;
   3. Vida, *Ars Poetica* Books 1-2.

30

35

12. Any other text or combination of texts approved by the Graduate Studies Committee in Classics.

In 1–11 passages for translation and comment will be set from the editions listed in the regulations for the Honour School of Literae Humaniores. The editions to be used for any option approved under 12 will be specified by the Graduate Studies Committee in Classics.

40

Section B

1. *The transmission of Greek texts, and the elements of palaeography and textual criticism,* with closer study of *Euripides,* Orestes 1-347 and 1246-1693. Candidates will be required (i) to presubmit two essays on some aspect of the transmission of Greek texts or textual criticism, (ii) sit a paper on Greek Palaeography (1.5 hours),

45

and (iii) to take a paper (Honour School of Literae Humaniores, option III.13: 3 hours) of transcription and of comment on passages in the set text.

2. *The transmission of Latin texts, and the elements of palaeography and textual criticism,* with closer study of either (*a*) Seneca, *Agamemnon* or Catullus 1–14, 27–39, 44–51, 65–7, 69–76, 95–101, 114–16[1]. Candidates will be required (i) to presubmit two   5
essays on some aspect of the transmission of Latin texts or textual criticism, (ii) sit a paper on Latin Paleography (1.5 hours), and (iii) to take a paper (Honour School of Literae Humaniores, Subject 514 or 515: 3 hours) of transcription and of comment on passages in the set text.

3. *Greek and Latin Papyrology, with special reference to literary papyri.* Candidates   10
will be required (i) to submit two essays that between them display more than a narrow range of the topic, and (ii) to undertake a practical test, in their own time, in deciphering and commenting on original papyri. (The examiners, in consultation with the supervisor and/or the teacher of the course, will assign each candidate a papyrus or small group of papyri not later than Saturday of sixth week in the Hilary   15
Full Term preceding the candidate's final term; he or she must prepare an edition of it, in proper scholarly form, and deliver two typed copies of this edition to the Examination Schools not later than noon on Thursday of sixth week in the Trinity Full Term in which the examination will be taken. The copies should be accompanied by a statement signed by the candidate to the effect that they are solely his or her own   20
work. This statement must be placed in a sealed envelope bearing the candidate's examination number and presented together with the copies.)

4. *Comparative Philology, with special reference to the history of the Greek and/or Latin language.* Two papers will be set. Paper (i), Essays, will cover (*a*) basic questions about the comparative and/or historical grammar of Greek and/or Latin, and (*b*)   25
questions about the history of the Greek and/or Latin language. Paper (ii), texts for translation and linguistic commentary, will include a compulsory question with passages from *either* Greek dialect inscriptions *or* Latin archaic inscriptions; other passages will be set from Greek and/or Latin literary texts; there will be an opportunity to show knowledge of Linear B and/or Oscan and Umbrian.   30

5. *Theory and methodology of classical literary studies.* Candidates will be expected to be familiar with the major theoretical and methodological issues that arise in the study of ancient literature, and with the major positions in contemporary critical theory and their relationship to classical studies. They will be required to show knowledge of a range of issues in these areas. Examination will be by means of four   35
pre-submitted essays.

6. Intermediate Greek. There will be one two-hour paper comprising unseen translation and grammatical questions on prescribed texts and one three-hour paper requiring translation from prescribed texts. A detailed specification and prescribed texts for the paper will be published in the M.St./M.Phil. course handbook not later   40
than Monday of Week 0 of the Michaelmas Term preceding the examination. Alternative texts for translation under this head may be offered by agreement with the Graduate Studies Committee.

7. Intermediate Latin. There will be one two-hour paper comprising unseen translation and grammatical questions on prescribed texts and one three-hour paper   45
requiring translation from prescribed texts. A detailed specification and prescribed texts for the paper will be published in the M.St./M.Phil. course handbook not later than Monday of Week 0 of the Michaelmas Term preceding the examination. Alternative texts for translation under this head may be offered by agreement with the Graduate Studies Committee.   50

---

[1] University classes will be given for only one of these options each year.

8. Any other subject approved by the Graduate Studies Committee in Classics, which will determine the method of examination.

Section C

A thesis of up to 25,000 words, on a subject to be proposed by the candidate in consultation with the supervisor, and approved by the Graduate Studies Committee in Classics. (The thesis word limit excludes the bibliography, any text that is being edited or annotated, any translation of that text, and any descriptive catalogue or similar factual matter, but includes quotations, notes and appendices. A note of the word-count must be included.) Supervisors or others are permitted to give bibliographical help and to discuss drafts.

The thesis (two typewritten or printed copies) must be delivered in a parcel bearing the words 'Thesis for the M.Phil. in Greek and/or Latin Languages and Literature' to reach the Examination Schools, High Street, Oxford OX1 4BG, by noon on Thursday of sixth week in the Trinity Full Term in which the examination is to be taken.

The examiners may invite a successful candidate to agree that one copy of his or her thesis be deposited in the Bodleian Library.]

[For students starting from MT 2015: 1. *Course.* Every candidate must follow for at least six terms a course of instruction in Greek and/or Latin Languages and Literature.

2. *Options.* See the schedule below. Candidates are required to offer a thesis (D) and any *two* options chosen from A, B, and C.

3. *Approval of Options.* The choice of options will be subject to the approval of the candidate's supervisor and of the Graduate Studies Committee in Classics, having regard to the candidate's previous experience, the range covered by the proposed options, and the availability of teaching and examining resources. Options under B7-B9 in disciplines other than Greek and/or Latin Languages and Literature require the approval of both the Graduate Studies Committee for Classical Languages and Literature and the Graduate Studies Committee responsible for the discipline concerned.

Candidates must submit their provisional choice of *options* to the Academic Administrative Officers, Ioannou Centre, 66 St. Giles', Oxford OX1 3LU not later than noon on Monday of Week 0 of Hilary Full Term in the first year of their course; the proposed *thesis title* not later than Tuesday of Week 1 in the Trinity Full Term of their first year; and the proposed titles of any *pre-submitted essays* (see §§ 4 and 6) no later than noon on the Monday of Week 0 of Hilary Full Term of the second year of the course (except that the titles of essays to be examined at the end of the *first year* of study in accordance with § 7 below should be submitted no later than the noon on the Monday of Week 0 of Hilary Full Term of the first year of the course).

Not all options may be available in any given year.

4. *Examination.* The texts for the options in Section A will appear in the M.St./M.Phil. handbook issued in Week 0 of the Michaelmas Term preceding the examination. Each of these options will be examined by (i) a written paper (three hours) of passages for translation and comment, in which the passages for comment will be set only from the books listed under α in each case, while passages for translation will be set from the books listed under both α and β in each case, and (ii) by three presubmitted essays (see § 6 below) which between them display knowledge of more than a narrow range of the topic. Passages for translation and comment will be set from the editions listed in the M.St./M.Phil. handbook: for any option approved under 11 the edition will be specified by the Graduate Studies Committee in Classical Languages and Literature.

5. Any candidate whose native language is not English may bring a bilingual (native language to English) dictionary for use in any examination paper where candidates are required to translate Ancient Greek and/or Latin texts into English.

6. *Presubmitted essays.* Essays should each be of between 5,000 and 7,500 words. The essay word limit excludes only the bibliography; quotations, notes and appendices are included. A note of the word-count must be included. Candidates who edit and annotate a substantial text, or compile a substantial descriptive catalogue, may apply to Graduate Studies Committee for permission to exclude the text or catalogue   5
in question from the word count.

Supervisors or others are permitted to give bibliographical help with, and to discuss a first draft of, such essays.

The essays (two typewritten or printed copies) must be delivered in a parcel bearing the words 'Essays submitted for the M.Phil. in Greek and/or Latin Languages and   10
Literature' to the Examination Schools, High Street, Oxford OX1 4BG, to arrive by noon on Wednesday of Week 6 in the appropriate Trinity Full Term.

7. One of the two options taken from A, B, and C must be completed by the end of the first year of study. If it is an option to be examined by presubmitted essays, these must be delivered as in § 6 above, but to arrive by noon on the Wednesday of Week 6   15
in the Trinity Full Term of the first year of study for the M.Phil.

8. In theses and pre-submitted essays all quotations from primary or secondary sources, and all reporting or appropriation of material from those sources, must be explicitly acknowledged. Each candidate must submit a signed declaration of authorship in a sealed envelope together with the thesis or pre-submitted essay.   20

9. *Oral Examination.* Candidates are required to present themselves for oral examination if summoned by the examiners.

10. *Distinction.* The examiners may award a distinction for excellence in the whole examination.

11. A candidate who fails to satisfy the examiners may enter for the examination on   25
one (but not more than one) subsequent occasion (as provided under the appropriate regulation). If it is the opinion of the examiners that the work done by a candidate, while not of sufficient merit to qualify for the degree of M.Phil., is nevertheless of sufficient merit to qualify for the degree of M.St. in Greek and/or Latin Languages and Literature, the candidate shall be given the option of resitting the M.Phil. or of   30
being granted leave to supplicate for the degree of Master of Studies.

SCHEDULE
Section A

1. Historiography
2. Lyric Poetry   35
3. Early Greek Hexameter Poetry
4. Greek Tragedy
5. Comedy
6. Hellenistic Poetry
7. Cicero   40
8. Ovid
9. Latin Didactic
10. Neronian Literature

The exact prescribed texts for each of options 1–10 will be as listed in the Student Handbook.   45

11. Any other text or combination of texts approved by the Graduate Studies Committee in Classics.

Section B

1. *The transmission of Greek texts, and the elements of palaeography and textual criticism*, with closer study of Euripides, *Orestes* 1–347 and 1246–1693. Candidates will be required (i) to presubmit two essays on some aspect of the transmission of Greek texts or textual criticism, (ii) sit a paper on Greek Palaeography (1.5 hours), and (iii) to take a paper (Honour School of Literae Humaniores, subject 513: 3 hours) of transcription and of comment on passages in the set text.

2. *The transmission of Latin texts, and the elements of palaeography and textual criticism*, with closer study of either (a) Seneca, *Agamemnon*: manuscripts, texts, interpretation: manuscripts, texts, interpretation or Catullus 1–14, 27–39, 44–51, 65–7, 69–76, 95–101, 114–16[1]: manuscripts, texts, interpretation. Candidates will be required (i) to presubmit two essays on some aspect of the transmission of Latin texts or textual criticism, (ii) to sit a paper on Latin Paleaography (1.5 hours), and (iii) to take a paper (Honour School of Literae Humaniores subjects 514 or 515: 3 hours) of transcription and of comment on passages in the set text.

3. *Greek and Latin Papyrology, with special reference to literary papyri.* Candidates will be required (i) to submit two essays that between them display more than a narrow range of the topic, and (ii) to undertake a practical test, in their own time. (They are to prepare and submit an edition, in proper scholarly form, of an original papyrus or small group or papyri. A papyrus or group of papyri will be assigned to each candidate not later than Saturday of Week 6 in the Hilary Full Term preceding the candidate's final term.)

4. *Comparative Philology, with special reference to the history of the Greek and/or Latin language.* Two papers will be set. Paper (i), Essays, will cover (a) basic questions about the comparative and/or historical grammar of Greek and/or Latin, and (b) questions about the history of the Greek and/or Latin language. Paper (ii), texts for translation and linguistic commentary, will include a compulsory question with passages from *either* Greek dialect inscriptions *or* Latin archaic inscriptions; other passages will be set from Greek and/or Latin literary texts; there will be an opportunity to show knowledge of Linear B and/or Oscan and Umbrian.

5. *Theoretical Approaches to Classical Literature*

6. *Reception: Theory and Methods*

Options B5 and B6 will be examined by means of four pre-submitted essays and require attendance at the associated classes.

7. Any option available in the M.Phil. in Classical Archaeology, Schedule B. This option will be examined *either* by two presubmitted essays *or* by a dissertation of not more than 10,000 words. The deadlines for submission of essays will be those of the M.Phil. in Greek and/or Latin Languages and Literature.

8. Any option available in the M.Phil. in Greek and/or Roman History, Lists B and C. This option will be examined by two presubmitted essays. The deadlines for submission will be those of the M.Phil. in Greek and/or Latin Languages and Literature.

9. Any other subject approved by the Graduate Studies Committee in Classics, which will determine the method of examination.

---

[1] University classes will be given for only one of these options each year.

Section C

1. *Intermediate Greek.* There will be one two-hour paper comprising unseen translation and grammatical questions on prescribed texts and one three-hour paper requiring translation from prescribed texts. A detailed specification and prescribed texts for the paper will appear in the M.St./M.Phil. handbook issued in Week 0 of the Michaelmas Term preceding the examination. Alternative texts for translation under this head may be offered by agreement with the Graduate Studies Committee.

2. *Intermediate Latin.* There will be one two-hour paper comprising unseen translation and grammatical questions on prescribed texts and one three-hour paper requiring translation from prescribed texts. A detailed specification and prescribed texts for the paper will appear in the M.St./M.Phil. handbook published in Week 0 of the Michaelmas Term preceding the examination.

Section D

A thesis of up to 25,000 words, on a subject to be proposed by the candidate in consultation with the supervisor, and approved by the Graduate Studies Committee in Classics. (The thesis word limit excludes only the bibliography; quotations, notes and appendices are included. A note of the word-count must be included. Candidates who edit and annotate a substantial text, or compile a substantial descriptive catalogue, may apply to Graduate Studies Committee for permission to exclude the text or catalogue in question from the word count. Supervisors or others are permitted to give bibliographical help and to discuss drafts.

The thesis (two typewritten or printed copies) must be delivered in a parcel bearing the words 'Thesis for the M.Phil. in Greek and/or Latin Languages and Literature' to reach the Examination Schools, High Street, Oxford OX1 4BG, by noon on Wednesday of Week 6 in the Trinity Full Term in which the examination is to be taken.

The examiners may invite a successful candidate to agree that one copy of his or her thesis be deposited in the Bodleian Library.]

Master of Philosophy in Greek and/or Roman History

(See also the general notice at the beginning of these regulations.)

1. Every candidate must follow, for at least six terms, a course of instruction in Greek and/or Roman History. Candidates will, when they enter for the examination, be required to produce from their society a certificate that they are following such a course.

2. Candidates may satisfy the Examiners in not more than three options in the Trinity Term of the first year of their course.

3. (*a*) In the case of options in languages, Schedule A below, candidates will be examined by written examination. Candidates taking options A (iii)-(vi) may bring a dictionary for their use in the examination. Any candidate taking either of options A (i) or A (ii) whose native language is not English may bring a bilingual (native language-English) dictionary for use in the examination.

(*b*) For options in topics and techniques, Schedules B and C below, candidates will be required to pre-submit two essays of not more than 5,000 words in length, which between them display knowledge of more than a narrow range of the topic covered by the course. (The essay word limit excludes the bibliography, any text that is being edited or annotated, any translation of that text, and any descriptive catalogue or similar factual matter, but includes quotations, notes and appendices.)

(*c*) For the Graduate Seminars, Schedule E below, candidates will be required to pre-submit one essay of not more than 5,000 words, based on a presentation to the Seminar, and one essay of not more than 5,000 words, based on other work done in connection with the Seminar. (The essay word limit excludes the bibliography, any text that is being edited or annotated, any translations of that text, and any descriptive catalogue or similar factual matter, but includes quotations, notes and appendices.)

Supervisors or others are permitted to give bibliographical help with and to discuss drafts of essays. Such essays (two typewritten or printed copies) must be sent in a parcel bearing the words 'Essays presubmitted for the M.Phil. in Greek and/or Roman History' to the Examination Schools, High Street, Oxford. OX1 4BG by noon on the **[For students starting before MT 2015:** Thursday of the sixth week**] [For students starting from MT 2015:** Wednesday of Week 6**]** of the Trinity Term in which the examination is to be taken.

4. *Oral Examination.* Candidates are required to present themselves for oral examination if summoned by the examiners.

5. If it is the opinion of the examiners that the work done by a candidate, while not of sufficient merit to qualify for the degree of M.Phil., is nevertheless of sufficient merit to qualify for the degree of Master of Studies in Greek and/or Roman History, the candidate shall be given the option of resitting the M.Phil. (as provided under the appropriate regulation) or of being granted leave to supplicate for the degree of Master of Studies.

6. *Syllabus*

Candidates must offer (1) an option from A below, (2) an option from B below (3) an option from B or C below, (4) a dissertation as described in D below, and must take, in the first year of their course, (5) one of the Graduate Seminars in Ancient History as described in E below. The option from A must be (i) or (ii), unless a candidate is dispensed from this requirement by the Graduate Studies Committee for Ancient History.

Not all options may be available in any given year.

A

(i) Intermediate Greek, as prescribed for the Master of Studies in Greek and/or Roman History. Paper A(ii)

(ii) Intermediate Latin, as prescribed for the Master of Studies in Greek and/or Roman History, Paper A(iv).

(iii) French

(iv) German

(v) Italian

(vi) Any other language which the candidate has satisfied the Graduate Studies Committee for Ancient History is relevant to their other papers including any dissertation.

B

(i) Greek Numismatics

(ii) Roman Numismatics

(iii) Greek Epigraphy

(iv) The Epigraphy of the Roman World

(v) Documentary Papyrology

[For students starting before MT 2015: (vi) Any of the following papers on the B list of the M.St. in Greek and/or Latin Language and Literature: B1–4; B7

(vii) Any of the papers from Schedule B of the M.St. in Classical Archaeology

(viii) Any other subject approved by the Graduate Studies Committee for Ancient History.]

[For students starting from MT 2015: (vi) Roman Law

(vii) Any of the following papers on the B list of the M.St. in Greek and/or Latin Languages and Literature: B1–4; B7. Presubmitted essays offered under this option will be subject to the normal regulations for the submission of pre-submitted essays in the M.Phil. in Greek and/or Roman History.

(viii) Any of the papers from Schedule B of the M.St. in Classical Archaeology. Presubmitted essays offered under this option will be subject to the normal regulations for the submission of presubmitted essays in the M.Phil. in Greek and/or Roman History.

(ix) Any other subject approved by the Graduate Studies Committee for Ancient History.]

C

(i) Greek history to *c*.650 BCE

(ii) Greek history to *c*.650–479 BCE

(iii) Greek history to *c*.479–336 BCE

(iv) Athenian democracy in the Classical age

(v) Alexander and his successors 336–301 BCE

(vi) The Hellenistic world 301–*c*.100 BCE

(vii) Rome and the Mediterranean world 241–146 BCE

(viii) Roman history 146–46 BCE

(ix) Cicero

(x) Roman history 46 BCE–54 CE

(xi) Roman history 54–138 CE

(xii) Roman history 138–312 CE

(xiii) The ecology, agriculture and settlement history of the ancient Mediterranean world

(xiv) The economy of the Roman Empire

(xv) The provinces of the Roman Empire

(xvi) Greek and/or Roman religion

(xvii) Gender and sexuality in the Greek and/or Roman world

(xviii) Greek and/or Latin historiography

[For students starting before MT 2015: (xix) Roman law

(xx) The Church in the Roman Empire from the beginnings to 312 CE

(xxi) The world of Augustine

(xxii) The City of Rome. This course is run in collaboration with the British School at Rome, and involves attendance at the residential course organised by the School annually in Rome; only those accepted by the School may take the option.

(xxiii) British School at Athens taught course (title and topic vary from time to time). This option is run in collaboration with the British School at Athens, and involves attendance at the residential course organised by the School in even-numbered years in Athens; only those accepted by the School may take the option.

(xxiv) Any other subject approved by the Graduate Studies Committee for Ancient History.]

[For students starting from MT 2015: (xix) The Church in the Roman Empire from the beginnings to 312 CE.

(xx) The world of Augustine.   5

(xxi) The City of Rome. This course is run in collaboration with the British School at Rome, and involves attendance at the residential course organised by the School annually in Rome; only those accepted by the School may take the option.

(xxii) British School at Athens taught course (title and topic vary from time to   10 time). This option is run in collaboration with the British School at Athens, and involves attendance at the residential course organised by the School in even-numbered years in Athens; only those accepted by the School may take the option.

(xxiii) Any other subject approved by the Graduate Studies Committee for Ancient   15 History.]

D

A dissertation of not more than 25,000 words on a subject to be approved by the Graduate Studies Committee for Ancient History. (The dissertation word limit excludes the bibliography, any text that is being edited or annotated, any translation of   20 that text, and any descriptive catalogue or similar factual matter, but includes quotations, notes and appendices.)

The dissertation (two typewritten or printed copies) must be sent in a parcel bearing the words 'Dissertation for the M.Phil. in Greek and/or Roman History' to The Chair of the Examiners, c/o Examination Schools, High Street, Oxford, to arrive no later   25 than noon on the Wednesday of Week 6 of the Trinity Full Term in which the examination is to be taken.

E

Graduate Seminars

(i) Greece and the East   30

(ii) Rome and the West

These working seminars, organised by members of the faculty in areas of current interest to them, run fortnightly in Michaelmas and Hilary Terms. The topics of the Seminars will vary from time to time. Details are announced in the Graduate handbook for the Degrees of M.St. and M.Phil. in Greek and/or Roman History.   35

7. All options, including the dissertation, require the approval of the candidate's supervisor and the Graduate Studies Committee for Ancient History, having regard to the candidate's previous experience, the range covered by the chosen options, and the availability of teaching and examining resources. **[For students starting from MT 2015:** Options under B (vii), (viii), (ix) and C (xxiii) in disciplines other than Ancient   40 History require the approval of both the Graduate Studies Committee for Ancient History and the Graduate Studies Committee responsible for the discipline concerned.] The options must be submitted for approval not later than the Friday of Week 5 of Michaelmas Term in the candidate's first academic year. Candidates will not normally be allowed to be examined in languages of which they are native   45 speakers or which they have previously studied in taught courses for more than two years.

Master of Philosophy in History of Science, Medicine, and Technology

(See also the general notice at the commencement of these regulations.)

The regulations of the Board of the Faculty of History are as follows:

(1) Every candidate must follow for at least six terms a course of instruction in   5
History of Science, Medicine, and Technology, and must upon entering for the
examination produce from his or her society a certificate to that effect.

(2) The examination will consist of the following parts:

Qualifying test

Every candidate must pass a qualifying test. The test shall consist of two courses on   10

1. Methods and themes in the history of science and technology.

2. Methods and themes in the history of medicine.

Candidates may be advised on the basis of their prospective individual research to
substitute one of the following courses from the Master of Philosophy in Economic
and Social History for (1) or (2) above: 15

(i) Methodological introduction to research in the social sciences and history.

(ii) Quantitative Methods and Computer Applications for Historians.

A paper from another established course within the University may be substituted
for one of the standard courses where this would provide a more appropriate training
for the candidate's dissertation focus. Such a choice will need formal approval from   20
both the Course Director and the Chair of the Graduate Studies Committee of the
Board of the Faculty of History.

The two methodological introduction courses will each be assessed by a methodological essay of up to 3,000 words. Two typewritten copies of each of the essays must
be submitted by noon on Monday of **[For students starting before MT 2015:** second   25
week of Hilary Term**] [For students starting from MT 2015:** Week 10 of Michaelmas
Term**]** of the candidate's first year to the Chair of Examiners for the M.Phil. in History
of Science, Medicine, and Technology, c/o Examination Schools, High Street, Oxford
OX1 4BG. In addition, convenors of qualifying courses will confirm in writing to the
chair of examiners not later than Friday of eighth week of Hilary Term the candidates'   30
satisfactory participation in their classes, including the completion of any assignments
for the weekly sessions. Any approved alternative qualifying course will be assessed
within the format and timetable of the paper's parent course. No candidate who has
failed the qualifying test of two courses will be permitted to supplicate for the degree.
Candidates who fail a qualifying course once will be permitted to take it again, not   35
later than one year after the initial attempt.

Final Examination

The examination shall consist of four papers and a dissertation.

I. Three advanced papers at least two of which must be selected from Schedule I
below ('Advanced Papers for the M.Phil. and M.Sc. in History of Science, Medicine,   40
and Technology'), and not more than one from any other M.Phil., the choice of which
must be approved by the Chair of the Graduate Studies Committee of the History
Board not later than Monday of the fourth week of the second Michaelmas Term of
the course.

Candidates must take at least two of their advanced papers as three-hour written   45
examinations. For each of their remaining advanced papers candidates must choose to
be assessed either by written examination or by two 5,000-word essays. Essays may

only be submitted in lieu of written papers for subjects in Schedule I or for papers from other M.Phil.s where similar provision exists in the regulations for those examinations. The essays must be the work of the candidates alone and they must not consult any other person including their supervisors in any way concerning the method of handling the themes chosen. The themes chosen by the candidate must be submitted for 5 approval by the chair of examiners by the examination entry date. Candidates will be informed within two weeks, by means of a letter directed to their colleges, whether the topics they have submitted have been approved. The finished essays must be delivered by the candidate to the Examination Schools, High Street, Oxford, by noon on Monday the sixth week of Trinity Term. The essays must be presented in proper 10 scholarly form, and two typed copies of each must be submitted.

    II. *Either* (i) one paper in a discipline or skill or sources or methods selected from Schedule II below.

       or   (ii) A fourth advanced paper selected from Schedule I or from any additional list of papers for the M.Phil. and M.Sc. in History of 15 Science, Medicine, and Technology approved by the Graduate Studies Committee of the Board of the Faculty of History and published in the definitive list of Advanced Papers as set out in Schedule I.

    III. A dissertation of not more than 30,000 words, including appendices but ex- 20 cluding bibliography on a topic approved by the candidate's supervisor. The dissertation must be delivered not later than noon on the Monday of the first week of the Trinity Term in which the examination is to be taken to the Examination Schools, High Street, Oxford. Dissertations submitted must not exceed the permitted length. If they do the examiners will reduce the marks awarded. The presentation and footnotes 25 should comply with the requirements specified in the Regulations of the Education Committee for the degree of M.Litt. and D.Phil. and follow the *Conventions for the presentation of dissertations and theses* of the Board of the Faculty of History.

    Each dissertation must include a short abstract which concisely summarises its scope and principal arguments, in about 300 words. 30

    Candidates must submit by the specified date three copies of their dissertation. These must be securely and firmly bound in either hard or soft covers. One copy of an M.Phil. dissertation which is approved by the examiners must be deposited in the Bodleian Library. This finalised copy should incorporate any corrections or amendments which the examiners may have requested. It must be in a permanently fixed 35 binding, drilled and sewn, in a stiff board case in library buckram, in a dark colour, and lettered on the spine with the candidate's name and initials, the degree, and the year of submission.

    3. Candidates may, if they so wish, be examined in up to two of their four papers (or submit essays in lieu of these papers as provided for above) at the end of their first 40 year.

    4. The examiners will permit the use of any hand-held pocket calculator subject to the conditions set out under the heading 'Use of calculators in examinations' in the *Regulations for the Conduct of University Examinations* .

    5. The examiners may award a distinction for excellence in the whole examination. 45

    6. If it is the opinion of the examiners that the work done by a candidate, while not of sufficient merit to qualify for the degree of M.Phil., is nevertheless of sufficient merit to qualify for the degree of Master of Science in History of Science, Medicine, and Technology, the candidate shall be given the option of resitting the M.Phil. (as provided under the appropriate regulation) or of being granted leave to supplicate 50 for the degree of Master of Science.

7. A candidate who fails the examination will be permitted to retake it on one further occasion only, not later than one year after the initial attempt.

Such a candidate whose dissertation has been of a satisfactory standard may resubmit the same piece of work, while a candidate who has reached a satisfactory standard on the written papers will not be required to retake that part of the examination.

Schedule I

Advanced Papers for the M.Phil. and M.Sc. in History of Science, Medicine, and Technology

A broad range of the course resources are shared with the corresponding courses in Economic and Social History, and Advanced Papers are therefore available in the subject areas listed here.

1. Economic and business history

2. History of science and technology

3. Social history

4. Historical demography

5. History of medicine

A descriptive list of Advanced Papers will be published by the Board of the Faculty of History in September for the academic year ahead (not all options may be available in every year). The definitive list of the titles of Advanced Papers for any one year will be circulated to candidates and their supervisors and posted on the Faculty notice board not later than Friday of third week of Michaelmas Term.

Schedule II

The paper in a relevant discipline or skill may be:

1. One of the papers from the M.Phil. in Economics.

2. One of the papers from the M.Phil. in Sociology or in Comparative Social Policy.

3. One of the papers from the M.Phil. in Russian and East European Studies.

4. One suitable paper from another Master's degree under the auspices of the Faculty of History approved from time to time by the Graduate Studies Committee of the Board of History.

5. One suitable paper from another Master's degree on the recommendation of the candidate's supervisor and endorsed by the Course Director.

Choices under Schedule II have to be approved by the Chair of the Graduate Studies Committee of the Board of the Faculty of History not later than Monday of the fourth week of the second Michaelmas Term of the course. Candidates wishing to take a paper under 1, 2, 3, or 5 will also need the approval of the appropriate course convenor and the Graduate Studies Committee of the relevant faculty board or inter-faculty committee who need to be satisfied that each candidate has an adequate background in the subject. Not all options may be available in any one year.

Master of Philosophy in International Relations

(*See also the general notice at the commencement of these regulations.*)

The regulations made by the International Relations Graduate Studies Committee are as follows:

First-Year Examination

Every candidate must pass a first-year examination before the end of the third term from commencement of the course unless given exemption by the International Relations Graduate Studies Committee. The first-year examination shall be set and administered by the examiners appointed to examine for the M.Phil. in International Relations. This test shall consist of three parts, as follows:

1. A formally assessed Research Design Proposal of 4,000 words, excluding bibliography, on the subject of the student's proposed M.Phil. thesis. Two hard copies, together with a copy on CD, must be submitted to the Examination Schools by noon on the Monday of sixth week of Trinity Term. It must be accompanied by a separate signed declaration that it is the candidate's own work except where otherwise indicated and that it has not previously been submitted for assessment, either at Oxford or at another institution. The scope and the format are as stated in the *Student Handbook*.

2. A single, three-hour examination paper covering material from the core papers as taught in the first year, namely:

The Development of the International System: The history of the relations between states in peace and war, and the development of the international system. It will include such topics as: major traditions of thought on International Relations; 19th century imperialism and euro-centrism; the concert system, the balance of power and the causes of the First World War; the peace settlement, collective security and the League of Nations; political and economic co-operation in the interwar period; the USA, Soviet Union, Middle East and Far East in the inter-war years; the impact of revolution, domestic politics and ideology on foreign policy; the causes of the Second World War; post-war reconstruction and the origins of the Cold War; the nuclear revolution and the impact of technological change; the evolution of the Cold War; decolonization, nationalism and self-determination; détente, arms control and regional conflicts; the end of the Cold War; the evolution of international economic institutions; the evolution of security institutions; and international relations in the post-Cold War world.

Contemporary Debates in International Relations Theory: Ideas about, and explanations of, international relations, concentrating mainly (but not exclusively) on the major theoretical approaches in the academic study of international relations since 1945. The key theories and approaches to be examined include: realism and neo-realism; theories about war, security, and the use of force in international relations; classical liberalism, globalization, and transformation in world politics; theories about inter-state co-operation and transnationalism; the concept of international society; constructivism and the impact of law and norms in international relations; neo-Marxist and critical theory approaches to international relations; normative theory and international ethics.

Details of the scope and coverage are given in the *Student Handbook*. **[For students starting before MT 2015:** The examination shall take place on the Friday of eighth week of Trinity Term, the exact time to be set by the examiners.]

3. The examiners must also be satisfied that candidates have satisfactorily completed their designated course of research training, and candidates must submit to the examiners all coursework completed as a part of their research methods training. The coursework requirements, including administrative arrangements and dates of submission, are set out in the *Student Handbook*. Candidates should note that the *Student Handbook* will set dates for the submission (and, where necessary resubmission) of work for individual research modules.

4. Candidates who fail the written examination part of the first-year examination will normally be allowed to retake it before the beginning of the next academic year. Candidates who fail the Research Design Proposal or the coursework submitted for the research modules may resubmit their work **[For students starting before MT 2015:** by the last Friday of August following the end of Trinity Full Term] **[For students starting from MT 2015:** , resubmission dates are set out in the Student Handbook].

Final Examination

No candidate shall enter the final examination unless he or she has already passed the first-year examination or has been granted exemption by the Graduate Studies Committee as stated above. In the final examination every candidate must offer:

1. A thesis of not more than 30,000 words, excluding bibliography, to be delivered   5
to the Examination Schools, High Street, Oxford, by noon on Monday in the first week of the Trinity Full Term in which the examination is to be taken. Two hard copies of the thesis, together with a copy on CD, must be accompanied by a separate signed declaration that it is the candidate's own work except where otherwise indicated and that it has not previously been submitted for assessment, either at Oxford or   10
at another institution. After the examination process is complete, each successful candidate must deposit one hardbound copy of their thesis in the Bodleian Library.

2. Two subject papers taken from the approved list of optional subjects in International Relations, as published in the *Student Handbook* by the International Relations Graduate Studies Committee on Monday of first week of Michaelmas Term   15
each academic year to apply to candidates being examined in the Trinity Term of that year. Candidates should note that the International Relations subjects available in any particular year will depend on the availability of teaching resources. Not all subjects will be available in every year and restrictions may be placed on the number of candidates permitted to offer certain subjects in any particular year. Candidates may, with the   20
special permission of the International Relations Graduate Studies Committee, offer subjects beyond the approved list of International Relations subjects. Applications must be made by the last Friday of the Trinity Term preceding that in which the examination is to be taken, and must be supported by the student's supervisor. Supervisors should ensure that applications are submitted as early as possible so that if approval is not   25
given, the candidate has sufficient time to choose an alternative.

3. Candidates must present themselves for viva voce examination when requested by the examiners. The examiners shall not normally fail any candidate without inviting him or her to attend such an examination. However, in the case of a failing mark in **[For students starting before MT 2015: three or more] [For students starting**   30
from MT 2015: two] of a candidate's final examination papers, the examiners shall not be obliged to ask the candidate for a viva.

The examiners may award a distinction for excellence in the whole examination.

Master of Philosophy in Judaism and Christianity in the Graeco-Roman World   35

(*See also the general notice at the commencement of these regulations.*)

The regulations made by the Boards of the Faculties of Oriental Studies and Theology are as follows:

Candidates will be admitted to take the examination as defined below in a specific year. In exceptional circumstances candidates may be allowed to take an examination   40
later than one to which they were admitted. Permission for this must be sought from the Faculty Board not later than Monday of the week before the first week of the Trinity Term in which the examination was to have been taken. The application must have the support of the candidate's college and be accompanied by a statement from the supervisor.   45

I. All candidates shall be required:

    (*a*) To satisfy the boards that they possess the necessary knowledge of Hebrew and Greek to profit by the course.

    (*b*) To present themselves for a written examination and to offer a thesis, as specified below.   50 (*c*) To present themselves for viva voce examination unless individually dispensed by the examiners. (No candidate will be failed without a viva.)

II. Candidates shall offer four papers and a thesis, not to exceed 20,000 words. Two papers must be taken on Judaism and two papers must be taken on Christianity, and A(1) and B(1) must be included, unless the boards shall otherwise determine.

A. Judaism

(1) Judaism from 200 BCE to 200 CE.

(2) Jewish historiography (with prescribed texts).

(3) Jewish Bible interpretation (with prescribed texts).

(4) Jewish eschatology (with prescribed texts).

(5) Jewish wisdom literature (with prescribed texts).

B. Christianity

(1) Christianity to 200 CE.

(2) The Gospels and the historical Jesus (with prescribed texts).

(3) Acts and the Pauline corpus (with prescribed texts).

(4) The Apostolic Fathers (with prescribed texts).

(5) The Apologists (with prescribed texts).

Note: Texts will be reported to the Faculty Board's second meeting of Michaelmas Full Term in the first year of the course.

III. The Examiners may award a Distinction for excellence in the whole examination.

Master of Philosophy in Late Antique and Byzantine Studies

(*See also the general notice at the commencement of these regulations.*)

1. Each candidate will be required to:

(a) follow for at least six terms a course of instruction in Late Antique and Byzantine Studies. Candidates will, when they enter for the examination, be required to produce from their society a certificate that they are following such a course.

(b) present a thesis of not more than 30,000 words on a subject approved by his/her supervisor; the thesis (three copies) must be typewritten and delivered to the Examination Schools, High Street, Oxford, by Monday of seventh week of Trinity Term of the candidate's second year at the latest.

(c) present himself/herself for a viva voce examination when required to do so by the examiners.

2. Candidates must take four of the following six papers. All candidates take the core paper on History, Art and Archaeology, *or*, if they already have the required linguistic competence, History and Byzantine Literature. For the remainder of their course they choose either the two Language and Literature papers and one other paper (which may be a second single language paper), or, if they already have considerable competence in their chosen language or languages, and their principal interests lie in History, Art and Archaeology, or Religion, they choose Auxiliary Disciplines and two Special Subjects.

I. Compulsory core paper on History, Art, and Archaeology, *or* History and Byzantine Literature:

Either

(a) Late Antiquity (covering the Roman Empire and adjoining regions)

or

(b) Byzantium

The core paper will be taught in classes in Michaelmas and Hilary Terms. Examination will be by two 5,000-word essays, to be submitted by Monday of seventh week of Trinity Term of the candidate's first year.

II. and III. Language and Literature (teaching in Greek, Latin, Slavonic, Armenian, Syriac, and Arabic will normally be available)

These papers are taught over three terms in classes, with reference to a selection of texts and/or extracts from texts which may vary from year to year according to the interests of candidates. Examination is by two three-hour papers: (candidates are permitted the use of relevant bilingual dictionaries, which will be provided by the faculty)

(a) translation, and

(b) set texts (with passages for translation and comment).

Candidates who are embarking on the study of one of the above languages will normally be expected to take both examinations in that language, but the Committee for Byzantine Studies may in special circumstances permit them to substitute another paper for one of these examination papers, taken at the end of the candidate's first year. Candidates taking a second language in their second year are only required to enter for examination in a single paper.

IV. Auxiliary Discipline(s):

Either

    (*a*) any two of the following: epigraphy, palaeography, numismatics, sigillography

or

    (*b*) papyrology: Greek, Coptic, or Arabic

or

    (*c*) artefact studies: one of ceramics, metalware, ivories, codices, carved marbles.

Paper IV will be taught by lectures/classes/tutorials. Examination will be by a three-hour paper, except for papyrology which is assessed by two 5,000-word essays on distinct aspects of the subject.

V. A Special Subject selected from the subject areas listed under 3. below.

Special Subjects will be taught by lectures/classes/tutorials. Examination will be either by two 5,000-word essays or by a 10,000-word dissertation (to be submitted by Monday of seventh week of Trinity Term of the candidate's first year).

VI. A second Special Subject selected from the subject areas listed under 3. below.

Special Subjects will be taught by lectures/classes/tutorials. Examination will be either by two 5,000-word essays or by a 10,000-word dissertation (to be submitted by Monday of seventh week of Trinity Term of the candidate's second year).

Note: both Special Subjects may be taken from the same section of the list below.

3. Overview of Special Subjects (for details, please consult the Course Handbook)

(*a*) History: Special Subjects on offer deal either with specific periods or with certain aspects of late Roman and Byzantine history (including military, diplomatic, political, social, economic and religious history) between the fourth and fifteenth centuries, as well as important developments in neighbouring regions.

(*b*) Art and Archaeology: Special Subjects on offer cover sculpture, portraiture, minor arts, monumental art and architecture of the late Roman, Byzantine, and Islamic spheres of influence as well as the archaeology of town and country throughout the Mediterranean and Near Eastern worlds.

(*c*) Literature (texts prescribed in translation): Special Subjects on offer range through historiography, hagiography, poetry and popular literature, and scholarship in the languages available for the degree programme.

(*d*) Religion: Special Subjects on offer cover theological debates and practical spirituality in the fields of Judaism, Christianity, and Islam.

(*e*) Such other subjects as may be approved on application to the Committee for Byzantine Studies.

Note: The list of Special Subjects detailed in the Course Handbook reflects the expertises and interests of current postholders. The list may be altered from time to time with developments of expertise and changes of interest on the part of the postholders.

4. Teaching in all the options may not be available each year, and applicants for admission will be advised whether teaching will be available in the options of their choice.

5. The examiners may award a distinction for excellence in the whole examination.

6. If it is the opinion of the examiners that the work done by a candidate, while not of sufficient merit to qualify for the degree of Master of Philosophy, is nevertheless of sufficient merit to qualify for the degree of M.St. in Late Antique and Byzantine Studies, the candidate shall be given the option of resitting the M.Phil. (as provided by the appropriate regulation) or of being granted leave to supplicate for the degree of Master of Studies.

Master of Philosophy in Latin American Studies

(*See also the general notice at the commencement of these regulations.*)

For the purposes of this examination, 'Latin America' will be interpreted as the eighteen Spanish-speaking republics of the Western Hemisphere, plus Brazil, Haiti, and Puerto Rico.

The regulations are as follows:

Year 1:

1. In the first year, candidates for the M.Phil. in Latin American Studies will:

(*a*) Follow for three terms a course of instruction in the M.Sc in Latin American Studies with the exception of the extended essay. Candidates will present three qualifying examinations, each of which counts for 16.6 per cent of the final degree mark. Examinations at the end of the first year will serve to qualify for entry onto the second year of the course.

(*b*) Develop a thesis topic, which will be the subject of fieldwork in the long vacation between the first and second year. A draft title for the thesis must be submitted for approval by the Latin American Centre Management Committee by 12:00 noon on the Friday of Week 0 of Hilary Term.

(*c*) Candidates may also be required to present themselves for an oral examination if requested to do so by the examiners. The oral examination will focus on the candidate's examination papers.

2. The list of examination papers will be published on the Latin American Centre website and in the *University Gazette* in Week 0 of Michaelmas Term. Candidates must take the core paper in Economics if they wish to take a further paper in that discipline. Specialisation on a single country or a combination of countries is permitted so long as the choice appears in the list of available papers published.

3. Candidates shall be deemed to have passed the qualifying examination if they have passed all three examination papers.

4. Candidates who fail one of the three papers taken at the end of the first year without compensating strengths on both of the other papers shall be deemed to have failed the qualifying examination. Such candidates will be required to retake the failed paper and pass it by the start of the Michaelmas Term of their second year, on a date stipulated by the Chair of Examiners, in order to continue the course without inter-   5
ruption.

5. Candidates who fail more than one paper shall be deemed to have failed the qualifying examination. Such candidates will be permitted to retake the papers failed on one (but not more than one) subsequent occasion, in Trinity Term, one year after the initial attempt. Such candidates must pass the papers that they have retaken in   10
order to continue onto the second year of the course.

Year 2:

6. In the second year, candidates for the M.Phil. in Latin American Studies will:

(*a*) Offer a thesis of not more than 30,000 words, including footnotes and appen-
    dices. Two typewritten copies of the thesis must be delivered to the Examination   15
    Schools and addressed to the Chair of Examiners for the M.Phil. in Latin
    American Studies, c/o Examination Schools, High Street, Oxford, by 12 noon
    on the Monday of Week 5 of Trinity Term in the calendar year in which the
    examination is to be taken. Successful candidates will be required to deposit one
    copy of their thesis in the Bodleian Library, and will be required to sign a form   20
    stating whether they will permit their thesis to be consulted. The thesis will be
    equivalent to two examination papers, and so will count for 33.3 per cent of the
    final degree mark.

(*b*) Take another examination paper from the list; or by agreement with the Latin
    American Centre Director of Graduate Studies and the relevant department,   25
    take a methodology or other paper from an appropriate M.Phil. elsewhere in
    the University of Oxford. The examination will count for 16.6 per cent of the
    final degree mark.

(*c*) Candidates will be required to present themselves for an oral examination. The
    oral examination may focus on the candidate's examination papers, thesis, or   30
    both.

7. Candidates shall be deemed to have passed the examination if they have passed all examination papers and the thesis.

8. Candidates who fail the second year examination paper (without compensating strengths on the thesis) or who fail the thesis shall be deemed to have failed the   35
examination. Such candidates will be permitted to resubmit the thesis or retake the examination paper on one (but not more than one) subsequent occasion, in Trinity Term, one year after the initial attempt. Such candidates must pass the thesis or examination paper in order to pass the examination.

9. Candidates who fail both the thesis and the examination paper shall be deemed   40
to have failed the examination. Such candidates will be permitted to retake the examination and resubmit the thesis on one (but not more than one) subsequent occasion, in Trinity Term, one year after the initial attempt. Such candidates must pass both the thesis and the examination paper in order to pass the examination.

10. The examiners may award a distinction for excellence in the whole examination.   45

Master of Philosophy in Law

(See the regulations for the Bachelor of Civil Law and Magister Juris)

Master of Philosophy in Medical Anthropology

(*See also the general notice at the commencement of these regulations.*)

Within the Division of Social Sciences, the course shall be administered by the School of Anthropology. The regulations made by the divisional board are as follows:

1. The Division of Social Sciences shall elect for the supervision of the course a Standing Committee, namely the Teaching Committee of the School of Anthropology, which shall have power to arrange lectures and other instruction. The course director shall be responsible to the Standing Committee.

The examination shall consist of the following:

1. *Qualifying Examination*

Every candidate will be required to satisfy the examiners in an examination for which, if he or she passes at the appropriate level, he or she will be allowed to proceed to the second year of the M.Phil. Candidates must follow a course of instruction in Medical Anthropology for at least three terms, and will, when entering for the examinations, be required to produce a certificate from their supervisor to this effect. Every candidate for the M.Phil. qualifying examination will be required to satisfy the examiners in four written papers to be taken in the Trinity Term of the academic year in which the candidate's name is first entered on the Register of M.Phil. Students or, with the approval of the Divisional Board, in a subsequent year. The following four papers shall be taken:

(1) *Concepts of disease, illness, health and medicine in global perspective*

The scope of this paper includes discussion of cross-cultural concepts of health, disease, sickness, pain, illness causation, diagnosis and treatment, from conjoined socio-cultural perspectives and human ecology. It explores metaphor and narrative at the interface of biological and cultural processes, the distribution of disease patterns in the light of environmental change, social inequality, global mobility and marginality, and the co-existence of conventional, alternative, and traditional health systems.

(2) *Theory and practice of bio-medicine and of other medical systems*

The scope of this paper includes issues of public health and policy on a comparative and global basis. It draws on ethnographies of particular societies to illustrate and test theoretical claims in medical anthropology. It discusses infectious diseases, specific health campaigns, evolutionary trends and life histories, alongside culturally defined concepts of risk, vulnerability, fate, evil, pollution, divination, religion, and shamanism.

(3) *Critical medical anthropology*

The scope of this paper comprises ecological and socio-cultural perspectives, and explores links to other fields and disciplines, including the place of material culture in medicine. It includes a critique of basic assumptions and methods in medical anthropology and consideration of the concept of well-being as being broader than conventional concepts of health. Themes for discussion include the phenomenology of the body, growth and personhood, gender, ageing and dying, notions of resistance and resilience, relationships between biodiversity and adaptability, reproduction, and fertility, and nutrition.

(4) *Option paper*

Candidates must select one option paper from those taught each year for the M.Sc in Social Anthropology. Titles of options will be made at the beginning of each academic year, and candidates may select their option from any of Lists A, B, or C.

2. *Final Examination*

Candidates must follow a course of instruction in Medical Anthropology for at least three terms, and will, when entering for the final examination, be required to produce a certificate from their supervisor to this effect. The final examination shall be taken in the Trinity Term of the academic year following that in which the candidate's name is first entered on the Register of M.Phil. Students or, with the approval of the Divisional Board, in a subsequent year.

Each candidate shall be required:

(1) to submit evidence of practical work and a research proposal in accordance with I below;

(2) to submit a thesis in accordance with II below;

(3) to present himself or herself for oral examination if required by the examiners. The oral examination may be on the candidate's written assignments, or dissertation, or both.

I. *Methods of fieldwork and social research*

[For students starting before MT 2015: The satisfactory completion of a course of practical work in (i) participant observation, in-depth interviewing, archival research, and qualitative data analysis; (ii) basic principles of statistical inference, and statistical models for the analysis of quantitative social science data, and (iii) methods of data collection, including questionnaire design, interviewing, and coding.] **[For students starting from MT 2015:** The satisfactory completion of a course of practical work in (i) qualitative methods, including participant observation, archival research, in-depth interviewing, questionnaire design, coding and qualitative data analysis; and (ii) basic principles in descriptive statistics and statistical inference for the analysis of quantitative social science data.]

The research proposal should not exceed 2,500 words. It need not be on the theme of the thesis, but should reflect the candidate's competence in conceiving and structuring an independent research project.

Candidates shall submit to the Examination Schools by noon on Tuesday of fifth week of the third term of the second year of the course reports of the practical work completed and the research proposal, accompanied by a statement that they are the candidate's own work except where otherwise indicated.

II. *Thesis*

Each candidate shall be required to submit a thesis of not more than 30,000 words (excluding references and appendices) on a subject approved by the supervisor. He or she shall send to the Teaching Committee of the School of Anthropology, with the written approval of his or her supervisor, the proposed title of the thesis, together with a paragraph describing its scope, for consideration by the School of Anthropology, by noon on the Monday of second week of Michaelmas Term in the academic year following that in which his or her name was entered on the Register of M.Phil. Students. The thesis (three copies) must be typewritten and delivered to the Examination Schools, High Street, Oxford, not later than noon on Tuesday of the fifth week of Trinity Term in the academic year in which the Final Examination is taken. The dissertation shall be provided with an abstract of up to 250 words, to be placed immediately after the title page. The word count shall be stated on the outside front cover of the thesis.

The Examiners shall require a successful candidate to deposit a copy of his or her thesis in the Tylor Library. If the thesis is superseded by a D.Phil. thesis by the same student partly using the same material, the Divisional Board of Social Sciences may authorise the withdrawal of the M.Phil. thesis from the Tylor Library. Such candidates will be required to sign a form stating whether they give permission for their thesis to be consulted.

The examiners may award a distinction for excellence in the whole examination.

III. *Resits*

In order to pass the degree, a student must pass all its assessed components. Where one or more components are failed, the student will be given the opportunity to re-sit or re-submit them once, as the case may be. Any subsequent award of the degree on successful completion of all the assessed components may be delayed by up to three terms, i.e. until the Examination Board next meets.

Master of Philosophy in Modern British and European History

(*See also the general notice at the commencement of these regulations.*)

The regulations of the Board of the Faculty of History are as follows:

1. Candidates for the Master of Philosophy in Modern British and European History must follow for at least six terms a course of instruction and directed research and must, upon entering the examination, produce from their society a certificate to that effect.

2. Candidates must attend such lectures, seminars and classes as their supervisor shall determine. In addition to the formally examined programme elements described below, each candidate will be expected to attend and complete in-course requirements for a series of skills and specialist options based on a schedule to be published from year to year by the Faculty's Graduate Studies Committee. The candidate's individual programme, agreed with her/his supervisor, will be subject to approval by the Director of Graduate Studies, in consultation with the programme convenor, by Friday of Week One of Michaelmas Term; subsequent changes must be agreed by the Director of Graduate Studies not later than Friday of Week Three of Hilary Term. Class teachers will report to the Chair of Examiners on the candidate's attendance and participation, and, where appropriate, test results, not later than Monday of Week Nine of Hilary Term, except in the case of three-term language classes where the respective reporting deadline will be Monday of Week Nine of Trinity Term.

3. The final examination shall comprise (i) one extended essay based on the programme's theory component, (ii) one extended essay based on an Advanced Option, (iii) one extended essay based on a class on the writing of History, and (iv) one dissertation proposal in the first year of the programme, and (v) one research methodology essay and (vi) a dissertation of not more than 30,000 words in the final year of the programme.

   I. During Michaelmas Term of the first year each candidate will attend core classes on historical theory and methodological approaches as well as a series of classes on sources and resources. The core classes will be assessed by an extended essay of between 4,000 and 5,000 words (the sources and resources component will feed into the preparation of a dissertation proposal in Trinity Term of the first year). Two copies of the essay, addressed to the Chair of Examiners for the Master of Philosophy in Modern British and European History, must be submitted to the Examination Schools by 12 noon on Monday of Week One of Hilary Term of the candidate's first year.

   II. In Hilary Term of the first year candidates must choose one Advanced Option, either from the joint Advanced Options for the Master of Studies in Modern British and European History and the Master of Philosophy in Modern British and European History, or from the Advanced Options for one of the Faculty of History's other Master's programmes. The choice of Advanced Option will depend on the candidate's training objectives or dissertation project. Details of available Advanced Options are published in course handbooks. Approval of the Advanced Option choice must be obtained from the programme convenor and Director of Graduate Studies by Friday of Week Four of Michaelmas Term. The request for approval must be sent to the History Graduate Office.

On recommendation from the candidate's supervisor, the Director of Graduate Studies, in consultation with the programme convenor, may approve relevant taught papers from Master's programmes offered by faculties other than History, provided   5
that the respective faculty's Graduate Studies Committee is satisfied that the candidate has an adequate background in the subject.

This part of the programme will be assessed by one extended essay of between 6,500 and 7,500 words. Two copies of the essay, addressed to the Chair of Examiners for the Master of Philosophy in Modern British and European History, must be submitted to   10
the Examination Schools by 12 noon on Monday of Week Nine of Hilary Term of the candidate's first year.

Essays should reflect skills and understanding the candidate has developed by following the approved choice of paper. The essay may complement but must not share significant content with the essay submitted under I. above.   15

Teaching may not be available for all the Advanced Options each year, and restrictions may be imposed on the combination of Advanced Options that may be taken in a particular year.

III. In Trinity Term candidates take a class on Writing History and finalise a proposal for their dissertation research during the Long Vacation and   20
Michaelmas Term of their second year. The Writing History classes will be assessed by an extended essay of between 4,000 and 5,000 words. The essay may complement but must not share significant content with the essays submitted under I. and II. above. Two copies of the extended essay on Writing History, addressed to the Chair of Examiners for the Master of Philosophy in   25
Modern British and European History, must be submitted to the Examination Schools by 12 noon on Monday of Week Nine of Trinity Term of the candidate's first year.

IV. Candidates must prepare an extended dissertation proposal of between 2,000 and 2,500 words. Two copies of the extended dissertation proposal, addressed   30
to the Chair of Examiners for the Master of Philosophy in Modern British and European History, must be submitted to the Examination Schools by 12 noon on Monday of Week Six of Trinity Term of the candidate's first year.

V. Candidates must prepare one methodological essay (of up to 7,000 words) and a seminar presentation for a class on 'Historical concepts and controversies',   35
to be examined in Trinity Term of the candidate's second year. Students may choose a topic for their essay and presentation in an area proximate to their dissertation subject, but may not replicate any other material submitted for examination.

Two typewritten copies of the extended essay, addressed to the Chair of Examiners   40
for the Master of Philosophy in Modern British and European History, must be submitted to the Examination Schools by 12 noon on Monday of first week of Trinity Term of the candidate's second year.

VI. A dissertation of not more than 30,000 words, including footnotes and appendices but excluding bibliography, on a topic approved by the candidate's   45
supervisor and the Programme Convenor of the M.Phil. in Modern British and European History. Candidates must apply in writing to the Programme Convenor for approval of the proposed topic of their dissertation. The application must be submitted to the History Graduate Office by 12 noon on Monday of Week Six of Trinity Term of the candidate's first year. Two copies   50
of the dissertation must be submitted to the Examination Schools by 12 noon

on Monday of Week Eight of Trinity Term of the candidate's second year. Dissertations submitted must not exceed the permitted length. If they do the Examiners will reduce the marks awarded. The presentation and footnotes should comply with the requirements specified in the Regulations of the Education Committee for the degrees of M.Litt. and D.Phil. and follow the *Conventions for the presentation of dissertations and theses* of the Faculty of History.

Each dissertation must include a short abstract which concisely summarises its scope and principal arguments, in about 300 words.

Each copy of the dissertation must be securely and firmly bound in either hard or soft covers. One copy of an M.Phil. dissertation which is approved by the examiners must be deposited in the Bodleian Library. This final copy should incorporate any corrections or amendments which the examiners may have requested. It must be hard bound, in a dark colour, and lettered on the spine with the candidate's name and initials, the degree, and the year of submission.

4. A candidate who, at the end of the first year of the course, is unable to continue on to the second year, may, with the support of his or her college and supervisor, apply to the Director of Graduate Studies in History for permission to transfer to the status of a student for the Master of Studies in Modern British and European History and to enter that examination in the current year.

5. The examiners may award a distinction to candidates who have performed with special merit in all parts of the examination for the Master of Philosophy in Modern British and European History.

6. A candidate who fails the examination will be permitted to retake the examination on one further occasion only, not later than one year after the initial attempt. A candidate whose dissertation has been of satisfactory standard will not be required to resubmit the dissertation. A candidate who has reached a satisfactory standard on the extended essays will not be required to retake those papers. If it is the opinion of the examiners that the work done by a candidate, while not of sufficient merit to qualify for the Degree of Master of Philosophy, is nevertheless of sufficient merit to qualify for the Degree of Master of Studies in Modern British and European History, the candidate shall be given the option of resitting the M.Phil. (as provided under the General Regulations § 2, cl. 4, and in accordance with this regulation) or of being granted leave to supplicate for the Degree of Master of Studies.

Master of Philosophy in Modern Japanese Studies

(*See also the general notice at the commencement of these regulations.*)

The regulations made by the School of Interdisciplinary Area Studies are as follows:

First year examinations

1. Candidates will be required to present themselves for examination EITHER in a compulsory paper in Japanese Language; and in two optional subjects at the end of Trinity Term in the year of registration; OR in three optional subjects at the end of Trinity Term in the year of registration.

2. Candidates taking the examination in Japanese Language will also be required to undertake a series of written tests and essays as specified by the M.Sc./M.Phil. Programme in Modern Japanese Studies Committee. The forms of assessment, and the dates and times of submission, where applicable, will be notified to students by not later than Friday of noughth week of Michaelmas Full Term.

In addition, all candidates will be required to undertake:

3. Research Methods for Area Studies: a series of assignments and/or an unseen written examination as specified by the M.Sc./M.Phil. Programme in Modern

Japanese Studies Committee. The forms of assessment, and the dates and times of submission, where applicable, will be notified to students by not later than Friday of noughth week of Michaelmas Full Term.

4. Candidates who pass these papers will proceed to the second year of the course and take the final examinations at the end of the second year. Candidates who fail one or more of the examination papers may, by permission of the M.Sc./M.Phil. in Japanese Studies Examination Board, proceed to the second year of the course and resit the failed papers during the final examination. Candidates who fail any item of coursework may, at the discretion of the M.Sc./M.Phil. in Japanese Studies Examination Board, be allowed to revise and resubmit that work no later than the Friday of sixth week of the Trinity Term in the academic year in which they begin the course.

5. In consultation with their supervisor and the Director of Graduate Studies, candidates may apply to change to the M.Sc. in Modern Japanese Studies degree no later than Friday of week 9 of Hilary Term of their first year.

Schedule

The structure of the first year of the course is as follows:

Eᴏᴛʜᴇʀ Mode A

   (*a*) *Compulsory core course in Japanese Language*

   (*b*) *Research Methods for Area Studies*

   (*c*) *Optional papers:* Candidates must choose two optional papers from a list published annually and distributed to students by Friday of noughth week of Michaelmas Full Term.

Oʀ Mode B

   (*a*) *Research Methods for Area Studies*

   (*b*) *Optional papers:* Candidates must choose three optional papers from a list published annually and distributed to students by Friday of noughth week of Michaelmas Full Term.

Final examination

6. No candidate shall enter the final examination unless he or she has already passed all the elements of the first year examination, save that the M.Sc./M.Phil. in Japanese Studies Examination Board may permit any candidates who has failed one or more of these elements to resit the papers at the same time as the final examination. In the final examination, every candidate must offer:

   (*a*) a thesis of not more than 30,000 words on a subject approved by the Director of Graduate Studies not later than fourth week of Michaelmas Full Term in the year in which the examination is to be taken, to be delivered to the Examination Schools, High Street, Oxford, by not later than 12 noon on Friday of the third week of Trinity Term in the year in which the examination is taken. The thesis must be accompanied by a statement that the thesis is the candidate's own work except where otherwise indicated.

   Two typewritten or word processed copies of the dissertation must be delivered to the Examination Schools, addressed to the Chair of Examiners for the M.Sc./M.Phil. in Modern Japanese Studies, c/o Examination Schools, High Street, Oxford at the times and days specified.

   Successful candidates will be required to deposit one copy of the thesis in the Bodleian Library.

   (*b*) Advanced Research Methods: a series of assignments and/or an unseen written examination as specified by the M.Sc./M.Phil. Programme in Modern Japanese Studies Committee. The forms of assessment, and the dates and times of submission, where applicable, will be notified to students by Friday of noughth week of Michaelmas Full Term.

(*c*) EITHER Mode A

(i) A compulsory paper in Advanced Japanese Language for candidates successfully passing the compulsory core course in Japanese at Upper Intermediate Level in the first year examinations, or for candidates successfully passing the compulsory core course in Japanese at Advanced Level in the first year examinations, a compulsory paper in Upper Advanced Japanese Language. Candidates taking the examination in Japanese language at either Advanced Level or Upper Advanced Level will also be required to undertake a series of written tests and essays as specified by the M.Sc./M.Phil. Programme in Modern Japanese Studies Committee. The forms of assessment, and the dates and times of submission, where applicable, will be notified to students by Friday of noughth week of Michaelmas Full Term.

(ii) One optional paper chosen from a list published annually and distributed to students by Friday of noughth week of Michaelmas Full Term, and taken at the end of Trinity Term of the second year of the course.

OR Mode B

(i) Two optional papers chosen from a list published annually and distributed to students by Friday of noughth week of Michaelmas Full Term, and taken at the end of Trinity Term of the second year of the course.

7. Candidates may be required to attend an oral examination on any part of the examination.

8. Candidates who fail one or more of the elements of the final examination will be permitted to resubmit the relevant work or retake the examination paper or papers, as applicable, on one further occasion only, not later than one year after the first attempt.

9. The examiners may award a distinction for excellence in the whole examination.

Master of Philosophy in Modern Languages

(*See also the general notice at the commencement of these regulations.*)

1. Candidates must follow a Programme chosen from those listed in the 'Handbook for Taught-Course Graduate Students'.

In order to gain admission to the course, applicants must show evidence of linguistic ability compatible with advanced literary study in the language(s) chosen to study. Comparative Literature candidates shall not be required to have reading fluency in more than two languages other than English. Unless otherwise stated, candidates will be expected to write in English unless explicit permission is obtained to write in the language (or one of the languages) studied. In the case of Comparative Literature candidates, writing in more than one language in addition to English will not be authorised.

All candidates must follow a course of instruction in Modern Languages at Oxford for a period of six terms. In exceptional circumstances, the Board of the Faculty of Medieval and Modern Languages may permit an extension of time. Candidates shall, when entering their name for the examination, be required to produce from their society a certificate stating that they are following the course of instruction for the period prescribed.

2. All candidates shall be required:

(a) To offer A, B, C, D, and E as defined in 3 below.

(b) To present themselves for viva voce examination at the time appointed by the examiners.

3. The examination shall consist of the following:

(A) *Either*

(i) Literary Theory. All candidates must attend such lectures, seminars, and classes as the course convener shall determine. All candidates must present one seminar paper during their course, and submit a written essay based on some aspect of the work done   5
for the seminar. This essay shall be written in English and must be of between 5,000 and 7,000 words in length, inclusive of a bibliography of works consulted. Candidates must submit three typed copies of the essay to the Head of Examinations and Assessments, Examination Schools, High Street, Oxford, by noon on Thursday of tenth week of Hilary Term of their first year. Each copy must have a cover sheet giving   10
the candidate's name, college, the title of the essay, the name of the candidate's supervisor, and the words 'Literary Theory', submitted in partial fulfilment of the requirements of the M.Phil. in Modern Languages'.

Or

(ii) History of Ideas in Germany from the Eighteenth to the Twentieth Centuries.   15
All candidates must attend such lectures, seminars, and classes as the course convener shall determine. All candidates must present one seminar paper during their course, and submit a written essay based on some aspect of the work done for the seminar. This essay may be written in English or German and must be of between 5,000 and 7,000 words in length. Candidates must submit three typed copies of the essay to the   20
Head of Examinations and Assessments, Examination Schools, High Street, Oxford, by noon on Thursday of tenth week of Hilary Term of their first year. Each copy must have a cover sheet giving the candidate's name, college, the title of the essay, the name of the candidate's course convener, and the words '[**Until 1 October 2014:** Methods of Criticism and] History of Ideas in Germany, submitted in partial fulfilment of the   25
requirements of the M.Phil. in Modern Languages'.

Or

(iii) Each candidate shall be required to offer either, (1) the History of the Book, or (2) Palaeography with Textual Criticism. Candidates will be examined on one or two essays on topics agreed by them with their course convener relating either to the   30
history of the book (for (1)) or to palaeography with textual criticism (for (2)). The essay or essays should be between 5,000 and 7,000 words in total. Candidates must submit three typed copies to the Head of Examinations and Assessments, Examination Schools, High Street, Oxford, by noon on Thursday of tenth week of Hilary Term of their first year. Each copy must have a cover sheet giving the   35
candidate's name, college, the title of the essay, the name of the candidate's supervisor, and the words 'History of the Book/Palaeography with Textual Criticism [either/or], submitted in partial fulfilment of the requirements of the Master of Philosophy in Modern Languages'. For (2), candidates will in addition be required to undertake a practical transcription test, made without reference to dictionaries or handbooks, on a   40
short manuscript text selected by the course convener, who will also mark, sign, and date the candidate's work. The test should take place by the end of the fourth week of the Trinity Term in which the examination is to be taken. The mark should be sent by the course convener to the Modern Languages Graduate Office.

Or   45

The work submitted under (i) must be written in English; the work submitted under (ii) may be written in English or German; the work submitted under (iii) may be written in English or, subject to the approval of the Medieval and Modern Languages Faculty Board, in a language appropriate to the literature concerned.

Approval must be sought for the choice of options in (A) by the end of the fourth   50
week of Michaelmas Term in the first year.

(B) A thesis, which may be written in English or, with the approval of the Medieval and Modern Languages Faculty Board, in the language appropriate to the literature concerned, of approximately 20,000 words and not more than 25,000 words, on a subject approved by the Board or by a person or persons to whom the Board may delegate this function. The subject of the thesis shall be related either to the fields of 5 study represented by (A) (i), (ii) or (iii) above or to one or more of the candidate's Special Subjects (C). When seeking approval for the subject of the thesis, every candidate shall submit with the proposed title a written statement of not more than 500 words explaining the scope of the topic and the manner in which it is proposed to treat it. Candidates are required to register the subject area or title of their dissertation 10 with the Modern Languages Graduate Office by the end of the fourth week of Hilary Term of their second year. The thesis must be presented in proper scholarly form. Three copies typed in double-spacing on one side only of quarto or A4 paper, each copy bound or held firmly in a stiff cover, must be delivered to the Head of Examinations and Assessments, Examination Schools, High Street, Oxford, by noon 15 on Thursday of the sixth week of Trinity Term of the second year.

Successful candidates will be required to deposit one copy of their thesis in the Bodleian Library.

(C) Three Special Subjects.

(i) and (ii) Candidates must select two Special Subjects from those listed in the 20 'Graduate Studies in Modern Languages' handbook associated with the programme which they are following; candidates may select a special subject from a different programme with approval from their supervisor; (iii) the third Special Subject must be of the candidate's own devising, worked out under supervisory guidance.

Candidates will normally offer two Special Subjects from the same language and 25 area, or from different areas in the same language. The Comparative Literature Programme will contain Special Subjects from two different languages, or one at least of the special subjects (C, D, and E) is comparative in scope.

Approval of Special Subjects (i) and (ii) must be sought, by application to the Modern Language Graduate Office, 41 Wellington Square, Oxford by the end of 30 the fourth week of Michaelmas Term of the first year. Approval of Special Subject (iii) and proposed title of the Dissertation must be sought, by application to the Modern Language Graduate Office, 41 Wellington Square, Oxford by the end of the fourth week of Hilary Term of the second year.

The Special Subjects must have the written support of the candidate's supervisor 35 and be approved by or on behalf of the Medieval and Modern Languages Faculty Board. A proposal for a Special Subject of the candidate's own devising shall be accompanied by a statement (of approximately 100 words) of the character and scope of the subject proposed.

Candidates will be assessed on an essay, or two essays (which may be written in 40 English, or, with the approval of the Medieval and Modern Languages Faculty Board, in the language appropriate to the literature concerned), on the topics they have agreed with the supervisor of each Special Subject.

The essay or essays submitted for each Special Subject should be between 5,000 and 7,000 words in total. 45

Students are required to submit work for assessment on all four of the non-dissertation components (A, C, D, and E). Of these four, the component gaining the lowest passing mark will be discounted in the final assessment. A fail mark must always be included in the final assessment.

The Special Subject essays shall be submitted to the Head of Examinations and 50 Assessments, High Street, Oxford, by noon on Thursday of the first week of Hilary

Term. However, candidates are strongly advised to complete their essays for the first two Special Subjects by the end of Hilary Term of their first year.

4. Candidates for Comparative Literature should ensure that either at least one of the special subjects (C, D, and E) is comparative in scope or the three special subjects are concerned with different languages. The dissertation must deal explicitly with comparative issues.

5. If it is the opinion of the examiners that the work done by a candidate, while not of sufficient merit to qualify for the degree of M.Phil., is nevertheless of sufficient merit to qualify for the Degree of Master of Studies in Modern Languages, the candidate shall be given the option of re-sitting the M.Phil. examination under the appropriate regulation, or of being granted permission to supplicate for the Degree of Master of Studies.

6. In the case of re-submission, candidates shall be required to submit all the material by noon on Thursday of the sixth week of the first Trinity Term following their first examination. Candidates may resubmit on one occasion only.

7. The examiners may award a Distinction for excellence in the whole examination.

Master of Philosophy in Music

(*See also the general notice at the commencement of these regulations.*)

The regulations made by the Board of the Faculty of Music are as follows:

Each candidate will be required:

1. To follow for at least six terms a course of study in music. Candidates will, when they enter for the examination, be required to produce from their society a certificate to that effect.

2. To have satisfied the examiners in a Qualifying Examination identical to that for the degree of Master of Studies in Music, and governed by the regulations for that degree, in the Trinity Full Term of the academic year in which their name is entered on the Register of graduate students. Candidates whose work in the Qualifying Examination is judged by the examiners to be of the standard required for the degree of Master of Studies in Music but not of the standard required to proceed to the second year of the M.Phil. in Music may supplicate for the degree of Master of Studies in Music. Candidates whose work in the Qualifying Examination is not judged by the examiners to be of the standard required for the degree of Master of Studies may retake the examination on one occasion only. Only candidates who reach the required standard to proceed to the second year at the first attempt may do so.

3. To specialise in musicology, performance or composition. The choice of specialism must correspond to that pursued for the Qualifying Examination, but the subject matter of work submitted must be different from that offered for examination in the first year.

4. To submit two substantial pieces of work, named 'Part 3' and 'Part 4' as a continuation of the numbering in the regulations for the degree of Master of Studies. The elements of the examination will be determined by the candidate's chosen specialism.

5. Candidates specialising in musicology will be required to submit:

Part 3: a written project of between 8,000 and 12,000 words in length (or equivalent), which may be *either* a short dissertation or an edition with commentary *or* an analysis *or* a portfolio of essays and ethnographic work. Music Ethnography portfolios may be submitted in a variety of formats, including recordings with commentary, video, photography, transcription and analysis. The topic of the project must be submitted for approval to the Masters' Course Convenor, Faculty of Music, by noon on Friday of the fourth week of Michaelmas Term. Two copies of the project must be submitted, not later than noon on Tuesday of the seventh week of Trinity Term, to the Chair of Examiners for the M.Phil. in Music, c/o Examination Schools, High Street, Oxford.

Part 4: *either* a dissertation of between 22,000 and 25,000 words in musicology or ethnomusicology *or* a substantial editorial exercise (edition), with prefatory matter, of comparable length. The topic for the dissertation or edition must be submitted for approval to the Masters' Course Convenor, Faculty of Music, by noon on Friday of the fourth week of Michaelmas Term. Subject to the approval of the Masters' Course Convenor, a dissertation may be a development of written work submitted for the M.St. Two typewritten copies of the dissertation or edition must be submitted, not later than noon Tuesday of Week 10 of Trinity term, to the Chair of Examiners for the M.Phil. in Music, c/o Examination Schools, High Street, Oxford. Successful candidates will be required to deposit one copy of the dissertation or edition in the Music Faculty Library; minor corrections, as required by the examiners, must be incorporated prior to deposit in the library.

6. Candidates specialising in performance will be required to submit:

Part 3: a recital of forty-five minutes' duration, vocal or instrumental, of at least two contrasted pieces. Two possible programmes must be submitted for approval to the Masters' Course Convenor, Faculty of Music, by Friday of third week of Hilary Term. Candidates will be informed of the examiners' choice of programme by the Friday of eighth week in the same term.

Part 4: *either* a dissertation of between 17,000 and 19,000 words in musicology or ethnomusicology *or* a substantial editorial exercise (edition), with prefatory matter, of comparable length. The topic for the dissertation or edition must be submitted for approval to the Masters' Course Convenor, Faculty of Music, by noon on Friday of the fourth week of Michaelmas Term. Subject to the approval of the Masters' Course Convenor, a dissertation may be a development of written work submitted for the M.St. Two typewritten copies of the dissertation or edition must be submitted, not later than noon on Tuesday of the seventh week of Trinity term, to the Chair of Examiners for the M.Phil. in Music, c/o Examination Schools, High Street, Oxford. Successful candidates will be required to deposit one copy of the dissertation or edition in the Music Faculty Library; minor corrections, as required by the examiners, must be incorporated prior to deposit in the library.

7. Candidates specialising in composition will be required to submit:

Part 3: a written project of between 8,000 and 12,000 words in length (or equivalent), which may be *either* a short dissertation *or* an edition with commentary *or* an analysis *or* a portfolio of essays and ethnographic work. Music Ethnography portfolios may be submitted in a variety of formats, including recordings with commentary, video, photography, transcription and analysis. The topic of the project must be submitted for approval to the Masters' Course Convenor, Faculty of Music, by noon on Friday of the fourth week of Michaelmas Term. Two copies of the project must be submitted, not later than noon on Tuesday of the seventh week of Trinity Term, to the Chair of Examiners for the M.Phil. in Music, c/o Examination Schools, High Street, Oxford.

Part 4: a portfolio of at least two well-contrasted compositions totalling between thirty-five and forty-five minutes in duration. The portfolio of compositions must be submitted, not later than noon on Tuesday of tenth week of Trinity term, to the Chair of Examiners for the M.Phil. in Music, c/o Examination Schools, High Street, Oxford.

8. The examiners may award a distinction for excellence in the whole examination. In this case the work will normally display an excellent command of the subject studied, evidence of critical understanding, and some demonstration of an original conceptual approach.

9. A candidate who fails the final examination will be permitted to retake it on one further occasion only, not later than one year after the initial attempt. Such a candidate whose work has been of satisfactory standard in one or more elements examined will be required to resubmit for examination the element(s) which fell below the passmark when originally examined.   5

Master of Philosophy in Oriental Studies

(*See also the general notice at the commencement of these regulations.*)

The regulations made by the Board of the Faculty of Oriental Studies are as follows:

1. Every candidate must present himself or herself for a written examination in one of the following subjects.   10

   (i) Cuneiform Studies.

   (ii) Egyptology (including Graeco-Roman and Christian Egypt).

  (iii) Modern Middle Eastern Studies.

  (iv) Classical Indian Religion.

   (v) Modern Jewish Studies.   15

  (vi) Jewish Studies in the Graeco-Roman Period.

 (vii) Islamic Art and Archaeology.

(viii) Ottoman Turkish Studies.

  (ix) Islamic Studies and History.

   (x) Modern Chinese Studies.   20

  (xi) Tibetan and Himalayan Studies.

 (xii) Modern South Asian Studies.

(xiii) Traditional East Asia: Classical, Medieval, and Early-Modern.

[For students starting from MT 2015: (xiv) Buddhist Studies.]

2. Candidates for subject (i) must satisfy the Oriental Studies Board by the time of   25
their qualifying examination that they possess a working knowledge of French and German; candidates for (ii) must satisfy the Oriental Studies Board by the time of their qualifying examination that they possess a working knowledge of French and German, and candidates who wish to offer Greek papyrology must possess a fluent knowledge of Greek; and for subject (v) candidates should possess a working knowl-   30
edge of either Hebrew or Yiddish, and a relevant European language. For subject (viii) and the Turkish option in subject (ix) candidates should possess a sound reading knowledge of Modern Turkish or Arabic or Persian. For subject (x) Modern Chinese Studies, candidates will normally have a first degree in a discipline relevant to their elective subject. For subject (xiii) Traditional East Asia: Classical, Medieval, and   35
Early Modern, candidates should possess a good proficiency (normally at least two years' study or equivalent) in modern Chinese, Japanese, or Korean.

[For students starting before MT 2015: A candidate who fails any part or parts of the Qualifying Examination may retake such part or parts during the Long Vacation prior to the second year of the course, except in the cases of the M.Phil. in Classical Indian   40
Religion, Modern Middle Eastern Studies, Modern Jewish Studies and Tibetan and Himalayan Studies. A candidate who fails any part or parts of the Qualifying Examination for these four courses may retake such part or parts during Trinity Term of the first year of study.

3. Subject to such regulations as the board may hereinafter make, every candidate must offer a thesis[1] on a subject approved by the board (or by a person or persons to whom it may delegate the power of giving such approval), and as far as possible falling within the scope of the subject offered by the candidate in the examination. Applications for approval of the thesis subject must reach the Board of the Faculty of Oriental Studies, Oriental Institute, on or before Monday of nought week of Hilary Term in the second year of the course. A title approval form is available on the Oriental Studies website. The thesis should be presented not later than noon on the Friday of the second week of the Trinity Term in which the examination is taken except in (ii) below, in which the thesis should be presented not later than noon on the Friday of the fourth week of the Trinity Term in which the examination is taken; (v) below, in which the thesis should be presented by noon on Friday of 6th week of Trinity Term; (vii) below, in which the thesis should be presented not later than noon on the Monday of seventh week of Trinity Term in which the examination is taken; (x) below, in which the thesis should be presented not later than noon of Monday of the second week of Trinity Term in which the examination is taken; and (xiii) below, in which the thesis should be presented not later than noon of Friday of the fifth week of Trinity Term in which the examination is taken.

Successful candidates will be required to deposit one copy of the thesis in the Bodleian.

4. Every candidate will be examined viva voce in the subjects of the school unless he or she shall have been individually excused by the examiners.

5. The examiners may award a distinction for excellence in the whole examination.]

[For students starting from MT 2015: 3. A candidate who fails any part or parts of the Qualifying Examination may retake such part or parts during the Long Vacation prior to the second year of the course, except in the cases of the M.Phil. in Classical Indian Religion, Modern Middle Eastern Studies, Modern Jewish Studies, and Tibetan and Himalayan Studies. A candidate who fails any part or parts of the Qualifying Examination for these four courses may retake such part or parts during Trinity Term of the first year of study except where stated otherwise in the particular regulations for individual courses in the following pages.

4. A candidate who fails any part or parts of the Final Examination may retake such part or parts on one occasion in the following academic year.

5. Subject to such regulations as the board may hereinafter make, every candidate must offer a thesis[1] on a subject approved by the board (or by a person or persons to whom it may delegate the power of giving such approval), and as far as possible falling within the scope of the subject offered by the candidate in the examination. Applications for approval of the thesis subject must reach the Board of the Faculty of Oriental Studies, Oriental Institute, on or before Monday of nought week of Hilary Term in the second year of the course. A title approval form is available on the Oriental Studies website. Two typewritten copies and an electronic copy in PDF format in a memory stick or CD, of the thesis must be submitted to the Chairman of the Examiners, name of degree, c/o Examination Schools, High Street, Oxford OX1 4BG, not later than noon on the Friday of the second week of the Trinity Term in which the examination is taken except in (ii) and (xiv) below, in which the thesis should be presented not later than noon on the Friday of the fourth week of the Trinity Term in which the examination is taken; (v) and (xiii) below, in which the thesis should be presented by noon on Friday of 6th week of Trinity Term; (vii) below, in which the

---

[1] See the general regulation concerning the preparation and dispatch of theses. Candidates are reminded that work submitted for the Degree of M.Phil. may subsequently be incorporated in a thesis submitted for the Degree of D.Phil.

thesis should be presented not later than noon on the Monday of seventh week of Trinity Term in which the examination is taken; The work must bear the candidates examination number (but not the candidates' name). Candidates must include a signed declaration sealed in an envelope addressed to the Chair of Examiners that the work is the candidates own.   5

Successful candidates will be required to deposit one copy of the thesis in the Bodleian.

6. Candidates may be required to attend a viva voce, except where stated otherwise in the particular regulations for individual courses in the following pages.

7. The examiners may award a distinction for excellence in the whole examination.]   10

Subjects

(i) Cuneiform Studies

A. *Qualifying Examination*

Each candidate will be required, unless exempted by the Oriental Studies Board, to pass a qualifying examination in the Sumerian and Akkadian languages not later than   15
the end of the third term after that in which his or her name has been placed on the register.

B. *Final Examination*

[For students starting from MT 2015: The following papers are assessed by a written examination paper at the end of Trinity Term except for paper 4.]   20

Each candidate(s) will be required to offer the following papers:

1. Prepared translations of Sumerian texts and related essay questions (1 paper)

2. Prepared translations of Akkadian texts and related essay questions (1 paper)

A list of prepared texts in the Sumerian and Akkadian languages will be provided to the candidate after he or she has successfully passed the qualifying examination. **[For   25
students starting before MT 2015:** The list of texts will be reported to the Faculty Board's second meeting of Michaelmas Term in the second year of the course.[1]**] [For students starting from MT 2015:** Lists of set texts must be submitted to the faculty office by Friday of seventh week of Michaelmas term.]

3. Unprepared translations of Akkadian (1 paper)   30

4. History and culture of ancient Mesopotamia (1 paper)

[For students starting before MT 2015: Candidates must demonstrate knowledge of the outlines of major aspects of Mesopotamian history, including political, social, economic, and cultural developments. They will be required to submit two essays each of not more than 5,000 words in length, which display knowledge of more than just a   35
narrow range of the topic.

Candidates are required to collect the subject of the essays from the Faculty Office, Oriental Institute, by noon, Friday of Week 1 of Michaelmas Term of the second year of the course for the first essay and by noon, Friday Week 1 of Hilary Term of the second year of the course for the second essay. The essays must be submitted to the   40
Examination Schools by the end of Weeks 8 of Michaelmas Term and Hilary Term respectively. For each essay two printed copies and a signed form certifying that the essay is the candidate's own work must be delivered in a parcel bearing the words 'Essay presubmitted for the M.Phil. in Cuneiform Studies' to the Examination Schools, High Street, Oxford OX1 4BG.']   45

[For students starting from MT 2015: Candidates are required to submit two essays each of not more than 5,000 words in length, which display knowledge of more than just a narrow range of the topic. The subject of the essays will be published by noon, Friday of Week 1 of Michaelmas Term of the second year of the course for the first

---

[1] Lists of set texts will be available in the Course Handbook.

essay and by noon, Friday Week 1 of Hilary Term of the second year of the course for the second essay. Candidates will be contacted with details on how to collect or access the question paper. The essays must be submitted to the Examination Schools by the end of Weeks 8 of Michaelmas Term and Hilary Term respectively. For each essay two printed copies and a signed form certifying that the essay is the candidate's own work must be delivered in an envelope marked 'Essay presubmitted for the M.Phil. in Cuneiform Studies' to the Examination Schools, High Street, Oxford OX1 4BG.]

5. The cuneiform world in context and approaches to the study of Assyriology;

[For students starting before MT 2015: (*a*) Cuneiform world in context (one half paper)

Candidates must be able to integrate the study of the cuneiform world into the wider context of the Near East. Three approaches may be pursued:

(1) The cuneiform world and the ancient Near East, i.e. the Hittite, Egyptian, or Biblical worlds.

(2) The cuneiform world and the ancient Mediterranean, i.e. Graeco-Roman antiquity.

(3) The cuneiform world and the later Near East, i.e. late antique and medieval periods.

Candidates must specify which of these approaches they will pursue not later than the end of the third term after that in which their name has been placed on the register. Not all options may be available every year.

(*b*) Approaches to the study of Assyriology (one half paper):

Questions will be set on the method, theory, bibliography, and history of Assyriology. Candidates will be expected to demonstrate knowledge of how to research any subject relating to cuneiform studies, and how to evaluate critically the contributions of disciplines, such as anthropology, archaeology, art history, history, and literary criticism, to the study of the cuneiform world.]

[For students starting from MT 2015: (*a*) Cuneiform world in context (one half paper)

A list of approaches will be published in the course handbook. Candidates must specify which of these approaches they will pursue not later than the end of the third term after that in which their name has been placed on the register. Not all options may be available every year.

(*b*) Approaches to the study of Assyriology (one half paper)]

C. *Thesis*

Each candidate will be required to present a thesis of not more than 20,000 words on a subject approved by the board. The thesis needs to include a substantial cuneiform-related element. **[For students starting before MT 2015:** The thesis should be presented not later than noon on the Friday of the second week of Trinity Term in which the final examination is taken.][1]

(ii) Egyptology

This course covers topics relating to dynastic, Graeco-Roman, and Christian Egypt.

A. *Qualifying Examination*

Each candidate will be required, unless exempted by the Oriental Studies Board, to pass a qualifying examination in Egyptian and/or Coptic not later than the end of the third term after he or she is admitted. Candidates offering options relating to the Graeco-Roman period may be required to pass a qualifying examination in Greek.

---

[1] See general regulations for theses and special regulations for theses in Oriental Studies.

B. *Final Examination*

1. Syllabus A: A candidate who has a first degree in Egyptology or equivalent qualification must offer Section I, *three* papers from Section II, and a thesis of not more than 30,000 words on a subject to be approved by the board.[1]

2. Syllabus B: All other candidates must offer Section I, *two* papers from Section II, Section III, and a thesis of not more than 20,000 words on a subject to be approved by the board.[1]

[For students starting before MT 2015: 3. All applications for approval of options must reach the Secretary, Board of the Faculty of Oriental Studies, Oriental Institute, on or before Monday in the sixth week of Trinity Full Term in the academic year preceding that in which the examination is to be taken. For options under Section II applicants must include a detailed definition of the topics offered and a list of primary sources, to be countersigned by their supervisors.

4. For the Final Examination the following papers will be set:

I. (i) A general paper on Egyptology.
   Questions will be set on method, theory, bibliography, and the history of Egyptology. Candidates will be expected to answer some questions outside the areas of their fields of specialisation.

   (ii) Unprepared translation from Egyptian texts.
   Passages may be set for translation from texts of all periods from the end of the Old Kingdom to the Conquest of Alexander. Texts of other periods may be set with the permission of the board.

II. Two (for candidates under 2 above, Syllabus B) or three (for candidates under 1 above, Syllabus A) papers in a special field selected from the list below, of which one will be on an appropriate category of primary source material.
   Since all special fields may not be available in every year, candidates must confirm with the Graduate Studies Committee of the Oriental Studies Board that the field they intend to offer is available by the end of the second term after they are admitted. Some related fields (e.g. demotic with Greek papyrology) may be combined with the permission of the board.

The following fields will normally be available:

Ancient Egyptian Art and Architecture

Archaeology

Christian Egypt

Demotic

Egyptian grammar

Graeco-Roman hieroglyphic texts

Greek papyrology

Hieratic texts

Egyptian literary or religious texts

Periods of history, from the early dynastic to the Byzantine.**]**

---

[1] See general regulations for theses and special regulations for theses in Oriental Studies.

3. All applications for approval of options must reach the Senior Academic Administrator, Oriental Institute, on or before Monday in the second week of Michaelmas Term in of the examination. For options under Section II applicants must include a detailed definition of the topics offered and a list of primary sources, to be countersigned by their supervisors.

5

Section I

For the Final Examination the following papers will be set:

(i) A general paper on Egyptology. Questions will be set on method, theory, bibliography, and the history of Egyptology. Candidates will be expected to answer some questions outside the areas of their fields of specialisation.

10

(ii) Unprepared translation from Egyptian texts.
Passages may be set for translation from texts of all periods from the end of the Old Kingdom to the Conquest of Alexander. Texts of other periods may be set with the permission of the board.

Section II

15

A special field selected from a list published in the course handbook of which one will be on an appropriate category of primary source material.

Some special fields may not be available every year.

Candidates for Syllabus A will be examined by unit (i), (ii), and (iii).

Candidates for Syllabus B will be examined by unit (i) and (ii).

20

The examination units are as follows:

(i) **[For students starting before MT 2015:** *Take-home examination.* One paper in the special field will be set as a take-home examination. The answer or answers for this examination should be typed and presented in proper scholarly form. Candidates will be informed as to which paper is to be examined as a take-home on Friday of eighth week of the Hilary Term preceding the Final examination; conventions for the setting of the paper will be released at the same time. The question paper for the take-home examination will be distributed to candidates in the Oriental Institute at 10 a. m. on Monday of first week in Full Term in the term in which the final examination is to be offered. The completed examination must be handed in to the Examination Schools, High Street, Oxford no later than 12 noon on Monday of second week. The completed paper should not exceed 5,000 words in length.] **[For students starting from MT 2015:** *Take-home examination.* One paper in the special field will be set as a take-home examination. The answer or answers for this examination should be typed and presented in proper scholarly form. Candidates will be informed as to which paper is to be examined as a take-home on Friday of eighth week of the Hilary Term preceding the Final examination; conventions for the setting of the paper will be released at the same time. The question paper for the take-home examination will be published to candidates in the Oriental Institute at 9 a.m. on Monday of first week in Full Term in the term in which the final examination is to be offered. Candidates will be contacted with details on how to collect or access the question paper. The completed examination must be handed in to the Examination Schools, High Street, Oxford no later than 12 noon on Monday of second week. The completed paper should not exceed 5,000 words in length.]

25

30

35

40

45

If candidates for a different degree are taking the same subject and are to be examined in a three-hour examination, M.Phil. candidates may instead take that examination. Applications to take the three-hour examination should be submitted to the faculty board by Friday of the first week in Michaelmas Term in the academic year of the final examination.

(ii) *Assessed essays.* For a second topic in the special field, candidates will be required to presubmit two essays of not more than 5,000 words each, which between them display command of more than a narrow range of the topic. Supervisors or others are permitted to give bibliographical help and to discuss drafts of essays. Such essays (two printed copies) must be delivered in a parcel bearing the words 'Essays presubmitted for the M.Phil. in Egyptology' to the Examination Schools, High Street, Oxford OX1 4BG by noon on the Thursday of the sixth week of Trinity Term in which the examination is to be taken.

(iii) *Examination paper* (Syllabus A only). One three-hour examination on an area within the special field. **[For students starting before MT 2015:** The subject of this examination is to be presented to the faculty board by Friday of the first week of Michaelmas Term in the academic year of the final examination.**]**

[For students starting before MT 2015: III. Prescribed texts in Middle and Late Egyptian (two papers). The list of texts to be offered will be reported to the Faculty Board's second meeting in Michaelmas Term in the second year of the course and subsequently published in the Course Handbook.**]**

[For students starting from MT 2015: Section III.

Prescribed texts in Middle and Late Egyptian (two papers). Lists of set texts must be submitted to the Faculty office by Friday of seventh week of Michaelmas Term and subsequently published in the Course Handbook.**]**

(iii) Modern Middle Eastern Studies

A. *Qualifying Examination*

Every candidate must pass a qualifying examination not later than the end of the second term from the commencement of the course. A candidate with an intermediate level of proficiency (the equivalent of 2–3 years of study) in Arabic, Persian or Turkish may offer respectively Advanced Arabic, Advanced Persian or Advanced Turkish. A candidate with native fluency or who has satisfied the examiners in the Second Public Examination in Arabic or Persian or Turkish or Hebrew, or has passed a similar examination in another university, must offer a different language for examination. The examination will consist of two papers:

(i) A language examination in Arabic or Advanced Arabic or Hebrew or Persian or Advanced Persian or Turkish or Advanced Turkish, (subject to the availability of teaching), based on grammar knowledge and reading comprehension.

(ii) A general methodological paper on the Middle East in the twentieth century.

Entries must be made on the appropriate form, obtainable from the University Offices, by Friday in the second week of Hilary Full Term following the candidate's admission. **[For students starting before MT 2015:** Candidates who fail the Qualifying Examination may at the discretion of the board be allowed to retake it in the first week after the following Full Trinity Term.**]**

B. *Final Examination*

[For students starting before MT 2015: It is strongly recommended that candidates for the Final Examination should, in the course of the Long Vacation preceding the year in which they propose to take the examination, attend a recognised language course in an appropriate Middle Eastern country.**]**

1. All candidates must offer

(*a*) one language paper in Arabic or Hebrew or Persian or Turkish, subject to the availability of teaching, based on knowledge of grammar, translation from the Oriental language to English, and reading comprehension or, for candidates who offered Advanced Arabic, Advanced Persian, or Advanced Turkish for the Qualifying Examination, one language paper in Arabic, Persian or Turkish respectively based on prose composition, translation from the Oriental language to English, and reading comprehension;

(*b*) a thesis of not more than 30,000 words on a subject to be approved by the board[1];

[For students starting before MT 2015: (*c*) three papers from (1)–(16), provided that instead of one of these papers, a candidate may offer a paper on a subject not included in the list below, with the approval of the board.

  (1) History of the Middle East, 1860–1970.

  (2) Politics of the Middle East.

  (3) Social anthropology of the Middle East.

  (4) International Relations of the Middle East.

  (5) Iranian History from the Constitutional to the Islamic Revolution, 1905–1979.

  (6) History of Turkey, 1908–80.

  (7) History and Politics of the Islamic Republic of Iran, 1979–2005.

  (8) Mass Media in the Middle East.

  (9) Politics of the Maghreb.

  (10) The Maghreb since 1830.

  (11) Israel: History, Politics and Society.

  (12) The Political Economy of the Middle East and North Africa.

  (13) Islam in the West.

  (14) Contemporary Islamic Ethics.

  (15) Political Islam, Islamism and Modern Islamic Movements.

  (16) Modern Turkish Literature: Texts and Contexts.

  (17) History from below in the Middle East and North Africa.

  (18) The Arab-Israeli Conflict**]**

[For students starting from MT 2015: (*c*) three papers from a list of options published in the course handbook. A candidate may offer a paper on a subject not included on the list, with the approval of the board.**]**

Teaching for some options may not be available in every year. Applicants for admission will be advised whether teaching will be available in the options of their choice.

2. All applications for approval must reach the **[For students starting before MT 2015:** Secretary, Board of the Faculty of Oriental Studies,**] [For students starting from MT 2015:** Senior Academic Administrator,**]** Oriental Institute, on or before the Monday in the second week of the Michaelmas Full Term preceding the examina-tion.un

(iv) Classical Indian Religion

A. *Qualifying Examination*

Candidates must pass a qualifying examination in Sanskrit not later than the end of the second term of the academic year in which the candidate's name is first entered on the register of M.Phil. students unless exempted by the Board of the Faculty of Oriental Studies.

B. *Final Examination*

Candidates will be required to offer the following four papers, but a candidate may submit a thesis of not more than 20,000 words on a subject approved by the board[1] instead of Paper (iv).

---

[1] See general regulations for theses and special regulations for theses in Oriental Studies.

[**For students starting before MT 2015:** (i) (*a*) Unprepared translation from epic and commentarial Sanskrit.

(*b*) Translation from the set books in two of the sections, as published in the Course Handbook. Lists of set texts will be reported to the Faculty Board's second meeting of Michaelmas Full Term in the second year of the course.   5

In Papers (ii) and (iii) candidates will be expected to show background knowledge of relevant social and political history. Emphasis will be laid on the study of primary sources, which may, however, be read in translation.

(iv) Approaches to the study of Indian religion:

Candidates will be asked to give a critical appreciation of the contributions of   10
different disciplines (theology, anthropology, philology etc.) and to discuss the application of various theoretical approaches (e.g. evolutionism, diffusionism, dialectical materialism, phenomenology, structuralism) to the subject.]

[**For students starting from MT 2015:** (i) Unprepared translation from epic and commentarial Sanskrit. This written examination will take place at the end of Trinity   15
Term.

(ii) and (iii) Translation from the set books in two of the sections. Lists of set texts must be submitted to the Faculty office by Friday of seventh week of Michaelmas Term. This written examination will take place at the end of Trinity Term.

In Papers (ii) and (iii), each of which is assessed by a three-hour examination,   20
candidates will be expected to show background knowledge of relevant social and political history. Emphasis will be laid on the study of primary sources, which may, however, be read in translation.

(iv) Approaches to the study of Indian religion: Candidates will be asked to give a critical appreciation of the contributions of different disciplines (theology, anthropol-   25
ogy, philology etc.) and to discuss the application of various theoretical approaches (e.g. evolutionism, diffusionism, dialectical materialism, phenomenology, structuralism) to the subject. This written examination will take place at the end of Trinity Term.]

(v) **Modern Jewish Studies**

A. *Qualifying Examination*   30

Candidates must pass a qualifying examination in Modern Hebrew or Yiddish not later than the end of the second term of the academic year in which the candidate's name is first entered on the Register of M.Phil. students unless exempted by the Board of the Faculty of Oriental Studies. The examination will consist of a language examination in Hebrew based on grammar knowledge and reading comprehension.   35
[**For students starting before MT 2015:** Candidates who fail the Qualifying Examination may be allowed to retake that part in Trinity Term of the first year of the course.]

Candidates, who will submit a take-home essay in their first year of the course to partially fulfil the requirements of (*b*) in the Final Examination, must enter for this   40
paper in their first year. Marks will not be moderated for Final Examination take-home essays taken in the first year of the course until the end of the second year of the course. [**For students starting before MT 2015:** Any failed Final Examination papers may be retaken on one occasion only, at the same time in the following academic year.]   45

B. *Final Examination*

All candidates must offer

(*a*) one language paper in Modern Hebrew or Yiddish based on grammar knowledge, reading comprehension, and translation into English, at a level equivalent to Intermediate or higher.   50 (*b*) Four papers [**For students starting before MT 2015:** from the following list] [**For students starting from MT 2015:** from a list published in the course handbook].

[**For students starting before MT 2015:** Candidates will present themselves for take-home essay examination. Essay examination will consist of the submission of two 5 essays of not more than 2,500 words each for each of the four papers chosen, which must be submitted to the Examination Schools, High Street, Oxford, by 12 noon on the Friday of noughth week of the term following that in which the paper was taught. Candidates will collect the essay topics from the Oriental Institute Faculty Office, on the Friday of eighth week of the term in which the paper is taught. When a paper 10 assessed by take-home essay is taught in the first year of the course, candidates must enter for the paper in the first year. Candidates proposing to offer a paper not included in the list below must obtain the permission of the Board of the Faculty of Oriental Studies. All applications for approval must be sent to the Secretary of the Board on or before the Monday in the second week of the Michaelmas Full Term preceding the 15 examination.

1. Modern Jewish History.
2. Modern Judaism: Arguments for Change.
3. Modern Jewish thought.
4. Modern Hebrew Literature. 20
5. Israel: History, Politics, Society.
6. The Holocaust: from History to Memory.
7. Jewish Literature in the nineteenth and twentieth centuries.
8. Modern Yiddish Literature.]

[**For students starting from MT 2015:** Candidates will present themselves for take- 25 home essay examination. Essay examination will consist of the submission of two essays of not more than 2,500 words each for each of the four papers chosen, which must be submitted to the Examination Schools, High Street, Oxford, by 12 noon on the Friday of noughth week of the term following that in which the paper was taught. The essay topics will be published, on Friday of eighth week of the term in which the 30 paper is taught. Candidates will be contacted with details on how to collect or access the question paper. When a paper assessed by take-home essay is taught in the first year of the course, candidates must enter for the paper in the first year. Candidates proposing to offer a paper not included in the list must obtain the permission of the Board of the Faculty of Oriental Studies. All applications for approval must be sent to 35 the Senior Academic Administrator on or before the Monday in the second week of the Michaelmas Full Term preceding the examination.]

Teaching for some options may not be available in every year. Applicants for admission will be advised whether teaching will be available in the options of their choice. Prescribed texts will be reported to the Faculty Board's second meeting of 40 Michaelmas Full Term in the first year of the course.

C. *Thesis*

A candidate shall submit a thesis of not more than 30,000 words on a topic selected in consultation with his or her supervisor and approved by the faculty Board.[1] [**For students starting before MT 2015:** Any failed Final Examination papers or thesis may 45 be retaken on one occasion only, at the same time in the following academic year.]

---

[1] See general regulations for theses and special regulations for theses in Oriental Studies.

(vi) Jewish Studies in the Graeco-Roman Period

A. *Qualifying Examination*

Candidates must pass a qualifying examination in Jewish Studies not later than the end of the third term after that in which the candidate's name is first entered on the register of M.Phil. students unless exempted by the Board of the Faculty of Oriental   5
Studies.

B. *Final Examination*

[For students starting before MT 2015: Every candidate shall submit a thesis of not more than 30,000 words[1] and present himself for a written examination. The written examination shall consist of Paper 1 and three further papers to be chosen from Papers   10
2 to 8.

(1) Jewish literature, history, and institutions from 200 BC to AD 425.
(2) Jewish historiography with prescribed texts.
(3) Jewish law with prescribed texts.
(4) Jewish Bible interpretation with prescribed texts.   15
(5) Jewish eschatology with prescribed texts.
(6) Jewish liturgy with prescribed texts.
(7) Jewish wisdom literature with prescribed texts.
(8) Jewish papyrology and epigraphy with prescribed texts.

Notes. 1. Candidates must satisfy the Board of the Faculty of Oriental Studies   20
before admission to the course that they possess the necessary qualifications in the Hebrew language to profit by the course. Those wishing to take options 2 or 8 must show evidence of their knowledge of Greek.]

[For students starting from MT 2015: Every candidate shall submit a thesis of not more than 30,000 words[1] and 4 written examinations. The written examina-   25
tions shall consist of one paper on Jewish literature, history, and institution from 200 BC to AD425 and three further papers from a list published in the course handbook.

Notes. 1. Candidates must satisfy the Board of the Faculty of Oriental Studies before admission to the course that they possess the necessary qualifications in the   30
Hebrew language to profit by the course.]

2. Papers 2–8 will contain passages for translation and comment as well as general questions relating to the prescribed texts.

3. Texts will be reported to the Faculty Board's second meeting of Michaelmas Full Term in the first year of the course.   35

(vii) Islamic Art and Archaeology

A. *Qualifying Examination*

Every candidate will be required to satisfy the examiners in a qualifying examina-
tion not later than the end of the third term after that in which the candidate's name is first entered on the Register of M.Phil. Students. The examination will include: 40

(*a*) a three-hour written examination: Introduction to Islamic Art and Archaeology, *c.550–c.190.*

(*b*) a portfolio, containing reports on the practical work completed during the year (according to the schedule given in the Course Handbook).

(*c*) a language examination in Arabic or Persian or Turkish.   45

---

[1] See general regulations for theses and special regulations for theses in Oriental Studies.

Candidates must submit the portfolio in (*b*) above not later than 12 noon on Monday of 7th Week of Trinity Term. Two printed copies and one digital copy on either a CD-ROM disc or a memory stick must be submitted in a securely sealed parcel clearly addressed to the Chair of Examiners, M. Phil. in Islamic Art and Archaeology (Oriental Studies), Examination Schools, High Street, Oxford. The parcel must bear the words 'QUALIFYING EXAMINATION FOR THE M. PHIL. IN ISLAMIC ART AND ARCHAEOLOGY (PORTFOLIO).' The portfolio must bear the candidate's examination number (but not the candidate's name, which must be concealed). Candidates must include a signed declaration sealed in an envelope addressed to the Chair of Examiners that the work is the candidate's own.

B. *Final Examination*

This shall be taken in the Trinity Term of the academic year following that in which the candidate's name is first entered on the Register of M.Phil. Students.

1. Every candidate must follow for at least six terms a course of instruction in Islamic Art and Archaeology.

2. The examination will include:

(*a*) A paper on a topic of Islamic art and archaeology or related fields (e.g. non-Islamic art, architecture and archaeology; Islamic studies; history; museology) to be selected by the candidate in consultation with the candidate's supervisor. This paper will be examined by an extended essay of between 5,000 and 6,000 words. Applications for the approval of the essay topic should be submitted to the Faculty office by Monday of **[For students starting before MT 2015:** sixth] **[For students starting from MT 2015:** second] week of Michaelmas Term and will be reported to the Faculty Board's second meeting of Michaelmas Term.

(*b*) Arabic or Persian or Turkish language examination.

(*c*) Arabic or Persian or Turkish prepared texts. **[For students starting from MT 2015:** This is a written examination paper.]

(*d*) A three-hour written examination: Approaches to Islamic Art and Archaeology.

(*e*) A **[For students starting before MT 2015:** dissertation] **[For students starting from MT 2015:** thesis][1] of not more than 30,000 words on a subject to be approved by the Faculty Board.

3. Candidates must submit the extended essay in (a) above not later than noon on the Monday of first week of Trinity Term of the year in which they sit the examination.

[For students starting before MT 2015: 4. Candidates must submit the dissertation in (e) not later than 12 noon on Monday of 7th Week of Trinity Term.

5. Both the extended essay and the dissertation must be submitted in printed form and as a digital copy on either a CD-ROM disc or a memory stick. Two printed copies and one digital copy of each must be submitted in a securely sealed parcel clearly addressed to the Chair of Examiners, M.Phil. in Islamic Art and Archaeology (Oriental Studies), Examination Schools, High Street, Oxford. The parcels must bear the words 'FINAL EXAMINATION FOR THE M.PHIL. IN ISLAMIC ART AND ARCHAEOLOGY (EXTENDED ESSAY [or DISSERTATION]).' Each piece of work must bear the candidate's examination number (but not the

---

[1] See general regulations for theses and special regulations for theses in Oriental Studies.

candidate's name, which must be concealed). Candidates must include a signed declaration sealed in a envelope addressed to the Chair of Examiners that the work is the candidate's own.]

[For students starting from MT 2015: 4. The extended essay must be submitted in printed form and an electronic copy in PDF on either a CD-ROM disc or a memory stick. Two printed copies and the CD-ROM disc or memory stick must be submitted in a securely sealed parcel clearly addressed to the Chair of Examiners, M.Phil. in Islamic Art and Archaeology (Oriental Studies), Examination Schools, High Street, Oxford. The parcels must bear the words 'FINAL EXAMINATION FOR THE M.PHIL. IN ISLAMIC ART AND ARCHAEOLOGY (EXTENDED ESSAY)'. Each piece of work must bear the candidate's examination number (but not the candidate's name, which must be concealed). Candidates must include a signed declaration sealed in an envelope addressed to the Chair of Examiners that the work is the candidate's own.]

If it is the opinion of the examiners that the work which has been required of a candidate is not of sufficient merit to qualify him or her for the Degree of M.Phil., the candidate shall be given the option of resitting the M.Phil. examination under the appropriate regulation, or of being granted permission to supplicate for the Degree of Master of Studies.

(viii) Ottoman Turkish Studies

A. *Qualifying Examination*

Every candidate will be required, unless exempted by the Oriental Studies Board, to pass a qualifying examination in Ottoman Turkish not later than the end of the third term after that in which his or her name has been placed on the register.

B. *Final Examination*

Every candidate will be required to offer the following four papers and a thesis[1] of not more than 30,000 words.

(1) Essay questions on Ottoman history and institutions, 1453–1699.

(2) Ottoman historical texts.

[For students starting before MT 2015: (Set texts will be reported to the Faculty Board's second meeting of Michaelmas Full Term in the second year of the course.)[2]]

(3) Ottoman texts in modern transcription and post-1928 Ottomanising texts.[2]

(4) Ottoman documents:

Ottoman Documents, ed. Repp (copies are available from the Oriental Institute).

Teaching for the course may not be available in every year: applicants for admission will only be accepted if teaching is available.

(ix) Islamic Studies and History

A. *Qualifying Examination*

[For students starting before MT 2015: Each candidate will be required, unless exempted by the Oriental Studies Board, to pass a qualifying examination in Arabic or Persian or Ottoman Turkish or any other language approved by the Faculty Board not later than the end of the third term after that in which the candidate's name has been placed on the register. The content of the examination shall be of such nature as to satisfy the board that the candidate is capable of using pre-modern texts in the respective language.

---

[1] See general regulations for theses and special regulations for theses in Oriental Studies.

[2] Lists of texts are available in the Course Handbook.

B. *Final Examination*

1. It is strongly recommended that candidates for the Final Examination attend a recognised language course in an appropriate Middle Eastern country during the long vacation between the third and fourth terms of their study.

2. The examination shall take place not later than the end of the third term of the second year from the candidate's admission to the M.Phil. degree programme. Full details of the examination will be provided in the examination conventions, which will be made available to the candidates in the second term of the second year of the course. Candidates must make their entries for the Final Examination by filling out the appropriate examination entry form by Friday of the first week of the second term of the second year from the candidate's admission to the course. The examiners may award a distinction to candidates who have performed with special merit. A candidate who fails this examination will be permitted to retake it on one further occasion only, not later than one year after the initial attempt. Such a candidate whose dissertation has been of a satisfactory standard may resubmit the same piece of work, while a candidate who has reached a satisfactory standard on the written papers will not be required to retake that part of the examination.

3. The Final Examination shall consist of these elements (a–c):

(*a*) All three of the following papers (1–3):

    (1) A language examination in Arabic, or Persian, or Ottoman Turkish, or any other language approved by the Faculty Board.[1]

    (2) A prescribed take-home essay on methods and research materials which must not exceed 4,000 words (on deadlines see below).

    (3) Islamic studies and history, 570–1500.

(*b*) Two of the following papers (5.1–5.22, at least one of which must involve translation into English of excerpts from a set text, or from a selection of set texts). Teaching for some options may not be available in every year. Applicants for admission will be advised whether teaching will be available in the options of their choice. All candidates must obtain the approval of the Board of the Faculty of Oriental Studies for the papers they wish to offer. All applications for approval must reach the Secretary, Board of the Faculty of Oriental Studies, Oriental Institute, not later than the Monday in the second week of Michaelmas Full Term preceding the examination.

5.1 From late antiquity to early Islam

5.2 Religion, politics and culture in the Umayyad period, 661–750

5.3 History, culture and society in the early Abbasid period, 750–925

5.4 Islamic historiography

5.5 The Seljuqs

5.6 Mamluk Egypt

5.7 History and culture during the Mongol Period

5.8 The rise of the Ottomans to 1566

5.9 Mughul India

5.10 Timurid History and Historiography

5.11 Safavid History

5.12 Arabic or Persian or Ottoman Palaeography

---

[1] Lists of texts are available in the Course Handbook.

5.13 Qur'an

5.14 Hadith

5.15 Islamic law

5.16 Sufism

5.17 Islamic theology   5

5.18 Muslim/non-Muslim relations

5.19 Arabic or Persian or Ottoman Turkish literature in any period prior to 1500

5.20 Topics in Arabic Philosophy

5.21 A paper chosen from the M.St. in Islamic Art and Archaeology

5.22 Other subject approved by the Board of the Faculty of Oriental Studies   10

All papers will be examined in the Examination Schools, High Street, Oxford at the end of Trinity Term except the prescribed essay on methods and research materials a (2). The topic of that paper will be announced by noon on Monday of the fifth week of the Trinity Term. The paper must be submitted to the Examination Schools, High Street, Oxford by noon on Monday of the sixth week of the Trinity Term.   15

(*c*) A thesis of 25,000 words on a subject approved by the Oriental Studies Faculty Board, of which two typed copies must be delivered to the Examination Schools, High Street, Oxford, by Noon of Monday of the fifth week of Trinity Term of the second year from the candidate's admission to the course. The thesis must be accompanied by a signed statement by the candidate that the   20 thesis is his or her own work except where otherwise indicated.]

[For students starting from MT 2015: Each candidate will be required, unless exempted by the Oriental Studies Board, to pass a qualifying examination in Arabic or Persian or Ottoman Turkish or any other language approved by the Faculty Board not later than the end of the third term after that in which the candidate's name has   25 been placed on the register. The content of the examination shall be of such nature as to satisfy the board that the candidate is capable of using pre-modern texts in the respective language.

B. *Final Examination*

1. The examination shall take place not later than the end of the third term of the   30 second year from the candidate's admission to the M.Phil. degree programme. Full details of the examination will be provided in the examination conventions, which will be made available to the candidates in the second term of the second year of the course. Candidates must make their entries for the Final Examination by filling out the appropriate examination entry form by Friday of the first week of the second term   35 of the second year from the candidate's admission to the course. The examiners may award a distinction to candidates who have performed with special merit. A candidate will be permitted to retake any failed papers on one further occasion only, not later than one year after the initial attempt.

2. The Final Examination shall consist of the following five units (1–5).   40

(1) A language examination in Arabic, or Persian, or Ottoman Turkish, or any other language approved by the Faculty Board. This written examination will take place at the end of Trinity Term.

(2) Islamic studies and history, 570–1500. This written examination will take place at the end of Trinity Term.   45

(3) and (4) Two optional papers which will be examined either as a written examination paper at the end of Trinity Term or by means of a take-home research paper of up to 5,000 words. A list of options and how they will be assessed will be available in the course handbook by noughth week of Michaelmas Term in the year of the exams.   Teaching for some options may not be available in every year. All   50 candidates must obtain the approval of the Board of the Faculty of Oriental Studies

for the papers they wish to offer. All applications for approval must reach the Senior
Academic Administrator, Oriental Institute, not later than the Monday in the second
week of Michaelmas Full Term preceding the examination.

For options assessed by means of a take-home research paper, the question paper
will be published by the examiners by noon Friday of eighth week of the term in which   5
the option is taught, and two copies of the essays must be submitted to the
Examination Schools, High Street, Oxford by noon on Friday of the following
week. Candidates will be contacted with details of how to collect or access the
questions. The examination for at least one of these optional papers, whether conducted in the Examination Schools or as a take-home essay, must require the student   10
to demonstrate the ability to use Arabic, Persian, or Turkish primary sources.

(5) A thesis of 25,000 words on a subject approved by the Oriental Studies Faculty
Board, of which two typed copies and an electronic copy in PDF format in a memory
stick or CD, of the thesis must be delivered to the Examination Schools, High Street,
Oxford, by noon of Friday of sixth week of Trinity Term of the second year from the   15
candidate's admission to the course. The thesis must be accompanied by a signed
statement by the candidate that the thesis is his or her own work except where
otherwise indicated.]

(x) Modern Chinese Studies

Candidates in Modern Chinese Studies must follow EITHER Track A (Social   20
Science) OR Track B (Humanities) throughout the entire course. Candidates are
required to spend a period of at least three months on an approved course of language
study in China or Taiwan after the qualifying examination at the end of the Trinity
Term of the first year, and before the start of the Hilary Term of the second year.

A. *Qualifying Examination*   25

The examination shall take place not later than the end of the third term from the
candidate's admission to the programme. **[For students starting before MT 2015:** Full
details of the Qualifying Examination will be provided in the examination conventions, which will be made available to the candidates from the eighth week of the first
term of the candidate's admission.] Candidates who fail one or more parts of the   30
Qualifying Examination may be allowed to retake that part or parts once at the end of
the Long Vacation of the first year of the course, except for **[For students starting
before MT 2015:** *Study of Modern China*] **[For students starting from MT 2015:** *Study
of Contemporary China*] which may be retaken at the end of Trinity Term of the first
year of the course. Candidates who fail the Final Examination elective paper taken   35
with the Qualifying Examination in the first year of the course may be allowed to
retake that part with the remainder of the Final Examination papers offered at the end
of the second year of the course.

The Qualifying Examination shall consist of three parts for Track A and two parts
for Track B, as follows: 40

(1) **[For students starting before MT 2015:** *Study of Modern China*] **[For students
starting from MT 2015:** *Study of Contemporary China*]

Each candidate will be required to follow a course of instruction on modern China.
Candidates will present themselves for examination in the core course Study of **[For
students starting before MT 2015:** Modern] **[For students starting from MT 2015:**   45
Contemporary] China at the beginning of Hilary Term of the first year.

(2) *Modern Chinese language (written and oral)*

All candidates must offer one written and one oral Chinese examination.
Candidates will be examined in Chinese I or Chinese II. Those who have followed
the Chinese II course will not be permitted to enter for the Chinese I examination.   50

Candidates shall present themselves for examination in Chinese language at the end of Trinity Term of the first year.

(3) *Research Methods for Area Studies* (Track A only)

[For students starting before MT 2015: All candidates are required to undertake an assessment in research methods for Asian studies, which is a series of assignments and/ or unseen written examinations as specified by the Oriental Studies Faculty Board. The forms of assessment, and the dates and times of submission, where applicable, will be notified to candidates by not later than Friday of noughth week of Michaelmas Full Term.] **[For students starting from MT 2015:** All candidates are required to undertake an assessment in research methods for Asian studies, which is a series of assignments and/or unseen written examinations as published in the course handbook. The forms of assessment, and the dates and times of submission, where applicable, will be published in the course handbook.]

Candidates shall also be required to offer one Final Examination Elective Paper at the end of Trinity Term of the first year (see below).

B. *Final Examination*

No candidate can pass the Final Examination unless he or she has already passed all parts of the first-year Qualifying Examination. The examination shall take place not later than the end of the third term of the second year from the candidate's admission to the M.Phil. degree programme, with the exception of the first of the two elective papers that shall be taken at the end of the first year of the programme. **[For students starting before MT 2015:** Full details of the examination will be provided in the examination conventions that will be made available to the candidates in the second term of the second year of the course. (see A. above).] In order to pass the degree all parts of the Final Examination must be passed. **[For students starting before MT 2015:** A candidate who fails the Final Examination will be permitted to retake it on one further occasion in the following year and only have to retake those parts of the examination that were failed.]

The Final Examination shall consist of:

(1) *Thesis*

The thesis will not be more than 20,000 words on a subject approved by the Oriental Studies Faculty Board.[1] **[For students starting before MT 2015:** Applications for approval of the thesis subject must reach the Secretary, Board of the Faculty of Oriental Studies, Oriental Institute, on or before Monday of nought week of Hilary Term in the second year of the course. Two typewritten or word-processed copies of the thesis must be delivered to the Examination Schools, High Street, Oxford, by Noon of Monday of the second week of Trinity Term of the second year from the candidate's admission to the programme. The thesis must be accompanied by a statement that it is the candidate's own work except where otherwise indicated. Successful candidates will be required to deposit one copy of the thesis in the Bodleian Library, and to sign a form stating whether they give permission for it to be consulted.]

(2) *Two Elective papers*

Candidates will be required to choose two elective papers offered as option courses under the M.Phil. or M.Sc. in **[For students starting before MT 2015:** Modern] **[For students starting from MT 2015:** Contemporary] Chinese Studies or under another Master's (M.Phil., M.Sc. or M.St.) degree programme in the University. The latter must be approved by the Board. The first elective paper will be taken at the end of the

---

[1] See general regulations for theses and special regulations for theses in Oriental Studies.

first year of the course, while the second paper will be taken at the end of the second year of the course. A list of papers approved for this purpose by the Oriental Studies Faculty Board will be available from the Course Director. The paper elected in the second year may not be the same as that taken in the first year. The examiners may, at their discretion, either require candidates to sit the standard examination paper for these elective papers, or offer a paper set specifically for students on the M.Phil. in Modern Chinese Studies.   5

(3) *Modern Chinese language (written and oral)*

Candidates will be required to take the written examination and an oral examination at the end of the Trinity Term of their final year. Candidates will be examined in Chinese I or Chinese II. Those who have followed the Chinese II course will not be permitted to enter for the Chinese I examination.   10

(4) *Modern China Humanities* (Track B only)

Candidates will be required to take a final written examination in the study of Modern China.   15

[For students starting before MT 2015: The examiners may examine any candidate viva voce.

The examiners may award a distinction for excellence in the final examination, but not in the qualifying examination.]

(xi) Tibetan and Himalayan Studies   20

A. *Qualifying Examination*

Candidates must pass a qualifying examination in Tibetan language at the end of the Hilary Term of their first year. This will consist of a written and an oral examination.

B. *Final Examination*   25

1. All candidates will be required to offer the following three papers, to offer a thesis of not more than 30,000 words, and to present themselves for an oral examination.

   (i) Unseen translation both from and into Tibetan.

   (ii) Translation from two set texts, which will include a modern Tibetan work   30
   and a classical work. The texts will be reported to the Faculty Board's
   second meeting of Trinity Full Term in the second year of the course[1].

   (iii) History and civilisation of Tibet and the Himalayas. Topics covered will
   include the history, politics, religion, and anthropology of the region.

C. *Thesis*   35

Candidates must submit a thesis of not more than 30,000 words on a topic selected by the candidate in consultation with his or her supervisor and approved by the faculty board.[1]

(xii) Modern South Asian Studies   40

A. *Qualifying Examination*

Candidates must pass a qualifying examination in Modern South Asian Studies not later than the end of the third term after that in which the candidate's name is first entered on the register of M.Phil. students. Unless exempted by the Board of the Faculty of Oriental Studies candidates will be required to offer the following papers: 45

1. A language examination in Hindi (Beginners or Advanced), Brajbhasha and Old Hindi Texts I, or a substitute core language, based on knowledge of grammar,

---

[1] See general regulations for theses and special regulations for theses in Oriental Studies.

translation and reading comprehension. (Teaching for some languages may not be available every year).

2. A general methodological paper on the history and culture of South Asia, to be assessed by three-hour examination.

Candidates, who will submit a take-home essay in their first year of the course to partially fulfil the requirements of (*c*) in the Final Examination, must enter for this paper in their first year. The mark for such essays will not be moderated until the candidate's final year of the course. **[For students starting before MT 2015:** Any failed Final Examination papers may be retaken on one occasion only, at the same time in the following academic year.]

B. *Final Examination*

1. All candidates must offer:

(*a*) one of the following language papers in Hindi (Advanced), Literary Hindi, Bengali, Brajbhasha & Old Hindi Texts, Sanskrit, Tibetan or Persian, based on knowledge of grammar, translation and reading comprehension. (Teaching for some languages may not be available every year).

(*b*) a thesis of not more than 20,000 words on a topic selected by the candidate in consultation with his or her supervisor and approved by the Faculty Board.[1] **[For students starting before MT 2015:** Applications for approval of the thesis subject must reach the Board of the Faculty of Oriental Studies, Oriental Institute, on or before Monday of nought week of Hilary Term in the second year of the course. Three typewritten copies of the thesis must be delivered to the Examination Schools, High Street, Oxford not later than noon on Friday of the third week of the Trinity Full Term in which the examination is to be taken.]

[For students starting before MT 2015: (*c*) three papers from (i)–(xvii) below. Instead of one of these papers, a candidate may offer a paper on a subject not included in the list below, with the approval of the board.

2. Optional Subjects

Courses marked with an asterisk are assessed by three-hour examination at the end of the second year. Others may be assessed either by three-hour examination at the end of the second year or on the basis of two essays of not more than 5,000 words each, on topics selected by the candidate from a list on the take-home examination paper, to be collected from the Faculty Office after 12 noon on the last Friday of term in which teaching for the paper is completed. The essays must be submitted to the Examination Schools, High Street, Oxford, by 12 noon on the Friday of noughth week of the term following that in which formal teaching for the Optional Subject is completed. When a paper assessed by essay is taught in the first year of the course, candidates must enter for the paper in the first year. Candidates are not allowed to enter for papers already chosen as unit 1 in the Qualifying Examination and I(a) in the Final Examination.

The Optional Subjects are:

    (i) Brajbhasha & Old Hindi Texts I

    (ii) Brajbhasha & Old Hindi Texts II

    (iii) Advanced Hindi

    (iv) Urdu Literary Texts

    (v) History and Civilisation of Tibet and the Himalayas (Paper (iii) in the M.Phil. in Oriental Studies (xi) *Tibetan and Himalayan Studies*)

    (vi) The Social Anthropology of a Selected Region: South Asia (Paper (i) in the M.Phil. in Social Anthropology)

    (vii) Societies and economies in India 1600–1800

    (viii) Aspects of social change in South Asia, c. 1860 to the Present (Advanced Option (ii) in the M.St. in Global and Imperial History)

---

[1] See general regulations for theses and special regulations for theses in Oriental Studies.

    (ix) Islamic History in South Asia
     (x) Scientific knowledge systems and their history in India
    (xi) History and Politics of South Asia (Paper (e) in the M.Phil. in Politics)
    (xii) Gender and Society in India, c. 1800 to the present
   (xiii) Material and visual culture of South Asia
   (xiv) Approaches to the history of Hinduism in India
    (xv) Shaivism
   (xvi) History of Medicine in South Asia
  (xvii) Gender and experience in Hindi Literature
 (xviii) History of Afghanistan c. 1900 to the present
   (xix) Any other subject approved by the faculty board
       Teaching for some optional subjects may not be available in every year.
3. The examiners may award a distinction for excellence in the whole examination.
4. A candidate who fails the examination will be permitted to retake it on one
further occasion only, not later than one year after the initial attempt. Such a
candidate whose thesis has been of a satisfactory standard may resubmit the
same piece of work, while a candidate who has reached a satisfactory standard
on the written papers will not be required to retake that part of the examination.]

[For students starting from MT 2015: (*c*) three papers from a list published in the
Course Handbook. Instead of one of the papers on the list, a candidate may offer a
paper on a subject with the approval of the board. Teaching for some optional subjects
may not be available in every year.

The papers can be assessed either by a three hour examination paper at the end of
the second year or a take-home examination paper. The method of examination will
be published in the course handbook. Candidates are required to submit two essays of
no more than 5000 words each, on topics selected by the candidate from a list on the
take-home examination paper. The list of topics will be published after 12noon on the
last Friday of term in which teaching for the paper is completed. Candidates will be
contacted with details of how to collect or access the questions. The essays must be
submitted to the Examination Schools, High Street, Oxford, by 12 noon on the Friday
of noughth week of the term following that in which formal teaching for the Optional
Subject is completed. When a paper assessed by essay is taught in the first year of the
course, candidates must enter for the paper in the first year. Candidates are not
allowed to enter for papers already chosen as unit 1 in the Qualifying Examination
and I(a) in the Final Examination.]

(xiii) Traditional East Asia: Classical, Medieval, and Early Modern

A. *Qualifying Examination*

Every candidate will be required, unless exempted by the Board of the Faculty of
Oriental Studies, to satisfy the examiners in an examination, to be known as the
Qualifying Examination for the M.Phil. in Traditional East Asia: Classical, Medieval,
and Early Modern, not later than the end of the third term after that in which the
candidate's name is first entered on the Register of M.Phil. Students. All candidates
must offer:

1. A language examination in modern Chinese or modern Japanese or modern
    Korean

2. A language examination in classical Chinese or classical Japanese or middle
    Korean

3. A written examination in Traditional East Asia

4. Three submitted essays on traditional East Asia. The essays, which must be of
    not more than 2,500 words each, must be written by the candidate, one in each of

the three terms of the first year, and must be chosen by the candidate to represent the candidate's best written performance in that term. Each essay must be submitted to the Examination Schools, High Street, Oxford, by 12 noon on the Friday of ninth week of the term in which the paper is taught.

B. *Final Examination*

This shall be taken in the Trinity Term of the academic year following that in which the candidate's name is first entered on the Register of M.Phil. Students or, with the approval of the faculty board, in a subsequent year. All candidates must offer:

1. Prescribed texts in one of the following: (i) Classical Chinese; (ii) Classical Japanese; (iii) Middle Korean; (iv) Classical Chinese and Classical Japanese; (v) Classical Chinese and Middle Korean.

2. Research Bibliography and Methodology on one of the following: (i) China; (ii) Japan; (iii) Korea. This paper will be set as a take-home examination. The answer or answers should be typed and presented in proper scholarly form. The question paper will be distributed to candidates in the Oriental Institute at 10 a.m. on **[For students starting before MT 2015:** Monday of eighth week] **[For students starting from MT 2015:** Tuesday of Week 9] of the Trinity Term in which the Final Examination is to be taken. The completed examination must be handed in to the Examination Schools no later than 12 noon on Friday of the same week.

3. Thesis. Candidates must submit a thesis of not be more than 30,000 words on a subject selected by the candidate in consultation with his or her supervisor and approved by the Board of the Faculty of Oriental Studies.[1]

4. The examiners will also examine every candidate viva voce unless excused.

[For students starting from MT 2015: (xiv) Buddhist Studies

A. *Qualifying examination*

Each candidate must pass a qualifying examination not later than the end of the third term from the commencement of the course. The examination will consist of two papers:

(i) A three-hour examination in the chosen primary Buddhist Language (either Sanskrit, Tibetan, or Classical Chinese).

(ii) A three-hour examination on basic aspects of Buddhist thought and history.

B. *Final examination*

In the Trinity Term of their second year, all candidates must offer:

(i) an advanced language paper consisting in a translation from seen and unseen texts in the chosen primary Buddhist Language, to be assessed by a three-hour examination

(ii) a thesis of not more than 20,000 words on a subject approved by the Board[1]

(iii) a paper on Approaches to the study of Buddhism, to be assessed by three-hour examination

(iv) *Either*

(*a*) a language paper in a second primary Buddhist language (either Sanskrit, Tibetan, or Classical Chinese), to be assessed by three-hour examination. The second primary Buddhist language can be studied either at a basic or at an advanced level. The former will be assessed by a three-hour examination in the chosen second primary Buddhist language (as for paper (ii) of the

---

[1] See general regulations for theses and special regulations for theses in Oriental Studies.

Qualifying examination); the latter by a translation from seen and unseen texts in the chosen second primary Buddhist language, to be assessed by a three-hour examination (as for paper (i) of the Final examination). Students who intend to study a second primary Buddhist language at an advanced level must satisfy the Faculty Board that they possess an adequate knowl-   5
edge of the chosen language.

Or

(*b*) A paper chosen from a list published in the course handbook, assessed as specified by the course instructor. Applications for approval of the chosen topic must be sent to the Senior Academic Administrator or before the   10
Monday in second week of Michaelmas Full Term preceding the examination.]

Master of Philosophy in Philosophical Theology

(*See also the general notice at the commencement of these regulations.*)

The regulations made by the Board of the Faculty of Theology and Religion are as follows: 15

Candidates will be admitted to take the examination as defined below in a specific year. In exceptional circumstances candidates may be allowed to take an examination later than one to which they were admitted. Permission for this must be sought from the faculty board not later than Monday of the week before the first week of the Trinity Term in which the examination was to have been taken. The application must   20
have the support of the candidate's college and be accompanied by a statement from the supervisor.

Candidates shall be required:

(*a*) To present themselves for a written examination in three of the papers pre-scribed below, the selection to depend on their previous qualifications;   25

(*b*) to present a thesis[1] of not more than 30,000 words on a topic in philosophical theology to be approved by the faculty board (the thesis must be accompanied by a signed statement by the candidate that the thesis is his or her own work except where otherwise indicated; successful candidates may be required to deposit one copy of the thesis in the Bodleian and to sign a form stating whether they give permission for the   30
thesis to be consulted);

(*c*) to present themselves for a viva voce examination unless individually dispensed by the examiners (no candidate will be failed without a viva).

1. *Philosophy of Religion*

with syllabus for examination the same as that for essays for the B.Phil. in   35
Philosophy.

2. *Either Moral Philosophy*

or Metaphysics and Theory of Knowledge

or Philosophical Logic and Philosophy of Language

or Philosophy of Science   40

or Philosophy of Mind and of Action

with syllabus for examination the same as that for essays for the B.Phil. in Philosophy.

3. *History of Philosophical Theology*

The paper will contain questions on philosophical influences on theology during the   45
patristic period, the early medieval period, and the period 1760–1860. Candidates are

---

[1] See general regulations for theses and special regulations for theses in Oriental Studies.

required to show knowledge of two of the three periods, and, within each of those two periods, of some of the principal relevant writings, viz. for the patristic period of works of Origen and Augustine, for the early medieval period of works of Anselm and Aquinas, and for the period 1760–1860 of works of Kant, Kierkegaard, and Schleiermacher. Study of texts in the original languages will not be required.

4. Either *The Development of Christian Doctrine to* AD *787* or *Theology in Western Europe from Gabriel Biel to Jacob Arminius*

as specified for the M.Phil. in Theology (paper 1 of Section A and paper 1 of Section C of the Christian Doctrine option).

The Examiners may award a Distinction for excellence in the whole examination.

If it is the opinion of the examiners that the work done by a candidate is not of sufficient merit to qualify him or her for the Degree of M.Phil. but is nevertheless of sufficient merit to qualify him or her for the Degree of Master of Studies in Philosophical Theology, the candidate shall be given the option of resitting the M.Phil. examination under the appropriate regulation, or of being granted permission to supplicate for the Degree of Master of Studies.

Master of Philosophy in Politics (Comparative Government, Political Theory, European Politics and Society)

(*See also the general notice at the commencement of these regulations. The current edition of the Student Handbook contains an elaborated version of these regulations.*)

The regulations made by the Politics Graduate Studies Committee are as follows:

[For students starting before MT 2015: *Qualifying Test*

Each candidate must pass a Qualifying Test at the end of the third term from the beginning of the course in the two *compulsory* papers specified for their course, unless given exemption by the Politics Graduate Studies Committee.

In *Comparative Government* the two compulsory papers are Comparative Government and Research Methods in Political Science.

In *European Politics and Society* the two compulsory papers are European Governance and Research Methods in Political Science.

In *Political Theory* the two compulsory papers are Theory of Politics and Research Methods in Political Theory.

Candidates who fail the written examination part of the Qualifying Test will normally be allowed to retake it before the beginning of the next academic year.

Compulsory papers:

(*a*) *Research Methods*

(i) *Research Methods in Political Science* (Compulsory paper for Comparative Government and European Politics and Society students only). Candidates will satisfactorily complete a programme of core and optional research methods training, as specified in the *Student Handbook*, and will also produce a Research Design Proposal of between 4,000 and 6,000 words, excluding bibliography, on the subject of the student's proposed M.Phil. thesis. Two hard copies of the Research Design Proposal, together with a copy on CD, must be submitted to the Examination Schools by noon on the Friday of sixth week of Trinity Term. It must be accompanied by a separate signed declaration that it is the candidate's own work except where otherwise indicated and that it has not previously been submitted for assessment, either at Oxford or at another institution. The Director of Graduate Studies in Politics shall draw the attention of the examiners to the names of any candidates who have failed to complete their research methods training to a satisfactory level of quality, and the examiners may require candidates to retake the course or a specified part thereof.

(ii) *Research Methods in Political Theory* (Compulsory paper for Political Theory students only). Candidates will satisfactorily complete a programme of core and optional research methods training, as specified in the *Student Handbook*, and will also produce a Research Design Proposal of between 4,000 and 6,000 words, excluding bibliography, on the subject of the student's proposed M.Phil. thesis. Two copies of the Research Design Proposal, together with a copy on CD, must be submitted to the Examination Schools by noon on the Friday of sixth week of Trinity Term. It must be accompanied by a separate signed declaration that it is the candidate's own work except where otherwise indicated and that it has not previously been submitted for assessment, either at Oxford or at another institution. The Director of Graduate Studies in Politics shall draw the attention of the examiners to the names of any candidates who have failed to complete their research methods training to a satisfactory level of quality, and the examiners may require candidates to retake the course or a specified part thereof.

Candidates in European Politics and Society will be required to have a working (i.e. good reading) knowledge of two of the following languages of the European Union: viz. English, and one of French, German, Italian, Polish, or Spanish. Unless exempted by the Politics Graduate Studies Committee, candidates will be tested in the language or languages they propose to offer by the end of their third term. Candidates who fail the test will normally be allowed to retake the test before the beginning of the next academic year.

(*b*) *Comparative Government*

(Compulsory paper for Comparative Government students only)

The theory and practice of government in modern states.

(*c*) *Theory of Politics*

(Compulsory paper for Political Theory students only)

A critical examination of political concepts and theories, including social concepts and theories with political relevance.

(*d*) *European Governance*

(Compulsory paper for European Politics and Society students only)

The constitutions and formal structure of governments in European states, including the UK, and the theory and practice of integration in Europe.

The marks achieved by candidates in the two compulsory papers of the Qualifying Test will be carried forward to be considered by the examiners in the second year alongside the marks achieved in the Final Examination.

Final examination

No candidate shall enter the final examination unless he or she has already passed the Qualifying Test. In the final examination every candidate must offer:

(1) A thesis[1] of not more than 30,000 words, excluding bibliography. Two hard copies, together with a copy on CD or USB flash drive, must be submitted to the Examination Schools by noon on the Monday of first week of Trinity Term. The thesis must be accompanied by a separate signed declaration that it is the

---

[1] See the general regulations concerning the preparation and dispatch of theses. Candidates are reminded that if after completing the M.Phil. they are accepted by the Politics Graduate Studies Committee for registration for the D.Phil., work submitted for the Degree of M.Phil. may subsequently be incorporated in a thesis submitted for the Degree of D.Phil.

candidate's own work except where otherwise indicated and that it has not previously been submitted for assessment, either at Oxford or at another institution. After the examination process is complete, each successful candidate must deposit one hardbound copy of their thesis in the Bodleian Library.

(2) Two subject papers taken from the approved list of optional subjects in Politics, as published in the *Student Handbook* by the Politics Graduate Studies Committee on Monday of first week of Michaelmas Term each academic year to apply to candidates being examined in the Trinity Term of that year. Candidates should note that the Politics subjects available in any particular year will depend on the availability of teaching resources. Not all subjects will be available in every year and restrictions may be placed on the number of candidates permitted to offer certain subjects in any particular year.

Candidates may, with the special permission of the Politics Graduate Studies Committee, offer subjects beyond the approved list of Politics subjects. Applications must be made by the last Friday of the Trinity Term preceding that in which the examination is to be taken, and must be supported by the student's supervisor. Supervisors should ensure that applications are submitted as early as possible so that if approval is not given, the candidate has sufficient time to choose an alternative.

The Examiners may award a distinction for excellence in the whole examination on the basis of the work submitted to them in both the Qualifying Test and the Final Examination.]

[**For students starting from MT 2015:** Each candidate must pass the Qualifying Test at the end of the third term from the beginning of the course. The Qualifying Test consists of two *compulsory* papers (unless a candidate is granted exemption by the Politics Graduate Studies Committee):

(1) A single three hour written examination paper testing knowledge of the candidate's core subject (*Theory of Politics* or *Comparative Government* or *European Governance*).

Theory of Politics

Compulsory paper for Political Theory students only. A critical examination of political concepts and theories, including social concepts and theories with political relevance.

Comparative Government

Compulsory paper for Comparative Government students only. The theory and practice of government in modern states.

European Governance

Compulsory paper for European Politics and Society students only. The theory and practice of government in European states, including the UK, and the theory and practice of integration in Europe.

(2) A research methods paper (*Research Methods in Political Science* or *Research Methods in Political Theory*).

Research Methods in Political Science

Compulsory paper for Comparative Government and European Politics and Society students only.

Research Methods in Political Theory

Compulsory paper for Political Theory students only.

Research Methods in Political Science and Research Methods in Political Theory are assessed in the following way. The candidate must submit:

(i) A Research Design Proposal of between 4000 and 6000 words, excluding bibliography, on the subject of the student's proposed M.Phil. thesis. Two copies of the Research Design Proposal, together with a copy on CD or USB flash drive, must be submitted to the Examination Schools by noon on the Friday of sixth week of Trinity Term. It must be accompanied by a separate signed declaration that it is the candidate's own work except where otherwise indicated and that it has not previously been submitted for assessment, either at Oxford or at another institution.

(ii) Research methods training coursework. Candidates will satisfactorily complete a programme of core and optional research methods training, as specified in the Student Handbook. Further details regarding these courses are provided in the Student Handbook.

For a candidate for the degree of M.Phil. to pass the Qualifying Test and proceed to the second year of study, the candidate must pass: the research methods paper (all elements of coursework and the Research Design Proposal) and the written examination.

Candidates who fail the written examination (paper (1) above) will normally be able to retake it before the beginning of the next academic year.

The mark for the written examination part of the Qualifying Test (paper (1) above) is carried forward and included in the final classification process for the degree of M.Phil.

Final Examination

No candidate shall enter the Final Examination unless he or she has already passed the Qualifying Test. In the Final Examination every candidate must offer:

(1) A thesis of not more than 30,000 words, excluding bibliography. Two hard copies, together with a copy on CD or USB flash drive, must be submitted to the Examination Schools by noon on the Monday of first week of Trinity Term. It must be accompanied by a separate signed declaration that it is the candidate's own work except where otherwise indicated and that it has not previously been submitted for assessment, either at Oxford or at another institution. After the examination process is complete, each successful candidate must deposit one hardbound copy of their thesis in the Bodleian Library.

(2) Two papers, taken from the approved list of optional subjects in Politics, as published in the *Student Handbook* by the Politics Graduate Studies Committee on Monday of first week of Michaelmas Term each academic year (to apply to candidates being examined in the Trinity Term of that year). Candidates should note that the Politics subjects available in any particular year will depend on the availability of teaching resources. Not all subjects will be available in every year, and restrictions may be placed on the number of candidates permitted to offer certain subjects in any particular year.

Candidates may, with special permission of the Politics Graduate Studies Committee, offer subjects outside this list. Applications must be made by the last Friday of the Trinity Term preceding that in which the examination is to be taken, and must be supported by the candidate's supervisor. Supervisors should ensure that applications are submitted as early as possible so that if approval is not granted the candidate has sufficient time to choose an alternative. When candidates sit optional papers offered at departments other than the Department of Politics and International Relations, they are bound by the regulations of the M.Phil. in Politics. The Examiners may award a distinction for excellence in the whole examination, on the basis of the work submitted to them in both the Qualifying Test and the Final Examination.]

Master of Philosophy in Russian and East European Studies

(*See also the general notice at the commencement of these regulations.*)

The regulations made by the Russian and East European Studies Management Committee are as follows:

First year examinations

There will be three compulsory papers to be taken at the end of the first year of the course.

1. An examination paper on *Twentieth Century Russian, Soviet and East European History.*

2. An examination paper on **[For students starting before MT 2015:** *Politics, Economics and International Relations of the Former Soviet Union and Eastern Europe.*] **[For students starting from MT 2015:** *Contemporary Russian and East European Studies Part 1.*]

3. An examination paper on **[For students starting before MT 2015:** *Society and Culture in the Former Soviet Union and Eastern Europe.*] **[For students starting from MT 2015:** *Contemporary Russian and East European Studies Part 2.*]

The papers shall be set and administered by the examiners appointed to examine the M.Phil. in Russian and East European Studies. The examination will be held in the eighth week of Trinity Full Term.

Candidates who pass these qualifying papers may proceed to the second year of the course and take the final examination at the end of the second year. Candidates who fail one or more of the examination papers may, by permission of the Russian and East European Studies Management Committee, proceed to the second year of the course and resit the failed papers during the final examination. All candidates will also be required to have demonstrated competence in Methods and Language as specified in Methods Requirement and Language Requirement.

Final Examination

(*a*) a thesis of at least 25,000 words but not more than 30,000 words on a subject approved by the Management Committee for Russian and East European Studies, to be delivered to the Examination Schools, High Street, Oxford, by Monday in the fourth week of Trinity Term in which the final examination is taken. The thesis must be accompanied by a statement that the thesis is the candidate's own work except where otherwise indicated.

(*b*) two subjects (optional courses) chosen from a list, which is approved annually by the Russian and East European Studies Management Committee. The selection of subjects have to be approved by the Russian and East European Studies Management Committee in Trinity Term, Year 1. A candidate who fails the Final Examination may enter again, on one subsequent occasion, usually in Trinity Term, provided that this is still within the twelve terms of his or her registration.

The examiners may award a distinction for excellence in the whole examination.

Methods Requirement. Each candidate will be required to participate in training in methodology (quantitative and qualitative) and research skills related to Russian and East European Studies and to have achieved pass marks for the assessed components, as specified in the Notes of Guidance of the year of Matriculation of the Candidates.

Language Requirement. Before admission to the final examination all candidates will be required to pass a language qualifying exam on the region, which is usually in Russian. In special circumstances permission may be granted for sitting an exam in another language. The specific arrangements for the provision and methods of assessment of language training are governed by the Examination Conventions and Notes of Guidance of the year of matriculation of the candidates.

Master of Philosophy in Slavonic Studies
(*See also the general notice at the commencement of these regulations.*)

The regulations made by the Board of the Faculty of Medieval and Modern Languages are as follows:

1. Candidates will be required to satisfy the examiners in a Qualifying Examination 5
identical with that for the M.St. in Slavonic Studies, in the academic year in which
their names are first entered on the Register of M.Phil. Students, before proceeding to
the final examination for the M.Phil. in the following year. Holders of the M.St. in
Slavonic Studies are exempt from this Qualifying Examination.

2. In the final examination for the M.Phil. each candidate will be required to take 10
two subjects from the Schedules listed for the M.St., excluding Schedule 2 v.
Candidates must take at least one subject from Schedule 2 i–iv, if they have not
already done so for the M.St. or for the Qualifying Examination. Candidates may
not repeat subjects which they have taken for the M.St. or for the Qualifying
Examination, nor take subjects from Schedules from which they have already taken 15
two subjects for the M.St. or for the Qualifying Examination. Candidates may not
take subjects which they have already studied in a first degree course.

3. Each candidate will be required to present a thesis of approximately 20,000
words and not more than 25,000 words. Candidates are required to register the subject
area or title of their thesis with the Modern Languages Graduate Office by the end of 20
the fourth week of Hilary Term of their second year. The subject of the thesis should
fall within the area of Slavonic languages and literatures. Three copies of the M.Phil.
thesis must be submitted to the Examination Schools by noon on Thursday of Week 6 of
Trinity Term of the second year. Work submitted in the thesis for the Degree of M.Phil.
may subsequently be incorporated in a thesis submitted for the Degree of D.Phil. 25

4. Candidates must present themselves for oral examination unless dispensed by the
examiners.

5. Candidates will be expected to be able to read secondary literature in at least one
European language other than English and the Slavonic languages, and may be
required to demonstrate this ability. Candidates will also be expected to attend a 30
course of lectures on bibliographical, library, and archival resources in the field of
Slavonic Studies.

6. If it is the opinion of the examiners that the work done by a candidate is not of
sufficient merit to qualify him for the Degree of M.Phil. but that nevertheless his or her
work in the Qualifying Examination was of sufficient merit to qualify him or her for 35
the Degree of M.St. in Slavonic Studies, the candidate shall be given the option of
resitting the M.Phil. examination under the appropriate regulation or of being granted
permission to supplicate for the Degree of Master of Studies.

7. The examiners may award a distinction for excellence in the whole examination.

Master of Philosophy in Social Anthropology 40
(*See also the general notice at the commencement of these regulations.*)

The Social Sciences Divisional Board shall elect for the supervision of the course a
Standing Committee, namely the Teaching Committee of the School of
Anthropology, which shall have power to arrange lectures and other instruction.
The course director shall be responsible to that committee. 45

The examination shall consist of the following:

1. *Qualifying Examination*

Every candidate will be required to satisfy the examiners in an examination for
which, if he or she passes at the appropriate level, he or she will be allowed to proceed
to the second year of the M.Phil. Candidates must follow a course of instruction in 50

Social Anthropology for at least three terms, and will, when entering for the examinations, be required to produce a certificate from their supervisor to this effect. The Qualifying Examination shall be taken in the Trinity Term of the academic year in which the candidate's name is first entered on the Register of M.Phil. students or, with the approval of the divisional board, in a subsequent year.

Each candidate will be required to satisfy the examiners in papers I-IV on the syllabus described in the Schedule for the M.Sc. in Social Anthropology, and governed by regulation 4 for that degree.

2. *Final Examination*

This shall be taken in the Trinity Term of the academic year following that in which the candidate's name is first entered on the Register of M.Phil. Students or, with the approval of the Teaching Committee, in a subsequent year.

Each candidate shall be required:

(i) to present himself or herself for written examination in one of the optional areas or topics available for that year, other than that taken by the candidate in the M.Phil. Qualifying Examination the previous year;

(ii) to submit to the Chair of Examiners not later than noon on Tuesday of the fifth week of Trinity Term an essay of 5,000 words (two copies) in the field of general Social Anthropology, on a topic to be selected from a list set by the examiners at the beginning of the third week of Trinity Term;

(iii) to submit a thesis in accordance with the regulations below;

(iv) to present himself or herself for oral examination if required by the examiners.

3. *Thesis*[1]

Each candidate shall be required to submit a thesis of not more than 30,000 words (excluding references and appendices) on a subject approved by the supervisor. He or she shall send to the Teaching Committee of the School of Anthropology, with the written approval of his or her supervisor, the proposed title of the thesis, together with a paragraph describing its scope, by noon on the Monday of second week of the Michaelmas Term in the academic year following that in which his or her name was entered on the Register of M.Phil. Students. The thesis (three copies) must be typewritten and delivered to the Examination Schools, High Street, Oxford, not later than noon on Tuesday of the second week of the Trinity Term in the academic year in which the Final Examination is taken. The dissertation shall be provided with an abstract of up to 250 words, to be placed immediately after the title page. The word count shall be stated on the outside front cover of the thesis.

The examiners shall require a successful candidate to deposit a copy of his or her thesis in the Tylor Library. If the thesis is superseded by a D.Phil. thesis by the same student partly using the same material, the Teaching Committee of the School of Anthropology may authorise the withdrawal of the M.Phil. thesis from the Tylor Library. Such candidates will be required to sign a form stating whether they give permission for their thesis to be consulted.

The examiners may award a distinction for excellence in the whole examination.

If it is the opinion of the examiners that the work which has been required of a candidate is not of sufficient merit to qualify him or her for the Degree of M.Phil. the candidate shall be given the option of resitting the M.Phil. examination under the appropriate regulation.

---

[1] See the general regulation concerning the preparation and dispatch of theses.

4. *Resits*

In order to pass the degree, a student must pass all its assessed components. Where one or more components are failed, the student will be given the opportunity to re-sit or re-submit them once, as the case may be. Any subsequent award of the degree on successful completion of all the assessed components may be delayed by up to three 5 terms, i.e. until the Examination Board next meets.

Master of Philosophy in Sociology and Demography

(*See also the general notice at the commencement of these regulations.*)

The regulations made by the Graduate Studies Committee of the Department of Sociology are as follows: 10

Qualifying test

Every candidate must pass a qualifying test at the end of the third term from the beginning of the course in the four compulsory papers, Methods of Social Research, Sociological Analysis, Demographic Analysis, Life Course Research and one Optional Paper from the list of optional papers, specified by the Department of 15 Sociology. This list will be published annually by Friday of the third week of Michaelmas Full Term in the Department of Sociology. Where coursework forms a part of the assessment, two typewritten copies must be delivered to the Examination Schools, High Street, Oxford, by noon on Friday of the eighth week of the Trinity Full Term in which the examination is to be taken unless otherwise specified in 20 the Graduate Studies Handbook, or, in the case of options taken outside the Department of Sociology, as specified by the department or faculty concerned. The examiners may examine candidates viva voce. Candidates who fail the qualifying test are allowed to retake the test before the beginning of the first week of the next academic year. Such candidates are required to retake only those elements of the 25 qualifying test that they have failed. Candidates who fail only one out of the five papers may, by permission of the Sociology Graduate Studies Committee, proceed to the second year of the course and re-sit the failed paper at the same time as the final examination. No candidate will be permitted to re-sit any of the compulsory papers more than once. 30

Final Examination

Every candidate must offer:

1. One further optional paper from the list of optional papers specified by the Department of Sociology;

2. A paper in the Replication project as specified in the Graduate Studies 35 Handbook;

3. A thesis[1] of not more than 30,000 words on a topic within the subject of the course, to be specified jointly by supervisor and student; two typewritten copies to be delivered to the Examination Schools, High St, Oxford, by noon on Friday of the sixth week of the Trinity Full Term in which the examination is to be taken. Successful 40 candidates will be required to deposit a copy of their thesis in the Department of Sociology. Candidates are warned that they should avoid repetition in their theses of material used in their option papers and that substantial repetition may be penalised.

The examiners may examine any candidate viva voce.

The examiners may award a Distinction for excellence in the whole examination on the 45 basis of the material submitted to them in both the qualifying and the final examination.

---

[1] See the general regulations concerning the preparation and dispatch of theses.

Compulsory Papers

Methods of Social Research

The satisfactory completion of a course of practical work including (i) statistical methods, and (ii) research design. Candidates shall submit reports of the practical work completed to the Examination Schools, High Street, Oxford, by the following   5
deadlines: for (i) statistical methods by 12 noon on Friday of the fifth week of the second term of the course; for (ii) research design by 12 noon on Monday of the first week of the third term of the course. The reports must be accompanied by a statement that they are the candidate's own work except where otherwise indicated. For (i) statistical methods, candidates will also be required to take a two-hour in-class test to   10
be held on the Friday preceding the first week of the second term of the course. The Director of Graduate Studies, or a deputy, shall draw to the attention of the examiners the names of any candidates who have failed to complete to a satisfactory level of quality the course of practical work, and the examiners may require candidates to retake the course or a specified part thereof. The reports of practical work shall be   15
available for inspection by the examiners.

Sociological Analysis

The object and objective of sociological analysis in relation to other social sciences. The nature of different sociological explanations, their possibilities and methodological implications. The relevance of rationality and of its limits with regard to both   20
individual agents and institutions. The interrelationships between description and explanation, theory and empirical data, macro- and micro-levels of analysis as they emerge from areas of major sociological enquiry.

Demographic Analysis

The object and objective of demographic analysis in relation to other social sciences.   25
Core demographic concepts, their related indicators and methods; and their application to the study of populations and population change. Demographic transition; the Second Demographic Transition; Fertility; Mortality; Migration; Life Tables; Temporal dimensions in demography; Demographic data.; Population projections.

Life Course Research   30

The theoretical foundation and practical implementation of the multilevel, actor-oriented life course approach in its application to demographic and sociological problems; the theoretical implications of life course designs; methods, design, and statistical techniques of life course research; key life course events (including births, deaths, migrations and relationship transitions); the role of the historical and geogra-   35
phical context for individual life courses; the role of kinship and network ties; and the role of human development (e.g. generalising the traditional demographic emphasis on period, cohort and age). Candidates shall submit research essay or reports as specified in the graduate studies handbook.

Master of Philosophy in Theology   40

[For students starting before MT 2015: 1. All candidates will be required to follow a course of instruction and directed research for six terms and present themselves for examination in one of the following subjects: Old Testament; New Testament; Christian Doctrine (one of seven subsections, as presented below); Ecclesiastical History; and Christian Ethics.   45

2. Candidates will be expected to attend such lectures and seminars as their supervisor shall recommend.

3. The examination shall consist of:
  (i) two three-hour written examinations (or in Old Testament, route II, one written examination), as prescribed in the regulations for each course.   50

(ii) *either* three essays of not more than 5,000 words each, *or* one long essay of not more than 15,000 words, on topics proposed by the candidate with the approval of his or her supervisor, and accepted by the Theology and Religion Faculty Board.

(iii) a dissertation of not more than 30,000 words on a topic proposed by the candidate with the approval of his or her supervisor, and accepted by the Theology and Religion Faculty Board. For candidates intending to proceed to doctoral study, the topic of the thesis should be such as to provide a foundation for doctoral research.

4. Proposals for essays must be submitted for consideration by the Faculty's Graduate Studies Committee (GSC) not later than Monday of Week 5 of Trinity Term in Year 1. The dissertation proposal must be submitted for consideration by the GSC by Monday of Week 0 of Michaelmas Term in Year 2. All of these proposals should comprise a title, a short statement of how the subject will be treated, a bibliography of core texts (both primary and secondary), and the signature of the supervisor indicating his or her approval. The titles and content of the essays and dissertation should not substantially overlap with each other.

5. Two copies of the completed essays, together with a signed statement by the candidate that it is his or her own work, must be submitted for examination not later than fourteen days before the first day of the written examination in Trinity Term of Year 2. The written examinations take place in Week 10 or 11 of Trinity Term in Year 2.

Two copies of the completed dissertation, together with a signed statement by the candidate that it is his or her own work, must be submitted for examination by Friday of Week 8 of Trinity Term.

Candidates must not put their names on the written examination papers or on any submitted work. All submitted work must be printed and sent in a parcel bearing the words, 'M.Phil. in Theology', to the Chair of Examiners, c/o the Examination Schools, High Street, Oxford.

Each candidate will be required to present himself or herself for an oral (viva voce) examination, which will take place within a few days of the written examination, and may include discussion of the candidate's work in any of the three elements listed above.

I OLD TESTAMENT

Two routes are possible, route I involving two written examinations and route II only one:

I.

(i) Candidates take a written examination in Prescribed Hebrew Texts, and then another in *either* unseen passages from the Hebrew Bible *or* the Aramaic portions of the Old Testament *or* passages from the Septuagint.

(ii) In addition they write *either* a long essay (up to 15,000 words) *or* three short essays (up to 5,000 words each) in one of the following subject areas: the Literature of the Old Testament and Apocrypha in its Historical Setting; Old Testament Theology; the History and Principles of Biblical Study.

II.

(i) Candidates take a written examination in Prescribed Hebrew Texts.

(ii) In addition they write *both* a long essay (up to 15,000 words) in one of the following subject areas *and* three short essays (up to 5,000 words) in another: the Literature of the Old Testament and Apocrypha in its Historical Setting; Old Testament Theology; the History and Principles of Biblical Study.

I. and II.

(iii) All candidates offer a dissertation of up to 30,000 words.

The prescribed texts will be listed in the Course Regulations for the Master of Philosophy in Theology for the year in which the candidates commenced their course.

II New Testament

(i) There will be two written examinations, one in the Religion and Literature of the New Testament: the Four Gospels and Acts in Greek, and the other in the Religion and Literature of the New Testament: The Epistles and Apocalypse in Greek. Candidates will be required to translate and to comment on matters of literary, historical and theological importance from a selection of these prescribed texts.

(ii) In addition they write *either* a long essay (up to 15,000 words) *or* three short essays (up to 5,000 words each) in one of the following subject areas: New Testament Theology. Varieties of Judaism, 200 BC–CE 200; the History and Principles of Biblical Study.

(iii) All candidates offer a dissertation of up to 30,000 words.

III Christian Doctrine

Section A. History of Doctrine: Patristic Theology
(i) There will be two written examinations:

1. The Development of Christian Doctrine to AD 451. Candidates will be expected to write three essays on different topics, showing knowledge of the main lines of development of Christian Doctrine, and discussing particular developments in relation to the historical conditions which influenced them.

2. *Either* (a) Hellenistic Philosophy and Christian Theology *or* (b) Christology of the Patristic Era. In each case the examination will consist of two essays on different topics and passages for translation and comment. Candidates may choose whether to translate and comment on Greek or Latin texts.

The prescribed texts for both examination papers will be listed in the Course Regulations for the Master of Philosophy in Theology for the year in which the candidates commenced their course.

(ii) Candidates will write *either* one long essay (up to 15,000 words) *or* three short essays (up to 5000 words each) on a topic or topics falling within the Patristic era.

(iii) All candidates offer a dissertation of up to 30,000 words.

Section B. History of Doctrine: Scholastic Theology
(i) There will be two written examinations:

1. Doctrine and Methods. Candidates will be expected to show knowledge of major theologians in the period 1050–1350 by commenting on passages from prescribed texts in Latin and writing two essays on different topics.

2. The Thought of Aquinas. Candidates will be expected to display knowledge of the thought of Thomas Aquinas by commenting on passages from prescribed texts in Latin and writing two essays on different topics.

The prescribed texts for both examination papers will be listed in the Course Regulations for the Master of Philosophy in Theology for the year in which the candidates commenced their course.

(ii) Candidates will write *either* one long essay (up to 15,000 words) *or* three short essays (up to 5000 words each) on a topic or topics falling within the Scholastic era.

(iii) All candidates offer a dissertation of up to 30,000 words.

Section C. History of Doctrine: Reformation Theology
(i) There will be two written examinations:

1. Theology in Western Europe from Gabriel Biel to Jacob Arminius. Candidates will be expected to write three essays on different topics, showing familiarity with the

tenets of the most seminal theologians of this era and discussing them in relation to the political, social and economic tendencies of the age.

2. Protestant and Tridentine Teaching on the Doctrines of Grace, Freewill and Predestination. Candidates will be expected to write three essays on different topics.

(ii) Candidates will write *either* one long essay (up to 15,000 words) *or* three short essays (up to 5,000 words each) on a topic or topics falling within the Reformation era;

(iii) All candidates offer a dissertation of up to 30,000 words.

Section D. Issues in Theology with special reference to Patristic Theology
(i) There will be two written examinations:

1. Methods and Styles in Theology from 1780 to the Present. Candidates will be expected to write three essays on different topics, discussing problems of theological method, showing a critical understanding of the main themes in systematic theology, and taking account of the impact on Christian theology of contemporary philosophy, critical historical studies, the natural and social sciences and non-Christian religions and ideologies.

2. *Either* (a) The Development of Christian Doctrine to AD 451 (as for (i) 1 of Section A above) or (b) Hellenistic Philosophy and Early Christian Thought (as for (i) 2(a) of Section A above) *or* (c) Christology in the Patristic Era (as for (i) 2(b) of Section A above). In (b) and (c) candidates will be expected to comment on passages from prescribed texts in English, which will be listed in the Course Regulations for the Master of Philosophy in Theology for the year in which the candidates commenced their course.

(ii) Candidates will write *either* one long essay (up to 15,000 words) *or* three long essays (up to 5000 words each) on a topic or topics falling within the Patristic era.

(iii) All candidates offer a dissertation of up to 30,000 words.

Section E. Issues in Theology with special reference to Scholastic Theology
(i) There will be two written examinations:

1. Methods and Styles in Theology from 1780 to the Present (as for (i).1 of Section D above);

2. *Either* (a) Doctrine and Methods (as for (i) 1 of Section B above) *or* (b) The Thought of Aquinas (as for (i) 2 of Section B above). In (b) candidates will be expected to comment on passages from prescribed texts in English, which will be listed in the Course Regulations for the Master of Philosophy in Theology for the year in which the candidates commenced their course.

(ii) Candidates will write *either* one long essay (up to 15,000 words) *or* three short essays (up to 5000 words each) on a topic or topics falling within the Scholastic era.

(iii) All candidates offer a dissertation of up to 30,000 words.

Section F. Issues in Theology with special reference to Reformation Theology
(i) There will be two written examinations:

1. Methods and Styles in Theology from 1780 to the Present (as for (i) 1 of Section D above).

2. *Either* (a) Theology in Western Europe from Gabriel Biel to Jacob Arminius (as for (i) 1 of Section C above) *or* (b) Protestant and Tridentine Teaching on the Doctrines of Grace, Freewill and Predestination (as for (i) 2 of Section C above).

(ii) Candidates will write *either* one long essay (up to 15,000 words) *or* three short essays (up to 5,000 words each) on a topic or topics falling within the Reformation era.

(iii) All candidates offer a dissertation of up to 30,000 words.

Section G. Modern Theology (1780–the present)

(i) There will be two written examinations:

1. Methods and Styles in Theology from 1780 to the Present (as for (i) 1 of Section D above).

2. *Either* (a) Modern Theology *or* (b) Theology and Modern European Thought from 1780 to the Present *or* (c) Theology and Literature from 1780 to the Present. In each case candidates will be expected to write three essays on different topics.

(ii) Candidates will write *either* three short essays (up to 5000 words each) *or* one long essay (up to 15,000 words) on a topic or topics falling within one of the three options specified under (i) 2 above;

(iii) All candidates offer a dissertation of up to 30,000 words.

IV Ecclesiastical History

(i) There will be two general papers, assessed either by two written exams, or by one written examination and three essays of up to 5,000 words in length

1. General paper on the Nature and Practice of Ecclesiastical History. Candidates will be expected to write three essays on different topics, discussing the nature of ecclesiastical history as a sub-discipline within History through study both of the writing of the history of the Church from the Early Church to the modern day and of shifts in historical method, with particular reference to methodological debates within History since the mid-nineteenth century.

2. A General paper, in which candidates will be expected to write three essays on different topics within one of the following fields: (a) The Early Church, AD 200–476; (b) The Western Church, AD 476–1050; (c) The Western Church, AD 1000–1400; (d) European Christianity AD 1400–1800; (e) European Christianity AD 1800–2000.

(ii) Candidates will write *either* one long essay (up to 15,000 words) *or* three short essays (up to 5,000 words each) on a topic or topics in ecclesiastical history.

(iii) All candidates offer a dissertation of up to 30,000 words.

V Christian Ethics

(i) There will be two written examinations:

1. Christian Moral Concepts and Methodology. Candidates will be expected to write three essays on different topics, showing understanding of basic conceptual and methodological issues as these are discussed in relevant classical and contemporary texts.

2. Select Texts and Practical Issues in Christian Ethics. Candidates will be expected to write three essays on different topics, showing careful interpretation of classic texts and a capacity to analyse a range of moral issues arising in practical fields.

(ii) Candidates will write three essays (up to 5,000 words each);

(iii) All candidates offer a dissertation of up to 30,000 words.]

[For students starting from MT 2015: (*See also the general notice at the commencement of these regulations.*)

The regulations made by the Board of the Faculty of Theology and Religion are as follows: Candidates for the M.Phil. in Theology are required to follow a course of instruction and directed research for six terms and to present themselves for examination in one of five subjects:

I. **Old Testament**

II. **New Testament**

III. **Christian Doctrine**, specialising in one of seven fields:

History of Doctrine: Patristic Theology (c. AD 100–787)

History of Doctrine: Scholastic Theology (c. AD 1050–1350)

History of Doctrine: Theology of the Reformation Period (c. AD 1500–1650)

Issues in Theology with special reference to Patristic Theology

Issues in Theology with special reference to Scholastic Theology

Issues in Theology with special reference to Reformation Theology

Issues in Theology with special reference to Theology from 1780 to the present day

IV. **Ecclesiastical History**, specialising in one of five fields:

The Early Church AD 200–476

The Western Church AD 476–1050

The Western Church AD 1000–1400

European Christianity AD 1400–1800

European Christianity AD 1800–2000

V. **Christian Ethics**

The examination consists of three elements:

A. Two written examinations (or in Old Testament, route II, one written examination) each of three hours' duration, which take place in Week 10 or 11 of Trinity Term in Year 2.

B. Three essays of not more than 5,000 words each **or one long essay** of not more than 15,000 words. Essay proposals must be submitted for consideration by the Faculty's Graduate Studies Committee *not later than Monday of Week 5 of Trinity Term in Year 1*. The completed essays (two copies of each), together with a signed statement by the candidate that it is his or her own work, must be submitted for examination *not later than fourteen days before the first day of the written examination in Trinity Term of Year 2*. The written examinations take place in Week 10 or 11 of Trinity Term in Year 2.

C. A dissertation of not more than 30,000 words.

The dissertation proposal must be submitted for consideration by the Faculty's Graduate Studies Committee *by Monday of Week 0 of Michaelmas Term in Year 2*. For candidates intending to proceed to doctoral study, the topic of the dissertation should normally be such as to provide a foundation for doctoral research. The completed dissertation (two copies), together with a signed statement by the candidate that it is his or her own work, must be submitted for examination *by Friday of Week 8 of Trinity Term*.

All essay and dissertation proposals should comprise a title, a short statement of how the subject will be treated, a bibliography of core texts (both primary and secondary), and the signature of the supervisor indicating his or her approval. The titles and content of the essays and dissertation should not substantially overlap with each other.

All submitted work should be double-spaced in font-size 12.

Candidates must not put their names on the written examination papers or on any submitted work. All submitted work must be printed and sent in a parcel bearing the words, 'M.Phil. in Theology', to the Chair of Examiners, c/o the Examination Schools, High Street, Oxford.

Each candidate is also required to present himself or herself for an oral (viva voce) examination, which takes place within a few days of the written examination, and may include discussion of the candidate's work in any of the three elements listed above.

Within this general pattern, the specific requirements of each subject may be found below.

I. OLD TESTAMENT

Two routes are possible, route I involving two written examinations and route II only one:

I.

   A. There will be two written examinations: 5

   1. **Prescribed Hebrew Texts**

   2. *Either* (a) **Unseen passages from the Hebrew Bible**

     or   (b) **The Aramaic portions of the Old Testament**

     or   (c) **Passages from the Septuagint**

   B. Candidates will write *either* one long essay (up to 15,000 words) *or* three short   10
essays (up to 5,000 words each) in one of the following subject areas: (1) The
Literature of the Old Testament and Apocrypha in its Historical Setting; (2) Old
Testament Theology; (3) the History and Principles of Biblical Study. The topic(s) will
be chosen by the candidates in liaison with the supervisor.

II.   15

   A. There will be one written examination in **Prescribed Hebrew Texts**.

   B. Candidates will write *both* one long essay (up to 15,000 words) in one of the
following subject areas, *and* three short essays (up to 5,000 words each) in another: (1)
The Literature of the Old Testament and Apocrypha in its Historical Setting; (2) Old
Testament Theology; (3) the History and Principles of Biblical Study. The topic(s) will   20
be chosen by the candidates in liaison with the supervisor.

I and II.

   C. All candidates offer a dissertation of up to 30,000 words. The topics of the essays
and the dissertation will be chosen by the candidate in liaison with the supervisor. The
candidate's progress will be supported by tutorials with the supervisor.   25

II. NEW TESTAMENT

   A. There will be two written examinations:

   1. **The Religion and Literature of the New Testament: the Four Gospels and Acts in
Greek**.

   2. **The Religion and Literature of the New Testament: The Epistles and Apocalypse**   30
in Greek.

   Candidates will be required to translate and to comment on matters of literary,
historical and theological importance from a selection of these prescribed texts.

   B. Candidates will write *either* one long essay (up to 15,000 words) *or* three short
essays (up to 5,000 words each) on a topic or topics in one of the following subject   35
areas: (1) New Testament Theology; (2) Varieties of Judaism, 200 BC–CE 200; (3) the
History and Principles of Biblical Study. The topic(s) will be chosen by the candidates
in liaison with the supervisor.

   C. All candidates offer a dissertation of up to 30,000 words. The topics of the essays
and the dissertation will be chosen by the candidate in liaison with the supervisor. The   40
candidate's progress will be supported by tutorials with the supervisor.

III. CHRISTIAN DOCTRINE

   Candidates will be required to offer one of the following sections:

   Section A. History of Doctrine: Patristic Theology

   Section B. History of Doctrine: Scholastic Theology   45

   Section C. History of Doctrine: Reformation Theology

   Section D. Issues in Theology with special reference to Patristic Theology

Section E. Issues in Theology with special reference to Scholastic Theology

Section F. Issues in Theology with special reference to Reformation Theology

Section G. Issues in Theology with special reference to Theology from 1780 to the present day

Section A. History of Doctrine: Patristic Theology

A. There will be two written examinations:

1. **The Development of Christian Doctrine to AD 451.** Candidates will be expected to write three essays on different topics, showing knowledge of the main lines of development of Christian Doctrine, and discussing particular developments in relation to the historical conditions which influenced them.

2. *Either* (a) **Hellenistic Philosophy and Christian Theology**

   Or (b) **Christology of the Patristic Era**

In each case the examination will consist of two essays on different topics and passages for translation and comment. Candidates may choose whether to translate and comment on Greek or on Latin texts. The prescribed texts for both examination papers will be listed in the Course Regulations for the M.Phil. in Theology for the year in which the candidates commenced their course.

B. Candidates will write *either* one long essay (up to 15,000 words) *or* three short essays (up to 5,000 words each) on a topic or topics falling within the Patristic era, chosen by each candidate in liaison with the supervisor; if necessary a special supervisor will be appointed in addition to the overall supervisor.

C. All candidates offer a dissertation of up to 30,000 words. The topics of the essays and the dissertation will be chosen by the candidate in liaison with the supervisor. The candidate's progress will be supported by tutorials with the supervisor.

Section B. History of Doctrine: Scholastic Theology

A. There will be two written examinations:

1. **Doctrine and Methods.** Candidates will be expected to show knowledge of major theologians in the period 1050–1350 by commenting on passages from prescribed texts in Latin and writing two essays on different topics.

2. **The Thought of Aquinas.** Candidates will be expected to display knowledge of the thought of Thomas Aquinas by commenting on passages from prescribed texts in Latin and writing two essays on different topics.

The prescribed texts for both examination papers will be listed in the Course Regulations for the M.Phil. in Theology for the year in which the candidates commenced their course.

B. Candidates will write *either* one long essay (up to 15,000 words) *or* three short essays (up to 5,000 words each) on a topic or topics falling within the Scholastic era, chosen by each candidate in liaison with the supervisor.

C. All candidates offer a dissertation of up to 30,000 words. The topics of the essays and the dissertation will be chosen by the candidate in liaison with the supervisor. The candidate's progress will be supported by tutorials with the supervisor.

Section C. History of Doctrine: Reformation Theology

A. There will be two written examinations:

1. **Theology in Western Europe from Gabriel Biel to Jacob Arminius.** Candidates will be expected to write three essays on different topics, showing familiarity with the tenets of the most seminal theologians of this era and to discuss them in relation to the political, social and economic tendencies of the age.

2. **Protestant and Tridentine Teaching on the Doctrines of Grace, Freewill and Predestination.**

Candidates will be expected to write three essays on different topics.

B. Candidates will write *either* one long essay (up to 15,000 words) *or* three short essays (up to 5,000 words each) on a topic or topics falling within the Reformation era, chosen by each candidate in liaison with the supervisor.

C. All candidates offer a dissertation of up to 30,000 words. The topics of the essays and the dissertation will be chosen by the candidate in liaison with the supervisor. The candidate's progress will be supported by tutorials with the supervisor.

Section D. Issues in Theology with special reference to Patristic Theology

A. There will be two written examinations:

1. **Methods and Styles in Theology from 1780 to the Present.** Candidates will be expected to write three essays on different topics, discussing problems of theological method, showing a critical understanding of the main themes in systematic theology, and taking account of the impact on Christian theology of contemporary philosophy, critical historical studies, the natural and social sciences and non-Christian religions and ideologies.

2. *Either* (a) **The Development of Christian Doctrine to 451 AD**, as in Section A.A.1 above;

   or   (b) **Hellenistic Philosophy and Early Christian Thought**, as in Section A. A.2(a) above;

   or   (c) **Christology in the Patristic Era**, as in Section A.A.2(b) above.

Passages for comment in (b) and (c) will be chosen from the same texts prescribed in Section A.A.2 above, but here in English only.

B. Candidates will write either one long essay (up to 15,000 words) or three short essays (up to 5,000 words each) on a topic or topics falling within the Patristic era, chosen by each candidate in liaison with the supervisor; if necessary a special supervisor will be appointed in addition to the overall supervisor.

C. All candidates offer a dissertation of up to 30,000 words. The topics of the essays and the dissertation will be chosen by the candidate in liaison with the supervisor. The candidate's progress will be supported by tutorials with the supervisor; if necessary a special supervisor will be appointed in addition to the overall supervisor.

Section E. Issues in Theology with special reference to Scholastic Theology

A. There will be two written examinations.

1. **Methods and Styles in Theology from 1780 to the Present**, as in Section D.A.1 above.

2. *Either* (a) **Doctrine and Methods**, as in Section B.A.1 above;

   or   (b) **The Thought of Aquinas**, as in Section B.A.2 above. In (b) candidates will be expected to comment on passages from the same texts prescribed in Section B. A.2, but here in English only.

B. Candidates will write *either* one long essay (up to 15,000 words) *or* three short essays (up to 5,000 words each) on a topic or topics falling within the Scholastic era, chosen by each candidate in liaison with the supervisor.

C. All candidates offer a dissertation of up to 30,000 words. The topics of the essays and the dissertation will be chosen by the candidate in liaison with the supervisor. The candidate's progress will be supported by tutorials with the supervisor.

Section F. Issues in Theology with special reference to Reformation Theology

A. There will be two written examinations:

1. **Methods and Styles in Theology from 1780 to the Present**, as in Section D.A.1 above.

2. *Either* (a) **Theology in Western Europe from Gabriel Biel to Jacob Arminius**, as in Section C.A.1 above;

   or   (b) **Protestant and Tridentine Teaching on the Doctrines of Grace, Freewill and Predestination**, as Section C.A.2 above.

B. Candidates will write *either* one long essay (up to 15,000 words) *or* three short essays (up to 5,000 words each) on a topic or topics falling within the Reformation era, chosen by each candidate in liaison with the supervisor.

C. All candidates offer a dissertation of up to 30,000 words. The topics of the essays and the dissertation will be chosen by the candidate in liaison with the supervisor. The candidate's progress will be supported by tutorials with the supervisor.

Section G. Issues in Theology with special reference to Theology from 1780 to the present day

A. The two written examinations will be:

1. **Methods and Styles in Theology from 1780 to the Present**, as in Section D.A.1 above.

2. *Either* (a) **Modern Theology**;

   or   (b) **Theology and Modern European Thought from 1780 to the Present**;

   or   (c) **Theology and Literature from 1780 to the Present**.

B. Candidates will write *either* one long essay (up to 15,000 words) *or* three short essays (up to 5,000 words each) on a topic or topics falling within one of 2 (a), (b) or (c) above, chosen by each candidate in liaison with the supervisor.

C. All candidates offer a dissertation of up to 30,000 words. The topics of the essays and the dissertation will be chosen by the candidate in liaison with the supervisor. The candidate's progress will be supported by tutorials with the supervisor.

IV. ECCLESIASTICAL HISTORY

A. There will be two general papers, assessed *either* by two written exams, *or* by one written examination and three essays (up to 5,000 words each).

1. **A General paper on the Nature and Practice of Ecclesiastical History**. Candidates will be expected to discuss the nature of ecclesiastical history as a sub-discipline within History through study of the writing of the history of the Church from the Early Church to the modern day and investigation of shifts in historical method, with particular reference to methodological debates within History since the mid-nineteenth century.

2. **A General paper** on *one* of the following, assessed *either* by unseen examination or *by* three essays (up to 5,000 words each):

(a) **The Early Church, AD 200–476**

(b) **The Western Church, AD 476–1050**

(c) **The Western Church, AD 1000–1400**

(d) **European Christianity AD 1400–1800**

(e) **European Christianity AD 1800–2000**

B. Candidates will write *either* one long essay (up to 15,000 words) *or* three short essays (up to 5,000 words each) on a topic or topics in ecclesiastical history, chosen by each candidate in liaison with the supervisor.

C. All candidates offer a dissertation of up to 30,000 words. The topics of the essays and the dissertation will be chosen by the candidate in liaison with the supervisor. The candidate's progress will be supported by tutorials with the supervisor.

V. CHRISTIAN ETHICS

A. There will be two written examinations:

1. **Christian Moral Concepts and Methodology**. Candidates will be expected to write three essays on different topics, showing an understanding of basic conceptual and methodological issues as these are discussed in relevant classical and contemporary texts.

2. **Select Texts and Practical Issues in Christian Ethics**. Candidates will be expected to write three essays on different topics, showing careful interpretation of classic texts and a capacity to analyse moral issues arising in practical fields.

B. Candidates will write *either* one long essay (up to 15,000 words) *or* three short essays (up to 5,000 words each) on a topic or topics in Christian ethics, chosen by each candidate in liaison with the supervisor.

C. All candidates offer a dissertation of up to 30,000 words. The topics of the essays and the dissertation will be chosen by the candidate in liaison with the supervisor. The candidate's progress will be supported by tutorials with the supervisor.]

Master of Philosophy in Visual, Material, and Museum Anthropology

1. The Social Sciences Board shall elect for the supervision of the course a Standing Committee, namely the Teaching Committee of the School of Anthropology, which shall have power to arrange lectures and other instruction. The course director shall be responsible to that committee. In order to pass the degree, a student must pass all its assessed components. Where one or more components are failed, the student will be given the opportunity to re-sit or re-submit them once, as the case may be. Any subsequent award of the degree on successful completion of all the assessed components may be delayed by up to three terms, i.e. until the Examination Board next meets.

2. The examinations shall consist of the following:

(1) Qualifying Examination Every candidate will be required to satisfy the examiners in an examination for which, if he or she passes at the appropriate level, he or she will be allowed to proceed to the second year of the M.Phil. Candidates must follow a course of instruction in Visual, Material, and Museum Anthropology for at least three terms, and will, when entering for the examinations, be required to produce a certificate from their supervisor to this effect. The Qualifying Examination shall be taken in the Trinity Term of the academic year in which the candidate's name is first entered on the Register of M.Phil. students or, with the approval of the divisional board, in a subsequent year. Each candidate will be required to satisfy the examiners in papers 1–4 on the syllabus described in the Schedule for the M.Sc. in

Visual, Material, and Museum Anthropology, and governed by regulation 4 for that degree, except that for Paper 3(a) an outline proposal for the M.Phil. thesis research of no more than 2,500 words should be submitted.

(2) Final Examination This shall be taken in the Trinity Term of the academic year following that in which the candidate's name is first entered on the register of M.Phil. students or, with the approval of the divisional board, in a subsequent year. Each candidate shall be required:

(i) to present himself or herself for written examination in one of the optional areas or topics available for that year in Lists A, B, or C, other than that taken by the candidate in the M.Phil. Qualifying Examination the previous year;

(ii) to submit to the Chair of Examiners not later than noon on Tuesday of the fifth week of Trinity Term an essay of 5,000 words (three copies) in the field of Visual, Material, and Museum Anthropology, on a topic to be selected from a list set by the examiners at the beginning of the third week of Trinity Term (candidates should not duplicate any material already used in their submission for paper 2 in the Qualifying Examination in the previous year);

(iii) to submit a thesis in accordance with the regulations below;

(iv) to present himself or herself for oral examination if required by the examiners.

Thesis

3. Each candidate shall be required to submit a thesis of not more than 30,000 words (excluding references and appendices) on a subject approved by the supervisor. The thesis may be based on the analysis of objects or photographs in the collections of the Pitt Rivers Museum, or a topic from one of the subject areas covered during the qualifying year, including option topics. The candidate shall send to the Teaching Committee of the School of Anthropology, with the written approval of his or her supervisor, the proposed title of the thesis, together with a paragraph describing its scope, by noon on Monday of the second week of Michaelmas Term in the academic year following that in which his or her name was entered on the register of M.Phil. students. The thesis (three copies) must be typewritten and delivered to the Chair of Examiners, M.Phil. in Visual, Material, and Museum Anthropology, c/o Examination Schools, High Street, Oxford, not later than Tuesday of the second week of Trinity Term in the academic year in which the Final Examination is taken. The dissertation shall be provided with an abstract of up to 250 words, to be placed immediately after the title page. The word count shall be stated on the outside front cover of the thesis.

4. The examiners shall require a successful candidate to deposit a copy of his or her thesis in the Balfour Library. If the thesis is superseded by a D.Phil. thesis by the same student partly using the same material, the Graduate Studies Committee of the School of Anthropology may authorise the withdrawal of the M.Phil. thesis from the Balfour Library. Such candidates will be required to sign a form stating whether they give permission for their thesis to be consulted.

5. The examiners may award a distinction for excellence in the whole examination.

NOTES

8

GENERAL REGULATIONS FOR THE DEGREE OF MASTER OF STUDIES

§1. Degree of Master of Studies

1. Any person who has

(*a*) been admitted as a student for the Degree of Master of Studies under the provisions of this section,

(*b*) satisfied the examiners in one of the examinations prescribed in this section, and

(*c*) kept three terms of statutory residence as a matriculated member of the University after admission as a Student for the Degree of Master of Studies,

may supplicate for the Degree of Master of Studies.

2. For the purpose of this section the words 'board' or 'faculty board' shall include any committee or other body authorised to admit candidates for the Degree of Master of Studies.

§2. Examinations for the Degree of Master of Studies

1. The examinations for the degree and the bodies responsible for the supervision of each examination shall be as listed below.

Examination	*Board*
Ancient Philosophy	Philosophy
Archaeological Science	Social Sciences
Archaeology	Social Sciences
Bible Interpretation	Oriental Studies
British and European History, from 1500 to the present (full-time)	History
British and European History, from 1500 to the present (part-time)	History
Celtic Studies	Modern Languages
Chinese Studies	Oriental Studies
Classical Archaeology	Social Sciences
Classical Armenian Studies	Oriental Studies
Classical Hebrew Studies	Oriental Studies
Creative Writing	Continuing Education
Diplomatic Studies	Continuing Education
English	English Language and Literature
English Language	English Language and Literature
Film Aesthetics	Modern Languages
General Linguistics and Comparative Philology	Faculty of Linguistics, Philology and Phonetics
Global and Imperial History	History
Greek and/or Latin Languages and Literature	Classics
Greek and/or Roman History	Classics

History of Art and Visual Culture	History	
History of Design	Continuing Education	
International Human Rights Law	Continuing Education	
Islamic Art and Archaeology	Oriental Studies	
Islamic Studies and History	Oriental Studies	5
Japanese Studies	Oriental Studies	
Jewish Studies	Oriental Studies	
Jewish Studies in the Graeco-Roman Period	Oriental Studies	
Korean Studies	Oriental Studies	10
Late Antique and Byzantine Studies	Classics and History	
Legal Research/Socio-Legal Research	Law	
Literature and Arts	Continuing Education	
Medieval History	History	
Medieval Studies	History	15
Mindfulness-Based Cognitive Therapy	Continuing Education	
Modern Jewish Studies	Oriental Studies	
Modern Languages	Modern Languages	
Modern South Asian Studies	History and Oriental Studies	
Music	Music	20
Oriental Studies	Oriental Studies	
Philosophical Theology	Theology	
Philosophy	Philosophy	
Philosophy of Physics	Philosophy	
Psychodynamic Practice	Continuing Education	25
Slavonic Studies	Modern Languages	
Study of Religions	Theology	
Syriac Studies	Oriental Studies	
Theology	Theology	
US History	History	30
Women's Studies	Modern Languages	
Yiddish Studies	Modern Languages	

2. The subjects of each examination shall be determined, subject to the approval of the Education Committee, by regulation of the board concerned, which shall have power to arrange lectures and courses of instruction for the examination.   35

3. No full-time student shall be admitted as a candidate for examination for the degree until he or she shall have spent at least three terms at work in Oxford after his or her admission as a student for the degree; time spent outside Oxford during term as part of an academic programme approved by Council shall count towards residence for the purpose of this clause.   40

4. Part-time students for the degree shall in each case be required to pursue their course of study for twice the number of terms required of an equivalent full-time student. Part-time students will not be required to keep statutory residence but must attend for such instruction and undertake such supervised fieldwork as the faculty board or committee concerned shall require. The Director of Graduate Studies of the   45
faculty board concerned, or the director of the department concerned, as the case may be, shall keep a register of attendance of part-time students. No student shall be granted leave to supplicate unless the register shows satisfactory attendance by him or her.

5. Final examination marks shall be released to candidates at the conclusion of the   50
examination. Exceptions to this may be made where assessment takes place through-out the course. In such cases, examination boards must meet formally, with all

members present, at interim points in the year in order to agree final marks for specified assessment components. Marks released as final marks may not subsequently be amended without permission of the Proctors.

6. A candidate who has failed to satisfy the examiners in any one of the examinations may enter again for that examination on one, but not more than one, subsequent occasion.

7. The examiners may award a distinction for excellence in the whole examination. Candidates who have initially failed any element of assessment shall not normally be eligible for the award of distinction.

§3. Admission of Candidates

1. Any person may be admitted by the board concerned as a candidate for an examination for the Degree of Master of Studies provided the following conditions have been satisfied:

(*a*) The application must be supported by the candidate's college.

(*b*) A candidate must either (i) have passed all the examinations required for the Degree of Bachelor of Arts and have obtained first or good second class honours in the Second Public Examination, or have obtained such honours in a degree examination of another university, such university having been approved by Council for the purpose of senior status, or (ii) in the opinion of the board, be otherwise adequately qualified to undertake the course.

2. An application for admission of a candidate who has passed the examinations required for the Degree of Bachelor of Arts shall be sent to the Registrar by the head or tutor of his or her college, and shall be accompanied by a statement of the subject which he or she proposes to study and evidence of his or her fitness to undertake a course of study therein.

3. An application for admission by a graduate of another university shall be sent to the Registrar by the head or tutor of the college to which he or she belongs or to which he or she has applied for admission, and shall be accompanied by all the necessary certificates from his or her previous university and by a statement of the subject which he or she proposes to study and evidence of his or her fitness to undertake a course of study therein.

4. An application for admission by any other candidate shall be sent to the Registrar by the head or tutor of the college to which he or she belongs or to which he or she has applied for admission, and shall be accompanied by evidence of his or her previous education and by a statement of the subject which he or she proposes to study and evidence of his or her fitness to undertake a course of study therein.

5. The Registrar shall bring any application submitted under cll. 2, 3, or 4 before the appropriate board for its approval. Such approval shall not be granted unless the board is satisfied that the candidate is well-fitted to enter on the course of study proposed by him or her.

6. A board shall have power to appoint a standing committee of its own members to consider the applications of candidates and to report to the board.

7. It shall be the duty of the Registrar to notify a candidate of the decision of a board as soon as may be.

8. A member of the University who holds the status of Probationer Research Student or the status of student for another higher degree or postgraduate diploma within the University may, with the approval of the board which admitted him or her, transfer to the status of Student for the Degree of Master of Studies, in which case the date of his or her admission as a Probationer Research Student or to the status of student for a higher degree or post-graduate diploma shall then be reckoned, unless

the board shall determine otherwise, as the date of his or her admission as a Student for the Degree of Master of Studies.

9. A candidate for the B.Phil. in Philosophy may, with the approval of the Board of the Faculty of Philosophy, transfer to the status of a Student for the Degree of Master of Studies in Philosophy. The application must be submitted not later than Friday of   5
the fourth week of the Hilary Full Term of the year in which he or she wishes to take the examination for the Degree of Master of Studies. The date of the candidate's admission as a B.Phil. Student shall then be reckoned as the date of his or her admission as a Student for the Degree of Master of Studies.

10. A student holding the status of Probationer Research Student may, with the   10
approval of the board which admitted him or her, be admitted as a candidate for an examination for the Degree of Master of Studies. Time spent as a student holding the status of Probationer Research Student shall count as time spent working for the Degree of Master of Studies.

11. A Student for the Degree of Master of Studies who is not a graduate of the   15
University may wear the same gown as that worn by Students for the Degree of Doctor of Philosophy.

12. A Student for the Degree of Master of Studies shall cease to hold such status if

(i) he or she shall have been refused permission to supplicate for the Degree of Master of Studies, or   20

(ii) the board concerned shall, in accordance with provisions set down by regulation by the Education Committee, and after consultation with the student's society and supervisor, have deprived the student of such status;

(iii) he or she shall have been transferred under the relevant provisions to another status;   25

(iv) he or she shall not have entered for the relevant examination within six terms for a full-time student and twelve terms for a part-time student.

§4. Supervision of Students

1. Every candidate on admission as a Student for the Degree of Master of Studies shall be placed by the board which admitted him or her under the supervision of a   30
graduate member of the University or other competent person selected by the board, and the board shall have power for sufficient reason to change the supervisor of any student.

2. It shall be the duty of a supervisor of a student to direct and superintend the work of the student for any part of the student's course in which supervision is   35
required and to undertake such duties as shall be from time to time set out in the relevant Policy and Guidance issued by the Education Committee.

3. The supervisor shall send a report on the progress of the student to the board at the end of each term and at any other time when the board so requests, or he or she deems it expedient. The supervisor shall communicate the contents of the report to the   40
student on each occasion that a report is made, so that the student is aware of the supervisor's assessment of his or her work during the period in question. In addition, he or she shall inform the board at once if he is of the opinion that the student is unlikely to reach the standard required for the Degree of Master of Studies.

The Registrar shall send a copy of each report by the supervisor to the student's   45
society.

Master of Studies in Ancient Philosophy

1. Every candidate must follow for at least three terms a course of instruction in Ancient Philosophy. Candidates will, when they enter for the examination, be required to produce from their society a certificate that they are following such a course.

2. Every candidate shall be required to offer (i) three essays in Ancient Philosophy: one on the first subject (refer to 4. below) and the other two on the second subject (refer to 5. below); and (ii) a thesis in Ancient Philosophy of 10,000–15,000 words.

3. The choice of subjects must be notified on the entry form for the examination, to be submitted by Friday of fourth week of Michaelmas Term.

4. The first subject shall be chosen from the list of undergraduate papers in ancient philosophy 0130–0135, as specified in the special regulations for *Philosophy in all Honour Schools including Philosophy*. The subject will be assessed by one 5,000 word essay on a topic (relevant to the subject) to be chosen by the candidate and approved by the Chair of Examiners no later than Friday of eighth week of Michaelmas Term. Two copies of the essay must be submitted to the Examination Schools, High Street, Oxford OX1 4BG by 10 a.m. on the Friday of noughth week of Hilary Term in the year in which the examination is taken. Essays must be typed or printed.

5. The second subject shall be a dedicated class taught across the Michaelmas and Hilary terms of the year of examination. The subject will be assessed by two 5,000 word essays on two topics (relevant to the subject) to be chosen by the candidate and approved by the Chair of Examiners no later than Friday of fifth week of Hilary Term. Two copies of each essay must be submitted to the Examination Schools, High Street, Oxford OX1 4BG, by 10 a.m. on Friday of ninth week of Hilary Term in the year in which the examination is taken. Essays must be typed or printed.

6. Candidates may not be permitted to offer certain combinations of subjects.

7. The reading lists for all subjects will include texts both in the original language and in translation; candidates' readings will be guided by their supervisor(s) according to their level of Ancient Greek. All reading lists will be posted on the Faculty website in Trinity Term preceding the year of examination.

8. Candidates must offer a thesis of no more than 10,000–15,000 words, exclusive of bibliographical references, on a subject proposed by the candidate in consultation with his or her supervisor and approved by the Graduate Studies Committee in Philosophy. A subject and thesis title must be submitted to the Committee no later than the fifth week of the Hilary Term of the year in which the examination is to be taken. Requests for permission to make later changes to the thesis title should be submitted, with the support of the candidate's supervisor to the Director of Graduate Studies in Philosophy *as soon as the candidate has decided to seek permission*. Two copies of the thesis must be submitted to the Examination Schools, High Street, Oxford OX1 4BG, by 10 a.m. on Friday of eighth week of Trinity Term in the year in which the examination is taken. The thesis shall be accompanied by a brief abstract and statement of the number of words it contains (exclusive of bibliographical references). Successful candidates will be required to deposit one copy of the thesis in the Bodleian Library (candidates will also be required to sign a form stating that they give permission for the thesis to be consulted).

9. Candidates who have not delivered the essays or the thesis as prescribed by the due date shall, unless they show exceptional cause, be deemed to have withdrawn from the examination.

10. Each essay shall be the candidate's own work. The candidate may discuss a draft (but not more than one) of each essay with his or her supervisor. The candidate's supervisor may provide bibliographical advice on essays throughout.

11. The examiners may award a distinction for excellence in the whole examination. A candidate who fails any one of the four elements of the examination (i.e. one of the three essays or the thesis) may apply to retake that element in the September immediately following the examination. A candidate who fails two or more elements may retake the examination in the year immediately following the failed examination.   5
It is necessary for a candidate to retake only the failed elements of the examination.

Master of Studies in Archaeological Science

1. Within the Division of Social Sciences, the course shall be administered by the Committee for the School of Archaeology. The regulations made are as follows:

2. Candidates for admission must apply to the Committee for the School of   10
Archaeology.

3. Candidates must follow a course of instruction in Archaeological Science for at least three terms and for a substantial part of the first two subsequent vacations, as determined by the course timetable.

4. The registration of candidates will lapse at the end of Trinity Term in the   15
academic year of their admission, unless it shall have been extended by the committee.

5. The written examination shall consist of:

(*a*) three papers on the syllabus described in the Schedule, to be taken in the second week of Trinity Term, *and*

(*b*) *either* one pre-set essay of approximately 10,000 words, *or* two pre-set essays of   20
approximately 5,000 words each. The subject and length of each essay must be approved by the examiners before the end of Michaelmas Full Term. Two copies of each essay must be delivered to the Examination Schools by noon on the Friday of first week of Trinity Term. Essays must be typed or printed, must bear the candidate's examination number but not his or her name, and   25
must include a statement of the number of words. Any illustrations must be included in both copies.

(*c*) in lieu of one of the three papers described in the Schedule, candidates may, with the permission of the School of Archaeology Committee for Graduate Studies, take one of the options from the M.St in Archaeology or M.St in Classical   30
Archaeology (Schedule B only). Candidates taking such an option would only be examined on one pre-set essay of approximately 5,000 words on Archaeological Science in lieu of the requirements laid out in b) above.

6. Each candidate will be required to submit a report of approximately 5,000 words, on a practical project selected in consultation with the supervisor and approved   35
by the Committee for the School of Archaeology.

7. Three typewritten copies of the report on the practical project must be sent, not later than noon on the Friday of ninth week of the Trinity Term in the year in which the examination is taken, to the M.St. Examiners (Archaeological Science), c/o Examination Schools, High Street, Oxford.   40

8. The examiners may require to see the records of practical work carried out during the first two terms of the course.

9. Candidates must present themselves for an oral examination as required by the examiners. This may be on the candidate's written papers, or practical work, or both.

10. The examiners may award a distinction for excellence in the whole examination.   45

11. In the case of failure in just one part of the examination, the candidate will be permitted to retake that part of the examination on one further occasion, not later than one year after the initial attempt. Written papers would be retaken the following year.

SCHEDULE

(i) *Principles and practice of scientific dating*

The principles of scientific dating methods including radiocarbon, luminescence, uranium series, and dendro-chronology. The practical aspects of these methods and the problems encountered in their application. The statistical analysis of chronological information in the study of archaeological sites and cultures.

(ii) *Bio-archaeology*

Scientific methods for the study of biological remains from archaeological sites; introduction to the analysis of plant and faunal remains including indicators of disease and artefactual analysis; theoretical and practical aspects of quantitative methods for diet reconstruction by isotopic analysis; introduction to ancient DNA studies; residue analysis.

(iii) *Materials analysis and the study of technological change*

Introduction to the history of technology; theoretical and practical aspects of materials analysis methods-SEM, microprobe, TIMS, ICP, ICP-MS, XRF, XRD, PIXE, FTIR, and NAA; application to analysis to different material types-stone, ceramics, vitreous materials, and metals; provenance of raw materials; case studies of application to archaeological problems.

Master of Studies in Archaeology

1. Within the Division of Social Sciences, the course shall be administered by the Committee for the School of Archaeology. The regulations made are as follows:

2. Candidates for admission must apply to the Committee for the School of Archaeology. They will be required to produce evidence of their appropriate qualifications for the proposed course, including their suitable proficiency in relevant ancient or modern languages.

3. Candidates must follow for three terms a course of instruction in Archaeology.

4. The registration of candidates will lapse on the last day of the Trinity Full Term in the academic year of their admission, unless it shall have been extended by the committee.

5. The written examination shall comprise three subjects: Not more than one subject of the three selected may normally be taken from either one of Schedule C or D.

(*a*) one subject selected from Schedule A below to be examined by written paper;

(*b*) one further subject selected from Schedules B–D, to be examined by two pre-set essays (each of 5,000 words). These subjects will be examined by two pre-set essays (each of 5,000 words) except that further subjects from Schedule A of the M.St. in Classical Archaeology will only be examined by written paper.

(c) a dissertation of not more than 10,000 words (excluding bibliography and descriptive catalogue or similar factual matter, but including notes and appendices) the subject to be selected from Schedules A–D.

The topic of the dissertation must be approved by the candidate's supervisor and by the School of Archaeology Committee for Graduate Studies. The topic of the dissertation must be clearly distinct from the pre-set essay titles. The dissertation must be the work of the candidate alone, and aid from others must be limited to prior discussion of the subject, bibliographic advice, help with access to study material and advice on presentation. The dissertation must be a new piece of work, substantially different from any dissertation previously submitted by the candidate for a degree of this or another university. When the dissertation is submitted, it must be

accompanied by a statement, signed by the candidate, confirming that these conditions have been met. The proposed title of the dissertation, countersigned by the
supervisor, must be submitted for approval by the committee by noon on the
Tuesday of the eighth week of the Michaelmas Full Term preceding the examination.
Two copies typed or printed (the second may be a photocopy) in double spacing on   5
one side only of A4 paper and bound simply or filed securely, must be delivered in a
parcel bearing the words 'Dissertation for the M.St. in Archaeology' to the
Examination Schools, High Street, Oxford, not later than noon on the Friday of the
sixth week of Trinity Full Term and should bear the candidate's examination number
but not his or her name. Candidates will be required to deposit one copy of the   10
dissertation with the Examination Schools.

Schedule A: Core Papers

   Ancient Maritime Societies
   Archaeological Method and Theory
   Archaeology of Asia   15
   Environmental Archaeology
   European Prehistory from the Mesolithic to the Bronze Age
   Europe in the Early Middle Ages AD 400–900
   Landscape Archaeology and Spatial Technology
   Transformation of the Celtic World 500 BC–AD 100   20
   Visual Cultures of the Ancient World

Schedule B: Options

   Archaeology of Colonialism
   Archaeology of Early Anglo-Saxon England
   Archaeology of Late Anglo-Saxon England   25
   Archaeology and Geographical Information Systems
   Archaeology and Material Culture
   Archaeology of Southern African Hunter-gatherers
   Body and Adornment Material Culture of Later Medieval Britain, AD 1000–1500
   Chinese Archaeology   30
   City, country and economy in the Late Roman Empire (fourth-seventh centuries AD)
   Coinage and Society in Anglo-Saxon England
   Cultural Heritage and Law: History
   Farming and States in Sub-Saharan Africa
   Formation of the Islamic World   35
   Hunter-gatherers in World Perspective
   Maritime Archaeology up to AD 1000
   Methods and Techniques in Maritime Archaeology
   Object Analysis and Research Methods
   Palaeolithic and Mesolithic Europe   40
   Palaeolithic Archaeology
   Palaeolithic Asia
   Practical Archaeobotany
   Regional studies in Australian and Pacific prehistory
   Topics in Aegean Prehistory   45

Schedule C: Archaeological Science

Any subject offered in the M.St. in Archaeological Science.

Schedule D: Classical Archaeology

Any subject offered in the M.St. in Classical Archaeology.

Candidates may apply for other subjects, to be taken under Schedule B, to be approved by the committee, which shall define their scope and inform both the candidate and the examiners of this definition in writing. Not all course options may be available in any given year.

6. Candidates will be expected to show a general knowledge of the appropriate history and geography, so far as they are concerned with their subjects.

7. Candidates must present themselves for an oral examination as required by the examiners.

8. The subjects to be offered by the candidates and their chosen method of examination, duly approved by their supervisors, must be submitted for approval to the committee in time for its meeting in eighth week of the Michaelmas Full Term preceding the examination. Notice of options to be offered by candidates must be given to the Registrar not later than Friday of the eighth week of that same term.

9. Where options are examined by pre-set essays as specified in 5 *(b)* above, candidates will normally select essay topics from a list offered by their supervisor. The proposed essay titles, countersigned by the supervisor, must be submitted for approval to the Chair of Examiners by noon on Friday of the seventh week of the Hilary Full Term preceding the examinations. Candidates must submit two copies of their essays by not later than noon on Monday of the second week of Trinity Full Term to the Examination Schools. Essays must be typed or printed.

10. The examiners may award a distinction for excellence in the whole examination.

11. In the case of failure in just one part of the examination, the candidate will be permitted to retake that part of the examination on one further occasion, not later than one year after the initial attempt. Written papers would be retaken the following year.

Master of Studies in Bible Interpretation

1. Before admission to the course, candidates must satisfy the Board of the Faculty of Oriental Studies that they possess the necessary qualification in Classical Hebrew, Aramaic or Syriac, to profit by the course. Teaching for a second language from these three will be provided during the course if required. Evidence of proficiency in Greek or Latin will be expected if options in either of these languages are chosen.

2. Every candidate must follow for at least three terms a course of study in Bible Interpretation.

3. *Syllabus*

There will be four Units. Units (i), (ii), and (iii) are each assessed by a written examination paper.

Unit (i) Essay questions on general background and methodology.

Unit (ii) Prescribed texts I. Passages for translation and comment, and essay questions on prescribed texts (a passage, or passages, for unprepared translation may also be set).

Unit (iii) Prescribed texts II. Passages for translation and comment, and essay questions on prescribed texts (a passage, or passages, for unprepared translation may also be set).

Units (ii) and (iii) must be chosen from two of the following:

(*a*) Hebrew biblical and exegetical texts
(*b*) Aramaic (Targum) texts
(*c*) Syriac biblical and exegetical texts
(*d*) Greek biblical and exegetical texts
(*e*) Latin biblical and exegetical texts

Unit (iv) A thesis of not more than 15,000 words (excluding bibliography), on a topic selected in consultation with the candidate's supervisor and approved by the Faculty Board. Applications for such approval should be submitted to the Faculty office by Monday of Week 0 of Hilary Term. Two typewritten copies and an electronic copy of the thesis in PDF format in a memory stick or CD, must be delivered to the Chair of Examiners, M.St. in Bible Interpretation, Examination Schools, High Street, Oxford, not later than 12 noon on Friday of fourth week of Trinity Term. The work must bear the candidates' examination number (but not the candidates' name.) Candidates must include a signed declaration sealed in an envelope addressed to the Chair of Examiners that the work is the candidates' own.

4. Lists of set texts must be submitted to the Faculty office by Friday of seventh week of Michaelmas Term.

5. Candidates may be required to attend a viva.

Teaching for some options may not be available in every year. Applicants for admission will be advised of this.

Master of Studies in British and European History, from 1500 to the present (full-time)

(See also the general notice at the commencement of these regulations.)

The regulations of the Board of the Faculty of History are as follows:

1. Candidates for this degree must follow for at least three terms a course of instruction and directed research and must, upon entering the examination, produce from their society a certificate to that effect.

2. Candidates must attend such lectures, seminars and classes as their supervisor shall determine. In addition to the formally examined programme elements described below, each candidate will be expected to attend and complete in-course requirements for a series of skills and specialist options based on a schedule to be published from year to year by the Faculty's Graduate Studies Committee. The candidate's individual programme, agreed with her/his supervisor, will be subject to approval by the Director of Graduate Studies, in consultation with the programme convenor, by Friday of Week One of Michaelmas Term; subsequent changes must be agreed by the Director of Graduate Studies not later than Friday of Week Three of Hilary Term. Class teachers will report to the Chair of Examiners on the candidate's attendance and participation, and, where appropriate, test results, not later than Monday of Week Nine of Hilary Term, except in the case of three-term language classes where the respective reporting deadline will be Monday of Week Nine of Trinity Term.

3. The final examination for candidates in British and European History shall comprise (i) one extended essay based on the programme's theory component, plus one annotated bibliography and one dissertation proposal, (ii) one extended essay based on an Advanced Option, and (iii) a dissertation of not more than 15,000 words.

I. During Michaelmas Term each candidate will attend core classes on historical theory and methodological approaches as well as a series of classes on sources and resources. The core classes will be assessed by an extended essay of between 4,000 and 5,000 words, and the sources and resources component by an annotated bibliography and a dissertation proposal of between 800 and 1,000 words. Two copies of the essay, annotated bibliography and proposal, addressed to the Chair of Examiners for the M.St. in British and European History, from 1500 to the present, must be submitted to the Examination Schools, High Street, Oxford by 12 noon on Monday of Week One of Hilary 5 Term. The assessment of the annotated bibliography and the dissertation proposal will be on a pass/fail basis only, and candidates who fail one of these elements will be given the opportunity to submit a revised version in the course of their programme.

II. In Hilary Term candidates must choose one Advanced Option, either from the 10 joint Advanced Options for the Master of Studies and the Master of Philosophy in British and European History, from 1500 to the present, or from the Advanced Options for one of the Faculty of History's other Master's programmes. The choice of Advance Option will depend on the candidate's training objectives or dissertation project. Details of available Advanced 15 Options are published in course handbooks. Approval of the Advanced Option choice must be obtained from the programme convenor and Director of Graduate Studies by Friday of Week Four of Michaelmas Term. The request for approval must be sent to the History Graduate Office. On recommendation from the candidate's supervisor, the Director of Graduate 20 Studies, in consultation with the programme convenor, may approve relevant taught papers from Master's programmes offered by faculties other than History, provided that the respective faculty's Graduate Studies Committee is satisfied that the candidate has an adequate background in the subject. This part of the programme will be assessed by one extended essay of between 6,500 25 and 7,500 words. Two copies of the essay, addressed to the Chair of Examiners for the M.St. in British and European History, from 1500 to the present, must be submitted to the Examination Schools, High Street, Oxford by 12 noon on Monday of Week Nine of Hilary Term. This essay should reflect skills and understanding the candidate has developed by following the 30 approved choice of Advanced Option paper. This essay may complement but must not share significant content with the essay submitted under I. above. *Teaching may not be available for all the Advanced Options each year, and restrictions may be imposed on the combination of Advanced Options that may be taken in a particular year.* 35

III. Each candidate must prepare a dissertation of not more than 15,000 words on a topic in his or her chosen subject area. The dissertation must include a short abstract which concisely summarises in about 300 words its scope and principal arguments. Two copies of the dissertation, addressed to the Chair of Examiners for the M.St. in British and European History, from 1500 to the 40 present, must be submitted to the Examination Schools by 12 noon of Monday of Week Eight of Trinity Term. Material submitted under I and II may be summarised or substantially further developed in the dissertation, but no significant part of the dissertation should reproduce or paraphrase other work submitted for examination. 45

4. The examiners may award a distinction to candidates who have performed with special merit in the whole examination.

5. A candidate who fails the examination will be permitted to retake it on one further occasion only, not later than one year after the initial attempt.

Master of Studies in British and European History, from 1500 to the present (part-time)

The regulations of the Board of the Faculty of History are as follows:

1. Candidates for this degree must follow for at least six terms a course of instruction and directed research and must, upon entering the examination, produce   5
from their society a certificate to that effect.

2. Candidates must attend such lectures, seminars and classes as their supervisor shall determine. In addition to the formally examined programme elements described below, each candidate will be expected to attend and complete in-course requirements for a series of skills and specialist options based on a schedule to be published from   10
year to year by the Faculty's Graduate Studies Committee. The candidate's individual programme, agreed with her/his supervisor, will be subject to approval by the Director of Graduate Studies, in consultation with the programme convenor, by Friday of Week One of each year's Michaelmas Term; subsequent changes must be agreed by the Director of Graduate Studies not later than Friday of Week Three of the following   15
Hilary Term. Class teachers will report to the Chair of Examiners on the candidate's attendance and participation, and, where appropriate, test results, not later than Monday of Week Nine of the Term in which the classes were held.

3. The final examination for candidates in British and European History, *from 1500 to the present*, shall comprise (i) one annotated bibliography and one dissertation   20
proposal, (ii) one extended essay based on an Advanced Option submitted in year one of the programme, (iii) one extended essay based on the programme's theory component, and (iv) a dissertation of not more than 15,000 words submitted in year two of the programme.

I. During the Michaelmas Term of the first year each candidate will attend a   25
series of classes on sources and resources. The sources and resources component will be assessed by an annotated bibliography and a dissertation proposal of between 800 and 1,000 words. Two copies of the annotated bibliography and the proposal, addressed to the Chair of Examiners for the *M.St. in British and European History, from 1500 to the present*, must be submitted to the   30
Examination Schools, High Street, Oxford by 12 noon on Monday of Week One of Hilary Term. These elements are assessed on a pass/fail basis only, and candidates who fail one of these elements will be given the opportunity to submit a revised version in the course of their first year on the programme.

II. In the Hilary Term of the first year candidates must choose one Advanced   35
Option, either from the joint Advanced Options for the Master of Studies and the Master of Philosophy in British and European History, from 1500 to the present, or from the Advanced Options for one of the Faculty of History's other Master's programmes. The choice of Advanced Option will depend on the candidate's training objectives or dissertation project. Details of available   40
Advanced Options are published on the programme pages in WebLearn handbooks. Approval of the Advanced Option choice must be obtained from the programme convenor and Director of Graduate Studies by Friday of Week Six of Michaelmas Term. The request for approval must be sent to the History Graduate Office. On recommendation from the candidate's super-   45
visor, the Director of Graduate Studies, in consultation with the programme convenor, may approve relevant taught papers from Master's programmes offered by faculties other than History, provided that the respective faculty's Graduate Studies Committee is satisfied that the candidate has an adequate background in the subject. This part of the programme will be assessed by one   50
extended essay of between 6,500 and 7,500 words. Two copies of the essay, addressed to the Chair of Examiners for the *M.St. in British and European History, from 1500 to the present*, must be submitted to the Examination

Schools, High Street, Oxford by 12 noon on Monday of Week One of the candidate's first Trinity Term. This essay should reflect skills and understanding the candidate has developed by following the approved choice of Advanced Option paper. *Teaching may not be available for all the Advanced Options each year, and restrictions may be imposed on the combination of* 5 *Advanced Options that may be taken in a particular year.*

III. During the Michaelmas Term of the second year each candidate will attend core classes on historical theory and methodological approaches. The core classes will be assessed by an extended essay of between 4,000 and 5,000 words. Two copies of the essay, addressed to the Chair of Examiners for the 10 *M.St. in British and European History, from 1500 to the present*, must be submitted to the Examination Schools, High Street, Oxford by 12 noon on Monday of Week Two of Hilary Term in the second year.

IV. Each candidate must prepare a dissertation of not more than 15,000 words on a topic in his or her chosen subject area. The dissertation must include a short 15 abstract which concisely summarises in about 300 words its scope and principal arguments. Two copies of the dissertation, addressed to the Chair of Examiners for the *M.St. in British and European History, from 1500 to the present*, must be submitted to the Examination Schools by 12 noon of Monday of Week Eight of their second Trinity Term. Material submitted under I, II, 20 and III may be complementary to the dissertation project but must not form a significant part of the dissertation itself.

4. The examiners may award a distinction to candidates who have performed with special merit in the whole examination.

5. A candidate who fails the examination will be permitted to retake it on one 25 further occasion only, not later than one year after the initial attempt.

Master of Studies in Celtic Studies

1. All candidates shall be required at the time of admission to satisfy the Board of the Faculty of Medieval and Modern Languages (if necessary, by written test) that they possess the appropriate qualifications for the proposed course, including suitable 30 proficiency in relevant languages. Normally the course will be restricted to candidates who have taken a first degree in a relevant subject area.

2. All candidates must follow a course of instruction in Celtic Studies at Oxford for a period of three terms, unless the Board of the Faculty of Medieval and Modern Languages in exceptional circumstances shall permit an extension of time, and they 35 shall, when they enter their names for the examination, be required to produce from their society a certificate stating that they are following the course of instruction for the period prescribed.

3. Candidates shall be required:

(*a*) to offer themselves for written examination as defined below. 40

(*b*) to offer themselves for viva voce examination at the time appointed by the examiners.

4. The subjects and papers of the examination shall be as follows:

(*a*) *Either*

(1) Two papers, one on each of two subjects selected from the following: 45

    (i) Historical and comparative Celtic linguistics.

    (ii) Irish literature up to the Cromwellian wars (4(*b*) for the M.Phil. in Celtic Studies).

    (iii) Welsh literature up to the Reformation (4(*c*) for the M.Phil. in Celtic Studies). 50

Or

(2) Two papers as follows:
  (i) One paper on a subject selected from those described in section (*a*) (1) above.
  (ii) One paper on a Special Subject to be chosen from the list given in section 4 (*d*) of the regulations for the M.Phil. in Celtic Studies. Candidates are allowed to offer a Special Subject of their own devising provided that it is similar in character and scope to those listed for the M.Phil. in Celtic Studies and that it is approved under the arrangements set out in section 7 of the regulations for that M.Phil. (Candidates shall, however, seek approval for their choice of Special Subject, whether it involves a title of their devising or not, by application to the Modern Languages Graduate Office, 41 Wellington Square, Oxford, by the end of the fourth week of their first term as a student for the examination).

(*b*) A dissertation of approximately 8,000 words and not more than 10,000 words on a topic approved by the Board of the Faculty of Medieval and Modern Languages or by a person or persons to whom the board may delegate the function of giving such approval. Candidates shall seek approval (by application to the Modern Languages Graduate Office, 41 Wellington Square, Oxford) for the proposed topic of their dissertation by the end of the fourth week of their second term as a student for the examination.

The dissertation must be the work of the candidate alone and aid from others must be limited to prior discussion as to the subject and advice on presentation. It must be presented in proper scholarly form. Two copies, typed in double-spacing on one side only of quarto or A4 paper, each copy bound or held firmly in a stiff cover, must be delivered to the Chair of the Examiners for the Degree of M.St. in Celtic Studies, c/o Examination Schools, High Street, Oxford, not later than Monday of the fourth week of the Trinity Full Term in which the examination is to be taken.

5. Other arrangements for the above papers and subjects shall be as specified for the M.Phil. in Celtic Studies.

6. The examiners may award a distinction for excellence in the whole examination.

Master of Studies in Chinese Studies

1. Before admission to the course, candidates must either have taken a degree in Chinese in the Honour School of Oriental Studies at Oxford or a comparable degree from another university, or must otherwise satisfy the Board of the Faculty of Oriental Studies that they possess the necessary qualifications in the Chinese language to profit by the course.

2. Every candidate must follow for at least three terms a course of instruction in Chinese Studies.

3. *Syllabus* There will be four Units.

4. Unit (i) Prescribed texts, with special reference to a subject approved by the Board. This is a written examination paper.

5. Unit (ii) Either Classical Chinese unprepared translation or Japanese or another Asian language approved by the Board. This is a written examination paper. Candidates may choose a language other than Classical Chinese only if the Board is satisfied that they possess a good knowledge of Classical Chinese. Candidates who have taken Chinese in the Honour School of Oriental Studies at Oxford are required to take Japanese or another Asian language.

6. Unit (iii) Bibliography and techniques of sinology, with special reference to the subject chosen in Unit (i). Exercises will be set after examinations for Units (i) and (ii) have taken place. Each candidate will be assigned one or more exercises set on a topic directly relating to the course of instruction he/she has followed, and will be required to submit a written answer to the Chair of Examiners by a date which the Chair will announce, but which shall, in any case, be not sooner than two days and not later than seven days following the examinations. Two copies of each typewritten essay must be submitted to the Chair of Examiners, M.St. in Chinese Studies, Examination Schools, High Street, Oxford. Candidates must include a signed declaration sealed in an envelope addressed to the Chair of Examiners that the work is the candidate's own.

7. Unit (iv) A thesis of not more than 15,000 words (excluding bibliography) on a topic selected in consultation with the candidate's supervisor and approved by the Faculty Board. Applications for such approval should be submitted to the Faculty office by Monday of Week 0 of Hilary Term. Two typewritten copies and an electronic copy of the thesis in PDF format in a memory stick or CD, must be submitted to the Chairman of the Examiners, name of degree, c/o Examination Schools, High Street, Oxford OX1 4BG. not later than 12 noon on Friday of Week 4 of Trinity Term. The work must bear the candidates' examination number (but not the candidates' name). Candidates must include a signed declaration sealed in an envelope addressed to the Chair of Examiners that the work is the candidates own.

8. Lists of set texts must be submitted to the Faculty office by Friday of seventh week of Michaelmas Term.

9. Candidates may be required to attend a viva.

Master of Studies in Classical Archaeology

1. Within the Division of Social Sciences, the course shall be administered by the Committee for the School of Archaeology. The regulations made are as follows:

2. Candidates for admission must apply to the Committee for the School of Archaeology. They will be required to produce evidence of their appropriate qualifications for the proposed course, including their suitable proficiency in relevant ancient or modern languages.

3. Candidates must follow for three terms a course of instruction in Classical Archaeology.

4. The registration of candidates will lapse on the last day of the Trinity Term in the academic year of their admission, unless it shall have been extended by the committee.

5. The written examination shall comprise three subjects:

(*a*) one subject on a period selected from Schedule A below, to be examined by written paper;

(*b*) two subjects selected from Schedules A–C [not more than one subject may normally be taken from Schedule C] examined by two pre-set essays (each of 5,000 words).

In lieu of one of the subjects in (*b*) above, M.St. (but not normally M.Phil.) candidates may offer, with the permission of the committee, a dissertation of not more than 10,000 words (excluding bibliography and descriptive catalogue or similar factual matter, but including notes and appendices).

The topic of the dissertation must be approved by the candidate's supervisor and by the School of Archaeology Committee for Graduate Studies. The topic of the dissertation must be clearly distinct from the pre-set essay titles. The dissertation must be the work of the candidate alone, and aid from others must be limited to prior discussion of the subject, bibliographic advice, help with access to study material and advice on presentation. The dissertation must be a new piece of work, substantially different from any dissertation previously submitted by the candidate for a degree of this or another university. When the dissertation is submitted, it must be accompanied by a statement, signed by the candidate, confirming that these conditions have been met. The proposed title of the dissertation, countersigned by the supervisor, must be submitted for approval by the committee by noon on the Tuesday of the eighth week of the Michaelmas Full Term preceding the examination. Two copies typed or printed (the second may be a photocopy) in double spacing on one side only of A4 paper and bound simply or filed securely, must be delivered in a parcel bearing the words 'Dissertation for the M.St. in Classical Archaeology' to the Examination Schools, High Street, Oxford, not later than noon on the Monday of the fifth week of Trinity Full Term and should bear the candidate's examination number but not his or her name. Candidates will be required to deposit one copy of the dissertation with the Examination Schools.

Schedule A: Periods

Aegean Area, 2000–1100 BC
Early Iron Age Greece, 1200–700 BC
Archaic, 800–480 BC
Classical, 500–300 BC
Hellenistic, 330–30 BC
Late Republican, 200–30 BC
Early Imperial, 30 BC–AD 120
Middle Imperial, AD 70–250
Late Antiquity, AD 280–650
Byzantine, AD 600–1453

Schedule B: Subjects

Aegean Bronze Age trade: interaction and identities
Aegean Bronze Age Scripts
Aegean Bronze Age religion
Topics in Aegean Prehistory
Aegean and the East, 1200–600 BC
Burials, settlements, and society in Early Greece, 1200–650 BC
Archaeology of the Early Greek polis, 800–450 BC
Early Ionia, 1000–450 BC Etruscan Italy
Greek sculpture
Greek vases
Achaeology of Athens and Attica 600–50 BC
The archaeology of ancient Macedonia, 600–100 BC
Greek funerary archaeology, 600–100 BC
Archaeology of Greek women
Greek coinage
Greek and Roman wallpainting
Roman sculpture
Historical narrative in Hellenistic and Roman art
Problems and methods in ancient art-history
Roman architecture
Topography of Rome (This may be taken in conjunction with the British School at Rome taught course only if accepted by the British School at Rome on its programme, and it involves attendance at the residential course organised by the British School at Rome in Rome.)
Pompeii and Ostia
Greek and Roman housing
Archaeology of the Roman economy
The archaeology of Roman urban systems
Roman North Africa

Landscape archaeology in the Greek and Roman world
Maritime archaeology of the Greek and Roman Mediterranean
Myth in Greek and Roman Art
Roman Britain
Roman coinage   5
Byzantine Constantinople
Late Roman and Byzantine mosaics and painting
Late Roman and Byzantine architecture
History of collections: classical art
Roman Portraits   10
Roman Provincial Art

Schedule C: Other subjects

Any subject offered in the M.St. in Archaeology, Byzantine Studies, Greek and/or Latin Languages and Literature, Greek and Roman History, History of Art, Women's Studies.   15

Candidates may apply for other subjects, to be taken under Schedule B, to be approved by the committee, which shall define their scope and inform both the candidate and the examiners of this definition in writing.

Not all subjects may be available in any one year.

6. Candidates will be expected to show a general knowledge of Ancient History and   20
Geography, so far as they are concerned with their periods and subjects.

7. Candidates must present themselves for an oral examination as required by the examiners.

8. The period and subjects to be offered by candidates and their chosen method of examination, duly approved by their supervisors, must be submitted for approval to   25
the committee in time for its meeting in eighth week of the Michaelmas Full Term preceding the examination. Notice of options to be offered by candidates must be given to the Registrar not later than Friday of the eighth week of that same term.

9. Candidates offering pairs of pre-set essays will propose essay topics in consulta-   tion with their supervisor or relevant course provider. The proposed essay titles,   30
countersigned by the supervisor, must be submitted for approval of the Chair of Examiners by no later than noon on Friday of the seventh week of the term in which the instruction for that subject is given. Candidates must deliver to the Examination Schools two copies of their essays by not later than noon on Monday of the first week of the term following that in which the instruction for that subject was   35
given. Essays must be typed or printed and should bear the candidate's examination number but not his or her name. Any illustrations must be included in both copies.

10. The examiners may award a distinction for excellence in the whole examination.

11. In the case of failure in just one part of the examination, the candidate will be permitted to retake that part of the examination on one further occasion, not later   40
than one year after the initial attempt. Written papers would be retaken the following year.

Master of Studies in Classical Armenian Studies

1. Before admission to the course, candidates must satisfy the Board of the Faculty of Oriental Studies that they possess the necessary qualifications to profit by the   45
course.

2. Every candidate must follow for at least three terms a course of instruction in Classical Armenian Studies.

3. *Syllabus*

There will be four Units. Each unit is examined by a written paper.

Unit (i). Essay questions on the language, literature, history, and culture of Ancient and Medieval Armenia.

Units (ii), (iii), (iv). Passages for translation and commentary, and essay questions on prescribed texts in Classical and, where relevant, post-Classical Armenian, with special reference to three of the following subjects (passages for unprepared translation from and into Classical Armenian will be set):

(1) Biblical texts.

(2) Homiletic and polemical literature.

(3) Hagiographic texts.

(4) Historical literature of the 5th-9th centuries.

(5) Historical literature of the 10th-14th centuries.

(6) Religious and secular verse.

(7) Any other subject approved by the Board.

4. Lists of set texts must be submitted to the Faculty office by Friday of seventh week of Michaelmas Term.

5. Candidates may be required to attend a viva.

Teaching for the course may not be available in every year. Applicants for admission will be advised of this.

Master of Studies in Classical Hebrew Studies

1. Before admission to the course, candidates must satisfy the Board of the Faculty of Oriental Studies that they possess the appropriate qualifications in Classical Hebrew to profit by the course.

2. Every candidate must follow for at least three terms a course of study in Classical Hebrew Studies.

3. *Syllabus*

There will be four Units. Each unit is examined by a written paper.

Unit (i) Essay questions on the history and literature of Israel and Judah in the Biblical period.

Unit (ii) Prepared and unprepared Biblical texts.

Units (iii) and (iv) *Two* of the following:

(1) Classical Hebrew Language;

(2) The principles and practice of textual criticism;

(3) North-west Semitic epigraphy;

(4) Aramaic;

(5) Dead Sea Scrolls;

(6) Any other subject approved by the Board.

4. Lists of set texts must be submitted to the Faculty office by Friday of seventh week of Michaelmas Term.

5. Candidates may be required to attend a viva.

Teaching for some options may not be available in every year. Applicants for admission will be advised of this.

Master of Studies in Creative Writing

1. Every candidate must follow for at least six terms a part-time course of instruction in Creative Writing.

2. The course will consist of lectures, seminars, workshops, individual tutorials, and a placement.

3. The examination will consist of the following parts:

(*a*) Two assignments selected from two of the genres listed in the schedule below. Assignments submitted for 1, 2, or 5 in the schedule should be no more than 2,500 words of prose. Assignments submitted for 3 in the schedule should be no more than 130 lines of poetry. Assignments submitted for 2 in the schedule should be: no more than 15 minutes (or *c*.2500 words) of Radio Drama; between 12 and 15 minutes stage play (no more than 2,500 words); approximately 15 minutes or no more than 2,500 words of screen play.

(*b*) Two critical appraisal assignments of no more than 2,500 words, selected from two of the genres listed in the schedule below.

(*c*) A portfolio of Creative Writing which may be no more than either approximately 7,000 words of prose or approximately 350 lines of poetry; or no more than *c*.7,000 words) of radio drama; or a stage play of between 35 and 40 minutes (no more than 7,500 words); or approximately 40 minutes or no more than 7,000 words of screenplay.

(*d*) Two extended critical essays, one of no more than 4,000 words and one of no more than 5,000 words, the latter related to the genre in which the final project is written, and both to be approved by the candidate's supervisor.

(*e*) A report on the candidate's Placement of no more than 2,500 words.

(*f*) A Final Project on a topic selected by the candidate in consultation with his or her supervisor and approved by the examiners. The final project may take the format of one of the following:

   (i) a piece of prose fiction or narrative non fiction of approximately 25,000 words;

   (ii) Radio Drama totalling 90 minutes or approximately 18,000 words;

   (iii) a 110-minute stage play (23,000–25,000 words);

   (iv) a screenplay of up to two hours in length (entire); approximately 110–120 pages (12pt Courier) 25,000 words;

   (v) a ninety-minute TV play (approximately 18,000 words);

   (vi) a collection of poetry of between 40 and 60 pages *and* between 600 and 1,200 lines.

Candidates may be required to attend a viva voce examination.

The second Extended Essay under 3(*d*) and the Final Project under 3(*f*) must be delivered not later than noon on the third Friday in September of the final year of the course to the Chair of Examiners for the Degree of M.St. in Creative Writing, c/o Examination Schools, High Street, Oxford.

All other elements of assessed work shall be forwarded to the examiners, c/o Registry, Department for Continuing Education, 1 Wellington Square, Oxford for consideration by such dates as the examiners shall determine and shall notify the candidates and tutors at the start of each academic year.

All assessed work (3(*a*) to 3(*f*)) must be accompanied by a statement that it is the candidate's own work.

4. The examiners may award a distinction for excellence in the whole examination.

5. A candidate who fails to satisfy the examiners in 3 may be permitted to resubmit work in respect of part or parts of the examination which they have failed for examination on one further occasion, not later than one year after the initial attempt.

SCHEDULE

1. Prose fiction   5
2. Drama
3. Poetry
4. Narrative non-fiction
5. Any other option approved by the Board of Study.

The schedule of assessment for any one year will be circulated to candidates and   10
supervisors by the second week of Michaelmas Term.

Master of Studies in Diplomatic Studies

1. Candidates for admission will be expected to have satisfactorily completed the Postgraduate Diploma in Diplomatic Studies not more than three terms before admission to the M.St.   15

2. The course will be taken on a part-time basis over a period of not fewer than three terms and not more than six terms. The total period of study for the Postgraduate Diploma in Diplomatic Studies and the M.St in Diplomatic Studies combined shall be not more than nine terms to be taken over a maximum of eighteen terms from the commencement of the Diploma.   20

3. In addition to having previously satisfied the examiners in all four modules and in the dissertation specified for the Postgraduate Diploma in Diplomatic Studies, every candidate will be required to satisfy the examiners in the following:

(*a*) participation in on-line dissertation supervisions;

(*b*) submission of a dissertation of no more than 15,000 words. The topic of the   25
dissertation, which should be related to one or more of the subject areas of the four modules in the Postgraduate Diploma, and which should be distinct from, though may be complementary to, the topic of the dissertation examined for the Postgraduate Diploma, must be approved by the course director not later than 12 noon on the Friday of first week of Michaelmas Full Term in the academic   30
year in which the examination is taken. Two typewritten or word processed copies of the dissertation must be delivered to the Registry, Department for Continuing Education, 1 Wellington Square, Oxford not later than 12 noon on Friday of sixth week of Trinity Full Term in the year in which the examination is taken.   35

4. Candidates may be required to attend a viva voce examination at the end of the course of study at the discretion of the examiners.

5. The examiners may award a distinction for excellence in the whole examination.

6. A candidate whose dissertation fails to satisfy the examiner may be permitted to resubmit on one further occasion only not later than one year after the initial failure.   40

7. If any candidate who is successful in the examination for the Degree of Master of Studies in Diplomatic Studies has previously successfully completed the Postgraduate Diploma in Diplomatic Studies, the Master of Studies will subsume his or her Diploma.

Master of Studies in English   45

Every candidate must follow for at least three terms a course of study in English.

Syllabus

The following subjects are prescribed:

A. Literature, Contexts, and Approaches

B. Bibliography, Palaeography, and Theories of Text

C. Special Options

The Faculty Board shall prescribe from year to year the particular courses which will be offered for each of these subjects. Courses under A will be taught over Michaelmas and Hilary Terms. Courses on bibliography and palaeography will be taught mainly in Michaelmas Term and courses on Theories of Text in Hilary Term. There will be two lists of Special Options, one for Michaelmas Term and one for Hilary Term. Options under C shall include an American Studies option. Entry to this option may be restricted by the faculty board.

Candidates must take A and four other subjects: two in Michaelmas Term (of which one at least must be a Special Option) and two in Hilary Term (of which one at least must be a Special Option). They must also offer a dissertation. Courses under A will be divided according to chronological period and candidates must take the course appropriate to their period of specialisation.

Candidates will be required to attend the lectures and classes prescribed by the Faculty Board for the courses they have chosen, and undertake such written work, exercises or presentations for those courses as the course tutors shall prescribe.

Essays

In Michaelmas Term candidates will be required to submit an essay of 5,000–7,000 words on a topic related to one of the special options taken under C in that term; two copies of the essay must be delivered to the Examination Schools, High Street, Oxford, not later than noon on Thursday of the tenth week of Michaelmas Term. In Hilary Term, candidates will be required to submit the following:

1. An essay of 5,000–7,000 words on a topic related to one of the special options taken under C in that term, to be submitted to the Examination Schools, High Street, Oxford, not later than noon on Monday of the tenth week of Hilary Term.

2. An essay of 5,000–7,000 words on a topic related either to an option taken under B (in either term) or to a second special option taken under C in that term, to be submitted to the Examination Schools, High Street, Oxford, not later than noon on Thursday of the tenth week of Hilary Term.

Candidates must gain approval of the topic of their essays by writing to the Chair of the M.St./M.Phil. Examiners, care of the English Faculty Office, by Friday of the sixth week of Michaelmas Term (for the first essay) and of Hilary Term (for the second and third essays).

Candidates offering the course in bibliography, palaeography and theories of text in the period up to 1550 under B will be required to pass a test in transcription and dating at the end of Hilary Term. Those who do not achieve a satisfactory mark in the test will be required to retake it at the start of Trinity Term. Any candidate not achieving a satisfactory mark at that stage will be deemed to have failed the whole examination. The test will not contribute to the final marks awarded by the examiners.

Candidates offering the course in bibliography in the period 1550 to the present day under B will be required also to attend a course in manuscript reading and transcription and to pass a test in transcription at the end of Michaelmas Term. Those who do not achieve a satisfactory mark in this test will be required to retake it at the start of Hilary Term. Any candidate not achieving a satisfactory mark at that stage will be deemed to have failed the whole examination. The test will not contribute to the final marks awarded by the examiners.

Not later than noon on Monday of the eighth week of Trinity Term, candidates must deliver to the Examination Schools, High Street, Oxford two copies of a dissertation (10,000–11,000 words) on a subject related to their course of study. The dissertation must be presented in proper scholarly form. Candidates must gain approval of the topic of their dissertation by writing to the Chair of the M.St./M.Phil. Examiners, care of the English Graduate Studies Office, by Friday of the sixth week of Hilary Term, providing an outline of the topic of not more than 200 words.

No candidate who has failed any of the above subjects will be awarded the degree in   5
that examination. Candidates who fail any part of the examination other than the test in bibliography in the period 1550 to the present day described above may resubmit that part by noon on the last Monday of the following Long Vacation. A candidate may resubmit a paper on only one occasion.

Candidates whose course of study includes the American Studies C Special Option   10
and a dissertation on a topic recognised by the English Graduate Studies Committee for English as being within the interdisciplinary field of English and American studies shall be awarded, if successful, degree of Master of Studies with the title English and American Studies.

Candidates whose course of study includes the World Literatures in English A and a   15
dissertation on a topic recognised by the English Graduate Studies Committee for English as being within the field of World Literatures in English shall be awarded, if successful, the degree of Master of Studies with the title World Literatures in English.

The examiners may award a distinction for excellence in the whole examination.

Master of Studies in English Language   20

Every candidate must follow for at least three terms a course of study in English Language.

Syllabus

The following subjects are prescribed:

A. Topics in English Language: History, Structure and Use   25

B. Research Methods for English Language

C. Special Options

The Faculty Board shall prescribe from year to year the particular courses which will be offered for each of these subjects. Courses under A and B will be taught over Michaelmas and Hilary Terms. There will be two lists of Special Options, one for   30
Michaelmas Term and one for Hilary Term. Students will also be able to choose any one option selected from those offered as B courses for the M.St./M.Phil. in General Linguistics and Comparative Philology, subject to the approval of the student's own Course Convenor and the tutor for the option. The teaching and assessment of the Linguistics B courses will follow the provisions and requirements as set by the Faculty   35
of Linguistics, Philology and Phonetics.

Candidates must take courses A, B and two C Option courses (one in each term). They must also offer a dissertation.

Candidates will be required to attend the lectures and classes prescribed by the Faculty Board for the courses they have chosen, and undertake such written work,   40
exercises or presentations for those courses as the course tutors shall prescribe.

Assessed written work

In Michaelmas Term candidates will be required to submit a piece of written work of 5,000–7,000 words on a topic related to one of the special options taken under C in that term; two copies must be delivered to the Examination Schools, High Street,   45
Oxford, not later than noon on Thursday of the tenth week of Michaelmas Term.

In Hilary Term, candidates will be required to submit the following:

    1. A piece of written work of 5,000–7,000 words on a topic related to one of the special options taken under C in that term, to be submitted to the Examination Schools, High Street, Oxford, not later than noon on Monday of   50
the tenth week of Hilary Term.

2. A piece of written work of 5,000–7,000 words on a topic related to the B course, to be submitted to the Examination Schools, High Street, Oxford, not later than noon on Thursday of the tenth week of Hilary Term.

'Written work' may consist of either an essay or a project which includes an analysis of linguistic data and/or an evaluation of a particular method of analysis. The three pieces of work submitted by candidates must include one piece of each type. Candidates must gain approval of the topic of their written work by writing to the Chair of M.St./M.Phil. Examiners, care of English Graduate Studies Office by Friday of the sixth week of Michaelmas Term (for the first essay) and of Hilary Term (for the second and third essays).

Candidates (as part of the B course) will be required to pass a test in English Language Analysis (assessing their competence in the phonetic transcription and grammatical analysis of English) by the end of Michaelmas Term. Those who do not achieve a satisfactory mark in this test will be required to retake it at the start of Hilary Term. Any candidate not achieving a satisfactory mark at that stage will be deemed to have failed the whole examination. The test will not contribute to the final marks awarded by the examiners.

Not later than noon on Monday of the eighth week of Trinity Term, candidates must deliver to the Examination Schools High Street, Oxford two copies of a dissertation (10,000–11,000 words) on a subject related to their course of study. The dissertation must be presented in proper scholarly form. Candidates must gain approval of the topic of their dissertation by writing to the Chair of the M.St./ M.Phil. Examiners, care of the English Graduate Studies Office, by Friday of the sixth week of Hilary Term, providing an outline of the topic of not more than 200 words.

No candidate who has failed any of the above subjects will be awarded the degree in that examination. Candidates who fail any part of the examination other than the English language analysis test may resubmit that part by noon on the last Monday of the following Long Vacation. A candidate may resubmit a paper on only one occasion.

The examiners may award a distinction for excellence in the whole examination.

Master of Studies in Film Aesthetics

1. In order to be considered for admission to the course, applicants must have completed a Bachelors degree, normally in a discipline from the Humanities, Fine Art or the Social Sciences.

2. Candidates must follow a course of instruction in Film Aesthetics at Oxford for a period of three terms, unless the Modern Languages Board in exceptional circumstances shall permit an extension of time, and shall when entering for the examination be required to produce from their society a certificate stating that they are following the course of instruction for the period prescribed.

3. The course shall comprise:

(a) A specified film workshop during the week preceding Week 0 of Michaelmas Term.

(b) Four classes during Michaelmas Term which explore fundamental aspects of film criticism, film analysis, film theory, film form, and film aesthetics.

(c) Four classes during Hilary Term on different, specialised areas of film aesthetics.

(d) A specified programme of films, to be screened publicly during Weeks 1–8 of Michaelmas and Hilary Terms.

(e) Dissertation supervision in Trinity Term.

4. Assessment shall comprise two 6,000 word essays, a 3,000 word essay, and a 10,000 word dissertation, two copies of each piece of written work should be submitted on every occasion.

5. Each essay topic should bear a clear and identifiable relation to a specified part of the course and there should not be substantial overlap between the essay topics.

6. The topic for the *first essay* shall be drawn from one or more of the four classes specified for Michaelmas Term. Each candidate shall submit their essay topic, to the chair of examiners by email for approval by noon on the Friday of Week 7 in Michaelmas Term. Written approval of essay topics will be given to candidates by noon on the Friday of Week 8 in Michaelmas Term. Essays shall be delivered to the Examination Schools, High Street, Oxford, by noon on Monday of Week 1 of Hilary Term. Essays will be marked by subject tutors and returned to candidates with comments by Week 4 of Hilary Term. Candidates may amend their essays in the light of these comments and shall resubmit their essays within the portfolio containing the first essay and the second essay, each clearly marked by noon on the Friday of Week 9 in Trinity Term.

7. The topic for the *second essay* shall be drawn from one or more of the four classes specified for Hilary Term. Each candidate shall submit their essay topic, to the chair of examiners by email for approval by noon on the Friday of Week 7 in Hilary Term. Written approval of essay topics will be given to candidates by noon on the Friday of Week 8 in Hilary Term. Essays shall be delivered to the Examination Schools, High Street, Oxford, by noon on Monday of Week 1 of Trinity Term. Essays will be marked by subject tutors and returned to candidates with comments by Week 4 of Trinity Term. Candidates may amend their essays in the light of these comments and shall resubmit their essays within the portfolio containing the first essay and the second essay, each clearly marked by noon on the Friday of Week 9 in Trinity Term.

8. Each candidate shall submit their *dissertation* topic, with the prior approval of the course coordinator, to the chair of examiners, for approval by noon on the Friday of Week 5 in Hilary Term. Written approval of dissertation topics will be given to candidates by noon on the Friday of Week 6 in Hilary Term. Dissertations shall be delivered to the Examination Schools, High Street, Oxford, by noon on the Friday of Week 6 in Trinity Term.

9. Candidates shall also submit an essay of 3,000 words entitled 'The Concept Essay' where they will examine an aspect of a concept from philosophical aesthetics or more specifically film aesthetics. This essay shall be submitted within the portfolio which also contains the first essay and the second essay, all of them clearly marked by noon on the Friday of Week 9 in Trinity Term.

10. The examiners may award a distinction for excellence in the whole examination.

11. Candidates must present themselves for an oral examination if required to do so by the examiners.

Master of Studies in General Linguistics and Comparative Philology

1. Candidates shall normally have a degree in a subject which has given them at least some experience of linguistic or philological work. Those intending to offer options chosen from C or D below should normally have, and may be required to demonstrate, some knowledge of the chosen (group of) language(s) and those intending to offer options chosen from C will normally be expected to be able to read secondary literature in French and German.

2. The names of all candidates for the M.St. must be registered with the Graduate Studies Assistant of the Faculty of Linguistics, Philology and Phonetics.

3. Every candidate shall pursue a course of study in General Linguistics and Comparative Philology for at least one academic year under the supervision of the faculty. Such study shall be pursued at Oxford.

4. Any person may be admitted to a course of study approved by the faculty, provided that he has *either* (*a*) passed the examinations required for the degree of Bachelor of Arts, *or* (*b*) taken a degree at some other university, such degree and such university having been approved by Council, and provided further that he has satisfied the faculty that he is qualified to pursue the study of General Linguistics and Comparative Philology.

5. The faculty shall have power in exceptional circumstances to admit a person not qualified under the provisions of clause 3 above, who has nevertheless satisfied the faculty that he is qualified to pursue the study of General Linguistics and Comparative Philology.

6. The examination shall consist of three parts:

(*a*) one general paper as indicated in A;

(*b*) two papers both of which must be chosen from those listed in B, or those listed in C (except that, at the discretion of the faculty, candidates may submit a paper from list B in place of one of those from list C), or those listed in D.

In lieu of one of the papers in list B or C or D candidates may offer with the permission of the faculty a thesis of no more than 15,000 words to be written on a subject within the field of the M.St. The word limit excludes the bibliography, appendices consisting of a catalogue of data, any extensive text which is specifically the object of a commentary or linguistic analysis, and any translation of that text, but includes quotations and footnotes.

The thesis (in two typewritten copies) must be sent in a parcel bearing the words 'Thesis for the M.St. in General Linguistics and Comparative Philology' to the Examination Schools, High Street, Oxford, not later than noon on the Friday of the first week of the Trinity Term in the academic year in which the examination takes place.

A. Linguistic Theory.

B. (i) Phonetics and Phonology.

(ii) Syntax.

(iii) Semantics.

(iv) Historical and comparative linguistics.

(v) Psycholinguistics and Neurolinguistics.

(vi) History and structure of a language.

(vii) Experimental Phonetics.

(viii) Sociolinguistics.

(ix) Computational Linguistics.

(x) English as World Language.

(xi) Any other subject which, from time to time, the Faculty of Linguistics, Philology and Phonetics at its own discretion may consider suitable.

C. (i) The comparative grammar of two Indo-European languages or language-groups.

(ii) The historical grammar of the two languages or language-groups selected.

(iii) Translation from, and linguistic comment upon, texts in the languages selected.

D.   (i) The history of one or two languages.

    (ii) The structure of the language or languages selected.

    (iii) *Either* (*a*) Translation from, and/or linguistic comment upon, texts in the language or languages selected, *or* (*b*) Any paper from B above except B (vi).

7. The general paper A and the papers in C and D are each assessed by three-hour written examination. The papers in B are assessed by:

Either (*a*) three-hour written examination.

Or (*b*) An essay of between 5,000 and 7,500 words (these limits to exclude symbols and diacritics, figures, the bibliography, appendices consisting of a catalogue of data, questionnaire, or other research instrument used to gather data, any extensive text which is specifically the object of a commentary or linguistic analysis, and any translation of that text, but include quotations and footnotes). For all B papers except for B(ix) and B(x), the essay (in two typewritten copies) must be sent in a parcel bearing the words 'Essay for the M.St./M.Phil. in General Linguistics and Comparative Philology' to the Chair of Examiners for the Degree of M.St./M.Phil. in General Linguistics, c/o Examination Schools, High Street, Oxford. Work for paper B(ix) is submitted as specified in the regulations for the M.Sc. in Computer Science, and work for papers under B(x) is submitted as specified in the regulations for the M.St. in English Language.

Or (*c*) A written report of between 5,000 and 7,500 words on the design and execution of an original research project (these limits exclude symbols and diacritics, figures, the bibliography, appendices consisting of a catalogue of data, questionnaire, or other research instrument used to gather data, any extensive text which is specifically the object of a commentary or linguistic analysis, and any translation of that text, but include quotations and footnotes). The research report (in two typewritten copies) must be sent in a parcel bearing the words 'Written work for the M.St./M.Phil. in General Linguistics and Comparative Philology' to the Chair of Examiners for the Degree of M.St./M.Phil. in General Linguistics, c/o Examination Schools, High Street, Oxford.

In addition, the lecturer on the course of instruction may require:

    (*a*) one or more practical problem set(s), to be completed and submitted at a time specified by the lecturer; and

    (*b*) one or more oral presentation(s) in a public forum.

For each paper in B, the lecturer on the course of instruction shall prescribe a suitable combination of these options, and shall make available to the Chair of Examiners evidence showing the extent to which each candidate has pursued an adequate course of work.

8. Of the two languages or language-groups selected by the candidates who wish to offer the papers listed in C above, one must be studied in greater depth than the other.

Combinations previously offered under the auspices of the Faculty of Linguistics, Philology and Phonetics are:

    (*a*) Greek with the elements of Sanskrit Philology.

    (*b*) Italic with the elements of Old Irish Philology.

    (*c*) Germanic with the elements of Greek Philology.

    (*d*) Greek with the elements of Anatolian Philology.

    (*e*) Romance with the elements of Italic Philology.

    (*f*) Italic with the elements of Greek Philology.

    (*g*) Sanskrit with the elements of Greek Philology.

(*h*) Greek with the elements of Slavonic Philology.

(*i*) Celtic with the elements of Italic Philology.

Other combinations are allowed subject to the approval of the faculty and the availability of teaching.

9. The language or languages selected by candidates who wish to offer the papers mentioned in D above may be ancient (e.g. Ancient Greek, Latin, Sanskrit, Akkadian, etc.) or modern (e.g. French, Italian, German, English, Turkish, etc.). Only languages for which teaching is available at the time can be offered.

10. The choice of the subjects for examination will be subject to the approval of the candidate's supervisor and the faculty, having regard to the candidate's previous experience and the availability of teaching. Not all options may be offered every year. The subjects which a candidate wishes to offer for examination must be submitted to the faculty for approval not later than Tuesday of the sixth week of the Michaelmas Term in the academic year in which the candidate is to be examined.

11. If a thesis is offered, the subject must be submitted for approval by the faculty not later than Tuesday of the sixth week of the Michaelmas Term in the academic year in which the candidate is to be examined.

12. Each candidate is required to present himself for an oral examination if and when required by the examiners.

13. The Examiners may award a distinction for excellence in the whole examination.

14. Candidates requesting re-examination should be required to resit or resubmit any paper in which they have failed to achieve a pass mark. The highest mark awarded for a re-examined paper should be the pass mark.

Master of Studies in Global and Imperial History

The regulations of the Board of the Faculty of History are as follows:

1. Candidates for this degree must follow for at least three terms a course of instruction and directed research and must, upon entering the examination, produce from their society a certificate to that effect.

2. Candidates must attend such lectures, seminars and classes as their supervisor shall determine. In addition to the formally examined programme elements described below, each candidate will be expected to attend and complete in-course requirements for a series of skills and specialist options based on a schedule to be published from year to year by the Faculty's Graduate Studies Committee.

3. The final examination shall comprise (i) two extended essays of between 4,000 and 5,000 words based on an Advanced Option, (ii) one three-hour examination paper based on the programme's conceptual and methodological component, and (iii) a dissertation of not more than 15,000 words.

I. The programme has three streams, providing the following distinct Advanced Options:

    (i) *Imperial History*: Empires in Global History 1750–2000;

    (ii) *South Asian History*: paper t.b.c.;

    (iii) *East Asian History*: history and historiography of modern China.

Two copies of the two essays, addressed to the Chair of Examiners for the M.St. in Global and Imperial History, must be submitted to the Examination Schools, High Street, Oxford by 12 noon on Monday of Week Nine of Hilary Term. The essays should reflect the skills and understanding acquired by the candidate through attending the Advanced Option classes. One of the essays may complement—but must not share significant content with—the dissertation, and the essays are also expected to be distinct from each other in period or issues covered.

II. Each candidate must sit a three-hour written examination on conceptual and methodological issues relating to their chosen stream through the course:

   (i) *Imperial History*: concepts and methods of imperial history;

   (ii) *South Asian History*: history and culture of South Asia;

   (iii) *East Asian History*: Research methods (East Asia).

III. Each candidate must submit a dissertation of not more than 15,000 words on a topic in the candidate's chosen subject area. The dissertation must include a short abstract which concisely summarises in about 300 words its scope and principal arguments.

Two copies of the dissertation, addressed to the Chair of Examiners for the M.St. in Global and Imperial History, must be submitted to the Examination Schools, High Street, Oxford, by 12 noon on Monday of Week Six of Trinity Term. Material submitted under I and II may be summarised or substantially further developed in the dissertation, but no significant part of the dissertation should reproduce or paraphrase other work submitted for examination.

4. The examiners may award a distinction to candidates who have performed with special merit in the whole examination.

5. A candidate who fails the examination will be permitted to retake it on one further occasion only, not later than one year after the initial attempt.

Master of Studies in Greek and/or Latin Languages and Literature

1. *Course.* Every candidate must follow for at least three terms a course of instruction in Greek and/or Latin Languages and Literature.

2. *Syllabus*

Candidates must take three options from lists A, B, C, and D below, at least one of which must be drawn from B or C. Not more than one dissertation (D) may be offered. Every candidate must offer at least one option that requires detailed study of Greek or Latin or of texts in those languages. Options which meet this criterion are specified in the Handbook.

A

The texts for each option will appear in the M.St./M.Phil. handbook issued in Week 0 of the Michaelmas Term preceding the examination. Each option will be examined by (*a*) one paper of translation (1½ hours) and (*b*) two pre-submitted essays. The texts listed in the handbook are those which should be studied in preparation for the pre-submitted essays. Passages will be set for translation only from those texts in section (α); the edition will be that listed in the handbook. For any option approved under A11 the edition will be specified by the Graduate Studies Committee in Classical Languages and Literature.

   1. Historiography

   2. Lyric Poetry

   3. Early Greek Hexameter Poetry

   4. Greek Tragedy

   5. Comedy

   6. Hellenistic Poetry

   7. Cicero

   8. Ovid

   9. Latin Didactic

10. Neronian Literature.

11. Any other text or combination of texts approved by the Graduate Studies Committee for Classical Languages and Literature.

B

1. *Methods and Techniques of Scholarship.* Candidates choosing this option are required to offer *two* of the following topics:

(*a*) Greek Literary Papyrology;

(*b*) Greek Palaeography;

(*c*) Latin Palaeography;

(*d*) Greek Metre;

(*e*) Latin Metre.

Each of these topics will be examined in one paper of 1½ hours, except for (a) Greek Literary Papyrology, which will be examined by a practical test taken in the candidate's own time (as prescribed for option B3 Greek and Latin Papyrology in the M.Phil. in Greek and/or Latin Languages and Literature). Option B1(a) may not be combined with option B10 below.

2. *Greek textual criticism*: Euripides, *Orestes* 1–347 and 1246–1693: papyri, manuscripts, text. (Honour School of Literae Humaniores, subject 513).

3. *Latin textual criticism. Either*

(*a*) Seneca, *Agamemnon*: manuscripts, text, interpretation (Honour School of Literae Humaniores, subject 514) *or*

(*b*) Catullus 1–14, 27–39, 44–51, 65–7, 69–76, 95–101, 114–16: manuscripts, text, interpretation (Honour School of Literae Humaniores, subject 515).

4. *Historical Linguistics and Comparative Philology.* This option includes an introduction to the methods and aims of historical and comparative linguistics, the reconstruction of the Indo-European protolanguage and its development into Latin and Greek. The questions set will require specific competence in one of the two classical languages but not necessarily in both. An opportunity will be given for (optional) commentary on Greek or Latin texts.

Each of options B2–B4 will be examined in one paper of three hours.

5. Any option available in the M.St. in Classical Archaeology, Schedule B. This option will be examined *either* by two presubmitted essays *or* by a dissertation of not more than 10,000 words. The deadlines for submission of essays will be those of the M.St. in Greek and/or Latin Languages and Literature.

6. Any option available in the M.St. in Greek and/or Roman History, Lists B, and C. This option will be examined by two presubmitted essays. The deadlines for submission will be those of the M.St. in Greek and/or Latin Languages and Literature.

7. *Theoretical Approaches to Classical Literature.*

8. *Reception: Theory and Methods.*

9. *Comparative Criticism.* This option may not be taken together with options 7. *Theoretical Approaches to Classical Literature* or 8. *Reception: Theory and Methods.*

Options B7, B8 and B9 will be examined by two presubmitted essays and require attendance at the associated classes.

10. *Greek and Latin Literary Papyrology.* This option will be examined by one presubmitted essay and by a practical test taken in the candidate's own time (as prescribed for Greek and Latin Papyrology in the M.Phil. for Greek and/or Latin Languages and Literature). This option may not be combined with option B1(*a*) above.

11. Any other subject proposed with the aim of developing skills needed for future research and approved by the Graduate Studies Committee in Classical Languages and Literature, which will determine the method of examination.

C

EITHER (1) Classical Greek:

either (*a*) *Elementary Greek.* There will be one three-hour paper, consisting of passages of Greek which will test knowledge of Attic grammar and competence in translation from Greek into English.   5

or (*b*) *Intermediate Greek.* There will be one two-hour paper comprising unseen translation and grammatical questions on prescribed texts and one three-hour paper requiring translation from prescribed texts. A detailed specification and prescribed texts for the paper will appear in the M.St./M.Phil. handbook issued in Week 0 of the Michaelmas Term preceding the examination. Alternative texts for translation under   10 this head may be offered by agreement with the Graduate Studies Committee in Classical Languages and Literature.

OR (2) Latin:

either Elementary Latin. There will be one three-hour paper, consisting of passages of Latin prose which will test knowledge of classical Latin grammar and competence in   15 translation from Latin into English.

or Intermediate Latin. There will be one two-hour paper comprising unseen translation and grammatical questions on prescribed texts and one three-hour paper requiring translation from prescribed texts. A detailed specification and prescribed texts for the paper will be published in the M.St./M.Phil. course handbook not later than   20 Monday of Week 0 of the Michaelmas Term preceding the examination.

D

A dissertation (if offered) should be of not more than 10,000 words on a subject to be proposed by the candidate in consultation with the overall supervisor or the supervisor for the dissertation, and approved by the Graduate Studies Committee in Classical   25 Languages and Literature. (The dissertation word limit excludes only the bibliography; quotations, notes and appendices are included. A note of the word-count must be included. Candidates who edit and annotate a substantial text, or compile a substantial descriptive catalogue, may apply to Graduate Studies Committee for permission to exclude the text or catalogue in question from the word count.) Supervisors or   30 others are permitted to give bibliographical help and to discuss drafts.

3. The choice of options and/or dissertation will be subject to the approval of the candidate's supervisor and the Graduate Studies Committee in Classical Languages and Literature, having regard to the candidate's previous experience, the range covered by the candidate's choices, and the availability of teaching and examining   35 resources. Options under B5, B6, and B11 in disciplines other than Greek and/or Latin Languages and Literature require the approval of both the Graduate Studies Committee for Classical Languages and Literature and the Graduate Studies Committee responsible for the discipline concerned. The options which the candidate wishes to offer must be submitted to the Academic Administrative Officer, Ioannou   40 Centre, 66 St. Giles', Oxford OX1 3LU, for approval not later than the Wednesday of Week 1 of Michaelmas Full Term. The candidate should also indicate by this date whether or not he or she wishes to offer a dissertation; the title of the dissertation need not be given until the Friday of Week 1 of Hilary Term (see under 7(i) below).

Not all options may be available in any given year.   45

4. In those options for which candidates are examined by presubmitted essays, two essays should be submitted, each of not more than 5,000 words in length, which between them display knowledge of more than a narrow range of the topic. (The essay word limit excludes only the bibliography; quotations, notes and appendices are included. A note of the word-count must be included. Candidates who edit and   50 annotate a substantial text, or compile a substantial descriptive catalogue, may apply to Graduate Studies Committee for permission to exclude the text or catalogue

in question from the word count.) Supervisors or others are permitted to give bibliographical help with, and to discuss a first draft of, such essays. Supervisors are also required to certify that, in their tutorial and class work, students have covered a wider range of topics within the overall subject.

5. Candidates are required to present themselves for oral examination if summoned by the examiners.

6. The examiners may award a distinction for excellence in the whole examination.

7. *Submission of proposed titles for essays and dissertations*:

(1) Those submitting two or more options examined by presubmitted essays must submit the proposed titles of two of those essays through their supervisors to the Academic Administrative Officer, Ioannou Centre, 66 St. Giles', Oxford OX1 3LU, not later than noon on Monday of Week 0 of Hilary Full Term. The proposed dissertation title, for those offering that option, must be submitted by the same date.

(2) Those offering only one option examined by presubmitted essays may, if they wish to submit their essays in Hilary Term, submit the proposed titles of their two essays through their supervisors to the Academic Administrative Officer, Ioannou Centre, 66 St. Giles', Oxford OX1 3LU, not later than noon on Monday of Week 0 of Hilary Full Term. Otherwise they must submit the proposed titles of their two essays through their supervisors to the Academic Administrative Officer, not later than Friday of Week 1 of Trinity Full Term.

(3) Those offering more than two presubmitted essays must offer their proposed titles for the remaining essays by Friday of Week 1 of Trinity Full Term.

(4) The final confirmation of the title of the dissertation, if different from that submitted under (1) above, must be submitted not later than Friday of Week 1 of Trinity Full Term.

8. *Delivery of final copies of essays and dissertations*:

(1) Two typewritten or printed copies of each presubmitted essay should be sent in a parcel bearing the words 'Essays submitted for the M.St. in Greek and/or Latin Languages and Literature' to the Examination Schools, High Street, Oxford OX1 4BG. If the candidates are offering only one option examined by presubmitted essays, the essays may be sent as above to arrive not later than noon on the Thursday of Week 5 of Hilary Full Term. Otherwise they must be sent as above to arrive not later than noon on the Wednesday of Week 6 of Trinity Full Term. If candidates are offering two options examined by presubmitted essays, at least two of the essays must be sent as above to arrive not later than noon on Thursday of Week 5 of Hilary Full Term; any others must be sent as above to arrive not later than noon on the Wednesday of Week 6 of Trinity Full Term.

In theses and pre-submitted essays all quotations from primary or secondary sources, and all reporting or appropriation of material from those sources, must be explicitly acknowledged. Each candidate must submit a signed declaration of authorship in a sealed envelope together with the thesis or pre-submitted essay.

(2) Two typewritten or printed copies of dissertations should be delivered in a parcel bearing the words 'Dissertation for the M.St. in Greek and/or Latin Languages and Literature' to the Examination Schools, High Street, Oxford OX1 4BG, to arrive not later than noon on the Wednesday of Week 6 of the Trinity Full Term in which the examination is to be taken.

9. *Use of bilingual dictionaries in examinations*:

Any candidate whose native language is not English may bring a bilingual (native language to English) dictionary for use in any examination paper where candidates are required to translate Ancient Greek and/or Latin texts into English.

Master of Studies in Greek and/or Roman History

1. Every candidate must follow, for at least three terms, a course of instruction in Greek and/or Roman History. Candidates will, when they enter for the examination, be required to produce from their society a certificate that they are following such a course.

2. (*a*) In the case of options in languages, Schedule A below, candidates will be   5
examined by written examination. Candidates taking options A (v)–(viii) may bring a dictionary for their use in the examination. Any candidate taking options A (i)–(iv) whose native language is not English may bring a bilingual (native language-English) dictionary for use in the examination.

(*b*) For options in topics and techniques, Schedules B and C below, candidates   10
will be required to pre-submit two essays of not more than 5,000 words in length, which between them display knowledge of more than a narrow range of the topic covered by the course. (The essay word limit excludes the bibliography, any text that is being edited or annotated, any translation of that text, and any descriptive catalogue or similar factual matter, but in-   15
cludes quotations, notes, and appendices.)

Supervisors or others are permitted to give bibliographical help with and to discuss drafts of essays. Such essays (two typewritten or printed copies) must be sent in a parcel bearing the words 'Essays presubmitted for the M.St. in Greek and/or Roman History' to the Examination Schools, High Street, Oxford, OX1 4BG, to reach there by noon on   20
the Wednesday of Week 6 of the Trinity Term in which the examination is to be taken.

3. *Oral Examination*. Candidates are required to present themselves for oral examination if summoned by the examiners.

4. *Syllabus*

Candidates must offer (1) an option from A below, (2) an option from B or C below,   25
and (3) a dissertation as described in D below. The option from A must be (i), (ii), (iii), or (iv), unless a candidate is dispensed from this requirement by the Graduate Studies Committee for Ancient History. In addition, all candidates must attend and partici-pate in one of the Graduate Seminars in Ancient History as described in E below, although this will not be a subject of examination.   30

A

(i) *Elementary Greek*. There will be one three-hour paper, consisting of passages of Greek which will test knowledge of Attic grammar and competence in translation from Greek into English.

(ii) *Intermediate Greek*. There will be one three-hour paper comprising passages   35
for translation from prescribed texts and a passage for unseen translation. A detailed specification and prescribed texts for the paper will be published in the M.St./M.Phil. course handbook not later than Monday of Week 0 of the Michaelmas Term preceding the examination. Alternative texts for transla-tion under this head may be offered by agreement with the Graduate Studies   40
Committee for Ancient History.

(iii) *Elementary Latin*. There will be one three-hour paper, consisting of passages of Latin prose which will test knowledge of classical Latin grammar and competence in translation from Latin into English.

(iv) *Intermediate Latin*. There will be one three-hour paper comprising passages   45
for translation from prescribed texts and a passage for unseen translation. A detailed specification and prescribed texts for the paper will be published in the M.St./M.Phil. course handbook not later than Monday of Week 0 of the Michaelmas Term preceding the examination. Alternative texts for transla-tion under this head may be offered by agreement with the Graduate Studies   50
Committee for Ancient History.

  (v) French

 (vi) German

(vii) Italian

(viii) Any other language which the candidate has satisfied the Graduate Studies
Committee for Ancient History is relevant to their other papers including any
dissertation.

B

   (i) Greek Numismatics.

  (ii) Roman Numismatics.

 (iii) Greek Epigraphy.

 (iv) The epigraphy of the Roman World.

  (v) Documentary papyrology.

 (vi) Roman Law.

(vii) Any of the following papers on the B list of the M.St. in Greek and/or Latin
Languages and Literature: B1–4; B7. Presubmitted essays offered under this
option will be subject to the normal regulations for the submission of presubmitted essays in the M.St. in Greek and/or Roman History.

(viii) Any of the papers from Schedule B of the M.St. in Classical Archaeology.
Presubmitted essays offered under this option will be subject to the normal
regulations for the submission of presubmitted essays in the M.St. in Greek
and/or Roman History.

 (ix) Any other subject approved by the Graduate Studies Committee for Ancient
History.

C

    (i) Greek history to *c.* 650 BCE

   (ii) Greek history *c.* 650–479 BCE

  (iii) Greek history 479–336 BCE

  (iv) Athenian democracy in the Classical age

   (v) Alexander and his successors 336–301 BCE

  (vi) The Hellenistic world 301–*c.* 100 BCE

 (vii) Rome and the Mediterranean World 241–146 BCE

(viii) Roman history 146–46 BCE

  (ix) Cicero

   (x) Roman history 46 BCE–54 CE

  (xi) Roman history 54–138 CE

 (xii) Roman history 138–312 CE

(xiii) The ecology, agriculture, and settlement history of the ancient
Mediterranean world

(xiv) The economy of the Roman Empire

 (xv) The provinces of the Roman Empire

(xvi) Greek and/or Roman religion

(xvii) Gender and sexuality in the Greek and/or Roman world

(xviii) Greek and/or Latin historiography

 (xix) The Church in the Roman Empire from the beginnings to 312 CE

 (xx) The world of Augustine

(xxi) The City of Rome. This course is run in collaboration with the British School at Rome, and involves attendance at the residential course organised by the School annually in Rome; only those accepted by the School may take the option.

(xxii) British School at Athens taught course (title and topic varies from time to time). This option is run in collaboration with the British School at Athens, and involves attendance at the residential course organised by the School in even-numbered years in Athens; only those accepted by the School may take the option.

(xxiii) Any other subject approved by the Graduate Studies Committee for Ancient History.

D

A dissertation of not more than 10,000 words on a subject to be approved by the Graduate Studies Committee for Ancient History. (The dissertation word limit excludes the bibliography, any text that is being edited or annotated, any translation of that text, and any descriptive catalogue or similar factual matter, but includes quotations, notes, and appendices.)

The dissertation (two typewritten or printed copies) must be sent in a parcel bearing the words 'Dissertation for the M.St. in Greek and/or Roman History' to The Chair of Examiners, c/o Examinations Schools, High Street, Oxford, to arrive no later than noon on the Wednesday of Week 6 of the Trinity Full Term in which the examination is to be taken.

E

Graduate Seminars
  (i) Greece and the East
  (ii) Rome and the West

These working seminars, organised by members of the faculty in areas of current interest to them, run fortnightly in Michaelmas and Hilary Terms. The topics of the Seminars will vary from time to time. Details are announced in the Graduate Handbook for the Degrees of Master of Studies and Master of Philosophy in Greek and/or Roman History.

5. All options, including the dissertation, require the approval of the candidate's supervisor and the Graduate Studies Committee for Ancient History, having regard to the candidate's previous experience, the range covered by the chosen options and the availability of teaching and examining resources. Options under B (vii), (viii), (ix) and C (xxiii) in disciplines other than Ancient History require the approval of both the Graduate Studies Committee for Ancient History and the Graduate Studies Committee responsible for the discipline concerned. The options must be submitted for approval not later than the Friday of Week 5 of the Michaelmas Term in the academic year in which the candidate intends to be examined. Candidates will not normally be allowed to be examined in languages of which they are native speakers or which they have previously studied in taught courses for more than two years.

Master of Studies in History of Art and Visual Culture

(*See also the general notice at the commencement of these regulations.*)
The regulations of the Board of the Faculty of History are as follows:

1. Every candidate must follow for at least three terms a course of instruction in the History of Art, and must, upon entering for the examination, produce from his or her society a certificate to this effect.

2. *Syllabus*

The course shall comprise: I, one compulsory paper; II, one optional paper chosen by the candidate; and III, a dissertation.

I. The compulsory paper entitled 'Theory and Methods in the History of Art' will be assessed by three essays of between 1,200 and 1,500 words each. A choice of topics for these essays as prescribed by the examiners will be published on the WebLearn pages for this degree programme by noon on Monday of ninth week of Trinity Term. Two copies of each essay submitted must be delivered to the Examination Schools, High Street, Oxford OX1 4BG, by noon on Thursday of ninth week of Trinity Term in the year in which the examination is to be taken.

II. Optional papers will cover topics and issues of art history and visual culture from the later Middle Ages to the present, as approved from time to time by the Committee of the History of Art. A definitive list of the optional papers available in any one year will be posted on the notice boards of the Faculty of History by Friday of fourth week of Michaelmas Term at the latest. Optional papers will be examined by two extended essays of between 4,000 and 5,000 words.

III. A dissertation of not more than 15,000 words on a topic in the history of art, to be approved by the candidate's supervisor and the Head of the Department of History of Art prior to the submission of essay and dissertation titles to the Chair of Examiners for the degree.

3. Candidates shall make written application for the approval of the titles of their extended essays in their optional paper, and also notify the examiners of the title of their dissertation by the examination entry date.

4. Two typewritten or printed copies of each extended essay for the optional paper must be sent to the Chair of the Examiners for the M.St in History of Art and Visual Culture, c/o Examination Schools, High Street, Oxford OX1 4BG by noon on Monday of Week One of Trinity Term. Two typewritten or printed copies of the dissertation must be sent to the Chair of Examiners at the same address by noon on Monday of Week Six of Trinity Term. The dissertation must include a short abstract which concisely summarizes its scope and principal arguments, in about 300 words. Both the essays and the dissertations must be (individually) securely and firmly bound in either hard or soft covers; and the presentation and footnotes should comply with the requirements specified in the Regulations of the Education Committee for the degrees of M.Litt. and D.Phil. and follow the *Conventions for the presentation of dissertations and theses* of the Board of the Faculty of History.

5. The examiners may award a distinction for excellence in the whole examination.

6. A candidate who fails the examination will be permitted to re-take the examination on one further occasion only, not later than one year after the initial attempt. Such a candidate whose dissertation has been of satisfactory standard will not be required to re-submit the dissertation, while a candidate who has reached a satisfactory standard on *both* the option and the prescribed theory and methods essays will not be required to re-take those parts of the examination.

Master of Studies in History of Design

[For students starting before MT 2015: 1. Candidates must follow a course of instruction in the History of Design. The course will be taken on a part-time basis over a period of not fewer than two years and not more than three years within a maximum period of five years.

2. The examination will consist of the following parts:

A Mandatory Course Papers

Every candidate must submit a written assignment for each of the three mandatory course papers taught in Year 1:

I. Techniques and Materials (Object Case Study: 2,500 words)

II. Historical Methods (Methodology and Critical Sources Review: 3,000 words)

III. Research Project (Extended Essay: 5,000 words)

B Advanced Papers

Every candidate must follow two Advanced Papers courses from the options listed in the Schedule below, and submit one written assignment of no more than 5,000 words in length for each paper. Candidates will select two Advanced Papers in Year 2   5
of the M.St from a list of available options.

C Dissertation

Every candidate must produce a dissertation of not more than 15,000 words, including appendices but excluding bibliography and endnotes, on a topic approved by the Course Director. The dissertation must be delivered not later than noon on the   10
last Monday in September of the second year of the course to the Chair of Examiners for the Degree of M.St in the History of Design, c/o Head of Examinations and Assessment, Examination Schools, High Street, Oxford.

3. Each candidate must attend a viva voce examination when required to do so by the examiners.   15

4. The examiners may award a distinction for excellence in the whole examination.

5. A candidate who fails a core topic or advanced paper, or whose dissertation fails to satisfy the examiners, may be permitted to retake the paper, or resubmit the dissertation, on one further occasion only, not later than one year after the initial attempt.   20

Schedule

Advanced Papers are available in the following areas:

• *Decoration in Modern France*

• *The Arts and Crafts Tradition in Modern Britain*

• *Design in the Machine Age*   25

• *Design, Body, Environment*

• *Visual Cultures of the World Wars*

• *Academic Writing and Contemporary Practice**

• *Medieval Period or Early Modern* Paper Option (shared with the proposed M.St Architectural History)   30

• Papers available to be shared with the existing M.Sc. English Local History:

A.7 *The social history of English architecture, 1870–1940*

A.8 *The English suburb, 1800–1939*

A.4 *English architecture 1500–1640*

* This Advanced Paper will be assessed by means of two written assignments: a   35
Documentation Project and a Critical Sources Review; each 1,500 words in length.

Not all advanced papers will be available in any one year and the definitive list of advanced papers available in any one year will be circulated to candidates and their supervisors during the second week of Michaelmas Term.

A Postgraduate Diploma will be available only to those registered as M.St students   40
but who for whatever reason are not continuing to complete the full M.St. To be awarded the Postgraduate Diploma in the History of Design students must successfully complete the Core papers in 2A(I-III) and the Advanced Papers in 2B.]

[**For students starting from MT 2015:** 1. Candidates must follow a course of instruction in the History of Design. The course is available on a part time basis   45
only to be followed over a period of six terms.

2. Every candidate will be required to satisfy the examiners in the following:

(*a*) Attendance at classes, individual tutorials, group seminars and other teaching sessions as required

(*b*) A written assignment for each of the three papers taught in Year 1
    (i) Materials and Techniques: an object case study of not more than 2,500 words
    (ii) Historical Methods: a methodology and critical sources review of not more than 3,000 words
    (iii) A research project of not more than 5,000 words.   5

(*c*) A written assignment of not more than 5,000 words for each of two Advanced papers selected from the Schedule below.

(*d*) A dissertation of not more than 15,000 words on a topic approved by the Course Director.

Assignments under 2(*b*) and (*c*) shall be submitted, to the examiners c/o the   10
Registry, Department for Continuing Education, 1 Wellington Square Oxford OX1 2JA, in for consideration by such dates as the examiners shall determine and of which they shall notify candidates. The dissertation under 2(*d*) must be submitted in hard copy and in digital copy not later than noon on the last Monday in September of the second year of the course to the Chairman of Examiners for the Degree of the M.St. in   15
History of Design c/o Examination Schools, High Street, Oxford OX1 4BG.

3. Each candidate must attend a *viva voce* examination when required to do so by the examiners.

4. The examiners may award a distinction for excellence in the whole examination.

5. Candidates who fail to satisfy the examiners in any part or parts of the examina-   20
tion may be permitted to resubmit work in respect of the part or parts of the examination which they have failed on not more than one occasion which shall normally be within one year of the original failure.

Schedule

Advanced Papers are available in the following areas: 25
  • *Decoration in Modern France*
  • *The Arts and Crafts Tradition in Modern Britain*
  • *Design in the Machine Age*
  • *Design, Body, Environment*
  • *Visual Cultures of the World Wars*   30
  • *Academic Writing and Contemporary Practice**
  • *Early Period*
  • Papers available to be shared with the existing M.Sc. English Local History:
    A.7 *The social history of English architecture, 1870–1940*
    A.8 *The English suburb, 1800–1939*   35
    A.4 *English architecture 1500–1640*

* This Advanced Paper will be assessed by means of two written assignments: a Documentation Project and a Critical Sources Review; each 1,500 words in length.

Not all advanced papers will be available in any one year and the definitive list of advanced papers available in any one year will be circulated to candidates and their   40
supervisors during the second week of Michaelmas Term.]

Master of Studies in International Human Rights Law

[For students starting before MT 2015: 1. Candidates must follow a course of instruction in International Human Rights Law. The course will be taken on a part-time basis over a period of not fewer than six terms and not more than twelve terms.   45

2. Every candidate will be required to satisfy the examiners in the following:
    (*a*)
        (i) Attendance at classes, individual tutorials, group seminars, and other teaching sessions as required;
        (ii) Participation in all parts of the course to the satisfaction of the Course   50
Director;

 (iii) Participation in (electronic) group discussions under the guidance, and to the satisfaction, of the student's academic tutor;

 (*b*) four written papers, each of three hours' duration, as set out below:

  (i) Fundamentals of International Human Rights Law II

  (ii) The Implementation and Development of International Human Rights Law I

  (iii) The Implementation and Development of International Human Rights Law II

  (iv) Populations at Risk

 (*c*) six essays, each of not more than 2,000 words in length, covering the Fundamentals of International Human Rights Law I;

 (*d*) a dissertation prospectus not to exceed 1,500 words in length that identifies the dissertation topic, central question, thesis and methodology; provides a summary of the dissertation; a schedule for completion and a working bibliography. The bibliography will not count towards the word length of the prospectus;

 (*e*) a dissertation of no more than 12,000 words on a topic selected by the student in consultation with the supervisor and agreed by the Board of Examiners.

The assignments under 2(*c–d*) and the dissertation under 2(*e*) will be forwarded to the examiners c/o Registry, Department for Continuing Education, Wellington Square, Oxford OX1 2JA, for receipt by such date as the examiners shall determine and shall notify the candidates and tutors.

3. Candidates may be required to attend a viva voce examination at the end of the course of study at the discretion of the examiners.

4. The examiners may award a distinction for excellence in the whole examination.

5. Candidates who fail to satisfy the examiners in the written examinations under 2 (b), the written portfolios under 2(*c–d*) or the dissertation under 2(*e*) may be permitted to resubmit work in respect of the part or parts of the examination which they have failed on not more than one occasion which shall normally be within one year of the original failure.]

[For students starting from MT 2015: 1. Candidates must follow a course of instruction in International Human Rights Law. The course will be taken on a part-time basis over six terms.

2. Every candidate will be required to satisfy the examiners in the following:

 (*a*)

  (i) Attendance at classes;

  (ii) Participation in all parts of the course to the satisfaction of the Course Director;

  (iii) Participation in (electronic) group discussions as prescribed in the course conventions;

 (*b*) Six assignments, each of not more than 2,000 words, on the subject of The Fundamentals of International Human Rights Law;

 (*c*) Four written examinations, each of three hours duration, to include two papers from each of:

  (i) Implementation and Development of International Human Rights Law;

  (ii) Populations at Risk.

Papers taken are to be chosen from a list in the handbook to be published by the first week of Michaelmas Term each year.

(*d*) Preparatory work associated with the dissertation consisting of a proposal of not more than 1,500 words. This is formative only and does not contribute to the final mark.

(*e*) A dissertation of not more than 12,000 words on a topic selected by the student in consultation with the supervisor and agreed by any two of the Examiners.]

Master of Studies in Islamic Art and Archaeology

1. Before admission to the course, candidates must satisfy the Board of the Faculty of Oriental Studies that they possess the necessary qualifications in Arabic or Persian or Ottoman Turkish to profit by the course.

2. Every candidate must follow for at least three terms a course of instruction in Islamic Art and Archaeology.

3. The examination will consist of the following four units:

Unit 1.

Candidates shall submit **either**

1A: two essays of between 5,000 and 7,000 words in length, which may be any two of the following:

   a. what might become part of a thesis for the M.Litt. or D.Phil.;

   b. an essay on the theoretical issues raised by the subject which the candidate is proposing for the thesis;

   c. an essay on a topic relevant to the subject;

   d. a discussion of the historical and literary background or of the source material which is relevant to the proposed subject.

or

1B: a thesis of between 12,000 and 15,000 words in length (excluding bibliography), which should be equivalent to a substantial draft chapter or chapters of a proposed thesis for the M.Litt. or the D.Phil. (For submission, see under 5 below.)

Unit 2

Candidates shall submit **either**

2A: a portfolio containing reports on the practical work completed during the course, according to the schedule given in the Course Handbook. (For submission, see under 5 below.)

   or

2B: a report or reports on practical work completed on an object or objects that will form the part of a proposed thesis for the M.Litt. or the D.Phil. (For submission, see under 5 below.)

Units 3 and 4.

Candidates shall take two three-hour examination papers, which may be any combination of language or non-language papers. When an elective paper is shared with another degree, the regulations for the paper follow that of the home degree.

4. Candidates must submit titles for their thesis or essay titles for Unit 1A or 1B by Monday noughth week of Hilary Term. The title for Unit 2A or 2B and subjects for the two elective papers (Units 3 and 4 of the examination, above) by Friday of second week of Michaelmas Term.

5. Lists of any set texts prescribed for the two elective papers (Units 3 and 4 of the examination, above) must be submitted to the Faculty Office by Friday of seventh week of Michaelmas Term.

6. All work submitted to the Chair of Examiners must be in typewritten form (except for figures, illustrations, and images). Two printed copies and one electronic copy in PDF (e.g. on a CD or a USB flash drive) of all the submitted work (Unit 1 and

Unit 2 of the examination, above) must be submitted, securely sealed and addressed to the Chair of Examiners, M.St. in Islamic Art and Archaeology, Examination Schools, High Street, Oxford, not later than 12 noon on Friday of fourth week of Trinity Term. The work must bear the candidate's examination number (but not the candidate's name, which must be concealed). Candidates must include a signed declaration sealed in an envelope addressed to the Chairman of Examiners that the work is the candidate's own.

7. Candidates may be required to attend a viva.

Master of Studies in Islamic Studies and History

The regulations of the Board of the Faculty of Oriental Studies is as follows:

1. Candidates for the M.St. in Islamic Studies and History must follow for at least three terms a course of instruction and directed research and must, upon entering the examination, produce from their society a certificate to that effect.

2. Candidates must attend such lectures, seminars, classes, and language classes as the convenors of the course shall determine, and must undertake any language tests set by the language teachers.

The final examination consists of the following four units, which all candidates must take:

(i) and (ii) Two optional papers chosen from the M.Phil. in Islamic Studies and History. Tuition for each of these two papers will take place either in Michaelmas or Hilary Term.

(iii) A prescribed take-home essay on methods and research materials related to one of the subjects studied under (i) and (ii). A choice of essay questions as prescribed by the examiners will be published on the WebLearn pages for this degree programme by noon on Friday of fourth Week of Hilary Term. They will be required to select one question from this paper, and prepare an essay of up to 4,000 words (excluding bibliography). Candidates must submit two typewritten copies of this essay in a sealed envelope addressed to the Chair of the Examiners of the M.St. in Islamic Studies and History, c/o Examination Schools, High Street, Oxford OX1 4BG, by noon on Friday of eighth week of the Hilary Term. The work must bear the candidates examination number (but not the candidates' name). Candidates must include a signed declaration sealed in an envelope addressed to the Chair of Examiners that the work is the candidates own.

(iv) A thesis of no more than 15,000 words (excluding bibliography), or two essays of no more than 6,000 words (excluding bibliography), on a topic (or topics) selected in consultation with the candidate's supervisor and approved by the Faculty Board. Candidates are required to submit two typewritten copies of the dissertation to the Chair of the Examiners, at the address above, by noon on Friday of fourth Week of Trinity Term.

3. The examiners may award a Distinction to candidates who have performed with special merit in the whole examination.

4. The examiners may examine any candidate by viva voce.

Master of Studies in Japanese Studies

1. Before admission to the course, candidates must *either* have taken Japanese in the Oxford Honour School of Oriental Studies *or* have taken a comparable degree from another university, *or* must satisfy the Board of the Faculty of Oriental Studies that they possess the necessary qualifications in the Japanese language to profit by the course.

2. Every candidate must follow for at least three terms a course of instruction in Japanese Studies with reference to one of the following subjects:

   (i) Japanese Linguistics

   (ii) Modern Japanese Literature

   (iii) Classical Japanese Literature

   (iv) another subject at the discretion of the Board of the Faculty of Oriental Studies.

The availability of subjects in a given year will be subject to the availability of teaching.

3. *Syllabus*

There will be four Units:

Unit (i) Context and Background. The examination will be by two take-home exercises, each comprising an essay of not more than 2,500 words on topics to be issued by the Oriental Institute Faculty Office, related directly to the course of instruction each candidate has followed. The exercises will be set not later than noon on Friday on each of Week 6 of Michaelmas Full Term and Week 6 of Hilary Full Term. At the same time as issuing each exercise, the Faculty Office will announce the date by which it is to be submitted, which shall be at least fourteen days later. Two copies of each typewritten essay must be submitted to the Chair of Examiners, M.St in Japanese Studies, Examination Schools, High Street, Oxford. The work must bear the candidates' examination number (but not the candidates' name.) Candidates must include a signed declaration sealed in an envelope addressed to the Chair of Examiners that the work is the candidates own.

Unit (ii) Texts, to be examined by written examination.

Unit (iii) Theory and Methodology, to be examined by written examination.

Unit (iv) A thesis of not more than 15,000 words (excluding bibliography), on a topic selected in consultation with the candidate's supervisor and approved by the Faculty Board. Applications for such approval should be submitted to the Faculty office by Monday of Week 0 of Hilary Term Two typewritten copies and an electronic copy in PDF format in a memory stick or CD, of the thesis must be submitted to the Chairman of the Examiners, name of degree, c/o Examination Schools, High Street, Oxford OX1 4BG. not later than 12 noon on Friday of fourth week of Trinity Term.

Candidates must include a signed declaration sealed in an envelope addressed to the Chair of Examiners that the work is the candidate's own.

4. Lists of set texts must be submitted to the Faculty office by Friday of seventh week of Michaelmas Term.

5. Candidates may be required to attend a viva.

Master of Studies in Jewish Studies

1. Before admission to the course, candidates must satisfy the Board of the Faculty of Oriental Studies that they possess the necessary qualifications to profit by the course.

2. Every candidate must follow for at least three terms a course of instruction in Jewish Studies.

3. There will be two tracks: Syllabus A and Syllabus B:

Syllabus A:

Unit (i) Three terms of *either* Biblical Hebrew, *or* Modern Hebrew, *or* Yiddish. Written examination will take place at the end of Trinity Term.

Unit (ii) Two options, one option to be taken in Michaelmas Term and one option to be taken in Hilary Term.

Unit (iii) A thesis of not more than 15,000-words (excluding bibliography), on a topic selected in consultation with the candidate's supervisor and approved by the Faculty Board. Applications for such approval should be submitted to the Faculty office by Monday of Week 0 of Hilary Term. Two typewritten copies and an electronic copy, in PDF format in a memory stick or CD, of the thesis must be submitted to the Chair of Examiners, M.St in Jewish Studies (Oriental Studies), Examination Schools, High Street, Oxford, not later than 12 noon on Friday of Week 6 of Trinity Term. The work must bear the candidate's examination number (but not the candidate's name, which must be concealed). Candidates must include a signed declaration sealed in an envelope addressed to the Chair of Examiners that the work is the candidate's own.

Syllabus B:

Unit (i): Three terms of *either* Biblical Hebrew, *or* Modern Hebrew, *or* Yiddish. Written examination will take place at the end of Trinity Term.

Unit (ii): Four options to be taken in Michaelmas Term, Hilary Term or Trinity Term. Options examined by essay must be taken in Michaelmas or Hilary Term.

4. A list of options for unit (ii) will be published in the Course Handbook.

The method of examination will be either by three-hour written examination held at the end of Trinity Term or by essay examination. The method of examination of each option will be determined in advance and will be published in the course handbook. The essay topics will be published on the Friday of Week 8 of the term in which the option is taught. Candidates will be contacted with details of how to collect or access the question paper. The essay examination will consist of two essays of not more than 2,500 words each for *Syllabus A* and not more than 3,000 words each for *Syllabus B*. Two type-written copies of each essay must be submitted to the Examination Schools, High Street, Oxford by 12 noon on the Friday of Week 0 of the term following that in which the option was taught. The work must bear the candidate's examination number (but not the canidate's name, which must be concealed). Candidates must include a signed declaration sealed in an envelope addressed to the Chair of Examiners that the work is the candidate's own.

5. Lists of set texts must be submitted to the Faculty office by Friday of Week 7 of Michaelmas Term.

6. Candidates may be required to attend a viva.

Master of Studies in Jewish Studies in the Graeco-Roman Period

1. Before admission to the course, candidates must satisfy the Board of the Faculty of Oriental Studies that they possess the necessary qualification in the Hebrew language to profit by the course. Those wishing to take options (*e*) or (*f*) must show evidence of their knowledge of Greek.

2. Every candidate must follow for at least three terms a course of study in Jewish Studies in the Graeco-Roman Period.

3. *Syllabus*

There will be four Units. Each unit is examined by a written paper.

Unit (i) Essay questions on Jewish history and institutions from 200 BCE to 135 CE.

Units (ii), (iii) and (iv) Prescribed texts. Select one paper for each unit from the following list:

(*a*) Dead Sea scrolls

(*b*) Mishnah

(*c*) Midrash

(*d*) Targum

(*e*) Septuagint

(*f*) Hellenistic Jewish literature

(*g*) Any other subject approved by the Board.

4. Lists of set texts must be submitted to the Faculty office by Friday of Week 7 of Michaelmas Term.

5. Candidates may be required to attend a viva.

Teaching for some options may not be available in every year. Applicants for admission will be advised of this.

Master of Studies in Korean Studies

1. Before admission to the course, candidates must satisfy the Board of the Faculty of Oriental Studies that they possess the necessary qualification to profit by the course. Candidates must have a knowledge of Korean at least up to the standard of a first degree.

2. Every candidate must follow for at least three terms a course of instruction in Korean Studies.

3. *Syllabus*

There will be four Units:

Unit (i) Set texts.

Unit (ii) *Either* Korean Language

or Classical Chinese

or Modern Japanese

Candidates who already possess a sufficient knowledge of Modern Korean will be required to choose Classical Chinese or Modern Japanese.

Unit (iii) Bibliography and techniques of Koreanology.

The examination will take the form of exercises to be set after examinations for Units (i) and (ii) have taken place. Each candidate will be assigned one or more exercises set on a topic directly relating to the course of instruction he or she has followed, and will be required to submit a written answer to the Chair of Examiners by a date which the Chair will announce at the conclusion of the written papers, but which shall, in any case, be not sooner than two days and not later than seven days from the date of the examination.

Unit (iv) A dissertation of not more than 15,000 words (excluding bibliography), on a topic selected in consultation with the candidate's supervisor and approved by the Faculty Board. Applications for such approval should be submitted to the Faculty office by Monday of nought week of Hilary Term.

The dissertation must be sent to the Chair of Examiners, M.St in Korean Studies (Oriental Studies), Examination Schools, High Street, Oxford, not later than 12 noon on Friday of fourth week of Trinity Full Term.

4. Lists of set texts must be submitted to the Faculty office by Friday of seventh week of Michaelmas Term and will be reported to the Faculty Board's second meeting of Michaelmas Term.

5. All work submitted to the Chair of Examiners must be in typewritten form. Two copies must be submitted, securely sealed and addressed. The work must bear the candidate's examination number (but not the candidate's name, which must be concealed). Candidates must include a signed declaration sealed in an envelope addressed to the Chair of Examiners that the work is the candidate's own.

6. Every candidate will be examined by oral examination unless he or she shall have been individually excused by the examiners.

Master of Studies in Late Antique and Byzantine Studies

(*See also the general notice at the commencement of these regulations.*)

1. Candidates must satisfy the Committee for Byzantine Studies and the appropriate Faculty Boards that they possess the necessary qualifications in Greek (ancient or modern) and/or Latin to profit by the course.   5

2. Every candidate must follow for at least three terms a course of instruction in Late Antique and Byzantine Studies. Candidates will, when they enter for the examination, be required to produce from their society a certificate that they are following such a course.

3. Candidates must take three of the following five papers. All candidates take the   10
core paper on History, Art and Archaeology, *or*, if they already have the required linguistic competence, History and Byzantine Literature. For the remainder of their course they choose either the two Language and Literature papers, or, Auxiliary Disciplines and one Special Subject.

I. Core paper on History, Art and Archaeology, *or* History and Byzantine   15
Literature:

Either

(*a*) Late Antiquity (covering the Roman Empire and adjoining regions)

or

(*b*) Byzantium   20

The core paper will be taught in classes in Michaelmas and Hilary Terms. Examination will be by two 5,000 word essays, to be submitted by Monday of seventh week of Trinity Term.

II. and III. Language and Literature (teaching in Greek, Latin, Slavonic, Armenian, Syriac, and Arabic will normally be available).   25

These papers are taught over three terms in classes, with reference to a selection of texts and/or extracts from texts which may vary from year to year according to the interests of candidates. Examination is by two three-hour papers (candidates are permitted the use of relevant bilingual dictionaries, which will be provided by the faculty):   30

(*a*) translation, and

(*b*) set texts (with passages for translation and comment).

Candidates who are embarking on the study of one of the above languages will normally be expected to take both examinations in that language, but the Committee for Byzantine Studies may in special circumstances permit them to substitute another   35
paper for one of these examination papers. Candidates cannot normally offer an examination in the language which qualified them for admission to the degree programme in the first instance.

IV. Auxiliary Discipline(s):

Either   40

(*a*) any two of the following: epigraphy, palaeography, numismatics, sigillography

or

(*b*) papyrology: Greek or Coptic or Arabic

or

(*c*) artefact studies: one of ceramics or metalware or ivories or codices or carved   45
marbles.

Paper IV will be taught by lectures/classes/tutorials. Examination will be by a three-hour paper, except for papyrology which is assessed by two 5,000 word essays on distinct aspects of the subject.

V. A Special Subject selected from the subject areas listed under 4. below.

Special Subjects will be taught by lectures/classes/tutorials. Examination will be either by two 5,000 word essays or by a 10,000 word dissertation (to be submitted by Monday of seventh week of Trinity Term).

    4. Overview of Special Subject (for details please consult the Course Handbook)   5

    (*a*) History: Special Subjects on offer deal either with specific periods or with certain aspects of late Roman and Byzantine history (including military, diplomatic, political, social economic and religious history) between the fourth and fifteenth centuries, as well as important developments in neighbouring regions.

    (*b*) Art and Archaeology: Special Subjects on offer cover sculpture, portraiture,   10 minor arts, monumental art and architecture of the late Roman, Byzantine and Islamic spheres of influence, as well as the archaeology of town and country throughout the Mediterranean and Near Eastern worlds.

    (*c*) Literature (texts prescribed in translation): Special Subjects on offer range through historiography, hagiography, poetry, popular literature and scholar-   15 ship in the languages available for the degree programme.

    (*d*) Religion: Special Subjects on offer cover theological debates and practical spirituality in the fields of Judaism, Christianity, and Islam.

    (*e*) Such other subjects as may be approved on application to the Committee for Byzantine Studies.   20

Note. The list of Special Subjects detailed in the Course Handbook reflects the expertise and interests of current postholders. The list may be altered from time to time with development of expertise and changes of interest on the part of the postholders.

5. Teaching in all the options may not be available each year, and applicants for admission will be advised whether teaching will be available in the options of their   25 choice.

6. The examiners may award a distinction for excellence in the whole examination.

Master of Studies in Legal Research/Socio-Legal Research

1. Candidates for admission to the course will be required to produce evidence of their appropriate qualifications for the course.   30

2. Candidates must follow a course of instruction in Legal Research Method approved by the Law Board, and must satisfy the examiners that they have completed to the required standard such tests or exercises in Legal Research Method as may be prescribed by the Law Board as part of such a course of instruction. Where the Law Board judges that it has sufficient evidence of a candidate's proficiency in legal   35 research method, it may in exceptional circumstances dispense a candidate from this requirement.

3. Every candidate on admission as a student shall be placed by the board of the Law Faculty under the supervision of a graduate member of the University or other competent person selected by the board, and the board shall have power for sufficient   40 reasons to change the supervisor of any student.

4. Examination for the Degree shall be by thesis, and by oral examination. The thesis must not exceed 30,000 words and should not normally be less than 25,000 words in length (the limit to include all notes but to exclude all tables and bibliography, and the candidate to state the number of words in the thesis to the nearest   45 hundred words). The thesis shall be wholly or substantially the result of work undertaken whilst registered for the degree of M.St. in Legal Research. The required format for this thesis is the common format prescribed for all law theses, which is printed in the Faculty of Law's Graduate Students' Handbook. The examiners must satisfy

themselves that the thesis affords evidence of serious study by the candidate and of ability to discuss a difficult problem critically; that the candidate possesses a good general knowledge of the field of learning within which the subject of the thesis falls; that the thesis is presented in a lucid and scholarly manner, and that the candidate has made a worthwhile contribution to knowledge or understanding in the field of learning within which the subject of the thesis falls to the extent that could reasonably be expected within the time normally spent as a student for the Degree.

5. At any time not earlier than the third nor later than the fifth term after the term of admission, a candidate may apply to the Board for examination. Such application shall be made to the Head of Examinations and Assessments and shall be accompanied by

(1) a statement as to what part, if any, of his or her thesis has already been accepted, or is being currently submitted, for any degree in this University or elsewhere;

(2) a statement that the thesis is the candidate's own work, except where otherwise indicated;

(3) two copies or, if leave has been obtained from the Board of the Faculty of Law, one copy of his or her thesis either at the same time as his or her application or at such later time as the Education Committee shall by regulation permit. The thesis must be securely and firmly bound in either hard or soft covers. Loose-leaf binding is not acceptable.

6. On receipt of any such application the Registrar shall submit it to the Board. The Board shall thereupon appoint two examiners whose duties shall be:

(1) to consider the thesis sent in by the student under the provisions of the preceding clause, provided that they shall exclude from consideration in making their report any part of the thesis which has already been accepted, or is being concurrently submitted, for any degree in this University or elsewhere, and shall have the power to require the candidate to produce for their inspection the complete thesis so accepted or concurrently submitted.

(2) to examine the candidate orally on the subject of his or her thesis and on subjects relevant to his or her field of study, and, if they wish on such matters as will enable them to discharge their duties under sub-paragraph (3) or (4);

(3) to report to the Board whether on the basis of the thesis submitted, the oral examination, and, where applicable, the report referred to in paragraph (7), the candidate:

   (i) should be awarded the Degree;
   (ii) should be awarded the Degree with Distinction; or
   (iii) should be given the opportunity to re-submit for the Degree within a further three terms.

The Education Committee shall have power, on the application of a faculty board in a special case, to authorise the appointment of a third examiner (or an assessor), upon such conditions and to perform such functions as the committee shall approve; any fee paid to such an additional examiner or assessor shall be met from the funds at the disposal of the committee.

The Education Committee shall have power to make regulations concerning the notice to be given of the oral examination and of the time and place at which it may be held.

7. On receipt of the report of the examiners, it shall be the duty of the board to decide whether the candidate is qualified to supplicate for the Degree of Master of Studies, with or without the award of a Distinction, and, if not, to indicate that the candidate should be given the opportunity to apply for re-examination.

The board may not permit the candidate to supplicate for the degree unless and until the Director of the Course in Legal Research Method, failing whom the Director of Graduate Studies (Research), has certified that the candidate has satisfied or been exempted from the requirements of that course.

8. If the board has adopted a recommendation that the candidate be given the opportunity to resubmit, and the candidate indicates the wish to take up that opportunity, the candidate shall retain the status and obligations of a Student for the Degree of Master of Studies and shall be permitted to apply to be re-examined within the period specified in para. 6 (3) (iii) above. Upon receiving such an application, the Board may reappoint the previous examiners, or may appoint different examiners instead of any or all of the previous examiners, as it shall judge appropriate.

9. The board may exempt any candidate who has re-submitted for the Degree from oral examination provided that the examiners are satisfied, without examining the candidate orally, that they can recommend to the board that the candidate has reached the standard required for the Degree.

Master of Studies in Literature and Arts

1. Every candidate must follow for at least six terms (and a maximum of eight terms) a part-time course of instruction in interdisciplinary study in the Humanities (Literature, History and History of Art).

2. The course will consist of lectures, seminars, on-line courses and individual tutorials.

3. Every candidate will be required to satisfy the examiners in the following parts:

(*a*) Four essays, each of no more than 5,000 words in length.

(*b*) Engagement with the on-line courses to the satisfaction of the Course Director.

(*c*) A dissertation on a topic selected by the candidate in consultation with the Course Director and his or her supervisor and approved by the examiners. The dissertation must be of no more than 11,000 words in length, and will need to demonstrate knowledge and awareness of more than one subject discipline.

Candidates may be required to attend a viva voce examination if the Examiners require further information in order to make a judgement on an individual candidate.

The dissertation under 3(*c*) must be submitted not later than noon on the third Friday in September of the final year of the course to the Chair of Examiners for the Degree of MLA, c/o Registry, 1 Wellington Square, Oxford. All other elements of assessed work shall be forwarded to the examiners, c/o Registry, 1 Wellington Square, Oxford for consideration by such dates as the examiners shall determine and shall notify the candidates and tutors at the start of each academic year.

The assessed work under 3(*a*) and 3(*c*) must be accompanied by a statement that it is the candidate's own work.

4. The examiners may award a Distinction for the MLA.

5. A candidate who fails to satisfy the examiners in 3 may be permitted to resubmit work in respect of part or parts of the examination which they have failed for examination on one further occasion. In the case of 3(*a*), candidates should resubmit work within one year, but normally not later than three months after the initial attempt. In the case of 3(*c*), candidates should resubmit work not later than twelve months after the initial attempt.

Master of Studies in Medieval History

The regulations of the Board of the Faculty of History are as follows:

1. Candidates for the M.St in Medieval History must follow for at least three terms a course of instruction and directed research and must, upon entering the examination, produce from their society a certificate to that effect.

2. Candidates must attend such lectures, seminars, classes, and language courses as his or her supervisor shall determine, and undertake any language tests set by language teachers. Language and class teachers will report to the Chair of Examiners on a candidate's attendance and participation, and where appropriate test results, not later than Friday of ninth week of Trinity Term.   5

3. Candidates will follow a core course in medieval history, focusing on historical methods and the interpretation of historical evidence, during Michaelmas Term. In consultation with the convenor of the core course they will select a historiographical or methodological problem in medieval history for individual in-depth study. On this agreed topic, candidates must submit to the Chair of the Examiners of the M.St. in   10
Medieval History, c/o Examination Schools, High Street, Oxford OX1 4BG, by noon on Monday of first week of Trinity Term two typewritten copies of an essay of between 3,000 and 5,000 words.

4. In Hilary Term candidates will be required to choose an option paper of historical study within the field of medieval history, as offered by the History   15
Faculty. A descriptive list of option papers will be published by the Faculty of History in September for the academic year ahead (not all options may be available in every year). The definitive list of option papers for any year will be posted on the Faculty's graduate notice board not later than Friday of third week of Michaelmas Term of the academic year in which the paper is to be taken. Candidates must submit   20
to the Chair of the Examiners of the M.St. in Medieval History, at the address above, by noon on Monday of first week of Trinity Term two typewritten copies of an extended essay (of between 8,000 and 10,000 words) based on an aspect of the chosen option paper.

5. The examiners may make the marks awarded to the candidates for the written   25
work known to the Director of Graduate Studies where necessary for the purpose of grant applications and progression assessments. However, the pass list shall be issued only following the completion of the whole examination, including submission and final assessment of the dissertation.

6. Candidates must choose, after due consultation with their supervisor, a topic for   30
a dissertation based on their individual research. Candidates are required to submit two typewritten copies of the dissertation, which shall not normally exceed 15,000 words, to the Chair of the Examiners, at the address above, at the latest by 12 noon on the last Friday in August of the academic year in which they are registered for the degree.   35

7. The examiners may award a distinction to candidates who have performed with special merit in the whole examination.

8. A candidate who fails the examination will be permitted to retake it on one further occasion only, not later than one year after the initial attempt.

Such a candidate whose dissertation has been of satisfactory standard may resubmit   40
the same piece of work, while a candidate who has reached a satisfactory standard on the written work will not be required to retake that part of the examination.

Master of Studies in Medieval Studies

The regulations of the Board of the Faculty of History are as follows:

1. Candidates for the M.St. in Medieval Studies must follow for at least three terms   45
a course of instruction and directed research and must, upon entering the examination, produce from their society a certificate to that effect.

2. Candidates must attend such lectures, seminars, classes as his or her supervisor, in consultation with the convenor of the M.St. in Medieval Studies, shall determine. These will include one compulsory language class over three terms, and candidates   50

must attend any language tests set by their language teachers. The choice of languages includes Latin, Old English, Old Norse, Old French, Old High German, Old Irish, Middle Welsh, Greek, Hebrew, and Arabic. Language and class teachers will report to the Chair of Examiners a candidate's attendance and participation, and where appropriate, test results not later than Monday of ninth week of Trinity Term.   5

3. In Michaelmas Term all candidates will follow, as directed by the programme convenor, a series of classes on research methods relevant to their particular combination of disciplines. In Hilary Term candidates will follow a compulsory interdisciplinary seminar, on a theme chosen by the convenor of the M.St. which will exemplify the different but complementary approaches to medieval sources offered by individual   10 disciplines. Candidates must provide evidence of attendance to the examiners.

4. In each Michaelmas and Hilary Term candidates will take one Option Paper of their choice, from the subject options made available by the participating faculties in any given year and term. A descriptive list of option papers will be published by the Faculty of History in September for the academic year ahead (not all options may be   15 available every year). The definitive list of option papers for any one year will be posted on the History Faculty's graduate notice board not later than Friday of third week of Michaelmas Full Term preceding the examination. For each of the two Option Papers candidates are to be assessed in the format prescribed by the procedures of the host programmes, provided the assessment does not exceed the equivalent of an   20 essay of between 5,000 and 7,000 words. Candidates should consult the convenor of the Option Paper on the modes and timetables of the prescribed assessment. Essay submissions must be addressed to the Chair of Examiners for the M.St in Medieval Studies, c/o Examination Schools, High Street, Oxford OX1 4BG, and handed in no later than 12 noon on Monday of first week of Trinity Term. Where the host   25 programme specifies an earlier deadline that deadline will apply.

5. Candidates will choose a course of palaeography and/or codicology classes in one of the participating faculties. Unless otherwise instructed through the host programme, they must submit two copies of the assessment portfolio prescribed by the host programme no later than 12 noon on Monday of first week of Trinity Term to   30 the Chair of Examiners, at the address above.

6. Candidates must choose, after due consultation with their supervisor, a topic for a dissertation based on their individual research. Candidates are required to submit two typewritten or printed copies of the dissertation, which shall not normally exceed 12,000 words, to the Chair of the Examiners, at the address above, at the latest by 12   35 noon on Monday of ninth week of Trinity Term. Each dissertation must include a short abstract which concisely summarises its scope and principal arguments, in about 300 words.

7. The examiners may award a distinction to candidates who have performed with special merit in the whole examination.   40

8. A candidate who fails the examination will be permitted to retake it on one further occasion only, not later than one year after the initial attempt.

Such a candidate whose dissertation has been of satisfactory standard may resubmit the same piece of work, while a candidate who has reached a satisfactory standard on the written work will not be required to retake that part of the examination.   45

Master of Studies in Mindfulness-Based Cognitive Therapy

1. Candidates must follow a course of instruction in Mindfulness-Based Cognitive Therapy (MBCT) for at least six terms. The course is designed to develop knowledge of the theoretical basis of MBCT and of related research and clinical principles, and to develop the competencies required in order to become an effective MBCT practitioner   50

and teacher. The course places equal emphasis on critical understanding of theory, on critical appreciation of research, and on candidates' capacity to demonstrate these through evidence of knowledge, understanding and the ability to apply these in practice. The course is available on a part-time basis only.

2. Candidates may be permitted under certain circumstances to suspend status for a maximum of six terms.

3. Every candidate will be required to satisfy the examiners in the following:

(*a*) Attendance at the teaching days, spread across two years, and including three residential training retreats;

(*b*) Written assignments as follows:

    (i) two essays, each of not more than 4000 words, demonstrating the capacity critically to appraise theory, research and clinical literature relevant to MBCT (Year I)

    (ii) one written reflective analysis of not more than 4,000 words of personal meditation practice, relating experience to theory, research, and clinical principles. (Year I)

    (iii) one written assignment, of no more than 4,000 words, describing the development, delivery and evaluation of a programme of MBCT teaching suitable for the student's client group, submitted with instructional materials as specified in the handbook

(*c*) Digital recordings of all MBCT classes, taught by the student in association with 4b)iii, to be examined for adherence to protocol and competence as an instructor (Year II);

(*d*) A dissertation of no more than 10,000 words on a topic selected by the student, related to the theory and practice of MBCT (Year II);

The written assignments under 3b) and the recordings of the MBCT classes under 3c) shall be forwarded to the examiners for consideration by such date as the examiners shall determine and shall notify candidates. Two hard copies and a digital copy of the dissertation under 3d) shall be delivered to the examiners for the M.St. in Mindfulness-Based Cognitive Therapy c/o Examination Schools, High Street Oxford OX1 4BG no later than noon on 31 July in the final year of the course, or the immediately preceding Friday if that date falls on a weekend.

4. Candidates may be required to attend a viva voce examination at the end of the course of study.

5. Candidates who fail to satisfy the examiners in any of the assignments, including the written assignments under 3b) and 3d) and the recorded performances under 3c), may be permitted to resubmit work in the part or parts of the examination which they have failed on one further occasion only which shall normally be within one year of the original failure.

6. The examiners may award a Distinction for the Master of Studies.

Master of Studies in Modern Jewish Studies

1. Before admission to the course, candidates must satisfy the Board of the Faculty of Oriental Studies that they possess the necessary qualification in the Hebrew or Yiddish languages to profit by the course.

2. Every candidate must follow for at least three terms a course of instruction in Modern Jewish Studies.

3. *Syllabus*

There will be four Units:

Unit (i) Passages for translation and comment and essay questions on prescribed texts in Hebrew or Yiddish. This paper will be examined by a three-hour written examination.

Units (ii) and (iii) Two papers from the following list, to be examined either by written examination or by take-home essay examination:

(*a*) Hebrew literature 1888–1948.

(*b*) The literature of the State of Israel.

(*c*) Jewish literature of the nineteenth and twentieth centuries.

(*d*) Major trends in Jewish religion and thought since 1789.

(*e*) Modern Jewish History.

(*f*) Israel: History, Politics and Society.

(*g*) Yiddish literature and culture.

(*h*) The Holocaust: from History to Memory.

(*i*) Any other subject approved by the Board.

Papers will be examined by two take-home essays of not more than 2,500 words each. Candidates will be notified of the essay topics on the Friday of eighth week of the term in which the paper is taught. Essays must be submitted to the Examination Schools, High Street, Oxford, by 12 noon on the Friday of noughth week of the term following that in which the paper was taught.

Unit (iv) A dissertation of not more than 15,000 words (excluding bibliography) on a topic selected in consultation with the candidate's supervisor and approved by the Faculty Board. Applications for such approval should be submitted to the Faculty office by Monday of nought week of Hilary Term.

Two copies of the dissertation must be submitted, to the Chair of Examiners, M.St. in Modern Jewish Studies (Oriental Studies), Examination Schools, by 12 noon on Friday of sixth week of Trinity Full Term.

4. Lists of set texts must be submitted to the Faculty office by Friday of seventh week of Michaelmas Term and will be reported to the Faculty Board's second meeting of Michaelmas Term.

5. All work submitted to the Chair of Examiners must be in typewritten form. Two copies must be submitted, securely sealed and addressed. The work must bear the candidate's examination number (but not the candidate's name, which must be concealed). Candidates must include a signed declaration sealed in an envelope addressed to the Chair of Examiners that the work is the candidate's own.

6. Every candidate will be examined by oral examination unless he or she shall have been individually excused by the examiners.

Teaching for some options may not be available in every year. Applicants for admission will be advised of this.

Master of Studies in Modern Languages

1. Candidates must follow a Programme chosen from those listed in the 'Handbook for Taught-Course Graduate Students'.

In order to gain admission to the course, applicants must show evidence of linguistic ability compatible with advanced literary study in the language(s) chosen to study. Comparative Literature candidates shall not be required to have reading fluency in more than two languages other than English. Unless otherwise stated, candidates will be expected to write in English unless explicit permission is obtained to write in the language (or one of the languages) studied. In the case of Comparative Literature candidates, writing in more than one language in addition to English will not be authorised.

All candidates must follow a course of instruction in Modern Languages at Oxford for a period of three terms, unless the Board of the Faculty of Medieval and Modern Languages in exceptional circumstances shall permit an extension of time, and candidates shall, when entering their name for the examination, be required to produce from their society a certificate stating that they are following the course of instruction for the period prescribed.

2. All candidates shall be required:

(*a*) To offer A, B, C, and D as defined in 3 below.

(*b*) To present themselves for viva voce examination at the time appointed by the examiners.

3. The examination shall consist of the following:

(A) *Either*

(i) Literary Theory. All candidates must attend such lectures, seminars, and classes as their course convener shall determine. All candidates must present one seminar paper during their course, and submit a written essay based on some aspect of the work done for the seminar. This essay shall be written in English and must be between 5,000 and 7,000 words in length. Candidates must submit three typed copies of their essay to the Head of Examinations and Assessments, Examination Schools, High Street, Oxford, by noon on Thursday of tenth week of Hilary Term. Each copy must have a cover sheet giving the candidate's name, college, the title of the essay, the name of the candidate's supervisor, and the words 'Literary Theory, submitted in partial fulfilment of the requirements of the M.St. in Modern Languages'.

Or

(ii) History of Ideas in Germany from the Eighteenth to the Twentieth Centuries. All candidates must attend such lectures, seminars, and classes as their course convener shall determine. All candidates must present one seminar paper during their course, and submit a written essay based on some aspect of the work done for the seminar. This essay may be written in English or German and must be between 5,000 and 7,000 words in length. Candidates must submit three typed copies to the Head of Examinations and Assessments, Examination Schools, High Street, Oxford, by noon on Thursday of tenth week of Hilary Term. Each copy must have a cover sheet giving the candidate's name, college, the title of the essay, the name of the candidate's supervisor, and the words 'History of Ideas in Germany, submitted in partial fulfilment of the requirements of the M.St. in Modern Languages'.

Or

(iii) Each candidate shall be required to offer either, (1) the History of the Book, or (2) Palaeography with Textual Criticism. Candidates will be examined on one or two essays on topics agreed by them with the course convener relating either to the history of the book (for (1)) or to palaeography with textual criticism (for (2)). The essay or essays should be between 5,000 and 7,000 words in total. Candidates must submit three typed copies to the Head of Examinations and Assessments, Examination Schools, High Street, Oxford, by noon on Thursday of tenth week of Hilary Term. Each copy must have a cover sheet giving the candidate's name, college, the title of the essay, the name of the candidate's supervisor, and the words 'History of the Book/Palaeography with Textual Criticism [either/or], submitted in partial fulfilment of the requirements of the M.St. in Modern Languages'. For (2), candidates will in addition be required to undertake a practical transcription test, made without reference to dictionaries or handbooks, on a short manuscript text selected by the course convener, who will also mark, sign, and date the candidate's work. The test should take place by the end of the fourth week of the Trinity Term in which the examination is to be taken.

Or

(iv) A methodological essay of between 5,000 and 7,000 words in length on a topic or issue related to one of the candidate's Special Subjects or dissertation. It might consist, for example, of a theoretical discussion of the candidate's approach to the material being studied, or a detailed analysis of existing approaches. If candidates choose this option, they will also be expected to attend a set of seminars in (i) or (ii) above, or a set of tutorials in (iii), and to make a presentation. Candidates must submit three copies to the Head of Examinations and Assessments, Examination Schools, High Street, Oxford, by noon on Thursday of tenth week of Hilary Term. Each copy must have a cover sheet giving the candidate's name, college, the title of the essay, the name of the candidate's supervisor, and the words 'Essay on Method, submitted in partial fulfilment of the requirements of the M.St. in Modern Languages'.

The work submitted under (i) must be written in English; the work submitted under (ii) may be written in English or German; the work submitted under (iii) may be written in English or, subject to the approval of the Medieval and Modern Languages Faculty Board, in a language appropriate to the literature concerned.

Approval must be sought for the choice of options in (A) by the end of the fourth week of Michaelmas Term.

(B) A dissertation of between 10,000 and 12,000 words written in English, or, with the approval of the Medieval and Modern Languages Faculty Board, in the language appropriate to the literature concerned, on a topic connected with those offered in (A) (i), (ii) or (iii) above or (C) below, but distinct from those covered by the essays submitted under (A) or (C), and approved by the Modern Languages Board. Candidates are required to register the subject area or title of their dissertation with the Modern Languages Graduate Office by the end of the fourth week of Hilary Term.

The dissertation must be presented in proper scholarly form. Three copies typed in double-spacing on one side only of quarto or A4 paper, each copy bound or held firmly in a cover, must be delivered to the Head of Examinations and Assessments, Examination Schools, High Street, Oxford, by noon on Thursday of the sixth week of Trinity Term.

(C and D) Two Special Subjects

Candidates may select two Special Subjects from those listed in the 'Graduate Studies in Modern Languages' handbook as associated with the programme which they are following; candidates may select a special subject from a different programme with the approval of their supervisor; or candidates may propose Special Subjects of their own devising, provided that each subject has the written support of the candidate's supervisor and is approved by or on behalf of the Medieval and Modern Languages Faculty Board. A proposal for a Special Subject of the candidate's own devising shall be accompanied by a statement (of approximately 100 words) of the character and scope of the subject proposed. Approval of all Special Subjects must be sought, by application to the Modern Languages Graduate Office, 41 Wellington Square, Oxford by end of the fourth week of Michaelmas Term. Approval of Special Subjects proposed will be dependent on the availability of teaching and examining resources at the relevant time.

Candidates will normally offer two Special Subjects from the same language and area or from different areas in the same language. The Comparative Literature Programme will contain Special Subjects from two different languages.

Candidates will be examined on an essay, or two essays (which may be written in English, or, with the approval of the Medieval and Modern Languages Faculty Board, in the language appropriate to the literature concerned), on the topics they have agreed with the supervisor of each Special Subject. The length of the work submitted for each Special Subject should be between 5,000 and 7,000 words in total.

4. Candidates for Comparative Literature should ensure that either at least one of the special subjects (C and D) is comparative in scope or the two special subjects are concerned with different languages. The dissertation must deal explicitly with comparative issues.

5. In addition to submitting the dissertation (B), students are required to submit work for assessment on all three of the non-dissertation components (A, C, and D). Of these three, the lowest passing mark will be discounted in the final assessment. A fail mark must always be included in the final assessment.

The Special Subject essays for Michaelmas Term shall be submitted to the Head of Examinations and Assessments, Examination Schools, High Street, Oxford, by noon on Thursday of the tenth week of Michaelmas Term. The Special Subject essays for Hilary Term shall be submitted to the Head of Examinations and Assessments, Examination Schools, High Street, Oxford, by noon on Thursday of the tenth week of Hilary Term.

In the case of resubmission, candidates shall be required to resubmit all the material by noon on Thursday of the sixth week of the first Trinity Term following their first examination. Candidates may resubmit on one occasion only.

6. The examiners may award a Distinction for excellence in the whole examination.

Master of Studies in Modern South Asian Studies

The regulations of the Boards of the Faculty of History and of Oriental Studies are as follows:

1. Candidates for the M.St. in Modern South Asian Studies must follow for at least three terms a course of instruction and directed research and must, upon entering the examination, produce from their society a certificate to that effect.

2. Candidates must attend such lectures, seminars, classes and language classes as the convenors of the course shall determine, and must undertake any language tests set by the language teachers.

The final examination consists of the following four units, which all candidates must take:

(i) A Language Paper in one of the following languages: Hindi, Literary Hindi, Bengali, Sanskrit, Persian, or Tibetan. The examination will be based on knowledge of grammar, translation and reading comprehension. Tuition for the language paper will be through classes, and will continue through all three terms of the academic year. Not all language options may be available every year.

(ii) A General Methodological Paper, 'The History and Culture of South Asia'. Tuition for this paper will be through weekly seminars held during Michaelmas and the first 4 weeks of Hilary Term. A choice of essay questions as prescribed by the examiners will be published on the WebLearn pages for this degree programme by noon on Friday of fourth week of Hilary Term. They will be required to select one question from this paper, and prepare an essay of up to 5,000 words (excluding bibliography). Candidates must submit two typewritten copies of this essay to the Chair of the Examiners of the M.St. in Modern South Asian Studies, c/o Examination Schools, High Street, Oxford OX1 4BG, by noon on Friday of 8th week of the Hilary Term.

(iii) An Optional Paper within the field of Modern South Asian Studies, from a list of options offered by the Faculties of History and Oriental Studies. The definitive list of options for the year ahead, together with short descriptions of each, will be published on Weblearn at the latest by the start of the Michaelmas Term. Tuition for this paper will be through a course of 8 weekly seminars held through the Hilary Term. A list of essay questions as prescribed by the examiners will be published on the WebLearn pages for this degree programme by noon on Friday of eighth week of Hilary Term. Candidates will be required to select one question from this paper, and prepare an essay of up to 5,000 words (excluding bibliography). Candidates must submit two typewritten copies of this essay to the Chair of the Examiners of the M.St. in Modern South Asian Studies, c/o Examination Schools, High Street, Oxford OX1 4BG, by noon on Friday of fourth week of the Trinity Term.

(iv) A Dissertation based on individual research. Candidates will choose their topics after due consultation with their supervisor. Candidates are required to submit two typewritten copies of the dissertation, which shall not normally exceed 15,000 words (excluding bibliography), to the Chair of the Examiners, at the address above, by noon on Friday of eighth week of Trinity Term. Each Dissertation must include a short abstract which concisely summarises its scope and principal arguments, in about 300 words.

3. The examiners may make the marks awarded to the candidates for the written work known to the Director of Graduate Studies where necessary for the purpose of grant applications and progression assessments. However, the pass list will be issued only following completion of the whole examination, including submission and final assessment of the dissertation.

4. The examiners may award a Distinction to candidates who have performed with special merit in the whole examination.

5. A candidate who fails the examination will be permitted to re-take it on one further occasion only, not later than one year after the initial attempt. Such a candidate whose thesis has been of a satisfactory standard may resubmit the same piece of work. A candidate who has reached a satisfactory standard on the written work will not be required to take that part of the examination. Candidates who have failed the language examination, but have otherwise satisfied the Examiners, will be required to re-sit the language examination only.

Master of Studies in Music

1. Each candidate will be required:

(*a*) to follow for at least three terms a course of study in music;

(*b*) to specialise in musicology, performance or composition;

(*c*) to take a two-part examination (Part 1 and Part 2).

2. The elements of the examination will be determined by the candidate's chosen specialism.

3. Candidates specialising in musicology will be required to submit:

Part 1a: an essay or exercise on issues and methods in musicology of 6,000 words (or equivalent in notation, visual documentation, or analytical diagrams), two copies of which must be submitted, not later than noon on Tuesday of the tenth week of

Michaelmas Term, to the Chair of Examiners for the M.St. in Music, c/o Examination Schools, High Street, Oxford.

Part 1b: an essay of 6,000 words, normally on a topic of the candidate's choice. Two copies of the essay must be submitted, not later than noon on Tuesday of Week 10 of Hilary Term to the Chair of Examiners for the M.St. in Music, c/o Examination   5
Schools, High Street, Oxford. A portfolio of appropriately assessed language work that is directly relevant to the candidate's intended field of research may substitute for Part 1b with the approval of the Masters' Course Convenor which must be sought by noon on Friday of the first week of Michaelmas Term.

Part 1c: an essay of 6,000 words, normally in response to an elective seminar. Two   10
copies of the essay must be submitted, not later than noon on Tuesday of Week 7 of Trinity Term to the Chair of Examiners for the M.St. in Music, c/o Examination Schools, High Street, Oxford.

Part 1d: an essay of 6,000 words, normally on a topic of the candidate's choice. Two copies of the essay must be submitted, not later than noon on Tuesday of Week 7 of   15
Trinity Term, to the Chair of Examiners for the M.St. in Music, c/o Examination Schools, High Street, Oxford.

Part 2: a dissertation of not more than 13,000 words (this word limit including footnotes but excluding bibliography and appendices) in musicology or ethnomusicology, or an editorial exercise (edition), with prefatory matter, of comparable length. The   20
topic for the dissertation or edition must be submitted for approval to the Masters' Course Convenor, Faculty of Music, by noon on Friday of the third week of Hilary Term. Two typewritten copies of the dissertation or edition must be submitted, not later than noon on the Tuesday of the tenth week of Trinity Term, to the Chair of Examiners for the M.St. in Music, c/o Examination Schools, High Street, Oxford.   25

4. Candidates specialising in performance will be required to submit:

Part 1a: a performance of not more than ten minutes' duration, to be given by the candidate in an examination in Week 0 or Week 1 of Hilary Term.

Part 1b: an essay of 6,000 words, normally on a topic of the candidate's choice. Two copies of the essay must be submitted, not later than noon on Tuesday of Week 10 of   30
Hilary Term to the Chair of Examiners for the M.St. in Music, c/o Examination Schools, High Street, Oxford.

Part 1c: an essay of 6,000 words, normally in response to an elective seminar. Two copies of the essay must be submitted, not later than noon on Tuesday of Week 7 of Trinity Term to the Chair of Examiners for the M.St. in Music, c/o Examination   35
Schools, High Street, Oxford.

Part 1d: an essay of 6,000 words, normally on a topic of the candidate's choice. Two copies of the essay must be submitted, not later than noon on Tuesday of Week 7 of Trinity Term, to the Chair of Examiners for the M.St. in Music, c/o Examination Schools, High Street, Oxford.   40

Part 2: a recital of not more than thirty minutes' duration, vocal or instrumental, of at least two contrasted pieces, to be performed not later than the tenth week of Trinity Term. Two possible programmes must be submitted for approval to the Masters' Course Convenor, Faculty of Music, by noon on Friday of third week of Hilary Term. Candidates will be informed of the examiners' choice of programme by Friday of   45
eighth week in the same term.

5. Candidates specialising in composition will be required to submit:

Part 1a: a musical composition of not more than eight minutes produced in response to techniques presented in composition seminars, two copies of which must be submitted, not later than noon on Monday of the tenth week of Michaelmas Term, to the   50

Chair of Examiners for the M.St. in Music, c/o Examination Schools, High Street, Oxford.

Part 1b: an essay of 6,000 words, normally on a topic of the candidate's choice. Two copies of the essay must be submitted, not later than noon on Tuesday of Week 10 of Hilary Term to the Chair of Examiners for the M.St. in Music, c/o Examination Schools, High Street, Oxford.

Part 1c: an essay of 6,000 words, normally in response to an elective seminar. Two copies of the essay must be submitted, not later than noon on Tuesday of Week 7 of Trinity Term to the Chair of Examiners for the M.St. in Music, c/o Examination Schools, High Street, Oxford.

Part 1d: a composition of not more than eight minutes produced in response to techniques presented in composition seminars. Two copies of the composition must be submitted, not later than noon on Tuesday of Week 7 of Trinity Term, to the Chair of Examiners for the M.St. in Music, c/o Examination Schools, High Street, Oxford.

Part 2: a musical composition or portfolio of compositions, of not more than twenty-five minutes' duration in total, two copies of which must be submitted, not later than noon on Tuesday of Week 10 of Trinity Term, to the Chair of Examiners for the M.St. in Music, c/o Examination Schools, High Street, Oxford.

6. The examiners may award a distinction for excellence in the whole examination. In this case the work will normally display an excellent command of the subject studied, evidence of critical understanding, and some demonstration of an original conceptual approach.

7. A candidate who fails the examination will be permitted to retake it on one further occasion only, not later than one year after the initial attempt. Such a candidate whose work has been of satisfactory standard in one or more elements examined will be required to resubmit for examination the element(s) which fell below the passmark when originally examined.

Master of Studies in Oriental Studies

1. Before admission to the course, candidates must satisfy the Board of the Faculty of Oriental Studies that they possess the necessary qualifications to profit by the course. The Board will not permit students to be admitted to the course if an M.St. in a particular subject under the aegis of the Board is considered more appropriate.

2. Candidates shall be required to attend for at least three terms such lecture courses and participate in such seminars as their supervisor shall specify.

3. *Syllabus*
There will be four Units:

Unit (i) Candidates shall submit either (A) two typed copies each of two essays of between 5,000 and 7,000 words in length, or (B) two typed copies of a thesis of between 12,000 and 15,000 words in length (excluding bibliography).

Option (A) may be any two of the following:

a. what might become part of a thesis for the M.Litt or D.Phil.;

b. an essay on the theoretical issues raised by the subject which the candidate is proposing for the thesis;

c. an essay on a topic relevant to the subject of the thesis;

d. a discussion of the historical and literary background or of the source material which is relevant to the proposed subject.

Option (B) should be equivalent to a substantial draft chapter or chapters of a proposed thesis for the M.Litt or the D.Phil.

The essays or thesis must be submitted to the Chair of Examiners, M.St in Oriental Studies, Examination Schools, High Street, Oxford, not later than 12 noon on Friday of fourth week of Trinity Term.

Units (ii) and (iii) Two three-hour examination papers, which may be any combination of language or non-language papers. When the elective papers are shared with another degree, the regulations for the paper follow that of the home degree.

Unit (iv) A prescribed essay, prepared in proper scholarly form, on research methods and materials relating to the area of study chosen under (i) above, of between 5,000 and 7,000 words. The topic of the essay will be set at the conclusion of the two examination papers Units (i) and (ii). The essay must be submitted to the Chair of Examiners, M.St in Oriental Studies, Examination Schools not later than seven days from the date on which the topic was set.

Candidates must submit titles for their written work (Unit (i) of the examination, above) and subjects for the two examinations (Units (ii) and (iii) of the examination, above) to the Faculty office by Monday of Week 0 of Hilary Term.

4. Lists of set texts must be submitted to the Faculty office by Friday of Week 7 of Michaelmas term.

5. All work submitted to the Chair of Examiners must be in typewritten form. Two copies must be submitted, securely sealed and addressed. An electronic copy of the thesis or essays for unit (i), must be submitted in PDF format in a memory stick or CD with the hard copies of the thesis. The work must bear the candidate's examination number (but not the candidate's name, which must be concealed). Candidates must include a signed declaration sealed in an envelope addressed to the Chair of Examiners that the work is the candidate's own.

6. Candidates may be required to attend a viva.

Master of Studies in Philosophical Theology

Candidates shall be required:

(*a*) to present themselves for a written examination in two of the papers prescribed below, the selection to depend on their previous qualifications;

(*b*) to present an essay of not more than 15,000 words on a topic in philosophical theology to be approved by the faculty board;

(*c*) to present themselves for a viva voce examination unless individually dispensed by the examiners (no candidate will be failed without a viva).

Candidates must make a written application for approval of the essay topic, to reach the Theology and Religion Graduate Studies Committee not later than Monday of noughth week in Hilary Term. In cases where there is some uncertainty about the acceptability of the proposal, candidates are advised to submit their applications earlier if possible. All applications should be accompanied by a recommendation from the candidate's supervisor. Two copies of the dissertation must be sent to the Chair of Examiners for the M.St in Philosophical Theology, c/o the Examination Schools, High Street, Oxford by the Friday of eighth week in Trinity Term of the year in which the examinations are taken. The dissertation must be accompanied by a signed statement by the candidate that the essay is the candidate's own work, except where otherwise indicated. The candidate's name should not appear on the dissertation itself.

Written examinations will be set in the tenth or eleventh week of Trinity Term.

The examiners may award a distinction to candidates who have performed with special merit in the whole examination.

1. *Philosophy of Religion*

As specified for Part B of the B.Phil. in Philosophy. See also regulations for Paper 1 of the M.Phil. in Philosophical Theology in the 'Course Regulations for the M.Phil. in Philosophical Theology' section of the course handbook.

2. *History of Philosophical Theology*

The paper will contain questions on philosophical influences on theology during the patristic period, the early medieval period, and the period 1760–1860. Candidates are required to show knowledge of two of the three periods and, within each of those two periods, of some of the principal relevant writings, viz. for the patristic period of works of Origen and Augustine, for the early medieval period of works of Anselm and Aquinas, and for the period 1760–1860 of works of Kant, Kierkegaard, and Schleiermacher. Study of texts in the original languages will not be required. Lectures, tutorials etc.: as for Paper 3 of the M.Phil. in Philosophical Theology.

3. Either *The Development of Christian Doctrine to AD 451*

or *Theology in Western Europe from Gabriel Biel to Jacob Arminus*

See regulations for Paper 1 of Section A and Paper 1 of Section C of the Christian Doctrine option of the M.Phil. in Theology in the 'Course Regulations for the M.Phil. in Theology' section of the course handbook.

Master of Studies in Philosophy

1. Every candidate must follow for at least three terms a course of instruction in Philosophy. Candidates will, when they enter for the examination, be required to produce from their society a certificate that they are following such a course.

2. Candidates will be required to attend the B.Phil. Pro-seminar. In addition, candidates will be required to attend two graduate classes in each of the three terms of their studies.

3. Candidates will be examined by submitting four essays of no more than 5,000 words each, in conformity with the following distribution requirement. One essay must be on a subject from Group 1 (Theoretical Philosophy), one on a subject from Group 2 (Practical Philosophy) and one on a subject from Group 3 (History of Philosophy).The one remaining essay may be assigned to a subject in any of the three Groups. The list of approved subjects in each Group will be the same as the list published for the B.Phil. in Philosophy in the Graduate Student Handbook.

4. Topics for the essays will be chosen by the candidates. Candidates may offer up to two essays on at most one subject not included in the list of approved subjects in the Graduate Student Handbook. Candidates wishing to offer an essay or essays on a subject not on the prescribed list must seek approval for the proposed subject from the Graduate Studies Committee in Philosophy *as soon as they decide they would like to offer it*, and in any case no later than the Friday of the fifth week of Trinity Term. Any such application must be supported by the relevant Course Coordinator. Where a subject is approved by the Graduate Studies Committee in Philosophy, the Committee will assign it to one of Groups 1–3.

5. Two printed copies of each essay must be delivered to the Examination Schools, High Street, Oxford OX1 4BG, by 10 a.m. on the Wednesdays of the following weeks: two essays are due in noughth week of Trinity Term and two essays must be submitted in noughth week of the Michaelmas Term following the year in which candidates are first entered on the Register of M.St. students. Candidates must give notice of the subject of each essay and the Group to which it will be assigned in accordance with the procedures and deadlines specified in the Graduate Student Handbook.

6. The examiners may award a distinction for excellence in the whole examination.

7. Candidates who fail up to two essays will be permitted to resubmit those essays; a resubmitted essay may be on a new topic, and may be on a new subject, provided that the distribution requirement is met. Candidates who choose to resubmit one or two failed essays must do so by 10 a.m. on Wednesday of noughth week of the following Michaelmas Term where the failed essay or essays had been submitted   5
during the first year of the degree, or by Wednesday of noughth week of the following Hilary Term where the essay or essays had been submitted in noughth week of Michaelmas Term. Candidates who fail three or more essays will be permitted to resubmit work for the failed elements of the examination during the following academic year. Candidates need only resubmit work for those elements of the examina-   10
tion that they failed. No resubmitted essay can receive a mark of more than 60. Candidates who fail to satisfy the examiners a second time in any part of the examination may not re-submit work for any part of the examination on any subsequent occasion.

Master of Studies in Philosophy of Physics   15

1. Every candidate must follow for at least three terms a course of instruction in Philosophy of Physics. Candidates will, when they enter for the examination, be required to produce from their society a certificate that they are following such a course.

2. Every candidate shall be required to offer the following subjects: 20

   (i) *Philosophy of Physics.*

   (ii) *Philosophy of Science.*

   (iii) One further subject chosen from the following list: Metaphysics and the Theory of Knowledge; Philosophy of Mind and Action; Philosophical Logic and the Philosophy of Language; Philosophy of Mathematics.   25

3. The choice of subjects must be notified on the entry form for the examination, to be submitted to the Examination Schools, High Street, Oxford by Friday of Week 7 of Hilary Term.

4. Candidates will be examined by submitting:

   (i) Two essays of no more than 5,000 words each on topics within the philosophy   30
   of physics. At most one essay may fall under each of the following subjects: (a) the philosophy of quantum theory; (b) the philosophy of space, time and symmetry; (c) the philosophy of statistical mechanics and thermodynamics; (d) other topics in the philosophy of physics.

   (ii) One essay of no more than 5,000 words on a topic in the philosophy of science   35
   (to be understood as excluding topics specifically in the philosophy of physics as specified under 4. (i) above).

   (iii) One essay of no more than 5,000 words, falling under one of the following subjects: (a) Metaphysics and the Theory of Knowledge; (b) Philosophy of Mind and Action; (c) Philosophical Logic and the Philosophy of Language;   40
   (d) Philosophy of Mathematics.

5. Topics for all essays will be chosen by the candidates.

6. Two printed copies of each of the essays in Philosophy of Physics must be delivered to the Examinations Schools, High Street, Oxford OX1 4BG, by 10am on Wednesday of Week 0 of Trinity Term in the year that the examination is to be taken.   45
Two printed copies of the Philosophy of Science essay must be delivered to the same address by 10am on Friday of Week 9 of Trinity Term in the year that the examination is to be taken. Two printed copies of the last essay (for Metaphysics and the Theory of Knowledge; Philosophy of Mind and Action; Philosophical Logic and

the Philosophy of Language; or Philosophy of Mathematics) must be delivered to the same address by 10am on Monday of Week 10 of Trinity Term in the year that the examination is to be taken. Essays must be typed or printed.

7. Candidates who have not delivered essays as prescribed by the due dates above shall, unless they show exceptional cause to the examiners, be deemed to have withdrawn from the examination. 5

8. The examiners may award a distinction for excellence in the whole examination.

9. A candidate will be deemed to have passed the examination if they obtain a passing mark on all four essays. In addition, a mark for the Philosophy of Science or elective paper (but not both) judged to be narrowly below passing quality may be 10 compensated for by strong performance on the Philosophy of Physics papers, provided that the candidate's average performance remains above the level judged sufficient for a pass by the Examiners.

10. A candidate who fails one element of the examination (i.e. one of the four essays), which has not been compensated in line with the provisions made under 15 paragraph 9. may apply to retake that element in the September immediately following the examination. A candidate who fails two or more elements may retake the examination in the year immediately following the failed examination. It is necessary for a candidate to retake only the failed elements of the examination.

11. In the case of candidates whose formal application to transfer to the second 20 year of the B.Phil. in Philosophy has been conditionally approved by the Graduate Studies Committee of the Faculty, the Board of Examiners for the M.St in Philosophy of Physics shall assess whether the candidate's overall performance meets the level of performance specified in the Graduate Student Handbook as a condition for entrance to the B.Phil. in Philosophy. If so, the candidate shall be deemed to have withdrawn 25 from the examination for the M.St. in Philosophy of Physics, and their M.St essays shall be deemed to have been submitted for the B.Phil. in Philosophy.

Master of Studies in Psychodynamic Practice

1. Candidates will be expected to have satisfactorily completed the Postgraduate Diploma in Psychodynamic Practice. 30

2. *Course*

The course will consist of Day Workshops, research methodology and application seminars, clinical seminars, individual clinical and research tutorials, and continuing personal therapy and supervised practice. The course will be taken on a part-time basis for a period of one year's duration. 35

3. Every candidate will be required to satisfy the examiners in the following:

   (*a*) attendance at Day Workshops, research methodology and application seminars, clinical seminars, individual clinical and research tutorials, and personal therapy and clinical placement sessions;

   (*b*) submission of a dissertation of no more than 15,000 words on a topic 40 selected by the student in consultation with the research tutor and course director and agreed by the external examiner. The dissertation must be forwarded to the examiners c/o Registry, Department for Continuing Education, Wellington Square, Oxford, OX1 2JA, for receipt not later than noon on the last Friday of September in the year in which the course 45 is studied. Material already submitted for the Postgraduate Diploma in Psychodynamic Practice may not be included;

    (*c*) participation in a minimum of 17 placement supervisions and at least 100 hours of client/patient contact, and submission of an end-of-year report by a candidate's placement supervisor;

    (*d*) participation in a minimum of 40 hours of personal therapy exceptions may be made for candidates who have had extensive personal therapy previously;   5

    (*e*) submission of annual reports from both research and clinical tutors;

    (*f*) a viva voce examination at the end of the course of study.

4. The examiners may award a distinction for excellence in the whole examination.

5. A candidate whose dissertation fails to satisfy the examiner may be permitted to resubmit on one further occasion only not later than one year after the initial failure.   10 Approval for deferral must be obtained from the relevant board of studies.

6. If any candidate who is successful in the examination for the Degree of Master of Studies in Psychodynamic Practice has previously successfully completed the Postgraduate Diploma in Psychodynamic Practice, the Master of Studies will subsume his or her diploma.   15

Master of Studies in Slavonic Studies

1. Candidates must have taken *either* Russian (as sole language *or* as one of two languages) *or* Czech (with Slovak) in the Oxford Honour School of Modern Languages, *or* have taken a comparable degree in a Slavonic language from another university, *or* must satisfy the committee that they possess the necessary qualifications   20 in a Slavonic language to profit by the course.

2. Candidates must follow for at least three terms a course of instruction in Slavonic Studies.

3. Each candidate will be required to take one language from Schedule 1 and three subjects from Schedules 2–10. Candidates may take no more than two subjects from   25 any one Schedule. Candidates may not take subjects which they have already studied in a first degree course.

4. Candidates will be examined by written examination, except:

    (i) for Schedule 2.iv (Methods of Criticism and the Theory of Literature) which will be examined under the regulations for the M.St./M.Phil. in Modern   30 Languages;

    (ii) for Schedule 6.i–ix which will be examined under the regulations for the M.St./M.Phil. in Modern Languages;

    (iii) that in lieu of written examination in one subject a candidate may elect under Schedule 2.v to submit an essay of 5,000 to 7,000 words on a subject of the   35 candidate's choice.

The subject of the essay should fall within the areas of Slavonic languages and literatures. Candidates are required to register the subject area or title of their essay with the Modern Languages Graduate Office by the end of the fourth week of Hilary Term. Three typed copies of the essay must be delivered to the Examination Schools,   40 High Street, Oxford by noon on Thursday of sixth week of Trinity Term. Work submitted in the form of an essay for the Degree of M.St. may subsequently be incorporated in a thesis submitted for the Degree of M.Phil., or may be used as the basis for the piece of written work required for admission to the status of student for the Degrees of M.Litt. or D.Phil.   45

5. Candidates must present themselves for oral examination unless dispensed by the examiners.

6. The examiners may award a distinction for excellence in the whole examination.

Schedule 1

Unseen translation from any one of the following languages (this must not be a language previously studied by the candidate to degree standard):

   i. Bulgarian

   ii. Croatian   5

   iii. Czech

   iv. Polish

   v. Russian

   vi. Serbian

   vii. Slovak   10

   viii. Slovene

   ix. Sorbian

   x. Ukrainian

Schedule 2

   i. Cyrillic Palaeography   15

   ii. Textual Criticism

   iii. Prague School of Linguistics

   iv. Methods of Criticism and the Theory of Literature (from the M.St. course in Modern Languages)

   v. A subject of the candidate's choice, approved by the committee.   20

Schedule 3

   i. Comparative Slavonic Philology

   ii. Old Church Slavonic

   iii. History of Church Slavonic.

Schedule 4   25

The History of:

   i. Ukrainian

   ii. Bulgarian *and* Macedonian

   iii. Croatian

   iv. Czech *and* Slovak   30

   v. Polish

   vi. Russian

   vii. Serbian

   viii. Slovene

   ix. Sorbian.   35

Schedule 5

The Structure and Present State of:

   i. Bulgarian

   ii. Croatian

   iii. Czech   40

   iv. Polish

   v. Russian

vi. Serbian

vii. Slovak

viii. Slovene

ix. Sorbian

x. Ukrainian.   5

Schedule 6

    i. Literature and Culture of the Russian Enlightenment (from the M.St. course in Modern Languages).

    ii. Pushkin and Romanticism (from the M.St. course in Modern Languages).

    iii. Gender and Representation in Russian Culture from 1800 (from the M.St.   10
course in Modern Languages).

    iv. Russian Modes of Lyric (1820–1940).

    v. The Rise of the Russian Novel (from the M.St. course in Modern Languages).

    vi. Russian Drama in the 19th and 20th Centuries (from the M.St. course in
Modern Languages).   15

    vii. The Russian Experience of Modernity, 1905–1945 (from the M.St. course in
Modern Languages).

    viii. The GULag and the Russian Literary Process (from the M.St. course in
Modern Languages).

    ix. Post-Soviet Russian Literature (from the M.St. course in Modern Languages).   20

Schedule 7

    i. Czech Poetry since 1774.

    ii. Czech Prose Fiction and Drama since 1774.

    iii. Polish Literature since 1798.

    iv. Slovak Literature since 1783.   25

Schedule 8

    i. Byzantine Civilization and its Expansion, 913–1204.

    ii. Bohemia from the Hussite Wars to the Battle of the White Mountain (1415–1620).

    iii. The History of Poland and Hungary, 1506 to 1795.   30

    iv. The Habsburg Monarchy, 1790–1918.

    v. The History of the Balkans, 1774–1918.

Schedule 9

    i. Russian Social and Political Thought, 1825–1917 (M.Phil. in Russian and
East European Studies B.1).   35

    ii. The History of Russia, 1861–1917 (M.Phil. in Russian and East European
Studies B.2).

    iii. The History since 1918 of either Poland or Czechoslovakia and its successor
states or Yugoslavia and its successor states.

Teaching for some options may not be available in every year. Applicants for admis-   40
sion will be advised whether teaching will be available in the options of their choice.

Master of Studies in Study of Religions

1. Each candidate will be required to follow a course of instruction for three terms and present himself or herself for examination in three subjects as set out in the syllabus.

2. A 10,000–15,000 word dissertation must be offered. All candidates must normally make a written application for approval of the topic no later than Monday of noughth week of Hilary Term. The application should be submitted to the Faculty of Theology and Religion for consideration by the Theology and Religion Graduate Studies Committee. In cases where there is some uncertainty about the acceptability of the proposal, candidates are asked to submit their applications earlier if possible. All applications should be accompanied by a recommendation from the candidate's supervisor. Two copies of the dissertation must be sent to the Chair of Examiners for the Degree of M.St in the Study of Religion, c/o the Examination Schools, High Street, Oxford before the end of eighth week of Trinity Term in the year of examination.

Titles for the two shorter essays must normally be submitted to the Faculty of Theology and Religion no later than Monday of noughth week of Hilary Term for consideration by the Graduate Studies Committee. Two copies of the essays must be submitted to the Examination Schools by the Friday before the beginning of Trinity Term in the year in which the examination is taken. Decisions on the suitability of titles for both dissertation and essays will be taken in consultation with the Chair of Examiners for that year.

The three-hour examination will be held in tenth or eleventh week of Trinity Term.

3. Each candidate will be required to present himself or herself for an oral (viva voce) examination unless individually dispensed by the examiners. This will take place within a few days of the written examination, and may include discussion of both the examination paper and any pre-submitted work.

4. The examiners may award a distinction to candidates who have performed with special merit in the whole examination.

5. A candidate who fails the examination will be permitted to retake it on one further occasion only, not later than one year after the initial attempt. Such a candidate whose 10,000–15,000 word essay has been of satisfactory standard may resubmit the same piece of work, while a candidate who had reached a satisfactory standard on the written papers will not be required to retake that part of the examination.

Syllabus

Candidates must offer the paper on the Nature of Religion and two papers selected from papers on the major texts and doctrines of (*a*) Buddhism, (*b*) Christianity, (*c*) Islam, (*d*) Judaism, or (*e*) Hinduism, or (*f*) any other paper that may from time to time be approved by the Board of the Faculty of Theology and Religion.

The paper on one of the candidate's two chosen religions will consist of a dissertation of 10,000–15,000 words. Essays and dissertations on the relations or comparisons between two religions, or approaches taken from one view towards others, are also welcomed, so long as they do not overlap with work done for any other elements of this degree. Decisions on the suitability of titles for both dissertation and essays will be taken in consultation with the Chair of Examiners for that year.

The paper on the other religion will consist of two essays of up to 5,000 words.

Candidates will not normally be allowed to substitute a long essay or two short essays for the paper on The Nature of Religion. Any candidate who believes that he or she has special grounds for seeking a dispensation must present a case to the Graduate Studies Committee, with the supervisor's approval, before the fifth week of Hilary Term.

The Nature of Religion

This paper will require that students demonstrate an advanced understanding of the main classical and contemporary approaches to the study of religions. It will cover the work of some of the most important scholars in the field, and consider the history of the field of the study of religion, through its methods and theories, over the 20th   5 century up to the present. The paper will also assess the work of these theoretical and methodological approaches as they influence our understanding of contemporary religious developments in the modern world.

(a) Buddhism

The paper will require that students investigate the fundamental aspects of Buddhist   10 thought, mainly as reflected by early Buddhist teaching. It will also explore the ways in which Buddhism has changed during the course of its history, adapting to diverse cultural contexts in the pre-modern and modern world.

(b) Christianity

For this paper, students may study any aspect of Christian life or thought at any   15 period of the Common Era and in any part of the world. Christianity is here understood to encompass groups and systems that are commonly deemed heterodox or heretical, together with those that are commonly regarded as offshoots of Christianity (e.g. Manichees, Latter-Day Saints, Jehovah's Witnesses). Topics may be historical, sociological or theological, but students taking theological texts as their principal   20 subject are strongly encouraged to take account of the historical and social background.

(c) Islam

The paper is a broad investigation of the historical origins and development of the theology, law and mysticism of Islam, from the classical to the modern period. Specific   25 topics will be established in consultation with students; possible subjects include: Prophethood of Muhammad; the Qur'an; the Hadith; Shi'ism; the theologies of the Mu'tazilis, Ash'aris, and Hanbalis; Islamic law (shari'a) and the Sunni schools of the Hanafis, Malikis, Shafi'is, and Hanbalis; Sufism (tasawwuf) and the major Sufi orders; Islam and other religions.   30

(d) Judaism

Jewish religion and thought since 70 ce with reference both to its historical development and to Judaism in the modern world. Selections from the texts listed in the student handbook will be assigned by the course tutor by the beginning of Michaelmas Term.   35

(e) Hinduism

This paper, for which the source material lies in Sanskrit texts read in English translation and in the context of reliable secondary sources, will be concerned with the main components of the brahminical tradition which, though of ancient origin, are still relevant today. Key areas include Vedic religion, nondualism, and traditional   40 (smarta) ritual practice. Particular attention will be paid to leading ideas developed in the listed primary texts read in translation, though the secondary sources provide necessary context. No attempt will be made to cover later theism or Hindu sects.

Master of Studies in Syriac Studies

1. Candidates must satisfy the Board of the Faculty of Oriental Studies before   45 admission to the course that they possess the necessary qualification in the Syriac language to profit by the course.

2. Every candidate must follow for at least three terms a course of study in Syriac Studies.

3. *Syllabus*

There will be four Units. Each unit is examined by a written paper.

Unit (i) Essay questions on the history, literature, and culture of the Syriac Churches.

Units (ii), (iii), and (iv) Passages for translation and comment, and essay questions   5
on prescribed texts in Syriac, with special reference to *three* of the following subjects (a passage, or passages, for unprepared translation may also be set):

  (1) Biblical versions;
  (2) Exegetical literature;
  (3) Early poetry;   10
  (4) Liturgy;
  (5) Historical literature;
  (6) Secular literature;
  (7) Monastic literature;
  (8) Hagiography;   15
  (9) Translations of Greek patristic texts;
  (10) Theological texts;
  (11) Any other subject approved by the Board.

4. Lists of set texts must be submitted to the Faculty office by Friday of Week 7 of Michaelmas Term.   20

5. Candidates may be required to attend a viva.

Teaching for the course may not be available in every year. Applicants for admission will be advised of this.

Master of Studies in Theology

Candidates for the M.St. in Theology are required to follow a course of instruction   25
and directed research for three terms and to present themselves for examination in one of seven subjects:

  I. **Old Testament**

 II. **New Testament**

III. **Christian Doctrine**, specialising in one of four fields: 30
    History of Doctrine: Patristic Theology (*c.* AD 100–787)
    History of Doctrine: Scholastic Theology (*c.* AD 1050–1350)
    History of Doctrine: Theology of the Reformation Period (*c.* AD 1500–1650)
    Modern Doctrine (post-1789), further specialising in one of three tracks:
      Modern Theology   35
      Theology & Modern European Thought
      Theology & Literature
IV. **Ecclesiastical History**, specialising in one of five fields:
    The Early Church AD 200–476
    The Western Church AD 476–1050   40
    The Western Church AD 1000–1400
    European Christianity AD 1400–1800
    European Christianity AD 1800–2000
  V. **Christian Ethics**
 VI. **Science & Religion**   45
VII. **Biblical Interpretation**

The examination consists of three elements:

A **Two essays** of not more than 5,000 words each

Essay proposals must be submitted for consideration by the Faculty's Graduate Studies Committee *by Monday of Week 0 of Hilary Term*. The completed essays (two copies of each) must be submitted for examination *by Friday of Week 0 of Trinity Term*.

B A dissertation of not more than 15,000 words   5

The dissertation proposal must be submitted for consideration by the Faculty's Graduate Studies Committee *by Monday of Week 0 of Hilary Term*. The completed dissertation (two copies) must be submitted for examination *by Friday of Week 8 of Trinity Term*.

C A written examination of three hours' duration   10

The written examination takes place *in Week 10 or 11 of Trinity Term*.

All essay and dissertation proposals should comprise a title, a short statement of how the subject will be treated, a bibliography of core texts (both primary and secondary), and the signature of the supervisor indicating his or her approval. The titles and content of the essays and dissertation should not substantially overlap with   15
each other. For candidates intending to proceed to doctoral study, the topic of the dissertation should normally be such as to provide a foundation for doctoral research.

All submitted work should be double-spaced in font-size 12.

Candidates must not put their names on the written examination papers or on any submitted work. All submitted work must be printed and sent in a parcel bearing the   20
words, 'M.St. in Theology', to the Chair of Examiners, c/o the Examination Schools, High Street, Oxford.

Each candidate is also required to present himself or herself for an oral (viva voce) examination, which takes place within a few days of the written examination, and may include discussion of the candidate's work in any of the three elements listed above.   25

Within this general pattern, particular requirements pertain to certain subjects, as indicated below.

I. **OLD TESTAMENT**

A and B (essays and dissertation) as above.

C (the written examination) is on prescribed Old Testament Texts in Hebrew.   30
Candidates are notified of the set texts at the beginning of Michaelmas Term.

II. **NEW TESTAMENT**

A and B (essays and dissertation) as above.

C (the written examination) is on prescribed New Testament Texts in Greek.
Candidates are notified of the set texts at the beginning of Michaelmas Term.   35

III. **CHRISTIAN DOCTRINE**

A and B (essays and dissertation): All work must fall within one of the four specialised fields listed above under Christian Doctrine. Candidates specialising in Modern Doctrine choose one of three tracks within that field (i.e. Modern Theology, Theology & Modern European Thought, or Theology & Literature); this determines   40
their attendance of seminars, and should influence their choice of titles for essays and the dissertation. In proposing their titles for such work, Modern Doctrine candidates should explain in which pieces of work they will demonstrate competence in (a) exploring the encounter between theology and some non-theological discipline, and (b) exploring a modern theological response to some theological reflection of the past.   45

C (the written examination) takes particular forms for the different fields. In the History of Doctrine specialisms, the examination includes passages for translation and comment from prescribed texts: Greek or Latin texts in the case of Patristic Theology; Latin texts in the case of Scholastic Theology; and Latin, German, or French texts in the case of Theology of the Reformation Period. In each of these cases essays will also   50 be set, both on the prescribed texts and on general topics within the same period. Candidates are notified of the set texts at the beginning of Michaelmas Term. In the Modern Doctrine field, the examination will be on Methods & Styles in Theology.

IV. ECCLESIASTICAL HISTORY

A and B (essays and dissertation): All work must fall within one of the five 5 specialised fields listed above under Ecclesiastical History.

C (the written examination) is a general paper on the Nature & Practice of Ecclesiastical History. Candidates will be expected to show knowledge of a range of historiographical approaches to key questions in ecclesiastical history and of the variety of approaches to historical method which have emerged as a result of the 10 professionalisation of teaching and research in history and of the introduction of new methods into the writing of history.

V. CHRISTIAN ETHICS

A and B (essays and dissertation): In proposing titles for essays and the dissertation, candidates should explain in which pieces of work they will demonstrate competence in 15 (a) exploring an ethical question, substantive or conceptual, in relation to contemporary discussion; (b) the interpretation of a biblical text of moral significance; and (c) the discussion of a non-biblical text of moral significance from a period of history prior to 1900.

C (the written examination) is on Christian Moral Concepts & Methodology: Contemporary & Historical Discussions. 20

VI. SCIENCE AND RELIGION

A and B (essays and dissertation) as above.

C (the written examination) is on topics in Science and Religion. In proposing titles for essays and the dissertation, candidates should explain in which pieces of work they will demonstrate competence in (a) exploring a historical debate in which scientific and 25 religious issues are involved; (b) exploring a philosophical debate with a bearing on the discussion of science and religion; (c) analysing a contemporary issue on the interface between science and religion.

VII. BIBLICAL INTERPRETATION

A and B (essays and dissertation): All work must fall within one period in the history 30 of biblical study. The period is selected by the student in consultation with his or her supervisor.

C (the written examination) is on the History & Principles of Biblical Study with special reference to a selected period. The period is the same one as that on which the student has worked for the essays and dissertation; where there is more than one 35 candidate in the examination, each will be able to answer on the period which he or she has studied.

Master of Studies in US History

The regulations of the Board of the Faculty of History are as follows: 40

1. Candidates for this degree must follow for at least three terms a course of instruction and directed research and must, upon entering the examination, produce from their society a certificate to that effect.

2. Candidates must attend such lectures, seminars and classes as their supervisor shall determine. In addition to the formally examined programme elements described 45 below, each candidate will be expected to attend and complete in-course requirements for a series of skills and specialist options based on a schedule to be published from year to year by the Faculty's Graduate Studies Committee.

3. The final examination shall comprise (i) two extended essays of between 4,000 and 5,000 words based on the Advanced Option, (ii) one examination paper based on the programme's conceptual and methodological component, and (iii) a dissertation of not more than 15,000 words.

I. There is currently only one Advanced Option in the 'History of the United States, and the colonies that preceded it, since 1600', which is supplemented by tutorial sessions which enable candidates and supervisors to tailor their studies to individual training needs.

Two copies of the two essays, addressed to the Chair of Examiners for the Master of Studies in US History, must be submitted to the Examination Schools, High Street, Oxford by 12 noon on Monday of Week Nine of Hilary Term. The essays should reflect skills and understanding the candidate has acquired through attending the Advanced Option classes, one of them may complement but must not share significant content with the dissertation, and the essays are also expected to be distinct from each other in period or issues covered.

II. The corresponding examination paper on conceptual and methodological issues is 'Methods and evidence in the History of the United States of America'.

III. Candidates must prepare a dissertation of not more than 15,000 words on a topic in his or her chosen subject area. The dissertation must include a short abstract which concisely summarises in about 300 words its scope and principal arguments.

Two copies of the dissertation, addressed to the Chair of Examiners for the Master of Studies in US History, must be submitted to the Examination Schools by 12 noon on Monday of Week Six of Trinity Term.

Material submitted under I. and II. may be summarised or substantially further developed in the dissertation, but no significant part of the dissertation should reproduce or paraphrase other work submitted for examination.

4. The examiners may award a distinction to candidates who have performed with special merit in the whole examination.

5. A candidate who fails the examination will be permitted to retake it on one further occasion only, not later than one year after the initial attempt.

Master of Studies in Women's Studies

1. Every candidate must follow, for at least three terms, a course of instruction in Women's Studies. Candidates will, when they enter for the examination, be required to produce from their society a certificate that they are following such a course.

2. Candidates are required to present themselves for viva voce examination if summoned by the examiners.

3. The examiners may award a distinction for excellence in the whole examination.

4. *Syllabus:*

Candidates must offer A and B below, two options from C, and a dissertation (D).

A. Feminist Theory

B. Approaches to Feminist Research

C. Options. Candidates must follow two of a range of option courses approved by the Joint Standing Committee for Women's Studies. A full list of the options available is given in the course handbook for the academic year in question.

D. A dissertation of up to 12,000 words (and not less than 10,000), including footnotes but excluding bibliography, on a subject proposed by the candidate in consultation with the dissertation supervisor. Appendices should be

avoided but must in any case be approved by the Chair of Examiners on an individual basis. Cases must be made on the basis that they are required for the examiners to understand the content of the dissertation. The approval form, detailing the title and subject of the dissertation, must be approved and forwarded electronically by the dissertation supervisor, to the Chair of   5
Examiners (c/o Graduate Studies Administrator for Women's Studies) not later than Friday of fifth week of Hilary Term. The subject matter of the dissertation may be related to that of either or both of the two pieces of written work submitted for the Options courses, but material deployed in such pieces of work may not be repeated in the dissertation.   10

5. In the case of C candidates will be examined by the submission of written work. The essays submitted under C should be of 6,000–7,000 words, including footnotes and excluding bibliography. The approval form detailing the topics of the written work proposed, countersigned by the dissertation supervisor must be submitted for approval to the Chair of Examiners (c/o Graduate Studies Administrator for Women's   15
Studies) not later than Friday of fifth week of Hilary Term.The two pieces of written work under C (three typewritten or printed copies of each piece, bearing on the front the candidate's examination number but neither his or her name or the name of his or her college) must be delivered in envelopes bearing the words: 'Option Essay sub-mitted for the M.St. in Women's Studies' to the Examination Schools, High Street,   20
Oxford. The first piece of written work under C must be delivered not later than noon on Friday of eighth week of Hilary Term; the second piece of written work under C must be delivered not later than noon on Friday of first week of Trinity Term. Candidates must themselves retain one typewritten or printed copy of each piece of work. Supervisors or others are permitted to give bibliographical help with and to   25
discuss drafts of written work submitted. Each envelope of written work must be accompanied, under a separate cover, by a signed statement by the candidate that it is his or her own work except where otherwise indicated.

6. In the case of D, the dissertation (three typewritten or printed copies, bearing on the front the candidate's examination number but neither his or her name nor the   30
name of his or her college) must be delivered in an envelope bearing the words: 'Dissertation submitted for the M.St. in Women's Studies' to the Examination Schools, High Street, Oxford, not later than noon on Friday of eighth week of Trinity Term. Students must also submit three copies of a brief abstract (no more than 500 words) outlining the rationale and approach of the thesis. Candidates must   35
themselves retain one typewritten or printed copy of their dissertation. Supervisors or others are permitted to give bibliographical help with and to discuss drafts of dis-sertations. The dissertation must be accompanied, under a separate cover, by a signed statement by the candidate that it is his or her own work, except where otherwise indicated.   40

7. In the case both of the submission of written work under C and of the submission of the dissertation (D), candidates must ensure that a separate receipt for each submission is received from the Examination Schools and is retained for future reference.

8. A candidate who fails to submit any of the three written elements (that is, the two   45
pieces of written work and the dissertation) by the dates specified above shall be deemed to have withdrawn from the examination.

9. If the two pieces of written work, submitted for C and/or the dissertation, submitted for D, fail the examination, the candidate shall not be granted leave to supplicate for the degree of M.St. Such a candidate is permitted to resubmit the   50
elements of the examination which have failed to satisfy the examiners, on one further occasion only. The two pieces of written work submitted for C shall be resubmitted by

noon on Friday of first week of the Trinity Term following their first examination. The dissertation (D) shall be resubmitted by not later than noon of Friday of eighth week of the Trinity Term following their first examination.

Master of Studies in Yiddish Studies

1. All candidates shall be required at the time of admission to satisfy the board (if necessary, by written and oral tests) that they possess the appropriate qualifications for the proposed course, including suitable proficiency in written and spoken Yiddish. Normally the course will be restricted to candidates who have taken a first degree in a relevant subject area.

2. All candidates must follow a course of instruction in Yiddish Studies at Oxford for a period of three terms, unless the Board of the Faculty of Medieval and Modern Languages in exceptional circumstances shall permit an extension of time and they shall, when they enter their names for the examination, be required to produce from their society a certificate stating that they are following the course of instruction for the period prescribed.

3. *Syllabus*

Candidates must offer both components of A below, one option from B, and a dissertation (C).

A. (i) Modern Yiddish Literature (1864–1939).
    (ii) History of the Yiddish Language.

Assessment of these subjects is by 'take-home' examination, one of which must be submitted by Friday of Week 9 of Hilary Term and one by Friday of Week 1 of Trinity Term. The examination papers will be distributed on the Friday of the preceding week.

B.   (i) Old Yiddish Literature (survey).
    (ii) Old Yiddish Literature: Secular and Religious Trends.
   (iii) Old Yiddish: Between Folklore and Literature.
   (iv) Nineteenth-Century Yiddish Literature.
    (v) Modern Yiddish Poetry.
   (vi) Yiddish Drama and Theatre.
  (vii) Twentieth-Century Centres of Yiddish Literature and Culture.
 (viii) Sociology of Yiddish.
   (ix) History of Yiddish Studies.
    (x) Yiddish Stylistics.
   (xi) Yiddish Bibliography and Booklore.
  (xii) Any other option approved by the board.

Unless the subject is governed by regulations laid down elsewhere, the subject is examined by submission of an essay of 5,000–7,000 words, to be submitted by Friday of Week 1 of Trinity Term.

Candidates shall seek approval (by application to the Modern Languages Graduate Office, 37 Wellington Square, Oxford) of their proposed option by the end of the fourth week of their first term.

Teaching for some options listed under B may not be available in every year. Applicants for admission will be advised of this.

C. A dissertation of approximately 10,000 words and not more than 12,000 words on a subject proposed by the candidate in consultation with the supervisor and approved by the Board of the Faculty of Medieval and Modern Languages. Candidates shall seek approval (by application to the Modern Languages Graduate Office, 41 Wellington Square, Oxford) for the proposed topic of their dissertation by the end of the fourth week of their second term.

The dissertation must be presented in proper scholarly form. Two copies, typed in double-spacing on one side only of A4 paper, each bound or held firmly in a stiff cover bearing on the front the candidate's examination number but neither his or her name nor the name of his or her college, must be delivered in a parcel bearing the words 'Dissertation submitted for the M.St. in Yiddish Studies' to the Examination Schools, High Street, Oxford, not later than noon on the Friday of the eighth week of Trinity Term. Candidates must themselves retain one copy of the dissertation.

Supervisors or others are permitted to give bibliographical help during the preparation of the dissertation and to discuss drafts.

5. The examiners may award a distinction for excellence in the whole examination.

NOTES

9

GENERAL REGULATIONS FOR THE DEGREE OF MASTER OF SCIENCE BY COURSEWORK

§1. Degree of Master of Science by Coursework

1. Any person who has been admitted to the status of student for the degree of Master of Science by Coursework, who has satisfied the conditions prescribed by this section, and has satisfied the examiners as required, may supplicate for the Degree of Master of Science by Coursework.

2. The Education Committee shall have power to make and vary such regulations as may be necessary for carrying out the duties laid upon it and upon the Registrar by this section.

3. For the purposes of this section, the words 'board', 'faculty board', or 'board of the faculty' shall include any committee authorised to admit candidates for the Degree of Master of Science by Coursework.

4. A Student for the Degree of Master of Science by Coursework who is not a graduate of the University may wear the same gown as that worn by Students for the Degree of Doctor of Philosophy.

§2. Admission of Candidates for the Degree of Master of Science by Coursework

1. A candidate seeking admission as a Student for the Degree of Master of Science by Coursework shall apply to the board under whose aegis the proposed course of study falls. Candidates for admission shall be required to provide such information as the board may determine from time to time by regulation. Applicants shall in addition be required to undertake such other tests and meet such conditions as, subject to the approval of the Education Committee, a board may determine by regulation.

2. Applications shall be made through the Registrar, and it shall be the duty of the Registrar to submit each application to the board concerned and to inform the candidate of the outcome, as soon as may be.

3. No person shall be admitted as a Student for the Degree of Master of Science by Coursework under these provisions unless he or she is also a member of a college, and unless the application for admission as a Student for the Degree of Master of Science by Coursework has the approval of that college. The Registrar shall forward the application to the candidate's college or to the college to which the candidate wishes to apply for membership, as appropriate; and admission by the faculty board shall be conditional upon admission by an approved society.

4. A student registered for any other higher degree or diploma in the University may apply for transfer to the status of Student for the Degree of Master of Science by

Coursework.[1] The board concerned shall have power to make such transfer, provided that it is satisfied that the student is well qualified and well fitted to undertake the course of study for which application is made, and that the application has the support of the candidate's society. A candidate who transfers status in this way shall be reckoned as having held the status of Student for the Degree of Master of Science by Coursework from the time of admission to his or her previous status, unless the board shall determine otherwise.

5. A student holding the status of Probationer Research Student may, with the approval of the board which admitted him or her, be admitted as a candidate for an examination for the Degree of Master of Science by Coursework. Time spent as a student holding the status of Probationer Research Student shall count as time spent working for the Degree of Master of Science.

§3. Supervision of Students for the Degree of Master of Science by Coursework

1. Every candidate on admission as a Student for the Degree of Master of Science by Coursework shall be placed by the board concerned under the supervision of a member of the University or other competent person selected by the board, and the board shall have power for sufficient reason to change the supervisor of any student or to arrange for joint supervision by more than one supervisor, if it deems it necessary.

2. It shall be the duty of the supervisor of a student entered upon a course of study to direct and superintend the work of the student, to meet the student regularly, and to undertake such duties as shall from time to time be set out in the relevant Policy and Guidance issued by the Education Committee.

3. The supervisor shall submit a report on the progress of a student to the board three times a year, and at any other time when the board so requests or the supervisor deems it expedient. The supervisor shall communicate the contents of the report to the student on each occasion that a report is made, so that the student is aware of the supervisor's assessment of his or her work during the period in question. In addition, the supervisor shall inform the board at once if he or she is of the opinion the student is unlikely to reach the standard required for the Degree of Master of Science by Coursework.

4. It shall be the duty of every Student for the Degree of Master of Science by Coursework to undertake such guided work and to attend such seminars and lectures as his or her supervisor requests; to attend such meetings with his or her supervisor as the supervisor reasonably arranges; and to fulfil any other requirements of the Education Committee as set out in relevant Policy and Guidance issued by the Education Committee.

§4. Residence and other Requirements for Students for the Degree of Master of Science by Coursework

1. No full-time Student for the Degree of Master of Science by Coursework shall be granted leave to supplicate unless, after admission, he or she has kept statutory residence and pursued his or her course of study at Oxford for at least three terms.

2. No full-time Student for the Degree of Master of Science by Coursework shall retain that status for more than six terms in all, except that any candidate for the Examination in Education may retain that status for nine terms in all.

---

[1] Students applying for the M.Sc in Advanced Cognitive Therapy Studies must commence by studying the Postgraduate Diploma in Advanced Cognitive Therapy Studies.

3. Part-time students for the Degree of Master of Science by Coursework shall in each case be required to pursue their course of study for twice the number of terms required of an equivalent full-time student. Part-time students shall not be required to keep statutory residence but must attend for such instruction and undertake such supervised fieldwork as the faculty concerned shall require. The Director of Graduate   5
Studies of the board concerned, or director of the department concerned, as the case may be, shall keep a register of attendance of part-time students. No student shall be granted leave to supplicate unless the register shows satisfactory attendance by him or her.

4. Part-time students may hold the status of Student for the Degree of Master of   10
Science by Coursework for up to twice the number of terms for which equivalent full-time students may hold that status except where an extension of time is permitted by special regulation.

5. A Student for the Degree of Master of Science by Coursework shall cease to hold that status if: 15

   (i) he or she shall have been refused permission to supplicate for the Degree of Master of Science by Coursework;

   (ii) the board concerned shall, in accordance with provisions set down by regulation by the Education Committee, and after consultation with the student's society and supervisor, have deprived the student of such status;   20

   (iii) he or she shall have been transferred under the relevant provisions to another status;

   (iv) he or she shall not have entered for the relevant examination within the time specified under this subsection.

§5. Examination of Students   25

1. The examinations for the Degree of Master of Science by Coursework shall be under the supervision of the boards authorised to admit candidates for the Degree of Master of Science by Coursework. The examinations for the degree and the bodies responsible for the supervision of each examination are listed below.

Examination	*Board*	
African Studies	Social Sciences	30
Applied Landscape Archaeology	Continuing Education	
Applied Linguistics and Second Language Acquisition	Social Sciences	
Applied Statistics	Mathematical, Physical and Life Sciences	35
Archaeological Science	Social Sciences	
Biodiversity, Conservation, and Management	Social Sciences	
Clinical Embryology	Medical Sciences	
Cognitive and Evolutionary Anthropology	Social Sciences	40
Cognitive Behavioural Therapy	Continuing Education	
Comparative Social Policy	Social Sciences	
Computer Science	Mathematical, Physical and Life Sciences	
Contemporary Chinese Studies	Social Sciences	45
Contemporary India	Social Sciences	
Criminology and Criminal Justice	Law	
Economic and Social History	History	
Economics for Development	Social Sciences	

Education	Social Sciences	
Endovascular Neurosurgery (Interventional Neuroradiology)	Medical Sciences	
English Local History	Continuing Education	
Environmental Change and Management	Social Sciences	5
Evidence-Based Health Care	Medical Sciences/Continuing Education	
Evidence-Based Social Intervention	Social Sciences	
Experimental Therapeutics	Medical Sciences/Continuing Education	10
Financial Economics	Social Sciences	
Global Governance and Diplomacy	Social Sciences	
Global Health Science	Medical Sciences	
History of Science, Medicine, and Technology	History	
Integrated Immunology	Medical Sciences	15
International Health and Tropical Medicine	Medical Sciences	
Latin American Studies	School of Interdisciplinary Area Studies	
Law and Finance	Social Sciences	
Learning and Teaching	Social Sciences	20
Major Programme Management	Social Sciences	
Management Research	Social Sciences	
Mathematical and Computational Finance	Mathematical, Physical and Life Sciences	
Mathematical and Theoretical Physics	Mathematical, Physical and Life Sciences	25
Mathematical Finance	Mathematical, Physical and Life Sciences	
Mathematical Modelling and Scientific Computation	Mathematical, Physical and Life Sciences	30
Mathematics and Foundations of Computer Science	Mathematical, Physical and Life Sciences	
Medical Anthropology	Social Sciences	
Migration Studies	Social Sciences	
Modern Japanese Studies	Social Sciences	35
Musculoskeletal Sciences	Medical Sciences	
Nature, Society, and Environmental Governance	Social Sciences	
Neuroscience	Medical Sciences	
Paediatric Infectious Diseases	Medical Sciences/Continuing Education	40
Pharmacology	Medical Sciences	
Political Theory Research	Social Sciences	
Politics Research	Social Sciences	
Psychological Research	Medical Sciences	45
Radiation Biology	Medical Sciences	
Refugee and Forced Migration Studies	Social Sciences	
Russian and East European Studies	Social Sciences	
Social Anthropology	Social Sciences	
Social Science of the Internet	Social Sciences	50
Sociology	Social Sciences	
Software and Systems Security	Mathematical, Physical and Life Sciences	

Software Engineering	Mathematical, Physical and Life Sciences
Software Engineering Programme	Mathematical, Physical and Life Sciences
Surgical Science and Practice	Medical Sciences/Continuing Education
Sustainable Urban Development	Continuing Education
Teacher Education (part time)	Social Sciences
Teaching English Language in University Settings	Social Sciences
Theoretical and Computational Chemistry	Mathematical, Physical and Life Sciences
Visual, Material and Museum Anthropology	Social Sciences
Water Science Policy and Management	Social Sciences

2. No candidate shall be permitted to take an examination under the preceding clause unless he or she has been admitted as a candidate for the examination in question by the body responsible for the course and has satisfied any other conditions prescribed in the regulations for that course.

3. Final examination marks shall be released to candidates at the conclusion of the examination. Exceptions to this may be made where assessment takes place throughout the course. In such cases, examination boards must meet formally, with all members present, at interim points in the year in order to agree final marks for specified assessment components. Marks released as final marks may not subsequently be amended without permission of the Proctors.

4. A candidate who has failed to satisfy the examiners in the examination may enter again for the examination on one, but not more than one, subsequent occasion.

5. The examiners may award a distinction for excellence in the whole examination. Candidates who have initially failed any element of assessment shall not normally be eligible for the award of distinction.

Master of Science by Coursework in African Studies

1. Each candidate will be required to follow a course of instruction in African Studies for three terms, and will, when they enter their names for the examination, be required to produce a certificate from their supervisors to this effect.

2. Candidates will be required to present themselves for examination in the compulsory paper in Themes in African History and the Social Sciences, and in one optional paper at the end of Trinity Term in the year of registration. In addition, each candidate will be required to submit the following written work:

   (i) One 4,500 word essay for the compulsory core course in Methodology, Ethics and Research Strategies selected from a list of questions approved by the African Studies Teaching Committee and made available to candidates by the last Friday of Michaelmas Term. The essay must be submitted not later than 12 noon on the first Monday of Hilary Term in the year in which the examination is taken.

   (ii) One 15,000 word dissertation, which must include discussion of the comparative reading, historiography, or theory relevant to the dissertation. The title of the dissertation must be approved by the African Studies Teaching Committee not later than 12 noon on the last day of eighth week of Michaelmas Full Term in the year in which the examination is taken. The dissertation must be submitted not later than 12 noon on Friday of sixth week of Trinity Full Term in the year in which the examination is taken.

Two typewritten or word processed copies of the written work detailed above must be delivered to the Examination Schools, addressed to the Chair of Examiners for the M.Sc. in African Studies, c/o Examination Schools, High Street, Oxford at the times and days specified.

3. A candidate must pass all components of the examination in order to pass the degree. A candidate who fails any element of the examination will be permitted to retake or resubmit it on one further occasion within six terms of his or her initial registration. A candidate who fails one or more of the compulsory or optional papers will be required to resit both papers. In the case of a failed essay or dissertation, the resubmitted dissertation can be on the same topic and include previously submitted work.

4. Candidates may be required to attend an oral examination on any part of the examination.

5. The examiners may award a distinction for excellence in the whole examination.

Schedule

The structure of the course is as follows:

(*a*) *Compulsory core course in Methodology, Ethics and Research Strategies*: ethics, politics; disciplinary approaches including history, politics, anthropology; conducting interviews: oral traditions, questionnaires, archives on and in Africa; visual materials, photographs and films; practical aspects of research.

(*b*) *Compulsory core course in Themes in African History and the Social Sciences*: key features of African states; social and economic change and the dilemmas of development; globalisation and conflict in the post-colonial era; environmental history and politics.

(*c*) *Optional paper*: Candidates must choose one optional paper from a list published annually and distributed to students by the last day of eighth week of Michaelmas Full Term.

Oxford 1+1 MBA programme

Candidates registered on the Oxford 1+1 MBA programme will follow an additional two or three month bridging programme at the end of their third term of the combined programme.

Each candidate will be appointed an academic advisor from the Saïd Business School to plan an individual course of study which will include as a minimum, the following three compulsory elements:

(i) Attendance of one of the summer elective programmes offered for the Master of Business Administration to be published by the MBA Director before the first Monday of the preceding term. Candidates would be required to undertake all assessments and receive feedback, but would not obtain credit towards the MBA. Candidates are not permitted to subsequently undertake the same elective as part of the MBA programme the following year.

(ii) A formatively assessed assignment of no more than 5,000 words (including all prefatory matter and appendices) supervised by the Saïd Business School academic advisor, which will relate the Master's degree learning to an appropriate area of the MBA programme. Candidates would also be required to present a work plan related to this assignment to the 1+1 programme class.

(iii) Attendance of the MBA pre-course as described in the joining instructions for the MBA class, unless granted exemption by the MBA Committee on the grounds of prior formal study or work experience.

Master of Science by Coursework in Applied Landscape Archaeology

1. Every candidate must follow for at least six terms a part-time course of instruction in Applied Landscape Archaeology and must upon entering for examination produce from his or her society a certificate to that effect.

2. The examination will consist of the following parts:

A Core Topics

Every candidate must submit two written assignments of no more than 2,500 words in length for each of the two core topic courses on:

   (1) Method and Theory in Landscape Archaeology;

   (2) Managing Twenty-first Century Landscapes.

One core topic will be taken in each year of the course.

B Advanced Papers

Every candidate must follow four of the six Advanced Paper courses listed in the Schedule below, and submit one written assignment of no more than 5,000 words in length for each paper. Candidates will take two Advanced Papers per year of the M.Sc.

C Dissertation

A dissertation of not more than 15,000 words, including appendices but excluding bibliography, on a topic approved by the candidate's supervisor. The dissertation must be delivered not later than noon on the last Monday in September of the second year of the course to the Chair of Examiners for the Degree of M.Sc. in Applied Landscape Archaeology, c/o Examination Schools, High Street, Oxford.

3. Candidates must attend one compulsory field training week (or in exceptional circumstances equivalent day or weekend schools) during their registration on the course.

4. Each candidate must attend a viva voce examination when required to do so by the examiners.

5. The examiners may award a distinction for excellence in the whole examination.

6. A candidate who fails a core topic or advanced paper, or whose dissertation fails to satisfy the examiners, may be permitted to retake the paper, or resubmit the dissertation, on one further occasion only, not later than one year after the initial attempt.

Schedule

Advanced Papers are available in the following areas:

   1. Archaeological prospection

   2. Reading the historic landscape

   3. Artefacts and Ecofacts in the landscape

   4. Digital landscapes

   5. Placement work

   6. Geoarchaeology

Not all advanced papers will be available in any one year and the definitive list of advanced papers available in any one year will be circulated to candidates and their supervisors during the second week of Michaelmas Term.

Master of Science by Coursework in Applied Linguistics and Second Language Acquisition

1. Candidates may normally only be admitted to the course if they have success-fully obtained an honours degree which contained a substantial element of second language learning and/or linguistics.

2. The course shall consist of eight taught modules (constituting Part 1 of the examination) and a dissertation (constituting Part 2 of the examination). Candidates shall be deemed to have passed the examination if they have satisfied the examiners in both Part 1 and Part 2.

3. Every candidate who is required to complete Part 1 will be required to complete all eight Modules of the course unless they can make a case for prior accreditation (by virtue of having successfully completed the Diploma in Education, Modern Foreign Languages), in which case they will be required to complete six Modules, and this will constitute Part 1 of the examination for these candidates. Candidates must pass Part 1 by examination or by prior accreditation before submitting a dissertation for Part 2. Interim marks for the first four Modules of Part 1 will be released to candidates following the first meeting of the Examination Board. At the close of the examination in Part 1, a list of candidates shall be published who have satisfied the examiners in that part of the examination.

4. Every candidate will be required to satisfy the examiners in the following:

    (i) Satisfactory attendance at the appropriate classroom-based courses;

    (ii) Satisfactory performance in both Part 1 and Part 2.

5. An electronic copy of each of the four Michaelmas Term assignments must be uploaded to the Assignments section of the Higher Degrees Weblearn no later than noon on the Friday of Week 0 Hilary Term, and an electronic copy of each of the four Hilary Term assignments must be uploaded to the Assignments section of the Higher Degrees Weblearn no later than Friday of Week 0 of Trinity Term. Part-time students must submit assignments for two modules on each of these occasions over a period of two years.

6. Candidates will be required to submit a dissertation of between 15,000 and 20,000 words (including footnotes/endnotes but excluding appendices and references or bibliography) on a subject selected by the candidate in consultation with the supervisor, which must be closely related to one or more of the themes of the course. The subject and title selected by the candidate must be approved by Departmental Board not later than the first day of the fifth week of Hilary Term of the course (for full-time candidates) and of the second year of the course (for part-time candidates).

7. Three word processed or printed copies of the dissertation must be delivered to the Chair of the Examiners, M.Sc. in Applied Linguistics and Second Language Acquisition, c/o Examination Schools, High Street, Oxford, OX2 6PY not later than noon on the last Friday of August of the year in which the final Module examination has been taken. One copy should be hard bound and two soft bound, the latter of which should be anonymous except for the candidate number. The hard bound copy of the dissertation of each candidate who passes the examination shall be retained by the department for deposit in the departmental library. The dissertation must be accompanied by a declaration indicating that it is the candidate's own work. Candidates will also be required to submit an electronic copy of the dissertation to Weblearn by noon on the same day. If Part 1 is failed, the candidate may retake the whole examination of Part 1 one further time on the next occasion when this is examined. If Part 2 is failed the candidate may resubmit the dissertation one further time on the next occasion when it is examined.

8. The candidate may also be examined orally. The oral examination may only be on the candidate's dissertation.

9. The examiners may award a distinction for excellence in the whole examination.

Schedule

Module A First Language Acquisition and Bilingualism   5
Module B Theories, Progression, and Methods
Module C Individual and Group Differences
Module D Input and Interaction
Module E Accessing Meaning
Module F Producing and Communicating Meaning   10
Module G Vocabulary Acquisition
Module H Error, Analysis, Interlanguage, and Testing
Optional Double Module: Teaching English as a Foreign Language Certificate.

Master of Science by Coursework in Applied Statistics

1. The Divisional Board of Mathematical, Physical and Life Sciences shall elect for   15
the supervision of the course a Standing Committee which shall have power to arrange lectures and other instruction.

2. Candidates shall follow for at least three terms a course of instruction in Statistics.

3. The examination will consist of: 20
    (i) a written examination consisting of two papers on the syllabus described in the schedule;
    (ii) a dissertation on a subject selected in consultation with the supervisor and approved by the chair of the committee.

4. Two typewritten or printed copies of the dissertation must be sent not later than   25
noon on the second Monday in September in the year in which the written examination is taken, to the M.Sc. examiners (Applied Statistics), c/o Examination Schools, High Street, Oxford. When submitting their M.Sc. dissertation, candidates must submit both paper and electronic versions which must be identical. The latter may be used by the examiners to check for plagiarism. See the Course Handbook for   30
further details. The examiners may retain one copy of the dissertation of each candidate who passes the examination for deposit in an appropriate departmental library.

5. Each candidate will be expected to have displayed evidence of the ability to apply statistical methods to real data.   35

The examiners will take into account the results of an assessment of ability to apply statistical methods to real data organised by the supervisory committee. The supervisory committee will be responsible for notifying the candidates of the arrangements for the assessment, and for forwarding the assessed material to the chair of the examiners before the end of the Trinity Term in the year in which the assessment is   40
made. The supervisory committee may specify that one of the practical assessments will be carried out as group projects, the details of which will be given in the Course Handbook.

6. In the written examination the examiners will permit the use of any hand-held pocket calculators subject to the conditions set out in Part 10 of the *Regulations for the*   45
conduct of Examinations.

7. In the written examination the examiners will permit the use of bilingual dictionaries.

8. The examiners may also examine any candidate viva voce.

9. The examiners may award a distinction for excellence in the whole examination.

10. If it is the opinion of the examiners that the work done by the candidate is not of sufficient merit to qualify for the Degree of M.Sc., but is nevertheless of sufficient merit to qualify for the Diploma in Applied Statistics, the candidate shall be given the option of retaking the M.Sc. examination on one further occasion, not later than one year after   5
the initial attempt, or of being issued with a diploma. In the event of a candidate's work not being of sufficient merit to qualify for the award of the M.Sc., the examiners will specify which of the components of the course may or must be redone.

Schedule

Paper 1: Principles of statistical analysis   10
Statistical distribution theory; statistical inference; statistical methods.
Paper 2: Further statistical methodology
Topics in statistical methodology chosen from a list approved by the Standing Committee and published in the Course Handbook by the beginning of Michaelmas Term of the academic year in which the written examination is to be taken.   15

Master of Science by Coursework in Archaeological Science

1. Within the Division of Social Sciences, the course shall be administered by the Committee for the School of Archaeology. The regulations made are as follows:

2. Candidates for admission must apply to the Committee for the School of Archaeology.   20

3. Candidates must follow a course of instruction in Archaeological Science for at least three terms and for a substantial part of the three subsequent vacations, as determined by the course timetable.

4. The written examination shall consist of:

   (*a*) three papers on the syllabus described in the Schedule, to be taken in the   25
   second week of Trinity Term, *and*

   (*b*) *either* one pre-set essay of approximately 10,000 words, *or* two pre-set essays of approximately 5,000 words each. The subject and length of each essay must be approved by the examiners before the end of Michaelmas Full Term. Two copies of each essay must be delivered to the Examination   30
   Schools by noon on the Friday of first week of Trinity Term. Essays must be typed or printed, must bear the candidate's examination number but not his or her name, and must include a statement of the number of words. Any illustrations must be included in both copies.

   (*c*) in lieu of one of the three papers described in the Schedule, and the extended   35
   essay(s), candidates may, with the permission of the School of Archaeology Committee for Graduate Studies, take one of the options from the M.St in Archaeology or M.St in Classical Archaeology (Schedule B only). Candidates taking such an option would only be examined on one pre-set essay of approximately 5,000 words on Archaeological Science in lieu of the   40
   requirements laid on in b) above.

5. Each candidate will be required to submit a dissertation of approximately 15,000 to 20,000 words, on a research area selected in consultation with the supervisor and approved by a person designated for this purpose by the Committee for the School of Archaeology.   45

6. Three typewritten copies of the dissertation must be sent, not later than noon on the Friday four weeks and two days before the start of the following Michaelmas Term, to the M.Sc. Examiners (Archaeological Science), c/o Examination Schools, High Street, Oxford. The examiners will retain one copy of the dissertation of each candidate for the departmental library.   50

7. The examiners may require to see the records of practical work carried out during the course.

8. Candidates must present themselves for an oral examination as required by the examiners. This may be on the candidate's written paper, or dissertation, or both.

9. The examiners may award a distinction for excellence in the whole examination.   5

10. In the case of failure in just one part of the examination (written papers, extended essay(s), dissertation), the candidate will be permitted to retake that part of the examination on one further occasion, not later than one year after the initial attempt. Written papers would be retaken the following year. Pass or failure in the written papers will be taken as an average of all written papers and in the case of   10 failure all written papers must be retaken. If the candidate passes all parts of the examination except the dissertation, the dissertation may be considered as a practical report as defined in the schedule for the M.St and, if of a sufficiently high standard, the candidate may be granted permission to supplicate for the degree of M.St.

Schedule   15

(i) *Principles and practice of scientific dating*

The principles of scientific dating methods including radiocarbon, luminescence, uranium series and dendro-chronology. The practical aspects of these methods and the problems encountered in their application. The statistical analysis of chronological information in the study of archaeological sites and cultures.   20

(ii) *Bio-archaeology*

Scientific methods for the study of biological remains from archaeological sites; introduction to the analysis of plant and faunal remains including indicators of disease and artefactual analysis; theoretical and practical aspects of quantitative methods for diet reconstruction by isotopic analysis; introduction to ancient DNA studies; residue analysis.   25

(iii) *Materials analysis and the study of technological change*

Introduction to the history of technology; theoretical and practical aspects of materials analysis methods—SEM, microprobe, TIMS, ICP, ICP-MS, XRF, XRD, PIXE, FTIR, and NAA; application of analysis to different material types—stone, ceramics, vitreous materials and metals; provenance of raw materials; case studies of   30 application to archaeological problems.

Master of Science by Coursework in Biodiversity, Conservation, and Management

1. The Social Sciences Divisional Board shall elect for the supervision of the course a Standing Committee.   35

2. Candidates must follow a course of instruction in Biodiversity, Conservation, and Management for at least three terms.

3. The examination will consist of:

(i) a written examination of three three-hour papers based on core courses as described in the schedule;   40

(ii) two assessed essays based on elective courses;

(iii) a dissertation on a subject selected in consultation with the supervisor and Course Director and approved by the Course and Academic Directors.

4. Candidates must submit to the Course Director by the end of Hilary Term in the year in which they enter the examination, the title and a brief statement of the form   45 and scope of their dissertation, together with the name of a person who has agreed to act as their supervisor during preparation of the dissertation.

5. The dissertation shall be of a maximum length of 15,000 words and accompanied by an abstract not exceeding 150 words. The maximum word count shall include footnotes, but exclude appendices, references and the abstract. The detailed format and specification of the dissertation shall be approved by the Standing Committee, and published in the course handbook.

6. The deadline for submission is noon on the first weekday of September in the year in which the written examination is taken. Two copies of the dissertation must be submitted, to the M.Sc examiners (Biodiversity, Conservation, and Management), c/o Examination Schools, High Street, Oxford OX1 4BG. The examiners may retain one copy of the dissertation of each candidate who passes the examination for deposit in an appropriate library. Both copies must bear the candidate's examination number but not his/her name.

7. All submitted work shall be accompanied by a separate statement certifying that the submitted work is the candidate's own work except where otherwise indicated.

8. In the written examination, the examiners will permit the use of hand-held pocket calculators subject to the conditions set out under the heading 'Use of calculators in examinations' in the *Regulations for the Conduct of University Examinations*.

9. The examiners may also examine any candidate viva voce on the candidate's written papers, dissertation, or both.

10. Arrangements for reassessment shall be specified by the Standing Committee and published in the course handbook.

11. The examiners may award a distinction for excellence in the whole examination.

Schedule

(*a*) *Core courses.*

Three core courses will be examined under the following heads:

(i) *Biodiversity science.*

Candidates will be expected to have knowledge of and a critical understanding of the major contemporary themes in biodiversity science and conservation including an appreciation of the various research methods used to collect scientific data.

(ii) *Conservation ethics and values.*

Candidates will be expected to have knowledge of the various ethical frameworks and value systems adopted by conservationists and how differing value systems can influence the development of effective conservation practice and policy.

(iii) *Biodiversity policy and management.*

Candidates will be expected to have knowledge of the techniques and conceptual basis of contemporary conservation planning and the international and national legal frameworks for implementing conservation policy.

(*b*) *Elective courses*

Candidates will be expected to show advanced knowledge of two of the option elective courses on offer in any one year.

Master of Science by Coursework in Clinical Embryology

1. The Divisional Board of Medical Sciences shall appoint for the supervision of the course an Organising Committee, which shall have the power to arrange lectures and other instruction.

2. The Organising Committee shall appoint for each candidate an academic adviser.

3. Each candidate shall follow a course of study in Clinical Embryology for at least three terms and for a substantial part of the three subsequent vacations, as determined

by the course timetable, and will, when entering for the examination, be required to produce a certificate from their academic adviser to this effect.

4. Candidates shall be examined in all of the following ways:

(i) Each candidate must submit to the Course Director by Monday of Week 8 of Michaelmas Term a skills checklist, initialled by the practical skills tutor, to verify that they have acquired the practical skills associated with the course. This checklist will be made available to the examiners. A candidate who submits an incomplete checklist will be required to undertake remedial training, and to resubmit the checklist by a specified date.

(ii) Each candidate must pass a qualifying examination at the end of Michaelmas Term. The examination shall normally consist of a two-hour computer-based assessment on the topics covered in modules I–V, as set out in the Schedule. Candidates who fail the qualifying examination shall be permitted to take it on one further occasion in Week 0 of Hilary Term. The Organising Committee shall submit to the examiners a list of candidates who have satisfactorily completed the qualifying examination not later than the end of the Hilary Term preceding the examination.

(iii) Each candidate must submit a typewritten or printed essay of between 3,000 and 4,000 words on a topic approved by the Organising Committee. The arrangements for approval will be notified to candidates not later than the start of Michaelmas Term of the academic year in which the examination is taken. The essay must be submitted by noon, Thursday of Week 9 of Hilary Term. In the event that they are deemed not to have achieved the required standard in this element of the examination, candidates will have the opportunity to revise and resubmit their essay by noon, Friday of Week 3 of Trinity Term.

(iv) Each candidate must pass a written examination in Week 0 of Trinity Term. The examination shall consist of a three-hour written paper on the topics covered in modules VI-X, as set out in the Schedule. Candidates who fail the examination shall be permitted to take it on one further occasion, no sooner than three weeks after the first occasion. Candidates must pass this examination in order to proceed with their research project.

(v) Each candidate must submit a typewritten or printed dissertation of not more than 10,000 words (excluding bibliography and appendices) on the research project as set out in the Schedule below. The research project and the subject of the dissertation must have been approved by the Organising Committee. The arrangements for approval will be notified to candidates not later than the start of Michaelmas Term of the academic year in which the examination is taken.

Candidates shall be examined viva voce on their dissertation, or on any other element of the examination, and shall also give poster and oral presentations on their research project. The viva voce examination will normally be conducted in September of the year in which the candidate is examined on dates to be determined by the examiners.

5. Each written submission (consisting of three hard copies plus an electronic copy) must be sent to the Chair of Examiners, M.Sc. in Clinical Embryology, c/o Examination Schools, High Street, Oxford on the following dates:

(*a*) The dissertation on the research project must be submitted by dates to be specified by the Organising Committee and published in the *University Gazette* not later than the start of Michaelmas Term of the academic year in which the examination is taken.

(*b*) The essay must be submitted by noon on Thursday of Week 9 of Hilary Term.

Each written submission must be accompanied (in a separate sealed envelope addressed to the Chair of Examiners) by a certificate indicating that it is the candidate's own work and a CD containing an electronic copy of each written submission.

6. The examiners may award a distinction for excellence in the whole examination.

7. The examiners shall retain one copy of each dissertation of each successful candidate for deposit in the Radcliffe Science library.

Schedule

(A) *Modules*

     I Essential Cellular and Molecular Biology

     II Laboratory Methods and Practical Skills

     III The Mammalian Reproductive System

     IV Fertilisation and Early Embryogenesis

     V Embryonic Development and Pregnancy

     VI Infertility

     VII Assisted Reproductive Technology (ART)

     VIII Assisted Conception: Skills and Techniques

     IX Micromanipulation in ART

     X Infertility and ART: Developments and Current Issues

(B) *Research project*

A research project under the supervision of a research supervisor. Students will undertake reading and research in relation to their research project during Trinity Term and the Long Vacation. The subject of each student's dissertation and the supervision arrangements for each student must be approved by the Organising Committee.

Master of Science by Coursework in Cognitive and Evolutionary Anthropology

1. Candidates must follow a course of instruction in Cognitive and Evolutionary Anthropology, including training in research, for at least three terms, and will, when entering for the examination, be required to produce a certificate from their supervisor to this effect.

2. Candidates will be required to present themselves for written and (if requested by the examiners) oral examinations and to submit three copies of a dissertation in a prescribed form on an approved topic as defined in (6) and (7) below.

3. The written examination will consist of four papers, one in each of the subjects listed in the Schedule.

4. For Paper 1, candidates will be required to submit three assignments (chosen from a list provided by the course convener not later than the Friday of eighth week of Hilary Term). The assignments must be submitted by the Friday before the start of Trinity Term to the Chair of Examiners, M.Sc. in Cognitive and Evolutionary Anthropology, c/o Examination Schools, High Street, Oxford.

5. For each of Papers 2, 3 and 4, candidates will be required to sit an examination.

6. Candidates will be required to submit a dissertation of no more than 15,000 words in length, on a topic agreed with their supervisors. The proposed title of the dissertation, together with a paragraph describing its scope and the supervisor's written endorsement, must be submitted to the Chair of Examiners by Tuesday of the second week of Trinity Term. Three typewritten copies of the dissertation must be

delivered not later than noon on the last Wednesday in August in the year in which the examination is taken, to the Chair of Examiners, M.Sc. in Cognitive and Evolutionary Anthropology, c/o Examination Schools, High Street, Oxford. The dissertation shall be provided with an abstract of up to 250 words, to be placed immediately after the title page. The word count shall be stated on the outside front cover of the thesis. 5

7. The four papers will be taken to constitute Part I of the degree and the dissertation to constitute Part II. At the close of the written examinations, the examiners will issue a list of those who have satisfied them in Part I.

8. The oral examination, if held, may be on any or all of the candidate's assessed essays, and/or the dissertation. 10

9. The examiners may award a distinction for excellence in the whole examination.

10. In order to pass the degree, a student must pass all its assessed components. Where one or more components are failed, the student will be given the opportunity to re-sit or re-submit them once, as the case may be. Any subsequent award of the degree on successful completion of all the assessed components may be delayed by up to three 15 terms, i.e. until the Examination Board next meets.

Schedule

Paper 1. *Quantitative Methods in the Human Sciences*
    (*a*) Hypothesis testing
    (*b*) Statistical analysis 20
    (*c*) Research design

Paper 2. *Principles of Evolution and Behaviour*
    (*a*) Primate and hominin phylogeny and evolution
    (*b*) Primate and hominin physiology
    (*c*) Primate and human diet and substance 25
    (*d*) Reconstructing past behaviour from primatology and archaeology

Paper 3. *Evolution and Human Behaviour*
    (*a*) Hominid evolutionary history
    (*b*) Human evolutionary psychology
    (*c*) Kinship and inheritance 30
    (*d*) Cultural evolutionary processes

Paper 4. *Mind and Culture*
    (*a*) Cognitive and evolutionary explanations in anthropology
    (*b*) Pan-human cognition: developmental and evolutionary perspectives
    (*c*) Cognitive origins of culture 35
    (*d*) Communication and transmission of culture.

Master of Science by Coursework in Cognitive Behavioural Therapy

1. Candidates will be expected to have satisfactorily completed either the Postgraduate Diploma in Cognitive Behavioural Therapy or the Postgraduate 40 Diploma in Advanced Cognitive Therapy Studies.

2. The course will consist of research seminars and supervision. The course will be taken on a part-time basis over a period of three terms.

3. Candidates may be permitted in certain circumstances to suspend status for a maximum of six terms. Any such period shall not count towards the maximum or minimum period of registration and no fee liability will be incurred against such periods.

4. Every candidate will be required to satisfy the examiners in the following:

(*a*) attendance at appropriate classroom-based courses including small group meetings.   5

(*b*) a research project of no more than 15,000 words on a topic approved by the Course Committee

The research project shall be submitted to The Registry, Department for Continuing Education, 1 Wellington Square, Oxford, OX1 2JD by such dates as the examiners shall determine. Research projects will be forwarded to the examiners for consideration.   10 Students are required to submit both a hard copy and an electronic copy.

5. Candidates may be expected to attend a viva voce examination at the end of the course of studies at the discretion of the examiners.

6. The examiners may award a distinction to candidates for the M.Sc.

7. A candidate whose research project fails to satisfy the examiners may be per-   15 mitted to resubmit on one further occasion only not later than one year after the initial failure.

8. If any candidate who is successful in the examination for the Degree of Master of Science in Cognitive Behavioural Therapy has previously successfully completed the Postgraduate Diploma in Cognitive Behavioural Therapy or the Postgraduate   20 Diploma in Advanced Cognitive Therapy studies, the Master of Science will subsume his or her diploma.

Master of Science by Coursework in Comparative Social Policy

Every candidate must follow, for at least three terms, a course of instruction in Comparative Social Policy.   25

The examination will be in four parts.

A. One compulsory papers in *Methods of Social Research*. As specified for the M.Phil. in Comparative Social Policy.

B. One compulsory paper in *Comparative Social Policy/Welfare States*. As specified for the M.Phil. in Comparative Social Policy.   30

C. One optional paper. This may be from the list of optional papers as specified for the M.Phil. in Comparative Social Policy. Teaching in some options may not be available every year. Candidates may, after special permission of the Social Policy and Intervention Graduate Studies Committee, offer subjects outside this list. This may include papers offered in other relevant master's degrees in the University,   35 subject to permission by the relevant Graduate Studies Committee as appropriate.

D. A thesis of not more than 10,000 words on a topic within the subject of the course, to be specified jointly by supervisor and student. The thesis should employ comparative method in the study of a social policy topic. Two typewritten copies of the thesis must be delivered to the Examination Schools, High Street, Oxford, by   40 noon of the weekday on or nearest to 15 August of the year in which the examination is to be taken. This word count applies to the text, but does not include graphs, tables and charts in the main text, or bibliography. An additional word limit of 2,000 words in total applies to the abstract, footnotes, endnotes and technical appendices (including graphs, tables and charts). Successful candidates may be   45 required to deposit a copy of their thesis in the Social Science Library.

The examiners may examine any candidate viva voce.

The examiners may award a Distinction for excellence in the whole examination on the basis of the material submitted to them.

Master of Science by Coursework in Computer Science

1. The Divisional Board of Mathematical, Physical and Life Sciences, in consultation with the Faculty of Computer Science, shall elect for the supervision of the course an Organising Committee which shall have power to arrange lectures and other instruction.

The committee shall elect a chair from its own members; the chair shall have power to approve applications on behalf of the committee. The committee shall be responsible for appointment of a supervisor for each student.

2. Candidates must follow a course of instruction in Computer Science for at least three terms and a substantial part of the three subsequent vacations, as determined by the course timetable, and will be required to produce a certificate from their supervisors to that effect.

3. The examination shall be in three parts, as follows:

  (i) Candidates shall be assessed on at least twenty-eight and no more than thirty-four units of topics chosen from a list of topics approved by the Organising Committee and published in the *University Gazette* by the beginning of Michaelmas Full Term in the academic year of the examination. The mode of assessment shall be either written assignment or written examination, as detailed in the Course Handbook and on the website www.cs.ox.ac.uk/teaching/MSCinCS/. The list of courses shall be divided into three sections: Schedule A, Schedule B and Schedule C, as detailed on the website www.cs.ox.ac.uk/teaching/MSCinCS/.

  (ii) Candidates shall submit a dissertation of not more than 30,000 words, plus not more than 30 pages of diagrams, tables, listing etc., on a subject selected by the candidate in consultation with the supervisor and approved by the director of the course.

  (iii) There shall be an examination viva voce, unless the candidate shall have been individually dispensed by the examiners, on the dissertation and on any of the topics for which he or she submitted a written assignment or written examination, to take place on the Thursday of week minus 1 of Michaelmas Term of the following academic year.

4. Every candidate must submit to the director of the course no later than the first Monday in Trinity Full Term in the year of the examination the title and a brief statement of the form and scope of his or her dissertation, together with an essay of not more than 3,000 words, describing the background of the project, its objectives and its plan of work. The submission must be approved by the person who has agreed to act as supervisor during the preparation of the dissertation.

Candidates will be expected to demonstrate in their dissertation an understanding of the topics studied in the course.

5. Two typewritten or printed copies of the dissertation must be delivered not later than noon of Monday of week minus 5 of Michaelmas Term of the following academic year to the M.Sc. Examiners (Computer Science), c/o Examinations Schools, High Street, Oxford.

One copy of the thesis of each successful candidate will normally be presented to the Department of Computer Science.

6. By a date in each term to be specified in the Course Handbook, each candidate in consultation with their supervisor must submit for approval by the director of the course a list of topics which will be taken in that term. At least twenty-eight units of topics must be selected with a maximum of 12 units to be taken from Schedule A; candidates shall be allowed to choose a maximum of thirty-four units of topics. The

choice must exclude any topics which substantially overlap the topics of the candidate's undergraduate degree or other recent academic study.

7. For each topic, the lecturer on the course of instruction shall prescribe a schedule of practical work, tutorial exercises and a written assignment or written examination, and shall make available to the Chair of Examiners evidence showing the extent to which each candidate has pursued an adequate course of practical and class work.

8. With the permission of the Organising Committee, a candidate may offer up to two alternative topics to replace any of the topics listed in Schedules B and C. An application for such replacement must be made to the director of the course by the end of the first week of the term in which the lecture course on the topic is given; it must be approved by the student's supervisor and by the lecturer on the course, who thereby undertakes to accept appointment as assessor for the topic.

9. Not later than noon on a date in each term to be determined by the examiners, who are responsible for making sure candidates are aware of that date and that the date is announced at the head of the assignment sheet, the completed assignment for each topic must be delivered to the M.Sc. Examiners (Computer Science), c/o Examination Schools, High Street, Oxford. Not later than noon on Monday of the fifth week of Trinity Term, practicals for all topics must be delivered to the M.Sc. Examiners (Computer Science), c/o the Post-Graduate Taught Course Administrator, Department of Computer Science, Oxford. Topics to be assessed by written examination will take place in Week 0 of the following term. No candidate shall attend classes or receive any form of individual tuition in the subject of an assignment between the time when the assignment is made available to the candidate and the time fixed for the delivery of the assignment to the examiners.

10. Any candidate who has not achieved an average of at least 50 in 24 units of topics by the beginning of Trinity Term shall be deemed to have failed the degree course and will not be permitted to submit a dissertation.

11. To satisfy the examiners for the degree of M.Sc. in Computer Science, a candidate must attain an average of at least 50 (pass) in the assignments or written examination in their best 28 units of topics, pass in the dissertation, pursue an adequate course of practical work and achieve an overall pass in practicals, and unless dispensed under cl.3 (iii) above satisfy the examiners in the viva voce examination.

12. The examiners may award a distinction for excellence in the whole examination.

13. A candidate who fails the examination will be permitted to retake it on one further occasion only, not later than one year after the initial attempt. Such a candidate whose dissertation has been of satisfactory standard may resubmit the same piece of work, while a candidate who has reached a satisfactory standard on the assignments or written examinations will not be required to retake that part of the examination.

Master of Science by Coursework in Contemporary Chinese Studies

1. Each candidate will be required to follow a course of instruction in Contemporary Chinese Studies for three terms.

2. Candidates will present themselves for examination in the core course Study of Contemporary China at the beginning of Hilary Term.

3. Candidates will choose two optional papers among the following:

Examination papers as part of option courses from the M.Sc. in Contemporary Chinese Studies or from another Master's (M.Phil., M.Sc., or M.St.) degree programme in the University. A list of papers approved for this purpose by the

Contemporary Chinese Studies Management Committee will be available from the Course Director and will be published at the beginning of each academic year. Students are free to elect any two of these papers in consultation with their supervisor, and must do so by filling out the examination entry form. Candidates may, after special permission of the Contemporary Chinese Studies Management Committee,   5
elect subjects outside this list. This may include papers offered in other relevant master's degrees in the University, subject to permission by the relevant Graduate Studies Committee as appropriate. The examiners may, at their discretion, either require candidates to sit the standard examination paper for this elective paper, or set a paper specifically for students on the M.Sc. in Contemporary Chinese Studies.   10

4. In addition, all candidates will be required to undertake the following assessment:

(i) Research Methods for Area Studies: a series of assignments and/or unseen written examinations as specified by the teaching committee for the M.Sc. in Contemporary Chinese Studies. The forms of assessment, and the dates and   15
times of submission, where applicable, will be notified to students by not later than Friday of noughth week of Michaelmas Full Term.

(ii) One 10,000 word dissertation: the title of the dissertation must be approved by the Director of Graduate Studies not later than 12 noon on Friday of the first week of Hilary Term in the academic year in which the examination is taken.   20
The dissertation must be submitted not later than 12 noon on Friday of sixth week of Trinity Term in the academic year in which the examination is taken. The dissertation must be accompanied by a statement that the dissertation is the candidate's own work except where otherwise indicated.

Two typewritten or word processed copies of each of the items of written work   25
detailed in 4 (i)–(ii) above must be delivered to the Examination School, addressed to the Chair of Examiners for the M.Sc. in Contemporary Chinese Studies, c/o the Examination Schools, High Street, Oxford at the times and days specified.

5. A candidate who fails the examination will be permitted to retake it on one further occasion within six terms of his or her initial registration. The candidate will be   30
permitted to resubmit the same item or items of written work that reached a satisfactory standard.

6. Candidates may be required to attend an oral examination on any part of the examination.

7. The examiners may award a distinction for excellence in the whole examination.   35

Schedule

The structure of the course is as follows:

(*a*) Compulsory Core course on The Study of Contemporary China

(*b*) Compulsory Core course in Research Methods for Area Studies

(*c*) Elective papers: Candidates must choose two optional papers from a list pub-   40
lished annually by the Contemporary Chinese Studies Management Committee. Candidates may, after special permission of the Contemporary Chinese Studies Management Committee, elect subjects outside this list. This may include papers offered in other relevant master's degrees in the University, subject to permission by the relevant Graduate Studies Committee as appropriate.   45

Oxford 1+1 MBA programme

Candidates registered on the Oxford 1+1 MBA programme will follow an additional two or three month bridging programme at the end of their third term of the combined programme.

Each candidate will be appointed an academic advisor from the Saïd Business School to plan an individual course of study which will include as a minimum, the following three compulsory elements:

(i) Attendance of one of the summer elective programmes offered for the Master of Business Administration to be published by the MBA Director before the first Monday of the preceding term. Candidates would be required to undertake all assessments and receive feedback, but would not obtain credit towards the MBA. Candidates are not permitted to subsequently undertake the same elective as part of the MBA programme the following year.

(ii) A formatively assessed assignment of no more than 5,000 words (including all prefatory matter and appendices) supervised by the Saïd Business School academic advisor, which will relate the Master's degree learning to an appropriate area of the MBA programme. Candidates would also be required to present a work plan related to this assignment to the 1+1 programme class.

(iii) Attendance of the MBA pre-course as described in the joining instructions for the MBA class, unless granted exemption by the MBA Committee on the grounds of prior formal study or work experience.

Master of Science by Coursework in Contemporary India

1. Each candidate will be required to follow a course of instruction in Contemporary India for three terms. Candidates must attend and satisfactorily complete the Induction Programme and the designated coursework for each compulsory module, specifically the 2,500 word essay per module. Candidates must also attend the course of lectures and classes for the Research Methods course.

2. Candidates will be required to present themselves for examination in two compulsory papers in Themes in Contemporary India at the end of Trinity Term of the year of registration.

3. In addition, all candidates will be required to undertake the following assessment:

(i) Research Methods: a series of assignments and/or unseen written examinations as specified by the teaching committee for the M.Sc. in Contemporary India. The forms of assessment, and the dates and times of submission, where applicable, will be notified to students by not later than Friday of noughth week of Michaelmas Full Term.

(ii) Critical theory of India essay: one 5,000 word essay on a topic in comparative theory, epistemology or historiography to be submitted no later than 12 noon on the Monday of the third week of Trinity Term in the year in which the examination is taken.

(iii) One 10,000 word dissertation: the title of the dissertation must be approved by the Director of Graduate Studies not later than 12 noon on Friday of fifth week of Hilary Full Term. The dissertation must be submitted not later than 12 noon on Monday of seventh week of Trinity Full Term in the year in which the examination is taken.

Two typewritten or word processed copies of each of the items of written work detailed in 3 (i)–(iii) above must be accompanied by a statement that the submission is the candidate's own work except where otherwise indicated, and be delivered to the Examinations Schools, addressed to the Chair of Examiners for the M.Sc. in Contemporary India, c/o the Examination Schools, High Street, Oxford at the times and days specified.

An identical electronic copy in word format of all submissions must be submitted to the Programme Administrator on or before the deadline.

4. A candidate who fails the examination will be permitted to retake it on one further occasion within six terms of his or her initial registration. The candidate will be permitted to resubmit the same item or items of written work that did not reach a satisfactory standard.

5. The examiners may award a distinction for excellence in the whole examination.

Schedule

The structure of the course is as follows:

(*a*) *Core course in Themes in Contemporary India*

i. Politics, International Relations and Political Economy

ii. Culture and Society, Human Development and Environment

(*b*) *Core course in Research Methods*

Oxford 1+1 MBA programme

Candidates registered on the Oxford 1+1 MBA programme will follow an additional two or three month bridging programme at the end of their third term of the combined programme.

Each candidate will be appointed an academic advisor from the Saïd Business School to plan an individual course of study which will include as a minimum, the following three compulsory elements:

(i) Attendance of one of the summer elective programmes offered for the Master of Business Administration to be published by the MBA Director before the first Monday of the preceding term. Candidates would be required to undertake all assessments and receive feedback, but would not obtain credit towards the MBA. Candidates are not permitted to subsequently undertake the same elective as part of the MBA programme the following year.

(ii) A formatively assessed assignment of no more than 5,000 words (including all prefatory matter and appendices) supervised by the Saïd Business School academic advisor, which will relate the Master's degree learning to an appropriate area of the MBA programme. Candidates would also be required to present a work plan related to this assignment to the 1+1 programme class.

(iii) Attendance of the MBA pre-course as described in the joining instructions for the MBA class, unless granted exemption by the MBA Committee on the grounds of prior formal study or work experience.

Master of Science by Coursework in Criminology and Criminal Justice

1. Every candidate must follow, for at least three terms, a course of instruction in Criminology and Criminal Justice.

2. There shall be a Board of Studies for the course, to be chaired by the Director of Graduate Studies for Criminology and also comprising all the members of the Board of Examiners for the Master of Science in Criminology and Criminal Justice for the current year, the Director or Assistant Director of the Centre for Criminology and a student representative (the latter for open business only).

3. The course will consist of four elements: core course in Explanation and Understanding in Criminology (Michaelmas Term) and Understanding Criminal Justice (Hilary Term); the course Research Design and Data Collection (Michaelmas Term); options; and dissertation. The core course will run for eight weeks throughout the first two terms (Michaelmas and Hilary). The Research Design and Data Collection course runs for eight weeks in the first term

(Michaelmas). Options will run for eight weeks in both Michaelmas and Hilary terms. Candidates will be required to choose two options in Michaelmas Term and three in Hilary Term. In Trinity Term students submit a dissertation 12,000–15,000 words long on a topic to be agreed by the Board of Studies. The required format for this dissertation is the common format prescribed for all law theses, which is printed in the   5
Faculty of Law's Graduate Students' Handbook.

4. The options are listed in the Schedule below.

5. Not all options will necessarily be taught or examined in any one year. Details of those which are available will be published in the Graduate Student Handbook produced by the Centre for Criminology for the year of the examination, subject to   10
any amendment posted on the designated notice board in the Centre for Criminology by Monday of Week Minus One of the Michaelmas Term before the examination is held.

6. In addition to the options set out in the Schedule, candidates may offer any other option that may be approved from time to time by regulation published in the *Gazette*   15
by the end of Monday of Week Minus One of the Michaelmas Term before the examination is held.

7. The course shall be assessed as follows:

(i) *Core Course*: There shall be 2 two hour examinations for the core course, the first to be taken in Week Nought of Hilary Term, and the second to be taken   20
in Week Nought of Trinity Term.

(ii) *Options and Research Design and Data Collection*: Courses other than Research Design and Data Collection, Social Explanation and Data Analysis, Quantitative Analysis for Social Scientists, and Qualitative Methods shall be examined by means of an assessed essay of no less than   25
3,500 and no more than 4,500 words (inclusive of footnotes, but excluding bibliography and appendices), for which time will be set aside during Weeks 8, 9 and 10 of Michaelmas and Hilary terms. A selection of three titles (as determined by the Board of Examiners), shall be posted on the designated noticeboard at the Centre for Criminology by noon on Thursday of Week   30
Seven of the relevant term. Candidates shall be required to submit two typewritten copies of each essay to the Examination Schools, High Street, Oxford, not later than Wednesday of Week Ten, by noon.

Research Design and Data Collection, Social Explanation and Data Analysis, Quantitative Analysis for Social Scientists, and Qualitative Methods shall be examined   35
by an assessed essay of 2,500 to 3,000 words (inclusive of footnotes, but excluding bibliography and appendices), to be written between Thursday of Week Seven and Wednesday of Week Ten of the term in which the course runs. A choice from three titles (as determined by the Board of Examiners) will be posted on the designated noticeboard at the Centre for Criminology by noon on Thursday of Week Seven of the   40
relevant term. Candidates shall be required to submit two copies of the essay to the Examination Schools, High Street, Oxford, not later than of Week 10, by noon. In addition, candidates taking Social Explanation and Data Analysis and/or Quantitative Analysis for Social Scientists and/or Qualitative Methods shall be required to complete to the satisfaction of the Course Tutor for the option a form of   45
continuous assessment, which will be approved by the Board of Studies and the details of which will be published in the Graduate Student Handbook for the relevant year.

(iii) *Dissertation*: Two typewritten copies of the dissertation shall be submitted to the Examination Schools by noon on Wednesday of Week Ten of Trinity Term. One bound copy of the dissertation of each candidate who passes the   50
examination shall be deposited in the Social Science Library, Manor Road.

8. The degree of M.Sc. shall be awarded to any candidate who achieves a mark of at least 50 per cent for (*a*) the five options and the Research Design and Data Collection course, (*b*) the core course paper, and (*c*) the dissertation, as well as satisfactory completion of the continuous assessment element of the Social Explanation and Data Analysis, and/or Quantitative Analysis for Social Scientists and/or Qualitative Methods.

9. The examiners may award a distinction for excellence in the whole examination.

10. Arrangements for reassessment shall be as follows:

(i) *Core Course*: Candidates who fail, or withdraw from, either core course examination may resit the examination according to the standard timetable for examinations in the following academic year. Such candidates who have completed successfully either or both of (*a*) the options and Research Design and Data Collection (i.e. have obtained an aggregate mark of 50 per cent or more) and (*b*) the dissertation, may carry forward the marks gained for the successfully completed components. Candidates may also carry forward their certificate of satisfactory completion of the continuous assessment element of Research Design and Data Collection, and, where relevant, those of Social Explanation and Data Analysis, and/or Quantitative Analysis for Social Scientists and/or Qualitative Methods.

(ii) *Options and Research Design and Data Collection*: Candidates who have failed to obtain an aggregate mark of 50 per cent for assessment for the options or who have withdrawn from any assessment, may resubmit assessments for which they obtained a mark of 49 per cent or less. Candidates may resubmit assessed essays in which they have obtained a mark of 49 per cent or less to the Examination Schools, High Street, Oxford, according to the standard time-table for submitting essays in the following academic year. Such candidates who have completed successfully (*a*) the core course examination, (*b*) the dissertation, and (*c*) any assessment for which they have received a mark of 50 per cent or more, may carry forward the marks gained for the successfully completed components. Candidates may also carry forward their certificate of satisfactory completion of the continuous assessment element of where relevant, that of Social Explanation and Data Analysis, and/or Quantitative Analysis for Social Scientists and/or Qualitative Methods.

(iii) *Continuous assessment element of Research Design ans Data Collection, Social Explanation and Data Analysis, Quantitative Analysis for Social Scientists and Qualitative Methods:* Candidates who fail to complete an assignment which forms part of the continuous assessment element of Social Explanation and Data Analysis and/or Quantitative Analysis for Social Scientists and/or Qualitative Methods to the satisfaction of the respective Course Tutor may be required to resubmit that assignment once by noon on Thursday of Week Ten of the relevant term.

(iv) *Dissertation*: Candidates who fail, or withdraw from, the dissertation may resubmit the dissertation by the required date in Trinity Term of the following academic year. Such candidates who have completed successfully (*a*) the core course and/or (*b*) the options may carry forward the marks gained for the successfully completed components. Candidates may also carry forward their certificate of satisfactory completion of the continuous assessment element of Social Explanation and Data Analysis and/or Quantitative Analysis for Social Scientists and/or Qualitative Methods.

Schedule

Comparative and Transnational Criminal Justice
Comparative Criminal Justice, Security and Human Rights
Crime and the Family
Criminal Justice in Transitional Settings   5
Criminal Justice, Migration and Citizenship
Desistance from Crime: The Role of Criminal Justice Agencies
Law, Economics and Crime
Mafias
News Media, Crime and Policy   10
Policing Global Insecurities
Prisons
Public and Private Policing
Public Opinion, Crime and Criminal Justice
Qualitative Methods   15
Race and Gender
Research Design and Data Collection
Restorative Justice
Risk, Security and Criminal Justice
Sentencing   20
Social Explanation and Data Analysis
Sociology of Punishment
The Death Penalty
The Politics of Crime Control
Transitional Justice   25
Victims
Victims and Restorative Justice
Violence and Civilisation
Youth Justice

Oxford 1+1 MBA programme   30
Candidates registered on the Oxford 1+1 MBA programme will follow an additional two or three month bridging programme at the end of their third term of the combined programme.

Each candidate will be appointed an academic advisor from the Saïd Business School to plan an individual course of study which will include as a minimum, the   35
following three compulsory elements:

(i) Attendance of one of the summer elective programmes offered for the Master of Business Administration to be published by the MBA Director before the first Monday of the preceding term. Candidates would be required to undertake all assessments and receive feedback, but would not obtain credit towards the MBA.   40
Candidates are not permitted to subsequently undertake the same elective as part of the MBA programme the following year.

(ii) A formatively assessed assignment of no more than 5,000 words (including all prefatory matter and appendices) supervised by the Saïd Business School academic advisor, which will relate the Master's degree learning to an appropriate area of the   45
MBA programme. Candidates would also be required to present a work plan related to this assignment to the 1+1 programme class.

(iii) Attendance of the MBA pre-course as described in the joining instructions for the MBA class, unless granted exemption by the MBA Committee on the grounds of prior formal study or work experience.

Master of Science by Coursework in Economic and Social History

The regulations of the Board of the Faculty of History are as follows:

1. Every candidate must follow for at least three terms a course of instruction in Economic and Social History and must upon entering for the examination produce from his or her society a certificate to that effect.

2. The examination will consist of the following parts:

Qualifying test

Every candidate must pass a qualifying test. The test shall consist of two courses on

(1) Methodological introduction to research in the social sciences and history.

(2) *Either* Quantitative methods and computer applications for historians

or A paper from another established course within the University where this would provide a more appropriate training for the candidate's dissertation focus. Such a choice will need formal approval from both the Course Director and the Chair of the Graduate Studies Committee of the Board of the Faculty of History.

The methodological introduction course will be assessed by an end of course essay of up to 4,000 words. Two copies of the essay must be submitted by noon on Friday of Week 10 of Michaelmas Term of the candidate's first year to the Chair of Examiners for the M.Sc. in Economic and Social History, c/o Examination Schools, High Street, Oxford OX1 4BG. A quantitative methods course is assessed by an assignment to be completed over the Christmas Vacation; two typewritten copies of the completed assignment must be submitted by noon on Monday of second week of Hilary Term to the Chair of Examiners for the M.Sc. in Economic and Social History at the above address. In addition, convenors of qualifying courses will confirm in writing to the Chair of Examiners not later than Friday of eighth week of Hilary Term the candidates' satisfactory participation in their classes, including the completion of any assignments for the weekly sessions. Any approved alternative qualifying course will be assessed within the format and timetable of the paper's parent course. No candidate who has failed the qualifying test of two courses will be permitted to supplicate for the degree. Candidates who fail a qualifying course once will be permitted to take it again, not later than one year after the initial attempt.

Final examination

The examination shall consist of two papers and a dissertation.

Candidates must take at least one of their papers as a three-hour written examination. For the remaining paper candidates must choose to be assessed either by written examination or by two 5,000 word essays. Essays may be only submitted in lieu of written papers for subjects in Schedule I below ('Advanced Papers for M.Phil. and M.Sc. in Economic and Social History') or for other papers permitted in Schedule II below where similar provision exists in the regulations for those examinations. The essays must be the work of the candidates alone and they must not consult any other person including their supervisors in any way concerning the method of handling the themes chosen. The themes chosen by the candidate must be submitted for approval by the chair of examiners by the examination entry date. Candidates will be informed within two weeks, by means of a letter directed to their colleges, whether the topics they have submitted have been approved. The finished essays must be delivered by the candidate to the Examination Schools, High Street, Oxford, by noon on Monday of sixth week of Trinity Full Term. The essays must be presented in proper scholarly form, and two typed copies of each must be submitted.

    I. One advanced paper selected from Schedule I below.

    II. *Either* (i) one paper in a relevant discipline or skill or sources or methods selected from Schedule II below;   5

    or (ii) a second advanced paper selected from Schedule I or from any additional list of papers for the M.Phil. and M.Sc. in Economic and Social History approved by the Graduate Studies Committee of the Board of the Faculty of History and published in the definitive list of Advanced Papers as set out in Schedule I.

    III. A dissertation of not more than 15,000 words, including appendices but   10
excluding bibliography, on a topic approved by the candidate's supervisor. The dissertation must be delivered not later than noon on the last Friday in August of the year in which the examination is taken to the Examination Schools, High Street, Oxford. Dissertations submitted must not exceed the permitted length. If they do the examiners will reduce the marks awarded.   15
The presentation and footnotes should comply with the requirements specified in the Regulations of the Education Committee for the degrees of M.Litt. and D.Phil. and follow the *Conventions for the presentation of dissertations and theses* of the Board of the Faculty of History.

Each dissertation must include a short abstract which concisely summarises its   20
scope and principal arguments, in about 300 words.

Candidates must submit by the specified date three copies of their dissertation. These must be securely and firmly bound in either hard or soft covers.

    3. The examiners will permit the use of any hand-held pocket calculator subject to the conditions set out below under the heading 'Use of calculators in examinations' in   25
the *Regulations for the Conduct of University Examinations*.

    4. The examiners may award a distinction for excellence in the whole examination.

    5. A candidate who fails the examination will be permitted to re-take it on one further occasion only, not later than one year after the initial attempt.

Such a candidate whose dissertation has been of satisfactory standard may   30
re-submit the same piece of work, while a candidate who has reached a satisfactory standard on the written papers will not be required to re-take that part of the examination.

SCHEDULE I

Advanced Papers for the M.Phil. and M.Sc. in Economic and Social History   35
A broad range of the course resources are shared with the corresponding courses in History of Science, Medicine, and Technology, and Advanced Papers are therefore available in the subject areas listed here.

    1. Economic and business history

    2. History of science and technology   40

    3. Social history

    4. Historical demography

    5. History of medicine

A descriptive list of Advanced Papers will be published by the Board of the Faculty of History in September for the academic year ahead (not all options may be available   45
in every year). The definitive list of the titles of Advanced Papers for any one year will be circulated to candidates and their supervisors and posted on the Faculty notice board not later than Friday of third week of Michaelmas Term.

SCHEDULE II

The paper in a relevant discipline or skill may be:

1. One of the papers from the M.Phil. in Sociology or in Comparative Social Policy.

2. One suitable paper from another Master's degree under the auspices of the Faculty of History approved from time to time by the Graduate Studies Committee   5
of the Board of the Faculty of History.

3. One suitable paper in a related skill or discipline other than those specified in paragraphs 1 to 2 above on the recommendation of the candidate's supervisor and endorsed by the Course Director.

Choices under Schedule II have to be approved by the chair of the Graduate Studies   10
Committee of the Board of the Faculty of History not later than Monday of the fourth week of Michaelmas Term. Candidates wishing to take a paper under 1 or 3 will also need the approval of the appropriate course convenor and the Graduate Studies Committee of the relevant faculty board or inter-faculty committee who need to be satisfied that each candidate has an adequate background in the subject. Not all   15
options may be available in any one year.

Master of Science by Coursework in Economics for Development

1. Every candidate for the M.Sc. must follow a course of instruction in Economics for Development for at least three terms. Candidates will, when entering for the examination, be required to produce a certificate from their society to this effect.   20

2. The examination will consist of:

(*a*) the following written papers, the syllabuses for which are given in the schedule:

    (i) Macroeconomic Theory

    (ii) Microeconomic Theory

    (iii) Development Economics   25

    (iv) Quantitative Methods

(*b*) an extended essay.

The extended essay shall be on a topic falling within the general field of development economics. The essay topic shall be selected by the student in consultation with the supervisor, and approved by the Course Director by the end of the first week of the   30
Trinity Full Term in which the examination is taken. The maximum length and form of the extended essay and instructions for submission will be communicated to candidates by the Chair of Examiners.

3. The candidate may also be examined orally.

4. The examiners may award a distinction for excellence in the whole examination.   35

Schedule

(i) *Macroeconomic Theory*

Questions will be set on aspects of macroeconomic theory, including questions related to international trade, central to the study of economic development. Full details of course content and structure will be provided in the *M.Sc. Economics for*   40
Development Handbook published at the beginning of Michaelmas Full Term of the academic year in which the examination is taken.

(ii) *Microeconomic Theory*

Questions will be set on aspects of microeconomic theory, including questions related to international trade, central to the study of economic development. Full   45
details of course content and structure will be provided in the *M.Sc. Economics for* *Development Handbook* published at the beginning of Michaelmas Full Term of the academic year in which the examination is taken.

(iii) *Development Economics*

Questions will be set on topics in development economics from a series of taught modules. The modules offered, which may vary from year to year, will normally be listed in the *M.Sc. Economics for Development Handbook* issued at the beginning of Michaelmas Full Term of the academic year in which the examination is taken, or as an addendum to the Handbook no later than 8th week of Michaelmas Full Term.

(iv) *Quantitative Methods*

Questions will be set on the theory and practice of quantitative methods used in the study of economic development. Full details of course content and structure will be provided in the *M.Sc. Economics for Development Handbook* published at the beginning of Michaelmas Full Term of the academic year in which the examination is taken.

Master of Science by Coursework in Education

1. Candidates must follow for three terms a course of instruction in Education, specialising in one of the following pathways: Comparative and International Education, Higher Education, Learning and Technology, Child Development and Education, or Research Training. The examination shall consist of six one-term papers and a dissertation.

2. Part 1 of the course consists of six papers. Candidates take a combination of required pathway-specific core papers and option papers, as determined in advance by each pathway convenor. Candidates will be informed of the available options, along with the assessment requirement, by Friday of 0th week of Michaelmas Term in the year in which the examination is taken. On some pathways, students are also required to successfully complete a research internship. Candidates following the 'Research Training' pathway will choose from a broader range of papers across the M.Sc. Education degree, in consultation with their supervisor and pathway convenor, of which at least half will be research methods focused.

3. Exceptionally, candidates may offer one paper from a relevant masters degree in another department in the University, in place of one option paper, subject to permission from the relevant pathway convenor and the Education Graduate Studies Committee. Applications to take such a paper must normally be made by Friday of the fifth week of Michaelmas Term.

4. Papers are normally assessed by one or more coursework assignments totalling no more than 3,000 words (inclusive of footnotes but excluding bibliography and appendices). All such assignments must be uploaded to the Assignments section of the Higher Degrees Weblearn site by the times and dates specified at the start of the course. Each submission must be accompanied by a declaration indicating that it is the candidate's own work. Exceptionally, candidates are assessed by unseen examination.

5. For Part 2 of the course, candidates will be required to submit a dissertation of 15,000–20,000 words (including footnotes/endnotes but excluding appendices and references or bibliography), the title to be selected in consultation with the supervisor, on a topic relevant to the pathway being followed. The subject and title selected by the candidate must be approved by the Course Director at a time to be announced at the beginning of the academic year in which the examination is taken.

6. Two soft bound, word-processed or printed copies of the dissertation must be delivered to the Chair of Examiners, M.Sc. Education, c/o Examination Schools, High Street, Oxford, not later than noon on the second Friday in August in the year in which the written examination is taken. These copies should be anonymous except for the candidate number, and accompanied by a declaration indicating that it is the candidate's own work. Candidates are also required to upload an electronic copy of the dissertation by noon on the same day and to submit a hardbound copy of the work to

the Department of Education no later than one week after submission of the soft bound copies. The hard bound copy of the dissertation of each candidate who passes the examination shall be retained by the department for deposit in the departmental library.

7. Every candidate will be required to satisfy the examiners in the following: (i) Satisfactory attendance at the appropriate classroom−based courses; (ii) Satisfactory performance in both Part 1 and Part 2.

8. Candidates may also be required to attend an oral examination. The oral examination may be on the candidate's written papers, dissertation, or both. Candidates shall be deemed to have passed the examination if they have satisfied the examiners in both Part 1 and Part 2. No candidate may progress to Part 2 unless they have passed a minimum of 4 papers in Part I. If Part 2 is failed the candidate may resubmit the dissertation one further time on the next occasion when this is examined.

9. The examiners may award a distinction for excellence in the whole examination.

Master of Science by Coursework in Endovascular Neurosurgery (Interventional Neuroradiology)

1. The Medical Sciences Board shall elect for the supervision of the course an Organising Committee which shall have the power to arrange lectures and other instruction.

2. Every candidate must follow for at least three terms or, in the case for part-time students, for at least six terms, a course of instruction in Endovascular Neurosurgery (Interventional Neuroradiology).

3. Candidates will be required to present themselves for written and oral examination and to submit a logbook and a dissertation in prescribed form on an approved topic.

4. Candidates will be required to take three papers of three hours each:

Paper 1: Pathology, Physiology, and Anatomy relevant to Endovascular Neurosurgery and Interventional Neuroradiology

Paper 2: Diagnosis in Endovascular Neurosurgery and Interventional Neuroradiology

Paper 3: Interventional Neuroradiological Techniques

Examination questions will reflect aspects of the subject as described in the schedule.

5. Candidates must be registered with the General Medical Council, hold an appropriate contract with the National Health Service, and have had appropriate experience in Diagnostic Radiology and/or Neurosurgery.

6. Each candidate will be required to submit a logbook to the Course Director by the end of their second term, or, in the case of part-time students, by the end of their fourth term. The logbook will subsequently be submitted to the examiners as part of the candidate's whole examination.

7. Each candidate will be required to submit a dissertation of no more than 15,000 words on a subject selected in consultation with the candidate's supervisor and approved by the Organising Committee. The dissertation may vary from an account of original research work to a survey of the literature. Dissertations which reproduce substantially work submitted in the other written assignments will not be admissible.

8. Three word-processed and appropriately bound copies of the dissertation must be delivered to the Course Director by a date prescribed by the examiners, together with the logbook as described above. The examiners shall retain two copies of the dissertation of each candidate who passes the examination, for deposit in the departmental library.

9. An oral examination will be held and this may include questions on the candidate's dissertation, logbook, or written papers.

10. The examiners may award a distinction for excellence in the whole examination.

Schedule

Paper 1: Pathology, Physiology, and Anatomy relevant to Endovascular Neurosurgery and Interventional Radiology

Pathology of lesions amenable to interventional neuroradiological techniques. The natural history of such conditions and the indications for interventional measures. Anatomy of the central nervous system with special reference to vascular anatomy including common variations to the normal pattern. The embryology and phylogeny of the blood supply of the head and spine. Vascular physiology with special reference to the cerebral and spinal circulations. Normal and potential sites of collateral circulation. Endovascular routes to lesion of the head and spine.

Paper 2: Diagnosis in Endovascular Neurosurgery and Interventional Neuroradiology

The clinical and radiological diagnosis of conditions amenable to interventional neuroradiological techniques including recognition of common symptoms and signs associated with such conditions.

Radiological and other imaging techniques for localisation and evaluation of cerebral and spinal lesion, including angiography, myelography, CT and MR scanning, Doppler ultrasound (transcranial and intra-operative), and the use of radiopharmaceuticals. Electrophysiological and cerebral blood flow measurement techniques as well as neurological and cardiovascular monitoring pertinent to interventional neuroradiological procedures.

Paper 3: Interventional Neuroradiological Techniques

Interventional techniques for biopsy, embolisation, thrombolysis, and angioplasty. Delivery systems: their construction and applications. Embolisation materials including balloons, coils, stents, particulate and liquid embolic agents and their advantages and disadvantages for different applications. Pre-and post-procedural precautions, including indications for treatment, informed consent, and the recognition and management of complications.

The official name, constitution pharmacology, modes of administration, clinical agents used in interventional neuroradiological techniques. Sedation and the provision of analgesia during procedures. In particular the use of anticoagulation, fibrinolytic, and anticonvulsant agents.

Master of Science by Coursework in English Local History

1. Every candidate must follow for at least six terms a part-time course of instruction in English Local History and must upon entering for examination produce from his or her society a certificate to that effect.

2. The examination will consist of the following parts:

Qualifying test

Every candidate must pass a qualifying test. The test shall consist of the satisfactory completion of a course on:

Concepts and methods: an introduction to research in local history

The organisers of the course shall, not later than the end of the Hilary Term in the first year of the course submit to the examiners a list of candidates who have satisfactorily completed the qualifying course. No candidate who has failed the qualifying test will be permitted to supplicate for the degree. Candidates who fail the qualifying course once will be permitted to take it again, not later than one year after the initial attempt.

Final Examinations

The final examination shall consist of three parts:

A. *Skills for local history*

Every candidate must submit two written assignments of no more than 2,500 words in length for each of two courses from the list below: 5

  (1) Sources, Methods and Foundations in Medieval Local History

  (2) Sources, Methods and Foundations in Early Modern Local History

  (3) Sources, Methods and Foundations in Modern Local History

B. *Advanced papers*

Every candidate must follow either   10

  (1) two advanced papers from Schedule A below,

  or

  (2) one advanced paper from Schedule A below and a second paper from Schedule B, which consists of papers also offered as part of the M.Sc. in Economic and Social History. Other Schedule B papers may be added   15 subject to the approval of the Chair of the Graduate Studies Committee of the History Faculty Board and of the Board of Studies of the Committee for Continuing Education.

Each candidate will submit two written assignments of not more than 5,000 words in length for each paper. Some Schedule B papers may be assessed by a three hour   20 unseen examination.

C. *Dissertation*

A dissertation of not more than 15,000 words, including appendices but excluding bibliography, on a topic approved by the candidate's supervisor. The dissertation must be delivered not later than noon on the last Monday in September of the second   25 year of the course to the Chair of Examiners for the M.Sc. in Local History, c/o Examination Schools, High Street, Oxford.

SCHEDULE A

Advanced Papers are available in the following areas:

  1. The development of rural society   30

  2. Social history

  3. Urban history

  4. History of religion

  5. Architecture and local society

SCHEDULE B   35

Advanced Papers are available in the following areas:

  1. Economic and business history

  2. History of science and technology

  3. Social history

  4. Historical demography   40

  5. History of medicine

A list of Advanced Papers will be published by the Board of Studies for the M.Sc. in English Local History in September for the academic year ahead (not all options may be available in every year). The definitive list of the titles of Advanced Papers for any one year will be circulated to candidates and their supervisors not later than Friday of   45 the third week of Michaelmas Term. Teaching for the Advanced Papers will take place in Hilary Term.

3. The examiners will permit the use of any hand-held pocket calculator subject to the conditions set out in *Regulations for the Conduct of University Examinations.*

4. Each candidate must attend an oral examination when required to do so by the examiners.

5. The examiners may award a distinction for excellence in the whole examination.

6. A candidate who fails an advanced paper, or whose dissertation fails to satisfy the examiners, may be permitted to retake the paper, or resubmit the dissertation, on one further occasion only, not later than one year after the initial attempt.

Master of Science by Coursework in Environmental Change and Management

1. The Social Sciences Divisional Board shall elect for the supervision of the course a Standing Committee. The Course Director will be responsible to the Standing Committee.

2. Candidates must follow a course of instruction in Environmental Change and Management for at least three terms, and will, when entering for the examination be required to produce a certificate from the Course Director to this effect.

3. The examination will consist of:

(i) a written examination of three papers on the syllabus described in the schedule:

(ii) a dissertation on a subject selected in consultation with the supervisor and Course Director and approved by the Course and Academic Directors.

(iii) two assessed essays based on Elective courses.

4. Candidates must submit to the Course Director by the end of the Hilary Term in the year in which they enter the examination, the title and a brief statement of the form and scope of their dissertation, together with the name of a person who has agreed to act as their supervisor during preparation of the dissertation.

5. The dissertation shall be of a maximum of 15,000 words and accompanied by an abstract not exceeding 150 words. The maximum word count shall include footnotes, but exclude appendices, references and the abstract. The detailed format and specification of the dissertation shall be approved by the Standing Committee, and be published in the course handbook.

6. Two typewritten or printed copies of the dissertation must arrive, not later than noon on the first weekday of September in the year in which the written examination is taken, to the M.Sc. Examiners (Environmental Change and Management), c/o Examination Schools, High Street, Oxford OX1 4BG. The examiners may retain one copy of the dissertation of each candidate who passes the examination for deposit in an appropriate department library.

7. In the written examination the examiners will permit the use of any hand-held pocket calculators subject to the conditions set out under the heading 'Use of calculators in examinations' in the *Regulations for the Conduct of University Examinations.*

8. The examiners may also examine any candidate viva voce on the candidate's written papers, dissertation, or both.

9. Arrangements for reassessment shall be specified by the Standing Committee and published in the course handbook.

10. The examiners may award a distinction for excellence in the whole examination.

Schedule

(i) *Understanding environmental change.* Candidates will be expected to have integrative knowledge of the critical issues in current and future environmental change as applied to terrestrial, aquatic, and atmospheric systems. Forces driving change including resource scarcity, competition, population, land use, pollution, technological   5
change, and climatic factors.

(ii) *Responding to environmental change.* Candidates will be expected to have knowledge of governance, economics, ethics, law, and sociocultural dimensions of mitigating and adapting to environmental change. Strategies appropriate for the management of changing environments.   10

(iii) *Methods and techniques for environmental management.* Candidates will be expected to have knowledge of methods for environmental appraisal and management. These may include: basic computing and modelling, experimental design, data acquisition and handling; remote sensing and GIS; methods of ecological economic and social analysis.   15

(iv) *Electives.* Candidates will be expected to show advanced knowledge of two of the elective courses on offer in any one year.

Master of Science by Coursework in Evidence-Based Health Care

(*old regulations for students registered on the M.Sc. EBHC before 1 October 2012*)

1. The Divisional Board of Medical Sciences, jointly with the Continuing   20
Education Board, shall elect for the supervision of the course a Standing Committee, which shall have the power to arrange lectures and other instruction.

2. Every candidate must follow for at least three and at most twelve terms a part-time course of instruction in the theory and practice of Evidence-Based Health Care, which shall normally take place over a period of no more than six years.   25

3. Every candidate will be required to satisfy the examiners in the following:

    (*a*) attendance at both of the modules listed in Schedule A (below);

    (*b*) attendance at four of the modules listed in Schedule B (below);

    (*c*) six written assignments, usually of no more than 5,000 words, one on each of the modules from 3(*a*) and 3(*b*) above;   30

    (*d*) a dissertation of not more than 30,000 words (including appendices and footnotes but excluding bibliography), on a subject selected by the candidate in consultation with the supervisor and approved by the Standing Committee.

The assessed work set out in clause 3(*c*) shall be forwarded to the examiners c/o   35
Registry, Department for Continuing Education, 1 Wellington Square, Oxford OX1 2JA, for consideration by such date as the examiners shall determine and of which they shall notify candidates. The dissertation set out in clause 3(*d*) shall be forwarded to the examiners c/o Examination Schools, High Street, Oxford OX1 4BG for consideration by such date as the examiners shall determine and of which they shall notify   40
candidates.

4. Candidates may be required to attend a viva voce examination at the end of the course of studies at the discretion of the examiners.

5. The examiners may award a distinction to candidates for the M.Sc.

6. Candidates who fail to satisfy the examiners in any of the six assignments under 3(*c*) may be permitted, normally within one year of the original failure, to resubmit work in respect of the part or parts they have failed on not more than one occasion for each assignment without being required to repeat attendance at the relevant module or modules under 3(*a*) and/or 3(*b*). Candidates who fail to satisfy the examiners   5
under 3(*d*) may be permitted to resubmit work in respect of the part or parts of the examination which they have failed, for examination on not more than one occasion which shall normally be within one year of the original failure.

7. The Standing Committee shall have the discretion to permit any candidate to be exempted, in exceptional circumstances, from attendance at a module under 3(*a*) or   10
3(*b*) and from submitting an assignment required under 3(*c*) above, provided that the Standing Committee is satisfied that such a candidate has undertaken equivalent study, or has appropriate work experience to an equivalent standard.

Schedule A

M1: Practice of EBHC   15

M2: Introduction to Study Design and Research Methods

Schedule B

M3: Knowledge into Action

M4: Clinical Epidemiology

M5: Evidence-Based Diagnosis and Screening   20

M6: Systematic Reviews

M7: Randomised Control Trials

M8: Essential Medical Statistics

M9: Patient-Based Evidence

M10: Ethics in Health Care   25

M11: Qualitative Research Methods

M12: Evidence-Based Dentistry

M13: Introduction to Statistics in Health Care Research

Any other module as defined by the Programme Director and approved by the Standing Committee.   30

Postgraduate Programme in Evidence-Based Health Care Studies
(*new regulations for students registering on any of the awards listed from 1 October 2012 and available to existing students*)

A. Definition of the Programme

1. The Continuing Education Board and the Medical Sciences Board shall jointly   35
offer a Programme in Evidence-Based Health Care Studies at postgraduate level.

2. The Continuing Education Board and the Medical Sciences Board shall jointly elect for the supervision of the Programme a Standing Committee which shall have the power to arrange lectures and other instruction.

3. The subject of the Programme shall be Evidence-Based Health Care Studies.   40

4. The policy of the Continuing Education Board on variable intensity part-time postgraduate study applies to this Programme.

5. The following awards shall be available within the Programme:

  i. M.Sc. in Evidence-Based Health Care

  ii. Postgraduate Diploma in Evidence-Based Health Care   45

  iii. Postgraduate Certificate in Evidence-Based Health Care

   iv. Postgraduate Diploma in Health Research

   v. Postgraduate Certificate in Health Research

B. Progression

6. Students admitted to the Programme with the intention of studying towards the award of the M.Sc. are required to matriculate, involving admission by a college of the University. Students admitted to the Programme intending to study towards a Postgraduate Certificate or Postgraduate Diploma who subsequently apply for admission to the M.Sc. will be required at that point to matriculate and to be admitted by a college.

7. Students who have satisfied the requirements for the award of the Postgraduate Certificate or the Postgraduate Diploma and who do not wish to continue their studies may end their registration at that point and be awarded the Postgraduate Certificate or Postgraduate Diploma as the case may be.

C. Duration

8. The minimum period of registration on the Programme shall be three terms.

9. The maximum period of registration shall be six terms for each of the Postgraduate Certificates, nine terms for each of the Postgraduate Diplomas and twelve terms for the M.Sc.

10. Candidates may be permitted in certain circumstances to suspend status, for a maximum of six terms. Any such period shall not count to the maximum or minimum permitted period of registration and no fee liability will be incurred during such periods.

D. Study criteria for eligibility for awards

11. The modules available in the Programme are specified in the Schedule below. Not all modules are available for each award. Every candidate for a given award will be required to satisfy the examiners in the following:

   i. M.Sc. in Evidence-Based Health Care

     (i) attendance at both of modules (i) and (ii);

     (ii) attendance at any four of modules (iii) to (xv) or (xx) of the schedule at H;

     (iii) submission of the required assessed work relating to each of the six modules in (i) and (ii) above, which shall be of not more than 4,000 words per module;

     (iv) submission of a dissertation of not more than 15,000 words, on a subject selected by the candidate in consultation with the supervisor and approved by the Standing Committee. Approval must be sought no later than the first day of the ninth term of registration. The dissertation must be submitted within three terms of the date of approval, notwithstanding the maximum permitted period of registration.

   ii. Postgraduate Diploma in Evidence-Based Health Care

     (i) attendance at both of modules (i) and (ii);

     (ii) attendance at any four of modules (iii) to (xv) or (xx) of the schedule at H;

     (iii) submission of the required assessed work relating to each of the six modules in (i) and (ii) above, which shall be of not more than 4,000 words per module.

   iii. Postgraduate Certificate in Evidence-Based Health Care

     (i) attendance at both of modules (i) and (ii);

     (ii) attendance at any one of modules (iii) to (xv) or (xx) of the schedule at H;

     (iii) submission of the required assessed work relating to each of the three modules in (i) and (ii) above, which shall be of not more than 4,000 words per module.

iv. *Postgraduate Diploma in Health Research*
  (i) attendance at modules (i) and (ii);
  (ii) attendance at any three of modules (iii) to (xi), or (xiv) to (xv), or (xx) of the schedule at H, or of the modules indicated as available in the regulations for the M.Sc. in Experimental Therapeutics;
  (iii) attendance at one additional module taken from under (ii) above, or (xii) of the schedule at H, or from those indicated in the regulations for the M.Sc. in Surgical Science and Practice;
  (iv) submission of the required assessed work, which shall be of not more than 4,000 words, relating to each of the six modules in (i) and (ii) and (iii) above.
v. *Postgraduate Certificate in Health Research*
  (i) attendance at modules (i) and (ii);
  (ii) attendance at one of modules (iii) to (x) or (xiv) to (xv) in the schedule at H, or one of the modules indicated as available from the regulations for the M.Sc. in Experimental Therapeutics;
  (iii) submission of the required assessed work, which shall be of not more than 4,000 words, relating to each of the three modules taken under (i) and (ii) above.

12. Assignments shall be forwarded (usually electronically via a specified online submission system) to the examiners c/o Registry, Department for Continuing Education, 1 Wellington Square, Oxford OX1 2JA, for consideration by such dates as the examiners shall determine and of which they shall notify candidates. Dissertations shall be submitted in hard copy and in electronic format to the Examiners c/o Examination Schools High Street Oxford OX1 4BG for consideration by such dates as the examiners shall determine and of which they shall notify candidates.

Assignments and dissertations must be accompanied by a statement that they are the candidate's work except where otherwise indicated.

13. Provided the Standing Committee is satisfied that a student on the Programme has undertaken equivalent study, of an appropriate standard, normally at another institution of higher education, or has appropriate work experience to an equivalent standard, the committee shall have the discretion to permit the candidate to be exempted from attendance and the submission of a written assignment in respect of one module for a Postgraduate Certificate, two modules for a Postgraduate Diploma and three modules for the M.Sc. In exercising this discretion the Standing Committee shall have consideration to the length of time that has elapsed since the study or work experience was undertaken.

E. The Examinations

14. Students on the Register shall enter for the examination for the award of the M.Sc. or the Postgraduate Diploma or the Postgraduate Certificate in Evidence-Based Health Care or the award of the Postgraduate Diploma or the Postgraduate Certificate in Health Research.

15. Candidates are required to attend a viva voce examination at the end of the course of studies leading to each award unless dispensed by the examiners.

16. The examiners may award a distinction for excellence in the overall examination for each award.

17. Candidates who fail to satisfy the examiners in any of the assignments or the dissertation under 11 above may be permitted, normally within one year of the original failure, to resubmit work in respect of the part or parts they have failed on

not more than one occasion for each assignment without being required to repeat attendance at the relevant module or modules.

F. Prior Undertaking of modules for credit

18. The Standing Committee shall have the discretion to deem satisfactory completion of a module including the associated assessment prior to registration for an award listed under 5 i–v above as having met the attendance and examination requirements in respect of that module under 11 above. Such discretion will normally only be exercised if the time elapsed between commencement of the accredited module concerned and registration for the award is not more than two years.

19. The maximum number of modules taken prior to registration for an award that can contribute to the achievement of the award shall be one for the Postgraduate Certificate, three for either of the Postgraduate Diplomas and three for the M.Sc.

G. Subsuming of previous modules and awards under the Programme

20. If any student who has previously successfully completed the Postgraduate Certificate and ended their registration on the Programme subsequently is re-admitted to another award listed under 5i-iv, the Standing Committee shall have the discretion to deem satisfactory completion of modules within the Postgraduate Certificate as having met the attendance and examination requirements in respect of the modules under 11 above. Such discretion will normally only be exercised if the time elapsed between first registration on a module contributing to the Postgraduate Certificate and registration for the higher award is not more than two years.

21. If any student who has previously successfully completed the Postgraduate Diploma and ended their registration on the Programme subsequently is re-admitted to the M.Sc., the Standing Committee shall have the discretion to deem satisfactory completion of modules within the Postgraduate Diploma as having met the attendance and examination requirements in respect of the modules under 11 above. Such discretion will normally only be exercised if the time elapsed between first registration on a module contributing to the Postgraduate Diploma and registering for the M.Sc. is not more than two years.

22. If a student who has been awarded a Postgraduate Diploma or Postgraduate Certificate is subsequently awarded a higher award then the M.Sc. or Postgraduate Diploma will subsume the lower award.

H. Schedule of Modules

    (i) Practice of Evidence-Based Health Care
    (ii) Introduction to Study Design and Research Methods
    (iii) Ethics for Biosciences
    (iv) Knowledge into Action
    (v) Clinical Epidemiology
    (vi) Evidence-Based Diagnosis and Screening
    (vii) Introduction to Statistics for Health Care Research
  (viii) Systematic Reviews
    (ix) Randomized Control Trials
    (x) Qualitative Research Methods
    (xi) Essential Medical Statistics
    (xii) Teaching Evidence-Based Practice
  (xiii) The History and Philosophy of Evidence-Based Health Care
  (xiv) Clinical Trial Management

(xv) Mixed Methods in Health Research

(xx) Any other module as defined by the Programme Director and approved by the Standing Committee.

Additional modules available (as specified above) from the regulations for the M.Sc. in Experimental Therapeutics   5
Structure of clinical trials and experimental therapeutics
Drug development, pharmacokinetics and imaging
Pharmacodynamics, biomarkers and personalised therapy
Adverse drug reactions, drug interactions, and pharmacovigilance
How to do research on therapeutic interventions: protocol preparation   10
Biological therapeutics

Additional modules available (as specified above) from the regulations for the M.Sc. in Surgical Science and Practice
Human factors, teamwork and communication
Becoming a medical educator   15
Quality improvement science and systems analysis

Master of Science by Coursework in Evidence-Based Social Intervention and Policy Evaluation (EBSIPE)

1. Candidates must follow for at least three terms a course of instruction in Evidence-Based Social Intervention and Policy Evaluation.   20

2. Every candidate will be required to satisfy the examiners in the following:

(i) A compulsory core paper, in either Evidence-Based Social Intervention or Policy Evaluation;

(ii) A compulsory Research Methods paper, for which students will be examined on the basis of a methods work book (consisting of two Quantitative and one   25
Statistics assignments each of up to 3,000 words, and a Qualitative assignment of up to 2,000 words) and a critical methods essay of up to 2,500 words.

(iii) One Option paper;

(iv) A thesis of not more than 10,000 words, on a topic related to, and attentive to the evidence-based intervention, policy evaluation or evaluation methods, and   30
decided jointly with, and approved by, the supervisor on behalf of the Department.

3. Two printed or word-processed copies of the Research Methods essay must be delivered to the M.Sc. Examiners (Evidence-Based Social Intervention), c/o Examination Schools, High Street, Oxford OX1 4BG, no later than 12 noon on   35
Friday of sixth week of the Trinity Term in which the examination has been taken.

4. Two printed or word-processed copies of the thesis must be delivered to the M.Sc. examiners (Evidence-Based Social Intervention and Policy Evaluation), c/o Examination Schools, High Street, Oxford OX1 4BG, no later than noon on 15 August or the weekday nearest to 15 August of the year in which the examination   40
has been taken. Successful candidates may be required to deposit a copy of their thesis in the Social Science Library.

5. A candidate who fails the examination may enter for one subsequent examination only, provided this is within six terms of his or her initial registration. A candidate who has attained a satisfactory mark in any one of the four components of the   45
examination in 2 above will not be required to retake the component(s) concerned.

6. Each candidate must attend a viva voce when required to do so by the examiners.

7. The examiners may award a distinction for excellence in the whole examination.

Schedule

(i) *Evidence-Based Social Intervention and Policy Evaluation* (core course): Candidates will be expected to have a knowledge of major theories underlying evidence-based social interventions or policy evaluation research. The course will use exemplary intervention and evaluation research studies to illustrate important theoretical, ethical, methodological, and practice issues.

(ii) *Research Methods* (core course): Candidates will be expected to have a knowledge of major quantitative and qualitative techniques, and research designs for understanding social problems and evaluating social interventions and policies.

(iii) *Option course*: This will enable students to link evidence-based solutions to a range of social problems. Not every option will be offered in any one year, and applicants for admission will be advised of this. Areas from which options may be offered include: promoting the welfare of children and families; multicultural mental health interventions; substance misuse and offending; interventions in relation to HIV and AIDS; community work; refugees and asylum seekers.

Master of Science by Coursework in Experimental Therapeutics

1. The Medical Sciences Board, in consultation with the Continuing Education Board, shall elect for the supervision of the course a Standing Committee that shall have the power to arrange lectures and other instruction.

2. The course is available on a part time basis only and shall consist of instruction in the theory and practice of Experimental Therapeutics.

3. The policy of the Continuing Education Board on variable intensity part-time postgraduate study shall apply to this award.

4. The minimum period of registration for the M.Sc. course shall be three terms and the maximum period of registration shall be twelve terms.

5. Candidates may be permitted in certain circumstances to suspend status, for a maximum of six terms. Any such period shall not count to the maximum or minimum permitted period of registration and no fee liability will be incurred during such periods.

6. Every candidate will be required to satisfy the examiners in the following:

(*a*) participation, to the satisfaction of the course director, in each of the modules listed below;

(*b*) six written assignments, each of not more than 4,000 words in length, one from each of the six modules specified;

(*c*) a dissertation of not more than 15,000 words (including tables, appendices, footnotes but excluding reference list) on a subject selected by the candidate in consultation with the supervisor and approved by the Standing Committee. Approval must be sought no later than the first day of the ninth term of registration. The dissertation must be submitted within three terms of the date of approval, notwithstanding the maximum permitted period of registration.

The assessed work set out in clause 6(*b* and *c*) shall be forwarded to the examiners c/o Registry, Department for Continuing Education, 1 Wellington Square, Oxford OX1 2JA, for consideration by such date as the examiners shall determine and shall notify candidates. The assessed work will, in normal circumstances, be submitted through an electronic submission system.

7. Candidates may be required to attend a viva voce examination at the end of the course of studies at the discretion of the examiners.

8. The examiners may award a distinction to candidates for the M.Sc.   5

9. Candidates who fail to satisfy the examiners in any of the assignments or the dissertation under 6 above may be permitted to resubmit work in respect of the part or parts they have failed on not more than one occasion for each assignment without being required to repeat attendance at the relevant module or modules. The resubmission shall normally be within one year of the original failure.   10

10. Provided the Standing Committee is satisfied that a student on the award has undertaken equivalent study, of an appropriate standard, normally at another institution of higher education, or has appropriate work experience to an equivalent standard, the committee may permit the candidate to be exempted from attendance and the submission of a written assignment in respect of up to three modules. In exercising   15
this discretion the Standing Committee shall take into consideration the length of time that has elapsed since the study or work experience was undertaken.

11. The Standing Committee may deem satisfactory completion of a module (including the associated assessment) undertaken prior to registration for the award as having met the attendance and examination requirements in respect of that module.   20
Such discretion will normally only be exercised if the time elapsed between commencement of the accredited module concerned and registration for the award is not more than two years. The maximum number of modules taken prior to registration for the award that may be counted in this way shall be three.

MODULE SCHEDULE   25

(1) Structure of clinical trials and experimental therapeutics*

(2) Drug development, pharmacokinetics and imaging*

(3) Pharmacodynamics, biomarkers and personalised therapy*

(4) Adverse drug reactions, drug interactions, and pharmacovigilance*

(5) How to do research on therapeutic interventions: protocol preparation*   30

(6) Biological therapeutics*

(7) Any other module as defined by the programme director and approved by the Standing Committee.

* Also available to students on the PG Certificate and Diploma in Health Research

Master of Science by Coursework in Financial Economics   35

1. Candidates must follow for at least three terms a course of instruction in Financial Economics. Candidates must complete:

(*a*) all courses from the Schedule, and satisfy the examiners in the assignment and/or examination associated with each course;

(*b*) five electives, of which one may be an individual project. Candidates must   40
satisfy the examiners in the assignment/examination/written report associated with each course, the list of electives to be published annually by the MFE Standing Committee before the first Monday of Hilary Term. If chosen, individual project written reports to be of not more than 10,000 words. Such projects must be approved by the MFE Standing Committee;   45

(*c*) candidates may be required to attend an oral examination on any of the above.

2. Assignments and written reports on projects must be presented not later than the time and date stipulated for each exercise; these will be published by the MFE Standing Committee before the first Monday of each term in which the assignment or project must be undertaken. The required number of copies must be delivered to the Examination Schools, and addressed to the Chair of Examiners for the M.Sc. in 5 Financial Economics, c/o Examination Schools, High Street, Oxford, except in the case of practical work, which should be submitted to the Saïd Business School, Park End Street, Oxford in the format advised by the MFE Standing Committee.

3. The examiners may award a distinction for excellence in the whole examination to candidates for the Degree. 10

4. In exceptional circumstances, a candidate wishing to take an examination later than the one to which he or she has been admitted may do so by application to the Chair of Examiners, via his or her College Senior Tutor or Tutor for Graduates.

5. Candidates are permitted on only one occasion to resubmit or retake failed assessment items on any course on which they have failed to achieve the required 15 standard.

Schedule

The following courses are required to be taken during Michaelmas and Hilary Terms. Details can be found in the course handbook:

(*a*) Corporate Finance 20

(*b*) Economics

(*c*) Asset Pricing

(*d*) Financial Econometrics.

Master of Science by Coursework in Global Governance and Diplomacy 25

1. Each candidate will be required to follow a course of instruction in Global Governance and Diplomacy for three terms, and will, when they enter their names for the examination, be required to produce a certificate from their supervisors to this effect. Candidates must offer:

(i) One of two foundation papers from the following list as detailed in the 30 Schedule:

(*a*) Global Governance

(*b*) International Diplomacy

(ii) A mandatory paper in Research Methods as detailed in the Schedule.

(iii) Two option papers to be selected from a list published annually by the Course 35 Director by Monday of Week Nought of Michaelmas Full Term.

(iv) One 10,000–12,000 word dissertation: the topic of the dissertation must be submitted to the Course Director for approval not later than 12 noon on Friday of seventh week of Michaelmas Term in the year in which the examination is taken. The dissertation must be submitted not later than 12 noon on 40 Thursday of sixth week of Trinity Full Term in the year in which the examination is taken. Two typewritten or word processed copies of the dissertation must be delivered to the Examination Schools, addressed to the Chair of Examiners for the M.Sc. in Global Governance and Diplomacy, c/o Examination Schools, High Street, Oxford at the time and date specified. 45

2. A candidate who fails the examination will be permitted to retake it on one further occasion within six terms of his or her initial registration. Such a candidate will be permitted to resubmit the same dissertation provided that this reached a

satisfactory standard, while a candidate who has reached a satisfactory standard on one or more examination papers will not be required to retake that part of the examination.

3. Candidates may be required to attend an oral examination on any part of the examination.

4. The examiners may award a distinction for excellence in the whole examination.

Schedule

(*a*) *Global Governance*: the sources, mechanisms, processes and practices of global governance at the subnational, national, international, and transnational levels: at the subnational, national, and transnational levels, the focus is on globalisation; at the international, transnational and supranational levels, the focus is on regional integration; at the level of inter-state governance, the focus is on international organisations, international regimes, and multilateralism.

(*b*) *International Diplomacy*: substantive knowledge and theoretical background concerning the institutions and processes of international diplomacy. The course reviews important themes of diplomatic thought and discusses their relevance for the current practice of diplomacy; examines the legal, organisational, communicational and cognitive underpinnings of diplomatic practice; studies processes and mechanisms of international negotiation, mediation, and public diplomacy; and focuses on how diplomacy is conducted in international and regional bodies;

(*c*) *Research Methods*: common research methods in the social sciences including but not limited to the topics of concept formation, causal analysis, single and comparative case study methods, case selection, qualitative interviewing, historical and ethnographic methods, genealogy, and statistical approaches and instruments.

Master of Science by Coursework in Global Health Science

1. The Divisional Board of Medical Sciences will appoint for the supervision of the course an Organising Committee, which will have the power to arrange lectures and other instruction.

2. The Organising Committee will appoint for each candidate an academic adviser.

3. Each candidate must follow a course of study in Global Health Science for at least three terms and for a substantial part of the three subsequent vacations, as determined by the course timetable.

4. Candidates shall be examined in all of the following ways:

 (i) A printed report of not more than 2,500 words (excluding bibliography) on an analysis of a dataset based on a research question approved by the Organising Committee. Additionally, candidates must submit an annotated copy of the STATA code used for their analysis.

 (ii) A printed essay of 3,000–4,000 words (excluding bibliography) selected from a choice of essay titles approved by the Organising Committee and based on the modules studied as set out in the Schedule.

 (iii) A written examination paper relating to the Principles of Epidemiology, and the Principles of Statistics.

 (iv) A written examination paper relating to the modules set out in the Schedule, with the exception of Principles of Epidemiology, and Principles of Statistics.

 (v) A printed dissertation of not more than 10,000 words (excluding bibliography and appendices) on the research project as set out in the Schedule below. The research project and the subject of the dissertation must have been approved by the Organising Committee.

5. Candidates may be examined viva voce and this examination will take place on dates to be determined by the examiners.

6. The arrangements for approval of written work for submission will be notified to candidates not later than the start of the Michaelmas Term of the academic year in which the examination is taken.

7. Three copies of each of the required written submissions must be sent to the Chair of Examiners, M.Sc. in Global Health Science, c/o Examination Schools, High Street, Oxford, by dates to be specified by the Organising Committee and published in the *University Gazette* not later than the start of Michaelmas Term of the academic year in which the examination is taken. Each submission must be accompanied by a declaration of the candidate's authorship.

8. The examiners may award a distinction for excellence in the whole examination.

9. The examiners will retain one copy of each dissertation of each successful candidate for deposit in the Radcliffe Science library.

Schedule

1. Introduction to Global Health Science
2. Principles of Epidemiology
3. Principles of Statistics
4. Non-Communicable Diseases
5. Communicable Diseases
6. Maternal and Child Health
7. Health Economics
8. Clinical Trials and Meta-Analyses
9. Nutritional Epidemiology
10. Implementation Strategies
11. Record Linkage and Bio-Informatics
12. Genetic Epidemiology
13. International Research Ethics

Research Project: A research project under the supervision of a research supervisor. Students will undertake reading and research in relation to their research project during Trinity Term. Following the written examinations students may elect to go on an overseas research placement during Trinity Term and the Long Vacation, though this is not a requirement of the course. The subject of each student's dissertation, an overseas placement, and the supervision arrangements for each student must be approved by the Organising Committee.

Master of Science by Coursework in History of Science, Medicine, and Technology

The regulations of the Board of the Faculty of History are as follows:

1. Every candidate must follow for at least three terms a course of instruction in History of Science, Medicine, and Technology, and must upon entering for the examination produce from his or her society a certificate to that effect.

2. The examination will consist of the following parts:

Qualifying test

Every candidate must pass a qualifying test. The test shall consist of two courses on

1. Methods and themes in the history of science and technology.
2. Methods and themes in the history of medicine.

Candidates may be advised on the basis of their prospective individual research to substitute one of the following courses from the Master of Science in Economic and Social History for (1) or (2) above:

(i) Methodological introduction to research in the social sciences and history.

(ii) Quantitative Methods and Computer Applications for Historians.   5

A paper from another established course within the University may be substituted for one of the standard courses where this would provide a more appropriate training for the candidate's dissertation focus. Such a choice will need formal approval from both the Course Director and the Chair of the Graduate Studies Committee of the Board of the Faculty of History.   10

The two methodological introduction courses will each be assessed by a methodological essay of up to 3,000 words. Two typewritten copies of each of the essays must be submitted by noon on Monday of Week 10 of Michaelmas Term to the Chair of Examiners for the M.Sc. in History of Science, Medicine, and Technology, c/o Examination Schools, High Street, Oxford, OX1 4BG. In addition, convenors of   15 qualifying courses will confirm in writing to the chair of examiners not later than Friday of eighth week of Hilary Term the candidates' satisfactory participation in their classes, including the completion of any assignments for the weekly sessions. Any approved alternative qualifying course will be assessed within the format and time-table of the paper's parent course. No candidate who has failed the qualifying test of   20 two courses will be permitted to supplicate for the degree. Candidates who fail a qualifying course once will be permitted to take it again, not later than one year after the initial attempt.

Final examinations

The examination shall consist of two papers and a dissertation.   25

Candidates must take at least one of their papers as a three-hour written examination. For the remaining paper candidates must choose to be assessed either by written examination or by two 5,000 word essays. Essays may only be submitted in lieu of written papers for subjects in Schedule I below ('Advanced Papers for M.Phil. and M.Sc. in History of Science, Medicine, and Technology') or for other papers permitted   30 in Schedule II below where similar provision exists in the regulations for those examinations. The essays must be the work of the candidates alone and they must not consult any other person including their supervisors in any way concerning the method of handling the themes chosen. The themes chosen by the candidate must be submitted for approval by the Chair of Examiners by the examination entry date.   35 Candidates will be informed within two weeks, by means of a letter directed to their colleges, whether the topics they have submitted have been approved. The finished essays must be delivered by the candidate to the Examination Schools, High Street, Oxford, by noon on Monday of sixth week of Trinity Full Term. The essays must be presented in proper scholarly form, and two typed copies of each must be submitted.   40

I. One advanced paper selected from Schedule I below.

II. *Either* (i) one paper in a relevant discipline or skill or sources or methods selected from Schedule II below;

    or (ii) a second advanced paper selected from Schedule I or from any additional list of papers for the M.Phil. and M.Sc. in History of   45 Science, Medicine, and Technology approved by the Graduate Studies Committee of the Board of the Faculty of History and published in the definitive list of Advanced Papers as set out in Schedule I.

III. A dissertation of not more than 15,000 words, including appendices but ex-   50 cluding bibliography, on a topic approved by the candidate's supervisor. The dissertation must be delivered not later than noon on the last Friday in August of the year in which the examination is taken to the Examination Schools, High Street, Oxford. Dissertations submitted must not exceed the permitted length. If they do the examiners will reduce the marks awarded. The presentation and footnotes should comply with the requirements specified in the Regulations of the Education Committee for the degrees of M.Litt. and D.Phil. and follow the *Conventions for the presentation of dissertations and theses* of the Board of the Faculty of History.

Each dissertation must include a short abstract which concisely summarises its scope and principal arguments, in about 300 words.

Candidates must submit by the specified date three copies of their dissertation. These must be securely and firmly bound in either hard or soft covers.

3. The examiners will permit the use of any hand-held pocket calculator subject to the conditions set out under the heading 'Use of calculators in examinations' in the *Regulations for the Conduct of University Examinations* .

4. The examiners may award a distinction for excellence in the whole examination.

5. A candidate who fails the examination will be permitted to retake it on one further occasion only, not later than one year after the initial attempt.

Such a candidate whose dissertation has been of satisfactory standard may resubmit the same piece of work, while a candidate who has reached a satisfactory standard on the written papers will not be required to retake that part of the examination.

Schedule I
Advanced Papers for the M.Phil. and M.Sc. in History of Science, Medicine, and Technology

A broad range of the course resources are shared with the corresponding courses in Economic and Social History, and Advanced Papers are therefore available in the subject areas listed here.

1. Economic and business history

2. History of science and technology

3. Social history

4. Historical demography

5. History of medicine

A descriptive list of Advanced Papers will be published by the Board of the Faculty of History in September for the academic year ahead (not all options may be available in every year). The definitive list of the titles of Advanced Papers for any one year will be circulated to candidates and their supervisors and posted on the Faculty notice board not later than Friday of third week of Michaelmas Term.

Schedule II

The paper in a relevant discipline or skill may be:

1. One of the papers from the M.Phil. in Sociology or in Comparative Social Policy.

2. One suitable paper from another Master's degree under the auspices of the Faculty of History approved from time to time by the Graduate Studies Committee of the Board of the Faculty of History.

3. One suitable paper in a related skill or discipline other than those specified in paragraphs 1 to 2 above on the recommendation of the candidate's supervisor and endorsed by the Course Director.

Choices under Schedule II have to be approved by the Chair of the Graduate Studies Committee of the Board of the Faculty of History not later than Monday of the fourth week of Michaelmas Term. Candidates wishing to take a paper under 1 or 3 will also need the approval of the appropriate course convenor and the Graduate Studies Committee of the relevant faculty board or inter-faculty committee who need   5 to be satisfied that each candidate has an adequate background in the subject. Not all options may be available in any one year.

Master of Science by Coursework in Integrated Immunology

1. The Divisional Board of Medical Sciences shall appoint for the supervision of the course an Organising Committee, which shall have the power to arrange the   10 teaching, assessment and other instruction.

2. The Organising Committee shall appoint an academic mentor for each candidate.

3. Each candidate shall:

    (*a*) follow a course of study in Integrated Immunology for at least three terms   15 and for a substantial part of the three vacations, as determined by the course timetable;

    (*b*) attend all organised sessions including lectures, tutorials, class-directed learning, problem-based learning and continuing professional development sessions which will be compulsory (a record of attendance is kept).   20

4. Candidates shall be examined in all of the following ways:

    (i) At the end of Michaelmas Term (normally in Week 10), each candidate must pass a computer-based examination on the topics in the Schedule for Term 1. Candidates who fail the examination once will be permitted to take it again on one further occasion normally in Week 0 of Hilary Term, in order to   25 proceed with the course.

    (ii) At the end of Hilary Term (normally in Week 10), each candidate must pass a computer-based examination on the topics in the Schedule for Term 2. Candidates who fail the examination once will be permitted to take it again on one further occasion normally in Week 0 of Trinity Term, in order to   30 proceed with the course.

    (iii) Each candidate will be required to submit to the examiners two copies of a printed essay of between 3,000–4,000 words by noon, Monday of Week 8 of Michaelmas Term. The subject of the essay must have been approved by the Examining Board. Each candidate shall make a public presentation on their   35 essay to the examiners and will be examined viva voce, at the end of Michaelmas Term at a time to be notified by the examiners. Candidates will have the opportunity to revise and re-submit their essay by noon, Friday of the week preceding Week 0 of Hilary Term, in the event that they are deemed not to have passed this element of the examination.   40

    (iv) Each candidate will be required to submit to the examiners two copies each of three clinical commentaries (printed) of 2,000 words each by noon, Monday of Week 8 of Hilary Term. The subjects of the clinical commentaries must have been approved by the Examining Board. Each candidate will be required to make a public presentation of one of their commentaries   45 and will be examined viva voce, at the end of Hilary Term at a time to be notified by the examiners. Candidates will have the opportunity to revise and re-submit their clinical commentaries by noon, Friday of the week preceding Week 0 of Trinity Term, in the event that they are deemed not to have passed this element of the examination.   50

(v) Each candidate will be required to submit to the examiners two copies of a printed research dissertation of not more than 10,000 words (excluding bibliography and appendices) on the research project selected for study as set out in the Schedule. The dissertation must be submitted by noon on the last Monday of July in the academic year in which the examination is taken.   5

(vi) Each candidate shall make a presentation of their research project and will be examined viva voce, normally in the first week of September in the year of examination on a date to be determined by the examiners. Under exceptional circumstances, candidates may be permitted to redo the research project and/or resubmit the research dissertation to an Examining Board   10 sitting in Michaelmas, Hilary or Trinity Term of the following year (and which will be according to the Examiners' discretion in each case), in the event they are deemed not to have reached the required standard.

5. The examiners may examine any candidate viva voce on any part of the examination.   15

6. Candidates must pass each element of the examination to pass overall.

7. Candidates must pass each element of the examination in each term before being permitted to progress to the next term.

8. Candidates will be allowed one opportunity to retake or resubmit each of the required elements should they fail to reach the necessary standard. Students failing to   20 pass any element on the second attempt will normally be judged to have failed to reach the necessary standard for the award.

9. The examiners may award a distinction for excellence in the whole examination.

10. The required written submissions must be sent to the Chair of Examiners, M.Sc. in Integrated Immunology, c/o Examination Schools, High Street, Oxford.   25

Schedule

The syllabus for study will be:

Term 1: Fundamental aspects of immunology

The dynamic anatomy of immunity

Innate immunity   30

Antigen presentation and recognition

Adaptive immunity

Phylogenetically ancient systems

Term 2: Clinical aspects of immunology

Infection and immunity   35

Failure of immunity

Aberrant and unwanted immunity

The immunology of cancer

Manipulation of immunity

Term 3: A basic or clinical research project   40

The project will be chosen in consultation with the Organising Committee. A research supervisor will be assigned who will provide regular supervision and guidance during the course of the 14-week laboratory-based research project in Oxford.

Master of Science by Coursework in International Health and Tropical Medicine

1. The Divisional Board of Medical Sciences will appoint for the supervision of the course an Organising Committee, which will have the power to arrange lectures and other instruction.

2. The Organising Committee will appoint for each candidate an academic adviser.

3. Each candidate must follow a course of study in International Health and Tropical Medicine for at least three terms and for a substantial part of the three subsequent vacations, as determined by the course timetable.

4. Candidates will be examined in all of the following ways:

   (i) A written examination paper relating to Paradigms and Tools for Global Health.

   (ii) A written examination paper relating to Challenges and Change in International Health, and Global Health Research and Practice.

   (iii) Two printed essays of 3,000–4,000 words each (excluding bibliography). The topic for each of the two essays must be selected from a choice of titles approved by the Organising Committee and based on the optional modules studied as set out in the Schedule.

   (iv) A printed dissertation of not more than 10,000 words (excluding bibliography and appendices) on the research project as set out in the Schedule below. The research project and the subject of the dissertation must have been approved by the Organising Committee.

5. Candidates may be examined viva voce and this examination will take place on dates to be determined by the examiners.

6. The arrangements for approval of written work for submission will be notified to candidates not later than the start of the Michaelmas Term of the academic year in which the examination is taken.

7. Three copies of each of the required written submissions must be sent to the Chair of Examiners, M.Sc. in International Health and Tropical Medicine, c/o Examination Schools, High Street, Oxford, by dates to be specified by the Organising Committee and published in the *University Gazette* not later than the start of Michaelmas Term of the academic year in which the examination is taken. Each submission must be accompanied by a declaration of the candidate's authorship.

8. A candidate who fails any of the written examination papers will be permitted to re-sit the failed component(s) on one further occasion, during September of the Long Vacation of the same academic year as their original examination attempt. A candidate who fails any of the submitted assessments will be permitted to re-submit the failed component(s) on one further occasion, at the time these assessments are submitted during the following academic year.

9. The examiners may award a distinction for excellence in the whole examination.

10. The examiners will retain one copy of each dissertation of each successful candidate for deposit in the Radcliffe Science library.

Schedule

A. *Core Modules*
   1. Paradigms and Tools for Global Health
   2. Challenges and Change in International Health
   3. Global Health Research and Practice

B. *Optional Modules*
1. Advanced Topics in Tropical Medicine
2. Vaccinology
3. Reproductive, Maternal, Newborn and Child Health
4. International Development and Health
5. Health, Environment and Development

C. *Research placement*: Students will produce a dissertation based on a research placement that will normally be undertaken overseas. A research placement supervisor will be assigned to each student in addition to their academic adviser. The subject of each student's dissertation, the research placement, and the supervision arrangements for each student must be approved by the Organising Committee.

Master of Science by Coursework in Latin American Studies

(*See also the the general notice at the commencement of these regulations.*)

For the purposes of this examination, 'Latin America' will be interpreted as the eighteen Spanish-speaking republics of the Western Hemisphere, plus Brazil, Haiti, and Puerto Rico.

The regulations are as follows:
1. Candidates for the M.Sc in Latin American Studies will:

(*a*) Follow a course of instruction for three terms and present three examination papers at the end of Trinity Term in the year of registration. These papers must include at least two of the core papers from among the following five disciplines: Economics, History, International Relations, Politics and Sociology. Each of the examination papers counts for 25 per cent of the final degree mark.

(*b*) Submit an extended essay, not exceeding 10,000 words, including footnotes and appendices. A draft title for the extended essay must be submitted for approval by the Latin American Centre Management Committee by 12:00 noon on the Friday of Week 0 of the Hilary Term preceding the written examination. Two typewritten copies of the extended essay must be delivered to the Examination Schools, addressed to the Chair of Examiners for the M.Sc in Latin American Studies, c/o Examination Schools, High Street, Oxford, by 12:00 noon on the Monday of Week 5 of Trinity Term in the calendar year in which the examination is taken. The extended essay will be equal to one examination paper, i.e. 25 per cent of the final degree mark.

(*c*) Candidates may also be required to present themselves for an oral examination if requested to do so by the examiners. The oral examination may focus on the candidate's examination papers, extended essay, or both.

2. The list of examination papers will be published on the Latin American Centre website and in the *University Gazette* in Week 0 of Michaelmas Term. Candidates must take the core paper in Economics if they wish to take a further paper in that discipline. Specialisation on a single country or a combination of countries is permitted so long as the choice appears in the list of available papers published.

3. Candidates shall be deemed to have passed the examination if they have passed all examination papers and the extended essay.

4. A mark of 48 or 49 in one of the exam papers or the extended essay can be compensated for with marks indicating clear ability on the remaining three components of the examination. Candidates who either (i) receive a mark of 48 or 49 in one exam paper or the extended essay which cannot be compensated for by the remaining three components, (ii) receive less than 48 in one of the four components of the examination, or (iii) receive two or more marks below 50 in the four components of the examination,

will be permitted to retake the paper(s)/resubmit the extended essay on one further occasion only, in Trinity Term, one year after the first attempt. Such candidates must pass the extended essay or examination paper(s) in order to pass the examination.

5. The examiners may award a distinction for excellence in the whole examination.

Oxford 1+1 MBA programme

Candidates registered on the Oxford 1+1 MBA programme will follow an additional two or three month bridging programme at the end of their third term of the combined programme.

Each candidate will be appointed an academic advisor from the Saïd Business School to plan an individual course of study which will include as a minimum, the following three compulsory elements:

(i) Attendance of one of the summer elective programmes offered for the Master of Business Administration to be published by the MBA Director before the first Monday of the preceding term. Candidates would be required to undertake all assessments and receive feedback, but would not obtain credit towards the MBA. Candidates are not permitted to subsequently undertake the same elective as part of the MBA programme the following year.

(ii) A formatively assessed assignment of no more than 5,000 words (including all prefatory matter and appendices) supervised by the Saïd Business School academic advisor, which will relate the Master's degree learning to an appropriate area of the MBA programme. Candidates would also be required to present a work plan related to this assignment to the 1+1 programme class.

(iii) Attendance of the MBA pre-course as described in the joining instructions for the MBA class, unless granted exemption by the MBA Committee on the grounds of prior formal study or work experience.

Master of Science by Coursework in Law and Finance

1. Candidates must follow for at least three terms a course of instruction in Law and Finance.

2. Candidates must complete the following courses, and satisfy the examiners in the summative assessment in each case:

(*a*) all courses from Schedule A; *and*

(*b*) either two law electives from Schedule B, or one law elective from Schedule B and an individual dissertation, or one elective from Schedule B and the Corporate Valuation course plus one further elective from Schedule C, as prescribed for the Master in Business Administration or Master of Science in Financial Economics.

3. Not all electives will necessarily be taught or examined in any one year. Details of those which are available will be published in the M.Sc. in Law and Finance Handbook for the year of the examination, subject to any amendment posted on the designated course website by Monday of week minus 1 of the Michaelmas Term before the examination is held.

4. With the consent of the MLF Academic Director and the Subject Group Convener of the Course in question, candidates may offer as an alternative to one or both law electives from Schedule B, any other course listed in Schedule A of the BCL/M.Jur regulations (subject to the same limitations imposed on BCL and M.Jur students).

5. With the consent of the MLF Academic Director, candidates may offer as an alternative to one or both electives from Schedule C, one or more courses from the list of electives prescribed for the Master in Business Administration or Master of Science in Financial Economics which are not already listed in Schedule C.

6. Candidates may offer a dissertation on a subject to be proposed by the candidate in consultation with the supervisor, and approved by the Chair of the Board of Examiners. The dissertation shall be wholly or substantially the result of work undertaken whilst registered for the degree of M.Sc. in Law and Finance. The required format for this dissertation is the common format prescribed for all law theses, which is printed in the Law Faculty Graduate Student Handbook and the M.Sc. in Law and Finance Handbook.

7. Course assignments, where set, must be submitted not later than the time and date stipulated for each exercise; these will be published by the Board of Examiners before the first Monday of each term in which the assignment or project must be undertaken.

8. The degree of M.Sc. shall be awarded to any candidate who achieves marks of at least 50 per cent in assessments for all courses (for which purposes a dissertation, if offered, shall count as one course), with satisfactory completion of pass/fail course assessment components where relevant.

9. The Board of Examiners may award a distinction for excellence in the examination.

10. Candidates are permitted on only one occasion to resubmit or retake failed assessment items on any course on which they have failed to achieve the required standard.

Schedule A

Law and Economics of Corporate Transactions
Finance
First Principles of Financial Economics

Schedule B

Comparative Corporate Law
Competition Law
Conflict of Laws
Corporate Tax Law and Policy
Corporate Finance Law
Corporate Insolvency Law
European Business Regulation
Intellectual Property Law
International Economic Law
Legal Concepts in Financial Law
Principles of Financial Regulation
Regulation
Transnational Commercial Law

Schedule C

Corporate Valuation
Asset Management
Capital Raising and Finance
Cases in Finance and Investment
Entrepreneurial Finance
Mergers, Acquisitions and Restructuring
Private Equity

Master of Science by Coursework in Learning and Teaching

1. Candidates for the M.Sc. in Learning and Teaching may only be admitted to the course if they are graduates who have been awarded Qualified Teacher Status in the United Kingdom, or an equivalent UK or overseas award recognised by the Departmental Board. They must also be employed in a teaching post within a school   5
or other educational setting. All candidates will be admitted initially for the Postgraduate Diploma in Learning and Teaching.

2. Every candidate must follow for at least three and at most nine terms a part-time course of instruction in Learning and Teaching.

3. The course will consist of one programme of study, covering four main topics,   10
and a research and development project. The examination shall be in three parts as follows:

Part 1 will be examined by two coursework assignments as described in clause 4 below.

Part II will be examined by one coursework assignment as described in clause   15
5 below.

Part III will be examined by a research and development project report as described in clause 6 below.

Those candidates who meet the criteria set out in clause 7 below will be exempt from Part I of the programme.   20

4. Part I of the M.Sc in Learning and Teaching shall be examined by means of two assignments relating to the content of the Part I elements of the topics of the programme of study taken by the candidate. Each assignment must be between 4,000 and 5,000 words in length, or their equivalent. Two printed copies of each assignment and one electronic copy (in a software format available in the department)   25
must be delivered to the Chair of Examiners, M.Sc in Learning and Teaching, c/o Department of Education, 15 Norham Gardens, Oxford OX2 6PY. The deadline for submission of assignments 1 and 2 will take place before Week 5 of Trinity Term of the candidate's first year of study, and will be no later than noon on a date specified by the examiners and published in the course handbook.   30

5. Part II of the M.Sc in Learning and Teaching shall be examined by means of one coursework assignment relating to the content of the Part II elements of the topics of the programme of study taken by the candidate. (Candidates may choose, in consultation with their supervisors, whether the assignment should be presented as a single piece of work, drawing explicitly on the learning from the two options, or as   35
two smaller scale pieces each carried out within different options but linked by a reflective introduction that brings the two studies together within the candidate's own practice of professional learning.) The assignment must be between 8,000 and 10,000 words in length, or their equivalent. Two printed copies of the assignment and one electronic copy (in a software format available in the department) must be delivered to   40
the Chair of Examiners, M.Sc in Learning and Teaching, c/o Department of Education, 15 Norham Gardens, Oxford OX2 6PY. The deadline for submission of assignments will take place before Week 5 of Trinity Term of the candidate's second year of study (or the first year if the candidate is exempted from part I), and will be no later than noon on a date specified by the examiners and published in the course   45
handbook.

6. Part III of the M.Sc. in Learning and Teaching shall be examined through a research and development project report, which presents a systematic account of a substantial practitioner research enquiry, focused on the design and implementation of a specific innovation in teaching and learning with a strong emphasis on the choice of   50
appropriate criteria, and relevant evidence for evaluating its impact. The research and

development work must involve a significant degree of collaboration with other adults, either engaging others in research; or enabling others to learn from research findings within the candidate's own school or educational setting. The research and development project report must be between 15,000 and 20,000 words in length, or their equivalent. Three printed copies of the project report and one electronic copy (in a software format available in the department) must be delivered to the Chair of Examiners, M.Sc. in Learning and Teaching, c/o Department of Education, 15 Norham Gardens, Oxford OX2 6PY, no later than noon on the third Friday in September of the candidate's third year on the course. One of the printed copies of the report must be hard bound and bear the name of the candidate. The hard bound copy of the research and development project report of each candidate who passes the examination will be retained by the Department of Education for deposit in the departmental library.

7. Those candidates who meet any of the following criteria will be exempt from Part I of the examination and will only be required to undertake Parts II and III. In such cases the assignment for Part II should relate to the content of Part II elements of the topics of the programme of study.

(*a*) Those candidates who have, since October 2007, successfully completed the course leading to the award of a Postgraduate Certificate in Education at the University of Oxford (i.e. the Oxford Postgraduate Certificate in Education examined at Master's level).

(*b*) Those candidates who have successfully completed a Postgraduate Certificate in Education at another university, assessed at Master's level and including an award equivalent to at least one third of a full Master's degree.

(*c*) Those candidates who have successfully completed the course leading to a Postgraduate Diploma in Educational Studies from the University of Oxford.

8. Candidates who fail to satisfy the examiners in an assignment or in the research and development project may be permitted to resubmit the assignment or project report on one occasion only. In each case the deadline for resubmission is normally the standard submission deadline for the following year.

9. Candidates who fail outright an assignment within either Part I or Part II of the examination will not normally be permitted to embark on the next year's programme of study within the M.Sc. in Learning and Teaching until they have successfully resubmitted their assignment. Candidates who are awarded a marginal fail will normally be permitted to embark on the next year's programme of study within the M.Sc. in Learning and Teaching, but will be required to resubmit the assignment.

10. The award of Distinction within the M.Sc. in Learning and Teaching is normally reserved for those candidates who receive distinction marks for both the assignment submitted for Part II of the examination, and for the final research and development project report. The examiners may also award a distinction on occasion to a candidate who has achieved a high pass for Part II of the examination, and an appropriately high distinction in Part III of the examination.

11. Candidates may also be examined orally on their final research and development project.

12. Candidates who successfully complete Parts I and II of the M.Sc. in Learning and Teaching (or who are exempt from Part I and successfully complete Part II) and who choose not to continue with their programme of study may be awarded a Postgraduate Diploma in Learning and Teaching.

Schedule

Programme of study:

Teachers and Learners

Part I: Teacher identity and agency

Part II: Pupil identity and agency

Curriculum, pedagogy and assessment

Part I: Curriculum, pedagogy and assessment - introduction

Part II: Mediation, alignment and assessment design

Responding to pupils

Part I: Learners, diversity and inclusion

Part II: Motivation and task design

Schools, equity and achievement

Part I: Educational research, professional communities and networks

Part II: Policy, schooling and research

Master of Science by Coursework in Major Programme Management

1. Candidates will follow for six terms (part time), a programme of instruction in Major Programme Management and will, when entering for the examination, be required to produce a certificate to this effect from a supervisor of the M.Sc. in Major Programme Management appointed for the purpose.

2. The programme will consist of eight compulsory courses, as prescribed in the schedule, and a dissertation of 10,000 words. Candidates must satisfy the examiners in the assessment (assignment/practical work) associated with each component. Modes of assessment and submission dates will be published by the M.Sc. Director and distributed to all candidates in the first week of the Michaelmas Term of the year in which the assessment takes place. The dissertation should demonstrate an ability to identify, formulate, implement and present a project in the area of Major Programme Management. Two typewritten copies of the dissertation, not exceeding 10,000 words in length (including endnotes, appendices, tables, but excluding references), must be submitted to the Examination Schools and addressed to the Chair of Examiners for the M.Sc. in Major Programme Management, c/o the Examination Schools, High Street, Oxford, by noon on the first Monday of September in the calendar year in which the examination is taken.

3. Candidates who fail to satisfy the Examiners in the assessment of any one of the components may retake/resubmit the failed assessment only once, no more than six months after the release of results for the original piece of assessment. Candidates who fail to satisfy the examiners in the dissertation may resubmit it on one, but no more than one, occasion which shall be by Week 10 of the Hilary Term in the following year.

4. The Examiners may choose to examine any candidate or group viva voce.

5. The Examiners may award a distinction for overall excellence in the examination.

Schedule of Core Courses

(i) Designing and Managing Successful Programmes

(ii) Systems Engineering

(iii) Financial Management

(iv) Contract Management

(v) Major Programme Risk

(vi) Research Methods

(vii) Managing Performance

(viii) Globalisation and Major Programmes

Master of Science by Coursework in Management Research

1. Candidates must follow for three terms a course of instruction in Management 5
Research and will, when entering for the examination be required to produce a
certificate from a supervisor for the M.Sc. in Management Research appointed for
the purpose to this effect.

2. The course will consist of two parts and candidates must satisfy the examiners
in the assessment (assignment/examination/practical work) associated with each 10
component in Part One and Part Two. Modes of assessment and submission dates
will be published by the M.Sc. Director and distributed to all candidates in the first
week of the term in which the assessment takes place.

(a) *Part One*

(i) *Introduction to Research Methods*, as prescribed in the Schedule. This course 15
has two components-Management Research Methods, and Statistical Research
Methods (both of which are assessed in Part One).

(ii) *Management and Organisational Theory*, (core course in Management
Research) as prescribed in the Schedule.

(b) *Part Two* 20

(i) *Advanced Research Methods.* One of two possible Advanced Research
Methods courses (Qualitative or Quantitative).

(ii) *Two elective courses.* Two required specialist elective courses, one elective to be
taken and assessed in Hilary Term, and one elective to be taken and assessed in
Trinity term, chosen from the list of subjects and rubrics approved by the 25
M.Sc. Director and published in the *Gazette* not later than the end of the
Trinity term of the academic year preceding the year of the examination.

(iii) *Dissertation.* Candidates are required to submit a dissertation in an agreed field
of management research. The dissertation should demonstrate an ability to
identify, formulate, implement and present a research project. Three typewrit- 30
ten copies of the dissertation, not exceeding 15,000 words in length (including
endnotes, appendices, tables, but excluding references), must be submitted to
the Examination Schools and addressed to the Chair of Examiners for the
M.Sc. in Management Research, c/o Examination Schools, High Street,
Oxford, by noon on the first Monday of August in the calendar year in 35
which the examination is taken.

3. Candidates who fail to satisfy the Examiners in any one of the *Part One*
Introduction to Research Methods components, or the Management and
Organisational Theory core course assessment may retake/resubmit the failed assessment only once, by Week 10 of Trinity Term in the year in which the examination is 40
taken. Candidates who fail to satisfy the examiners in *Part Two* the Advanced
Research Methods course or in either one of the two required electives my resit or
resubmit the failed elective only once, by Week 0 of Hilary Term in the following year.
Candidates who fail to satisfy the Examiners in Part Two in the dissertation may
resubmit it on one, but no more than one, subsequent occasion, which shall be by 45
Week 0 of Hilary term in the following year.

4. The Examiners may choose to examine any candidate or group viva voce.

5. The Examiners may award a distinction for excellence for the overall examination of the course.

Schedule

(*a*) *Research Methods (Introduction to Research Methods and Advanced Research Methods)*   5

The two components address and discuss the nature of research in management studies and its relation to other social sciences, epistemology, strategies for literature review, research design, qualitative methods, interviewing, questionnaire design and ethnography, data sources and data collection, statistical methods, statistical and econometric modelling, analysis and interpretation of qualitative and quantitative   10
data and the presentation of research results.

(*b*) *Management and Organisational Theory*

The course aims to demonstrate and introduce the wide range of social science perspectives which can be brought to bear in the study of management and organisations. It will explore a range of epistemological and ontological interpretations of   15
management in organisations, especially emphasising recent developments in theory. It will do so by treating a series of key substantive issues and topics-for example, trust and accountability; rationality; language and discourse, technology-from each of two broadly contrasting theoretical commitments. The first commitment comprises those perspectives and frameworks that focus on structure and institutionalised arrange-   20
ments. A second comprises those approaches that emphasise action and process.

By the end of the course students should be equipped to identify and evaluate the relative merits of a diversity of theoretical perspectives. A second and complementary purpose of the course is to provide sufficient understanding of key concepts within management and organisation theory to enable the student to make informed deci-   25
sions on optional areas of study offered in subsequent terms.

Master of Science by Coursework in Mathematical and Computational Finance

1. The Divisional Board of Mathematical, Physical and Life Sciences shall appoint for the supervision of the course a supervisory committee, which shall have the power   30
to approve lectures and other instruction. The committee shall appoint a course organiser who will be responsible for ensuring that the programme is set up and the decisions of the committee are carried out.

2. The course organiser shall arrange for the appointment of a supervisor for each candidate.   35

3. Each candidate shall follow a course of study in Mathematical and Computational Finance for at least three terms and for a substantial part of the intervening vacations.

4. The examination will consist of the following parts:

(i) Two written examinations, and one take-home project, which will cover the   40
Michaelmas Term core courses in mathematical methods and numerical analysis, based on the schedule below. The written examinations will be organised within the department.

(ii) Candidates will be assessed on either the 'Modelling' Stream (covering Hilary Term modelling courses) or the 'Data Driven' Stream (covering Hilary Term   45
data driven courses). The 'Modelling' Stream will be assessed by a written examination. The 'Data Driven' Stream will be assessed by a written examination and a computer based practical examination. Further details will be specified in the Course Handbook on the Course Website. Examinations will be organised within the Department.   50

(iii) Candidates will be assessed on a 'Tools' Stream (covering Hilary Term courses on tools). The 'Tools' Stream will be assessed by a written examination. Further details will be specified in the Course Handbook on the Course Website. The examination will be organised within the Department.

(iv) One course in Quantitative Risk Management which will assessed by a take-home project.

(v) Two courses in Financial Computing with C++ which will be assessed by two practical examinations arranged within the Department. The details will be specified in the Course Handbook on the Course Website.

(vi) A dissertation of between twenty-five and forty pages on a topic approved by the examiners.

More detail on these requirements will be set out each year in the Course Handbook on the Course Website.

5. Take-home projects shall be submitted electronically. Submission shall be in accordance with both the details given in the Course Handbook on the Course Website and with the deadlines which the examiners shall determine and notify candidates of. In exceptional cases where a candidate is unable to submit work electronically, he or she must apply to the Standing Committee for permission to submit the work in paper form to the Examiners, c/o the Academic Administrator for Mathematical Finance, Mathematical Institute. Such applications must reach the Mathematical Institute not less than two weeks before the deadline for submitting the work.

6. Three copies of the dissertation must be delivered not later than noon on a date to be specified by the examiners which will normally be in late June, to the Examiners, M.Sc. in Mathematical and Computational Finance, c/o Examination Schools, High Street, Oxford OX1 4BG. A copy of the dissertation in pdf or other machine-readable format shall also be made available, in accordance with instructions which the examiners shall determine and notify candidates of. Candidates will also be required to give an oral presentation based on their dissertation.

7. The examiners may award a distinction for excellence in the whole course.

8. A candidate who fails the examination will be permitted to retake it on one further occasion only, not later than one year after the initial attempt. In such a case the examiners will specify at the time of failure which components of the examination may or must be redone.

Schedule

Mathematical methods including stochastic analysis, partial differential equations, probability and statistics. Mathematical models of financial markets; associated topics in financial economics. The numerical solution of ordinary, partial and stochastic differential equations. Monte Carlo methods. Numerical methods for optimisation. Programming in appropriate languages, and use of relevant packages.

Master of Science by Coursework in Mathematical and Theoretical Physics

1. The Examination in Mathematical and Theoretical Physics shall be under the supervision of the Mathematical, Physical and Life Sciences Board.

2. The Divisional Board of Mathematical, Physical and Life Sciences shall appoint for the supervision of the course a supervisory committee, which shall have the power to approve lectures and other instruction. The committee shall appoint a Director of Studies who will be responsible for ensuring that the programme is set up and the decisions of the committee are carried out.

3. The subject of the M.Sc. of Mathematical and Theoretical Physics shall be Mathematical and Theoretical Physics and related subjects.

4. In the following 'the Course Handbook' refers to the Mathematical and Theoretical Physics Handbook and supplements to this published by the Joint Supervisory Committee for Mathematical and Theoretical Physics.

5. Each candidate shall follow a course of study in Mathematical and Theoretical Physics for at least three terms.

6. Candidates will complete and be assessed on the following parts:

    (i) Candidates will offer 10 units with one unit corresponding to a 16 hour lecture course.

    (ii) At least four units will be assessed by written, invigilated examinations which will take place. Examination details will be published in the Course Handbook.

    (iii) Candidates may offer one unit which is a dissertation. The dissertation will follow the guidelines and procedures of the Part C Mathematics course outlined in the Special Regulations for the Honour School of Mathematics.

    (iv) The other units will be assessed by marked course work, take-home papers or mini-projects. The Course Handbook will specify which units will be assessed by each method mentioned above and sets out the rules governing submission of coursework. In addition, for certain courses, an electronic copy may be required. Details of the courses to which this applies, and instructions for the online submission process will be included in the Notice to Candidates that applies to the candidates of the M.Sc. of Mathematical and Theoretical Physics.

    (v) Candidates will be required to attend an oral examination at the end of the course of studies.

7. The examiners may award a distinction for excellence in the whole examination.

8. A candidate who fails to satisfy the Examiners may retake the examination on at most one subsequent occasion, not later than one year after the initial attempt. In such a case the examiners will specify at the time of failure which components of the examination may or must be redone.

9. Syllabus and examination details will be published each year in the Course Handbook and on the course web pages by the beginning of the Michaelmas Full Term in the academic year of the examination.

Master of Science by Coursework in Mathematical Finance

For students registering on the M.Sc. in Mathematical Finance in or after January 2012 and available to those who enrolled on the M.Sc. or PGDip. in Mathematical Finance in or before January 2011 and who have not already been awarded the relevant qualification.

1. Every student must follow a part-time course of instruction in the theory and practice of Mathematical Finance.

2. The Mathematical, Physical and Life Sciences Board shall elect for the supervision of the M.Sc. a Supervisory Committee which shall have the power to arrange lectures and other instruction.

3. The following awards shall be available to students registering on the M.Sc. in Mathematical Finance:

    (i) M.Sc. in Mathematical Finance

    (ii) Postgraduate Diploma in Mathematical Finance

4. Admission is only to the M.Sc. in Mathematical Finance.

5. Exceptionally, a candidate for the M.Sc. in Mathematical Finance may apply to be awarded the Postgraduate Diploma in Mathematical Finance, subject to such a candidate having satisfied the criteria for that award as set out in clauses 7 and 10 below. Candidates so awarded the Postgraduate Diploma cease, at that point, to be registered for the M.Sc. in Mathematical Finance, and may not normally be re-admitted to the M.Sc.

6. To be eligible for the award of an M.Sc., a student must be on the Register for the M.Sc. for at least seven terms.

7. To be eligible for the Postgraduate Diploma, a student must be on the Register for the M.Sc. for at least four terms.

8. A student may apply to extend for five further terms up to a maximum of twelve terms in total.

9. Every candidate will be required to satisfy the examiners in the following:

(*a*) *M.Sc. in Mathematical Finance*

    (i) attendance at each core module as detailed in Section A, and three advanced modules from Section B, of the Schedule below;

    (ii) two written examinations, covering material relevant to the core modules in Section A of the Schedule;

    (iii) three assignments chosen from the advanced modules in Section B of the Schedule. Assignments should be of no more than ten sides of A4 in length (excluding tables, appendices, footnotes and bibliography);

    (iv) a dissertation of not more than forty five sides of A4 in length (excluding the abstract, tables, appendices, footnotes and bibliography), on a subject selected by the candidate in consultation with the supervisor and approved by the Supervisory Committee.

(*b*) *Postgraduate Diploma in Mathematical Finance*

    (i) attendance at each core module as detailed in Section A, and three advanced modules from Section B, of the Schedule below;

    (ii) two written examinations, covering material relevant to the core modules in Section A of the Schedule;

    (iii) three assignments chosen from the advanced modules in Section B of the Schedule. Assignments should be of no more than ten sides of A4 in length (excluding tables, appendices, footnotes and bibliography).

The assignments under (*a*) (iii) and (*b*) (iii) above, and the dissertation under (*a*) (iv) above, shall usually be submitted electronically, in accordance with details given in the handbook, by such date as the examiners shall determine and shall notify candidates.

Any candidate who is unable, for some reason, to submit work electronically must apply to the Supervisory Committee for permission to submit the work in paper form to the examiners c/o the Academic Administrator for Mathematical Finance, Mathematical Institute. Such applications must reach the Mathematical Institute two weeks before the deadline for submitting the work.

10. Candidates may be required to attend a viva voce examination at the end of the course of studies (for the M.Sc. or the Postgraduate Diploma) at the discretion of the examiners.

11. The examiners may award a distinction to candidates for the M.Sc. or Postgraduate Diploma.

12. Candidates who fail to satisfy the examiners in the written examinations under 9 (*a*) (ii) or (*b*) (ii), the assignments under 9 (*a*) (iii) or (*b*) (iii), or the dissertation under 9 (*a*) (iv) may be permitted to resubmit work in respect of the part or parts of the examination which they have failed on one further occasion. In the case of the written

examinations, this shall normally be on the occasion of the written examinations next following; in the case of assignments or the dissertation, the work shall normally be resubmitted within one year of the decision of the examiners.

13. In the exceptional circumstances that a candidate previously awarded the Postgraduate Diploma is re-admitted to the M.Sc. and is successful in the examination for the M.Sc. having for that examination incorporated the assignments submitted for the Postgraduate Diploma, then the subsequent award will subsume his or her previous award.

Schedule

Section A: Core Modules

The Supervisory Committee shall approve the content of four core modules to be given each year which shall be published in the handbook. The following components will be covered: Mathematical Techniques; Derivative Pricing; Portfolio Theory and Asset Pricing; Numerical Methods; Interest Rates.

Candidates may, in exceptional circumstances, and with the permission of the Supervisory Committee, be exempt from attendance at part of the first core module undertaken.

Section B: Advanced Modules

The Supervisory Committee shall approve the content of at least three advanced modules to be given each year which shall be made known to students by the end of Week Eight of the Trinity term in the calendar year in which the written examination is held.

Master of Science by Coursework in Mathematical Modelling and Scientific Computing

1. The Divisional Board of Mathematical, Physical and Life Sciences shall appoint for the supervision of the course a supervisory committee, including a member from outside the University, which shall have the power to approve lectures and other instruction. The committee shall appoint a course organiser who will be responsible for ensuring that the programme is set up and the decisions of the committee are carried out.

2. The course organiser shall arrange for the appointment of a supervisor for each candidate.

3. Each candidate shall follow a course of study in Mathematical Modelling and Scientific Computing for three terms and their corresponding vacations.

4. Candidates will complete and be assessed on all the following parts:

  (i) Four written examinations on core course material in mathematical methods and numerical analysis. These examinations will be organised within the department [1 unit each];

  (ii) Two Special Topics chosen from a list that will be published each year. One special topic should be labelled 'Modelling' and one should be labelled 'Scientific Computing'. These special Topics will be assessed by a written project [1 unit each];

  (iii) Case Studies in Mathematical Modelling and Scientific Computing. Students will submit a project on each of these courses for assessment [1 unit each];

  (iv) One further Special Topic or one further Case Study in either Mathematical Modelling or Scientific Computing [1 unit];

  (v) A dissertation on a topic approved by the examiners. The dissertation need not necessarily contain original research to pass. [4 units].

The detailed requirements will be set out each year on the course website.

5. Three copies of the dissertation must be delivered not later than noon on a date to be specified by the examiners which will normally be a Friday in early September to the Examiners, M.Sc. in Mathematical Modelling and Scientific Computing, c/o Examination Schools, High Street. The examiners may also direct that a copy of the dissertation in pdf or other machine-readable format be made available.   5

6. Candidates will be required to attend an oral examination at the end of the course of studies.

7. In addition to the academic elements of the course there will be a programme of career development activities requiring participation from each student.

8. The examiners may award a distinction for excellence in the whole course.   10

9. A candidate who fails the course will be permitted to retake it on one further occasion only, not later than one year after the initial attempt. In such a case the examiners will specify at the time of failure which of the assessed components of the course may or must be redone.

Schedule   15

Mathematical methods including ordinary and partial differential equations, transforms, applications of complex variable theory, distributions and asymptotics. Mathematical modelling and application of mathematics to problems in physical sciences, biology and medicine, industry and other areas.

The numerical solution of ordinary and partial differential equations. Finite element methods, numerical linear algebra, numerical methods for optimisation and approximation.   20

Master of Science by Coursework in Mathematics and Foundations of Computer Science

1. The Divisional Board of Mathematical, Physical and Life Sciences shall elect for the supervision of the course a Standing Committee which shall have power to arrange lectures and other instruction.   25

2. Candidates shall follow for at least three terms a course of instruction in Mathematics and Foundations of Computer Science.

3. The examination shall be in three parts, as follows: 30

(*a*) Candidates shall successfully complete a written assignment on each of five courses chosen from a list of courses approved by the Standing Committee and published in the course handbook. The list of courses shall be divided into two sections: Section A (Mathematical Foundations) and Section B (Applicable Theories). Each section shall be divided into schedule I (basic) and schedule II   35
(advanced). Candidates shall be required to satisfy the examiners in at least two courses taken from Section B and in at least two courses taken from schedule II (these need not be distinct).

(*b*) Candidates shall submit a short dissertation on a topic selected by the candidate in consultation with the supervisor and approved by the Standing Committee.   40
The dissertation must bear regard to course material from Sections A or B. Between thirty-five and sixty-five typed pages is the preferred length.

(*c*) There shall be an oral examination on the dissertation and its background material, and the candidate shall normally be expected to give a short presentation on the dissertation.   45

4. Candidates must submit to the chair of the Standing Committee by the end of the second week of Trinity Term in the year in which they enter the examination, the title and a brief statement of the form and scope of their dissertation, together with the name of a person who has agreed to act as their supervisor during the preparation of the dissertation.   50

5. Two typewritten copies of the dissertation must be delivered not later than noon on 1 September in the year in which the examination is taken, to the M.Sc. Examiners (Mathematics and Foundations of Computer Science), c/o Examination Schools, High Street, Oxford. The examiners may retain one copy of the dissertation of each candidate who passes the examination for deposit in an appropriate departmental library.

6. Each candidate in consultation with their supervisor shall notify the director of the course of their intention to offer a written assignment for a lecture course not later than the Friday of the third week of each term. No candidate may offer more than four courses in one term. There will be a written assignment for each course. The topics in the assignment will be suggested by the relevant lecturer not later than the Monday of eighth week of the term during which the course is given. These topics will be sufficient to offer options appropriate to the course. The choice of topics will vary from year to year. Completed assignments must be delivered not later than noon on the Monday of the eleventh week of the term during which the course is offered, to the M.Sc. Examiners (Mathematics and Foundations of Computer Science), c/o Examination Schools, High Street, Oxford, together with a signed statement that the work offered for assessment is the candidate's own.

7. A candidate who does not submit a written assignment on a course for which he or she has entered, by noon on the Monday of the eleventh week of the relevant term, shall be deemed to have failed the course in question.

8. If a candidate is deemed to have failed a particular course, he or she shall not be permitted to re-enter for examination in that course in the same year.

Any candidate who has not satisfied the examiners in four courses, at least one of which shall have been taken from schedule II and at least one from Schedule B, by the beginning of the Trinity Term shall be deemed to have failed the degree course.

9. A candidate who has failed to satisfy the examiners in the examination may be admitted to, and examined on, the course as offered in the year subsequent to the initial attempt. No piece of written work shall be submitted for examination on more than one occasion.

10. The examiners may award a distinction for excellence in the whole examination.

Master of Science by Coursework in Medical Anthropology

1. The Social Sciences Divisional Board shall elect for the supervision of the course a Standing Committee, namely the Teaching Committee of the School of Anthropology, which shall have power to arrange lectures and other instruction. The course director will be responsible to this committee.

2. Candidates must follow a course of instruction in Medical Anthropology for at least three terms, and will, when entering for the examination, be required to produce a certificate from their supervisor to this effect.

3. Candidates will be required to present themselves for written and, where invited, oral examinations, and to submit three copies of a dissertation in prescribed form on an approved topic as defined below.

4. The written examination will consist of four papers on the syllabus described in the Schedule.

5. Each candidate will be required to submit a dissertation of no more than 10,000 words, on a subject selected in consultation with the supervisor and approved by the Chair of Examiners. The proposed title of the dissertation together with a paragraph describing its scope and the supervisor's written endorsement, must be submitted to the Chair of Examiners by Tuesday of the second week of Trinity Term.

6. Three typewritten copies of the dissertation must be delivered not later than noon on the last Wednesday in August in the year in which the examination is taken, to the Chair of the Examiners, M.Sc. in Medical Anthropology, c/o Examination Schools, High Street, Oxford. The dissertation shall be provided with an abstract of up to 250 words, to be placed immediately after the title page. The word count shall be stated on the outside front cover of the thesis.

7. An oral examination, if held, may be on the candidate's written papers, or dissertation, or both.

8. The examiners may award a distinction for excellence in the whole examination.

The four papers will be taken to constitute Part I of the degree and the dissertation to constitute Part II. At the close of the written examinations, the examiners will publish a list of those who have satisfied them in Part I.

9. In order to pass the degree, a student must pass all its assessed components. Where one or more components are failed, the student will be given the opportunity to re-sit or re-submit them once, as the case may be. Any subsequent award of the degree on successful completion of all the assessed components may be delayed by up to three terms, i.e. until the Examination Board next meets.

Schedule

Every candidate will be required to satisfy the examiners in four papers as follows:

1. *Concepts of disease, illness, health and medicine in global perspective*

The scope of this paper includes discussion of cross-cultural concepts of health, disease, sickness, pain, illness causation, diagnosis and treatment, from conjoined sociocultural perspectives and human ecology. It explores metaphor and narrative at the interface of biological and cultural processes, the distribution of disease patterns in the light of environmental change, social inequality, global mobility and marginality, and the coexistence of conventional, alternative and traditional health systems.

2. *Theory and practice of bio-medicine and of other medical systems*

The scope of this paper includes issues of public health and policy on a comparative and global basis. It draws on ethnographies of particular societies to illustrate and test theoretical claims in medical anthropology. It discusses infectious diseases, specific health campaigns, evolutionary trends and life histories, alongside culturally defined concepts of risk, vulnerability, fate, evil, pollution, divination, religion, and shamanism.

3. *Critical medical anthropology*

The scope of this paper comprises ecological and socio-cultural perspectives, and explores links to other fields and disciplines, including the place of material culture in medicine. It includes a critique of basic assumptions and methods in medical anthropology and consideration of the concept of well-being as being broader than conventional concepts of health. Themes for discussion include the phenomenology of the body, growth and personhood, gender, ageing and dying, notions of resistance and resilience, relationships between biodiversity and adaptability, reproduction and fertility, and nutrition.

4. *Option paper*

Candidates must select one option paper from those taught each year for the M.Sc. in Social Anthropology. Titles of options will be made available by the end of the third week of Michaelmas Term at the beginning of each academic year, and candidates may select their option from any of Lists A, B, or C.

Master of Science by Coursework in Migration Studies

1. The Social Sciences Board shall elect for the supervision of the course a Standing Committee, which shall consist of the Directors of the Centre on Migration, Policy and Society (COMPAS) and of the International Migration Institute (IMI) ex officio, the course director, and two other members of the teaching staff drawn from the Oxford Department of International Development and the School of Anthropology, which shall have the power to arrange lectures and other instruction. The course director shall be responsible to that committee.

2. Candidates must follow a course of instruction in Migration Studies for at least three terms and will, when entering for the examinations, be required to produce a certificate from their supervisor to this effect. Candidates will be expected to attend such lectures and seminars as their supervisor/course director shall recommend.

3. The final examination shall be taken in Trinity Term of the academic year in which the candidate's name is first entered on the Register of M.Sc Students or, with the approval of the Board, in a subsequent year.

4. The examiners may at their discretion require any candidate to attend for a viva voce examination.

5. Each candidate will be required to satisfy the examiners in five papers in accordance with I, II, III, IV, and V below.

I *International Migration in the Social Sciences: An Interdisciplinary Introduction*

6. The paper will cover theories and approaches in migration studies; basic concepts in migration studies; types of human migration and mobility; the history and development of migration studies. Assessment of this paper will take place in the form of one written essay of a maximum of 5,000 words (excluding notes and bibliography). This essay will be expected to display an understanding of key concepts and analysis in the economics, politics, sociology and anthropology of migration. Candidates shall submit their essay to the Examination Schools no later than 12 noon on Tuesday of the first week of the Hilary Term of the course, accompanied by a statement that the essay is the candidate's own work except where otherwise indicated.

II *Migration, Globalisation and Social Transformation*

7. This paper will be examined by means of a three-hour written examination to be taken during Trinity Term. Candidates will be expected to display understanding of the major debates in contemporary migration, including theoretical and practical questions and issues that currently drive research in the field of migration studies. Topics to be covered will vary from year to year, depending on changes in the focus of migration studies.

III *Elective paper*

8. Candidates' understanding of the two options they choose will be assessed through two sets of questions in an options paper. A list of papers approved for this purpose by the Standing Committee will be available from the course director by Monday of sixth week of Michaelmas Term. Students are free to elect any one of these papers in consultation with their supervisor. The examiners may, at their discretion, either require candidates to sit the standard examination paper for this elective paper, or else set a paper specifically for students on the M.Sc. in Migration Studies.

IV *Methods in Social Research*

9. Each student must display an understanding of research methods relevant to migration studies, which will be assessed by satisfactory completion of a course of practical work. This paper will cover (i) participant observation, in-depth interviewing, archival research, and qualitative data analysis; (ii) basic principles of statistical inference, and statistical models for the analysis of quantitative social science data; (iii)

methods of data collection, including questionnaire design, interviewing and coding; and (iv) basic principles of statistical modelling in the social sciences.

10. Assessment of this paper shall take the form of three pieces of coursework, written during Michaelmas Term and Hilary Term. Candidates shall submit a portfolio consisting of copies of all coursework to the Examination Schools no later than 12 noon on Tuesday of noughth week of the Trinity Term of the course, accompanied by a statement that the coursework is the candidate's own work except where otherwise indicated.

V *Dissertation*

11. Each candidate shall be required to submit a dissertation of not more than 15,000 words (excluding references and appendices) on a subject approved by the supervisor. The candidate shall send to the Standing Committee, with the written approval of his or her supervisor, the proposed title of the dissertation for consideration by the Standing Committee, by noon on the Friday of the first week of Hilary Term in the academic year in which his or her name was entered on the Register of M.Sc. Students.

12. The dissertation (three copies) must be typewritten and delivered to the Examination Schools, High Street, Oxford, not later than noon on Thursday of eighth week of Trinity Term in the year in which the examination is taken. An electronic copy must also be submitted to the M.Sc. in Migration Studies Course Coordinator, again by the date and time specified above. The dissertation must be presented in proper scholarly form, in 1.5 line spacing and double-sided on A4 paper, each copy bound or held firmly in a stiff cover. The dissertation must be marked for the attention of the Chair of Examiners, M.Sc. in Migration Studies, c/o Examination Schools, High Street, Oxford. The word count shall be stated on the outside front cover of the dissertation. The examiners shall retain a copy of the dissertation of each candidate who passes the examination for deposit in the Social Sciences Library.

13. The examiners may award a distinction for excellence in the whole examination.

14. If it is the opinion of the examiners that the work done by a candidate is not of sufficient merit to qualify for the degree of M.Sc., the candidate shall be given the option of re-sitting the M.Sc. examination on one further occasion only, normally not later than one year after the first attempt.

Master of Science by Coursework in Modern Japanese Studies

1. Candidates will be required to present themselves for examination EITHER in a compulsory paper in Japanese Language; and in two optional subjects at the end of Trinity Term in the year of registration; OR in three optional subjects at the end of Trinity Term in the year of registration.

Candidates taking the examination in Japanese Language will also be required to undertake a series of written tests and essays as specified by the M.Sc./M.Phil. Programme in Modern Japanese Studies Committee. The forms of assessment, and the dates and times of submission, where applicable, will be notified to students not later than Friday of noughth week of Michaelmas Full Term.

2. In addition, all candidates will be required to undertake the following assessment:

(i) Research Methods for Area Studies: a series of assignments and/or an unseen written examination as specified by the M.Sc./M.Phil. Programme in Modern Japanese Studies Committee. The forms of assessment, and the dates and times of submission, where applicable, will be notified to students by not later than Friday of noughth week of Michaelmas Full Term.

(ii) One 10,000 word dissertation: the title of the dissertation must be approved by the Director of Graduate Studies by not later than 12 noon on Friday of fourth week of Hilary Full Term in the year in which the examination is taken. The dissertation must be submitted by not later than 12 noon of the weekday on or nearest to 1 September in the year in which the examination is taken. The dissertation must be accompanied by a statement that the dissertation is the candidate's own work except where otherwise indicated.

Two typewritten or word processed copies of the dissertation must be delivered to the Examination Schools, addressed to the Chair of Examiners for the M.Sc. in Modern Japanese Studies, c/o Examination Schools, High Street, Oxford at the times and days specified. Successful candidates will be required to deposit one copy of the dissertation in the Bodleian Library.

3 Candidates who fail one or more of the elements of the final examination will be permitted to resubmit the relevant work or retake the examination paper or papers, as applicable, on one further occasion only, not later than one year after the first attempt.

4. Candidates may be required to attend an oral examination on any part of the examination.

5. The examiners may award a distinction for excellence in the whole examination.

6. In consultation with their supervisor and the Director of Graduate Studies, candidates may apply to change to the M.Phil. in Modern Japanese Studies degree no later than Friday of Week 9 of Hilary Term.

Schedule

The structure of the course is as follows:
EITHER Mode A

    (a) *Compulsory core course in Japanese Language*

    (b) *Research Methods for Area Studies*

    (c) *Optional papers:* Candidates must choose two optional papers from a list published annually and distributed to students by not later than Friday of noughth week of Michaelmas Full Term.

OR Mode B

    (a) *Research Methods for Area Studies*

    (b) *Optional papers:* Candidates must choose three optional papers from a list published annually and distributed to students by not later than Friday of noughth week of Michaelmas Full Term.

Master of Science by Coursework in Musculoskeletal Sciences

1. The Medical Sciences Board shall elect for the supervision of the course an Organising Committee, which shall have the power to arrange teaching, assessments and other instruction.

2. The Organising Committee shall appoint for each candidate an academic supervisor.

3. Candidates will hold a first degree in medicine, or exceptionally a biomedical science degree.

4. Candidates shall follow a course of study in Musculoskeletal Sciences on a part-time basis for at least six terms, and including vacations, as determined by the course timetable. The course commences every two years in January and runs until December of the following year.

5. Candidates shall be examined in all of the following ways:

(i) Year 1 (January to December)

    (*a*) Each candidate shall submit a literature review of no more than 4,000 words on a topic selected by the candidate and approved by the Organising Committee. The review must be submitted during Week 2 of Michaelmas term on a date to be specified in the course handbook.   5

    (*b*) Each candidate must pass an examination in Michaelmas Term. The examination will comprise two elements: the first of these will consist of a one-hour computer-based assessment comprising multiple-choice questions; the second of these will constitute a two-hour written paper. The dates of the examination will be specified in the course handbook.   10

(ii) Year 2 (January to December)

    (*a*) Each candidate must submit, for assessment of their progress, an outline research proposal. The outline must be submitted in Hilary Term on a date to be specified in the course handbook.

    (*b*) Each candidate will be assessed on their presentation skills by means of a public oral presentation on his or her research topic. The presentation must take place in Trinity Term on a date to be specified in the course handbook.   15

    (*c*) Each candidate must submit a written research proposal of no more than 10,000 words on a topic selected by the candidate and approved by the Organising Committee. The proposal must be submitted in Michaelmas Term on a date to be specified in the course handbook.   20

    (*d*) Each candidate must pass an examination in Michaelmas Term. The examination will comprise two elements: the first of these will consist of a one-hour computer-based assessment comprising multiple-choice questions; the second of these will constitute a two-hour written paper. The dates of the examination will be specified in the course handbook.   25

6. Candidates may be examined viva voce on their research proposal. The viva voce examination will normally be conducted at the end of the course.

7. Candidates must pass each examination or written assignment in order to pass overall.   30

8. Candidates will be allowed one opportunity to retake or resubmit each of the required elements, normally within six months of the original failure, should they fail to reach the necessary standard. Candidates failing to pass any element at the second attempt will normally be judged to have failed to reach the necessary standard for the award and will not be permitted to continue.   35

9. The required written submissions must be sent to the Chair of Examiners, M.Sc. in Musculoskeletal Sciences, c/o Examination Schools, High Street, Oxford. Submissions must be accompanied by a declaration of authorship and originality.

10. The examiners may award a distinction for excellence in part of or in the whole examination.   40

11. The examiners may award a postgraduate diploma to candidates who have satisfied the requirements for the award of the Postgraduate Diploma (comprising all assessments with the exception of the written research proposal) and who do not wish to continue their studies, or who fail to meet the required standard for the written research proposal.   45

Schedule

The syllabus for study will include the following components:

Core Subjects

    Candidates are required to complete all of the following modules:

1. Principles of Musculoskeletal Diseases
2. Research, Statistics and Epidemiology
3. Scientific Aspects of Common Musculoskeletal Diseases

Specialist Subjects
Candidates are required to complete one of the following modules: 5
1. Advanced Rheumatology
2. Advanced Orthopaedics

Master of Science by Coursework in Nature, Society, and Environmental Governance

1. The Social Sciences Divisional Board shall elect for the supervision of the course   10
a Standing Committee. The Academic Director(s) and Course Director will be responsible to the Standing Committee.

2. Candidates must follow a course of instruction in Human Geography for at least
three terms, and will, when entering for the examination, be required to produce a
certificate from the Course Director to this effect.   15

3. The examination will consist of:

   (i) a written examination of three three-hour papers as described in the schedule;

   (ii) two assessed essays based upon elective courses;

   (iii) a dissertation on a subject selected in consultation with the supervisor and the
        Course Director and approved by the Course and Academic Directors.   20

4. Candidates must submit to the Course Director by the end of Hilary Term in the
year in which they enter the examination, the title and a brief statement of the form
and scope of their dissertation, together with the name of a person who has agreed to
act as their supervisor during preparation of the dissertation.

It may be (*a*) a theoretical argument related to themes in contemporary human   25
geography and/or environmental governance, or (*b*) a piece of empirically based
research, or (*c*) an extended treatment of an issue which is intended to be the basis
for future research for the degree of M.Litt. or D.Phil. In that case (*c*), it may be part
of a proposal and/or application for further degree study.

5. The dissertation shall be of a maximum length of 15,000 words and accompanied   30
by an abstract not exceeding 150 words. The maximum word count shall include
footnotes, but exclude appendices, references and the abstract. The detailed format
and specification of the dissertation shall be approved by the Standing Committee,
and published in the course handbook.

6. The deadline for submission is noon on the first weekday of September in the   35
year in which the written examination is taken. Two copies of the dissertation must be
submitted, to the M.Sc examiners (Nature, Society and Environmental Governance),
c/o Examination Schools, High Street, Oxford OX1 4BG. The examiners may retain
one copy of the dissertation of each candidate who passes the examination for deposit
in an appropriate library. Both copies must bear the candidate's examination number   40
but not his/her name.

7. All submitted work shall be accompanied by a separate statement certifying that
the submitted work is the candidate's own work except where otherwise indicated.

8. In the written examination the examiners will permit the use of hand-held pocket calculators subject to the conditions set out under the heading 'Use of calculators in examinations' in the *Regulations for the Conduct of University Examinations.*

9. The examiners may also examine any candidate viva voce on the candidate's written papers, dissertation, or both.

10. Arrangements for reassessment shall be agreed by the Standing Committee and published in the course handbook.

11. The examiners may award a distinction for excellence in the whole examination.

Schedule

(*a*) *Core courses*

The core courses will be examined under the following heads:

1. *Research Skills*

Candidates will be expected to have a knowledge of research methods in social, environmental, and geographical research. These will include qualitative and quantitative methods relevant to contemporary research themes.

2. *Theory and Analysis*

Candidates will be expected to have knowledge of relevant debates in human geography and related disciplines concerning the relations between nature and society, science and environmental politics, and global and local political and economic processes.

3. *Policy and Governance*

Candidates will be expected to have knowledge of relevant debates and issues concerning environmental policy and governance, and corporate environmental management.

(*b*) *Elective courses*

Candidates will be expected to show advanced knowledge of two of the elective courses on offer in any one year.

Master of Science by Coursework in Neuroscience

1. The Divisional Board of Medical Sciences shall elect for the supervision of the course an Organising Committee which shall have power to arrange lectures and other instruction.

2. The Organising Committee shall appoint for each candidate an academic advisor.

3. Each candidate shall follow a course of study in Neuroscience for at least three terms and for a substantial part of the three subsequent vacations, as determined by the course timetable, and will, when entering for the examination, be required to produce a certificate from the Organising Committee to this effect.

4. Candidates shall be examined in all of the following ways:

   (i) each candidate must pass a qualifying examination at the end of the first term from the beginning of the course. The test shall consist of the satisfactory completion of the Neuroscience Introductory Course and one three-hour written paper on the topics covered in that course, as set out in the Schedule; the Organising Committee shall not later than the end of the Hilary Term preceding the examination submit to the examiners a list of candidates who have satisfactorily completed the qualifying examination. Candidates who fail the qualifying examination once shall be permitted to take it again in the first week of Hilary Term of the year of the final examination;

(ii) each candidate will be required to submit to the examiners *either* two copies of a typewritten or printed essay of not more than 3,000 words on a topic approved by the Organising Committee in each of the five modules chosen for study, as set out in the Schedule, *or* in the case of the modules specified by the Organising Committee one practical notebook in each module chosen for study; candidates must submit their titles for approval by deadlines determined by the Organising Committee and posted in the *Gazette* no later than the end of the preceding term;

(iii) each candidate will be required to submit to the examiners three copies of a typewritten or printed dissertation of not more than 10,000 words (excluding bibliography and appendices) on each of the two research projects chosen for study, as set out in the Schedule;

(iv) each candidate will be required to give a public oral presentation on each of his or her research projects, on dates to be determined by the Organising Committee.

5. Each candidate will be examined viva voce.

6. Before being given leave to supplicate, candidates must have demonstrated understanding of and competence in the topics covered by the professional development programme as set out in the Schedule, to the satisfaction of the programme organisers, who shall submit a certificate to the examiners to this effect.

7. The required written submissions must be sent to the Chair of Examiners, M.Sc. in Neuroscience, c/o Examination Schools, High Street, Oxford, on the following dates:

(*a*) The dissertations on the first and second research projects must be submitted by dates to be specified by the Organising Committee and which will be published in the *University Gazette* not later than the start of Michaelmas Term of the academic year in which the examination is taken.

(*b*) The essays or the practical notebooks for each module must be submitted by deadlines determined by the Organising Committee and posted in the *Gazette* no later than the end of the preceding term.

Each submission must be accompanied by a certificate indicating that it is the candidate's own work.

8. The viva voce examinations will be conducted in September in the year in which the candidate is examined on dates to be determined by the examiners.

9. The examiners may award a distinction for excellence in the whole examination.

10. The examiners shall retain one copy of each dissertation of each successful candidate for deposit in the most appropriate departmental library.

Schedule

The syllabus for study will include four principal components:

(*a*) *Professional Development Programme for Neuroscientists*

Candidates will be required to follow a programme of Professional Development courses to provide transferable skills for a career in scientific research. The programme will consist of practical exercises and taught classes with interactive discussions and practical assignments in the following areas:

(i) Presentation skills, verbal and written;

(ii) Career planning, assessing personal skills and values, curricula vitae, and interview techniques;

(iii) Exploitation of science: patents and intellectual property;

(iv) Ethical and social issues in science.

(*b*) *Introduction to Neuroscience*

Five module introduction to neuroscience, each consisting of lectures and practicals. Candidates who have already received training in neuroscience may, at the discretion of the Organising Committee, be exempted from attendance at one or more of the introductory modules. Such candidates will be required to pass the qualifying examination which will cover the topics covered in the Introduction to Neuroscience. They will be required to follow an alternative course of instruction approved by the Organising Committee.

Module I: Introduction to the brain

Module II: Neuroanatomy

Module III: Neuronal Cell and Molecular Biology

Module IV: Synapses and transduction

Module V: Systems overview.

Candidates will also be required to take courses on experimental design, computing, and statistics, approved by the Organising Committee.

(*c*) *Specialist neuroscience courses*

This will consist of five taught courses consisting of lectures, seminars, practicals, and demonstrations, chosen from a list of courses in neuroscience to be approved annually by the Organising Committee. These will be grouped under three headings: molecular, cellular, and systems, and candidates will be required to choose at least one course under each of the three headings. Details of the courses available in each academic year will be published in the *Gazette* in the preceding Trinity Term.

(*d*) *Laboratory research projects*

Two research projects based on the candidate's laboratory placements, each under the supervision of a research supervisor, on subjects selected in consultation with the Organising Committee. The research projects shall be in separate areas of neuroscience.

Master of Science by Coursework in Paediatric Infectious Diseases

1. The Divisional Board of Medical Sciences, jointly with the Continuing Education Board, shall elect for the supervision of the course a Standing Committee, which shall have the power to arrange lectures and other instruction.

2. Candidates for admission will be required to have completed the assessment and participation requirements for the Postgraduate Diploma in Paediatric Infectious Diseases not more than six terms before admission to the M.Sc. A candidate who is subsequently unsuccessful in the Postgraduate Diploma in Paediatric Infectious Diseases will not be permitted to remain on the register for the M.Sc.

3. The course may be taken on a part-time basis over a period of three terms.

4. Candidates may be permitted under certain circumstances to suspend status, for a maximum of six terms. Any such period shall not count towards the maximum or minimum permitted period of registration and no fee liability will be incurred during such periods. Any period of suspension taken during the Postgraduate Diploma shall count towards the maximum permitted.

5. Every candidate shall be required to satisfy the examiners in the following:

(*a*) Participation in dissertation supervisions

(*b*) A dissertation of not more than 15,000 words on a research project selected by the candidate in consultation with the supervisor and approved by the Standing Committee

The dissertation under clause 5(*b*) shall be submitted in hard copy and on disc (or equivalent media) to the examiners for the M.Sc in Paediatric Infectious Diseases c/o   5
Examination Schools High Street Oxford OX1 4BG, no later than noon on the 30th September in the final year of the course, or the immediately preceding Friday if that date falls on a weekend.

6. Candidates may be required to attend a viva voce examination at the end of the course of studies at the discretion of the examiners.   10

7. The examiners may award a distinction to candidates for the M.Sc.

8. A candidate who fails to satisfy the examiners in the dissertation may be permitted to resubmit on one further occasion only, not later than one year after the initial failure.

9. A candidate who is successful in the examination for the M.Sc. in Paediatric   15
Infectious Diseases and has previously completed the Postgraduate Diploma in Paediatric Infectious Diseases shall have his or her Diploma subsumed by the M.Sc.

Master of Science by Coursework in Pharmacology

1. The Divisional Board of Medical Sciences shall appoint for the supervision of the course an Organising Committee, which shall have the power to arrange lectures   20
and other instruction.

2. The Organising Committee shall appoint for each candidate an academic advisor (*mentor*).

3. Each candidate shall:

(*a*) follow a course of study in Pharmacology for at least three terms and for a   25
substantial part of the three subsequent vacations, as determined by the course timetable;

(*b*) attend practical classes which will be compulsory (a record of attendance will be kept);

(*c*) when they submit their dissertations in September, produce a certificate   30
from their academic advisor to the effect that they have fulfilled the requirements of (*a*) and (*b*).

4. Candidates shall be examined in all of the following ways:

(i) each candidate must pass a qualifying examination at the end of Michaelmas Term. The test shall consist of one three-hour written paper   35
on the topics covered by the Pharmacology Introductory Course, as set out in the Schedule. The Organising Committee shall not later than the end of the Hilary Term preceding the final examination submit to the examiners a list of candidates who have satisfactorily completed the qualifying examination. Candidates who fail the qualifying examination   40
once shall be permitted to take it again in the first week of the Hilary Term of the year of the final examination.

(ii) each candidate must pass a three-hour data handling and experimental design examination (also known as the quantitative examination) during Hilary Term. Candidates must pass the examination in order to proceed   45
with the course, and those who fail shall be permitted to sit the examination on one further occasion only.

(iii) each candidate must pass an essay examination at the beginning of Trinity Term on the material covered in the Advanced Pharmacology courses. Candidates must pass the examination in order to proceed with the course, and those who fail shall be permitted to sit the examination on one further occasion only. 5

(iv) each candidate will be required to submit to the examiners two copies of a printed Critical Literature Review of not more than 3,000 words which will be an extended introduction to their approved research project. One practical notebook in which all practical class experiments are recorded will also be submitted. 10

(v) each candidate will be required to submit to the examiners three copies of a printed dissertation of not more than 10,000 words (excluding bibliography and appendices) on the research project selected for study as set out in the Schedule. The arrangements for approval will be notified to candidates not later than the start of Michaelmas Term of the academic 15 year in which the examination is taken.

(vi) each candidate will be expected to give a public oral presentation on his or her research project, on dates to be determined by the Organising Committee.

5. Each candidate shall be examined viva voce. 20

6. Before being given leave to supplicate, candidates must have demonstrated understanding of and competence in the topics covered by the professional development programme as set out in the Schedule, to the satisfaction of the programme organisers, who shall submit a certificate to the examiners to this effect.

7. The required written submissions must be sent to the Chair of Examiners, M.Sc. 25 in Pharmacology, c/o Examination Schools, High Street, Oxford on the following dates:

(*a*) The dissertation on the research project must be submitted by dates to be specified by the Organising Committee and which will be published in the *University Gazette* not later than the start of Michaelmas Term of the academic 30 year in which the examination is taken.

(*b*) The essay and the practical notebook must be submitted by deadlines determined by the Organising Committee and posted in the *Gazette* no later than the end of the term preceding submission.

Each submission must be accompanied by a certificate indicating that it is the 35 candidate's own work.

8. The viva voce examination will normally be conducted in September in the year in which the candidate is examined on dates to be determined by the examiners.

9. The examiners may award a distinction for excellence in part of or in the whole examination. 40

10. The examiners shall retain one copy of each dissertation of each successful candidate for deposit in the Radcliffe Science Library.

Schedule

The syllabus for study will include four principal components:

(*a*) *Professional Development Programme for Pharmacologists* 45

To provide transferable skills for a career in scientific research, this programme will consist of classes, exercises and interactive discussions in the following areas:

(i) Presentation skills, verbal and written;

 (ii) Career planning, assessing personal skills and values, curricula vitae and interview techniques;

 (iii) Exploitation of science: getting ideas to the marketplace, patents, intellectual property rights; the relationship between academic and industrial research; government science policy and research funding; 5

 (iv) Ethical and social issues in science.

Creativity and teamwork are integral components of the learning undertaken during the practical classes and research projects. Time management and learning skills are developed as part of the structured timetable of examinations and coursework submission deadlines throughout the year. 10

(b) Introduction to Pharmacology

Three module introduction to pharmacology, each consisting of lectures and practical classes. Candidates who have already received training in some of the topic areas covered may, at the discretion of the Organising Committee, be exempted from attendance at one or more of the introductory lecture series. Such candidates will be 15
required to pass the qualifying examination, which will cover the topics covered in the Introduction to Pharmacology.

 Module I: Cell & Receptor Pharmacology

 Module II: Tissue and Organ Pharmacology

 Module III: Neuropharmacology 20

Candidates will also be required to take courses on experimental design, data interpretation, computing and statistics, approved by the Organising Committee. Candidates will be required to obtain a Home Office licence and will follow the course of study required for modules 1 to 4 of this.

(c) Advanced pharmacology courses 25

This will consist of the following five taught courses consisting of lectures, seminars and practical classes: Cardiovascular & Systems Pharmacology, Cell Signalling, Neuropharmacology I, Neuropharmacology II, Drug Discovery & Personalised Medicine.

(d) Research Project Dissertation 30

Candidates shall submit a dissertation on a research project undertaken under the supervision of a research supervisor. The subject of each dissertation and the supervision arrangements for each student must be approved by the Organising Committee. The research project will normally be laboratory-based, but in exceptional circumstances students may undertake a library-based project, subject to approval from the 35
Organising Committee.

Master of Science by Coursework in Political Theory Research

(*See also the general notice at the commencement of these regulations. The current edition of the Student Handbook contains an elaborated version of these regulations.*)

 The regulations made by the Politics Graduate Studies Committee are as follows: 40
M.Sc. Examination

A candidate for the M.Sc. in Political Theory Research shall follow a course of instruction in Political Theory Research for twelve months. Each candidate must pass the M.Sc. Examination at the end of Trinity Term in the two compulsory papers. Each candidate must also submit a thesis during the Long Vacation. Compulsory papers 45
 (1) *Theory of Politics*

 (Compulsory paper taken from the M.Phil. in Politics)

A critical examination of political concepts and theories, including social concepts and theories with political relevance. The paper is assessed by a single three hour written examination at the end of Trinity Term.

(2) *Research Methods in Political Theory*

(Compulsory paper taken from the M.Phil. in Politics)

The paper is assessed in the following way. The candidate must submit:

(i) A Research Design Proposal of between 4000 and 6000 words, excluding bibliography, on research design as it bears on the subject of the candidate's proposed M.Sc. thesis. Two copies of the Research Design Proposal, together with a copy on CD or USB flash drive, must be submitted to the Examination Schools by noon on the Friday of sixth week of Trinity Term. It must be accompanied by a separate signed declaration that it is the candidate's own work except where otherwise indicated and that it has not previously been submitted for assessment, either at Oxford or at another institution.

(ii) Research methods training coursework. Candidates will satisfactorily complete a programme of core and optional research methods training, as specified in the *Student Handbook*. Candidate who fail elements of the research methods training coursework are normally permitted to submit a second time (or, if the coursework is assessed by a test, to resit that test) by a date specified in the *Student Handbook*.

The Thesis

Each candidate must submit a thesis of not more than 15,000 words, excluding bibliography. Two hard copies, together with a copy on CD or USB flash drive, must be submitted to the Examination Schools by noon on the last Friday of August following the end of Trinity Full Term. It must be accompanied by a separate signed declaration that it is the candidate's own work except where otherwise indicated and that it has not previously been submitted for assessment, either at Oxford or at another institution. The thesis must be clearly marked with the candidate's examination number, the title of the thesis and the words M.Sc. in Political Theory Research. After the examination process is complete, each successful candidate must deposit one hardbound copy of their thesis in the Bodleian Library.

For a candidate to pass the degree of M.Sc. in Political Theory Research, the candidate must pass: the *Research Methods in Political Theory* paper (all elements of coursework and the Research Design Proposal), the *Theory of Politics* paper, and the thesis.

The examiners may award a distinction for excellence in the whole examination.

Master of Science by Coursework in Politics Research

(*See also the general notice at the commencement of these regulations. The current edition of the Student Handbook contains an elaborated version of these regulations.*)

The regulations made by the Politics Graduate Studies Committee are as follows:

M.Sc. Examination

A candidate for the M.Sc. in Politics Research shall follow a course of instruction in Politics Research for twelve months. Each candidate must pass the M.Sc. Examination at the end of Trinity Term in the two compulsory papers. Each candidate must also submit a thesis during the Long Vacation. Compulsory papers

(1) A single three hour written examination paper testing knowledge of the candidate's core subject (*Comparative Government or European Governance*).

Comparative Government

Compulsory paper taken from the M.Phil. in Politics

The theory and practice of government in modern states.   5

European Governance

Compulsory paper taken from the M.Phil. in Politics

The constitutions and formal structure of governments in European states, including the UK, and the theory and practice of integration in Europe.

(2) *Research Methods in Political Science*   10

(Compulsory paper taken from the M.Phil. in Politics)

The paper is assessed in the following way. The candidates must submit:

(i) A Research Design Proposal of between 4000 and 6000 words, excluding bibliography, on research design as it bears on the subject of the candidate's proposed M.Sc. thesis. Two copies of the Research Design Proposal, together   15 with a copy on CD or USB flash drive, must be submitted to the Examination Schools by noon on the Friday of sixth week of Trinity Term. It must be accompanied by a separate signed declaration that it is the candidate's own work except where otherwise indicated, and that it has not previously been submitted for assessment, either at Oxford or at another institution.   20

(ii) Research methods training coursework. Candidates will satisfactorily complete a programme of core and optional research methods training, as specified in the *Student Handbook*. Candidates who fail elements of the research methods training coursework are normally permitted to submit a second time (or, of the coursework is assessed by a test, to resit that test) by a date specified in the   25 *Student Handbook*.

The Thesis

Each candidate must submit a thesis of not more than 15,000 words, excluding bibliography. Two hard copies, together with a copy on CD or USB flash drive, must be submitted to the Examination Schools by noon on the last Friday of August   30 following the end of Trinity Full Term. It must be accompanied by a separate signed declaration that it is the candidate's own work except where otherwise indicated and that it has not previously been submitted for assessment, either at Oxford or at another institution. The thesis must be clearly marked with the candidate's examination number, the title of the thesis and the words M.Sc. in Politics Research. After the   35 examination process is complete, each successful candidate must deposit one hardbound copy of their thesis in the Bodleian Library.

For a candidate to pass the degree of M.Sc. in Politics Research, the candidate must pass: the *Research Methods in Political Science* paper (all elements of coursework and the Research Design Proposal), the written examination paper (*Comparative*   40 *Government* or *European Governance*), and the thesis.

The examiners may award a distinction for excellence in the whole examination.

Master of Science by Coursework in Psychological Research

1. The Divisional Board of Medical Sciences shall appoint for the supervision of the course an Organising Committee, which shall have the power to arrange lectures   45 and other instruction.

2. The Organising Committee shall appoint an academic adviser for each candidate.

3. Each candidate shall follow a course of study in Psychological Research for at least three terms and for a substantial part of the three subsequent vacations, as determined by the course timetable, and shall, when entering for the examination, be required to produce a certificate from their academic adviser to this effect.

4. The examination shall consist of the following parts:

A. Core Modules

Candidates shall be examined in each of six core modules:

I. *Research Evaluation*

Each candidate shall be required to submit a 2,000 word review of a journal article assigned by the Organising Committee. The deadline for submission shall be notified to students at the start of the course.

II. *Statistical Theory and Methods*

    (*a*) Each candidate shall be required to submit a series of reports based on SPSS data analyses carried out during statistical workshops. Each of the reports will be assessed on a pass/fail basis. The deadline for each submission shall be notified to students at the start of the course.

    (*b*) Each candidate shall also be required to sit a two-hour written examination. The examination will be marked on a pass/fail basis and candidates failing to reach the required standard will have one further opportunity to enter for the examination before the end of the academic year.

III. *MatLab Programming for Experimental Psychology*

Each candidate shall be required to submit a piece of MatLab code that they have produced, which shall be accompanied by a report of no more than 2,000 words that explains the code. The deadline for submission shall be notified to students at the start of the course.

IV. *Computer Modelling of Brain Function*

Each candidate shall be required to submit an essay of no more than 3,000 words. Essay topics must be approved by the Organising Committee. The deadline for submission shall be notified to students at the start of the course.

V. *Project Design*

Each candidate shall be required to submit a 3,000 word review of relevant literature and methods relating to their chosen research project. The deadline for submission shall be notified to students at the start of the course.

VI. *Mini Project*

Each candidate shall be required to submit a written report of activities conducted in the mini-project. The deadline for submission shall be notified to students at the start of the course.

B. Optional Modules

Candidates shall be assessed in each of three optional modules, selected from the following list:

    I. *Philosophical Foundations of Psychology*

    II. *Brain and Cognition*

    III. *Emotion, Personality and Social Behaviour*

    IV. *Language and Development*

For each optional module undertaken, candidates shall be required to submit an essay of no more than 3,000 words. Essay topics must be approved by the Organising Committee. The deadlines for submission shall be notified to students at the start of the course.

C. Research Project

Candidates shall be required to submit not later than noon on the first Monday in September, three copies of a typewritten or printed dissertation of not more than 10,000 words in length (excluding bibliography and any appendices) on his or her research project.   5

Candidates shall also be required to deliver a poster presentation based on their research project. However, this shall not contribute to the overall result for this module. The date on which candidates are required to deliver their presentations will be in the Long Vacation.

5. Candidates must achieve a pass in each of the modules in order to pass the   10
examination overall. In the event that a candidate is deemed not to have achieved the required standard in an element of the examination, he or she will have the opportunity to re-submit or re-sit the relevant assessment on one further occasion before the end of the academic year.

6. Written submissions must be sent to the Chair of Examiners, M.Sc. in   15
Psychological Research, c/o Examination Schools, High Street, Oxford:

    (*a*) two copies of each of the required written submissions for the assessment of core and optional modules must be submitted by the times and dates specified at the start of the course.

    (*b*) three copies of the dissertation on the research project must be submitted not   20
later than noon on the first Monday in September.

Each written submission must be accompanied by a statement signed by the candidate confirming that it is his or her own work.

7. Candidates may be required to attend an oral examination at the discretion of the examiners and this may include questions on the candidate's dissertation, or on   25
any other element of the examination.

8. The examiners may award a distinction for excellence in the whole examination.

Schedule

A. Core Modules

I. *Research Evaluation* This module is delivered as a series of oral presentations   30
collaboratively prepared by groups of students followed by group discussions. The focus is on research articles that illustrate the use of particular kinds of methodology and/or design.

II. *Statistical Theory and Methods* This module comprises a series of statistical lectures and complementary statistical workshops.   35

III. *MatLab Programming for Experimental Psychology* This module provides practical training in MatLab programming for psychologists. This will provide students with programming skills early on in the course, which can then be used in research projects.

IV. *Computer Modelling of Brain Function* This module provides an introduction to   40
the goals and methods of computational modelling in the context of cognitive neuroscience, covering the architecture, function, and properties of a number of basic prototypical classes of neural network. It also looks at how these basic neural networks provide building blocks for larger-scale models of brain function. Lectures will be supplemented by practical sessions providing hands-on experience of computa-   45
tional modelling.

V. *Project Design* This module provides practical instruction in research and presentation skills. Students will undertake detailed planning of the Research Project.

VI. *Mini Project* Small groups of 2–4 students will be assigned to research teams within the Department of Experimental Psychology and guided through research   50 tasks involving, for example, setting up equipment and procedures for a study, collection of pilot data, coding and processing of data, and statistical analysis.

B. Optional Modules

I. *Philosophical Foundations of Psychology* This module begins with historical and foundational issues and progresses to philosophical issues arising from areas of con-   5
temporary research in psychology. Topics studied will include some of: the subject matter of psychology; levels of description; the epistemology of psychology; psychological understanding; cognitive science; the study of neuropsychological and psychiatric disorders; the scientific study of consciousness; and philosophical issues arising from areas of contemporary research.   10

II. *Brain and Cognition* This module covers methods used in research in cognitive psychology and neuropsychology. It presents foundational knowledge from neuroanatomy, neurological disorders, neurological and psychological assessment and the use of experimental methods, to familiarise students with the diverse methodologies which contribute to cognitive neuropsychology. Methodologies deployed in the in-   15
vestigation of perception and cognition are discussed and evaluated.

III. *Emotion, Personality, and Social Behaviour* This module provides a critical analysis of the range of methods and approaches used in social psychology and the study of individual differences.

IV. *Language and Development* This module addresses methods used in selected   20
areas of developmental psychology with a particular emphasis on language. Longitudinal designs, and observational and experimental methods are reviewed and evaluated with examples from recent research. Attention is also given to studies of brain function during development and to the uses of fMRI and EEG data. Particular issues arising from the study of infants lacking verbal skills are identified.   25

C. Research Project

Each student shall carry out a project involving data collection and analysis under the supervision of a research supervisor, on a subject selected in consultation with the academic advisor and approved by the Organising Committee. The Organising Committee shall be responsible for the appointment of the research supervisor.   30

Master of Science by Coursework in Radiation Biology

1. The Medical Sciences Board shall elect for the supervision of the course an Organising Committee, which shall have the power to arrange lectures and other instruction.

2. The Organising Committee shall appoint an academic adviser for each candi-   35
date.

3. Each candidate shall follow a course of study in Radiation Biology for at least three terms and for a substantial part of the three subsequent vacations, as determined by the course timetable, and produce a certificate from their academic adviser to this effect when they submit their dissertation.   40

4. Candidates shall be examined in all of the following ways:

(i) Each candidate must pass a qualifying examination at the end of Michaelmas Term. The examination shall be on modules 1–6 in the Schedule. Candidates who fail the qualifying examination once, shall be permitted to take it again in Week 0 of Hilary Term.   45

(ii) Each candidate will be required to submit to the examiners two copies of a typewritten or printed assignment of 3,000 words by noon, Friday of Week 8 of Hilary Term. A choice of assignment titles will be provided to students by

Week 8 of Michaelmas Term and will have been approved by the Organising Committee. The assignment will account for 15 per cent of the final marks.

(iii) Each candidate must pass a three-hour written examination at the end of Hilary Term (normally in Week 9). The examination shall be on the modules set out in the Schedule. Candidates who fail the examination once, will be permitted to take it again in Week 0 of Trinity Term. The examination will account for 25 per cent of the final marks.

(iv) Each candidate shall undertake an original laboratory research project of approximately six months. Candidates will be examined on their project in three ways:

a. Each
candidate will be required to submit to the examiners three copies of a typewritten or printed research dissertation of not more than 10,000 words (excluding bibliography and appendices) based on the research project. The dissertation must be submitted by a date to be specified by the Organising Committee and which will be published in the student handbook not later than the start of Michaelmas Term of the academic year in which the examination is taken.

b. Each
candidate will be expected to give a presentation to the examiners and assessors on his or her research project after submission of the dissertation.

c. Each
candidate will be examined viva voce by the examiners. The dissertation, presentation and viva voce will be given a single grade and account for 60 per cent of the final marks.

5. Candidates must pass the written examination in Hilary Term in order to pass the examination overall. In addition candidates must achieve an overall pass mark on the written assignment and dissertation combined.

6. The examiners may award a distinction for excellence in the whole examination.

7. The required written submissions must be sent to the Chair of Examiners, M.Sc. in Radiation Biology, c/o Examination Schools, High Street, Oxford.

8. The examiners shall retain one copy of each dissertation of each successful candidate for deposit in the Radcliffe Science Library.

Schedule

The modules for study will be:
1. Physics and Chemistry of Radiation Action
2. Molecular Radiation Biology
3. Cellular and Tissue Radiation Biology
4. Whole Body Exposure and Carcinogenesis
5. Radiation Epidemiology
6. Radiation Protection
7. Imaging Technologies
8. Tumour Microenvironment

9. Principles of Clinical Radiation Biology
10. Applications of Radiation Therapy
11. Translational Radiation Biology
12. Clinical Radiation Biology.

Master of Science by Coursework in Refugee and Forced Migration Studies

1. Candidates will be expected to attend such lectures and seminars as their supervisor/course director shall recommend.

2. Candidates will, when they enter for their examination, be required to produce a certificate from their society that they are following a course of study in the field which they have pursued in Oxford for at least three terms.

3. Candidates must present themselves for an oral examination if requested by the examiners.

4. The examiners may award a distinction for excellence in the whole examination. Every candidate will be required to satisfy the examiners in two papers and two essay papers as follows:

Paper I: International Legal and Normative Framework

International legal and normative framework in relation to refugees and displaced persons. International and domestic application of individual and group rights to displaced persons and refugees. Activities and involvement of the relevant international organs, governments, and intergovernmental and non-governmental organisations relevant to forced migration. Concepts of migration and intervention and their justifications. Evolution of humanitarian responses to forced migration. Organisational culture of assistance.

Paper II: Causes and Consequences of Forced Migration

Theories of the causes of forced migration and humanitarian crises. Historical dimensions, political and social dynamics of forced migration. Social, political and cultural constructions of place and space. Impact of forced migration on gender relations and age structures. Coercion and conflict. Implications of forced migrants for conceptualising the modern state and the international order. Security and stability of states. Environmental and development-induced displacement. Poverty and vulnerability. Impact of forced migrants on host populations and governments. Ethical issues raised by migration. Agency, coping mechanisms and survival strategies of affected populations. Nationalism, ethnicity and group identity. Consequences of resettlement programmes for livelihood and economic autonomy. Repatriation and local-level social reconstruction. Institutional responses to forced migrants.

Multidisciplinary Thesis

Each student will be required to write a thesis of not less than 10,000 and not more than 15,000 words on a topic relevant to forced migration. The purpose of this thesis is to ensure that the students have engaged in a multidisciplinary analysis of a single issue in forced migration to gain an awareness of the complex interrelations in the field.

The topic of the thesis will require approval by the chair of examiners. This thesis must be the work of the candidate alone and aid from others must be limited to prior discussion as to the subject and advice on presentation. The thesis (three copies) must be typewritten and delivered to the Examination Schools, High Street, Oxford, not later than noon on Thursday of Week Eight of Trinity Term. An electronic copy must also be submitted to the M.Sc. in Refugee and Forced Migration Studies Coordinator, again by the date and time specified above. The thesis must be presented in proper scholarly form, in double-spacing and on one side only of quarto or A4 paper, each copy bound or held firmly in a stiff cover. The examiners shall retain a copy of the thesis of each candidate who passes the examination for deposit in the Social Sciences Library.

Research Methods Group Essay

Each student must display an understanding of research methods relevant to forced migration. This will be in the form of a group essay of approximately, but no more than 5,000 words, based on directed field research conducted during a four-week period in Hilary Term. The essay will present findings and engage with topics which include: epistemology of social science; social science paradigms; ethics and values; quantitative, qualitative, and participatory methods of data collection; the presentation of statistical information; research design; sampling theory; hypothesis testing; questionnaire design; participant observation; participatory learning and action; and evaluative research.

The essay must be presented in a proper scholarly form and delivered to the Examination Schools, High Street, Oxford, no later than Friday noon in Week Seven of Hilary Term.

A candidate who fails the examination will be permitted to retake it on one further occasion only, not later than one year after the initial attempt. A candidate who has reached a satisfactory standard on any of the three components of the examination: (i) the thesis; (ii) the two written papers; (iii) the research methods group essay, will not be required to retake that part of the examination. Candidates may also be required to attend an oral examination, which may be on one or more of the candidate's written examinations, thesis or group essay. Any candidate who fails a group assignment may be considered for a pass on the basis of an oral examination.

5. Candidates may be provided with selected international legal materials for use during some examinations, as published annually in the Course Handbook.

Master of Science by Coursework in Russian and East European Studies

1. Each candidate will be required to follow a course of instruction for three terms and to present himself or herself for examination in the three compulsory papers in Week Eight of Trinity Term, as well as to present a thesis for examination. In addition, each candidate will be required to participate in training in methodology (quantitative and qualitative) and research skills related to Russian and East European Studies and to have achieved pass marks for the assessed components, as specified in the Notes of Guidance of the year of matriculation of the candidate. Two copies of a thesis should be delivered to the Chair of Examiners for the M.Sc. in Russian and East European Studies, c/o Examination Schools, High Street, Oxford, by noon on the Friday of the sixth week of Trinity Term in the calendar year in which the examination is taken.

2. Candidates who fail a written examination may be allowed to retake it in the following year. In the case of a failed thesis, this may be resubmitted in Trinity Term

of the following year. Only one resubmission is permitted. In special circumstances, the Examiners may allow a marginal failure in one component in accordance with the rules outlined in the Examination Conventions.

3. The examiners may award a distinction for excellence in the whole examination.

SCHEDULE OF PAPERS

1. *Twentieth-Century Russian, Soviet and East European History.*
2. *Contemporary Russian and East European Studies Part 1.*
3. *Contemporary Russian and East European Studies Part 2.*
4. A thesis of at least 12,000 words but not more than 15,000 words.

Oxford 1+1 MBA programme
Candidates registered on the Oxford 1+1 MBA programme will follow an additional two or three month bridging programme at the end of their third term of the combined programme.

Each candidate will be appointed an academic advisor from the Saïd Business School to plan an individual course of study which will include as a minimum, the following three compulsory elements:

(i) Attendance of one of the summer elective programmes offered for the Master of Business Administration to be published by the MBA Director before the first Monday of the preceding term. Candidates would be required to undertake all assessments and receive feedback, but would not obtain credit towards the MBA. Candidates are not permitted to subsequently undertake the same elective as part of the MBA programme the following year.

(ii) A formatively assessed assignment of no more than 5,000 words (including all prefatory matter and appendices) supervised by the Saïd Business School academic advisor, which will relate the Master's degree learning to an appropriate area of the MBA programme. Candidates would also be required to present a work plan related to this assignment to the 1+1 programme class.

(iii) Attendance of the MBA pre-course as described in the joining instructions for the MBA class, unless granted exemption by the MBA Committee on the grounds of prior formal study or work experience.

Master of Science by Coursework in Social Anthropology

1. The Social Sciences Divisional Board shall elect for the supervision of the course a Standing Committee, namely the Teaching Committee of the School of Anthropology, which shall have power to arrange lectures and other instruction. The course director shall be responsible to that committee.

2. Candidates must follow a course of instruction in Social and Cultural Anthropology for at least three terms, and will, when entering for the examinations, be required to produce a certificate from their supervisor to this effect.

3. Candidates will be required to present themselves for written and (if requested) oral examinations and to submit three copies of a dissertation in prescribed form on an approved topic as defined below.

4. The written examination will consist of four papers on the syllabus described in the Schedule.

5. Each candidate will be required to submit a dissertation of no more than 10,000 words, on a subject selected in consultation with the supervisor and approved by the Chair of Examiners. The proposed title of the dissertation, together with a paragraph

describing its scope and the supervisor's written endorsement, must be submitted to the Chair of Examiners by Tuesday of the second week of Trinity Term.

6. Three typewritten copies of the dissertation must be delivered not later than noon on the last Wednesday in August in the year in which the examination is taken, to the Chair of the Examiners, M.Sc. in Social Anthropology, c/o Examination   5
Schools, High Street, Oxford. The dissertation shall be provided with an abstract of up to 250 words, to be placed immediately after the title page. The word count shall be stated on the outside front cover of the thesis.

7. The oral examination (if requested) may be on the candidate's written papers, or dissertation, or both.   10

8. The examiners may award a distinction for excellence in the whole examination.

9. In order to pass the degree, a student must pass all its assessed components. Where one or more components are failed, the student will be given the opportunity to re-sit or re-submit them once, as the case may be. Any subsequent award of the degree on successful completion of all the assessed components may be delayed by up to three   15
terms, i.e. until the Examination Board next meets.

10. The four papers will be taken to constitute Part I of the degree and the dissertation to constitute Part II. At the close of the written examinations, the examiners will publish a list of those who have satisfied them in Part I.

Schedule   20

Students must satisfy the examiners in four papers, two of a general nature and two options; one option paper must be selected from List A (below). The syllabuses for the two general papers are as follows:

I. *Culture and Identity*

This paper will focus on the following topics: history and politics of anthropology;   25
anthropology, ethnography and colonialism; gift and exchange; production and consumption; aesthetics, poetics, music and dance; material culture and museums; landscape and the built environment; personhood and the body; identity, ethnicity and nationalism.

II. *Kinship, Power, and Change*   30

This paper will focus on the following topics: family, kinship, and relatedness; gender and age; ritual and religion; myth, history, memory and time; symbolism; representations of misfortune, including witchcraft, possession and healing; politics, law and the state; multiculturalism, migration and globalisation; language and literacy; classification; power, violence, resistance, and agency.   35

The two option papers are as follows:

III. *Option Paper I: The Social Anthropology of a Selected Region*

This option paper must be selected from List A (below).

IV. *Option Paper II: Open Choice*

This option paper must be selected from any of the lists below: 40

    List A. Anthropology of a Selected Region

    List B. Topics in Material Anthropology

    List C. Anthropology and Topical Issues

Options offered in any of the three lists may vary from year to year. Lists for the current academic year will be issued by the Director of Graduate Studies or his or her   45
delegate by the end of the third week of Michaelmas term.

Master of Science by Coursework in Social Science of the Internet

1. Candidates must follow for three terms a course of instruction in Social Science of the Internet.

2. The examination will be in eleven parts, as follows:

   A. Compulsory core paper in 'Social Dynamics of the Internet', assessed by examination.

   B. Compulsory core paper in 'Internet Technologies and Regulation', assessed by examination.

   C. Compulsory core methods paper in 'Digital Social Research Methods: Methods Core' assessed by written coursework. Details of and arrangements for submission of the written course work shall be notified to candidates by the first Monday of Michaelmas Term.

   D. Compulsory core paper in 'Digital Social Research Methods: Statistics Core' assessed by examinations.

   E. Four (4) methods option modules, to be chosen from a list to be published on the Oxford Internet Institute annually by the first Monday of Michaelmas Term. Students will normally select two modules from the first four-week period and two modules from the second four-week period of the list. Students wishing to take three options during a single four-week period must first seek permission from the Director of Graduate Studies. Not all methods options may be available every year. The methods option papers will be assessed by arrangements which are specified in the reading lists for each module, details and arrangements for submission of which shall be notified to candidates by the first Monday of Michaelmas Term.

   F. Two (2) option papers, to be chosen from a list to be published on the Oxford Internet Institute website annually by the first Monday of Michaelmas Term. Not all options may be available every year. The option papers will be assessed by written coursework, details of and arrangements for submission of which shall be notified to candidates by the first Monday of Michaelmas Term.

   G. A thesis of between 10,000 and 15,000 words on a topic within the subject of the course, to be specified jointly by supervisor and student, and approved by the programme director. Two written copies of the thesis must be delivered to the Examination Schools, High Street, Oxford, by noon of the weekday on or nearest to the 1st of August of the year in which the degree is to be taken. Successful candidates will be required to deposit a copy of their thesis in the Oxford Internet Institute Library.

3. The examiners may examine any candidate viva voce.

4. The examiners may award a Distinction for excellence in the whole examination on the basis of the material submitted to them.

Oxford 1+1 MBA programme

Candidates registered on the Oxford 1+1 MBA programme will follow an additional two or three month bridging programme at the end of their third term of the combined programme.

Each candidate will be appointed an academic advisor from the Saïd Business School to plan an individual course of study which will include as a minimum, the following three compulsory elements:

(i) Attendance of one of the summer elective programmes offered for the Master of Business Administration to be published by the MBA Director before the first

Monday of the preceding term. Candidates would be required to undertake all assessments and receive feedback, but would not obtain credit towards the MBA. Candidates are not permitted to subsequently undertake the same elective as part of the MBA programme the following year.

(ii) A formatively assessed assignment of no more than 5,000 words (including all   5
prefatory matter and appendices) supervised by the Saïd Business School academic advisor, which will relate the Master's degree learning to an appropriate area of the MBA programme. Candidates would also be required to present a work plan related to this assignment to the 1+1 programme class.

(iii) Attendance of the MBA pre-course as described in the joining instructions for   10
the MBA class, unless granted exemption by the MBA Committee on the grounds of prior formal study or work experience.

Master of Science by Coursework in Sociology

Every candidate must follow, for at least three terms, a course of instruction in Sociology.   15
The examination will be in four parts:

A. A compulsory paper in *Methods of Social Research*.

B. A compulsory paper in *Sociological Analysis*.

C. Two optional papers. These will be from a list published annually by Friday of the third week of Michaelmas Full Term in the Department of Sociology.   20

D. A thesis of not more than 10,000 words on a topic within the subject of the course to be specified jointly by supervisor and student. Candidates are warned that they should avoid repetition in their theses of material used in their option papers and that substantial repetition may be penalised. Two typewritten copies of the thesis must be delivered to the Examination Schools, High Street, Oxford, by noon of the week-   25
day on or nearest to 1 September of the year in which the examination is to be taken. Successful candidates will be required to deposit a copy of their thesis in the Department of Sociology.

The examiners may examine any candidate viva voce.

The examiners may award a Distinction for excellence in the whole examination on   30
the basis of the material submitted to them.

Oxford 1+1 MBA programme

Candidates registered on the Oxford 1+1 MBA programme will follow an additional two or three month bridging programme at the end of their third term of the combined programme.   35

Each candidate will be appointed an academic advisor from the Saïd Business School to plan an individual course of study which will include as a minimum, the following three compulsory elements:

(i) Attendance of one of the summer elective programmes offered for the Master of Business Administration to be published by the MBA Director before the first   40
Monday of the preceding term. Candidates would be required to undertake all assessments and receive feedback, but would not obtain credit towards the MBA. Candidates are not permitted to subsequently undertake the same elective as part of the MBA programme the following year.

(ii) A formatively assessed assignment of no more than 5,000 words (including all   45
prefatory matter and appendices) supervised by the Saïd Business School academic advisor, which will relate the Master's degree learning to an appropriate area of the MBA programme. Candidates would also be required to present a work plan related to this assignment to the 1+1 programme class.

(iii) Attendance of the MBA pre-course as described in the joining instructions for the MBA class, unless granted exemption by the MBA Committee on the grounds of prior formal study or work experience.

Software Engineering Programme

For students registering on the M.Sc. in Software Engineering or the M.Sc. in Software and Systems Security on or after 1 April 2010.

A. Definition of the Programme

1. The Mathematical, Physical and Life Sciences Divisional Board shall offer a Programme of Studies in Software Engineering at postgraduate level.

2. The subjects of the Programme shall be Software Engineering, Software and Systems Security, and Object Technology.

3. The following awards shall be available within the Programme:

  i. M.Sc. in Software Engineering

  ii. M.Sc. in Software and Systems Security

  iii. Postgraduate Diploma in Software Engineering

  iv. Postgraduate Diploma in Software and Systems Security

  v. Postgraduate Certificate in Software Engineering

  vi. Postgraduate Certificate in Software and Systems Security

  vii. Postgraduate Certificate in Object Technology

4. The Mathematical, Physical and Life Sciences Divisional Board shall elect for the supervision of the Programme a Supervisory Committee which shall have the power to arrange lectures and other instruction.

B. Progression

5. Entry to the Programme is to the M.Sc. in Software Engineering or the M.Sc. in Software and Systems Security.

6. With the approval of the Programme Director, a candidate may transfer from the M.Sc. in Software Engineering to the M.Sc. in Software and Systems Security, or from the M.Sc. in Software and Systems Security to the M.Sc. in Software Engineering, subject to being eligible to study for the relevant award as set out in sections C and D below.

7. With the approval of the Programme Director, a candidate for the M.Sc. in Software Engineering or for the M.Sc. in Software and Systems Security may be awarded one of the Postgraduate Certificates or Postgraduate Diplomas set out in clause 3 above, subject to such a candidate having satisfied the criteria for the award of the relevant Postgraduate Certificate or Postgraduate Diploma as set out in sections C and D below.

C. Eligibility for awards: duration of study

8. To be eligible for the award of an M.Sc., a student must have been on the Register for the Programme for a period of not less than two years, and not more than four years.

9. To be eligible for the award of a Postgraduate Diploma, a student must have been on the Register for the Programme for a period of not less than one year, and not more than three years.

10. To be eligible for the award of a Postgraduate Certificate, a student must have been on the Register for the Programme for a period of not less than one year, and not more than two years.

11. The Programme Director shall have power

    a. to grant suspension from the Register for a period or periods totalling not   5
more than three terms during each of the maximum periods given in clauses 8, 9, and 10 above;

    b. to approve an extension of time of not more than three terms to each of the maximum periods given in clauses 8, 9, and 10 above;

subject to the total periods of suspensions and extensions not exceeding six terms   10
overall.

D. Eligibility for awards: study and examinations

12. Students on the Register shall enter for the examination for the award of the M.Sc., unless they have been given approval under clause 7 above to be awarded one of the Postgraduate Certificates or Postgraduate Diplomas.   15

13. Schedules A-C of modules will be published at http://www.cs.ox.ac.uk/softeng/ handbook/schedules.html. If insufficient students register for a module the Programme Director may make the decision not to offer that module.

14. Every candidate will be required to satisfy the examiners in the following:

a. M.Sc. in Software Engineering   20

    (i) attendance at a minimum of ten modules chosen from those in the Schedule, comprising a programme of study approved by the Supervisory Committee;

    (ii) submission of at least ten written assignments corresponding to those modules;

    (iii) participation in a project module   25

    (iv) submission of a dissertation of not more than 20,000 words (including appendices and footnotes but excluding bibliography) on a subject selected by the candidate in consultation with the supervisor and approved by the Supervisory Committee. In preparation for the dissertation, candidates will be required to submit a proposal following participation in the project   30
module. Dissertations submitted which differ from the topic approved by the Supervisory Committee may not be marked by the examiners;

b. M.Sc. in Software and Systems Security

    (i) attendance at a minimum of ten modules chosen from those in the Schedule, of which at least six should come from Schedule C, together comprising a   35
programme of study approved by the Supervisory Committee;

    (ii) submission of at least ten written assignments corresponding to those modules attended;

    (iii) participation in a project module;

    (iv) submission of a dissertation of not more than 20,000 words (including   40
appendices and footnotes but excluding bibliography) on a subject selected by the candidate in consultation with the supervisor and approved by the Supervisory Committee. In preparation for the dissertation, candidates will be required to submit a proposal following participation in the project module. Dissertations submitted which differ from the topic approved by   45
the Supervisory Committee may not be marked by the examiners;

    (v) the subject of the projects and dissertation shall relate to software and systems security, and must have been approved as such by the Supervisory Committee.

c. Postgraduate Diploma in Software Engineering

    (i) attendance at a minimum of eight modules chosen from those in the Schedule,   50
comprising a programme of study approved by the Supervisory Committee;

(ii) submission of at least eight written assignments corresponding to those modules attended.

d. Postgraduate Diploma in Software and Systems Security
(i) attendance at a minimum of eight modules chosen from those in the Schedule, of which at least five should come from Schedule C, comprising a programme of study approved by the Supervisory Committee;
(ii) submission of at least eight written assignments corresponding to those modules attended.

e. Postgraduate Certificate in Software Engineering
(i) attendance at a minimum of four modules, chosen from the Schedule, together comprising a programme of study approved by the Supervisory Committee;
(ii) submission of at least four written assignments, corresponding to those modules attended.

f. Postgraduate Certificate in Software and Systems Security
(i) attendance at a minimum of four modules, chosen from the Schedule, at least three of which chosen from Schedule C, together comprising a programme of study approved by the Supervisory Committee;
(ii) submission of at least four written assignments, corresponding to those modules attended.

g. Postgraduate Certificate in Object Technology
(i) attendance at a minimum of four modules, chosen from the Schedule, at least three of which chosen from Schedule B, together comprising a programme of study approved by the Supervisory Committee;
(ii) submission of at least four written assignments, corresponding to those modules attended.

The assignments and, for the M.Sc., two typewritten or printed copies of the dissertation, shall be forwarded to the examiners for consideration by such dates as the examiners shall determine and shall notify to candidates, supervisors and tutors. The assignments and the dissertation must be accompanied by a statement that it is the candidate's work except where otherwise indicated. Candidates are usually required to submit the assignments electronically. Details will be given in the programme handbook. Any candidate who is unable, for some reason, to submit practical work electronically must apply to the Programme Director for permission to submit the work in paper form. Such applications must reach the Programme Director two weeks before the deadline for submitting the work. The two copies of the dissertation shall be addressed to the Chair of Examiners, Software Engineering Programme, c/o Examination Schools, High Street, Oxford, OX1 4BG.

15. Provided the Supervisory Committee is satisfied that a candidate has undertaken equivalent study, of an appropriate standard, normally at another institution of higher education, the committee shall have the discretion to permit the candidate to be exempted from attending, and submitting the written assignment for, modules chosen from Schedule A, B, or C, as required under clause 13 above as follows:

a. For the M.Sc.: up to two of the total of ten modules for which written assignments are required;
b. For the award of the Postgraduate Diploma: up to two of the total of eight modules;
c. For the award of the Postgraduate Certificate: up to one of the total of four modules.

16. Candidates may be required to attend a viva voce examination as part of the examination for each award at the discretion of the examiners.

17. The examiners may award a distinction for excellence in the whole examination for each award.

18. Candidates who fail to satisfy the examiners in the assignments under clause 14   5
above may be permitted to resubmit work in respect of part or parts of the examination which they have failed for examination on not more than one occasion which shall normally be within one year of the initial failure. No written assignment shall be submitted to the examiners on more than one occasion.

E. Subsuming of previous awards under the Programme   10

19. In the exceptional circumstances that a candidate granted approval under clause 7 above to be awarded of one of the Postgraduate Certificates or Postgraduate Diplomas (set out in clause 3 above) is readmitted to one of the M.Scs (set out in clause 3 above), then the following apply:

    a. If any candidate who is successful in the examination for the Postgraduate   15
    Diploma has previously successfully completed the Postgraduate Certificate, and for that examination has incorporated the assignments submitted for the Postgraduate Certificate into the Postgraduate Diploma, then the Postgraduate Diploma will subsume his or her Certificate.

    b. If any candidate who is successful in the examination for the M.Sc. has   20
    previously successfully completed the Postgraduate Diploma or the Postgraduate Certificate, and for that examination has incorporated the assignments submitted for the Postgraduate Certificate or Postgraduate Diploma into the M.Sc., then the subsequent award will subsume his or her previous award.   25

F. Examination Conventions and Readmission

20. In the case of a candidate who is readmitted they will be subject to the Examination Conventions in force at the date of their readmission.

Master of Science by Coursework in Surgical Science and Practice (old regulations)   30

1. The Divisional Board of Medical Sciences, jointly with the Continuing Education Board, shall elect for the supervision of the course a Standing Committee, which shall have the power to arrange lectures and other instruction.

2. Candidates must follow for at least six terms and no more than nine terms, a part-time course of instruction in the theory and practice of Surgical Science and   35
Practice, which shall normally take place over a period of two years and no more than four years.

3. Every candidate will be required to satisfy the examiners in the following:

    (*a*) Attendance at the modules in Schedule A and Schedule B below and other teaching sessions as required.   40

    (*b*) Active participation in all parts of the course to the satisfaction of the Course Director.

    (*c*) Four written assignments related to the modules in Schedule A, each of not more than 4,000 words in length.

    (*d*) Two assignments consisting of multiple choice questions or structured short   45
    questions, online project working and practical tests related to the modules in Schedule B.

(*e*) A dissertation of not more than 20,000 words (excluding tables, appendices, footnotes and bibliography), on a subject selected by the candidate in consultation with the supervisor and approved by the Course Director.

The assignments set out in clauses 3(*c–e*) shall be forwarded, usually through a specified electronic submission system, to the examiners c/o Registry, Department for Continuing Education, 1 Wellington Square, Oxford OX1 2JA, for consideration by such date as the examiners shall determine and of which they shall notify candidates.

4. Candidates may be required to attend a viva voce examination at the end of the course of studies at the discretion of the examiners.

5. The examiners may award a distinction to candidates for the M.Sc.

6. Candidates who fail to satisfy the examiners in any part of the examination may be permitted to resubmit work in respect of the part or parts of the examination that they have failed, for examination on not more than one occasion which shall normally be within one year of the original failure.

7. The Standing Committee shall have the discretion to permit any candidate to be exempted, in exceptional circumstances, from attendance at any module under 3(*a*) and from submitting the associated assignment required under 3(*c*) and 3(*d*) above, provided that the Standing Committee is satisfied that such a candidate has undertaken equivalent study, or has appropriate work experience to an equivalent standard.

Schedule A

The practice of evidence-based health care
Quality improvement science and systems analysis
Introduction to surgical management and leadership
Becoming a medical educator
Any other module as defined by the Course Director and approved by the Standing Committee.

Schedule B

Human factors, teamwork and communication
Surgical technology and robotics.

Master of Science by Coursework in Surgical Science and Practice

(*new regulations for students registering on any of the awards listed from 1 October 2012 and available to existing students*)

1. The Medical Sciences Board, jointly with the Continuing Education Board, shall elect for the supervision of the course a Standing Committee, which shall have the power to arrange lectures and other instruction.

2. The course is available on a part time basis only and shall consist of instruction in the theory and practice of Surgical Science and Practice.

3. The policy of the Continuing Education Board on variable intensity part time study shall apply to this award.

4. The minimum period of registration on the M.Sc. shall be three terms and the maximum period of registration shall be twelve terms.

5. Candidates may be permitted in certain circumstances to suspend status, for a maximum of six terms. Any such period shall not count to the maximum or minimum permitted period of registration and no fee liability will be incurred during such periods.

6. Every candidate will be required to satisfy the examiners in the following:

    (*a*) Attendance at the modules in Schedule A and Schedule B below and other teaching sessions as required.

    (*b*) Participation in all parts of the course to the satisfaction of the Course Director.

    (*c*) Four written assignments related to the modules in Schedule A, each of not more than 4,000 words in length.

    (*d*) Two assignments consisting of multiple choice questions or structured short questions, online project working and practical tests related to the modules in Schedule B.

    (*e*) A dissertation of not more than 15,000 words (including tables, appendices and footnotes but excluding reference list), on a subject selected by the candidate in consultation with the supervisor and approved by the Standing Committee. Approval must be sought no later than the first day of the ninth term of registration. The dissertation must be submitted within three terms of the date of approval, notwithstanding the maximum permitted period of registration.

The assignments set out in clauses 6(*c–e*) shall be forwarded, usually through a specified electronic submission system, to the examiners c/o Registry, Department for Continuing Education, 1 Wellington Square, Oxford OX1 2JA, for consideration by such date as the examiners shall determine and shall notify candidates.

7. Candidates may be required to attend a viva voce examination at the end of the course of studies at the discretion of the examiners.

8. The examiners may award a distinction to candidates for the M.Sc.

9. Candidates who fail to satisfy the examiners in any part of the examination under 6 (*c–e*) above may be permitted to resubmit work in respect of the part or parts of the examination that they have failed, on not more than one occasion for each assignment without being required to repeat attendance at the relevant module or modules. The resubmission will normally be within one year of the original failure.

10. Provided the Standing Committee is satisfied that a student on the award has undertaken equivalent study, of an appropriate standard, normally at another institution of higher education, or has appropriate work experience to an equivalent standard, the committee may permit the candidate to be exempted from attendance and the submission of a written assignment in respect of up to three modules. In exercising this discretion the Standing Committee shall take into consideration the length of time that has elapsed since the study or work experience was undertaken.

11. The Standing Committee may deem satisfactory completion of a module (including the associated assessment) prior to registration for the award as having met the attendance and examination requirements in respect of that module. Such discretion will normally only be exercised if the time elapsed between commencement of the accredited module concerned and registration for the award is not more than two years. The maximum number of modules taken prior to registration for the award that may count in this way shall be three.

Schedule A

The practice of evidence-based health care

Quality improvement science and systems analysis*

Introduction to surgical management and leadership

Becoming a medical educator*

Any other module as defined by the Course Director and approved by the Standing Committee.

Schedule B

Human factors, teamwork and communication*

Surgical technology and robotics 5

*Also available to students registered for the PG Diploma in Health Research

Master of Science by Coursework in Sustainable Urban Development

1. The Continuing Education Board shall elect for the supervision of the course a course committee that shall have the power to arrange lectures and other instruction in the theory and practice of Sustainable Urban Development. 10

2. The course may be taken on a part-time basis over a period of not less than six and not more than nine terms.

3. Candidates may be permitted under certain circumstances to suspend status, for a maximum of six terms. Any such period shall not count towards the maximum or minimum permitted period of registration and no fee liability will be incurred during 15 such periods.

4. Every candidate will be required to satisfy the examiners in the following:

    (*a*) Attendance at classes, tutorials, group seminars and other teaching sessions;

    (*b*) seven written assignments, each being on one of the units listed in the Schedule below, and each of not more than 3,000 words in length; 20

    (*c*) a dissertation of not more than 15,000 words (excluding tables, appendices, footnotes and bibliography), on a subject selected by the candidate in consultation with the supervisor and approved by the course committee.

The assessed work set out in clause 4(*b*) shall be forwarded in normal circumstances through an electronic submission system to the examiners c/o Registry, Department 25 for Continuing Education, 1 Wellington Square, Oxford OX1 2JA, for consideration by such date as the examiners shall determine and of which they shall notify candidates. The assessed work set out in clause 4(*c*) shall be submitted in hard copy and on a USB stick to the examiners c/o, Examination Schools, High Street, Oxford OX1 4BG for consideration by such date as the examiners shall determine and of which they 30 shall notify candidates.

4. Candidates may be required to attend a viva voce examination at the end of the course of studies at the discretion of the examiners.

5. The examiners may award a distinction to candidates for the M.Sc.

6. Candidates who fail to satisfy the examiners in any part of the examination may 35 be permitted to resubmit work in respect of the part or parts of the examination that they have failed for examination on not more than one occasion which shall normally be within one year of the original failure.

7. The course committee shall have the discretion to permit any candidate to be exempted, in exceptional circumstances, from submitting an assignment, provided 40 that the committee is satisfied that such a candidate has undertaken equivalent study, or have appropriate work experience to an equivalent standard.

Schedule

Concepts of the City and Environmental Change

Climate Change and the Built Environment 45

Place-making and Urban Design

Financing Sustainability

Sustainable Transport
Urbanism, Community and City-building
Leadership, Governance and Future Cities
Urbanisation and the Global South
Any other subject approved by the course committee.   5
Not all units will be available in any one year.

Master of Science by Coursework in Teacher Education (part-time)

1. All candidates will be initially admitted for the Postgraduate Diploma in
Teacher Education.

2. Every candidate must follow for six terms a part-time course of instruction in   10
Teacher Education, approved by the Academic Committee of the Department of
Education. All candidates on the course will be required to complete four summatively
assessed units of study, two formatively assessed residential units and a research and
development dissertation.

3. The M.Sc in Teacher Education shall be examined by means of four assignments   15
relating to the content of each of the four units and a research and development
dissertation. Each assignment must be between 4,000 and 5,000 words in length, or
their equivalent in tables, charts and diagrams in accordance with guidance given in
the unit. One electronic copy (in a software format available in the department) must
be submitted online to the Chair of Examiners, M.Sc in Teacher Education, c/o   20
Department of Education, 15 Norham Gardens, Oxford OX2 6PY who will provide
the digital address. The deadline for the submission of assignments will be no later
than noon on Monday of Week 1 of Hilary and Trinity terms.

4. The research and development dissertation will present a systematic account of a
substantial practitioner research enquiry, focused on the design and implementation of   25
a specific innovation in teacher education with a strong emphasis on the choice of
appropriate criteria, and relevant evidence for evaluating its impact. The dissertation
must be between 15,000 and 20,000 words in length. One electronic copy (in a software
format available in the department) must be submitted to the Chair of Examiners,
M.Sc. in Teacher Education, c/o Department of Education, 15 Norham Gardens,   30
Oxford OX2 6PY who will provide a digital address, no later than noon on the third
Friday in September in the candidate's second year on the course. One printed copy of
the report must also be provided hard bound bearing the name of the candidate, and
proof of posting by the submission date must be scanned and sent to the Chair of
Examiners. The hard bound copy of the research and development project report of   35
each candidate who passes the examination will be retained by OUDE for deposit in
the departmental library.

5. Candidates who fail to satisfy the examiners in an assignment or in the research
and development dissertation will be permitted to resubmit on one occasion only. The
deadline for resubmission of unit assessments will be noon on the Monday falling   40
8 weeks after the initial submission date, following the term in which the unit is taken.
To transfer successfully from the Postgraduate Diploma to the M.Sc. candidates must
have passed both assessment units in the first year.

6. The award of Distinction within the M.Sc. in Teacher Education is normally
reserved for those candidates who receive distinction marks for at least two of the four   45
assignments, and over 60 for the other two, and also achieve distinction for the
dissertation.

7. Candidates may also be examined orally on their final research and development
dissertation before the Michaelmas term Examination Board meeting. All candidates
will be informed of the date at the start of the second year, as they will be required to   50
attend Oxford in person.

8. If the dissertation is awarded a failing mark, the candidate may resubmit the dissertation one further time on the next occasion when it is examined. If having passed the four assessments a failing mark is received for the dissertation, either at the time of the original submission (and the candidate does not wish to re-sit) or after re-submission, students may apply to exit the programme with a Postgraduate Diploma. 5

Master of Science by Coursework in Teaching English Language in University Settings

1. The course is open only to candidates who are currently enrolled upon or have recently completed the Postgraduate Diploma in Teaching English Language in University Settings (PGDip TELUS) who have passed the first six modules of their 10 course, and who have submitted a satisfactory dissertation proposal. Candidates will normally apply in Hilary Term of their second PGDip TELUS year.

2. Candidates will be required to complete the final two summatively assessed online modules as defined for the PGDip TELUS by carrying out tasks and participating in discussions as directed by the Course Director. Candidates will also be 15 required to submit a dissertation of between 15,000 and 20,000 words (including footnotes/endnotes but excluding appendices and references or bibliography) on a subject selected by the candidate in consultation with the supervisor, which must be closely related to one or more of the themes of the course.

3. Three word processed or printed copies of the dissertation must be delivered to the 20 Chairman of the Examiners, M.Sc. Teaching English Language in University Settings, c/o Examination Schools, High Street, Oxford, OX2 6PY no later than noon of the last Friday in August of the year in which they have been enrolled on the M.Sc. TELUS. An additional electronic copy must also be uploaded to the appropriate Weblearn site.

4. One copy should be hard bound and two soft bound, the latter of which should 25 be anonymous except for the candidate number. The hard bound copy of the dissertation of each candidate who passes the examination shall be retained by the department for deposit in the departmental library. The dissertation must be accompanied by a declaration indicating that it is the candidate's own work.

5. To be awarded the Master of Science, candidates must pass a minimum of seven 30 of the eight taught modules, and must pass the dissertation. The pass mark for the taught modules and the dissertation is fifty. Sixty percent of the overall mark for the M.Sc. will be based on the mean of the best seven marks of the eight taught modules, and forty percent on the dissertation mark. The examiners may award a distinction for excellence in the examination. 35

6. The candidate may also be examined orally. The oral examination will only be on the candidate's dissertation.

7. If a candidate receives a failing mark on any of the taught modules, they may be re-examined on those modules on one further occasion, which will normally be in the following year. If the dissertation is awarded a failing mark, the candidate may 40 resubmit the dissertation one further time on the next occasion when it is examined. If a failing mark is received on the dissertation, either at the time of the original submission or upon re-sit, and the mean of the mark for the best seven taught modules is fifty or above, the student may be awarded the PGDip TELUS as an exit award.

Master of Science by Coursework in Theoretical and Computational Chemistry

1. An Organising Committee shall be appointed which shall have power to arrange lectures and other instruction.

2. Candidates shall follow for at least three terms a course of instruction in Theoretical and Computational Chemistry, as determined by the course timetable.

3. The following routes shall be available:

   (*a*) M.Sc. in Theory and Computational Chemistry with progression to Probationer Research Student Status at the University of Oxford for a maximum of a further three terms in the Centre for Doctoral Training in Theory and Modelling in Chemical Sciences;

   (*b*) M.Sc. in Theory and Computational Chemistry with progression to doctoral study at a partner institution in the Centre for Doctoral Training in Theory and Modelling in Chemical Sciences;

   (*c*) M.Sc. in Theory and Computational Chemistry with no further progression to doctoral study at Oxford or with partner universities in the Centre for Doctoral Training in Theory and Modelling in Chemical Sciences.

4. The examination shall be in two parts, as follows:

   (*a*) Candidates shall successfully complete the prescribed coursework and/or tests on each of the taught modules offered, as specified below.

   (*b*) Candidates shall submit a project report on each of two short projects selected by the candidate in consultation with the supervisor, and approved by the organising committee. One of these projects shall be at Oxford and the other at one of the other partner institutions. The project report shall be assessed by the supervisor and one other academic appointed by the organising committee.

5. The Director of the Centre for Doctoral Training in Theory and Modelling in Chemical Sciences or an appointed deputy shall make available to the examiners a certificate showing the extent to which the candidate has an adequate command of the topics in the modules offered and the assessments of the two short projects.

6. The nature of the assessed work for each module will depend on the nature of the module and will be specified in the course handbook. Completed assignments must be submitted, via the Administrator for the Centre for Doctoral Training in Theory and Modelling in Chemical Sciences, by the corresponding deadline specified in the course handbook.

7. Any candidate who has failed four or more modules of any type at the first attempt will not be permitted to progress to the second year of the doctoral programme in the Centre for Doctoral Training in Theory and Modelling in Chemical Sciences.

8. Assessed work for any failed module may be resubmitted before noon on 1st September for consideration by the board of examiners.

9. A candidate who has failed to satisfy the examiners may enter again for the examination on one, but not more than one, subsequent occasion, not later than one year after the initial attempt, and need only resubmit the assessed work for failed modules. Such candidates will not be permitted to progress to the second year of the doctoral training programme in the Centre for Doctoral Training in Theory and Modelling in Chemical Sciences.

10. Candidates may be examined viva voce at the Examiners' discretion.

11. The examiners may award a distinction for excellence in the whole examination.

12. The Director of the Centre for Doctoral Training in Theory and Modelling in Chemical Sciences or an appointed deputy shall have power to delete courses and to add other lecture courses to this list, and shall publish full details of any such changes in the *University Gazette* by not later than the Friday of the eighth week of the Trinity Term in the year preceding the examination.   5

13. The organising committee shall decide to which of the participating universities the student will transfer for their doctoral project in the second year, based on consultation with students and prospective doctoral supervisors, together if required with the results of the M.Sc.

List of taught modules   10

14. The following eight modules shall be designated *core courses* and must be offered by all candidates: Quantum Mechanics, Statistical Mechanics, Mathematics 1, Statistics, Computer Programming and Numerical Methods, Methods of Computer Simulation, Electronic Structure Theory, Software Development Training.

15. The following nine modules shall be designated *option courses* and candidates   15
must offer five of these for assessment: Applied Computational Chemistry, Biomolecular Simulation, Mathematics 2, Quantum Mechanics in Condensed Phases, Intermolecular Potentials, Chemical Informatics, Chemical Reaction Dynamics, Advanced Statistical Mechanics, Advanced Quantum Mechanics.

Master of Science by Coursework in Visual, Material,   20
and Museum Anthropology

1. The Social Sciences Divisional Board shall elect for the supervision of the course a Standing Committee, namely the Teaching Committee of the School of Anthropology, which shall have power to arrange lectures and other instruction. The course director will be responsible to that committee.   25

2. Candidates must follow a course of instruction in Visual, Material and Museum Anthropology for at least three terms, and will, when entering for the examination, be required to produce a certificate from their supervisor to this effect.

3. Four papers will be taken to constitute Part I of the degree, as follows. Paper 1 will be examined by coursework essay; Paper 2 will be examined either by coursework   30
essay or one three-hour paper; Paper 3 will be examined by a portfolio of coursework notes and a research proposal; Paper 4 will be examined by one three-hour paper. The dissertation will be taken to constitute Part II of the degree. A candidate who fails any of the component parts of the examination may re-take or re-submit that part of the examination on one occasion only. At the close of the written examinations, the   35
examiners will publish a list of those who have satisfied them in Part I.

4. Candidates will be required to submit three copies of written work, required for Papers 1 and 3 comprising an essay for Paper 1 and a portfolio of coursework notes and a research proposal for Paper 3; to present themselves for a written examination for Papers 2 and 4 (where relevant), and to submit three copies of a dissertation in   40
prescribed form on an approved topic as defined below.

5. The assessed written work will consist of:

(i) one essay of no more than 5,000 words for Paper 1 on the syllabus described in the Schedule; for Paper 1 a list of essay titles will be announced no later than Monday of the fourth week of Michaelmas Term. Three typewritten copies of   45
the essay, together with three copies of any associated non-print materials, must be delivered not later than noon of the Tuesday of the first week of Hilary Term to the Chair of the Examiners, M.Sc. in Visual, Material, and Museum Anthropology, c/o Examination Schools, High Street, Oxford. Non-print materials shall not constitute more than fifteen minutes of viewing/read-   50
ing time in the case of video or multimedia submissions.

(ii) an outline proposal for the M.Sc. dissertation research of no more than 2,500 words for Paper 3(a) on the syllabus described in the Schedule. A template wil be provided for the proposal on Friday of 8 week of Hilary Term. Three typewritten copies of the research proposal or essay, together with three copies of any associated non-print materials, must be delivered not later than noon of the Tuesday of the fifth week of Trinity Term to the Chair of the Examiners, M.Sc. in Visual, Material, and Museum Anthropology, c/o Examination Schools, High Street, Oxford. Non-print materials shall not constitute more than fifteen minutes of viewing/reading time in the case of video or multimedia submissions.

(iii) The portfolio must be delivered not later than noon on the Tuesday of the fifth week of Trinity Term to the Chair of Examiners, M.Sc. in Visual, Material, and Museum Anthropology, c/o Examination Schools, High Street, Oxford. Non-print materials shall not constitute more than fifteen minutes of viewing/reading time in the case of video or multimedia submissions.

(iv) a dissertation of no more than 10,000 words, on a subject selected in consultation with the supervisor and approved by the Chair of Examiners. The proposed title of the dissertation together with a paragraph describing its scope and the supervisor's written endorsement, must be submitted to the Chair of Examiners by Tuesday of the second week of Trinity Term. Three typewritten copies of the dissertation, together with three copies of any associated non-print materials, must be delivered not later than noon of the last Wednesday in August in the year in which the examination is taken to the Chair of the Examiners, M.Sc. in Visual, Material, and Museum Anthropology, c/o Examination Schools, High Street, Oxford. The dissertation shall be provided with an abstract of up to 250 words, to be placed immediately after the title page. The word count shall be stated on the outside front cover of the thesis. Non-print materials shall not constitute more than fifteen minutes of viewing/reading time in the case of video or multimedia submissions.

6. The written examination will consist of one three-hour paper for Paper 4 (Fundamental Concepts in Visual, Material and Museuam Anthropology) on the syllabus described in the Schedule. Paper 2 (option) may be assessed either by one three-hour paper or by coursework essay. For those doing Paper 2 assessed by coursework essay, three copies of the essay, together with three copies of any associated non-print materials, must be delivered not later than noon of Tuesday of the second week of Trinity Term to the Chair of Examiners, M.Sc. in Visual, Material, and Museum Anthropology, c/o Examination Schools, High Street, Oxford.

7. There will be no oral examination.

8. The examiners may award a distinction for excellence in the whole examination.

9. In order to pass the degree, a student must pass all its assessed components. Where one or more components are failed, the student will be given the opportunity to re-sit or re-submit them once, as the case may be. Any subsequent award of the degree on successful completion of all the assessed components may be delayed by up to three terms, i.e. until the Examination Board next meets.

Schedule

Every candidate will be required to satisfy the examiners in four papers as follows, and a dissertation:

1. *Contemporary themes in Visual, Material, and Museum Anthropology*

Topics central to this paper include: the changing roles and meanings of artefacts over time; the legacies of anthropology's history in the present—with special reference to museums and material culture; issues of representation, politics and power; theoretical and methodological shifts in the analysis of material culture, museums and

display; fieldwork, collecting, archival processes and other methodologies central to the production of anthropological knowledge. Case studies may focus on topics such as; visual culture (including photography, the internet, art and aesthetics); music and performance; museum ethics and relationships with 'source communities'; landscape and the built environment; religion, identity, and material culture; dress and body 5
modification; mass production and trade; debates concerning tradition, modernity and authenticity; transnational cultural flows; the wider issues of cross-cultural investigation; phenomenological, semiotic and post-structuralist approaches to visual media and material culture; time, memory and perception; film and photographs as material culture; social uses and local practices of visual media use, including indi- 10
genous media and indigenous curation; professional visual media production; visual media and contemporary arts practices; image ethics; digital media practice; audience response and reception theory; art, performance, and display; detailed study of the work of one or more contemporary ethnographic filmmaker, artist, or photographer. *[Note: some topics may vary slightly from year to year].* 15

2. *Option paper*

Candidates must select one option paper from those taught each year for M.Sc. candidates at the Institute of Social and Cultural Anthropology. Titles of options will be made known at the beginning of each academic year and candidates may select their option from any of Lists A, B, or C. 20

3. *Research Methods in Visual, and Material Anthropology and Museum Ethnography*

This paper focuses on visual, material, or museum-related anthropological theory and methods. The scope of this paper includes: fieldwork and data collection methods, visual and non-visual, including photo-, object- and film/video-elicitation; qualitative 25
and quantitative techniques; cultural property and indigenous rights; preparing research proposals; museum display and design; ethical problems; curating exhibitions, artefacts and photographs; working with artists, curators, 'culture brokers' and 'source communities'; elementary still photographic, video and digital multimedia production; exhibition design, analysis and presentation techniques. 30

4. *Fundamental Concepts in Visual, Material, and Museum Anthropology*

This paper focuses on anthropology's distinctive contribution to understanding social and cultural form and process, and the role of human creativity within them, with particular reference to artefacts of material and visual culture, and to the collection, display, production, circulation and consumption of such artefacts. 35
Attention will be paid to the subject's history and its place within broader concerns of politics, colonialism, and culture; issues of power and identity in relation to visual, material and museum anthropology; the formation of museum collections and visual archives; and also to the place of the socio-cultural in constituting such 'natural' phenomena as ecology, landscape, and population. The scope of this paper includes 40
the following topics: the history and development of anthropological photography and object analysis, of documentary and ethnographic film, and of visual display in and beyond museums; an introduction to film and photographic theory, to material culture theory and to anthropological theories of representation, exchange and consumption; the Colonial archive and Colonial documentary practices; the ethnography 45
of film, photography and other visual representational practices.

Master of Science by Coursework in Water Science, Policy and Management

1. The Social Sciences Divisional Board shall elect for the supervision of the course a Standing Committee. The Academic Director and Course Director will be responsible to the Standing Committee. 5

2. Candidates must follow a course of instruction in Water Science, Policy and Management for at least three terms, and will, when entering for the examination, be required to produce a certificate from the Course Director to this effect.

3. The examination will consist of:

    (i) a written examination of three papers based on core courses as described in the 10 schedule;

    (ii) two assessed essays based on elective courses;

    (iii) a dissertation on a subject selected in consultation with the supervisor and Course Director and approved by the Course and Academic Directors.

4. Candidates must submit to the Course Director by the end of Hilary Term in the 15 year in which they enter the examination, the title and a brief statement of the form and scope of their dissertation, together with the name of a person who has been agreed by the Course Director or Academic Director to act as their supervisor during preparation of the dissertation.

5. The dissertation shall be of a maximum length of 15,000 words and accompanied 20 by an abstract not exceeding 150 words. The maximum word count shall shall include footnotes, but exclude appendices, references and the abstract. The detailed format and specification of the dissertation shall be approved by the Standing Committee, and published in the course handbook.

6. The deadline for submission of the dissertation is noon on the first weekday of 25 September in the year in which the written examination is taken. Two copies of the dissertation must be submitted, to the M.Sc Examiners (Water Science, Policy and Management) c/o Examinations Schools, High Street, Oxford OX1 4BG. The examiners may retain one copy of the dissertation of each candidate who passes the examination for deposit in an appropriate library. Both copies must bear the candi- 30 date's examination number but not his/her name.

7. All submitted work shall be accompanied by a separate statement certifying that that the submitted work is the candidate's own work except where otherwise indicated.

8. In the written examination, the examiners will permit the use of hand-held pocket calculators subject to the conditions set out under the heading 'Use of calcu- 35 lators in examinations' in the Special Regulations concerning Examinations.

9. The examiners may also examine any candidate viva voce on the candidate's written papers, dissertation or both.

10. Arrangements for reassessment shall be specified by the Standing Committee and published in the course handbook. 40

11. The examiners may award a distinction for excellence in the whole examination.

Schedule

(a) *Core courses*

The core courses will be examined under the following heads: 45

1. *Water Science*

Candidates will be expected to have knowledge and a critical understanding of the physical, chemical and biological processes, and interactions across the hydrological cycle at the global, basin/catchment and hillslope scale, of the relationship of water to health and disease, and of the engineering and technological solutions to water supply and sanitation.

2. *Water and Society*

Candidates will be expected to have knowledge and a critical understanding of the   5
arguments and issues related to the legal, social, political and institutional dimensions of water decision-making. Along with the economic approaches, modelling tools, and analysis techniques that can be used to support policy.

3. *Water Management*

Candidates will be expected to have knowledge and a critical understanding of   10
relevant debates and issues concerning water management.

(*b*) *Elective courses*

Candidates will be expected to show advanced knowledge of two of the elective courses on offer in any year.

NOTES

10

MASTER OF THEOLOGY (IN APPLIED THEOLOGY) AND POSTGRADUATE DIPLOMA IN APPLIED THEOLOGY

1. The Board of the Faculty of Theology and Religion shall have power to award Postgraduate Diplomas in Applied Theology. Any person who has been admitted under the provisions of this section as a Student for the Postgraduate Diploma in Applied Theology, who has satisfied the conditions prescribed in the relevant regulations made by the faculty board under Section B below, and who has satisfied the examiners for the Diploma may be awarded the Postgraduate Diploma in Applied Theology.

2. Any person who has been admitted under the provisions of this section as a Student for the Degree of Master of Theology, who has satisfied the conditions prescribed in the relevant regulations made by the faculty board under Section A below, and who has satisfied the examiners for the degree may supplicate for the Degree of Master of Theology. Alternatively, such persons may be awarded the Postgraduate Diploma in Applied Theology if they have satisfied the conditions prescribed in the relevant regulations made by the faculty board under Section B below and have satisfied the examiners for the Diploma.

3. The examinations for the Degree of Master of Theology and for the Postgraduate Diploma in Applied Theology shall be under the supervision of the Board of the Faculty of Theology and Religion which shall have power to make regulations governing the examinations. The examiners may award a distinction for excellence in the whole examination. Candidates who have initially failed any element of assessment shall not normally be eligible for the award of distinction.

4. There shall be a Committee for the supervision of arrangements for the Degree of Master of Theology and for the Postgraduate Diploma in Applied Theology which shall be called the Master of Theology Studies Committee. This Committee shall consist of two representatives of the Board of the Faculty of Theology and Religion (at least one of whom shall be a member of the board's Graduate Studies Committee) and one representative of each of the participating institutions, as listed in the Schedule below. The Committee may co-opt up to three additional members. The Committee shall have such powers and duties in respect of the Degree of Master of Theology and the Postgraduate Diploma in Applied Theology as may from time to time be prescribed by the Board of the Faculty of Theology and Religion.

5. The Board of the Faculty of Theology and Religion shall have the power to admit as students for the Degree of Master of Theology and for the Postgraduate Diploma in Applied Theology candidates nominated by the institutions listed in the Schedule below.

6. Each of the institutions listed in the Schedule below shall make a return to the Registrar by the end of the first week of Michaelmas Full Term, showing the names of all persons nominated in that term as Students for the Degree of Master of Theology and for the Postgraduate Diploma in Applied Theology, and the Registrar shall keep a register of such students.

7. The Board of the Faculty of Theology and Religion shall have power, on the advice of a student's society or other institution, to remove temporarily or permanently the name of a student from the register.

Schedule

The participating institutions for the Degree of Master of Theology and for the Postgraduate Diploma in Applied Theology are: Blackfriars; Campion Hall; Harris Manchester College; Mansfield College; Regent's Park College; Ripon College, Cuddesdon; St Benet's Hall; St Stephen's House; and Wycliffe Hall.

A. **Regulations for the course of instruction for the Master of Theology (in Applied Theology) at the participating institutions listed in the Schedule.**

1. Candidates, who must be members of the University, shall be graduates in theology, or shall hold an equivalent theological qualification.

2. Full-time residential candidates will complete Part I of the course in *one* year and *one* additional residential year for Part II [dissertation]. Submission of Unit 2 may be delayed until the April submission after the first year of the course.

3. Part-time non-residential candidates will complete Part I of the course in *two* years part-time and *two* additional years for Part II [dissertation].

4. Candidates may change from full-time to part-time after the first year of study.

5. Part-time candidates shall be required to attend courses of instruction organised by the participating institutions equivalent to one day a week over six terms.

6. For part-time students there shall be no residential requirement for Part II.

7. In Part I, all candidates will take the first two units and any two others. All units in Part I are examined by extended essays of not more than 7,000 words. In addition, Unit 2 will normally be supplemented with a portfolio of supporting materials.

8. Part II will consist of a dissertation of between 15,000 and 20,000 words on an aspect of applied theology. All Candidates for Part II are required to present themselves for a viva voce examination unless individually dispensed by the examiners.

9. A request for approval for the specific titles of the extended essays submitted in Part I, written on the appropriate form, must reach the Graduate Studies Assistant, Humanities Division by the final Friday in February (for essays to be submitted in the following late April), and by the first Friday in June (for essays to be submitted in the following late September). In the case of Unit 2, the application should include a brief description of any portfolio of material to be submitted. Proposed topics for Part II dissertations may be submitted to the M.Th. Studies Committee before the completion of Part 1, and must have been submitted by the final Friday in December (for submissions in the following late April) and by the final Friday in March (for submissions in the following late September).

10. Extended essays must be the candidate's own work, and must be typed or printed on one side of the paper. Essays must include a bibliography and footnotes (only the latter being included in the word count). Candidates may receive tutorial guidance in the preliminary stages of composition; tutors may also read or comment on a first draft, giving the candidate not more than one tutorial session at this further stage. Normal graduate supervision shall be provided for the preparation of the dissertation in Part II. When submitted, the extended essays must be accompanied by a certificate signed by the candidate indicating that it is the candidate's own work. This certificate must be submitted separately in a sealed envelope addressed to the Chair of the Examiners for the M.Th. in Applied Theology at the address below.

11. Extended essays may be submitted to the Chair of the Examiners, M.Th. in Applied Theology, c/o Examination Schools, High Street, Oxford OX1 4BG, by 12 noon on the Friday before 1 May and 1 October in any year, provided that all

extended essays must have been submitted by 12 noon on the Friday before 1 October following the third term in which a candidate's name has been on the register if the course is being taken full-time, or the sixth term if part-time. Candidates may delay the submission of their extended essay for Unit 2 until the April following the end of the first year of their course.   5

12. In Part I, a candidate whose extended essay fails to reach the level which the examiners have determined to be the pass mark (or the required average for passing Part I) may be allowed at the discretion of the examiners to resubmit that work on one further occasion only, within the next two examination periods, provided that (save in the case envisaged in 16. below) no extended essay is submitted later than the   10
submission of the dissertation. Permission to resubmit a unit must be sought in writing from the Chair of Examiners by the final Friday in February (for essays to be submitted in the following late April), and by the final Friday in June (for essays to be submitted in the following late September).

13. In Part II, if the examiners are satisfied that the dissertation has reached the   15
required level for the M.Th., but minor corrections are needed, they shall require the candidate to make these corrections before they submit their report. If the dissertation fails to reach the required level, the examiners may, but are not obliged to, give a candidate permission to revise and resubmit a dissertation at one further examination period, not later than three terms after the first submission.   20

14. Full-time students for the M.Th. must submit their dissertation within six terms of beginning the course; part-time students must submit their dissertation within twelve terms of beginning the course; students who change from full-time to part-time status after three terms must submit their dissertation within nine terms of beginning the course. This regulation is not affected by a student's need to resubmit   25
a Part I Unit, except in the case covered by 16. below.

15. No full-time student for the degree shall normally retain that status for more than six terms. No part-time student for the degree shall normally retain that status for more than twelve terms; and no student who changes from full-time to part-time status after the first year of study shall normally retain student status for more than nine   30
terms.

16. In the event of a full-time student needing to resubmit Unit 2 following a first examination in the Trinity Term of the student's second year of study, the M.Th. Studies Committee will review the case. It may at its absolute discretion grant permission, either for the resubmission to occur after the submission of the disserta-   35
tion (notwithstanding 12. above), or for the submission of the dissertation to be delayed until the Trinity Term examination in the following academic year.

Part I (and Postgraduate Diploma in Applied Theology)
Candidates will take the first two units and any two others.
1. *Doctrine, Context and Practice*   40
Candidates will explore the interrelationship between Christian doctrine and Christian practice in historical and social context. They will be able to demonstrate an understanding of Christian doctrine and practice as these have been developed in scripture, tradition and in the modern world.

2. *Experiential project with theological reflection*   45
Candidates will be expected to offer a theological evaluation of a project under-taken in either a church or secular setting in which the candidate shares in the concerns and experiences of those involved. They should normally submit a portfolio of material which should include relevant documentation and one or more case studies based upon contact made over a period of not less than twenty-one days and should   50
offer a theological reflection based on this evidence. Full-time candidates may delay

submission of this unit until the April submission following the end of the first year of their course.

3. *Sociology of Religion*

Candidates will be expected to demonstrate an understanding of the main methods of the study of religion in relation to modern society. They should consider such topics as secularisation, religious organisation, civil religion, and fundamentalism. They may also address the relationship between sociology and the different areas of theological study including biblical studies, doctrine and church history.

4. *Pastoral Psychology*

Candidates will study the contribution of psychological studies to pastoral understanding and practice; the principles of psychological explication with particular reference to the psychology of religious experience; the importance of the psychological dimension in particular areas of pastoral concern, for instance human development, marriage, sickness, death and bereavement.

5. *Science and Faith in the Modern World*

Candidates will explore the interrelationships between Christian theology and the natural sciences, with special reference to the implications for contemporary Christian practice. They will consider methodological issues in their own right, and such specific topics as the implications of evolutionary theory, or developments in fundamental physics, for the Christian doctrine of creation.

6. *The use of the Bible*

Candidates will be expected to study the use of the Bible in preaching, worship, and ethics, the phenomenon of diversity in the Bible; the contribution of hermeneutics to the use of the Bible in pastoral ministry; and the quest for a critical standpoint in contextual study of the Bible.

7. *Christian Spirituality*

Candidates will explore critically the theological issues raised by selected well-established traditions of Christian prayer and devotion, drawing when appropriate on insights from the human sciences and from other academic disciplines. They should also consider different models of spiritual growth and spiritual guidance, drawing out the theology of ministry implicit within these.

8. *Liturgy and Worship*

Candidates will explore theologically the role of liturgy within Christian life, mission and discipleship, drawing when appropriate on insights from the human sciences and from other academic disciplines. They should consider such topics as the role of symbols, the relationship between the verbal and the non-verbal in worship, the relationship between liturgy and creativity, and the interaction between liturgy and culture.

9. *Christian Ethics*

Candidates will consider the interrelationships between Christianity and the theory and practice of the moral life. They will explore questions of fundamental moral theology, and also address selected specific ethical issues.

10. *Mission in the Modern World*

Candidates will study the mission of the Church in the light of the mission of God and in the context of contemporary societies and cultures. They should consider the inter-relationship of various aspects of mission such as evangelism; social and political action; dialogue with other faiths and ideologies. Candidates should evaluate the implications on mission of issues such as secularisation, urbanisation, post-colonialism, and post-modernity.

11. *Inter-Faith Dialogue*

Candidates will study the encounter of faith communities and the development of inter-faith dialogue in plural societies. They will critically examine models of dialogue and may, if they wish, focus on the relationship of Christianity to one other faith tradition.

12. *Ecclesiology in an Ecumenical Context*

Candidates will examine the doctrines of the Church, the ministry and the sacraments in their relationship to the concrete realities of the life of the Church and the nature of its authority. The study will be made in the light of current thought across the Christian traditions.

Part II

1. The title of the proposed dissertation, together with a summary, must be submitted for approval by the Master of Theology Studies Committee in the final term of Part I of the course. The Committee shall approve a supervisor for the writing of the dissertation.

2. The dissertation (two copies) shall be submitted to the Chair of the Examiners, M.Th. in Applied Theology, c/o Examination Schools, High Street, Oxford OX1 4BG, not later than 12 noon on the Friday before 1 October following the ninth term in which a candidate's name has been on the register if the course is being taken full-time, or the twelfth term if part-time.

3. The thesis must be printed or typed on one side of the paper only, with a margin of 3 to 3.5 cms on the left-hand edge of each page, and must be securely and firmly bound in either hard or soft covers. Loose-leaf binding is not acceptable.

4. The completed dissertation must be accompanied by a signed statement by the candidate that it is his or her own work except where otherwise indicated. This statement must be submitted separately in a sealed envelope addressed to the Chair of Examiners for the M.Th. in Applied Theology at the above address.

5. All candidates are required to present themselves for a viva voce examination unless individually dispensed by the examiners.

6. Certain successful theses, on the recommendation of the examiners, should be deposited in the Theology Faculty Library. The library copy of thesis must be in a permanently fixed binding, drilled and sewn, in a stiff board case in library buckram, in a dark colour, and lettered on the spine with the candidate's name and initials, the degree, and the year of submission.

B. **Regulations for the course of instruction for the Postgraduate Diploma in Applied Theology at the participating institutions listed in the Schedule.**

1. The entry requirements for the course are as prescribed at A.1. above.

2. A candidate may complete the course either in ONE year full-time (residential) *or* TWO years part-time (non-residential).

3. Part-time candidates shall be required to attend courses of instruction organised by the participating institutions for one day a week during six terms, together with one three-day residential study conference organised by the M.Th. Studies Committee in each of the two years of their course.

4. The examination will consist of an extended essay of up to 7,000 words on each of the two compulsory and two optional units of Part I of the M.Th. course as set out above. The regulations concerning extended essays are as prescribed at A.4. above.

5. **[For students starting before MT 2015:** No full-time student for the Diploma shall retain that status for more than six terms in all, and no part-time student for that award shall retain that status for more than nine terms in all.] **[For students starting from MT 2015:** No full-time student for the Diploma shall normally retain that status

for more than three terms in all, and no part-time student for that award shall normally retain that status for more than six terms in all.]

6. Candidates who have successfully completed the Diploma at an appropriate level may subsequently proceed to Part II of the M.Th. on the recommendation of the M.Th. Studies Committee. At the discretion of the Committee, transfer of   5
Diploma candidates to Part II of the M.Th. course may be allowed to those candidates who have reached the required standard in the four papers submitted by the end of their first year.

NOTES

11

MASTER OF BUSINESS ADMINISTRATION

§1. Degree of Master of Business Administration (Full-time and Part-time)

1. Any person who has been admitted to the status of student for the Degree of Master of Business Administration, who has satisfied the conditions prescribed by this section, and who has satisfied the examiners as required, may supplicate for the Degree of Master of Business Administration.

2. The Social Sciences Board with the concurrence of the Education Committee shall have power to make and vary such regulations as may be necessary for carrying out the duties laid upon it and upon the Registrar by this section.

3. A Student for the Degree of Master of Business Administration who is not a graduate of the University may wear the same gown as that worn by Students for the Degree of Doctor of Philosophy.

§2. Admission of Candidates

1. A candidate seeking admission as a Student for the Degree of Master of Business Administration shall apply to the MBA Committee. Candidates for admission shall be required to provide such information as the committee may determine from time to time by regulation. Applicants shall in addition be required to undertake such other tests and meet such conditions as, subject to the approval of the Social Sciences Board, the committee may determine by regulation.

2. No person shall be admitted as a Student for the Degree of Master of Business Administration under these provisions unless he or she is also a member of some college, hall, or other approved society, and unless the application for admission as a Student for the Degree of Master of Business Administration has the approval of that society. The Head of Admissions shall forward the application to the candidate's society or to the society to which the candidate wishes to apply for membership, as appropriate; and admission by the committee shall be conditional upon admission by an approved society.

3. A student registered for any other higher degree or diploma in the University may apply for transfer to the status of Student for the Degree of Master of Business Administration. The committee shall have power to make such transfer, provided that it is satisfied that the student is well qualified and well fitted to undertake the course of study for which application is made, and that the application has the support of the candidate's society. A candidate who transfers status in this way shall be reckoned as having held the status of Student for the Degree of Master of Business Administration from the time of admission to his or her previous status, unless the committee shall determine otherwise.

§3. Supervision of Students

1. Every candidate on admission as a Student for the Degree of Master of Business Administration shall be placed by the MBA Committee under the supervision of a

5

10

15

20

25

30

35

40

member of the University or other competent person selected by the committee, and the committee shall have power for sufficient reason to change the supervisor of any student or to arrange for joint supervision by more than one supervisor, if it deems necessary.

2. It shall be the duty of the supervisor of a student entered upon a course of study to direct the work of the student, to meet the student regularly, and to undertake such duties as shall be from time to time set out in the Divisional Board's memorandum of guidance for students and supervisors.

3. The supervisor shall submit a report on the progress of a student to the committee three times a year, and at any other time when the committee so requests or the supervisor deems expedient. The supervisor shall communicate the contents of the report to the student on each occasion that a report is made, so that the student is aware of the supervisor's assessment of his or her work during the period in question. In addition, the supervisor shall inform the committee at once if he or she is of the opinion that the student is unlikely to reach the standard required for the Degree of Master of Business Administration.

4. It shall be the duty of every Student for the Degree of Master of Business Administration to undertake such guided work and to attend such seminars and lectures as his or her supervisor requests; to attend such meetings with his or her supervisor as the supervisor reasonably arranges; and to fulfil any other requirements of the Divisional Board as set out in its memorandum of guidance for students and supervisors.

§4. Residence and other Requirements

1. No full-time Student for the Degree of Master of Business Administration shall be granted leave to supplicate unless, after admission, he or she has kept statutory residence and pursued his or her course of study at Oxford for at least thirty-seven weeks.

2. No full-time Student for the Degree of Master of Business Administration shall retain that status for more than six terms in all.

3. Part-time students for the Degree of Master of Business Administration shall in each case be required to pursue their course of study over an elapsed time of 21 months. Part-time students shall not be required to keep statutory residence but must attend for such instruction and undertake such supervised coursework as the MBA committee shall require. The part-time MBA Director shall keep a register of attendance of part-time students. No student shall be granted leave to supplicate unless the register shows satisfactory attendance by him or her.

4. Part-time students may hold the status of Student for the Part-time Degree of Master of Business Administration for a period not exceeding 48 months.

5. A Student for the Degree of Master of Business Administration shall cease to hold that status if:

   (*a*) he or she shall have been refused permission to supplicate for the Degree of Master of Business Administration;

   (*b*) the MBA Committee shall, in accordance with provisions set down by regulation by the Divisional Board, and after consultation with the student's society and supervisor, have deprived the student of such status;

   (*c*) he or she shall have been transferred under the relevant provisions to another status; or

   (*d*) he or she shall not have entered for the relevant examination within the time specified under this sub-section.

§5. **Examination of Students**

1. The examination for the Degree of Master of Business Administration shall be under the supervision of the MBA Committee. The subjects of each examination shall be determined by regulation by the committee, which shall have power to arrange lectures and courses of instruction for the assessment. The assessment shall consist of:

(*a*) course assignments;

(*b*) written examinations;

(*c*) oral presentations;

(*d*) written or oral reports on a business project approved by the committee;

(*e*) class participation; and

(*f*) an oral examination; provided that the committee shall have power by regulation to authorise the examiners to dispense individual candidates from the oral examination. This provision notwithstanding, the examiners may, if they deem expedient, set a candidate a further written examination after examining the candidate orally.

2. No candidate shall be permitted to take an examination under the preceding clause unless he or she has been admitted as a candidate for the examination in question by the committee and has satisfied any other conditions prescribed in the regulations for that course.

3. Unless otherwise provided in this sub-section, the number and distribution of examiners shall be as set out in the relevant regulation.

4. A candidate who has failed to satisfy the examiners in the examination may enter again on one, but not more than one, subsequent occasion for that part of the examination which he or she failed.

A. Full-time students

1. Candidates must follow for at least three terms a course of instruction in Management Studies. Candidates must complete components (*a*)–(*e*) below:

(*a*) all eight courses from the Schedule;

(*b*) EITHER nine electives, a maximum of two of which can be completed by taking equivalent (up to four) half electives;

OR seven electives, a maximum of two of which can be completed by taking equivalent (up to four) half electives, and a summer project, which must be approved by the MBA Director.

A list of electives will be published by the MBA Director no later than the first Monday of the preceding term.

(*c*) the integration modules on Global Rules of the Game, Responsible Leadership, and Entrepreneurship;

(*d*) an Entrepreneurship Project (EP);

(*e*) Global Opportunities & Threats Oxford (GOTO).

2. Students must satisfy the examiners in all assessments associated with components (*a*)–(*e*) above, but may fail one of the eight courses from component (a) or one of the elective courses from component (b) and still pass the programme as a whole. Candidates may be required to attend an oral examination on any part.

3. The examiners may award a distinction for excellence in the whole examination to candidates for the Degree.

4. In exceptional circumstances, a candidate wishing to take an examination later than the one to which he or she has been admitted may do so by application to the Chair of Examiners.

B. Part-time students

1. Candidates taking the course on a part-time basis must follow for not less than 21 months a course of instruction in Management Studies. Candidates must complete components (*a*) to (*g*) below:

    (*a*) all eight courses from the Schedule;   5

    (*b*) six electives, a maximum of two of which can be completed by taking equivalent (up to four) half electives. The list of electives will be published by the Director of the part-time MBA not later than the first day of the first module of the second year of the programme;

    (*c*) an Entrepreneurship Project (EP);   10

    (*d*) the Global Rules of the Game integrative module;

    (*e*) the Strategic Leader integrative module;

    (*f*) the Business in Emerging Markets module;

    (*g*) Global Opportunities & Threats Oxford (GOTO).

2. Students must satisfy the examiners in all assessments associated with compo-   15
nents (a)–(g) above, but may fail one of the eight courses from component (a), or one of the elective courses from component (b), or one of the components (d) to (g) and still pass the programme as a whole. Candidates may be required to attend an oral examination on any part.

3. The MBA Committee shall have the discretion to permit any candidate to the   20
part-time MBA to be exempted from up to four courses providing that the Committee is satisfied that such a candidate has completed equivalent study of an appropriate standard, and has passed the assessment associated with that equivalent study, on either the Postgraduate Diploma in Financial Strategy, the Postgraduate Diploma in Global Business, the Postgraduate Diploma in Organisational Leadership, or the   25
Postgraduate Diploma in Strategy and Innovation (previously the Postgraduate Diploma in Advanced Strategy) no more than five years before initial registration for the part-time MBA. Application for exemptions will only be permitted until 31st December 2017, after which candidates on any Postgraduate Diploma may only transfer onto the part-time MBA under clause 4 below.   30

4. The MBA Committee shall have the discretion to permit any candidate to transfer onto the part-time MBA from either the Postgraduate Diploma in Financial Strategy, the Postgraduate Diploma in Global Business, the Postgraduate Diploma in Organisational Leadership, or the Postgraduate Diploma in Strategy and Innovation, providing that the Committee is satisfied that such a candidate has   35
completed equivalent study of an appropriate standard on the four courses on the respective Postgraduate Diploma, and has passed the assessment associated with these four courses.

5. With the approval of the Director of the part-time MBA, a candidate may substitute core courses or electives on the part-time MBA with core courses from   40
the Postgraduate Diploma in Financial Strategy, the Postgraduate Diploma in Global Business, the Postgraduate Diploma in Organisational Leadership, the Postgraduate Diploma in Strategy and Innovation, or M.Sc. in Major Programme Management, assuming that core course falls within the permitted registration period for the part-time MBA.   45

6. The examiners may award a distinction for excellence in the whole examination to candidates for the Degree.

7. In exceptional circumstances, a candidate wishing to take an examination later than the one to which he or she has been admitted may do so by application to the Chair of Examiners.   50

Schedule

(*a*) Analytics
(*b*) Firms & Markets
(*c*) Accounting
(*d*) Strategy 5
(*e*) Business Finance
(*f*) Leadership Fundamentals
(*g*) Technology & Operations Management
(*h*) Marketing

NOTES

12

MASTER OF FINE ART

§1. Degree of Master of Fine Art

1. Any person who has been admitted to the status of Student for the Degree of Master of Fine Art, who has satisfied the conditions prescribed by this section, and who has satisfied the examiners as required, may supplicate for the Degree of Master of Fine Art.

2. The Education Committee shall have power to make and vary such regulations as may be necessary for carrying out the duties laid upon it and upon the Registrar by this section.

3. A Student for the Degree of Master of Fine Art who is not a graduate of the University may wear the same gown as that worn by Students for the Degree of Doctor of Philosophy.

§2. Admission of Candidates

1. A candidate seeking admission as a Student for the Degree of Master of Fine Art shall apply to the Committee for the Ruskin School of Art. Candidates for admission shall be required to provide such information as the Committee may determine from time to time by regulation. Applicants shall in addition be required to undertake such other tests and meet such conditions as, subject to the approval of the Education Committee, the Committee may determine by regulation.

2. A student registered for any other higher degree or diploma in the University may apply for transfer to the status of Student for the Degree of Master of Fine Art. The Committee shall have power to make such transfer, provided that it is satisfied that the student is well-qualified and well-fitted to undertake the course of study for which application is made, and that the application has the support of the candidate's society. A candidate who transfers status in this way shall be reckoned as having held the status of Student for the Degree of Master of Fine Art from the time of admission to his or her previous status, unless the Committee shall determine otherwise.

§3. Supervision of Students

1. Every candidate on admission as a Student for the Degree of Master of Fine Art shall be placed by the Committee for the Ruskin School of Art under the supervision of a member of the University or other competent person selected by the Committee, and the Committee shall have power for sufficient reason to change the supervisor of any student or to arrange for joint supervision by more than one supervisor, if it deems necessary.

2. It shall be the duty of the supervisor of a student entered upon a course of study to direct and superintend the work of the student, to meet the student regularly, and to undertake such duties as shall be from time to time set out in the relevant Policy and Guidance issued by the Education Committee.

3. The supervisor shall submit a report on the progress of a student to the Committee three times a year, and at any other time when the Committee so requests or the supervisor deems expedient. The supervisor shall communicate the contents of the report to the student on each occasion that a report is made, so that the student is aware of the supervisor's assessment of his or her work during the period in question. In addition, the supervisor shall inform the Committee at once if he or she is of the opinion that the student is unlikely to reach the standard required for the Degree of Master of Fine Art.

4. It shall be the duty of every Student for the Degree of Master of Fine Art to undertake such guided work and to attend such seminars and lectures as his or her supervisor requests; to attend such meetings with his or her supervisor as the supervisor reasonably arranges; and to fulfil any other requirements of the relevant Policy and Guidance issued by the Education Committee.

§4. Residence and other Requirements

1. No full-time Student for the Degree of Master of Fine Art shall be granted leave to supplicate unless, after admission, he or she has kept statutory residence and pursued his or her course of study at Oxford for at least forty weeks. No part-time Student for the Degree of Master of Fine Art shall be granted leave to supplicate unless, after admission, he or she has pursued his or her course of study at Oxford for at least six terms on a part-time basis, including attendance for university-based work for a minimum of 30 days annually, ten days per term.

2. No full-time Student for the Degree of Master of Fine Art shall retain that status for more than two years in all. No part-time students shall retain that status for more than four years in all.

3. A Student for the Degree of Master of Fine Art shall cease to hold that status if:

(*a*) he or she shall have been refused permission to supplicate for the Degree of Master of Fine Art;

(*b*) the Committee for the Ruskin School of Art shall, in accordance with provisions set down by regulation by the Education Committee, and after consultation with the student's society and supervisor, have deprived the student of such status;

(*c*) he or she shall have been transferred under the relevant provisions to another status; or

(*d*) he or she shall not have entered for the relevant examination within the time specified under this sub-section.

§5. Examination of Students

1. The examination for the Degree of Master of Fine Art shall be under the supervision of the Committee for the Ruskin School of Art. The subjects of each examination shall be determined by regulation by the Committee, which shall have power to arrange lectures and courses of instruction for the examination.

2. No candidate shall be permitted to take an examination under the preceding clause unless he or she has been admitted as a candidate for the examination in question by the Committee and has satisfied any other conditions prescribed in the regulations for that course.

3. Unless otherwise provided in this sub-section, the number and distribution of examiners shall be as set out in the relevant regulation.

4. A candidate who has failed to satisfy the examiners in the examination may enter again on one, but not more than one, subsequent occasion for that part of the examination which he or she failed.

1. The examination shall include both practical and written work.

2. Every candidate for the examination must follow a programme of study in the practice of art, which will include the development of individually determined projects of artwork, presented for discussion in a series of group seminars.

3. Every candidate for the examination must follow a programme of seminars for the discussion of contemporary art and cultural theory.

4. Syllabus

(*a*) Every candidate must submit an exhibition or other presentation as appropriate of completed artworks in any medium including 2D, 3D installation, performance, moving image, writing and sound. Full time candidates must submit this by noon of Friday of the Week 6 in Trinity term. Part time candidates must submit this by noon of Friday of Week 6 in Trinity term of their second year.

(*b*) Every candidate must submit full documentation of their studio project work.

Full time candidates must submit this as a document of not more than 30 pages, to include images. It should incorporate a text of not more than 2,000 words to annotate and explicate the visual documentation and may be accompanied by up to 20 minutes of moving image in a universal file of digital format, on DVD or hard-drive. This should be submitted by noon of Friday of Week 8 in Trinity Term.

Part time candidates must submit documentation of studio project work completed in the 1st year by noon on Friday of Week 8 of Trinity Term of that year. They must submit documentation of studio project work completed in the 2nd year by noon on Friday of Week 8 of Trinity Term of that year. In each case it must be submitted as a document of not more than 15 pages, to include images. It should incorporate a text of not more than 1,000 words to annotate and explicate the visual documentation and may be accompanied by up to 10 minutes of moving image in a universal file of digital format on DVD or hard-drive. It should be submitted to the Chairman of the Examiners, MFA in Fine Art, c/o Examination Schools, High Street, Oxford OX1 4BG.

(*c*) Every candidate must, after consultation with his or her supervisor, submit an extended text of at least at least 4,000 words in support of their studio work. This may be an account of the methodology used in the studio project, an exposition of its theoretical framework, or an essay on another topic of direct relevance to the practice. The completed essay should be submitted as a PDF plus 3 printed copies. Full time candidates must submit not later than noon of Monday of Week 1 in Trinity Term. Part time candidates must submit it not later than noon of Monday of Week 1 in Trinity Term of their 2nd year. It should be submitted to the Chairman of the Examiners, MFA in Fine Art, c/o Examination Schools, High Street, Oxford OX1 4BG.

5. Candidates must present themselves for an oral examination unless individually dispensed from this requirement by the examiners. In this examination the essay referred to in 4(c) the submission in 4(b) and the candidate's general command of their field will be discussed.

6. A candidate who fails the examination may re-sit at the end of the following Michaelmas Term.

7. The examiners may award a distinction for excellence in the examination.

NOTES

13

MASTER OF PUBLIC POLICY

GENERAL REGULATIONS

§1. Degree of Master of Public Policy

1. Any person who has been admitted to the status of student for the Degree of Master of Public Policy, who has satisfied the conditions prescribed by this section, and who has satisfied the examiners as required, may supplicate for the Degree of Master of Public Policy.

2. The Social Sciences Board with the concurrence of the Education Committee shall have power to make and vary such regulations as may be necessary for carrying out the duties laid upon it and upon the Registrar by this section.

3. A student for the Degree of Master of Public Policy who is not a graduate of the University may wear the same gown as that worn by Students for the Degree of Doctor of Philosophy.

§2. Admission of Candidates

1. A candidate seeking admission as a Student for the Degree of Master of Public Policy shall apply to the BSG Graduate Studies Committee. Candidates for admission shall be required to provide such information as the committee may determine from time to time by regulation. Applicants shall in addition be required to undertake such other tests and meet such conditions as, subject to the approval of the Social Sciences Board, the committee may determine by regulation.

2. No person shall be admitted as a Student for the Degree of Master of Public Policy under these provisions unless he or she is also a member of some college, hall, or other approved society, and unless the application for admission as a Student for the Degree of Master of Public Policy has the approval of that society. The Academic Director shall forward the application to the candidate's society or to the society to which the candidate wishes to apply for membership, as appropriate; and admission by the committee shall be conditional upon admission by an approved society.

3. A student registered for any other higher degree or diploma in the University may apply for transfer to the status of Student for the Degree of Master of Public Policy. The committee shall have power to make such transfer, provided that it is satisfied that the student is well qualified and well fitted to undertake the course of study for which application is made, and that the application has the support of the candidate's society. A candidate who transfers status in this way shall be reckoned as having held the status of Student for the Degree of Master of Public Policy from the time of admission to his or her previous status, unless the committee shall determine otherwise.

§3. Supervision of Students

1. Every candidate on admission as a Student for the Degree of Master of Public Policy shall be placed by the BSG Graduate Studies Committee under the supervision of a member of the University or other competent person selected by the committee, and the committee shall have power for sufficient reason to change the supervisor of any

student or to arrange for joint supervision by more than one supervisor, if it deems necessary.

2. It shall be the duty of the supervisor of a student entered upon a course of study to direct and superintend the work of the student, to meet the student regularly, and to undertake such duties as shall be from time to time set out in the Divisional Board's   5
memorandum of guidance for students and supervisors.

3. The supervisor shall submit a report on the progress of a student to the committee three times a year, and at any other time when the committee so requests or the supervisor deems expedient. The supervisor shall communicate the contents of the report to the student on each occasion that a report is made, so that the student is   10
aware of the supervisor's assessment of his or her work during the period in question. In addition, the supervisor shall inform the committee at once if he or she is of the opinion that the student is unlikely to reach the standard required for the Degree of Master of Public Policy.

4. It shall be the duty of every Student for the Degree of Master of Public Policy to   15
undertake such guided work and to attend such seminars and lectures as his or her supervisor requests; to attend such meetings with his or her supervisor as the supervisor reasonably arranges; and to fulfil any other requirements of the Divisional Board as set out in its memorandum of guidance for students and supervisors.

§4. Residence and other Requirements   20

1. No full-time Student for the Degree of Master of Public Policy shall be granted leave to supplicate unless, after admission, he or she has kept statutory residence and pursued his or her course of study at Oxford for at least thirty-two weeks.

2. No full-time Student for the Degree of Master of Public Policy shall retain that status for more than six terms in all.   25

3. A Student for the Degree of Master of Public Policy shall cease to hold that status if:

   (*a*) he or she shall have been refused permission to supplicate for the Degree of Master of Public Policy;

   (*b*) the BSG Graduate Studies Committee shall, in accordance with provisions set down by regulation by the Divisional Board, and after consultation with   30
   the student's society and supervisor, have deprived the student of such status;

   (*c*) he or she shall have been transferred under the relevant provisions to another status; or

   (*d*) he or she shall not have entered for the relevant examination within the time specified under this sub-section.   35

§5. Examination of Students

1. The examination for the Degree of Master of Public Policy shall be under the supervision of the BSG Graduate Studies Committee. The subjects of each examination shall be determined by regulation by the committee, which shall have power to arrange lectures and courses of instruction for the assessment. The assessment shall consist of: 40

   (*a*) course assignments;

   (*b*) written examinations;

   (*c*) written reports on a summer project approved by the committee; and

   (*d*) an oral examination; provided that the committee shall have power by regulation to authorise the examiners to dispense individual candidates from the oral   45
   examination. This provision notwithstanding, the examiners may, if they deem expedient, set a candidate a further written examination after examining the candidate orally.

2. No candidate shall be permitted to take an examination under the preceding clause unless he or she has been admitted as a candidate for the examination in question by the committee and has satisfied any other conditions prescribed in the regulations for that course.

3. Unless otherwise provided in this sub-section, the number and distribution of examiners shall be as set out in the relevant regulation.

4. A candidate who has failed to satisfy the examiners in the examination may enter again on one, but not more than one, subsequent occasion for that part of the examination which he or she failed.

SPECIAL REGULATIONS

1. Candidates must follow for at least three terms a course of instruction in Public Policy. Candidates must complete:

    (*a*) all courses from the Schedule, and satisfy the examiners in the assignment and/or examination associated with each course;

    (*b*) two electives. Candidates must satisfy the examiners in the assignment/ examination/written report associated with each course, the list of electives to be published annually by the BSG Graduate Studies Committee before the first Monday of Hilary Term;

    (*c*) a summer project. Candidates must satisfy the examiners in the written report associated with the summer project;

    (*d*) candidates may be required to attend an oral examination on any of the above.

2. Assignments and written reports on projects must be presented not later than the time and date stipulated for each exercise; these will be published by the BSG Graduate Studies Committee before the first Monday of each term in which the assignment or project must be undertaken. The required number of copies must be delivered to the Examination Schools, and addressed to the Chair of Examiners for the Masters in Public Policy, c/o Examination Schools, High Street, Oxford.

3. The examiners may award a distinction for excellence in the whole examination to candidates for the Degree.

4. In exceptional circumstances, a candidate wishing to take an examination later than the one to which he or she has been admitted may do so by application to the Chair of Examiners, via his or her College Senior Tutor or Tutor for Graduates.

5. Candidates are permitted on only one occasion to resubmit or retake failed assessment items on any course on which they have failed to achieve the required standard.

Schedule

The following courses are required to be taken. Details can be found in the course handbook:

    1. Major policy challenge introduction

    2. Core I Foundations

    3. Core II Economics

    4. Core III The Organization and Practice of Government

    5. Core IV Science and Public Policy

    6. Core V Law and Public Policy

    7. Core VI Policy Evaluation

    8. Applied Policy I - Strategy and Communication

    9. Applied Policy II - Public Budgeting and Private Finance

    10. Applied Policy III - Major Programme Management

    11. Applied Policy IV - Negotiation

NOTES

14

GENERAL REGULATIONS GOVERNING RESEARCH DEGREES

§1. Probationer Research Students

1. Any person intending to work for the Degree of Master of Letters or of Master   5
of Science by research or of Doctor of Philosophy must apply in the first instance for
admission as a Probationer Research Student, except as provided in the appropriate
regulation.

2. The Education Committee shall have power to make and vary such regulations
as may be necessary for carrying out the duties laid upon it and upon the Registrar by   10
this section.

3. For the purposes of this section the words 'board', 'faculty board', 'board of the
faculty' or 'divisional board' shall include any body with powers to admit students to
the status of Probationer Research Student.

4. A Probationer Research Student who is not a graduate of the University may   15
wear the same gown as that worn by Students for the Degree of Doctor of Philosophy.

§2. Admission of Candidates as Probationer Research Students

1. The board to which a prospective student's branch of study belongs may admit
any person as a Probationer Research Student provided that the board is satisfied:
   (1) that the candidate is well-fitted and well-qualified to conduct work for a   20
   research degree,
   (2) that the branch of study proposed by the candidate is one which may profitably
   be pursued under the superintendence of the board,
   (3) that supervision will be available, and
   (4) that the faculty board or department under whose aegis the research is to be   25
   conducted has adequate facilities to enable the research to be undertaken.

2. Applications for admission shall be forwarded to the Registrar, according to
such timetables as the Education Committee shall determine. The Registrar shall be
responsible for transmitting the candidate's application to the faculty board or department concerned, together with a statement of the branch of study which the candidate   30
intends to pursue, and such evidence of his or her fitness to undertake the proposed
study as may be required by the board or department.

3. No person shall be admitted as a Probationer Research Student unless he or she
is also a member of a college, and unless the application for admission as a
Probationer Research Student has the approval of his or her college. The Registrar   35
shall forward the application to the candidate's college or to the college to which the
candidate wishes to apply for membership, as appropriate; and admission by the
board shall be conditional upon admission by an approved society.

4. A student already on the register of graduate students and holding the status
of student for another degree, and who wishes to read for the M.Sc. by Research,   40

M.Litt., or D.Phil. may apply for transfer to the status of Probationer Research Student, provided that before admitting the student to that status the board concerned shall be satisfied that he or she fulfils the conditions set out in clause 1 above. Students who transfer in this way shall be reckoned as having been admitted as Probationer Research Students from the time they were admitted to their previous status.   5

5. It shall be the duty of the Registrar to notify candidates of the decision of the board as soon as may be and to inform a candidate whose application has been approved by the board of the term from which his or her admission as a Probationer Research Student is to be reckoned.

6. It shall be the duty of the Registrar to keep a Register of those admitted to the   10
status of Probationer Research Student.

7. A board may grant a student suspension from the Register or deprive a student of his or her status; and in such cases it shall at all times follow procedures determined by the Education Committee by regulation. A board may also reinstate a student to the Register, provided that the total number of terms a student has spent as a   15
Probationer Research Student has not exceeded five terms in the case of a full-time student, or ten terms in the case of a part-time student.

§3. Supervision of Probationer Research Students

1. Every candidate, on admission as a Probationer Research Student, shall be placed by the board concerned under the supervision of a member of the University   20
or other competent person selected by the board, and the board shall have power for sufficient reason to change the supervisor of any student or to arrange for joint supervision by more than one supervisor, if it deems it necessary.

2. It shall be the duty of a supervisor to advise a student as to the courses of instruction and classes, if any, which he or she should attend, and generally to direct   25
and superintend the student's work. It shall also be the supervisor's duty to assist a student, when satisfied of his or her competence, in the selection of a subject for his or her thesis.

3. The supervisor shall submit a report on the progress of the student to the board three times each year, and at any other time when the board so requests or the   30
supervisor deems it expedient; and shall undertake such other duties as shall be from time to time set out in the relevant Policy and Guidance issued by the Education Committee. The supervisor shall communicate the contents of the report to the student on each occasion that a report is made, so that the student is aware of the supervisor's assessment of his or her work during the period in question. In addition,   35
the supervisor shall inform the board at once if he or she is of the opinion that a student is unlikely to reach the standard required for admission at least to the status of student for the Degree of Master of Letters or of Science.

The Registrar shall send a copy of each report by the supervisor to the student's college, and to the Director of Graduate Studies or other nominated person under the   40
board concerned.

4. It shall be the duty of a Probationer Research Student to pursue any course of study preparatory to research recommended by his or her supervisor, and in particular to attend such courses of instruction as the supervisor may advise or the board concerned may require. A board may award a certificate of graduate attainment at   45
the end of the Trinity Term in the year of the student's admission as Probationer Research Student. Subject to the approval of the Education Committee, each board shall have power to determine by regulation what test or condition, if any, it may require before awarding such a certificate.

§4. Residence and other Requirements of Probationer Research Students

1. A full-time Probationer Research Student who has been admitted under the provisions of the preceding sub-section shall normally keep statutory residence and pursue his or her course of study at Oxford during the period in which he or she holds the status of Probationer Research Student. Time spent outside Oxford during term as part of an academic programme approved by Council shall count towards residence for the purpose of this clause.

2. A board may, on application from a candidate, and with the support of his or her college and supervisor, grant dispensation from such residence in exceptional circumstances, on the grounds that it is necessary to the student's work that he or she should be allowed to study at some other place than Oxford.

3. Part-time students holding the status of Probationer Research Student shall in each case be required to pursue their course of study for a minimum of four terms, and a maximum of eight terms. (*For students admitted before 1 October 2011*, a minimum of six terms and maximum of twelve terms), prior to an application for transfer of status, save that students who have completed the requirements for the Degrees of Master of Studies or Master of Science (by Coursework) by part-time study may, with the permission of the board or other relevant body, apply for transfer of status after three terms. Part-time students shall not be required to keep statutory residence, but must attend for such instruction as the board or other relevant body shall require, subject to the approval of the Education Committee. No student may apply to the relevant faculty board or other body for the appointment of examiners unless his or her supervisor has certified that the student has fulfilled the requirements for part-time students laid down by the board or other relevant body.

4. Any student may, with the permission of the board, alter the subject of research approved by the board, provided that the conditions of suitability set out in §2, cl. 1 of this section continue to be met. In such cases the date of the student's admission for all the purposes of this section shall remain unchanged, unless the board shall determine otherwise.

For Probationer Research students admitted after 1 October 2011

5. A full-time student (other than students to whom cl.9 and 10 in this section may apply) may hold the status of Probationer Research Student for up to four terms and a part-time student for up to eight terms, including the term in which he or she was admitted.

6. A candidate whose first application for transfer to D.Phil. status is not approved shall be permitted to make one further application, following the procedures laid down in clauses 1-4 above, and shall be granted an extension of time for one term if this is necessary for the purposes of making the application.

7. Subject to the approval of the responsible divisional board or the CE Board as appropriate, and for good cause, a full-time student may be permitted to hold the status of PRS (prior to the first application for transfer of status) for a further one or two terms, and a part-time student for a further one or four terms. A first application for transfer of status must have been submitted and assessed within the six term limit of PRS status. Any application outside those limits (other than in clause 6 above) must be approved by or on behalf of Education Committee.

8. A Probationer Research Student (other than a student to whom cl. 9 and 10 in this section apply shall cease to hold such status if:

(i) (*a*) he or she shall not have gained admission to another status within four terms of admission as a full-time student to the status of Probationer Research Student, or within eight terms for a part-time student, and

(*b*) he or she has not been given approval under clause 6 above to hold Probationer Research Student status for a further one or two terms as a full-time student or one to four terms as a part-time student;

(ii) he or she has failed to gain admission to either doctoral status or to the status of the applicable lower degree after the two transfer applications allowed under clause 7 above;

(iii) the board concerned shall in accordance with provisions set down in section 5.2 below, and after consultation with the student's college and supervisor, have deprived the student of such status.

9. For a full-time Probationer Research Student registered on a doctoral training programme listed in the special regulations for the Mathematical, Physical and Life Sciences and the Medical Sciences Division. Found in the 'Research Degrees in the Mathematical, Physical and Life sciences Division' and 'Research Degrees in the Medial Sciences' sections, the maximum number of terms for which he or she may hold that status is as specified in the special regulations.

10. A Probationer Research Student registered on a Doctoral Training Centre Programme or the Doctoral Training Partnership Programme shall cease to hold such status if:

(i) (*a*) he or she shall not have gained admission to another status within the number of terms specified in the special regulations for that programme and

(*b*) he or she has not been given approval as specified in the special regulations or under clause 7 above to hold Probationer Research Student status for a further one or two terms as a full-time student or one to four terms as a part-time student;

(ii) he or she has failed to gain admission to either doctoral status or to the status of the applicable lower degree after the two transfer applications allowed under clause 7 above;

(iii) the board concerned shall in accordance with provisions set down in and after consultation with the student's college and supervisor, have deprived the student of such status.

§5. Register of Graduate Students

1. Suspension of Graduate Research Students from the Register

1. If, for good cause, a student is temporarily unable to carry out his or her research, the board concerned may grant him or her a request for a temporary suspension of status, for not less than one and not more than three terms at any one time. Applications for suspension of status should be made to the board concerned, c/o the relevant Graduate Studies Assistant; and should be accompanied by statements of support from a student's supervisor and society. No student may be granted more than six terms' suspension of status in this way by a board.

2. A board may for sufficient reason, and after consultation with the student's supervisor and college, temporarily suspend him or her from the Register on its own initiative.

2. Removal of Graduate Research Students from the Register

1. A board which considers that it may be necessary to consider the removal of a student from the Register on academic grounds shall, except in cases requiring immediate action, follow the procedures for counselling and warnings set out in paras. 4–6.

2. A board shall not be required to follow the procedures for the removal of a graduate research student from the Register where a student ceases to hold the status of a student for a degree through failure to meet the requirements laid down in the decrees and regulations governing that degree. In particular where a student fails to achieve transfer within the prescribed time his or her status automatically lapses, and his or her name is removed from the Register.

3. A board shall not be required to follow the procedures for counselling and warnings set out below in cases of particular gravity and/or urgency or where it considers, for whatever reason, that immediate action is required, and in such circumstances a board may immediately notify the Education Committee as set out at paragraph 6 below and the matter will proceed as set out in that and subsequent paragraphs. In these circumstances, the board should indicate to the Education Committee why the procedures for counselling and warnings are not to be followed in that instance.

4.1. Subject to para. 3 above, wherever practicable, the formal procedures for the removal of a student from the Register should be preceded by private and informal counselling involving the student's supervisor and college, with the object of establishing the cause of any problem and advising appropriate remedial action.

4.2. If informal means are not effective in producing the necessary improvement, the student will be invited to a formal interview. Written notice of a formal interview should be given at least seven days before it takes place. Such notice will include an indication of the nature and purpose of the interview and the problem or problems that the interview is intended to address. The student will have the right to put his or her case and to be accompanied by a friend. The formal interview will be conducted by the head of department or Director of Graduate Studies who on conclusion of the interview and if further action is considered necessary will issue either (a) a first formal warning, to be confirmed in writing to the student and to his or her supervisor and society, setting out the reason for which it is given, and specifying a period of time for improvement to be made (which period should in no case be less than one month or more than three months); or (b) a final warning as set out in 5 below.

4.3. If the student unreasonably fails to attend the formal interview, a formal warning in writing may be issued without interview, and the student shall be required to acknowledge receipt of the formal warning.

5.1. If the first formal warning issued under 4.2 above is not effective in producing the necessary improvement, the head of department or Director of Graduate Studies shall invite the student to a second formal interview. The procedure will be as for the first formal interview. At the conclusion of the interview the head of department or Director of Graduate Studies shall, if further action is required, issue a final warning, which shall be confirmed in writing to the student and to his or her supervisor and society.

5.2. Where a final warning is issued under 4.2 or 5.1 above the warning itself and the written confirmation should make it clear that if the necessary improvement is not achieved within the specified period, the board may initiate action for the removal of the student from the Register of Graduate Students.

6. Where a final written warning is issued to a graduate student, a copy of the written warning shall be sent to the Education Committee. Where, following a final

written warning, the necessary improvement is not achieved within the specified period and further action is indicated, the Education Committee shall be informed by the Secretary of the board concerned. A full report of the action taken by the board in relation to the student shall be made to the Proctors who shall decide whether further action should be taken and, if so, whether under the relevant disciplinary procedures of the University or under the board's power to remove a student from the Register of Graduate Students on academic grounds. The Proctors' ruling (which may include a decision that no further action is to be taken) shall be taken without reference to the Education Committee, and shall be final.

7.1. Where the Proctors determine that it is appropriate for the matter to be considered under the board's power to initiate action for the removal of a student from the Register of Graduate Students, the board shall seek the approval of the Chair of the Education Committee to undertake any such action. Where such approval is given, the board shall inform the student and the student's college and supervisor, in writing, with a minimum of seven days' notice, of its intention to consider the removal of the student from the Register, set out its reasons and invite comments. In particular the board shall inform the student of his or her right under paragraph 7.3 to present his or her case.

7.2. A board shall delegate the task of hearing the student's case to a panel comprising at least three of its members and shall set out the terms of reference to be followed by the panel. The board shall not appoint any member who has had a previous connection with the student or his or her work.

7.3. The student may be accompanied by a friend and shall have the right to hear and to challenge any evidence presented to the panel. The student may present his or her case in writing or orally, or both, as the student wishes, and the student's society and supervisor shall have the same rights. (All written evidence shall be circulated to the student, the student's supervisor, and the student's college not less than four days before the panel considers the case.) In conducting a hearing, the panel shall ensure that the student has every opportunity to hear and to challenge the case made out by the board for the removal of the student from the Register including any evidence (written or oral) which the panel will consider in reaching a conclusion. Where the student fails to appear without good cause, the panel may proceed in the student's absence.

8. The panel shall then determine its decision as to whether the student's name shall, or shall not, be removed from the Register of Graduate Students. The decision shall be communicated to the student, college, and supervisor. The student shall also be advised in writing of the reasons for the decision and of his or her rights of appeal. The board shall also inform the Education Committee of all cases where the board has decided to deprive a student of his or her status.

9.1. A student or his or her society may appeal in writing against the decision of the faculty board within fourteen days of the date of the letter from the board conveying its decision. The appeal shall be addressed to the Education Committee (c/o the Secretary, Education Committee, University Offices, Wellington Square, Oxford OX1 2JD), which shall appoint a sub-committee to conduct a hearing of the student's appeal.

9.2. The sub-committee shall include a minimum of three members of the Education Committee, which shall appoint one of the chosen members as chair, with the power to cast an additional vote if necessary. The sub-committee may seek such legal advice as it believes to be necessary for the proper conduct of its duties, and shall have power to require any members of the University to assist it in the hearing.

9.3. The sub-committee shall give the board, the student, the student's college, and the student's supervisor, not less than seven days' notice in writing, of the date and time of the hearing, and shall give them the opportunity to make representations to the sub-committee orally and/or in writing. The student may be accompanied by a friend and shall have the right to hear and to challenge any evidence (written or oral) presented to the sub-committee; the student may present his or her case in writing, or orally, or both, as the student wishes: the board, the student's college, and the student's supervisor shall have the same rights. (All written evidence shall be circulated to the faculty board, the student, the student's supervisor, and the student's college not less than four days before the sub-committee considers the case.)

9.4. At the conclusion of a hearing, the sub-committee shall have power to:

(i) confirm the board's decision to remove the student's name from the Register of Graduate Students;

(ii) uphold the student's appeal and direct that the student's name shall remain on the Register of Graduate Students;

(iii) impose such lesser penalty or requirement in place of the removal of the student's name from the Register of Graduate Students as it deems appropriate.

9.5. In reaching its decision, the sub-committee shall have regard to:

(*a*) whether the board correctly followed the required procedures, and, in the case of procedural irregularity or irregularities, whether any irregularity or irregularities were such as to have materially prejudiced the board's inquiry;

(*b*) whether the board's decision could reasonably have been reached on the evidence before it;

(*c*) any evidence presented to the sub-committee which was not available to the board's panel;

(*d*) any mitigating circumstances offered by or on behalf of the student;

(*e*) any other factors which in the opinion of the sub-committee are relevant to a fair consideration of the student's appeal.

9.6. The sub-committee shall communicate its decision to the student, to the student's society and supervisor, and to the board, in writing, within two months of the conclusion of any hearing. The decision of the sub-committee will be final, subject only to a complaint to the Proctors.

3. Reinstatement of Graduate Research Students to the Register

A student who has lapsed from the Register or has withdrawn or whose name has been removed from the Register by the board concerned may apply for reinstatement to his or her former status on the Register. Such applications shall be addressed by the student to the board concerned, and shall be accompanied by written statements commenting on the application from the candidate's college and former supervisor. The board shall reach a decision on such applications and shall determine the date from which any reinstatement granted under these provisions shall be effective. No reinstatement may be granted under these provisions if the student's name has been on the Register of students of the relevant status for the maximum number of terms allowed under the decree governing that status.

§6. Students with Disabilities

1. This part is concerned with candidates for research degree assessments who have a physical or mental impairment which has a substantial and long-term adverse effect on their ability to carry our normal activities.

2. Candidates may apply for alternative arrangements where the impairment which they have significantly affects their ability to undertake the following assessments in the manner in which they are normally undertaken by candidates.

3. Research degree assessments are taken to include interviews, presentations, and oral examinations for Transfer of Status, Confirmation of Status, and the final oral examination for the degrees of M.Litt., M.Sc. by Research, and D.Phil.

4. Candidates may apply for alternative assessment arrangements to the appropriate Board in advance of, or at the same time as, submitting their application for assessment.

5. The relevant Director of Graduate Studies will determine whether the arrangement is one that they can approve, or one that must be approved by the Proctors. The Proctors shall issue guidance periodically on the adjustments to assessments that the DGS may approve, and those that should be referred to the Proctors.

6. The application must be supported by evidence as set out on the application form. If the DGS is not satisfied that the evidence supports the request, the application must be forwarded to the Proctors for determination.

7. Decisions on applications shall be communicated to the department or faculty who shall be responsible for putting the approved arrangements into place.

8. Alternative assessment arrangements approved by the DGS or the Proctors under these regulations shall normally apply to all assessments for the duration of the candidate's course of study. It shall be the responsibility of the candidate to apply for any subsequent change to these arrangements which he or she may wish, and to inform the DGS of any material change in his or her circumstances which might affect the suitability of these arrangements.

Appeals

9. A candidate who is dissatisfied with any decision made by the Proctors under these regulations, may appeal against it in accordance with the following provisions.

10. An appeal must be made in writing within 14 days of the date of the Proctors' decision, addressed to the Chair of the Education Committee.

11. The appeal shall be determined expeditiously by the Chair or another member of the Committee, other than one of the Proctors, nominated by the Chair.

§7. Regulations concerning the Examination of Graduate Research Students

1. Regulations governing the content and length of theses

(i) *Material for transfer or submission*

Material submitted for transfer to, or for the award of, the degrees of M.Litt., M.Sc. by Research, and D.Phil., shall be wholly or substantially the result of work undertaken while the student holds the status of Probationer Research Student or the status of a student for the degree concerned, except that a candidate may make application for a dispensation from this requirement to the Education Committee.

(ii) *Prior publication*

Prior publication of material arising from research undertaken while holding the status of Probationer Research Student or the status of a student for the M.Litt., M.Sc. by Research, or D.Phil., is fully acceptable, but the inclusion of published papers within a thesis may be subject to special regulation by the board concerned. Candidates should note that the acceptance of such material for publication does not of itself constitute proof that the work is of sufficient quality or significance to merit the award of the degree concerned. This remains a judgement of the relevant board on the recommendation of its examiners.

(iii) *Thesis length*

If a thesis exceeds the permitted length, the board concerned may decline to appoint examiners or to forward the thesis to examiners already appointed, and may return it   5
to the candidate for revision. If the examiners find that a thesis which has been forwarded to them exceeds the permitted length, they should report the fact to the relevant board and await further instructions before proceeding with the examination.

2. Preparation and submission of theses for the Degrees of M.Litt., M.Sc. by Research, and D.Phil.   10

(i) *Text and footnotes*

Candidates should note that the purpose of these regulations is not only to ease the task of the examiners (which is obviously in the candidates' interests), but also to ensure that the copy finally deposited in the Bodleian or other university library is of a standard of legibility which will allow it (subject to applicable copyright rules) to be   15
photocopied or microfilmed if required in future years.

The thesis must be printed or typed with a margin of 3 to 3.5 cm on the left-hand edge of each page (or on the inner edge, whether left-hand or right-hand, in the case of a thesis which is printed on both sides of the paper). Theses in typescript should present the main text in double spacing with quotations and footnotes in single   20
spacing. In the case of word-processed or printed theses, where the output resembles that of a typewriter, double spacing should be taken to mean a distance of about 0.33 inch or 8 mm between successive lines of text. Candidates are advised that it is their responsibility to ensure that the print of their thesis is of an adequate definition and standard of legibility.   25

Footnotes should normally be placed at the bottom of each page. Where they are given at the end of each chapter or at the end of the thesis, two separate unbound copies of footnotes should also be presented, for the convenience of the examiners.

Candidates should carefully note the regulations concerning word limits which individual boards have made. In such cases, candidates should state the approximate   30
number of words in their theses.

Theses must be submitted in English unless for exceptional reasons a board otherwise determines in the term in which the candidate is first admitted as a research student.

The pages of the thesis must be numbered. Each copy should have an abstract   35
included (see below).

(ii) *Examiners' copies: binding and presentation*

At the time of their examination, candidates must submit two copies of their thesis, which must be securely and firmly bound in either hard or soft covers. Loose-leaf binding is not acceptable. Candidates are responsible for ensuring that examiners'   40
copies are securely bound and should note that theses which do not meet this requirement will not be accepted.

Fine Art candidates offering studio practice as part of their submission must submit, together with the written portion of their thesis, documentation in appropriate form of the exhibition or portfolio of works to be examined. Wherever possible, this docu-   45
mentation should be bound with the written portion of the thesis.

Candidates should pack each copy of the thesis intended for the examiners into a separate but unsealed parcel or padded envelope, ready in all respects, except the address, to be posted to the examiners when appointed. Each parcel should bear the candidate's name and society and the words 'M.LITT./M.SC./D.PHIL. (as appropriate) THESIS AND ABSTRACT' in BLOCK CAPITALS in the bottom left-hand corner. A slip giving the address to which the examiners should write in order to contact the candidate about arrangements for the oral examination should be enclosed with each copy of the thesis. Candidates are responsible for ensuring that their examiners have no difficulty in communicating with them. The separate copies thus packed should be submitted to the Examination Schools, High Street, Oxford. If sent or posted they should be enclosed in one covering parcel.

The theses of candidates who fail to follow this advice are liable to delay in being forwarded to the examiners.

(iii) *Date of submission of examiners' copies*

Candidates may submit the examiners' copies of their thesis, prepared as described above, at the same time as they apply for the appointment of their examiners. If they intend, however, to submit the examiners' copies at a later date, they will be required to state, at the time of their application for appointment of examiners, the date by which they will submit. This should be as soon as possible after the date of application and may in no case be later than the last day of the vacation immediately following the term in which application for the appointment of examiners has been made.

(iv) *Library copies: binding and presentation*

Once the board has granted a candidate leave to supplicate, he or she must submit a finalised copy of the thesis, as approved by the examiners, to the Examination Schools for deposit in the relevant university library. [For candidates admitted on or after 1 October 2007: The candidate must also submit an electronic copy to the Oxford Research Archive. (Candidates whose thesis has been prepared in non-standard media such as to make electronic submission impracticable may apply to the Proctors for exemption from this requirement.)] These should incorporate any corrections or amendments which the examiners may have requested of the candidate. The examiners must confirm in writing in their report to the board that any corrections required have been made.

The library copy of the thesis must be in a permanently fixed binding, drilled and sewn, in a stiff board case in library buckram, in a dark colour, and lettered on the spine with the candidate's name and initials, the degree, and the year of submission.

Fine Art candidates offering studio practice as part of their submission must submit the written portion of their thesis together with documentation in appropriate form of their exhibition or portfolio of works. Wherever possible, this documentation should be bound with the written portion of the thesis.

Candidates should note that leave to supplicate is conditional upon receipt by the Examination Schools of the library copy of their thesis and [for candidates admitted on or after 1 October 2007, receipt by the Oxford Research Archive of an electronic copy and [for candidates supplicating on or after 1 July 2013] receipt by the Examination Schools of the library copy of the thesis and receipt by the Oxford Research Archive of the electronic copy of the thesis no later than by the end of the fifth day before the date of the degree ceremony booked by the candidate for conferral of their degree and that candidates may not proceed to take their degree until they have fulfilled the requirement [by the stipulated deadline for those supplicating on or after 1 July 2013] to submit a library copy of the thesis and [for candidates admitted on or after 1 October 2007]: an electronic copy (unless an exception to the requirement to submit an electronic copy of the thesis has been granted by the Proctors)].

(v) *Abstracts*

The abstract of the thesis should concisely summarize its scope and principal arguments, in about 300 words. It should be printed or typewritten, on one side only, of A4-sized paper. Each copy of the abstract should be headed with the title of the thesis, the name and college of the candidate, the degree for which it is submitted, and the term and year of submission.

One copy of the abstract prepared at the time of the examination should be bound into each of the examiners' copies of the thesis. Subsequently, when the examination is 5 completed, candidates should also arrange for a copy of the abstract to be bound into the library copy of their thesis, and should submit with the library copy a separate, unbound copy of their abstract which may be despatched to ASLIB and published. The copy of the abstract which is earmarked for dispatch to ASLIB should be presented separately in a form suitable for microfilming, i.e. it should be (1) on one 10 side of a single sheet of A4 paper, (2) a typed, single-spaced top copy, a clear photocopy, or a printed copy (i.e. it should not be a carbon or poor photocopy), and (3) headed up with name, college, year and term of submission, and the title of the thesis.

It should be noted that some boards have made regulations requiring the submis- 15 sion of more detailed abstracts in addition to the general requirement of an abstract not normally exceeding 300 words.

3. Conduct of Oral Examinations for the Degrees of M.Litt., M.Sc. by Research, and D.Phil.

(i) The oral examination shall be held at Oxford in a suitable university or college 20 building, unless the Proctors give special permission for it to be held at some other place. In the case of Fine Art candidates offering studio practice as part of their submission, where it does not take place in the presence of the exhibition or portfolio of works, the candidate's supervisor must arrange for the examiners to view this part of the submission prior to the commencement of the oral examination. It shall, except 25 in special circumstances, begin not earlier than 9 a.m. nor later than 5 p.m. and may be held in term or vacation. The student or his or her college, other society, or approved institution, may within fourteen days of the date of the Proctors' decision in respect of the granting of consent, appeal in writing to the Chair of the Education Committee (who may nominate another member of the committee, other than one of the Proctors, 30 to adjudicate the appeal).

(ii) The examination may be attended by any member of the University in academic dress. No person who is not a member of the University may attend it except with the consent of both examiners.

(iii) The place and time of the examination shall be fixed by the examiners, who 35 shall be responsible for informing the candidate of the arrangements made. It shall be the duty of candidates to ensure that any letter addressed to them at their college or any other address which they have given is forwarded to them if necessary. The examiners shall allow reasonable time for receiving an acknowledgement from the candidate of their summons. 40

(iv) Except as provided in clause (v) below, the day shall be fixed by the examiners to suit their convenience. So that candidates may know what arrangements for absence from Oxford they may safely make, the examiners shall inform candidates within a reasonable time of the date fixed.

(v) Candidates may apply to the board concerned for the oral examination to be 45 held not later than a certain date, provided that this date shall not be earlier than one calendar month after the date on which the thesis has been received at the Examination Schools or after the date on which the examiners have agreed to act, whichever is the later. If the board is satisfied that there are special circumstances justifying this application, it will ask the examiners to make arrangements to enable 50 the oral examination to be held within the period specified.

In such cases the examiners, when invited to act, will be informed that the candidate has asked that the oral examination should be held not later than a certain date, and acceptance of the invitation to examine will be on the understanding that they would seek to meet this request. If is not practicable to meet the student's request, then the board shall decide how to proceed.   5

(vi) Notice of the examination shall be given in one of the following ways:

1. It may be published in the University Gazette not later than the day before it is due to take place;

2. Not later than two days before the examination the examiners may:

   (*a*) inform the Graduate Studies Office in writing; and   10

   (*b*) post a notice in the Examination Schools; and

   (*c*) if the examination is to be held at a place other than the Examination Schools, post a notice also at the place of the examination.

The notice shall state the name of the candidate, the subject of the thesis, the place, day, and hour of the examination, and the names of the examiners.   15

If an examination is held without the giving of the notice required by this regulation it shall be invalid, unless the Proctors, on receipt of a written application from the examiners, shall determine otherwise. The student or his or her college, other society, or approved institution, may within fourteen days of the date of the Proctors' decision in respect of the granting of consent, appeal in writing to the Chair of the Education   20 Committee (who may nominate another member of the committee, other than one of the Proctors, to adjudicate the appeal).

(vii) If, owing to illness or other urgent and unforeseen cause, an examiner is unable to attend the examination, it shall be postponed to a later date, provided that, if the Proctors are satisfied that postponement would be a serious hardship to the   25 candidate, they may authorize another member of the board concerned to attend the examination as a substitute, but such substitute shall not be required to sign the report. The Proctors shall determine what payment, if any, the substitute examiner shall receive.

(viii) Candidates are strongly recommended to take a copy of their thesis to the   30 examination. In the case of Fine Art candidates offering studio practice as part of their submission, where the oral examination is not taking place in the presence of the exhibition or portfolio of works, it is recommended they attend with the written portion of their thesis together with documentation of the work.

(ix) An oral examination shall be held in Oxford as prescribed in clause (i). In   35 exceptional circumstances, normally affecting the ability of the external examiner to take part in an Oxford-based oral examination, application may be made to the relevant board for special permission to hold the examination using audiovisual electronic communication with the external examiner concerned. The board concerned may approve the application only where: 40

   (i) it accepts that no alternative and timely arrangements may reasonably be put in place;

   (ii) the proposed arrangements are acceptable to both examiners and to the candidate;

   (iii) it involves remote communication with only one of the examiners (normally the external);   45

   (iv) it is content to bear the additional cost of the necessary arrangements;

   (v) an oral examination of this type takes place according to arrangements and in premises approved by the Proctors;

(vi) the oral examination takes place according to the protocol approved by the Education Committee;

(vii) in the event of any technical or other problems, the validity of the process used to conduct the oral examination and to determine the outcome will be decided by the Proctors.   5

NOTES

15

GENERAL REGULATIONS FOR THE DEGREE OF MASTER OF LETTERS

§1. Degree of Master of Letters

1. Any person who has been admitted to the status of Student for the Degree of Master of Letters and who has satisfied the conditions prescribed by this decree may supplicate for the Degree of Master of Letters.

2. The Education Committee shall have power to make and vary such regulations as may be necessary for carrying out the duties laid upon it and upon the Registrar by this section.

3. For the purposes of this section the words 'board', 'faculty board', 'board of the faculty', 'divisional board' shall include any body with powers to admit students to read for the Degree of Master of Letters.

4. A Student for the Degree of Master of Letters who is not a graduate of the University may wear the same gown as that worn by Students for the Degree of Doctor of Philosophy.

§2. Status of Student for the Degree of Master of Letters

1. The following may be admitted to the status of Student for the Degree of Master of Letters:

(i) a member of the University who, having held the status of Probationer Research Student under the provisions of the appropriate regulation has successfully completed the relevant qualifying test or tests and fulfilled the other requirements for transfer to M.Litt. status prescribed in §3 of this section;

(ii) a member of the University who, having held the status of student for another higher degree within the University, has successfully completed the relevant qualifying test or tests and fulfilled the other requirements for transfer to M.Litt. status prescribed in §3 of this section;

(iii) a member of the University who has successfully completed the examination for the Degree of Bachelor or Master of Philosophy or Master of Science by Coursework or of Bachelor of Civil Law and who has fulfilled the conditions laid down in §3 of this section for applicants in that category.

2. It shall be the duty of the Registrar to keep a register of those admitted to the status of Student for the Degree of Master of Letters.

3. A board may grant a student suspension from the Register or deprive a student of his or her status; and in such cases it shall at all times follow the procedures determined by the Education Committee by regulation. A board may also reinstate a student to the Register, provided that the number of terms a student has spent with the status of Student for the Degree of Master of Letters shall not have exceeded

fifteen in all in the case of a full-time student, or eighteen terms in the case of a part-time student.

§3. Admission of Candidates to the Status of Student for the Degree of Master of Letters

1. Candidates qualified under §2 of this section may apply for admission as a   5
Student for the Degree of Master of Letters to the board concerned through the
Registrar. Such applications shall be accompanied by:
  (i) a statement from the supervisor that he or she approves the proposed subject
      for a thesis and considers the candidate well qualified to undertake research in
      that subject;   10
  (ii) a statement of support for the application from the candidate's college;
  (iii) a statement of the subject of the thesis and of the manner in which the
      candidate proposes to treat it.

2. Candidates qualified under §2, cl. 1 (i) and (ii) of this section shall in addition be
required to submit written work, the precise manner and form of which shall be   15
determined by regulation by each board. This shall be considered by two assessors
appointed by the board, neither of whom shall normally be the candidate's supervisor,
and who shall examine the candidate orally. Upon completion of their examination of
the candidate's application, the assessors shall make a recommendation as to whether
it should be granted. In each case the assessors shall make a reasoned written report to 20
the board in support of their recommendation.

3. The board shall consider the candidate's application together with the material
supplied in accordance with clauses 1 and 2 above. No application shall be granted
unless the board is satisfied that the candidate is capable of carrying out research, that
the subject of the thesis and the manner of its treatment proposed by the candidate are 25
acceptable, that the subject is one which may profitably be pursued under the superintendence of the board, and that the board or department concerned is satisfied that it
has adequate facilities to enable the research to be undertaken.

4. Subject to the approval of the Education Committee, each board may determine
by regulation what other test or condition, if any, it requires before admitting a   30
candidate to M.Litt. status. Each board shall be empowered, without further authority, to require from the supervisor any further confidential report on an applicant's
suitability to pursue research towards the Degree of Master of Letters.

5. It shall be the duty of the Registrar to submit any application made under these
provisions to the board concerned, and to notify the candidate of the outcome as soon   35
as may be.

6. A student qualified under §2, cl. 1 (i) or (ii) of this section whose application for
transfer to M.Litt. status is successful shall be reckoned as having been admitted to the
status of student for the Degree of Master of Letters with effect from the date of
admission to his or her previous status, unless the board determines otherwise.   40

7. A student qualified under §2, cl. 1 (iii) of this section whose application for
admission to M.Litt. status is successful shall be admitted as a Student for the Degree
of Master of Letters from the beginning of the term in which admission takes place.

§4. Supervision of Students for the Degree of Master of Letters

1. Every candidate on admission as a Student for the Degree of Master of Letters   45
shall be placed by the board concerned under the supervision of a member of the
University or other competent person selected by the board, and the board shall have

power for sufficient reason to change the supervisor of any student or to arrange for joint supervision by more than one supervisor, if it deems it necessary.

2. It shall be the duty of a supervisor to direct and superintend the work of the student, to meet the student regularly, and to undertake such duties as shall from time to time be set out in the relevant Policy and Guidance issued by the Education Committee.

3. The supervisor shall submit a report on the progress of the student to the board three times a year, and at any other time when the board so requests or he or she deems it expedient. The supervisor shall communicate the contents of the report to the student on each occasion that a report is made, so that the student is aware of the supervisor's assessment of his or her work during the period in question. In addition, the supervisor shall inform the board at once if he or she is of the opinion that the student is unlikely to reach the standard required for the Degree of Master of Letters.

The Registrar shall send a copy of each report by the supervisor to the student's college, and to the Director or other nominated person under the faculty board concerned.

4. It shall be the duty of every Student for the Degree of Master of Letters to undertake such guided work as his or her supervisor requests; to attend such meetings with his or her supervisor as the latter reasonably arranges; and to fulfil any other requirements of the General Board set out from time to time in the relevant Policy and Guidance issued by the Education Committee.

§5. Residence and other Requirements for Students for the Degree of Master of Letters

1. Except as provided in clause 3 of this sub-section, a Student for the Degree of Master of Letters who has been admitted for full-time study under the provisions of §3 of this section shall be required to be on the Register for at least six terms, and during this period shall keep statutory residence and pursue his or her course of study at Oxford. Time spent outside Oxford during term as part of an academic programme approved by Council shall count towards residence for the purpose of this clause.

2. The board concerned may dispense a student on application through his or her college and with the support of the supervisor from not more than three terms of such residence and study in Oxford, provided that such dispensation shall be granted only on grounds that it is necessary to the student's work that he or she should be allowed to study at some other place than Oxford.

3. A student who has successfully completed the examination for the Degree of Master or Bachelor of Philosophy or of Master of Studies or of Master of Science by Coursework, or a student under the supervision of the Board of the Faculty of Law admitted under the provisions of §2, cl. 1 (iii) of this section, shall keep statutory residence and pursue his or her course of study at Oxford for not less than three terms after such admission.

4. Any student who, after admission under §3 of this section, has kept statutory residence and studied at Oxford for a period of forty-two days, not necessarily consecutive, but falling within the same academic year, may apply to the board concerned for leave to reckon such period as one term towards the total required under clause 1 of this sub-section. The board shall have power to grant such leave provided that:

(i) no day so reckoned which falls within any term shall also be reckoned for the purpose of keeping that term;

(ii) no student who has kept the Michaelmas, or the Hilary, or the Trinity Term shall be allowed to reckon in this manner any day that falls within the eight weeks beginning on the first day of Full Term in Michaelmas, or Hilary, or Trinity Term, as the case may be;

(iii) no student shall be allowed to reckon in this manner more than one such period in the same academic year;

(iv) no student shall be allowed to reckon more than three terms in the same academic year.

For the purposes of this clause, the academic year shall begin on the first day of Michaelmas Term and end on the day preceding the first day of Michaelmas Term in the following calendar year.

Applications for leave to reckon any period as a term under the provisions of this clause shall be made to the board, through the Registrar, by the student's college.

5. Part-time students holding the status of student for the Degree of Master of Letters shall in each case be required to pursue their course of study for a minimum of twelve terms, subject to the provisions of §3, cl. 6. Part-time students shall not be required to keep statutory residence, but must attend for such instruction as the board or other relevant body shall require, subject to the approval of the Education Committee. No student may apply to the relevant faculty board or other body for the appointment of examiners unless his or her supervisor has certified that the student has fulfilled the requirements for part-time students laid down by the board or other relevant body.

6. Any student may, with the permission of the board, alter the subject of research approved by the board, provided that the conditions of suitability set out in §2 above continue to be met. In such cases the date of the student's admission for all the purposes of this section shall remain unchanged, unless the board shall determine otherwise.

7. If a full-time Student for the Degree of Master of Letters has held that status for nine terms, or a part-time student for fifteen terms, but has been prevented by exceptional circumstances from completing his or her thesis, the board shall have power to grant an extension of time for a period or periods not exceeding three terms in all for a full-time student, or three terms in all for a part-time student, to be determined by the board. Applications for such extension of time shall be made through the Registrar not later than the term in which the student is due to apply for permission to supplicate, and must be accompanied by statements of support from the student's society and supervisor.

8. A Student for the Degree of Master of Letters shall cease to hold such status if:

(i) he or she shall have been refused permission to supplicate for the Degree of Master of Letters;

(ii) the board concerned shall in accordance with §2 cl. 3 of this section, and with the provisions set down by regulation by the Education Committee, and after consultation with the student's college and supervisor, have deprived the student of such status;

(iii) he or she shall have been transferred under the relevant provisions to another status;

(iv) he or she shall have failed to complete his or her thesis within nine terms for a full-time student, or fifteen terms for a part-time student or within such further extension of time as may have been granted by the board concerned.

§6. Examination of Students for the Degree of Master of Letters

1. A Student for the Degree of Master of Letters who has fulfilled the applicable residence and other requirements set out in §5, and whose status has not expired, may apply for the appointment of examiners and for leave to supplicate for the Degree of Master of Letters.

2. Such applications should be made to the board concerned through the Registrar. They shall include:

    (i) a certificate from the student's college that the application has the approval of that college;

    (ii) a certificate from the supervisor that the candidate has pursued his or her course of study in Oxford in accordance with the provisions of §5 of this section;

    (iii) a statement by the candidate of what part, if any, of the thesis has already been accepted, or is being concurrently submitted, for any degree or diploma or certificate or other qualification in this University or elsewhere;

    (iv) a statement by the candidate that the thesis is his or her own work, except where otherwise indicated.

3. The supervisor shall consult with the candidate concerning possible examiners, and forward to the board the names of suggested examiners with details of any special considerations which the candidate wishes to make known about any potential examiners.

4. The student shall also submit for examination, at such time as the Education Committee shall by regulation require:

    (i) two printed or typewritten copies of a thesis;

    (ii) two printed or typewritten copies of an abstract of the thesis, which shall not normally exceed 300 words.

5. On receipt of an application for the appointment of examiners the board concerned shall appoint two examiners, neither of whom shall be the candidate's supervisor, and whose duties shall be:

    (i) to consider the thesis and the abstract of it submitted by the student under the provisions of the preceding clause, provided that they shall exclude from consideration in making their report any part of the thesis which has already been accepted, or is being concurrently submitted, for any degree or other qualification in this University or elsewhere (except for the Degree of Bachelor of Civil Law of this University) and shall have the power to require the candidate to produce for their inspection the complete thesis so accepted or concurrently submitted;

    (ii) to examine the student orally, and also, if they think fit, by a written examination, in the subject of the thesis and in other relevant subjects;

    (iii) to report to the board through the Registrar;

    (iv) to return to the student the copies of the thesis and of the abstract thereof submitted for examination.

The Education Committee shall have power to make regulations concerning the notice to be given of the oral examination and of the time and place at which it may be held. The examination may be attended by any member of the University in academic dress, while non-members may attend only with the consent of the examiners. In the case of theses submitted to the Divisional Boards of Social Sciences, Mathematical, Physical and Life Sciences, and Medical Sciences, the Proctors after consultation with the relevant faculty board may decide (either at their own discretion or at the request

of the candidate or the supervisor or department) to forbid the attendance of any
person or all persons (other than the examiners and the candidate) or to impose any
condition on attendance if and to the extent that such action is in their view necessary
to protect the interests of the University or the candidate or both, and the examiners
shall be informed accordingly and shall include this information in the notice of   5
examination. The student, or his or her college, may within fourteen days of the
date of the Proctors' decision appeal in writing to the Chair of the Education
Committee (who may nominate another member of the committee, other than one
of the Proctors, to adjudicate the appeal).

6. Having completed the examination of a candidate for the first time, the exam-   10
iners may make recommendation (i) or (ii) below only. Having completed the examination of a candidate who has revised and re-submitted his or her thesis, the
examiners may make any one of recommendations (i) to (iii). The recommendations
are:

(i) that the candidate should be granted leave to supplicate for the Degree of   15
Master of Letters. In this case the examiners must include in their report
statements that:

1. the candidate possesses a good general knowledge of the field of learning
within which the subject of the thesis falls;

2. that the candidate has shown competence in investigating the chosen topic;   20

3. that the candidate has made a worthwhile contribution to knowledge or
understanding in the field of learning within which the subject of the thesis
falls;

4. that the thesis is presented in a lucid and scholarly manner;

5. that it merits of the award of the Degree of Master of Letters.   25

Examiners shall bear in mind that their judgement of the extent of the candidate's
contribution to knowledge or understanding of the relevant field of learning shall take
into account what may reasonably be expected of a capable and diligent student after
two years of full-time study in the case of a full-time student, or twelve terms in the
case of a part-time student.   30

If the examiners are satisfied that the candidate's thesis is of sufficient merit for the
degree but consider, nevertheless, that before the thesis is deposited the candidate
should make minor corrections (which are not sufficiently substantial to justify
reference back for re-examination), they must require the candidate to correct the
thesis to their satisfaction before they submit their report. If the candidate has not   35
completed these corrections within one calendar month of the date of the oral
examination, his or her name shall be removed by the Registrar from the Register
of Students for the Degree of Master of Letters, provided that the board may, on good
cause shown by the candidate, grant an extension of time of one further calendar
month in which the candidate may fulfil this requirement before the removal of his or   40
her name from the Register. No subsequent extension shall be granted, but it shall be
open to a candidate who has failed to fulfil this requirement within those one or two
months in total, as the case may be, to apply to the board for reinstatement as a
Student for the Degree of Master of Letters, with the support of his or her society and
supervisor, upon submission to the Registrar of a copy of his or her thesis incorporat-   45
ing the required corrections, and upon payment of such reinstatement fee as may from
time to time be prescribed by Council by decree. Permission to supplicate shall not be
granted until this fee has been paid;

(ii) that the board should refer the thesis back to the student in order that he or she
may revise it for re-examination. If the examiners so recommend they shall   50
annex to their report to the board a statement (for transmission to the student)

setting out the respects in which the thesis falls below the standard required for the degree. If the board adopts this recommendation the student shall retain the status and obligations of a Student for the Degree of Master of Letters, and may apply again for the appointment of examiners, in accordance with the procedure laid down in this subsection, not later than the third term after that in which the board gave permission so to reapply. If such permission shall have been given by a board during a vacation, it shall be deemed to have been given in the term preceding that vacation. On re-submission of the thesis, students should submit a separate report indicating the specific changes made. The word limit for the accompanying report shall be 1,000 words;

(iii) that the board should refuse the candidate's application for leave to supplicate.

7. In each case the examiners must embody in their report, in support of their recommendation, an account of the scope, character, and quality of the candidate's work.

8. On receipt of the examiners' report the board shall reach a decision on whether to accept the examiners' recommendation, provided that no candidate shall be given leave to supplicate unless the examiners have made the statements required in clause 6 (i) above.

9. A candidate who has been granted leave to supplicate by a board shall be required to submit to the Examination Schools a copy of his or her thesis, incorporating any amendments or corrections required by the examiners and approved by the board, with a view to deposit in the Bodleian or other appropriate university library. [For candidates admitted on or after 1 October 2007: candidates are also required to submit an electronic copy of their thesis to the Oxford Research Archive, unless an exception to this requirement has been granted by the Proctors.] [For candidates supplicating on or after 1 July 2013: candidates are also required to submit the library copy to the Examination Schools and where applicable the electronic copy of the thesis to the Oxford Research Archive no later than the end of the fifth day before the date of the degree ceremony booked by the candidate for conferral of their degree.] Permission to supplicate shall in all cases be conditional upon fulfilment of these requirements.

10. In an exceptional case in which a board is unable to accept the examiners' recommendation, or in which the examiners cannot reach an agreed recommendation, the board shall have power to appoint one or two new examiners as it deems necessary, to conduct such further examination of the candidate as the board may require. The board shall make a report on any such case to the Education Committee.

11. The board may exempt a candidate who is being re-examined under the provisions of clause 6 (ii) above from the oral examination, provided that the examiners are able to certify that they are satisfied, without examining the candidate orally, that they can recommend to the board in the terms required by clause 6 (i) above that he or she be given leave to supplicate for the Degree of Master of Letters.

12. It shall be the duty of the Registrar to notify the candidate of the board's decision as soon as may be. The Registrar shall also be responsible for publishing at the end of each academic year the names of those candidates to whom permission to supplicate has been granted during that year, together with a statement of the subject of the thesis written by each.

13. When, on the conclusion of the investigation of a complaint made by a candidate, the Proctors recommend that a candidate be re-examined, the board shall have power to hold a new examination.

NOTES

16

GENERAL REGULATIONS FOR THE DEGREE OF MASTER OF SCIENCE BY RESEARCH

§1. Degree of Master of Science by Research

1. Any person who has been admitted to the status of Student for the Degree of Master of Science by Research and who has satisfied the conditions prescribed by this decree, may supplicate for the Degree of Master of Science.

2. The Education Committee shall have power to make and vary such regulations as may be necessary for carrying out the duties laid upon it and upon the Registrar by this section.

3. For the purpose of this section the words 'board', 'faculty board', 'board of the faculty' or 'divisional board' shall include any committee with powers to admit candidates for the Degree of Master of Science by Research.

4. A Student for the Degree of Master of Science by Research who is not a graduate of the University may wear the same gown as that worn by Students for the Degree of Doctor of Philosophy.

§2. Status of Student for the Degree of Master of Science by Research

1. The following may be admitted to the status of Student for the Degree of Master of Science by Research:
  (i) a member of the University who, having held the status of Probationer Research Student under the provisions of the appropriate regulation, has successfully completed the relevant qualifying test for transfer to M.Sc. status prescribed in §3 of this section;
  (ii) a member of the University who, holding the status of student for another higher degree within the University, has successfully completed the relevant qualifying test for transfer to M.Sc. status prescribed in §3 of this section.

2. It shall be the duty of the Registrar to keep a Register of those admitted to the status of Student for the Degree of Master of Science by Research.

3. A board may grant a student suspension from the Register or deprive a student of his or her status; and in such cases it shall at all times follow procedures determined by the Education Committee by regulation. A board may also reinstate a student to the Register, provided that the number of terms a student has spent as a Student for the Degree of Master of Science shall not have exceeded fifteen in all in the case of a full-time student, or eighteen terms in the case of a part-time student.

§3. Admission of Candidates for the Degree of Master of Science by Research

1. A candidate qualified under §2 of this section may apply for admission as a Student for the Degree of Master of Science by Research to the board under whose aegis the proposed subject of research falls. Such applications should be made through   5
the Registrar, and must be accompanied by:

    (i) a statement from the supervisor (where appropriate) that he or she approves the proposed subject for a thesis and considers the candidate well fitted to undertake research;

    (ii) a statement of the subject of the proposed thesis and details of the manner in   10
which the candidate proposes to treat it;

    (iii) a statement of support for the application from the candidate's society.

2. Applicants shall in addition be required to undertake such other tests and meet such other conditions as, subject to the approval of the Education Committee, a board may determine by regulation.   15

3. The board shall consider the candidate's application together with the material supplied in accordance with clauses 1 and 2 above. No application shall be granted unless the board is satisfied that the candidate is capable of carrying out research, that the subject of the thesis and the manner of its treatment proposed by the candidate are acceptable, that the subject is one which may profitably be pursued under the super-   20
intendence of the board, and that the board or department concerned is satisfied that it has adequate facilities to enable the research to be undertaken.

4. It shall be the duty of the Registrar to submit any application made under these provisions to the board concerned and to inform a candidate of the outcome as soon as may be.   25

5. A candidate who is admitted to the status of Student for the Degree of Master of Science by Research shall be reckoned as having held that status from the time of admission to his or her previous status, unless the board shall determine otherwise.

§4. Supervision of Students for the Degree of Master of Science by Research   30

1. Every candidate on admission as a Student for the Degree of Master of Science by Research shall be placed by the board concerned under the supervision of a member of the University or other competent person selected by the board, and the board shall have power for sufficient reason to change the supervisor of any student or to arrange for joint supervision by more than one supervisor, if it deems   35
it necessary.

2. It shall be the duty of a supervisor to direct and superintend the work of the student, to meet the student regularly, and to undertake such duties as shall be from time to time set out in Policy and Guidance issued by the Education Committee. The supervisor shall submit a report on the progress of the student to the board three times   40
a year, and at any other time when the board so requests or the supervisor deems it expedient; and shall carry out such other duties as are set out in Policy and Guidance issued by the Education Committee. The supervisor shall communicate the contents of the report to the student on each occasion that a report is made, so that the student is aware of the supervisor's assessment of his or her work during the period in question.   45
In addition, the supervisor shall inform the board at once if he or she is of the opinion the student is unlikely to reach the standard required for the Master of Science by Research.

The Registrar shall send a copy of each report by the supervisor to the student's college and to the Director of Graduate Studies or other nominated person under the faculty board concerned.

3. It shall be the duty of every Student for the Degree of Master of Science by Research to undertake such guided work as his or her supervisor requests; to attend such meetings with his or her supervisor as the latter reasonably arranges; and to fulfil any other requirements set out in Policy and Guidance issued by the Education Committee.

§5. Residence and other Requirements for Students for the Degree of Master of Science by Research

1. A Student for the Degree of Master of Science by Research shall, after admission for full-time study, keep statutory residence and pursue his or her work at Oxford for at least three terms. Time spent outside Oxford during term as part of an academic programme approved by Council shall count towards residence for the purpose of this clause.

2. Any student who, after admission under §3 of this regulation, has kept statutory residence and studied at Oxford for a period of forty-two days, not necessarily consecutive, but falling within the same academic year, may apply to the board concerned for leave to reckon such period as one term towards the total required under the preceding clause. The board shall have power to grant such leave provided that:

(i) no day so reckoned which falls within any term shall also be reckoned for the purpose of keeping that term;

(ii) no student who has kept the Michaelmas, or the Hilary, or the Trinity Term shall be allowed to reckon in this manner any day that falls within the eight weeks beginning on the first day of Full Term in Michaelmas, or Hilary, or Trinity Term, as the case may be;

(iii) no student shall be allowed to reckon in this manner more than one such period in the same academic year;

(iv) no student shall be allowed to reckon more than three terms in the same academic year.

For the purposes of this clause, the academic year shall begin on the first day of Michaelmas Term and end on the day preceding the first day of Michaelmas Term in the following calendar year.

3. Applications for leave to reckon any period as a term under the provisions of the preceding clause shall be made to the board, through the Registrar, by the student's society.

4. Part-time students holding the status of Student for Degree of Master of Science by Research shall in each case be required to pursue their course of study for a minimum of twelve terms, subject to the provisions of § 3, cl. 5. Part-time students shall not be required to keep statutory residence, but must attend for such instruction as the board or other relevant body shall require, subject to the approval of the Education Committee. No student may apply to the relevant board or other body for the appointment of examiners unless his or her supervisor has certified that the student has fulfilled the requirements for part-time students laid down by the board or other relevant body.

5. Any student may, with the permission of the board, alter the subject of research approved by the board, provided that the conditions of suitability set out in §2 above continue to be met. In such cases the date of the student's admission for all the

purposes of this section shall remain unchanged, unless the board shall determine otherwise.

6. If a full-time Student for the Degree of Master of Science by Research has held that status for nine terms, or a part-time student for fifteen terms but has been prevented by exceptional circumstances from completing his or her thesis, the board   5
shall have power to grant an extension of time for a period or periods not exceeding three terms in all for a full-time student, or three terms in all for a part-time student, to be determined by the board. Applications for such an extension of time shall be made through the Registrar not later that the term in which the student is due to apply for permission to supplicate.   10

7. A Student for the Degree of Master of Science by Research shall cease to hold such status if:

(i) he or she shall have been refused permission to supplicate for the Degree of Master of Science;

(ii) the board concerned shall, in accordance with provisions set down by regula-   15
tion by the Education Committee, and after consultation with the student's society and supervisor, have deprived the student of such status;

(iii) he or she shall have failed to complete his or her thesis within nine terms for a full-time student, or fifteen terms for a part-time student, or within such further extension of time as may have been granted by the board concerned.   20

§6. Examination of Students for the Degree of Master of Science by Research

1. Candidates who have fulfilled the applicable residence and other requirements set out in §5 of this section, and whose status has not expired, may apply for the appointment of examiners and for leave to supplicate for the Degree of Master of   25
Science by Research.

2. Applications for the appointment of examiners should be made to the board concerned through the Registrar. They shall include:

(i) a certificate from the student's society that the application has the approval of that society;   30

(ii) a certificate from the supervisor that the candidate has pursued his or her course of study in Oxford in accordance with the provisions of §5 of this section;

(iii) a statement by the candidate what part, if any, of the thesis has already been accepted, or is being concurrently submitted for any degree or diploma or   35
certificate or other qualification in this University or elsewhere;

(iv) a statement by the candidate that the thesis is his or her own work, except where otherwise indicated.

3. The supervisor shall consult with the candidate concerning possible examiners, and forward to the board the names of suggested examiners with details of any special   40
considerations which the candidate wishes to make known about any potential examiners.

4. The student shall also submit for examination, at such time as the Education Committee shall by regulation require:

(i) two printed or typewritten copies of a thesis;   45

(ii) two printed or typewritten copies of an abstract of the thesis, which shall not normally exceed 300 words.

5. On receipt of an application for the appointment of examiners the board concerned shall appoint two examiners neither of whom shall be the candidate's supervisor, and whose duties shall be:

    (i) to consider the thesis and the abstract of it submitted by the student under the provisions of the preceding clause, provided that they shall exclude from consideration in making their report any part of the thesis which has already been accepted, or is being concurrently submitted, for any degree or other qualification in this University or elsewhere and shall have the power to require the candidate to produce for their inspection the complete thesis so accepted or concurrently submitted;

    (ii) to examine the student orally, and also, if they think fit, by a written examination, in the subject of the thesis and in other relevant subjects;

    (iii) to report to the board through the Registrar;

    (iv) to return to the student the copies of the thesis and of the abstract thereof submitted for examination.

The Education Committee shall have power to make regulations concerning the notice to be given of the oral examination and of the time and place at which it may be held. The examination may be attended by any member of the University in academic dress, while non-members may attend only with the consent of the examiners. In the case of theses submitted to the Social Sciences, Mathematical, Physical and Life Sciences, and Medical Sciences Boards, the Proctors after consultation with the relevant divisional board may decide (either at their own discretion or at the request of the candidate or the supervisor or department) to forbid the attendance of any person or all persons (other than the examiners and the candidate) or to impose any condition on attendance if and to the extent that such action is in their view necessary to protect the interests of the University or the candidate or both, and the examiners shall be informed accordingly and shall include this information in the notice of examination. The student, or his or her college, may within fourteen days of the date of the Proctors' decision appeal in writing to the Chair of the Education Committee (who may nominate another member of the committee, other than one of the Proctors, to adjudicate the appeal).

6. Having completed the examination of a candidate for the first time, the examiners may make recommendation (i) or (ii) below only. Having completed the examination of a candidate who has revised and re-submitted his or her thesis, the examiners may make any one of recommendations (i) to (iii). The recommendations are:

    (i) that the candidate should be granted leave to supplicate for the Degree of Master of Science by Research. In this case the examiners must include in their report statements that:

        1. the candidate possesses a good general knowledge of the field of learning within which the subject of the thesis falls;

        2. that the candidate has shown competence in investigating the chosen topic;

        3. that the candidate has made a worthwhile contribution to knowledge or understanding in the field of learning within which the subject of the thesis falls;

        4. that the thesis is presented in a lucid and scholarly manner;

        5. that it merits of the award of the Degree of Master of Science.

Examiners shall bear in mind that their judgement of the extent of the candidate's contribution to knowledge or understanding of the relevant field of learning shall take into account what may reasonably be expected of a capable and diligent student after two years of full-time study in the case of a full-time student, or twelve terms in the case of a part-time student.

If the examiners are satisfied that the candidate's thesis is of sufficient merit for the degree but consider, nevertheless, that before the thesis is deposited the candidate should make minor corrections (which are not sufficiently substantial to justify reference back for re-examination), they must require the candidate to correct the thesis to their satisfaction before they submit their report. If the candidate has not completed these corrections within one calendar month of the date of the oral examination, his or her name shall be removed by the Registrar from the Register of Students for the Degree of Master of Science by Research, provided that the board may, on good cause shown by the candidate, grant an extension of time of one further calendar month in which the candidate may fulfil this requirement before the removal of his or her name from the Register. No subsequent extension shall be granted, but it shall be open to a candidate who has failed to fulfil this requirement within those one or two months in total, as the case may be, to apply to the board for reinstatement as a Student for the Degree of Master of Science by Research, with the support of his or her society and supervisor, upon submission to the Registrar of a copy of his or her thesis incorporating the required corrections, and upon payment of such reinstatement fee as may from time to time be prescribed by Council by decree. Permission to supplicate shall not be granted until this fee has been paid;

(ii) that the board should refer the thesis back to the student in order that he or she may revise it for re-examination. If the examiners so recommend they shall annexe to their report to the board a statement (for transmission to the student) setting out the respects in which the thesis falls below the standard required for the degree. If the board adopts this recommendation the student shall retain the status and obligations of a Student for the Degree of Master of Science, and may apply again for the appointment of examiners, in accordance with the procedure laid down in this subsection, not later than the third term after that in which the board gave permission so to reapply. If such permission shall have been given by a board during a vacation, it shall be deemed to have been given in the term preceding that vacation. On re-submission of the thesis, students should submit a separate report indicating the specific changes made. For students in the Medical Sciences Division and the Department for Continuing Education, the word limit for the accompanying report shall be 1,000 words; for students in the Mathematical, Physical and Life Sciences Division, the word limit shall be 2,000 words;

(iii) that the board should refuse the candidate's application for leave to supplicate.

7. In each case the examiners must embody in their report, in support of their recommendation, an account of the scope, character, and quality of the candidate's work.

8. On receipt of the examiners' report the board shall reach a decision on whether to accept the examiners' recommendation, provided that no candidate shall be given leave to supplicate unless the examiners have made the statements required in clause 6 (i) above.

9. A candidate who has been granted leave to supplicate by a board shall be required to submit to the Examination Schools a copy of his or her thesis, incorporating any amendments or corrections required by the examiners and approved by the board, with a view to deposit in the Bodleian or other appropriate university library. [For candidates admitted on or after 1 October 2007: candidates are also required to submit an electronic copy of their thesis to the Oxford Research Archive, unless an exception to this requirement has been granted by the Proctors.] [For candidates supplicating on or after 1 July 2013: candidates are also required to submit the library

copy to the Examination Schools and where applicable the electronic copy of the thesis to the Oxford Research Archive no later than the end of the fifth day before the date of the degree ceremony booked by the candidate for conferral of their degree.] Permission to supplicate shall in all cases be conditional upon fulfilment of these requirements. 5

10. In an exceptional case in which a board is unable to accept the examiners' recommendation, or in which the examiners cannot reach an agreed recommendation, the board shall have power to appoint one or two new examiners as it deems necessary, to conduct such further examination of the candidate as the board may require. The board shall make a report on any such case to the Education Committee. 10

11. The board may exempt a candidate who is being re-examined under the provisions of clause 6 (ii) above from the oral examination, provided that the examiners are able to certify that they are satisfied, without examining the candidate orally, that they can recommend to the board in the terms required by clause 6 (i) above that he or she be given leave to supplicate for the Degree of Master of Science. 15

12. It shall be the duty of the Registrar to notify the candidate of the board's decision as soon as may be. The Registrar shall also be responsible for publishing at the end of each academic year the names of those candidates to whom permission to supplicate has been granted during that year, together with a statement of the subject of the thesis written by each. 20

13. When, on the conclusion of the investigation of a complaint made by a candidate, the Proctors recommend that a candidate be re-examined, the board shall have power to hold a new examination.

NOTES

17

GENERAL REGULATIONS FOR THE DEGREE OF DOCTOR OF PHILOSOPHY

§1. Degree of Doctor of Philosophy

1. Any member of the University who has been admitted to the status of Student for the Degree of Doctor of Philosophy and who has satisfied the conditions prescribed by this decree may supplicate for the Degree of Doctor of Philosophy.

2. The Education Committee shall have power to make and vary such regulations as may be necessary for carrying out the duties laid upon it and upon the Registrar by this section.

3. For the purposes of this section the words 'board', 'faculty board', 'board of the faculty', or 'divisional board' shall include any body which has power to admit students to read for the Degree of Doctor of Philosophy.

4. Students for the Degree of Doctor of Philosophy who are not graduates of the University may wear a long gown of black stuff, whose shape and ornaments shall be in accordance with a pattern approved by the Vice-Chancellor and Proctors and preserved in the University Offices, Wellington Square.

§2. Status of Student for the Degree of Doctor of Philosophy

1. The following may be admitted to the status of Student for the Degree of Doctor of Philosophy:

   (i) a member of the University who, having held the status of Probationer Research Student under the provisions of the appropriate regulation, or having held the status of student for another higher degree within the University, or having completed the requirements for another higher degree within the University, has successfully completed the relevant qualifying test for entry to D.Phil. status prescribed in §3 of this section;

   (ii) a member of the University who has been given leave to supplicate for the Degree of Master or Bachelor of Philosophy, or of Master of Science by Research, or of Master of Letters, provided that the subject of the thesis offered by the candidate in the examination for that degree shall be in the broad field of research proposed for the D.Phil.

2. It shall be the duty of the Registrar to keep a Register of those admitted to the status of Student for the Degree of Doctor of Philosophy.

3. A board may grant a student suspension from the Register or deprive a student of his or her status; and in such cases it shall at all times follow procedures determined by the Education Committee by regulation. A board may also reinstate a student to the Register, provided that the number of terms a student has spent with the status of Student for the Degree of Doctor of Philosophy shall not have exceeded eighteen in all in the case of a full-time student, or twenty-seven terms in the case of a part-time student.

§3. Admission of Candidates to the Status of Student for the Degree of Doctor of Philosophy

1. Candidates qualified under §2 of this section may apply for admission as Student for the Degree of Doctor of Philosophy to the board concerned through the Registrar. Such applications shall be accompanied by:

    (i) a statement from the supervisor that he or she approves the proposed subject for a thesis[1] and considers the candidate well-fitted to undertake advanced research;

    (ii) a statement of support for the application from the candidate's society;

    (iii) a statement of the subject of the proposed thesis and details of the manner in which the candidate proposes to treat it.

2. Save for those applying under the provisions of §2, cl. 1 (ii) of this section, applicants shall in addition be required to submit written work to the board, which work shall be assessed by two assessors appointed by the board, neither of whom shall normally be the candidate's supervisor. The precise manner and form of the written work shall be determined by regulation by each board. In the case of Fine Art candidates offering studio practice, and in the case of Music candidates offering a portfolio of musical compositions as part of their submissions, this will include such studio or compositional work as the board requires. The process of assessment must always include an interview with the applicant. Upon completion of their assessment of the candidate's work, the assessors shall make a recommendation as to whether the application for transfer to D.Phil. status should be granted. In each case the assessors shall make a reasoned written report to the board in support of their recommendation.

3. The board shall consider the candidate's application together with the material supplied in accordance with clauses 1 and 2 above. No application for transfer shall be granted unless the assessors shall have certified and the board is satisfied that the candidate is capable of carrying out advanced research, and that the subject of the thesis and the manner of its treatment proposed by the candidate are acceptable; and unless the board or department under whose aegis the research is to be conducted has adequate facilities to enable the research to be undertaken.

4. Subject to the approval of the Education Committee, each board shall have power to determine by regulation what other test or condition, if any, it may require before approving admission to D.Phil. status. Each board shall be empowered, without further authority, to require from the supervisor any further confidential report on an applicant's suitability to pursue research towards the D.Phil.

5. It shall be the duty of the Registrar to submit any application made under these provisions to the board concerned, and to inform the candidate of the outcome as soon as may be.

6. A candidate whose first application for transfer to D.Phil. status is not approved shall be permitted to make one further application, following the procedures laid down in clauses 1–4 above, and shall be granted an extension of time for one term if this is necessary for the purposes of making the application.

7. An applicant who transfers to the status of Student for the Degree of Doctor of Philosophy shall be reckoned as having held that status from the time he or she was admitted to his or her previous status unless the board shall determine otherwise.

---

[1] Here and hereafter in these regulations, in the case of Fine Art candidates offering studio practice as part of their submission, and in the case of Music candidates offering a portfolio of musical compositions as part of their submission, 'thesis' shall be understood to include the totality of the candidate's submission.

§4. Confirmation of Status as a Student for the Degree of Doctor of Philosophy

1. A candidate who has been admitted to the status of Student for the Degree of Doctor of Philosophy must, not later than the ninth term or normally earlier than the sixth term after that in which he or she was initially admitted to the status of a Probationer Research Student or to the status of a student for another higher degree of the University, or the eighteenth and twelfth terms respectively in the case of a part-time student, complete the assessment process prescribed by the relevant board for confirmation of his or her status as a D.Phil. Student. A board or committee may, for good reason, permit a candidate to defer for a maximum of three terms his or her application for confirmation of status. A student who has been admitted to the status of Student for the Degree of Doctor of Philosophy after successfully completing the requirements for the Degree of Master (or Bachelor) of Philosophy, or having held the status of Student for the M.Litt. or M.Sc. by Research, may be exempted by the board or committee concerned from the requirement for confirmation of status. With the exception of students who have been exempted under this provision, all Students for the Degree of Doctor of Philosophy must have their status confirmed before making an application for the appointment of examiners.

2. Candidates applying for confirmation of their status shall submit their application to the board concerned, through the Registrar; and such applications shall be accompanied by:

(i) certification from the supervisor that the candidate's progress has been such as to warrant confirmation of status;

(ii) a statement of support for the application from the candidate's society.

3. Each faculty board shall, subject to the approval of the Education Committee, determine by regulation any other conditions which a student must fulfil before his or her status may be confirmed.

4. A candidate whose first application for confirmation of their status is not approved shall be permitted to make one further application following the procedures laid down in this section normally within one term of the original application, and shall be granted an extension of time for one term if this is necessary for the purposes of making the application.

5. A Student for the Degree of Doctor of Philosophy shall cease to hold such status unless it has been confirmed within nine terms of his or her admission to that status (or within a maximum of twelve terms where deferral has been approved in accordance with paragraph 4.1) in the case of a full-time student, or eighteen terms (or a maximum of twenty-four terms where deferral has been approved in accordance with paragraph 4.1) in the case of a part-time student, in accordance with the provisions of this section.

6. If, after considering a candidate's second application for confirmation of status, a board concludes that the student's progress does not warrant this, the board may approve his or her transfer to the status of Student for the Degree of Master of Science by Research or of Master of Letters, as appropriate.

§5. Supervision of Students for the Degree of Doctor of Philosophy

1. Every candidate on admission as a Student for the Degree of Doctor of Philosophy shall be placed by the board which approved his or her application under the supervision of a member of the University or other competent person selected by the board, and the board shall have power for sufficient reason to change

the supervisor of any student or to arrange for joint supervision by more than one supervisor, if it deems it necessary.

2. It shall be the duty of a supervisor to direct and superintend the work of the student, to meet the student regularly, and to undertake such duties as shall be from time to time set out in Policy and Guidance issued by the Education Committee. The supervisor shall submit a report on the progress of the student to the board three times a year as required, and at any other time when the board so requests or the supervisor deems it expedient; and shall carry out such other duties as are set out in Policy and Guidance issued by the Education Committee. The supervisor shall communicate the contents of the report to the student on each occasion that a report is made, so that the student is aware of the supervisor's assessment of his or her work during the period in question. In addition, the supervisor shall inform the board at once if he or she is of the opinion the student is unlikely to reach the standard required for the Degree of Doctor of Philosophy.

The Registrar shall send a copy of each report by the supervisor to the student's college, and to the Director of Graduate Studies or other nominated person under the board concerned.

3. It shall be the duty of every Student for the Degree of Doctor of Philosophy to undertake such guided work as his or her supervisor requests; to attend such meetings with his or her supervisor as the latter reasonably arranges; and to fulfil any other requirements of the Education Committee set out in its memorandum of guidance for students and supervisors.

§6. Residence and other Requirements for Students for the Degree of Doctor of Philosophy

1. Except as provided in clause 2 of this subsection, a Student for the Degree of Doctor of Philosophy shall after admission for full-time study keep statutory residence and pursue his or her course of study at Oxford for at least six terms, provided that a Student for the Degree of Doctor of Philosophy who is also a Bachelor or Master of Philosophy or Master of Science or Master of Letters or Master of Studies or Bachelor of Civil Law or Magister Juris or Master of Theology (except for those who hold the degree having studied for it at Westminster College) shall keep statutory residence and pursue his or her course of study at Oxford for at least three terms after admission as a Student for the Degree of Doctor of Philosophy. Time spent outside Oxford during term as part of an academic programme approved by Council shall count towards residence for the purpose of this clause.

2. The board concerned may dispense a student for the Degree of Doctor of Philosophy, on application through his or her society and with the support of his or her supervisor, from not more than three terms of residence and study in Oxford either on the ground that it is necessary to the student's work that he or she should be allowed to pursue his or her course of study at some other place than Oxford, or for other good cause.

3. Students exceptionally permitted to undertake their research in a well-found laboratory outside Oxford shall not be required to keep statutory residence, but must attend for such instruction as the board shall require.

4. Any student who, after admission under §3 of this section, has kept statutory residence and studied at Oxford for a period of forty-two days, not necessarily consecutive, but falling within the same academic year, may apply to the board concerned for leave to reckon such period as one term towards the total required under the preceding clause. The board shall have power to grant such leave provided that:

(i) no day so reckoned which falls within any term shall also be reckoned for the purpose of keeping that term;

(ii) no student who has kept the Michaelmas, or the Hilary, or the Trinity Term shall be allowed to reckon in this manner any day that falls within the eight weeks beginning on the first day of Full Term in Michaelmas, or Hilary, or Trinity Term, as the case may be;

(iii) no student shall be allowed to reckon in this manner more than one such period in the same academic year;

(iv) no student shall be allowed to reckon more than three terms in the same academic year.

For the purposes of this clause, the academic year shall begin on the first day of Michaelmas Term and end on the day preceding the first day of Michaelmas Term in the following calendar year.

Applications for leave to reckon any period as a term under the provisions of this clause shall be made to the board, through the Registrar, by the student's society.

5. Part-time students holding the status of Student for the Degree of Doctor of Philosophy shall in each case be required to pursue their course of study for a minimum of twelve terms, subject to the provisions of §3, cl. 6. Part-time students shall not be required to keep statutory residence, but must attend for such instruction as the board or other relevant body shall require, subject to the approval of the Education Committee. No student may apply to the relevant faculty board or other body for the appointment of examiners unless his or her supervisor has certified that the student has fulfilled the requirements for part-time students laid down by the faculty board or other relevant body.

6. Any student may, with the permission of the board alter the subject of the research originally approved provided that the conditions of suitability set out in §3 of this section continue to be met. In such cases the date of the student's admission for all the purposes of this section shall remain unchanged, unless the board shall order otherwise.

7. If a full-time Student for the Degree of Doctor of Philosophy has held that status for twelve terms, or a part-time student for twenty-four terms, but has been prevented by exceptional circumstances from completing his or her thesis, the board shall have power to grant an extension of time for a period or periods, not exceeding six terms in all for a full-time student, or three terms in all for a part-time student, to be determined by the board. Applications for such extension of time shall be made through the Registrar not later than the term in which the student is due to apply for permission to supplicate.

8. A Student for the Degree of Doctor of Philosophy shall cease to hold that status if:

(i) he or she shall have been refused permission to supplicate for the Degree of Doctor of Philosophy; or

(ii) the board concerned shall in accordance with §2, cl. 3 of this section, and with the provisions set down by regulation by the Education Committee and after consultation with the student's college and supervisor, have deprived the student of such status;

(iii) he or she shall have been transferred under the relevant provisions to another status;

(iv) he or she shall have failed to complete his or her thesis within twelve terms for a full-time student, or twenty-four terms for a part-time student or within such further extension of time as may have been granted by the board concerned.

§7. Examination of Students for the Degree of Doctor of Philosophy

1. A Student for the Degree of Doctor of Philosophy who has fulfilled the applicable residence and other requirements set out in §6 of this section and whose status has not expired, may apply to the board concerned for the appointment of examiners and for leave to supplicate for the Degree of Doctor of Philosophy.

2. Such applications should be made to the board concerned through the Registrar. They shall include:

(i) a certificate from the student's college that the application has the approval of that college;

(ii) a certificate from the supervisor that the student has pursued his or her course of study in Oxford in accordance with the provisions of §6 of this section;

(iii) a statement by the candidate of what part, if any, of the thesis has already been accepted, or is concurrently being submitted, for any degree or diploma or certificate or other qualification in this University or elsewhere;

(iv) a statement by the candidate that the thesis is his or her own work, except where otherwise indicated.

3. The supervisor shall consult with the candidate concerning possible examiners, and forward to the board the names of suggested examiners together with details of any special considerations which the candidate wishes to make known about any potential examiners.

4. The candidate shall also submit for examination, at such time and in such format as the Education Committee shall by regulation permit:

(i) two printed or typewritten copies of a thesis; or (in the case of Fine Art candidates offering studio practice as part of their submission) two printed or typewritten copies of the written portion of the thesis, and a portfolio or exhibition of work, together with documentation of that work;

(ii) two printed or typewritten copies of an abstract of the thesis, which shall not normally exceed 300 words.

5. On receipt of an application the board concerned shall appoint two examiners, neither of whom shall be the candidate's supervisor, and whose duties shall be:

(i) to consider the thesis and the abstract of it submitted by the student, provided that they shall exclude from consideration in making their report any part of the thesis which has already been accepted, or is being concurrently submitted, for any degree or other qualification in this University or elsewhere otherwise than as part of the requirements of this University for the Degree of Bachelor of Philosophy or of Master of Philosophy or of Bachelor of Civil Law, or as part of the dissertation submitted by a Student for the Degree of Master of Science by Coursework or of Master of Studies, and shall have the power to require the candidate to produce for their inspection the complete thesis so accepted or concurrently submitted;

(ii) (in the case of Fine Art candidates offering studio practice as part of their submission) to consider the portfolio or exhibition of work documented under section 4 (i) of these regulations, and presented or mounted by the candidate in partial satisfaction of the examination requirements;

(iii) to examine the student orally in the subject of his or her thesis;

(iv) to satisfy themselves by examination (oral, written, or both) whether the student possesses a good general knowledge of the particular field of learning within which the subject of the thesis falls;

(v) to report to the board through the Registrar on the scope, character, and quality of the work submitted;

(vi) to return to the student the copies of the thesis and the abstracts thereof.

The Education Committee shall have power to make regulations concerning the notice to be given of the oral examination, and of the time and place at which it may be held. The examination may be attended by any member of the University in academic dress, while non-members may attend only with the consent of the examiners. In the case of theses submitted to the Social Sciences, Mathematical, Physical and Life Sciences, and Medical Sciences Boards, the Proctors after consultation with the relevant Divisional Board may decide (either at their own discretion or at the request of the candidate or the supervisor or department) to forbid the attendance of any person or all persons (other than the examiners and the candidate) or to impose any condition on attendance if and to the extent that such action is in their view necessary to protect the interests of the University or the candidate or both, and the examiners shall be informed accordingly and shall include this information in the notice of examination. The student, or his or her college, may within fourteen days of the date of the Proctors' decision appeal in writing to the Chair of the Education Committee (who may nominate another member of the committee, other than one of the Proctors, to adjudicate the appeal).

6. Having completed the examination of a candidate for the first time, the examiners may make any one of recommendations (i), (ii), or (iv) below only. Having completed the examination of a candidate who has revised and re-submitted his or her thesis, the examiners may make any one of recommendations (i)–(vi). The recommendations are:

(i) that the board should grant the candidate leave to supplicate for the Degree of Doctor of Philosophy. In making this recommendation, the examiners must include in their report statements that:

1. the student possesses a good general knowledge of the particular field of learning within which the subject of the thesis falls;

2. the student has made a significant and substantial contribution in the particular field of learning within which the subject of the thesis falls;

3. the thesis is presented in a lucid and scholarly manner;

4. in their opinion the thesis merits the Degree of Doctor of Philosophy;

5. the student has presented a satisfactory abstract of the thesis.

Examiners shall bear in mind that their judgement of the substantial significance of the work should take into account what may reasonably be expected of a capable and diligent student after three or at most four years of full-time study in the case of a full-time student, or eight years in the case of a part-time student.

(i) (*a*) **Minor corrections**

If the examiners are satisfied that the candidate's thesis is of sufficient merit to qualify for the degree but consider, nevertheless, that before the thesis is deposited the candidate should make minor corrections (which are not sufficiently substantial to justify reference back for re-examination and which should be capable of completion within one month), they must require the candidate to correct the thesis to their satisfaction before they submit their report. If the candidate has not completed these corrections within one calendar month of the date of receipt of the list of minor corrections from the examiners, his or her name shall be removed by the Registrar from the Register of Students for the Degree of Doctor of Philosophy, provided that the board may, on good cause shown by the candidate, grant an extension of time of one further calendar month in which the candidate may fulfil this requirement before the removal of his or her name from the Register. No subsequent extension shall be granted, but it shall be open to a candidate who has failed to fulfil this requirement within those one or two months in total, as the case may be, to apply to the board for reinstatement as a Student for the Degree of Doctor of Philosophy, with the support of his or her society and supervisor, upon submission to the Registrar of a copy of his or her thesis incorporating the required corrections, and upon payment of such reinstatement fee as may from time to time be prescribed by Council by decree. Permission to supplicate shall not be granted until this fee has been paid;

(i) (*b*) **Major corrections**

If the examiners are satisfied that the candidate's thesis is of sufficient potential merit to qualify for the degree but consider, nevertheless, that before the thesis is deposited the candidate should make major corrections (which are not sufficiently substantial to justify reference back for re-examination and which should be capable of completion within six months), they should report this preliminary recommendation to the board with a description of the major corrections which they require the candidate to make before they confirm their recommendation.

Where the examiners make this recommendation, and the board, considering the extent and nature of the major corrections, takes the view that the recommendation ought to be reference of the thesis back to the candidate in order that he or she may revise it for re-examination, the board may, exceptionally, ask the examiners to review their recommendation.

If the candidate has not completed these corrections within six calendar months of the date of receipt of the list of major corrections from the examiners, his or her name shall be removed by the Registrar from the Register of Students for the Degree of Doctor of Philosophy, provided that the board may, on good cause shown by the candidate, grant an extension of time of up to three further calendar months in which the candidate may fulfil this requirement before the removal of his or her name from the Register. No subsequent extension shall be granted, but it shall be open to a candidate who has failed to fulfil this requirement within those six or nine months in total, to apply to the board for reinstatement as a Student for the Degree of Doctor of Philosophy, with the support of his or her society and supervisor, upon submission to the Registrar of a copy of his or her thesis incorporating the required corrections, and upon payment of such reinstatement fee as may from time to time be prescribed by Council by decree. Permission to supplicate shall not be granted until this fee has been paid.

Where a recommendation of approval subject to major corrections has been made, the examiners, on receipt of the corrected thesis on the first occasion, may conclude and report one of the following:

(*a*) the original recommendation is now fully substantiated;

(*b*) the work as submitted still requires minor corrections prior to confirmation of the original recommendation and a further one month may be allowed for this from that date;

(*c*) the work as now submitted still requires major corrections prior to confirmation of the original recommendation and a further six months may be allowed for this from that date.

Recommendation (*a*) or (*b*) may be made without a further oral examination on condition that both examiners have reviewed and approved the major corrections. A further oral examination must be held if either of the examiners requires it or if the recommendation is likely to be (*c*).

In the exceptional instance where (*c*) applied and the outcome of the second and final submission of corrections still remained unsatisfactory, the examiners will amend their original recommendation to (ii) below.

(ii) that the board should offer the candidate a choice between (a) reference of the thesis back to him or her in order that he or she may revise it for re-examination for the Degree of Doctor of Philosophy, and (b) leave to supplicate for the Degree of Master of Letters or of Master of Science, as appropriate, on the basis that the thesis has not reached the standard required for the Degree of Doctor of Philosophy but has nevertheless reached that required for the Degree of Master of Letters or of Master of Science.

    (*a*) If the board adopts this recommendation, and the student chooses to revise the thesis for re-examination for the Degree of Doctor of Philosophy, the student shall retain the status and obligations of a Student for the Degree of Doctor of Philosophy and shall be permitted to apply again for the appointment of examiners, in accordance with the procedure laid down in this subsection, not later than the sixth term after that in which the board gave permission so to reapply. If such permission shall have been given by a board during a vacation, it shall be deemed to have been given in the term preceding that vacation. Accompanying the revised thesis at re-submission should be a separate report indicating the specific changes made. For students in the Humanities, Medical Sciences and Social Sciences Divisions and the Department for Continuing Education, the word limit for the accompanying report shall be 1,000 words; for students in the Mathematical, Physical and Life Sciences Division, the word limit shall be 2,000 words;

    (*b*) If the board adopts this recommendation and the student chooses leave to supplicate for the Degree of Master of Letters or Master of Science by Research, the examiners may still determine that before the thesis is deposited the candidate should make minor corrections in accordance with the regulations under (i) above.

(iii) that the board should refer the student's thesis back in order that he or she may present it for re-examination for the Degree of Master of Letters or of Master of Science, as determined by the examiners (if appropriate), only. If the board adopts the recommendation the student shall be transferred forthwith to the status of Student for the Degree of Master of Letters or Student for the Degree of Master of Science as the case may be, and shall be permitted to apply for permission to supplicate for the Degree of Master of Letters or Master of Science in accordance with the provisions of the appropriate regulation. If such permission shall have been given by a board during a vacation, it shall be deemed to have been given in the term preceding that vacation. The word limit for a thesis resubmitted under this provision shall be that specified by the D.Phil regulations under which it was originally submitted;

(iv) that the board should refer the student's thesis back in order that he or she may present it for re-examination either under (ii) above for the Degree of Doctor of Philosophy or, if the student chooses, under (iii) above for the Degree of Master of Letters or of Master of Science only. The board shall adopt such a recommendation only if it is fully satisfied that the thesis as it stands is not of the standard required for the Degree of Doctor of Philosophy, nor for the Degree of Master of Letters or of Master of Science as the case may be, but that the candidate could reach the standard required for the Degree of Doctor of Philosophy. If such permission shall have been given by a board during a vacation, it shall be deemed to have been given in the term preceding that vacation;

(v) that the thesis has not reached the standard required for the Degree of Doctor of Philosophy but has nevertheless reached that required of the Degree of Master of Letters or of Master of Science, and that the candidate may be granted leave to supplicate for one of the latter degrees on the basis of the thesis as it stands;

the examiners may still determine that before the thesis is deposited the candidate should make minor corrections in accordance with the regulations under (i) above.

(vi) that the student's application for leave to supplicate should be refused.

7. If the examiners recommend reference back of the student's application under clause 6 (ii) or (iii) or (iv) above, they shall annex to their report to the board a statement (for transmission to the candidate) setting out the respects in which the thesis falls below the standard required for the degree in question, and what changes are necessary for it to reach that standard, save that examiners of a thesis submitted for the first time may, in exceptional circumstances, and notwithstanding a recommendation under clause 6 (ii) or (iv) above, certify that they are unable to indicate how the thesis might be changed, within the time allowed, in order to reach the required standard for the degree of Doctor of Philosophy.

8. On receipt of the examiners' report the board shall reach a decision on whether to accept the examiners' recommendation, provided that no candidate shall be given leave to supplicate for the Degree of Doctor of Philosophy unless the examiners have made the statements required in clause 6 (i) above.

9. A candidate who has been granted leave to supplicate by a board shall be required to submit to the Examination Schools a copy of his or her thesis, incorporating any amendments or corrections required by the examiners and approved by the board, with a view to deposit in the Bodleian or other appropriate university library. [For candidates admitted on or after 1 October 2007: candidates are also required to submit an electronic copy of their thesis to the Oxford Research Archive, unless an exception to this requirement has been granted by the Proctors.] [For candidates supplicating on or after 1 July 2013: candidates are also required to submit the library copy to the Examination Schools and where applicable the electronic copy of the thesis to the Oxford Research Archive no later than the end of the fifth day before the date of the degree ceremony booked by the candidate for conferral of their degree.] Permission to supplicate shall in all cases be conditional upon fulfilment of these requirements.

10. In an exceptional case in which a board is unable to accept the examiners' recommendation, or in which the examiners cannot reach an agreed recommendation, the board shall have power to appoint one or two new examiners as it deems necessary, to conduct such further examination of the candidate as the board may require. The board shall make a report on any such case to the Education Committee.

11. The board may exempt a candidate who is being re-examined under the provisions of clause 6 (ii)–(v) above from the oral examination, provided that the examiners are able to certify that they are satisfied without examining the candidate orally that they can recommend to the board in the terms required by clause 6 (i) above that he or she be given leave to supplicate for the Degree of Doctor of Philosophy.

12. It shall be the duty of the Registrar to notify the candidate of the board's decision as soon as may be. The Registrar shall also be responsible for publishing at the end of each academic year the names of those candidates to whom permission to supplicate has been granted during that year, together with a statement of the subject of the thesis written by each.

13. When, on the conclusion of the investigation of a complaint made by a candidate, the Proctors recommend that a candidate be re-examined, the board shall have power to hold a new examination.

NOTES

18

RESEARCH DEGREES IN THE HUMANITIES DIVISION

TRANSFER OF STATUS AND CONFIRMATION OF STATUS

1. *Transfer of Status*

Purpose and criteria

(i) To assess whether the candidate is capable of carrying out advanced research, and has had suitable preparation in terms of subject-specific research training.

(ii) To assess whether the subject of the thesis and the manner of its treatment as proposed by the candidate are acceptable and potentially of D.Phil. quality.

(iii) To assess whether the thesis can reasonably be completed in no more than 6 to 9 terms from transfer.

Applying for transfer of status

(i) **Students admitted to Probationer Research Student (PRS) status**

Students who have completed a one-year Master's degree at the University of Oxford or elsewhere, or a two-year M.Phil. degree at a university other than the University of Oxford are admitted to Probationer Research Student (PRS) status. Transfer of status from PRS to D.Phil. must take place in Trinity Term of Year 1 or Michaelmas Term of Year 2 as measured from the admission to PRS status.

(ii) **Students admitted to D.Phil. status**

Students who have completed a two-year M.Phil. degree at the University of Oxford and who have already commenced work on their doctoral thesis will be admitted either as a Probationer Research Student or as a student with D.Phil. status. The decision will be made by the relevant University Admitting Body based on the proposed doctoral research and on previous qualifications, including research undertaken at Master's level. For students who are admitted to PRS status, transfer of status from PRS to D.Phil. must take place in Trinity Term of Year 1 or Michaelmas Term of Year 2 as measured from the admission to PRS status.

The relevant University Admitting Body may only admit students directly to D.Phil. status if the Admitting Body is satisfied that the student meets the three conditions described under 'purpose of transfer of status' above. In such cases, the admissions process should follow the same pattern as the transfer of status process, and normally all candidates who are admitted directly to D.Phil. status must be interviewed. For students who are admitted directly to D.Phil. status, the transfer of status process is waived.

Material normally required for applications for transfer of status

Entries for individual Faculty Boards below indicate exactly which materials students studying for a D.Phil. degree in that faculty should submit to apply for transfer of status.

Candidates applying for transfer of status from Probationer Research Student (PRS) to D.Phil. should normally submit the following documents:

    (i) GSO.2 form: Application to transfer status.

    (ii) A detailed outline (not exceeding 1,000 words) of the proposed thesis subject and of the manner in which it will be treated, including a provisional list of chapters and their proposed coverage.

    (iii) Written work (or equivalent, e.g. a portfolio, score or CD/DVD), to be specified by the faculty. The submitted work should be on the topic of the proposed thesis, and if this consists of written work, should be about 10,000 words long (usually a draft chapter of the thesis; if the submitted work is not a draft chapter, then the candidate should provide a written explanation of the written work's relationship to the thesis).

    (iv) A reference from the supervisor: the supervisor (or supervisors, if there is more than one) must provide a full and detailed assessment of the student and the student's application for transfer in the 'Comment' section of the GSO.2 form. Where there are two supervisors, either each one must submit an assessment report or both must sign a joint assessment.

    (v) Information about subject-specific research or other training completed by the student, e.g. proof of linguistic competence. The faculty should specify any research training/research skills (e.g. linguistic competence, ability to use archives, handling of ancient documents) which students are expected to have acquired by this stage of their doctoral studies.

Assessment

    (i) Assessors: the faculty must appoint two assessors, neither of whom must be the candidate's supervisor.

    (ii) Interview: an interview by both assessors, based on the submitted written materials, is compulsory.

    (iii) Report: the assessors must submit a joint written report, making a clear recommendation to the relevant faculty Graduate Studies Committee (or equivalent) of 'transfer' or 'not transfer', and providing reasons for their recommendation. The report should note any subject-specific research training still required by the student successfully to complete their doctorate.

Outcome of assessment

    (i) The assessors may recommend that the candidate be transferred to D.Phil. status.

    (ii) The assessors may judge that the candidate is not (yet) ready to transfer, in which case they may:

        (*a*) recommend that the candidate should reapply after undertaking further preparatory work, which should be clearly described in their report, or

        (*b*) recommend that the candidate should transfer to a lower level of research degree, such as the Master of Letters (M.Litt.).

Unsuccessful applications

    (i) A candidate whose first application for transfer to D.Phil. status is not approved shall be permitted to make one further application, and will be granted an extension of time for one term if this is necessary for the purposes of making the application. Normally the assessors should be the same as for the original application.

    (ii) If, after considering a candidate's second application for transfer of status, the relevant board concludes that the student's progress does not warrant transfer, the board must consider whether to approve his or her transfer to the status of Student for the Degree of Master of Letters (M.Litt.).

Reporting

The report of the assessors must be considered by the Faculty Graduate Studies Committee (or equivalent), which may delegate authority to the Director of Graduate Studies. Where authority is delegated, the Director of Graduate Studies must report his or her decision to the Faculty Graduate Studies Committee (or equivalent). A copy 5
of the transfer report must also be sent to the student, supervisor and college.

Appeals

Candidates who wish to contest the outcome of the transfer assessment, either on procedural or academic grounds, should first discuss the matter with their Director of Graduate Studies. Where a concern is not satisfactorily settled by that means, the 10
candidate, their supervisor or their college authority may make an appeal directly to the Proctors. In accordance with the University's complaints and appeals processes, the Proctors can only consider whether the procedures for reaching an academic decision were properly followed, and cannot challenge the academic judgement of the assessors. 15

Loss of Probationer Research Student status

Candidates will lose their Probationer Research Student status if they have not gained admission to another status (e.g. D.Phil. or M.Litt.) within six terms of admission as a full-time student to the status of Probationer Research Student, or if the faculty board concerned deprives them of such status (after consultation with the 20
college/hall and supervisor). If a candidate loses his or her status as a Probationer Research Student and has not gained admission to another status, the candidate is no longer registered as a student of the University.

2. *Confirmation of Status*

Purpose and criteria 25

The purpose of confirmation is to:

(i) assess the progress of the student's research, and

(ii) to ensure that the student's research progress is such that the student may reasonably be expected to submit within six months to one year.

Applying for confirmation of status 30

(i) Candidates who were admitted to Probationer Research Student (PRS) status must apply for confirmation of status between Trinity Term of Year 2 and Trinity Term of Year 3 as measured from their admission to PRS status.

(ii) Application for confirmation of status should be made at least *six months* (i.e. two terms, or Trinity Term plus the summer vacation) prior to submission of 35
the thesis.

Material normally required for applications for confirmation of status

Entries for individual faculty boards below indicate exactly which materials students studying for a D.Phil. degree in that faculty should submit to apply for confirmation of status. 40

Candidates applying for confirmation of D.Phil. status should normally submit the following documents:

(i) GSO.14 form: Application to Confirm D.Phil. status.

(ii) An abstract of the thesis, a list of chapters with a paragraph describing each chapter, a clear statement indicating which chapters have been written, and a 45
detailed timetable for the completion of the remaining chapters.

(iii) Written work (or equivalent, e.g. a portfolio, score or CD/DVD), to be specified by the faculty. The submitted work should be on the topic of the proposed thesis, and if this consists of written work, should be about 10,000 words long (usually a draft chapter of the thesis including all footnotes, bibliography etc.; if the submitted work is not a draft chapter, then the candidate should provide a written explanation of the written work's relationship to the thesis).   5

(iv) A reference from the supervisor: the supervisor (or supervisors, if there is more than one) must provide a confidential assessment of the student and their application (this must be in addition to, or instead of, the 'Comment' section of GSO.14). The faculty may specify additional references.

(v) Confirmation material should normally include copies of the report(s) from   10
the transfer process.

Assessment

(i) Assessors: the faculty must appoint at least one assessor, who must not be the candidate's supervisor. Ideally two assessors should be appointed.

(ii) Interview: an interview by at least one assessor who is not the supervisor,   15
based on the submitted written materials, is compulsory.

(iii) Report: the assessor(s) must submit a written report on both the written and interview components of the application, making a clear recommendation to the relevant Faculty Graduate Studies Committee (or equivalent).

Outcome of assessment   20

(i) The assessor(s) may recommend that the candidate's D.Phil. status be confirmed.

(ii) The assessor(s) may judge that the candidate does not (yet) satisfy the purpose of the confirmation process as described above, and may:

(*a*) recommend resubmission of the application at a later date within the   25
normal timetable;

(*b*) recommend that the candidate should transfer to a lower level of research degree, such as the M.Litt.

Unsuccessful applications

If the candidate's first application for confirmation of status is not approved, the   30
candidate is permitted to make one further application, normally within one term of the orginal application. The candidate will be granted an extension of time for one term if this is necessary for the purposes of making the application. If, after considering a candidate's second application for confirmation of status, a board concludes that the student's progress does not warrant confirmation, the board may approve his or   35
her transfer to the status of Student for the Degree of Master of Letters (M.Litt.).

Deferral of confirmation

In exceptional circumstances where unforeseen and unavoidable obstacles have arisen since transfer of status so as to delay a student's research progress, the student may apply to their faculty board for deferral of confirmation of status up to a   40
maximum of three terms. An application for deferral must consist of:

(i) a clear and detailed description of the obstacles;

(ii) a statement of support from the student's supervisor;

(iii) a statement of support from the Director of Graduate Studies.

Reporting   45

The report of the assessor(s) must be considered by the Faculty Graduate Studies Committee (or equivalent), which may delegate authority to the Director of Graduate Studies. Where authority is delegated, the Director of Graduate Studies must report their decisions to the Faculty Graduate Studies Committee (or equivalent). A copy of the transfer report must also be sent to the student, supervisor, and college.

RESEARCH DEGREES IN LINGUISTICS, PHILOLOGY, & PHONETICS

1. *Probationer Research Students*   5

Candidates for admission will normally be expected to have a first or upper second class degree. They will be required to submit evidence (in the form of essays written in English) of their competence in the broad subject of their intended research and should have a basic knowledge of the language(s) in which the main secondary literature is written.   10

2. *Theses*

Theses submitted for the Degree of M.Litt. in Comparative Philology and General Linguistics should not exceed 50,000 words. The word limit excludes the bibliography, appendices consisting of a catalogue of data, any extensive text which is specifically the object of a commentary or linguistic analysis, and any translation of that text, but   15
includes quotations and footnotes.

Theses submitted for the Degree of D.Phil. in Comparative Philology and General Linguistics should not exceed 100,000 words. The word limit excludes the bibliography, appendices consisting of a catalogue of data, any extensive text which is specifically the object of a commentary or linguistic analysis, and any translation of that   20
text, but includes quotations and footnotes.

RESEARCH DEGREES IN CLASSICS

1. *Admission to M.Litt. status*

Applications from Probationer Research Students for transfer to the status of Student for the Degree of Master of Letters will not normally be considered before   25
the beginning of the candidate's third term as a Probationer Research Student. Transfer will normally take place in the third or fourth term.

The written work to be submitted should be a single essay, preferably typed, on a subject relevant to the candidate's proposed thesis. For candidates in *Languages and Literature* the essay should not be more than 10,000 words in length; for candidates in   30
Ancient History it should not be more than 5,000 words in length.

2. *Admission to D.Phil. status*

Applications from Probationer Research Students for transfer to the status of Student for the Degree of Doctor of Philosophy will not normally be considered before the beginning of the candidate's third term as a Probationer Research   35
Student. The board regards the end of the third, or the beginning of the fourth, term as the normal time for this application to be made.

The written work to be submitted should be a single essay, preferably typed, and should be close in content to a chapter or part of a chapter of the candidate's proposed thesis.   40

For candidates in *Languages and Literature* the essay should not be more than 5,000 words in length; for candidates in *Ancient History* it should not be more than 10,000 words in length.

In *Languages and Literature* candidates will also be required to have attended such classes as the Graduate Studies Committee shall from time to time determine.

3. *Confirmation of D.Phil. status*

Applications from Students for the Degree of Doctor of Philosophy for confirmation of status should be accompanied by a reasoned statement of the nature of the 5 proposed thesis. Candidates in *Ancient History* are required to submit in addition a single essay of between 5,000 and 10,000 words in length, which should be close in content to a chapter or part of a chapter of the proposed thesis; candidates in Languages and Literature should be required to submit an essay, of approximately 5,000 words in length. Candidates may also be required to attend an interview. 10

In Languages and Literature candidates will also be required to provide evidence of reading competence in German and a second modern language by the time of confirmation. Further details on the modern language policy are set out in the Faculty's D.Phil. handbook.

The board regards the end of the sixth, or the beginning of the seventh, term from 15 the candidate's admission as a Probationer Research Student as the normal time for this application to be made except in the case of candidates who have been admitted directly to the status of Student for the Degree of Doctor of Philosophy of Philosophy after taking the M.Phil. and whose admission as Probationer Research Student is thereafter deemed to have begun when they began the M.Phil.: in this case the normal 20 time is the end of the ninth term after admission to the Status of Probationer Research Student.

4. *Theses*

All candidates when they submit their theses must state the approximate number of words therein both (*a*) including citations and, if they have been granted permission to 25 count citations separately, (*b*) excluding citations. Theses exceeding the limit are liable to be returned unexamined for reduction to the proper length. Candidates who have submitted in their final term may be allowed a maximum period of two terms to effect the necessary reduction.

Theses submitted for the Degree of M.Litt. in *Ancient History and Archaeology* 30 should not exceed 50,000 words, and those submitted for the Degree of D.Phil. should not exceed 100,000 words, excluding the bibliography, any text that is being edited or annotated, and any descriptive catalogue, but including footnotes and appendices. Leave to exceed these limits will only be given in exceptional cases, and upon the presentation of a detailed explanation by the candidate, together with a statement of 35 the excess length required and the written support of the supervisor. Such applications should be made immediately it becomes clear that authorisation to exceed the limit will be required, and in any case not later than the Friday of the fifth week of the term before that in which application is made for appointment of examiners. Every candidate submitting a thesis must state the number of words therein. 40

A thesis submitted for the Degree of M.Litt. in Classical Languages and Literature should not exceed 60,000 words. There is no minimum word limit but approximately 50,000 words would be accepted as a guideline. A thesis submitted for the Degree of D.Phil. should not exceed 100,000 words. There is no minimum word limit but approximately 80,000 words would be accepted as a guideline. The word limit 45 excludes the bibliography, any text that is being edited or annotated, translations of Greek or Latin quoted, and any descriptive catalogue, but includes Greek or Latin quoted, footnotes and appendices.

Candidates submitting archaeological theses incorporating photographs are required to present original photographs in one copy of the thesis only, provided 50 that the copies in the other two are adequately reproduced.

The copy of the thesis containing the original photographs should be the one deposited in the Bodleian Library.

5. *Written Examination for the D. Phil.*

The board recommends that, when a written examination is held, two papers be set, three hours being allowed for each.

Questions should be set testing candidates' knowledge of matters germane to, but not specifically included in, their treatment of the subject of their thesis, and command of the methods appropriate to the handling of them. Where submitted work is professedly based upon evidence, literary, material, or monumental, candidates should be required in the written examination to satisfy the examiners that they have adequately studied the original sources of such evidence.

The examiners are requested to include in their report to the board a statement of their judgement upon the qualifications shown in these regards by candidates.

RESEARCH DEGREES IN ENGLISH

General

Candidates for admission to D.Phil. and M.Litt. status, must have been interviewed by one of the persons appointed by the Board for this purpose, unless the Board determines otherwise.

1. *Transfer to M.Litt. and D.Phil. status*

(i) All research candidates are initially registered as Probationer Research Students and will be required to submit an application to transfer to M.Litt. or D.Phil. status no later than Friday of noughth week in the Trinity Term of their first year as a Probationer Research Student. In exceptional cases the English Graduate Studies Committee may permit the candidate to postpone submission; candidates seeking such postponement must apply to the Director of Graduate Studies well in advance, and no later than Monday of fifth week of Hilary Term.

(ii) Candidates must write to the English Graduate Studies Office by Friday of the eighth week of Hilary Term of their first year as a Probationer Research Student, giving notice of their intention to apply for transfer to D.Phil. status, and providing the title of their proposed thesis.

(iii) Candidates must submit the following materials: (1) The transfer of status application form, endorsed by the candidate's society and supervisor. (2) Two copies of a detailed outline (not exceeding 1,000 words) of the proposed subject and the manner in which it will be treated, including a provisional list of chapters and their proposed coverage. (3) Two copies of a piece of written work on the topic of their proposed thesis (of about 10,000 words).

(iv) A confidential report from the supervisor should be sent by the supervisor directly to the English Graduate Studies Office. The Graduate Studies Office shall send the outline, written work and the confidential report to two assessors appointed by the Director of Graduate Studies. The Director of Graduate Studies shall not appoint the candidate's supervisor as an assessor.

(v) The assessors shall then examine the candidate orally and report to the English Graduate Studies Committee in writing whether the candidate's subject is satisfactory for the degree in question and whether he or she is competent to undertake it. If they think this is not the case, they may recommend resubmission after a set period of probation; such resubmission will constitute the second attempt at Transfer of Status provided for in the General Regulations for the degree. If the assessors disagree, the Graduate Studies Committee shall decide what should be done.

2. *Confirmation of D.Phil. status*

   (i) Application for confirmation of D.Phil. status, with endorsements by the candidate's society and supervisor, shall normally be presented to the English Studies Office not later than Monday of fifth week in the eighth term after admission to the D.Phil. programme. In exceptional cases the   5 English Graduate Studies Committee may permit the candidate to postpone submission by up to one term: candidates seeking such postponement should apply to the Committee through the Director of Graduate Studies well in advance.

  (ii) Application for confirmation of D.Phil. status shall be accompanied by: (1)   10 Two copies of a full outline of chapters (*c*.100 words per chapters), summarising the scope of individual chapters and their state of completion, including a timetable for completion of the work which remains to be done before submission of the thesis; (2) Two copies of a draft abstract of the thesis as a whole, of approximately 1,000 words; (3) Two copies of a sample chapter, of 10,000   15 words; (4) a confidential report from the supervisor which should be sent direct to the Graduate Studies Office. The English Graduate Studies Office will send the written work and the confidential report as well as any previous reports on transfer to the interviewer appointed by the English Graduate Studies Committee on behalf of the English Faculty Board.   20

  (iii) The interviewers shall examine the candidate orally. If the interviewer considers it necessary, a second assessor may be appointed in consultation with the Director of Graduate Studies.

  (iv) The interviewers shall report to the English Graduate Studies Committee in writing whether the candidate's subject is satisfactory and whether he or she is   25 competent to tackle it. If confirmation is not recommended the interviewers may (1) recommend reapplication after a further period of study or (2) recommend transfer to M.Litt. status.

  (v) Any candidate whose first application for confirmation is refused may reapply on one (only) further occasion, normally within one term of the original   30 application. The candidate may be granted an extension of time for one term if this is necessary for the purposes of making the application. The material required will be the same as (ii) above.

3. *Theses*

    Theses submitted to the Board of the Faculty of English Language and Literature   35 for the Degree of M.Litt. should normally be around 40,000 words in length and should in no case exceed 50,000 words, exclusive of the bibliography and of any text that is being edited but including notes, glossary, appendices, etc. Theses submitted for the Degree of D.Phil. should normally be around 80,000 words in length and should in no case exceed 100,000 words, exclusive of the bibliography and of any text being   40 edited, but including notes, glossary, appendices, etc. Leave to exceed these limits will be given only in exceptional cases (e.g. when the subject of the thesis requires extensive quotation from unpublished or inaccessible material, or where substantial and supplementary bibliographical or biographical listings are essential or helpful for an understanding of the arguments of the thesis) and on the recommendation of the   45 supervisor. Applications to exceed the limit of 50,000 words for the M.Litt. or 100,000 words for the D.Phil. must be made in writing to the English Graduate Studies Committee in advance of the application for appointment of examiners. Each application should include a detailed explanation, a statement of the excess length requested, and a covering letter from the supervisor.   50

RESEARCH DEGREES IN FINE ART

1. *Admission*

Candidates may elect to pursue research by thesis alone, or by a combination of thesis and studio practice; where the latter course is proposed, the studio work produced must be original work developed and realised in respect of the stated aims 5 of the research programme, exemplifying and locating the ideas that have been developed in conjunction with the written part of the thesis. Fine Art candidates are initially admitted as Probationer Research Students. Depending on whether they wish to pursue research by thesis alone, or through a combination of thesis and studio practice, candidates should support their application with: 10

EITHER

(A) 1. a sample of recent written work (4,000–6,000 words), preferably but not necessarily related to the proposed topic or area of research, such as an undergraduate or Master's dissertation (or part of it) or a substantial essay;

    2. a proposal for a research topic or area (about 1,000 words), which should include 15 a statement why this work should be carried out at Oxford.

OR

(B) (For those intending to offer studio practice as part of the final submission)

    1. a sample of written work (2,000–3,000 words);

    2. a portfolio of recently completed studio work with slides or other documen- 20 tation of work not available for inclusion;

    3. a plan of work to be completed in Oxford.

All candidates should expect to attend for interview.

Part-time study

In assessing applications from candidates seeking to undertake a research degree 25 through part-time study, the Committee for the Ruskin School of Art shall have regard to evidence that:

  (i) the candidate is suitable to undertake research at doctoral level;

  (ii) the candidate's personal and professional circumstances are such that it is both practicable for him or her to fulfil the requirements of the course, and neces- 30 sary for him or her to study on a part-time basis;

  (iii) if appropriate, the candidate has the written support of his or her present employer for his or her proposed course of study and its obligations;

  (iv) the candidate's proposed topic of research is suitable for part-time study;

  (v) the candidate can meet the attendance requirements relating to part-time 35 study.

Attendance requirements for part-time study

Part-time students are required to attend for a minimum of thirty days of university-based work each year, to be arranged with the agreement of their supervisor, for the period that their names remain on the Register of Graduate Students unless individu- 40 ally dispensed by the committee.

2. *Transfer of status to M.Litt. or D.Phil.*

During the first year of study, Probationer Research Students are required to attend lectures, seminars, and classes within the University as directed by their supervisor(s). Students will also undertake foundation work related to their research area. 45

Applications for transfer to M.Litt. or D.Phil. status should normally be made by the end of the third term, and must be made by the end of the sixth term. Students must satisfy the committee that (*a*) they have followed and completed their prescribed courses of study, (*b*) they have undertaken preparatory research (and, where applicable, studio work) to the satisfaction of their supervisor(s), (*c*) the proposed research topic is acceptable, and that they are competent to undertake it, (*d*) (in the case of those intending to offer studio practice as part of the final submission) the proposed work to be undertaken is of sufficient substance.   5

In the case of part-time students, applications for transfer should normally be made by the end of the sixth term, and must be made by the end of the twelfth term.

Candidates for transfer should submit a brief statement (1,000 words) on the topic of their research and the manner in which they propose to treat it. This should be accompanied by: 10

EITHER

(A) an essay of about 5,000 words relevant to the topic proposed for the thesis.

OR

(B) (for those intending to offer studio practice as part of the final submission) a portfolio or exhibition of studio work with slides or other documentation of work not available for inclusion and a related essay of 3,000 words.   15

Application for transfer (including all the submitted material) should be submitted no later than the third term and accompanied by a report from the student's supervisor(s). (Upon the recommendation of the supervisor(s), a student may be permitted to submit no later than Monday of the week before full term in the fourth term.) On receiving the submissions the committee shall appoint two assessors, both of whom shall consider the submitted material, and conduct the oral examination. Transfer to D.Phil. student status is dependent on satisfactory reports from assessors and confirmation of (*a*)–(*d*) above.   20

25

3. *Confirmation of D.Phil. status*

Applications for confirmation of D.Phil. status should normally be made by the end of the eighth term as a research student at Oxford, and must be made by the end of the ninth term; or, in the case of part-time students, normally by the end of the eighteenth term (and must be made by the end of the twenty-fourth term).   30

Every student seeking confirmation of status should make a submission consisting of:

EITHER

(A) 1. a thesis title, together with an outline of the thesis, and an essay of about 6,000 words on the current state of the student's research, or a portion of the thesis of comparable length.   35

OR

(B) 1. a portfolio or exhibition of studio work, accompanied by a statement of future plans;

2. an essay on a related topic (3,000 words).   40

All candidates will be examined orally by two assessors. In the case of those intending to offer studio practice as part of the final submission, both assessors will view the portfolio or exhibition of studio work prior to the oral examination. Confirmation of status may take place only when the committee has received satisfactory reports from the assessors, and from the student's supervisor(s).   45

4. *Final submission*

EITHER

(A) For the Degree of M.Litt. a thesis not exceeding 40,000 words, or for the Degree of D.Phil., a thesis not exceeding 80,000 words, including notes, bibliography, glossary, appendices, etc.   50

OR

(B) For the Degree of M.Litt. an exhibition of studio work and a written thesis of up to 20,000 words. For the Degree of D.Phil. an exhibition of studio work and a written thesis of up to 40,000 words.

In the case of those offering studio practice as part of the final submission, both assessors will view the portfolio or exhibition of studio work prior to the oral examination. The supervisor will ensure that the assessors view the studio work. This may take place in a different venue from, and on a day prior to the oral examination. There should normally be no more than three months between the dates of the viewing and the oral examination. In conducting the oral examination, the assessors will be concerned to establish that the studio work has been clearly presented in relation to the argument of the written thesis, and that it has been set in its relevant theoretical, historical, or critical context.

RESEARCH DEGREES IN HISTORY

1. Admission/First year course work

In History (which includes medieval history, economic and social history, history of science, and history of art) graduate students are initially admitted *either* as candidates for a taught programme *or* as candidates for a research programme. The requirements for all taught programmes are laid out in detail under their individual regulations above.

Research students are admitted as Probationer D.Phil. students, and are required to undertake the following work in their probationary period:

(*a*) attend such lectures, seminars and classes as his or her supervisor shall determine; and

(*b*) present one seminar paper during the first year. Such paper shall normally be assessed by two assessors. Such assessors should not include the candidate's supervisor. The work done for the seminar paper may form the basis of the essay required under (2) below.

Applications for admission/transfer to M.Litt. or D.Phil. status shall be accompanied by:

(1) two copies of a statement (of 500 to 1,000 words) of the subject of the thesis and the manner in which the candidate proposes to treat it; such a statement will also normally include a descriptive title for the research project, an indication of identified or envisaged primary sources, an outline of the time table for background reading, archival or field work, and writing-up; also an account of how the research project relates to work done for any relevant master's dissertation;

(2) two copies of a piece of written work, normally 3,000–5,000 words long, being *either* (*a*) a section of the proposed thesis, *or* (*b*) an essay on a relevant topic, or (*c*) an augmented version of the statement required under (1) above; candidates should note that if they adopt alternative (c) they must also submit separately the statement required under (1) above;

(3) two copies of a confidential report from the supervisor, which should be sent by the supervisor directly to the Faculty's Graduate Office.

Successful completion of the work prescribed above is not in itself sufficient qualification for students to advance to M.Litt. or D.Phil. status.

2. Readmission after completion of a taught programme

Students who are currently entered as candidates for the examination in the M.St. in Medieval History, M.St. or M.Phil. in Late Antique and Byzantine Studies, M.St. in Medieval Studies, M.St. or M.Phil. in Modern British and

European History, M.St. in Global and Imperial History, M.St. in US History, M.St. in History of Art and Visual Culture, M.Sc. in English Local History, M.Sc. or M.Phil. in Economic and Social History, M.Sc. or M.Phil. in History of Science, Medicine, and Technology, or another relevant Master's programme may apply for admission to the M.Litt. or D.Phil. programme in the year in which they enter the   5
final examination for their M.Sc., M.St., or M.Phil. programme. Readmission may be made conditional on such requirements as the Graduate Studies Committee may impose, and successful completion of their current degree is not in itself sufficient qualification for students to be admitted to a research programme.

3. *Special provisions for part-time students*[1]   10
In assessing applications from candidates seeking to undertake a research degree through part-time study, the Graduate Studies Committee of the Board of the Faculty of History shall have regard to evidence that:
  (i) the candidate is suitable to undertake research at doctoral level;
  (ii) the candidate's proposed topic of research is suitable for part-time study;   15
  (iii) the candidate's personal and professional circumstances are such that it is both practicable for him or her to fulfil the requirements of the course, and necessary for him or her to study on a part-time basis;
  (iv) if appropriate, the candidate has the written support of their present employer for their proposed course of study and its obligations;   20
  (v) the candidate can meet the following attendance requirements for their period of part-time study: attendance for a minimum of thirty days of university-based work each year, normally coinciding with the full terms of the academic year, to be arranged with the agreement of their supervisor, for the period that their names remain on the Register of Graduate Students unless individually   25
dispensed by the Graduate Studies Committee on the Board of the Faculty of History. During a candidate's probationary period the attendance arrangements must take account of relevant induction and training events scheduled by the Faculty.

4. *Transfer to full M.Litt. or D.Phil. status*   30
  (i) The application form, endorsed by the candidate's society and supervisor, and the supporting material as outlined under 1. above shall normally be presented to the Faculty's Graduate Office not later than Friday of eighth week in the candidate's first Hilary Term (or Friday of eighth week in the candidate's second Hilary Term in the case of part-time students). In exceptional cases the Graduate Studies Committee may   35
permit the candidate to postpone submission: candidates seeking such postponement should apply to the Director of Graduate Studies well in advance.
  (ii) Two copies of a confidential report from the supervisor should be sent by the supervisor directly to the Faculty's Graduate Office. The Graduate Office shall send both copies of the written work and the confidential report to the candidate's inter-   40
viewer who will pass on one copy to the second assessor nominated as below.
  (iii) The interviewer shall then, together with a second assessor appointed in conjunction with the Director of Graduate Studies, examine the candidate orally. The interviewer shall be entitled, after consultation with the Director of Graduate Studies, to appoint a deputy to act instead. When the interviewer is also the supervisor, the   45
Director of Graduate Studies shall act as if he or she were the interviewer and shall have power to appoint a deputy and the second assessor.

---

[1] It should be noted that admission or change to study on a part-time basis in History is reviewed on an annual basis, and is subject to decisions by the University on the availability of doctoral research by means of part-time study.

(iv) The assessors shall report to the Graduate Studies Committee in writing whether the candidate's subject is satisfactory for the degree in question and whether he or she is competent to tackle it.[2] If they think this is not the case, they may recommend resubmission after a set period of further probation; such resubmission will constitute the second attempt at Transfer of Status provided for in the General Regulations for the degree. If the assessors disagree, the Graduate Studies Committee shall decide what should be done.

(v) Candidates holding the status of M.Litt. student may apply for transfer to D.Phil. status at any time, within the statutory limit of nine terms. Their Transfer of Status application will be considered according to the procedure laid down for confirmation of D.Phil. status (see below). The interviewer appointed by the Faculty Board shall follow that procedure, except that the interviewer will be asked to state explicitly whether in addition to this procedure a subsequent formal confirmation of D.Phil. status would be desirable, or not.

5. *Confirmation of D.Phil. status*

(i) Application for confirmation of D.Phil. status, with endorsements by the candidate's society and supervisor, shall normally be presented to the Faculty's Graduate Office not later than Monday of third week in the eighth term after admission to the D.Phil. programme (or in the candidate's twelfth term after transfer to full D.Phil. status in the case of part-time students). In exceptional cases the Graduate Studies Committee may permit the candidate to postpone submission by up to one term: candidates seeking such postponement should apply to the Committee through the Director of Graduate Studies well in advance.

(ii) Application for confirmation of D.Phil. status shall be accompanied by: (1) a full outline of chapters (1–2 pages), summarising the scope of individual chapters and their state of completion, including a timetable for completion of the work which remains to be done before submission of the thesis; (2) a draft abstract of the thesis as a whole, of between 1,000 and 2,000 words; (3) a sample chapter, of between 6,000 and 10,000 words; (4) a confidential report from the supervisor which should be sent direct to the Faculty's Graduate Office. The Graduate Office shall send the written work and the confidential report to the interviewer appointed by the Faculty Board.

(iii) The interviewer shall then examine the candidate orally. If the interviewer considers it necessary, a second assessor may be appointed in conjunction with the Director of Graduate Studies. In cases where the interviewer is also the supervisor, the Director of Graduate Studies shall act as if he or she were the interviewer and shall have power to appoint a deputy and, if necessary, a second assessor.

---

[2] Assessors are asked to note the important distinction in the criteria for the two degrees. In the case of the M.Litt. candidates are required to have made 'a worthwhile contribution to knowledge or understanding in the field of learning within which the subject of the thesis falls', while for the D.Phil. it is necessary to have made 'a significant and substantial contribution in the particular field of learning within which the subject of the thesis falls'. The phrase 'a significant and substantial contribution', in the case of doctoral theses, is interpreted as work that displays stature, judgement, and persuasiveness in historical exposition and the shaping of conclusions. But examiners are explicitly requested to bear in mind that their judgement of the significance of the work submitted should be based on what may reasonably be expected of a capable and diligent graduate student after three or, at most, four years of full-time study. Similarly, the requirement that candidates for the M.Litt. should make 'a worthwhile contribution to knowledge or understanding' in their chosen field is qualified by the request that examiners should take into account what may be expected after two years of full-time study.

(iv) The interviewer shall report to the Graduate Studies Committee in writing whether the candidate's subject is satisfactory and whether he or she is competent to tackle it. If confirmation is not recommended the interviewer may recommend re-application after a further period of study (within the timeframe provided for in the General Regulations) or alternatively transfer to M.Litt. status, subject to the general   5
regulations governing confirmation of status.

6. Theses

Theses submitted for the Degree of M.Litt. should not exceed 50,000 words and those submitted for the Degree of D.Phil. should not exceed 100,000 words, *including* all notes, appendices, any source material being edited, and all other parts of the thesis whatsoever,   10
excluding only the bibliography; any thesis exceeding these limits is liable to be rejected on that ground. Any application for permission to exceed the limit should be submitted with a detailed explanation and statement of the amount of excess length requested, and with a covering letter from the supervisor. Applications should be made as soon as possible and may not be made later than the last day of the fifth week of the term before that in which   15
application is made for appointment of examiners. The presentation and footnotes should comply with the requirements specified in the Regulations of the Education Committee for the degrees of M.Litt. and D.Phil. and follow the *Conventions for the presentation of essays, dissertations and theses* of the Faculty of History.

All candidates must submit with their thesis two printed or typewritten copies of an   20
abstract of the thesis, which shall not normally exceed 1,500 words for the M.Litt. or 2,500 words for the D.Phil., prepared by the student. This is in addition to the requirement to submit an abstract of not more than 300 words in length required by the Education Committee's regulations. Copies of both abstracts shall be bound into the copy of the thesis which shall be deposited in the Bodleian Library. One loose copy   25
of the 300 words abstract, printed on a single page, must be submitted together with the Library copy to the Examination Schools.

RESEARCH DEGREES IN MEDIEVAL & MODERN LANGUAGES

1. *Application for admission as a Probationer Research Student*   30

General

Applicants from the United Kingdom for admission as Probationer Research Students will normally be expected to attend for interview; other applicants required for inter-view will be notified as appropriate. The interviews will be conducted by or on behalf of a member of the board or its Graduate Studies Committee.   35

1. *Transfer to M.Litt. and D.Phil. status*

Unless they have successfully completed the M.Phil. in European Literature or the M.Phil. in Medieval and Modern Languages, research students are normally registered in the first instance for the degree of Master of Studies in Medieval and Modern Languages, and follow the requirements laid down for that degree. Transfer to M.Litt. or D.Phil. status   40
normally takes place at the end of the first year and is dependent on successful completion of the M.St. course though this is in itself not a sufficient condition for transfer.

The board may however (i) permit candidates to register in the first instance for another degree of M.St. or for the degree of M.Phil., or (ii) permit those who have already obtained an equivalent qualification to the degree of M.St. in Medieval and   45
Modern Languages to register as Probationer Research Students for the first year, following such courses as the board may require.

2. *Admission to M.Litt. status*

Candidates must give notice of intention to apply for transfer in writing to the Modern Languages Graduate Office, 41 Wellington Square, Oxford, by the end of the fourth week of the third term before they seek entry to M.Litt. status, giving the title of the proposed thesis. By Friday of the sixth week they shall submit an application form together with (i) three copies of a statement (not more than 500 words) of the title of the proposed thesis and of the manner in which the subject will be treated, and of the way in which the proposed treatment relates to existing work relevant to the chosen topic, the statement to include a provisional scheme of the contents of the thesis, and (ii) two typed copies of a piece of written work normally not more than about 10,000 words long (which will usually be the same as the dissertation submitted for the degree of M.St. in Medieval and Modern Languages). The material shall be sent to two assessors, neither of whom shall normally be the candidate's supervisor and who, in the case of students for the M.St. in Medieval and Modern Languages, shall normally be acting as assessors in that examination also. The assessors shall examine the candidate orally (if appropriate in the course of the examination for that degree).

The assessors will be asked to report to the Graduate Studies Committee for its meeting in July.

3. *Admission to D.Phil. status*

Candidates must give notice of intention to apply for transfer in writing to the Modern Languages Graduate Office, 41 Wellington Square, Oxford, by the end of the fourth week of the third term before they seek entry to D.Phil. status, giving the title of the proposed thesis. By Friday of the sixth week they shall submit an application form together with (i) three copies of a statement (not more than 500 words) of the title of the proposed thesis and of the manner in which the subject will be treated, and of the way in which the proposed treatment relates to existing work relevant to the chosen topic, the statement to include a provisional scheme of the contents of the chosen topic, and (ii) two typed copies of a piece of written work normally not more than about 10,000 words long (which will usually be the same as the dissertation submitted for the degree of M.St. in Modern Languages).

No application for admission within the terms of §3 of the general regulations for the Degree of Doctor of Philosophy will normally be considered by the Graduate Studies Committee of the board unless the applicant has previously been interviewed by a member of the Faculty invited to act in this capacity by the committee. The application form must be signed by the person who interviews the candidate.

The material shall be sent to two assessors, neither of whom shall normally be the candidate's supervisor and who, in the case of students for the M.St. in European Literature, shall normally be acting as assessors in that examination also. The assessors shall examine the candidate orally (if appropriate in the course of the examination for that degree).

The assessors will be asked to report to the Graduate Studies Committee for its meeting in July.

The requirements for the submission of a piece of written work at (ii) above and for action by assessors will not apply in the case of candidates who have been given leave to supplicate for the degree of M.Phil. or of M.Litt. whose subject of thesis for that degree is in the broad field of research proposed for the D.Phil.

Any candidate whose application for transfer to M.Litt. or D.Phil. Status is refused may reapply on one (only) further occasion.

4. The board will award a Certificate of Graduate Attainment to a Probationer Research Student whose application for transfer to the status of student for the degree of D.Phil. or M.Litt. is approved by the committee. In exceptional circumstances the committee may recommend the award of the certificate to other Probationer Research Students who are strongly supported by their supervisor.

2. *Application for confirmation of status as a student for the Degree of Doctor of Philosophy*

(*a*) **Candidates other than those who have already been given leave to supplicate for the Degree of M.Phil.**

(i) Each applicant for confirmation of D.Phil. status must submit two copies of a   5
piece of written work of 15,000 words in length (except where text is accompanied by graphs or statistical material), being a draft of a chapter or chapters of the thesis (excluding the introductory or concluding chapters and any section submitted for the first transfer examination). The student shall show on a provisional list of the contents of the thesis the place he or she plans for   10
the draft chapter(s). This piece of work must be substantially different from that submitted on application for admission to D.Phil. status. Each applicant must also submit, at the time of application, three copies of a statement (of not more than 1,000 words) of the title of the proposed thesis and of the manner in which the subject will be treated, and of work achieved on other parts of the   15
thesis and work remaining to be done.

(ii) Unless permission is given otherwise by the committee, the application for confirmation of D.Phil. status shall be submitted to the Modern Languages Graduate Office, 41 Wellington Square, Oxford, not later than the Friday of the fourth week of the applicant's ninth term from admission to graduate   20
status, and copies of the written work by not later than 30 June. The written work shall be read by two assessors appointed by the Graduate Studies Committee of the board. Neither of the assessors shall normally be the candidate's supervisor. The assessors shall examine the candidate orally.

(iii) The assessors shall report to the committee in writing whether they recom-   25
mend that the candidate's status as a D.Phil. student should be confirmed. They shall also make a written report, in support of their recommendation, covering the following points: whether the subject of the thesis and the manner of its treatment proposed by the candidate are acceptable; and whether the thesis can reasonably be completed in three or at most four years of full-time   30
study from the date of the candidate's admission as a research student, (Note: students reading for the M.St. in Modern Languages are considered to be taught-course students). On receipt of the report, the committee shall decide whether to approve the candidate's application. If it reaches the conclusion that the candidate's subject for a thesis is unsatisfactory and/or that the   35
candidate is unlikely to be able to complete the thesis proposed, it may permit resubmission by a date which the committee shall specify. If, after a second application, the committee continues to be unable to give approval, it will *either* admit the candidate to M.Litt. status *or* take appropriate action under the regulations made by the Education Committee for the removal of a   40
student from the Register.

(*b*) **Candidates who have already been given leave to supplicate for the degree of M.Phil. (Candidates who propose a topic for their D.Phil. which is different from their M.Phil. topic shall be subject to the regulations under (*a*) above).**

Applicants must submit to the Modern Languages Graduate Office, 41 Wellington   45
Square, Oxford with their applications three copies of a statement (of not more than 1,000 words) of the title of the proposed thesis and of the manner in which the subject will be treated, and of the way in which the proposed treatment relates to existing work relevant to the chosen topic, and of work achieved on other parts of the thesis and work remaining to be done. The statement should include a provisional scheme of   50
the contents of the thesis, which identifies the place of the M.Phil. thesis in the scheme. Confirmation will be subject to the Graduate Studies Committee of the board being

satisfied, on the evidence of the statement and of the examiners of the M.Phil., that the student is capable of carrying out advanced research; that the M.Phil. thesis is in the field of research proposed for the D.Phil.; that the subject can be profitably pursued under the superintendence of the board; and that the thesis can reasonably be expected to be completed in three or at the most four years of full-time study from the date of the candidate's admission as an M.Phil. student. If the committee is not satisfied, it may permit one further application by a date which it shall specify.

3. *Theses*

Theses submitted for the Degree of M.Litt. should not exceed 50,000 words and those submitted for the Degree of D.Phil. should not exceed 80,000 words, excluding the bibliography and any text that is being edited but including notes, glossary, appendices, etc. Leave to exceed these limits will be given only in exceptional cases. Any application for permission to exceed the limit should be submitted with a detailed explanation and statement of the amount of excess length requested, and with a covering letter from the supervisor. Application must be made immediately it seems clear that authorisation to exceed the limit will be sought and normally not later than six months before the intended date of submission of the thesis.

Every candidate who is editing a text must also state the length of the text being edited.

In addition to the arrangements for an abstract of the thesis set out in the Education Committee's regulations above, three printed or typewritten copies of a fuller abstract of the thesis (which shall not normally exceed 1,500 words for the M.Litt. and 2,500 words for the D.Phil.) prepared by the student is required. A copy of the fuller abstract must be bound into the copy of the thesis which, if the application for leave to supplicate for the degree is successful, will be deposited in the Bodleian Library. The fuller abstract may be bound into the two examiners' copies of the thesis if the candidate so desires.

RESEARCH DEGREES IN MUSIC

1. *Probationer Research Student*

(*a*) **Admission**

(i) Each candidate for admission as a Probationer Research Student should support the application with:

EITHER

(A)

    1. a sample of recent written work (4,000–6,000 words), preferably but not necessarily related to the proposed topic or area of research, such as an undergraduate dissertation (or part of it) or a substantial essay;

    2. a proposal for a research topic or area (about 1,000 words), which should include a statement why this work should be carried out at Oxford.

OR

    (B) (For those intending to offer compositions as part of the final submission)

        1. a sample of written work (2,000–3,000 words);

        2. one or two recently completed compositions;

        3. a plan of work to be completed in Oxford.

Candidates should expect to attend for interview if required.

(*b*) **Course of study**

Candidates seeking admission in order to read for the M.Litt. or D.Phil. are normally registered as Probationer Research Students and as such, unless specifically exempted by the board must follow the requirements laid down for the Degree of Master of Studies in Music. Such exemption will not normally be granted except to candidates who have already obtained a qualification of equivalent status and breadth elsewhere. Transfer to M.Litt. or D.Phil. status normally takes place at the end of the first year and is dependent on successful completion of the M.St. course (though this in itself is not a sufficient condition of transfer).

Probationer Research Students who have been exempted from the requirements laid down for the Degree of Master of Studies in Music must attend courses as recommended by their supervisors and approved by the Director of Graduate Studies. In most instances these courses of study will be undertaken in the Faculty of Music, but exemptions will be made where more appropriate courses are offered in other faculties.

Students will also undertake foundation work related to their research area or topic under the direction of a supervisor.

(*c*) **Transfer to the status of M.Litt. or D.Phil. Student**

    (i) Probationer research students seeking to transfer to the status of M.Litt. or D.Phil. Student must satisfy the Board of the Faculty of Music that (*a*) they have followed and completed their prescribed courses of study, (*b*) they have undertaken preparatory research work to the satisfaction of their supervisor, (*c*) the proposed research topic is acceptable, and (*d*) they are competent to handle the research topic.

A candidate for transfer to the new status must make a submission in the manner prescribed in the University's *Examination Regulations*.

The faculty board requires that the written work submitted shall be:

EITHER

(A)

an essay of about 5,000 words relevant to the topic proposed for the thesis, and a bibliographic essay of the same length reviewing the historical and/or theoretical literature relevant to the thesis topic and its field.

OR

(B)

(For those intending to offer compositions as part of the final submission) a portfolio of two significantly contrasted compositions (together lasting between ten and fifteen minutes maximum), a proposed work-schedule for the following year, and a related essay of 5,000-10,000 words.

Two copies of the thesis title, thesis outline, essays and compositions must be submitted. The essay must be typewritten in double spacing, and placed in a temporary form of binding. The submissions must be made through the Registrar no later than seven days before the second meeting of the Graduate Studies Committee of the board in the student's third term from admission. Upon the recommendation of the supervisor, the board may permit a student to submit no later than seven days before the second meeting in the fourth term of study.

    (ii) On receiving the submissions the board shall appoint two assessors, both of whom shall read the scripts and conduct the oral examination, provided that the board may appoint additional assessors should the need arise.

    (iii) Transfer to the new status shall only take place when the board has received satisfactory reports from the assessors, from those who conducted the prescribed courses of study, and from the student's supervisor.

    (iv) M.St. students admitted to the status of Probationer Research Students must apply for transfer to M.Litt. or D.Phil. status in their fourth term of graduate study. The submissions required may consist of all or part of the work submitted for the Degree of M.St. provided that it is relevant to the research topic.

(v) Students for the M.Phil. who intend to take the degree may seek admittance to the status of M.Litt. or D.Phil. Student, provided that they satisfy the general 5 regulations of the university, and that they submit a provisional thesis title and outline of the manner in which it is intended to treat the research topic which is acceptable to the board.

2. *M.Litt. Students*

(*a*) **Admission** 10

The procedure for the admission of a Probationer Research Student to the status of M.Litt. Student is outlined in section (*c*) of the faculty board's regulations for Probationer Research Students in Music.

(*b*) **Supervision**

The Graduate Studies Committee of the board will receive a report on each 15 student's progress from his or her supervisor at the end of each term. The committee may request or receive an additional report at the end of the Long Vacation.

3. *D.Phil. Students*

(*a*) **Admission**

The procedure for the admission of a Probationer Research Student to the status of 20 D.Phil. Student is outlined in section (*c*) of the faculty board's regulations for Probationer Research Students in Music.

(*b*) **Supervision**

The Graduate Studies Committee of the board will receive a report on each student's progress from his or her supervisor at the end of each term. The committee 25 may request or receive an additional report at the end of the Long Vacation.

(*c*) **Confirmation of Status**

The status of D.Phil. Student shall normally be confirmed in the sixth term as a research student at Oxford. In addition to the general requirements of the regulations, the Board of the Faculty of Music requires that every student seeking confirmation of 30 status must make a submission consisting of:

EITHER

(A) 1. thesis title, together with an annotated outline of the thesis (both title and outline may be altered or revised forms of those submitted for the examination for admission to D.Phil. status); 35

2. an essay of about 6,000 words on the current state of the student's research, or a portion of the thesis of comparable length.

OR

(B) 1. an annotated inventory of the proposed contents of the final portfolio of compositions and title of the supporting dissertation; 40

2. a portfolio of two or more well-contrasted compositions, with a total duration of approximately 25 minutes;

3. a critical or analytical essay of 5,000–10,000 words.

(i) Candidates will be examined orally. Two copies of the thesis title, thesis outline and essay (or thesis extract), or inventory, thesis title, portfolio, and 45 essay must be submitted. The essay (or thesis extract) must be typewritten in double spacing, and placed in a temporary form of binding. The submissions must be made through the Registrar no later than seven days before the second meeting of the Graduate Studies Committee in the student's fifth term from admission. Upon the recommendation of the supervisor, the board may permit a student to submit no later than seven days before the second meeting in a subsequent term of study, provided that this falls within the limits set down in the University's *Examination Regulations.*

(ii) On receiving the submissions the board shall appoint two assessors, both of whom shall read the scripts and conduct the examination, provided that the board may appoint additional assessors should the need arise.

(iii) Confirmation of status may only take place when the board has received satisfactory reports from the assessors, and from the student's supervisor.

4. *Final submission for the Degree of M.Litt.*
EITHER a thesis of not more than 50,000 words.

OR (Musical Composition) a portfolio of between three and six musical compositions, totalling approximately 45 minutes' duration, and a dissertation of not more than 15,000 words either on the candidate's own music or on some aspect of music related to the candidate's compositional concerns.

5. *Final submission for the Degree of D.Phil.*
EITHER a thesis of not more than 100,000 words, exclusive of any text being edited but including notes, bibliography, glossary, appendices, etc.

OR (Musical Composition) (*a*) a portfolio of between three and six musical compositions, totalling between 45 and 90 minutes' duration, with at least one composition being of large scale (defined as for large-scale forces, such as orchestra, and/or of more than 30 minutes' duration); and (*b*) a dissertation of between 20,000 and 25,000 words either on the candidate's own music or on some aspect of music related to the candidate's compositional concerns.

RESEARCH DEGREES IN ORIENTAL STUDIES

1. *M.Litt. in Oriental Studies*

The first year of study in the Oriental Studies Faculty will be regarded as a qualifying period, during which the student shall be registered as a Probationer Research Student. Application for transfer to M.Litt. status should be made by the end of the third term. All students will normally be expected to submit:

(*a*) a piece of formal written work related to the field of their proposed thesis of approximately 5,000 words in length;

(*b*) a satisfactory outline (of not more than 500 words) of the proposed subject of the thesis.

The written work shall be assessed by two assessors (neither of whom may be the supervisor), appointed by the board, and they shall normally be expected also to discuss the submission with the student in person. They must do so if they are not able to make a positive recommendation. When examiners make a positive recommendation to the board, they shall be required explicitly to state in their report that they have satisfied themselves on the basis of their discussion with the student and/or their consideration of the submitted material that the student has the linguistic competence necessary to carry out the proposed research. If on the basis of the evidence available to them they are not able to make such a statement, they shall recommend to the board that the results of a formal written language test arranged by the board for this purpose should be submitted to them for consideration before their recommendation on the student's application is made.

On the basis of the results of the examination the faculty board will decide whether the student should be accepted for admission to M.Litt. status.

Candidates who have successfully completed the M.St. in Oriental Studies may be recommended for admission to M.Litt. status on the basis of the results of the examination, subject to the submission of a satisfactory outline (of not more than 500 words) of the proposed subject of the thesis.

2. *D.Phil. in Oriental Studies*

5

The first year of study in the Oriental Studies Faculty will be regarded as a qualifying period, during which the student shall be registered as a Probationer Research Student. Application for transfer to D.Phil. status should be made by the end of the third term. All students will normally be expected to submit:

(*a*) a piece of formal written work related to the field of their proposed thesis of 10
between 5,000 and 10,000 words in length;

(*b*) a satisfactory outline (of not more than 500 words) of the proposed subject of the thesis.

The written work shall be assessed by two assessors (neither of whom may be the supervisor), appointed by the board, and they shall normally be expected also to 15 discuss the submission with the student in person. They must do so if they are not able to make a positive recommendation. When examiners make a positive recommendation to the board, they shall be required explicitly to state in their report that they have satisfied themselves on the basis of their discussion with the student and/or their consideration of the submitted material that the student has the linguistic competence 20 necessary to carry out the proposed research. If on the basis of the evidence available to them they are not able to make such a statement, they shall recommend to the board that the results of a formal written language test arranged by the board for this purpose should be submitted to them for consideration before their recommendation on the student's application is made. 25

Candidates who have successfully completed the M.St. in Oriental Studies may be recommended for admission to D.Phil. status on the basis of the results of the examination, subject to the submission of a satisfactory outline (of not more than 500 words) of the proposed subject of the thesis.

Candidates who have successfully completed the M.Phil. in Oriental Studies may be 30 recommended for admission to D.Phil. status on the basis of the results of the examination, subject to the submission of a satisfactory outline (of not more than 500 words) of the proposed subject of the thesis. In exceptional cases, such candidates may be recommended for admission to confirmed D.Phil. status.

The board requires from each applicant for confirmation of D.Phil. status a written 35 statement of the manner in which he or she proposes to treat the subject. The board will approve such applications only if the assessors appointed by the board shall have certified that a piece of work written by the applicant (of 10,000-15,000 words in length) is of the requisite standard to justify the confirmation. Assessment of the application shall include a viva voce examination of the candidate by two persons 40 appointed by the board.

3. *Theses*

Theses submitted for the Degree of M.Litt. should not exceed 50,000 words and those for the Degree of D.Phil. should not exceed 100,000, exclusive of any text that is being edited, and of bibliography, but including notes, glossary, appendices, etc. 45 Leave to exceed this limit will be given only in exceptional cases.

RESEARCH DEGREES IN PHILOSOPHY

1. *Admission as Probationer Research Student*

Candidates for admission are required to submit with their application one piece of written work of between 4,500 and 5,000 words, on a subject related to the proposed 50 research topic. The piece must be typed and in English, unless by special permission.

2. *Admission to M.Litt. or D.Phil. status*

Applications from Probationer Research Students for transfer to the status of Student for the Degree of Master of Letters or Doctor of Philosophy will not normally be considered before the beginning of the candidate's third term as a Probationer Research Student. The board regards the third term as the normal time for this application to be made and expects applications to be made by the end of the second week of the third term.

Applications should be accompanied by a thesis outline of about two pages and a piece of written work of approximately 5,000 words in the area and philosophical style of the proposed thesis. The board will appoint two assessors, who will read the submissions and conduct an interview with the candidate.

Candidates admitted as Probationer Research Students after completing the Master of Studies degree in Ancient Philosophy at the University of Oxford must complete all of the following requirements by the end of Week 8 of their third term as a Probationer Research Student:

(*a*) Attend two graduate classes with at least one from the following subject areas: moral philosophy; metaphysics; theory of knowledge; philosophical logic and philosophy of language; philosophy of mind and action.

(*b*) Submit one 5,000 word essay on a topic of the student's choice for one of the above listed classes, the pass mark for which is 68.

(*c*) Submit a thesis outline of about two pages.

(*d*) Submit a piece of written work of approximately 5,000 words in the area and philosophical style of the proposed thesis.

The board will appoint two assessors, who will read the submissions and conduct an interview with the candidate. If the mark for the essay mentioned in (*b*) above is between 60 and 67 (inclusive) then the assessors may, depending on the quality of the candidate's other submitted work, recommend approval or refusal of the Transfer of Status application.

The Philosophy Graduate Studies Committee may, depending on the student's prior experience and education, waive requirements (*a*) and/or (*b*). If it waives both requirements then the student must complete the requirements by the end of Week 2 of their third term as a Probationer Research Student.

Candidates admitted as Probationer Research Students after completing the Master of Studies degree in Philosophy of Physics at the University of Oxford must complete the following requirements by the end of the Week 0 before the start of their fourth term as a Probationer Research Student:

(*a*) Attend two graduate classes (which cannot be in the subject area of their M.St. in Philosophy of Physics elective option, Philosophy of Physics or Philosophy of Science) with at least one from the following subject areas: moral philosophy; metaphysics; theory of knowledge; philosophical logic and philosophy of language; philosophy of mind and action.

(*b*) Submit one 5,000 word essay on a topic of the student's choice for one of the above listed classes, the pass mark for which is 68.

(*c*) Submit a thesis outline of about two pages.

(*d*) Submit a 20,000 word dissertation on a topic of their choice, preferably in the area and philosophical style of their thesis.

The board will appoint two assessors, who will read the submissions and conduct an interview with the candidate. If the mark for the essay mentioned in (*b*) above is between 60 and 67 (inclusive) then the assessors may, depending on the quality of the candidate's other submitted work, recommend approval or refusal of the Transfer of Status application.

The Philosophy Graduate Studies Committee may, depending on the student's prior experience and education, waive requirements (*a*) and/or (*b*), and it has the power to replace requirement (d) by requirement 5

    (*e*) Submit a piece of written work of approximately 5,000 words in the area and philosophical style of the proposed thesis.

If it waives (*a*) and (*b*) and replaces (*d*) by (*e*) then the student must complete the requirements by the end of Week 2 of their third term as a Probationer Research Student. 10

3. *Confirmation of D.Phil. status*

Applications from Students for the Degree of Doctor of Philosophy for confirmation of status will not normally be considered before the beginning of the candidate's third term after transfer to D.Phil. status. The board regards the third term after transfer as the normal time for this application to be made and expects applications to 15 be made by the end of the second week of the third term. It also expects that students should normally have their D.Phil. status confirmed at least one year before the submission of their thesis.

Applications should be accompanied by a thesis outline of about two pages and a piece of written work of approximately 5,000 words, intended as a part of the thesis, in 20 final or near-final draft. The board will appoint two assessors. The application will be considered, in the first instance, by the first assessor. If the first assessor is satisfied that the application should be approved, then he or she will interview with the candidate and recommend approval to the board. If the first assessor is not satisfied that the application should be approved, the application will be sent to the second assessor. 25 Both assessors will interview the candidate and a joint recommendation will be made. The assessors may not recommend that the application be refused unless they have first interviewed the candidate.

4. *Theses*

M.Litt. theses should not exceed 50,000 words, and D.Phil. theses should not exceed 30 75,000 words, exclusive of bibliographical references, unless the candidate has, with the support of his or her supervisor, secured the leave of the board to exceed this limit.

All candidates when they submit their theses must state the approximate number of words therein both (*a*) including citations and, if they have been granted permission to count citations separately, (*b*) excluding citations. Theses exceeding the limit are liable 35 to be returned unexamined for reduction to the proper length. Candidates who have submitted in their final term may be allowed a maximum period of two terms to effect the necessary reduction.

RESEARCH DEGREES IN THEOLOGY AND RELIGION 40

1. *Admission to the status of Probationer Research Student*

Applicants may be admitted to M.Litt. or D.Phil. student status either (1) from M.St. status; (2) from M.Phil. status; (3) from Probationer Research Student Status. The Board expects most applicants seeking to pursue doctoral research in the Faculty to seek M.St. Student status first. 45

2. *Admission to M.Litt. or D.Phil. Student status from M.St. or M.Phil. student status*

    (i) Applicants holding M.St. or M.Phil. Student status shall apply for admission to M.Litt. or D.Phil. status in the year of their M.St. or M.Phil. examination at the times announced for graduate admissions applications. 50

  (ii) In either case the application shall include a description in about 500 words of the research which it is intended to undertake, supported by the proposed supervisor.

  (iii) The Board may indicate a provisional readiness to admit to M.Litt. or D.Phil. Student status, which will then be subject to a report from the Examiners of the M.St. or M.Phil.

3. *Admission by the route of Probationer Research Student*

  (i) Admission to the status of Probationer Research Student will normally be granted only to applicants who have already completed a Master's level graduate degree, including a dissertation or thesis, in a theological subject.

  (ii) Application for admission as a Probationer Research Student, which shall be made at the times and in the manner announced for graduate admissions applications, will normally be accompanied by an interview with a member of the Graduate Studies Committee, though the Board may dispense from this.

  (iii) A Probationer Research Student is normally expected to apply for transfer within three terms (or six terms in the case of part–time students). A Probationer Research Student who has not successfully transferred by the end of the six terms for which such status may be held in total (twelve terms in the case of part–time students) shall lapse from the register of Graduate Students.

  (iv) The application for transfer must include two typewritten copies of a description in about 500 words of the research which it is intended to undertake and two typewritten copies of a piece of original written work of about 5,000 words relevant to the subject of the proposed research.

  (v) There shall be an oral examination with a competent person appointed by the Board as assessor, which may treat of the description of the proposed research, the submitted piece of work and any other aspect of the applicant's progress towards research. The candidate's supervisor may attend this examination. If the candidate fails to satisfy the assessor, the Board may appoint a date by which a further oral examination must be held, with such conditions as it sees fit, and grant extension of Probationer Research Student status up to that date, subject to the overall limit in 1(iii) above.

4. *Admission directly to M.Litt. or D.Phil. Student status by former M.St. or M.Phil. students*

  (i) The Board may admit directly to M.Litt. or D.Phil. Student status applicants who within the past five years have received permission from the Board of the Faculty of Theology and Religion to supplicate for the degrees of M.St. or M.Phil.

  (ii) Application for admission, which shall be made at the times and in the manner announced for graduate admissions applications, will normally require an interview with a member of the Graduate Studies Committee, though the Board may dispense from this.

  (iii) The application shall be accompanied by the dissertation or thesis which formed part of the Master's degree.

5. *Special Provisions for part-time students*

In assessing applications from candidates seeking to undertake a research degree through part-time study, the Graduate Studies Committee of the Board of the Faculty of Theology and Religion shall have regard to evidence that:

  (i) the candidate is suitable to undertake research at doctoral level;

(ii) the candidate's personal and professional circumstances are such that it is both practicable for him or her to fulfil the requirements of the course, and necessary for him or her to study on a part-time basis;

(iii) if appropriate, the candidate has the written support of their present employer for their proposed course of study and its obligations;

(iv) the candidate's proposed topic of research is suitable for part-time study;

(v) the candidate can meet the attendance requirements relating to part-time study.

6. *Attendance requirements (for part-time students)*

Part-time students are required to attend for a minimum of thirty days of university-based work each year, to be arranged with the agreement of their supervisor, for the period that their names remain on the Register of Graduate Students unless individually dispensed by the Graduate Studies Committee on the Board of the Faculty of Theology and Religion.

7. *Confirmation of D.Phil. status*

Applications should be accompanied by one short abstract of approximately 300 words and one long abstract of 1,500–2,000 words, a draft chapter, and an outline of the thesis, indicating what has been completed to date and a timetable for completion. The written work shall be read by two assessors appointed by the Graduate Studies Committee. Neither of the assessors shall normally be the candidate's supervisor. The assessors shall examine the candidate orally.

8. *Preparation of theses for the Degrees of M.Litt. and D.Phil.*

(i) Theses submitted for the Degree of M.Litt. should not exceed 50,000 words, or 100,000 for the D.Phil., excluding only the bibliography in both cases. The faculty board is prepared to consider an application for a relaxation of this limit in special circumstances.

(ii) All candidates must submit an abstract of the thesis, of between 1,000 and 1,500 words for an M.Litt., and between 1,500 and 2,500 for a D.Phil., prepared by the candidate. This is in addition to the requirement to submit an abstract of not more than 300 words in length required by the Education Committee's regulations. One copy of each abstract prepared at the time of the examination should be bound into each of the examiners' copies of the thesis. Copies of both abstracts shall be bound into the copy of the thesis which shall be deposited in the Bodleian Library. In addition one loose copy of the 300 word abstract, printed on a single page, must be submitted together with the Library copy.

NOTES

19

RESEARCH DEGREES IN THE MATHEMATICAL, PHYSICAL AND LIFE SCIENCES DIVISION

1. Permission to Work in a Well-Found Laboratory Outside the University

Applicants who are admitted to undertake research under the supervision of the Mathematical, Physical and Life Sciences Divisional Board may, exceptionally, be permitted by the divisional board to undertake their research in a well-found laboratory outside the University. Such candidates shall be dispensed from the residence requirements, but shall be required to attend the University for such instruction as the division and department concerned shall require. Before admitting a candidate on this basis, the department concerned shall be required to satisfy itself and the divisional board that appropriate arrangements are in place for approving all aspects of the student's academic work, including the following:

(i) the availability of the equipment and facilities necessary for the project in the agency concerned;

(ii) the existence of a wider collaboration between the department and the agency in which the student is based;

(iii) the subject of their doctoral studies;

(iv) satisfactory induction procedures;

(v) satisfactory health and safety arrangements;

(vi) satisfactory supervision arrangements, to include specification of a minimum number of contact hours between student and supervisor, which shall include not less than two face-to-face meetings between student and supervisor, for a total of at least 8 hours, each term;

(vii) satisfactory arrangements for monitoring the student's progress within the department;

(viii) provision for the student to attend the University for such instruction as the division and department shall require.

Dispensation from these rules shall be sought from the Head of the Mathematical, Physical and Life Sciences Division through the departmental Director of Graduate Studies.

2. Transfer of Status and Confirmation of Status

1. *Transfer of Status*

All research students will be admitted to the status of Probationer Research Student in the first instance. The status of Probationer Research Student may be held for a maximum of four terms (other than students registered on the doctoral training programmes listed in the Doctoral Training Programmes in MPLS section). Probationer Research Students should normally apply to transfer status to M.Sc. by Research or D.Phil. status before the end of the fourth full-term from admission, subject to the further guidance below. Cases to defer applications for the transfer of status must be made by the candidate with the supervisor's support to the departmental Director of Graduate Studies by the end of the fourth full-term after admission. Approval will only be granted in exceptional circumstances, in accordance with the General Regulations Governing Research Degrees, set out in §4.

In the Biological Sciences (the Departments of Plant Sciences and Zoology), candidates should apply to transfer from the status of Probationer Research Student by the end of the fourth full-term after admission as a research student.   5

In the Mathematical Sciences (the Departments of Computer Science, Mathematics and Statistics) students in Category A (those who have had no previous experience of research work, and normally all candidates in the Department of Computer Science)   10
should apply to transfer from the status of Probationer Research Student between the second and fourth full-term after admission as a research student. Students with no previous experience of research work are advised to apply in the third full-term after admission. Students in Category B (those who have had previous experience of research work who may have completed a taught master's course) should apply to   15
transfer immediately after admission to Probationer Research Student status. (This category is only available to candidates in the Department of Computer Science in exceptional circumstances with the approval of the Director of Graduate Studies.)

In the Physical Sciences (the Departments of Chemistry, Earth Sciences, Engineering Science, Materials and Physics), candidates should apply to transfer   20
from the status of Probationer Research Student in the third or fourth full-term after admission as a research student.

In the *Biological Sciences, Mathematical Sciences,* and *Physical Sciences,* a first application for transfer of status must take place within the six term limit of PRS status, as set out in the General Regulations Governing Research Degrees, §4. Any application   25
outside those limits (other than in the General Regulations Governing Research Degrees, §4, cl.6), must be approved by or on behalf of Education Committee.

Doctoral training programmes, the regulations applying to research students following doctoral training programmes are set out in the Doctoral Training Programmes in MPLS Section.   30

Advice on the timing of transfer of status in each department will be provided by the departmental Director of Graduate Studies.

Applications to transfer status should be considered by a minimum of two assessors on behalf of the Board of the Mathematical, Physical and Life Sciences Division, one of whom may be the student's academic advisor, but neither of whom should normally   35
be the student's supervisor or a member of his/her supervisory team. Each department has its own assessment procedures, which should include as a minimum the following four components:

(i) completion of the appropriate graduate studies application forms to be submitted to the Divisional Graduate Studies Office, 9 Parks Road;   40

(ii) submission of written work by the student. For example: a progress report; a literature review; any required course work; a plan for the development of the student's research; any published papers. Each department will set out its own requirements in this area;

(iii) an interview between the student and his/her assessors. The process of assessment must always include an interview with the candidate if the assessors   45
cannot recommend transfer to D.Phil. status;

(iv) the student should have made a brief presentation or talk whilst a Probationer Research Student. This need not be part of the transfer interview.

A report will be written to provide feedback to the student, their supervisor, and college. The report will include an assessment of the viability and suitability of the proposed research, and of its completion on a reasonable timescale.

A candidate whose first application for transfer to D.Phil. status is not approved, shall be permitted to make one further application, and shall be granted an extension of time for one term if this is necessary for the purposes of making the application.

These procedures are also set out in the Division's Postgraduate Research Student Handbook.

2. *Confirmation of Status*

Confirmation of status for D.Phil. students must take place no later than nine terms after admission to graduate status. Students are advised to apply for their first attempt at confirmation of D.Phil. status by the end of the eighth full-term after admission as a graduate research student.

Doctoral training programmes, the regulations applying to research students following doctoral training programmes are set out in the Doctoral Training Programmes in MPLS Section.

Students are encouraged very strongly to apply for confirmation of status at least six–twelve months before they expect to submit their thesis for examination to make this process a constructive part of the development of the student's research. The application for confirmation of status must be made and approved before requesting the formal appointment of examiners.

The requirements for confirmation of status may vary for each department within the following framework:

(i) completion of the appropriate graduate studies application forms to be submitted to the Divisional Graduate Studies Office, 9 Parks Road. The candidate and their supervisor are required to provide a clear indication of progress to date, and the timetable for submission of the thesis;

(ii) all applications must be reviewed by one or more assessors, one of whom may be the departmental Director of Graduate Studies. If there is only one assessor this should not be the candidate's supervisor;

(iii) the candidate should produce a brief written report about their research achievements to date. The specific requirements will be set out by the department, for example a publication(s) or draft chapter(s) from the candidate's thesis, a plan and the timetable for submission of the thesis;

(iv) the assessor(s) may request to interview the candidate, and the candidate may request to have an interview with the assessor(s). The process of assessment must always include an interview with the candidate if the assessor(s) are unable to recommend confirmation of D.Phil. status.

The assessor(s) will write a brief report to provide feedback to the candidate, the supervisor, and college. The report will include an assessment of progress and submission of the thesis within the planned timescale.

A candidate whose first application for confirmation of status is not approved, shall be permitted to make one further application, normally within one term of the original application, and shall be granted an extension of time for one term if this is necessary for the purposes of making the application.

If a candidate's application for confirmation of status is unsuccessful, the board may approve a transfer from D.Phil. to M.Sc. by Research status.

Cases to defer applications for the confirmation of status must be made by the candidate with the supervisor's support to the departmental Director of Graduate Studies by the end of the ninth full-term after admission. Approval will only be granted in exceptional circumstances. Students may apply to defer confirmation of status for a maximum of three terms. The Director of Graduate Studies in each department may decide how many terms, up to the maximum, a candidate may be allowed to defer.

These procedures are also set out in the Division's Postgraduate Research Student   5
Handbook.

3. Appointment of Examiners

In applying for appointment of examiners, candidates should note that a supervisor is disqualified from appointment, and that the divisional board will not normally appoint as examiner individuals previously closely associated with the candidate or   10
his or her work, representatives of any organisation sponsoring the candidate's research, representatives of any organisation at which a candidate dispensed from residence under the provisions of cl.1 above, is based, or former colleagues of the candidate. In particular, an examiner, whether internal or external, who has played a significant part in advising the candidate is inappropriate and particularly so where the   15
collaboration has led to the publishing of joint papers by the candidate and the examiner. It is accepted that examiners will usually be acquainted with the supervisor, and sometimes the candidate, and that this in itself is not a bar to acting as an examiner. Dispensation from this rule should be sought from the Head of Division through the departmental Director of Graduate Studies.   20

RESEARCH DEGREES IN BIOLOGICAL SCIENCES (PLANT SCIENCES AND ZOOLOGY)

All research students will be admitted to the status of Probationer Research Student in the first instance. Individuals may hold this status for a maximum of four terms. The provisions for extension to this time limit are set out in the General Regulations   25
Governing Research Degrees, §4. Candidates should discuss with their supervisors whether to apply for transfer to M.Sc. status or to D.Phil. status, and the most appropriate time at which to apply. It is possible to transfer to M.Sc. status initially and thereafter to D.Phil. status if this is appropriate.

1. *Admission of students to the status of Student for the M.Sc. by Research*   30

Applicants should submit the material specified in Regulations for the Degree of Master of Science by Research, §3, cl. 1; the board does not normally require any further test under §3, cl. 2. Candidates may obtain full details from the Director of Graduate Studies.

2. *Admission of students to the status of Student for the Doctor of Philosophy*   35

The form of written work to be submitted by candidates for admission as Students for the Doctor of Philosophy, and the manner of its examination, as required by Regulations for the Degree of Doctor of Philosophy, §3, cl. 2, shall be determined by the board acting through the candidate's department or sub-department. Details may be obtained from the Director of Graduate Studies.   40

3. *Confirmation for Status of Student for the Doctor of Philosophy*

The status of Students for the Doctor of Philosophy will be confirmed by the board under the provisions of Regulations for the Degree of Doctor of Philosophy, §4, cl. 2, when it has received a certificate from the candidate's head of department that he or she is continuing satisfactorily to conduct research. Details may be obtained from the   45
Director of Graduate Studies.

4. *Theses*

D.Phil. theses should normally be not more than 50,000 words in length (approximately 170 sides of A4 paper), exclusive of bibliography, appendices, diagrams, and tables. In exceptional circumstances the permission of the board can be sought to exceed this limit, but in no case may a thesis be longer than 75,000 words.

A set of scientific papers prepared as for publication, but not necessarily yet published, that concern a common subject may constitute an acceptable thesis, provided that with the addition of an Introduction, General Discussion, and General Conclusions they constitute a coherent body of work. Such papers should either be incorporated as typescript pages or as offprints bound in to the body of the thesis. Papers written in collaboration should not be included unless the greater part of the work is directly attributed to the candidate himself or herself, and the supervisor so certifies. Joint papers may however be included as appendices in a thesis.

Candidates with some published work may also include that as part of a traditional thesis, normally as an appendix.

Approval to submit a thesis using this format must be sought in advance from the appropriate Director of Graduate Studies.

RESEARCH DEGREES IN MATHEMATICAL SCIENCES (COMPUTER SCIENCE, MATHEMATICS AND STATISTICS)

1. *Admission to the status of Probationer Research Student*

Applicants (other than those from overseas) will be notified individually if they are required to attend for interview before a decision is taken on an application for admission.

2. *Admission to the status of Student for the Degree of Master of Science by Research*

A Probationer Research Student may apply for transfer to M.Sc. status at any time within four terms of admission to the status of Probationer Research Student. Assessment for transfer shall be by oral examination. Two persons appointed by the board shall conduct the examination.

3. *Admission to the status of Student for the Degree of Doctor of Philosophy*

(i) Any person seeking transfer to the status of D.Phil. student must apply to the board, which will approve such application only if two (or, in exceptional cases, three) assessors appointed by the board shall have certified

    (*a*) that they have considered the written work submitted by the applicant and are satisfied that it demonstrates a capability of producing research work of the requisite standard and presenting the findings clearly; and

    (*b*) that together they have interviewed the candidate and satisfied themselves that the planned programme of research is one that may be profitably undertaken at Oxford and that the candidate has a good knowledge and understanding of the work that is likely to be needed to embark on the programme.

(ii) Before making application to the board for transfer to the status of D.Phil. student, the applicant shall, in consultation with his or her supervisor, prepare a body of written work which shall be submitted as evidence of suitability for transfer.

(iii) Applications shall be in one of two categories:

Category A (open to students who have had no previous experience of research work, and normally all candidates in the Department of Computer Science.)

In this category the written work submitted shall consist of a short dissertation on a topic selected in consultation with the supervisor, the preferred length being of between twenty-five and fifty typed pages (or fifteen to thirty printed pages of TEX, depending on font used).   5

Students in Category A should apply to transfer from the status of Probationer Research Student to the status of Student for the degree of Doctor of Philosophy between the second and fourth term after admission as a research student. Students with no previous experience of research work are advised to apply in the third term   10 after admission. Cases to defer application for the transfer of status must be made by the candidate's supervisor to the departmental Director of Graduate Studies by the end of the fourth full-term after admission. Approval will only be granted in exceptional cases. The provisions governing deferral are set out in the General Regulations Governing Research Degrees, §4. A form of application for the assessment together   15 with a form of application for transfer should be sent to the relevant departmental administrator. The applicant should include with the application a brief description of the proposed subject of research for the D.Phil. degree and a brief statement (courses attended, texts and publications studied etc.) setting out the steps taken to ensure that he or she has the knowledge and understanding likely to be necessary to embark on the   20 planned research work. The applicant should also name a date (not later than four weeks before the start of the Full Term following the date of application (applications made in vacation to be counted as if they had been made in the following term)) by which time he or she undertakes to make available two (or in exceptional cases three) copies of the written work supporting the application.   25

A student whose first application for transfer to D.Phil. status under Category A is not approved, shall be permitted to make one further application, and shall be granted an extension of time for one term if this is necessary for the purposes of making the application. A candidate failing to secure a Category B transfer to D.Phil. status will be allowed to apply for transfer under Category A.   30

Category B (open to applicants who have had previous experience of research work; it is expected that this will include many students who have successfully completed a taught master's course. This category is only available to candidates in the Department of Computer Science in exceptional circumstances with the approval of the Director of Graduate Studies.)   35

In this category the written work submitted with the application may consist of either

(*a*) a thesis or dissertation produced in connection with another course of research or study; or

(*b*) work that has been accepted for publication in a learned journal or journals; or   40

(*c*) other work which is in the opinion of the supervisor of comparable standing.

Students under Category B will make applications immediately after admission to Probationer Research Student status. A form of application for assessment together with a form of application for transfer together with two copies of the written work, should be sent to the relevant departmental administrator. In exceptional cases a third   45 copy may be required. The applicant should include with the application a brief description of the proposed subject of research for the D.Phil. degree and a brief statement (courses attended, texts and publications studied, etc.) setting out the steps taken to ensure that he or she has the knowledge and understanding likely to be necessary to embark on the planned research work.   50

(iv) In both types of application, on receipt of a form of application for assessment the board will appoint two (or in exceptional cases, three) members of the faculty to advise the board on the suitability of the applicant for transfer. Having considered the work submitted they shall arrange to interview the applicant to assess his/her suitability. They shall subsequently report to the board as to whether or not they are satisfied that the conditions described in clause 3(i) above have been met.   5

(v) On receipt of the report from the board's advisers, and after due consideration of any supervisor's reports that are available the board shall determine

    (*a*) that the application be approved; or   10

    (*b*) that the application be rejected, but that the student be allowed to apply for transfer to the status of Student for the Degree of M.Sc. by Research; or

    (*c*) that the candidate make one further application (under Category A).

4. *Transfer from status of Student for the Degree of Master of Science by Research to status of Student for the Degree of Doctor of Philosophy*   15

(i) Any person seeking transfer to the status of a D.Phil. student must apply to the board, which will approve such application only if two (or, in exceptional cases, three) persons appointed by the board shall have certified:

    (*a*) that they have considered written work submitted by the applicant and are satisfied that it demonstrates a capability of producing research work of   20
the requisite standard and presenting the findings clearly; and

    (*b*) that together they have interviewed the candidate and satisfied themselves that the planned programme of research is one that may be profitably undertaken at Oxford and that he or she has a good knowledge and understanding of the work that is likely to be needed to embark on the   25
programme.

(ii) Before making application to the board for transfer to the status of D.Phil. student, the applicant shall in consultation with his/her supervisor prepare a body of written work which shall be submitted as evidence of suitability for transfer.   30

(iii) Application for transfer from M.Sc. status to D.Phil. student status shall consist of a short dissertation on a topic selected in consultation with the supervisor, the preferred length being of between twenty-five and fifty typed pages (or fifteen to thirty printed pages of TEX, depending on fount used), or a part-written thesis.   35

Application may be made at any time up to the ninth term after admission. A form of application for assessment together with a form of application for transfer should be sent to the relevant departmental administrator. The applicant should include with the application a brief description of the proposed subject of research for the D.Phil. degree and a brief statement (courses attended, texts and publications studied etc.)   40
setting out the steps taken to ensure that he or she has the mathematical knowledge and understanding likely to be necessary to embark on the planned research work. The applicant should also name a date (not later than four weeks before the start of the Full Term following the date of application (applications made in vacation to be counted as if they had been made in the following term)) by which time he or she   45
undertakes to make available two (or in exceptional cases three) copies of the written work in support of the application.

A student whose first application for transfer from M.Sc. by Research status to D.Phil. status is not approved, shall be permitted to make one further application, and shall be granted an extension of time for one term if this is necessary for the purposes   50
of making the application.

(iv) On receipt of a form of application for assessment the board will appoint two (or in exceptional cases, three) members of the faculty, neither of whom shall normally be the applicant's supervisor, to advise the board on the suitability of the applicant for transfer. Having considered the work submitted they shall arrange to interview the applicant to assess suitability. They shall subsequently   5
report to the board as to whether or not they are satisfied that the conditions described in clause (i) above have been met.

(v) On receipt of the report from the board's assessors, and after due considera- tion of any supervisor's reports that are available the board shall determine that the application be approved; or that the application be rejected.   10

5. *Confirmation of D.Phil. status*

Confirmation of D.Phil. Student status, which will normally take place by the end of the eighth term after that in which the candidate was admitted as a Probationer Research Student, will take the form of an oral examination with two assessors appointed by the board, based on the candidate's own written report of progress.   15

The assessors shall recommend to the board either that D.Phil. status be confirmed or that one further application may be made, normally within one term of the original application. An extension of time for one term shall be granted if this is necessary for the purposes of making the application. If D.Phil. status is not confirmed, the second application shall normally be made by the end of the tenth term after that in which the   20
candidate was admitted as a Probationer Research Student. Two assessors appointed by the board shall require evidence of progress such as written work and shall indicate to the student precisely what is required. A second oral examination may be held.

If, after considering a candidate's second application for confirmation of status, the board concludes that the student's progress does not warrant this, it may approve his   25
or her transfer to the status of Student for the Degree of Master of Science by Research.

6. *Thesis*

Where some part of the thesis is not solely the work of the candidate or has been carried out in collaboration with one or more persons, the candidate shall submit a   30
clear statement of the extent of his or her own contribution.

In *Computer Science*, the text of a thesis submitted for the Degree of D.Phil. shall not exceed 250 pages of A4, single-spaced in normal size type, but there is no limit in references, diagrams, tables of empirical data or other forms of computer output, etc. Most theses are between 150 and 200 pages, though what is normal depends on the   35
topic. Theses on certain topics in theoretical computer science tend to be shorter; those that rely on the collection and interpretation of empirical data presented as evidence may be closer to the upper limit.

In *Mathematics* and in *Statistics*, the text of theses submitted for the Degree of D.Phil. shall not exceed 200 pages, A4 size, double-spaced in normal-size type, but   40
there is no limit on references, numerical tables, diagrams, computer output, etc. The normal length of a thesis, however, is nearer 100 pages (exclusive of the material defined above).

RESEARCH DEGREES IN PHYSICAL SCIENCES

1. *Master of Science by Research*   45

Applicants for admission as students for the Degree of Master of Science by Research shall in addition to the requirements of Regulations for the Degree of Master of Science by Research, §3, cl. 1, be required to undertake such other tests as the department concerned, acting through the candidate's head of department or sub-department shall determine. The Notes of Guidance provided by the department or sub-department will give details of these requirements.

2. *Doctor of Philosophy*

The form of written work to be submitted by candidates for admission as Students for the Degree of Doctor of Philosophy, and the manner of its examination, as required by Regulations for the Degree of Doctor of Philosophy, §3, cl. 2, shall be determined by the department concerned, acting through the candidate's head of department or sub-department. The notes of guidance provided by the department or sub-department will give details of these requirements. All candidates will be examined orally.

3. *Confirmation of status of students for the Degree of Doctor of Philosophy*

The status of Students for the Degree of Doctor of Philosophy will be confirmed by the board under the provisions of Regulations for the Degree of Doctor of Philosophy, §4, cl. 1, when it has received a certificate from the candidate's head of department or sub-department that he or she is continuing satisfactorily to conduct research. The candidate and the supervisor will be required to provide a clear indication of the proposed time-table for submission of the thesis.

4. *Theses*

(*a*) **Longer abstracts: Earth Sciences, Chemistry, and Engineering**

Candidates for the Degrees of M.Sc. and D.Phil. in Earth Sciences must submit with their theses, in addition to the abstracts of them required of all candidates of up to 300 words, three copies of a longer abstract of not more than 1,500 words for the M.Sc. and 2,500 for the D.Phil., one copy of which shall be bound into the copy of the thesis which, if the application for leave to supplicate for the degree is successful, will be deposited in the Bodleian Library.

Candidates for the Degrees of M.Sc. and D.Phil. in *Chemistry* or *Engineering* may if they wish submit with their theses, in addition to the abstract of them required of all candidates, a longer abstract of not more than 1,500 words for the M.Sc. and 2,500 for the D.Phil.. Should such an abstract be submitted, a copy of it must be bound into the copy of the thesis which, if the application for leave to supplicate for the degree is successful, will be deposited in the Bodleian Library. The fuller abstract may be bound into the other two copies of the thesis if candidates so desire.

(*b*) **Word limits**

Theses submitted by candidates in *Materials* shall not exceed 25,000 words for the M.Sc. and 40,000 words for the D.Phil., A4 size, double-spaced, but there is no limit on references, diagrams, tables, photographs, computer programmes, etc.

Theses submitted by candidates for the Degree of D.Phil. in *Physics* (except *Theoretical Physics*) must not exceed 250 pages, A4 size, double spaced in normal-size type (elite), the total to *include* all references, diagrams, tables, etc.

The text of theses submitted for the degree of D.Phil. in *Theoretical Physics* must not exceed 150 pages as defined above.

Theses submitted by candidates for the Degree of M.Sc. in Physics must not exceed 150 pages as defined above.

Theses submitted by candidates in *Engineering Science* must not exceed 250 pages for the Degree of D.Phil. or 200 pages for the Degree of M.Sc. They should be double spaced on A4 paper, in normal size type (Times New Roman, 12 point), the total to *include* all references, diagrams, tables, appendices, etc.

The text of theses submitted for the Degree of D.Phil. in *Earth Sciences* must not exceed 250 pages as defined above, but there is no limit on diagrams, tables, etc.

In special circumstances the Graduate Studies Committee of the appropriate department or sub department may, on application made *before* the thesis is submitted, grant
leave to exceed the limit by a stated amount. Applications to exceed these limits must
explain why the candidate believes the nature of the thesis is such that an exception
should be made, and must be supported by the supervisor.   5

DOCTORAL TRAINING PROGRAMMES
IN MPLS

1. *Programmes covered by these regulations*

(a) The regulations in cl. 2, 3, and 4 shall apply to all research students registered on
the following doctoral training programmes, irrespective of the division or department   10
they are based within for their research project:

(i) Centres for Doctoral Training in: Autonomous Intelligent Machines and
    Systems; Biomedical Imaging; Cyber Security; Healthcare Innovation;
    Industrially Focused Mathematical Modelling; Oil and Gas; Partial
    Differential Equations: Analysis and Applications; Renewable Energy   15
    Marine Structures; Science and Application of Plastic Electronic Materials;
    Science and Technology of Fusion Energy; Statistical Science; Systems
    Approaches to Biomedical Science; Synthesis for Biology and Medicine; and
    Synthetic Biology;

(ii) Doctoral Training Centres in: Life Sciences Interface; and Systems Biology;   20

(iii) Doctoral Training Partnership in Environmental Research;

(iv) Doctoral Training Partnership in Interdisciplinary Bioscience;

(v) Students for the D.Phil. in Cardiovascular Medicinal Chemistry.

The programmes listed in (i), (ii) and (v) shall be under the supervision of the Board
of the Mathematical, Physical, and Life Sciences Division.   25

The programmes listed in (iii) shall be under the joint supervision of the Boards of
the Mathematical, Physical, and Life Sciences Division, and the Social Sciences
Division. They shall appoint a Management Board to run the programme.

The programme listed in (iv) shall be under the joint supervision of the Boards of
the Mathematical, Physical, and Life Sciences Division, and the Medical Sciences   30
Division. They shall appoint a Management Board to run the programme.

(b) The regulations in cl. 2, 3, and 4 shall not apply to the doctoral training
programmes listed below. Students shall be registered for the first year of their
programme as follows:

(i) Centre for Doctoral Training in Gas Turbine Aerodynamics: students shall be   35
    registered for the first year of this programme at the University of Cambridge,

(ii) Centre for Doctoral Training in Science and Application of Plastic Electronic
     Materials: students shall be registered for the first year of this programme at
     the Imperial College of Science and Technology,

(iii) Centre for Doctoral Training in Diamond Science and Technology: students   40
      shall be registered for the first year of this programme at the University of
      Warwick,

(iv) Centre for Doctoral Training in Theory and Modelling in Chemical Sciences
     shall be registered for the first year of this programme on the M.Sc. in
     Theoretical and Computational Chemistry.   45

These programmes shall be under the supervision of the Board of the Mathematical,
Physical, and Life Sciences Division.

Students on the programmes listed in b (i)–(iii) must pass the postgraduate taught course that they are registered on for the first year in order to be admitted to the status of Probationer Research Student. Students on the programme listed in b (iv) must meet the conditions specified in the regulations for the M.Sc. in Theoretical and Computational Chemistry in order to be admitted to the status of Probationer Research Student. Students listed in b (i) to (iv) who are admitted to the status of Probationer Research Student may hold that status for up to four terms. The General Regulations Governing Research Degrees and the regulations for Research Degrees in Physical Sciences shall then apply.

2. *Probationer Research Student Status*

(a) Students admitted to the doctoral programmes listed in (1) (a) shall hold the status of Probationer Research Student for a maximum of six terms.

(b) Students admitted by The University of Warwick to the Centre for Doctoral Training in Statistical Science, and students admitted by the University of Bristol or the University of Warwick to the Centre for Doctoral Training in Synthetic Biology, and students admitted by the University of Nottingham to the Centre for Doctoral Training in Biomedical Imaging shall be matriculated and hold the status of Probationer Research Student Status at the University of Oxford for the first three terms of their doctoral training programme.

(c) A Probationer Research Student on a doctoral training programme listed in (1) (a) shall apply for admission to D.Phil. status normally before the end of the fifth term, and no later than the eighth week of the sixth term.

(d) A Probationer Research Student registered on the Centre for Doctoral Training in Renewable Energy Marine Structures programme may choose to apply for admission to either the degree of Doctor of Engineering or the degree of Doctoral of Philosophy. A Student must choose which degree to apply for no later than the end of the third full-term. The Regulations below apply to students seeking to apply for and supplicate for the degree of Doctor of Philosophy. For students seeking to apply for the degree of Doctor of Engineering, the Regulations for the Doctor of Engineering shall apply.

(e) The Education Committee regulations applying to a Probationer Research Student on a doctoral training programme that govern applications for transfer from Probationer Research Student Status are set out under General Regulations Governing Research Degrees §4 cl.6; and extensions to the maximum number of terms specified above are set out under General Regulations Governing Research Degrees §4 cl.7.

(f) A Probationer Research Student on a doctoral training programme shall cease to hold such status in accordance with General Regulations Governing Research Degrees §4.10 (i)–(iii).

(g) The board may grant a student suspension from the Register of those admitted to the status of Probationer Research Student or deprive a student of his or her status; and in such cases it shall at all times follow procedures determined by the Education Committee by regulation. The board may also reinstate a student to the Register, provided that the total number of terms a Student has spent as a Probationer Research Student has not exceeded eight terms in the case of a Student on a doctoral training programme listed in (1) (a).

3. *Confirmation of Status as a Student for the Degree of Doctor of Philosophy*

A candidate on a doctoral training programme listed in (1) (a) who has been admitted to the status of Student for the Degree of Doctor of Philosophy must apply to the board for confirmation of his or her status as a D.Phil. Student no later than the eighth week of the tenth term after admission as a research student; and not normally earlier than the ninth term after that in which he or she was initially admitted to the status of a Probationer Research Student or to the status of a student for another higher degree of the University.

A Student for the Degree of Doctor of Philosophy on a doctoral training programme listed in 1(a) shall cease to hold such status unless it has been confirmed within ten   5
terms of his or her admission to Probationer Research Student status.

4. *Other requirements for students for the Degree of Philosophy following a doctoral training programme*

A full-time Student for the Degree of Doctor of Philosophy following a doctoral training programme may hold that status for twelve terms from admission to   10
Probationer Research Student status.

NOTES

20

RESEARCH DEGREES IN THE MEDICAL SCIENCES DIVISION

1. ADMISSION OF RESEARCH STUDENTS

All research students will be admitted to the status of Probationer Research Student in   5
the first instance.

2. PROBATIONER STATUS

Students may hold the status of Probationer Research Students for a maximum of four
terms. Candidates should discuss with their supervisors whether to apply for transfer
to M.Sc. status or D.Phil. status, and the most appropriate time at which to apply. In   10
exceptional circumstances the Board may grant up to two terms' extension to this
deadline.

Students on the programmes listed below may hold Probationer Research Student
status for a maximum of six terms:

D.Phil. in Cardiovascular Science (BHF)   15

D.Phil. in Chromosome and Developmental Biology

D.Phil. in Genomic Medicine and Statistics

D.Phil. in Infection, Immunology and Translational Medicine

D.Phil. in Ion Channels and Disease

D.Phil. in Structural Biology   20

In exceptional circumstances the Board may grant up to one term's extension to this
deadline.

3. ADMISSION OF STUDENTS TO THE STATUS OF STUDENT FOR THE DEGREE OF MASTER OF SCIENCE BY RESEARCH

Candidates should submit the statement from the supervisor and the statement from   25
the candidate's society as specified by the regulations governing the degree of Master
of Science by Research. In addition, candidates should submit an outline of their
project of no more than 500 words and a timetable for completion. Candidates will be
required to give a presentation on their work. Further guidance on the form of the
written submission and the form of the presentation should be sought from the   30
departmental Director of Graduate Studies.

4. ADMISSION OF STUDENTS TO THE STATUS OF STUDENT FOR THE DEGREE OF DOCTOR OF PHILOSOPHY

Candidates should submit the statement from the supervisor and the statement from
the candidate's society as specified by the regulations governing the degree of Doctor   35
of Philosophy. In addition, candidates should submit a report of no more than 3,000
words which should include an abstract, introduction, results, discussion and future
plans including a proposed timetable for completion. Students may add appendices as
necessary of up to a further 2,000 words including methods, figure legends, and
references. Further guidance on the form of report should be sought from the depart-   40
mental Director of Graduate Studies.

5. PERMISSION TO WORK IN A WELL-FOUND LABORATORY OUTSIDE OF OXFORD

Applicants who are admitted to undertake research under the supervision of the Medical Sciences Divisional Board may, exceptionally, be permitted by the Divisional Board to undertake their research in a well-found laboratory outside of Oxford. Such candidates shall be dispensed from the residence requirements, but shall be required to attend Oxford for such instruction as the Division and department concerned shall require. Before admitting a candidate on this basis, the department concerned shall be required to satisfy itself and the Divisional Board that appropriate arrangements are in place for approving all aspects of the student's academic work, including the following:

  (i) the availability of the equipment and facilities necessary for the project in the agency concerned;
 (ii) the existence of a wider collaboration between the department and the agency in which the student is based;
(iii) the subject of their doctoral studies;
(iv) satisfactory induction procedures;
 (v) satisfactory health and safety arrangements;
(vi) satisfactory supervision arrangements, to include specification of a minimum number of contact hours between student and supervisor, which shall include not less than two face-to-face meetings between student and supervisor, for a total of at least 8 hours, each term;
(vii) satisfactory arrangements for monitoring the student's progress within the department;
(viii) provision for the student to attend Oxford for such instruction as the division and department shall require.

6. CONFIRMATION OF STATUS OF STUDENTS FOR THE DEGREE OF DOCTOR OF PHILOSOPHY

Candidates shall normally apply for confirmation of status in the eighth term from their admission as a research student, and no later than the ninth term from their admission as a research student. The Board strongly advises candidates to apply for confirmation of status a minimum of one term before they intend to submit their thesis.

Candidates should submit the statement from the supervisor and the statement from the candidate's society as specified by the regulations governing the degree of Doctor of Philosophy. Candidates must include a statement detailing the skills training that they have undertaken. This paperwork should be accompanied by a full contents list for the thesis, and include the milestones of any remaining work to be undertaken, and dates for the submission of draft chapters to the supervisor(s) for comment.

Candidates shall be required to deliver a formal, oral presentation of their work. The presentation will be attended by two assessors who are deemed to have the appropriate expertise to comment on the content of the project. The assessors will be appointed by the candidate's department; at least one assessor will have had no direct supervisory involvement with the student. Following the presentation the assessors will conduct an interview with the candidate.

The assessors will report to the Board on the candidate's suitability for confirmation of D.Phil. status. This report will be based on the information provided in the statement from the supervisor and the statement from the candidate's society as specified by the regulations governing the degree of Doctor of Philosophy, and in the supplementary statement from the candidate in conjunction with their presentation and interview. In cases where confirmation of status is not recommended the assessors will attach a short written report detailing where the work submitted falls below the standard required.

7. THESES

For students admitted prior to 1 October 2009.

A set of scientific papers that concern a common subject may exceptionally con- 5
stitute an acceptable thesis, but only if with the addition of an introduction, general discussion, and general conclusion they constitute a continuous theme. Joint papers may not be included unless the supervisor certifies the extent of the candidate's own contribution. Joint papers may be included as appendices in a thesis. Approval to submit a thesis using this format should be sought from the divisional board (via the 10 Chair, Medical Sciences Graduate School Committee, c/o Medical Sciences Office, Level 3 John Radcliffe Hospital, Oxford OX3 9DU) as soon as possible after admission and not later than the date at which the appointment of examiners is requested.

Candidates with some published work may also include that as part of a traditional thesis, normally as an appendix. 15

The length and scope of theses in each subject area in the Division is set out in the Graduate School Weblearn site https://weblearn.ox.ac.uk/portal/hierarchy/medsci/department/grad_school.

BIOCHEMISTRY: JOINT DOCTORAL
PROGRAMME WITH THE SCRIPPS 20
RESEARCH INSTITUTE

1. General

(*a*) The University may, in collaboration with The Scripps Research Institute, La Jolla, California (TSRI), through the Department of Biochemistry, admit a candidate to the full-time status of Probationer Research Student, and, on successful transfer of 25 status, of Student for the Degree of Doctor of Philosophy (or, exceptionally, Master of Science) jointly with TSRI and permit such a student to supplicate for the degree of Doctor of Philosophy (or, exceptionally, Master of Science by Research) jointly awarded with TSRI.

(*b*) The Board shall, in consultation with TSRI, elect for the supervision of the 30 programme a Joint Programme Committee, which shall have the power to arrange research supervision, lectures, and other instruction, and shall be responsible to both institutions. The programme directors in each institution will be responsible to the Oxford-Scripps Joint Programme Committee ('the Joint Programme Committee'), membership of which will consist of faculty members from both institutions. 35

(*c*) All students accepted on this programme will be admitted simultaneously as students of both institutions, and will be subject to the regulations and guidelines of both institutions, **except** as provided in the following regulations. Students admitted to the programme will be matriculated as students of the University of Oxford at the beginning of the programme, which is of five years' duration, irrespective of whether 40 they begin their studies at Oxford or at TSRI; and, for the purpose of University of Oxford regulations, numbers of terms shall be reckoned from the term in which the student is admitted to the joint programme, irrespective of whether they begin their studies at Oxford or at TSRI.

(*d*) The joint programme shall be subject to the following detailed regulations for 45 the conduct of the programme and the admission of students, and the granting of leave to supplicate shall be subject to those regulations and any other relevant provisions agreed by the University and TSRI.

(*e*) For the purposes of these regulations 'Board' shall mean the Medical Sciences Divisional Board of the University of Oxford or any body or person authorised to act on its behalf in these matters.

(*f*) For the purposes of these regulations, 'term' shall mean a term as prescribed in the University of Oxford's Regulations on the Number and Length of Terms, and when the required time in these regulations is reckoned in years, a year shall be deemed to be the equivalent of three terms. (For example, if five years are required, fifteen terms shall be understood.)

(*g*) In the event of a conflict between the regulations and guidelines of the two institutions, the procedure for resolution described in the Inter-Institutional Agreement between the two institutions will apply.

2. Admission

(*a*) All students will be admitted to the status of Probationer Research Student (Joint Oxford/TSRI) in the first instance. The provisions of the University of Oxford Regulations for Admission as a Probationer Research Student, §§1, 2, relating to the Status of Probationer Research Student and to the Admission of Candidates as Probationer Research Students, apply **except** that the Board will discharge its duties under these regulations following consultation with TSRI, through the Joint Programme Committee.

(*b*) Although students may hold this status for a maximum of six terms, candidates should normally apply to transfer from Probationer Research Student (Joint Oxford/TSRI) status in the third term after admission as a research student.

3. Induction

All students admitted to the programme will undertake an induction session at TSRI, and thereafter will start the full programme of study at Oxford or TSRI in accordance with the regulations set out above and below. Students starting at Oxford will be required to attend the induction course in the Department of Biochemistry.

4. Residence and other requirements

(*a*) With the exception of the references to part-time students, the provisions of the University of Oxford Regulations for Admission as a Probationer Research Student, §4, relating to the Residence and other Requirements of Probationer Research Students, apply to Probationer Research Students (Joint Oxford/TSRI).

(*b*) With the exception of the references to part-time students, the provisions of the University of Oxford Regulations for the Degree of Doctor of Philosophy, §6, relating to Residence and other Requirements for Students for the Degree of Doctor of Philosophy, apply to Doctor of Philosophy (Joint Oxford/TSRI) students **except** that he or she shall be deprived of that status if he or she shall have failed to complete his or her thesis within fifteen terms or within such further extension of time as may have been granted by the Board (see 7(*f*) below).

(*c*) In line with the regulations referred to in (*a*) and (*b*) above which make provision that 'time spent outside Oxford during term as part of an academic programme approved by Council shall count towards residence for the purpose of this clause', study at TSRI shall qualify as residence under these regulations; the normal patterns of study, after completion of the induction session under 3. above, shall be as follows:

(i) *For students commencing the programme at Oxford*: Students will study in Oxford for up to the first three years of the programme, during which period they will be subject to the regulations and disciplinary procedures of the University of Oxford, and for the remaining years at TSRI.

(ii) *For students commencing the programme at TSRI*: Students will study at TSRI for up to the first three years of the programme, and for the remaining years in Oxford, during which period they will be subject to the regulations and disciplinary procedures of the University of Oxford.

5. Fees

The following provisions of Appendix I, Regulations on Financial Matters, apply:

§ 1 *Fees payable at matriculation*

§ 2 *Fees payable by candidates on registration, entry for an examination, application for leave to supplicate, or resubmission of a thesis for certain degrees*   5

§ 5 *In respect of certificates and personal data*

§ 6 *Composition fees payable by members of the University*, except that students who begin their study at TSRI shall pay no composition fee in respect of the first two years of their programme.

Students who begin their study at Oxford will therefore be liable for composition   10
fees at the HomeEU or Overseas rate as appropriate in respect of their first nine terms of residence under the terms of section 3, thereafter being exempt under the terms of section 4, of §6; and students who begin their study at TSRI will be liable for composition fees at the HomeEU or Overseas rate as appropriate in respect of their final nine terms of residence (noting in both cases that residence, under the terms of 4   15
(*c*) above, includes study at TSRI).

6. Supervision

The Department of Biochemistry and TSRI, in consultation through the Joint Programme Committee, will each appoint academic supervisors for each student, who will be required to make termly reports on students' progress while the student   20
remains in the joint degree programme, i.e. until the thesis has been accepted for the award of the Doctor of Philosophy (Joint Oxford/TSRI).

(i) For Probationer Research Students (Joint Oxford/TSRI), the provisions of the University of Oxford Regulations for Admission as a Probationer Research Student, §3, relating to Supervision of Probationer Research Students, apply.   25

(ii) For Doctor of Philosophy (Joint Oxford/TSRI) Students, the provisions of the University of Oxford Regulations for the Degree of Doctor of Philosophy, §5, relating to Supervision of Students for the Degree of Doctor of Philosophy, apply.

(iii) For all students, the provisions of the Memorandum of Guidance for Supervisors and Research Students will apply (see 11 below).   30

7. Student progress

(*a*) *Completion of coursework at TSRI*

   (i) All students will be required to undertake a sequence of taught coursework in connection with the proposed field of research at TSRI and to pass the associated examinations in accordance with the TSRI requirements unless   35
exempted from this requirement under (ii) following.

   (ii) Candidates may, in advance of registration for the joint degree programme, apply to the Joint Programme Committee for exemption from all or part of this requirement in recognition of study and examinations previously undertaken.   40

   (iii) A student who fails any element of the coursework will be required to resit the examination, or to pass an equivalent element, before proceeding to the next stage of the programme.

(*b*) *Admission of students to the status of Student for the Degree of Doctor of Philosophy (Joint Oxford/TSRI)*   45

   (i) Students who begin their programme of study at TSRI will apply for transfer of status according to the stated requirements, i.e. by entering the TSRI qualifying examination for PhD candidacy, having completed and passed the taught coursework elements as provided under (*a*)(i) and (*a*)(iii) above.

(ii) For students who begin their programme of study at the University of Oxford, the provisions of the University of Oxford Regulations for the Degree of Doctor of Philosophy, §3, Admission of Candidates to the Status of Student for the Degree of Doctor of Philosophy, shall apply, and **in addition**, unless exempted under the provisions of (*a*)(ii) above, such students will be required   5
to undertake the sequence of taught coursework at TSRI, and to pass the coursework examinations, as provided under (*a*)(i) and (*a*)(iii) above, when they have moved to TSRI.

(iii) Application for transfer of status should normally take place during the third term after admission to the programme. However, if a student undertakes   10
work in two or more different laboratories within the particular institution during the first year, application for transfer of status may be delayed until after the third term, but *must* be made before the end of the sixth term. A candidate whose first application for transfer to Doctor of Philosophy (Joint Oxford/TSRI) status is not approved shall be permitted to make one further   15
application, following the procedures laid down in the University of Oxford Regulations for the Degree of Doctor of Philosophy, §3, cll.1 to 4, and shall be granted an extension of time for one term if this is necessary for the purposes of making the application.

(iv) The recommendations open to the assessors of the application for the *first time*   20
shall be:

Transfer to Doctor of Philosophy (Joint Oxford/TSRI) status; or

Transfer to Master of Science by Research (Joint Oxford/TSRI) status; or

Rejection of application to transfer to either Doctor of Philosophy (Joint Oxford/TSRI) status or Master of Science by Research (Joint Oxford/TSRI)   25
status, with the opportunity for submission of a second application, if the candidate chooses.

(v) The recommendations open to the assessors of the application for the *second time* shall be:

Transfer to Doctor of Philosophy (Joint Oxford/TSRI) status; or   30

Transfer to Master of Science by Research (Joint Oxford/TSRI) status; or

Rejection of application to transfer to either Doctor of Philosophy (Joint Oxford/TSRI) status or Master of Science by Research (Joint Oxford/TSRI) status, with consequent removal from the Register of Graduate Students.

(vi) It is possible to transfer to M.Sc. (Joint Oxford/TSRI) status initially and   35
thereafter apply to transfer to Doctor of Philosophy (Joint Oxford/TSRI) status if this is appropriate.

(*c*) *Admission of students to the status of Student for the Degree of Master of Science by Research (Joint Oxford/TSRI): Guidelines for transfer to M.Sc. status*

If, exceptionally, it is agreed that the student should apply for transfer to the status   40
of student for the degree of Master of Science by Research (Joint Oxford/TSRI), the procedures set out in the programme guidelines will be followed.

The decision to work towards the Degree of M.Sc. by Research (Joint Oxford/TSRI) should be reached in discussion with the supervisor(s) concerned and agreed by the Director of Graduate Studies at Oxford and the Dean of Graduate Studies at   45
TSRI.

(*d*) *Confirmation of Status of Student for the Degree of Doctor of Philosophy (Joint Oxford/TSRI)*

With the exception of the references to part-time students, the provisions of the University of Oxford Regulations for the Degree of Doctor of Philosophy, **§4**,   50
Confirmation of Status as a Student for the Degree of Doctor of Philosophy, will

apply to Doctor of Philosophy (Joint Oxford/TSRI) students. The status of a Student for the Degree of Doctor of Philosophy (Joint Oxford/TSRI) will be confirmed under the provisions above, on the basis of supporting statements from the supervisors from both institutions, when it has been confirmed by the Director of Graduate Studies in consultation with the Dean of Graduates at TSRI that the student is continuing satisfactorily to conduct research. Confirmation of Doctor of Philosophy (Joint Oxford/TSRI) status exists to give faculties and departments an opportunity to monitor the direction and progress of a student's work in the period between transfer of status and submission of thesis. It intends both to assess the progress of the research work and to support the work of a student and his or her supervisor(s) by ensuring that the Director of Graduate Studies and the Dean of Graduates at TSRI are aware of the state of the research in progress, and the likely timetable for submission. Application for confirmation of Doctor of Philosophy (Joint Oxford/TSRI) status should be made normally after the ninth term, and *must* be made before the fifteenth term; the detailed arrangements for application at Oxford and at TSRI are as set out in the programme guidelines.

A candidate whose first application for confirmation of his or her status is not approved shall be permitted to make one further application following the procedures laid down in this section, normally within one term of the original application, and shall be granted an extension of time for one term if this is necessary for the purposes of making the application. If, after considering a candidate's second application for confirmation of status, the Board concludes that the student's progress does not warrant this, the Board may approve his or her transfer to the status of Student for the Degree of Master of Science by Research (Joint Oxford/TSRI).

(*e*) *Termination of status*

(i) *Probationer Research Student (Joint Oxford/TSRI)*

The provisions of the University of Oxford Regulations for Admission as a Probationer Research Student, §4, cl.6, apply. Decisions made under these provisions will be the subject of consultation between the two institutions through the Joint Programme Committee.

(ii) *Student for the Degree of Doctor of Philosophy (Joint Oxford/TSRI)*

The provisions of the University of Oxford Regulations for the Degree of Doctor of Philosophy, §6, cl.8, apply **except** that he or she shall be deprived of that status if he or she shall have failed to complete his or her thesis within fifteen terms or within such further extension of time as may have been granted by the Board (see (*f*) below). Decisions made under these provisions will be the subject of consultation between the two institutions, through the Joint Programme Committee.

(*f*) *Extension of time*

Student for the Degree of Doctor of Philosophy (Joint Oxford/TSRI)

If a full-time Student for the Degree of Doctor of Philosophy (Joint Oxford/TSRI) has held that status for fifteen terms, but has been prevented by exceptional circumstances from completing his or her thesis, the Board shall have power to grant an extension of time for a period or periods, not exceeding nine terms in all, to be determined by the Board. Applications for such extension of time shall be made through the relevant Graduate School Assistant at the University of Oxford not later than the term in which the student is due to apply for permission to supplicate; applications made under these provisions will be the subject of consultation between the two institutions through the Joint Programme Committee.

8. Suspension of Graduate Students from the Register

The provisions of the General Regulations of the Education Committee Governing Research Degrees §5.1, apply; action proposed under these provisions will be the subject of consultation between the two institutions through the Joint Programme Committee.

9. Removal of Graduate Students from the Register

The provisions of the General Regulations of the Education Committee Governing Research Degrees §5.2, apply; action proposed under these provisions will be the subject of consultation between the two institutions through the Joint Programme Committee.

10. Reinstatement of Graduate Students to the Register

The provisions of the General Regulations of the Education Committee Governing Research Degrees §5.3, apply; action proposed under these provisions will be the subject of consultation between the two institutions through the Joint Programme Committee.

11. Complaints and appeals

(*a*) While at Oxford students may seek advice on matters of concern from a number of individuals who have responsibility for different aspects of the well-being of graduate students; these include supervisors, Director of Graduate Studies, college tutors, the student's college and departmental advisors, head of department, and college head. If resolution of a complaint or appeal is not possible by means of procedures in place within the Department of Biochemistry, then a student may refer the matter to the Proctors for formal consideration, under the Statutes and Regulations of the University of Oxford relating to the powers of the Proctors.

(*b*) While at TSRI, students may seek advice on matters of concern from numerous individuals and a committee who have responsibility for aspects of the well-being of graduate students. These individuals include the thesis research advisor, the student-chosen Advisory and Qualifying Examination Committee (consisting of at least two members of the TSRI faculty, one Oxford representative, and the student's advisor at TSRI) that meets annually or when requested by the student or a faculty member, and the Dean and the Associate Deans. In the absence of a resolution of a conflict, the student is permitted to present his or her case to the President of TSRI who will make every reasonable effort to resolve the conflict.

12. Appointment of examiners

(*a*) A Student for the Degree of Doctor of Philosophy (Joint Oxford/TSR) who has fulfilled the applicable requirements set out in the preceding clauses of this section and whose status has not expired, may apply to the Board for the appointment of examiners and for leave to supplicate for the Degree of Doctor of Philosophy (Joint Oxford/TSRI).

(*b*) Such applications should be made to the Board through the relevant Graduate School Assistant at the University of Oxford. They shall include:

(i) a certificate from the student's college that the application has the approval of that college;

(ii) a certificate from the supervisors that the student has pursued his or her course of study in Oxford and at TSRI in accordance with the preceding clauses of this section;

(iii) a statement by the candidate of what part, if any, of the thesis has already been accepted, or is currently being submitted, for any degree or diploma or certificate or other qualification in the University of Oxford, TSRI, or elsewhere;

(iv) a statement by the candidate that the thesis is his or her own work, except where otherwise indicated.

(*c*) The supervisors shall consult with the candidate concerning possible examiners, and forward to the Board the names of suggested examiners together with details of any special considerations which the candidate wishes to make known about any potential examiners.

(*d*) The candidate shall also submit, to the University of Oxford, for examination, at such time and in such format as provided by the General Regulations Governing Research Degrees, and by the Special Regulations of the Board as set out in this section:

  (i) two printed or typewritten copies of a thesis;

  (ii) two printed or typewritten copies of an abstract of the thesis, which shall not normally exceed 300 words.

Submission of additional copies of the thesis, and abstract as appropriate, to the Thesis Committee at TSRI shall be according to the TSRI guidelines.

(*e*) On receipt of an application the Board shall appoint two examiners, in consultation with The Scripps Research Institute, neither of whom shall be the candidate's supervisor. The appointment of examiners by the Board shall be in accordance with the provisions of the Education Committee's Notes of Guidance for Research Degrees, i.e. that it is an absolute requirement for examinations for the Degree of Doctor of Philosophy that one examiner should be external to the University of Oxford, and that this is the preferred convention for the Degree of M.Sc. by Research. In addition, both the examiners appointed by the Board for the Degree of Doctor of Philosophy (Joint Oxford/TSRI) and for the Degree of Master of Science by Research (Joint Oxford/TSRI) should be external to TSRI. For examinations which are undertaken at TSRI (see 15(*a*) below), the examiners shall act together with such members of the candidate's Thesis Committee as shall be determined by TSRI, and for examinations which are undertaken at Oxford, up to two members of the candidate's Thesis Committee, as determined by TSRI, shall take part in the examination; the student's TSRI thesis advisor may attend the examination on a non-participatory basis.

The duties of the examiners (jointly with the members of the Thesis Committee) shall be:

  (i) on behalf of the University of Oxford and TSRI, to consider the thesis and the abstract of it submitted by the student, provided that they shall exclude from consideration in making their report any part of the thesis which has already been accepted, or is being concurrently submitted for any degree or other qualification in this University or TSRI or elsewhere, and shall have the power to require the candidate to produce for their inspection the complete thesis so accepted or concurrently submitted;

  (ii) to examine the student orally in the subject of his or her thesis;

  (iii) to satisfy themselves by examination (oral, written, or both) whether the student possesses a good general knowledge of the particular field of learning within which the subject of the thesis falls;

  (iv) to report to the Board through the relevant Graduate School Assistant at the University of Oxford on the scope, character, and quality of the work submitted;

  (v) to return to the student the copies of the thesis and the abstracts thereof.

13. Theses

The provisions of the General Regulations of the Education Committee Governing Research Degrees §6. cll. 1, and 2, apply.

Theses for the Degree of Doctor of Philosophy (Joint Oxford/TSRI) should not normally be more than 50,000 words in length (amounting to approximately 170 sides of A4 paper), exclusive of bibliography, appendices, diagrams, and tables. In exceptional circumstances the permission of the Board can be sought to exceed this limit, but in no case may a thesis be longer than 75,000 words.

14. Conduct of Oral Examinations

(*a*) The oral examination may be held in either institution, as agreed by the student, the supervisors, and the Thesis Committee in consultation and as endorsed by the Joint Programme Committee, in a suitable institutional or college building. It shall, except in special circumstances, begin not earlier than 9 a.m. nor later than 5 p.m., and may be held in term or vacation. The examiners shall be responsible for informing the candidate of the final arrangements made and shall give reasonable time for the candidate to make himself or herself available. It shall be the duty of candidates to ensure that any letter addressed to them at their college or any other address which they have given is forwarded to them if necessary. The examiners shall allow reasonable time for receiving an acknowledgement from the candidate of their summons.

(*b*) Candidates may apply to the Board for the oral examination to be held not later than a certain date, provided that this date shall not be earlier than one calendar month after the date on which the thesis has been received at Oxford by the Examination Schools, or after the date on which the examiners have agreed to act, whichever is the later. If the Board is satisfied that there are special circumstances justifying this application, it will ask the examiners to make arrangements to enable the oral examination to be held within the period specified. In such cases the examiners, when invited to act, will be informed that the candidate has asked that the oral examination be held not later than a certain date, and acceptance of the invitation to examine will be on the understanding that they would seek to meet this request. If it is not practicable to meet the student's request, then the Board shall decide how to proceed.

(*c*) Notice of the examination shall be given in the University of Oxford in one of the following ways:

(i) It may be published in the *University Gazette* not later than the day before it is due to take place;

(ii) Not later than two days before the examination the examiners may inform the relevant Graduate School Assistant in writing; and post a notice in the Examination Schools; and if the examination is to be held in Oxford in a place other than the Examination Schools, post a notice also at the place of examination.

(*d*) The notice shall state the name of the candidate, the subject of the thesis, the place, day, and hour of the examination, and the names of the examiners. If an examination is held without the giving of notice required by this regulation it shall be invalid, unless the Proctors, on receipt of a written application from the examiners, shall determine otherwise. The student or his or her college, other society, or approved institution, may within fourteen days of the date of the Proctors' decision in respect of the granting of consent, appeal in writing to the Education Committee (who may nominate another member of the committee, other than one of the Proctors, to adjudicate the appeal).

(*e*) An examination held in Oxford may be attended by any member of the University in academic dress. Up to two members of the candidate's Thesis Committee, as determined by TSRI, may take part in the examination, and the student's TSRI thesis advisor may attend on a non-participatory basis, but otherwise no person who is not a member of the University may attend it except with the consent of the examiners. The Proctors, after consultation with the Board, may decide (either at their own discretion or at the request of the candidate or the supervisor(s) or the department) to forbid the attendance of any person or all persons (other than the examiners, including the agreed members of the candidate's Thesis Committee, and the candidate) or to impose any condition on attendance if and to the extent that such action is in their view necessary to protect the interests of the University or the candidate or both, and the examiners shall be informed accordingly and shall include this information in the notice of examination. The student or his or her college may   5 within fourteen days of the date of the Proctors' decision appeal in writing to the Chair of the Education Committee (who may nominate another member of the committee, other than one of the Proctors, to adjudicate the appeal).

(*f*) Candidates are strongly recommended to take a copy of their thesis to the examination.   10

(*g*) If, owing to illness or other urgent and unforeseen cause, an examiner is unable to attend the examination, it shall be postponed to a later date; however, if, after appropriate consultation between the Department of Biochemistry and TSRI through the Joint Programme Committee, the Proctors are satisfied that postponement would be a serious hardship to the candidate, they may authorise another member of the   15 Board to attend the examination as a substitute but such substitute shall not be required to sign the report containing the recommendation as described in 16 below. The Proctors shall determine what payment, if any, the substitute examiner shall receive.

(*h*) Oral examinations held at The Scripps Research Institute shall be subject to   20 such detailed regulations of that institute as are relevant.

15. Recommendation of the examiners

Having completed the examination of a candidate *for the first time*, the examiners appointed by the Board and by TSRI may make any one of the recommendations (*a*), (*b*) or (*d*) below *only*. Having completed the examination of a candidate *who has*   25 *revised and resubmitted his or her thesis*, the examiners may make any one of the recommendations (*a*) to (*f*). The recommendations are:

(*a*) That the Board should grant the candidate leave to supplicate for the Degree of Doctor of Philosophy (Joint Oxford/TSRI). In making this recommendation, the examiners must include in their report statements that: 30

- the student possesses a good general knowledge of the particular field of learning within which the subject of the thesis falls;
- the student has made a significant and substantial contribution in the particular field of learning within which the subject of the thesis falls;
- the thesis is presented in a lucid and scholarly manner;   35
- in their opinion the thesis merits the Degree of Doctor of Philosophy (Joint Oxford/TSRI);
- The student has presented a satisfactory abstract of the thesis.

Examiners shall bear in mind that their judgement of the substantial significance of the work should take into account what may reasonably be expected of a capable and   40 diligent student after completing the five-year joint programme. If the examiners are satisfied that the candidate's thesis is of sufficient merit to qualify for the degree but consider, nevertheless, that before the thesis is deposited the candidate should make minor corrections (which are not sufficiently substantial to justify reference back for re-examination), they must require the candidate to correct the thesis to their satisfac-   45 tion before they submit their report. If the candidate has not completed these corrections within three calendar months of the date of receipt of the list of minor corrections from the examiners, his or her name shall be removed by the relevant Graduate School Assistant at the University of Oxford on behalf of the Registrar from the Register of Students for the Degree of Doctor of Philosophy (Joint Oxford/TSRI);   50 however, the Board may, on good cause shown by the candidate, grant an extension of time of three further calendar months in which the candidate may fulfil this requirement before the removal of his or her name from the Register. No subsequent extension shall be granted, but it shall be open to a candidate who has failed to fulfil this requirement within those three or six months in total, as the case may be, to apply to the Board for reinstatement as a Student for the Degree of Doctor of Philosophy (Joint Oxford/TSRI), with the support of his or her society and supervisor(s), upon submission to the relevant Graduate School Assistant of a copy of his or her thesis incorporating the required corrections, and upon payment of such reinstatement fee as is prescribed by Council at that time. Permission to supplicate shall not be granted until this fee has been paid.

(*b*) That the Board should offer the candidate a choice between (i) reference of the thesis back to him or her in order that he or she may revise it for re-examination for the Degree of Doctor of Philosophy (Joint Oxford/TSRI), and (ii) leave to supplicate for the Degree of Master of Science (Joint Oxford/TSRI), as appropriate, on the basis that the thesis has not reached the standard required for the Degree of Doctor of Philosophy (Joint Oxford/TSRI) but has nevertheless reached that required for the Degree of Master of Science (Joint Oxford/TSRI). If the Board adopts this recommendation, and the student chooses to revise the thesis for re-examination for the Degree of Doctor of Philosophy (Joint Oxford/TSRI), the student shall retain the status and obligations of a Student for the Degree of Doctor of Philosophy (Joint Oxford/TSRI) and shall be permitted to apply again for the appointment of examiners in accordance with the provisions of the University of Oxford Regulations for the Degree of Doctor of Philosophy, §7, relating to Examination of Students for the Degree of Doctor of Philosophy. If such permission shall have been given by the Board during a vacation, it shall be deemed to have been given in the term preceding that vacation.

(*c*) That the Board should refer the student's thesis back in order that he or she may present it for re-examination for the Degree of Master of Science (Joint Oxford/TSRI) only. If the Board adopts the recommendation the student shall be transferred forthwith to the status of Student for the Degree of Master of Science (Joint Oxford/TSRI), and shall be permitted to apply for permission to supplicate for the Degree of Master of Science (Joint Oxford/TSRI) in accordance with the provisions of the University of Oxford Regulations for the Degree of Master of Science by Research, §6, relating to Examination of Students for the Degree of Master of Science by Research. If such permission shall have been given by the Board during a vacation, it shall be deemed to have been given in the term preceding that vacation. The word limit for a thesis submitted under this provision shall be that specified for the Doctor of Philosophy (Joint Oxford/TSRI) under 14 above.

(*d*) That the Board should refer the student's thesis back in order that he or she may present it for re-examination either under (*b*) above for the Degree of Doctor of Philosophy (Joint Oxford/TSRI) or, if the student chooses, under (*c*) above for the Degree of Master of Science (Joint Oxford/TSRI) only. The Board shall adopt such a recommendation only if it is fully satisfied that the thesis as it stands is not of the standard required for the Degree of Doctor of Philosophy (Joint Oxford/TSRI), nor for the Degree of Master of Science (Joint Oxford/TSRI), but that the candidate could reach the standard required for the Degree of Doctor of Philosophy (Joint Oxford/TSRI). If such permission shall have been given by the Board during a vacation, it shall have been deemed to have been given in the term preceding that vacation.

(*e*) That the thesis has not reached the standard required for the Degree of Doctor of Philosophy (Joint Oxford/TSRI) but has nevertheless reached that required for

Master of Science (Joint Oxford/TSRI), and that the candidate may be granted leave to supplicate for that degree on the basis of the thesis as it stands.

(*f*) That the student's application for leave to supplicate should be refused.

If the examiners recommend reference back of the student's application under (*b*), (*c*), or (*d*) above, they shall annex to their report to the Board a statement for 5 transmission to the candidate setting out the respects in which the thesis falls below the standard for the degree in question, and what changes are necessary for it to reach that standard. In exceptional circumstances, examiners of a thesis submitted *for the first time*, and notwithstanding a recommendation under (*b*) or (*d*) above, may certify that they are unable to indicate how the thesis might be changed, within the time 10 allowed, in order to reach the standard required for the degree of Doctor of Philosophy (Joint Oxford/TSRI).

On receipt of the examiners' report, the Board shall reach a decision on whether to accept the examiners' recommendation; no candidate shall be given leave to supplicate for the degree of Doctor of Philosophy (Joint Oxford/TSRI) unless the examiners have 15 made the statements required in clause (*a*) above. A candidate who has been granted leave to supplicate by the Board shall be required to submit to the Examination Schools a copy of his or her thesis, incorporating any amendments or corrections required by the examiners and approved by the Board, with a view to deposit in the Bodleian or other appropriate library of the University of Oxford. Permission to 20 supplicate shall in all cases be conditional upon fulfilment of this requirement.

In an exceptional case in which the Board is unable to accept the examiners' recommendation, or in which the examiners cannot reach an agreed recommendation, the Board shall have power to appoint one or two new examiners as it deems necessary (subject to consultation with the Joint Programme Committee), to conduct such 25 further examination of the candidate as the Board may require. The Board shall make a report on any such case to the Education Committee.

The Board may exempt a candidate who is being re-examined under the provisions of clauses (*b*)–(*e*) above from the oral examination, provided that the examiners are able to certify that they are satisfied without examining the candidate orally that they 30 can recommend to the Board in the terms required by clause (*a*) above that he or she be given leave to supplicate for the Degree of Doctor of Philosophy (Joint Oxford/ TSRI).

It shall be the duty of the relevant Graduate School Assistant, on behalf of the Registrar, to notify the candidate of the Board's decision as soon as may be. The 35 relevant Graduate School Assistant shall also be responsible for publishing at the end of each academic year the names of those candidates to whom permission to supplicate has been granted during that year, together with a statement of the subject of the thesis written by each.

When, on the conclusion of the investigation of a complaint made by a candidate, 40 the Proctors recommend that a candidate be re-examined, the Board shall have power to hold a new examination.

MEDICAL SCIENCES DOCTORAL TRAINING CENTRE

1. General regulations 45

These regulations shall apply to all students registered for
1. D.Phil. in Biomedical and Clinical Sciences
2. D.Phil. in Cardiovascular Science (BHF)
3. D.Phil. in Chromosome and Developmental Biology

4. D.Phil. in Genomic Medicine and Statistics

5. D.Phil. in Infection, Immunology and Translational Medicine

6. D.Phil. in Ion Channels and Disease

7. D.Phil. in Structural Biology

within the Medical Sciences Doctoral Training Centre, irrespective of the division   5
or department they are based within for their research project.

Programme 1 above is a three-year programme. Programmes 2–7 above are four-year programmes.

The provisions of the following regulations shall apply, except as specifically provided below: General Regulations Governing Research Degrees; Regulations for   10
the Degree of Master of Science by Research, Regulations for the Degree of Doctor of Philosophy (§1–7); and the Special Regulations of Divisional and Faculty Boards concerning the status of Probationer Research Student and the degrees of M.Litt., M.Sc. by Research, and D.Phil.

For the purposes of these regulations 'Board' shall mean the Medical Sciences   15
Divisional Board.

2. Register of Probationer Research Students

The Board may grant a student suspension from the Register of those admitted to the status of Probationer Research Student or deprive a student of his or her status; and in such cases it shall at all times follow procedures determined by the Education   20
Committee by regulation. The Board may also reinstate a student to the Register, provided that the total number of terms a student has spent as a Probationer Research Student has not exceeded six terms in the case of a student on a four-year Medical Sciences Doctoral Training Centre programme.

3. Probationer Research Student Status   25

A student on a four-year Medical Sciences Doctoral Training Centre programme may hold the status of Probationer Research Student for a maximum of six terms, including the term in which the student was admitted. In exceptional circumstances the Board may grant up to one term's extension to this deadline.

4. Confirmation of Status as a Student for the Degree of Doctor of Philosophy   30

A student on a four-year Medical Sciences Doctoral Training Centre programme who has been admitted to the status of Student for the Degree of Doctor of Philosophy must apply to the Board for confirmation of his or her status as a D.Phil. Student not later than the tenth term and normally during the ninth term after admission to the programme. In all other respects the procedure for confirmation of status of such   35
students will follow the procedures for confirmation of status of students within the Medical Sciences Division.

5. Other requirements for students for the Degree of Doctor of Philosophy following a Medical Sciences Doctoral Training Centre four-year D.Phil. Programme

A full-time Student for the Degree of Doctor of Philosophy following a four-year   40
Medical Sciences Doctoral Training Centre programme may hold the status of a registered research student for a maximum of twelve terms. If such a student has been prevented by exceptional circumstances from completing his or her thesis by that time, the Board shall have power to grant an extension of time for a period or periods, not exceeding six terms in all, to be determined by the Board. Applications for such   45
extension of time shall be made through the Registrar not later than the term in which the student is due to apply for permission to supplicate.

A full-time Student for the Degree of Doctor of Philosophy following a four-year Medical Sciences Doctoral Training Centre Programme shall cease to hold that status if: (i) he or she shall have been refused permission to supplicate for the Degree of   50

Doctor of Philosophy; or (ii) the Board concerned shall in accordance with the Regulations for the Degree of Doctor of Philosophy, Part A., §2, cl. 3, and with the provisions set down by regulation by the Education Committee and after consultation with the student's college supervisor, have deprived the student of that status; (iii) he or she shall have been transferred under the relevant provisions to another status; (iv)   5
he or she shall have failed to complete his or her thesis within twelve terms or within such further extension of time as may have been granted by the Board concerned.

NOTES

21

RESEARCH DEGREES IN THE SOCIAL SCIENCES DIVISION

RESEARCH DEGREES IN ANTHROPOLOGY

1. Transfer from M.Phil. status to D.Phil. status

A student who has obtained an M.Phil. may only be admitted direct to D.Phil. status on condition that the research topic is a development of the research contained in the M.Phil. thesis or if the student can otherwise demonstrate his or her competence to undertake the proposed research, and that appropriate supervision can be provided.

2. Transfer from Probationer Research Student status to M.Litt. or D.Phil. status

For transfer of status, the student should submit two copies in typescript of a substantial piece of written work relevant to the proposed thesis. The work should not exceed 20,000 words excluding bibliography and any appendixes, but including notes, and should consist of, or incorporate, a detailed research proposal. The student will be required to show that the research already undertaken shows promise of the ability to produce a satisfactory M.Litt. or D.Phil. thesis, as the case may be, on the intended topic. Students should submit their work to the Departmental Office, Institute of Social and Cultural Anthropology, not later than the end of Trinity *full term* after the Michaelmas Term in which they were admitted. An extension of one term (i.e. to the end of the Michaelmas full term in the year after the student was admitted) may be granted in exceptional circumstances. In the case of students admitted in other terms, submission should take place by the end of the third term (i.e. full term) after admission, with the possibility of an extension for a further one term (i.e. to the end of full term) in exceptional circumstances. (NB: alternative provisions apply to probationer research students with coursework, as described in paragraph 3, below). The student's submission will be assessed by two assessors appointed by the Teaching Committee of the School of Anthropology and Museum Ethnography, to which they will submit a written report. A student whose first application is unsuccessful may be given one further opportunity to apply for transfer of status, for which an extension of one term is automatically granted.

All probationer research students must give presentations on their proposed research projects to the class designated for that purpose or an agreed equivalent to qualify for transfer of status. They will also be expected to attend relevant courses on training and methods, as agreed with, and directed by, their supervisor(s).

3. Probationer research students with coursework

Probationer research students entering the Institute of Social and Cultural Anthropology should normally have a prior, full taught-course degree in social or cultural anthropology at either the graduate or undergraduate levels before being admitted to this status. Exceptionally, however, students who have earned a distinction in either (1) a degree in a closely related subject that includes some social or cultural anthropology, or (2) a mixed degree in social or cultural anthropology and another closely related subject may be admitted directly to the status of probationer research student in anthropology. In addition to the standard requirements for probationer research students in anthropology (and except as varied below), students entering the above Institute via this route should satisfy the following conditions:

(1) they enter the Institute as research students in the Michaelmas term of their first academic year and not in any other term;

(2) the topic of their proposed research lies in the general thematic or geographical area covered by their prior degree;

(3) they undertake a full course of eight tutorials in general anthropology, with essays, in the first Michaelmas term of their admission as probationer research students. Three of the essays produced for these tutorials are to be submitted for assessment as described below;

(4) they follow a course in an option (area or topic) offered to master's students in the above Institute in the first Hilary and, where provided for, Trinity terms after their admission as research students. The option must be relevant to their proposed research if one is available (area or topic), except that they may not repeat an option in which they have been examined as part of a prior degree in the University of Oxford. If the student cannot take such an option for either of these reasons, a free choice may be allowed with the agreement of the Director of Graduate Studies for Anthropology or his or her delegate. The student shall write one essay of tutorial standard on the option for assessment as described below;

(5) the proposed supervisor has given his or her approval of this course of action in writing to the Director of Graduate Studies for anthropology or, in case the latter is the proposed supervisor, to the Director of the Institute of Social and Cultural Anthropology.

Note: the work specified in (3) and (4) above shall constitute Part I of the assessment for transfer from probationer research student to full D.Phil. student, and the text for transfer that the student will be required to prepare on the basis of his or her proposed research (in the same manner as for ordinary probationer research students in anthropology) shall constitute Part II of the said assessment.

Students following these arrangements must pass an assessment of the work they have carried out under (3) and (4) above (Part I), which shall normally involve scrutiny of three tutorial essays and the option essay. This assessment shall be carried out at the same time as the standard assessment of the text on the proposed research (Part II). An extra assessor or assessors, one of whom in special cases may be the student's supervisor, may but need not be appointed to scrutinise the work carried out for Part I. The extra assessor(s), if any, need not be present at the assessment interview with the student, but should advise the assessors conducting the interview in writing beforehand of the standard of work achieved by the student in Part I.

Both parts of the assessment, i.e. Parts I and II as specified above, must be passed by the student, though not necessarily on the same occasion. If the student fails in either Part I or Part II, or both, he or she will be required to resubmit materials for, and pass, the relevant part(s) within one term of the original submission. Both elements in Part I, as described under (3) and (4) above, must be passed by the student.

The deadline for a student following this path to submit materials for assessment for upgrade to full status as a doctoral student shall normally be the fourth term after admission as a research student (i.e. the Michaelmas Term of the second year in the status of probationer research student). Such students are expected to start work on their text for upgrade during the Hilary term after their admission as probationer research students at the latest.

4. Confirmation of Status as a student for the Degree of Doctor of Philosophy

The provisions of the Regulations for the Degree of Doctor of Philosophy (§4) shall apply, except as specifically provided below.

Application for confirmation of D.Phil. status shall normally be made not earlier than the sixth term and not later than the ninth term from admission as a research 5
student in the case of a student admitted first to the status of Probationer Research Student, and normally not earlier than the third term and not later than the sixth term from readmission in the case of a student admitted directly to D.Phil. status from an M.Phil. degree within the School of Anthropology and Museum Ethnography.

For students admitted directly to D.Phil. status from an M.Phil. degree within the 10
School of Anthropology and Museum Ethnography before 1 October 2012:

(i) Application for confirmation of D.Phil. status shall normally be made not earlier than the sixth term and not later than the ninth term from readmission.

For students admitted directly to D.Phil. status from an M.Phil. degree within the
School of Anthropology and Museum Ethnography before 1 October 2011: 15

(i) Application for confirmation of D.Phil. status shall normally be made not earlier than the fourth term and not later than the tenth term from readmission.

The Teaching Committee of the School of Anthropology and Museum Ethnography may in addition, and for good reason, permit a candidate to defer for a maximum of three terms his or her application for confirmation of status. 20

A student for the Degree of Doctor of Philosophy shall cease to hold such status unless it has been confirmed within nine terms of his or her admission if first admitted as a Probationer Research Student, or within six terms from readmission directly to D.Phil. status from an M.Phil. degree within the School of Anthropology and Museum Ethnography (or within a maximum of twelve terms or nine terms respec- 25
tively where deferral has been approved in accordance with the paragraph above).

The student will be required to give evidence confirming that the research already carried out gives promise of the ability to produce a satisfactory D.Phil. thesis on the intended topic. For this purpose the applicant must submit: (a) a detailed outline of the whole of the proposed thesis, including an indication of the topics, theories, 30
arguments etc. to be covered in individual chapters (as applicable); and (b) at least one and not more than two sample chapters. In the latter case, the student is advised to submit one chapter that is basically ethnographic in type (if applicable), the other concerning the more general comparative and/or theoretical issues with which the thesis deals, though this advice may be varied in consultation with the supervisor(s). 35
The outline should not exceed 4,000 words, and the submitted chapters should not exceed 20,000 words in total. If these materials do exceed these limits, the assessors are under no obligation to read beyond them, though they are permitted to require the student to submit extra materials to help them in reaching a recommendation. The materials should be submitted, in two copies, to the Departmental Office, Institute of 40
Social and Cultural Anthropology.

On receiving the application the Teaching Committee of the School of Anthropology and Museum Ethnography shall appoint two assessors. The assessors shall read the script and interview the candidate before submitting to the Teaching Committee of the School of Anthropology and Museum Ethnography a reasoned 45
written report supporting their recommendation. A student whose first application is unsuccessful may be given one further opportunity to apply, following the procedures laid down, normally within one term of the original application, and may apply for an extension of time for one term if necessary for the purpose of making the application.

All D.Phil. students must give presentations on their research projects to the class 50
designated for that purpose or an agreed equivalent to qualify for confirmation of status.

5. *Submission of theses*

D.Phil. theses submitted by the students in Anthropology must not exceed 100,000 words, including notes (but excluding bibliography, glossary, and appendices containing ethnographic material and archaeological evidence), unless for exceptional reasons and on the recommendation of the candidate's supervisor the Teaching Committee of the School of Anthropology and Museum Ethnography otherwise determines.

RESEARCH DEGREES IN ARCHAEOLOGY

1. General regulations

These regulations shall apply to all students registered for the D.Phil. in Archaeology, the D.Phil. in Archaeological Science, and the D.Phil. in Classical Archaeology.

2. Transfer from Probationer Research Student status to D.Phil. status

This transfer shall normally take place not later than the fourth term after admission as a research student. The student will be required to show that the research already accomplished shows promise of the ability to produce a satisfactory D.Phil. thesis on the intended topic. For this purpose, the candidate must make an oral presentation of their work, and submit to the Archaeology Graduate Studies Committee two copies in typescript of a substantial piece of written work (of between 10,000 and 12,000 words) relevant to the proposed thesis, together with a research proposal. These should normally be submitted to the Graduate Studies Assistant at the School of Archaeology, by the Monday of the fifth week in the term in which the application is made. On receiving the application the Archaeology Graduate Studies Committee shall appoint two assessors, of whom neither shall normally be the student's supervisor. The assessors shall read the scripts and interview the candidate before submitting to the committee a reasoned written report supporting their recommendation. A student whose first application is unsuccessful may be given one further opportunity to apply for transfer, following the procedures laid down, and may apply for an extension of time for one term if necessary for the purpose of making the application.

3. Confirmation of D.Phil. status

The status of student for the Degree of Doctor of Philosophy shall be confirmed by the committee under the provisions of Regulations for the Degree of Doctor of Philosophy § 4, cl. 1. Candidates should normally apply for confirmation of status by week five of their seventh term after admission as a research student. Candidates must make an oral presentation of their work, and submit a research outline, of approximately 1,000 words, a table of contents indicating how much work has been done on each section of the thesis to date, and a draft chapter or chapters of the thesis of no more than 10,000 words. The committee will appoint two assessors who will consider the applications and will normally interview candidates. A student whose first application is unsuccessful may be given one further opportunity to apply, following the procedures laid down, normally within one term of the original application, and may apply for an extension of time for one term if this is necessary for the purpose of making the application.

4. Length of D.Phil. theses

Theses submitted for the Degrees of D.Phil. in Archaeology, Archaeological Science and Classical Archaeology should not normally exceed 80,000 words, excluding bibliography and descriptive catalogue or similar factual matter.

RESEARCH DEGREES IN EDUCATION

1. Admission

All students (whether studying on a full or part-time basis) are normally admitted as Probationer Research Students. A student admitted to study on a full-time basis is not permitted to change the basis of his or her study from full-time to part-time at any stage of his or her registration as a graduate student.

In assessing applications from candidates seeking to undertake a research degree through part-time study, the Department shall have regard to evidence that:

(i) the candidate has a minimum of three years' experience as a professional educator and is currently employed in an established post within an educational institution;

(ii) the candidate can meet the attendance requirements relating to part-time study and lives locally to the University;

(iii) the candidate has the written support of their present employer for their proposed course of study and its obligations;

(iv) the candidate's proposed topic of research is related to their present or intended professional work.

Attendance requirements (for part-time students)

Part-time research students are required to attend for a minimum of thirty days of university-based work each year, to be arranged with the agreement of their supervisor, for the period that their names remain on the Register of Graduate Students unless individually dispensed by the Department's Departmental Board.

2. Candidates with Probationer Research Student status, unless or until they have entered upon another status, or have been otherwise dispensed from some or all of the following requirements by the Director of Doctoral Research, are required to undertake the work set out below during the first year.

A first year student shall be expected to satisfactorily complete a course of lectures, seminars and classes, as set out on the pages of WebLearn and in agreement with the Director of Doctoral Research.

3. Transfer from Probationer Research Student status to D.Phil. status

This transfer shall normally take place not later than the fourth term after admission as a Probationer Research Student. The student will be required to show that the research already accomplished shows promise of the ability to produce a satisfactory D.Phil. thesis on the intended topic. For this purpose the student must submit to the Higher Degrees Office of the Department of Education two word-processed, soft bound copies of a substantial piece of written work as follows:

The submission should be about 10,000 words in length and must include:

(i) A current thesis title;

(ii) Current thesis abstract: max 400 words;

(iii) A document of up to 10,000 words that includes a background to the proposed research, including a review of the relevant literature and theoretical perspectives; the conceptual framework and rationale informing the research design; key research questions; and a reflective discussion of methods, access, research ethics and analysis;

(iv) The Transfer document should provide evidence of a convincing and realistic research design; this may include a discussion of the pilot study. It should also highlight potential challenges or difficulties that may be encountered.

The following are also required, though they are not included in the 10,000 word limit

(v) CUREC form(s) as required and clear evidence of how commitment to responsible (ethical) conduct of research will be realised

(vi) Risk assessment form including evidence that the student has considered carefully issues of safety in fieldwork

(vii) A clear timetable for the research which demonstrates that the project is feasible and practicable and can be completed within the timeframe of 3 years

(viii) A list of references

(ix) Evidence of presentation of work at a seminar (e.g. RTS, Work in Progress, Research Group Seminar, STORIES Conference etc.)

(x) A Skills Review and Training Analysis

In consultation with the student and supervisor, the Director of Doctoral Research acting on behalf of the Academic Committee shall appoint two assessors who will interview the student and make a recommendation to the committee in an agreed written report. Candidates seeking to transfer to D.Phil. Status will be expected during the interview to show evidence of research training through successful completion of the requirements of the Department's educational research methods course, unless specifically exempted from all or part of it. A candidate whose first application for transfer to D.Phil. status is unsuccessful shall be permitted to make one further application to apply for transfer within one term. Those students who fail at the second attempt may be approved for transfer to M.Litt. status, or transfer to M.Sc. by Research status.

4. Confirmation of Status

Confirmation of Status shall normally take place not later than the seventh term after admission as a Probationer Research Student. It is intended to be a comprehensive monitoring of progress towards the final thesis.

Students' application for Confirmation of Status will be examined by two assessors appointed for this purpose. The student must submit to the Higher Degrees Office of the Department of Education two printed, soft bound copies of a substantial piece of written work of about 30,000 words as follows:

(i) Current Thesis Title.

(ii) Thesis Abstract (Up to 300 words).

(iii) Proposed Thesis table of contents (indicating progress on each chapter).

(iv) A draft Introduction to the thesis, setting out the overall argument and/or contribution of the thesis. The introduction should also describe the proposed contents of each chapter, explaining how they link together and develop the thesis. These statements should normally be up to 500 words for each chapter. An extended literature review (but not the full chapter) can be submitted as Appendix A (This is important if neither of your Confirmation of Status examiners were your Transfer of Status examiners).

(v) One fully developed methods chapter that documents how the research questions were addressed in practice, and reflects on how the initial research designs were refined or developed in the field.

(vi) One draft Findings chapter. This chapter should show how the research questions are being addressed and describe the emergent findings.

(vii) A list of references for the confirmation document.

(viii) a list of references being used in the thesis more broadly.

(xi) A clear assessment of progress made, and a timetable leading up to thesis submission.

The Confirmation submission should normally be up to 30,000 words (not including abstract, references or Appendix A). Further supporting materials can be provided in appendices, for the examiners to consult if they so wish. 5

Candidates whose first application for confirmation of status is not approved shall be permitted to make one further application within one term.

5. Thesis

Theses submitted for the degree of D.Phil. should build on and develop the material submitted for Transfer of Status and Confirmation of Status. 10

A thesis for the Degree of M.Sc. by Research which exceeds 30,000 words, or a thesis for the Degree of M.Litt. which exceeds 50,000 words, or a thesis for the Degree of D.Phil. which exceeds 100,000 words, in each case including footnotes/endnotes but excluding appendices and references or bibliography, is liable to be rejected by the board unless the candidate has, with the support of his or her supervisor, secured the 15 leave of the Department's Departmental Board to exceed this limit.

RESEARCH DEGREES IN ECONOMICS, SOCIAL POLICY AND INTERVENTION, SOCIOLOGY, AND INTERNATIONAL DEVELOPMENT

1. Transfer to M.Litt. (or M.Sc. by Research) or D.Phil. status 20

Students in these subject areas will normally be expected to transfer out of Probationer Research status in their third or fourth term after admission. Applications should be submitted to the departmental Graduate Studies Committee and will comprise the following:

(a) a transfer of status form, obtainable from the relevant Graduate Studies 25 Assistant, signed by the candidate's supervisor and an appropriate college officer. The candidate should indicate clearly on the form the status to which he or she wishes to transfer; and

(b) a provisional thesis title and a short outline statement of the proposed research topic, which should include sources and methods to be used; and 30

(c) a piece of written work relevant to the thesis of between 5,000 and 7,000 words.

The Graduate Studies Committee will appoint two assessors, one of whom will normally be a member of the committee, except in cases where neither of the two most appropriate assessors is a member of the committee, who will read the work, examine the candidate orally, and submit a written report to the committee. 35

The committee will then decide whether transfer to the status applied for will be approved. In the case of applications to transfer to D.Phil. status where the committee is not satisfied that the candidate should be allowed to make the transfer it may approve admission to M.Litt. status, (or exceptionally to M.Sc. by Research Status) or approve an extension of time in order to allow the candidate to resubmit at a later date 40 (but before the end of the sixth term after admission to Probationer Research status). The committee may request additional written work or other evidence, or appoint an additional assessor, whenever it is considered necessary.

Individual Graduate Studies Committees may require additional tests or forms of assessment to be completed. Candidates are advised to consult the Notes of Guidance 45 for Graduate Students issued by each Graduate Studies Committee.

Any candidate who is admitted to M.Litt. status (or M.Sc. by Research Status) may subsequently apply for transfer to D.Phil. status before the end of the sixth term after admission to Probationer Research status. The committee will expect to see evidence of substantial developments in the progress of the research since the transfer to M.Litt. status (or M.Sc. by Research Status) before this further transfer is approved.   5

Additional regulations for the Department of Economics

Probationer Research Students in Economics are required to take a qualifying examination, unless exempted from all or part of the examination by the appropriate Graduate Studies Committee, on the grounds of an appropriate previous graduate degree or substantial professional experience since graduation. The examination con-   10
sists of the equivalent of five second year papers in the M.Phil. examination, where one first year M.Phil. paper is the equivalent of two second year papers, taken at the times set for that examination in Trinity Term. A student who does not achieve the required mark on a paper is automatically granted a two term extension to Probationer Research Student status and is allowed to resit that paper once in the following   15
Trinity Term examination, unless a special dispensation is obtained from the Graduate Studies Committee.

Probationer Research Students are required to achieve a mark of 64 on each of the papers they sit in order to pass the Qualifying Examination. In exceptional circumstances the Graduate Studies Committee may exempt a student from having to pass   20
the examination is he/she receives marks of 50 or above on each paper. All requests for exemption will require the strong support of the supervisor.

Additional regulations for International Development

Probationer Research Students in International Development who have been admitted to this status but who have not received appropriate postgraduate training in a   25
relevant aspect of development studies or of research techniques for the social sciences may, with the formal approval of the Director of Graduate Studies, the Course Director of the course concerned, and the Graduate Studies Committee for the Department of International Development, be required to attend and pass successfully any course listed for the M.Phil. in Development Studies or appropriate course from   30
another postgraduate degree at Oxford University.

This condition shall be conveyed to the student when the offer of a place is made and in such cases transfer to D.Phil. status shall not normally be permitted until this condition has been fulfilled.

2. Confirmation of D.Phil. status   35

Students who have been admitted to D.Phil. status must, not later than the ninth term or normally earlier than the sixth term after that in which he or she was initially admitted to the status of a Probationer Research Student or to the status of a student for another higher degree of the University, apply for confirmation of that status. Students would normally be expected to apply for confirmation of D.Phil. status   40
before the end of their ninth term after admission to Probationer Research status.

Requirements for confirmation of status are:

(*a*) completion of the appropriate form, obtainable from the relevant Graduate Studies Assistant, signed by the supervisor and an appropriate college officer.

(*b*) a comprehensive outline of the treatment of the thesis topic including details of   45
progress made and an indication of the anticipated timetable for submission.

(*c*) two draft chapters intended to form part of the final thesis.

The application must be submitted to the relevant Graduate Studies Committee, who will appoint assessors as appropriate. A written report on the application will be made to the committee before confirmation of D.Phil. status is approved.   50

If the committee does not consider that the candidate's progress warrants confirmation of status it may either (*a*) recommend resubmission of the application at a later date within the normal timetable (not later than six terms after admission to D.Phil. status) or (*b*) approve an extension of D.Phil. status in order to allow time for resubmission of the application or (*c*) approve transfer to M.Litt. status, or (*d*) reject   5
the application.

Individual departments may require candidates to complete other tests or assessments before confirmation is approved. Candidates are advised to consult the Notes of Guidance for Graduate Students issued by each Graduate Studies Committee.

Additional regulations for International Development   10

Probationer Research Student entrants must confirm status by the end of the ninth term after arrival in Oxford, and entrants from the M.Phil in Development Studies must do so by the end of their eleventh term after arrival in Oxford. The comprehensive outline should be up to 3,000 words. The main submission should be between 15,000 and 20,000 words of the main thesis, which can be one chapter or parts of two   15
or more chapters. It should be core material based on the writing up of fieldwork or other research.

Additional regulations for the sub-faculty of Economics

Those applying for confirmation of D.Phil. status in Economics shall present the preliminary results of their research at a departmental seminar or workshop as part of   20
the confirmation process, under arrangements to be approved by the Director of Graduate Studies.

D.Phil. students coming from the M.Phil. in Economics must confirm status by the end of their eleventh term as a graduate student in Economics at the University of Oxford, inclusive of the time spent on the M.Phil.   25

3. Theses

M.Sc. by Research

Where, exceptionally, transfer has been allowed to M.Sc. by Research status, candidates are required to submit either a thesis or two written papers not exceeding in total 25,000 words in length.   30

Theses for the Degree of M.Litt. which exceed 50,000 words, theses or written papers for the M.Sc. by Research which exceed in total 25,000 words, and those for the Degree of D.Phil. which exceed 100,000 words, excluding the bibliography, are liable to be rejected unless candidates have, with the support of their supervisors, secured the leave of the appropriate Academic Studies Committee to exceed this limit.   35
These figures are strictly *maxima*. It is not the board's intention that they should be construed as norms, and candidates are advised that many successful theses have been significantly shorter.

Additional regulations for the Department of Social Policy and Intervention

Social Policy D.Phil. Pathway: 40

A D.Phil. thesis may be accepted for examination if it consists of a minimum of four academic papers of publishable quality, framed by an introduction and a conclusion. Only one of the four academic papers may be a co-authored piece of work, with the candidate having contributed at least 70 percent of the work [to be confirmed by the co-author(s)]. Such a body of work shall be deemed acceptable provided it represents a   45
coherent and focused body of research, addressing one overarching research question. Current overall word limits and conditions are detailed in the D.Phil. Notes for Guidance. Candidates wishing to proceed in this manner must be approved at the time of confirmation of D.Phil. status.

Social Intervention D.Phil. Pathway: 50

A D.Phil. thesis may be accepted for examination if it consists of a minimum of three academic papers of publishable quality. Such a body of work shall be deemed acceptable provided it represents a coherent and focused body of research. It should include an Introduction, a Survey of Literature, and a Conclusion. Current word limits and conditions are detailed in the D.Phil. Notes for Guidance. A D.Phil. Thesis   5
submitted under this rubric may include joint publications. Where joint publications are included, all co-authors must certify in writing to the Director of Graduate Studies that the majority of that work represents the work of the candidate. Candidates wishing to proceed in this manner must obtain permission from their supervisor, from the Director of Graduate Studies, and must be approved at the time of con-   10
firmation for D.Phil. status. Evidence must be submitted at the time permission is sought that at least one of the three academic papers has been submitted to an identified journal, if not yet accepted or published. If, after a petition is accepted, a candidate wishes to revert to a standard D.Phil. thesis format, the candidate must lodge a petition with his or her supervisor to be approved by the Director of Graduate   15
Studies, showing good cause for the change.

DOCTORAL TRAINING PROGRAMME IN SCIENCE AND ENGINEERING IN ARTS, HERITAGE AND ARCHAEOLOGY

(a) Students admitted to the centre for doctoral training with the intent to pursue a   20
research project based at the University of Oxford, will be registered in the first year of the doctoral training programme at University College London, where they will complete an MRes degree. Students will also hold Recognised Student status at the University of Oxford for their first year of study. Students are required to pass the MRes in order to progress onto the second year of the doctoral training programme.   25

(b) Students transferring to the University of Oxford from the start of their second year of the doctoral training programme will be admitted to the status of Probationer Research Student. Status will be back-dated to their commencement on the doctoral training programme.

(c) Transfer of Status from Probationer Research Student to D.Phil., M.Litt. or   30
M.Sc. by research should be achieved not later than the third term following transfer to Oxford. Students are required to demonstrate that the research already accomplished shows promise of the ability to produce a satisfactory D.Phil., M.Litt. or M.Sc. by Research thesis on the intended topic. Students are required to submit to the Director of Graduate Studies a report title and abstract (of no more than 300 words/   35
one side of A4) by Friday of eighth week Michaelmas Term. Each student will also give a Transfer of Status Presentation of fifteen minutes (plus ten minutes of questions) during noughth week of Hilary Term. Students should submit two copies (and one electronic copy) of a research proposal of no more than 7,500 words, including an outline of research plans, a preliminary review of the literature, methodology progress   40
to date, bibliography and a timetable for completion to the Director of Graduate studies by Friday of eighth week Hilary Term. On receiving the application, the Director of Graduate studies will, on behalf of the Graduate Studies Committee, appoint two assessors neither of whom will normally be the student's supervisor. The assessors will read the script before submitting to the Board their reports and a joint   45
summary statement supporting their recommendation. Students will be required to attend a Transfer of Status Assessment Meeting with their supervisor(s) and assessors to discuss their report. These meetings will be held during 1st week of Trinity Term. A student whose first application is unsuccessful may be given one further opportunity

to apply for transfer, following the procedures laid down in the General Regulations Governing Research Degrees.

(d) Confirmation of D.Phil. Status should normally be achieved not later than the ninth term from commencement on the Doctoral Training Programme. The department expects that, in most cases, the application for confirmation will be made 5 immediately after return from field-work and no later than eighth week Trinity Term of the student's third year on the doctoral training programme. No candidate may submit a thesis for the doctoral degree without having first obtained confirmed doctoral status. Any student who does not confirm by the end of their ninth term, will be required to apply for a deferral of confirmation of status and may be allowed up to 10 three terms for this purpose. Any student who fails to confirm status within nine terms from commencement on the Doctoral Training Programme (or within a maximum of twelve terms where deferral has been approved) will have their student status lapsed. The purpose of the submission for confirmed status is to ensure that the student is working to a doctoral standard. The confirmation report should show evidence that 15 the research already accomplished gives promise of the ability to produce a satisfactory D.Phil. thesis on the intended topic. For this purpose the candidate must submit to the Director of Graduate Studies two copies (together with an electronic version) of a report describing in approximately 3,000 words the aims and methods of the projected thesis. The student will also be required to include with the written work 20 an outline of the proposed thesis, including the topics to be covered in individual chapters, and a timetable for completion. In addition, two substantive chapters of no more than 10,000 words each must also be submitted. Students wishing to undertake the D.Phil. via scientific papers should substitute the chapters of the thesis with two papers. On receiving the application the Director of Graduate Studies will appoint two 25 assessors (normally two academic members of staff) neither of whom will normally be the student's supervisor. The assessors will read the script before submitting to the Board their written reports and a joint summary statement supporting their recommendation. Students will be required to meet with their assessors and supervisor(s) at an assessment interview to discuss their report. A student whose first application is 30 unsuccessful may be given one further opportunity to apply for confirmation, following the procedures laid down, normally within one term if necessary for the purpose of making the application. Students will be notified of the outcome and they should receive advice from their supervisor(s) on their confirmation assessment.

(e) A full-time Student for the Degree of D.Phil. in the Centre for Doctoral 35 Training in Science and Engineering in Arts, Heritage and Archaeology, may hold status for twelve terms from commencement on the doctoral training programme. A full-time student for the Degree of M.Litt. or M.Sc. by Research may hold that status for nine terms from commencement on the doctoral training programme (six terms from transfer to Oxford). Candidates for the Degrees of D.Phil., M.Litt., or M.Sc. by 40 Research are required to submit at least two sets of all maps, diagrams, and other illustrations, one of which should be a reproduction of the original set. The copy of the thesis deposited in the Bodleian should be one of those with a complete set of maps and illustrations. Applications for leave to present only one set of maps, diagrams and other illustrations may be granted in exceptional circumstances, but such concessions 45 will be granted only very sparingly. M.Sc. by Research theses should be approximately 40,000 words, inclusive of appendices but exclusive of tables, figures, and references. M.Litt. theses should not exceed 50,000 words, exclusive of the bibliography, unless for exceptional reasons and on the recommendation of the candidate's supervisor the board otherwise determines. D.Phil. theses submitted by students in Geography must 50 not exceed 100,000 words, exclusive of the bibliography but including notes, glossary, appendices, etc., unless for exceptional reasons and on the recommendation of the candidate's supervisor the Board otherwise determines. A D.Phil. thesis may be accepted for examination if comprised of a minimum of four scientific papers submitted for publication if not yet accepted or published. Such a body of work will be deemed acceptable provided it represents a coherent and focused body or research. It should include an Introduction, a Survey of Literature, and a Conclusion. Current word limits and conditions remain in place. A D.Phil. thesis submitted under this rubric may include joint publications. In that case, all co-authors must certify in writing to the Director of Graduate Studies that the majority of the work represents that of the candidate. Candidates wishing to proceed in this manner must obtain permission from his/her supervisor(s), and the School, and must be approved at the time of confirmation for D.Phil. status. Evidence must be submitted at the time permission is sought that the scientific papers have been submitted to identified journals. If, after a petition is accepted, a candidate wishes to revert to a standard D.Phil. thesis format, the candidate must lodge a petition with his/her supervisor(s), and the School.

RESEARCH DEGREES IN GEOGRAPHY

For students admitted before 1 October 2015

1. Transfer from Probationer Research Student status to M.Litt., M.Sc., or D.Phil. status

The transfer of status normally takes place not later than the third term after admission as a research student. Students are required to demonstrate that the research already accomplished shows promise of the ability to produce a satisfactory M.Litt, M.Sc, or D.Phil. thesis on the intended topic. Students are required to submit to the director of Graduate Studies a report title and abstract (of no more than 300 words/one side of A4) by Friday of eighth week Michaelmas Term. Each student will also give a Transfer of Status Presentation of fifteen minutes (plus ten minutes of questions) during noughth week of Hilary Term. Students should submit two copies (and one electronic copy) of a research proposal of no more than 7,500 words, including an outline of research plans, a preliminary review of the literature, methodology progress to date, bibliography and a timetable for completion to the Director of Graduate studies by Friday of eighth week Hilary Term. On receiving the application, the Director of Graduate studies will, on behalf of the Graduate studies Committee, appoint two assessors (normally two members of the academic staff) neither of whom will normally be the student's supervisor. The interviewers will read the script before submitting to the board their reports and a joint summary statement supporting their recommendation. Students will be required to attend a Transfer of Status Assessment Meeting with their supervisor(s) and transfer of status assessors to discuss their report. These meetings will be held during 1st week of Trinity Term. A student whose first application is unsuccessful may be given one further opportunity to apply for transfer, following the procedures laid down, and may apply for an extension of time for one term if this is necessary for the purpose of making the application.

2. Confirmation of D.Phil. status

Application for Confirmation of D.Phil. status should normally be made not earlier than the sixth term from admission as a research student and not later than the ninth term. The department expects that, in most cases, the conformation will be made immediately after return from field-work and no later than eighth week Trinity Term of the student's third year. No candidate may submit a thesis for the doctoral degree without having first obtained confirmed doctoral status. Any student who does not confirm by the end of their ninth term, will be required to apply for a deferral of confirmation of status and may be allowed up to three terms for this purpose. Any student who fails to confirm status within nine terms of registering as a PRS (or within a maximum of twelve terms where deferral has been approved) will have their student status lapsed. Students who have taken an M.Phil. first and were admitted directly to D.Phil. status, should confirm status within three terms of starting the D.Phil. Any student who fails to confirm within nine terms of starting the M.Phil. (or within a maximum of twelve terms where deferral has been approved) will have their status lapsed. The purpose of the submission for confirmed status is to ensure that the candidate is working to a doctoral standard.

The confirmation report should show evidence that the research already accomplished gives promise of the ability to produce a satisfactory D.Phil. thesis on the intended topic. For this purpose the candidate must submit to the Director of Graduate Studies two copies (together with an electronic version) of a report describing in approximately 3,000 words the aims and methods of the projected thesis. The student will also be required to include with the written work an outline of the proposed thesis, including the topics to be covered in individual chapters, and a timetable for completion. In addition, two substantive chapters of no more than 10,000 words each must also be submitted. Candidates wishing to undertake the D.Phil. via scientific papers should substitute the chapters of the thesis with two papers.

On receiving the application the Director of Graduate studies will appoint two assessors (normally two academic members of staff) neither of whom will normally be the student's supervisor. The assessors will read the script before submitting to the board their written reports and a joint summary statement supporting their recommendation. Students will be required to meet with their assessors and supervisor at an assessment interview to discuss their report. A student whose first application is unsuccessful may be given one further opportunity to apply for confirmation, following the procedures laid down, normally within one term if necessary for the purpose of making the application. Students will be notified of the outcome and they should receive advice from their supervisor(s) on their confirmation assessment.

3. Submission of theses

Candidates for the Degrees of M.Sc., M.Litt., and D.Phil. are required to submit at least two sets of all maps, diagrams, and other illustrations, one of which should be a reproduction of the original set. The copy of the thesis deposited in the Bodleian should be one of those with a complete set of maps and illustrations.

Applications for leave to present only one set of maps, diagrams and other illustrations may be granted in exceptional circumstances, but such concessions will be granted only very sparingly.

M.Sc. theses should be approximately 40,000 words, inclusive of appendices but exclusive of tables, figures, and references.

M.Litt. theses should not exceed 50,000 words, exclusive of the bibliography, unless for exceptional reasons and on the recommendation of the candidate's supervisor the board otherwise determines.

D.Phil. theses submitted by students in Geography must not exceed 100,000 words, exclusive of the bibliography but including notes, glossary, appendices, etc., unless for exceptional reasons and on the recommendation of the candidate's supervisor the board otherwise determines.

A D.Phil. thesis may be accepted for examination if comprised of a minimum of four scientific papers submitted for publication if not yet accepted or published. Such a body of work will be deemed acceptable provided it represents a coherent and focused body or research. It should include an Introduction, a Survey of Literature, and a Conclusion. Current word limits and conditions remain in place.

A D.Phil. thesis submitted under this rubric may include joint publications. In that case, all co-authors must certify in writing to the Director of Graduate Studies of the School that the majority of the work represents that of the candidate.

Candidates wishing to proceed in this manner must obtain permission from his/her supervisor, the School, and the Divisional Board and must be approved at the time of confirmation for D.Phil. status. Evidence must be submitted at the time permission is sought that the scientific papers have been submitted to identified journals.

If, after a petition is accepted, a candidate wishes to revert to a standard D.Phil. thesis format, the candidate must lodge a petition with his/her supervisor, the School, the Divisional Board showing good cause for the change.

For students admitted after 1 October 2015

1. Transfer from Probationer Research Student status to M.Litt., M.Sc., or D.Phil. status

The transfer of status normally takes place not later than the third term after admission as a research student. Students are required to demonstrate that the research already accomplished shows promise of the ability to produce a satisfactory M.Litt., M.Sc., or D.Phil. thesis on the intended topic. Students are required to submit to the director of Graduate Studies a report title and abstract (of no more than 300 words/one side of A4) by Friday of eighth week Michaelmas Term. Each student will also give a Transfer of Status Presentation of fifteen minutes (plus ten minutes of questions) during noughth week of Hilary Term. Students should submit two copies (and one electronic copy) of a research proposal of no more than 7,500 words, including an outline of research plans, a preliminary review of the literature, methodology progress to date, bibliography and a timetable for completion to the Director of Graduate studies by Friday of eighth week Hilary Term. On receiving the application, the Director of Graduate studies will, on behalf of the Graduate studies Committee, appoint two assessors (normally two members of the academic staff) neither of whom will normally be the student's supervisor. The interviewers will read the script before submitting to the board their reports and a joint summary statement supporting their recommendation. Students will be required to attend a Transfer of Status Assessment Meeting with their supervisor(s) and transfer of status assessors to discuss their report. These meetings will be held early in Trinity Term. A student whose first application is unsuccessful may be given one further opportunity to apply for transfer, following the procedures laid down, and may apply for an extension of time for one term if this is necessary for the purpose of making the application.

2. Confirmation of D.Phil. status

Application for Confirmation of D.Phil. status should normally be made not earlier than the sixth term from admission as a research student and not later than the ninth term. The department expects that, in most cases, the conformation will be made immediately after return from field-work and no later than eighth week Trinity Term of the student's third year. No candidate may submit a thesis for the doctoral degree without having first obtained confirmed doctoral status. Any student who does not confirm by the end of their ninth term, will be required to apply for a deferral of confirmation of status and may be allowed up to three terms for this purpose. Any student who fails to confirm status within nine terms of registering as a PRS (or within a maximum of twelve terms where deferral has been approved) will have their student status lapsed. Students who have taken an M.Phil. first and were admitted directly to D.Phil. status, should confirm status within three terms of starting the D.Phil. Any student who fails to confirm within nine terms of starting the M.Phil. (or within a maximum of twelve terms where deferral has been approved) will have their status lapsed. The purpose of the submission for confirmed status is to ensure that the candidate is working to a doctoral standard.

The confirmation report should show evidence that the research already accomplished gives promise of the ability to produce a satisfactory D.Phil. thesis on the intended topic. For this purpose the candidate must submit to the Director of Graduate Studies two copies (together with an electronic version) of a report describing in approximately 3,000 words the aims and methods of the projected thesis. The student will also be required to include with the written work an outline of the proposed thesis, including the topics to be covered in individual chapters, and a timetable for completion. In addition, two substantive chapters of no more than 10,000 words each must also be submitted. Candidates wishing to undertake the D.Phil. via scientific papers should substitute the chapters of the thesis with two papers.

On receiving the application the Director of Graduate studies will appoint two assessors (normally two academic members of staff) neither of whom will normally be the student's supervisor. The assessors will read the script before submitting to the board their written reports and a joint summary statement supporting their recommendation. Students will be required to meet with their assessors and supervisor at an assessment interview to discuss their report. A student whose first application is unsuccessful may be given one further opportunity to apply for confirmation, following the procedures laid down, normally within one term if necessary for the purpose of making the application. Students will be notified of the outcome and they should receive advice from their supervisor(s) on their confirmation assessment.

3. Submission of theses

Candidates for the Degrees of M.Sc, M.Litt, and D.Phil. are required to include a complete sets of all maps, diagrams, and other illustrations, bound into the copy of the thesis deposited in the Bodleian.

M.Sc. theses should not exceed 40,000 words, M.Litt. theses should not exceed 50,000 words, and D.Phil. theses should not exceed 100,000 words. In all case word counts are inclusive of notes, glossary, appendices etc. but exclusive of tables, figures, and bibliography, unless for exceptional reasons and on the recommendation of the candidate's supervisor the board otherwise determines.

A D.Phil. thesis may be accepted for examination if comprised of a minimum of four academic papers submitted for publication in peer review journals. The papers do not have to be accepted or published. The papers must be accompanied by a framing document that will normally be between 15,000 and 20,000 words and which comprises an Introduction, Literature Review, Methodology, and Conclusion. Current word limits and conditions remain in place.

A D.Phil. thesis submitted under this rubric may include joint publications. In that case, the student should normally be the first author for papers submitted as part of their D.Phil. thesis. Where this is not the case, a clear justification should be given and all co-authors must certify in writing that the majority of the work represents that of the candidate and a letter to this effect must be submitted with the application for appointment of examiners to the Director of Graduate Studies. There are no restrictions on the number, or order, of other co-authors, reflecting the variation in established academic practice. Papers should be either incorporated as typescript pages or as offprints bound into the body of the thesis.

Candidates wishing to proceed in this manner must obtain permission from his/her supervisor and the School and must be approved at the time of confirmation for D.Phil. status. Evidence must also be submitted at this time that at least one academic paper has been submitted to an identified journals, if not yet accepted or published.

If, after an application is accepted, a candidate wishes to revert to a standard D.Phil. thesis format, the candidate must submit an application to his/her supervisor, and the School showing good cause for the change.

RESEARCH DEGREES IN LAW

1. The First Research Year

(i) All those admitted to a research degree in the Faculty of Law must in the first year follow a course of instruction in Legal Research Method approved by the Law Board (or, for students registered for the D.Phil. in Criminology, a course of instruction in Criminal Research Methods), and must satisfy the examiners that they have completed to the required standard such tests or exercises as may be prescribed by the Law Board as part of such a course of instruction. Where the Law Board judges that it has sufficient evidence of a candidate's proficiency in research methods, it may in exceptional circumstances dispense a candidate from this requirement.

(ii) Candidates admitted in the first instance as Probationer Research Students may, with the consent of the Faculty Board, transfer to the status of a student for the M.St. in Legal Research.

2. Special provisions for part-time D.Phil. Criminology students

(i) Candidates are required to meet the following attendance requirements for their period of part-time study: attendance for a minimum of 30 days of university-based work each year, normally coinciding with the full terms of the academic year, to be arranged with the agreement of their supervisor, for the period that their names remain on the Register of Graduate Students unless individually dispensed by the Graduate Studies Committee on the Board of the Faculty of Law. During a candidate's probationary period the attendance arrangements must take account of relevant induction and training events scheduled by the Centre for Criminology.

3. Transfer to the D.Phil. or M.Litt.

(i) Candidates wishing to transfer to the status of student for the degree of D.Phil. or M.Litt. must, subject to sub-paragraphs (ii) and (iii) below, undertake both parts of the Qualifying Test (paragraph 3 below).

(ii) It is not possible to transfer to M.Litt. status, having successfully completed the M.Phil. or M.St. in Legal Research, unless the candidate proposes to write an entirely new thesis. A candidate transferring to D.Phil. status is entitled to incorporate the thesis presented for the M.Phil. or M.St. in Legal Research within the D.Phil. thesis.

(iii) Candidates who at the time of the transfer will have successfully completed the M.Phil. in Law or the M.Phil. in Criminology and Criminal Justice or the M.St. in Legal Research shall submit for Part B of the Qualifying Test their successful M.Phil. or M.St. thesis. In such a case the word limits for Part B in sub-paragraph (ii) of paragraph 3 below do not apply.

(iv) Students who have previously been registered for the M.St. in Legal Research or for the M.Phil. in Law or M.Phil. in Criminology and Criminal Justice, and have been granted leave to supplicate for either of these degrees, but have been referred on their application to transfer to D.Phil. status, may conditionally hold the status of Probationer Research Student, provided that the Faculty Board is satisfied that the student fulfils the conditions set out in the appropriate regulation. Probationer Research Student status in this instance may not be held for more than six terms beyond the date at which they first held the status of a student for the M.St. in Legal Research or for the M.Phil. in Law or M.Phil. in Criminology and Criminal Justice.

4. The Qualifying Test

   (i) Part A of the Qualifying Test requires that the candidate shall submit to the Faculty of Law Graduate Studies Office (or, for students registered for the D.Phil. in Criminology, to the Graduate Studies Administrator within the Centre for Criminology) two typescript or printed copies of a statement of the subject of the proposed thesis and details of the manner in which the candidate proposes to treat it. This statement shall not exceed 2,000 words.

   (ii) Subject to sub-paragraph (iii) of paragraph 2 above, Part B of the Qualifying Test requires that the candidate shall submit to the Faculty of Law Graduate Studies Office (or, for students registered for the D.Phil. in Criminology, to the Graduate Studies Administrator within the Centre for Criminology) two typescript or printed copies of a substantial piece of written work which may or may not be intended to form part of the proposed thesis but must be relevant to its subject. For transfer to the D.Phil., this Part B submission must not exceed 10,000 words, for the M.Litt., 6,000 words. In each case the candidate must state the number of words used. The required format for this submission is the common format prescribed for all law theses which is printed in the Faculty of Law's Graduate Students' Handbook.

   (iii) Supervisors of candidates offering Part B are required to discuss with the candidate the names of possible assessors, and to provide the Board (or, for students registered for the D.Phil. in Criminology, the Director of Graduate Studies (Research)) with the names of three suitable persons who have indicated their willingness to act as assessors if called upon to do so. This notification may be made before the submission of the material, but must be made, at the latest, on the day the material is submitted. (For students registered for the D.Phil. in Criminology, two assessors will be appointed by the Director of Graduate Studies (Research) in consultation with the supervisor).

   (iv) Subject to sub-paragraph (v) below, candidates admitted as Probationer Research Students to the doctoral or M.Litt. programmes, must submit all materials for the Qualifying Test by the end of the fourth week of Full Term in the third term after the candidate's admission. Candidates enrolled on the part-time D.Phil. in Criminology shall submit their materials by the end of the fourth week of Full Term in the sixth term after the candidate's admission.

   (v) Subject to the general time-limit in sub-paragraph (vi) below, the Graduate Studies Committee, having consulted with the supervisor, may, for good cause, allow the Qualifying Test to be deferred. Applications for deferral must be made through the Faculty of Law Graduate Studies Office (or, for students registered for the D.Phil. in Criminology, to the Graduate Studies Administrator within the Centre for Criminology) in time to allow the Graduate Studies Committee to consider the matter in the second week of the candidate's third term. For candidates enrolled on the part-time D.Phil. in Criminology, applications for deferral must be made in time to allow the Graduate Studies Committee to consider the matter in the second week of the candidate's sixth term.

   (vi) In no case may the materials for the Qualifying Test be submitted or resubmitted after the end of the fourth term from the admission of the student to the doctoral or M.Litt. programmes. A student will in any case cease to hold PRS status if he or she does not gain admission to another status within four terms of admission as a full-time student. In the case of candidates enrolled on the part-time D.Phil. in Criminology, materials for the Qualifying Test may not be submitted or resubmitted after the end of the eighth term from the admission of the student to the doctoral programme.

5. Assessing the Qualifying Test

(i) The Director of Graduate Studies shall appoint two assessors and shall report their appointments to the Board.

(ii) The assessors shall interview the candidate.

(iii) The assessors shall report in writing as to (a) the suitability of the candidate's subject for the kind of thesis in question and (b) the competence of the candidate to handle it at the required level; and, in accordance with their report, the assessors shall make a recommendation.

(iv) On the original submission for the Qualifying Test, the assessors may recommend (a) that the candidate be granted the transfer which has been applied for, or (b) that the candidate be permitted to resubmit Part A or, in the case in which the candidate is a Probationary Research Student, Part B or both Part A and Part B; in the case in which the candidate offers a successful M.Phil. or M.St. thesis for Part B within sub-paragraph (iii) of paragraph 2 above, there can be no reference back except in relation to Part A. Hence in a case in which, despite having earned the degree for which it was submitted, the thesis fails to satisfy the assessors of Part B of the Qualifying Test, the permission to transfer must be refused.

(v) Unless, for good cause shown, the Director of Graduate Studies, after consultation with the supervisor, agrees to an extension of time, the assessors must lodge their report and recommendation with the Faculty of Law Graduate Studies Office (or, for students registered for the D.Phil. in Criminology, to the Graduate Studies Administrator, the Centre for Criminology) within one calendar month of the date on which the materials are sent out to them.

(vi) The Faculty of Law Graduate Studies Office (or, for students registered for the D.Phil. in Criminology, to the Graduate Studies Administrator, the Centre for Criminology) shall pass the report and recommendation to the Director of Graduate Studies (or, for students registered for the D.Phil. in Criminology, the Director of Graduate Studies (Research)), who has the authority of the Board to inform the candidate without further delay of the nature of the recommendation and to inform the supervisor of the contents of the report.

(vii) Where the assessors have recommended resubmission, the candidate should normally resubmit at any time before the end of the subsequent term following the original submission. On resubmission the assessors may recommend (a) that the candidate be granted the transfer requested or (b) that the candidate be refused permission to transfer. In the case of a Probationary Research Student the effect of the latter recommendation is to entitle the candidate to apply for transfer to the M.St. in Legal Research under the appropriate regulation, with effect retrospective to the original registration as a Probationary Research Student. Such applications will be considered by the Graduate Studies Committee. For candidates enrolled on the part-time D.Phil. in Criminology, the candidate should normally resubmit at any time before the end of the second term following the original submission.

(viii) The Director of Graduate Studies shall place the report of the assessors before the meeting of the Graduate Studies Committee next following its receipt by The Faculty of Law Graduate Studies Office (or, for students registered for the D.Phil. in Criminology, to the Graduate Studies Administrator at the Centre for Criminology).

6. Confirmation of D.Phil. status

    (i) Applications for confirmation of status shall normally be made not earlier than the sixth term, and confirmation of status must normally be completed no later than three terms after the Qualifying Test. Candidates enrolled on the part-time D.Phil. in Criminology shall normally apply for confirmation of   5 status not earlier than the twelfth term following their admission, and confirmation of status must normally be completed not later than six terms after the Qualifying Test.

    (ii) Application for confirmation of D.Phil. status shall be accompanied by (a) a statement giving the title of the thesis, and summarising each component   10 chapter in approximately 100 words per chapter, (b) an overview of the intended thesis, of approximately 1,000 words, stating how much of the thesis is complete and how much remains to be done (with an estimate of the probable date of completion), and (c) a piece of written work, which shall normally be of 20,000–30,000 words in length and intended to form part of the   15 thesis.

    (iii) The candidate's supervisor shall provide a report on the candidate's application upon the form provided for this purpose or in a separate communication sent directly to the Graduate Studies Administrator. The report shall comment upon the accuracy of the account and feasibility of the timetable, and upon the   20 candidate's progress, together with an estimate of the probable date of completion.

    (iv) The documents described above under (ii) and (iii) shall be considered by two assessors, appointed by the Graduate Studies Committee, one of whom shall, wherever practicable, be one of those who acted at the time of the candidate's   25 transfer to D.Phil. status. The assessors shall interview the candidate and submit a joint written report to the Graduate Studies Committee, normally within one month of receiving the application. The report shall include a recommendation as to whether the application should be approved. The faculty may grant the application or refer it back for resubmission. Only one   30 resubmission for confirmation may be submitted, and no such resubmission will normally be permitted after the end of the candidate's ninth term. For candidates enrolled in the part-time D.Phil. in Criminology, resubmission will not normally be permitted after the end of the candidate's eighteenth term.

7. All theses and dissertations in law must conform to the statement which appears   35 in the Law Faculty's Graduate Students' Handbook under the title 'Format of Theses in the Faculty of Law'.

RESEARCH DEGREES IN POLITICS AND INTERNATIONAL RELATIONS

(See also the general notice at the commencement of these regulations. The current   40 *edition of the relevant Student Handbook contains an elaborated version of these regulations.)*

Candidates with Probationer Research Student status, unless or until they have entered upon another status, or have been otherwise dispensed from some or all of the following requirements by the relevant Graduate Studies Committee, are required to   45 undertake the work set out below during the first year.

1. A first-year student shall:

    (i) satisfactorily complete a course of lectures, seminars, and classes, as determined in the relevant Student Handbook and supplemented by his or her supervisor;   50

(ii) satisfactorily complete a course of research methods training, as determined in the relevant Student Handbook and supplemented by his or her supervisor and/or by the relevant Director of Research Training.

2. Applications for transfer from Probationer Research Student status to D.Phil. or M.Litt. status must be submitted in accordance with the requirements in the relevant   5
Student Handbook. Applicants in their fourth and final term of Probationer Status must submit their completed application including all written work not later than 5 p.m. on the Friday of sixth week of that term, except in Trinity Term when the accompnying written work must be submitted no later than 5 p.m. on the last Friday in August. Students unable to meet these deadlines may apply for up to two terms of   10
deferral of transfer of status. In addition to satisfying the above requirements (i) and (ii), the transfer of status application must include two copies of an outline of the proposed research topic and two copies of the written work-all as specified in the relevant Student Handbook. The relevant Graduate Studies Committee will appoint two assessors. Upon receiving the report of the assessors, the GCS will then decide   15
whether to approve the transfer. In the case of applications to transfer to D.Phil. status where the committee does not so approve, it may authorise an extension of one term in order to allow the candidate to resubmit.

3. Applications for confirmation of D.Phil. status must be submitted in accordance with the requirements in the relevant Student handbook. Applicants in their ninth   20
term must submit their completed application including all written work not later than 5 p.m. on the Friday of sixth week of that term, except in trinity when the accompanying written work must be submitted no later than 5 p.m. on the last Friday in August. Students unable to meet these deadlines may apply for up to three terms of deferral of confirmation of D.Phil. status. The confirmation of status application must   25
include two copies of the written work - all as specified in the relevant Student Handbook. The relevant Graduate Studies Committee will appoint two assesssors. Upon receiving the report of the assessors, the GSC will then decide whether to approve confirmation of D.Phil. status. In the case of applications to confirm D.Phil. status where the committee does not so approve, it may authorise an extension   30
of one term in order to allow the candidate to resubmit.

4. Students admitted directly to D.Phil. status having completed an Oxford M.Phil. and whose M.Phil. thesis was in the same broad field as the D.Phil. research proposal must confirm D.Phil. status within ten terms as a graduate student, inclusive of time spent on the M.Phil. Applications for confirmation of D.Phil. status must be sub-   35
mitted in accordance with the requirements of the relevant Student Handbook. Applicants in their tenth term must submit the completed application including all written work not later than 5 p.m. on the Friday of the sixth week of that term, except in Trinity Term when the accompanying written work must be submitted no later than 5 p.m. on the last Friday in August. Students unable to meet these deadlines may   40
apply for up to two terms of deferral of confirmation of D.Phil. status. The confirmation of status application must include two copies of the written work - all as specified in the relevant Student Handbook. The relevant Graduate Studies Committee will appoint two assassors. Upon receiving the report of the assessors, the GSC will then decide whether to approve confirmation of D.Phil. status. In the case of applications   45
to confirm D.Phil. status where the committee does not approve, it may authorise an extension of time in order to allow the candidate to resubmit.

5. Though not in itself sufficient qualification for students wishing to advance to M.Litt. or D.Phil. status, the successful completion of the M.Sc. in Politics Research or the M.Sc. in Political Theory Research may serve in place of 1. (i) and (ii) above,   50
and material submitted as part of the requirements for the M.Sc. may also be used in the transfer application.

6. Four paper route

A D.Phil. thesis may be accepted for examination if it consists of a minimum of four academic papers of publishable quality, framed by an introduction, a survey of literature and a conclusion. Such a body of work shall be deemed acceptable provided it represents a coherent and focused body of research, addressing one overarching research question. Current overall word limits and conditions are detailed in the D.Phil. Student Handbook. Candidates wishing to proceed in this manner must be approved at the time of Transfer of status.

If, after a petition is accepted, a candidate wishes to revert to a standard D.Phil. thesis format, the candidate must lodge a petition with his or her supervisor to be approved by the Director of Graduate Studies, showing good cause for the change.

RESEARCH DEGREES IN THE SAÏD BUSINESS SCHOOL

1. Probationer Research Students

All students are normally admitted as Probationer Research Students (PRS).

Unless granted a dispensation by the D.Phil. Committee of the Saïd Business School, during their first year, Probationer Research Students shall:

(*a*) attend such lectures, seminars and classes as his or her supervisor and/or the committee shall determine;

(*b*) satisfactorily complete such courses and coursework as the supervisor and/or the committee shall determine, dependant upon which course the student has already taken prior to commencing the D.Phil.;

(*c*) applications to D.Phil. Committee for exemption from the above will be considered.

2. Transfer of status

Students who have taken the M.Sc. in Management Research or MFE prior to commencing their D.Phil. study as a PRS are normally expected to transfer status in their third term. All students must transfer status by the end of their fourth term.

Applications for transfer of status must be submitted to the D.Phil. Committee and should be comprised of the following:

(*a*) a transfer of status form (GSO.2), signed by the student's supervisor and an appropriate college officer. The candidate should indicate clearly on the form the status to which he or she wishes to transfer;

(*b*) a good pass in all of the courses and coursework as stated in 1.(b) above, approved by the student's supervisor;

(*c*) a satisfactory research proposal or research outline;

(*d*) where appropriate, one draft chapter of the thesis.

Further details of these requirements are set out in the D.Phil. Notes for Guidance.

Two assessors nominated by the student and his/her supervisor and appointed by the D.Phil. Committee will examine the student by viva voce and submit a written transfer report to the D.Phil. Committee with recommendations as to whether or not the student should be allowed to transfer to D.Phil. status.

The D.Phil. Committee will consider the application and the recommendations of the assessors and in light of this will decide whether to approve the transfer of status, or approve admission to M.Litt. status (in the case that the Committee is not satisfied that the candidate should be allowed to transfer), or approve an extension of time in order to allow the candidate to carry out further research and make revisions to his/

her proposal and to resubmit at a later date (but before the PRS status period expires). The committee may request additional written work (such as a revised research proposal) or other evidence, and/or appoint an additional assessor, and/or state that the student should be re-examined.

3. Confirmation of D.Phil. status

Students will normally be expected to apply for their Confirmation of Status by the end of their sixth term after admission. They must apply for their Confirmation of Status by the end of their ninth term.

Applications for confirmation of status as a Student for the Degree of Doctor of Philosophy shall comprise the following:

(*a*) a confirmation of status application form (GSO14) signed by the candidate's supervisor and an appropriate officer of the candidate's college;

(*b*) a comprehensive outline of the treatment of the thesis topic including details of progress made and an indication, where possible, of the anticipated time-table for submission;

(*c*) two draft chapters totalling no more than 25,000 words which include mate-rial particularly central to the thesis.

Further details of these requirements are set out in the D.Phil. Notes for Guidance.

The application must be submitted to the D.Phil. Committee and will be considered by two assessors nominated by the student and supervisor and appointed by D.Phil. Committee. These may be the same assessors as were chosen for the transfer of status, but assessors selected at this stage may not be chosen for the final viva voce. The assessors will read the work, interview the candidate (examine viva voce) and make a recommendation to the committee in a written report.

If the committee does not consider that the candidate's progress warrants confirma-tion of status it may either recommend resubmission of the application at a later date within the normal timetable, or approve an extension of D.Phil. status in order to allow time for resubmission of the application, or recommend transfer to M.Litt. status, or reject the application.

4. Three paper route

A D.Phil. thesis may be accepted for examination if comprised of a minimum of three academic papers of publishable quality. Such a body of work shall be deemed acceptable provided it represents a coherent and focused body of research. It should include an Introduction, a Survey of Literature, and a Conclusion. Current word limits and conditions are detailed in the D.Phil. Notes for Guidance.

A D.Phil. Thesis submitted under this rubric may include joint publications, pro-viding that, aside from the candidate, none of the named co-authors is a student. Where a joint publication with another student is included, this must be in addition to the minimum of three academic papers required to be included in the D.Phil. thesis. Where joint publications are included, all co-authors must certify in writing to the Director of Graduate Studies of the School that the majority of that work represents the work of the candidate.

Candidates wishing to proceed in this manner must obtain permission from his/her supervisor, the Director of Graduate Studies, and the D.Phil. Committee and must be approved at the time of confirmation for D.Phil. status. Evidence must be submitted at the time permission is sought that at least one of the three academic papers has been submitted to an identified journal, if not yet accepted or published.

If, after a petition is accepted, a candidate wishes to revert to a standard D.Phil. thesis format the candidate must lodge a petition with his/her supervisor, the School and D.Phil. Committee showing good cause for the change.

5. Thesis

Theses for the Degree of M.Litt. which exceed 50,000 words and those for the Degree of D.Phil. which exceed 100,000, excluding the bibliography, are liable to be rejected unless candidates have, with the support of their supervisors, secured the prior dispensation of the board of Graduate Studies to exceed this limit. 5

RESEARCH DEGREES IN THE OXFORD INTERNET INSTITUTE

1. Admissions

Applicants shall be required to satisfy the Graduate Studies Committee of the Oxford Internet Institute that they have: 10

(*a*) a Master's degree or other advanced degree, normally in one of the social sciences, and normally passed with a mark of at least 67 per cent or an equivalent level of distinction;

(*b*) achieved at least a 2.1 (or its equivalent) at first degree level;

(*c*) for students whose first language is not English, have met the higher level of the 15 University's English language requirements; and that they are;

(*d*) well-fitted to undertake research at doctoral level.

2. Probationer Research Students

All students are normally admitted as Probationer Research Students.

Unless granted a dispensation by the Graduate Studies Committee of the Oxford 20 Internet Institute, Probationer Research Students during their first year shall:

(*a*) attend such lectures, seminars, and classes as his or her supervisor and/or the committee shall determine;

(*b*) attend and satisfactorily complete such courses or classes from the Institute's Research Methods Training Programme as directed by the committee; 25

(*c*) attend and satisfactorily complete the Institute's Social Dynamics of the Internet course.

3. Transfer to M.Litt. or D.Phil. status

Students will normally be expected to transfer to D.Phil. (or M.Litt.) status in their third or fourth term as a Probationer Research Student at the Oxford Internet 30 Institute. Applications should be submitted to the Graduate Studies Committee of the Oxford Internet Institute and will comprise the following:

(*a*) a transfer of status form, signed by the candidate's supervisor and an appropriate officer of the candidate's college;

(*b*) confirmation from the candidate's supervisor that such courses as the candidate 35 has been required to undertake have been satisfactorily completed;

(*c*) an outline of their research (one side of A4 paper);

(*d*) a detailed research proposal of no more than 6,000 words. This should:

(i) draw upon relevant literature to discuss the background to the research, theoretical perspectives, and possible outcomes to the research; 40

(ii) state key research questions;

(iii) discuss the overall methodological approach, and specific strategies, to be employed in answering these research questions, paying particular attention to practical and ethical issues relevant to the research.

(*e*) a preliminary timetable for the research; 45

(*f*) a list of references;

(*g*) OII Training Needs Assessment Form.

The application will be considered by a specially constituted panel of two assessors appointed by the Graduate Studies Committee of the Oxford Internet Institute. The panel will read the work, interview the candidate and make a recommendation to the committee in a reasoned written report.

Candidates will be expected during the interview to show evidence of their under-   5
standing of general theory and research methods in the social sciences applicable to their proposed study and specific research methods appropriate to the study of social aspects of the Internet and related ICTs.

A student whose first application is unsuccessful may be given one further opportunity to apply for transfer, following the procedures laid down, and may apply for an   10
extension of time for one term if this is necessary for the purpose of making the application.

4. Confirmation of status

Applications for confirmation of status as a Student for the Degree of Doctor of Philosophy should be made not earlier than the sixth term from admission as a PRS.   15
Any student who does not confirm status by the end of the ninth term, will be required to apply for deferral of confirmation of status and may be allowed up to three terms for this purpose. Applications submitted to the Graduate Studies Committee of the Oxford Internet Institute shall comprise the following:

(*a*) a confirmation of status application form signed by the candidate's supervisor   20
and an appropriate officer of the candidate's college;

(*b*) an abstract of the thesis (one side of A4 paper);

(*c*) an outline structure of the thesis, consisting of chapter headings, and a brief statement of the intended content;

(*d*) an outline timetable detailing what work has already been carried out and what   25
activities are planned for the remaining stages;

(*e*) two completed draft chapters intended to form part of the final thesis;

(*f*) OII Training Needs Assessment Form.

The application will be considered by a specially constituted panel of two assessors appointed by the Graduate Studies Committee of the Oxford Internet Institute. The   30
panel will read the work, interview the candidate and make a recommendation to the committee in a written report.

A student whose first application is unsuccessful may be given one further oppor-
tunity to apply for confirmation, following the procedures laid down, and may apply for an extension of time for one term if this is necessary for the purpose of making the   35
application.

5. Thesis

The thesis must not exceed 100,000 words for D.Phil., or 50,000 for M.Litt., the limit to include abstract, all notes and appendices but not the bibliography. Any thesis exceeding this limit is liable to be rejected on that ground unless prior dispensation has   40
been granted by the Graduate Studies Committee on the advice of the candidate's supervisor.

RESEARCH DEGREES IN THE BLAVATNIK SCHOOL OF GOVERNMENT

1. Admissions   45

Applicants shall be required to satisfy the Graduate Studies Committee of the Blavatnik School of Government that they have:

(*a*) a good 2.1 (or equivalent) undergraduate degree;

(*b*) a relevant Master's degree or other advanced degree, and normally passed with a mark of at least 70 per cent or an equivalent level of distinction both for the thesis and the overall degree;

(*c*) for students whose first language is not English, have met the higher level of the University's English language requirements; and that they are:

(*d*) well-suited to undertake research at doctoral level.

2. Transfer to D.Phil. status

Students will normally be admitted as Probationer Research Students. Applications for Transfer of Status should be submitted to the Graduate Studies Committee of the Blavatnik School of Government no later than the end of Trinity *full term* after the Michaelmas Term in which they were admitted. An extension of one term (i.e. to the end of the Michaelmas full term in the year after the student was admitted) may be granted in exceptional circumstances. Should students be admitted in other terms, submission should take place by the end of the third term after admission, with the possibility of an extension for a further one term in exceptional circumstances.

The student will be required to show that the research already accomplished shows promise of the ability to produce a satisfactory D.Phil. For this purpose, applications will comprise the following:

(*a*) a transfer of status form, signed by the candidate's supervisor and an appropriate officer of the candidate's college;

(*b*) confirmation from the candidate's supervisor that such courses as the candidate has been required to undertake have been satisfactorily completed;

(*c*) two copies in typescript of a brief, single paragraph summary of the project, including information on methodological and theoretical approach.

(*d*) two copies in typescript of a research proposal of no more than 4,000 - 6,000 words. This should consist of:

    i. a short description of the project, including the research question and a provisional list of chapter headings;

    ii. a brief account of the relevant literature, and an account of how the research question and data analysis fit into it;

    iii. an account of the proposed research methods including (a) data sources (for theoretical theses this should be a list of books and articles), (b) proposals for data handling, (c) proposals for data analysis, and (d) an account of how the proposed research and analysis are envisaged to bear on the question posed;

    iv. a tentative timetable for the research;

(*e*) two copies in typescript of a draft chapter (for example the literature review) of between 5,000 and 7,000 words

The application will be considered by two assessors appointed by the Graduate Studies Committee of the Blavatnik School of Government. The panel will read the work, interview the candidate and make a recommendation to the committee in a written report.

The committee will decide in the light of the assessors' report whether to grant the application. In cases where the committee is not satisfied that the transfer to D.Phil. status should be allowed, it may either (a) approve admission to M.Litt. status or (b) approve an extension of time in order to allow the candidate to carry out further research and make revisions to his/her proposal and to resubmit it at a later date (but before the PRS status period expires). The committee may request additional written work (such as a revised research proposal or revised literature review) or other evidence, and/or appoint an additional assessor, and/or state that the student should be re-examined.

3. Confirmation of status

Application for Confirmation of D.Phil. status should normally be made not later   5
than the seventh term from admission as a research student. No candidate may submit a thesis for the doctoral degree without having first obtained confirmed doctoral status. Any student who does not confirm by the end of their ninth term will be required to apply for deferral of confirmation of status and, in exceptional circumstances, may be allowed up to three terms for this purpose.   10

The student will be required to show that the research already accomplished shows promise of the ability to produce a satisfactory D.Phil. Applications should be submitted to the Graduate Studies Committee of the Blavatnik School of Government and will comprise the following:

(*a*) a confirmation of status application form signed by the candidate's supervisor   15
and an appropriate officer of the candidate's college;

(*b*) two copies in typescript of an abstract of the thesis (one side of A4 paper);

(*c*) two copies in typescript of an outline structure of the thesis, consisting of chapter headings, and a brief statement of the intended content;

(*d*) two copies in typescript of an outline timetable detailing what work has already   20
been carried out and what activities are planned for the remaining stages;

(*e*) two copies in typescript of two completed draft chapters (other than the literature review) intended to form part of the final thesis.

The application will be considered by a specially constituted panel of two assessors appointed by the Graduate Studies Committee of the Blavatnik School of   25
Government. The panel will read the work, interview the candidate and make a recommendation to the committee in a written report.

If, in the light of the assessors' report, the committee does not consider that the candidate's progress warrants confirmation of status, it may either (a) recommend resubmission of the application at a later date within the normal timetable (not later   30
than six terms after admission to D.Phil. status) or (b) approve an extension of D.Phil. status in order to allow time for resubmission of the application, or (c) approve transfer to M.Litt. status, or (d) reject the application.

4. Thesis

The D.Phil. thesis must not exceed 80,000 words, the limit to include abstract, all   35
notes and appendices but not the bibliography.

M.Litt. theses should not exceed 50,000 words, the limit to include all notes and appendices but not the bibliography.

NOTES

22

RESEARCH DEGREES IN THE DEPARTMENT OF CONTINUING EDUCATION

1. For the purposes of this section the word 'board' shall include any body that has been authorised by the Continuing Education Board with power to act on its behalf to admit students to read for the Degree of Doctor of Philosophy; and to assess students with PRS or D.Phil. status.

2. *Admission*

(*a*) Students are admitted to study on part-time basis only.

(*b*) Students are admitted *either*

    (i) as Probationer Research Students, *or*

    (ii) as a D.Phil. student. Students may, at the discretion of the Continuing Education Board, be admitted to D.Phil. status under the provisions of Sect. 15, para. 2, cl. 1(i). Students who have successfully completed the M.Sc. in Advanced Cognitive Therapy, the M.Sc. in Applied Landscape Archaeology, the M.Sc. in English Local History, the M.Sc. in Evidence-Based Health Care, the M.St. in Mindfulness-Based Cognitive Therapy, the M.Sc. in Professional Archaeology, the M.Sc. in Sustainable Urban Development, or any other relevant Oxford Masters degree deemed an acceptable prerequisite by the board, may be admitted under these provisions.

(*c*) In assessing applications from candidates seeking to undertake a research degree through part-time study, the board shall have regard to evidence that:

    (i) the candidates can meet the attendance requirements relating to part-time study;

    (ii) the candidates are well-fitted to undertake research at doctoral level;

    (iii) the candidate's personal and professional circumstances are such that it is both practicable for them to fulfil the requirements of the course, and necessary for them to study on a part-time basis;

    (iv) if appropriate, the candidates have the written support of their present employer for their proposed course of study and its obligations;

    (v) the proposed field of research can be appropriately supervised under the auspices of the Continuing Education Board.

3. *Attendance requirements*

Students are required to attend for a minimum of thirty days of university-based work each year, to be arranged with the agreement of their supervisor, for the period that their names remain on the Register of Graduate Studies unless individually dispensed by the Continuing Education Board.

4. *Probationer Research Student*

A research student in Archaeology or Architectural History or Cognitive-Behavioural Therapy or English Local History or Evidence-Based Health Care or

Sustainable Urban Development admitted to Probationer Research Student status shall normally be required to:

(i) attend such lectures, seminars, and classes as his or her supervisor shall determine, and provide evidence of his or her attendance; and

(ii) present one seminar paper which shall be assessed by one or two assessors. Such assessors should not normally include the candidate's supervisor; and

(iii) submit an essay of between 3,000 and 5,000 words, being either a section of the candidate's proposed thesis or an essay on a relevant topic, and a brief statement limited to 500 words, of the subject of the thesis and the manner in which the candidate proposes to treat it.

5. *Admission/transfer to D.Phil. status*

(*a*) Applicants must demonstrate that they are capable of producing research work of the requisite standard and presenting the findings clearly; and that their planned programme of research is one that may be profitably undertaken at Oxford; and that they have a good knowledge and understanding of the work that is likely to be needed to embark on the programme.

(*b*) Students who have successfully completed the M.Sc in Advanced Cognitive Therapy, M.Sc. in Applied Landscape Archaeology, the M.St. or M.Sc. in English Local History, the M.Sc. in Evidence-Based Health Care, the M.St. in Mindfulness-Based Cognitive Therapy, the M.St. or M.Sc. in Professional Archaeology, the M.Sc. in Sustainable Urban Development, or any other relevant Oxford Masters degree deemed an acceptable prerequisite by the board, shall normally apply for admission to D.Phil. status up to the twelfth term after their initial admission as a graduate student.

(*c*) Students who hold the status of Probationary Research Student, shall normally apply for admission to D.Phil. status after a minimum of six terms and no longer than eight terms.

(*d*) A student may be permitted to hold the status of Probationary Research Student for up to a further four terms subject to the provisions of Chapter 12, Section 4 cl.7.

(*e*) Admission to D.Phil. status may be made conditional on such requirements as the board may impose.

(*f*) Applicants should specify the date by which they undertake to make available two (or in exceptional cases, three) copies of the written work in support of the application. Applicants should do so not later than four weeks before the start of the full term in which they wish to be assessed. Application for transfer should be sent to the Registry, Department for Continuing Education, 1 Wellington Square.

(*g*) Applications for transfer to D.Phil. status shall be accompanied by:

(1) a brief statement, limited to 500 words, of the subject of the thesis and the manner in which the candidate proposes to treat it.

(2) a report from the supervisor, which should be sent by the supervisor direct to the Registry of the Department for Continuing Education.

(3) *either*, **for research students in Archaeology, Architectural History, Cognitive-Behavioural Therapy, English Local History, and Evidence-Based Health Care**:

a piece of written work, normally 3,000 to 5,000 words long, being *either* (a) a section of the proposed thesis, *or* (b) an essay on a relevant topic, *or* (c) an augmented version of the statement under (1) above;

[Candidates should note that if they adopt alternative (c) above they must also submit the required 500 word statement.]

or, **for research students in Sustainable Urban Development**:

(*a*) a proposal of not more than 7,500 words, which includes: thesis title; outline of research plans; preliminary review of the literature; preliminary review of methodology; progress to date; timetable to completion; fieldwork design; bibliography; *and*

(*b*) a presentation (of 15 minutes duration, plus 10 minutes for questions) outlining the aims and objectives of the research, the literature used, the proposed methodologies, and the progress to date.

The Registry shall send the written work and the supervisor's report to the assessors appointed by the board.

(*h*) Candidates should also note that while as precise a definition of the subject should be given as is possible at this stage of their work, they are not bound to follow the statement precisely, but may reformulate their plan in the light of further study. If reformulation goes so far as to require alteration of the title of the thesis as approved, however, they should seek permission of the relevant board to alter it.

(*i*) Candidates shall be assessed by two assessors appointed by the board, neither of whom will normally be the student's supervisor. The assessors shall certify that they have considered the written work submitted by the applicant and interviewed the applicant. The assessors should also provide a written report of the application to the board for approval of their recommendation. In cases where the assessors decide that the application is not of the required standard to transfer to D.Phil. status their written report should outline the areas in which the application is judged to fall short of the required standard.

(*j*) A candidate who is unsuccessful may be given one further opportunity to apply for transfer (within the limit of eight terms). A candidate whose second application for transfer is unsuccessful shall cease to hold the status of a Probationary Research Student.

6. *Confirmation of D.Phil. status*

(*a*) Assessors are appointed by the board to assess whether a candidate's work on their thesis is developing satisfactorily and that they may be considered ready to be examined within three further terms. D.Phil. status must be confirmed before a candidate may submit their thesis for examination for the degree of D.Phil.

(*b*) Application for confirmation of D.Phil. status, with statements of support from the candidate's society and supervisor, shall normally be presented to the Registry of the Department for Continuing Education not earlier than four weeks before the end of the twelfth term, and at the latest by four weeks before the end of the eighteenth term, after admission to the status of Probationer Research Student or to status of student for another higher degree of the University.

(*c*) Application for confirmation of D.Phil. status shall normally be accompanied by:

(1) a report from the supervisor which should be sent directly to the Registry of the Department for Continuing Education.

(2) either, **for research students in Archaeology, Architectural History, Cognitive-Behavioural Therapy, English Local History, and Evidence-Based Health Care**:

(*a*) a statement of the title of the thesis and of the manner in which the candidate proposes to treat it. This should include a proposed chapter structure; and

(*b*) a specimen chapter or part of a chapter not longer than 10,000 words in the case of Archaeology, and Cognitive-Behavioural Therapy and Evidence-Based Health Care or 6,000 words in the case of Architectural History and English Local History; 5

or, **for research students in Sustainable Urban Development**:

(*a*) a report of not more than 3,000 words that includes: the thesis title; a thesis outline (including contents page and a brief summary of the content of individual chapters); the aims and methods of the thesis; a timetable for completion; and 10

(*b*) two substantive chapters, each of no more than 10,000 words, based on the research findings.

The Registry should send the written work and the supervisor's report to the interviewer appointed by the board. 15

(*d*) Candidates shall be assessed by two assessors appointed by the board, at least one of whom will not be the student's supervisor. The assessment shall include an oral examination. The assessors shall also provide a written report of the application to the board for approval of their recommendation. In cases where the assessors decide that the application is not of the required standard to 20 warrant confirmation of D.Phil. status, their written report should outline the areas in which the application is judged to fall short of the required standard.

(*e*) A student who is unsuccessful may be given one further opportunity to apply for confirmation (within the statutory limit).

7. *Theses* 25

Theses submitted for the degree of D.Phil. in *Archaeology* should not normally exceed 80,000 words, *excluding* bibliography and descriptive catalogue or similar factual matter.

Theses submitted for the degree of D.Phil. in Cognitive-Behavioural Therapy shall not exceed 80,000 words. This shall *include* all notes, appendices, any source 30 material being edited, and all other parts of the thesis whatsoever *excluding only* the bibliography.

Theses submitted for the degree of D.Phil. in *Architectural History* and in *English Local History* and *Evidence-Based Health Care* and *Sustainable Urban Development* shall not exceed 100,000 words. This shall *include* all notes, appendices, any source 35 material being edited, and all other parts of the thesis whatsoever *excluding only* the bibliography.

Any thesis exceeding these limits is liable to be rejected on that ground. It is recognised that in special circumstances it will be necessary for leave to be granted to exceed this limit by a stated amount. In particular it is recognised that the inclusion 40 of essential edited source material, whether as an appendix or as a main part of the thesis, presents special problems in regard to length; and the board will be prepared to consider applications for edited material to be excluded from the word limit otherwise placed on the thesis. Leave to exceed these limits for other reasons will be given only in the most special cases and on the recommendation of the supervisor. Any application 45 for permission to exceed the limit should be submitted with a detailed explanation and statement of the amount of excess length requested, and with a covering letter from the supervisor. Applications should be made as soon as possible and may not be later than the last day of the fifth week of the term before that in which applications made for appointment of examiners. 50

Theses submitted for the degree of D.Phil. in *Archaeology* , *Architectural History*, *Cognitive-Behavioural Therapy, English Local History, Evidence Based Health Care* and *Sustainable Urban Development* must be accompanied with two printed or type-written copies of an abstract of the thesis, which shall not normally exceed 2,500 words for the D.Phil., prepared by the student. One copy of the abstract shall be   5
bound into the copy of the thesis which shall be deposited in the Bodleian Library. (This is in addition to the requirement to submit an abstract of not more than 300 words in length required by the Education Committee's Regulations.)

8. Candidates admitted exceptionally under Council Regulations 15 of 2002 shall normally be subject to the provisions of (2)–(7) above. Theses submitted for the degree   10
of D.Phil. by students admitted under this provision shall not normally exceed 100,000 words inclusive of all notes, appendices, any source material being edited, and all other parts of the thesis whatsoever excluding only the bibliography. The Continuing Education Board may, in individual cases, determine that alternative provisions shall apply, and in such cases shall notify the candidate on admission.   15

NOTES

23

DOCTOR OF ENGINEERING

1. Any member of the University who has been admitted to the status of student for the degree of Doctor of Engineering by the Mathematical, Physical and Life Sciences Board and who has satisfied the conditions prescribed by these regulations may supplicate for the degree of Doctor of Engineering. 5

2. Candidates shall follow a programme of study consisting of (*a*) coursework and (*b*) research, in engineering or applied science, in the context of industrial or other professional practice. Each candidate must pass a specified number of coursework modules during the programme of study, as detailed in the Special Regulations for the 10 degree of Doctor of Engineering in Renewable Energy Marine Structures. Each candidate shall submit for examination a thesis, or portfolio of a coherent set of linked research projects.

3. A student for the degree of Doctor of Engineering shall normally pursue his or her course of study at Oxford for 12 terms. 15

4. A student for the degree of Doctor of Engineering may be permitted by the Mathematical, Physical and Life Sciences Divisional Board to undertake their research in a well-found research environment outside the University. Before admitting a candidate on this basis, the conditions set out in the Research Degrees in the Mathematical, Physical and Life Sciences Division shall be met. 20

5. Candidates shall be admitted initially with the status of Probationer Research Student. Students shall hold the status of Probationer Research Student for a maximum of six terms, and shall apply for admission to the status of student for the degree of Doctor of Engineering normally before the end of the fifth term, and no later than the eighth week of the sixth term. 25

6. A member of the University who has held the status of Probationer Research Student and has completed the qualifying test for entry to Doctor of Engineering status prescribed in the Special Regulations for the degree of Doctor of Engineering in Renewable Energy Marine Structures may be admitted to the status of student for the degree of Doctor of Engineering. 30

7. A candidate should normally apply for confirmation of his or her status as a student for the degree of Doctor of Engineering no later than the eighth week of the tenth term after that in which he or she was initially admitted to the status of Probationer Research Student. Candidates applying for confirmation of status must have fulfilled the requirements as specified for the specific programme. 35

8. Examiners of the thesis submitted for the degree of Doctor of Engineering shall bear in mind that their judgement of the substantial significance of the work should take into account what may reasonably be expected of a capable and diligent student after four years of full-time study.

9. If, after considering a candidate's second application for transfer of status, or a 40 candidate's second application for confirmation of status, the responsible body considers that the student's progress does not warrant this, the responsible body may approve his or her transfer to the status of student for the Degree of Master of Science by Research.

10. Except as specifically provided above, and as provided in the Regulations for the degree of Doctor of Engineering in Renewable Energy Marine Structures, the provisions of the following regulations shall apply: Regulations for Admission as a Probationer Research Student; General Regulations for the Degree of Doctor of Philosophy (§1-7); General Regulations of the Education Committee governing the examination of students for the degrees of M.Sc. by Research, M.Litt., and D.Phil. and concerning the maintenance of the register; Regulations for Research Degrees in the Mathematical, Physical and Life Sciences Division; provided that, in all cases, 'Doctor of Engineering' shall be substituted for 'Doctor of Philosophy'.

Doctor of Engineering in Renewable Energy Marine Structures

1. A Probationer Research Students registered on the Centre for Doctoral Training in Renewable Energy Marine Structures programme may choose to apply for admission to either the degree of Doctor of Engineering or the degree of Doctoral of Philosophy. A Student must choose which degree to apply for no later than the end of the third full-term. The Regulations below apply to students seeking to apply for and supplicate for the degree of Doctor of Engineering. For students seeking to apply for the degree of Doctor of Philosophy, the Regulations set out in Doctoral Training Programmes in MPLS shall apply.

2. Candidates shall follow a programme of study in Engineering and related disciplines, consisting of (a) coursework and (b) research, and shall have an industrial or other external sponsor.

3. The University of Oxford shall appoint an academic supervisor for each student. The sponsor shall appoint both an external supervisor and a professional mentor for each student. The student shall meet with their academic supervisor normally at least four times per term, at least one of these meetings taking place in Oxford.

4. In order successfully to fulfil the coursework requirements, candidates are required to pass a specified number of coursework modules in each academic year, as detailed in the Course Handbook. The list of permitted courses is detailed in the Course Handbook, and will be updated annually. If a candidate fails any coursework module they are permitted to re-sit the module according to the details as stipulated in the Course Handbook.

5. Admission to Doctor of Engineering status: Candidates must fulfil the specific conditions as detailed in the Course Handbook. The academic supervisor and external supervisor shall each provide a report on the student's progress. A candidate whose first application for transfer to Doctor of Engineering status is not approved shall be permitted to make one further application, following the procedures laid down above, and shall be granted an extension of time for one term (beyond the six term maximum) if this is necessary for the purposes of making the application.

6. Confirmation of status: Candidates will be required to fulfil the specific conditions, as detailed in the course Handbook, before applying for confirmation of status. A candidate whose first application for confirmation of Doctor of Engineering status is not approved shall be permitted to make one further application, following the procedures laid down above, normally within one term of the original application, and shall be granted an extension of time for one term (beyond the normal maximum of ten terms) if this is necessary for the purposes of making the application.

7. In order to supplicate for the degree of Doctor of Engineering, candidates will be required to pass a specified number of coursework modules, as detailed in the Course Handbook. They will also submit for examination a thesis, or portfolio of a coherent set of linked research projects, as described in the course handbook.

8. The coursework modules shall be provided under arrangements approved by the Mathematical, Physical and Life Sciences Division and the Education Committee, as set out in the Course Handbook. Coursework modules offered by another institution shall be provided under the arrangements approved by the Mathematical, Physical and Life Sciences Division and the Education Committee and set out in a collaboration agreement with that institution. Variation of arrangements for the provision of modules will require the approval of the Mathematical, Physical and Life Sciences Division and the Education Committee.

NOTES

24

DOCTOR OF LETTERS AND DOCTOR OF SCIENCE

1. Any person belonging to one of the following classes may become a candidate for the Degree of Doctor of Letters or of Doctor of Science under the conditions set forth in this Section:[1]

(*a*) Masters of Arts or Masters of Biochemistry or Chemistry or Earth Sciences or Engineering or Mathematics or Physics (including Masters of Arts or Masters of Engineering of the University of Cambridge, and Masters of Arts of the University of Dublin, who have been incorporated in this University) who have entered upon the thirtieth term from their matriculation (at this University or, if earlier, at Cambridge or Dublin as the case may be);

(*b*) Undergraduates or Bachelors of Arts of the University of Cambridge or Dublin who have been incorporated and have incepted in the Faculty of Arts in this University and have entered upon the thirtieth term from their matriculation at Cambridge or Dublin;

(*c*) Persons on whom the Degree of Master of Arts has been conferred by decree or special resolution, other than a degree *honoris causa,* and who have entered upon the ninth term from their admission to that degree;

(*d*) Doctors of Philosophy, Masters of Science or of Letters, and Bachelors of Letters or of Science who have entered upon the twenty-first term from their matriculation.

2. Any such person may apply for permission to supplicate for the Degree of Doctor of Letters or of Doctor of Science, submitting, with the application, evidence of his fitness. This evidence must consist of published papers or books, and one year at least must elapse between the publication of any such paper or book and its submission as evidence in support of an application.[2] The candidate, in his application, shall state whether any part of the work submitted has previously been accepted for a degree.

3. The application shall be made through the Registrar to the board to which the subject of the papers or books in question belongs, and at least two copies of each of such papers or books shall, where possible, be sent with it. The application must further be accompanied by the fee prescribed in the appropriate regulation (see Appendix I) and by a certificate, signed by some officer of, or some person deputed by, the college to which the candidate belongs, showing that his application has the approval of the college. A candidate who submits papers or books which have been produced in collaboration shall state in respect of each item the extent of his own contribution.

---

[1] If papers or books published in the calendar year preceding that in which application is made are submitted, the applicant should specify the exact date of publication.

[2] All applications must be on the agenda of the meeting of the board at which they are to be considered. They should therefore reach the Registrar not less than eight days before the board's meeting.

Applications for permission to supplicate for the Degree of Doctor of Letters shall be made to one of the following bodies only:

Board of the Faculty of:

Classics;

English Language and Literature;   5

Law;

Linguistics, Philology and Phonetics;

Management.

Medieval and Modern Languages and Literature;

History;   10

Music;

Oriental Studies;

Philosophy;

Theology.

Divisional Board: 15

Social Sciences.

Applications for permission to supplicate for the Degree of Doctor of Science shall be made to one of the following boards only:

Divisional Board:

Social Sciences;   20

Mathematical, Physical and Life Sciences;

Medical Sciences.

Committee for:

Archaeology.

4. The board shall appoint judges to consider the evidence submitted by any   25
candidate, and to report thereon to the board. In making their report the judges
shall state whether the evidence submitted constitutes an original contribution to the
advancement of knowledge of such substance and distinction as to give the candidate
an authoritative status in some branch or branches of learning.

5. If the board approves the evidence as of sufficient merit for the degree, it shall   30
give leave to the candidate to supplicate for the degree, and shall notify its decision in
the *University Gazette.* One copy of each of the papers and books submitted as
evidence shall remain in the possession of the University for deposit in Bodleian
Library, provided that no book or paper of which the Library already possesses a
copy shall be so deposited except with the consent of the candidate and of the   35
Librarian, unless the copy submitted by the candidate shall be of a different issue or
shall contain alterations or additions.

6. The boards shall have power to make, and to vary from time to time, such
regulations for carrying out the provisions of this Section as they may deem expedient,
provided that all such regulations and any variations in them shall be submitted to the   40
Education Committee for approval.

NOTES

25

DEGREES IN CIVIL LAW, MAGISTER JURIS, AND MASTER OF PHILOSOPHY IN LAW

§1. Admission of Candidates for the Degrees of Bachelor of Civil Law, Magister Juris, and Master of Philosophy in Law

1. Any person may be admitted by the Board of the Faculty of Law as a candidate for the Degrees of Bachelor of Civil Law, Magister Juris, or Master of Philosophy in Law provided that the following conditions have been satisfied:

(*a*) A candidate must either (i) have passed all the examinations required for the Degree of Bachelor of Arts and have obtained honours in the Second Public Examination, or have obtained honours in a degree examination of another university, such university having been approved by Council for the purpose of the status of Senior Student, or (ii) in the opinion of the Board of the Faculty of Law, be otherwise adequately qualified to undertake the course.

(*b*) A candidate must satisfy relevant provisions prescribed in the regulations made by the board, and any conditions the board may impose.

2. Any student for these degrees who is not a graduate of the University may wear the same gown as that worn by Students for the Degree of Doctor of Philosophy.

§2. Degrees of Bachelor of Civil Law and Magister Juris

Any person who has been admitted under the provisions of §1 above may supplicate for the Degree of Bachelor of Civil Law or the Degree of Magister Juris provided:

(i) that he or she has satisfied the examiners in the examinations prescribed in this section; and

(ii) that he or she has kept three terms of statutory residence as a matriculated member of the University after admission as a Student for the Degree of Bachelor of Civil Law or Magister Juris, whichever is the earlier.

§3. Degree of Master of Philosophy in Law

Any person who has been admitted under the provisions of §1 above may supplicate for the Degree of Master of Philosophy in Law provided:

(i) that he or she has satisfied the examiners in the examinations prescribed in this section; and

(ii) that he or she has kept six terms of statutory residence as a matriculated member of the University after admission as a Student for the Degree of Bachelor of Civil Law or Magister Juris.

§4. Examinations for the Degrees of Bachelor of Civil Law, Magister Juris, and Master of Philosophy in Law

1. The examinations for the Degrees of Bachelor of Civil Law, Magister Juris, and Master of Philosophy in Law shall comprise such subjects as the Board of the Faculty of Law shall from time to time by regulation determine.   5

2. The examinations shall be under the supervision of the board.

§5. Supervision of Students

Every candidate who elects to offer a thesis or dissertation shall seek approval from the Board of the Faculty of Law as prescribed in the regulations made by the board. Subject to such approval, supervision shall be provided as prescribed in the appro-   10
priate regulation, provided that references to the Degree of Master of Studies shall be deemed to refer to the Degrees of Bachelor of Civil Law, Magister Juris, or Master of Philosophy in Law as the case may be.

§6. Admission of Bachelors of Civil Law and Holders of the Degree of Magister Juris or the Degree of   15 Master of Philosophy in Law to the Degree of Doctor of Civil Law

1. Any person who has been admitted to the Degree of Bachelor of Civil Law or to the Degree of Magister Juris or Master of Philosophy in Law, and who has completed fifteen terms from the date of such admission, may apply to the Board of the Faculty   20
of Law for leave to supplicate for the Degree of Doctor of Civil Law. The application shall be made through the Registrar, and shall be accompanied by

(1) evidence that the candidate's application has the approval of his or her college;

(2) the fee prescribed in the appropriate regulation (see Appendix I);

(3) evidence of the candidate's fitness for the degree. This evidence must consist of   25
three copies of a published book or of published books or papers, treating in a scientific manner of one or more legal subjects and consisting of an original contribution to the advancement of knowledge of such substance and distinction as to give the candidate authoritative status in some branch or branches of legal learning. A candidate who submits papers or books which have been produced in collaboration shall   30
state in respect of each item the extent of the candidate's own contribution.

2. On receipt of the application the Board of the Faculty of Law, having deter-
mined that the evidence submitted is of the appropriate kind, shall appoint not fewer than two judges, who shall report to the board on the sufficiency of the evidence.

3. If the board, after consideration of the reports of the judges, shall approve the   35
evidence as sufficient for the degree, it shall give leave to the candidate to supplicate for the degree, and shall notify its decision in the *University Gazette*. One copy of the evidence shall remain in the possession of the University for deposit in Bodleian Library, provided that no book or paper of which the Library already possesses a copy shall be so deposited except with the consent of the candidate and of the   40
Librarian, unless the copy submitted by the candidate shall be of a different issue or shall contain alterations or additions.

§7. Admission to the Degrees of Bachelor of Civil Law and Doctor of Civil Law by Accumulation

1. Any person belonging to one of the following classes may apply to the Board of the Faculty of Law for permission to supplicate for the Degrees of Bachelor of Civil Law and Doctor of Civil Law at the same time under the conditions set forth in this sub-section:

    (*a*) Masters of Arts, except those on whom the degree has been conferred by decree or special resolution, who have entered upon the sixty-sixth term from their matriculation at this University, or, if they have been incorporated in this University, the sixty-sixth term from their matriculation at the University of Cambridge or of Dublin;

    (*b*) persons on whom the Degree of Master of Arts has been conferred by decree or special resolution, other than a degree *honoris causa*, and who have entered upon the forty-fifth term from their admission to that degree;

    (*c*) Doctors of Philosophy, or Masters of Letters or of Science or of Studies, who have entered upon the sixty-sixth term from their matriculation at this University.

2. The application of any such person shall be made to the board, and dealt with by the board, in the manner prescribed in §6 above.

3. If the board approves the evidence as sufficient for the Degree of Doctor of Civil Law, it shall give leave to the candidate to supplicate for the Degrees of Bachelor of Civil Law and Doctor of Civil Law at the same time, although the candidate shall not have passed the examination for the former degree.

Degrees of Bachelor of Civil Law and Magister Juris

1. *Admission criteria*

    BCL The Law Board will normally admit to the BCL only candidates whose previous legal training is primarily in the common law.

    M.Jur. The Law Board will normally admit to the M.Jur. only candidates whose previous legal training is not primarily in the common law.

2. *Residence*

    Candidates for the BCL and M.Jur. must keep three terms statutory residence.

3. *Courses and subjects*

    The subjects of the examination are listed in Schedule A below. The details of the courses are set out in the Law Faculty Student Handbook.

    Candidates for the BCL and M.Jur. must offer four papers. A dissertation counts as one paper.

    Not all subjects will necessarily be taught or examined in any one year. Depending on the availability of teaching resources, the Law Faculty may limit the number of candidates that may offer a subject. Details of those subjects which are available will be published in the Law Faculty Student Handbook for the year of the examination, subject to any amendment posted in the Law Faculty Office by Monday of week minus 1 of the Michaelmas Term before the examination is held.

    In addition to the subjects in Schedule A, candidates may offer any other subject that may be approved from time to time by regulation published in the *Gazette* by the end of the Monday of week minus 1 of the Michaelmas Term before the examination is held.

No candidate for the BCL or M.Jur. may:

(*a*) offer a subject with the same title and/or the same syllabus as one which he or she has previously offered in the Final Honour School of Jurisprudence or Diploma in Legal Studies;

(*b*) offer two subjects having the same syllabus.   5

BCL Subject to compliance with the regulations above, candidates for the BCL may offer:

(*a*) any subject in List I which is offered in the year in question;

(*b*) a dissertation under the provisions in Schedule B below.

M.Jur. Subject to compliance with the regulations above, candidates for the M.Jur.   10
may offer:

(*a*) any subject in List I which is offered in the year in question;

(*b*) any subject in List II which is offered in the year in question;

(*c*) a dissertation under the provisions in Schedule B below.

4. *Examinations*   15

Candidates offering Jurisprudence and Political Theory will be examined under the provisions of Schedule C.

The examiners may award a distinction for excellence in the examination.

Candidates who fail or withdraw from the examination may with the permission of the faculty board and subject to such conditions as it imposes offer themselves for re-   20
examination. Candidates offering themselves for re-examination must retake all of the papers, except that:

(*a*) if all of the written papers are passed and the dissertation failed then only the dissertation need be resubmitted;

(*b*) if the dissertation is passed and one or more of the written papers failed then   25
only the written papers need be re-taken;

provided that nothing in this clause shall prejudice the powers of the Education Committee and Proctors to permit partial resits in exceptional circumstances.

If a candidate, having failed or withdrawn from an examination, successfully applies to sit the examination at a later date, and one or more of the subjects studied   30
by that candidate are not available when the candidate comes to be examined, papers shall nevertheless be set for that candidate in those subjects. These papers may not be taken by other candidates.

5. *Statutes and Other Source Material*

Details of the statutes and other source material which will be available to candi-   35
dates in the examination room for certain papers will be given in a notice circulated to candidates by the examiners.

6. *Notice of options*

The date for notification of the options to be offered by candidates is the fourth week of the Michaelmas Full Term preceding the examination with the exception of   40
the dissertation option [see Schedule B].

7. *Change of option choice*

Save in exceptional circumstances, no student may change their choice of option later than Friday of the first week of Hilary Term.

8. *Examiners*   45

The examiners appointed to examine subjects in List II shall be those appointed to examine the same subjects in the Honour School of Jurisprudence and shall examine those papers in the examination for the Honour School of Jurisprudence.

Degree of M.Phil. in Law

1. *Admissions*

Candidates may signify their intention to take the M.Phil. in Law when they apply for the BCL or M.Jur. or M.Sc. Law and Finance or after they have been admitted. In either case a formal application must then be made in the Hilary Term preceding the Michaelmas Term in which they wish to study for the M.Phil. The appropriate form, obtainable from the The Faculty of Law Graduate Studies Office, must be returned to the Law Faculty's Student Administration Officer on the same date as that office specifies for the receipt of applications for the M.St. in Legal Research. Admission of those whose thesis topics are approved by the Law Faculty's Graduate Studies Committee and for whom that Committee certifies the availability of supervision will always be conditional on a specified level of performance in the BCL or M.Jur. or M.Sc. Law and Finance.

2. *Residence*

Candidates for the M.Phil. in Law must keep 6 terms statutory residence, which may include periods spent in residence while studying for the BCL or M.Jur. or M.Sc. Law and Finance.

3. *Courses and examination*

Candidates for the M.Phil. in Law shall satisfactorily complete Part 1 and Part 2. Part 1 and Part 2 shall be taken in that order and shall normally be taken in successive years. A candidate wishing to take Part 2 but not to proceed directly from Part 1 to Part 2 in successive years must seek permission from the Graduate Studies Committee for Law. Part 1 shall consist of the BCL or M.Jur. or M.Sc. Law and Finance as the case may be.

In Part 2, candidates for the M.Phil. in Law shall follow a course of instruction in Legal Research Method, satisfy the examiners that they have completed to the required standard such tests or exercises in Legal Research Method as may be prescribed as part of such a course of instruction, and be examined by thesis which must not exceed 30,000 words and should not normally be less than 25,000 words, and by oral examination, under the provisions of cll. 1 to 9 of the regulations for the M.St. in Legal Research, provided that:

(*a*) references to the Degree of Master of Studies shall be deemed to refer to Part 2 of the M.Phil. in Law;

(*b*) in cl. 5, the date of application for examination shall be during the Trinity Term after the candidate began Part 2 of the M.Phil. in Law. A candidate who wishes to apply for examination at a later date must seek the approval of the Graduate Studies Committee for Law by the end of Week Four of the same Trinity Full Term. Only in exceptional circumstances will the Committee extend the M.Phil. deadline. Unless the deadline has been extended, a thesis submitted after the required date will normally be eligible only to be examined for an M.St.

The thesis may cover the same area of Law as a dissertation offered in the BCL or M.Jur. or M.Sc. Law and Finance, but the text of the dissertation must not be incorporated into the thesis.

SCHEDULE A

List I

Advanced Property and Trusts;
Commercial Remedies;
Comparative Corporate Law;
Comparative and Global Environmental Law;

Comparative Equality Law;
Comparative Human Rights;
Comparative Public Law;
Competition Law;
Conflict of Laws;   5
Constitutional Principles of the EU;
Constitutional Theory;
Corporate Tax Law and Policy;
Corporate Finance Law;
Corporate Insolvency Law;   10
Criminal Justice, Security and Human Rights;
Dissertation;
European Business Regulation (the law of the EU's internal market);
European Private Law: Contract;
European Private Law: Tort;   15
European Union as Actor in International Law;
Evidence;
Intellectual Property Law;
International and European Criminal Law;
International and European Employment Law;   20
International Commercial Arbitration;
International Dispute Settlement;
International Economic Law;
International Law and Armed Conflict;
International Law of the Sea;   25
Jurisprudence and Political Theory;
Law and Society in Medieval England;
Law in Society;
Legal Concepts in Financial Law;
Medical Law and Ethics;   30
Personal Taxation;
Philosophical Foundations of the Common Law;
Principles of Civil Procedure;
Principles of Financial Regulation;
Private Law and Fundamental Rights;   35
Punishment, Security and the State;
Regulation;
Restitution of Unjust Enrichment;
Roman Law (Delict);
The Roman and Civilian Law of Contracts;   40
Transnational Commercial Law.
List II
Commercial Law;
Company Law;
Comparative Law: Contract;   45
Contract;
European Union Law (may not be taken in conjunction with Constitutional Principles
    of the EU from list I);
European Human Rights Law;
Family;   50
Land;
Public International Law;
Tort;

Trusts (may not be taken in conjunction with Advanced Property and Trusts from list I);
Copyright, Patent and Allied Rights (may not be taken in conjunction with European
Intellectual Property Law from List I, or with Copyright, Trade Marks, and Allied
Rights);
Copyright, Trade Marks and Allied Rights (may not be taken in conjunction with 5
European Intellectual Property Law from List I, or with Copyright, Patent, and
Allied Rights).

SCHEDULE B

Dissertations

Candidates for the BCL and M.Jur. may offer a dissertation, which must be written 10
in English and must not exceed 12,500 words and should not normally be less than
10,000 words (including notes, but excluding tables of cases or other legal sources) on
a subject to be proposed by the candidate in consultation with the supervisor, and
approved by the Graduate Studies Committee in Law. The dissertation shall be wholly
or substantially the result of work undertaken whilst registered for the degree of 15
Bachelor of Civil Law or Magister Juris. In deciding whether to give approval, the
committee shall take into account the suitability of the subject matter and availability
of appropriate supervision. Candidates should submit the proposed title of the dissertation and a synopsis of its scope in not more than 500 words not later than
Monday of Week Minus One of Michaelmas Full Term to the board's Director of 20
Graduate Studies (Taught Courses) who shall, when the topic and supervisor have
been confirmed by or on behalf of the board's Committee for Graduate Studies,
communicate that information to the Chair of the Examiners for the BCL and M.Jur.
Supervisors or others are permitted to give bibliographical help and to discuss
drafts. Every candidate offering a dissertation is entitled to six sessions of supervision, 25
each of approximately one hour, not counting meetings to settle the shape of the
dissertation before it was approved.
The examiners must judge the extent to which the dissertation affords evidence of
significant analytical ability on the part of the candidate. The required format for this
dissertation is the common format prescribed for all law theses, which is printed in the 30
Faculty of Law's Graduate Student's Handbook.

Submission

No later than noon on Friday of the fifth week of Trinity Full Term two copies of your
dissertation must be delivered to the Examination Schools, High Street, Oxford OX1
4BG. The package must be clearly marked 'Dissertation for BCL/M.Jur.'. In order to 35
ensure anonymity, the dissertation must bear your examination number. Neither your
name nor the name of your college must appear. You must include with the thesis (i) a
signed statement that, except where otherwise indicated, the thesis is entirely your own
work, and (ii) a second statement indicating which part or parts of the dissertation
have formed or will form part of a submission in accordance with the requirements of 40
another course at this or another university. To ensure anonymity these statements
must be placed in a sealed envelope. The examiners shall exclude from consideration
any part of your dissertation which is not your own work or which has been or will
be submitted to satisfy the requirements of another course, and the examiners shall
have power to require you to produce for their inspection the work so submitted or 45
to be submitted.

SCHEDULE C

Candidates offering Jurisprudence and Political Theory will be examined in that
subject by the submission of three essays. Essay questions will be published by the
Board of Examiners on the morning of the Friday of the eighth week of the Hilary 50

Term preceding the examination. Candidates will be contacted with details of how to collect or access the questions. The examiners shall offer a choice of six topics from which candidates shall be required to select three. The total length of the three essays submitted shall be not less than 5,000 words, nor more than 8,000. The essays shall be wholly or substantially the result of work undertaken whilst registered for the degree   5
of Batchelor of Civil Law or Magister Juris. Two copies of each essay submitted must be delivered to the Chair of the BCL/M.Jur. Examiners, Examination Schools, High Street, Oxford OX1 4BG, by noon on the Friday preceding the beginning of the Trinity Full Term in which the examination is to be taken. The essays must bear the candidate's examination number, but not his or her name or the name of his or her   10
college. Every candidate shall sign a Declaration of Authorship to the effect that the essays are his or her own work. Candidates shall further state the total number of words used in their essays. This Declaration of Authorship shall be presented together with the essays. To ensure anonymity the Declaration of Authorship must be placed in a sealed envelope.   15

NOTES

26

REGULATIONS FOR DEGREES IN MEDICINE AND SURGERY

GENERAL REGULATIONS
Qualifications of Candidates for the Degree of Bachelor of Medicine

1. A student who has been admitted to the Degree of Bachelor of Arts with Honours may supplicate for the Degree of Bachelor of Medicine, provided that they shall have passed the examinations hereinafter prescribed.

2. A candidate who has been admitted to the Second Examination for the Degree of Bachelor of Medicine by the Medical Sciences Board under the provisions of clause 1 of the special regulations for the Second Examination for the Degree of Bachelor of Medicine may supplicate for the Degree of Bachelor of Medicine without having been admitted to the Degree of Bachelor of Arts with Honours, provided that they shall have passed the Second Examination and shall have kept statutable residence for six terms.

3. A candidate for the Preliminary Examination in Medicine or for the Degree of Bachelor of Medicine who has been admitted under the provisions of clause 1 of the special regulations for the Second Examination for the Degree of Bachelor of Medicine and who is not a graduate of the University may wear the same gown as that worn by Students for the Degree of Doctor of Philosophy.

Degree of Bachelor of Surgery

Any person admitted to the Degree of Bachelor of Medicine shall *ipso facto* be admitted also to the Degree of Bachelor of Surgery.

FIRST BM PARTS I AND II

First Examination for the Degree of Bachelor of Medicine

1. The First Examination for the Degree of Bachelor of Medicine shall be under the supervision of the Medical Sciences Board.

2. The subjects of the First Examination shall be:

Part I

1. Organisation of the Body
2. Physiology and Pharmacology
3. Biochemistry and Medical Genetics
4. Population Health 1: Medical Sociology

Part II

5. Applied Physiology and Pharmacology
6. The Nervous System
7. Principles of Pathology
8. Psychology for Medicine

3. The syllabus of each subject shall be as prescribed from time to time by the Medical Sciences Board by regulation.

4. Subjects 1, 2, 3, 5, 6, and 7 shall each be examined in three Parts: A, B, and C. In each of these subjects, a candidate must offer Parts A, B, and C at one examination, provided that a candidate who has failed at his or her first attempt to satisfy the examiners in one Part only of a subject may offer that Part alone at a subsequent examination. In each of these subjects, a candidate must pass all three Parts, or have accumulated passes in all three Parts, in order to pass in that subject. When a candidate who at the first attempt passed only one or two Part(s) of a subject subsequently passes the remaining Part(s) of that subject, the examiners shall publish his or her name as having passed in that subject.

5. A candidate must offer all four subjects in Part I at one examination, provided that a candidate who has failed at his or her first attempt in any subject or subjects may offer subject 4 or any Part or Parts of subjects 1, 2, or 3 at a subsequent examination (in accordance with clause 4 above), and provided that the Medical Sciences Board may dispense candidates who have already passed a First Public Examination in any subject from the requirement to offer all four subjects at one examination. In Part I, the examiners may publish the name of a candidate as having passed one, two, three, or four subjects, and the examiners may in addition publish the name of a candidate as having passed one or two Part(s) only of any of the subjects 1, 2, or 3. In Part II, a candidate must offer all four subjects at one examination, provided that a candidate who has failed at his or her first attempt in any subject or subjects may offer subject 8 or any Part or Parts of subjects 5, 6, or 7 at a subsequent examination (in accordance with clause 4 above). In Part II, the examiners may publish the name of a candidate as having passed one, two, three, or four subjects, and the examiners may in addition publish the name of a candidate as having passed one or two Part(s) only of any of the subjects 5, 6, or 7.

6. A candidate shall be deemed to have passed the First Examination if he or she has satisfied the examiners in all the subjects of Parts I and II as specified in clause 2 above.

7. A candidate who has passed Part I of the First Examination shall be deemed to have passed the First Public Examination.

8. No candidate shall be admitted to the examination for Part II of the First Examination without first having passed all the subjects of Part I, save in exceptional circumstances at the discretion of the Medical Sciences Board following application from the candidate's society.

9. No candidate may offer any subject or Part of a subject in Parts I and II of the First Examination on more than two occasions, save in exceptional circumstances. A further exceptional opportunity to offer any subject or Part of a subject for Part I of the First Examination shall require application to and approval on behalf of the Education Committee of the University, in accordance with the *General Regulations for the First and Second Public Examinations*. A further exceptional opportunity to offer any subject or Part of a subject for Part II of the First Examination shall require application to and approval on behalf of the Educational Policy and Standards Committee of the Medical Sciences Board, according to the procedure set out in the handbook for medical students in Years 1–3.

10. The examiners may award a Distinction to candidates of special merit in either Part I or Part II of the examination, provided that all examinations for all four subjects specified for that Part in clause 2 above have been offered in their entirety and passed at one examination at the first scheduled opportunity which shall be the candidate's first attempt, except in exceptional circumstances at the discretion of the Board of Examiners following application from the candidate's society.

11. The examiners may award a Pass with Merit to candidates of special merit in any of the individual subjects 1, 2, 3, 5, 6, or 7, provided that all four subjects of Part I or of Part II of the examination have been offered in their entirety at one examination.

The award of Pass with Merit shall be based on performance in Part B of a subject and shall be confined to candidates who have passed Parts A and C of that subject at the same sitting which shall be the first scheduled opportunity and the candidate's first attempt, except in exceptional circumstances at the discretion of the Board of Examiners following application from the candidate's society.

12. No candidate shall be admitted to the First Examination unless he or she has been through the standard selection procedures for the standard medical course (including sitting the Biomedical Admissions Test—BMAT), has met the published entry requirements for admission to the standard medical course, and his or her name has been entered on the University Register of Medical Students.

Regulations for Part C of subjects 1, 2, 3, 5, 6 and 7

For each subject, the Director of Pre-Clinical Studies or his or her deputy may request practical notebooks from any candidate in order to subsequently make available to the examiners evidence (in the form of a list of names, signed by the Director or his or her deputy) showing the extent to which each candidate has a satisfactory attendance record at practical classes in that subject and the extent to which each candidate has a satisfactory record of practical work in that subject. The examiners may also request practical notebooks from any candidate; such candidates will be named in a list posted in the foyer of the Medical Sciences Teaching Centre one week before the day of the first examination paper. Each notebook submitted shall be accompanied by a statement signed by the candidate indicating that the notebook is the candidate's own work.

The practical course for subject 2 includes the course in elementary statistics defined in the Composite Syllabus for Part I.

Candidates whose attendance record and/or record of practical work is unsatisfactory will normally be required by the examiners to submit to further examination. Failure to satisfy the examiners that the candidate has a satisfactory knowledge and understanding of the practical course shall result in the candidate being failed in Part C of the relevant subject of the examination.

Evidence of satisfactory practical work and of attendance at a practical course is normally admissible by the examiners for a period extending no longer than to the end of the academic year following the year in which the course was pursued.

Candidates may be required to undergo oral examination.

Regulations for the Patient and Doctor Course

The Director of Pre-Clinical Studies or his or her deputy will make available to the examiners evidence (in the form of a list of names, signed by the Director or his or her deputy) to certify that each candidate has participated satisfactorily in the *Patient and Doctor Course*.

Part I

Part I

1. *Organisation of the Body*
2. *Physiology and Pharmacology*
3. *Biochemistry and Medical Genetics*
4. *Population Health 1: Medical Sociology*

A Composite Syllabus (Core plus Extension) for Part I will be published annually at the start of Michaelmas Term by the Medical Sciences Board. The syllabus will make appropriate reference to related issues of clinical significance. In each subject, candidates will be expected to have a general understanding of the components specified in the syllabus, including methods of study and quantitative analysis of experimental results.

In subjects 1, 2, and 3 two papers will be set, Paper A and Paper B. Paper A shall be no longer than 1 hour and 15 minutes in duration, and shall be a computer-based assessment of breadth of knowledge and understanding of the Core Syllabus. Paper B shall be set to examine deeper knowledge and understanding of a choice of topics included in or closely relating to the Composite Syllabus. For Subjects 1, 2, and 3, Paper B shall be two hours in duration.

In subject 4, one one-and-a-half-hour paper will be set, assessing knowledge and understanding of the Composite Syllabus.

Part II

Part II

5. *Applied Physiology and Pharmacology*

6. *The Nervous System*

7. *Principles of Pathology*

8. *Psychology for Medicine*

A Composite Syllabus (Core plus Extension) for Part II will be published annually at the start of Michaelmas Term by the Medical Sciences Board. The syllabus will make appropriate reference to related issues of clinical significance. In each subject, candidates will be expected to have a general understanding of the components specified in the syllabus, including methods of study and quantitative analysis of experimental results.

In subjects 5, 6, and 7 two papers will be set, Paper A and Paper B. Paper A shall be no longer than 1 hour and 15 minutes in duration, and shall be a computer-based assessment of breadth of knowledge and understanding of the Core Syllabus. Paper B shall be set to examine deeper knowledge and understanding of a choice of topics included in or closely relating to the Composite Syllabus. For Subjects 5, 6, and 7, Paper B shall be three hours in duration.

In subject 8, one one-and-a-half hour paper will be set. The paper shall consist of two sections: (1) multiple-choice questions (45 minutes), assessing breadth of knowledge and understanding of the Core Syllabus; (2) essay questions (45 minutes), examining deeper knowledge and understanding of a choice of topics included in or closely related to the Composite Syllabus.

PRINCIPLES OF CLINICAL ANATOMY

A

There shall be a Qualifying Examination in the Principles of Clinical Anatomy for medical students who have passed the First Examination for the Degree of Bachelor of Medicine and who are seeking admission to a course in clinical medicine in Oxford or elsewhere. The examination shall be governed by the following provisions.

(*a*) The examination shall be under the supervision of the Medical Sciences Board.

(*b*) No candidate shall be admitted to this Qualifying Examination unless his or her name has been entered on the Register of University Medical Students and he or she has previously passed the First Examination for the Degree of Bachelor of Medicine.

(*c*) Candidates for the Qualifying Examination in the Principles of Clinical Anatomy are required to keep statutory residence and pursue their studies at Oxford, extending to no more than two weeks beyond the end of Trinity Full Term, provided that the divisional board shall have power to permit candidates to vary the dates of their residence so long as the overall programme requirement is met.

(*d*) The syllabus and obligations required of candidates, and the method of examination, shall be as prescribed from time to time by regulations of the Medical Sciences Board.

B

The syllabus shall be published annually in Trinity Term by the Medical Sciences Board.

Candidates shall submit notebooks, initialled as satisfactory by the demonstrators, or other certified evidence of satisfactory practical work associated with the course.

The examination will consist of in-course assessment of a form approved by the Medical Sciences Board. Any candidate whose performance in any part of this assessment is judged to be unsatisfactory may be reassessed during the course or at some duly advertised time during the Long Vacation by such means as may be deemed appropriate by the examiners. In determining whether a candidate has passed the examination, the examiners will take account of the candidate's overall record of assessment without necessarily requiring a satisfactory performance in every constituent part.

The Director of Pre-Clinical Studies or his or her deputy is required to make available to the examiners evidence (in the form of a list of names, signed by the Director or his or her deputy) to certify that each candidate has a satisfactory attendance record at the course in the Principles of Clinical Anatomy. Any candidate whose record of attendance is deemed unsatisfactory by the examiners shall be liable to undergo additional examination by such means as may be deemed appropriate by the examiners, or he or she may be failed at the discretion of the examiners.

Candidates may be required to undergo oral examination.

PRELIMINARY EXAMINATION IN MEDICINE

1. A candidate may be admitted to the Preliminary Examination in Medicine provided that his or her name is on the Register of Clinical Students and he or she has been admitted to the Degree of Bachelor of Arts with Honours or has obtained a degree of another university deemed adequate for the purpose by the Medical Sciences Board, and that he or she has satisfied such additional qualifications as the Medical Sciences Board may from time to time prescribe in its regulations.

2. Candidates for the Preliminary Examination in Medicine are required to pursue their studies during a period of: normally 30 weeks in Year 1; normally 39 weeks in Year 2; provided that the Medical Sciences Board shall have power to permit candidates to vary the dates of their studies so long as the overall programme requirement is met.

3. The examination shall be under the supervision of the Medical Sciences Board.

4. The examination shall comprise such subjects and papers as the Medical Sciences Board shall from time to time by regulation determine.

5. The Preliminary Examination in Medicine shall consist of two parts. Part I may be offered not earlier than three terms, and Part II not earlier than six terms, from the date of entry onto the Register of Clinical Students.

6. A core syllabus and an extension syllabus for each of Parts I and II will be published annually at the start of the Michaelmas Term prior to the examination by the Medical Sciences Board.

7. The examiners may award a Distinction to candidates of special merit in either Part I or Part II of the examination, provided that all the subjects in that Part have been offered and passed at one examination.

Part I

The examination will assess candidates' core knowledge and understanding of core material, and clinical skills and critical-appraisal skills.

Candidates must pass all seven components listed below in order to pass the examination.   5

Candidates who fail any component(s) of the examination at the first attempt need re-sit only the component(s) that they have failed, provided that all components are passed within a single academic year; except that, where a candidate has been granted leave by the Board to sit a component or components for a third time (under the provisions of the General Regulations for Part I of the Preliminary Examination in   10 Medicine), the Board may also, at its discretion, waive the requirement for the candidate to pass all components within a single academic year.

The examination will be set at the end of the extended Trinity Term and at the end of the Long Vacation.

Examiners may award Distinctions for outstanding performance in Papers 3, 4, and   15 5, together with the Submitted Essay and Behavioural Sciences element of the Longitudinal Case Study, by candidates sitting the examination for the first time.

Candidates may be required, at the discretion of the examiners, to undergo an oral examination which may include a further clinical examination.

No candidate may enter for the examination on more than two occasions, save in   20 exceptional circumstances at the discretion of the Medical Sciences Board following application from the candidate's society.

1. *Core Material*

Candidates will be required to demonstrate their knowledge and understanding of the principles of basic medical science as defined in the core syllabus for Part I. Two   25 papers will be set.

Paper 1 (one hour) will be a computer-based assessment consisting of multiple-choice questions.

Paper 2 (two hours) will be in the format of problem-based questions.

Each question will be marked pass or fail, and a cumulative pass/fail mark will be   30 given for a candidate's overall performance in the two papers. The marks from these papers will not contribute to the award of a Distinction.

2. *Paper 3: Ethics (one hour)*

Candidates will be required to write one essay in response to a choice of question topics.   35

3. *Paper 4: Systems of the Body (one and a half hours)*

Candidates will be required to write one essay from a choice of questions, which will relate to extension topics notified to candidates at the start of the academic year.

Candidates will be given credit for demonstrating their breadth of reading beyond the core syllabus, for their ability to synthesise evidence from different sources and   40 produce a coherent argument, and for discussion of experimental evidence from primary literature.

During the examination, candidates will have access to such databases of medical literature as may be prescribed from time to time by the Medical Sciences Board and notified to candidates at the beginning of the academic year.   45

4. *Paper 5: Critical Appraisal (two hours)*

This paper will assess candidates' ability to critically appraise primary research material.

The primary research paper, or extracts from a number of papers, may report laboratory-based or clinical research. The literature will contain experimental, public health, or clinical data for interpretation but may also include descriptions of experimental methods.

Candidates may be required to offer criticism of the experimental method, or of the 5
interpretation of the results, or to draw their own inferences from the published data.

Candidates must attempt all questions.

5. *Clinical Skills*
Candidates will be required to demonstrate, in a practical examination, their ability to take a clinical history and to perform a clinical examination of the systems of the 10
body specified in the core curriculum and, to apply such practical skills as may be defined in the core syllabus published by the Medical Sciences Board.

The examination will include an assessment of candidates' communication skills with patients, orally and/or in writing, and of their professional behaviour.

6. *Submitted Essay: Systems of the Body* 15
(i) *Form and subject of the essay*
Candidates will be required to submit an essay on a topic approved by the examiners. The submitted essay shall be of not more than 3,000 words, excluding any tables, figures, diagrams, or references. It must be in a format prescribed by the Graduate-entry Education Committee and published in the *Notes of Guidance for* 20
the Preliminary Examination in Medicine.

A list of suggested essay titles, and the topics to which they relate, approved by the Chair of Examiners in consultation with the module organisers, shall be published no later than the end of Week 5 of the Michaelmas Term in the academic year of the examination. Candidates may also propose their own titles. The essay may 25
relate to any of the topics set out in the Notes of *Guidance for the Preliminary Examination in Medicine* except that candidates may not submit an essay that closely relates to work that they have previously submitted for any university examination.

A candidate wishing to offer an essay with a title not on the approved list must 30
apply for approval of their proposed title by no later than the end of Week 0 of Hilary Term in the academic year of the examination. Application shall be made via the Course Administrator in the Medical School Office and shall include the proposed title, a brief outline of the subject matter, and the topic or topics to which it relates. Decision on the application shall be made by the Chair of 35
Examiners in consultation with the module organisers and shall be communicated to the candidate as soon as possible and in any case not later than Week 2 of Hilary Term in the academic year of the examination.

(ii) *Registration*
No later than the end of Week 0 of Hilary Term in the academic year of the 40
examination, every candidate must register the title of their essay via the Course Administrator in the Medical School Office.

(iii) *Authorship*
The essay must be the candidate's own work. Candidates' tutors, or their deputies nominated to act as advisors, may discuss with candidates the proposed 45
field of study, the sources available, and the method of treatment, but on no account may they read or comment on any written draft. Every candidate shall sign a certificate to the effect that this rule has been observed and that the essay is their own work. The certificate, sealed in a separate envelope, should be addressed to the Chair of Examiners for the Preliminary Examination in Medicine Part I 50
and submitted alongside the essay.

(iv) *Submission*

The essay (two paper copies and an electronic copy) must be submitted to the Chair of Examiners for the Preliminary Examination in Medicine Part I, c/o the Examination Schools, High Street, Oxford, not later than noon on the Friday of Week 0 of Trinity Term.   5

7. *Longitudinal Case Study combined with Behavioural Sciences Commentary*

Candidates will be required to complete a Longitudinal Case Study during their clinical course, details of which will be published each year in the clinical course handbook. This coursework must be submitted to the candidate's GP Tutor by the first Friday following the end of Week 9 of Hilary Term.   10

The clinical course organiser will then forward each case study to the Chair of Examiners by the end of Week 0 of Trinity Term, together with a certificate, signed by the relevant clinical supervisor, of satisfactory performance by the candidate in the Longitudinal Case Study.

Candidates will separately submit an essay covering an aspect of Behavioural   15
Sciences, which will relate to the longitudinal case study. This essay will contribute to the award of a Distinction.

(i) *Form and subject of the essay*

Candidates will be required to submit a Behavioural Sciences commentary, relating to the patient described in the Longitudinal Case Study, in the form of   20
an essay of not more than 3,000 words, excluding any tables, figures, diagrams, or references. It must be in a format prescribed by the Graduate-entry Education Committee and published in the *Notes of Guidance for the Preliminary Examination in Medicine*.

The essay must refer to aspects of Behavioural Sciences from a list published at   25
the beginning of the academic year by the Graduate-entry Education Committee and included in the Notes of Guidance for the *Preliminary Examination in Medicine*. The number of such topics to be covered in the essay will be determined from time to time by the Graduate-entry Education Committee and will be published with the list and included in the *Notes of Guidance*.   30

(ii) *Authorship*

The essay must be the candidate's own work. Candidates' tutors, or their deputies nominated to act as advisors, may discuss with candidates the proposed field of study as it relates to the patient, the sources available, and the method of treatment, but on no account may they read or comment on any written draft.   35
Every candidate shall sign a certificate to the effect that this rule has been observed and that the essay is their own work; and the candidate's tutor or advisor shall countersign the certificate confirming that, to the best of their knowledge and belief, this is so. The certificate, sealed in a separate envelope, should be addressed to the Chair of Examiners for the Preliminary Examination in Medicine Part I and   40
submitted alongside the essay.

(iii) *Submission*

The essay (two paper copies and an electronic copy) must be submitted to the Chair of Examiners for the Preliminary Examination in Medicine Part I, c/o the Examination Schools, High Street, Oxford, not later than noon on the Friday of   45
Week 0 of Trinity Term.

Part II

The examination will consist of seven components. Candidates must pass all seven components listed below in order to pass the examination.

Candidates who fail any component(s) of the examination at the first attempt need   50
re-sit only the component(s) that they have failed, provided that all components are

passed within a single academic year; except that, where a candidate has been granted leave by the Board to sit a component or components for a third time (under the provisions of the General Regulations for Part II of the Preliminary Examination in Medicine), the Board may also, at its discretion, waive the requirement for the candidate to pass all components within a single academic year. 5

The examination will be set towards the end of Trinity Term and at a time to be specified by the examiners during the Long Vacation.

Examiners may award Distinctions for outstanding performance in Papers 2 and 3, and the two extended essays, by candidates sitting the examination for the first time.

Candidates may be required, at the discretion of the examiners, to undergo an oral 10 examination which may include a further clinical examination.

No candidate may enter for the examination on more than two occasions, save in exceptional circumstances at the discretion of the Medical Sciences Board following application from the candidate's society.

1. *Paper 1: Medicine (two hours)* 15
This paper will test core knowledge and understanding through problem-based questions. This material may include basic and applied science, differential diagnosis of common diseases and simple first-line clinical investigations.

The paper will be marked pass/fail only. The marks from this paper will not contribute to the overall mark in the examination, nor to the award of a Distinction. 20

2. *Paper 2: Clinical Science (two hours)*
This paper will relate to extension topics notified to candidates at the start of the academic year and will require candidates to answer two questions.

Candidates will be given credit for demonstrating their breadth of reading beyond the core syllabus, for their ability to synthesise evidence from different sources and 25 produce a coherent argument, and for discussion of primary literature.

3. *Paper 3: Data Interpretation (two hours)*
This paper will assess candidates' ability to critically appraise primary research material.

The primary research paper, or papers (normally not more than two), will report 30 clinical research. The literature will contain experimental, epidemiological, or clinical data for interpretation, including public health data.

Candidates may be required to offer criticism of the experimental method, or of the interpretation of the published data (including epidemiological data), or to draw their own inferences from the published data. 35

Candidates must attempt all questions.

4. *Extended Essay on a Public Health topic*
   (i) *Form and subject of the essay*
   Candidates will be required to submit an essay on a topic related to Public Health aspects of the diagnosis or management of a clinical case they have seen 40 during their clinical attachments in the second year of the course. The submitted essay shall be of not more than 3,000 words, excluding any tables, figures, diagrams, or references. It must be in a format prescribed by the Graduate-entry Education Committee and published in the *Notes of Guidance for the Preliminary Examination in Medicine*. 45

   The essay must refer to aspects of Public Health from a list published at the beginning of the academic year by the Graduate-entry Education Committee and included in the Notes of Guidance for the *Preliminary Examination in Medicine*. The number of such topics to be covered in the essay will be determined from time to time by the Graduate-entry Education Committee and will be published with the 50 list and included in the *Notes of Guidance*.

(ii) *Validity*

Candidates must submit with their essay a certificate from the Clinical Tutor in Medicine or in Surgery, or from a consultant in charge of the patient, confirming that the student has seen the patient described in the essay.

As a prologue to the essay, candidates should include a summary of the clinical   5
case to which the essay refers. The summary should not usually exceed 250 words, but will not be included in the overall word count for the essay.

(iii) *Authorship*

The essay must be the candidate's own work. Candidates' tutors, or their deputies nominated to act as advisors, may discuss with candidates the proposed   10
field of study, the sources available, and the method of treatment, but on no account may they read or comment on any written draft. Every candidate shall sign a certificate to the effect that this rule has been observed and that the essay is their own work. The certificate, sealed in a separate envelope, should be addressed to the Chair of Examiners for the Preliminary Examination in Medicine Part II   15
and submitted alongside the essay.

(iv) *Submission*

The essay (two paper copies and an electronic copy) must be submitted to the Chair of Examiners for the Preliminary Examination in Medicine Part II, c/o the Examination Schools, High Street, Oxford, not later than noon on the Friday of   20
Week 1 of Trinity Term.

5. *Extended Synoptic Essay on a Science topic*
  (i) *Form and subject of the essay*

Candidates will be required to submit an essay on a topic approved by the examiners, illustrating a technique or scientific application across several fields of   25
clinical or basic science. The submitted essay shall be of not more than 3,000 words, excluding any tables, figures, diagrams, or references. It must be in a format prescribed by the Graduate-entry Education Committee and published in the *Notes of Guidance for the Preliminary Examination in Medicine*.

A list of suggested essay titles, and the topics to which they relate, approved by   30
the Chair of Examiners in consultation with the Chair of the Graduate-entry Education Committee, shall be published no later than the end of Week 5 of the Michaelmas Term in the academic year of the examination. Candidates may also propose their own titles. Candidates may not submit an essay that closely relates to work that they have previously submitted for any university examination.   35

A candidate wishing to offer an essay with a title not on the approved list must apply for approval of their proposed title by no later than the end of Week 0 of Hilary Term in the academic year of the examination. Application shall be made via the Course Administrator in the Medical School Office and shall include the proposed title, a brief outline of the subject matter, and the topic or topics to which   40
it relates. Decision on the application shall be made by the Chair of Examiners in consultation with the Chair of the Graduate-entry Education Committee and shall be communicated to the candidate as soon as possible and in any case not later than Week 2 of Hilary Term in the academic year of the examination.

(ii) *Registration*   45

No later than the end of Week 0 of Hilary Term in the academic year of the examination, every candidate must register the title of their essay via the Course Administrator in the Medical School Office.

(iii) *Authorship*

The essay must be the candidate's own work. Candidates' tutors, or their   50
deputies nominated to act as advisors, may discuss with candidates the pro-

posed field of study, the sources available, and the method of treatment, but on no account may they read or comment on any written draft. Every candidate shall sign a certificate to the effect that this rule has been observed and that the essay is their own work. The certificate, sealed in a separate envelope, should be addressed to the Chair of Examiners for the Preliminary Examination in 5 Medicine Part II and submitted alongside the essay.

(iv) *Submission*
The essay (two paper copies and an electronic copy) must be submitted to the Chair of Examiners for the Preliminary Examination in Medicine Part II, c/o the Examination Schools, High Street, Oxford, not later than noon on the 10 Friday of Week 1 of Trinity Term.

6. *A clinical long case, followed by a viva*
Candidates will be assessed on their clinical history and examination skills, including their communication skills and professional behaviour, and knowledge of differential diagnosis and firstline investigations. 15

7. *An Objective Structured Clinical Examination or similar problem-based clinical assessment*
Candidates will be assessed on their ability to perform a clinical examination of the systems of the body specified in the core curriculum, and on their practical skills, and on their ability to interpret and use clinical data. 20

8. In addition to the above examination, candidates will be required to have satisfactorily completed the following courses of instruction during Year 2:
  (a) practical skills and procedures (defined in the core curriculum) to be assessed in course. A completed checklist of these skills and procedures, signed by the appropriate Clinical Tutor or other representative nominated by the Course 25 Director, is required as a qualification for entry to the examination. These skills may be re-sampled during the end-of-year clinical assessment.
  (b) the Laboratory Medicine course (as prescribed for the Second Examination for the Degree of BM, Year 1).
  (c) Medicine (as prescribed for the Second Examination for the Degree of BM, 30 Year 1).
  (d) Surgery (as prescribed for the Second Examination for the Degree of BM, Year 1).

SECOND BM

Second Examination for the Degree of Bachelor of Medicine 35

1. A candidate may be admitted to the Second Examination if his or her name has been entered on the University Register of Clinical Students and he or she has satisfied one of the following conditions:
  (*a*) he or she has passed in all the subjects of the First Examination and the Qualifying Examination in the Principles of Clinical Anatomy and has either been 40 admitted to the Degree of Bachelor of Arts with Honours or obtained a bachelor's degree at another university; or
  (*b*) he or she has passed in all the subjects of the Preliminary Examination in Medicine; or
  (*c*) he or she has both 45
    (i) successfully completed at a university in the United Kingdom a GMC-approved course of study in medical sciences that has included the subjects of the First Examination and the Principles of Clinical Anatomy, and is deemed by the Medical Sciences Board to qualify the candidate for admission; and

(ii) obtained a bachelor's degree in science or arts at a university, such degree having been approved by the Board.

2. Candidates for the Second Examination for the Degree of Bachelor of Medicine are required to pursue their studies during a period of: normally 38 weeks in Year 1; normally 45 weeks in Year 2; normally 46 weeks in Year 3; provided that the Medical Sciences Board shall have power to permit candidates to vary the dates of their studies so long as the overall programme requirement is met.

3. The Second Examination for the Degree of Bachelor of Medicine shall be under the supervision of the Medical Sciences Board. The Board shall have power to require candidates for admission to any part of the Second Examination to produce certificates of attendance at courses of practical instruction, and such other certificates as the Board may from time to time determine, and to define the form of such certificates. It shall be the duty of the Registrar to see that these conditions are observed.

4. The subject of the Second Examination shall be clinical medicine in all its aspects.

(*a*) The Second Examination shall cover three years, the subjects for each year being prescribed by regulation of the Medical Sciences Board.

(*b*) Each of Years 1 and 2 shall involve a form of assessment prescribed by regulation of the Board which shall be notified to candidates. No candidate shall commence Year 2 or 3 until he or she has satisfactorily completed Year 1 or 2 respectively (except that a candidate shall be permitted to commence Year 2 if he or she has passed in all the subjects in the Preliminary Examination in Medicine), unless the Director of Clinical Studies and the Associate Director of Clinical Studies, at their discretion and in exceptional circumstances, decide that the candidate may proceed to the next year of study on condition that he or she should undertake remedial work and if necessary be reassessed at a later date.

(*c*) Year 3 shall involve written and clinical examinations and may involve oral examinations. No candidate shall be examined on the Year 3 Vocational Skills Course until he or she has passed the assessments for Years 1 and 2 and the Year 3 General Clinical Studies Course.

5. A candidate who has passed in all the subjects of the Preliminary Examination in Medicine shall be exempted from the Year 1 assessments of the Second Examination and shall be permitted to proceed directly to commence Year 2.

6. The examiners may award a Distinction for outstanding performance over the three years. Criteria for Distinctions will be determined by the Medical Sciences Board.

7. The examiners may award merits in each of the examined subjects in Years 1, 2 and 3.

8. Breach of the Code of Conduct for Medical Students, as approved and from time to time amended by Council's General Purposes Committee on the recommendation of the Medical Sciences Board, may be deemed to be a ground for removal of a student's name from the University Register of Clinical Students according to procedures which shall always be subject to approval by Council's General Purposes Committee on the recommendation of the Medical Sciences Board.

9. The provisions of the appropriate regulations, concerning the times of holding examinations and the entry of names, and the special regulation concerning dress shall not, unless otherwise prescribed by regulation of the board, apply to Years 1 and 2, except in the case of a formal examination set by the examiners of these stages, as prescribed by regulation of the Board.

Regulations for Assessment in Years 1, 2, and 3

Proposals for the assessment of candidates in Years 1, 2, and 3 of the examination shall be drawn up by each specialty group, or in the case of Year 3 by the Board's Clinical Education Committee and submitted for approval to the Medical Sciences

Board, at such times as the Board shall determine. The form or forms of assessment
are chosen from among the following:

    (*a*) clinical examination including long and short cases;

    (*b*) competency check sheets, logbooks, or portfolios;

    (*c*) examination and comment (written or viva voce) on specimens;   5

    (*d*) objective structured clinical examinations;

    (*e*) poster presentations;

    (*f*) case presentations;

    (*g*) written tests, which may consist in whole or in part of, for example, multiple
choice questions, short answer questions, extended matching questions or essays;   10

    (*h*) case histories and commentaries;

    (*i*) prepared essays;

    (*j*) viva voce examinations; and

    (*k*) other tests individually approved by the Board.

In clinical subjects, all assessments shall include a test of clinical competence. In   15
addition, reports on candidates' attendance and general aptitude shown during the
course of instruction shall be made by those responsible for the course and taken into
consideration in association with the performance of candidates in the assessment.

A candidate shall be warned (in writing with a copy to the Director of Clinical
Studies) by those responsible for the course in question before the assessment takes   20
place, if his or her attendance and general aptitude are such as seems likely to
jeopardise his or her chances of passing the assessment.

The first assessment of candidates shall be carried out during or at the conclusion of
each component of the course by the staff, as appointed by the head of the relevant
department, or, in the case of Year 3, by the examiners and/or assessors. Candidates in   25
Years 1 and 3 shall be permitted a maximum of three attempts to pass an assessment.
In Year 2 the Examination Board may require candidates to be assessed in a specified
module or modules on one further occasion. Candidates in Year 2 shall be permitted a
maximum of two attempts in order to pass Year 2.

It shall be the responsibility of the staff concerned, under the supervision of the   30
Medical Sciences Board, to give the candidates and the relevant examiners and/or
assessors, reasonable notice of the dates on which the assessments will take place, to
decide on the outcome of each assessment, and to keep departmental records of each
assessment. A candidate should not normally be assessed exclusively by staff members
who have been responsible for his or her instruction.   35

Year 1

Syllabus and Examination

In Year 1, students are required to satisfy the examiners in:

    (*a*) the Laboratory Medicine course (concerning the application to human disease of
the principles of Laboratory Medicine, including Histopathology, Microbiology   40
and Infection, Clinical Biochemistry, Immunology, and Haematology);

    (*b*) Medicine;

    (*c*) Surgery.

Each candidate will be assessed according to the methods approved by the Medical
Sciences Board and notified to candidates before the commencement of each course of   45
instruction.

Candidates must satisfy the relevant head of department or his or her deputy, or the
Director of Clinical Studies and the Associate Director of Clinical Studies, that they

have attended a course of instruction, and attained the necessary skills, knowledge and understanding in:

(a) The Patient Doctor 2 Course (being an introduction to clinical methods, history taking and physical examination);

(b) Anaesthetics;   5

(c) Clinical Pharmacology;

(d) Communication Skills;

(e) Medical Ethics and Law;

(f) Primary Health Care;

(g) Radiology;   10

(h) Special Study approved on behalf of the Medical Sciences Board.

No candidate shall commence Year 2 until he or she has satisfactorily completed Year 1, unless the Director of Clinical Studies and the Associate Director of Clinical Studies at their discretion should, in exceptional circumstances, decide that the candidate may proceed to Year 2 on condition that he or she should undertake remedial   15
work and if necessary be reassessed at a later date.

Assessment

A candidate in Year 1 who fails to reach a satisfactory standard in any part of the assessment at the first attempt may offer himself or herself for reassessment on one further occasion and will only be required to be reassessed in the part or parts of the   20
assessment they have failed.

If a candidate fails to reach a satisfactory standard at the second attempt in any part of the assessment, the head of department concerned, or his or her deputy, shall require the candidate to be reassessed in the part or parts of the assessment previously failed after completing the necessary coursework; this assessment shall be carried out   25
and adjudged by the staff appointed by the relevant head of department and in the presence of an external examiner. In the event that a candidate's performance is judged to be unsatisfactory at this third attempt then his or her name shall be removed from the Register of Clinical Students subject to appeal to the Medical Sciences Board.   30

Duties of the Examiners

In the first assessment of candidates in Year 1 each relevant pair of examiners shall be required to attend, and if they so wish participate, on at least one occasion each year.

In the reassessment of any candidate who has been deemed to have failed the whole assessment in Year 1, the external examiner shall be present and may participate if he   35
or she wishes.

Year 3 examiners may assist with the assessment in Year 1.

Year 2

Syllabus and Examination

In Year 2, students are required to satisfy the examiners in: 40

(a) Neurology and Neurosurgery;

(b) Obstetrics and Gynaecology (including Genito-Urinary Medicine);

(c) Orthopaedics, Rheumatology, Trauma and Emergency Medicine;

(d) Paediatrics;

(e) Community-based Subjects (encompassing Geratology, Dermatology,   45
Palliative Care, Primary Care and Population Health 2: Public Health);

(f) Psychiatry.

Each candidate will be assessed according to the methods approved by the Medical Sciences Board and notified to candidates before the commencement of each course of instruction.   50

Candidates must satisfy the relevant head of department or his or her deputy, that they have attended a course of instruction in, and attained the necessary skills, knowledge and understanding in:

 (*a*) Ophthalmology;

 (*b*) Otolaryngology. 5

No candidate shall commence Year 3 until he or she has satisfactorily completed Year 2, unless the Director of Clinical Studies and the Associate Director of Clinical Studies at their discretion should, in exceptional circumstances, decide that the candidate may proceed to Year 3 on condition that he or she should undertake remedial work and if necessary be reassessed at a later date. 10

Assessment
A candidate in Year 2 who fails to reach a satisfactory standard in any individual course module assessment at the first attempt and is required by the Examination Board to be reassessed, will only be required to be reassessed in the part or parts of the assessment they have failed. 15

A candidate must reach the threshold pass mark for Year 2 (from the sum of cumulative marks awarded from each course module assessment) and satisfy the Examination Board in a minimum of five out of the six modules, or the candidate will be deemed to have failed the second year of the course. A candidate who has been deemed to have failed will be allowed only one further attempt to pass Year 2 and will 20
be required to repeat the second year of the course in its entirety. In the event that a candidate's performance is judged to be unsatisfactory at this second attempt then his or her name shall be removed from the University Register of Clinical Students subject to appeal to the Medical Sciences Board.

Duties of the Examiners 25
In the first assessment of candidates in the individual course module assessments of Year 2 each relevant pair of examiners/specialty advisors shall be required to attend, and if they so wish participate, on at least one occasion in each year.

Year 3

Syllabus and Examination 30
In Year 3, students are required to satisfy: (a) the examiners in General Clinical Studies; and (b) the Director of Clinical Studies and the Associate Director of Clinical Studies in Vocational Skills. Each candidate will be assessed according to the methods approved by the Medical Sciences Board and notified to candidates before the commencement of each course of instruction. Students who fail an assess- 35
ment will have to forfeit part or all of the elective for a period of intensive clinical training.

1. General Clinical Studies
Students are required to satisfy the examiners in:

 (*a*) Medicine and Surgery encompassing Communication Skills, Radiology, and 40
Clinical Pharmacology; and

 (*b*) Specialties studied but not previously formally examined (namely Ophthalmology and Otolaryngology).

Candidates must satisfy the Director of Clinical Studies and the Associate Director of Clinical Studies that they have attended a course of instruction in Special Study and 45
Clinical Options approved by the Medical Sciences Board.

2. Vocational Skills

Students are required to satisfy the Director of Clinical Studies and the Associate Director of Clinical Studies that they have provided work to a satisfactory standard in:

   (*a*) Special Study and Clinical Options as approved by the Medical Sciences Board;

   (*b*) A Course to prepare students for work as a Foundation 1 doctor;   5

   (*c*) An Elective (students who fail an assessment may be required to complete remedial clinical work. These students will forfeit part, or all, of the elective and instead will be required to produce a satisfactory report at the end of an additional clinical attachment);

   (*d*) A student assistantship with a clinical team; and   10

   (*e*) An assessment in procedural skills.

Assessment

A candidate in Year 3 who fails to reach a satisfactory standard at the first attempt in any part of the assessment in medicine and surgery will be deemed, normally, to have failed the complete assessment and may offer himself or herself for reassessment   15
on one further occasion. This reassessment will be undertaken in the presence of an external examiner. A candidate in this position will usually be required to be reassessed in all parts of the assessment, unless the examiners specifically direct that there be reassessment only in the part or parts in which the candidate has failed to reach a satisfactory standard.   20

If a candidate fails to reach a satisfactory standard at the second attempt in any part of the assessment, then the candidate shall be deemed to have failed the complete assessment. The examiners shall require the candidate to be reassessed after completing the necessary coursework; this assessment shall be carried out and adjudged by the examiners, which shall include an external examiner. In the event that a candidate's   25
performance is judged to be unsatisfactory at this third attempt then his or her name shall be removed from the University Register of Clinical Students subject to appeal to the Medical Sciences Board.

Duties of the Examiners

1. General Clinical Studies   30

The examination shall be arranged and conducted by the Year 3 Examination Board under the direction of the Chair of Examiners and the Principal Examiners in Medicine and Surgery.

When fewer than ten candidates present themselves the examination shall be arranged and conducted by the Chair of Examiners and the Principal Examiners in   35
Medicine and Surgery.

In considering whether a candidate has passed the assessment, the examiners may fail a candidate who does not satisfy them in one part of the assessment, even if he or she has satisfied them in other parts at that stage.

2. Vocational Skills   40

Candidates shall be required to submit to the Director of Clinical Studies and the Associate Director of Clinical Studies such evidence as they require of the successful completion of their work.

In considering whether candidates shall have passed the assessment, the Director of Clinical Studies and the Associate Director of Clinical Studies may fail a candidate   45
who has provided either none or insufficient evidence of satisfactory completion of one part of the course, even if he or she has satisfied them in other parts of the course.

MASTER OF SURGERY
A

1. Any person may supplicate for the Degree of Master of Surgery provided that:
(*a*) *either*

  (i) he or she has been admitted to the Degree of Bachelor of Surgery and has 5
  entered upon the thirtieth term from his or her matriculation, or in the case of a
  person who has incorporated as a Bachelor of Surgery, the thirtieth term from
  the date of matriculation at the University of Cambridge, or in the case of a
  person who has been admitted to the Second Examination for the Degree of
  Bachelor of Medicine under the provisions of the appropriate regulation, the 10
  twenty-first term from his or her matriculation;

or

  (ii) he or she holds the Degree of Master of Arts of the University (other than a
  degree by decree or special resolution or a degree honoris causa), has previously
  been entered in the Register of University Medical Students and has passed the 15
  First Examination for the Degree of Bachelor of Medicine of this University,
  holds a medical degree of another British university qualifying him or her to
  practise medicine, and has entered upon the thirtieth term from his or her
  matriculation;

(*b*) he or she has passed the FRCS or equivalent examination, and passed the 20
examination hereinafter prescribed.

2. The examination shall consist of a thesis, and may include a viva voce examination to test the candidate's general competence in his or her own field.

3. No candidate shall be admitted to the examination earlier than the sixteenth
term from the date of passing the Second Examination for the Degree of Bachelor of 25
Medicine or an equivalent final medical examination from a university approved by
Council i.e. a university approved for the purpose of senior status or a university
especially approved for the purpose of this clause.

4. A candidate shall submit as evidence of his or her fitness to supplicate for the
degree a thesis upon a subject previously approved by the Medical Sciences Board, or 30
with the previous approval of that board a book or papers which have already been
published under his or her own name. A candidate may submit joint publications
provided that a substantial portion of the work submitted has been written solely by
him or her. He or she shall make his application to the Medical Sciences Board
through the Registrar, and shall at the same time submit: 35

(*a*) evidence that the subject of his or her thesis or published work has been
approved by the Medical Sciences Board;

(*b*) four printed or typewritten copies of an abstract, of around 400 to 450 words
and not exceeding 600 words, summarising the scope of the thesis or other evidence,
the techniques used, and the principal findings; 40

(*c*) a certificate from the proper officer of his or her society that his or her application has the approval of that society;

(*d*) the fee prescribed in the appropriate regulation;

(*e*) such number of copies of his or her evidence in such form as the board may by
regulation direct. 45

The thesis or other evidence shall be accompanied by a certificate signed by the
candidate indicating that it is the candidate's own work except where otherwise
indicated. If the thesis or published work has not been submitted for examination

before the sixteenth term after approval has been given under this clause, the candidate is required to seek reapproval of his or her submission.

5. On receipt of any such application, the Registrar shall submit it to the Medical Sciences Board. The board shall thereupon appoint two examiners whose duties shall be:

(1) to consider the evidence sent in by the candidate under the provisions of the preceding clause; provided that they shall exclude from consideration in making their report any part of the evidence that *either*

(*a*) has already been accepted, or is being concurrently submitted for any degree in this or any other University, and shall have the power to require the candidate to produce for their inspection the complete thesis so accepted or concurrently submitted; or

(*b*) does not represent the candidate's own work;

(2) if they think fit to examine the candidate orally;

(3) to report to the board through the Registrar;

(4) to return to the Registrar, with their report, the copy or copies of the evidence submitted by the candidate.

6. On receipt of the report of the examiners, it shall be the duty of the board to decide whether to permit the candidate to supplicate for the Degree of Master of Surgery, but permission shall in no case be given unless the examiners have reported that the work as embodied in his or her evidence and tested by his or her examination has resulted in an original contribution to knowledge deserving publication (whether or not already published) based on clinical and/or experimental observations, and that it is in their opinion of sufficient merit to entitle the candidate to supplicate for the Degree of Master of Surgery.

7. If the board approves the evidence as of sufficient merit for the degree, the board shall notify its decision in the University Gazette and one copy of the thesis or of each of the papers and books submitted as evidence shall remain in the possession of the University for deposit in Bodley's Library.

B

M.Ch.

1. Dissertations, theses, or published work for the M.Ch. must be submitted in *English* unless for exceptional reasons the Medical Sciences Board otherwise determines at the time of approving the subject of a dissertation or thesis, or granting leave to submit published work, as the case may be.

2. Candidates are required to send three copies of any dissertation, thesis, book, or papers submitted. Dissertations or theses must be either printed or typewritten and should not normally exceed 50,000 words (excluding appendices and case reports). Only in exceptional circumstances and with the approval of the Medical Sciences Board is it permitted to exceed this limit.

3. Candidates are required to submit at the same time as their application four printed or typewritten copies of an abstract, of around 400 to 450 words and not exceeding 600 words, summarising the scope of the dissertation, thesis, or published work, the techniques used, and the principal findings. One copy of the abstract will be used for the appointment of judges or examiners. One copy must be bound into the copy of the dissertation or thesis which, if the applicant is successful, will be deposited in the Bodleian Library. The abstract may also be bound into the other two copies of the dissertation, thesis, or published work if the candidate so desires. Each copy of the abstract shall be headed with the title of the dissertation, thesis, or published work, the name and college of the candidate, the degree for which it is submitted, and the term of submission.

4. Unless the board has excused the candidate from this requirement, the dissertation or thesis must be typed on one side of the paper only with a margin of 3 to 3.5 cms on the left-hand edge of each paper. The dissertation, thesis, or published work must have a stabbed binding with covers of stout manila or stiff cardboard and a canvas back, or must be stitched and bound in a stiff case. (It should be noted that the 5 dissertation, thesis, or published work must be bound and that a loose-leaf binder of the screw-in type is not acceptable.)

Candidates are advised to pack each copy of the dissertation, thesis, or published work into a separate parcel, ready in all respects, except the address, to be posted to the judges or examiners when appointed. Each parcel should bear the candidate's 10 name and college and the words 'M.Ch. THESIS' as appropriate in BLOCK CAPITALS in the bottom left-hand corner. The separate copies thus packed should be sent to the Examination Schools, High Street, Oxford OX1 4BG, in one covering parcel.

5. Oral Examination for the M.Ch. 15

(1) The examination may be attended by any member of the University in academic dress. No person who is not a member of the University may attend it except with the consent of both judges or examiners.

(2) The place, day, and hour of the examination shall be fixed by the judges or examiners, who shall be responsible for informing the candidate thereof by post 20 prepaid, and it shall be the duty of the candidate to ensure that any letter addressed to him is forwarded to him if away. The judges or examiners shall allow reasonable time for receiving an acknowledgement from the candidate of their summons. The day shall be fixed by the judges or examiners to suit their own convenience, but they are asked, in order that the candidate may know what 25 arrangements he may safely make, to give the candidate early information of the date fixed, even though it may be some considerable time ahead.

(3) Notice of the examination shall be given by the judges or examiners to the Registrar.

(4) If, owing to illness or other urgent and unforeseen cause, a judge or 30 examiner is unable to attend the examination, it shall be postponed to a later date, provided that, if the Vice-Chancellor is satisfied that postponement will be a serious hardship to the candidate, he may authorise another person to attend the examination as a substitute. Such substitute shall not be required to sign the report, but he shall receive such remuneration as the Vice-Chancellor and 35 Proctors shall determine.

DOCTOR OF MEDICINE

Status of Student for the Degree of Doctor of Medicine

1. Any person may supplicate for the Degree of Doctor of Medicine if *either*:

(1) he or she has been admitted to the Degree of Bachelor of Medicine and has 40 entered upon the thirty-sixth term from his or her matriculation, or, in the case of a person who has been admitted to the Oxford Graduate Entry Medical Course, the thirtieth term from the date of his or her matriculation, or, in the case of a person who has incorporated as a Bachelor of Medicine, the thirty-sixth term from the date of his or her matriculation at the 45 University of Cambridge, or, in the case of a person who has been admitted to the Second Examination for the Degree of Bachelor of Medicine under the provisions of clause 1 of the special regulations for the Second Examination for the Degree of Bachelor of Medicine, the twenty-seventh term from his or her matriculation; *or* 50

(2) he or she holds the Degree of Master of Arts of the University (other than a degree by decree or resolution or an honorary degree), has previously been entered in the Register of University Medical Students and has passed the First Examination for the Degree of Bachelor of Medicine of this University, holds a degree qualifying him or her to be placed on the Medical Register,   5
and has entered upon the thirty-sixth term from his or her matriculation.

2. It shall be the duty of the Registrar to keep a Register of those admitted to the status of Student for the Degree of Doctor of Medicine.

3. On application for admission to the status of Student for the Degree of Doctor of Medicine, the applicant shall state whether he or she will wish to submit as his or her   10
dissertation a series of papers or books, as permitted under clause 3 of the regulations for the Examination of Students for the Degree of Doctor of Medicine.

Registration for the Degree of Doctor of Medicine
1. Except in the case of submission of published work as a dissertation for the degree, no student shall submit a dissertation until at least the beginning of the sixth   15
term after the Medical Sciences Board has granted his or her admission.

2. A student must carry out the bulk of the research for the dissertation during the period in which he or she is registered.

3. If the dissertation, including published work submitted as a dissertation, has not been submitted for examination before the fifteenth term after admission has been   20
granted, a student shall be required to seek readmission.

Advisers of Students for the Degree of Doctor of Medicine
1. (1) Except in the case of students submitting published work as a dissertation for the degree, every student on admission as a Student for the Degree of Doctor of Medicine shall be allocated to an Adviser in Oxford appointed by the   25
Medical Sciences Board in the student's area of research.

(2) In the case of students working outside Oxford, each student shall be required to seek additional advice from a senior member of the academic or clinical staff at the institution at which the research is to be pursued; and the student shall notify the Medical Sciences Board of the name of that   30
person and provide a written statement signed by that person confirming that he or she is willing to undertake the role of an additional Adviser.

2. (1) It shall be the duty of the Adviser to offer support and assistance to the student in the manner prescribed in the *Memorandum of Guidance for Advisers and Students for the Degree of Doctor of Medicine* as published   35
from time to time by the Medical Sciences Board.

(2) The Adviser shall submit reports on the progress of the student's work at the beginning of each Michaelmas and Trinity Term, and the reports of Advisers outside Oxford shall, in the case of the relevant students, also be received by the Adviser in Oxford.   40

(3) It shall be the responsibility of the Adviser at the host institution (whether that is Oxford or elsewhere) to inform the Medical Sciences Board if he or she is of the opinion that the student is unlikely to reach the standard required for the Degree of Doctor of Medicine.

3. (1) Except when approval has been given for submission of published work as a   45
dissertation for the degree, it shall be the duty of every Student for the Degree of Doctor of Medicine to seek the advice of the Adviser (or, in the case of students working outside Oxford, both Advisers) at an early stage of the proposed research and to seek comments on his or her dissertation before its submission.   50

(2) During the course of the research the student shall maintain contact with the Adviser or Advisers in the manner prescribed in the *Memorandum of Guidance for Advisers and Students for the Degree of Doctor of Medicine.*

Confirmation of status as a Student for the Degree of Doctor of Medicine

1. (1) Except in the case of submission of published work as a dissertation, a student registered for the Degree of Doctor of Medicine must, not later than the sixth term and not earlier than the third term after that in which he or she was admitted to the status of Student for the Degree of Doctor of Medicine, apply to the Medical Sciences Board for confirmation of that status.

   (2) Except in the case of students submitting published work as a dissertation, all Students for the Degree of Doctor of Medicine shall have their status confirmed before they may make an application for the appointment of examiners.

2. Students applying for confirmation of status shall submit their application to the Medical Sciences Board through the Registrar; and each application shall be accompanied by:

   (1) a report on the work undertaken since registration;

   (2) a statement from the Adviser at the place where the work is being undertaken commenting on whether the student's progress provides firm evidence that the work when completed is likely to reach the standard required for the Degree of Doctor of Medicine.

3. (1) If, after considering a student's application for confirmation of status, the Medical Sciences Board concludes that the student's progress does not warrant confirmation, the board may permit the submission of a further application not later than the third term after the original application.

   (2) If the second application is unsuccessful, the student's name shall be removed from the Register of Students for the Degree of Doctor of Medicine.

4. Except in the case of submission of published work as a dissertation for the degree, a Student for the Degree of Doctor of Medicine shall cease to hold that status unless it has been confirmed within nine terms of his or her admission to that status.

Examination of Students for the Degree of Doctor of Medicine

1. A Student for the Degree of Doctor of Medicine who has, where applicable, fulfilled the requirements set out in the regulations for Registration for the Degree of Doctor of Medicine and Confirmation of Status as a Student for the Degree of Doctor of Medicine respectively, and whose status has not expired, may apply to the Medical Sciences Board for the appointment of examiners and for leave to supplicate for the Degree of Doctor of Medicine.

2. Students admitted to the Degree of Doctor of Medicine prior to April 2002 will be given the option of examination under the regulations introduced in April 2002.

3. (1) A Student for the Degree of Doctor of Medicine may

   either

   (*a*) submit a dissertation upon a subject which, together with the proposed manner of treating it, has previously been approved by the Medical Sciences Board;

   or

   (*b*) in exceptional circumstances, submit as his or her dissertation a series of papers or books published at least twelve months before the proposed date of submission, if the previous approval of the Medical Sciences

Board has been given after considering the seniority of the student (who shall be required to have held a career-grade post for a period of at least fifteen years prior to submission), and the opinions of any referees who may be consulted.

(2) Submission of published works as a dissertation shall be permitted only when there is evidence of outstanding quality in the scientific papers or other works intended for submission; it shall also be a requirement that the published works be accompanied by a general introduction and a general conclusion and that they form a continuous theme.

4. Applications for the appointment of examiners and for leave to supplicate shall be made to the Medical Sciences Board through the Medical Sciences Graduate School Office and shall include:

(1) a statement by the candidate that the thesis is his or her own work, except where otherwise indicated;

(2) a statement by the candidate of what part, if any, of the thesis has already been accepted, or is concurrently being submitted, for any degree or diploma or certificate or other qualification in this University or elsewhere;

(3) a statement, where applicable, from the Adviser at the place where the research was undertaken certifying that the candidate has sought his or her advice as appropriate;

(4) a statement from the candidate's college in support of the application;

(5) two printed or typewritten copies of an abstract of the thesis, which shall not normally exceed 300 words in length.

5. Where the Medical Sciences Board has given approval for submission of published work as a dissertation, two printed or typewritten copies of the thesis may be submitted by the student immediately after approval, in a format which is in accordance with the instructions obtainable from the Medical Sciences Board through the Medical Sciences Graduate School Office.

6. In all other cases, students shall submit an application in accordance with clause 4 above up to four months in advance of submitting two printed or typewritten copies of the thesis in a format which is in accordance with the instructions obtainable from the Medical Sciences Board through the Medical Sciences Graduate School Office.

7. If a student has not submitted his or her thesis for examination within twelve months from submission of the application under the provisions of clause 4 above, then the application shall lapse.

8. (1) On receipt of an application the Medical Sciences Board shall appoint two examiners, neither of whom shall be the student's Adviser, and one of whom shall be external to the University.

(2) The duties of the examiners shall be:

(*a*) to consider the thesis and the abstract of it submitted by the candidate, except that they shall exclude from consideration in making their report any part of the thesis that either has already been accepted, or is concurrently being submitted, for any degree or diploma or certificate or other qualification in this University or elsewhere, or does not represent the candidate's own work;

(*b*) to examine the candidate orally in the subject of his or her thesis, unless, in exceptional circumstances in the case of submission of published work as a dissertation, the board agrees, on the recommendation of the examiners, to dispense with this requirement;

(*c*) to report to the Medical Sciences Board through the Registrar on the scope, character, and quality of the work submitted, in the manner prescribed in clause 10 below;

(*d*) to return to the candidate the copies of the thesis and abstract.

9. (1) The Medical Sciences Board shall have power to make regulations concerning the notice to be given of the oral examination, and of the time and place at which it may be held.

(2) The examination may be attended by any member of the University in academic dress, while non-members may attend only with the consent of the examiners.

(3) The Vice-Chancellor and Proctors after consultation with the board may decide (either at their own discretion or at the request of the student or the supervisor or department) to forbid the attendance of any person or all persons (other than the examiners and the candidate) or to impose any condition on attendance if and to the extent that such action is in their view necessary to protect the interests of the University or the candidate or both, and the examiners shall be informed accordingly and shall include this information in the notice of examination.

10. Having completed the examination, the examiners may make one of the following recommendations in their report to the Medical Sciences Board, or they may alternatively proceed in accordance with the provisions of clause 11 below:

(1) that the board grant the student leave to supplicate for the Degree of Doctor of Medicine, if making this recommendation, the examiners shall include in their report statements that:

(*a*) the student possesses a comprehensive knowledge of the particular field of learning in which the thesis falls;

(*b*) the thesis embodies original observations on either clinical or experimental material;

(*c*) the work done by the student and embodied in the thesis has resulted in an original and substantial contribution to medical science;

(*d*) the thesis is presented in a lucid and scholarly manner;

(*e*) the student has presented a satisfactory abstract of the thesis;

(*f*) in their opinion the thesis merits the award of the Degree of Doctor of Medicine;

(2) that the board offer the student the option of reference of the thesis back to him or her in order that he or she may revise it for re-examination for the Degree of Doctor of Medicine on not more than one occasion, on the basis that the thesis has not reached the standard required for the Degree of Doctor of Medicine; if making this recommendation, the examiners shall annex to their report to the board a statement, for transmission to the student, setting out the respects in which the thesis falls below the standard required for the degree and what changes are necessary for it to reach that required standard, and setting a deadline (subject to the agreement of the board) for resubmission;

(3) that, in the case of a student whose thesis has already been referred back on one occasion, the student's application for leave to supplicate be refused; if making this recommendation, the examiners shall annex to their report a statement, for transmission to the student, setting out the respects in which the thesis falls below the standard required for the degree.

11. (1) If the examiners are satisfied that the student's thesis is of sufficient merit to qualify for the degree but consider, nevertheless, that before the thesis is

deposited the student should make minor corrections (which are not sufficiently substantial to justify reference back for re-examination), they shall
require the student to correct the thesis to their satisfaction before they
submit their report.

(2) If the student has not completed these corrections within three calendar   5
months of the date of the oral examination, his or her name shall be
removed by the Registrar from the Register of Students for the Degree of
Doctor of Medicine, except that the board may, on good cause shown by
the student, grant an extension of time of three further calendar months in
which the student may fulfil this requirement before the removal of his or   10
her name from the Register.

(3) No subsequent extension shall be granted, but it shall be open to a student
who has failed to fulfil this requirement within those three or six months in
total, as the case may be, to apply to the board for reinstatement as a
Student for the Degree of Doctor of Medicine, with the support of his or her   15
college and Adviser(s), upon submission to the Registrar of a copy of his or
her thesis incorporating the required corrections, and upon payment of such
reinstatement fee as may from time to time be prescribed by Council by
decree; leave to supplicate shall not be granted until this fee has been paid.

12. The Medical Sciences Board may exempt a candidate who is being re-examined   20
under the provision of clause 10(2) above from a further oral examination, if the
examiners are able to certify that they are satisfied without examining the candidate
orally that they can recommend to the board in the terms required by clause 10(1)
above that he or she be given leave to supplicate for the Degree of Doctor of Medicine.

13. In an exceptional case in which the Medical Sciences Board is unable to accept   25
the examiners' recommendation, or in which the examiners cannot reach an agreed
recommendation, the board shall have power to appoint one or two new examiners, as
it deems necessary, to conduct such further examination of the candidate as the board
may require.

14. (1) A student who has been granted leave to supplicate by the board shall be   30
required to submit to the Registrar a copy of his or her thesis, incorporating
any amendments or corrections required by the examiners and approved by
the board, with a view to deposit in the Bodleian or other appropriate
university library.

(2) Leave to supplicate shall in all cases be conditional upon fulfilment of this   35
requirement.

15. (1) It shall be the duty of the Registrar to notify the student of the board's
decision as soon as may be.

(2) The Registrar shall also be responsible for publishing at the end of each
academic year (except in so far as it may be necessary not to publish any   40
name in order to comply with the provisions of the Data Protection Act
1998) the names of those students to whom permission to supplicate has
been granted during that year, together with a statement of the subject of
the thesis written by each.

16. When, on the conclusion of an investigation of a complaint made by a student,   45
the Proctors recommend that a student be re-examined, the board shall have power to
hold a new examination.

DM

1. *Admission*

Students qualified under the appropriate regulation may apply for admission as a Student for the Degree of Doctor of Medicine to the Medical Sciences Board through the Registrar. Such application shall be accompanied by:　　　　　　　　　　　5

(i) a completed application form (obtainable from the Medical Sciences Graduate School Office);

(ii) a statement of not more than 1,500 words outlining the proposed scope of the research to be undertaken and provisional thesis title;

and, in the case of students wishing to submit published work, the following　　10
additional information:

(iii) a list of the works to be submitted, details of their publication, and a statement on whether any part of the work to be submitted has previously been accepted for a degree. A student who submits work that has been produced in collaboration shall state in respect of each item the extent of his or her own contribu-　　15
tion. This statement must be certified by each of the senior and primary authors (where he or she is not the student) in the case of each piece of collaborative work submitted.

A set of published works may constitute an acceptable dissertation but only if with the addition of a general introduction and general conclusion they form a continuous　　20
theme.

2. *Confirmation of Status*

Students who have been admitted to DM status, and intend to submit a dissertation for a thesis, must, not later than six terms and not earlier than three terms after admission to DM status, apply for confirmation of that status.　　　　　　　　25

The requirements for confirmation of status are:

(i) completion by the student of the appropriate form (obtainable from the Medical Sciences Graduate School Office);

(ii) submission by the student of a report of no more than 2,500 words on the work undertaken since registration, including a comprehensive outline of the　　30
research topic, details of progress made, and the anticipated timetable for submission of the thesis;

(iii) completion of the appropriate form (obtainable from the Medical Sciences Graduate School Office) by the Adviser at the place where the work is being undertaken.　　　　　　　　　　　　　　　　　　　　　　　　35

The application shall be directed to the Graduate School Committee of the Medical Sciences Board, which shall appoint two assessors competent in the student's area of research (who may include the Adviser in Oxford in the case of students working outside Oxford). The assessors shall submit to the board's Graduate School Committee a report (using a form obtainable from the Medical Sciences Graduate　　40
School Office) after considering the student's report and, if necessary, interviewing the student. Before a decision is reached on whether or not confirmation of status should be approved the Graduate School Committee shall take into account the comments made on the application by the Adviser at the place of work and that Adviser's biannual reports.　　　　　　　　　　　　　　　　　　　　　　45

If the Graduate School Committee does not consider that the student's progress warrants confirmation of status it may either: (a) permit the resubmission of the application on one further occasion not later than the third term after the original application; or (b) reject the application.

A copy of the assessors' report, amended as necessary by the Graduate School　　50
Committee, will normally be made available to the student.

3. *Theses*

The requirements for the submission of a thesis are as follows:

(i) The completion by the student of the appropriate form (obtainable from the Medical Sciences Graduate School Office). The form may be submitted immediately in the case of students submitting published work as a dissertation and up to four months in advance of submitting the thesis in the case of other students.

(ii) The submission of two printed or typewritten copies of the thesis and two printed or typewritten copies of an abstract, formatted and supplied according to the instructions obtainable from the Medical Sciences Board through the Medical Sciences Graduate School Office.

4. *Oral Examination*

(i) The place, day, and hour of examination shall be fixed by the examiners, who shall be responsible for informing the student by post, and it shall be the duty of the student to ensure that any letter addressed to him or her is forwarded to him or her if away. The examiners shall allow reasonable time for receiving an acknowledgement from the student of their summons. The day shall be fixed by the examiners to suit their own convenience but they are asked, in order that the student may know what arrangements he or she may safely make, to give the student early information of the date fixed, even though it may be some considerable time ahead.

(ii) Notice of the examination shall be given by the examiners to the Research Degrees Team at the Examination Schools, High Street, Oxford, OX1 4BG.

(iii) If, owing to illness or other urgent or unforeseen cause, an examiner is unable to attend the examination, it shall be postponed to a later date, except that, if the Proctors are satisfied that postponement will be a serious hardship to the student, the Proctors may authorise another person to attend the examination as a substitute. The substitute shall not be required to sign the report, but he or she shall receive such remuneration as the Vice-Chancellor and Proctors shall determine.

NOTES

27

DOCTOR OF DIVINITY

1. Any person belonging to one of the following classes may become a candidate for the Degree of Doctor of Divinity under the conditions set forth in this section:

(a) Masters of Arts who have incepted in this University and have entered upon the thirtieth term from their matriculation;

(b) Masters of Arts of the University of Cambridge or Dublin who have been incorporated in this University and have entered upon the thirtieth term from their matriculation at Cambridge or Dublin;

(c) Undergraduates or Bachelors of Arts of the University of Cambridge or Dublin who have been incorporated and have incepted in the Faculty of Arts in this University and have entered upon the thirtieth term from their matriculation at Cambridge or Dublin;

(d) Persons on whom the Degree of Master of Arts has been conferred by decree or special resolution, other than a degree *honoris causa*, and who have entered upon the ninth term from their admission to that degree;

(e) Doctors of Philosophy, Masters of Letters or of Science, and Bachelors of Letters or of Science who have entered upon the twenty-first term from their matriculation.

2. A candidate for the Degree of Doctor of Divinity shall apply to the board through the Registrar and shall submit with his or her application work dealing with some subject or subjects in the area of Theology or the Study of Religions. At least three printed copies of all the work submitted shall be provided by the candidate. This evidence must consist of published papers or books and one year at least must elapse between the publication of any such paper or book and its submission as evidence in support of an application. The evidence may include published work previously submitted successfully by the candidate for the Degree of Bachelor of Divinity.

A candidate who submits work which has been produced in collaboration shall state in respect of each item the extent of his own contribution.

3. The application shall also be accompanied by the fee prescribed in the appropriate regulation (see Appendix I) and by a certificate signed by some officer of, or some person deputed by, the society to which the candidate belongs, and showing that his or her application has the approval of such society.

4. The work submitted by the candidate shall be examined by at least two judges appointed by the board. They shall report to the board through the Registrar, and it shall be the duty of the board to consider their report, and to decide whether the evidence submitted constitutes an original contribution to the advancement of theological knowledge of such substance and distinction as to give the candidate an authoritative status in this branch of learning.

5. If the board, after consideration of the reports of the judges, shall approve the evidence as sufficient for the degree, it shall give leave to the candidate to supplicate for the degree, and shall notify its decision in the *University Gazette*. One copy of each of the papers and books submitted as evidence shall remain in the possession of the

University for deposit in Bodleian Library, provided that no book or paper of which the library already possesses a copy shall be so deposited except with the consent of the candidate and of the librarian, unless the copy submitted by the candidate shall be of a different issue or shall contain alterations or additions.

5

NOTES

28

EXAMINATIONS FOR DIPLOMAS
AND CERTIFICATES

POSTGRADUATE DIPLOMA IN APPLIED
STATISTICS

GENERAL REGULATIONS

1. The Divisional Board of Mathematical, Physical and Life Sciences shall have power to grant Postgraduate Diplomas in Applied Statistics to candidates who have satisfied the conditions prescribed in this section.

2. The examination for the Postgraduate Diploma in Applied Statistics shall be under the supervision of the Divisional Board of Mathematical, Physical and Life Sciences.

3. Subject to the provisions of this section, any member of the University may be admitted to the course and to the examination who has obtained the leave of the Divisional Board of Mathematical, Physical and Life Sciences, provided that

   (*a*) he or she has passed all the examinations required for the Degree of Bachelor of Arts and has obtained First or good Second Class Honours in the Second Public Examination, or has obtained such honours in a degree examination of another university, such university having been approved by Council for the purposes of Senior Status, or

   (*b*) he or she is, in the opinion of the board, otherwise adequately qualified to undertake the course.

4. Applications for leave under the preceding clauses shall be sent to the Registrar through the head or tutor of the society to which the applicant belongs or desires to belong. The board shall have power to determine the character and length of a course of study to be followed by the applicant before he may be admitted to the examination.

5. On admitting an applicant as a candidate for the postgraduate diploma, the board shall appoint a supervisor who shall direct and superintend the work of the candidate. The supervisor shall submit a report on the progress of the candidate to the board at the end of each term (except the term in which the student enters for the examination) and at any other time when the board so requests or the supervisor believes it expedient. In particular the supervisor shall inform the board at once if he or she is of the opinion that a student is unlikely to reach the standard required for the postgraduate diploma.

6. After admission as a Postgraduate Diploma Student, a candidate must have kept statutory residence and pursued a course of study at Oxford for at least three terms before taking the examination, provided that a candidate for the Degree of Master of Science (Applied Statistics) may, with the approval of the Divisional Board of Mathematical, Physical and Life Sciences, transfer to the status of a Student for the Postgraduate Diploma in Applied Statistics not later than the last day of Hilary Term in the year in which the written examination is to be taken, in which case the date of

his or her admission as a Student for the Degree of Master of Science shall be reckoned as the date of his or her admission as a postgraduate diploma student; time spent outside Oxford during term as part of an academic programme approved by Council shall count towards residence for the purpose of this clause.

7. A Student reading for the postgraduate diploma who is not a graduate of the University may wear the same gown as that worn by Students for the Degree of Doctor of Philosophy.

8. The examiners may award a distinction for excellence in the whole examination. Candidates who have initially failed any element of assessment shall not normally be eligible for the award of distinction.

9. A candidate who failed to satisfy the examiners in any one of the examinations, may enter again for that examination on one, but not more than one, subsequent occasion.

SPECIAL REGULATIONS

1. The Divisional Board of Mathematical, Physical and Life Sciences shall elect for the supervision of the course a standing committee which shall have power to arrange lectures and other instruction.

2. Candidates shall follow for at least three terms a course of instruction in Statistics.

3. The examination will consist of a written examination consisting of two papers on the syllabus described in the schedule.

4. In the written examination the examiners will permit the use of bilingual dictionaries.

5. Each candidate will be expected to have displayed evidence of the ability to apply statistical methods to real data.

The examiners will take into account the results of an assessment of ability to apply statistical methods to real data organised by the standing committee. The committee will be responsible for notifying the candidates of the arrangements for the assessment, and for forwarding the assessed material to the Chair of Examiners before the end of the Trinity Term in the year in which the assessment is made. The supervisory committee may specify that one of the practical assessments will be carried out as group projects, the details of which will be given in the Course Handbook.

SCHEDULE

Paper 1: Principles of statistical analysis
Statistical distribution theory; statistical inference; statistical methods.
Paper 2: Further statistical methodology
Topics in statistical methodology chosen from a list approved by the standing committee and published in the Course Handbook by the beginning of Michaelmas Term of the academic year in which the written examination is to be taken.

DIPLOMA IN LEGAL STUDIES

GENERAL REGULATIONS

1. The Board of the Faculty of Law shall have power to grant Diplomas in Legal Studies to members of the University who have kept residence and pursued a course of study at Oxford for not less than three terms; time spent outside Oxford during term as part of an academic programme approved by Council shall count towards residence for the purpose of this clause.

2. The examination for the Diploma in Legal Studies shall be under the supervision of the Board of the Faculty of Law.

3. The examiners for the diploma shall be such of the Public Examiners in the Honour School of Jurisprudence as shall be required.

4. A Diploma Student must keep statutory residence and pursue a course of study at Oxford for three terms, and may not take the examination for the Diploma earlier or later than in the second term after that with effect from which he or she was admitted as a Diploma student.

5. The examiners may award a distinction to a candidate for the Diploma in Legal Studies.

SPECIAL REGULATIONS

1. The Diploma will normally only be granted to candidates who on admission had no significant previous education in the common law.

2. The examination for the diploma shall be in each Trinity Term.

3. The examination shall consist of any three standard subjects selected by the candidate from such standard subjects specified for the Honour School of Jurisprudence as notified as available in the Diploma in Legal Studies. Notice of these subjects will be given in the edition of the Law Faculty Handbook for Undergraduate Students for the relevant year, which will be published and made available on the Faculty website by Monday of noughth week of Michaelmas Term that year.

4. Candidates in examinations will not be required to answer more than three questions.

5. Candidates may be required to attend a viva voce examination.

6. The Law Board will approve and offer a Legal Research Skills Programme, as outlined in the Special Regulations for the Honour School of Jurisprudence. Candidates for the Diploma are required to undertake unit one of the course and an additional print resources class (details of which will be notified to the students) and to complete the associated assessments to the satisfaction of the Programme Coordinator appointed by the Law Board.

POSTGRADUATE DIPLOMA IN THEOLOGY

GENERAL REGULATIONS

1. It shall be lawful for the Board of the Faculty of Theology and Religion to grant Postgraduate Diplomas in Theology to candidates who have satisfied the conditions prescribed in this Section.

2. The examination shall be under the supervision of the Board of the Faculty of Theology and Religion.

3. Subject to the provisions of this Section, any member of the University who has obtained the leave of the Board of the Faculty of Theology and Religion normally may be admitted to the examination for the Postgraduate Diploma in Theology provided that he or she has passed all the examinations required for the Degree of Bachelor of Arts and has obtained First or upper Second Class Honours in the Second Public Examination, or has attained such honours in a degree examination of another university, such university having been approved by Council for the purposes of Senior Status.

4. Applications for leave under cl. 3 shall be sent to the Registrar, through the Head or tutor of the society to which the applicant belongs or desires to belong. The board shall have power to determine the character and length of a course of study in Theology to be followed by the applicant before he or she may be admitted to the examination.

5. The examiners may award a distinction in any subject in the examination.

6. A student reading for the diploma who is not a graduate of the University shall wear the same gown as that worn by Students for the Degree of Doctor of Philosophy.

SPECIAL REGULATIONS

1. Every candidate is required to follow for at least three terms a course of instruction in Theology, and he or she will, when he or she enters his or her name for the examination, be required to produce from his or her Society a certificate that he or she is following a course of instruction in Theology for at least three terms.

2. Candidates may complete the course either in nine months as a full-time student, or in twenty-one months as a part-time student.

3. All candidates will be required to offer three papers (and not more than four) from those specified in the schedule of papers prescribed for the Final Honour School of Theology and Religion, apart from those listed below;

    (i) Further Studies in History and Doctrine

    (ii) Selected Topics (Old Testament) I

        (i) Prophecy

        (ii) Apocalyptic

    (iii) Selected Topics (Old Testament) II

        (i) Wisdom

        (ii) Worship and Liturgy

    (iv) The Hebrew of the Old Testament

    (v) Archaeology in Relation to the Old Testament

    (vi) Religions and Mythology of the Ancient Near East

    (vii) Christian Liturgy

    (viii) Early Syriac Christianity

(ix) History and Theology of the Church in the Byzantine Empire from AD1000 to 1453

 (x) Mysticism

(xi) Psychology of Religion

(xii) English Church and Mission 597–754

4. Part-time students will study two papers in their first year of study, and the third (and fourth, if this option is chosen) in their second year of study. Examination will be at the second year of study.

5. Not all papers will be available every year.

6. Candidates may choose to offer either two short essays of 3,000 to 4,000 words or one long essay of 7,000 to 8,000 words in place of one of their chosen papers, except for paper (27) The New Testament in Greek. The essay word limit is inclusive of notes and appendices, but excludes the bibliography.

7. Any candidate may be examined viva voce.

Regulations concerning essays

In the Michaelmas Term of each year, the Board of the Faculty of Theology and Religion will publish a list of topics, from which candidates may choose to write either two short essays or one long essay in place of one of their chosen papers. The topics offered may vary from year to year and will be related to the research interests of the teachers concerned.

The candidate is advised to have an initial discussion with his or her supervisor regarding the proposed field of study, the sources available, and the method of presentation. He or she should have further discussions with his or her supervisor during the preparation of the essay. His or her supervisor may read and comment on drafts of the essay.

Every candidate shall sign a letter declaring the essay to be his or her own work. This letter, which can be found in the Handbook for Graduate Studies or collected from the Theology and Religion Faculty Office, Gibson Building, ROQ, Woodstock Road, shall be presented together with the essay, in a separate sealed envelope.

The candidate must submit two typed copies of the essay (bound or held firmly in a stiff cover), addressed to the Chair of the Examiners, Postgraduate Diploma in Theology, Examination Schools, High Street, Oxford not later than noon on the Friday of the first week of Trinity Term. Candidates must not put their names on the examination paper or on any pre-submitted work.

POSTGRADUATE CERTIFICATE IN EDUCATION

GENERAL REGULATIONS

1. The Departmental Board of the Department of Education shall have power to grant Postgraduate Certificates in Education to candidates who have satisfied the relevant conditions prescribed in this section.

2. The examination for the Postgraduate Certificate in Education shall be under the supervision of the Departmental Board which shall have the power to make regulations concerning the examination and arrange lectures and courses of instruction for the Certificate.

3. (*a*) All applicants for the Postgraduate Certificate in Education must have obtained on entry to the course a grade C or above in GCSE English Language and in GCSE Mathematics, or their equivalent.

   (*b*) Applicants must be graduates. Candidates for admission should normally have at least a good upper second class degree in a subject appropriate for the curriculum area to which they are applying.

4. After admission as a certificate student, a candidate must have kept statutory residence and pursued a course of study in Oxford for at least three terms before taking the examination.

5. A student reading for the Postgraduate Certificate in Education, who is not a graduate of the University, may wear the same gown as that worn by Students reading for the degree of Doctor of Philosophy.

SPECIAL REGULATIONS

1. *Course*

(*a*) The course will consist of lectures, tutorials, seminars, and classes in the theory and practice of education, together with a serial placement and two extended periods of practical experience in schools or other educational settings.

(*b*) The subjects of the course of study are as follows:

Curriculum studies related to the professional knowledge, understanding and skills required for teaching a specific subject across the 11–18 age range: the place of the subject in the school curriculum; the establishment and maintenance of a purposeful learning environment; lesson planning, teaching, and evaluation; formative and summative assessment; the promotion of young people's health and well-being; professional team work and collaboration In each of the seven subjects offered (English, Geography, History, Mathematics, Modern Foreign Languages, Religious Education, and Science) an integrated programme requires students to set theoretical and research-based understandings alongside classroom observation and teaching experience, subjecting both the educational theory and the practice to rigorous critical evaluation.

A Professional Development Programme presented through an integrated programme taught within the University and across the partnership schools, concerned with issues of policy and professional practice which transcend individual subjects. This programme is structured around a number of core themes which include: the changing nature of education and the role of schools; the developing school curriculum (secondary phase) and assessment; adolescence, learners and learning; inclusion and issues of social justice; teacher professionalism and collaborative working. It also includes training in research methods appropriate to the conduct of small scale practitioner research studies.

School Experience. The course includes 120 days' experience in a school or other educational setting nominated for this purpose by the Department of Education.

Candidates are required to keep statutory residence and pursue their studies at Oxford during a period of at least 35 weeks in three terms for the dates shown at: http://www.ox.ac.uk/about_the_university/university_year/dates_of_term.html. 5

2. *Examination*

Every candidate will be required to satisfy the examiners in the following:

(*a*) an assignment of 4,000 to 5,000 words (including footnotes/endnotes but excluding appendices, references or bibliography) on an issue of professional practice which transcends individual subjects. 10

One electronic copy of the assignment (in a software format available in the department) must be submitted online to a digital address provided by the PGCE Examiners, at such dates and times as the examiners shall determine. Both copies of the assignment should be anonymous except for the candidate number.

(*b*) two curriculum assignments of 4,000-5,000 words each (including footnotes/ 15 endnotes but excluding appendices, references or bibliography), related to the theory and practice of teaching and learning within the candidate's own subject discipline.

One electronic copy of the assignment (in a software format available in the department) must be submitted online to a digital address provided by the PGCE 20 Examiners, at such dates and times as the examiners shall determine. Both copies of each assignment should be anonymous except for the candidate number.

(*c*) an assessment of the candidate's professional attributes, knowledge, under-standing and skills in relation to the Teachers' standards as determined by the Department for Education. This assessment is carried out by persons represent- 25 ing both the University and its partnership schools who are appointed for this purpose by the Departmental Board of the Department of Education.

Details of submission deadlines for the assignments set out under (*a*) and (*b*) above and of the deadlines for the assessment of candidate's professional attributes, knowl-edge, understanding and skills as set out in (*c*) above shall be published annually in the 30 PGCE course handbook distributed to candidates at the start of the course.

The determination of any candidate's fitness to teach during the course of the Postgraduate Certificate of Education programme must be carried out in accordance with the Regulations for procedures concerning fitness to teach during the PGCE programme published annually in the PGCE course handbook and made available to 35 students on the first day of the PGCE term.

Candidates may also be called for viva voce examination.

If it is the opinion of the examiners that any or all of the candidate's written assignments are not of the standard required for the award of the Postgraduate Certificate in Education, but that all assignments are nevertheless of sufficient merit 40 to meet the standards required for the Professional Graduate Certificate in Education, then the board may recommend that the candidate should be awarded the Professional Graduate Certificate in Education, provided that the candidate's professional attri-butes, knowledge, skills, and understanding are also assessed as having met the Teachers Standards. 45

Candidates who fail the examination may apply to the Departmental Board to be re-examined on not more than one occasion which should normally be within one year of their initial failure.

Those candidates who have failed the examination, but whose assignments meet the standards required for the Professional Graduate Certificate in Education, may apply 50 for re-examination for the Postgraduate Certificate in Education within one academic year. In such cases the Departmental Board may recommend candidates to the Department for Education for the Award of Qualified Teacher Status even before their assignments have been resubmitted provided that they have satisfied the examiners in 2(*c*) above.   5

Candidates who fail to satisfy the examiners in 2(*c*) above shall not be granted permission to re-enter for the examination.

PROFESSIONAL GRADUATE CERTIFICATE IN EDUCATION

GENERAL REGULATIONS

1. The Departmental Board of the Department of Education shall have power to grant Professional Graduate Certificates in Education to candidates who have satisfied the relevant conditions prescribed in this section.

2. The examination for the Professional Graduate Certificate in Education shall be under the supervision of the Departmental Board which shall have the power to make regulations concerning the examination and arrange lectures and courses of instruction for the Certificate.

3. (*a*) All candidates for the Professional Graduate Certificate in Education must have obtained on entry to the course a grade C or above in GCSE English Language and in GCSE Mathematics, or their equivalent.

    (*b*) All candidates must be graduates. They should normally have at least a good upper second class degree in a subject appropriate for the curriculum area to which they are applying.

4. After admission as a certificate student, a candidate must have kept statutory residence and pursued a course of study in Oxford for at least three terms before taking the examination.

5. A student reading for the Professional Graduate Certificate in Education, who is not a graduate of the University, may wear the same gown as that worn by Students reading for the degree of Doctor of Philosophy.

SPECIAL REGULATIONS

1. *Course*

(*a*) The course will consist of lectures, tutorials, seminars, and classes in the theory and practice of education, together with a serial placement and two extended periods of practical experience in schools or other educational settings.

(*b*) The subjects of the course of study are as follows:

Curriculum studies related to the professional knowledge, understanding, and skills required for teaching a specific subject across the 11–18 age range: the place of the subject in the school curriculum; the establishment and maintenance of a purposeful learning environment; lesson planning, teaching, and evaluation; formative and summative assessment; the promotion of young people's health and well-being; professional team work and collaboration In each of the seven subjects offered (English, Geography, History, Mathematics, Modern Foreign Languages, Religious Education, and Science) an integrated programme requires students to set theoretical and research-based understandings alongside classroom observation and teaching experience, subjecting both the educational theory and the practice to rigorous critical evaluation.

A Professional Development Programme presented through an integrated programme taught within the University and across the partnership schools, concerned with issues of policy and professional practice which transcend individual subjects. This programme is structured around a number of core themes which include: the changing nature of education and the role of schools; the developing school curriculum (secondary phase) and assessment; adolescence; learners and learning; inclusion and issues of social justice; teacher professionalism and collaborative working. It also includes training in research methods appropriate to the conduct of small scale practitioner research studies.

School Experience The course includes 120 days' experience in a school or other educational setting nominated for this purpose by the Department of Education.

2. *Examination*

Every candidate will be required to satisfy the examiners in the following:

    (*a*) an assignment of 4,000 to 5,000 words (including footnotes/endnotes but ex-   5
        cluding appendices, references, or bibliography) on an issue of professional
        practice which transcends individual subjects.

One electronic copy of the assignment (in a software format available in the department) must be submitted online to a digital address provided by the PGCE Examiners, at such dates and times as the examiners shall determine. Both copies of   10 the assignment should be anonymous except for the candidate number.

    (*b*) two curriculum assignments of 4,000-5,000 words each (including footnotes/
        endnotes but excluding appendices, references or bibliography), related to the
        theory and practice of teaching and learning within the candidate's own subject
        discipline.   15

One electronic copy of the assignment (in a software format available in the department) must be submitted online to a digital address provided by the PGCE Examiners, at such dates and times as the examiners shall determine. Both copies of each assignment should be anonymous except for the candidate number

    (*c*) an assessment of the candidate's professional attributes, knowledge, under-   20
        standing and skills in relation to the Teachers Standards as determined by the
        Department for Education. This assessment is carried out by persons represent-
        ing both the University and its partnership schools who are appointed for this
        purpose by the Departmental Board of the Department of Education.

Details of submission deadlines for the assignments set out under (*a*) and (*b*) above   25 and of the deadlines for the assessment of candidate's professional attributes, knowledge, understanding and skills as set out in (*c*) above shall be published annually in the PGCE course handbook distributed to candidates at the start of the course.

The determination of any candidate's fitness to teach during the course of the Professional Certificate of Education programme must be carried out in accordance   30 with the Regulations for procedures concerning fitness to teach during the PGCE programme published annually in the PGCE course handbook and made available to students on the first day of the PGCE term.

Candidates may also be called for viva voce examination.

Candidates who fail the examination may apply to the Departmental Board to be   35 re-examined on not more than one occasion which should normally be within one year of their initial failure.

Candidates who fail to satisfy the examiners in 2(*c*) above shall not be granted permission to re-enter for the examination.

   40

CERTIFICATE AND DIPLOMA IN THEOLOGICAL AND PASTORAL STUDIES

GENERAL REGULATIONS

1. The Board of the Faculty of Theology and Religion shall have the power to grant the following awards to candidates who have satisfied the conditions prescribed in this section and any further conditions which the board may prescribe by regulation:

Certificate in Theological and Pastoral Studies

Diploma in Theological and Pastoral Studies

2. The examinations for these qualifications shall be under the supervision of the Board of the Faculty of Theology and Religion.

3. Candidates who have been admitted under such conditions as the Board of the Faculty of Theology and Religion shall prescribe, to courses at Blackfriars, Campion Hall, Harris Manchester College, Mansfield College, Regent's Park College, Ripon College, Cuddesdon, St Benet's Hall, St Stephen's House, and Wycliffe Hall may be admitted by the board to the examinations for the above mentioned qualifications, provided that they have paid to the Curators of the University Chest, through their colleges or other institutions, the fees prescribed in the appropriate regulation (see Appendix 1).

4. The supervision of the arrangements for the above mentioned qualifications shall be the responsibility of the Supervisory Committee for the Degree of Bachelor of Theology. The committee shall have such powers and duties in respect of the above mentioned qualifications as may from time to time be prescribed by the Board of the Faculty of Theology and Religion.

5. Part-time students for the above mentioned qualifications shall in each case be required to pursue their course of study for twice the number of terms required of an equivalent full-time student.

6. On successful completion of the Certificate in Theological and Pastoral Studies, candidates may offer the remaining papers necessary to complete the Diploma in Theological and Pastoral Studies.

SPECIAL REGULATIONS

Admission Requirements

Candidates will normally be expected to have five GCSE passes at grades A–C, one of which must be in English Language, and two passes at Advanced Level (A2); they will normally be expected to meet University residence requirements. Exemptions from these requirements for mature student candidates or those otherwise qualified may be made at the discretion of the BTh Supervisory Committee. Candidates must demonstrate aptitude and vocation for ministry or other church work. Students who can demonstrate completed and accredited previous academic achievement equivalent to the Certificate in Theological and Pastoral Studies may, at the discretion of the Supervisory Committee for the Bachelor of Theology, be admitted directly to study for the Diploma in Theological and Pastoral Studies.

Course Requirements

Candidates for the Certificate in Theological and Pastoral Studies will take at least *four papers* at Level 4[1] from the syllabus as outlined for the Bachelor of Theology, including at least one of A1 and A2.

---

[1] As defined in the Framework for Higher Education Qualifications (2008).

Candidates who have satisfied the examiners in four papers including A1 or A2 may supplicate for the Certificate or may take at least *four further papers* at Level 5[1] from the syllabus as outlined for the Bachelor of Theology, including at least one of C1 and C4.

Candidates for the Certificate or Diploma in Theological and Pastoral Studies may   5
not transfer to the CTh or BTh courses, or to any other University of Oxford degree programme.

Examinations

Examination will take place by continuous assessment within colleges, supervised and moderated by the BTh Supervisory Committee and a Faculty Board moderator   10
on behalf of the Faculty Board. Two summative pieces of work will be assessed for each paper. These will take the form of two essays or, alternatively, one essay plus one project. Essays at Level 4 should not exceed 2,500 words, and essays at Level 5 should not exceed 3,000 words. Guidelines for the project will be published in the course handbook issued by the Faculty of Theology and Religion. In addition to submitting   15
these two moderated pieces of work for each paper, candidates must complete a form, countersigned by a college officer, stating that they have attended the relevant course of instruction and passed the required formative, internally assessed work for that paper.

The Examiners may award the Certificate and the Diploma at the following grades: 20
Distinction, Merit, and Pass.

---

[1] As defined in the Framework for Higher Education Qualifications (2008).

POSTGRADUATE DIPLOMA IN MUSCULOSKELETAL SCIENCES

GENERAL REGULATIONS

1. The Medical Sciences Board shall have the power to grant Postgraduate Diplomas in Musculoskeletal Sciences to candidates who have satisfied the conditions prescribed in this Section.

2. The Examination shall be under the supervision of the Medical Sciences Board.

SPECIAL REGULATIONS

1. The Medical Sciences Board shall elect for the supervision of the course an Organising Committee, which shall have the power to arrange teaching, assessments, and other instruction.

2. The Organising Committee shall appoint for each candidate an academic supervisor.

3. Candidates will hold a first degree in medicine, or exceptionally a biomedical science degree.

4. Candidates shall follow a course of study in Musculoskeletal Sciences on a part-time basis for at least six terms, and including vacations, as determined by the course timetable. The course commences every two years in January and runs until December of the following year.

5. Candidates shall be examined in all of the following ways:

(i) Year 1 (January to December)

   (*a*) Each candidate shall submit a literature review of no more than 4,000 words on a topic selected by the candidate and approved by the Organising Committee. The review must be submitted during Week 2 of Michaelmas Term on a date to be specified in the course handbook.

   (*b*) Each candidate must pass an examination in Michaelmas Term. The examination will comprise two elements: the first of these will consist of a one-hour computer-based assessment comprising multiple-choice questions; the second of these will constitute a two-hour written paper. The dates of the examination will be specified in the course handbook.

(ii) Year 2 (January to December)

   (*a*) Each candidate must submit, for assessment of their progress, an outline research proposal. The outline must be submitted in Hilary Term on a date to be specified in the course handbook.

   (*b*) Each candidate will be assessed on their presentation skills by means of a public oral presentation on his or her research topic. The presentation must take place in Trinity Term on a date to be specified in the course handbook.

   (*c*) Each candidate must pass an examination in Michaelmas Term. The examination will comprise two elements: the first of these will consist of a one-hour computer-based assessment comprising multiple-choice questions; the second of these will constitute a two-hour written paper. The dates of the examination will be specified in the course handbook.

6. Candidates may be examined viva voce on their research proposal. The viva voce examination will normally be conducted at the end of the course.

7. Candidates must pass each examination or written assignment in order to pass overall.

8. Candidates will be allowed one opportunity to retake or resubmit each of the required elements, normally within six months of the original failure, should they fail to reach the necessary standard. Candidates failing to pass any element at the second attempt will normally be judged to have failed to reach the necessary standard for the award and will not be permitted to continue.   5

9. The required written submissions must be sent to the Chair of Examiners, M.Sc. in Musculoskeletal Sciences, c/o Examination Schools, High Street, Oxford. Submissions must be accompanied by a declaration of authorship and originality.

10. The examiners may award a distinction for excellence in part of or in the whole examination.   10

SCHEDULE

The syllabus for study will include the following components:
Core Subjects
Candidates are required to complete all of the following modules:
1. Principles of Musculoskeletal Diseases   15
2. Research, Statistics and Epidemiology
3. Scientific Aspects of Common Musculoskeletal Diseases

Specialist Subjects
Candidates are required to complete one of the following modules:
1. Advanced Rheumatology   20
2. Advanced Orthopaedics

NOTES

29

GENERAL REGULATIONS FOR EXAMINATIONS FOR DIPLOMAS AND CERTIFICATES OPEN TO NON-MEMBERS OF THE UNIVERSITY

GENERAL REGULATIONS

1. A Register shall be kept by the Registrar of the University of all students who are studying with a view to obtaining a diploma or certificate granted under the provisions of this Decree and who are not members of the University. The Register shall be entitled the Register of Diploma Students.

2. For the purpose of this Register, each of the bodies empowered to grant diplomas or certificates shall make to the Registrar each term, not later than the end of the second week of Full Term, a return of the names and addresses of all students who have been admitted by such body in that term and who are studying with a view to a diploma or certificate and who are not members of the University.

3. No student shall have his or her name entered, replaced, or retained on the Register unless *either* (1) he or she is more than twenty-five years of age and has satisfied the Vice-Chancellor and Proctors that he or she is of good character, *or* (2) he or she is a graduate of a university approved by Council under the appropriate regulation, *or* (3) he or she has been admitted as a student for a Diploma or Certificate by the Continuing Education Board, *or* (4) he or she is a member of a society or institution in Oxford established for the purpose of higher study and approved for the purpose of this decree by Council,[1] *or* (5) he or she is a member of the Public Service, naval, military, or civil, engaged on a course of higher study or research.

4. Before the name of any person is entered or replaced on the Register, he or she shall pay to the Registrar of the University, through the body returning his or her name in pursuance of clause 2 above, a fee as prescribed in the appropriate regulation (see Appendix I). The Registrar shall pay all fees so received to the University Chest. This clause shall not apply to students admitted as candidates for the Special Diploma in Educational Studies, for Postgraduate Diplomas or Postgraduate Certificates awarded by the Continuing Education Board, for the Diploma in Jewish Studies or for the Diploma in Management Studies.

5. The name of any diploma student may be removed, either temporarily or permanently, from the Register either by the Proctors or by the body by which his or her name was returned. No name which has been removed shall be replaced on the Register except with the consent of the authority which removed it. Nothwithstanding the earlier provisions of this clause, the student may within fourteen days of the date of the Proctors' decision appeal in writing to the Chair of the Education Committee (who may nominate another member of the committee, other than one of the Proctors, to

---

[1] The following bodies have been approved under this clause: Ruskin College, Green-Templeton College, Ripon College Cuddesdon, St Stephen's House, Wycliffe Hall, and the Oxford Centre for Hebrew and Jewish Studies.

adjudicate the appeal). If the Proctors' decision is not upheld, the Education Committee may replace the student's name on the Register.

6. No one whose name is not on the Register, except a member of the University, shall be entitled to attend any lecture or course of instruction given under arrangements made by a body which grants any such diploma or certificate as aforesaid.   5

7. No one except a member of the University shall be permitted to be a candidate in the examination, or any part of the examination, for any such diploma or certificate unless his or her name (1) is on the Register in the term in which such examination or part of an examination is held, or, if the examination is held in vacation, in the term immediately preceding such examination, (2) has been on the Register during at least   10 one previous term or such longer period as may be prescribed by the body under whose authority the examination is held, provided that such body may dispense from this second requirement any candidate who before registration has attended only lectures or courses of instruction given in vacation under arrangements made by such body, or who is a member of the Public Service, naval, military, or civil, engaged   15 on a course of higher study or research.

8. The bodies empowered to grant diplomas or certificates shall cause lists of candidates in the examinations or any parts of examinations for any such diplomas or certificates to be distributed in the usual manner at least three days before the day fixed for the beginning of any such examination.   20

NOTES

30

GENERAL REGULATIONS FOR POSTGRADUATE DIPLOMAS IN EDUCATION

1. The Departmental Board of the Department of Education shall have power to grant Postgraduate Diplomas in Education and Postgraduate Diplomas in Learning and Teaching in Higher Education and Postgraduate Diplomas in Teaching English in University Settings and Postgraduate Diplomas in Teacher Education to candidates who have satisfied the conditions prescribed in this section and any further conditions which the committee may prescribe by regulation.

2. The examinations for the diplomas shall be under the supervision of the Departmental Board which shall have power subject to the approval of the Education Committee to make regulations governing the examinations.

3. Candidates, whether members of the University or not, may be admitted as students for the diplomas under such conditions as the committee shall prescribe, provided that

   (i) before admission to a course of study approved by the committee, candidates have satisfied the committee that they have received a good general education, that they have had appropriate educational experience acceptable to the committee, and are well qualified to enter the proposed course of study;

  (ii) any person so admitted who is not a member of the University, shall be required to pay to the Curators of the University Chest through the committee the composition fee payable under the provisions of the appropriate regulation, notwithstanding that he or she is not a member of the University.

4. The Departmental Board shall make a return to the Registrar by the end of the sixth week of Michaelmas Term, showing the names of all persons admitted in that term as students for the diplomas, and the Registrar shall add the names of non-members of the University to the Register of Diploma Students.

5. Any person who has been accepted as a candidate for the diplomas and who has satisfactorily pursued a course, whose character and length have been approved by the committee, may be admitted to the examinations.

6. A candidate must apply to the committee for admission to the examinations at such time as the committee shall, by regulation, prescribe. His or her application must be accompanied by:

   (*a*) a certificate from the Secretary of the Committee that he or she is satisfactorily pursuing a course of study approved by the committee;

   (*b*) such other information as the committee may, by regulation, require.

POSTGRADUATE DIPLOMA IN EDUCATION

1. Candidates for the Postgraduate Diploma in Education shall be qualified teachers in the United Kingdom, or recognised by the Graduate Studies Committee as being of equivalent status overseas. They shall normally have had not less than three years' educational experience acceptable to the committee. The committee may in exceptional cases admit to the examination candidates with other qualifications.

2. Each candidate for the Postgraduate Diploma in Education will follow a course of study approved by the Graduate Studies Committee. Each candidate shall be required to follow *one* of the following options:

(*a*) A full-time course involving a programme of study of three terms in duration which will consist of: an introduction to research methods; an individual programme of study leading to the submission of the dissertation; and a common programme of studies embracing topics from amongst the following areas of study upon which he will be required to submit essays; the development of the educational system of England and Wales; the nature and control of the curriculum; the organisation, administration, and management of schools; contemporary work in sociology and psychology in relation to the practice of pedagogy in schools; assessment in education; teacher education; comparative education.

(*b*) A course involving a programme of study of three terms in duration in which each candidate will spend at least 40 per cent of the days of these terms in university-based study, and the remainder of these terms working in his or her own school or local education authority and engaged in a research and development project. Each programme of study will consist of an introduction to research methods, a research and development project concerned with a signficant aspect of educational practice, which will lead to the submission of the dissertation, and a programme of studies which shall be equivalent in weight to the common programme of studies indicated in 3(*a*) above, which shall incorporate part of that common programme and which shall be related to the research and development project being undertaken by the candidate. The whole programme for each candidate shall be approved by the Graduate Studies Committee, which shall satisfy itself that the programme is suitable in its standards and scope for the Postgraduate Diploma in Education and is practically viable for the candidate for whom it is proposed. Application for approval of programmes is to be received not later than six weeks before the beginning of the term in which the course starts. The Committee, having considered a proposed programme, will inform the candidate of its decision not later than two weeks before the beginning of that term.

(*c*) A course extending over a minimum period of two years and a maximum period not normally exceeding three years from the beginning of the term in which the candidate is admitted for the Postgraduate Diploma course, with no requirements for full-day attendance, but otherwise involving the same requirements as those prescribed in 3(*b*) above.

3. Each student for the Postgraduate Diploma in Education will be assigned to a supervisor, who will be responsible for directing the student's course of study, including the dissertation. The title of the dissertation is to be submitted to the examiners for approval. The examiners shall notify candidates of the date by which the title must be submitted for approval.

4. All candidates for admission as students for the Postgraduate Diploma in Education and must apply to the department not later than two weeks before the start of the term in which the Postgraduate Diploma Courses start.

5. Every candidate for admission to the examination must apply to the Graduate Studies Committee for entry to the examination by the first day of Hilary Full Term in the academic year in which he wishes to take the examination. Candidates for the Postgraduate Diploma in Education must, at the same time, state the subject on which he or she proposes to submit the dissertation.

6. Candidates for the Postgraduate Diploma in Education must offer a dissertation of between 15,000 and 20,000 words. Two typewritten copies of the dissertation must be delivered to the Postgraduate Diploma Examiners, Department of Education, 15 Norham Gardens, Oxford, OX2 6PY, not later than noon on 30 September after the completion of the course of studies. Candidates wishing to submit dissertations later than 30 September must obtain the approval of the Departmental Board by the last day of the preceding Trinity Term, but no dissertation may be submitted later than noon on 30 September in the year following, unless the Departmental Board approves a later date for submission. One bound copy of the dissertation of each candidate who passes the examination shall be retained by the department for deposit in the departmental Library.

7. Candidates for the Postgraduate Diploma in Education may also be required to attend an oral examination.

8. The examiners for the Postgraduate Diploma in Education shall also consider, as part of the examination, reports on the candidate's work submitted by his or her supervisor. Reports shall be submitted at the end of each Full Term except that, in the term in which the candidate takes the examination, a report shall be submitted by the end of the seventh week of Full Term.

9. Candidates for the Postgraduate Diploma in Education who fail the examination may be re-examined on not more than one occasion which normally shall be within one year of their initial failure.

POSTGRADUATE DIPLOMA IN LEARNING AND TEACHING IN HIGHER EDUCATION

1. Candidates for the Postgraduate Diploma in Learning and Teaching in Higher Education ('the Diploma') shall be engaged as teachers in higher education.

2. All candidates for admission as students for the Diploma must apply to the Course Director at the Oxford Learning Institute not later than March 31st in the calendar year in which they wish to start the course. The Course Director shall forward his or her recommendations for decision to the Academic Committee of the Department of Education.

3. All candidates for the Diploma shall follow a course of study approved by the Academic Committee of the Department of Education.

4. Every candidate for admission to the examination must apply to the Academic Committee of the Department of Education by submitting an examination entry form to the Course Director at the Oxford Learning Institute no later than the first day of Hilary Full Term preceding the Michaelmas Term in which he or she wishes to be examined. No candidate shall be examined later than in the seventh term following the start of his or her course of study except with the approval of the Academic Committee of the Department of Education following written application via the Oxford Learning Institute.

5. Candidates for the Diploma must submit a portfolio of written work of between 12,000 and 15,000 words in total. Two typewritten copies of the portfolio and a certificate from the Oxford Learning Institute confirming that the candidate has participated in no fewer than six of the full-day seminars in the Diploma programme must be delivered to the Postgraduate Diploma Examiners, Department of Education, 15 Norham Gardens, Oxford OX2 6PY, not later than noon on the Monday of the first week of the Michaelmas Full Term in which the candidate is to be examined. In exceptional circumstances, following written application in advance via the Oxford Learning Institute, the Academic Committee of the Department of Education may allow late submission by specifying a revised deadline not later than noon on the Friday of the first week of that Michaelmas Term. One bound copy of the dissertation of each candidate who passes the examination shall be retained for deposit in the Oxford Learning Institute.

6. Candidates for the Diploma in Learning and Teaching in Higher Education may be awarded a distinction.

7. Notwithstanding the provisions in clause 4 above regulating the time allowed for completion of the course, candidates for the Diploma who fail the examination may be re-examined on not more than one occasion which shall be in the Michaelmas Term following their initial failure.

POSTGRADUATE DIPLOMA IN LEARNING AND TEACHING (PART-TIME)

1. The Postgraduate Diploma in Learning and Teaching is open only to candidates who are admitted to follow the required programme of study with the intention of proceeding to the M.Sc. in Learning and Teaching. The required programme of study will comprise Part I and Part II of the M.Sc. in Learning and Teaching (or Part II for those candidates who are exempt from Part I), as specified in the examination regulations pertaining to the programme for the degree of Master of Science in Learning and Teaching.

2. As candidates registered for the Diploma, students will follow a course of study that will allow them to progress, on successful completion of Part II, to the M.Sc. in Learning and Teaching. Students who, having successfully completed Part II, choose not to continue with their programme of study will be awarded the Diploma. Those who progress to, and successfully complete Part III of the M.Sc. programme, will be awarded the degree of Master of Science which will subsume the award of the Diploma.

POSTGRADUATE DIPLOMA IN TEACHER EDUCATION (PART-TIME)

1. Every candidate must follow for five terms a part-time course of instruction in Teacher Education approved by the Graduate Studies Committee of the Department of Education.

2. All candidates on the course will be required to complete four summatively assessed units of study and one formatively assessed residential unit. Two units are taught each academic year on an alternating basis.

3. The Postgraduate Diploma shall be examined by means of four assignments relating to the content of each of the four units. Each assignment must be between 4,000 and 5,000 words in length, or their equivalent in tables, charts and diagrams in accordance with guidance given in the unit. One electronic copy (in a software format available in the department) must be submitted online to the Chair of Examiners, M.Sc. in Teacher Education, c/o Department of Education, 15 Norham Gardens, Oxford OX2 6PY who will provide the digital address. The deadline for the submission of assignments will be no later than noon on Monday of Week 1 of Hilary and Trinity terms.

4. Candidates who fail to satisfy the examiners in an assignment will be permitted to resubmit on one occasion only. The deadline for resubmission of unit assessments will noon on the Monday falling 8 weeks after the initial submission date, following the term in which the unit is taken.

5. The award of Distinction within the Postgraduate Diploma is normally reserved for those candidates who receive distinction marks for at least two of the four assessed assignments, and over 60 for the other two.

POSTGRADUATE DIPLOMA IN TEACHING
ENGLISH LANGUAGE IN UNIVERSITY SETTINGS

1. Candidates for the Postgraduate Diploma in Teaching English Language in University Settings (the Diploma) shall normally have successfully obtained an honours degree. They shall normally be engaged as teachers of English as a second or foreign language at the time of application, and shall expect to continue this engagement during the Diploma course.

2. Every candidate will be required to complete all eight summatively assessed online modules of the course by carrying out tasks and participating in discussions as directed by the Course Director. Every candidate will also be required to complete both formatively assessed residential modules, or, in exceptional cases and as determined by the Course Director, to give evidence of equivalent learning for one of these two modules.

3. Every candidate will be required to satisfy the examiners in the following:

(i) Satisfactory participation in the appropriate web-based tasks and discussions for each module.

(ii) Satisfactory performance in the take-home examinations. Every candidate must complete all eight take-home examinations, each examination consisting of an essay which will be given a numerical mark; and a reflective portfolio which will be marked on a pass/fail basis.

4. The overall mark for the Diploma shall be the mean of the seven best marks of the eight essays completed in the take-home examinations. Failure on a portfolio will result in a maximum mark of forty nine on the corresponding module. Marks will be released to candidates during Hilary Term and Trinity Term of each year after a meeting of the Examination Board for the Diploma.

5. In each of the two years of this part-time course, an electronic copy of each of two module Michaelmas Term take-home examinations and accompanying portfolios must be uploaded to Weblearn, no later than noon on the Friday of Week 0 of Hilary Term, and an electronic copy of each of two module Hilary Term take-home examinations must be uploaded in the same fashion no later than noon on the Friday of Week 0 of Trinity Term. Each take-home examination must be accompanied by a declaration indicating that it is the candidate's own work.

6. Candidates for the Diploma who fail any part of the examination may be re-examined on not more than one occasion which shall be in the year following their initial failure.

7. The pass mark for each take home examination is fifty. The examiners may award a distinction for excellence on the overall examination.

NOTES

31

GENERAL REGULATIONS FOR POSTGRADUATE CERTIFICATES (CONTINUING EDUCATION)

1. The Continuing Education Board shall have power to grant Postgraduate   5
Certificates to candidates who have satisfied the conditions prescribed in this section
and any further conditions which the board may prescribe by regulation.

2. The examination for each Postgraduate Certificate shall, in consultation with
representatives of collaborating departments or faculties, be under the supervision of
the Continuing Education Board which shall have power, subject to the approval of   10
the Education Committee, to make regulations governing the examination.

3. Candidates, whether members of the University or not, may be admitted as
students for a Postgraduate Certificate under such conditions as the board shall
prescribe, provided that before admission to a course of study approved by the
board, candidates shall have satisfied the board that they have had appropriate   15
educational and professional experience acceptable to the board, and are well-
equipped to enter the proposed course of study.

4. Any person who has been accepted as a candidate for a Postgraduate Certificate,
and who has satisfactorily pursued a course, the character and length of which have
been approved by the board, may be admitted to the examination.   20

POSTGRADUATE CERTIFICATE
IN ARCHAEOLOGY

1. (*a*) The course will consist of lectures, classes, seminars, and tutorials in Archaeology. The course, which is available on a part-time basis only, is normally be taken over a period of one year and over a maximum of two years.   5

(*b*) The subjects of the course of study will include topics relevant to archaeological research methods, landscape archaeology, material culture, and analytical techniques.

2. Every candidate will be required to satisfy the examiners in the following:

(*a*) attendance at the taught courses;

(*b*) three assignments of between 2,000 and 2,500 words based on the taught   10
courses;

(*c*) a practical logbook of up to 5,000 words;

(*d*) a dissertation of up to 10,000 words (including bibliography, appendices, foot-notes, figure captions and descriptive catalogues but excluding external reference data under the heading of 'supplementary information') on a topic agreed   15
by the Board of Examiners.

The assignments under 2(*b*), the logbook under 2(*c*) and the dissertation under 2(*d*) shall be submitted electronically to the examiners c/o the Registry, Department for Continuing Education, Wellington Square, Oxford OX1 2JA for consideration by such date as the examiners shall determine and shall notify candidates. The logbook   20
under 2(*c*) and dissertation under 2(*d*) must also be submitted in hard copy.

3. Candidates may be required to attend a viva voce examination at the end of the course of studies.

4. The examiners may award a distinction to candidates for the Postgraduate Certificate.   25

5. Candidates who fail to satisfy the examiners in the assignments under 2(*b*), or the logbook under 2(*c*) or the dissertation under 2(*d*), may be permitted to resubmit work in respect of the part or parts of the examination which they have failed for examination on not more than one occasion which shall normally be within one year of the initial failure.   30

POSTGRADUATE CERTIFICATE IN ARCHITECTURAL HISTORY

1. *Course*

    (*a*) The course will consist of lectures and classes on architectural history and on site evaluation and survey. The course may be taken on a part-time basis over a period which shall normally be of one year's duration and shall not exceed two years.

    (*b*) The course will consist of three taught units, two of which will be on architectural history and one of which will be on site evaluation and survey, which will be offered in three ten-week terms.

2. Every candidate will be required to satisfy the examiners in the following:

    (*a*) attendance at the classroom-based courses;

    (*b*) submission of the following portfolio of written work:

        (i) three essays or projects linked to unit one each of which shall not exceed 1,500 words in length;

        (ii) two essays linked to unit two, each of which shall not exceed 2,000 words in length;

        (iii) a workbook linked to unit three;

        (iv) a dissertation which shall not exceed 8,000 words in length on a topic agreed by the Board of Studies.

    The assignments under (i)–(iii) and the dissertation under (iv) will be forwarded to the examiners c/o the Registry, Department for Continuing Education, Wellington Square, Oxford OX1 2JA by such dates as the examiners shall determine and shall notify to candidates.

3. Candidates may be required to attend a *viva voce* examination at the end of the course of studies at the discretion of the examiners.

4. The examiners may award a distinction to candidates for the certificate.

5. Candidates who fail to satisfy the examiners in the assignments under 2(i)–(iii), or the dissertation under 2(iv), or both, may be permitted to resubmit work in respect of part or parts of the examination which they have failed for examination on not more than one occasion which shall normally be within one year of the initial failure.

POSTGRADUATE CERTIFICATE IN COGNITIVE BEHAVIOURAL THERAPY FOR PSYCHOLOGICAL TRAUMA

1. The course will consist of lectures, tutorials, seminars, and classes on the principle and practice of cognitive behavioural therapy for psychological trauma, together with clinical practice in cognitive behavioural therapy for psychological trauma. The course will be taken on a part-time basis over a period of not less than three terms and not more than nine terms.

2. Every candidate will be required to satisfy the examiners in the following:

(*a*) attendance at the appropriate classroom-based courses including small group case supervisions;

(*b*) one essay of no more than 4,000 words, to assess critical appreciation of theory, research and practice on topics provided by course tutors and approved by the examiners;

(*c*) one written case report of 4,000 to 6,000 words;

(*d*) one video or audio (-tape or digital equivalent) recording of a therapy session;

(*e*) close clinical supervision of two 'training clients' as evidenced by a log book of supervised clinical practice.

The essay under (*b*), the case report under (*c*) and the audio/video recording under (*d*) shall be forwarded to the examiners for consideration by such date as the examiners shall determine and shall notify the candidates and tutors.

The audio/video- recording will be accompanied by a written reflective analysis on topics provided by course tutors, and students will also be required to keep a log book to provide evidence of their supervised CBT practice with two 'training' clients by the end of block 4.

3. The examiners may award a distinction to candidates for the Postgraduate Certificate.

4. Candidates who fail to satisfy the examiners in the essay under 2(*b*), the case report under 2(*c*) and the audio/video- recording under 2(*d*) may be permitted to resubmit work in respect of the part or parts of the examination that they have failed for examination on not more than one occasion, which shall normally be within three months of the original failure.

POSTGRADUATE CERTIFICATE IN COGNITIVE BEHAVIOURAL THERAPY (INTRODUCTORY LEVEL)

1. The course will consist of lectures, tutorials, seminars, and classes on the principle and practice of cognitive behavioural therapy, together with clinical practice in cognitive behavioural therapy. The course will be taken on a part-time basis over a period of not less than three terms and not more than nine terms.

2. Every candidate will be required to satisfy the examiners in the following:

(*a*) attendance at the appropriate classroom-based courses including small group case supervisions;

(*b*) two essays, each of no more than 4,000 words, to assess critical appreciation of theory, research and practice on topics provided by course tutors and approved by the examiners;

(*c*) one written case report of 2,000 to 4,000 words;

(*d*) one audio/visual tape (or digital equivalent) recording of a therapy session;

(*e*) close clinical supervision of three 'training clients' as evidenced by a log book of supervised clinical practice.

The essays under (*b*), the case report under (*c*) and the one audio/videotape (or digital equivalent) recording under (*d*) shall be forwarded to the examiners for consideration by such date as the examiners shall determine and shall notify the candidates and tutors.

The audio/videotape (or equivalent recording) will be accompanied by a written reflective analysis on topics provided by course tutors, and students will also be expected to keep a log book to provide evidence of their supervised CBT practice with three 'training' clients in module 3.

3. The examiners may award a distinction to candidates for the Postgraduate Certificate.

4. Candidates who fail to satisfy the examiners in meeting their attendance requirements under 2(*a*), the essays under 2(*b*), the case report under 2(*c*) and the audio/videotape (or digital equivalent) recording under 2(*d*) may be permitted to resubmit work in respect of the part or parts of the examination that they have failed for examination on not more than one occasion, which shall normally be within three months of the original failure.

POSTGRADUATE CERTIFICATE
IN DIPLOMATIC STUDIES

1. Students for the Certificate may hold that status for no more than six terms.

2. Each student will follow a course of study comprising four core courses. The four core courses are: 5

International Politics;

Economics;

International Law;

Diplomatic Practice.

3. *Examinations.* All candidates will be required to satisfy the examiners in four   10
separate three-hour written examinations covering each of the core areas listed in the
preceding paragraph demonstrating that they have mastered the substance of the
subjects listed and (where appropriate), that they are able to apply them in their
continuing professional careers in the international field.

4. The examiners may award a distinction to candidates for the Certificate.   15

5. A candidate whose overall average mark falls below 50 shall be eligible to resit
the failed elements during the following academic year.

6. Candidates who fail to satisfy the examiners in the written examinations in all
four of the core elements of the Certificate course, will not be eligible to qualify for the
Certificate.   20

POSTGRADUATE CERTIFICATE IN ECOLOGICAL SURVEY TECHNIQUES

1. The course will consist of instruction in the theory and practice of Ecological Survey Techniques. The course will be taken on a part time basis.

2. The policy of the Continuing Education Board on variable intensity part-time postgraduate study applies to this award.

3. The minimum period of registration for the award of the Postgraduate Certificate shall be three terms and the maximum period shall be six terms.

4. Candidates may be permitted by the Continuing Education Board in certain circumstances to suspend status for a maximum of six terms. Any such period shall not count to the maximum or minimum permitted period of registration and no fee liability will be incurred during such periods.

5. Where a candidate undertakes a module under 10 below, the date of registration for the award shall retrospectively be deemed to be the first day of the term in which the module was taken.

6. Every candidate will be required to satisfy the examiners in the following:

   (*a*) attendance at the one-week module in Schedule A in the candidate's first term of registration;

   (*b*) engagement with and contribution to both online modules in Schedule B;

   (*c*) engagement with and contribution to two online modules chosen from those listed in Schedule C;

   (*d*) participation in and completion of a Field Project module;

   (*e*) participation to the satisfaction of the Programme Director in all other parts of the course;

   (*f*) one written assignment of not more than 2,500 words based on the module in Schedule A. This is formative only and the marks do not contribute to the final award;

   (*g*) four written assignments of not more than 2,000 words, one from each of the modules from 6(*b*) and one from each of the modules chosen from 6(*c*) above. Depending on the modules chosen, up to two of the written assignments on the modules from 6(*c*) may be replaced by presentations in a media specified by the examiners;

   (*h*) One field project of not more than 5,000 words and an associated journal of not more than 1,000 words.

The assessed work under Clauses 6 (*f*), (*g*) and (*h*) will be submitted to examiners, in normal circumstances through an electronic submission system, for consideration by such date as the examiners shall determine and of which they shall notify candidates.

7. Candidates may be required to attend a viva voce examination at the end of the course at the discretion of the examiners.

8. The examiners may award a Distinction to candidates for the Certificate.

9. Candidates who fail to satisfy the examiners in any part of the assessment listed under 6(*g*) or 6(*h*) may be permitted to resubmit work in respect of the part or parts of the examination which they have failed on not more than one occasion shall normally be within one year of the original failure.

10. The Course Committee shall have the discretion to deem satisfactory completion of a module including the associated assessment prior to registration for the award as having met the attendance and examination requirements in respect of that

module. Such discretion will normally only be exercised if the time elapsed between commencement of the module concerned and registration for the award is not more than two years. The maximum number of modules taken prior to registration for the award that can contribute to the achievement of the award of the Postgraduate Certificate in this way shall be two.   5

Core Module Schedule A

Introduction to ecological survey techniques

Core Modules Schedule B

Data analysis
Field techniques for surveying vegetation   10

Optional Modules Schedule C

Field techniques for surveying mammals and reptiles
Field techniques for surveying birds
Field techniques for surveying invertebrates
Field techniques for surveying fish and amphibians   15

POSTGRADUATE CERTIFICATE IN EVIDENCE-BASED HEALTH CARE

1. The Divisional Board of Medical Sciences, jointly with the Continuing Education Board, shall elect for the supervision of the course a Standing Committee, which shall have the power to arrange lectures and other instruction. 5

2. Candidates must follow for at least three and at most nine terms a part-time course of instruction in the theory and practice of Evidence-Based Health Care, which shall normally take place over a period of no more than four years. The postgraduate certificate is only available to students admitted for the degree of M.Sc. in Evidence-Based Health Care. 10

3. Every candidate will be required to satisfy the examiners in the following:

(*a*) attendance at both of the modules listed in Schedule A (below);

(*b*) attendance at one of the modules listed in Schedule B (below);

(*c*) three written assignments, usually of no more than 5,000 words, one on each of the modules from 3(*a*) and 3(*b*) above. 15

The assessed work set out in clause 3(*c*) shall be forwarded to the examiners c/o Registry, Department for Continuing Education, 1 Wellington Square, Oxford OX1 2JA, for consideration by such date as the examiners shall determine and of which they shall notify candidates.

4. Candidates may be required to attend a viva voce examination at the end of the 20 course of studies at the discretion of the examiners.

5. The examiners may award a distinction to candidates for the Postgraduate Certificate.

6. Candidates who fail to satisfy the examiners in any of the three assignments under 3(*c*) may be permitted, normally within one year of the original failure, to 25 resubmit work in respect of the part or parts they have failed on not more than one occasion for each assignment without being required to repeat attendance at the relevant module or modules under 3(*a*) and/or 3(*b*).

7. The Standing Committee shall have the discretion to permit any candidate to be exempted, in exceptional circumstances, from attendance at one module under 3 30 (*a*) or 3(*b*) and from submitting the associated assignment required under 3(*c*) above, provided that the Standing Committee is satisfied that such a candidate has undertaken equivalent study, or has appropriate work experience to an equivalent standard.

SCHEDULE A 35

M1: Practice of EBHC

M2: Introduction to Study Design and Research Methods

SCHEDULE B

M3: Knowledge into Action

M4: Clinical Epidemiology 40

M5: Evidence-Based Diagnosis and Screening

M6: Systematic Reviews

M7: Randomised Control Trials

M8: Essential Medical Statistics

M9: Patient-Based Evidence 45

M10: Ethics in Health Care

M11: Qualitative Research Methods

M12: Evidence-Based Dentistry

M13: Introduction to Statistics in Health Care Research

Any other module as defined by the Programme Director and approved by the Standing Committee.

POSTGRADUATE CERTIFICATE IN HEALTH RESEARCH

1. The Medical Sciences Board, jointly with the Continuing Education Board, shall elect for the supervision of the course a Standing Committee, which shall have the power to arrange lectures and other instruction.

2. Candidates must follow for at least three and at most nine terms, a part-time course of instruction in the theory and practice of Health Research, which shall normally take place over a period of no more than three years.

3. Every candidate will be required to satisfy the examiners in the following:

 (*a*) attendance at three of the modules listed in the Schedule (below);

 (*b*) three written assignments, usually of no more than 5,000 words, one on each of the modules from 3(*a*) above.

The assignments set out in clause 3(*b*) shall be forwarded, usually electronically via a specified online submission system, to the examiners c/o Registry, Department for Continuing Education, 1 Wellington Square, Oxford OX1 2JA, for consideration by such date as the examiners shall determine and of which they shall notify candidates.

4. Candidates may be required to attend a viva voce examination at the end of the course of studies at the discretion of the examiners.

5. The examiners may award a distinction to candidates for the Postgraduate Certificate.

6. Candidates who fail to satisfy the examiners in any of the three assignments under 3(*b*) may be permitted, normally within one year of the original failure, to resubmit work in respect of the part or parts they have failed on not more than one occasion for each assignment without being required to repeat attendance at the relevant module or modules under 3(*a*).

7. The standing committee shall have the discretion to permit any candidate to be exempted, in exceptional circumstances, from attendance at any module under 3(*a*) and from submitting the associated assignment required under 3(*b*) above, provided that the standing committee is satisfied that such a candidate has undertaken equivalent study, or has appropriate work experience to an equivalent standard.

Schedule

M1: Practice of EBHC
M2: Introduction to Study Design and Research Methods
M3: Bioethics and Good Clinical Practice
Any other module as defined by the Programme Director and approved by the Standing Committee replacing one of the three above.

POSTGRADUATE CERTIFICATE IN
HISTORICAL STUDIES

1. Each candidate shall follow for at least three terms and a maximum of six terms a part- time course of instruction in historical studies.

2. The course will consist of seminars, classes, tutorials, and on-line distance learning.

3. The course will consist of five units listed in the schedule below.

4. Every candidate will be required to satisfy the examiners in the following:

(*a*) a minimum of 75 per cent attendance at the classroom-based sessions and active participation in all parts of the course to the satisfaction of the course director;

(*b*) four assignments that shall not exceed 2,500 words based on units one to four in the schedule below;

(*c*) two primary source evaluations of not more than 1,500 words each;

(*d*) a dissertation of not less than 8,000 words and not exceeding 10,000 words.

The assignments under 4(*b*)–(*c*) shall be submitted electronically and the dissertation under 4(*d*) shall be submitted in hard copy and on disc (or equivalent) to the examiners c/o Registry, Department for Continuing Education, Wellington Square, Oxford OX1 2JA for consideration by such date as the examiners shall determine and shall notify candidates.

5. Candidates may be required to attend a viva voce examination at the end of the course of studies at the discretion of the examiners.

6. The examiners may award a distinction to candidates for the Certificate.

7. A candidate who fails to satisfy the examiners in the assignments under 4(*b*)–(*c*) or in the dissertation under 4(*d*) above may normally be permitted to resubmit work in respect of the part or parts of the examination which they have failed on not more than one occasion which shall normally be within one year of the original failure.

SCHEDULE

Unit One: Princes, States and Revolutions

Unit Two: European Court Patronage

Unit Three: Religious Reformations and Movements

Unit Four: Memory and Conflict

Unit Five: Special Subjects

POSTGRADUATE CERTIFICATE IN NANOTECHNOLOGY

1. The Continuing Education Board shall elect for the supervision of the course a Steering Committee that shall have the power to arrange lectures and other instruction.

2. Every candidate must follow for at least three terms a part-time course of instruction in the theory and practice of Nanotechnology normally over a period of one year and no more than three years.

3. Every candidate will be required to satisfy the examiners in the following:

(*a*) participation, to the satisfaction of the Course Director, in all parts of the three modules in the Schedule;

(*b*) a portfolio of assignments (written reports, problem sheets and presentations) for each of the modules in the Schedule, totalling not more than 2,500 words in length for Module 1, and not more than 6,000 words for each of Modules 2 and 3.

The assessed work set out in clause 3(*b*) shall be forwarded to the examiners c/o Registry, Department of Continuing Education, 1 Wellington Square, Oxford OX1 2JA, for consideration by such date as the examiners shall determine and of which they shall notify candidates.

4. Candidates may be required to attend a *viva voce* examination at the end of the course of studies at the discretion of the examiners.

5. The examiners may award a distinction to candidates for the certificate.

6. Candidates who fail to satisfy the examiners in any part of the examination may be permitted to resubmit work in respect of the part or parts of the examination which they have failed for examination on not more than one occasion which shall normally be within one year of the original failure.

7. The Steering Committee shall have the discretion to permit any candidate to be exempted from one of the three modules in the Schedule, provided that the steering committee is satisfied that such a candidate has undertaken equivalent study, or has appropriate work experience to an equivalent standard.

SCHEDULE

1. The Wider Context of Nanotechnology
2. The Fundamental Science of Nanotechnology
3. Fundamental Characterisation for Nanotechnology.

POSTGRADUATE CERTIFICATE IN PSYCHODYNAMIC COUNSELLING

1. *Course*

   (*a*) The course will consist of lectures, tutorials, seminars, classes, and workshops on psychodynamic theory, philosophy, and techniques. Self exploration will be undertaken in small experiential groups. The course will be taken on a part-time basis over a period which shall be of one year's duration.

   (*b*) The course will consist of three study terms, each of ten weeks, covering respectively: (i) The Psychodynamic Approach-Definition: (ii) Process and Skills in Early Sessions: (iii) Practicalities, Technique, and Ethical Implications.

2. Every candidate will be required to satisfy the examiners in the following:

   (*a*) attendance at weekly classes, a weekend school, individual tutorials, and review and revision days;

   (*b*) two written assignments, each of no more than 3,000 words and each on one key psychodynamic concept;

   (*c*) one written assignment, of no more than 4,000 words, to provide a critique of interpersonal processes and techniques in action;

   (*d*) an extract from the student's Reflective Journal, of no more than 5,000 words;

   (*e*) annual reports from a candidate's course tutor.

   The assignments under (*b*)–(*d*) will be forwarded to the examiners c/o Registry, Department for Continuing Education, Wellington Square, Oxford OX1 2JA, for consideration by the examiners by such date as the examiners shall determine and shall notify candidates before the start of the academic year in which the assignment is due.

3. Candidates may be required to attend a viva voce examination at the end of the course of studies.

4. Candidates who fail to satisfy the examiners in 2(*b*)–(*d*) above may be permitted to resubmit work in the part or parts of the examination which they have failed for examination on not more than one occasion which shall normally be within one year of the original failure. Approval for deferral must be obtained from the relevant board of studies.

5. The examiners may award a distinction to candidates for the certificate.

POSTGRADUATE CERTIFICATE IN SURGICAL SCIENCE AND PRACTICE (EXIT AWARD ONLY) (NEW REGULATIONS)

1. The Medical Sciences Board, jointly with the Continuing Education Board, shall elect for the supervision of the course a Standing Committee, which shall have the power to arrange lectures and other instruction.

2. The Postgraduate Certificate is only available to students admitted for the degree of M.Sc. in Surgical Science and Practice. The course is available on a part time basis only and shall consist of instruction in the theory and practice of Surgical Science and Practice.

3. The policy of the Continuing Education Board on variable intensity part time study shall apply to this award.

4. The minimum period of registration on the Postgraduate Certificate shall be three terms and the maximum period of registration shall be twelve terms.

5. Every candidate will be required to satisfy the examiners in the following:

    (*a*) Participation, to the satisfaction of the Course Director, in any three of the modules selected from either Schedule A or Schedule B below.

    (*b*) Written assignments related to each of the modules selected from Schedule A, each of not more than 4,000 words in length.

    (*c*) Assignments consisting of multiple choice questions or structured short questions, online project working and practical tests related to each of the modules selected from Schedule B.

The assignments set out in clause 5(*b*) and (*c*) shall be forwarded, usually through a specified electronic submission system, to the examiners c/o Registry, Department for Continuing Education, 1 Wellington Square, Oxford OX1 2JA, for consideration by such date as the examiners shall determine shall notify candidates.

6. Candidates may be required to attend a viva voce examination at the end of the course of studies at the discretion of the examiners.

7. The examiners may award a distinction to candidates for the Postgraduate Certificate.

8. Candidates who fail to satisfy the examiners in any of the assignments under 5(*b*) or (*c*) above may be permitted to resubmit work in respect of the part or parts they have failed on not more than one occasion for each assignment without being required to repeat attendance at the relevant module or modules. The resubmission shall normally be within one year of the original failure.

9. Provided the Standing Committee is satisfied that a student on the award has undertaken equivalent study, of an appropriate standard, normally at another institution of higher education, or has appropriate work experience to an equivalent standard, the committee may permit the candidate to be exempted from attendance and the submission of a written assignment in respect of up to three modules. In exercising this discretion the Standing Committee shall take into consideration the length of time that has elapsed since the study or work experience was undertaken.

10. The Standing Committee may deem satisfactory completion of a module (including the associated assessment) prior to registration for the award as having met the attendance and examination requirements in respect of that module. Such discretion will normally only be exercised if the time elapsed between commencement of the accredited module concerned and registration for the award is not more than two

years. The maximum number of modules taken prior to registration for the award that may count in this way shall be three.

SCHEDULE A

The practice of evidence-based health care
Quality improvement science and systems analysis   5
Introduction to surgical management and leadership
Becoming a medical educator
Any other module as defined by the Course Director and approved by the Standing
Committee.

SCHEDULE B   10

Human factors, teamwork and communication
Surgical technology and robotics.

NOTES

32

GENERAL REGULATIONS FOR POSTGRADUATE DIPLOMAS (CONTINUING EDUCATION)

1. The Continuing Education Board shall have power to grant Postgraduate   5
Diplomas to candidates who have satisfied the conditions prescribed in this section
and any further conditions which the board may prescribe by regulation.

2. The examination for each Postgraduate Diploma shall be under the supervision
of the Continuing Education Board which shall have power, subject to the approval of
the Education Committee, to make regulations governing the examination.   10

3. Candidates, whether members of the University or not, may be admitted as
students for a Postgraduate Diploma under such conditions as the board shall prescribe,
provided that before admission to a course of study approved by the board, candidates
shall have satisfied the board that they have had appropriate educational experience
acceptable to the board, and are well-equipped to enter the proposed course of study.   15

4. Any person who has been accepted as a candidate for a Postgraduate Diploma,
and who has satisfactorily pursued a course, the character and length of which have
been approved by the board, may be admitted to the examination.

POSTGRADUATE DIPLOMA IN ADVANCED COGNITIVE THERAPY STUDIES (NEW REGULATIONS)

1. The course will consist of lectures, tutorials, seminars, and classes on the principles and practice of advanced cognitive therapy studies, together with clinical supervision and practice in the supervision and training of cognitive therapists. The course will be taken on a part-time basis.

2. The policy of the Continuing Education Board on variable intensity part-time postgraduate study applies to this award.

3. The minimum period of registration for the award of the Postgraduate Diploma shall be three terms and the maximum period shall be nine terms.

4. Candidates may be permitted by the Continuing Education Board in certain circumstances to intermit for a maximum of six terms. Any such period shall not count to the maximum or minimum permitted period of registration and no fee liability will be incurred during such periods.

5. Where a candidate undertakes a module for credit under Cl. 10 below the date of registration for the award shall retrospectively be deemed to be first day of the term in which the module was taken.

6. Every candidate will be required to satisfy the examiners in the following:

   (*a*) attendance at the modules listed below;

   (*b*) attendance at two independent advanced level clinical therapy training workshops;

   (*c*) one video of a supervision session together with a reflective commentary and a written critique of no more than 2,000 words in respect of Module 1;

   (*d*) one written report of no more than 4,000 words covering the design, delivery and evaluation of a CBT training event in respect of Module 2;

   (*e*) one recorded clinical session of a 'complex case' together with a written case study of no more than 4,000 words of that patient in respect of Module 3;

   (*f*) one written research proposal of no more than 1,500 words in respect of Module 4;

   (*g*) one written assignment of no more than 4,000 words describing and evaluating the development of a service initiative in respect of Module 5.

The assessed work under (*c*), (*d*), (*e*), (*f*), and (*g*), shall be forwarded to the examiners for consideration by such dates as the examiners shall determine and shall notify the candidates and tutors.

7. Candidates may be required to attend a viva voce examination at the end of the course of studies at the discretion of the examiners.

8. The examiners may award a distinction to candidates for the Postgraduate Diploma.

9. Candidates who fail to satisfy the examiners in any of the assignments under 6 (*c*) to (*g*) above may be permitted to resubmit work in respect of the part or parts they have failed on not more than one occasion for each assignment without being required to repeat attendance at the relevant module or modules. The resubmission shall normally be within one year of the original failure.

10. Provided the Programme Committee is satisfied that a student on the award has undertaken equivalent study, of an appropriate standard, normally at another institution of higher education, or has appropriate work experience to an equivalent stan-

dard, the Committee shall have the discretion to permit the candidate to be exempted from attendance and the submission of a written assignment in respect of up to two modules. In exercising this discretion the Programme Committee shall have consideration to the length of time that has elapsed since the study or work experience was undertaken. 5

11. The Programme Committee shall have the discretion to deem satisfactory completion of a module including the associated assessment prior to registration for the award as having met the attendance and examination requirements in respect of that module. Such discretion will normally only be exercised if the time elapsed between commencement of the accredited module concerned and registration for the 10 award is not more than two years. The maximum number of modules taken prior to registration for the award that can contribute to the achievement of the award of the Postgraduate Diploma shall be two.

MODULES

Module 1. Supervision theory, principles and practice 15
Module 2. Training skills, in the context of adult learning theory
Module 3. Updates in clinical theory, research and practice in Anxiety Disorders and Depressive Disorders
Module 4. Research methodology and skills for the practicing clinician
Module 5. Organisational development, particularly as it relates to establishing, 20 maintaining and developing cognitive therapy service.

POSTGRADUATE DIPLOMA IN COGNITIVE BEHAVIOURAL THERAPY

1. The course will consist of lectures, tutorials, seminars, and classes on the principle and practice of cognitive behavioural therapy, together with clinical practice in cognitive behavioural therapy. The course will be taken on a part-time basis over a period of not less than three terms and no more than nine terms.   5

2. Every candidate will be required to satisfy the examiners in the following:

(*a*) attendance at the appropriate classroom-based courses including small group case supervisions;

(*b*) supervised treatment of at least five patients by cognitive behavioural therapy;   10

(*c*) six audio- or videotape presentations of behavioural therapy sessions;

(*d*) three written case presentations, each of no more than 4,000 words;

(*e*) a dissertation of no more than 10,000 words on a topic approved by the examiners.   15

The six audio- or videotape presentations under (*c*), the three case presentations under (*d*), and the dissertation under (*e*) shall be forwarded to the examiners for consideration by such date as the examiners shall determine and shall notify candidates and tutors.

3. Candidates may be required to attend a viva voce examination at the end of the course of study at the discretion of the examiners.   20

4. The examiners may award a distinction to candidates for the Diploma.

5. Candidates who fail to satisfy the examiners in the audio- or videotape presentations under 2(*c*), the three case presentations under 2(*d*), or the dissertation under 2(*e*) may be permitted to resubmit work in respect of the part or parts of the examination which they have failed for examination on not more than one occasion which shall normally be within one year of the original failure.   25

POSTGRADUATE DIPLOMA IN DIPLOMATIC STUDIES

1. Students for the Diploma may hold that status for no more than six terms.

2. Candidates are only eligible to be admitted to the Diploma in Diplomatic Studies if they have achieved a satisfactory standard in the first term of study for the Certificate in Diplomatic Studies. Admission to the Diploma will take place at the end of the first term in the year of study, on the basis of a transfer proposal and the first term's assessed written work, as approved by the Admissions Committee for the programme.

3. Each student will follow a course of study comprising four core courses. The four core courses are:

International Politics. Key concepts in international relations leading to central issues in world politics, with particular emphasis on change in the international system and the evolving role of diplomacy in consequence.

Economics. Basics of international trade theory and macroeconomics, focusing on such applied and political economy topics as trade liberalisation, globalisation, and international resource transfers.

International Law. Principles of international law and the processes of legal reasoning, and their application to current world problems ranging from the nature of international law to the use of force and conflict settlement.

Diplomatic Practice. Overview of different regions of the world, major international organisations, and current world problems as they affect diplomats. Review of practical aspects of diplomacy and their application to discussion of practical action by means of which governments can address these problems.

In addition, candidates will be required to submit a dissertation of between 10,000 and 12,000 words.

4. *Examinations.* Candidates will be required to take papers in International Politics, International Law, Economics, and Diplomatic Practice.

5. *Syllabus*

    I. Four core modules: International Politics, Economics, International Law, and Diplomatic Practice.

    II. Each candidate will be required to present a dissertation of not more than 12,000 words, on a subject approved by the examiners, to the examiners c/o the Registry, Department for Continuing Education, 1 Wellington Square, Oxford OX1 2JA, by 12 noon on Friday of sixth week of Trinity Term in the year in which he or she completes the course. All material submitted for the dissertation shall be accompanied by a certificate signed by the candidate indicating that it is the candidate's own work.

6. The examiners may award a distinction to candidates for the Diploma. To be awarded a distinction, a candidate must obtain **either** an average of 70 overall in the five programme elements; **or** a mark of 70 or above in three of the five programme elements, of which one shall normally be the dissertation.

7. A candidate for the Diploma who fails to meet the standard required for award of the Diploma, but who has met the examination standards and requirements stipulated in the regulations governing the Certificate in Diplomatic Studies, may be offered the option of resitting the examination for the Diploma, or (having satisfied the examination standards and requirements of that qualification) of being awarded the Certificate.

8. A candidate whose overall average mark falls below 50 shall be eligible to resit the failed elements on one occasion during the following academic year. Compensation in one paper is allowed.

9. Candidates who fail to satisfy the examiners in the written examinations in all four of the core elements of the Certificate course, or who fail to submit a dissertation of the necessary standard will be eligible to resit on one occasion.

POSTGRADUATE DIPLOMA IN EVIDENCE-BASED HEALTH CARE

1. The Divisional Board of Medical Sciences, jointly with the Continuing Education Board, shall elect for the supervision of the course a Standing Committee, which shall have the power to arrange lectures and other instruction.

2. Candidates must follow for at least three and at most nine terms a part-time course of instruction in the theory and practice of Evidence-Based Health Care, which shall normally take place over a period of no more than four years. The postgraduate diploma is only available to students admitted for the degree of M.Sc. in Evidence-Based Health Care.

3. Every candidate will be required to satisfy the examiners in the following:

  (*a*) attendance at both of the modules listed in Schedule A (below);

  (*b*) attendance at four of the modules listed in Schedule B (below);

  (*c*) six written assignments, usually of no more than 5,000 words, one on each of the modules from 3(*a*) and 3(*b*) above.

The assessed work set out in clause 3(*c*) shall be forwarded to the examiners c/o Registry, Department for Continuing Education, 1 Wellington Square, Oxford OX1 2JA, for consideration by such date as the examiners shall determine and of which they shall notify candidates.

4. Candidates may be required to attend a viva voce examination at the end of the course of studies at the discretion of the examiners.

5. The examiners may award a distinction to candidates for the Postgraduate Diploma.

6. Candidates who fail to satisfy the examiners in any of the six assignments under 3(*c*) may be permitted, normally within one year of the original failure, to resubmit work in respect of the part or parts they have failed on not more than one occasion for each assignment without being required to repeat attendance at the relevant module or modules under 3(*a*) and/or 3(*b*).

7. The Standing Committee shall have the discretion to permit any candidate to be exempted, in exceptional circumstances, from attendance at a module under 3(*a*) or 3 (*b*) and from submitting an assignment required under 3(*c*) above, provided that the Standing Committee is satisfied that such a candidate has undertaken equivalent study, or has appropriate work experience to an equivalent standard.

SCHEDULE A

M1: Practice of EBHC

M2: Introduction to Study Design and Research Methods

SCHEDULE B

M3: Knowledge into Action

M4: Clinical Epidemiology

M5: Evidence-Based Diagnosis and Screening

M6: Systematic Reviews

M7: Randomised Control Trials

M8: Essential Medical Statistics

M9: Patient-Based Evidence

M10: Ethics in Health Care

M11: Qualitative Research Methods

M12: Evidence-Based Dentistry

M13: Introduction to Statistics in Health Care Research

Any other module as defined by the Programme Director and approved by the Standing Committee.

POSTGRADUATE DIPLOMA IN EXPERIMENTAL THERAPEUTICS (EXIT AWARD ONLY)

(old regulations for students registered on the M.Sc. Experimental Therapeutics before 1 October 2012)

1. The Medical Sciences Board, in consultation with the Continuing Education Board, shall elect for the supervision of the course a Standing Committee that shall have the power to arrange lectures and other instruction.

2. Every candidate must follow for at least six terms a part-time course of instruction in the theory and practice of Experimental Therapeutics, which shall normally take place over a period of two years and no more than four years.

3. Every candidate will be required to satisfy the examiners in the following:

(*a*) active participation, to the satisfaction of the Programme Director, in each of the modules listed below.

(*b*) six written assignments of not more than 5,000 words in length, one from each of the six modules specified.

The assessed work set out in cl. 3(*b*) shall be forwarded to the examiners c/o Registry, Department for Continuing Education, 1 Wellington Square, Oxford OX1 2JA, for consideration by such date as the examiners shall determine and of which they shall notify candidates. The assessed work will, in normal circumstances, be submitted through an electronic submission system.

4. The examiners may award a distinction to candidates for the Postgraduate Diploma.

5. Candidates who fail to satisfy the examiners in any part of the examination may be permitted to resubmit work in respect of the part or parts of the examination that they have failed, for examination on not more than one occasion which shall normally be within one year of the original failure.

6. The Standing Committee shall have the discretion to permit any candidate to be exempted from submitting an assignment of the total of six written assignments required under 3(*b*) above, provided that the Standing Committee is satisfied that such a candidate has undertaken equivalent study, or has appropriate work experience to an equivalent standard.

SCHEDULE

(1) Structure of clinical trials and experimental therapeutics

(2) Pharmacokinetics and Drug Therapy

(3) Pharmacodynamics, Biomarkers and Personalised Therapy

(4) Adverse drug reactions, drug interactions, and pharmacovigilance

(5) How to do research on therapeutic interventions: protocol preparation

(6) Biological Therapeutics

(7) Any other module as defined by the Programme Director and approved by the Standing Committee.

POSTGRADUATE DIPLOMA IN EXPERIMENTAL THERAPEUTICS (EXIT AWARD ONLY) (NEW REGULATIONS)

1. The Medical Sciences Board, in consultation with the Continuing Education Board, shall elect for the supervision of the course a Standing Committee that shall have the power to arrange lectures and other instruction.

2. The Postgraduate Diploma is only available to students admitted for the degree of M.Sc. in Experimental Therapeutics. The course is available on a part time basis only and shall consist of instruction in the theory and practice of Experimental Therapeutics.

3. The policy of the Continuing Education Board on variable intensity part-time postgraduate study shall apply to this award.

4. The minimum period of registration on the PG Diploma shall be three terms and the maximum period of registration shall be twelve terms.

5. Candidates may be permitted in certain circumstances to suspend status, for a maximum of six terms. Any such period shall not count to the maximum or minimum permitted period of registration and no fee liability will be incurred during such periods.

6. Every candidate will be required to satisfy the examiners in the following:

(*a*) participation, to the satisfaction of the course director, in each of the modules listed below;

(*b*) six written assignments of not more than 4,000 words in length, one from each of the six modules specified.

The assessed work set out in clause 6(*b*) shall be forwarded to the examiners c/o Registry, Department for Continuing Education, 1 Wellington Square, Oxford OX1 2JA, for consideration by such date as the examiners shall determine and shall notify candidates. The assessed work will, in normal circumstances, be submitted through an electronic submission system.

7. Candidates may be required to attend a viva voce examination at the end of the course of studies at the discretion of the examiners.

8. The examiners may award a distinction to candidates for the PG Diploma.

9. Candidates who fail to satisfy the examiners in any of the assignments under 6*b* above may be permitted to resubmit work in respect of the part or parts they have failed on not more than one occasion for each assignment without being required to repeat attendance at the relevant module or modules. The resubmission shall normally be within one year of the original failure.

10. Provided the Standing Committee is satisfied that a student on the award has undertaken equivalent study, of an appropriate standard, normally at another institution of higher education, or has appropriate work experience to an equivalent standard, the committee may permit the candidate to be exempted from attendance and the submission of a written assignment in respect of up to three modules. In exercising this discretion the Standing Committee shall take into consideration the length of time that has elapsed since the study or work experience was undertaken.

11. The Standing Committee may deem satisfactory completion of a module (including the associated assessment) undertaken prior to registration for the award as having met the attendance and examination requirements in respect of that module. Such discretion will normally only be exercised if the time elapsed between commencement of the accredited module concerned and registration for the award is not more

than two years. The maximum number of modules taken prior to registration for the award that may be counted in this way shall be three.

Module Schedule

(1) Structure of clinical trials and experimental therapeutics[1]

(2) Drug development, pharmacokinetics and imaging[1]   5

(3) Pharmacodynamics, biomarkers and personalised therapy[1]

(4) Adverse drug reactions, drug interactions, and pharmacovigilanc[1]

(5) How to do research on therapeutic interventions: protocol preparation[1]

(6) Biological therapeutics[1]

(7) Any other module as defined by the programme director and approved by the   10
Standing Committee.

---

[1] Also available to students on the PG Certificate and Diploma in Health Research.

POSTGRADUATE DIPLOMA
IN HEALTH RESEARCH

1. The Medical Sciences Board, jointly with the Continuing Education Board, shall elect for the supervision of the course a Standing Committee, which shall have the power to arrange lectures and other instruction.

2. Candidates will normally be expected to have satisfactorily completed the Postgraduate Certificate in Health Research. Applications for dispensation from this requirement will be considered, in exceptional circumstances only, by the Standing Committee. To be dispensed from this requirement, candidates must demonstrate that they have undertaken equivalent study, or have appropriate work experience to an equivalent standard.

3. Candidates must follow for at least three and at most six terms, a part-time course of instruction in the theory and practice of Health Research. For candidates who have successfully completed the Postgraduate Certificate in Health Research, the number of terms in excess of three taken to complete the study of the Postgraduate Certificate will count towards the maximum number of terms permitted to complete the study of the Postgraduate Diploma. The period of study for the Postgraduate Diploma shall normally be no more than two years, so long as, for candidates who completed the Postgraduate Certificate in Health Research, the total period of study on the Postgraduate Certificate and Diploma in Health Research shall be no longer than three years from the commencement of the Postgraduate Certificate.

4. Every candidate will be required to satisfy the examiners in the following:

   (*a*) attendance at three of the modules listed in the Schedule (below);

   (*b*) three written assignments, usually of no more than 5,000 words, one on each of the modules from 4(*a*) above.

The assignments set out in clause 4(*b*) shall be forwarded, usually electronically via a specified online submission system, to the examiners c/o Registry, Department for Continuing Education, 1 Wellington Square, Oxford OX1 2JA, for consideration by such date as the examiners shall determine and of which they shall notify candidates.

5. Candidates may be required to attend a viva voce examination at the end of the course of studies at the discretion of the examiners.

6. The examiners may award a distinction to candidates for the Postgraduate Diploma.

7. Candidates who fail to satisfy the examiners in any of the three assignments under 4(*b*) may be permitted, normally within one year of the original failure, to resubmit work in respect of the part or parts they have failed on not more than one occasion for each assignment without being required to repeat attendance at the relevant module or modules under 4(*a*).

8. The standing committee shall have the discretion to permit any candidate to be exempted, in exceptional circumstances, from attendance at any module under 4(*a*) and from submitting the associated assignment required under 4(*b*) above, provided that the standing committee is satisfied that such a candidate has undertaken equivalent study, or have appropriate work experience to an equivalent standard.

SCHEDULE

M4: Evidence in Practice (Clinical Epidemiology and Decision Making)
M5: Systematic Reviews
M6: Randomized Control Trials
M7: Qualitative Research Methods

M8: Introduction to Statistics in Health Care Research
M9: The power of bioinformatics in modern research
M10: Evidence-Based Diagnosis
M11: Knowledge into Action

Any other module as defined by the Programme Director and approved by the 5
Standing Committee.

POSTGRADUATE DIPLOMA IN HISTORY
OF DESIGN (EXIT AWARD ONLY)

[For students starting before MT 2015: 1. Candidates must follow a course of instruction in History of Design. The course will be taken on a part-time basis over a period of not fewer than two years and not more than three years within a maximum   5
period of five years. The postgraduate diploma is only available to students admitted for the degree of M.St. in the History of Design.

2. The examination will consist of the following parts:

A Core Papers

Every candidate must submit a written assignment for each of the three core course   10
papers taught in Year 1:

    I. Techniques and Materials (Object Case Study: 2,500 words)

    II. Historical Methods (Methodology and Critical Sources Review: 3,000 words)

    III. Research Project (Extended Essay: 5,000 words)   15

B Advanced Papers

Every candidate must follow two Advanced Papers courses form the options listed in the Schedule below, and submit one written assignment of no more than 5,000 words in length for each paper. Candidates will select two Advanced Papers in Year 2 of the M.St. from a list of available options.   20

3. Each candidate must attend a viva voce examination when required to do so by the examiners.

4. The examiners may award a distinction for excellence in the Postgraduate Diploma.

5. A candidate who fails the assessment for a core module or advanced paper, may   25
be permitted to resubmit the written work, on one further occasion only, not later than one year after the initial attempt.

SCHEDULE

Advanced Papers are available in the following areas:
- Decoration in Modern France   30
- The Arts and Crafts Tradition in Modern Britain
- Design in the Machine Age
- Design, Body, Environment
- Visual Cultures of the World Wars
- Academic Writing and Contemporary Practice*   35
- Medieval Period or Early Modern Option
- Papers from the existing M.Sc. English Local History:

A.7 The social history of English architecture, 1870–1940

A.8 The English suburb, 1800–1939

A.4 English architecture 1500–1640   40

* This Advanced Paper will be assessed by means of two written assignments: a Documentation Project and a Critical Sources Review; each 1,500 words in length

Not all advanced papers will be available in any one year and the definitive list of advanced papers available in any one year will be circulated to candidates and their supervisors during the second week of Michaelmas Term.]   45

[**For students starting from MT 2015:** 1. Candidates must follow a course of instruction in the History of Design. The course is available on a part time basis only to be followed over a period of six terms. The postgraduate diploma is only available to students admitted for the degree of M.St. in the History of Design.

2. Every candidate will be required to satisfy the examiners in the following: 5

(*a*) Attendance at classes, individual tutorials, group seminars and other teaching sessions as required

(*b*) A written assignment for each of the three papers taught in Year 1

i. Materials and Techniques: an object case study of not more than 2,500 words

ii. Historical Methods: a methodology and critical sources review of not more than   10
3,000 words

iii. A research project of not more than 5,000 words

(*c*) A written assignment of not more than 5,000 words for each of two Advanced papers selected from the Schedule below

Assignments under 2(*b*) and (*c*) shall be submitted, to the examiners c/o the   15
Registry, Department for Continuing Education, 1 Wellington Square Oxford OX1 2JA, in for consideration by such dates as the examiners shall determine and of which they shall notify candidates.

3. Each candidate must attend a viva voce examination when required to do so by the examiners.   20

4. The examiners may award a distinction for excellence in the Postgraduate Diploma.

5. Candidates who fail to satisfy the examiners in any part or parts of the examination may be permitted to resubmit work in respect of the part or parts of the examination which they have failed on not more than one occasion which shall   25
normally be within one year of the original failure.

SCHEDULE

Advanced Papers are available in the following areas:

- *Decoration in Modern France*
- *The Arts and Crafts Tradition in Modern Britain*   30
- *Design in the Machine Age*
- *Design, Body, Environment*
- *Visual Cultures of the World Wars*
- *Academic Writing and Contemporary Practice**
- *Early Period*   35
- *Papers available to be shared with the existing M.Sc. English Local History:*

A.7 The social history of English architecture, 1870–1940

A.8 The English suburb, 1800–1939

A.4 English architecture 1500–1640

* This Advanced Paper will be assessed by means of two written assignments: a   40
Documentation Project and a Critical Sources Review; each 1,500 words in length

Not all advanced papers will be available in any one year and the definitive list of advanced papers available in any one year will be circulated to candidates and their supervisors during the second week of Michaelmas Term.]

RECANATI-KAPLAN CENTRE POSTGRADUATE DIPLOMA IN INTERNATIONAL WILDLIFE CONSERVATION PRACTICE

1. The Mathematical, Physical and Life Sciences Board, jointly with the Continuing Education Board, shall elect for the supervision of the course a Standing Committee that shall have the power to arrange lectures and other instruction.

2. The diploma shall be entitled the Recanati-Kaplan Centre Postgraduate Diploma in International Wildlife Conservation Practice.

3. Candidates must follow for a period of eight months a course of instruction in International Wildlife Conservation Practice.

4. Every candidate will be required to satisfy the examiners in the following:

    (*a*) the submission of five written assignments of not more than 2,000 words each, one on each of the modules listed in the Schedule below; and

    (*b*) the attendance on two projects approved by the Standing Committee, and the submission of two reports of not more than 7,000 words each, one on each of the projects.

The assignments under (*a*) and the reports under (*b*) shall be forwarded to the examiners c/o the Registry, Department for Continuing Education, 1 Wellington Square, Oxford OX1 2JA, for consideration by such date as the examiners shall determine and of which they shall notify candidates.

5. Candidates may be required to attend a viva voce examination at the end of the course of studies at the discretion of the examiners.

6. The examiners may award a distinction to candidates for the Postgraduate Diploma.

7. Candidates who fail to satisfy the examiners in any part of the examination may be permitted to resubmit work in respect of the part or parts of the examination which they have failed for examination on not more than one occasion which shall normally be within one year of the original failure.

SCHEDULE OF MODULES

(*a*) Wildlife Ecology and Behaviour

(*b*) Species and Biodiversity Monitoring

(*c*) Population Management

(*d*) Habitat Assessment

(*e*) Human Populations/Actions and Conservation

Any other module as defined by the Programme Director and approved by the Standing Committee.

POSTGRADUATE DIPLOMA IN PAEDIATRIC INFECTIOUS DISEASES

1. The Divisional Board of Medical Sciences, jointly with the Continuing Education Board, shall elect for the supervision of the course a Standing Committee, which shall have the power to arrange lectures and other instruction.

2. The course may be taken on a part-time basis over a period of not less than six and not more than nine terms.

3. Candidates may be permitted under certain circumstances to suspend status, for a maximum of six terms. Any such period shall not count towards the maximum or minimum permitted period of registration and no fee liability will be incurred during such periods.

4. Every candidate shall be required to satisfy the examiners in the following:

    (*a*) Attendance at two residential courses over two years held annually in Oxford entitled 'Infection and Immunity in Children' (with a different course programme each year).

    (*b*) Attendance at the residential PENTA-ESPID (Tr@inforPedHIV) training course in paediatric HIV medicine.

    (*c*) Completion of the Online PENTA-ESPID (Tr@inforPedHIV) module in paediatric HIV medicine.

    (*d*) Participation in seven ESPID Online Case Rounds.

    (*e*) Participation in one four-week PENTA-ESPID (Tr@inforPedHIV) Online Case Discussion in paediatric HIV medicine.

    (*f*) Participation in six online multiple choice sessions.

5. Every candidate shall be required to satisfy the examiners in the following:

    (*a*) A written assignment consisting of a case study and literature review of no more than 4000 words;

    (*b*) A short oral presentation;

    (*c*) A written assignment of no more than 4,000 words, taking the form of an in-depth review and critical analysis of a topic from the syllabus;

    (*d*) A written assignment of no more than 4,000 words, taking the form of either:

    i. An audit project written in the format of a scientific paper;

    or

    ii. A project report describing a small-scale research study in the field of paediatric infectious diseases undertaken by the candidate of no more than 4000 words written in the style of a scientific paper;

    or

    iii. An in-depth literature review and research project protocol.

    (*e*) An examination consisting of multiple choice questions in paediatric infectious diseases.

The assignments under 5(*a*), 5(*c*), and 5(*d*) shall be forwarded to the examiners c/o Registry, Department of Continuing Education, 1 Wellington Square, Oxford OX1 2JA, for consideration by such date as the examiners shall determine and of which they shall notify candidates. The assessed work will, in normal circumstances, be submitted through an electronic submission system.

6. Candidates may be required to attend a viva voce examination at the end of the course of studies at the discretion of the examiners.

7. The examiners may award a distinction to candidates for the Postgraduate Diploma.

8. A candidate who fails to satisfy the examiners in the assessed work detailed under clause 5 above may be permitted one further attempt at an assessment or assessments only, not later than one year after the initial failure.   5

POSTGRADUATE DIPLOMA IN PSYCHODYNAMIC PRACTICE

1. *Course*

    (*a*) The course will consist of lectures, tutorials, seminars, classes, and supervised practice on the theory and practice of Psychodynamic Practice. Candidates will be required to undertake personal therapy. The course will be taken on a part-time basis over a period which shall be of two years' duration.

    (*b*) The course places equal emphasis on theory, practice, and the candidate's personal and professional development. In the first year candidates will study the Historical and Theoretical Perspective, the Psychiatric Perspective, the Contemporary Perspective, and the Developmental Perspective, and be introduced to core clinical models. The organisational perspective will be taught to complement candidates' clinical placements. Candidates will study long term counselling and psychotherapy. The second year will include the study of time limited counselling and psychotherapy and the application of the core theoretical model to varied contexts and clinical populations.

2. Every candidate will be required to satisfy the examiners in the following:

    (*a*) attendance at weekly classes, sensitivity group sessions, individual tutorials, a weekend school, and review sessions and revision days;

    (*b*) five written assignments as follows:

         (i) an initial case study of no more than 3,000 words.

         (ii) a second case study, of no more than 3,000 words.

         (iii) an extract from a candidate's placement log of no more than 3,000 words.

         (iv) an extract from the candidate's Reflective Journal, of no more than 3,000 words.

         (v) an essay, of no more than 3,000 words, based on theoretical material covered in the course.

    (*c*) a dissertation of no more than 10,000 words (including appendices and footnotes but excluding bibliography). The subject of the dissertation must be submitted for approval by the external examiner following consultation with the course director by noon of Friday of fourth week of Hilary Full Term in the second year of the course.

    (*d*) participation in a minimum of 17 placement supervisions to include at least 100 hours of client/patient contact;

    (*e*) participation in a minimum of 80 hours of personal therapy and submission of a statement of hours completed from the candidate's personal therapist;

    (*f*) submission of annual reports from the candidate's course tutor and clinical seminar leader;

    (*g*) confirmation from the sensitivity group conductor that there are no ethical reasons why the candidate should be discouraged from commencing professional work.

The assignments under (*b*) and three typewritten or printed copies of the dissertation under (*c*) will be forwarded to the examiners c/o Registry, Department for Continuing Education, Wellington Square, Oxford OX 1 2JA for consideration by such date as the examiners shall determine and shall notify candidates before the start of the academic year in which the assignment is due.

3. Candidates may be required to attend a viva voce examination at the end of the course of studies.

4. Candidates who fail to satisfy the examiners in any of the assignments in 2(*b*) or the dissertation may be permitted to resubmit work in the part or parts of the examination which they have failed for examination on not more than one occasion which shall normally be within one year of the original failure. Approval for deferral must be obtained from the relevant board of studies. Candidates who fail to obtain a satisfactory report of their placement at the end of the first year will be given additional support. Candidates who fail to obtain a satisfactory report at the end of the second year may be permitted by the examiners to continue in the placement until the required standard is reached, for a period of no more than one year after the end of the second year.

5. The examiners may award a distinction to candidates for the diploma.

POSTGRADUATE DIPLOMA IN SURGICAL SCIENCE AND PRACTICE (EXIT AWARD ONLY) (NEW REGULATIONS)

1. The Medical Sciences Board, jointly with the Continuing Education Board, shall elect for the supervision of the course a Standing Committee, which shall have the power to arrange lectures and other instruction.

2. The Postgraduate Diploma is only available to students admitted for the degree of M.Sc. in Surgical Science and Practice. The course is available on a part time basis only and shall consist of instruction in the theory and practice of Surgical Science and Practice.

3. The policy of the Continuing Education Board on variable intensity part time study shall apply to this award.

4. The minimum period of registration on the Postgraduate Diploma shall be three terms and the maximum period of registration shall be twelve terms.

5. Every candidate will be required to satisfy the examiners in the following:

    (*a*) Attendance at the modules in Schedule A and Schedule B below and other teaching sessions as required.

    (*b*) Active participation in all parts of the course to the satisfaction of the Course Director.

    (*c*) Four written assignments related to the modules in Schedule A, each of not more than 4,000 words in length.

    (*d*) Two assignments consisting of multiple choice questions or structured short questions, online project working and practical tests related to the modules in Schedule B.

The assignments set out in clauses 5(*c*) and (*d*) shall be forwarded, usually through a specified electronic submission system, to the examiners c/o Registry, Department for Continuing Education, 1 Wellington Square, Oxford OX1 2JA, for consideration by such date as the examiners shall determine and shall notify candidates.

6. Candidates may be required to attend a viva voce examination at the end of the course of studies at the discretion of the examiners.

7. The examiners may award a distinction to candidates for the Postgraduate Diploma.

8. Candidates who fail to satisfy the examiners in any of the assignments under 5 (c) or (d) above may be permitted to resubmit work in respect of the part or parts they have failed on not more than one occasion for each assignment without being required to repeat attendance at the relevant module or modules. The resubmission shall normally be within one year of the original failure.

9. Provided the Standing Committee is satisfied that a student on the award has undertaken equivalent study, of an appropriate standard, normally at another institution of higher education, or has appropriate work experience to an equivalent standard, the committee may permit the candidate to be exempted from attendance and the submission of a written assignment in respect of up to three modules. In exercising this discretion the Standing Committee shall take into consideration the length of time that has elapsed since the study or work experience was undertaken.

10. The Standing Committee may deem satisfactory completion of a module (including the associated assessment) prior to registration for the award as having met the attendance and examination requirements in respect of that module. Such discretion will normally only be exercised if the time elapsed between commencement of the

accredited module concerned and registration for the award is not more than two years. The maximum number of modules taken prior to registration for the award that may count in this way shall be three.

Schedule A

The practice of evidence-based health care   5
Quality improvement science and systems analysis
Introduction to surgical management and leadership
Becoming a medical educator
Any other module as defined by the Course Director and approved by the Standing
Committee.   10

Schedule B

Human factors, teamwork and communication
Surgical technology and robotics.

POSTGRADUATE DIPLOMA IN SUSTAINABLE URBAN DEVELOPMENT

1. The Continuing Education Board shall elect for the supervision of the course a course committee that shall have the power to arrange lectures and other instruction in the theory and practice of Sustainable Urban Development. The postgraduate diploma is only available to students admitted to the degree of M.Sc. in Sustainable Urban Development.

2. The course may be taken on a part-time basis over a period of not less than six and not more than nine terms.

3. Candidates may be permitted under certain circumstances to suspend status, for a maximum of six terms. Any such period shall not count towards the maximum or minimum permitted period of registration and no fee liability will be incurred during such periods.

4. Every candidate will be required to satisfy the examiners in the following:

    (*a*) Attendance at classes, tutorials, group seminars and other teaching sessions;

    (*b*) seven written assignments, each being on one of the units listed in the Schedule below, and each of not more than 3000 words in length;

The assessed work set out in clause 4(*b*) shall be forwarded in normal circumstances through an electronic submission system to the examiners c/o Registry, Department for Continuing Education, 1 Wellington Square, Oxford OX1 2JA, for consideration by such date as the examiners shall determine and of which they shall notify candidates.

4. Candidates may be required to attend a viva voce examination at the end of the course of studies at the discretion of the examiners.

5. The examiners may award a distinction to candidates for the Postgraduate Diploma.

6. Candidates who fail to satisfy the examiners in any part of the examination may be permitted to resubmit work in respect of the part or parts of the examination that they have failed for examination on not more than one occasion which shall normally be within one year of the original failure.

7. The course committee shall have the discretion to permit any candidate to be exempted, in exceptional circumstances, from submitting an assignment, provided that the committee is satisfied that such a candidate has undertaken equivalent study, or have appropriate work experience to an equivalent standard.

SCHEDULE

Concepts of the City and Environmental Change
Climate Change and the Built Environment
Place-making and Urban Design
Financing Sustainability
Sustainable Transport
Urbanism, Community and City-building
Leadership, Governance and Future Cities
Urbanisation and the Global South
Any other subject approved by the course committee.
Not all units will be available in any one year.

NOTES

33

GENERAL REGULATIONS FOR UNDERGRADUATE CERTIFICATES (CONTINUING EDUCATION)

1. The Continuing Education Board shall have the power to grant Certificates to 5
candidates who have satisfied the conditions prescribed in this section and any further
conditions which the board may prescribe by regulation.

2. The examination for each Certificate (Continuing Education) shall be under the
supervision of the Continuing Education Board, which shall have power, subject to
the approval of the Education Committee, to make regulations governing the exam- 10
ination.

3. Candidates, whether members of the University or not, may be admitted as
students for an Undergraduate Certificate (Continuing Education) under such conditions as the board shall prescribe, provided that before admission to a course of study
approved by the board, candidates shall have satisfied the board that they have 15
appropriate educational experience acceptable to the board, and are well-equipped
to enter the proposed course of study.

4. Any person who has been accepted as a candidate for an Undergraduate
Certificate (Continuing Education), and who has satisfactorily pursued a course, the
character and length of which have been approved by the board, may be admitted to 20
the examination.

UNDERGRADUATE CERTIFICATE IN ARCHAEOLOGY

1. *Course*

    (*a*) The course will consist of lectures, tutorials, seminars and classes on the subject of Archaeology. The course, which is available on a part-time basis only, may be taken over a period of a minimum of two, and no more than three years.

    (*b*) The subjects of the course will be taught in two one-year modules. One module shall be offered each year. Candidates must complete the introductory module *Discovering Archaeology: its purpose and practice* (Module A) before proceeding to Module B. To qualify for the award of the Certificate, candidates must satisfy the examiners in modules A and B.

2. Every candidate will be required to satisfy the examiners in the following:

    (*a*) Attendance at a minimum of 75 per cent of class-based sessions;

    (*b*) Attendance at one week of fieldwork (and associated written work) and study visits to the satisfaction of the Course Director;

    (*c*) Attendance at a minimum of two one-hour tutorials in the second year of the course;

    (*d*) Three practical assignments, of which two shall be between 1,000 and 1,500 words in length, and one shall be between 2,000 and 2,500 words, based on the practical work undertaken in Module A;

    (*e*) Three written assignments of normally between 1,400 and 1,600 words in length, based on the subjects taught in Module A;

    (*f*) Three practical assignments, each of which shall be between 1,000 and 1,500 words in length, based on the practical work undertaken in Module B;

    (*g*) Three written assignments of normally between 1,800 and 2,000 words in length, based on the subjects taught in Module B;

    (*h*) One written assignment totalling no more than 1,000 words in length, and a field notebook, covering work done in the fieldwork week;

    (*i*) One two-hour written examination, covering the subjects taught in Module A;

    (*j*) One extended project of between 4,500 and 5,500 words in length consisting of a subject of the candidate's choice relating to the course material in Module B and agreed with the Course Director.

The written work under clauses 2(*b*), (*d*)–(*j*) will be forwarded to the examiners for consideration by such dates as the examiners shall determine and shall notify candidates.

3. Candidates may be required to attend a viva voce examination at the end of the course.

4. The examiners may award a distinction to candidates for the Certificate.

5. Candidates who fail to satisfy the examiners in the assessed work specified in clauses (*b*), (*d*) to (*j*) may be permitted to resubmit work in respect of the part or parts of the examination which they have failed on not more than one occasion which shall normally be within one year of the initial failure.

UNDERGRADUATE CERTIFICATE IN HIGHER EDUCATION

1. The Certificate shall consist of accredited classes and other courses of study provided by the Department for Continuing Education. The Certificate is available on a part-time basis and may be taken over a period of not fewer than two years and no more than four years.

2. The main subjects for the Certificate shall be Archaeology, Art History, Architectural History, Creative Writing, History, Italian, Literature, Philosophy, and Spanish, together with such other subjects as may be approved by the Continuing Education Board. Candidates must select one of these as their main subject. A list of classes and other courses available in any one year that can be taken for the Certificate, including those identified as qualifying courses, will be published annually by the Department.

3. Every candidate will be required to satisfy the examiners in the following:

    (*a*) accumulation of 120 Credit Accumulation and Transfer Scheme (CATS) points from classes and courses provided by the Department for Continuing Education. These 120 points must include the following:

        (i) 5 points from either three study skills day schools or the online study skills course;

        (ii) 10 points from a course approved as a qualifying course in the candidate's main subject;

        (iii) no fewer than 50, and no more than 70, additional points, in the candidate's main subject;

        (iv) no fewer than 30 points, and no more than 50 points, from eligible classes or courses in other subjects;

        (v) a reflective learning journal of not more than 2,000 words submitted in two parts (5 CATS points).

    (*b*) Two assignments, each of no more than 2,500 words or equivalent, based on topics relating to two separate classes or courses in the candidate's main subject area.

    (*c*) One assignment of not more than 3,500 words or equivalent based on a topic relating to a class or course in the candidate's main subject area other than those referred to in 3(*b*) above.

    (*d*) Attendance at a minimum of 70 per cent of each class or course.

4. Timing

    (*a*) The study skills day schools or online study skills course referred to in 3(*a*)(i) above must normally be undertaken during the first term of registration;

    (*b*) The first part of the reflective journal referred to in 3(a)(v) above shall normally be submitted after completion of the first 60 CATS points of study and the second part after completion of at least 100 CATS points.

    (*c*) The assignment referred to in 3(*c*) above shall normally be submitted during the last year of registration for the Certificate.

5. Credit may not be counted as part of the Certificate of Higher Education if it contains a significant proportion of material (normally 30 per cent or more) duplicated from a class or course already counted towards any certificate, diploma or other award of the University.

6. The Director of the Certificate shall have the discretion to permit any candidate to count towards the Certificate up to 30 CATS points from any class or course offered by the Department for Continuing Education so long as these shall have been obtained no more than four years before formal registration on the Certificate.

7. Candidates may count up to 105 CATS points towards the Certificate of Higher Education from courses studied online.

8. A candidate may be required to attend a viva voce examination.

9. The examiners may award a distinction to candidates for the Certificate.

10. Candidates who fail any accredited class or course they intent to count towards the Certificate under 3(*a*) above, or who fail to satisfy the examiners in the reflective journal under 3(*a*)(v) may be permitted to resubmit work in respect of that class or course, or resubmit the reflective journal on not more than one occasion.This shall normally be within one month of the initial failure. Candidates who fail to satisfy the examiners in the assignments under 3(*b*) or 3(*c*) above may be permitted to resubmit the assignment or assignments on not more than one occasion. This shall normally be within three months of the initial failure. All resubmissions of work must be within one year of the initial failure.

UNDERGRADUATE CERTIFICATE IN HISTORY OF ART

1. Course

   (*a*) The course shall consist of lectures, tutorials, seminars, and classes on the subjects of the History of Art. The course, which is available on a part-time basis only, may be taken over a period of a minimum of two, and no more than three years.

   (*b*) The subjects of the course will be taught in two one-year modules. One module shall be offered each year. Students must complete Module 1 before proceeding to Module 2.

2. Every candidate will be required to satisfy the examiners in the following:

   (*a*) Attendance at the theoretical courses; students must attend a minimum of 75 per cent of the equivalent of sixty two-hour sessions;

   (*b*) Attendance at six study visits;

   (*c*) Four written assignments of not more than 1,500 words and four of not more than 2,000 words based on the subjects taught;

   (*d*) Two long essays one of 3,000 words and one of 5,000 words on a subject approved by the Course Director;

   (*e*) Six class tests.

The written work under (*c*) and (*d*), and the class tests under (e), will be forwarded to the examiners for consideration by such dates as the examiners shall determine and shall notify candidates.

3. Candidates may be required to attend a viva voce examination at the end of the course.

4. The examiners may award a distinction to candidates for the Certificate.

5. Candidates who fail to satisfy the examiners in the written work under (*c*) and (*d*), or the class tests under (*e*), may be permitted to resubmit work in respect of part or parts of the examination which they have failed on not more that one occasion which shall normally be within one year of the initial failure.

UNDERGRADUATE CERTIFICATE IN
THEOLOGICAL STUDIES

1. The course shall consist of lectures, tutorials, seminars and/or classes on the subject of Theology. The course is available on a full-time basis, taken over a period of three terms, or on a part-time basis taken over a period of six terms.

2. Candidates may be permitted under certain circumstances to suspend status for a maximum of six terms. Any such period shall not count towards the minimum and maximum periods of registration, and no fee liability will be incurred during such periods.

3. Every candidate will be required to satisfy the examiners in the following:

    (*a*) Attendance at classes and other sessions as indicated in the course handbook

    (*b*) Written assignments or examination papers, as specified, for six papers, to include:

        i. At least one of A1 or A2 from Part 1 of the Schedule for the Degree of Bachelor of Theology;

        ii. At least one of A3 or A4 from the Part 1 schedule;

        iii. At least one of A5–A10 from the Part 1 schedule;

        iv. Three other papers from the Part 1 schedule.

The written work under (*b*) will be submitted to the Examiners for the Certificate in Theological Studies, Examination Schools, High Street, Oxford, for consideration by such dates as the examiners shall determine and shall notify candidates.

4. Candidates may be expected to attend a viva voce examination at the end of the course.

5. The examiners may award a distinction to candidates for the Certificate.

6. Candidates who fail to satisfy the examiners in the written work or the examinations under 3(*b*) may be permitted to resubmit work in respect of part or parts of the examination which they have failed, on not more than one occasion, which shall normally be within one year of the initial failure.

UNDERGRADUATE CERTIFICATE IN THEOLOGY AND RELIGIOUS STUDIES

1. The course shall consist of lectures, tutorials, seminars, and classes on the subject of Theology and Religious Studies. The course, which is available on a part-time basis only, may be taken over a period of a minimum of one, and no more than two, years.

2. Every candidate will be required to satisfy the examiners in the following:

   (*a*) Attendance at the theoretical courses, including study visits; students must attend a minimum of 75 per cent of the equivalent of 30 two-hour sessions;

   (*b*) One written assignment of not more than 1,000 words. This assignment is formative only and marks do not contribute to the final award.

   (*c*) Five written assignments of not more than 1,500 words based on the subjects taught.

   (*d*) One case study of not more than 3,000 words on a subject approved by the course director. The written work under (*c*) and (*d*) will be forwarded to the examiners for consideration by such dates as the examiners shall determine and shall notify candidates.

3. Candidates may be expected to attend a viva voce examination at the end of the course.

4. The examiners may award a distinction to candidates for the Certificate.

5. Candidates who fail to satisfy the examiners in the written work under 2(*c*) and (*d*) may be permitted to resubmit work in respect of part or parts of the examination which they have failed on not more that one occasion which shall normally be within one year of the initial failure.

NOTES

34

GENERAL REGULATIONS FOR UNDERGRADUATE DIPLOMAS (CONTINUING EDUCATION)

1. The Continuing Education Board shall have the power to grant Diplomas to candidates who have satisfied the conditions prescribed in this section and any further conditions which the board may prescribe by regulation.

2. The examination for each Diploma (Continuing Education) shall be under the supervision of the Continuing Education Board, which shall have power, subject to the approval of the Education Committee, to make regulations governing the examination.

3. Candidates, whether members of the University or not, may be admitted as students for an Undergraduate Diploma (Continuing Education) under such conditions as the board shall prescribe, provided that before admission to a course of study approved by the board, candidates shall have satisfied the board that they have appropriate educational experience acceptable to the Board and are well-equipped to enter the proposed course of study.

4. Any person who has been accepted as a candidate for an Undergraduate Diploma (Continuing Education), and who has satisfactorily pursued a course, the character and length of which have been approved by the committee, may be admitted to the examination.

UNDERGRADUATE DIPLOMA IN
BRITISH ARCHAEOLOGY

1. *Course*

   (*a*) The course shall consist of class-based sessions, tutorials, fieldtrips, and fieldwork on the subject of British archaeology. The course is available on a part-time basis only. It may be taken over a period of six terms normally within a nine term period.

   (*b*) The subjects of the course will be taught in three one-year modules. One module is offered each year. Modules currently available are:

   Module 1: Early Prehistoric Britain;

   Module 2: Later Prehistoric and Roman Britain;

   Module 3: Anglo-Saxon, Viking and Medieval Britain.

2. Every candidate will be required to satisfy the examiners in the following:

   (*a*) Attendance at class sessions, tutorials, field trips, and practical training;

   (*b*) Ten coursework assignments, each of which shall be no more than 2,500 words in length, based on the theoretical courses;

   (*c*) In the first module, one practical logbook of no more than 8,000 words;

   (*d*) In the second module, one practical logbook of no more than 8,000 words or an extended project of no more than 8,000 words on a topic approved by the course director.

Assignments under (b)–(d) will be forwarded to the examiners for consideration by such dates as the examiners shall determine and shall notify candidates.

3. Candidates may be required to attend a viva voce examination at the end of the course.

4. The examiners may award a distinction to candidates for the Diploma.

5. Candidates who fail to satisfy the examiners in the assignments under 2(b)–(d), may be permitted to resubmit work in respect of the part or parts of the examination which they have failed on not more than one occasion which shall normally be within one year of the initial failure.

UNDERGRADUATE DIPLOMA IN CREATIVE WRITING

1. *Course*

   (*a*) The course shall consist of lectures, tutorials, seminars and classes on the subject of Creative Writing. The course, which is available on a part-time basis only, may be taken over a period of a minimum of two, and no more than five years.

   (*b*) The course will cover the study and practice of the craft of writing. A range of literary genres and sub-genres will be considered, and directed approaches to the analytical reading of work by other writers will be undertaken.

2. Every candidate will be required to satisfy the examiners in the following:

   (*a*) Attendance at the theoretical courses; students must attend a minimum of 75 per cent of the class based sessions;

   (*b*) Attendance at twelve forty-five minute individual tutorials, six day schools and one one-week summer school;

   (*c*) Nine written assignments, each of no more than 2,000 words in length of prose, or 15 pages of drama, or 100 lines of poetry;

   (*d*) Two end-of-year portfolios of written work, each of not more than 6,000 words of prose, or 30 pages of drama or 300 lines of poetry.

   Assignments under (*c*) and (*d*) will be forwarded to the examiners for consideration by such dates as the examiners shall determine and shall notify candidates.

3. Candidates may be required to attend a viva voce examination at the end of the course.

4. The examiners may award a distinction to candidates for the Diploma.

5. Candidates who fail to satisfy the examiners in the assignments under 2(*c*)–(*d*) may be permitted to resubmit work in respect of the part or parts of the examination which they have failed on not more than one occasion which shall normally be within one year of the initial failure.

UNDERGRADUATE DIPLOMA IN ENGLISH LOCAL HISTORY

REGULATIONS

1. The course shall consist of lectures, seminars and classes on the subject of English Local History. The course is available on a part time basis only, to be taken over a period of six terms. The subjects of the course will be taught in two one year modules, offered in alternate years:

Module 1: English Local History up to 16thC

Module 1: English Local History up to 16^{th}C

Module 2: English Local History since the 16^{th}C

2. Every candidate will be required to satisfy the examiners in the following:

(*a*) attendance at classes;

(*b*) six coursework assignments, each of which shall not exceed 2,500 words in length;

(*c*) two extended essays, each of which shall not exceed 5,000 words in length, based on material taught during the course;

(*d*) two portfolios which shall not exceed 4,000 words in length commenting on selected primary sources.

Assignments under (*b*), (*c*), and (*d*) will be forwarded to the examiners for consideration by such dates as the examiners shall determine and shall notify candidates.

3. Candidates may be required to attend a viva voce examination at the end of the course.

4. The examiners may award a distinction to candidates for the Diploma.

5. Candidates who fail to satisfy the examiners in the assignments under 2 (b), (c), or (d), may be permitted to resubmit work in respect of the part or parts of the examination which they have failed on not more than one occasion which shall normally be within one year of the initial failure.

UNDERGRADUATE DIPLOMA IN HISTORY OF ART

1. *Course*

(*a*) The course shall consist of lectures, tutorials, seminars and classes on the subject of the History of Art. The course, which is available on a part-time basis only, may be taken over a period of a minimum of two, and no more than five years.

(*b*) The subjects of the course will be taught in four one-year modules of which candidates must offer two. Two modules will be available each year. Modules currently available are:

Module 1: The Late Middle Ages and the Early Renaissance

Module 2: The High Renaissance and Baroque

Module 3: Revolution to Modernity: 1848–1914

Module 4: Modern Art and Contemporary Visual Culture

2. Every candidate will be required to satisfy the examiners in the following for each of the two modules to be offered:

(*a*) Attendance at the theoretical courses; students must attend a minimum of 75 per cent of the equivalent of 30 two-hour sessions;

(*b*) Attendance at five Saturday Study Days;

(*c*) i) Two essays, each of which shall not exceed 3,000 words in length;

ii) A research project consisting of no more than 8,000 words in length each, based on a subject of the candidate's choice relating to the course material and agreed with the Course Director;

iii) A written three-hour examination paper.

The essays under (*c*)i and the project under (*c*)ii will be forwarded to the examiners for consideration by such dates as the examiners shall determine and shall notify candidates.

3. Candidates may be required to attend a viva voce examination at the end of the course.

4. The examiners may award a distinction to candidates for the Diploma.

5. Candidates must achieve a pass mark (40 per cent) in each element of assessment in each module: the two essays under 2(*c*)i taken together; the research project under 2(*c*)ii and the examination under 2(*c*)iii. Candidates who fail to satisfy the examiners in any element may be permitted to resubmit work in respect of that element on not more than one occasion which shall normally be within one year of the initial failure.

UNDERGRADUATE DIPLOMA IN THEOLOGICAL STUDIES

1. The course shall consist of lectures, tutorials, seminars and/or classes on the subject of Theology. The course is available on a full-time basis, taken over a period of three terms, or on a part-time basis taken over a period of six terms.   5

2. Candidates may be permitted under certain circumstances to suspend status for a maximum of six terms. Any such period shall not count towards the minimum and maximum periods of registration, and no fee liability will be incurred during such periods.

3. Candidates will normally be expected to have satisfactorily completed the   10 Undergraduate Certificate in Theological Studies. Applications for dispensation from this requirement will be considered, in exceptional circumstances only, by the Continuing Education Board. To be dispensed from this requirement, candidates must demonstrate that they have undertaken equivalent study to an equivalent standard.

Part One   15

4. Every candidate will be required to satisfy the examiners in the following:

   (*a*) Attendance at classes and other sessions as indicated in the course handbook

   (*b*) Written assignments or examination papers as specified, for six papers, to include:

       i. At least one of A1 or A2 from Part 1 of the Schedule for the Degree of   20 Bachelor of Theology;

       ii. At least one of A3 or A4 from the Part 1 schedule;

       iii. At least one of A5–A10 from the Part 1 schedule;

       iv. Three other papers from the Part 1 schedule.

Part Two   25

5. Every candidate will be required to satisfy the examiners in the following:

   (*a*) Attendance at classes and other sessions as indicated in the course handbook

   (*b*) Written assignments or examination papers as specified, for a further six papers, to include:

       i. Paper B1 or B2 of Part 2 of the Schedule for the Degree of Bachelor of   30 Theology;

       ii. Paper C1 or C2 from the Part 2 schedule;

       iii. At least one of papers D1–D7 from Section D of the Part 2 schedule;

       iv. Three other papers from papers B1 or B2, C1 or C2, or D1–7 of the Part 2 schedule, or A11 or A12 from the Part 1 schedule, unless already   35 offered for the Undergraduate Certificate.

The written work under 4(*b*) and 5(*b*) will be submitted to the Examiners for the Diploma in Theological Studies, Examination Schools, High Street, Oxford, for consideration by such dates as the examiners shall determine and shall notify candidates.   40

6. Candidates may be expected to attend a viva voce examination at the end of the course.

7. The examiners may award a distinction to candidates for the Diploma.

8. For any candidate who is successful in the examination for the Undergraduate Diploma in Theological Studies and who has already successfully completed the Undergraduate Certificate in Theological Studies (and for the diploma examination has incorporated the assignments submitted or examinations taken for the Undergraduate Certificate) the Undergraduate Diploma will subsume his or her Certificate. 5

9. Candidates who fail to satisfy the examiners in the written work or the examinations under 4(*b*) or 5(*b*) may be permitted to resubmit work in respect of part or parts of the examination which they have failed, on not more than one occasion, which shall normally be within one year of the initial failure. 10

NOTES

35

GENERAL REGULATIONS FOR UNDERGRADUATE ADVANCED DIPLOMAS (CONTINUING EDUCATION)

1. The Continuing Education Board shall have power to grant Advanced Diplomas   5
(two-year part-time), Advanced Diplomas (one-year full-time), and Advanced
Diplomas (one-year part-time) to candidates who have satisfied the conditions prescribed in this section and any further conditions which the Board may prescribe by
regulation.

2. The examination for each Advanced Diploma (Continuing Education) shall be   10
under the supervision of the Continuing Education Board, which shall have power,
subject to the approval of the Education Committee, to make regulations governing
the examination.

3. Candidates, whether members of the University or not, may be admitted as
students for an Advanced Diploma (Continuing Education) under such conditions as   15
the Board shall prescribe, provided that before admission to a course of study
approved by the Board, candidates shall have satisfied the board that they have
appropriate educational experience acceptable to the committee and are well-
equipped to enter the proposed course of study.

4. Any person who has been accepted as a candidate for an Advanced Diploma   20
(Continuing Education), and who has satisfactorily pursued a course, the character
and length of which have been approved by the Board, may be admitted to the
examination.

UNDERGRADUATE ADVANCED DIPLOMA IN BRITISH ARCHAEOLOGY

1. The course shall consist of lectures, tutorials, seminars and classes on the subject of British archaeology. The course, which is available on a part-time basis only, will be followed over one year.

2. The subjects of the course will be taught in a single one-year module from the schedule below. Candidates may not follow a module which they have previously undertaken as part of the Diploma in British Archaeology.

3. Candidates may be permitted under certain circumstances to suspend status.Any period suspended shall not count towards the maximum or minimum permitted period of registration and no fee liability will be incurred during such periods.

4. Every candidate will be required to satisfy the examiners in the following:

    (*a*) Attendance at the class sessions and the practical training;

    (*b*) Attendance at tutorials;

    (*c*) Three coursework assignments, each of which shall not exceed 2,500 words in length, based on the theoretical courses;

    (*d*) One practical logbook which shall not exceed 4,000 words;

    (*e*) A dissertation on a topic in British Archaeology which shall not exceed 10,000 words on a topic approved by the course director, based on one or more of the modules studied during the Diploma and the Advanced Diploma.

Assignments under 4 (*c*), and (*d*), and (*e*) will be forwarded to the examiners, for consideration by such dates as the examiners shall determine and shall notify candidates. The assessed work will, in normal circumstances, be submitted through an electronic submission system.

5. Candidates may be required to attend a viva voce examination at the end of the course.

6. The examiners may award a distinction to candidates for the Advanced Diploma.

7. Candidates who fail to satisfy the examiners in the assignments under 4(*c*)–(*e*), may be permitted to resubmit work in respect of the part or parts of the examination which they have failed on not more than one occasion which shall normally be within one year of the initial failure.

UNDERGRADUATE ADVANCED DIPLOMA IN BRITISH AND EUROPEAN STUDIES

1. The course will consist of lectures, tutorials, and classes in the culture and civilisation of Britain and Europe, with accompanying study of English language and academic literacy, to be followed over a period of one year.

2. Candidates may be permitted under certain circumstances to suspend status for a maximum of two years.

3. The subjects of the course shall be:

   a. British and European Studies

   b. English language and academic literacy

Candidates who demonstrate to the satisfaction of the course director that they have a command of the English language at least equivalent to the higher level required for admission to postgraduate study at Oxford may substitute a course of study and examination relating to an aspect or aspects of the culture and civilisation of Britain and/or Europe for the study of English Language and academic literacy.

4. Each candidate must satisfy the examiners in:

   (*a*) Attendance at the lectures, tutorials and classes;

   (*b*) A portfolio of exercises of not more 10,000 words in total, based on the contents of the English language and academic literacy unit. Students who do not follow the English language and academic literacy unit must submit three assignments, each of not more than 3,000 words, based on the courses followed relating to the culture and civilisation of Britain and/or Europe.

   (*c*) Six assignments, each of a maximum of 2,000 words, based on the courses in British and European Studies;

   (*d*) An extended tutorial essay of not more than 5,000 words normally on a topic related to one of the theoretical courses studied under (*c*) above.

Candidates offering the culture and civilisation of Britain and/or Europe assignments under (*b*) should not offer material for assignments under (*c*) or (*d*) that substantially reworks that submitted for those assignments.

Assignments under 3(*b*)–3(*d*) will be forwarded to the examiners for consideration by such dates as the examiners shall determine and shall notify candidates.

6. Candidates may be required to attend a viva voce examination at the end of the course of studies.

7. The examiners may award a distinction to candidates for the Advanced Diploma.

8. Candidates who fail to satisfy the examiners in any part or parts of the examination may be permitted to re-submit work in respect of the part or parts of the examination which they have failed on not more than one occasion which shall normally be within one year of the initial failure.

UNDERGRADUATE ADVANCED DIPLOMA IN DATA AND SYSTEMS ANALYSIS

1. *Course*

    (*a*) The course will comprise four taught units and a project.

    (*b*) The course is available on a part-time basis and will normally be taken over a period of one year, and may not be taken over a period of more than two years.

2. Every candidate will be required to satisfy the examiners in the following:

    (*a*) participation in all parts of the course;

    (*b*) participation in group discussions under the guidance, of the student's tutor;

    (*c*) four assignments of 4,000 words each (or equivalent), based on the units 1-4 below;

    (*d*) a team project report of 4,000 words (or equivalent).

Assignments under 2(*c*) and 2(*d*) above will be forwarded to the examiners for consideration by such dates as the examiners shall determine and shall notify candidates.

3. Candidates will be required to achieve an overall pass for the four assignments under 2(*c*) above and the report under 2(*d*) above. All assignments under 2(*c*) and the project report under 2(*d*) carry equal weight.

4. Candidates may be required to attend a viva voce examination at the end of the course.

5. The examiners may award a Distinction to candidates for the Advanced Diploma.

6. Candidates who fail to satisfy the examiners in the requirements under 2(*c*)–2(*d*) and 3 may be permitted to resubmit work in respect of the part or parts of the examination which they have failed for examination on not more than one occasion which shall normally be within one year of the examiners' decision to permit the candidate the opportunity to resubmit the work.

SCHEDULE

Unit 1: The System Development Life-cycle and Management

Unit 2: Systems Analysis and Design—Data Driven and Procedural Techniques

Unit 3: Systems Analysis and Design—Data Organisation

Unit 4: Systems Analysis and Design—Objects and Architectures

Unit 5: Team Project

UNDERGRADUATE ADVANCED DIPLOMA IN LOCAL HISTORY

1. *Course*

The course will comprise two modules:

Module 1 Concepts and Methods for Local History 5

Module 2 Databases for Historians

The course, which is available on a part-time, distance learning basis only, will normally be taken over a period of one year, and may not be taken over a period of more than two years.

2. Every student will be required to satisfy the examiners in the following: 10

(*a*) participation in all parts of the course to the satisfaction of the Course Director;

(*b*) participation in electronic group discussions under the guidance, and to the satisfaction, of the student's academic tutor;

(*c*) one assignment of not more than 2,000 words, one assignment of not more 15 than 2,500 words, one assignment of not more than 2,000 words plus supporting tables, and one assignment of not more than 3,000 words, based on the work covered in the Concepts and Methods module (Module 1);

(*d*) one assignment of not more than 2,500 words, based on the work covered in the Databases module (Module 2); 20

(*e*) one assignment of not more than 5,000 words, which will be a Local History project involving the use of a database of historical data.

Assignments under 2(*c*)–(*e*) above will be forwarded to the examiners for consideration by such dates as the examiners shall determine and shall notify students.

3. Students will be required to pass all assignments in both modules to be awarded 25 the Advanced Diploma. Students who fail to satisfy the examiners in the assignments under 2(*c*)–(*e*) may be permitted to resubmit work which they have failed for examination on not more than one occasion which shall normally be within in one year of the date on which the assignment was first due to be submitted.

4. Students may be required to attend a viva voce examination at the end of the 30 course of studies.

5. The examiners may award a Distinction to candidates for the Advanced Diploma.

NOTES

36

DIPLOMAS AND CERTIFICATES OPEN TO NON-MEMBERS OF THE UNIVERSITY

POSTGRADUATE DIPLOMA IN MANAGEMENT STUDIES

GENERAL REGULATIONS

1. The Executive Committee of the Saïd Business School shall have power to grant Postgraduate Diplomas in Management Studies to candidates who have satisfied the conditions prescribed in this section and any further conditions which the Committee may prescribe by regulation.

2. The examination for the Postgraduate Diploma shall be under the supervision of the Executive Committee of the Saïd Business School which shall have power, subject to the approval of the Social Sciences Divisional Board, to make regulations governing the examination.

3. Candidates, whether members of the University or not, may be admitted as students for the Postgraduate Diploma under such conditions as the committee shall prescribe, provided that before admission to a course of study approved by the Committee, candidates shall have satisfied the committee that they have had appropriate educational experience acceptable to the committee, have relevant industrial or commercial experience and are well-equipped to enter the proposed course of study.

4. Any person who has been accepted as a candidate for the Postgraduate Diploma, and who has satisfactorily pursued the course prescribed by the Committee, may be admitted to the examination.

SPECIAL REGULATIONS

1. Students of the diploma may hold that status for no more than nine terms.

2. The Standing Committee shall appoint an academic supervisor to supervise the work of the candidate. The supervisor shall send a report of the work of the candidate to the board at the end of each period of study. The supervisor will inform the board if it is thought that the student is unlikely to reach the standard required by the diploma.

3. Each student will follow a course of study comprising four core courses and a business project. The four core courses are: Managing the organisation: Functional and cross-functional management, finance and accounts, information management, operations management, and human resources. Managing strategically: Corporate strategy, securing competitive advantage, strategic approaches to leadership, investment, product development, and human resources. Managing change: Managing personnel and organisational change, reward strategies for change, leading change and change through teamwork, change in manufacturing and services. A fourth core course from a range of options to be notified to candidates at the start of the course. Each candidate must submit a business project to be undertaken as part of a group assignment on a subject to be approved by their supervisor. Candidates must submit,

no later than Friday of the sixth week of the Michaelmas Term in the year after their Part I examination, a report of no more than 6,000 words to their supervisor.

4. The examination will be in three parts:

(a) Part I The examination shall be held after the first two core courses. It shall consist of one written paper covering elements of the first two core courses.   5

(b) Part II No candidate shall enter the Part II examination unless he or she has already passed Part I. The Part II examination shall consist of one written paper covering elements of the third and fourth core courses.

(c) Each candidate will be required to propose, research, and submit a dissertation not exceeding 10,000 words on a topic agreed by the examiners. The dissertation   10
must be submitted to the Chairman of Examiners, c/o the Postgraduate Secretary, Saïd Business School, by Friday of the first week of July in the year in which it is intended to finish the course.

5. The examiners shall also consider, as part of the examination, a report on the candidate's business project submitted by his or her supervisor.   15

6. The examiners, of whom two shall be appointed, shall have a duty to examine the student in accordance with any regulations prescribed by regulation and to submit a written report to the Graduate Studies Committee of the Saïd Business School which shall decide whether the diploma should be awarded.

7. Candidates may also be required to attend a viva voce examination.   20

8. The examiners may award a distinction to candidates for the diploma.

9. Candidates who fail an examination may be re-examined on not more than one occasion which normally shall be within one year of their initial failure.

POSTGRADUATE DIPLOMA IN INTELLECTUAL PROPERTY LAW AND PRACTICE

GENERAL REGULATIONS

1. The Board of the Law Faculty shall have the power to grant Postgraduate Diplomas in Intellectual Property Law and Practice to candidates who have satisfied the conditions prescribed in this section and any further conditions which the Board may prescribe by regulation.

2. The examination for the Postgraduate Diploma shall be under the supervision of the Board of the Law Faculty which shall have power, subject to the approval of the Divisional Board, to make regulations governing the examination.

3. Persons may be admitted to read for the Postgraduate Diploma under such conditions as the Board shall prescribe, provided that before admission candidates shall have satisfied the Board that they have appropriate educational experience acceptable to the Board, and are well equipped to enter the proposed course of study.

4. Any person who has been accepted as a candidate for the Postgraduate Diploma, and who has satisfactorily pursued the course prescribed by the Board, may be entered for the examination.

SPECIAL REGULATIONS

1. Each candidate will follow a course of study comprising a two-week residential programme in Intellectual Property Law and Practice and five Legal Practice workshops in the area of Intellectual Property.

2. The examination will be in two parts:

(a) *Part I*

Each candidate will be required to complete and submit five written coursework assignments of at least 3,000 words each in response to questions set by the examiners. Those coursework assignments must be submitted to the Chair of Examiners for the Diploma in Intellectual Property Law and Practice, Examination Schools, High Street, Oxford, OX1 4BG, on the date stipulated in the year in which the written examination is taken. The submission date will be published in the course handbook before the first Monday on the first term in which students commence the course.

(b) *Part II*

The Part II examination shall consist of two written papers covering elements of the courses covered in the residential programme.

3. The examiners may award a distinction to candidates for the Diploma.

4. Candidates who fail an examination may be re-examined on not more than one occasion which shall normally be within one year of their initial failure.

POSTGRADUATE CERTIFICATE IN MANAGEMENT STUDIES

GENERAL REGULATIONS

1. The Academic Policy Committee of the Saïd Business School shall have the power to grant Postgraduate Certificates in Management Studies to candidates who have satisfied the conditions prescribed in this section and any further conditions which the Committee may prescribe by regulation.

2. The examination for the Postgraduate Certificate in Management Studies shall be under the supervision of the Academic Policy Committee of the Saïd Business School which shall have the power, subject to the approval of the Social Sciences Divisional Board, to make regulations governing the examination.

3. Candidates may be admitted as students for the Postgraduate Certificate of Management Studies under such conditions as the committee shall prescribe, providing that before admission, candidates shall have satisfied the committee that they have appropriate educational experience acceptable to the committee, have relevant professional experience, and are well equipped to enter the proposed course of study.

4. Any person who has been accepted as a candidate for the postgraduate certificate, and who has satisfactorily pursued the course prescribed by the committee, may be admitted to the examination.

5. Every person who has been accepted as a candidate for the postgraduate certificate shall be placed by the committee under the supervision of a member of the University or other competent person selected by the committee. It shall be the duty of the supervisor to direct and superintend the work of the candidate and to submit a report to the examiners on the candidate's work.

SPECIAL REGULATIONS

1. Candidates of the postgraduate certificate may hold that status for no more than three terms.

2. Candidates are only eligible to be admitted to the Postgraduate Certificate of Management Studies if they have first satisfactorily completed a programme of study approved for this purpose by the Executive Committee of the Saïd Business School.

3. Every candidate for the postgraduate certificate shall pursue a course of study approved by the Academic Policy Committee of the Saïd Business School.

4. Every candidate will be required to satisfy the examiners in the following:

   (*a*) An extended project of no more than 20,000 words on a subject falling within any field of Management Studies to be agreed by the Programme Director. Three typewritten/word-processed copies of the project must be submitted to the Chair of Examiners c/o Examinations Office, Said Business School, Park End Street, Oxford, not later than 12 noon on the first Friday of September. The project must be accompanied by a statement by the candidate indicating that it is the candidate's own work;

   (*b*) A report by the supervisor on the candidate's work;

   (*c*) A viva voce examination.

5. Candidates who fail to satisfy the examiners may re-submit their project on not more than one occasion which shall normally be within six months of the initial failure.

6. (*a*) If for good cause a student is temporarily unable to carry out his or her coursework, the Executive Committee may grant him or her temporary suspension of status for a minimum of one term and a maximum of three terms. Applications for suspension of status should be made to the Diploma and Accredited Programmes Committee c/o the relevant Graduate Studies Assistant and should be accompanied by a statement of support from the student's supervisor.

    5

    10

  (*b*) The Academic Policy Committee may for sufficient reason, and after consultation with the student's supervisor, temporarily suspend him or her from the Register on its own initiative.

POSTGRADUATE DIPLOMA IN FINANCIAL STRATEGY (PART-TIME)

GENERAL REGULATIONS

1. The Executive Committee of the Saïd Business School shall have the power to grant Postgraduate Diplomas in Financial Strategy to candidates who have satisfied the conditions prescribed in this section and any further conditions which the Committee may prescribe by regulation.

2. The examination for the Postgraduate Diploma shall be under the supervision of the Executive Committee of the Saïd Business School which shall have power, subject to the approval of the Social Sciences Divisional Board, to make regulations governing the examination.

3. Candidates may be admitted as students for the Postgraduate Diploma under such conditions as the Committee shall prescribe, provided that before admission candidates shall have satisfied the Committee that they have appropriate educational experience acceptable to the Committee, have relevant professional experience, and are well equipped to enter the proposed course of study.

4. Any person who has been accepted as a candidate for the Postgraduate Diploma, and who has satisfactorily pursued the course prescribed by the Committee, may be admitted to the examination.

SPECIAL REGULATIONS

1. Candidates must follow a course of instruction in Financial Strategy for at least twelve months and not more than fourteen months. Candidates must complete:

(*a*) Four core courses, and satisfy the examiners in the assessment associated with each course. The four core courses are:

Strategy;

Business Finance I;

Business Finance II;

Corporate Valuation.

Details can be found in the course handbook.

(*b*) Courses may be assessed by one or more of the following: written examinations, individual assignments, and group assignments, subject to the constraint that at least 50 per cent of marks in any course must be assigned to individual work.

(*c*) A project report not exceeding 10,000 words on a topic agreed by the examiners. Three typewritten/word-processed copies of the project report must be submitted to the Chair of Examiners for the Postgraduate Diploma in Financial Strategy, c/o Saïd Business School, Park End Street, Oxford, not later than 12 noon *on the date stipulated in the year in which the written examination is taken. The submission date will be published by the Course Director before the first Monday of the first term in which students commence the course.* All material submitted for the project report shall be accompanied by a statement signed by the candidate indicating that it is the candidate's own work.

2. Candidates may be examined viva voce on any assessment, the project report, or both.

3. The examiners may award a distinction for excellence in the whole examination.

4. Candidates who fail an assessment may be re-examined on not more than one occasion which normally shall be within one year of their initial failure.

5. With the approval of the Programme Director, a candidate may substitute core courses on the Postgraduate Diploma with core courses from the part-time MBA, the Postgraduate Diploma in Global Business, the Postgraduate Diploma in Organisational Leadership, the Postgraduate Diploma in Strategy and Innovation, or M.Sc. in Major Programme Management, assuming that core course falls within the permitted registration period for the original Postgraduate Diploma.

POSTGRADUATE DIPLOMA IN STRATEGY AND INNOVATION (PART-TIME)

For candidates admitted after 1 October 2009; candidates admitted before this date will be examined according to the regulations in the Examination Regulations *2008*   5

GENERAL REGULATIONS

1. The Executive Committee of the Saïd Business School shall have the power to grant Postgraduate Diplomas in Strategy and Innovation to candidates who have satisfied the conditions prescribed in this section and any further conditions which the Committee may prescribe by regulation.   10

2. The examination for the Postgraduate Diploma shall be under the supervision of the Executive Committee of the Saïd Business School which shall have power, subject to the approval of the Social Sciences Divisional Board, to make regulations governing the examination.

3. Candidates may be admitted as students for the Postgraduate Diploma under   15
such conditions as the Committee shall prescribe, provided that before admission candidates shall have satisfied the Committee that they have appropriate educational experience acceptable to the Committee, have relevant professional experience, and are well equipped to enter the proposed course of study.

4. Any person who has been accepted as a candidate for the Postgraduate Diploma,   20
and who has satisfactorily pursued the course prescribed by the Committee, may be admitted to the examination.

SPECIAL REGULATIONS

1. Candidates must follow a course of instruction in Strategy and Innovation either
for at least twelve months and not more than fourteen months, or for at least twenty-   25
four months and not more than twenty-six months. Candidates must complete:

(*a*) four courses, and satisfy the examiners in the assessment associated with each course. The four courses are:

> Strategy
> Innovation Strategy   30
> Globalisation and Strategy
> Strategy in Action

(*b*) Courses may be assessed by one or more of the following: written examinations, individual assignments, and group assignments, subject to the constraint that at least 50 per cent of marks in any course must be assigned to individual work.   35

(*c*) a project report not exceeding 10,000 words on a topic agreed by the examiners. Three typewritten/word-processed copies of the project report must be submitted to the Chair of Examiners for the Postgraduate Diploma in Strategy and Innovation, c/o Saïd Business School, Park End Street, Oxford, not later than 12 noon on the date stipulated in the year in which the written examination   40
is taken. The submission date will be published by the Course Director before the first Monday of the first term in which students commence the course. All material submitted for the project report shall be accompanied by a statement signed by the candidate indicating that it is the candidate's own work.

2. Candidates may be examined viva voce on one or more of the written examinations, assignments, and the project report.

3. The examiners may award a distinction for excellence in the whole examination.

4. Candidates who fail an examination may be re-examined on not more than one occasion which shall normally be within one year of their initial failure. 5

5. With the approval of the Programme Director, a candidate may substitute core courses on the Postgraduate Diploma with core courses from the part-time MBA, the Postgraduate Diploma in Global Business, the Postgraduate Diploma in Organisational Leadership, the Postgraduate Diploma in Financial Strategy, or M.Sc. in Major Programme Management, assuming that core course falls within the permitted registration period for the original Postgraduate Diploma. 10

POSTGRADUATE DIPLOMA IN ORGANISATIONAL LEADERSHIP (PART-TIME)

GENERAL REGULATIONS

1. The Executive Committee of the Saïd Business School shall have the power to grant Postgraduate Diplomas in Organisational Leadership to candidates who have satisfied the conditions prescribed in this section and any further conditions which the Committee may prescribe by regulation.

2. The examination for the Postgraduate Diploma shall be under the supervision of the Executive Committee of the Saïd Business School which shall have power, subject to the approval of the Divisional Board, to make regulations governing the examination.

3. Candidates may be admitted as students for the Postgraduate Diploma under such conditions as the Committee shall prescribe, provided that before admission candidates shall have satisfied the Committee that they have appropriate educational experience acceptable to the Committee, have relevant professional experience, and are well equipped to enter the proposed course of study.

4. Any person who has been accepted as a candidate for the Postgraduate Diploma, and who has satisfactorily pursued the course prescribed by the Committee, may be admitted to the examination.

SPECIAL REGULATIONS

1. Candidates must follow a course of instruction in Organisational Leadership for at least twelve months and not more than fourteen months. Candidates must complete:

(*a*) Four courses, and satisfy the examiners in the assessment associated with each course. The four courses are:

Leadership Fundamentals;

The Strategic Mindset;

Meeting the Organisational Challenge;

The Strategic Leader.

Details can be found in the course handbook.

(*b*) Courses may be assessed by one or more of the following: written examinations, individual assignments, and group assignments, subject to the constraint that at least 50 per cent of marks in any course must be assigned to individual work.

(*c*) A project report not exceeding 10,000 words on a topic agreed by the examiners. Three typewritten/word-processed copies of the project report must be submitted to the Chair of Examiners for the Postgraduate Diploma in Organisational Leadership, c/o Saïd Business School, Park End Street, Oxford, not later than 12 noon *on the date stipulated in the year in which the written examination is taken. The submission date will be published by the Course Director before the first Monday of the first term in which students commence the course.* All material submitted for the project report shall be accompanied by a statement signed by the candidate indicating that it is the candidate's own work.

2. Candidates may be examined viva voce on any assessment, the project report, or both.

3. The examiners may award a distinction for excellence in the whole examination.

4. Candidates who fail an assessment may be re-examined on not more than one occasion which normally shall be within one year of their initial failure.   5

5. With the approval of the Programme Director, a candidate may substitute core courses on the Postgraduate Diploma with core courses from the part-time MBA, the Postgraduate Diploma in Global Business, the Postgraduate Diploma in Strategy and Innovation, the Postgraduate Diploma in Financial Strategy, or M.Sc. in Major Programme Management, assuming that core course falls within the permitted regis-   10 tration period for the original Postgraduate Diploma.

POSTGRADUATE DIPLOMA IN GLOBAL BUSINESS (PART-TIME)

GENERAL REGULATIONS

1. The Executive Committee of the Saïd Business School shall have the power to grant Postgraduate Diplomas in Global Business to candidates who have satisfied the conditions prescribed in this section and any further conditions which the committee may prescribe by regulation.

2. The examination for the Postgraduate Diploma shall be under the supervision of the Executive Committee of the Saïd Business School which shall have power, subject to the approval of the Divisional Board, to make regulations governing the examination.

3. Candidates may be admitted as students for the Postgraduate Diploma under such conditions as the committee shall prescribe, provided that before admission candidates shall have satisfied the committee that they have appropriate educational experience acceptable to the committee, have relevant professional experience, and are well equipped to enter the proposed course of study.

4. Any person who has been accepted as a candidate for the Postgraduate Diploma, and who has satisfactorily pursued the course prescribed by the committee, may be admitted to the examination.

SPECIAL REGULATIONS

1. Candidates must follow for at least twelve months and not more than fourteen months a course of instruction in Global Business. Candidates must complete:

(*a*) Four courses, and satisfy the examiners in the assessment associated with each course. The four courses are:

Global Strategy

Risk and Reputation

Corporate Diplomacy in a Global Context

The Challenges of Business in Emerging Markets

Details can be found in the course handbook.

(*b*) Courses may be assessed by one or more of the following: written examinations, individual assignments, and group assignments, subject to the constraint that at least 50 per cent of marks in any course must be assigned to individual work.

(*c*) A project report not exceeding 10,000 words on a topic agreed by the examiners. Three typewritten/word-processed copies of the project report must be submitted to the Chair of Examiners for the Postgraduate Diploma in Global Business, c/o Saïd Business School, Park End Street, Oxford, not later than 12 noon *on the date stipulated in the year in which the written examination is taken. The submission date will be published by the Course Director before the first Monday of the first term in which students commence the course.* All material submitted for the project report shall be accompanied by a statement signed by the candidate indicating that it is the candidate's own work.

2. Candidates may be examined viva voce on any assessment, the project report, or both.

3. The examiners may award a distinction for excellence in the whole examination.

4. Candidates who fail an assessment may be re-examined on not more than one occasion which normally shall be within one year of their initial failure.

5. With the approval of the Programme Director, a candidate may substitute core courses on the Postgraduate Diploma with core courses from the part-time MBA, the Postgraduate Diploma in Organisational Leadership, the Postgraduate Diploma in Strategy and Innovation, the Postgraduate Diploma in Financial Strategy, or M.Sc. in Major Programme Management, assuming that core course falls within the permitted registration period for the original Postgraduate Diploma.

CERTIFICATE IN THEOLOGY AND CERTIFICATE FOR THEOLOGY GRADUATES

1. The Board of the Faculty of Theology and Religion shall have power to grant the following certificates to candidates who have satisfied the conditions prescribed in this section and any further conditions which the board may prescribe by regulation:

Certificate in Theology;

Certificate for Theology Graduates.

2. The examinations for the above mentioned certificates shall be under the supervision of the Board of the Faculty of Theology and Religion.

3. Candidates, both members of the University and others, who have been admitted, under such conditions as the Board of the Faculty of Theology and Religion shall prescribe, to courses at Campion Hall, Mansfield College, Regent's Park College, St. Benet's Hall, Blackfriars, Ripon College Cuddesdon, St. Stephen's House, Wycliffe Hall, and Harris Manchester College may be admitted by the board to the examinations for the above mentioned certificates, provided that they have paid to the Curators of the University Chest, through their colleges or other institutions, the fee or fees prescribed in the appropriate regulation (see Appendix I).

4. The supervision of the arrangements for the above mentioned certificates shall be the responsibility of the Supervisory Committee for the Degree of Bachelor of Theology and the Theology Certificates. The committee shall have such powers and duties in respect of the above mentioned certificates as may from time to time be prescribed by the Board of the Faculty of Theology and Religion.

5. Part-time students for the above mentioned certificates shall in each case be required to pursue their course of study for twice the number of terms required of an equivalent full-time student.

6. On successful completion of part I or of the entire course, candidates for the Certificate in Theology may, with the approval of the Supervisory Committee, offer the remaining papers necessary to meet the requirements for the award of the Bachelor of Theology.

A. THE CERTIFICATE IN THEOLOGY

A. 1. *Admission requirements*

Candidates will normally be expected to have five GCSE passes, one of which must be in English Language and two of which must be at Advanced Level. Exemptions from this requirement for mature student candidates or those otherwise qualified may be made at the discretion of the Supervisory Committee.

A. 2. *Course requirements*

The length of the course is two years. A minimum of eight papers must be taken from the syllabus as outlined for the Bachelor of Theology. In Part 1 candidates must take all four papers. In Part 2 they must take one paper each from sections B, C, and D. The Supervisory Committee may dispense a candidate from individual compulsory papers on the basis of previous academic work, but not from the total number of papers required.

B. THE CERTIFICATE FOR THEOLOGY GRADUATES

B. 1. *Admission requirements*

Candidates for the Certificate for Theology Graduates must have obtained an Honours or Joint Honours Degree in Theology. Candidates for the one-year course must have obtained at least second class honours. Candidates for the one-year course who have not taken the Honour School of Theology in Oxford must apply to the Supervisory Committee.

B. 2. *Course requirements*

One-year candidates must take at least four papers. Two-year candidates must take at least eight papers. There are no compulsory papers. All papers will be examined at the same level. Each paper will be examined by an essay of 7,000 words, except that:

- (*a*) candidates may integrate two papers in a single essay of 12,000 words (which will still count as two papers);
- (*b*) one-year candidates may substitute a written examination in one paper, and two-year candidates in up to three papers, except for paper D.1;
- (*c*) candidates may take papers additional to the minimum requirement by written examination, except for paper D.1.

C. REGULATIONS OF GENERAL APPLICATION

C. 1. *Registration and fees*

Not later than the end of the second week of Michaelmas Term, colleges shall forward the names of non-members of the University who wish to be registered as candidates for either of the two certificates, together with the registration fee prescribed (see Appendix I) in accordance with the appropriate regulation. No registration fee is payable for matriculated members of the University, but colleges shall, by the stated time, notify the Registrar of all such students commencing certificate courses.

C. 2. *Examination*

Further provisions governing the examination for the Certificates in Theology are given in the regulations for the Bachelor of Theology.

NOTES

37

GENERAL REGULATIONS FOR FOUNDATION CERTIFICATES

1. The Continuing Education Board shall have power to grant Foundation Certificates to candidates who have satisfied the conditions prescribed in this section and any further conditions which the Committee may prescribe by regulation.

2. The examination for each certificate shall be under the supervision of the Continuing Education Board which shall have the power subject to the approval of the Education Committee, to make regulations governing the examination.

3. The Director of the Department for Continuing Education shall keep a register of attendance of students for the Certificate. No student shall be granted leave to take the examination unless the register shows satisfactory attendance by him or her.

4. Candidates, whether members of the University or not, may be admitted as students for the Certificate under such conditions as the Continuing Education Board shall prescribe provided that, before admission to the course, candidates have satisfied the Committee that they are well qualified to enter the proposed course of study.

5. Examination for the certificate shall be by written examination, by coursework essays, and (if the examiners think fit) by oral examination, under such conditions as the Continuing Education Board may by regulation prescribe.

FOUNDATION CERTIFICATE IN ENGLISH LITERATURE

1. The course shall consist of lectures, classes and tutorials on the subject of English Literature. The course is available on a part-time basis only, to be followed over a period of two years.

2. Candidates may be permitted under certain circumstances to suspend status for a maximum of two years.

3. Every candidate will be required to satisfy the examiners in the following:

    i. Attendance at a minimum of 80% of face to face classes, attendance at the day schools, a summer school and at six tutorials;

    ii. Four written papers, two on each of the topics below, each of three hours' duration;

       a. Early Modern Literature

       b. Victorian and Modern Literature

    iii. Two portfolios of written work demonstrating critical approaches to language and literature, the first to be of not more than 3,000 words and the second to be of not more than 5,000 words;

    iv. Thirteen coursework essays, each of not more than 2,000 words in length.

The portfolios and assignments under 3 iii and iv will be forwarded to the examiners for consideration by such dates as the examiners shall determine and shall notify candidates.

4. Candidates may, at the discretion of the examiners, be required to attend a viva voce examination at the end of the course of studies.

5. The examiners may award a distinction to candidates for the Certificate.

6. Candidates who fail to satisfy the examiners in the assessed work specified in clause 3 may be permitted to resubmit work in respect of the part or parts of the examination which they have failed on not more than one occasion which shall normally be within one year of the initial failure.

FOUNDATION CERTIFICATE IN HISTORY

1. The course which is available on a part-time basis only, may be taken over a period of two, and no more than four years.

2. The examination will consist of:

    (i) Four papers as set out below, each of three hours' duration: 5

        (*a*) Two papers on British History, 1485–1603 and 1900–1979;

        (*b*) One paper on European History, 1815–1914;

        (*c*) One optional paper (source-based) to be chosen from a list to be published annually before the end of the last week of Trinity Term.

    (ii) Nine coursework essays, each of up to 2,000 words in length.   10

    (iii) One extended essay of up to 4,000 words on a candidate's optional subject.

    (iv) Candidates may be required to attend a viva voce examination at the end of the course of studies at the discretion of the examiners.

The coursework essays in 2 (ii) and the extended essay in 2 (iii) will be forwarded to the examiners for consideration by such dates as the examiners shall determine and   15 shall notify the candidates. Essays must be the candidate's own work and every candidate must submit a statement to that effect.

3. The examiners may award a distinction to candidates for the Certificate.

4. Candidates who fail to satisfy the examiners in the assessed work specified in clause 2 may be permitted to resubmit work in respect of the part or parts of the   20 examination which they have failed on not more than one occasion which shall normally be within one year of the initial failure.

NOTES

38

EXAMINATIONS FOR DEGREES AND CERTIFICATES IN CLINICAL PSYCHOLOGY

DOCTOR OF CLINICAL PSYCHOLOGY

GENERAL REGULATIONS

1. The Oxford Institute of Clinical Psychology Training shall have power, on behalf of the Medical Sciences Board, to admit Students for the Degree of Doctor of Clinical Psychology.

2. The Oxford Institute of Clinical Psychology Training shall make a return to the Registrar by the end of the first week of Michaelmas Full Term, showing the names of all persons admitted in that term as Students for the Degree of Doctor of Clinical Psychology, and the Registrar shall keep a register of such students.

3. The Medical Sciences Board shall have power, on the recommendation of the Oxford Institute of Clinical Psychology Training, to remove temporarily or permanently the name of a student from the register. This power shall include cases where students have been found under the procedures of the course and the Oxford Health NHS Foundation Trust guilty of gross misconduct or in breach of the British Psychological Society's Code of Ethics and Conduct.

4. Students shall be admitted to the doctoral programme for a probationary period. The external examiner shall conduct a formal mid-course review during the second half of the second year of the course (i.e. between eighteen and twenty-four months after the commencement of the course). Candidates shall be required to complete successfully all elements of the work required before they are permitted to progress onto the second part of the course.

5. Subject to the provisions of clauses 3 and 4 above, students for the Degree of Doctor of Clinical Psychology may hold that status for a maximum of five years.

6. The Proctors shall be responsible for overseeing the proper conduct of the examinations for the Degree in Clinical Psychology. They shall have power to investigate any concern regarding the conduct of any candidate for the examination and to impose any penalty equivalent to that which may be imposed upon a member of the University in similar circumstances.

7. An appeal against a decision of the Board of Examiners for the Doctorate in Clinical Psychology must be made to the Complaints & Academic Appeals Panel of the Oxford Institute of Clinical Psychology Training in the first instance, through procedures laid down in the course handbook. A candidate who is dissatisfied with the decision of the Institute's Complaints & Academic Appeals Panel may submit an appeal through the University's Procedures for Handling Complaints (including Academic Appeals) laid down and published by the Proctors under section 22 of Statute IX. No procedures arising from a candidate's status as employee or former employee of the Oxford Health NHS Foundation Trust may affect a decision of the examiners.

8. Should any Students for the Degree of Doctor of Clinical Psychology have access to University services and facilities, they will be required to observe the appropriate statutes, regulations, and/or rules governing the use of such services and facilities. The Proctors shall have power to investigate any alleged breaches of those statutes, regulations, and/or rules and to deal with the matter and impose any penalty equivalent to that which they would have been empowered to impose upon a member of the University in similar circumstances.

Special Regulations

1. Candidates shall follow a course of training in Clinical Psychology for a period of at least three years. The training shall consist of Clinical, Academic, and Research elements, and candidates will be required to demonstrate their competence in all three elements. The precise periods of training, and the amount of time to be spent on each element, will be notified to candidates by the Course Director prior to the commencement of the course.

2. Candidates shall be examined in all of the following ways:

    (*a*) Clinical Activity

    Each candidate shall develop competence in five or six supervised clinical areas normally including the following:

    (i) Adult; (ii) Child; (iii) Disabilities; (iv) Older People; (v) Specialist (to be chosen by the candidate in consultation with the course tutors, subject to the availability of appropriate supervision. Final year candidates will normally either develop competence in one (twelve month) or two (six month) elective areas).

    Candidates shall submit to the Board of Examiners a report on five of the above clinical areas. Normally, at least one report will concern clinical work which is other than individually based. Each report shall consist of not more than 6,000 words including tables and diagrams but excluding references and appendices. Candidates shall also submit to the Clinical Tutor a notebook (Log Book) for each clinical area. The candidate's supervisor in each clinical area shall complete, in consultation with the Clinical Tutor, an Evaluation of Clinical Competence (ECC). The Reports and ECC Forms shall be assessed as part of the examination. The notebooks shall be available to the examiners.

    (*b*) Academic Activity

    Candidates shall be required to follow a programme of study, as prescribed by the Director of the Course, normally in each of the following areas:

    (i) Adult mental health; (ii) Children; (iii) Disabilities; (iv) Older People; (v) Specialist teaching.

    Candidates are required to submit an extended essay in three of these areas. The essay shall not exceed 5,000 words including tables and diagrams but excluding references, and shall be on a subject approved in advance by the Institute. One essay will take the form of a Critical Review.

    (*c*) Research Activity

    Candidates shall offer the following:

    (i) One service-related project of approximately 4,500 words in length including tables and diagrams but excluding references and appendices. The project shall normally be carried out within a clinical context within the first two years of training and shall be of direct relevance to the clinical work.

    (ii) A research dissertation of between 15,000 and 25,000 words, including tables, diagrams, references, and appendices. The Research Dissertation shall consist of a research report of a significant and substantial investigation with human participants and shall be of clinical relevance. The subject of the Research Dissertation must be approved in advance by the Institute. All candidates will be examined on the Dissertation viva voce.

3. Candidates shall be required to satisfy examiners in each of the assessment units   5
described in clause 2 above.

4. Guidelines on the preparation and submission of all written work will be updated annually as required and will be included in the Course Handbook.

5. Deadlines for the submission of all assessed work (i.e. essay titles, essays, service-related projects, integrated clinical reports, critical reviews, dissertation proposals and   10
dissertations) will be published annually by the Institute in the 'Annual Course Syllabus Book' at the start of the academic year. They will also be posted in the Course Office.

6. All material submitted for examination must be sent to the Chair of Examiners for the Doctorate in Clinical Psychology, c/o the Course Manager, Isis Education   15
Centre, Warneford Hospital, Headington, Oxford. It shall be accompanied by a certificate signed by the candidate indicating that it is the candidate's own work, except where otherwise specified. In the case of the integrated clinical report, service-related project, and dissertation, this must be supported by a signed statement from the candidate's supervisor indicating that the material submitted is the candi-   20
date's own work. These certificates must be submitted separately in a sealed envelope addressed to the Chair of Examiners for the Doctorate in Clinical Psychology.

POSTGRADUATE CERTIFICATE IN SUPERVISION OF APPLIED PSYCHOLOGICAL PRACTICE

GENERAL REGULATIONS

1. The Oxford Institute of Clinical Psychology Training shall have power, on behalf of the Medical Sciences Board, to admit students for the Postgraduate Certificate in Supervision of Applied Psychological Practice.

2. The Oxford Institute of Clinical Psychology Training shall make a return to the Registrar by the end of the first week of Michaelmas Full Term, showing the names of all persons admitted in that term as students for the Postgraduate Certificate in Supervision of Applied Psychological Practice, and the Registrar shall keep a register of such students.

3. The Medical Sciences Board shall have power, on the recommendation of the Oxford Institute of Clinical Psychology Training, to remove temporarily or permanently the name of a student from the register. This power shall include cases where students have been found under the procedures of the course guilty of gross misconduct or in breach of relevant regulations, codes or standards of their associated professional or registration body.

4. Students will hold a professional postgraduate qualification as an applied psychologist, or as a qualified psychotherapist or counsellor with an Honours degree, or another relevant professional qualification in health and social care or education, and will be registered with a professional body as deemed appropriate by the Oxford Institute for Clinical Psychology Training. Students will have been professionally qualified for at least one year and will have experience of providing clinical supervision, or exceptionally will be at the point of taking on clinical supervisory responsibilities.

5. The Oxford Institute of Clinical Psychology Training shall have power, on behalf of the Medical Sciences Board, to elect for the supervision of the programme a Steering Committee to arrange teaching, assessments and other instruction.

6. Every student must follow a one year course of study on a part-time basis, and attend teaching days which will normally take place monthly, as determined by the programme timetable. The programme commences in October and runs until September of the following year.

7. Students shall normally be required to attend a minimum of 10 of the 13 teaching days across the programme.

8. Students will be required to undertake a minimum of 40 hours of clinical supervision of their own supervisees (on an individual, group or peer basis) during the duration of the programme, and arrangement of this prior to joining the programme shall be the responsibility of each student.

9. Students will be required to receive regular supervision themselves for their own professional practice, and arrangement of this prior to joining the programme shall be the responsibility of each student.

10. Students who are unable to attend the minimum number of teaching days, or to complete the minimum number of clinical supervision hours will be able to defer completion of the course until the following year, until the programme requirements have been satisfied. Subject to the provisions of clauses 3, 6, 7, and 8 above, Students

for the Postgraduate Certificate in Supervision of Applied Psychological Practice may hold that status for a maximum of two years.

11. The Proctors shall be responsible for overseeing the proper conduct of the examinations for the Postgraduate Certificate in Supervision of Applied Psychological Practice. They shall have power to investigate any concern regarding   5 the conduct of any candidate for the examination and to impose any penalty equivalent to that which may be imposed upon a member of the University in similar circumstances.

12. An appeal against a decision of the Board of Examiners for the Postgraduate Certificate in Supervision of Applied Psychological Practice must be made to the   10 Complaints & Academic Appeals Panel of the Oxford Institute of Clinical Psychology Training in the first instance, through procedures laid down in the course handbook. A candidate who is dissatisfied with the decision of the Institute's Complaints & Academic Appeals Panel may submit an appeal through the University's Procedures for Handling Complaints (including Academic Appeals)   15 laid down and published by the Proctors under section 22 of Statute IX.

13. Should any Students for the Postgraduate Certificate in Supervision of Applied Psychological Practice have access to University services and facilities, they will be required to observe the appropriate statutes, regulations, and/or rules governing the use of such services and facilities. The Proctors shall have power to investigate any   20 alleged breaches of those statutes, regulations, and/or rules and to deal with the matter and impose any penalty equivalent to that which they would have been empowered to impose upon a member of the University in similar circumstances.

Special Regulations

1. Students shall follow a course of training in the supervision of applied psycho-   25 logical practice. This training is designed to provide a thorough grounding in the understanding and application of supervision theory, drawing on the evidence base, and to provide opportunities to develop key supervision skills. A number of theories, models and frameworks will be covered, as well as a critical review of the evidence base for supervision. Key concepts and principles will be reviewed including effective   30 supervisory relationships, ethical issues, power and difference in supervision. There will be opportunities to practice important supervision skills such as developing supervision contracts, assessing competence and giving feedback, as well as promoting learning and reflective practice. There will be opportunities for students to learn from programme staff and from one another. Methods of learning will incorporate a   35 combination of didactic lectures, small and large group discussion, experiential exercises (including role play and personal reflection), self-assessment and facilitated supervision groups. The details and format of the training will be notified to students by the Course Director, prior to the commencement of the course.

2. Candidates shall be examined in all of the following ways: 40

    (*a*) One 4,000 word essay on an aspect of supervision covered in the curriculum. The essay must be submitted in March on a date to be specified in the programme Handbook.

    (*b*) Recording of supervision (video or audio) with a 2,000 word critical commentary and completed outcome measure of the supervisory relationship.   45 The recording and accompanying material must be submitted in July on a date to be specified in the programme Handbook.

    (*c*) Reflective log (3,000 words) of supervision practice and learning and development as a supervisor, including a record of the number of supervisory hours undertaken as a supervisor and as a supervisee. The log must be   50 submitted in September on a date to be specified in the programme Handbook.

3. Guidelines for the preparation and submission of all assessed work will be included in the programme Handbook.

4. Candidates must pass all of the examined components in order to pass overall.

5. Should they fail to reach the required standard candidates will be permitted one opportunity to re-take each of the required examined components, normally within 3 months of the original failure. Candidates failing to pass any examined component at the second attempt will normally be judged to have failed to reach the required standard for the award of the Postgraduate Certificate and will not be permitted to continue.

6. Candidates shall be required to satisfy the examiners in all of the examined components within 2 years of registering for the Postgraduate Certificate.

7. The required submissions must be:

   (*a*) sent to the Chair of Examiners for the Postgraduate Certificate in Supervision of Applied Psychological Practice, c/o the Programme Administrator, Isis Education Centre, Warneford Hospital, Headington, Oxford OX3 7JX by the required date.

   (*b*) accompanied by a declaration of authorship signed by the candidate, and for assignment 2(c), must be countersigned by the candidate's practice supervisor.

   (*c*) accompanied by a declaration that no clinical or supervisory material has been included, without ensuring that it: (i) has been fully anonymised, (ii) does not enable identification, and (iii) has been obtained and used with consent.

Declarations must be submitted separately in a sealed envelope addressed to the Chair of Examiners for the Postgraduate Certificate in Supervision of Applied Psychological Practice.

8. The Board of Examiners will meet three times a year, will decide upon the outcome of the examined components, and will recommend to the University the award of the Postgraduate Certificate for successful candidates.

9. There is no alternative award for candidates who fail to meet the required standard or who do not complete the programme.

NOTES

39

RECOGNIZED STUDENTS

1. There shall be a Register of Recognized Students who are not members of the University.

2. The Board of a faculty or divisional board may place the name of any applicant 5
on the Register of Recognized Students:

Provided that the applicant:

(*a*) is not a member of the University,

(*b*) possesses the qualifications required from candidates for admission to the status
of Senior Student except that persons not so qualified may in exceptional cases 10
be admitted,

(*c*) is placed under an academic adviser appointed by the board. It shall be the duty
of the academic adviser to advise on the work of the student but not to give
systematic instruction. He or she shall submit a report on the progress of the
student to the Board at the end of each term. 15

3. Application for admission as a Recognized Student shall be made to
the Registrar for submission to the appropriate faculty board and shall be accompanied by

(*a*) evidence of the degrees previously obtained by the applicant,

(*b*) a statement of the proposed subject of study, 20

(*c*) a certificate from a professor or head of a department of the University of
Oxford supporting the application.

4. If an applicant for admission as a Recognized Student shall propose a subject of
study which is outside the scope of the board of any faculty or divisional board but
which may in the opinion of the Education Committee be profitably studied at 25
Oxford, that committee may, on the recommendation of a delegacy or committee
constituted under the provisions of the appropriate regulation, deal with his or her
case as if it were the board of a faculty.

5. For each term for which his or her name is on the Register, every Recognized
Student shall pay to the Curators of the University Chest, within fourteen days from 30
the beginning of Full Term (or from the date of the decision to place his or her name
on the Register, in the case of a decision taken during Full Term and applying to that
term), a fee at the annual rate specified in the appropriate regulation.

6. A Recognized Student shall cease to hold that status

(*a*) if he or she shall have failed to pay the fees required under clause 5, 35

(*b*) if his or her name shall have been removed from the Register by the faculty
or divisional board concerned.

7. Every Recognized Student shall be entitled

(i) to use the University Libraries subject to the provision of the statutes governing particular Libraries, 40

    (ii) to attend lectures advertised in the lists of boards of faculties and other bodies:

Provided that attendance

        (*a*) at lectures described as seminars or classes or informal instruction shall be subject to the permission of the holder,   5

        (*b*) at lectures given in any college building shall be subject to the right of the college concerned to refuse admission.

    (iii) to work in any University department or institution subject to the agreement of the head of that department or institution.

8. No Recognized Student shall have his or her name on the Register of Recognized   10
Students for more than three terms.

9. A faculty or divisional board shall have power to remove from the Register the name of any Recognized Student which it has placed on the Register.

NOTES

40

VISITING STUDENTS

1. There shall be a Register of Visiting Students who are members of a college or other society but who are not members of the University. Council may determine from time to time conditions for admission to the Register and the maximum numbers of the members of each college or other society who may be admitted as Visiting Students in any one year.

2. Application for admission as a Visiting Student shall be made to the Registrar through the candidate's society within fourteen days after the society has admitted the candidate. The application shall provide such particulars as Council shall from time to time specify, and shall include an undertaking by the candidate, in terms approved from time to time by Council, (i) as to conduct and (ii) as to payment when due of the fees payable to the University while holding the status of Visiting Student.

3. For each term in which his or her name is on the Register, every Visiting Student shall pay: to his or her college or other society for transmission to the Curators of the University Chest, within fourteen days from the beginning of Full Term (or, in the term of admission, within fourteen days from the day on which his or her name was entered on the Register), a fee at the annual rate specified in the appropriate regulation.

4. A Visiting Student shall cease to hold that status (i) after three terms, or (ii) forthwith if:

   (*a*) he or she shall have failed to pay the fees required under cl. 3;

   (*b*) he or she ceases to be a member of a college or other society;

   (*c*) he or she is matriculated, or his or her name is placed on the Register of Diploma Students or the Register of Recognized Students; or

   (*d*) in accordance with the prescribed procedure, he or she is found to have committed a breach of his or her undertaking as to conduct and it is held that his or her status is to cease as a consequence.

5. Every Visiting Student shall be entitled:

   (*a*) to use the university libraries subject to the provisions of the statutes or decrees governing particular libraries, and to the general regulations and rules of the libraries concerned.

   (*b*) to attend lectures advertised in the lists of boards of faculties and other bodies, provided that:

   (i) attendance at lectures described as seminars or classes or informal instruction shall be subject to the permission of the holder, and

   (ii) attendance at lectures given in any college building shall be subject to the right of the college concerned to refuse admission.

6. A Visiting Student may be permitted to work, and receive teaching or supervision, in any university laboratory, subject to prior arrangement agreed between his

or her society and the head of department, and subject to such conditions as may be determined, by the head of department in accordance with arrangements approved from time to time by Council.

7. No Visiting Student shall be eligible to be a candidate for any examination, or scholarship, prize, or other award of the University.

COMMON AWARD STUDENTS

1. St Stephen's House and Wycliffe Hall are authorised to offer the Common Award, to be validated by the University of Durham, for the training of Church of England ordinands admitted to the Permanent Private Halls for that purpose.

2. There shall be a Register of Common Award Students who are members of a 5
Permanent Private Hall but who are not members of the University.

3. The Permanent Private Hall shall place on the Register the name of any student it has admitted to study for the Common Award of the University of Durham.

4. Subject to the approval of the Education Committee, the Permanent Private Halls Supervisory Committee may determine from time to time conditions for inclu- 10
sion on the Register and the maximum numbers of the members of each Permanent Private Hall who may be admitted as Common Award Students in any one year.

5. Application for inclusion on the register of Common Award Students shall be made to the Registrar through the candidate's Permanent Private Hall within fourteen days after the Hall has admitted the candidate. The application shall provide such 15
particulars as the Education Committee shall from time to time specify, and shall include an undertaking by the candidate, in terms approved from time to time by the Education Committee, as to conduct while holding the status of a Common Award Student.

6. Subject to the approval of the Education Committee, the Permanent Private 20
Halls Supervisory Committee may specify the University facilities and services and determine the level of access to their use which shall be made available to Common Award Students, as well as determining the charge paid by the Permanent Private Halls for these facilities and services.

7. A Common Award Student shall cease to hold that status (i) after he or she 25
completes the necessary period of study for the Common Award, or (ii) after he or she ceases to be a member of a Permanent Private Hall prior to the completion of his or her period of study for the Common Award, or (iii) forthwith if, in accordance with the prescribed procedure, he or she is found to have committed a breach of his or her undertaking as to conduct and it is held that his or her status is to cease as a consequence. 30

8. No Common Award Student shall be eligible to be a candidate for any examination, or scholarship, prize, or other award of the University.

APPENDIX I

REGULATIONS ON FINANCIAL MATTERS

Section I. Fees and Dues payable to the University

§1. *University fees payable by members of the University*   5

1. All fees payable under this Section are set by Council's Planning and Resource Allocation Committee on an annual basis and are available from www.ox.ac.uk/feesandfunding/fees/information/universityrates/ or from the Planning and Resource Allocation Section. Fees are payable at one of four rates, 'home', 'ELQ', 'islands', and 'overseas'. The 'home' rate is payable by students who meet   10 the criteria given in Schedule 1 of the Education (Fees and Awards) (England) Regulations 2007 and subsequent amendments. The 'ELQ' rate is payable by students who meet the criteria for the 'home' rate but who are reading for a qualification of an equivalent or lower level to one they already hold. The 'islands' rate is payable by residents of the Channel Islands or the Isle of Man who meet the requirements laid   15 down by the respective Islands governments. Where a course does not have a separate 'ELQ' or 'islands' rate, the 'ELQ' or 'islands' rate will be the same as the 'home' rate. All students not meeting these criteria shall pay fees at the 'overseas' rate unless otherwise exempted.

  2. (*a*) Every member of the University shall pay a University fee at the appro-   20 priate annual rate for each academic year in which he or she is working in Oxford:

      (i) For the Degree of BA or the Degree of M.Biochem. or the Degree of M.Chem. or the Degree of M.Math.Comp.Sci. or the Degree of M.Earth Sc. or the Degree of M.Eng. or the Degree of M.Math. or   25 the Degree of M.Comp.Sci. or the Degree of M.Comp.Phil. or the Degree of M.Phys. or the Degree of M.Phys.Phil. or the Degree of M.Math.Phil. (Those working for an honour school requiring the study of one or more languages for an academic year outside Oxford or for Law with Law Studies in Europe, or for an honour school   30 requiring a period of study shorter than a year outside Oxford, or for Part II in Chemistry or Materials Science or Molecular and Cellular Biochemistry, or for Part II in the Honour Schools of Engineering Science **[Until MT 2017:** or Engineering, Economics, and Management] **[Until MT 2018:** or Materials, Economics, and   35 Management]**, shall be deemed for all the purposes of this clause to be working in Oxford for the degree of BA or the Degree of M.Biochem. or the Degree of M.Chem. or the Degree of M.Eng., whether or not their work is being undertaken in Oxford);

      (ii) for the Degree of BFA;   40

      (iii) for the Degree of BCL or Magister Juris;

  (iv) for a second Final Honour School;

  (v) for the First Examination for the Degree of BM;

  (vi) for the Diploma in Theology;

  (vii) for the Diploma in Legal Studies;

  (viii) for the Certificate in Diplomatic Studies;

  (ix) for the Postgraduate Diploma in Diplomatic Studies;

  (x) for the Postgraduate Diploma in Education; or

  (xi) for the Postgraduate Certificate in Education (those working for the certificate shall be deemed for all the purposes of this clause to be working in Oxford, whether or not their work is being undertaken in Oxford).

(*b*) The fees shall be paid as follows:

  (i) in the case of those members of the University whose fees are paid under the terms of the Education (Student Support) Regulations (or under corresponding arrangements approved by the Scottish Executive, Northern Ireland Assembly, Welsh Assembly or the States Assembly of Jersey, States Assembly of Guernsey or Isle of Man Government) the fees shall be paid in accordance with the arrangements laid down in those regulations;

  (ii) in all other cases, fees shall be collected in accordance with the provisions of §3 below;

  (iii) on application by their society, and subject to the approval of Council's Education Committee, some part of the University fee for an academic year may subsequently be returned to those who do not work in Oxford for the whole of that year. The general rule agreed by Council is that, for each complete term not spent working in Oxford, one third of the annual fee shall be returned.

3. Every member of the University shall pay a University fee at the appropriate annual rate for each term from and including the term in which he or she begins to work for the Second Examination for the Degree of Bachelor of Medicine up to and including the term in which he or she completes all the stages of the examination, or ceases to work for the examination.

4. (*a*) Subject to the provisions of cl. 5 below, every member of the University shall pay a University fee at the appropriate annual rate for each term in which he or she is registered as a Probationer Research Student or is working for one of the qualifications listed below, from and including the term in which he or she is first so registered or begins working for such qualification, up to and including the term in which he or she takes the final examination or (in the case of a degree or diploma by thesis only) submits his or her thesis:

  (i) the Degree of B.Phil.;

  (ii) the Degree of M.Sc.;

  (iii) the Degree of M.St.;

  (iv) the Degree of MBA;

  (v) the Degree of MPP;

  (vi) the Degree of M.Litt.;

  (vii) the Degree of M.Phil.;

  (viii) the Degree of M.Th.;

  (ix) the Degree of M.F.A.;

(x) the Degree of D.Phil.;

(xi) the degree of D.Eng.;

(xii) any diploma or certificate other than:

    (*a*) the Diploma in Theology;

    (*b*) the Diploma in Legal Studies;   5

    (*c*) the Postgraduate Diploma in Education;

    (*d*) the Postgraduate Certificate in Education;

    (*e*) the Certificate in Management Studies;

    (*f*) the Certificate in Theology;

    (*g*) the Certificate in Diplomatic Studies;   10

    (*h*) the Postgraduate Diploma in Diplomatic Studies; or

    (*i*) certificates issued by the Board of Studies in Education under the provisions of the appropriate regulation.

(*b*) In the case of a degree or diploma that is not be thesis only, the term in which the students tales the final examination is that in which the published sub-   15
mission due date or examination date falls for the final piece of work (which may consist of a dissertation, thesis, essay, other assessed exercise, or written examination). A thesis or other assessed exercise for which the published due date falls other than during Full Term shall be deemed for the purposes of this clause to have been due for submission during the preceding term.   20

(*c*) In the case of a degree of diploma by thesis only, a thesis submitted other than during Full Term shall be deemed for the purposes of this clause to have been submitted during the preceding term.

(*d*) Candidates who continue to work for one of the qualifications listed in this clause after attempting an examination shall pay a University fee for each   25
term in which they receive tuition or supervision; but if they receive no further tuition or supervision, they shall pay no further University fees but shall pay the fee prescribed in §7 below when they re-enter. Candidates whose thesis submitted for the degree of M.Litt., M.Sc., or D.Phil., has been referred back shall pay no further University fees, but shall pay the fee   30
prescribed in §7 below when they apply for re-examination; and candidates whose dissertation for the degree of M.Sc. in Education did not satisfy the examiners shall pay the fee prescribed in §7 below before a revised or new dissertation for Part II of the examination is examined. For the purposes of this clause, 'term' shall include any period of forty-two days' residence   35
reckoned as a term of residence under the Regulations for Residence in the University provided that not more than three University fees shall be payable in the same academic year.

(*e*) The fee shall be collected in accordance with §3 below.

5. (*a*) The number of termly University fees payable under cl. 4 above by those   40
working for the degree of D.Phil. shall not exceed nine provided that:

    (i) [for candidates admitted for a D.Phil. from 1 September 2006 on-wards] Candidates for the D.Phil. may count towards this figure up to three termly University fees paid while working for the degree of M.Phil., M.St. in Legal Research, or B.Phil. provided that the candi-   45
date has been given leave to supplicate for that degree;

    (ii) Candidates for the D.Phil. who have held the status of Probationer Research Student, or of Student for the Degree of M.Sc. by Research or M.Litt. or for the Diploma in Law, before transferring to work for the degree of D.Phil. shall be deemed for the purpose of this subsection to have been working for the D.Phil. from the term in which they began working for the course from which they have transferred, and may count towards their D.Phil. fee liability any fees paid while holding their previous status, subject to the payment on transfer of 5 any consequent additional fees for which they are liable. A candidate is not deemed to be 'transferring to work for the Degree of D.Phil.', when he or she is admitted for the Diploma in Law or as a D.Phil. student after satisfying the examiners for the Degree of M.Sc. by Research or M.Litt.; 10

(*b*) The number of termly University fees payable by candidates for the Doctor of Engineering shall not exceed twelve.

(*c*) The number of termly University fees payable under cl. 4 above by those working for any qualification other than the degree of D.Phil. or D.Eng. shall not exceed six in respect of each qualification, provided that: 15

  (i) Candidates who transfer from the D.Phil. to the M.Litt. or M.Sc. by Research may count up to six University fees paid while working towards the D.Phil. (including fees paid while holding the status Probationer Research Student) towards this figure;

  (ii) Candidates receiving tuition or supervision after attempting an exam- 20 ination shall continue to pay University fees for each term in which they receive tuition or supervision;

  (iii) Candidates under (iv) and (v) below who receive tuition or supervision after failing an examination or who require an extension of time shall continue to pay University fees for each term in which they receive 25 tuition or supervision;

  (iv) Students for the Degree of Master of Science in Evidence-Based Health Care, Experimental Therapeutics, Software and System Security, Software Engineering, Surgical Science and Practice, or Sustainable Urban Development shall pay all applicable module fees and not 30 more than four annual registration fees;

  (v) Part-time students for the Degree of Master of Theology shall not pay more than six University fees (at the half rate) while working for Part II of that degree; and

  (vi) Part-time students for the M.Sc. in Mathematical Finance shall pay not 35 more than two tuition fees covering seven terms of study, payable at the start of the first and second years of the course respectively; students requiring an extension of time shall pay a fee of £530 for each term in which they continue to receive tuition or supervision.

(*d*) the number of termly University fees payable by candidates registered for a 40 D.Phil. through one of the following doctoral training programmes shall not exceed twelve: Autonomous Intelligent Machines and Systems; Cardiovascular Medicinal Chemistry; Cyber Security; Environmental Research; Healthcare Innovation; Industrially Focused Mathematical Modelling; Interdisciplinary Bioscience; Life Sciences Interface; New and 45 Sustainable Photovoltaics; Oil and Gas; Partial Differential Equations: Analysis and Applications; Science and Technology of Fusion Energy; Synthesis for Biology and Medicine; Systems Approaches to Biomedical Science; Systems Biology;

(*e*) the number of termly University fees payable by candidates registered for a 50 D.Phil. through one of the following doctoral training programmes shall not exceed twelve: Biomedical Imaging; Statistical Science; Synthetic Biology. Candidates registered for one of these doctoral training programmes, who are admitted by the University of Warwick, Bristol, or Nottingham, and who hold the status of Probationer Research Student at Oxford, shall not normally pay more than three termly University fees while at Oxford;   5

(*f*) the number of termly University fees payable by candidates registered for a D.Phil. through one of the following doctoral training programmes shall not exceed twelve: Diamond Science and Technology; Gas Turbine Aerodynamics; Renewable Energy Marine Structures; Science and Application of Plastic Electronic Materials. Candidates for these pro-   10 grammes may count towards this figure up to the equivalent of three termly University fees paid to the relevant partner university;

(*g*) the number of termly University fees payable by candidates registered for a D.Phil. through the doctoral training programme in Theory and Modelling in Chemical Sciences shall not exceed twelve. Candidates registered for a   15 D.Phil. through this doctoral training programme may count up to three termly University fees paid while working for the M.Sc. in Theoretical and Computational Chemistry towards this figure;

(*h*) Fee requirements relating to full-time students undertaking graduate study shall also apply to part-time students holding the same status, save that part-   20 time students shall be required to pay half the applicable full-time fee over twice the applicable length of time for full-time students, except where the fee for the part-time programme is otherwise specified in the regulations, and except where the applicable period is otherwise specified under cl. 5(*c*) above.

(*i*) (i) Where admission as a graduate student is reckoned from a term earlier   25 than that in which the application for admission was approved, on the grounds that:

   (*a*) A term or terms had been spent at another university on a course of study directly relevant to the work subsequently undertaken for the degree of M.Litt., M.Sc., or D.Phil., and   30

   (*b*) The earlier study had not led to the award of a qualification of any university, and was under the supervision of a person who has subsequently taken up an appointment at Oxford,

   (ii) Subject to the approval of Council's Education Committee, any fees payable under cl. 4 above in respect of such term or terms may be   35 remitted either wholly or in part. For the purposes of determining the appropriate fee level, the student will usually be deemed to have commenced the programme of study in the term to which their admission has been antedated.

(*j*) The number of termly University fees payable by candidates for a D.Phil. in   40 the Medical Sciences Doctoral Training Centre who have been admitted to a four-year doctoral programme shall not exceed twelve.

(*k*) The number of termly University fees payable by candidates for a D.Phil. in Biomedical Sciences under the NIH-Oxford programme shall not exceed six.

6. Subject to the approval of Council's Education Committee, where a clinical   45 student has already spent at least three terms working full-time for the Degree of M.Sc. by research and has paid at least three University fees in respect thereof, any further fees payable in respect of the M.Sc. course for terms in which he or she is also working as a clinical student at a university clinical school outside Oxford may be remitted.   50

7. Every member of the University shall pay such other fees applicable to him or her as may be prescribed by any statute or regulation.

§2. *Visiting, Recognized, and Matriculated Non-Award Students*

1. Every member of the University who, not holding an academic appointment in the University or the colleges, has been matriculated in order to study in the University otherwise than for a degree, diploma, or certificate of the University shall pay a University fee at the appropriate annual rate published at www.ox.ac.uk/feesandfunding/fees/information/universityrates/ or available from the Planning and Resource Allocation Section for each term in which he or she is studying in the University.

2. Every person on the Register of Recognized Students or on the Register of Visiting Students shall pay a University fee at the appropriate annual rate on the basis set out below, and as published at www.ox.ac.uk/feesandfunding/fees/information/universityrates/ or available from the Planning and Resource Allocation Section for each term in which he or she is studying in the University.

(*a*) For Recognised Students, fees shall be payable at 50% of the 'overseas' graduate research fee rate specified for the relevant subject area; in cases where a Recognised Student is studying across subject areas with different fee rates, the applicable fee rate shall be that which applies to the larger portion of their studies; in the case of two subjects equally weighted, the fee rate shall be that which applies to the subject that carries the higher fee; in the case of three subjects weighted equally, the fee rate shall be that which applies to the subject that carries the mid-level fee.

(*b*) For Visiting Students, fees shall be payable at 50% of the 'overseas' undergraduate fee rate specified for the relevant subject area; in cases where the subject is not offered at undergraduate level, fees shall be payable at 50% of the 'overseas' graduate research fee rate as specified for the relevant subject area; in cases where a Visiting Student is studying across subject areas with different fee rates, the applicable fee rate shall be that which applies to the larger portion of their studies; in the case of two subjects equally weighted, the fee rate shall be that which applies to the subject that carries the higher fee; in the case of three subjects weighted equally, the fee rate shall be that which applies to the subject that carries the mid-level fee.

3. Every person described in cll. 1 and 2 above shall pay such other fees applicable to him or her as may be prescribed by any statute or regulation.

§3. *Arrangements relating to the payment of University fees*

1. (*a*) Not later than the fourteenth day after the last day of every Full Term, the Head or Bursar of every society, or the Head of the student's department for programmes where fees are usually paid directly to the department, shall send to the Secretary of the Chest a schedule signed by himself or herself containing the names of all members of the society who were liable to pay the University fees referred to in §1 and §2 above, in respect of that term.

(*b*) The Head or Bursar of every society shall pay to the Secretary of the Chest such University fees as were due for that term in accordance with the mechanisms agreed between the colleges and the University from time to time. Where University fees are collected by a department these shall be paid to the Secretary of the Chest in accordance with the mechanisms that are agreed from time to time.

2. Annual University fees shall be paid on or before the seventh day of Michaelmas Full Term (or of the term in which the student commences his or her course, as the case may be) unless the Bursar of the student's college or the Head of the student's department for programmes where fees are usually paid directly to the department, certifies in writing that:

    (*a*) The college has approved the student's application to pay by instalments, the first such instalment having been paid; and/or

    (*b*) The student has applied for, and is prima facie eligible for, a contribution to his or her fee from his or her local authority (or other fee-paying body), and the college is of the opinion that no contribution will be required from the student;

    (*c*) The student's programme did not commence on the first day of the relevant term, and payment is due on the seventh day after the actual commencement of the student's programme.

3. (*a*) In the event that any fee or continuation charge payable by the student, or the relevant instalment towards such a fee, remains unpaid after the due date of payment it shall be the duty of the Bursar of the student's college, or the Registrar for programmes where fees or charges are usually paid directly to the University, or the Head of the student's department for programmes where fees or charges are usually paid directly to the department, to notify the student concerned that, in the event that the fees or charges due have not been paid in full within four weeks from the date of such notification, the student shall ordinarily be liable for suspension from access to the premises and facilities of the University (including the Examination Schools and other places of examination). The student shall be informed that, apart from in exceptional circumstances, they will be suspended from the end of such four-week period until such time as outstanding fees or charges have been paid, at which point they may apply for reinstatement, or until two terms have elapsed, at which point they will be removed from the Register of Students. The Bursar or Head shall also inform the Registrar that he or she has so notified the student concerned; and if the fees or charges due have not been paid in full within the specified four-week period, the Bursar or Head shall inform the Registrar of the position, whereupon, subject to the other provisions of this clause, the University shall have the right, having considered the circumstances of the case, to suspend the student concerned from access to the premises and facilities of the University. If the fees or charges due have not been paid in full within two terms of the date of any suspension imposed under this clause, the University shall have the right, having first considered the circumstances of the case, to remove the student from the Register of Students. A student may apply to Education Committee for reinstatement to the Register of Students. Any such reinstatement, which is not automatic, will be conditional upon payment of all outstanding fees.

    (*b*) On application by their society, or by the Head of the student's department for programmes where fees are usually paid directly to the department, and subject to the approval of Council's Education Committee, some part of the fee for an academic year may subsequently be returned to those who do not work in Oxford as a result of suspension or withdrawal, for the whole of that year. The general rule agreed by Council is that, for each complete term not spent working in Oxford, one third of the annual fee shall be returned. In addition, if a student withdraws or suspends their status on or before Monday of Week 4 of any term the fees payable in respect of that term will generally be reimbursed to the student. Certain programmes which have been granted permission to charge non-refundable deposits and programmes within the Department for Continuing Education, the Mathematical Institute, and the Saïd Business School may operate different refund policies.

(c) Applications for the remission or waiver of University fees, for the resolution of issues relating to the non-payment of University fees, and for all other questions of doubt or difficulty relating to the liability of individual students 5 for University fees, including those covered under cll. 2 and 3 (a) and (b) above, and for questions of doubt or difficulty relating to the charging of deposits for course fees, or for tuition fee reductions or bursaries as covered in §6, or for liability for the continuation charge as covered in §4 shall be determined by the Fees Panel. The Panel shall be chaired by the Assessor and 10 consist of two members nominated by Conference of Colleges, two members nominated by Council's Education Committee, and the Assessor-elect. Applications for dispensation from residence requirements, other than those specified above, shall be determined by the Proctors, on condition that if the Fees Panel or the Proctors, as the case may be, are unable to 15 agree on how to deal with any individual application they shall refer the application to Council's Education Committee for decision.

(d) There shall be no appeal against a decision of the Fees Panel. A student may, however, make a further application under the procedures outlined above for relief from suspension or such terms as may have been imposed by a Fees 20 Panel if the Bursar of his or her college supports an application on the basis that the student's financial circumstances have changed for reasons beyond his or her control.

§4. *Regulations relating to the University continuation charge*

1. A candidate admitted to graduate research study (that is, a student for the 25 D.Phil., D.Eng., M.Litt., M.Sc.(Res), or any other programme of study designated as a research programme) who commenced their current programme of study in or after September 2011 and who has reached the end of the period of fee liability, as defined at §1, cl. 5, and who thereafter remains registered as a graduate research student, shall pay a continuation charge for each subsequent term up to and including 30 the term in which the thesis is submitted. Candidates whose thesis has been referred back shall pay no further University fee or continuation charge, but shall pay the fee prescribed in §7 below when they apply for re-examination.

2. A student who is paying University fees in respect of any given term shall not be liable for a continuation charge in the same term. 35

3. The continuation charge first became payable in 2013–14 and the rate will be reviewed on an annual basis. The rate for the current academic year is available from www.ox.ac.uk/feesandfunding/fees/information/maxlib/otherfees/ or from the Planning and Resource Allocation Section. Divisions may remit the continuation charge (subject to approval by Council's Planning and Resource Allocation 40 Committee) for graduate research students on a specified course or courses of study, provided that the remission applies to all students on that course in a specified term or terms of study.

§5. *Regulations relating to the fees for certain scholarship and exchange agreements*

1. Notwithstanding the provisions of §1 above, the University shall remit three- 45 fifths of the prescribed University fees payable by any overseas student who estab- lishes, by information certified to the Secretary of the Chest by an officer of the student's college or society, that at least half of the cost of the student's maintenance (as distinct from university or college fees) in the relevant year has been provided by

resident Junior Members of the University (otherwise than from funds of common rooms contributed directly or indirectly by local education authorities or other grant-paying authorities in payment of membership fees); provided that the number of students whose fees are remitted under this clause shall not in any one year exceed thirty-five and that any arrangements required for determining the allocation between　5 colleges or other societies of the benefits available under this clause shall be subject to approval from time to time by Council's Education Committee.

2. Council's Education Committee shall have power to approve exchange arrange-ments with other universities under which no fees are payable on either side. Any of the University fees prescribed in §1 or §2 above, which would otherwise have been　10 payable by any person working in Oxford under those exchange arrangements shall be remitted.

§6. *Regulations for Oxford Bursaries and Tuition Fee Reductions*

1. The arrangements described in this section apply to members of the University, entitled, in accordance with the criteria set out in §1, cl. 1, to be charged University　15 fees at the appropriate 'home' (and EU) rate, who are working in Oxford:

- (*a*) for the Degree of BA or the Degree of MBiochem or the Degree of MChem or the Degree of MMathCompSci or the Degree of MEarthSc or the Degree of MEng or the Degree of MMath or the Degree of MCompSci or the Degree of MCompPhil or the Degree of MPhys or the Degree of MPhysPhil or the Degree　20 of MMathPhil, or the degree of MMathPhys (4-year course only), or the degree of BTh (full-time mode only);
- (*b*) for the degree of BFA;
- (*c*) for the First Examination for the Degree of BM;
- (*d*) for the Preliminary Examination in Medicine;　25
- (*e*) for the Second Examination for the degree of BM;
- (*f*) for the full-time Undergraduate Certificate or Diploma in Theological Studies;
- (*g*) for the Postgraduate Certificate in Education.

2. All students described in cl.1 above, who are entitled to receive support from a funding agency as described in cl. 6 below, will be eligible to be assessed for an　30 Oxford bursary, subject to cl. 4. Bursary levels will be at the rates determined from time to time by Council's Education Committee and Planning and Resource Allocation Committee. Bursary amounts are set out on the University website. Special regulations for members of the University described in cl.1 (*d*), (*e*), and (*g*) are set out in cll. 11 to 13.　35

3. All students described in cl. 1, who are entitled to receive support from a funding agency as described in cl. 6 below, who commenced their programme of study on or after 1 September 2012, and who would otherwise be liable for full University fees as described in §1,will be eligible to be assessed for a reduction in University fees, hereafter referred to as a 'tuition fee reduction' subject to cl. 4. The level of the tuition　40 fee reduction will be at the rates determined from time to time by Council's Education Committee and Planning and Resource Allocation Committee. The different levels of tuition fee reduction are set out on the University website. Special regulations for members of the University described in cl. 1 (*d*) and (*g*) are set out in cll. 11–134. Students will not be entitled to a cash equivalent of a tuition fee reduction.　45

4. If a student who is eligible to be charged University fees at the 'home' (and EU) rate is not entitled to means-tested maintenance support from his or her funding agency, he or she will not be eligible to be assessed for a bursary or tuition fee reduction in that academic year. Students who are entitled to be assessed by the

Student Finance Services Non UK Team, and who are entitled, in accordance with the criteria set out in §1, cl. 1, to be charged fees at the appropriate 'home' (and EU) rate, are eligible to be assessed for a bursary or tuition fee reduction, subject to the conditions referred to in cl. 10 below.

5. Students who are repeating a year of their studies at Oxford will be eligible to be   5
assessed for a bursary and/or tuition fee reduction, subject to cl. 4. Students repeating their first year or transferring to year one of a new course described in cl. 1 who were eligible for an additional start-up bursary in their first year of study will not be eligible for any further start-up bursary.

6. Requirements for the assessment of a student's household income are as follows: 10

(*a*) A member of the University as described in cl. 1 can only be considered for a bursary or tuition fee reduction if he or she is first financially assessed by his or her funding agency and if consent has been given for the University to access this information. Financial assessments will only be accepted from Student Finance England, Student Finance Northern Ireland, Student Finance Wales,   15
the Student Awards Agency for Scotland, the Student Finance Services Non UK Team, the Student Loans Company (SLC) or the National Health Service (NHS). The University will only base a student's bursary and/or tuition fee reduction upon income information provided to it via the above agencies;

(*b*) Special regulations for financial assessments apply to members of the University   20
who are working in Oxford for the Preliminary Examination in Medicine and Second Examination for the degree of BM. These are set out in cll. 11 and 12;

(*c*) 'Home' students are obliged to accept any maintenance grant they become eligible for as a result of financial assessment by their funding agency in order to be eligible to be assessed for a bursary and/or a tuition fee reduction. 'Home'   25
(and EU) students are not required by the University to take out a maintenance loan or tuition fee loan from their funding agency to be eligible to be assessed for a bursary or for a tuition fee reduction respectively.

7. The annual deadlines for the assessment of bursaries and tuition fee reductions shall be as follows: 30

(*a*) To be assessed for an Oxford bursary and/or tuition fee reduction students must comply with the application deadlines set by their funding agency. Students who fail to comply with requests to provide information to their agency will not be assessed by the University after the deadlines listed in (*b*) and (*c*) below;

(*b*) To be assessed, or reassessed, for an Oxford bursary students must ensure that   35
they have provided all information to their funding agency in time to ensure their assessment is complete and available to the University from the SLC or other approved agency by 30 May of the academic year in which they wish to be considered for a bursary;

(*c*) To be assessed, or reassessed, for a tuition fee reduction students must ensure   40
that they have provided all information to their funding agency in time to ensure their assessment is complete and available to the University from the SLC or other approved agency by 20 December of the academic year in which they wish to be considered for a tuition fee reduction;

(*d*) Any student who wishes to be considered for a bursary and/or tuition fee   45
reduction, or for a change in their bursary and/or tuition fee reduction after the dates listed in (*b*) and (*c*) above must submit a case to the Student Fees and Funding section (Examination Schools, Oxford OX1 4BG) detailing the delay relating to their financial assessment by 30 May of that academic year. The student must confirm when he or she applied for funding, what difficulties he or   50
she had in being assessed correctly, the action he or she took to rectify this, and

provide any corresponding evidence. The student will be expected to respond in a timely manner to any requests for further information from Student Fees and Funding. The student must also provide the final financial notification for that year as soon as it is available and no later than 20 December of the following academic year. If the student is in their final year of study, the deadline for submission of the financial support notification is Friday of Week 9 of Trinity Term of that year.

8. The arrangements for adjustments to bursaries during an academic year are as follows:

(*a*) Each of the regulations in this clause will be subject to the dates and regulations listed in cl. 7;

(*b*) Students who have received an overpayment of their bursary following a revised household income assessment will not be asked to repay any funds, unless the bursary was obtained due to incorrect information being knowingly submitted to the student's funding agency by the student or his or her sponsor;

(*c*) If a student's revised household income assessment results in an increased bursary entitlement, subsequent bursary payments will be adjusted upwards to reflect the student's increased entitlement for the whole year. The increased bursary payments will be calculated as if the student had been eligible for that level from the start of the academic year;

(*d*) If a student fails to provide information requested by their funding agency, as a result of which the financial assessment is withdrawn, the University will suspend bursary payments until the student's assessment has been completed by the funding agency, at which point their bursary entitlement will be re-assessed;

(*e*) The amount paid per term will be one third of the total annual bursary to which the student is eligible. Students will be expected to repay their bursary for any term where they have suspended or withdrawn before the bursary payment date, currently Week 4 in Michaelmas term and Week 2 in Hilary and Trinity terms.

9. The arrangements for adjustments to fee liability and tuition fee reductions during an academic year are as follows:

(*a*) Each of the regulations in this clause will be subject to the dates and regulations listed in cl. 7;

(*b*) Students whose revised household income assessment has increased will not be liable for increased University fees, unless the initial tuition fee reduction was obtained due to incorrect information being knowingly submitted to the student's funding agency by the student or his or her sponsor;

(*c*) If a student's revised household income assessment has reduced, resulting in an entitlement to a larger tuition fee reduction, he or she will receive an additional tuition fee reduction. The level of the tuition fee reduction will calculated as if the student had been eligible for that level from the start of the academic year.

10. The arrangements for changes to bursary and tuition fee reduction entitlement between years are as follows:

(*a*) Students entitled, in accordance with the criteria set out in §1, cl. 1, to be charged University fees at the appropriate 'home' (and EU) rate, and who are entitled to be financially assessed by Student Finance England, Student Finance Northern Ireland, Student Finance Wales, the Student Awards Agency for Scotland, the SLC or the NHS, are required by these funding agencies to apply for financial support each year if they wish to access means-tested support. The assessment of their household income by their funding agency may change from year to year, and consequently their entitlement to a bursary and/

or tuition fee reduction is subject to change each year. Special regulations are set out in cll. 11 and 12 for financial assessments for members of the University working for the Preliminary Examination in Medicine (Part II) and Bachelor of Medicine (Second Examination);

(*b*) Students entitled, in accordance with the criteria set out in §1, cl. 1, to be charged fees at the appropriate 'home' (and EU) rate, and who are entitled to be financially assessed by the Student Finance Services Non UK Team may have their household income assessed in the first year of study only. Students who wish to have their household income reassessed or continuing year students who wish to be financially assessed for the first time must submit a request to the Student Fees and Funding section, Examination Schools, Oxford, OX1 4BG.

(*c*) Students will only be eligible to be assessed for a bursary and/or tuition fee reduction for the period in which they are entitled, in accordance with the criteria set out in §1, cl. 1, to be charged University fees at the appropriate 'home' (and EU) rate.

11. Special regulations apply for members of the University who are working in Oxford for the Preliminary Examination in Medicine (Part II) and Bachelor of Medicine (Second Examination) where these students were admitted on the accelerated four-year course. These are as follows:

(*a*) The household income of students in years two to four of their course will be estimated on the basis of the financial assessment of their household income in year one of their course or from their latest NHS (or corresponding authority) bursary assessment as evidenced by the student;

(*b*) Students not eligible for fee support from the NHS/SLC because their funding agency does not provide fee support for this course will be eligible to be assessed for a tuition fee reduction in all years of their course where household income will be estimated on the basis of the financial assessment of their household income in year one of their course. A tuition fee reduction is not available to those students who are eligible for fee support from the NHS/SLC after the first year of their course;

(*c*) Students will be eligible to be assessed for a bursary for all years of the course.

12. Special regulations apply for members of the University who are working in Oxford for the Bachelor of Medicine (Second Examination) in years four to six of the six-year medicine course:

(*a*) The household income of students in years five and six of the six-year medicine course will be estimated on the basis of the financial assessment of their household income in year four of their course or from their latest NHS (or corresponding authority) bursary assessment as evidenced by the student;

(*b*) Students in year four of the course will be eligible to be assessed for a tuition fee reduction;

(*c*) Students will be eligible to be assessed for a bursary for all years of the course.

13. Members of the University working in Oxford for the Postgraduate Certificate in Education will only be eligible to be assessed for an Oxford bursary if their full entitlement to government maintenance support (including a government teacher training bursary or affiliated scholarship) amounts to less than £9,000.

14. If a student believes that his or her bursary or tuition fee reduction has not been processed according to these regulations and/or the bursary and tuition fee reduction rates approved by Council's Education Committee and Planning and Resource Allocation Committee, he or she should contact the Student Fees and Funding section, Examination Schools, Oxford OX1 4BG. Any question of doubt or difficulty

relating to the eligibility of individual students for tuition fee reductions and/or Oxford bursaries shall be determined by the Fees Panel, as described in §3, cl. 3.

§7. *Fees payable by candidates on registration, entry for an examination, application for leave to supplicate, resubmission of a thesis for certain degrees, or supplicating for admission to or accumulation of certain degrees*   5

1. Fees are payable in the following circumstances. Fees are reviewed on an annual basis with the fees for the current academic year available from www.ox.ac.uk/feesandfunding/fees/information/maxlib/otherfees/ or from the Planning and Resource Allocation Section. In the case of circumstances described in (a)–(c) below and if University fees as defined in §1 are payable in respect of the same term, fees for   10 (a)–(c) below do not apply.

(*a*) On entering for certain university examinations:
   (i) Certificates in Theology;
   (ii) Certificate and Diploma in Theological and Pastoral Studies;
   (iii) Degree of B.Mus;   15

(*b*) On re-entering the university examination for the Degrees of B.Phil., M.Phil., M.Th., M.Sc. (by Coursework), M.St., MBA, MFA, MPP, or any diploma or certificate (other than those listed under §1 cl. 4(*a*)(xii) (*a*)–(i);

(*c*) On resubmission of a thesis for the degree of M.Litt., M.Th., M.Sc. (by Research), D.Phil., or D.Eng., or on reinstatement on the Register of Students   20 for the degree of M.Litt., M.Sc. (by Research), D.Phil. or D.Eng.;

(*d*) For late entry for examinations:
   (i) where a candidate proposes to offer a subject or part of the examination which has already been offered by a candidate who entered by the due date and no change in the conduct of the examination is involved;   25
   (ii) where the provisions of (i) are not satisfied but the chair of examiners is willing to consent;

(*e*) For late alteration of options:
   (i) where a candidate proposes to offer a subject or part of the examination which has already been offered by a candidate who entered by the due date   30 and no change in the conduct of the examination is involved;
   (ii) where the provisions of (i) are not satisfied but the chair of examiners is willing to consent;

(*f*) For late submission of a thesis or other exercise;

(*g*) On admission to the Status of Student for the Degree of DM and for each   35 subsequent year that the name of the student remains on the register of students for the degree;

(*h*) On resubmission for the degree of DM;

(*i*) On resubmission of a thesis for the Degree of M.Ch.;

(*j*) On applying for leave to supplicate: 40
   for the degree of M.Ch.;
   for the degree of DM;
   for the degrees of DD, DCL, D.Litt., D.Sc., and D.Mus.

2. Every person shall pay £10 on supplicating for admission to the degree of MA, provided that: 45

(*a*) No fee shall be payable by any person on whom a degree has been conferred by special resolution or who incorporates in virtue of having obtained an educational position in the University;

(*b*) No fee shall be payable by a Master of Surgery on supplicating for admission to the Degree of Master of Arts.

3. A fee shall be paid by every person accumulating the Degrees of Bachelor and Doctor of Civil Law. The fee for the current academic year is available from www.ox.ac.uk/feesandfunding/fees/information/maxlib/otherfees/ or from the Planning and Resource Allocation Section.

§8. *Fees payable by candidates for fieldwork*

1. In the following programmes of study, additional charges will be made for fieldwork that is a requirement of the programme:

BA Archaeology;

BA Biological Sciences;

BA Classical Archaeology & Ancient History;

BA Geography;

BA Geology (pre-2012 entrants only);

MEarthSci (pre-2012 entrants only);

M.Phil. Latin American Studies; and

M.Sc. Water Science, Policy and Management.

2. Other programmes of study may carry additional charges for optional fieldwork, projects or placements that are not a requirement of the programme.

§9. *Fees payable by candidates on registration for courses validated by the University*

1. A registration fee is payable for the degree of Doctor of Clinical Psychology and for the Postgraduate Certificate in Supervision of Applied Psychological Practice. The fee for the current academic year is available from www.ox.ac.uk/feesandfunding/fees/information/maxlib/otherfees/ or from the Planning and Resource Allocation Section.

§10. *Fees payable by certain students working in departments or faculties who are not members of the University nor Recognized students nor Visiting Students*

1. If a person who is not a member of the University is admitted to work, and receive instruction or supervision, in any university department by the head of the department, he or she shall pay to the Secretary of the Chest such fee or fees as shall be prescribed by the head of the department in accordance with arrangements approved from time to time by Council's Education and Planning and Resource Allocation Committees.

2. The head of each department shall have discretion to fix a fee or fees for any member of the University who is working in his or her department, unless that member is liable to pay University fees under the provisions of §1 or §2 cl. 1 or would be liable but for the provisions of §1 cl. 5 thereof.

3. The head of each department shall maintain, and on request send to the Secretary of the Chest not later than the end of the third week of Full Term, or in the case of students working in the vacation only, as soon as may be, a list of the names of the students attending lectures or working in his or her department other than those liable to pay a fee covering that term under §1 or §2.

4. No fee shall be payable under the provisions of this subsection by any person who is paying a fee under the provisions of §4, or whose name is on the Register of Recognized Students or the Register of Visiting Students, or by any salaried employee who is receiving instruction or supervision in the department in which he or she is working.   5

5. For the purposes of this subsection the word 'Term' shall include the vacation following.

§11. *Fees payable by certain Clinical Students*

1. Every person attached to the clinical school under regular instruction for a qualifying medical examination of another university or of a recognised professional   10
institution shall, unless liable to pay University fees under the provisions of §1, pay to the Regius Professor of Medicine a fee of £10 on admission and a University fee every three months at the annual rate published at www.ox.ac.uk/feesandfunding/fees/information/universityrates/ or available from the Planning and Resource Allocation Section which would be applicable to him or her if liable for fees under §1 cl. 3.   15

2. The Regius Professor of Medicine shall have discretion to fix fees for persons attached to the clinical school who are not under regular instruction but who would otherwise be liable to pay a fee or fees under cl.1 above.

3. Within fourteen days of the last day of every Full Term the Regius Professor of Medicine shall: 20

(*a*) Send to the Secretary of the Chest a schedule specifying (a) the names of all the persons who were liable to pay any of the fees referred to in cll. 1 and 2 above since the preparation of the previous schedule, and (b) the particular fees payable by such persons, and

(*b*) Account to the curators for the fees so specified between those at the 'home' and   25
'overseas' rates, for the remainder of the course then being undertaken.

§12. *Fees in respect of certificates, transcripts and personal data*

1. Every person shall pay the fee prescribed below in each case for certificates issued, on request, to Degree Conferrals Office, Examination Schools, Oxford OX1 4BG: 30

(*a*) for the first certificate attesting admission to any degree, which shall include a statement of the class obtained, no charge

(*b*) for each replacement certificate attesting admission to any degree (the request must be accompanied by a written statement declaring the original lost, stolen or damaged) £30   35

2. Every person shall pay the fee prescribed below in each case for transcripts issued, online or by request to University of Oxford, c/o Examination Schools, High Street, Oxford OX1 4BG:

(*a*) for the first transcript provided upon successful completion: no charge

(*b*) for each transcript provided during the course and any subsequent transcripts   40
upon completion: £5

3. Every person making a request to be supplied with personal data under Section 7 of the Data Protection Act 1998 shall pay the fee determined from time to time by Council. Such requests should be addressed to the Data Protection Officer, University Offices, Wellington Square, Oxford OX1 2JD, from whom details of the current fee   45
can be obtained. The fee is subject to a maximum prescribed from time to time by the Home Secretary under the Act.

INDEX